The Adventures in Literature Program
Olympic Edition

Adventures for Readers: Book 1

Reading Workshop with Tests
Teacher's Manual
*Many Voices 1**

Adventures for Readers: Book 2

Reading Workshop with Tests
Teacher's Manual
Many Voices 2

Adventures in Reading

Reading Workshop with Tests
Teacher's Manual
Many Voices 3

Adventures in Appreciation

Reading Workshop with Tests
Teacher's Manual
Many Voices 4

Adventures in American Literature

Reading Tests
Teacher's Manual
Many Voices 5

Adventures in English Literature

Reading Tests
Teacher's Manual
Many Voices 6

* 33⅓ rpm twelve-inch longplay record album for each book.

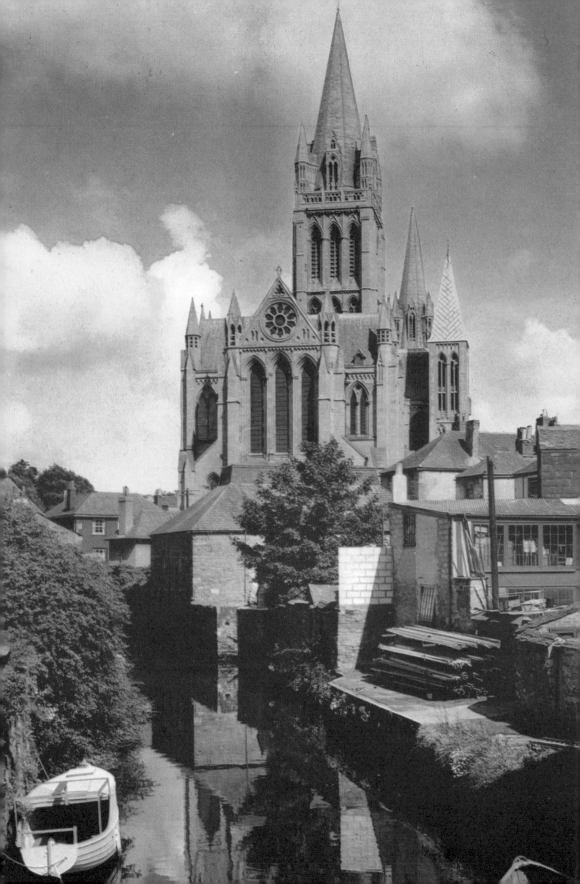

ADVENTURES

IN

ENGLISH

LITERATURE

Rewey Belle Inglis

Formerly University High School, University of Minnesota

Josephine Spear

Chairman of English Department, University School, Indiana University

Harcourt, Brace and Company   New York   Chicago

Truro Cathedral in Cornwall

THE POETS' CORNER IN WESTMINSTER ABBEY

Acknowledgments for permissions and illustrations are covered by the present copyright
for this edition as well as copyrights for the 1931, 1938, 1941, 1946, 1949,
and 1952 editions of Adventures in English Literature.

REWEY BELLE INGLIS *has twenty-five years of teaching experience, which includes not only
high-school English but Methods and Practice Teaching in English. She is a past president of
the National Council of Teachers of English. Her interest in English literature has led her
to make three extensive tours of the British Isles.* DR. JOSEPHINE SPEAR *has been teaching
secondary-school English for nineteen years. She also has taught graduate and undergraduate
courses in English Literature and Methods.*

DRAWINGS BY:
Edwin Brooks, Milton Glaser, Witold Mars, Ray Porter, Susanne Suba, Johannes Troyer.

Printed in the United States of America [h · 1 · 60]

PICTURE CREDITS: *Above* — Galloway. *Cover* — Photo by Cecil Beaton from *Life* Magazine. © 1956, *Time*, Inc.
Title page — British Travel Association.

CONTENTS

THE ANGLO-SAXON PERIOD

It is almost a miracle that we have firsthand knowledge of the earliest period of English literature. The 3,000 lines of *Beowulf*, the poem that is most expressive of the Anglo-Saxon spirit, are known to us by mere chance. The only existing manuscript was discovered in the collection of Sir Robert Cotton in the year 1705. This same manuscript barely escaped destruction in the British Museum fire of 1731. It is thus that, more than twelve centuries after they were recorded, we are able to read of the lives of these sea-going warriors of long ago.

THE MEDIEVAL PERIOD

In feudal Britain, a rigid class structure defined positions in society, from nobles to serfs. In the towns, commerce grew and craftsmen and merchants became important. The medieval church exerted a powerful influence. Chivalry, the picturesque social code of the nobility, lent aspects of grace, romance, and idealism to the era. Ballads were the oral literature of the people. The most famous book of the time, Geoffrey Chaucer's *The Canterbury Tales,* shows this diversity of life through characters who are so realistic that they remind us of ourselves.

THE ELIZABETHAN AGE

In Elizabethan England, the men who bore the arms, sat in the councils of the queen, brawled in the taverns, sailed the seven seas, and carried on the commerce of the nation were the same men who wrote the love lyrics, the romantic epics, the adventure-laden prose, and the immortal dramas. The age that bears Elizabeth's name was a glorious one not only because of the dramatic queen but also because of men like the intrepid explorers Drake and Raleigh; the great scholar, Francis Bacon; and the supremely gifted poet-dramatist, Shakespeare.

THE SEVENTEENTH CENTURY

Dissension and calamity marked the seventeenth century. The people were divided by partisan positions in politics and religion; they were united by the common catastrophes of the Civil War, the Black Plague, and the great fire of London. Out of the conflicting tempers of the times came writers who had as little in common as the elegant courtier Sir John Suckling and the learned poet and pamphleteer John Milton. The moods competing for dominance, in life and literature, were lightheartedly Cavalier or solemnly Puritan.

THE EIGHTEENTH CENTURY

The eighteenth century in England is appropriately called the Age of Reason, for it was a secure and confident time. London was a bustling city, where cheerful coffeehouses were focal points for business, social, and literary gatherings. The literature of the century revealed intelligence, sophistication, and originality. It was mainly prose. Dramatists produced mannered comedies that still sparkle with wit. Two significant new forms of writing appeared and flourished — the periodical, which fostered the informal essay, and the novel.

THE ROMANTIC AGE

This golden age of lyric poetry belongs to youth. Never in English literature have young men looked so searchingly into their own souls and at the world around them and expressed their responses in language of such beauty and power. In the early decades of the nineteenth century Britain was stirred by new feelings about the world of nature, about liberty — both personal and political — and about the common man. Here is a literature of vigor and courage, love and wisdom, despair and hope.

THE VICTORIAN AGE

"Eminent Victorians" is what Lytton Strachey called several of the dominant figures of this century. Victoria, the long-reigning queen, set the pervading mood of seriousness. Discoveries in science revealed new wonders for the intellectually curious. Industry was changing the face of the nation and altering the pattern of living of thousands. Meanwhile, poets, essayists, and novelists were writing thoughtfully of manners and moral values, while a few of their contemporaries were moved to make lighthearted fun of Victorian earnestness.

THE MODERN AGE

Twentieth-century English literature displays masters in all its forms: Shaw as playwright extraordinary, Galsworthy as versatile writer of fiction and drama, Yeats and Eliot as deeply inquiring poets, and Winston Churchill as eloquent historian. Each of these men has won not only a Nobel prize but worldwide eminence as well. Young writers growing up in this century have written about contemporary values and changes in social structure with a clarity comparable to that of the writers of the eighteenth century.

MODERN BIOGRAPHY

MODERN ESSAYS

MODERN DRAMA

A Guide to
BRITAIN

J. B. PRIESTLEY

Let me first introduce myself, in my present capacity as a guide. I know Britain well because it is my native country and I have lived in it sixty-three years. Furthermore — and this seems to me important — I happen to know America fairly well too. I have been visiting your country for twenty-five years, have traveled widely in it, have stayed in places as far apart as Providence and San Diego, Seattle and New Orleans, and indeed have seen more of the United States than many of my friends in New York. I have often been sharply critical of America, just as I have often been even more sharply critical of Britain; but such criticism, like that of a brother or sister, comes from an affectionate concern.

Charming in its rustic English setting, Anne Hathaway's cottage recalls the time of the supreme genius of English literature, William Shakespeare.

Galloway

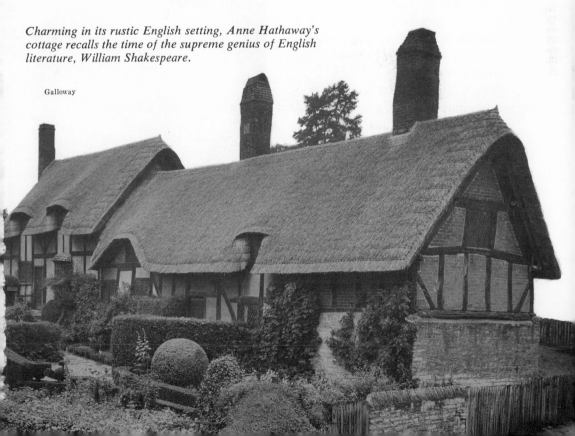

"This sceptered isle" is small and old

When you leave America for Britain, you leave a very large new country for a small old one. Nearly everything that surprises you in Britain stems from that difference. Let us take some obvious examples, some things you would notice at once. The English fields are small because the land has been highly cultivated for a long time, with a rotating system of crops, ranging from wheat, barley, oats, to roots or grass, grown to feed cattle and sheep. This variety of crops is most successful with small fields. And nearly all the farms you will see are "mixed," that is, engaged both in growing cereals and in raising stock. The intense green of the pastures is of course the result of the damp climate that rarely reaches very high or low temperatures.

You will notice that roads in Britain are much narrower and more winding than yours, far less suitable for automobile traffic. The reason is that these roads were being used long before the automobile was invented. Actually the straightest roads in England were made by the Romans.

The unsurpassed beauty of the English countryside is evident in this peaceful summertime view of a valley in Devon. Lush grazing fields make this an outstanding area for dairy farming.

2   British Travel Association.

The later roads grew out of paths and tracks winding their way through forests and between marshes. You may ask why these have not been set aside in favor of straight, wide motor *Modern traffic* roads. Is it simply lack of enterprise or old-fashioned prejudice *crowds the* in favor of narrow lanes? To some extent, it may be both; but *narrow,* bold civil engineering is far more difficult in a small, congested *winding roads* country like England, where the ownership of every piece of land goes back centuries and an elaborate tangle of rights is always involved.

Along these winding roads, hooting round every corner, go processions of cars strange to American eyes. They are much more varied in size and general appearance than your cars are, ranging from giant shining Rolls Royces and Daimlers to absurd midgets that seem to bounce along the road. There is not the fairly uniform speed that you find on most American main roads, and this British mixture of powerful giants and limping midgets, fast sports cars and ancient family vehicles, all crowded together on narrow winding roads, makes

A few tiny passenger cars are trapped in a rush-hour traffic jam of the big red double-decker buses that are such a familiar sight on London streets.

Acme

driving in England a far more hazardous business than it is in America. It is also more expensive, for the cars themselves cost more, pay more in taxes, and the price of gasoline is higher. Because there are far more towns and villages along the roads in England, there is not the elaborate roadside catering for the needs of the traveler that there is now almost everywhere in the States. This can be inconvenient, but it does mean that driving through open country is pleasanter in Britain. And because of the comparatively small distances between towns, and the elaborate system of public transport by bus or local train, you can easily get along without a car at all in Britain. I have not driven a car myself for many years, and by using trains, buses, taxis, I am free of the worry about parking, which is becoming one of the nightmares of our age.

At first our railroad trains will look to you almost like toys. They seem about half the size of yours, although the gauge of the track is exactly the same. When I was young, we regarded our railroads as the best in the world; the locomotives, in spite of their size, were fast and powerful; the track was smooth; the ride was swift and comfortable. Now I must confess that our whole railroad system, chiefly because of the strain of two long hard wars, is not what it was, either in comparative speed or comfort. At one time we had three classes of tickets, first, second, and third, but then the second dropped out of use, and now we have, rather absurdly, first and third. Our stations were nearly all built a long time ago, and look it. The best that can be claimed for them is that, if you have not to wait too long in them and it is not pouring with rain, they are not without a vaguely romantic charm, suggesting the atmosphere of the later Dickens novels or perhaps the earlier Sherlock Holmes stories.

I shall now deal, fairly I hope, with some grumbles about Britain that I have heard over and over again from American visitors. To begin with, when you travel in Britain you are, so to speak, traveling *in time* (like a character in science fiction) as well as in space. The life of twenty centuries and more is all round you. I am writing this in my house on the tiny Isle of Wight, a few miles off the South Coast. From my study windows I can see, on the hill opposite, the burial mounds of Bronze Age chieftains; half-an-hour's drive would bring me to the remains of the Roman governor's villa; a quarter of an hour away is Carisbrooke Castle, where Charles the First was imprisoned; and I used to own a seventeenth-century manor house, a few miles away, that was supposed

British Information Service

The Rows in Chester are open galleries that continue from one building to the next, surrounding the main square. This is an ancient city, with a medieval wall that still stands.

to be haunted by his ghost. Every fine Sunday morning I walk through the countryside described by Tennyson (who lived near here) in *Maud* and other poems, and so it goes on, a rich thickness in time. When we were threatened invasion by Hitler in the summer of 1940, as a member of the Home Guard I spent nights on watch, at the summit of a neighboring hill, with the same kind of men, probably bearing the same family names, who were on watch there for the Spanish Armada and then for Napoleon's fleet. Here, then, you are in history, up to the neck in it.

Every spot is steeped in centuries of history

Now you cannot be in history, in a rich thickness of time, with so much that is old all round you, and yet have everything new and up to date, with all the latest devices for efficiency and comfort. If an inn is two or three centuries old, it cannot have all the advantages of a hotel built last year, cannot at one and the same time be charmingly old-fashioned, quaint, and rambling, and be all bright and new and super-efficient. You may have to choose between good plumbing, refrigeration, and air conditioning, on the one hand, and a romantic sense of

In the Cotswold Hills, a trainer starts on a sixteen-mile morning walk with his pack of hounds. He knows and calls each dog by name.

the past, on the other. Many English hotels have not enough bathrooms, partly because they were built before bathrooms were thought of (you took a bath in your bedroom, as I did when I was in college at Cambridge, where a round tin thing was filled with cans of warm water), and also because there is a building bylaw in England that all bathrooms must have access to the outer air.

Most British houses still do not have central heating, nor the large stoves found in Central and Northern Europe, but are warmed (sometimes rather tepidly) by old-fashioned open fireplaces. Some of them are so big that you can sit inside the chimney opening. American visitors, accustomed to houses and apartments being warmed throughout, soon begin to feel chilly in Britain if they move away from the fire.

Cornell Capa from *Magnum*

A title in a bookstall catches Mr. Priestley's eye as he walks along a London street.

Black Star

But there is another reason for the complaints about feeling cold in Britain. The truth is — and here I believe I release a secret never divulged before — that more than half of such complaints arise from one simple fact: the visitors are wearing thin, light clothes intended for American temperatures and quite wrong for normal British temperatures, indoors and outdoors. At this moment (it is the middle of January) I am probably wearing twice the thickness and weight of clothes that the average American man wears. But why not lighten my clothing and heighten the temperature of the room? Because I feel uncomfortable if I have to breathe warmer air. In the same way, I cannot sleep in a very warm bedroom but enjoy a warm weight of blankets in a very cold bedroom. All this, I agree, is partly mere habit, on both sides of the Atlantic.

I will now reveal a far more important secret, which is the essential clue to mysteries that have bewildered almost every visitor to England. Ever since the Industrial Revolution, England (not Britain, because we must leave Scotland and Wales out of this) has been the most urban country in the world, with a higher proportion of its population living and working in towns than any other country has, and yet *the English refuse to believe they have to live in towns.* Believe me, this is the great clue. It explains why the average English town is so dull, so dreary, so dark and shut-up at night, and why so much of the English countryside is so enchantingly beautiful. There are of course plenty of English towns that are very attractive indeed: for example, old cathedral cities like Canterbury, Salisbury, Wells; magnificent Oxford and Cambridge; an exquisite eighteenth-century inland resort like Bath; or that fine Regency seaside resort, Brighton. But the average market town is dull, and the industrial towns are nearly all horribly dreary. The visitor from America or the continent of Europe, compelled to spend the night in one of these towns, stares at the dismal sights and the darkening streets with grow-

Englishmen live in towns, but love the country

ing dismay and longs to be anywhere else. What can one do, where does one go? The shops are closed; there is no welcome glitter of neon lighting; there are no cheerful restaurants, no dance floors, no sounds of music.

What is the matter with these people? Do they hate life? No, they do not. But they have never really faced the fact that they are townsfolk and must make the very best out of living in a town. If they are not actually planning to remove into the country, they are at least vaguely dreaming of the day when they will leave the town forever, so they do not feel it is worth while making the town a cheerful, attractive place to live in. Moreover, they like to spend far more time at home, behind drawn blinds and curtains, than most other peoples do, and so do not care how unattractive their streets are, because all they want to do with the streets is to hurry along them to get home. There are of course plenty of inns, taverns, " pubs " (our short name for " public houses," that is, build-ings licensed to sell liquor), but even these, though often very snug and cozy inside, seem gloomily curtained and shuttered, withdrawn, from the outside.

All these English, a very large proportion of the total population, probably long influenced by the example of a landowning aristocracy, are countrymen at heart. As soon as they can afford a house out in the country, they will acquire one. And once out in the country, the neglected town left far behind, the whole picture magically changes. For the unspoiled English countryside (and much of it was ruined by nineteenth-century industry) is beyond question the finest in the world, with whole villages, manor houses, cottages, that look as if they came from some idyllic dream of life. (It is this dream that is haunt-ing the townsfolk.) The gardens blaze with flowers, for the English are born gardeners. The meadows, the woods, the smooth lawns, the in-numerable singing birds, the masses of wild flowers, the mossy ancient walls, the very graveyards: all is exquisite, an enchantment. It is the landscape of the great lyrical poets. It is for this reason that so many of us here detest the whole Industrial Revolution and all the more recent developments, industrial and social, that so rapidly turn fields and woods into cement and concrete, for they have gone far to ruin the most beautiful countryside on earth.

Drawings by Beuville

Historic Tower Bridge spans the mouth of the Thames, overlooking London docks that are crowded with foreign commerce. Visible at the right is the Tower of London.

A glance at the map of Europe shows the island of Britain, some six hundred miles long and not more than three hundred at its widest, anchored, so to speak, off the north coast of France. Actually only twenty-one miles of water separate Dover from Calais, but these are perhaps the most significant twenty-one miles in the world. Time after time they have saved Britain from invasion, and so have helped to preserve the liberties of Western Man.

*English
weather
suits the
English
temperament*

Britain is farther north than the United States, on the same latitude as Labrador. The reason that it has a very different climate from Labrador is that it is an island, not part of any great land mass, that it is partly washed by the Gulf Stream, and that the close proximity to the sea protects the island from any extremes of heat and cold. It used to be said that the climate of Britain was almost ideal, simply because there were hardly any days when a man could not move around out

of doors. But this man must have been either a robust farmer or a sporting squire, for English weather provides plenty of discomfort for modern and less hardy types of humanity. It has in fact too many coldish, dampish, gray days, though a really good English day either in early summer or early autumn still seems to me incomparable.

Many Americans find these damp, gray days or the raw and foggy winter weather very depressing, at the opposite extreme from the exhilarating days so often found in the States. I do not blame them, but our climate has its compensations: it tends to feed and soothe the nerves, not making the demands the electric atmosphere of America so often tends to make; and if the British are famous for their ease and calm in a crisis, I suspect they have been much helped by their climate. Again, on the vast dramatic continent of America, with its floods, droughts, blizzards, heat waves, hurricanes, tornadoes, Nature displays too often a frightening hostility, as if she sharply resented the presence of Man on the scene; and this hardly exists in Britain, where sun and wind and rain seem scaled down to a companionable and helpful degree.

Finally, nobody in Britain is really very far from the sea, that marvelous combined doorway-and-window. I am no enthusiastic seaman myself, yet there have been times, in the Middle West, in Eastern Europe, or in Africa, when I have begun to feel a strange sense of oppressiveness and melancholy, and then I have suddenly realized that I was in a place much too far from the sea.

Scotland, Wales, and Northwest England are mountainous. The more important peaks are only between 2,500 and 4,000 feet high; but the best of them are genuine craggy mountains, offering good sport for climbers, and claiming a few lives every year. The famous Lake District, home of the poets, is like a miniature Switzerland, and offers an astonishing variety of scenery all in a day's walk. I used to spend much time there, just after the First World War, scrambling up and down the peaks; but my later taste, rejoining that of my early youth, preferred the moors, narrow green valleys, the white streams, and gray stone villages, or the Yorkshire Dales, near where I was born.

The grazing flock at the edge of Lake Buttermere typifies the romantic beauty of the Lake District. Here, scenery and literary associations combine to delight the visitor.

A forest of smokestacks gives this Yorkshire town a grim and sooty aspect. In the heart of an industrial area, Halifax has a thriving carpet factory.

The center and the east of England consist of two plains; and then further south, roughly parallel with the South Coast, are the rounded, grassy chalk hills known as the Downs. The highly industrialized areas are largely in the center, called the Midlands, and in the North, for it was in these regions that the largest deposits of coal were found. Here, during the Industrial Revolution and throughout the nineteenth century, sprang up the foundries and factories and warehouses and thousands of mean, dark streets so often described and denounced by Victorian writers like Dickens, Carlyle, Ruskin. During the last thirty years or so, many of the newer industries, the so-called " light industries,"

have built their factories, no longer dependent on coal, away from the old industrial areas, either in the Southwest (where most of the new airplane works are, near Bristol and Gloucester) or within fifty miles of London.

Industry produces goods for export

The richest farming country is in the flat Eastern districts, which are drier than those in the West; and there is a magnificent tradition of good agriculture, dating back to the eighteenth century, running from Suffolk up to East Yorkshire. But nearly everywhere the pasture is good, so that British cattle, sheep, and pigs are among the very best in the world. If the population could be reduced by a half, the British people could live superbly off their own produce; but we have over fifty million persons living on this island and so cannot feed ourselves. Thus we have to export manufactured goods to pay for both the foodstuffs and the various raw materials of industry that we have to buy abroad. This makes our situation far more difficult and precarious than yours.

Who are these people? Like Americans, they are a mixture of races, but in Britain the chief mixing happened a long time ago, over a thousand years. The principal ingredients in the mixture were the Celts, who were here first (though preceded by other peoples in smaller numbers), and successive waves of Nordic peoples — Angles, Saxons, Jutes, Danes. It would not be difficult to explain the English character in terms of this mixture. The Englishman outside is a cool,

British Information Service

The iron and steel industry has long been important in Britain's economy. This blast furnace in Lincolnshire is the largest in Europe.

obstinate, practical Anglo-Saxon. Inside he is a moody, romantic, imaginative Celt. These two different strains can be discovered throughout English life and literature. Other people looking at the English from the outside overlook and forget the Celtic strain. They are encouraged to do this often by the English themselves, who are romantic and imaginative people pretending hard to be unromantic and unimaginative.

The most foolish thing ever said about the English came from Napoleon, when he called us " a nation of shopkeepers." That is just what we are not. We are among the worst shopkeepers in the world. Our salesmanship is notoriously bad. Other nations continually overtake us and outsell us. How do we keep going then, fifty million of us on our crowded island? Not by hard work, because many other nations habitually work harder than we do. Actually we are not very fond of steady hard work. On the other hand, we are capable of making sudden prodigious efforts if the occasion, preferably a very dramatic one, calls for it — thus, after Dunkirk, these people worked miracles of production, staying at their machines and benches until they dropped. Winston Churchill, himself a romantic, imaginative man, succeeded as war leader just because he knew how to appeal to the imaginative side of the British, the hidden romantic who comes out and takes charge when told that ruin threatens him and that his back is against the wall.

Opposing elements make up the character of Englishmen

It is not the calm, practical, outer man but the inner, secret, imaginative man, the Celt within, who really keeps us going. For other nations beat us at routine production and salesmanship, the practical jobs. What we are best at are precisely those tasks that demand imagination and inventiveness. If we were not a highly inventive people we could no longer exist on this island, not after taking the full fury of two terrible wars, into which we flung all our manpower and savings. Thus, this new age is dominated by things like radar, jet engines, television, penicillin; and these are all British discoveries. It is more than likely that we are closer to the peaceful use of atomic power than any other country; and indeed we are making great sacrifices to this end.

If all this begins to sound like boasting, I offer you my apologies, but what I am trying here to establish is the supreme importance of the imaginative side of the British character, so often carefully concealed by the British themselves as individuals. But of course it is largely the secret of English literature, so rich in lyrical poetry, drama, romance, humor. If the British were what other peoples often think they are — utterly prosaic, cautious, calculating, dull — then where did this wonderful literature come from? I do not blame anybody for misjudging my fellow countrymen. They ask to be misjudged. They are rather proud and rather shy, so all too often they turn a blank mask on the world, carefully hiding the essential imaginative, romantic, inventive Briton. But he is there all the time, and our earth has been vastly enriched by his innumerable creations.

Our political and social system is different from yours. This is not a very profound or original observation, but there is rather more in it than first meets the eye. By declaring at once that the two systems are different, I am really announcing that here there will be no competition between them, that we shall not have to decide which is the better system. Men can live a reasonably good life under either system. It is my experience that most Americans are curious about British political and social life but often have very strange ideas about it. I know because I have answered questions in all manner of places between New York and San Francisco. The British system is harder to explain than the American, just as a gnarled old tree is harder to draw than a pole or a pylon. The American Constitution is not two hundred years old; it was designed by enlightened and public-spirited men; it is the product of a rational age. The British Constitution has grown like the old tree. It is crammed with apparent contradictions and absurdities. But then, so are most people. And nobody can deny that this political and social Crazy Castle suits the British.

Now you are American citizens. But I am not a British *citizen;* I am a British *subject,* a subject of Her Majesty Queen Elizabeth the Second. You might say that I live here in England by her gracious permission. This country belongs to her. The navy, army, air force are all hers. Nearly everything crimson or scarlet one sees here, from the robes of the judges to the round boxes (known as " pillar boxes ") for posting letters in the streets, belongs to her. Nearly all important official announcements and declarations are made in her name. All titles are given by her. Newly appointed Cabinet ministers

British scientists and technicians have been responsible for many of the discoveries that have shaped the twentieth century. Today they are pioneers in aircraft engineering.

have to go to Buckingham Palace to kiss her hand. Yes, we are all her subjects, millions and millions and millions of us — in all possible shades of human coloring. And no doubt at this point your republican blood is up; you feel a contempt for a man who will submit to such tyranny. But there is no

An important moment following the coronation of Elizabeth II. Leaving Westminster Abbey, the queen enters the golden state coach, attended by her maids of honor.

tyranny. This royal ownership (which must not be confused with what the queen really owns as a person) is a kind of fiction. There has to be an official head of the state, and in Britain, whose official name is The United Kingdom, this head is the reigning monarch.

Contingents of the Royal Air Force (left) and the Brigade of Guards stand by. The elaborate pomp and ceremony of the coronation are rooted in centuries of tradition.

From Elizabeth the First, who possessed enormous personal powers and made full use of them, to our own smiling Elizabeth the Second, across four centuries of intrigue and strife, trial and error, the real power of the Crown has been whittled away, so that now we may truthfully say that the monarch reigns but does not rule. All genuine power to rule the country is now vested in Parliament and Cabinet. The queen, whose name appears on all important state documents, whose head is to be seen on

The queen's likeness appears on coins.

coins and stamps, is really a symbolic figure, representing the State in its executive capacity. Her direct political power and influence, as a person, are negligible.

This does not mean that she does nothing but appear in processions and show herself like a super-movie star. She has a great number of serious duties to perform, as titular head of the State: she presides at certain councils; the prime minister and his senior ministers frequently report to her; she sees all very important documents and dispatches; she takes a genuine interest in the many appointments she has to make officially, even though she makes them on the advice of the politicians or the heads of the fighting services. But she cannot behave, as kings and queens did long ago, as if the country really belonged to her. And because she is so comparatively powerless, is hedged about by all manner of restrictions, she is never subjected to savage criticism and bitter personal attacks by politicians and the press, as our kings and queens used to be. Because she has to be dutiful, polite, charming, then we, her so-called subjects, try to be on our best behavior with her. She is the living symbol — and a good-looking young woman makes an excellent living symbol — of our feeling for, and attachment to, our country. So when the London crowds are in an exalted patriotic mood, they can mass themselves densely in front of Buckingham Palace, and shout and cheer for the queen until she and her husband and perhaps her small children come out on the balcony to smile and wave in response to this mood.

Royalty has influence and glamour

Now all this will seem foolish or delightful to you, according to your temperament. But the system has certain advantages that are worth pointing out. For example, members of a special family, who have been trained to carry out their special duties, cut a better figure as a representative head of the State than do elderly politicians, retired soldiers, and the like. They are more glamorous. Some of the old magic of kingship still illuminates them. They remain much longer on the job. (Queen Victoria reigned sixty years, and in the last part of her reign the fabulous old lady restored the popularity of the monarchy that it had lost earlier.) And unless a country has a very strong republican feeling and tradition, as America has, this system, a limited monarchy, is safer than any other. It is almost a guarantee against any form of dictatorship. The reason for this is not hard to discover. In a limited monarchy like ours, all the glamour and magic, all the showmanship and publicity, all the romantic traditional ceremonies and the grandest parades, are attached to, and associated with, a person whose power from the outset is strictly limited and cannot be increased. This leaves no room for an unscrupulously ambitious politician to capture all this glamour and excitement for himself. He cannot begin to compete with the Crown.

But is it possible to have a king or queen at the head of a truly democratic society steadily moving nearer and nearer to social equality? Something like this has been achieved in the Scandinavian countries, which have comparatively small and highly progressive communities. But in my opinion it has not been achieved yet in Britain, where the presence and great popularity of the royal family, at the apex of the social pyramid, do tend to preserve a class structure of society, just because they strengthen that pyramid and save it from collapse. Though royalty no longer has any political power, it has a good deal of social and cultural influence. The socially ambitious, the climbers and snobs, delight in attending functions at which royalty will be present, and like to share the same tastes and amusements.

Britain is often said to have " the Mother of Parliaments." She is rather an untidy old lady. She has a House of Lords and a House of Commons. The House of Lords, to which nobody is elected and in which all the members are peers of the realm, is more at home in Gilbert and Sullivan's *Iolanthe* than it is in modern political life. The real seat of government is the House of Commons, which consists at present of six hundred and thirty members, all elected by and representing their own districts, known in Britain as " constituencies." They are paid, not handsomely, and receive some expense money. All but a few belong to one or other of our two great political parties, Conservative or Labor. After every general election the party that has the majority of members forms a government, headed by the prime minister, who chooses his ablest colleagues as Cabinet ministers, each of them responsible for one of the more

The queen attracts crowds wherever she goes. Often they are not only curious but friendly and affectionate as well.

Kemsley Picture Service

Arnold Newman

The dignity of English courts is enhanced by the traditional robes and wigs of lawyers and judges.

important state departments. One party can be in power for a maximum term of five years, after which there must be another election; but often during this term the government is defeated in the House of Commons — that is, it is outvoted by the other party, known as the Opposition — or it obviously loses all its support in the country, is savagely attacked in the newspapers and at meetings everywhere, and then the prime minister offers the king or queen his resignation, the government dissolves, and there is another general election.

Much of the time in the House of Commons is spent on replies to questions put down in advance by members, especially members of the opposing party.

"The Mother of Parliaments"

Ministers (or their assistants, known usually as undersecretaries) must answer publicly on behalf of their particular ministries or departments. This system of public questioning-and-answering is one of the best features of Parliament, because it compels the government to explain itself and is an effective check on any abuse of power. During the summer of 1940, when Britain faced Hitler alone, was threatened by invasion, was turning itself upside down to arm itself, and Churchill's government had been compelled to take over vast emergency powers, Ernest Bevin, then Minister of Labor and busy performing prodigies of hasty reorganization, was faced with a Question in the House of Commons. " Did the Minister realize that many of his officials in Labor Exchanges were now behaving in a very brusque, rude fashion? " That was the question put to Bevin, while the fate of the whole Empire hung in the balance, while at any moment the German bombers might darken the sky and send London up in smoke and flame. And Bevin stood up, said he was glad his attention had been called to this incivility on the part of his officials, who would be instructed to improve their manners, no matter how busy they might be. I often grumble about Parliament — all Englishmen do — but when I find myself beginning to despair, I remember that story: the wonderful old " Mother of Parliaments " at her best.

For a long time after the Norman Conquest there were two languages in England — the Anglo-Saxon of the common folk and the Norman French of

The House of Commons is the real seat of government, and it has been a model for legislative bodies all over the world. Its sessions are often marked by lively exchanges between Conservatives and Laborites, but a strong sense of fair play prevails.

the court and the barons and their followers. The difference in both language and social status is reflected in English usage to this day. Thus, when we wish to refer to the animals themselves, we say " sheep," like the Anglo-Saxons who had to look after them. But when we think of them in terms of the kitchen and the dining hall, then we say " mutton," borrowing it from the language of the conquerors, who ate the animals but did not look after them. So the Saxon tended the " swine "; his Norman lord ate the " pork." And in this and a thousand other ways, wherever you are, if you speak English, you are still entangled with English history. The language you use, like all the nations that use it, is itself a marvelously rich mixture. It has its earthy " sheep and swine " side, its more artificial and cultivated " mutton and pork " side. It is a magnificent reservoir of words, chiefly fed originally by two great streams, one from the North, the other from the South by way of Rome and Normandy. (But with some ves-

This characteristic scene in Kent contrasts the ethereal beauty of blossoming fruit trees with the sturdy plainness of the farm buildings.

tiges of older tongues still remaining: in my boyhood I heard shepherds counting their flocks, muttering the ancient Celtic numerals.) The Northern and the Southern, the earthy and the cultivated, the Celt and the Saxon, the poetical and the prosaic, the dreamily imaginative and the stoutly practical, the Monarchy and the Parliament, the traditional and the boldly inventive — notice how in English language, society, character, we keep coming upon these pairs of opposites!

English literature has immense richness and vitality

It is the existence of all these pairs of opposites (and we could have found plenty more of them) that makes nearly everything characteristically English so difficult to define exactly, so easy to misunderstand. And because English literature is the expression of what is essentially English — I do not say " British " now because we never talk about " British literature," but what is meant is in fact the literature of Britain, not of England alone — all these and other pairs of opposites have been at work in it, complicating its character but also giving it immense variety, richness, vitality. The language itself, so large and confused, was a long time settling down into something that could be easily written and easily understood. Chaucer, a genius, is the first master of the newly fashioned instrument, and even in him, right at the outset, you can find double, opposing strains — a wistful delicacy and a gross, ribald humor. Then, with a leap to the later Elizabethans, we find the instrument in full pitch and force, piping and thundering in the hands of the dramatists and lyric poets. Shakespeare himself is at their head, Shakespeare who can move swiftly and surely from the extreme of tragedy, black and bitter as death, to the opposing extreme of uproarious, bawdy farce, from King Lear and Hamlet to bully Bottom and Falstaff.

Later, descending from this supreme height of poetical and dramatic achievement, the stream, never as magically fresh again, broadens out into a majestic river of lyrical verse and persuasive prose, and the names and the books multiply and become legion. And always we discover, whether we survey whole centuries or some brief period, an age of writers or one single man of genius, some pair of opposites at work again, creating variety, richness, vitality, like electricity flashing between two poles. (And now the river has divided into two, for you have of course an American literature, fed far back from the same source but now expressing another place, another people, another dream of life.)

Fiction, prose drama, the essay, bring us increasingly to whatever is down-to-earth or found in the market place, to the homely and the humorous, to the sturdy old Saxon strain. Yet the poets, still haunted by the ancient Celt, listen to the songbirds and to the cries of agony and ecstasy from their own hearts, stare at the wild flowers and deep into their own troubled minds, and, out of it all, make music. All the opposites, all the strange contrasts, are here in this literature, from a long, long time ago to this very day: the black mills and dark towns and, only an hour away, the exquisite, hazy countryside; Parliament arguing and voting on its crowded benches and, 'round the corner, a queen riding a white horse.

A Literary Map of
BRITAIN

NORTH

ENGLAND

Whitby
YORKSHIRE
Jarrow
TYNE
DURHAM
SWALE MOORS
YORK
PENNINE CHAI
NORTHUMBERLAND
Lancaster
CHEVIOT HILLS
BAY
Grasmere
LAKE DISTRICT
CUMBERLAND
Berwick
TWEED
Abbotsford
HOLYROOD
LEITH
Ecclefechan
Aberdeen
KINCAR
DEE
GRAMPIAN MTS.
Dunsinane
Kirriemuir
Dundee
Banff
BANFF
SPEY
MORAY
Forres
Birnam Wood ×
Scone
Perth
BIRTH
TAY
FIRTH OF FORTH
FIFE
Dunfermline
Edinburgh
MIDLOTHIAN
BLYTHE
DUMFRIES
SOLWAY FIRTH
MORAY FIRTH
NAIRN
Inverness
INVERNESS
LOCH NESS
ROSS AND CROMARTY
SCOTLAND
ARGYLL
Bannockburn
Glasgow
CLYDE
RENFREW
AFTON
KIRKCUD-BRIGHT
ISLE OF MAN
Ayr
Auchinleck
DOON
AYR
GTOWN
FIRTH OF CLYDE
SKYE
MULL
ISLAY
NORTH CHANNEL
HEBRIDES
GIANT'S CAUSEWAY
Belfast
ANTRIM
DOWN
BANN
NORTHERN
LONDONDERRY
LOUGH NEAGH
ARMAGH
LO
IRELAND
TYRONE
MONAGHAN
CAVAN
DON

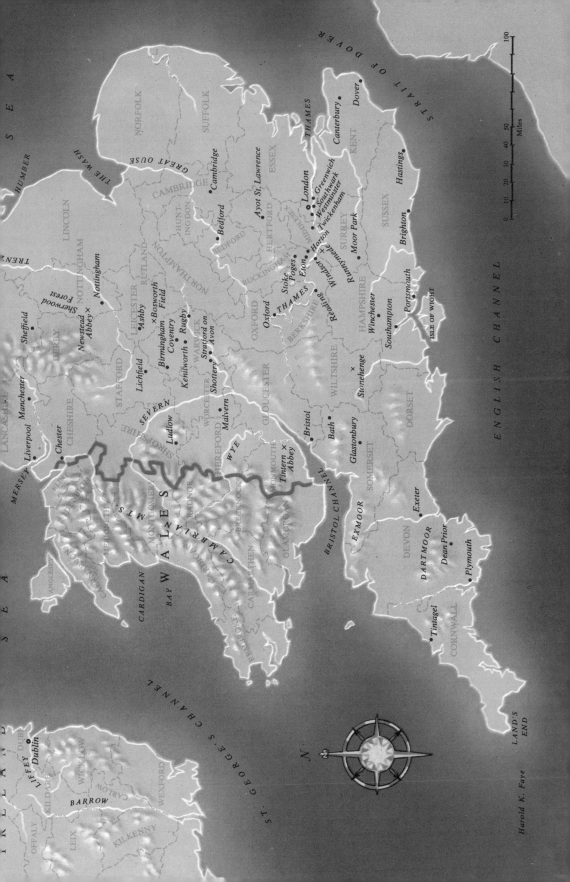

STRAIT OF DOVER

ENGLISH CHANNEL

NORTH SEA

IRISH SEA

ST. GEORGE'S CHANNEL

CARDIGAN BAY

BRISTOL CHANNEL

LAND'S END

NORFOLK

SUFFOLK

GREAT OUSE

THE WASH

HUMBER

TRENT

LINCOLN

NOTTINGHAM

DERBY

CHESHIRE

LANCASHIRE

MERSEY

CAMBRIDGE

HUNT.INGDON

RUTLAND

NORTHAMPTON

LEICESTER

STAFFORD

SHROPSHIRE

WORCESTER

HEREFORD

BEDFORD

ESSEX

HERTFORD

BUCKINGHAM

OXFORD

MIDDLESEX

KENT

SURREY

SUSSEX

BERKSHIRE

HAMPSHIRE

WILTSHIRE

DORSET

SOMERSET

EXMOOR

DEVON

DARTMOOR

CORNWALL

GLOUCESTER

MONMOUTH

GLAMORGAN

BRECKNOCK

RADNOR

MONTGOMERY

CARDIGAN

CARMARTHEN

PEMBROKE

ANGLESEY

CARNARVON

DENBIGH

FLINT

MERIONETH

CAMBRIAN MTS.

WALES

SEVERN

WYE

THAMES

THAMES

RUNNIMEDE

ISLE OF WIGHT

Dublin
LIFFEY
DUB.

WICKLOW
KILDARE
CARLOW
WEXFORD
OFFALY
LEIX
KILKENNY
BARROW

Sheffield
Manchester
Liverpool
Chester
Nottingham
Newstead × Abbey
Sherwood Forest
Ashby ×
Bosworth Field
Birmingham
Coventry
Rugby
Kenilworth × Warwick
Stratford on Avon
Shottery
Lichfield
Ludlow
Malvern
Cambridge
Bedford
Ayot St. Lawrence
London
Greenwich
Southwark
Westminster
Twickenham
Horton
Moor Park
Stoke Poges
Eton
Windsor
Reading
Oxford
Canterbury
Dover
Hastings
Brighton
Portsmouth
Southampton
Winchester
Stonehenge ×
Bristol
Bath
Glastonbury
Tintern × Abbey
Exeter
Dean Prior
Plymouth
Tintagel

Harold K. Faye

100
90
80
70
60
50
40
30
20
10
0
Miles

N.

THE ANGLO-SAXON

W HEN THE Anglo-Saxon tribes migrated from northern Europe to the British Isles in the fifth century, they probably found ruins of towns and a few roads, for the Romans had withdrawn from England only fifty years before. In the three hundred years of their occupation, the Romans had made slow progress against the forests, swamps, and moors. Before their arrival, the native Celts inhabited the island, and their civilization continued side by side with that brought by the Roman invaders. Since the Celts had no written language, their myths and legends were not recorded for many centuries. English literature thus begins with the first inhabitants after the Romans — the Anglo-Saxons.

Why do we choose 449 and 1066 as the dates for this period? In 449 a band of Jutes from the peninsula of Jutland, or Denmark, crossed the stormy North Sea in their ships to settle in Kent. They were followed by wave after wave of

Stonehenge, pictured above, is a group of gigantic stones arranged at some prehistoric time in a series of four circles on Salisbury Plain.

PERIOD · 449-1066

Jutes, Angles (or " hookmen "), and Saxons (or " swordsmen "). Until an
" Anglia " or " Angle-land " came into existence, we cannot really speak of
England or an English period at all. The second date, 1066, marks the invasion by the Norman-French, the last invasion of England. With that date begins a new ruling class, a new way of life, and a new language.

ROMAN RULE IN BRITAIN

Let us look back about five hundred years from the date 449.

Julius Caesar raided Britain in 55 and 54 B.C.; within a hundred years the
Romans had conquered the island. They held it with a relatively small number of soldiers for more than three centuries. During this time, civilization
advanced and commerce flourished. The people built solid stone villas and
towns. They had sunken baths, glass windows, and a kind of central heating.
Ruins of a Roman public bath are to be seen today in the city of Bath.

The Romans were in Britain on military assignment (the Latin word for
camp — *castra* — may still be seen in the names of Chester, Manchester, and

Lancaster). Although Hadrian's wall, a great fortification running across the island near the Scottish border, was built around A.D. 123 to prevent raids from the savage Picts and Scots, life was mainly peaceful and prosperous.

In the fourth and fifth centuries the Roman Empire started crumbling. When its legions were called home to protect Rome from hostile invaders, the Roman imprint on Britain began to fade.

GERMANIC INVASIONS

Although they were called by different names, the Jutes, the Angles, and the Saxons belonged to the same Germanic race. They came to Britain for conquest and settlement. For a brief time they met resistance from the native Britons (Celts) under the leadership of the half-legendary King Arthur; eventually some of those tribes fled to Wales and Ireland. The Angles and Saxons were left to make themselves at home. Of their many kingdoms, the greatest was Mercia, formed of several smaller kingdoms and occupying the central part of Britain. The names of the Saxon kingdoms still persist in the counties of Essex, Sussex, and Middlesex.

In the eighth and ninth centuries the Danes threatened to destroy the Saxon rule by pillaging villages, seizing booty, and demanding tribute. They came in their ships, plundered and burned as they swept across the land, and then were gone again. Later, however, they conquered and made permanent settlements, controlling most of the territory in the northeast. In this area, the " Danelaw," the Danish invaders remained to become a part of the mixture of races that was to make England.

WHAT WERE THE ANGLO-SAXONS LIKE?

The Angles and Saxons, hardy and athletic, were wandering, seafaring tribes. When they arrived in Britain, they were yet semibarbarous, worshipers of Odin. The great ocean, the cold winter, the thunder, and the sun were their gods. They had a grim sense of Fate, which they called Wyrd (from which our word " weird " comes). During a storm at sea, in the middle of a fierce battle, the Anglo-Saxon called upon his gods, did the best he could do, and then left the outcome in the hands of Wyrd.

Their superstitions and religious beliefs were part of their daily lives. Even now our weekdays are named after those ancient gods: Tuesday for the dark god Tiw; Wednesday for the warlike Woden; Thursday for Thor, the god of thunder; Friday for Frigga, the goddess of love and the home.

The Anglo-Saxons were pagan and cruelly ferocious, but they possessed noble qualities, too. They were faithful; they were earnest; they were brave. They were not afraid of anything — a whale or a dragon or a sea monster, a Celt or a Roman. They liked action and fighting and contests of physical strength. Fair play and good sportsmanship were guiding motives among them.

A leader was admired most for his generosity and was called a " ring giver " or " bracelet bestower." In a thane (noble), the greatest virtue was loyalty, even until death. The Anglo-Saxons did not let one another down; truth, frankness, and straight dealing were practiced as well as preached.

These roving tribes were used to hardships. The wintry, lonely seas, the gray skies, and the mist of the British Isles made an environment similar to that of their homes along the Baltic and the North Seas, where the forests were dark and the fog rose from the water. They were a melancholy race, and their gloom and moodiness persisted through later English literature.

They admired endurance, which has remained a part of the English character from the time of Beowulf's seven-day swimming match to the air bombardment of England during World War II. There is little difference between Winston Churchill encouraging the English in those darkest months of the war, when England stood alone, and the old East Saxon leader who nearly a thousand years ago said to his men:

> " Heart must be keener, courage the hardier,
> Bolder our mood as our band diminisheth."

HOW DID THE ANGLO-SAXONS LIVE?

As the years passed and the tribes and kingdoms prospered, Anglo-Saxon life reached the level described in *Beowulf*, the English national epic. After the hunt or battle, the followers of the king or chieftain would meet in the mead hall, which was a banquet room attached to the living quarters of the king. There thanes and athelings (nobles) would gather

to receive gifts from the king, to eat with their comrades, and to boast of their exploits.

Down the center of the mead hall ran a shallow trench in which fires were built. Flanking the fires were two long tables, where the guests sat on the outer side in order to face the warmth. The meat was eaten from communal dishes, catch-as-catch-can, with fingers and hunting knives. Scraps and bones were thrown to the dogs at their feet. The favorite drink was mead, a powerful brew of water and honey, fermented with malt and yeast.

In the middle of the hall stood the Saxon scop (poet) or gleeman (singer) with his harp to entertain the warriors. His memory had to be unusual, and his job of holding the attention of both the old and the young called forth all his skill. He gave news, sang songs, told stories, and asked riddles. For the Anglo-Saxon, the riddle was an intellectual exercise. Can you guess the subject of this one?

> I'm prized by men, in the meadows I'm found,
> Gathered on hill-sides, and hunted in groves;
> From dale and from down, by day I am brought.
> Airy wings carry me, cunningly store me,
> Hoarding me safe. Yet soon men take me;
> Drained into vats, I'm dangerous grown.
> I tie up my victim, and trip him, and throw him;
> Often I floor a foolish old churl.
> Who wrestles with me, and rashly would measure
> His strength against mine, will straightway find himself
> Flung to the ground, flat on his back,
> Unless he leave his folly in time,
> Put from his senses and power of speech,
> Robbed of his might, bereft of his mind,
> Of his hands and feet. Now find me my name,
> Who can bind and enslave men so upon earth,
> And bring fools low in broad daylight.

ANGLO-SAXON GOVERNMENT

The Anglo-Saxons governed themselves democratically by war councils when they were on the move and by village meetings when they settled down. The war chief and even the king were elected, though family connections as well as abilities were considered. The king had around him his followers or thanes to whom he gave protection and allegiance. In turn, the thanes watched over the farmlands and collected the taxes — in grain, in cheese, or in meat.

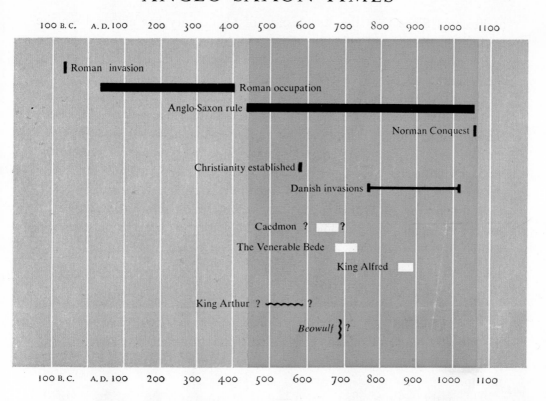

Decisions were made in town meetings or folkmoots — meetings called to talk things over. (Today a "moot point" means a question that can be argued.) Tribes and even small kingdoms were hardly more than large groups of interconnected families; but in his folkmoot a man was independent, and he was able to cast a vote.

BEGINNINGS OF CHRISTIANITY

Christianity existed in England side by side with the paganism of roving Germanic tribes, for Roman Britain had been largely Christian. That religion continued to flourish in the Celtic settlements in Ireland and Wales. The Jutes, Angles, and Saxons invaded England by force; Christian monks later invaded it peacefully.

The story is told that in 587 a certain abbot, seeing some English boys being sold as slaves in Rome, asked who they were. "Angles," he was told. "Not Angles," he answered, admiring their fresh complexions and fair hair, "but angels." When the abbot later became Pope Gregory, he sent Augustine in 597 as a missionary to England to Christianize these "angels." Augustine subsequently built a church at Canterbury, where he later became the first archbishop. Since then the Archbishop of Canterbury has always been the leading churchman of England.

But no one year or one man brought Christianity to the island. Throughout the seventh and eighth centuries churches and monasteries were set up in northern England, where Christianity had spread from Ireland, as it had come to the southern ports of Ireland from Rome. (See the map on page 35.) Here the monks laboriously copied old manuscripts, wrote new ones, and preserved much of what we know about those times. Especially are we indebted to the monk known as the Venerable Bede, who wrote in Latin a *Church History of the English People*. In it he tells of Caedmon, an unlearned keeper of cows in the monastery of Whitby, who in a sudden vision received the power of song. The fragment of Caedmon's hymn quoted by Bede is the most ancient Old English poem that has an identified date and author.

ANGLO-SAXON LITERATURE

The Anglo-Saxons brought from their homes on the continent stories which they told repeatedly — stories of personal achievement and endeavor which they hoped would be imitated. Thus the first literature of these people was preserved in their memories and was passed on to later generations by word of mouth.

This oral literature was in verse — long narratives of heroes, stories of the wanderings of minstrels, pagan charms sung at harvest time, and riddles recited in the mead hall. Today we can read a few battle poems, some short pieces about explorers, several songs like " The Seafarer " filled with the Old English loneliness and restless wandering, and the great epic *Beowulf,* high point of Anglo-Saxon literature. Their forms of verse were easy to invent, easy to memorize. The typical line has a swinging, four-beat rhythm; and the repetition of similar sounds makes it as unforgettable as " Peter Piper picked a peck of pickled peppers."

BEGINNINGS OF UNITY

When the Danes burst upon England in the eighth and ninth centuries, they were a terrible menace to the kingdoms of Northumbria, Mercia, East Anglia, and those of the Saxons. (See the map on page 35.) Finally, King Alfred of Wessex (871–900), a wise Saxon leader, was able to unite his people and to force the Danes to the northeast part of England. He then attempted to revive the education of his countrymen, for it had been interrupted by the Danish raids. Alfred, stressing the importance of using the native tongue in writing, was influential in getting Bede's *Church History of the English People* translated and in starting the *Anglo-Saxon Chronicle* to record British history.

BRITAIN
1066-1485

BRITAIN
IN ALFRED'S TIME

SCOTLAND

NORTHUMBRIA

SCOTLAND

YORK

Danelaw

WALES

MERCIA

EAST
ANGLIA

ESSEX

WESSEX

SUSSEX

KENT

Bannockburn [1]
Dumfermline [2]
Edinburgh

Hadrian's Wall [3]

Jarrow [4]

Whitby [5]

IRELAND

Lancaster

York

Dublin

Manchester

Chester

Sherwood
Forest

Bosworth
Field [6]

Ashby [7]

Coventry

Cambridge [8]

WALES

ENGLAND

Oxford [9]

Bath [10]

Runnymede [11]

Westminster [12]

London

Canterbury [16]

Stonehenge [13]

Southwark [15]

SOUTH BRITAIN [14]

Hastings [17]

1 Robert the Bruce won a significant victory over the English here. **2** Setting for "Sir Patrick Spens." **3** Built in 123 A.D., against raids by Picts and Scots. **4** The Venerable Bede lived in the monastery here. **5** Caedmon entered the monastery at Whitby. **6** Richard III was slain here in 1485, ending the Wars of the Roses. **7** Site of famous tournaments. **8** Cambridge University dates from the twelfth and thirteenth centuries. **9** Oxford University was organized

of a Roman public bath. **11** Magna Charta signed 1215. **12** Caxton set up his printing press here. **13** Prehistoric monuments. **14** Traditionally, the region of King Arthur and his knights. **15** Chaucer's pilgrims stayed overnight here, at the Tabard Inn. **16** Chaucer's pilgrims traveled on this road to Canterbury. The Cathedral here was the scene of the murder of Thomas à Becket in 1170. **17** In the last invasion of England, William of Normandy defeated

King Alfred united England, if only for about thirty years, against great odds. Alfred's successors, neither so wise nor so fortunate as he, had a century and a half of unrest before the Norman-French conquered England and brought the Anglo-Saxon period to an end in 1066.

SUMMARY

After the Jutes came to England in 449, they were followed by larger tribes of Angles and Saxons — all belonging to the same Germanic race. The traces of Roman occupation of many centuries had begun to disappear, and the Anglo-Saxons, after driving the native Celts into Wales and Ireland, set up small kingdoms from which England (" Angle-land ") finally developed.

When the Anglo-Saxons arrived in England, they were semibarbarous and pagan. Only fragments of their early writings exist: some anonymous short poems, riddles, and the epic *Beowulf*. They reflect the admiration of physical endurance, the melancholy disposition, devotion to duty, and sense of loyalty that were characteristic of these hardy people. Modern Englishmen, recognizing some of these qualities in themselves today, are glad to claim part of their heritage from the Anglo-Saxons.

Christianity invaded England peacefully. Later Christian influences are shown in the manuscripts composed or copied in the monasteries. Through these writings, individual writers appear: Bede (writer of a church history in Latin) and Caedmon (writer of religious poems in Old English).

King Alfred probably was the greatest force in unifying England. Not only did he force the Danes to the northeast part of England, but he also revived the education of his countrymen, and welded them into one people.

The Seafarer

Translated by J. Duncan Spaeth

From earliest times to the present day, English literature reflects the vital part played by the sea in English life. " The Seafarer " may be called the ancestor of the many poems about the sea in this volume. It was written by an unknown author in the fifth or sixth century, but its powerful descriptions, metrical charm, and flowing alliteration please a modern reader. These qualities have been skillfully preserved by the translator. He has, however, made one interesting change. The original poem is not written as a

"The Seafarer," from *Old English Poetry*, translated by J. Duncan Spaeth, published by Princeton University Press. Reprinted by permission of the publisher.

dialogue, but Dr. Spaeth sensed in it two opposite attitudes. His arrangement shows the enthusiasm of a youth for new adventure, in spite of the warnings from an old sailor of the hardships to be faced on the sea.

THE OLD SAILOR

True is the tale that I tell of my travels,
Sing of my seafaring sorrows and woes;
Hunger and hardship's heaviest burdens,
Tempest and terrible toil of the deep,
Daily I've borne on the deck of my boat.   5
Fearful the welter of waves that encompassed me,
Watching at night on the narrow bow,
As she drove by the rocks, and drenched me with spray.
Fast to the deck my feet were frozen,
Gripped by the cold, while care's hot surges   10
My heart o'erwhelmed, and hunger's pangs
Sapped the strength of my sea-weary spirit.

Little he knows whose lot is happy,
Who lives at ease in the lap of the earth,
How, sick at heart, o'er icy seas,   15
Wretched I ranged the winter through,
Bare of joys, and banished from friends,
Hung with icicles, stung by hailstones.
Nought I heard but the hollow boom
Of wintry waves, or the wild swan's whoop.   20
For singing I had the solan's° scream;
For peals of laughter, the yelp of the seal;
The sea-mew's cry, for the mirth of the mead hall.
Shrill through the roar of the shrieking gale
Lashing along the sea-cliff's edge,   25
Pierces the ice-plumed petrel's° defiance,
And the wet-winged eagle's answering scream.
Little he dreams that drinks life's pleasure,
By danger untouched in the shelter of towns,
Insolent and wine-proud, how utterly weary   30
Oft I wintered on open seas.
Night fell black, from the north it snowed
Harvest of hail.

THE YOUTH

Oh, wildly my heart
Beats in my bosom and bids me to try   35
The tumble and surge of seas tumultuous,
Breeze and brine and the breakers' roar.

21. *solan* (sō'lăn): a sea bird, like a gull. (The small circle° is used in poetry throughout this book to indicate a footnote, which is identified by the number of the line in which the footnoted word appears.) 26. *petrel:* a sea bird.

Daily, hourly, drives me my spirit
Outward to sail, far countries to see.
Liveth no man so large in his soul,   40
So gracious in giving, so gay in his youth,
In deeds so daring, so dear to his lord,
But frets his soul for his sea adventure,
Fain to try what fortune shall send.
Harping he needs not, nor hoarding of treasure;   45
Nor woman can win him, nor joys of the world.
Nothing does please but the plunging billows;
Ever he longs, who is lured by the sea.
Woods are abloom, the wide world awakens,
Gay are the mansions, the meadows most fair;   50
These are but warnings, that haste on his journey
Him whose heart is hungry to taste
The perils and pleasures of the pathless deep.

THE OLD SAILOR

Dost mind the cuckoo mournfully calling?
The summer's watchman sorrow forebodes.   55
What does the landsman that wantons in luxury,
What does he reck the rough sea's foe,
The cares of the exile, whose keel has explored
The uttermost parts of the ocean ways!

THE YOUTH

Sudden my soul starts from her prison house,   60
Soareth afar o'er the sounding main;
Hovers on high, o'er the home of the whale;
Back to me darts the bird sprite and beckons,
Winging her way o'er woodland and plain,
Hungry to roam, and bring me where glisten   65
Glorious tracts of glimmering foam.
This life on land is lingering death to me,
Give me the gladness of God's great sea.

AN ANCIENT SEA POEM

1. You will recognize in this poem a number of the characteristics of the Anglo-Saxons described on pages 30–32. To what aspects of Anglo-Saxon life do the following phrases refer:

line 23 — " the mirth of the mead hall "
line 42 — " so dear to his lord "
line 45 — " harping he needs not "

2. Summarize the points that influence the moods of the old sailor and the youth. Could these conflicts be within the mind of a single person? Discuss.

3. What different seasons of the year are described? On what seas do you think the old man has sailed? In what type of ship?

SUGGESTIONS FOR WRITING

1. If you have had experience on the sea, write a description showing your feeling about it.

2. Write a dialogue between father and son, showing different points of view as to the use of the family car, or some other matter of everyday life.

Beowulf

Translated by J. Duncan Spaeth

Beowulf is the greatest piece of literature to come down to us from the Anglo-Saxons. Much that we would like to know about it is lost in the distant past and will probably never be discovered: Who wrote it? When? Where? Scholars have found enough evidence in the poem itself to determine that it was probably composed by a single gifted poet sometime during the seventh or eighth century. The existing manuscript of a later date is no doubt a copy of an earlier one. The author was perhaps a Christianized West Saxon who drew his story from old pagan legends brought over from the continent; or perhaps monks substituted Christian references for pagan ones when they copied the manuscript. The character of Beowulf seems to be a blending of a historical figure with various mythical heroes of an earlier day.

The theme is universal — the age-old story of a great leader who saves or tries to save a people in grave danger. The action takes place in Sweden and Denmark. The characters — all people of noble birth — are Danes, Geats, Franks, and Frisians. Though persons of low rank are introduced into the poem, their individual names are not given.

Beowulf is the hero of the story. Strong, fearless, an advocate of freedom and justice, he typifies the Anglo-Saxon ideals of personal conduct. The villains are the firedrake or dragon from the dark caves and the cannibal-ogre Grendel [1] and his mother who live in the miasma of swamps in the land of mists and cold nights. The tone is dark, melancholy, austere. In simple, direct, majestic verse, *Beowulf* relates an exciting story.

The poem begins. From an unknown country a mysterious ship one day comes into harbor. It brings the infant Scyld [2] to the homeland of the Spear-Danes. This child later becomes their king, and a good king he is, reigning long and successfully. When he dies, his subjects spare no pains in honoring him. As was the custom in Scandinavia, they clothe him in armor, surround him with treasure, place him on a ship, and send him back to the sea.

Years pass. Scyld's descendant, Hrothgar,[3] wins great fame and wealth in battles with enemies. He builds the greatest of mead halls, called Heorot,[4] where his loyal warriors may gather. He feels that he has earned peace, rest, and enjoyment of the riches he has won. But fate has other things in store for him. Now appears on the scene a villain, a superhuman monster named Grendel.

[1] *Grendel* (grĕn′dĕl).
[2] *Scyld* (shĭld).
[3] *Hrothgar* (hrŏth′gȧr).
[4] *Heorot* (hā′ō·rŏt): literally, Hart Hall, because the horns of a stag or hart adorned its gables. The site of Heorot may be identified with Leire in Seeland, Denmark.

Selections from *Beowulf* from *Old English Poetry*, translated by J. Duncan Spaeth, published by Princeton University Press. Reprinted by permission of the publisher.

In the darkness dwelt a demon-sprite,
Whose heart was filled with fury and hate,
When he heard each night the noise of revel
Loud in the hall, laughter and song.
To the sound of the harp the singer chanted   5
Lays he had learned, of long ago;
How the Almighty had made the earth,
Wonder-bright lands, washed by the ocean;

All is happiness How he set, triumphant, sun and moon
in the new home To lighten all men that live on the earth.   10
until the angry He brightened the land with leaves and branches;
fiend Grendel
comes from his Life he created for every being,
lair. Each in its kind, that moves upon earth.
So, happy in hall, the heroes lived,
Wanting naught, till one began   15
To work them woe, a wicked fiend.

The demon grim was Grendel called,
Marsh stalker huge, the moors he roamed.
The joyless creature had kept long time
The lonely fen,° the lairs of monsters,   20
Cast out from men, an exile accurst.
The killing of Abel, brother of Cain°
Was justly avenged by the Judge Eternal.

When night had fallen, the fiend crept near
To the lofty hall, to learn how the Danes   25
In Heorot fared, when the feasting was done.
The athelings all within he saw
Asleep after revel, not recking of danger,
And free from care. The fiend accurst,
Grim and greedy, his grip made ready;   30
Snatched in their sleep, with savage fury,
Grendel enters Thirty warriors; away he sprang
the main hall
at night and Proud of his prey, to repair to his home,
carries off thirty His blood-dripping booty to bring to his lair.
warriors. At early dawn, when daybreak came,   35
The vengeance of Grendel was revealed to all;
Their wails after wassail° were widely heard,
Their morning woe. The mighty ruler,
The atheling brave, sat bowed with grief.

So Grendel wrongfully ruled the hall,   40
One against all till empty stood
That lordly mansion, and long remained so.
For the space of twelve winters the Scyldings' Friend°

20. *fen:* low marshland, a moor. 22. This is one of a number of passages which indicate that the author of the epic in its present form was a Christian. For the story of Cain and Abel see Genesis 4. 37. *after wassail* (wŏs″l): after the festive drinking of the night before. 43. *Scyldings' Friend:* Hrothgar.

The murders continue for twelve years, and gleemen spread the news abroad.

Bore in his breast the brunt of this sorrow,
Measureless woe. In mournful lays   45
The tale became known; 'twas told abroad
In gleemen's songs, how Grendel had warred
Long against Hrothgar, and wreaked his hate
With murderous fury through many a year.

The wise men take counsel together, erect altars to their heathen gods, and pray for relief from the monster, all to no avail. At last, from an unexpected source, Hrothgar and his people are given new hope of deliverance.

THE COMING OF BEOWULF

Thus boiled with care the breast of Hrothgar;   50
Ceaselessly sorrowed the son of Healfdene,°
None of his chieftains might change his lot.
Too fell was the foe that afflicted the people
With wrongs unnumbered, and nightly horrors.
Then heard in his home King Hygelac's thane,°   55
The dauntless Jute, of the doings of Grendel.
In strength he outstripped the strongest of men
That dwell in the earth in the days of this life.
Gallant and bold, he gave command

Beowulf makes plans to go to the aid of the Danes.

To get him a boat, a good wave-skimmer.   60
O'er the swan-road,° he said, he would seek the king
Noble and famous, who needed men.
Though dear to his kin, they discouraged him not;
The prudent in counsel praised the adventure,
Whetted his valor, awaiting good omens.   65

51. *Healfdene* (hā′ălf·dĕn·nà): half-Dane; that is, his mother was a foreigner. 55. *Hygelac's* (hĭg′ĕ·lăks) *thane:* Beowulf. Hygelac is a historical character — king of the Jutes, a people who lived in southern Sweden, according to most authorities, or in northern Denmark. 61. *swan-road:* sea.

He with fourteen followers hardy
Went to embark; he was wise in seamanship,
So Beowulf chose from the band of the Jutes
Heroes brave, the best he could find;
Showed them the landmarks, leading the way.   70
Soon they descried their craft in the water,
At the foot of the cliff. Then climbed aboard
The chosen troop; the tide was churning
Sea against sand; they stowed away
In the hold of the ship their shining armor,   75
War gear and weapons; the warriors launched
Their well-braced boat on her welcome voyage.
Swift o'er the waves with a wind that favored,
Foam on her breast, like a bird she flew;
A day and a night they drove to seaward,   80
Cut the waves with the curving prow,
Till the seamen that sailed her sighted the land,
Shining cliffs and coastwise hills,
Headlands bold. The harbor opened,
Their cruise was ended. Then quickly the sailors,   85
The crew of Weder folk,° clambered ashore,
Moored their craft with clank of chain mail,
And goodly war gear. God they thanked
That their way was smooth o'er the surging waves.

At the coast, Beowulf and his men are met by a guard, who, after
being convinced of their good intentions, conducts them toward the
palace. They enter the hall, and Beowulf introduces himself to
Hrothgar and his thanes. His last words voice a characteristic German attitude.

" Hail, King Hrothgar: Hygelac's thane   90
And kinsman am I. Known is the record
Of deeds of renown I have done in my youth.
Far in my home, I heard of this Grendel;
Seafarers tell the tale of the hall:
How bare of warriors, this best of buildings   95
Deserted stands, when the sun goes down
And twilight deepens to dark in the sky.
By comrades encouraged, I come on this journey.
The best of them bade me, the bravest and wisest,
To go to thy succor, O good King Hrothgar;   100
For well they approved my prowess in battle,
They saw me themselves come safe from the conflict
When five of my foes I defeated and bound,
Beowulf declares Beating in battle the brood of the monsters.
the prowess that At night on the sea with nickers° I wrestled,   105
makes him a fit Avenging the Weders, survived the sea peril,
opponent for
Grendel. And crushed in my grip the grim sea monsters

86. *Weder* (wā′dĕr) *folk:* another name for the Jutes. 105. *nickers:* sea demons, probably walruses
or whales.

That harried my neighbors. Now I am come
To cope with Grendel in combat single,
And match my might against the monster alone.   110
I pray thee therefore, prince of the Scyldings,
Not to refuse the favor I ask,
Having come so far, O friend of the Shield-Danes,
That I alone with my loyal comrades,
My hardy companions, may Heorot purge.   115

Moreover they say that the slaughterous fiend
In wanton mood all weapons despises.
Hence — as I hope that Hygelac may,
My lord and king, be kind to me —
Sword and buckler° I scorn to bear,   120
Gold-adorned shield, as I go to the conflict.
With my grip will I grapple the gruesome fiend,
Foe against foe, to fight for our life.
And he that shall fall his faith must put
In the judgment of God. If Grendel wins,   125
He is minded to make his meal in the hall
Untroubled by fear, on the folk of the Jutes,
As often before he fed on the Danes.
No need for thee then to think of my burial.
If I lose my life, the lonely prowler   130
My blood-stained body will bear to his den,
Swallow me greedily, and splash with my gore
His lair in the marsh; no longer wilt then
Have need to find me food and sustenance.
To Hygelac send, if I sink in the battle,   135
This best of corselets that covers my breast,
Heirloom of Hrethel, rarest of byrnies,
The work of Weland.° So Wyrd will be done."

---

120. *buckler:* a kind of shield worn on one arm. 138. *Weland* (wā′lănd): the celestial blacksmith
of the Northmen, corresponding to Vulcan of classical mythology.

Hrothgar replies with complimentary reference to Beowulf's father,
and then once more recounts the horrors cf Grendel's visits to
Heorot. A banquet is prepared, with the usual eating and drinking
and minstrel's song. Unferth,[1] a jealous Danish courtier, belittles
Beowulf by sarcastic comment on his defeat in a swimming match
with Breca, a young prince of another tribe. Beowulf replies by giving his version of this adventure, in which he had killed nine sea
demons. Then Beowulf goes on to accuse Unferth of murdering his
own brothers.

  After this tilt the banquet proceeds. The queen, Wealhtheow,[2]
passes the ale cup. The noisy revel continues until at last Hrothgar
and his followers leave Heorot to Beowulf and his men. After once
more asserting that he will meet Grendel unarmed, Beowulf and his
men lie down and go to sleep.

---

[1] *Unferth* (ŭn′fârth). [2] *Wealhtheow* (wā′ĕl·thā·ō).

BEOWULF'S FIGHT WITH GRENDEL

Now Grendel came, from his crags of mist
Across the moor; he was curst of God.   140
The murderous prowler meant to surprise
In the high-built hall his human prey.
He stalked 'neath the clouds, till steep before him
The house of revelry rose in his path,
The gold-hall of heroes, the gaily adorned.   145
Hrothgar's home he had haunted full often,
But never before had he found to receive him
So hardy a hero, such hall guards there.
Close to the building crept the slayer,
Doomed to misery. The door gave way,   150
Though fastened with bolts, when his fist fell on it.
Maddened he broke through the breach he had made;
Swoln° with anger and eager to slay,
The ravening fiend o'er the bright-paved floor
Furious ran, while flashed from his eyes   155
An ugly glare like embers aglow.
He saw in the hall, all huddled together,
The heroes asleep. Then laughed in his heart
The hideous fiend; he hoped ere dawn
To sunder body from soul of each;   160
He looked to appease his lust of blood,
Glut his maw° with the men he would slay.
But Wyrd had otherwise willed his doom;
Never again should he get a victim
After that night.

          Narrowly watched   165
Hygelac's thane how the horrible slayer
Forward should charge in fierce attack.
Nor was the monster minded to wait:
Sudden he sprang on a sleeping thane.
Ere he could stir, he slit him open;   170
Bit through the bone-joints, gulped the blood,
Greedily bolted the body piecemeal.

Grendel devours Soon he had swallowed the slain man wholly,
a sleeping man, Hands and feet. Then forward he hastened,
then attacks Sprang at the hero, and seized him at rest;   175
Beowulf. Fiercely clutched him with fiendish claw.
But quickly Beowulf caught his forearm,
And threw himself on it with all its weight.
Straight discovered that crafty plotter,
That never in all mid-earth had he met   180
In any man a mightier grip.
Gone was his courage, and craven fear
Sat in his heart, yet helped him no sooner.

153. *Swoln:* swollen. 162. *maw:* stomach.

Fain° would he hide in his hole in the fenland,
His devil's den. A different welcome   185
From former days he found that night!
Now Hygelac's thane, the hardy, remembered
His evening's boast, and bounding up,
Grendel he clenched, and cracked his fingers;
The monster tried flight, but the man pursued;   190
The ravager hoped to wrench himself free,
And gain the fen, for he felt his fingers
Helpless and limp in the hold of his foe.

'Twas a sorry visit the man-devourer
Made to the Hall of the Hart that night.   195
Dread was the din, the Danes were frighted
By the uproar wild of the ale-spilling fray.
The hardiest blenched as the hall foes wrestled
In terrible rage. The rafters groaned;
'Twas wonder great that the wine hall stood   200
Firm 'gainst the fighters' furious onslaught,

The mead hall is Nor fell to the ground, that glorious building.
almost wrecked With bands of iron 'twas braced and stiffened
in the fury of the Within and without. But off from the sill
battle. Many a mead-bench mounted with gold   205
Was wrung where they wrestled in wrath together.
The Scylding nobles never imagined
That open attack, or treacherous cunning,
Could wreck or ruin their royal hall,
The lofty and antlered, unless the flames   210
Should someday swallow it up in smoke.
The din was renewed, the noise redoubled;
Each man of the Danes was mute with dread,
That heard from the wall the horrible wail,
The gruesome song of the godless foe,   215
His howl of defeat, as the fiend of hell
Bemoaned his hurt. The man held fast;
Greatest he was in grip of strength,
Of all that dwelt upon earth that day.

Loath in his heart was the hero-deliverer   220
To let escape his slaughterous guest.
Of little use that life he deemed
To human kind. The comrades of Beowulf
Unsheathed their weapons to ward their leader,
Eagerly brandished their ancient blades,   225
The life of their peerless lord to defend.
Little they deemed, those dauntless warriors,
As they leaped to the fray, those lusty fighters,
Laying on boldly to left and to right,
Eager to slay, that no sword upon earth,   230

184. *Fain:* gladly.

No keenest weapon, could wound that monster:
Point would not pierce, he was proof against iron;
'Gainst victory blades the devourer was charmed.
But a woeful end awaited the wretch,
That very day he was doomed to depart,   235
And fare afar to the fiends' domain.

Beowulf tears
Grendel's arm
from its socket,
and the mortally
wounded Grendel
crawls to his lair.

Now Grendel found, who in former days
So many a warrior had wantonly slain,
In brutish lust, abandoned of God,
That the frame of his body was breaking at last.   240
Keen of courage, the kinsman of Hygelac
Held him grimly gripped in his hands.
Loath was each to the other alive.
The grisly monster got his death wound:
A huge split opened under his shoulder;   245
Crunched the socket, cracked the sinews,
Glory great was given to Beowulf.
But Grendel escaped with his gaping wound,
O'er the dreary moor his dark den sought,
Crawled to his lair. 'Twas clear to him then,   250
The count of his hours to end had come,
Done were his days. The Danes were glad,
The hard fight was over, they had their desire.
Cleared was the hall, 'twas cleansed by the hero
With keen heart and courage, who came from afar.   255

ANGLO–SAXON VERSE FORM

Anglo-Saxon, or Old English, verse has three characteristics:

a. Each line has *four principal beats* but may have any number of syllables.

b. Some of the four beats *alliterate* — that is, begin with the same sound. (In original Old English verse the third beat *always* alliterates with the first, or second, or both. The translation by Dr. Spaeth is very close to the original in this respect.)

c. The verse is *not rhymed.*

This form is admirably suited for narrative poetry to be recited aloud. It is simple to understand, easy to listen to, easy to catch in its alliteration (which is its principal ornament), easy to compose. The jingle about Old King Cole might sound like this in the Anglo-Saxon verse form:

Cole was the king; he was keen and merry;
Mirthful he was, with minstrels in mead hall.
He called for his cup; he called for his pipe.
His fiddlers were three, and fine was their
    trilling.

The beat of the line is hypnotizing, yet its elasticity keeps it from becoming boring. It has been used a number of times by later poets. Coleridge, for example, was influenced by the Old English rhythms. The American poet Edna St. Vincent Millay wrote her operatic play *The King's Henchman* in this style. T. S. Eliot in his play *The Cocktail Party* returns to the native English principle of a four-beat loose line, though he has given up the alliteration. In *Beowulf* the line moves fast, and its hammer strokes make the battles and the boasting forceful. When chanting the poem, the ancient gleeman probably struck a chord on his harp with each accented syllable.

ANGLO–SAXON ADVENTURES

1. In what ways does the poem bring out the following Anglo-Saxon ideals of conduct: (*a*) love of personal freedom, (*b*) allegiance to lord or king, (*c*) repression of feelings, (*d*) open-handed hospitality, (*e*) love of glory as the ruling mo-

tive of every noble life? Which of these remain as ideals in America today? Which have been changed or modified?

2. Do you think that such monstrous creatures as Grendel or such supermen as Beowulf really existed? If not, how do you explain the frequent appearance of such beings in early literature? If possible, give examples of such exaggerated characters in modern literature. What purpose do they serve?

3. Practice reading parts of the poem aloud in order to get the swing of the four-accent lines.

CREATIVE ACTIVITIES

1. Write an account of an evening in an Anglo-Saxon mead hall, if possible illustrating it with a sketch of the hall; or write an account of a corresponding social event of modern life, picturing the kind of room in which it takes place.

2. Make a small model of a mead hall, or draw sketches of Anglo-Saxon dwellings and costumes.

THE POWER OF WORDS

COMPOUND WORDS

Did you notice the use of compound words in *Beowulf?* This condensed way of expressing an idea is a feature of Old English and is still in active operation in modern English. Words are joined with a hyphen; then, years later perhaps, the hyphen is dropped and the two words are fused into one. Thus we have *lighthearted,* but *light-footed* still wears its hyphen.

Make a list of all the compound words you find in *Beowulf.* Explain what each word on your list is really saying. You will find that some of them are figurative expressions for commonplace words.

From now on, pay attention to compound words in your reading, even of newspapers. Sports reporters are especially fond of coining such words to give variety and snap to their style. Individually or as a class you might start a collection of modern compound words. It's an inexpensive hobby! Or you might write an account of a sports contest using compound words effectively.

READING LIST FOR THE ANGLO–SAXON PERIOD

Bryher, Winifred, *Roman Wall*

Though the scene of this excellent novel is the Continent, it illuminates the situation faced by the Romans in Britain just before their withdrawal.

Chesterton, G. K., *The Ballad of the White Horse*

A poem on how Alfred inspired his troops to victory over the Danes; to commemorate this triumph, a white horse, the Saxon emblem, was carved in a chalky hillside.

Costain, Thomas B., *The Conquerors*

The first volume of his history, *The Pageant of England,* into which he puts the color and vitality that mark his novels.

Farnol, Jeffrey, *The King Liveth*

A novel filled to the brim with action, as Alfred the Great drives the Danes back from Wessex.

Hosford, Dorothy, *By His Own Might, the Battles of Beowulf*

Modern prose makes it easier to concentrate on the excitement and suspense of Beowulf's adventures.

Kipling, Rudyard, *Puck of Pook's Hill* and *Rewards and Fairies* (sequel)

Fanciful stories and poems of the early days of Britain, told to children, but not a child's book.

Longfellow, Henry W., " The Discoverer of the North Cape " (in his *Collected Poems*)

In this short poem a seafaring Northman brings a walrus tooth to King Alfred. What does it signify?

Muntz, Hope, *The Golden Warrior*

The story of Harold, the last Saxon king, is told with rich color and authentic detail. The leading characters seem swept along by forces they cannot control.

Tennyson, Alfred, " The Battle of Brunnanburh " (in his *Collected Poems*)

The poet translates a famous Saxon battle song into modern English, but retains the unusual swing of the original meter.

FOR LISTENING

A selection from *Beowulf,* lines 90–138, has been recorded and is available on *Many Voices 6A.*

THE GROWTH OF THE ENGLISH LANGUAGE

The Old English Period

Today more people speak English than any other language in the world. It may become the universal language of the future. As you progress through the centuries in this book you will see how our language, which had its beginnings more than fifteen hundred years ago, has gradually changed. The language we use today no more resembles its original form than a grown man resembles the baby he once was.

A page of Old English in the early runic alphabet would be a complete mystery to you. Later forms of writing, like that in the sample from the *Beowulf* manuscript reproduced below, still look

much like a foreign alphabet. Even printing it in our present alphabet would not clarify its meaning. But scholars, by long study of language forms and histories, have been able to translate the Old English writings so that we can recognize the actual roots of our present English in those strange-looking manuscripts. A short passage from *Beowulf* describing Grendel's gloomy abode well illustrates this point:

OLD ENGLISH
(*Printed in the modern alphabet*)

Hie dygel lond
Warigeath, wulf-hleothu, windige naessas,
Frecne fen-gelad, thaer fyrgen-stream
Under naessa genipu, nither gewiteth
Flod under foldan.

LITERAL TRANSLATION
(*Language similarities become evident.*)

They [a] darksome land
Ward, wolf-cliff, windy nesses.
Frightful fen-paths, where mountain-stream
Under nesse's mists nether wanders,
A flood under earth.

FREE POETIC TRANSLATION
(*The lines take on meaning and present a vivid picture.*)

Lonely and waste is the land they inhabit,
Wolf-cliffs wild and windy headlands,
Ledges of mist, where mountain torrents
Downward plunge to dark abysses
And flow unseen.

While many other languages have contributed extensively to present-day English, the *basic* words are derived chiefly from the speech of the Anglo-Saxons. An interesting study has shown that of the *one thousand words that recur most frequently in our speaking and writing,* 61.7 per cent come from Old English, 30.9 per cent come from French, 2.9 per cent come from Latin, and the small residue comes from various North Germanic tongues.

It is not only in vocabulary that this kinship with Old English is shown, but also in the very structure of sentences. If you have studied the elaborate declension of nouns and conjugation of verbs in Latin, you realize how much simpler English word forms are. We have few changes within a word itself to express case, number, and tense, but show most relationships by little words such as *to, for, of, have, had, will,* and many others. Old English was originally more highly inflected than modern English is, for there was always a tendency in England to simplify grammar, to shorten words, and to drop forms that seemed unnecessary. Some dialects of Old English were more highly inflected than others. It was usually the plainer, easier dialect that survived in speech and consequently influenced the later development of the language. A good example of this long process of simplification is the changes in the verb *had.*

OLD ENGLISH	MIDDLE ENGLISH	MODERN ENGLISH
Singular	*Singular*	*Singular*
1. haefde	1. hadde	1. had
2. haefdes(t)	2. haddest	2. had
3. haefde	3. hadde	3. had
Plural 1, 2, 3	*Plural* 1, 2, 3	*Plural* 1, 2, 3
haefdon	hadde(n)	had

Some of the irregular forms of our present language, such as the plural *en* in *oxen* and *children,* are survivals from Old English inflections.

Contributions from other languages were few during the Anglo-Saxon period. They came chiefly from two sources. The Danes, who finally occupied the northeast half of England, supplied many words, especially sea terms and place names. The names of about six hundred towns in the east of England still end in *by,* Danish for *town,* and the same word is preserved in *by-law.* Other common words from the same source are *fellow, skin, happy, ugly,* and *knife.* To the Danes we also owe the tendency to put a strong accent on the first syllable and slur over the vowels in following syllables. This characteristic of English speech is called " the law of recessive accent." Words

later adopted from a tongue with quite a different accent system, like French, often became Anglicized by a shift in accent as well as by changes in sound. The French word *quantité,* equivalent to the English *quantity,* is a case in point.

The second foreign influence, that of Latin, accompanied Christianity to England, naturally introducing many church terms. In a few centers of learning, such as King Alfred's court, Latin played a part, but the widespread adoption of Latin words into English came during later periods. Perhaps the most significant change in these early centuries was the gradual substitution of the Latin alphabet for the crude Germanic runes, which are still to be found in ancient inscriptions recently excavated.

For six hundred years the English language was narrow and isolated like a river near its source. Later chapters will show how it gradually widened as it received new tributaries until it eventually enriched the whole world.

THE MEDIEVAL

WHILE Alfred the Great was unifying the English against the attacks of the Danes in the ninth century, other ruthless Norsemen were seizing a French province on the English Channel. In France the people used to pray in their churches: " From the fury of the Northmen, O Lord, deliver us! " These wild Norsemen intermarried with the conquered French; within a hundred years they had become civilized Normans with a Christian faith, a different language, and a new social system.

Intermarriage of the families of Norman dukes and Saxon kings gave William, the Duke of Normandy, a questionable claim to the English throne. On the pretext that he had been promised the throne, he invaded England in 1066 and defeated the Saxon king Harold at the Battle of Hastings. William, now called " The Conqueror," made the English people his subjects and gave most of their land to his Norman followers. This occupation by the French was the last invasion of England.

"The Benjamites Win Their Wives" is an illustration from an illuminated Bible of the thirteenth century, one which the Crusaders carried to spread knowledge of Christianity.

PERIOD 1066-1485

The date of the Saxons' defeat — 1066 — is as unforgettable to an Englishman as 1492 is to an American. The Saxons feared the end of Angle-land, but in time they mingled with the Norman-French to form a new England. Each group made distinctive contributions to this new race of Englishmen. The Celts of Ireland and Scotland, together with the Welsh, had strong emotions and vivid imaginations. The Angles and Saxons and Danes exemplified courage, endurance, and pleasure in physical action. The Normans, touched by the Mediterranean civilization which stretched back to the Romans and the Greeks, had learned to think logically and to organize complete systems, whether in politics, religion, or social life. In their enjoyment of luxurious and refined living, they brought wit and color and gaiety to England. From these varied racial strains, the character of the Englishman was built up.

The Norman nobles formed a new ruling class, to which the Anglo-Saxon peasants were subservient. However, they shared their authority with the Church, whose influence was steadily growing.

THE POWERFUL MEDIEVAL CHURCH

Religion was a strong, stabilizing force in the life of medieval man. The Church helped to calm his fear of death and to give him the hope of happiness after death. It nourished his trust in God, his belief that all living beings, from the lowest to the highest, had an assigned place in God's great plan of creation.

The peasants might live in thatched hovels and cottages, the burghers in narrow streets where upper stories jutted out over dark lanes below; but in erecting their parish churches and magnificent cathedrals, all of the people united to build beautiful buildings in which to house the symbols of their spirit. The cathedrals remain as England's greatest architectural glory — from the rounded arches and heavy stone walls of the Romanesque and Norman churches to the later pointed arches, high-springing vaults, and enormous stained-glass windows of the Gothic style.

In a period when government was a struggle for power — and when fighting was a highly respected pastime — the Church carried the torch of civilization. Books and learning were preserved by the clergy in a time when the knights and nobles had little interest in learning. Teaching and the copying of manuscripts (there was as yet no printing) flourished in monasteries throughout England. Though even in King Alfred's time young scholars had gathered at Oxford to listen to lectures by the monks and priests, the official organization of the two great universities, Oxford and Cambridge, took place in the twelfth and thirteenth centuries.

As wealth increased in the monasteries, some of the clergy became worldly and unprincipled, as Chaucer points out. In general, however, the Church stood for high ideals, and even kings claimed their " divine right " to rule because they had been crowned as God's lieutenants by the Church. The very shrine to which Chaucer's pilgrims are traveling in *The Canterbury Tales* shows the power of the Church over rulers of state. Two hundred years before Chaucer's time, Thomas à Becket, the Archbishop of Canterbury, was murdered before the altar of his own cathedral because he would not yield to King Henry II in a struggle between church and state. For his indirect part in this murder, Henry had to do heavy penance; and Canterbury became a saint's shrine which pilgrims visited every spring.

Aerofilms Ltd.

Canterbury Cathedral, built in the twelfth through the fifteenth centuries.

THE CRUSADES

The strong religious enthusiasm of the medieval period is most easily recognized in the Crusades — a dramatic expression of the influence of the Church over the minds of men. During the eleventh, twelfth, and thirteenth centuries, great international expeditions were undertaken to recapture Jerusalem and the Holy Land from the infidel Moslems. Even kings rode forth in the Crusades, among them Richard the Lion-Hearted. Although the movement began in religious zeal, traders and adventurers accompanied the crusaders. Traveling abroad made them familiar not only with Europe but also with Asia. Thus Englishmen learned of far horizons, developed trade, and familiarized themselves with Eastern science, literature, and art.

FEUDALISM: ORDERED SOCIAL CLASSES

Like a modern dictator, the conquering William stamped out rebellion. To hold the unwilling and disunited country, William needed an army; and this was made possible by the feudal system which he enforced. The word *feudalism* comes from *feud* or *fief,* the name of the land a person held under the king. William introduced the idea that all the land belonged to the king, to be portioned out to his followers. They in return promised him personal loyalty, a unit of fighting men, and a certain sum of money. The simple Anglo-Saxon idea of a leader protecting his followers, of followers obeying their leader, was now attached to the ownership of the land. Nobles, knights, men of rank down to the lowliest tenants parceled out their land to their followers, who in turn gave certain services to their masters. Thus, the Normans became landholders and gentlemen; many of the original Anglo-Saxons, dispossessed of their land, became laborers and serfs who tilled the soil and turned over most of their produce to the feudal lords above them. The system resulted in a class society so rigid that members of the lowest class, the serfs, were bound to the land on which they worked and could even be sold with it.

CHIVALRY: THE FLOWER OF FEUDALISM

Along with feudalism the Normans introduced chivalry, the social code practiced by the nobility. The word *chivalry* comes from the French *cheval,* horse. It stood for the behavior of the knight, who originally was an armed warrior on horseback. Chivalry prescribed the training for a young nobleman first as a page, then as a squire, and finally as a knight. He was taught reverence toward women, service to the church, allegiance to the king. Such a system yielded a trained group of gentlemen-soldiers whose ideals were knightly honor, Christian principles, and romantic love. In practice, the actions of

knights often fell short of these ideals; despite this fact, the institutions of chivalry softened the fierceness of medieval times and guided men to a better life.

A knight chose a lady for whom he fought in the jousts or tournaments, which were the athletic events of the period. These military games were held in lists, comparable to modern stadiums; and in spite of chain mail, and later, plate armor, the lances and swords inflicted bloody wounds and often fatally injured a combatant. According to the popular legends and tales of the times, wandering knights or knights-errant rode through the countryside in quest of adventure. Many knights were interested only in perilous enterprises, not their vows.

There were many stories of chivalry — of knights in love and war. Popular in England was Malory's *Morte d'Arthur,* in which the adventures of King Arthur and the Knights of the Round Table were told as if Arthur and his soldiers had lived in the days of chivalry. The romance, a favorite form of literature throughout these centuries, glorified adventurous heroes in a setting of medieval splendor. The word *romance,* meaning a story from the lands settled by the Romans, suggested that chivalry came from southern France, where the troubadours sang of courtesy, tenderness, and loyalty in love.

TOWN LIFE

Along with the romantic splendor of feudal chivalry, a solid middle class was formed. While not as colorful as the aristocratic knight, townsfolk were, nevertheless, just as important in medieval life. With the expansion of trade, the towns grew and the laborers began to gain independence. In the trades, the idea of organization developed into what is called the guild system. A guild, in some ways like a trade union, guaranteed a good product, protected its members from unchecked competition, trained new workmen as apprentices, and set wages and prices. Weavers, dyers, carpenters, butchers — all had their guilds.

The guilds were part of the social life as well as the business life of the times. From the churches, they took over the production of miracle plays, as these early forms of the drama were called. The first plays had been little more than dialogues dramatizing a religious festival. But as they developed, the clergy began to suspect that the desire for entertainment rather than religious instruction drew people to church.

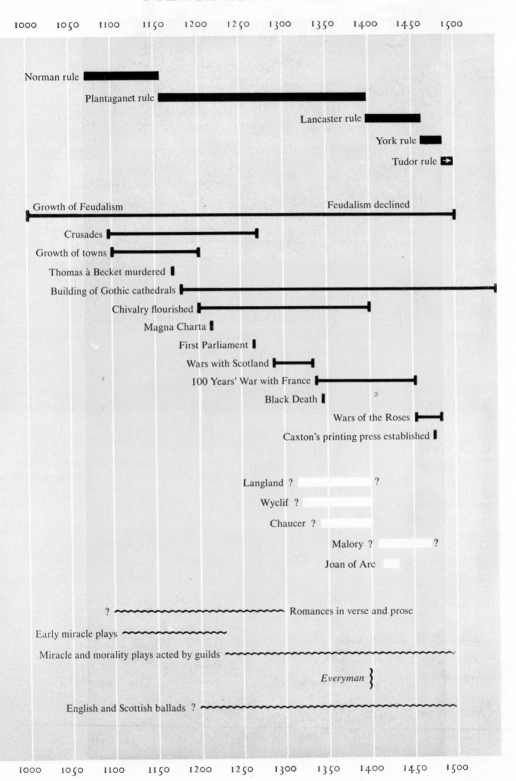

1000 1050 1100 1150 1200 1250 1300 1350 1400 1450 1500

Norman rule

Plantaganet rule

Lancaster rule

York rule

Tudor rule

Growth of Feudalism   Feudalism declined

Crusades

Growth of towns

Thomas à Becket murdered

Building of Gothic cathedrals

Chivalry flourished

Magna Charta

First Parliament

Wars with Scotland

100 Years' War with France

Black Death

Wars of the Roses

Caxton's printing press established

Langland ?   ?

Wyclif ?

Chaucer ?

Malory ?   ?

Joan of Arc

?   Romances in verse and prose

Early miracle plays

Miracle and morality plays acted by guilds

Everyman }

English and Scottish ballads ?

The trade guilds presented their plays on platforms or double-decker wagons in courtyards of inns or public squares. Many episodes, acted by different guilds, formed a collection of plays that spanned the whole story of the Bible. The boatbuilders' guild might give the shipbuilding of Noah; the fishmongers, the Flood; the bakers, the Last Supper. Often there were broadly humorous passages with the Devil as the leading buffoon.

The morality plays, a later development of the miracle plays, were allegorical, with characters personifying virtues and vices: Charity, Pride, Truth, Falsehood. More originality of plot was possible than in a miracle play, but the manner of presentation was much the same.

The towns had their amusements, but they also had their tragedies. The badly cured meat, the open sewers, and the lack of cleanliness everywhere resulted in epidemics of disease. The Black Death, a mysterious plague that spread from Asia, ravaged England in 1348 with a death toll estimated at two-fifths of the population.

CHANGES IN GOVERNMENT

By the middle of the thirteenth century England no longer was a French province but an English nation. The Norman line, set up by William the Conqueror, was followed by the Plantagenets, a name given by the founder of the family because he wore a sprig of *planta genesta,* or broom flower, in his helmet. Henry II (1154–1189) brought order out of a period of anarchy, and reduced the power of the unruly barons and independent princes. He was responsible for the beginnings of the English Common Law. After dividing his realm into six districts, he appointed three judges to each district. Since the same justice was administered in each of the six districts of his realm, a common law evolved.

Another step toward law and justice came during the reign of the cruel and craven King John (1199–1216). Not only had King John lost the French possessions and antagonized the nobles but he also had offended the Pope to such a degree that England was placed under an interdict. Indignation at the king's tyrannical acts finally united the barons, knights, and town representatives. They forced King John to sign the Magna Charta or Great Charter in 1215. This document laid the foundations for personal and political liberty for all Englishmen: trial by jury, fines fixed by law, taxes assessed with consent of council.

Fifty years later a powerful baron, Simon de Montfort, summoned two knights from each county and two citizens from each town to meet as a parliament (from the French *parler,* to talk). Their object was to control the king still further. This first group of representatives was the forerunner of the House of Commons.

WARS OF THE MIDDLE AGES

Hunger and disease took a deadly toll, but many died upon the battlefield. Efforts to subdue Scotland ran intermittently through the reigns of the first three Edwards. The Hundred Years' War was fought with France to win control of commerce and to gain territory on the continent. Although Joan of Arc rescued her country and had the Dauphin (heir to the French throne) crowned at Reims, an English patriotism was created. Many spectacular battles were fought, and a new weapon was introduced — the longbow, which made knights in armor ineffective.

After the foreign wars, England was torn by a civil war between two royal families quarreling over the kingship. This thirty years' dispute was known as the Wars of the Roses because the white rose was the emblem of one family, the House of York, and the red rose was the symbol of the other, the House of Lancaster. The last of the York kings, Richard III, whom Shakespeare portrays as a ruthless tyrant, was killed at the battle of Bosworth Field in 1485. It was he who shouted, in the last moments of that battle, the now-famous cry, " A horse! a horse! my kingdom for a horse! "

Union of the two families through marriage founded the Tudor family, whose rulers were to bring to England a new period of growth and strength and confidence. Feudalism was dying out as a social system. Englishmen were advancing toward the modern periods of English history. Thus the date 1485, when the first Tudor, Henry VII, came to the throne, is a suitable milestone for the end of the medieval period.

RICHNESS OF MEDIEVAL LITERATURE

Medieval literature presents a bright panorama of the period. Hundreds of ballads kept poetry and singing alive in the homes of the ordinary people and at their festivals. For the nobility there were the long romances of chivalry. You will read a short selection from Malory's *Morte d'Arthur,* which is part of that great realm of medieval romance in which King Arthur and his knights appear as central figures in heroic legends.

After the miracle plays, based on Bible stories and produced by the Church and later the guilds, the morality plays became popular. These were allegorical stories in which the characters were symbols, usually representing an abstract quality like a vice or virtue. *Everyman,* the best of these plays, has been staged several times in our own day. The hero, who might be any one of us, finds that only one of his friends, Good Deeds — not Fellowship or Riches or Strength — will accompany him when he is summoned by Death.

Most of the early medieval literature is by unknown writers, but by the fourteenth century individual authors had become known. Chaucer, " the father of English literature," is the greatest. In picturing colorful, pageant-loving England he made his various medieval characters come alive as real men and women. John Wyclif opened a new realm of literature when scholars working under his direction translated the Bible from Latin into English so that the common folk could read it for themselves.

William Langland, of whom we know little personally, wrote *The Vision of Piers the Plowman.* His long poem protested against the social injustices of his time which already had produced revolts among the peasants. Though he wrote in the metrical style of Old English poetry, Langland pointed toward the future by striking the first literary blow for the rights of the ordinary individual.

SUMMARY

After the Norman Conquest — the last invasion of England — there was a gradual blending of peoples and languages. By the end of the medieval period, England was becoming the unified nation we know today. One of the great forces of the age, the Church, helped to develop civilized living. It brought man closer to religion, fostered beauty in architecture and art, preserved literature, and promoted education. The religious enthusiasm of the people is reflected in the Crusades.

An equally powerful force was feudalism, a system whereby the king and the nobles entrusted land to men of lower rank in return for loyalty and military service. This system, resulting in a rigid class society, stamped out rebellion and brought order to the country.

Beneath the splendor of feudal chivalry, a powerful new middle class developed in the towns. This class organized trade and craft guilds to regulate the conditions of their work. The town guilds also produced the miracle and morality plays of that time.

By the end of the period, consideration was being given to personal and political liberty. England was approaching a new era of confidence and growth and strength.

Literary output was tremendous. Early in the period it was chiefly anonymous; later four great names emerge: Chaucer, outstanding poet and student of human nature; Wyclif, translator of the Bible into English; Langland, protestor against social injustice; and Malory, recorder of the Arthur legends.

EARLY ENGLISH
AND SCOTTISH BALLADS

From the common people came the ballads of early England and Scotland. Generation after generation sang them before they were, after many centuries, recorded in written form; therefore, it is impossible to date them or to identify their original authors. As they were told and retold, the ballads changed — listeners forgot lines or improvised their own — and so gradually there grew to be many versions of a single story.

Unlike the literary ballads of later times, such as those by Walter Scott and Samuel Coleridge, this early poetry of the people resembles modern " popular songs." It deals with the comedies and tragedies of everyday life: quarrels among members of a family or lovers or friends, death, war, fear of the unknown, and the adventures of outlaws. Wherever the English and Scottish people went, they carried with them their old ballads. Early settlers brought them to North America; some versions are still sung in the mountain sections of the South. They have crept into our folklore, influenced the work of our writers and musicians, and become a part of our heritage.

The old ballads use common devices in telling a story. Most often the ballad is simple and direct — it usually stresses a single incident and plunges into the narrative with little or no introduction of background. The narrative is often hinted at rather than told in detail. You must do considerable guessing as to what happens between stanzas, or who is the speaker of certain stanzas. The story is developed largely through dialogue. Often standard speeches have a definite meaning, as if they were part of a code. For example, calling upon his mother to " make the bed soft and narrow " means that the speaker is dying.

As you read the ballads, you will easily recognize that they are meant to be sung. There is much use of refrains, as when the last line of a stanza is repeated. This suggests the way in which ballads were often sung or recited to a group, with a single voice carrying the main part of the stanza, and everyone chiming in on the chorus. Perhaps in old times the group danced to these rhythms, for the French word from which *ballad* is derived once meant *to dance*.

Robin Hood Rescuing Three Squires

Old ballads are the chief source of the many legends clustering about the name of Robin Hood. What historical basis there is for such a person is only guesswork. Some think he was the last Saxon to take a stand against the Norman overlords, some that he was merely a symbol of the ideal yeoman. In him the Saxons could center their wishful thinking and could express their glee at the trouble he caused the upper classes.

Robin Hood is represented as a skilled archer, an outlaw who robbed the rich and strong to help the poor and weak. A brave leader who aroused the devoted loyalty of his followers, he was a true sportsman, recognizing worth and skill even when he was defeated. Later in Elizabethan times he was represented as the disguised Earl of Huntingdon, who had forfeited his estate to the Normans. One writer carefully prepared a family tree to prove Robin's title. Maid Marian was introduced where the feminine element was needed for the May Day dances based on old ballads. Through additions such as these it was easy to supply a happy ending to Robin's life. The older tales never had this; in the early versions Robin Hood bleeds to death when betrayed by a false cousin. One of the best-known later treatments of Robin Hood is in Scott's *Ivanhoe,* where the merry outlaw is disguised under the name Locksley. Light opera, motion pictures, and television have also made his story familiar in our own century.

> Bold Robin Hood ranging the forest all round,
>   The forest all round ranged he;
> O there did he meet with a gay lady,°
>   She came weeping along the highway.°

In a long conversation with this lady it comes out that she is sad because her three sons are condemned to die. Robin Hood then enumerates several possible crimes, asking whether any of these are the cause of the sentence. The lady denies all of them.

> " What have they done then? " said jolly Robin,
>   " Come tell me most speedily."
> "Oh! it is for killing the king's fallow deer,
>   And they all are condemned to die."

5

> " Get you home, get you home," said jolly Robin,
>   " Get you home most speedily,
> And I will unto fair Nottingham go,
>   For the sake of the squires all three."

10

3. *gay lady:* Under the circumstances, she could hardly be gay in our common meaning of the word. Originally the word referred to great excitement from any cause. 4. *highway:* As the word is found in this and other ballads in a position to rhyme with *he* or some other *ee* sound, we may infer that the North Country pronunciation of *highway* gave it more of an *ee* sound. In line 8 *die* is pronounced *dee.* This is still common Scottish pronunciation. A familiar example is the last line of "Annie Laurie" — "I'd lay me doon and dee."

Then bold Robin Hood for Nottingham goes,
   For Nottingham town goes he,
O there did he meet with a poor beggar-man,   15
   He came creeping along the highway.

" What news, what news, thou old beggar-man?
   What news, come tell unto me ":
" O there is weeping and wailing in fair Nottingham,
   For the death of the squires all three."   20

This beggar-man had a coat on his back,
   'T was neither green, yellow, nor red;
Bold Robin Hood thought 't was no disgrace
   To be in a beggar-man's stead.

" Come, pull off thy coat, you old beggar-man,   25
   And you shall put on mine;
And forty good shillings I'll give thee to boot,
   Besides brandy, good beer, ale and wine."

Bold Robin Hood then unto Nottingham came,
   Unto Nottingham town came he;   30
O there did he meet with great master sheriff
   And likewise the squires all three.

" One boon, one boon," says jolly Robin,
   " One boon I beg on my knee;
That for the deaths of these three squires,   35
   Their hangman I may be."

" Soon granted, soon granted," says great master sheriff,
   " Soon granted unto thee;
And you shall have all their gay clothing,
   Aye, and all their white money."   40

" O I will have none of their gay clothing,
   Nor none of their white money,
But I'll have three blasts on my bugle-horn,
   That their souls to heaven may flee."

Then Robin Hood mounted the gallows so high,   45
    Where he blew loud and shrill,
Till an hundred and ten of Robin Hood's men,
    They came marching all down the green hill.

" Whose men are all these? " says great master sheriff,
    " Whose men are they? Tell unto me."
" O they are mine, but none of them thine,   50
    And they're come for the squires all three."

" O take them, O take them," says great master sheriff,
    " O take them along with thee;
For there's never a man in all Nottingham   55
    Can do the like of thee."

Bonny Barbara Allan

There are many versions of this tragic love ballad in England, Scotland, and America; ninety-two different versions have been discovered in Virginia alone. The selection given here is one of the oldest versions, and it is probably as near to the original Scottish story as any that can be found. One of the interesting characteristics of these old ballads is that their telling and retelling has caused details to be changed. For instance, in " Bonny Barbara Allan " the hero's name has become in various versions Sir James of the Grave, Jemmy Grove, and John Green. Sometimes Barbara dies repentant of her cruelty; sometimes she maintains her hurt pride and scorn to the end. The last two stanzas here printed originally belonged to another love ballad but became grafted on this one. This little tragedy has many musical settings.

It was in and about the Martinmas time,
    When the green leaves were a-falling,
That Sir John Graeme, in the West
        Country,
    Fell in love with Barbara Allan.   4

He sent his men down through the town
    To the place where she was dwelling:
" O haste and come to my master dear,
    Gin° ye be Barbara Allan."

8. *Gin:* if.

O hooly, hooly° rose she up,
    To the place where he was lying,   10
And when she drew the curtain by,
    " Young man, I think you're dying."

" O it's I'm sick, and very, very sick,
    And it's a' for Barbara Allan ";
" O the better for me ye's never be,   15
    Though your heart's blood were a-
        spilling.

9. *hooly:* slowly.

"O dinna ye mind,° young man," said
  she,
  "When the red wine ye were fillin',
That ye made the healths gae round and
  round,
  And slighted Barbara Allan?"   20

He turned his face unto the wall,
  And death was with him dealing;
"Adieu, adieu, my dear friends all,
  And be kind to Barbara Allan."

And slowly, slowly raise she up,   25
  And slowly, slowly left him,
And, sighing, said she could not stay,
  Since death of life had reft him.

She had not gane a mile but twa,°   29
  When she heard the dead-bell ringing,
And every jow° that the dead-bell geid,°
  It cried, "Woe to Barbara Allan!"

"O mother, mother, make my bed!
  O make it saft and narrow!
Since my love died for me today,   35
  I'll die for him tomorrow."

They buried her in the old churchyard,
  And Sir John's grave was nigh her.
And from his heart grew a red, red rose,
  And from her heart a brier.   40

They grew to the top o' the old church
  wall,
  Till they could grow no higher,
Until they tied a true love's knot —
  The red rose and the brier.

17. *dinna ye mind:* don't you remember.
29. *gane a mile but twa:* gone only two miles.
31. *jow:* stroke; *geid:* gave.

Sir Patrick Spens

Good old Sir Patrick Spens, who obeyed orders and braved the ocean at the stormiest, most dangerous time of year, was a man who would obviously appeal to the people of the rugged north.

It is not clear whether Sir Patrick is an actual historical figure, for he is not mentioned in any of the documents of the time. In some versions of this ballad, however, there are references to Norwegian lords; and it is known that in the thirteenth century a group of Norwegians did come to Scotland to escort home their king, Eric, and his bride, Margaret, daughter of Alexander III of Scotland. So perhaps there is some historical background for the ballad.

The king sits in Dumferling° toune,
  Drinking the blude-reid wine:
"O whar will I get a skilly° skipper,
  To sail this new schip of mine?"

O up and spak an eldern knicht,°   5
  Sat at the kings richt kne:
"Sir Patrick Spens is the best sailor,
  That ever sailed the se."

The king has written a braid° letter,
  And sealed it wi his hand,   10
And sent it to Sir Patrick Spens,
  Was walking on the strand.

The first line that Sir Patrick red,
  A loud lauch lauched he;
The next line that Sir Patrick red,   15
  The teir blinded his ee.°

1. *Dumferling* (dŭm·fĕr'lĭng): a town near Edinburgh, now Dumfermline. 3. *skilly:* skillful. 5. *eldern knicht:* older knight. 9. *braid:* on a broad sheet, or long. 16. *ee:* eye.

" O wha is this has don this deid,
  And told the king o' me,
To send us out at this time o' the yeir,
  To sail upon the se!   20

" Mak ready, mak ready, my mirry men
    all,
  Our guid schip sails the morne."
" Now, ever alake,° my master deir,
  I feir a deadlie storme.

" I saw the new moone late yestreen,
  Wi' the auld moone in hir arme,   26
And if we gang to se, master,
  I feir we'll cum to harme."

O laith,° laith wer our guid Scots lords
  To weet their cork-heild schoone;°
Bot lang owre° a' the play was playd,
  They wat their hats aboone.°   32

O lang, lang may their ladies sit,
  Wi their fans into their hand;
Before they se Sir Patrick Spens   35
  Cum sailing to the strand.

And lang, lang may their maidens sit,
  Wi their gold kems° in their hair,
All waiting for their ain deir loves,
  For thame they'll se na mair.   40

Haf owre,° haf owre to Aberdour,°
  'Tis fiftie fadom deip,
And thair lies guid Sir Patrick Spens,
  Wi the Scots lords at his feit.

23. *alake:* alack, alas. 29. *laith:* loath, unwilling. 30. To wet their cork-heeled shoes.
31. *owre:* ere, before. 32. Their hats floated
above them. 38. *kems:* combs. 41. *Haf owre:*
half over, halfway; *Aberdour:* a small town near
Edinburgh.

Get Up and Bar the Door

Most medieval ballads are concerned with
a tragic theme in which love and death
play important roles. But there are a few
that strike a lighter note. Usually these
humorous poems tell of some amusing conflict between a husband and wife in which
the man is the victor. In the following ballad the tables are turned, and the wife wins
the argument.

It fell about the Martinmas time,°
  And a gay time it was then,
When our goodwife got puddings to
    make,
  She's boild them in the pan.

The wind sae cauld blew south and
    north,   5
  And blew into the floor;
Quoth our goodman to our goodwife,
  " Gae out and bar the door."

" My hand is in my hussyfskap,°
  Goodman, as ye may see;   10
An it shoud nae be barrd this hundred
    year,
  It's no be barrd for me."°

They made a paction° tween them twa,
  They made it firm and sure,
That the first word whaeer° shoud
    speak,   15
  Shoud rise and bar the door.

1. *Martinmas time:* November 11. 9. *hussyfskap:* household duties. 11–12. "The door
will not be barred in a hundred years if I have
to bar it." 13. *paction:* agreement. 15. *whaeer:*
whoever.

Then by there came two gentlemen,
    At twelve o'clock at night,
And they could neither see house nor
    hall,
Nor coal nor candlelight.   20

" Now whether is this a rich man's house,
    Or whether it is a poor? "°
But neer a word wad ane o' them° speak,
    For barring of the door.

And first they° ate the white puddings,
    And then they ate the black;   26
Tho muckle° thought the goodwife to
    hersel,
    Yet neer a word she spake.

Then said the one unto the other,
    " Here, man, tak ye my knife;   30
Do ye tak aff the auld man's beard,
    And I'll kiss the goodwife."

" But there's nae water° in the house,
    And what shall we do than? "
" What ails ye at the pudding broo,°   35
    That boils into° the pan? "

O up then started our goodman,
    An angry man was he:
" Will ye kiss my wife before my een,
    And scad° me wi pudding bree? "°

Then up and started our goodwife,   41
    Gied three skips on the floor:
" Goodman, you've spoken the foremost
    word;
    Get up and bar the door."

21–22. The strangers ask the question.
23. *them:* the man and his wife. 25. *they:* the
strangers. 27. *muckle:* much. 33. *water:* probably to scald the beard in order to scrape it off.
35. "What's the matter with using the pudding
water?" 36. *into:* in. 40. *scad:* scald; *bree:* broth,
liquor.

BALLADS GAY AND TRAGIC

1. What characteristic of Robin Hood is
emphasized in the first ballad? Does he
appear in a favorable or unfavorable light?
How do you know that the sheriff had encountered Robin Hood and his men before
this incident? What features of this ballad
are characteristic of Robin Hood's exploits?

2. What reasons can you find for the
popularity of " Bonny Barbara Allan "? If
you have access to other versions, compare
them for differences.
3. What superstitious belief in evil
omens is brought out in " Sir Patrick
Spens "? What other sea poems and stories
have you read in which similar beliefs are
revealed? At what place in the narrative
do you first realize that the poem will end
tragically?
4. What does " Get Up and Bar the
Door " tell you about the lives of common
folk in long-ago England? In what way is
this humorous situation applicable to family life today?

CLASS ACTIVITIES

1. Write a ballad using a modern theme.
2. Plan a program of ballad music including, if possible, transcriptions of old
and modern ballads.
3. Dramatize informally " Get Up and
Bar the Door " by having one student read
the narrative and four actors come in with
their lines in the right places.

THE POWER OF WORDS

SCOTTISH DIALECT

Naturally enough, with the limited communication of ancient days, many different
dialects developed within the small territory of the British Isles. The amazing thing
is that so much of this variety of speech
persists today. In the old Scottish ballads
there are many words that you will find in
literature of the twentieth century.
One of the commonest differences between dialects and standard English is the
pronunciation of internal vowels. *O* sometimes becomes *a* as in *lang,* or *au* as in
auld, cauld, or *ae* as in *gae, sae.* Find other
good examples in these ballads of internal
vowel change to show pronunciation differences.
There are occasional consonant changes,
such as *knicht* and *richt* for *knight* and
right. This shows that these words were
pronounced with a guttural sound like that
in German. Over the centuries this sound
became silent in standard English. Watch
for these same words in Chaucer.

THE GROWTH OF THE ENGLISH LANGUAGE

The Middle English Period

After the Norman Conquest in 1066, England became a land of three tongues, and it took several centuries for these to fuse into what might be truly called the *English* language. The conquered English spoke Old English; the Norman overlords spoke French; churchmen used Latin. Since the country was without a common national language, it is no wonder that chaos prevailed for many years.

What little writing was done was in the language of the class for which it was intended. The ballads, some of which you have just read, were the literature of the common people. If they do not *look* like Old English, remember that these songs and tales were passed on largely by word of mouth. The versions that you see here were written down in later centuries after many language changes had taken place. The castle people were interested primarily in long tales of chivalry, composed at first in French and often celebrating a French hero, such as Roland or Charlemagne. In the monasteries, monks were writing in Latin about church doctrines, philosophy, and the lives of saints. But people of all classes had to communicate with one another, and so there developed a kind of common tongue, with an Old English basis enriched by French and Latin words. Gradually this hybrid language gained standing. In 1362, three centuries after the conquest, Parliament was for the first time opened by a speech in English instead of French.

In the fourteenth century a few individual authors emerged from the great mass of anonymous writing. The most important of these was Geoffrey Chaucer, whom you are about to study. The short passage on page 83 gives you the first chance you have had in this volume to read English just as it was written six centuries ago.

At about the same time came Wyclif's translation of the Bible into the vernacular. Earlier the Bible had been available only in Latin and was therefore a closed book to all except the clergy. But now, even though a man could not read or write, he could listen to a reading of the life of Christ in language that he understood.

Both Chaucer and Wyclif used the Midland dialect, which was the speech of London and central England. The island was dotted with dialects. Men of the South and men of the North probably understood each other with difficulty, if at all. Which of these forms of speech would win out in the end? Chaucer and Wyclif had much to do with the answer to this question. Later they were ably seconded by William Caxton, who brought to London in 1476 that amazing new invention from the Continent — the printing press. He produced hundreds of copies of the works of Chaucer and other writers. Until then it had often taken years of a scribe's life to write out a single manuscript, a treasure that few could afford. Since printing always gives stability, permanence, and wide circulation to any form of language, it is easy to see why the Midland dialect, rather than one of the others, eventually became the accepted standard.

It is also easy to see why certain spellings which were originally phonetic were retained long after their pronunciation had changed with the passing of time. As English has always had a tendency to clip and shorten pronunciation, there remains in our spelling a great residue of silent letters which originally were pronounced. A most striking example is our final silent *e*, which you will find usually pronounced in Chaucer's writing as a separate syllable. Some of these final *e*'s have disappeared from modern English; others have been retained, chiefly to indicate that the preceding vowel is, or was originally, "long." Other familiar silent letters are in *often, knight, cough, drought*, etc.

With printing, language now crystallized so quickly that by the end of the fifteenth century a page of English prose seems almost modern, compared with a page of Chaucer. A quick glance at the selection from Malory on page 95 will convince you of this. *Morte d'Arthur* too is in the Midland dialect.

The other dialects never died out completely but became the backbone of dialects most noticeable today in southwestern, western, and northern England, and in Scotland. In fact, the Scottish and northern dialects produced a rich literature of their own. Examples of its use in modern times are the poems by Robert Burns (page 332) and the story of Yorkshiremen by Eric Knight (page 593).

Just how did the impact of French and Latin during the Middle Ages affect English? Not in sentence structure, for, unlike the French, we still put the adjective before the noun. Latin might have influenced us to retain the complex inflections of Old English, but it didn't. During the Middle Ages the gradual changes that took place in syntax seemed to grow out of native English tendencies. We still use the little linking words like *of, to, for* to glue our sentences together. We generally follow the subject-verb-object order in our sentences. It has been said that we could write natural and idiomatic sentences today using only words of Old English derivation, whereas we could not compose an acceptable sentence using only words from French or Latin.

Nouns alone can tell us a great deal about the social history of the Middle Ages. What conclusions can you draw from the following groups of words?

Of Anglo-Saxon derivation: *man, woman, child, house, home, horse, dog, cow, king, sheriff, outlaw, arrow.*

Of French derivation: *chivalry, armor, homage, government, nobility, madam, mansion, tournament, royalty, banquet.*

Of Latin derivation: *cathedral, chaplain, charity, miracle, paradise, apostle, saint, sacrament, salvation.*

The close contacts between England and France throughout the Middle Ages made French the most influential outside language. These early borrowings have become so intimately a part of our language that we are not immediately aware of their origin, but regard them as native English words. Some good examples are *place, large, change, pay, state, rule, judge.*

Our stream of English, which ran its narrow course during Anglo-Saxon times, has now been broadened by two great tributaries, Latin and French. Just as the Mississippi becomes a different kind of river after the great waters of the Missouri and the Ohio flow into it, so Middle English became a quite different language from Old English.

GEOFFREY CHAUCER 1340?—1400

Chaucer is often called "the Father of English literature," and to him goes the honor of being the first great English humorist and realist. He was born into the home of a well-to-do wine merchant of London who was able to place his son when a mere lad in a noble household as a page. He later became a court favorite and married one of the ladies in waiting to the queen.

Chaucer served his country and his king loyally as soldier, courtier, diplomat, civil administrator, and translator of books into the English language — a language which he, more than any other writer, helped to "create." Some of his experiences were as dramatic as the fictional stories he wrote. In 1359, when the English invaded France, Chaucer was captured and the king contributed sixteen pounds toward his ransom! Later, he made several trips to France and Italy on government affairs.

Following his journeys abroad, Chaucer became Comptroller of the Port of London and later a Member of Parliament. But after the death of his influential patron, John of Gaunt, Chaucer may have felt the sting of poverty. He won a pension from the king but did not enjoy it long, for he died within a year. He lies buried in the Poets' Corner of Westminster Abbey, the first of many great English writers to find a resting place in that famous shrine.

Throughout his active public life Chaucer was also a diligent scholar. He collected about sixty volumes which he kept hidden away in a chest, for in the days before printing such a library was a treasure.

In his earlier writings, Chaucer borrowed French styles of verse and frequently used classical themes and references. But in his masterpiece *The Canterbury Tales* he drew on his own times as a setting for stories and thereby helped to establish a realistic pattern of English writing that was to persist for centuries. Each story is appropriate in subject matter, language, and general style to its teller.

The Canterbury Tales is our first real collection of short stories in English literature, though they are in poetry rather than in prose like the modern short story. Chaucer ties his tales together by having the storytellers travel as a group on a journey to the shrine of a well-known saint, Thomas à Becket. Each was to tell two stories en route to Canterbury and two on the way back. But Chaucer died before the work was completed, and instead of the proposed one hundred and twenty-four stories only twenty-four were written. Parts of the *Prologue* to the whole work and one of the stories, *The Nun's Priest's Tale*, are given here.

Prologue to The Canterbury Tales

Turn back the clock of time to the year 1387. Approaching Tabard Inn in the town of Southwark [1] across the river from London is a band of pilgrims. Traveling on horseback, they will have a long, slow journey to Canterbury, about sixty-five miles to the southeast. Although it is only midafternoon, the air from the Thames River is chilly. Since the travelers are tired and hungry, they decide to spend the night at the inn and travel on the morrow.

Inside the inn the landlord bustles about preparing for the comfort of his approaching guests. As they come across London Bridge, he hears the shrieking bagpipe played by one of the pilgrims, and the jingling bells on the bridle reins of the horses. He orders firewood, food, boards for the trestles in the main room, and wooden trenchers to be placed upon them. Now all is tumult and confusion as the travelers come clattering into the innyard. Stable boys shout as they rub down the horses; serving men rush to and fro with bowls so that the travelers may wash their hands.

[1] *Southwark* (sŭth'ẽrk).

Since forks are unknown and two people generally use a trencher, or platter, between them, clean hands are doubly necessary. The cooks bring in food and place it on the boards — fish and fowl and meats cooked in garlic, onions, mustard, vinegar, and spices; bacon and pea soup; puddings and pastries; wine and Southwark ale.

The landlord seats himself in the place of honor by one of the wooden pillars, while the travelers find places around the boards. After eating, everybody is in a gay mood and eagerly agrees to follow the landlord's suggestion: that each relate two stories en route to Canterbury and two on the way back. The best storyteller will receive a free dinner at the expense of the others at the end of the journey. They also accept the landlord's proposal that he accompany them as their leader and judge of the stories. But it is getting late, and a long, hard day lies ahead. The travelers pay for their food and lodging and retire. Now let Chaucer continue with the *Prologue,* which follows in a modern English version by Ruth M. Stauffer.

The illustration below and those on pages 72–82 are from woodcuts that appeared in the second edition of The Canterbury Tales, *printed by William Caxton about 1484.*

hen April showers with sweetness pierce the root
Of droughts of March, and make the buds upshoot,
And bathe the veins in sap, wherefrom the flowers
Are born to blossom in these vernal showers;
When soft west winds have breathed upon the trees,   5
And tender sprouts appear on all the leas,
And when the youthful sun has run his course
Half through the Ram° — the sign of springtime's force —
When little birds — so stirred by nature's might
They seem with open eyes to sleep all night —   10
Make melody at dawn; then folk also
On pleasant pilgrimages long to go,
And palmers° want to seek some far-off strands
And distant shrines, well known in many lands;
Especially from every county's end   15
Of England down to Canterbury they wend;
The holy blessed martyr° there they seek,
That help will give if they are sick or weak.

Befell that in that season, on a day
In Southwark at the Tabard, as I lay   20
Ready upon my pilgrimage to start
To Canterbury with a pious heart,
At night there came into that hostelry
Full nine and twenty in a company
Of sundry folk, by chance together there   25
In fellowship; and pilgrims, too, they were
That on to Canterbury meant to ride.
The rooms were spacious, and the stables wide,
And comfortable indeed we all were made.
And shortly, ere the sun his head had laid   30
To rest, I spoke with all the fellowship,
And so they let me join them on their trip;
And we made compact then to rise betimes,
And take our way there, as I've told in rimes.
But now, while still I have the time and space,   35
Ere that I farther in this story pace,
I think it only reasonable and fair
To tell you what each one was like: his air,
His rank, his bearing, what he traveled in,
And at a knight then will I first begin.   40

THE KNIGHT

A *Knight* there was, and that a worthy man,
That from the very time he first began
To ride abroad, had loved high chivalry,

---

8. *Ram:* the first of the twelve signs of the zodiac. The time indicated by the passage is about April 11. The year is 1387. 13. *palmers* (päm′ērz): pilgrims who had visited the Holy Land and wore two crossed palms to indicate this. 17. *martyr:* Thomas à Becket, Archbishop of Canterbury, murdered in 1170; canonized in 1172 (see page 52).

Truth, and all honor, freedom, and courtesy;   45
And thus he rode out in his liege lord's war
In Christian lands and heathen — none so far.
In fifteen mortal battles had he been —
Crusades against the Turk and Saracen;
And fought in tournaments, and won the prize;   50
And yet, although most worthy, he was wise,
And in his bearing meek as is a maid.
He never had in all his lifetime said
An ill-bred word to serf or man of might:
He was a very perfect gentle knight.

THE SQUIRE

With him there was his son, a youthful *Squire;*   55
To be a knight was now his heart's desire.
He tried to train his hair to curliness!
Of twenty years of age, he was, I guess,
And singularly quick, and very strong.
In France and Flanders he had served full long,   60
And valiant been, considering his years:
He hoped his fame would reach his lady's ears.
He wore the latest clothes: the gown, indeed,
Quite short, and all embroidered like a mead°
Of springtime flowers; the sleeves hung down his side,   65
Extremely long and very, very wide.
He played the flute or sang the livelong day.
He was as fresh as is the month of May.
A well-trained squire, one skilled in horsemanship,
He sat a horse with just the expert's grip,   70
Could ride in jousts, and make his charger prance,
Compose love songs, and draw, and write, and dance.
This lad had fallen in love; by moonlight pale
He slept no more than does the nightingale!
Courteous he was, willing and meek; and able   75
To carve before his father at the table.°

THE YEOMAN

One servant had the knight — no retinue;
For straight from war he went to pay his due
Of thanks for safe return. This servingman
Had close-cropped hair, and face of swarthy tan;   80
And he was clad in coat and hood of green;
A sheaf of peacock arrows, bright and keen,
Under his belt he carried thriftily;
And in his hand a mighty bow had he;
A sword and buckler° by his side were hung,   85

64. *mead* (mēd): meadow. 76. This line refers to the custom of the time for the son to carve his
father's meat and wait upon him. 85. *buckler* (bŭk'lēr): a shield.

A hunting horn across his shoulder slung;
The baldric° was of green; and on his breast
Saint Christopher° in silver kept him blest.
A *Yeoman* was he, and a forester,
And knew the ways of woodcraft, I aver.

THE NUN

There was a Nun, a pleasant *Prioress.*
This lady's smile was coy, I must confess.
And she was known as Madame Eglantine.
She liked to chant the services divine;
But then, in truth, she sang straight through her nose!
And as a court-bred dame she liked to pose:
She spoke fair French, but with an accent queer,
For Paris she had never come anear.
Her mien was stately, and her courtesy
So overnice it strained gentility.
Her table manners were indeed a treat:
With dainty grace she reached to take her meat;
Her upper lip she wiped so very clean
That never was the slightest fraction seen
Of grease within the rim upon her cup;   105
She never let a morsel she took up
Drop down upon her breast; nor did she wet
Her fingers in her sauce too deep. And yet,
In spite of all her social poise and art,
She had a very, very tender heart.   110
Upon my word, this Prioress would cry
To see a mouse caught in a trap and die!
Pet dogs she had, which she herself saw fed
Upon roast beef and milk and sweetened bread:
But if one died, she wept till she was sick;   115
Or if you struck them smartly with a stick,
When they got underfoot as pets will do.
Well built and tall she was, and handsome, too:
Her eyes as gray as glass; a noble head;
Her mouth was winsome — small and soft and red.   120
Her cloak was modish, and her wimple,° note,
Was pleated carefully about her throat.
Her rosary was coral; it was strung
With green; a golden locket from it hung,
Engraved in Latin: first, the letter *A;*   125
Then followed, *Amor vincit omnia.*°
She was an amiable and gentle dame.
Another Nun and three priests° with her came.

87. *baldric* (bôl'drĭk): a belt, worn over one shoulder, to support a bugle or sword. 88. *Saint Christopher:* patron saint of travelers, whose figure on a brooch or medal is believed to shield the wearer from danger. 121. *wimple* (wĭm'p'l): a covering of silk or linen material for head, neck, and chin. It is still worn by nuns, but in medieval times it was worn by all women. 126. *Amor vincit omnia:* Love conquers all things. 128. *three priests:* It is supposed that "and three priests" was added by some scribe to fill out a line left incomplete by Chaucer. Only one priest is mentioned again, and the count of "nine and twenty" allows for only one.

THE MONK

A *Monk* rode with us on a palfrey° brown.
He wore fine boots and fur bands on his gown;   130
A bowknot held his hood, a curious jewel.
He loved to hunt. What matter if the rule°
Said monks must stay at home and labor? Faugh!
He didn't give a plucked hen for that law.
He thought that text was not worth even an oyster   135
Which says that monks must not stray out of cloister!
For all such strict old forms he just passed by!
And right he was! The world needs men, say I.
Why should a man do nought but pore o'er books,
And study all the time until he looks   140
Just like a ghost? Or in a monastery
Stay all day long, and never find life merry?
A stable full of thoroughbreds, he owned;
And coursing greyhounds, swift and silver-toned.
And when he rode, men might his bridle hear   145
Jingling in a whistling wind as clear
And just as loud as do the chapel bells
In the far abbey where this fat monk dwells.

THE FRIAR

One Hubert came along, a jolly *Friar*.
He knew the taverns well in every shire: 150
The barmaids and the landlords were his friends.
He said one never seemed to gain his ends
By helping sick and poor — such vulgar scum!
They never made it worth his while to come.
To have to deal with those who beg their bread   155
Would never get you anywhere, he said.
And so he kept in touch with richer folk
And prosperous country squires. His yoke
Of penance was not harsh to men of thrift:
The sign of *true* repentance was a gift   160
Of alms and dole to humble friars, you know!
So pleasant was his " *In principio* "°
That even a poor widow with no shoe
Would give a farthing° without more ado.
Of double worsted was his semicope,°   165
Handsome enough for abbot or for pope.
No threadbare cope of poverty for him!
He played the fiddle well and sang with vim.
His eyes, like stars upon a frosty night,
Would twinkle as he trilled with all his might.   170

---

129. *palfrey* (pôl'frĭ): a saddle horse. 132. *the rule:* the regulations of the Benedictine monastic order, to which the monk probably belonged. 162. "*In principio*" (ĭn prĭn·sĭp'ĭ·ō): "In the beginning," the opening of the Gospel of John, a favorite passage used by begging friars. 164. *farthing:* quarter of a cent. 165. *semicope* (sĕm'ĭ·cōp): a short cape.

He lisped a little when he talked or sung,
To make his English sweet upon his tongue.

THE MERCHANT

There was a *Merchant,* rich, as you'd suppose,
With well-trimmed beard, and fine imported clothes.
He watched the market and a profit made   175
When he exchanged his gold in foreign trade.
And it was his opinion, spoken free,
That England ought to guard the Northern Sea
'Twixt Harwich° and The Netherlands, and rout
The pirates, when he sent his ventures out.   180
He was a self-made man, and talked you blue
With all the business deals that he'd put through.
So pompous was he, and so shrewd, I bet
That no one guessed he really was in debt.

THE OXFORD SCHOLAR

A *Clerk* — that is, an Oxford scholar — who   185
Looked hollow to his bones, and threadbare, too,
Rode with us on a nag lean as a rake.
The youth was poor, and starved for learning's sake.
He'd rather spend his gold on books than food,
Or on gay clothes or fun, as others would.   190
Of ethics and philosophy he read,
Kept Aristotle° right beside his bed.
He seldom spoke; but what he said was clear,
And full of sense, so that you wished to hear;
Of high ideals and virtue was his speech;   195
And gladly would he learn, and gladly teach.

THE LAWYER

A famous *Lawyer* on the trip did go —
A learned man, at least he sounded so;

179. *Harwich* (hăr′ĭj): an important seaport on the North Sea. 192. *Aristotle* (ăr′ĭs·tŏt′′l): Greek philosopher (384–322 B.C.), regarded by medieval scholars as the highest authority on all matters of learning.

In jurisprudence wise; knew all the laws;
And in the best-made wills could pick out flaws.
He knew by heart decisions and decrees
From William° down. Codes, statutes — these
Were play to him; in litigation, skilled;
With presents and with fees his chests were filled.
A busier man than he you'd find nowhere,   205
Yet he seemed busier than he was, I'd swear.

THE FRANKLIN

He brought with him a hearty *Country Squire,*
Whose jovial face shone red as any fire
Through beard as white as is a daisy. He
Enjoyed good food, loved hospitality;   210
Kept open house back home — in fact, you'd say
It snowed both meat and drink there every day!
His greatest joy was eating all the while:
Good meats, good wines, and all in hearty style;
For Epicurus'° son he seemed to be,   215
So sure good meals meant true felicity!
He kept his table standing always set
Ready to entertain whome'er he met.
He bragged of having dishes out of season.
His cook was scolded far beyond a reason   220
If anything was wrong, or dinner late!
In his own shire° he was a man of weight:
Had sat in Parliament, been judge at court;
Had held all county offices, in short.

THE GUILDSMEN

There were five members of a city guild,°   225
Who rolled in wealth because they were so skilled.
They all were dressed alike, for their attire
Must match their guild: *Upholsterer* and *Dyer,*

202. *William:* William the Conqueror (see page 50). 215. *Epicurus* (ĕp'ĭ·kū′rŭs): Greek philosopher (342?–270 B.C.), who taught that happiness is the goal of life. 222. *shire* (shīr): county.
225. *guild:* For a discussion of guilds, see page 54.

75

A *Carpenter,* a *Hatter, Weaver* — these
Had silver-mounted daggers, if you please!   230
To be an alderman, each one seemed fit,
And how their wives would have rejoiced at it!
To have a mantle carried like a queen,
Be called " *ma dame!* "° and frequently be seen
At vigils° leading all the company,   235
Would flatter any woman's vanity.

THE COOK

They had a *Cook* along, whose skill was known
In boiling chicken with the marrow bone;
The king he was of culinary art:
He knew the use of flavorings, keen and tart;   240
Could roast and bake and broil and boil and fry;
Could make good soup, and triumphed at a pie!
It seemed a pity that upon his shin
He had a running sore, for he could win
At making rich blancmange,° and never fail   245
To judge the different grades of London ale.

THE SHIPMAN

A *Shipman* rode his horse as best he could!
Bad gales and storms at sea he had withstood:
His weather-beaten face made this quite plain.
He knew the coast from Jutland° down to Spain,   250
Or Hull° to Carthage° — dangers and the tides,
The harbors and the pilotings besides;
With many a tempest had his beard been shaken.
Full many a draft of wine he'd deftly taken
While merchant slept, and many a mother's son
Had walked the plank in sea fights he had won.
Smuggler and pirate both he'd been, in fine,
This hardy skipper of the *Madeline.*

THE PHYSICIAN

And various others took this pilgrimage:
A skilled *Physician,* pompous, rich, and sage;
Astrology he knew, and by the spell
Of stars, his patients' ailments he could tell;
And his prescriptions gave the druggist trade —
For each, brisk business for the other made!
His fad was dieting and moderate fare;

234. "*ma dame*" (mà·dàm'): French for "my lady." 235. *vigils:* The eves of some church festivals often became social gatherings where women showed off their finery. 245. *blancmange* (blà·mänzh'): French for "white food"; not a dessert as today, but a concoction of minced chicken, rice, milk, sugar, and almonds. 250. *Jutland* (jŭt'lănd): peninsula on the mainland of Denmark. 251. *Hull:* a seaport in northern England; *Carthage* (kär'thĭj): a port in North Africa.

He did not read his Bible much, I'd swear!°
Though fine his clothes, he hoarded well the pence
That he'd collected in the pestilence;°
For gold° is used in doses, I've heard tell:
That must be why he loved his gold so well.   270

THE WIFE OF BATH

A *Wife of Bath*° did much to keep us gay
With tales of love and love charms, on the way —
A lively soul, who knew the inmost art
Of how to win a spouse and hold his heart;
For she had had five husbands in her time,   275
Not counting scores of lovers in her prime!
She'd grown a little deaf, but nought she cared:
Now forth to foreign lands each year she fared,
Since fate decreed she seek out every shrine.
(Her teeth grew far apart — a certain sign   280
That she should travel far!) She'd seen Boulogne,°
And Rome, and Palestine, Spain, and Cologne.°
Abundant gold she had, for she could weave
So well, that even in Flanders,° I believe,
You could not find her match. She liked fine gear,   285
And o'er the parish wives to domineer.
She took precedence on the relic days°
In offering alms to manifest her praise.
If any dame went first, so wroth was she
That in her heart she lost all charity!   290
The towering headdress worn upon her hair
On Sunday weighed a full ten pounds I'd swear!
But now she wore a wimple and a hat
As broad as any buckler, and as flat.
The mantle round her waist did not conceal   295
Red stockings, and a spur upon each heel.
She kept the other pilgrims all in gales
Of laughter, listening to her merry tales.

THE PARSON

A kindly *Parson* took the journey too.
He was a scholar, learned, wise, and true   300
And rich in holiness though poor in gold.
A gentle priest: whenever he was told

266. In medieval times, doctors, and other men interested in science, were commonly thought to be skeptical of religion. 268. *pestilence:* the Black Death, which ravaged all Europe in the fourteenth century (see page 56). 269. *gold:* It was an actual medieval belief that gold dissolved in medicine was a remedy for certain ailments. 271. *Wife of Bath:* A wife was a matron, or married woman. Bath is a town in the southwest of England known for its medicinal springs. 281. *Boulogne* (bōō'lōn'): a city in northern France on the English Channel. 282. *Cologne* (kŏ·lōn'): a German city on the Rhine River. 284. *Flanders* (flăn'dērz): old name for Belgium. 287. *relic days:* Certain Sundays were set apart for offering gifts to religious relics, such as the bones of dead saints (see *The Pardoner,* page 80).

That poor folks could not meet their tithes° that year,
He paid them up himself; for priests, it's clear,
Could be content with little, in God's way.   305
He lived Christ's gospel truly every day,
And taught his flock, and preached what Christ had said.
And even though his parish was widespread,
With farms remote, and houses far asunder,
He never stopped for rain or even for thunder;   310
But visited each home where trouble came:
The rich or poor to him were all the same.
He always went on foot, with staff in hand;
For as their minister, he took this stand:
No wonder that iron rots if gold should rust!   315
That is, a priest in whom the people trust
Must not be base, or what could you expect
Of weaker folk? The Shepherd must perfect
His life in holiness that all his sheep
May follow him, although the way is steep,   320
And win at last to heaven. Indeed, I'm sure
You could not find a minister more pure.
He was a Christian both in deed and thought;
He lived himself the Golden Rule he taught.

THE PLOWMAN

The brother of the Parson came along: 325
A *Plowman* used to work, and very strong.
A kindly, simple laboring man was he,
Living in peace and perfect charity.
With all his heart he loved God best, and then
His neighbor as himself. For poorer men   330
He'd thresh and dig and plow — work all the day
In heavy toil without expecting pay:
It was enough if Christ approve his deed.
He rode a mare, the poor man's humble steed.

THE MILLER

The *Miller,* Robin, was a thickset lout,   335
So big of bone and brawn, so broad and stout
That he was champion wrestler at the matches.
He'd even break a door right off its latches
By running at it with his burly head!
His beard, broad as a spade, was fiery red;   340
His mouth, a yawning furnace you'd suppose!
A wart with bristly hairs stood on his nose.
A clever scamp he was, with " thumb of gold "
To test the flour he ground; for when he tolled
His share of grain, he sneaked the payment thrice!   345

---

303. *tithes* (tīthz): taxes for the Church, consisting of one-tenth of the individual's yearly income
or production.

The jokes and tales he told were not so nice.
A drunk and vulgar rogue he proved to be.
But yet he played the bagpipe cleverly,
And to its tune he led us out of town.
A blue hood wore he, and a short white gown.   350

THE MANCIPLE

There was a *Manciple*° among the band:
He bought provisions, as I understand,
For thirty lawyers at an Inn of Court.
This steward was a canny man; in short,
Shrewd as the lawyers were, he fooled them all,   355
Got rich on fat commissions — made a haul!

THE REEVE

The *Reeve,*° or bailiff, rode a horse called Scot.
Tall, thin, clean-shaven, and his temper hot,
He was the despot of his lord's estate,
And hounded all the tenants into hate.   360
They feared him like the plague; but yet, you see,
Farming he understood from A to Z;
For he knew by the drought and by the rain
The yielding of his seed and of his grain;
His master's sheep, his stock, his horses too,   365
His poultry, swine, and cows, this bailiff knew.
He managed all so well that he himself
Was slowly gathering in the lord's own wealth —
Contrived to lend his master craftily
What was his own and rightful property!   370
A Norfolk° man, he came from Baldeswell.°
A carpenter he'd been, so I've heard tell.

THE SUMMONER

A *Summoner* whose duties are to search,
And bring to court, offenders 'gainst the Church —
A kind of church policeman — joined us there.   375
He had a fiery face — enough to scare
The children with its blotched and pimpled skin,
Its scurfy eyebrows, and its beardless chin.
His eyes were little, and were much too narrow;
His temper quick; he peered just like a sparrow.   380
Garlic and onions were his special taste;
And when with drafts of wine his wits were braced,
He shouted Latin phrases learned in court,
And "*Questio quid juris!*"° he'd exhort.

351. *Manciple* (măn′sĭ·p'l): a servant who bought provisions for a college or an Inn of Court. The latter was a society of lawyers and law students. 357. *Reeve* (rēv): estate manager. 371. *Norfolk* (nôr′fŭk): a county in eastern England; *Baldeswell* (bôld′ĭs·wĕl): a town in Norfolk. 384. "*Questio quid juris!*": "The question is, what is the law?"

(For like a parrot he was really dense;   385
He'd learned the words, but could not grasp the sense.)
He'd set a garland on his round bald head,
And made a buckler out of cake and bread!

THE PARDONER

The *Pardoner,*° who came along with him,
Carried a wallet° filled up to the brim   390
With pardons hot from Rome, and relics old
(At least, he said they were), and these he sold
To poor believers back in lonely towns,
And priests as stupid as the country clowns:
A pillowcase he called Our Lady's veil;   395
He showed a fragment of the very sail
Of Peter's boat;° a cross weighed down with stones;
And in a glass he had pig's-knuckle bones!
And yet in church he read the lesson well,
And sang the offertory like a bell: 400
He knew that when that anthem had been sung,
He then must preach, and polish up his tongue
To make the silver tinkle in the plate.
A noble churchman this, the reprobate!
His hair hung down in stringy yellow locks: 405
His priest's hood he had trussed up in his box,
For he observed the new bare-headed style.
He and the Summoner did the way beguile
By brisk duets: they sang the latest hit,
" Come hither, love, to me! " Our ears were split!   410
The Pardoner's voice was shrill as any goat;
The other sang the bass deep in his throat.

Now that I've told you shortly, in a clause,
The rank, the dress, the number, and the cause
Why these were all assembled at the inn   415
Called Tabard — near the Bell — I must begin
And tell you what we did that selfsame night,
And later of the pilgrimage I'll write.
But first I pray you of your courtesy
If they appear ill-bred, do not blame me;   420
For anyone, you know, who tells a tale
He heard another speak, should never fail
To use the selfsame words and matter too,
Or else be found a liar and untrue:
Plato° himself has said — if Greek you read —   425
The words must be the cousin to the deed.

389. *Pardoner:* a preacher licensed to grant indulgences for sins in return for offerings to the church. 390. *wallet:* a sack. 397. *Peter's boat:* St. Peter was, of course, a fisherman before he became a disciple of Christ. 425. *Plato:* a Greek philosopher (427?–347 B.C.). Chaucer could not read Greek, but he knew Plato through Latin translations.

So even if the language be not fine,
But rude or coarse, the fault is theirs not mine;
And if some questions of their rank arise
Through my poor wit, I here apologize.°   430

THE HOST

Our *Host*° gave us good cheer. He served a meal
That gratified us all, and made us feel
(Especially when we had drunk his wine)
In high good humor, genial and benign.
A handsome man this host was, I declare;   435
A fine official he'd be anywhere;
A portly, keen-eyed man, whose speech was bold,
But such as sound experience would uphold
In common sense; a merry fellow, too;
For when the feast was ended, and he knew   440
That each of us had settled our account,
His amiability began to mount,
And in a jovial mood, he had his say:
    " Well, gentlemen, I have enjoyed your stay.
To tell the truth, I have not seen this year   445
A group so jolly as you've gathered here.
In fact I'd like to conjure up some scheme
That would amuse, and win me your esteem.
Ha! of a plan I've just this moment thought:
A good pastime — and it shall cost you naught.   450
    " You go to Canterbury. Heaven speed you!
The blissful martyr's self reward and heed you!
You mean, I'm sure, unless my memory fails,
To liven up the way by telling tales;
For certainly to ride along alone
In utter dumbness, silent as a stone,
Is not a bit of fun in pilgrimages.
Now by my father's soul (he's dead, these ages),
In truth I've hit upon the very thing!
Don't be afraid; it hasn't any string.   460
Just take a vote and let me know your mind."
    We did not think it worth our while to find
Objections to his friendliness, and so
Declared we all desired his plan to know.
    " Well, this it is, my lords. Suppose we say   465
That each of you tell four tales by the way,
Two as you go, and two as you return;
And then the one whose tale is best will earn
A festive supper here at Tabard Inn,
Paid by the rest. Now that's a prize to win! "   470

430. Chaucer is here apologizing for the fact that the pilgrims do not tell their tales in order of rank, as would have been considered proper in medieval society. 431. The Host has been almost certainly identified with a real innkeeper named Harry Bailly who had an inn at Southwark in Chaucer's time.

We heartily agreed, and took him up.
But first we set the price at which we'd sup
On our return; you see, we thought it wise
To fix beforehand, just how much the prize
Should cost us all. And it was understood   475
That he should manage all, for well he could.
   So then we went to bed. And next we knew
The dawn had come; and all our motley crew
The busy Host assembled, like a cock
That gathers all his hens and leads the flock.   480
   Then forth we ambled at a snail-like pace
Until we reached St. Thomas' watering place;°
And here our Host pulled up his horse, and said:
   " Well, here we are. Now you have made me head;
If evensong and morning song agree,°   485
You must obey the orders given by me.
Whoever is a rebel to my will,
We'll cast accounts, and make him foot the bill.
Here are the lots: who gets the shortest straw
Must be the first to speak. Now let us draw.   490
" Sir Knight," he said, " my master and my lord,
Let's see how Lady Luck will you award.
Come near," quoth he, " my lady prioress;
And you, sir clerk, don't be so modest — yes,
We'll all take turns. Here, sir, the first is yours.   495
Now, mind, the shortest cut first tale ensures."
   We drew the lots; and, as was only right,
The shortest straw of all fell to the Knight.
It was good luck, indeed, a happy choice;
It made us all applaud and much rejoice.   500
When this good man perceived that it was true,
He did not " Hem! " and " Ha! " as lesser do,
But said: " Well, since I must begin the game,
Why, welcome be the lot, in God's good name!
Now let us ride, and hark to what I say."   505
And with that word we rode along the way;
And he began a pleasant tale in rhyme;
He told it thus: " Now, once upon a time . . ."

Heere endeth the prolog of this book; and
heere bigynneth the first tale which is the Knyghtes Tale.

482. *St. Thomas' watering place:* less than two miles from the Tabard Inn. 485. If you feel this morning as you did last night.

Parts of the Prologue

IN THE ORIGINAL MIDDLE ENGLISH

Now that you have read the *Prologue* in a modern English version, you will be curious to see the language in which Chaucer wrote. It is Middle English, the language which emerged from the mixture of Anglo-Saxon dialects and Norman French and which became the foundation of the later English speech that we use. At first glance it looks almost like a foreign language, but you will soon recognize words here and there that resemble our modern English. The pronunciation, too, seems strange when you first hear it, and you may feel embarrassed on trying to speak it. But have a try! Read the words freely and openly, enjoying their poetic qualities — musical sounds and rhythmic combinations.

Probably the best way to learn to read Chaucerian English is to hear and imitate an experienced reader. But you can work out the pronunciations yourself quite well, by using the pronunciation table on page 85. Read a few passages first to get the " feel " of the language, and then turn to this table for specific help. Practice aloud until you can read smoothly, enjoying the sense of the lines as well as the sounds.

Whan that Aprille with his shourës sootë
The droghte of March hath percëd to the rootë,
And bathëd every veyne in swich licour,
Of which vertu° engendrëd is the flour;
Whan Zephirus eek with his swetë breeth 5
Inspirëd hath in every holt and heeth
The tendrë croppës, and the yongë sonnë
Hath in the Ram his halfë cours y-ronnë,
And smalë fowlës maken melodyë,
That slepen al the night with open yë, 10
(So priketh° hem nature in hir corages°):
Than longen folk to goon on pilgrimages,
And palmers for to seken straungë strondës,
To fernë halwës,° couthe° in sondry londës;
And specially, from every shirës endë 15
Of Engelond, to Caunterbury they wendë,
The holy blisful martir for to sekë,
That hem hath holpen, whan that they were sekë.
    Bifel that, in that sesoun on a day,
In Southwerk at the Tabard as I lay 20

4. *vertu:* power, strength. 11. *priketh:* stirs, arouses; *corages:* hearts. 14. *fernë halwës:* distant shrines; *couthe:* known.

Redy to wenden on my pilgrimagë
To Caunterbury with ful devout coragë,
At night was come in-to that hostelryë
Wel nyne and twenty in a compaignyë,
Of sondry folk, by aventure y-fallë   25
In felawshipe, and pilgrims were they allë,
That toward Caunterbury wolden rydë;
The chambrës and the stablës weren wydë,
And wel we weren esëd attë bestë.
And shortly, whan the sonnë was to restë,   30
So hadde I spoken with hem everichon,
That I was of hir felawshipe anon,
And madë forward erly for to rysë,
To take our wey, ther as I yow devysë.
    But natheles, whyl I have tyme and spacë,   35
Er that I ferther in this talë pacë,
Me thinketh it acordaunt to resoun,
To tellë yow al the condicioun
Of ech of hem, so as it semëd me,
And whiche they weren, and of what degree;°   40
And eek in what array that they were innë;
And at a knight than wol I first beginnë. . . .

                        THE SQUIRE

    With him ther was his sone, a yong Squyer,
A lovyer, and a lusty bachelor,
With lokkës crulle, as they were leyd in pressë.
Of twenty yeer of age he was, I gessë.
Of his stature he was of evenë lengthë.°   5
And wonderly delivere,° and greet of strengthë.
And he hadde been somtyme in chivachyë°
In Flaundrës, in Artoys, and Picardyë,°
And born him wel, as of so litel spacë,
In hopë to stonden in his lady gracë.   10
Embroudëd was he, as it were a medë
Al ful of fresshë flourës, whyte and redë.
Singinge he was, or floytinge,° al the day;
He was as fresh as is the month of May.
Short was his goune, with slevës longe and wydë.   15
Wel coude he sitte on hors, and fairë ryde.
He coudë songës make and wel endytë,°
Juste° and eek daunce, and well purtreye and wrytë
So hote he lovedë, that by nightertalë°
He sleep namore than doth a nightingalë.   20
Curteys he was, lowly, and servisablë,
And carf biforn his fader at the tablë. . . .

40. *degree:* rank. 5. *evenë lengthë:* moderate height. 6. *delivere:* agile. 7. *chivachyë:* military expeditions. 8. *Flaundrës . . . Artoys . . . Picardyë:* place names, all concerned with Edward III's war with
France. 13. *floytinge:* playing the flute. 17. *endytë:* write. 18. *juste:* engage in a joust, or single combat.
19. *nightertalë:* nighttime.

PRONUNCIATION TABLE

The exact pronunciation of Chaucerian English is a difficult and uncertain matter. Nevertheless, if you follow these rules, you will produce something very close to what Chaucer himself must have said.

VOWELS

a — always the sound *ah*. It may be prolonged as in *bathëd* (bahth·ed), line 3, and *maken* (mahken), line 9; or shortened in *at, and*. Note that *a* is never pronounced as in modern *hate* or *hat*, but always with the *ah* sound.

ai, ay, ei, ey — as in *day*. *Veyne*, line 3; *array*, line 41.

au, aw, — as in *house*. *Straungë*, line 13; *Caunterbury*, line 16; *felawshipe*, line 26.

oo — usually pronounced like modern *ō*. See sootë, line 1; rootë, line 2.

e, long — as in *hate, they*. *Swetë* (swā-ta), line 5. A vowel doubled is always long. *Eek* (āke), line 5; *breeth* (brāth), line 5.

e, short — as in *men*. *Hem*, line 11; second syllable of *slepen*, line 10, and *priketh*, line 11.

Note that the final *e* — printed as *ë* — which would usually be silent in modern English, is almost always pronounced in Middle English. Its sound is like the final *a* in modern words. Thus *sootë*, line 1, is like the last two syllables of *Minnesota*.

When the final *e* precedes a vowel or *h*, it is not pronounced, as in line 2, *droghte of March*. In this text the *e* which is to be pronounced as another syllable is indicated thus: ë.

CONSONANTS

Most of the consonants are as in modern English. A few show foreign influence.

g — as in *get*, except in French words before *e* and *i* where it is like *zh*. *Corages*, line 11; *pilgrimages*, line 12 (similar to modern *garages*).

gh, ch — never silent as in modern English. Pronounced like the German *ch* in *nicht*. *Droghte*, line 2; *night*, line 10. In *knight*, line 42, the *k* is also pronounced as in German (k·nicht). Before a vowel or at the end of a word *ch* is pronounced as in *church*.

c and t are never blended with a following *i* as in modern *condition*, or *special;* but the *i* is pronounced as a separate syllable. (*C* has the sound of *s* when it comes before *i*.) *Specially* (four syllables), line 15; *condicioun* (four syllables), line 38.

CHAUCER'S PILGRIMS

1. Chaucer is acclaimed for his realistic portrayal of people in his own times, rich and poor alike. You can find in *The Canterbury Tales* a cross section of English society of medieval times. Place the pilgrims under their appropriate classes, as follows:

The Feudal System — Knight, Squire, etc.
The Church — Prioress, Nun's Priest, etc.
Town and Trades — Lawyer, Cook, etc.

How many of the professions represented in the *Prologue* have survived to this day? How many have ceased to exist?

2. Try to form a mental picture of each character and a clear impression of his personality.

3. Not only do you learn about people in Chaucer's time from the *Prologue* but also about Chaucer himself. Find passages that reveal (*a*) his genial sense of humor, (*b*) his good-natured acceptance of people, even if they are not particularly distinguished, (*c*) his appreciation of loyalty and honesty in people. Which of the characters in the *Prologue* do you think Chaucer himself most resembles? Whom does he most admire? least admire?

4. Compare a passage of fifteen or twenty lines in the original Middle English with the same lines in the modernized version. How would you describe the differences you may find in (*a*) meaning and (*b*) poetic rhythm and rhyme?

5. Chaucer is a great *satirist*, though he is almost never malicious, bitter, or savage when he pokes fun at the foibles and weaknesses of people. Point out examples of satire in the *Prologue* that particularly amused you, or struck you as a true appraisal of human character.

CLASS ACTIVITIES

1. Have members of the class draw pictures of the travelers. Several modern artists have illustrated Chaucer. Collect a display of prints, by class members and

outside artists, for your English classroom.

2. Select a committee to write a short radio play based on the *Prologue,* and then stage it with members of the class taking the various roles. Use a public address system or a screen to separate the actors from the class audience.

3. Form groups to study and report on medieval life. Make comparisons between modern and medieval customs and conditions of (*a*) travel, (*b*) table manners, (*c*) the practice of medicine, (*d*) commerce and manufacturing, (*e*) religious observances.

4. Prepare a talk to give in class on (*a*) Thomas à Becket, (*b*) Canterbury Cathedral and the town of Canterbury, (*c*) the French influence on Chaucer's English. Students of French will want to try the last of these topics, using several passages of the original Middle English to point out French words.

5. Write a prologue of your own, based upon some " pilgrimage " of modern life, such as an athletic event, a speech tournament, a district or state meeting of some club. Chaucer's *Prologue* will furnish you with numerous ideas, and so will these similar but later works: Longfellow's *Tales of a Wayside Inn,* Whittier's *The Tent on the Beach,* and John Masefield's *Reynard the Fox.* Chaucer himself may have borrowed the idea for *The Canterbury Tales* from the *Decameron,* a collection of tales by the fourteenth-century Italian writer Boccaccio. In the *Decameron* a group of young people withdraw to a country place to avoid the plague raging in their city, and in this way fall to telling tales.

THE POWER OF WORDS

METAPHOR AND SIMILE

The terms *metaphor, figures of speech, simile,* and *figurative language* all refer to the use of words to make *comparisons* between unlike things. Metaphor is used in everyday speech constantly (the " heart of the matter," the " seat of our troubles " are metaphors, and so is " make hay while the sun shines "). In poetry, metaphor allows the writer to express himself imaginatively and colorfully. Chaucer, for example, compares the young Squire to the month of May, his embroidered gown to a meadow of flowers, and his sleeplessness to that of a nightingale.

When the comparison is expressed with *like* or *as,* it is called a *simile.* The poverty of the Oxford scholar is impressed upon us by the description of his horse as " lean as a rake." What picture of the horse do you see? Find other examples of figurative language in which Chaucer pokes fun at the characters.

The Nun's Priest's Tale

CHANTICLEER AND PERTELOTE

The first of the Canterbury Pilgrims to relate a tale is the Knight. He tells of two noble young captives of war who fall madly in love with a beautiful young girl whom they watch as she walks to and fro in the garden beneath their prison window. It is a sad tale of broken friendship and unrequited love. After several of the other travelers tell their stories, the Monk proceeds to bore everyone with no less than seventeen gloomy tales about tragedies that befell illustrious men. Wishing to offset the depressing effect of these on the listeners, the Host asks the Nun's Priest, Sir John, to cheer the travelers with something bright and lively. And this — in a modern version by Rewey Belle Inglis — is the story he tells them.

Once on a time a widow old and frail
Lived in a tiny cottage in a dale.
Her life was simple and her income slight;
She and two daughters lived as best they might
5   By frugal planning and hard work. Three cows,
A sheep called Molly, chickens, and three sows
Formed all her fortune. She could not afford
To serve rare morsels at her humble board;
But all the dainties that she went without
10 Kept her from apoplexy and the gout.
She drank no wine — no, neither white nor red —
But never had she dizziness of head.
The color of her meals was white and black —
Milk and brown bread — of these she had no lack.
15 Sometimes an egg or two, or bacon slice,
Would give a special meal an added spice.
    A yard she had, protected all about
With sticks, and just beyond a ditch dug out.
Here lived her cock, a bird named Chanticleer.°
20 No other cock in crowing was his peer.
His merry voice outdid the organ's swell,
And every hour of day he knew so well
That the poor widow had no need of clock —
She timed her actions by her faithful cock.
25 His ruddy comb like coral was in hue;
His bill jet black, his legs and toes of blue.
His nails like whitest lilies; and like gold
His burnished body flashed in perfect mold.
This noble cock o'er seven hens was lord.
30 They followed at a distance and adored.
Of these the fairest was named Pertelote,°
On whom Lord Chanticleer did truly dote.
So courteous, discreet, and debonair,
Companionable was she, and so fair
35 That from the day when she was seven nights old
She truly had his heart within her hold.
What joy it was at sunrise in fair weather
To hear them sing " My Love's Away " together.
For in those days, I'd have you understand,
40 The birds and beasts could speak in every land.
    One day just as the sun was to appear,
The seven wives surrounding Chanticleer
Were startled by a groaning in his throat
As if from troubled dreams. Then Pertelote
45 Aghast cried out, "What ails you, my heart's dear,
That you should groan in sleep as if in fear?
You a fine sleeper! " quoth she. " Fie! For shame! "
Then Chanticleer awoke and answered, " Dame,

19. *Chanticleer* (chăn′tǐ·klēr): from the French meaning
"clear singer." 31. *Pertelote* (pĕr′tǐ·lōt).

Think not amiss that I have suffered fright,
50 For such an evil dream I've had this night
That I pray God I may its meaning read,
To keep my body from foul prison freed.
Methought that in the yard I roamed around,
When suddenly I saw a fearful hound
55 That would have seized me and have left me dead.
His color was between yellow and red,
But both his ears and tail were tipped with black.
His piercing eyes would slay me. O alack!
This was the horrid sight that made me start."
60   " Away! " quoth she. " Shame on you, faint of heart!
Have you a beard and call yourself a man?
I cannot love a coward; no woman can.
We want our husbands hardy, wise, and free.
What is a dream? Nothing but vanity.
65 It may arise from eating too rich food.
No doubt this came from choler of the blood,°
Which often makes men dream of arrows, fires,
Great beasts of prey, and hideous vampires.
Just so, if melancholia should attack,
70 You then would dream of bears and bulls of black.
Lo, Cato,° wise man, as the world must deem,
Has bid us take no notice of a dream.
Now when we leave the perch, I strongly urge
That you a laxative shall take to purge
75 Yourself of choler and of melancholy.
To fail to do so would be utter folly.
Although our town has no apothecary,
I can instruct you so you need not tarry.
Here in our own yard I am very sure
80 You'll find the herbs to bring about your cure.
But if you scorn my counsel — or forget —
A tertian fever° may develop yet.
Now for a day or two eat worms alone,
And this will give your system just the tone
85 To take the centaury° and hellebore,°
Or caper spurge,° or several doses more
Of fumitory,° then the gay-tree° berry,
And our ground ivy, sure to make you merry.
Just peck at these wherever they are found,
90 And you need fear no nightmares, I'll be bound.

---

66. *choler* (kŏl'ẽr) *of the blood:* an excess of yellow bile in the blood. According to medieval medical theory, the individual's temperament and physical condition were determined by the predominance of one of the four "humors" (blood, phlegm, black bile, yellow bile), or fluids, which existed in the body. The dominance of blood made one cheerful (sanguine); phlegm, sluggish (phlegmatic); black bile, melancholy; yellow bile, choleric, or irritable. 71. *Cato:* In the fourth century some unknown author compiled four books of popular maxims in Latin. The work was attributed to Cato the Elder (234–149 B.C.). 82. *tertian* (tûr'shăn) *fever:* a fever recurring every other day. 85–87. *centaury* (sĕn'tô·rĭ), *hellebore* (hĕl'ĕ·bōr), *caper spurge* (kā'pēr spûrj), *fumitory* (fū'mĭ·tō'rĭ): medicinal plants; *gay-tree:* dogwood.

Cheer up now, husband, and I'll say no more."
  " Madame," quoth he, " I thank you for your lore,
But this Lord Cato, though he may be wise
Opposes greater minds when he denies
95 The prophecy of dreams, for joys or woes
Are often forecast thus, experience shows.
One of the greatest authors° men may read
Tells of two friends, and both devout indeed,
Who on a pilgrimage came to a town
100 Where lodgings there were none, though up and down
They walked inquiring at each hostelry.
At last they found they must part company
If they would have a place to sleep at all.
Now one of them found quarters in a stall
105 Where he beside the oxen had to rest.
The other man was luckier in his quest,
And found a room where he could have a bed.
But in his dreams his friend appeared and said,
' Dear brother, in an ox's stall I lie,
110 And by a murderer's hand I soon must die
If you come not to save me from this fate.'
The man awoke, but then bethought him straight
That dreams are vanity, and slept once more;
But then he had the same dream as before.
115 Again he woke, and then he slept again.
This time the friend reproached, ' Now I am slain.
Behold my bloody wounds are deep and wide.
Now rise up early in the morningtide
And at the west gate stand until you see
120 A farmer's cart which has apparently
Nothing upon it but a load of dung.
Here underneath my murdered corpse is flung.
Now stop that cart and you will learn the truth.
It was my gold they killed me for, in sooth.'
125 Then rose the man and sought his comrade's inn.
' Your friend left just as daylight did begin,'
The landlord said. The man's suspicion grew.
He sought the west gate, and there soon came through
A farmer's cart exactly as foretold.
130 The man was now convinced and made so bold
As to cry justice for his murdered friend.
The folk rushed forth and tipped the cart on end.
There was the body cut with gashes new!
Murder will out, and dreams come surely true! "

    Chanticleer offers several other examples to convince his wife, quot-
    ing the life of St. Kenelm, stories of the Old Testament, and legends
    of Greek mythology.

---

97. *One of the greatest authors:* Cicero (106–43 B.C.), a Latin orator.

135   " Now let us speak of mirth and stop all this;
       Dear Madam Pertelote, as I have bliss,
       In one thing God has sent me wondrous grace,
       For when I see the beauty of your face,
       Your lovely eyes all rimmed with scarlet-red,
140   Then suddenly is scattered all my dread;
       For certainly as *In principio*
       Mulier est hominis confusio° —
       Now the true meaning of this Latin is
       ' Woman is man's delight and all his bliss ' —
145   And such a joy to me your bright eye's beam
       That I defy the warning of the dream."
          Then down he flew and found a grain of corn,
       Chucked at his hens and blithely hailed the morn.
       No longer fearful, like a lion grim
150   He paced about the yard, his hens with him.
       He strutted on his toes scarce touching ground,
       And crowed with every grain of corn he found.
       Thus see we Chanticleer a royal king,
       But later there befalls a dreadful thing.
155   A coal-black fox, full of iniquity,
       That in the grove, for three years secretly
       Had lived, now saw a chance to do his worst,
       And through the hedge that very night he burst
       Into the yard where Chanticleer the fair
160   Would with his wives be likely to repair.
       Concealed among the herbs the villain lay
       Until about eleven the next day,
       Waiting to fall upon poor Chanticleer,
       Just as a human murderer lingers near
165   His victim. O thou false Iscariot!°
       Thou Sinon° who took Troy with subtle plot!
       Poor Chanticleer! Accursèd be that hour
       That brought thee from thy perch to this brute's power!
       Venus, thy patron goddess, was away,
170   And it was Friday, that ill-fated day!
       The warning dream he quite ignored, alas!
       What God foreknows, however, comes to pass,
       Although the scholars still have great dispute
       Upon this point, and some would quite refute
175   The argument that God's foreknowledge still
       Can make us act contrary to our will.°
       In metaphysics° I take little stock,
       So let's proceed. My tale is of a cock —

141–142. *In principio*, etc.: "In the beginning, woman is man's destruction." Note the contrast to Chanticleer's interpretation. 165. *Iscariot* (ĭs·kăr′ĭ·ŏt): Judas Iscariot, who betrayed Christ. 166. *Sinon* (sī′nŏn): the designer of the wooden horse by which the Greeks captured Troy in the Trojan War. 176. Scholars of religion in Chaucer's day were deeply concerned with the relation of the individual's freedom of will to God's omnipotence and omniscience. 177. *metaphysics* (mĕt′-ȧ·fĭz′ĭks): the philosophy of first principles which asks such questions as "What exists?" "What is real?" and "How do we know?"

A cock who took his wife's ill-timed advice.
180 'Twas Eve drove Adam out of Paradise!
(But think not I would slander woman's wit;
'Tis but in jest I gave that little hit.
Some authors like to cast on woman a slur,
But I have never seen the harm in her.)

185   Fair Pertelote was bathing in the sand
With all her sisters six; the air was bland,
And Chanticleer was singing lustily,
As merry as a mermaid in the sea.
It then befell that as his roving eye
190 Followed the flutter of a butterfly,
It saw the visage of the hidden fox,
Hereditary foe of all the cocks.
Then the poor bird no longer wished to crow.
"Cok, cok," he cried in fright and turned to go.
195 But quickly said the fox, "O gentle sir,
I am your loyal friend. Why all this stir?
My presence here no harm to you can bring.
I simply came to hear your lordship sing.
How like an angel's voice from heaven each note

200 That flows melodious from your noble throat!
My lord your father (may God rest his name!)
Also your mother to my house once came,
And truly I would like to please their son.
But as to singing I have known no one
205 Save you, your father's equal. By my eyes,
How he could sing to help the sun arise!
He'd crane his neck and stretch upon his toes,
And singing from the heart, his eyes he'd close.
I'm sure his son to match him must aspire;
210 Let's see if you can imitate your sire."
   Poor Chanticleer, intrigued by flattery,
Began to flap his wings and shut his eye
And stand on tiptoe, but before a note
Was voiced, the fox had seized him by the throat
215 And dragged him to the wood without pursuit.
The lady hens, however, were not mute:
They raised such outcry as was made in vain
By Trojan women for King Priam° slain,
And Pertelote shrieked louder than the rest
220 Because among the seven she loved him best.
No louder shrieked the great Hasdrubal's° wife
When she at Carthage saw him lose his life
And threw herself into the deadly flames.
No greater wailing among Roman dames

218. *King Priam* (prī'ăm): the last king of Troy, who was slain when the Greeks conquered the
city. 221. *Hasdrubal* (hăz'drōō'băl): the defender of Carthage when the Romans destroyed the
city in 146 B.C.

225   When Nero° had the guiltless senators slain,
      But to our story let's return again.
          When the poor widow and her daughters two
      Heard the hens making such a great to-do,
      They rushed outdoors, saw the fox disappear
230   Within the grove, bearing their Chanticleer.
      They rushed pell-mell to save the frightened prey.
      " Out! Out! " they shouted. " Harrow!° Weylaway!°
      Ha, ha, the fox! " and after him they ran.
      Out dashed with staves their neighbors to a man.
235   The dogs ran barking, Collie and Gerland;
      Then Malkin° followed, distaff still in hand.
      The cows and calves ran too, and even hogs
      So frightened by the barking of the dogs
      And shouts of men and women at their backs,
240   Scampered till due to fall right in their tracks.
      They yelled like fiends in hell; the ducks quacked shrill,
      Thinking the men with sticks were out to kill.
      The geese went flapping up into the trees,
      And from the hive out flew a swarm of bees.
245   Such sights and sounds, ah *benedicite!*°
      I hope I ne'er again may hear and see.
      Some came with horns of brass, and some of box,°
      And some of bone, and blew to scare the fox.
      They whooped and hollered, blew and bellowed all,
250   Until you'd think the very heavens would fall.
          Now listen while I tell to your amaze
      How fortune may reverse her tricky plays.
      The cock who helpless lay upon the back
      Of Master Fox, though frightened, had no lack
255   Of ready wit, and said, " If in your place,
      Safe by the entrance to the wood, I'd face
      Around, and to these silly men and girls
      I'd shout, ' Turn back, turn back, you haughty churls!
      A plague upon you all! The cock is mine.
260   I'll eat him up. Just think how well I'll dine! ' "
      The fox, quite blind to methods he'd begun,
      Replied at once, " In faith, it shall be done! "
      And thus to speak, unthinking spread his jaws.
      The cock, I can assure you, did not pause
265   For second thought, but flapped his wings in glee,
      And presto! perched upon a lofty tree.
          Now when the fox discovered he'd been duped,
      A second time to trickery he stooped.
      " Alas, my friend," quoth he, " did I alarm
270   By holding you so tight? I meant no harm.
      Surely you can't suspect some base intent.

225. *Nero* (nē′rō): a Roman Emperor (A.D. 54–68), famous for his brutal tyrannies. 232. *Harrow* (hăr′ō): an ancient Norman cry to arouse pursuit of a thief; *Weylaway* (wāl′à·wā′): alas. 236. *Malkin* (mäl′kĭn): one of the widow's daughters. 245. *benedicite* (bĕn′ē·dĭs′ĭ·tē): bless you. 247. *box:* boxwood.

Come down and let me tell you what I meant.
I'll speak the truth to you this time, I swear."
" Nay then," quoth Chanticleer, " you speak me fair,
275 But let me be accursed, both blood and bone,
If from experience I've no wiser grown.
You fooled me once, you shall not fool me twice.
If I came down you'd eat me in a trice.
Who shuts his eyes when he should watchful be
280 Need never hope from God prosperity."
" Nay," quoth the fox, " and God shall never cease
To plague the chattering tongue that should keep peace."
     Lo, thus it goes with carelessness, you see,
And with too great a trust in flattery.
285 Now do not judge as folly, my good men,
This simple tale of fox and cock and hen.
It has a moral hidden in a laugh;
Be wise and take the grain, but leave the chaff.

THE TALE OF CHANTICLEER AND PERTELOTE

1. Over and over again in the world's literature, writers have chosen to teach a moral — or make some statement of belief — by clothing it in the form of a story. We call such stories by the terms *fable, allegory,* and *parable.* Make sure you know the meaning of these terms. Someone in the class should read a book-length — and highly entertaining — fable that satirizes Communist dictatorship, George Orwell's *Animal Farm.* Report to the class on the comparison between Orwell's modern English and Chaucer's Middle English fables.

2. Describe the difference in personality between Chanticleer and Pertelote. What amusing characteristics of husband and wife are given to the cock and hen?

3. What is the moral of the tale? Is the story told primarily to teach a moral or to poke fun at some typical family situations? Quote passages to support your argument.

4. Chaucer uses a dream to present " a story within a story." Do you know of any current novels, plays, or short stories in which this device is used? How does Chanticleer's dream bear on the main story? How does Pertelote interpret it?

5. The story of the cock and hen is one of the oldest and most popular in the arts. Read Aesop's fable on this theme and note similarities and differences, or look up the French writer La Fontaine's version for a comparison. You may also enjoy reading a modern drama based on the cock story, Edmond Rostand's *Chantecler.*

THE POWER OF WORDS

WORD FAMILIES

In the opening lines of the *Prologue* in the original language on page 83, we find such forthright Anglo-Saxon words as *eek, holt, heeth,* side by side with such graceful French terms as *licour, vertu,* and *melodye.* Pick out six other terms on this page that you judge to be Anglo-Saxon, and six you think are French. Verify your choices in a dictionary.

In the story of the cock there are many illustrations of the social significance of the two parent languages. Since this is a farm story it is filled with Saxon nouns: *herb, hoard, stitch, cart, distaff, churls, chaff.* But part of the humor of the story lies in the portrayal of the cock and his favorite hen as nobility — like the Normans in England, as a matter of fact. The very names Chanticleer and Pertelote are French. The cock addresses the hen as *Madame,* and he is called *royal* and *debonair.*

In this story, find at least ten Saxon and ten French derivatives that are used in modern English, beyond those quoted here. You may be fooled by words like *lord* (Saxon) and *grain* (Latin), so use a dictionary to make sure.

SIR THOMAS MALORY ?—1471

All of us know King Arthur and his Round Table through the countless stories that make him, of all the medieval heroes, the most familiar in English literature. The real Arthur is a shadowy figure in history. He was probably a Celtic chieftain of the sixth century, known for his bravery in war and his just rule of an ancient tribe of Britons. No contemporary records or accounts of him exist, yet in the centuries that followed his reign many writers celebrated him in song and story.

In the twelfth century the story of Arthur was told in Latin by Geoffrey of Monmouth and in French by Wace, who added the Round Table legend. The first version in English is the *Brut,* a poem by Layamon. But by far the most important of the early accounts is *Morte d'Arthur* (Death of Arthur) by Sir Thomas Malory. Because it is a long story in prose, it has sometimes been called the forerunner of the novel, though it bears only a faint resemblance to novels as we know them today. *Morte d'Arthur* has served as the inspiration for many later writers. Tennyson's *The Idylls of the King* and the American poet E. A. Robinson's series of Arthurian legends are based on it, as are poems by Masefield and others.

Little is known of Sir Thomas Malory himself. He was a knight who fought in the Hundred Years' War in France. Recently, evidence has been uncovered that he was several times arrested for robbing and assaulting his neighbors. Malory apparently undertook his great story while serving a twenty-year sentence. He died in 1471, one year after completing *Morte d'Arthur.* Fourteen years later it was published by William Caxton, who introduced printing into England.

Morte d'Arthur

The legends told by Malory begin with the birth of Arthur and end with his mysterious death. According to Malory, one day Arthur pulls the famous sword Excalibur from a block of stone, thus proving his right to rule England. He further establishes this right by subduing twelve rebellious princes and winning twelve great battles against Saxon invaders. Far and wide he becomes known as a brave, just, and wise ruler. At his Round Table he gathers a group of knights, among them Sir Launcelot, Sir Percivale, Sir Gawaine, and other familiar figures. The knights go on dangerous missions, fight in tournaments, and pledge their honor to ladies of the court, all in the spirit of chivalry. But after a time the glory of the court declines. Queen Guinevere is faithless to her husband and loves Sir Launcelot secretly. One after another, the knights grow disillusioned. Finally, the court is threatened by attack from without. During King Arthur's absence on a conquest, Sir Mordred, his traitorous nephew, organizes a plot against him. In a final battle, Arthur's knights are defeated; Sir Gawaine, his faithful nephew, is killed, and Arthur himself is borne away on a barge to his last rest by three mysterious ladies.

The following selection is taken from an earlier part of Arthur's life, when he was winning his reputation as the flower of chivalry. One of his constant companions was Merlin, the court magician. Here you will find an excellent picture of the knight-errant, who roams the woods in search of wrongs to right, and you will get a sense of the superstition and mysticism of medieval days.

HOW ARTHUR FOUGHT WITH KING PELLINORE AND HOW MERLIN SAVED ARTHUR'S LIFE, AND ARTHUR BY THE MEAN OF MERLIN GAT HIS SWORD EXCALIBUR.

THEN ON the day there came in the court a squire on horseback, leading a knight before him wounded to the death, and told him how there was a knight in the forest had reared up a pavilion [1] by a well, and hath slain my master, a good knight, his name was Miles; wherefore I beseech you that my master may be buried, and that some knight may revenge my master's death. Then the noise was great of that knight's death in the court, and every man said his advice. Then came Griflet that was but a squire, and he was but young, of the age of the king Arthur, so he besought the king for all his service that he had done him to give the order of knighthood.

Thou art full young and tender of age, said Arthur, for to take so high an order on thee.

Sir, said Griflet, I beseech you to make me knight.

Sir, said Merlin, it were great pity to lose Griflet, for he will be a passing [2] good man when he is of age, abiding with you the term of his life. And if he adventure his body with yonder knight at the fountain, it is in great peril if ever he come again, for he [3] is one of the best knights of the world, and the strongest man of arms.

Well, [4] said Arthur.

So at the desire of Griflet the king made him knight.

Now, said Arthur, unto Sir Griflet, sith [5] I have made you knight thou might give me a gift.

What ye will, said Griflet.

Thou shalt promise me by the faith of thy body, when thou hast jousted with the knight at the fountain, whether it fall [6] ye be on foot or on horseback, that right so ye shall come again unto me without making any more debate.

I will promise you, said Griflet, as you desire. Then took Griflet his horse in great haste, and dressed his shield [7] and took a spear in his hand, and so he rode a great wallop till he came to the fountain, and thereby he saw a rich pavilion, and thereby under a cloth stood a fair horse well saddled and bridled, and on a tree a shield of divers colors and a great spear. Then Griflet smote on the shield with the butt of his spear, that the shield fell down to the ground.

With that the knight came out of the pavilion, and said, Fair knight, why smote ye down my shield?

For [8] I will joust with you, said Griflet.

It is better ye do not, said the knight, for ye are but young, and late made knight, and your might is nothing to mine.

As for that, said Griflet, I will joust with you.

That is me loath, said the knight, but sith I must needs, I will dress me thereto. [9]

Of whence be ye? said the knight.

Sir, I am of Arthur's court.

So the two knights ran together that Griflet's spear all to-shivered; and therewithal he smote Griflet through the shield and the left side, and brake the spear that the truncheon [10] stuck in his body, that horse and knight fell down.

When the knight saw him lie so on the ground, he alighted, and was passing heavy, [11] for he weened [12] he had slain

[6] *fall:* happen.

[7] *dressed his shield:* took up his shield in position for combat.

[8] *For:* because.

[9] *That . . . thereto:* I am reluctant to do so, but, since I must, I will get ready.

[10] *truncheon* (trŭn′chŭn): spear shaft.

[11] *passing heavy:* exceedingly grieved; weighed down with sorrow.

[12] *weened:* supposed.

[1] *pavilion* (pȧ·vĭl′yŭn): a tent.

[2] *passing:* exceedingly.

[3] *he:* the knight at the fountain.

[4] *Well:* It is well, or so be it. Arthur was replying to Griflet's request, not to Merlin.

[5] *sith:* since.

him, and then he unlaced his helm and gat him wind, and so with the truncheon he set him on his horse, and so betook him to God,[1] and said he had a mighty heart, and if he might live he would prove a passing good knight. And so Sir Griflet rode to the court, where great dole [2] was made for him. But through good leeches [3] he was healed and saved.

Then King Arthur was passingly wroth for the hurt of Sir Griflet. And so he commanded a privy man of his chamber that ere it be day his best horse and armor, with all that longeth [4] unto his person, be without the city or tomorrow day.[5] Right so on tomorrow day he met with his man and his horse, and so mounted up and dressed his shield and took his spear, and bade his chamberlain tarry there till he came again. And so Arthur rode a soft pace till it was day, and then was he ware of three churls [6] chasing Merlin, and would have slain him. Then the king rode unto them, and bade them: Flee, churls! then were they afeard when they saw a knight, and fled. O Merlin, said Arthur, here hadst thou been slain for all thy crafts [7] had I not been.

Nay, said Merlin, not so, for I could save myself an I would; and thou art more near thy death than I am, for thou goest to the deathward, an God be not thy friend.[8]

So as they went thus talking they came to the fountain, and the rich pavilion there by it. Then King Arthur was ware where sat a knight armed in a chair.

Sir knight, said Arthur, for what cause abidest thou here, that there may no knight ride this way but if he joust with thee? I rede thee leave [9] that custom, said Arthur.

This custom, said the knight, have I used and will use maugre [10] who saith nay, and who is grieved with my custom let him amend it that will.

I will amend it, said Arthur.

I shall defend [11] thee, said the knight. Anon [12] he took his horse and dressed his shield and took a spear, and they met so hard either in other's shields, that all to-shivered their spears. Therewith anon Arthur pulled out his sword.

Nay, not so, said the knight; it is fairer, said the knight, that we run more together with sharp spears.

I will well, said Arthur, an I had any more spears.

I have enow, said the knight; so there came a squire and brought two good spears, and Arthur chose one and he another; so they spurred their horses and came together with all their mights, that either brake their spears to their hands. Then Arthur set hand on his sword.

Nay, said the knight, ye shall do better, ye are a passing good jouster as ever I met withal, and for the love of the high order of knighthood let us joust once again.

I assent me, said Arthur.

Anon there were brought two great spears, and every knight gat a spear, and therewith they ran together that Arthur's spear all to-shivered. But the other knight hit him so hard in the midst of the shield, that horse and man fell to the earth, and therewith Arthur was eager, and pulled out his sword, and said, I will assay [13] thee, sir knight, on foot, for I have lost the honor on horseback. Then the knight alighted and dressed his shield unto Arthur. And there began

[1] *betook him to God:* left him to the care of God.

[2] *dole:* grieving.

[3] *leeches:* doctors.

[4] *longeth:* belongs.

[5] *without . . day:* outside the city before daylight tomorrow.

[6] *churls:* peasants.

[7] *crafts:* magic arts.

[8] *thou goest . . . friend:* You are going to your death unless God favors you.

[9] *rede thee leave:* advise you to give up.

[10] *maugre* (mô'gĕr): in spite of.

[11] *defend:* prohibit, prevent.

[12] *Anon:* at once.

[13] *assay* (ă·sā'): test, try.

a strong battle with many great strokes, and so hewed with their swords that the cantels [1] flew in the fields. So at the last they smote together that both their swords met even together. But the sword of the knight smote King Arthur's sword in two pieces, wherefore he was heavy.

Then said the knight unto Arthur, Thou art in my danger whether me list to save thee or slay thee, and but thou yield thee as overcome and recreant, thou shalt die. [2]

As for death, said King Arthur, welcome be it when it cometh, but to yield me unto thee as recreant I had liefer die than to be so shamed. And therewithal the king leapt unto Pellinore, [3] and took him by the middle and threw him down, and raced off [4] his helm. When the knight felt that, he was adread, and anon he brought Arthur unto him, for he was a passing big man of might, and raced off his helm and would have smitten off his head.

Then came Merlin and said, Knight, hold thy hand, for an thou slay that knight thou puttest this realm in the greatest damage that ever was realm: for this knight is a man of more worship than thou wotest of. [5]

Why, who is he? said the knight.

It is King Arthur.

Then would he have slain him for dread of his wrath, and heaved up his sword, and therewith Merlin cast an enchantment to the knight, that he fell to the earth in a great sleep. Then Merlin took up King Arthur, and rode forth on the knight's horse.

Alas! said Arthur, what has thou done, Merlin? Hast thou slain this good knight by thy crafts? There liveth not so worshipful a knight as he was; I had liefer than the stint of my land a year that he were alive. [6]

Care ye not, said Merlin, for he is wholer than ye; for he is but asleep, and will awake within three hours. I told you, said Merlin, what a knight he was; here had ye been slain had I not been.

Right so the king and he departed, and went unto an hermit that was a good man and a great leech. So the hermit searched all his wounds and gave him good salves; so the king was there three days, and then were his wounds well amended that he might ride and go, and so departed. And as they rode, Arthur said, I have no sword.

No force, [7] said Merlin, hereby is a sword that shall be yours, an I may.

So they rode till they came to a lake, the which was a fair water and broad, and in the midst of the lake Arthur was ware of an arm clothed in white samite, [8] that held a fair sword in that hand.

Lo! said Merlin, yonder is that sword that I spake of. With that they saw a damsel going upon the lake.

What damsel is that? said Arthur.

That is the Lady of the Lake, said Merlin; and within that lake is a rock, and therein is as fair a place as any on earth, and richly beseen; [9] and this damsel will come to you anon, and then speak ye fair to her that she will give you that sword. Anon withal came the damsel unto Arthur, and saluted him, and he her again.

Damsel, said Arthur, what sword is that, that yonder the arm holdeth above the water? I would it were mine, for I have no sword.

Sir Arthur, king, said the damsel,

---

[1] *cantels* (kăn't'lz): pieces or fragments cut or sliced off, presumably from their shields.

[2] *Thou art . . . die:* You are at my mercy whether I wish to save or slay you, and unless you admit that you are defeated and a coward (*recreant:* rĕk'rē-ănt) you shall die.

[3] *Pellinore:* the knight of the fountain.

[4] *raced off:* tore off.

[5] *more . . . wotest of:* more importance than you know.

[6] *liefer . . . alive:* I had rather have him alive than have a year's income from my land.

[7] *No force:* no matter.

[8] *samite* (săm'īt): heavy silk, interwoven with gold and silver.

[9] *beseen:* decorated.

that sword is mine, and if ye will give me a gift when I ask it you, ye shall have it.

By my faith, said Arthur, I will give you what gift ye will ask.

Well! said the damsel, go ye into yonder barge, and row yourself to the sword, and take it and the scabbard with you, and I will ask my gift when I see my time. So Sir Arthur and Merlin alighted and tied their horses to two trees, and so they went into the ship, and when they came to the sword that the hand held, Sir Arthur took it up by the handles, and took it with him, and the arm and the hand went under the water. And so they came unto the land and rode forth.

Then Sir Arthur looked on the sword, and liked it passing well.

Whether [1] liketh you better, said Merlin, the sword or the scabbard?

Me liketh better the sword, said Arthur.

Ye are more unwise, said Merlin, for the scabbard is worth ten of the sword, for whiles ye have the scabbard upon you, ye shall never lose no blood, be ye never so sore wounded; therefore keep well the scabbard always with you. So they came unto Carlion,[2] whereof his knights were passing glad. And when they heard of his adventures, they marveled that he would jeopard [3] his person so, alone. But all men of worship said it was merry to be under such a chieftain, that would put his person in adventure as other poor knights did.

---

[1] *Whether:* which.

[2] *Carlion:* Arthur's residence; it has been identified with the modern town of Caerleon in southwest England.

[3] *jeopard* (jĕp′ērd): risk.

This story of how Arthur received his famous sword, Excalibur, is contradictory to the account given earlier in the book that Arthur as a boy drew the sword from a stone and thus proved his right to the throne. There are many such contradictions throughout the Arthur stories because the legends grew up at different times.

MEDIEVAL ROMANCE

1. Many of the traits that made Arthur an ideal leader in his day are shown in this selection. What are they? Compare him with Beowulf in this respect. Which of these traits make for good leadership even today?

2. What can you find in this legend that reveals medieval rather than sixth-century customs, material goods, and standards of conduct? How much do you learn about the " code of chivalry "?

3. As you did with Chaucer's tales, select words of Saxon and of French origin from Malory's writing. Which of the two languages seems to prevail in the conversations?

4. Students who have read Mark Twain's *A Connecticut Yankee in King Arthur's Court* may tell incidents from it showing how Mark Twain satirizes medieval chivalry and magic.

CLASS ACTIVITY

" How the Arthurian legends have influenced our literature, music, and art " would make a valuable co-operative study. Let students choose their field of special interest and illustrate their talks with readings, phonograph records, and slides.

READING LIST FOR THE MEDIEVAL PERIOD

Chute, Marchette, *Geoffrey Chaucer of England*

Chaucer has come to mean more to the public at large since this very readable account appeared; it is both historically accurate and lively in style.

Converse, Florence, *Long Will*

The title refers to William Langland of *Piers the Plowman* fame. Wat Tyler, who stirred up a revolt, and Chaucer are also characters in the story.

Costain, Thomas B., *The Magnificent Century*

Second volume of his history, *The Pageant of England,* covering the time from the Magna Charta, 1215, to 1272.

Douglas, Ronald MacDonald, *The Scots' Book*

If you like folklore, and have a warm feeling for Scotland, this is the book for you.

Doyle, A. Conan, *Sir Nigel*

Edward III and the Black Prince are actors in this stirring tale, which includes the Battle of Poitiers in France, and the tragic results of the Black Death. Doyle's *The White Company* is a sequel.

Eaton, Jeanette, *Jeanne d'Arc*

A biography of Joan of Arc, who, more than any other French person of the Middle Ages, has become a favorite subject in English literature.

Gilbert, Jane, *Imps and Angels*

Boys of the thirteenth century, as well as those of the twentieth, could answer to those names. Here the mischief is closely tied to building a cathedral. (Easy reading.)

Eliot, T. S., *Murder in the Cathedral*

A poetic drama on the martyrdom of Thomas à Becket by an outstanding poet and dramatist of our day. (Mature.)

MacLeod, Mary, *King Arthur and His Noble Knights*

If you wish to read more about the Knights of the Round Table, you will find this modernization easier than Malory.

Malcolmson, Anne Burnett, *The Song of Robin Hood*

The authentic ballads presented in new and attractive form with accompanying music and drawings. An artistic edition.

Noyes, Alfred, " Sherwood," in *Collected Poems*

Poetic drama romantically picturing Robin Hood's band in Sherwood forest.

Oman, Carola, *Crouchback*

The end of the medieval period as hastened by the Wars of the Roses. The complex character of Richard III comes alive.

Porter, Jane, *Scottish Chiefs*

The struggle for Scottish independence from England so stirringly told that this book, written in the last century, is still highly popular.

Pyle, Howard, *Men of Iron* and *Merry Adventures of Robin Hood*

If you have never read these two classics of youth, now is a good time to begin.

Scott, Sir Walter, *Ivanhoe*

One of the best pictures of the Middle Ages in fiction, featuring a tournament, the siege of a castle, Robin Hood (under the name of Locksley), and a witchcraft trial. Probably you have read it. If not, why not?

——, *Quentin Durward*

Medieval life on the Continent. A plain Scotsman becomes involved in French plots under Louis XI, and finally wins the hand of an aristocratic lady.

——, *The Talisman*

The scene is the Holy Land, where Richard the Lion-Hearted is fighting the Moslem Saladin to win back the Holy Sepulcher.

Shaw, George Bernard, *Saint Joan*

A tense drama of the famous Joan of Arc's rise to power, her trial, and her martyrdom. The unusual theme of the last act: what would we do with Joan today? (Mature.)

Sterne, E. G., *Loud Sing Cuckoo*

Chaucer, Wat Tyler, and John Ball are all characters in this novel which takes its title from an old song of the Middle Ages.

Stevenson, Robert Louis, *The Black Arrow*

A message foretelling the death of others is attached to the arrow that kills one of the soldiers. This is just one incident in a long series of thrillers. Time: the Wars of the Roses.

Tennyson, Alfred, *The Idylls of the King*

Classic tales in verse of the Knights of King Arthur. If you have missed these during your high school career, now is the time to make up for it.

Twain, Mark, *A Connecticut Yankee in King Arthur's Court*

One ridiculous incident after another shows the superiority of modern common sense over the false glamour of chivalry.

FOR LISTENING

The following selections have been recorded and are available on *Many Voices 6A: Prologue to the Canterbury Tales,* lines 1–42, in Middle English; " Sir Patrick Spens "; and " Get Up and Bar the Door."

THE ELIZABETHAN

N O AGE in England was more vigorous and colorful than the Elizabethan. The pronounced intellectual and artistic stirring of Europe in the past two centuries, known as the Renaissance, had begun to affect England at the end of the fifteenth century. Inquisitive Englishmen set out to discover this rebirth of civilization — in books, in music, in painting, in sculpture, and on the seas. This was a complex and changing age, one of great discoveries and great individuals. It became important to be an Englishman.

The first Tudor kings, Queen Elizabeth's grandfather, Henry VII (1485–1509), and her father, Henry VIII (1509–1547), ushered in a period of progress which reached its brilliant climax under Elizabeth herself (1558–1603). There was a culmination of great writing during her reign, and several of the best writers survived her. In a literary sense the whole period from 1485 to 1625 may be called the Elizabethan Age.

The picture of a great gathering of English ships at Dover is by a sixteenth-century artist, painted in the days of Henry VIII, when England's sea power was just beginning.

AGE 1485-1625

THE GROWTH OF A POWERFUL CENTRAL GOVERNMENT

In the sixteenth century, England changed from a medieval to a modern country. Medieval England had been governed by feudalism, and chivalry had been a colorful feature of its life. Education had been confined largely to the monasteries, and in religion the country was directed by the Church of Rome. Now Elizabethan England was struggling toward parliamentary representation in government and was breaking away from established religious authorities. The drama was becoming a new kind of entertainment, and the world of nature was a new area of study.

The Wars of the Roses, which set half the English barons against the other half, established the Tudor family on the throne. Henry VII — shrewd of mind and cold of heart — united the nation and gave it peace, wealth, and trade during his twenty-five-year reign. His son Henry VIII was one of England's strongest and most colorful kings. His headstrong career included six marriages.

When the Church refused to allow Henry to divorce Catherine of Aragon in order to marry Anne Boleyn, lady in waiting to the queen, Henry precipitated a quarrel with the Pope. From this break with Rome there emerged an English national church. With the complete separation of the Church of England from papal authority, English clergymen and Parliament declared the king to be the temporal head of the Church of England. Henry ordered the monasteries destroyed and their wealth and property transferred to the royal coffers. The power of the state, centralized in one figure, was growing and making itself felt.

THE REFORMATION

Even after his break with the Roman Catholic Church, Henry VIII cherished the title Defender of the Faith, which had been conferred on him by the Pope for publicly opposing Martin Luther. Luther, in Germany, was the first to preach openly against a flagrant abuse of the Roman Catholic Church: the sale of indulgences. In protesting other practices of the Church, Luther spearheaded what was to become a general movement, known as the Protestant Reformation. In this movement, John Calvin in Switzerland and John Knox in Scotland led Protestants in expressing the independent thought of the new age.

The position of the Church of England resembled in many ways the religious position of Luther. Although Henry VIII's break with Rome was largely personal, the medieval idea of one religious order gave way to the ideas of individual differences and personal conviction.

THE REIGN OF ELIZABETH

At the age of twenty-five, Elizabeth, the last and the greatest of the Tudor rulers, began her reign of forty-five years. With shrewdness and diplomacy, she endeared herself to the English people. She knew when to be stern and when to be tolerant; she knew how to keep power in balance and in her own hands.

Elizabeth — after whom the poet Spenser modeled Gloriana, the Faerie Queene — coquettishly kept all her courtiers and nobles dangling on strings for her favors. Extravagant in her clothes yet stingy in government expenditures, demanding flattery yet never carried away by it, a patron of artists and explorers, an admirer of handsome men as well as wise ones — she was a symbol of national glory to the English.

By firmly establishing the rule of the monarchy, she made the power of the government felt throughout the land. She swung England back to Protestantism (Queen Mary had attempted to re-establish Catholicism); but, for the most part, Elizabeth left the Catholics in peace. Adroitly she broke up an alliance between Scotland and France, which would have been dangerous to England. To stop the rise in prices and restore prosperity, she had all the money reminted. Taxation was reduced, and the laborers were cared for by the poor laws. English national power was dramatically demonstrated in 1588 when the Spanish Armada was defeated by a combination of bad English weather and superb English seamanship.

Although Elizabeth possessed a violent temper and could scold like a fishwife, she had deep worldly wisdom, great personal magnetism, and grandeur of spirit.

The Metropolitan Museum of Art

QUEEN ELIZABETH
By an unknown artist

She said of herself, " I know I have but the body of a weak and feeble woman, but I have the heart and stomach of a king, and a king of England too." Under Queen " Gloriana " England became wealthy, happy, and safe.

DISCOVERY OF THE NEW WORLD

This was the era of the voyager, the golden age of the sea rover. In 1581, down the river from London, on the deck of the *Golden Hind,* Queen Elizabeth knighted Francis Drake for sailing around the world. The great age of geographical discoveries and colonial expansion was under way.

On the roll of illustrious Elizabethan voyagers are Sir Martin Frobisher, who reached Labrador; Sir Humphrey Gilbert, who discovered his New-foundland; and his more famous half brother, Sir Walter Raleigh, who settled colonists in Virginia. For the curious public at home, the wide-ranging discoveries of the English navigators were collected and published by Richard Hakluyt in the many volumes of his *Voyages.*

The navigators sailed for different reasons: for the sheer excitement of discovery, for trade or booty, and for new regions to colonize. All the nations of Europe set out on a race for empire. England's greatest antagonist was Spain, who built up her riches from the Americas. In a kind of undeclared war, with the private support of Elizabeth, the British privateers did not hesitate to plunder the great gold-laden Spanish galleons or to pillage the Spanish settlements.

Written on our eastern coastline are names of English rulers. In Virginia, named for the Virgin Queen Elizabeth, the first permanent English settlement, Jamestown, was named in honor of James I. The Carolinas and Georgia show that the later kings, Charles II (Carolus in Latin) and George II, are also remembered in American geography.

A New World had been discovered, in which the Old World could reproduce itself and expand. The beckoning horizon of that new world gave men chances for action and adventure. It also roused in their imaginations the possibilities of ways of life not yet known.

EXPANSION OF IDEAS

The boundaries of men's thoughts were expanding along with the boundaries of the physical world. The spirit of the age was confident and optimistic. Man's thinking was developing in science, first on the Continent and later in England.

Francis Bacon's curiosity about the world led him to study everything in nature as well as in books. His quest for knowledge eventually brought about his death: after stuffing a chicken with snow to see if cold acted as a preservative, Bacon caught a fatal chill. Because he advocated careful experimenting instead of accepting knowledge on unsupported theory, Bacon has been called the " father of modern science." The age of scientific experiment was beginning, and the discoveries of the scientists were enlarging the area of man's knowledge.

THE CLASSICS AND HUMANISM

Actually, in its civilizing effects upon the Elizabethans, the discovery of the new world was less important than the discovery of the ancient world. A new culture based on many past civilizations was being born. This rebirth of learning was kept aflame by new acquaintance with the old Greek and Roman works of literature: the classics.

The Greeks and the Romans created works in literature and thought that have never been surpassed for balance and beauty. During the Middle Ages, however, the classics were partially lost to men. When the Roman Empire

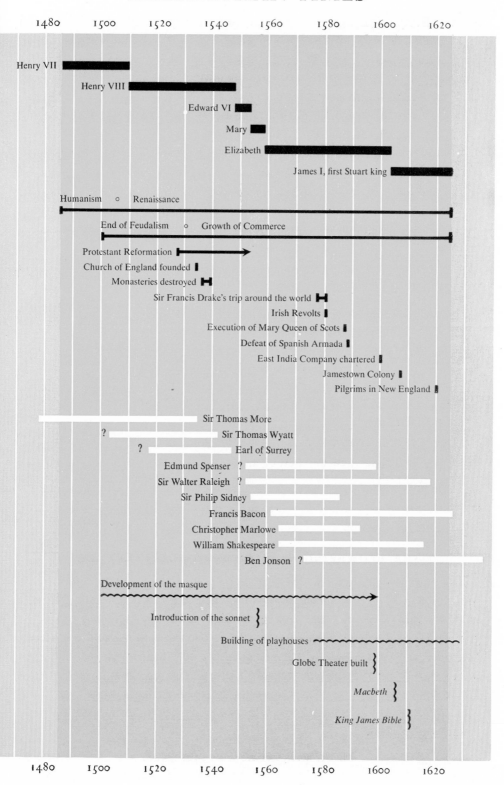

1480   1500   1520   1540   1560   1580   1600   1620

Henry VII

Henry VIII

Edward VI

Mary

Elizabeth

James I, first Stuart king

Humanism   ○   Renaissance

End of Feudalism   ○   Growth of Commerce

Protestant Reformation

Church of England founded

Monasteries destroyed

Sir Francis Drake's trip around the world

Irish Revolts

Execution of Mary Queen of Scots

Defeat of Spanish Armada

East India Company chartered

Jamestown Colony

Pilgrims in New England

Sir Thomas More

?   Sir Thomas Wyatt

?   Earl of Surrey

Edmund Spenser   ?

Sir Walter Raleigh   ?

Sir Philip Sidney

Francis Bacon

Christopher Marlowe

William Shakespeare

Ben Jonson   ?

Development of the masque

Introduction of the sonnet   }

Building of playhouses

Globe Theater built   }

Macbeth   }

King James Bible   }

fell and Europe was overrun by primitive tribes, men turned to the Church for guidance. The life of the physical world was held to be unimportant; men were more concerned with the world after death. But when the classics were rediscovered in Italy and France, and somewhat later introduced into England, this medieval interest shifted.

If God was the center of the universe for the Middle Ages, man became the center for the Renaissance. The movement which centered on man in this world is often called Humanism — the striving to perfect all *human* possibilities. Sir Thomas More, the greatest of the English Humanists, studied Greek and Latin at Oxford. While on a diplomatic mission to the Continent, he wrote his *Utopia,* which describes a country ideally governed. Today the word " utopia " signifies a perfect, although seemingly unattainable, state for mankind.

This ambitious quest to expand and to perfect earthly life rings out in the words of the Elizabethan dramatist Christopher Marlowe:

> Our souls, whose faculties can comprehend
> The wondrous architecture of the world,
> And measure every wandering planet's course,
> Still climbing after knowledge infinite,
> And always moving as the restless spheres,
> Will us to wear ourselves and never rest
> Until we reach the ripest fruit of all,
> That perfect bliss and sole felicity,
> The sweet fruition of an earthly crown.

These lines sum up all that we have said so far about the Elizabethan Renaissance: the desire for worldly power, the search for knowledge, the seeking after human perfection.

THE FLOWERING OF ELIZABETHAN LITERATURE

The new learning was the inspiration of great prose, poetry, and drama. Many of the selections which follow show that the Elizabethans were fascinated by ideals — they wanted to know how to be the perfect courtier, or gentleman, or governor. Spenser stated that his purpose in writing *The Faerie Queene* was " to fashion a gentleman or noble person in virtuous and gentle discipline." Most Elizabethan poems picture nature and human beings in a graceful and idealized manner. Surely the Elizabethans believed in perfection, when Shakespeare could write that if he is mistaken in thinking that true love is unchanging, then

> I never writ, nor no man ever loved.

BRITAIN
1485-1700

SCOTLAND

Forres [1]
Inverness [2]

Birnam Wood
Scone [3]
Fife [4]
Firth of Forth
Edinburgh

IRELAND

Dublin

WALES

ENGLAND

COUNTY [14]
CORK

Kenilworth [5]
Stratford
on Avon [6]
Oxford
R. Lea [8]
Thames
Westminster
Southwark [11]

Cambridge
Bedford [7]

London [9]
Horton [10]

DEVONSHIRE

Dean Prior [12]
Plymouth [13]

1 Royal palace in *Macbeth*. 2 Macbeth's castle. 3 Scene of the coronation of kings in *Macbeth*. 4 Macduff's castle. 5 Elizabeth's visit to this castle is the subject of Sir Walter Scott's novel *Kenilworth*. 6 Shakespeare born, 1564. 7 John Bunyan wrote part of *The Pilgrim's Progress* in Bedford jail. 8 Setting for Izaak Walton's *The Compleat Angler*. 9 Many writers lived and worked in London. The Royal Society was founded, the Sons of Ben flourished, and Pepys kept his famous diary here. 10 Milton wrote his minor poems here. 11 Here stood the Globe Theater, where Shakespeare was playwright and actor, and where *Macbeth* was performed. 12 Robert Herrick was vicar here. 13 Pilgrims sailed for America. 14 Spenser wrote *The Faerie Queene* in "exile," as he thought, in Kilcolman Castle.

The Englishmen of the Renaissance were in love with human beauty, which they considered the outward sign of man's spirit striving for perfection. For the English were not content to write about perfection; they tried to achieve it in their lives. Sir Philip Sidney — soldier, scholar, horseman, poet, courtier — when wounded fatally on the battlefield, passed his cup of water to a common soldier with these words: " Thy necessity is greater than mine." His generous act revealed the spirit of an ideal gentleman.

One of Sir Philip's many accomplishments was the writing of an essay called *The Defense of Poesy,* in which he wondered why England should be " so hard a stepmother to poets," considering that " our tongue is most fit to honor poesy, and to be honored by poesy." Sidney died in 1586, a few years too soon to witness the achievements of Spenser, Marlowe, Shakespeare, and Jonson.

Yet even before Sidney's birth, Sir Thomas Wyatt brought the sonnet from Italy, and the Earl of Surrey for the first time used blank verse, which has been a standard English meter ever since. Furthermore, lyric (or " singing ") poetry was developed, for England was becoming a nation of musicians and singers. Lutes hung in every barbershop — a waiting patron might take one down from its peg and start up some " barbershop harmony." The Elizabethans also began complicated part singing in madrigals. Tottel's *Miscellany* (1557) became the first of many collections of songs and lyrics of the sort that you will find in the pages that follow. Some of the collections had such flamboyant titles as *The Paradise of Dainty Devices* and *A Gorgeous Gallery of Gallant Inventions.*

SIR PHILIP SIDNEY,
poet and soldier,
scholar and courtier —
was the ideal
Elizabethan gentleman.
This portrait,
by an unknown painter,
shows that he was
elegant and poised as well.

More poets in England sang and published in the seventy-five years after 1550 than in the thousand years that preceded. By 1625, English literature had been enriched by:

1. The prodigious outpouring of the Elizabethan sonneteers, principally celebrating beauty and love.

2. The publication of Spenser's epic romance, *The Faerie Queene,* a many-pictured, chivalric allegory of incredibly beautiful dreams.

3. The development of the *masque,* a kind of court pageant combining poetry, dancing, singing, lavish costumes, and extravagant settings.

4. A multiplying variety of English prose styles. London pamphleteers wrote in the hard-hitting and vivid fashion of London rogues and middle-class craftsmen. Raleigh and Bacon composed stately histories. Holinshed put together historical chronicles in which Shakespeare found many plots for his plays. A large number of scholars, convened by James I in 1604, translated into English an authorized version of the Bible (1611), called the King James Version. Its beautiful style has influenced English writers for hundreds of years. English prose writing varied from the clipped sentences of Bacon's essays to the ample flowing movements of the King James Bible.

Printing had been brought to England by William Caxton even before the Tudor period began. Now came a torrent of printed books. For the ordinary man who was bored with the old romances and ballads, a sudden wealth of literature appeared: histories, biographies, travel books, love poems.

DRAMA: THE GLORY OF THE ELIZABETHAN AGE

Although books were available, the common people found a still richer literary entertainment in the theater. The theater flourished largely because of popular support. Originally, the companies of actors were protected by nobles, but much of their financial success came from the paying public. Since the middle-class governors of London were often strict, the ordinary citizen found much of his amusement outside the city walls — north of London where the first theater was erected in 1576, or across the Thames at Southwark, where he could watch bull- and bearbaiting or see the latest play.

At first, plays were given by traveling companies on platforms set up in innyards. When the first theaters were built, therefore, they looked much like Elizabethan inns, with galleries on all sides and an open courtyard below — just as our first automobiles resembled carriages, and for no better reason. As the playwrights gradually learned to use blank verse effectively, the audience became accustomed to poetry and did not feel that it was artificial or unmanly. To see a play, citizens would take the chance of picking up the plague in the crowded theaters, or of getting into a riot among turbulent and hot-headed spectators. So great was the appeal of drama that sailors on far voyages would themselves put on performances of Shakespeare.

Marlowe's poetry told stories of grim adventurers like Doctor Faustus, who sold his soul to the devil. Shakespeare, the master of them all, gave every man and woman what seemed to fit his own inner needs. Ben Jonson wrote tragedies based on classical stories, as well as realistic comedies crowded with the characters and the talk of the times. These three were the leaders in a host of dramatists. In the theater more than anywhere else, the Elizabethan could see that he was living in a " brave new world," bustling with action, thronged with people ranging from the vulgar to the noble.

SUMMARY

The Elizabethan Age was of great importance to England and to the world. The nation began increasing her wealth and power under Henry VII and Henry VIII. When the Church of England was set up as a part of the Reformation, the new power of the state became evident.

Queen Elizabeth, a dominating and wise woman, possessed a grandeur of spirit. She restored English pride and position by extending the boundaries of the known physical world. Her explorers, merchant adventurers, and colonizers began to establish an empire.

Man's thinking also expanded. Englishmen shared in the rebirth of classical learning called the Renaissance. They also helped to advance the new movement of Humanism, a belief in man's possibilities and in his striving toward perfection.

This new learning was the inspiration for such writers as Spenser, Sidney, Bacon, Marlowe, Shakespeare, Jonson, and the translators of the Bible. They created one of the most brilliant ages of literature ever known.

EDMUND SPENSER 1552–1599

Because he had an astonishing control of the poet's craft and great creative imagination, Edmund Spenser is often called " the poet's poet." Unlike Shakespeare, who was concerned with the problems and mixed emotions of real human beings, Spenser created a dream world in which his knights move as symbols of noble ideals.

Spenser, the son of a London cloth-maker, attended school on a scholarship set up for poor boys. While still a student, he became adept at translating and introducing classical meters into English poetry. Shortly after taking degrees from Cambridge University, he published *The Shepherd's Calendar*, which consists of twelve descriptive poems, one for each month, about the beauties of the countryside. This series won Spenser court recognition and began the vogue for pastoral poetry.

Encouraged by Sir Walter Raleigh, a court favorite, Spenser next wrote his greatest work, *The Faerie Queene*. The title so obviously referred to Queen Elizabeth that the flattered patron ordered a generous pension for the poet. Spenser did not receive all his money, however, from the unwilling treasurer; and, feeling out of favor, he returned to his home in Ireland, a picturesque old castle. After a native rebellion broke out, the castle, together with his belongings and some manuscripts, was burned. Spenser returned to London, broken and impoverished, and died not long after. He was buried in the Poet's Corner in Westminster Abbey, next to that other great early poet, Chaucer.

Spenser's masterpiece, *The Faerie Queene,* is the longest poem in the English language. It is not as long as Spenser origi-

nally intended it to be, however. He set out to write twelve books, each recounting the story of a knight who personifies one of the virtues of a perfect gentleman. But only six of the adventures were completed — those of the knights representing Holiness, Temperance, Chastity, Friendship, Justice, and Courtesy.

The poem is written in a stanza of his own invention, ever since called the Spenserian stanza. It consists of eight lines in iambic pentameter and a ninth line containing two extra syllables. The rhyme scheme always follows the form given in the stanza below. This stanza was widely imitated by later poets whom you will be reading — Burns, Byron, Shelley, and Keats. To enable you to recognize it and remember its origin when you meet it again, a stanza from *The Faerie Queene* is quoted here. It is a famous description of the House of Morpheus (sleep), stanza 41 from Book I, Canto I. Notice the skillful handling of sound effects.

	Rhyme scheme	
And more, to lulle him in his slumber soft,	*a*	
A trickling streame from high rock tumbling downe,	*b*	
And ever-drizzling raine upon the loft,°	*a*	
Mixt with a murmuring winde, much like the sowne	*b*	
Of swarming Bees, did cast him in a swowne:°	*b*	5
No other noyse, nor peoples troublous cryes,	*c*	
As still are wont t'annoy the wallèd towne,	*b*	
Might there be heard: but carelesse Quiet lyes,	*c*	
Wrapt in eternall silence farre from enemyes.	*c*	

3. *upon the loft:* upon the roof. 5. *swowne:* swoon, fainting spell.

Amoretti

As a young man Spenser was sent to Ireland to help suppress an Irish rebellion, and many years of his life were spent there. There he met and married Elizabeth Boyle, of whom little is known except as she is described in Spenser's sonnet sequence *Amoretti* (little love poems).

After Sir Thomas Wyatt introduced the sonnet from Italy, it became the vogue in the English court to honor one's lady in this form of verse. Spenser, Sidney, and Shakespeare all wrote famous sonnet sequences. A sonnet is always fourteen lines long,

each line in iambic pentameter, that is, ten syllables with stress on every other syllable. The rhyme scheme of a sonnet may vary according to the preference of the poet. The Elizabethans created their own order of rhymes, but later poets returned to the original Italian rhyme scheme, which became the standard for English sonnets. (Elizabeth Barrett Browning's sonnets, on pages 490–91, follow this form.) In this volume you will find many examples of these varied forms. The sonnet is still a popular type of poem.

Sonnet 26

Rhyme scheme

Sweet is the rose, but grows upon a briar;	*a*
Sweet is the juniper, but sharp his bough;°	*b*
Sweet is the eglantine, but pricketh near;	*a*
Sweet is the fir-bloom, but his branch is rough;	*b*
Sweet is the cypress, but his rind is tough;	*b* 5
Sweet is the nut, but bitter is his pill;°	*c*
Sweet is the broom-flower, but yet sour enough;	*b*
And sweet is moly, but his root is ill.	*c*
So every sweet with sour is tempered still,	*c*
That maketh it be coveted the more:	*d* 10
For easy things, that may be got at will,	*c*
Most sorts of men do set but little store.	*d*
Why then should I account of little pain,	*e*
That endless pleasure shall unto me gain!°	*e*

2. *his bough:* In the sixteenth century *his* was still used where today we use *its.* "Bough" was probably pronounced to rhyme with "rough" in medieval times, to which Spenser likes to refer. 6. *pill:* center or core. 13, 14. Why then should I be disturbed by a little trouble that will bring me endless pleasure?

Sonnet 37

What guile is this, that those her golden tresses
    She doth attire under a net of gold;
    And with sly skill so cunningly them dresses,
    That which is gold, or hair, may scarce be told?
Is it that men's frail eyes, which gaze too bold,   5
She may entangle in that golden snare;
And, being caught, may craftily enfold
Their weaker hearts, which are not well aware?
Take heed, therefore, mine eyes, how ye do stare
Henceforth too rashly on that guileful net,   10
In which, if ever ye entrappèd are,
Out of her hands ye by no means shall get.
    Fondness° it were for any, being free,
    To covet fetters, though they golden be!

13. *Fondness:* foolishness.

CHRISTOPHER MARLOWE
1564–1593

and SIR WALTER RALEIGH
1552?–1618

Christopher Marlowe is one of the most romantic and tragic figures of Elizabethan England. He was killed in a tavern brawl at the age of twenty-nine, at the height of his poetic powers. He had grown up in Canterbury and had studied at Cambridge, where it is said he engaged in secret governmental work, much to the displeasure of his tutors. "Kit" Marlowe was an impetuous young man, endowed with a genius that poured out, during six short years, into magnificent tragic dramas. *Tamburlaine* pictures a great Asiatic conqueror of the fourteenth century. *Dr. Faustus* tells the age-old legend of the man who sells his soul to the devil, a story used by the German poet Goethe in *Faust* and also in Gounod's opera *Faust*. In his plays Marlowe perfected blank verse, which Shakespeare later used. He was admired by many poets; Ben Jonson speaks of his ability to write a "mighty line" with sonorousness and power.

SIR WALTER RALEIGH

Sir Walter Raleigh is known chiefly as the English explorer who tried to start a colony in America. He called it Virginia in honor of Elizabeth, the Virgin Queen. He was one of the bright stars of a bright age, a friend of Spenser and Marlowe, and a favorite of the queen. Raleigh was handsome, ambitious, vigorous, hot-tempered, and sometimes unscrupulous, and he led an adventurous life — in and out of favor with the queen, in and out of prison. Finally he died under the executioner's ax. While imprisoned in the Tower of London for thirteen years, Raleigh wrote a lengthy *History of the World;* earlier he had written an account of his journey to the Americas. Like other courtiers of the time, he was also a poet and could write a pastoral lyric, like the following one, with grace and wit.

"The Passionate Shepherd to His Love" and "The Nymph's Reply to the Shepherd" are a famous pair of lyrics in English literature. In the first pastoral, Marlowe pictures a perfect, idyllic love. It expresses the Elizabethan ideal of courtship. In the second, Raleigh replies in a way that shows that the Elizabethans were realistic as well as romantic. Notice how the passionate shepherd is suddenly brought down to earth by a very practical nymph.

The Passionate Shepherd
to His Love

CHRISTOPHER MARLOWE

Come live with me and be my love,
And we will all the pleasures prove
That hills and valleys, dales and fields,
Or woods or steepy mountain yields.

And we will sit upon the rocks,   5
Seeing the shepherds feed their flocks,
By shallow rivers, to whose falls
Melodious birds sing madrigals.

And I will make thee beds of roses,
And a thousand fragrant posies,   10
A cap of flowers, and a kirtle°
Embroidered all with leaves of myrtle;

A gown made of the finest wool,
Which from our pretty lambs we pull;
Fair linèd slippers for the cold,   15
With buckles of the purest gold;

A belt of straw and ivy buds
With coral clasps and amber studs;
And if these pleasures may thee move,
Come live with me and be my love.   20

Thy silver dishes for thy meat
As precious as the gods do eat,
Shall on an ivory table be
Prepared each day for thee and me.

The shepherd swains shall dance and
   sing   25
For thy delight each May morning;
If these delights thy mind may move,
Then live with me and be my love.

11. *kirtle* (kûr′t′l): a dress.

The Nymph's Reply to the Shepherd

SIR WALTER RALEIGH

If all the world and love were young,
And truth in every shepherd's tongue,
These pretty pleasures might me move
To live with thee and be thy love.   4

Time drives the flocks from field to fold,
When rivers rage, and rocks grow cold;
And Philomel° becometh dumb;
The rest complains of cares to come.

The flowers do fade, and wanton fields
To wayward Winter reckoning yields;
A honey tongue, a heart of gall,   11
Is fancy's spring, but sorrow's fall.

Thy gowns, thy shoes, thy beds of roses,
Thy cap, thy kirtle, and thy posies,
Soon break, soon wither, soon forgotten,   15
In folly ripe, in reason rotten.

Thy belt of straw and ivy buds,
Thy coral clasps and amber studs,
All these in me no means can move
To come to thee and be thy love.   20

But could youth last, and love still breed,
Had joys no date,° nor age no need,
Then these delights my mind might move
To live with thee and be thy love.

7. *Philomel* (fĭl'ō·mĕl): the nightingale.
22. *no date:* no final date; no end.

ELIZABETHAN LOVE POEMS

1. What bit of wisdom does Spenser use as the principal thought in Sonnet 26? How does he apply this to his own life in the last two lines? What kind of troubles do you think he might have had in mind? Which of the plants mentioned are familiar to you? Which do not grow in your vicinity? You can probably find pictures of these plants in a good botany reference book.

2. In Sonnet 37 what do you learn of ladies' hairdressing styles of that day? In what double sense does the poet use the word *net* in line 10? At what stage in his love affair does he seem to be?

3. Review what was said about the Spenserian stanza on page 111; then study the stanza given on that page until you are familiar with its form — rhythm, line length, and rhyme scheme. Point out specific words and phrases that reveal Spenser as a sensuous poet.

4. Why is Marlowe's poem called a pastoral lyric? How do you picture the shepherd and his love? What promises of the shepherd are obviously far-fetched? Which might be possible?

5. In Raleigh's poem show how the nymph answers each of the shepherd's statements. How would you describe her attitude, especially if you were to think of her as a modern woman?

THE POWER OF WORDS

CHANGING FASHIONS

The literature of early centuries gives interesting evidence of how words take on new shades of meaning over long periods of time. Two such words in the preceding lyrics are *nymph* and *swain*. In ancient Greek mythology, nymphs were immortal maidens who lived in streams, woodlands, or mountains. The Renaissance brought the word *nymph* to England, where it came to be used in pastoral poetry for a beautiful young country girl. Later, in the eighteenth century, you will find it applied to the artificial belles of London society. In modern times the word has reverted almost entirely to its original meaning in mythology, although it is still sometimes used in poetry to mean a beautiful girl.

Swain, on the other hand, began humbly as an old Norse term for a serving boy. Pastoral poetry elevated him to a young shepherd, usually pictured as courting a maiden. In later usage the word sometimes means just a country fellow, without suggesting anything of courtship. But earlier in our own century the suggestion of courtship dominated that of rural life, and for a while *swain* became a slang term which later gave way to *boy friend.*

THE GROWTH OF THE
ENGLISH LANGUAGE

The Elizabethan Age

Just as we say that the Elizabethan Age marked the flowering of English literature, so too we can see a parallel flowering of the English language. The two are inseparable. That buoyant, searching, investigating spirit that sent some men out to explore a New World, sent others back into the ancient world to relive the great days of antiquity, particularly Greek antiquity, through reading about them. New experiences need new words. When the Elizabethans could not find the words they wanted in an existing language, they coined new ones. They loved extravagant expression, elaborate figures of speech, and frequent allusions to classical mythology. The poets brought in new verse forms like the sonnet and blank verse, both developed in Italy, and created new forms like the Spenserian stanza. The great vogue of poetry in the sixteenth century brought into English the words *poem, ode, elegy, lyric, epic,* and *satire,* and, in fact, most of the terminology we now use in classifying poetry. Some of these were adopted directly from France or Italy, but all hark back to Greek roots, for ancient Greece was the cradle of our poetry.

The sudden popularity of drama tended to accentuate florid language. One of the best examples is in *Macbeth,* page 154, line 63 of Act II, Scene ii: "The multitudinous seas incarnadine." Two long words almost fill the line. In *Hamlet,* however, Shakespeare has the prince warn a strolling company of actors against mouthing great words and overacting.

One of Shakespeare's greatest gifts to our language was the tremendous number of phrases which have become familiar to our tongue. Here are a few:

laugh myself to death
brave new world
thereby hangs a tale
the tooth of time
the milk of human kindness
more in sorrow than in anger
more honored in the breach than the observance
one may smile and smile and be a villain
brevity is the soul of wit
the slings and arrows of outrageous fortune
the glass of fashion and the mold of form
we have seen better days.

A short session with Bartlett's *Familiar Quotations* would reveal dozens of others.

Like dress, language is subject to change of fashion. A great style-setter of Elizabethan days was a book by John Lyly called *Euphues* (ū′fū·ēz), intended to teach elegance of deportment and conversation to young courtiers. In language it was as full of frills and furbelows as one of Queen Elizabeth's costumes. At first Shakespeare, like everyone else, imitated its artificiality, but later he helped to laugh it out of style by his parodies on it. From the title of this book came the term *euphuism* applied later to any highly mannered writing.

The scholars and scientists used language with more restraint and orderliness than was customary among the poets and playwrights. Bacon's essays, one of which you will read, show admirable neatness and balance of sentence structure. His thought is packed into small space and requires thinking over. Don't test your reading speed on a Bacon essay.

As a result of the work of the Humanists, education came to be more and more respected. Most people today remember Henry VIII as the man with six wives, but it is well to remember too that he was said to be the best-educated monarch that England had had up to that time. His daughter Elizabeth, who was well versed in Latin and Greek, carried on that tradition and proved that women were capable of higher learning. Schools where the study of Latin prevailed were now being rapidly established. The compiler of a Latin-English dictionary introduced Latin words into English as a means of expanding and beautifying the English tongue. Scholarly Sir Thomas More wrote his famous *Utopia* in Latin, and expected his family to write letters to him in this language. The Humanists found English lacking in the abstract terms they needed for expressing their ideas, but Latin could supply them. Thus most of our abstract nouns come from Latin. The interest in man's relationship to other men and to the physical world around him brought in a whole new vocabulary. With innumerable Latin roots, prefixes, and suffixes to draw on, the possibilities for forming abstract words were endless. A few by way of illustration are *premise, deduction, reference, conclusion.*

In the schools Greek was now running a close second to Latin, and derivatives from Greek were appearing more and more. We have already mentioned poetic terms. *Criticism, rhetoric, philosophy* suggest other fields planted with Greek seeds. In fact most English words that begin with *rh* or that contain the roots *philo* (love), *tele* (far), *phon* (sound), to mention only a few, come from Greek sources. Ever since the Renaissance, Greek has been the gold mine from which to dig out scientific terms. He who discovers a species or makes an invention is likely to try a combination of Greek roots to name it.

Other languages that were drawn into the English stream in the sixteenth century were Spanish and American Indian. They entered chiefly by way of the New World. Spain had a foothold there before England, and had already gathered names from the Indian tribes for various products. The best known in English today are *chocolate, cocoa, potato,* and *tobacco,* which have a flavor of both Indian and Spanish. Direct from Indian dialects strange words like *tomahawk, wampum,* and *wigwam* began to make their way across the Atlantic in the reports of the early settlers. Think of the new words that were to come pouring into English as discovery, commerce, and colonization developed in the centuries to come!

WILLIAM SHAKESPEARE

1564–1616

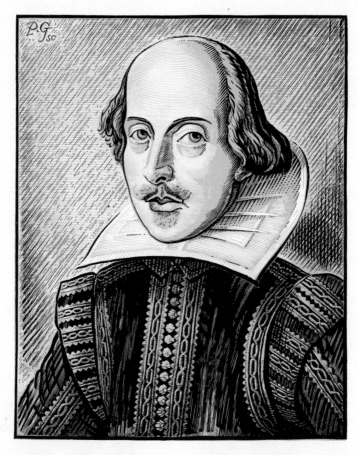

It is impossible to talk about Shakespeare without using superlatives. Critics never tire of saying that he is the greatest of English writers and perhaps the greatest poet in all world literature.

Yet for all his glory, and despite the efforts of several generations of scholars, Shakespeare's life is shrouded in mystery and may never be clarified. We do know that he was born in a little English town, Stratford on Avon. The house assumed to be his birthplace still stands and has been converted into a museum filled with mementos and first editions of his works. Near by stands the grammar school he probably attended as a boy, and the guild

hall where in all likelihood he enjoyed the plays presented by traveling actors during his boyhood. Shakespeare's mother was a member of the gentry; his father was prominent in Stratford: a high bailiff, alderman, and justice of the peace. With the passage of time he became a squire and was granted a coat of arms.

At the village of Shottery near Stratford is the cottage of Anne Hathaway, who at twenty-six was married to Shakespeare, then only eighteen. After the birth of their three children, Shakespeare went up to London alone to seek his fortune. Whether he and his wife were estranged or whether he saw his family at intervals has been a subject of great conjecture, but there is no actual proof for either theory. After about twenty years as an actor and playwright in London, he returned to Stratford and apparently took up the life of a wealthy squire. Today it is possible to see the site of the handsome house he bought there, though the building itself no longer stands. At fifty-two he died, leaving provision in his will that he be buried in the chancel of Trinity Church in Stratford. Wishing to avert the practice of that day, whereby the bones of those long interred were often removed from burial places, Shakespeare had this last poem placed on his tomb:

Good friend, for Jesus' sake forbeare
To dig the dust enclosèd heare;
Bleste be the man that spares these stones,
And curst be he that moves my bones.

With all these concrete evidences, in Stratford, Shakespeare seems like a real person; but in London, where he spent most of his life and did his most important work, he seems almost like a myth. A few records show that he acted minor parts in the theaters across the Thames and owned a share in the old Globe Theater.

After his death, his friends and co-workers collected and published his plays in what is known as *The First Folio* (1623). This was a difficult task, for Shakespeare had taken no steps to preserve his writings. Fortunately most of them could be found in old theater records.

Shakespeare's name is now given to one hundred and fifty-four sonnets, five long poems, and thirty-seven plays of all types — farce, history, romantic comedy, and tragedy. Not all the writings attributed to him have been verified as his, but most of them bear his unmistakable mark: versatility, a power over words, and a wide and deep understanding of human nature such as no other English writer has equaled.

It is impossible to give exact dates for the writing of Shakespeare's plays, but they can be placed in four general groups that could conceivably represent periods in his life from youth to an approaching old age.

The plays of the first period are marked by youthful dreams and exuberant spirits. Paramount among them are *A Midsummer Night's Dream,* loveliest of poetic fantasies; *The Merchant of Venice,* with its dramatic trial scene; *The Taming of the Shrew,* his most popular farce; and *Romeo and Juliet,* a romantic tragedy of ageless beauty and world renown.

The second period is that of the great chronicles and romantic comedies. The fat, rollicking Falstaff rolls through the two plays of *King Henry IV* and recurs in *The Merry Wives of Windsor,* said to have been written at the queen's request to see Falstaff in love. By this time Shakespeare had a proprietary interest in the Globe Theater, for which he wrote three great comedies: *Much Ado about Nothing, As You Like It,* and *Twelfth Night.* They have certain elements in common, such as the profusion of choice lyrics, the plot turning on concealed identity, the witty, self-reliant heroines (in the last two disguised as boys), and the highly individualized comic characters.

Depression and tragedy mark the plays of the third period. What sorrow or disillusionment in Shakespeare's life may have darkened his spirit we can only guess, for there is no definite record. Among several plays laid in ancient Greece and Rome, the best known is *Julius Caesar,* analyzing man's relation to the state. Even greater are four tragedies which touch the depths of human experience in various stages of life. The young prince in *Hamlet* shows a sensitive and subtle intellect struggling against the adverse circumstances of life and against elements in his own nature. *Othello* is a powerful study of love in middle life destroyed by overmastering jealousy and suspicion. *King Lear* gives an unforgettable picture of an aged, childish king driven mad by the ingratitude of his daughters. *Macbeth* analyzes the soul of the mature, grasping ruler who sacrifices everyone to gratify his personal ambition.

With the fourth period the storm and stress of Shakespeare's inner spirit seems to have passed away. *A Winter's Tale* and *The Tempest* are plays of warmth and reconciliation. Old wrongs are righted and forgiven in the end. He returns to the spirited fantasy and tender romance of the earlier comedies, suffused with a mellow philosophy, especially in his last play, *The Tempest.*

Thus Shakespeare's genius completes its full circle with no lessening of poetic power, and with an almost godlike return of poise.

Songs from the Plays

In Shakespeare's day, music was a familiar part of the theater. Shakespeare himself wrote 124 beautiful songs for his plays. These were all set to music in his lifetime; over the centuries many composers (notably Schubert) have given them new musical settings. A few of the original settings are still known today.

Three Songs FROM The Tempest

Here are three songs from one of Shakespeare's best comedies, *The Tempest*. A party of Italian nobles is shipwrecked on a strange enchanted island. Over them hovers Ariel, a delicate invisible spirit, whose songs are a significant part of the play. By the first song the young prince Ferdinand is convinced that his father is drowned (Act I, Scene ii). The second song expresses Ariel's happiness as he thinks of the freedom his master has promised him (Act V, Scene i). In the third song Ariel warns the honest counselor, Gonzalo, that a plot is brewing (Act II, Scene i).

I

Full fathom five thy father lies.
  Of his bones are coral made;
Those are pearls that were his eyes;
  Nothing of him that doth fade
But doth suffer a sea change   5
Into something rich and strange.
Sea nymphs hourly ring his knell:
                Dingdong!
Hark! now I hear them — Dingdong,
  bell!

II

Where the bee sucks, there suck I;
In a cowslip's bell I lie;
There I couch when owls do cry.
On the bat's back I do fly
After summer merrily.   5
Merrily, merrily, shall I live now
Under the blossom that hangs on the
  bough.

III

While here you do snoring lie,
Open-eyed conspiracy
  His time doth take.
If of life you keep a care,
Shake off slumber, and beware.   5
  Awake, awake!

Hark, Hark, the Lark *

Hark, hark! the lark at heaven's gate sings,
   And Phoebus° 'gins arise,
His steeds to water at those springs
   On chaliced° flowers that lies;
And winking Marybuds° begin   5
   To ope their golden eyes.
With everything that pretty is,
     My lady sweet, arise!
       Arise, arise!

* In the play *Cymbeline* (Act II, Scene iii), the musicians of her
lover sing this song to Princess Imogen.
2. *Phoebus* (fē′bŭs): the sun, personified as the driver of a chariot.
4. *chaliced* (chăl′ĭst): cup-shaped.
5. *Marybuds:* marigolds.

O Mistress Mine

In *Twelfth Night* (Act II, Scene iii) we find this quaint love song. It is one of the few Shakespeare songs for which we still have sixteenth-century music.

O Mistress mine, where are you roaming?
O stay and hear! your true love's coming
    That can sing both high and low;
Trip no further, pretty sweeting,
Journeys end in lovers' meeting —   5
    Every wise man's son doth know.

What is love? 'tis not hereafter;
Present mirth hath present laughter;
    What's to come is still unsure;
In delay there lies no plenty, —   10
Then come kiss me, Sweet-and-twenty,
    Youth's a stuff will not endure.

Who Is Silvia?

This serenade from *The Two Gentlemen of Verona* (Act IV, Scene ii) is better known than the play itself. Of the more than twenty musical settings for it, Schubert's is the most famous. He is especially skillful in building up each stanza, by repeating the last line, to a climax of melody.

Who is Silvia? What is she,
    That all our swains commend her?
Holy, fair, and wise is she;
    The heaven such grace did lend her,
That she might admirèd be.   5

Is she kind as she is fair?
    For beauty lives with kindness.
Love doth to her eyes repair,
    To help him of his blindness,
And, being helped, inhabits there.   10

Then to Silvia let us sing,
    That Silvia is excelling;
She excels each mortal thing
    Upon the dull earth dwelling:
To her let us garlands bring.   15

Blow, Blow, Thou Winter Wind

This song from *As You Like It* (Act II, Scene vii) is sung by Amiens to the banished Duke in the Forest of Arden.

Blow, blow, thou winter wind!
Thou are not so unkind
  As man's ingratitude;
Thy tooth is not so keen,
Because thou art not seen,   5
Although thy breath be rude.

Heigh ho! sing, heigh ho! unto the green
  holly;
Most friendship is feigning, most loving
  mere folly.
  Then, heigh ho, the holly!
  This life is most jolly.   10

Freeze, freeze, thou bitter sky!
That dost not bite so nigh
  As benefits forgot;
Though thou the waters warp,
Thy sting is not so sharp   15
  As friend remembered not.°

Heigh ho, sing, heigh ho! unto the green
  holly;
Most friendship is feigning, most loving
  mere folly.
  Then, heigh ho, the holly!
  This life is most jolly.   20

16. As what a forgotten friend feels.

SHAKESPEARE'S LYRICS

1. What is the mood of each lyric? What does this show about the range of Shakespeare's powers?

2. As you would expect, the most effective way to approach these songs is to hear them in their musical settings. Try to obtain recordings of the songs. Listen carefully to the music and then reread the songs. Does the music enhance them in any way? Does it detract from them?

3. Because there is no set form for a song, great variety in rhythmical pattern may be found. Are any two of these alike in pattern? Note rhyme schemes and variations in length of line. Show examples of refrain and of alliteration.

SUGGESTION FOR WRITING

Try writing a short lyric of your own. Poets and musicians in the class might collaborate on original words and music.

Sonnets

Of all the sonnet sequences written by Elizabethan poets, none can equal the sonnets of Shakespeare in perfect form and depth of thought and feeling; nor have they been excelled in all English literature. No one knows whether Shakespeare's sonnets — one hundred and fifty-four in all — reflect the poet's own emotional experiences or imaginary situations. Many of them seem to be addressed to a young friend and another group to a mysterious " dark lady " with whom he apparently is deeply in love. The identity of these persons has been guessed at but never proved by Shakespearean scholars.

Shakespeare does not use the Italian rhyme scheme but a form preferred by many of the Elizabethan sonneteers. You will notice that there are three four-line stanzas with an alternate rhyme in each. Then the thought is summarized in a rhymed couplet at the end. In comparing the rhyme scheme with the one Spenser used (see page 111), you will see a slight difference, though in general they follow the same plan.

Sonnet 18

	Rhyme scheme	
Shall I compare thee to a summer's day?	*a*	
Thou art more lovely and more temperate:	*b*	
Rough winds do shake the darling buds of May,	*a*	
And summer's lease hath all too short a date;	*b*	
Sometimes too hot the eye of heaven shines,	*c*	5
And often is his gold complexion dimmed;	*d*	
And every fair from fair sometime declines,°	*c*	
By chance, or nature's changing course, untrimmed.°	*d*	
But thy eternal summer shall not fade	*e*	
Nor lose possession of that fair thou owest;°	*f*	10
Nor shall Death brag thou wanderest in his shade,	*e*	
When in eternal lines to time thou growest —°	*f*	
So long as men can breathe, or eyes can see,	*g*	
So long lives this,° and this gives life to thee.	*g*	

7. Every beautiful thing will eventually lose some of its beauty. 8. *untrimmed:* deprived of its beauty. 10. *owest:* own. 12. When through these lines, your fame will increase with time, and you will have immortality. 14. *this:* this poem.

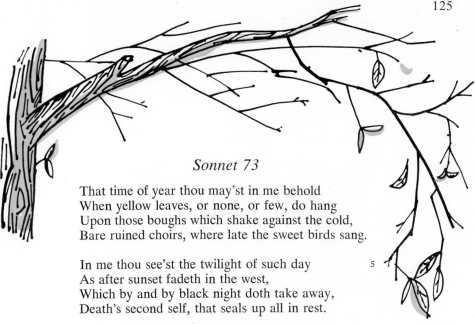

Sonnet 73

That time of year thou may'st in me behold
When yellow leaves, or none, or few, do hang
Upon those boughs which shake against the cold,
Bare ruined choirs, where late the sweet birds sang.

In me thou see'st the twilight of such day 5
As after sunset fadeth in the west,
Which by and by black night doth take away,
Death's second self, that seals up all in rest.

In me thou see'st the glowing of such fire,
That on the ashes of his youth doth lie 10
As the deathbed whereon it must expire,
Consumed with that which it was nourished by.°

— This thou perceiv'st, which makes thy love more strong,
To love that well which thou must leave ere long.

12. Choked by the ashes of the wood that fed the flame.

Sonnet 29

When in disgrace with fortune and men's eyes
I all alone beweep my outcast state,
And trouble deaf heaven with my bootless° cries,
And look upon myself, and curse my fate;

Wishing me like to one more rich in hope, 5
Featured like him, like him with friends possessed,
Desiring this man's art, and that man's scope,
With what I most enjoy contented least;

Yet in these thoughts myself almost despising,
Haply I think on thee — and then my state, 10
Like to the lark at break of day arising
From sullen earth, sings hymns at heaven's gate;

For thy sweet love remembered such wealth brings
That then I scorn to change my state with kings.

3. *bootless:* useless.

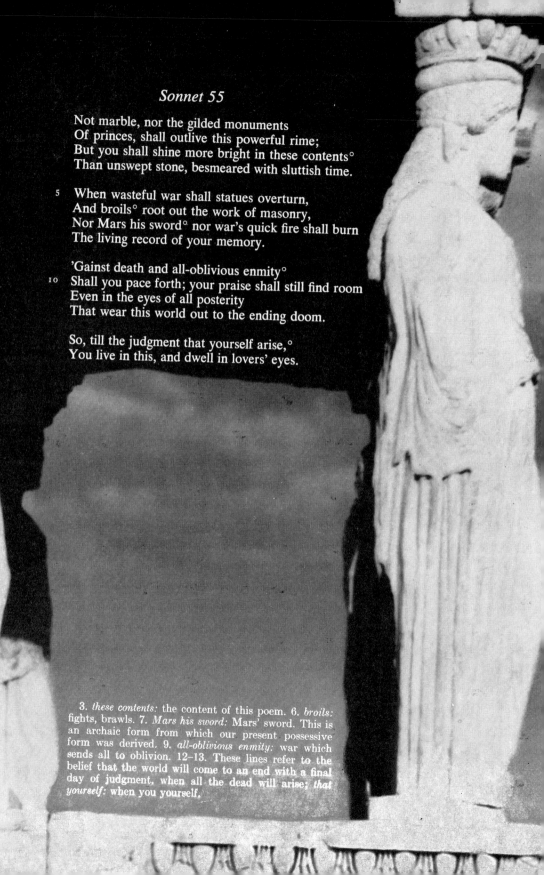

Sonnet 55

Not marble, nor the gilded monuments
Of princes, shall outlive this powerful rime;
But you shall shine more bright in these contents°
Than unswept stone, besmeared with sluttish time.

5 When wasteful war shall statues overturn,
And broils° root out the work of masonry,
Nor Mars his sword° nor war's quick fire shall burn
The living record of your memory.

'Gainst death and all-oblivious enmity°
10 Shall you pace forth; your praise shall still find room
Even in the eyes of all posterity
That wear this world out to the ending doom.

So, till the judgment that yourself arise,°
You live in this, and dwell in lovers' eyes.

3. *these contents:* the content of this poem. 6. *broils:*
fights, brawls. 7. *Mars his sword:* Mars' sword. This is
an archaic form from which our present possessive
form was derived. 9. *all-oblivious enmity:* war which
sends all to oblivion. 12–13. These lines refer to the
belief that the world will come to an end with a final
day of judgment, when all the dead will arise; *that
yourself:* when you yourself.

Sonnet 116

Let me not to the marriage of true minds
Admit impediments. Love is not love
Which alters when it alteration finds,
Or bends with the remover to remove —°

O, no! it is an ever-fixèd mark   5
That looks on tempests, and is never shaken;
It is the star to every wandering bark,
Whose worth's unknown, although his height be taken.°

Love's not Time's fool,° though rosy lips and cheeks
Within his bending sickle's compass come;   10
Love alters not with his brief hours and weeks,
But bears it out ev'n to the edge of doom —

If this be error, and upon me proved,
I never writ, nor no man ever loved.

4. Or ceases to love because the other has ceased. 7–8. The true value of love, like the star by which the sailor takes his bearings, is not wholly known or understood by the lover, although it furnishes a clear guide. 9. *Love's . . . fool:* Love endures despite the changes wrought by time.

SHAKESPEARE'S SONNETS

1. Although these sonnets are as musical as many songs, they are densely packed with thought; each one presents what is almost an " argument " in verse. Write a brief statement in your own words of the central idea in each sonnet.

2. In Sonnet 29 (one of the most famous), what two moods are contrasted? What causes each mood? To what element in the world of nature does Shakespeare compare this change of mood? Look up information on the English skylark — you will run across this bird in many poems of later periods — to see why the lines here and in " Hark, Hark, the Lark," on page 121, are especially meaningful.

3. In Sonnet 55, why does the poet think that his poem is a more permanent tribute than a stone monument? Do you think the time that has elapsed since then proves or disproves his point?

4. What is the mood in Sonnet 73?

5. In Sonnet 116, what characteristics of love are emphasized? To what is love compared in the second quatrain? How is Time pictured in the third? How many words or phrases can you find that emphasize permanence? Contrast this with the emphasis on change in the three preceding sonnets.

SUGGESTION FOR WRITING

Try writing a sonnet yourself — many high school students have written good ones. Read yours to the class or record it for playing in class. To get some ideas on themes in sonnets, read a few by the American poets Edna St. Vincent Millay and Henry Wadsworth Longfellow.

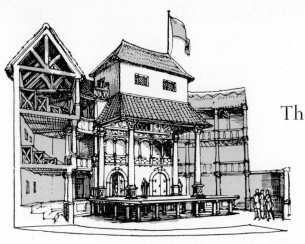

The Theater

in Shakespeare's Tim

There was excitement in the theater in Shakespeare's time. Never before had drama flourished with such gusto in England; never had so many people flocked to the playhouses to enjoy such superb dramas. The Globe, where Shakespeare was part owner and actor as well as playwright, was built in 1599, in Southwark. The Rose and the Swan, two older theaters, were its neighbors. On fine days, flags flew from the roofs, announcing that a play would be performed that afternoon.

What kinds of people crowded the theaters? They were a motley collection of Londoners: ordinary citizens, town idlers, seafarers ashore, travelers out to see the sights, and a few bold women. They carried their lunches, or bought fruit from girls selling apples and oranges at the door. There were men of higher rank in the audience, too: noblemen and students, country squires, masked women with men escorts. Entrance to the theater cost a penny; another penny entitled one to a seat in one of the galleries. Young dandies, who enjoyed admiring glances from the audience, sometimes sat on the stage!

In its structure, the Elizabethan theater was far different from the ones we know today. The Globe was an eight-sided building, open to the sky in the center. The sides, covered by a thatched roof, held three tiers of galleries. The acting platform, surrounded on three sides by standing spectators, projected into the pit, which was the open area in the center. An inner stage at the rear of this platform was hidden by a curtain which could be drawn aside when indoor scenes were portrayed. There was a balcony above the stage, used for the second story of a house in a street scene, or for the appearance of a supernatural being, and for the musicians. At the sides of the inner stage, and behind it, were the actors' dressing rooms. No actresses appeared in the Elizabethan theater; women's roles were taken by boys, and the audience would have been shocked to see a woman on the stage. There were props and costumes but little scenery — the spectators used their imaginations.

Imagine, then, that you are at the Globe, waiting for the play to begin. There is no dimming of lights — for the light comes from the sun; no curtain going up — for there is no curtain. Actors appear on the stage, the audience grows quiet, and you are ready for the first act of *Macbeth*.

WILLIAM SHAKESPEARE'S "MACBETH" is a powerful drama of a man whose weakness brought him first power, then defeat. The story is based on historical fact; Shakespeare adapted it from a contemporary history book, Holinshed's *Chronicles*. The play was probably written in 1606 as a tribute to James I, who traced his ancestry to the Scottish nobleman Banquo. Alive with the passions of eleventh-century Scotland, yet timeless in its impact, *Macbeth* is one of the most gripping of Shakespeare's tragedies.

Photographs by Paul George Schutzer

All pictures on pages 129–35 are from the production of *Macbeth* by the Rooftop Theatre, 111 East Houston St., New York, N.Y., Ray Boyle and Yolande Betbeze, producers. Directed by Ray Boyle, designed by Macdonald Eaton, costumes by Jeanne Button. Used through the courtesy of the producers and Roger Sullivan.

Macbeth, Thane of Glamis

BETH

LADY MACBETH   Art thou afeard?

LADY MACBETH   Why did you bring these daggers from the place?
They must lie there; go carry them; and smear
The sleepy grooms with blood.

MACBETH   I'll go no more.
I am afraid to think what I have done;
Look on 't again I dare not.

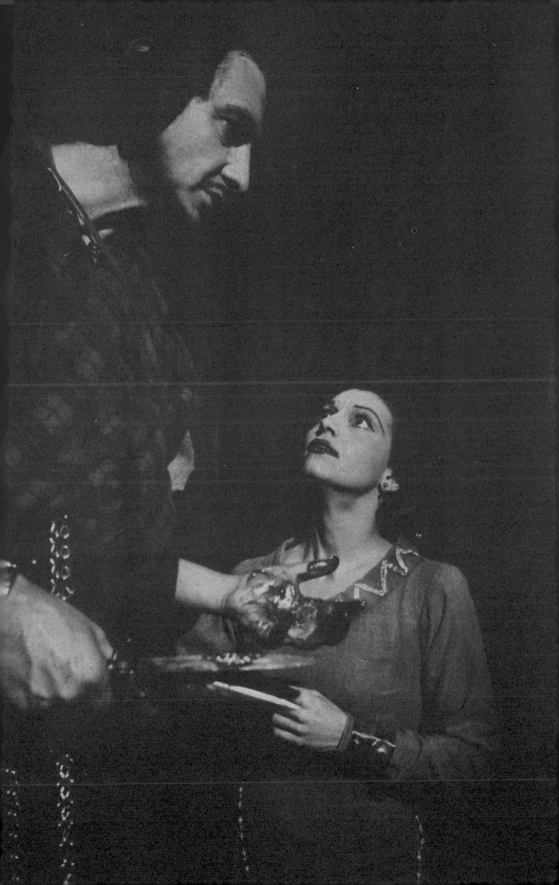

MACBETH Of all men else I have avoided thee.
But get thee back; my soul is too much charged
With blood of thine already.

MACDUFF   I have no words;
My voice is in my sword . . .

MACBETH

Lay on, Macduff,
And damned be him
that first cries
" Hold, enough! "

Dramatis Personae

ACT

DUNCAN, *king of Scotland*

MALCOLM
DONALBAIN } *his sons*

MACBETH } *generals of the*
BANQUO } *king's army*

MACDUFF
LENNOX
ROSS
MENTEITH } *noblemen of Scotland*
ANGUS
CAITHNESS

LADY MACBETH

LADY MACDUFF

Gentlewoman attending
   on Lady Macbeth

HECATE, *goddess of witchcraft*

Three Witches

FLEANCE, *son to Banquo*

SIWARD, *Earl of Northumberland,*
   general of the English forces

Young SIWARD, *his son*

SEYTON, *an officer attending*
   on Macbeth

BOY, *son to Macduff*

An English Doctor

A Scotch Doctor

A Sergeant

A Porter

An Old Man

Apparitions

Lords, Gentlemen, Officers,
   Soldiers, Murderers, Attendants,
   and Messengers

SCENE: *Scotland; England*
TIME: *the eleventh century*

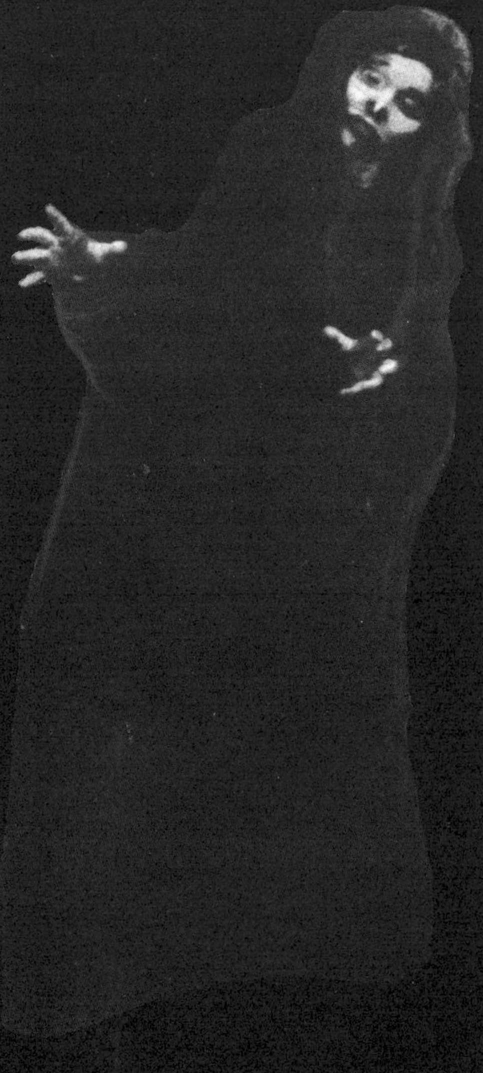

SCENE I. *A desert place.*

[*Thunder and lightning. Enter three* WITCHES.]

FIRST WITCH. When shall we three meet again
    In thunder, lightning, or in rain?
SECOND WITCH. When the hurly-burly's done,
    When the battle's lost and won.
THIRD WITCH. That will be ere the set of sun.   5
FIRST WITCH. Where the place?
SECOND WITCH.   Upon the heath.
THIRD WITCH. There to meet with Macbeth.
FIRST WITCH. I come, Graymalkin!°
SECOND WITCH. Paddock° calls.
THIRD WITCH. Anon.°   10
ALL. Fair is foul, and foul is fair:°
    Hover through the fog and filthy air.   [*Exeunt.*

8. *Graymalkin:* cat. 9. *Paddock:* toad. According to the superstition of the times, the cat and the toad were animals which the witches used to obtain knowledge. 10. *Anon:* at once. 11. *Fair . . . fair:* To mix things up thus is a witch's delight. The line suggests that the witches completely reverse accepted standards.

SCENE II. *A camp near Forres.**

[*Alarum* † *within. Enter* DUNCAN, MALCOLM, DONALBAIN,‡ LENNOX, *with* ATTEND-
ANTS, *meeting a bleeding* SERGEANT.]

DUNCAN. What bloody man is that? He can report,
    As seemeth by his plight, of the revolt
    The newest state.

MALCOLM.   This is the sergeant
    Who like a good and hardy soldier fought
    'Gainst my captivity. Hail, brave friend!   5
    Say to the king the knowledge of the broil°
    As thou didst leave it.

SERGEANT.   Doubtful it stood,
    As two spent swimmers, that do cling together
    And choke their art.° The merciless Macdonwald —
    Worthy to be a rebel, for to that   10
    The multiplying villainies of nature
    Do swarm upon him — from the western isles
    Of kerns and gallowglasses° is supplied;
    And fortune, on his damnèd quarrel smiling,
    Showed like a rebel's wench. But all's too weak;   15
    For brave Macbeth — well he deserves that name —
    Disdaining fortune, with his brandished steel,
    Which smoked with bloody execution,
    Like valor's minion° carvèd out his passage
    Till he faced the slave;   20
    Which ne'er shook hands, nor bade farewell to him,
    Till he unseamed him from the nave to the chaps,
    And fixed his head upon our battlements.

DUNCAN. O valiant cousin! worthy gentleman!

SERGEANT. As whence the sun 'gins his reflection   25
    Shipwrecking storms and direful thunders break,
    So from that spring whence comfort seemed to come
    Discomfort swells.° Mark, king of Scotland, mark:
    No sooner justice had with valor armed
    Compelled these skipping kerns to trust their heels,   30
    But the Norweyan° lord, surveying vantage,
    With furbished arms and new supplies of men
    Began a fresh assault.

DUNCAN.   Dismayed not this
    Our captains, Macbeth and Banquo?

SERGEANT.   Yes;
    As sparrows eagles, or the hare the lion.°   35
    If I say sooth, I must report they were

---

* *Forres* (fŏr'ĭs): a town in northeast Scotland. † *Alarum:* a trumpet call, sounded off stage.
‡ *Donalbain* (dŏn'ăl·bān). 6. *broil:* battle. 9. *choke their art:* prevent each other from swimming.
13. *kerns and gallowglasses:* light-armed and heavy-armed troops. 19. *minion:* favorite. 27–28. *So
. . . swells:* On the heels of good news, comes bad news. 31. *Norweyan* (nôr·wā'yăn): old form of
Norwegian. 35. *As sparrows . . . lion:* No more than eagles are dismayed by sparrows, or lions by
hares, were Macbeth and Banquo upset by the Norwegian lord's new men.

As cannons overcharged with double cracks, so they
Doubly redoubled strokes upon the foe.
Except they meant to bathe in reeking wounds,
Or memorize another Golgotha,°   40
I cannot tell.
But I am faint, my gashes cry for help.

DUNCAN. So well thy words become thee as thy wounds;
They smack of honor both. Go get him surgeons.

                                               [*Exit* SERGEANT, *attended.*

Who comes here?

                                [*Enter* ROSS.]

MALCOLM.   The worthy thane° of Ross.   45
LENNOX. What a haste looks through his eyes! So should he look
    That seems to speak things strange.
ROSS.   God save the king!
DUNCAN. Whence camest thou, worthy thane?
ROSS.   From Fife, great king;
Where the Norweyan banners flout the sky
And fan our people cold. Norway himself,   50
With terrible numbers,
Assisted by that most disloyal traitor,
The thane of Cawdor,° began a dismal conflict;
Till that Bellona's bridegroom,° lapped in proof,°
Confronted him with self-comparisons,   55
Point against point rebellious, arm 'gainst arm,
Curbing his lavish° spirit; and, to conclude,
The victory fell on us.
DUNCAN.   Great happiness!
ROSS.   That now
Sweno, the Norways' king, craves composition;°
Nor would we deign him burial of his men   60
Till he disbursèd at Saint Colme's inch°
Ten thousand dollars to our general use.
DUNCAN. No more that thane of Cawdor shall deceive
Our bosom interest.° Go pronounce his present° death,
And with his former title greet Macbeth.   65
ROSS. I'll see it done.
DUNCAN. What he hath lost, noble Macbeth hath won.   [*Exeunt.*

              SCENE III. *A heath near Forres.*

         [*Thunder. Enter the three* WITCHES.]

FIRST WITCH. Where hast thou been, sister?

---

40. *memorize another Golgotha* (gŏl'gō·thȧ): cause a slaughter of the enemies that would make the
place as memorable as Golgotha, where Christ was crucified. 45. *thane:* a Scottish title of rank,
similar to the English earl. 53. *Cawdor* (kô'dẽr). 54. *Bellona's* (bĕ·lō'nȧz) *bridegroom:* Bellona was
the Roman goddess of war. Macbeth, as a great soldier, is called her bridegroom; *lapped in proof:*
dressed in armor. 57. *lavish:* insolent. 59. *craves composition:* desires peace. 61. *Saint Colme's inch:*
an island near Edinburgh, Scotland (now called Inchcolm). 64. *bosom interest:* most vital concerns;
present: immediate.

SECOND WITCH. Killing swine.°
THIRD WITCH. Sister, where thou?
FIRST WITCH. A sailor's wife had chestnuts in her lap.
     And munched, and munched, and munched. " Give me," quoth I.   5
     " Aroint thee,° witch! " the rump-fed ronyon° cries.
     Her husband's to Aleppo° gone, master o' the *Tiger;*
     But in a sieve I'll thither sail,
     And, like a rat without a tail,
     I'll do, I'll do, and I'll do.   10
SECOND WITCH. I'll give thee a wind.
FIRST WITCH. Thou'rt kind.
THIRD WITCH. And I another.
FIRST WITCH. I myself have all the other,
     And the very ports they blow,   15
     All the quarters that they know
     I' the shipman's card.°
     I will drain him dry as hay;
     Sleep shall neither night nor day
     Hang upon his penthouse lid;°   20
     He shall live a man forbid.°
     Weary se'nnights° nine times nine
     Shall he dwindle, peak,° and pine;
     Though his bark cannot be lost,
     Yet it shall be tempest-tost.   25
     Look what I have.
SECOND WITCH. Show me, show me.
FIRST WITCH. Here I have a pilot's thumb,
     Wrecked as homeward he did come.   *[Drum within.*
THIRD WITCH. A drum, a drum!   30
     Macbeth doth come.
ALL. The weird sisters, hand in hand,
     Posters° of the sea and land,
     Thus do go about, about;
     Thrice to thine and thrice to mine   35
     And thrice again, to make up nine.
     Peace! the charm's wound up.

         [Enter MACBETH *and* BANQUO]

MACBETH. So foul and fair a day I have not seen.
BANQUO. How far is 't called to Forres? What are these
     So withered and so wild in their attire,   40
     That look not like the inhabitants o' the earth,
     And yet are on 't? Live you? or are you aught
     That man may question? You seem to understand me,
     By each at once her choppy finger laying
     Upon her skinny lips. You should be women,   45
     And yet your beards forbid me to interpret
     That you are so.

---

     2. *killing swine:* a practice attributed to witches by superstition. 6. *Aroint thee:* Begone; *ronyon:* mangy creature. 7. *Aleppo:* city in Syria. 17. *card:* compass. 20. *penthouse lid:* eyelid; literally, the roof of a shed. 21. *forbid:* accursed. 22. *se'nnights:* weeks. 23. *peak:* grow thin. 33. *Posters:* couriers.

MACBETH.   Speak, if you can. What are you?
FIRST WITCH. All hail, Macbeth! hail to thee, thane of Glamis!°
SECOND WITCH. All hail, Macbeth! hail to thee, thane of Cawdor!
THIRD WITCH. All hail, Macbeth, that shalt be king hereafter!   50
BANQUO. Good sir, why do you start, and seem to fear
     Things that do sound so fair? I' the name of truth,
     Are ye fantastical,° or that indeed
     Which outwardly ye show? My noble partner
     You greet with present grace and great prediction   55
     Of noble having and of royal hope,
     That he seems rapt° withal; to me you speak not.
     If you can look into the seeds of time,
     And say which grain will grow and which will not,
     Speak then to me, who neither beg nor fear   60
     Your favors nor your hate.
FIRST WITCH. Hail!
SECOND WITCH. Hail!
THIRD WITCH. Hail!
FIRST WITCH. Lesser than Macbeth, and greater.   65
SECOND WITCH. Not so happy, yet much happier.
THIRD WITCH. Thou shalt get kings, though thou be none;
     So all hail, Macbeth and Banquo!
FIRST WITCH. Banquo and Macbeth, all hail!
MACBETH. Stay, you imperfect speakers, tell me more.   70
     By Sinel's death° I know I am thane of Glamis;
     But how of Cawdor? The thane of Cawdor lives,
     A prosperous gentleman; and to be king
     Stands not within the prospect of belief,
     No more than to be Cawdor. Say from whence   75
     You owe this strange intelligence,° or why
     Upon this blasted heath you stop our way
     With such prophetic greeting? Speak, I charge you.   [WITCHES *vanish.*
BANQUO. The earth hath bubbles, as the water has,
     And these are of them. Whither are they vanished?   80
MACBETH. Into the air; and what seemed corporal° melted
     As breath into the wind. Would they had stayed!
BANQUO. Were such things here as we do speak about?
     Or have we eaten on the insane root
     That takes the reason prisoner?°   85
MACBETH. Your children shall be kings.
BANQUO.   You shall be king.
MACBETH. And thane of Cawdor too: went it not so?
BANQUO. To the selfsame tune and words. Who's here?

        [*Enter* ROSS *and* ANGUS.]

ROSS. The king hath happily received, Macbeth,

---

48. *Glamis* (glämz). 53. *fantastical:* creation of the imagination. 57. *rapt:* absorbed, or lost in his own thoughts. 71. *Sinel's* (sī'nĕlz) *death:* Sinel was Macbeth's father. 76. *intelligence:* knowledge. 81. *corporal:* material, of bodily substance. 84–85. *Or have . . . prisoner:* a common superstition of the times, that eating of a certain herb caused insanity.

The news of thy success; and when he reads   90
Thy personal venture in the rebels' fight,
His wonders and his praises do contend
Which should be thine or his.° Silenced with that,
In viewing o'er the rest o' the selfsame day,
He finds thee in the stout Norweyan ranks,   95
Nothing afeard of what thyself didst make,
Strange images of death.° As thick as hail
Came post with post; and every one did bear
Thy praises in his kingdom's great defense,
And poured them down before him.

ANGUS.   We are sent   100
To give thee from our royal master thanks;
Only to herald thee into his sight,
Not pay thee.

ROSS. And, for an earnest° of a greater honor,
He bade me, from him, call thee thane of Cawdor;   105
In which addition,° hail, most worthy thane!
For it is thine.

BANQUO. [*Aside*] What, can the devil speak true?

MACBETH. The thane of Cawdor lives; why do you dress me
In borrowed robes?

ANGUS.   Who was the thane lives yet;   110
But under heavy judgment bears that life
Which he deserves to lose. Whether he was combined
With those of Norway, or did line° the rebel
With hidden help and vantage, or that with both
He labored in his country's wreck, I know not;   115
But treasons capital,° confessed and proved,
Have overthrown him.

MACBETH. [*Aside*] Glamis, and thane of Cawdor!
The greatest is behind.° [*To* ROSS *and* ANGUS] Thanks for your pains.
[*To* BANQUO] Do you not hope your children shall be kings, 120
When those that gave the thane of Cawdor to me
Promised no less to them?

BANQUO.   That, trusted home,°
Might yet enkindle you unto the crown,
Besides the thane of Cawdor. But 'tis strange;
And oftentimes, to win us to our harm,   125
The instruments of darkness tell us truths,
Win us with honest trifles, to betray 's
In deepest consequence.
Cousins, a word, I pray you.

MACBETH.   [*Aside*] Two truths are told,
As happy prologues to the swelling act   130
Of the imperial theme.° — I thank you, gentlemen.

93. *Which . . . his:* whether he should praise you or wonder at you. 96–97. *Nothing . . . death:*
Macbeth killed many of his enemies and saw them die, but he was not afraid of death for himself.
104. *earnest:* pledge, or assurance. 106. *addition:* title. 113. *line:* support. 116. *capital:* deserving
death. 119. *behind:* yet to come. 122. *home:* fully. 131. *imperial theme:* that Macbeth would eventually be king.

[*Aside*] This supernatural soliciting
Cannot be ill, cannot be good. If ill,
Why hath it given me earnest of success,
Commencing in a truth? I am thane of Cawdor.   135
If good, why do I yield to that suggestion
Whose horrid image doth unfix my hair
And make my seated heart knock at my ribs,
Against the use of nature?° Present fears
Are less than horrible imaginings;   140
My thought, whose murder yet is but fantastical,
Shakes so my single state of man that function
Is smothered in surmise;° and nothing is
But what is not.
BANQUO.   Look, how our partner's rapt.
MACBETH. [*Aside*] If chance will have me king, why, chance may crown me,   145
    Without my stir.
BANQUO.   New honors come upon him,
    Like our strange garments, cleave not to their mold
    But with the aid of use.°
MACBETH.   [*Aside*] Come what come may,
    Time and the hour runs through the roughest day.
BANQUO. Worthy Macbeth, we stay upon your leisure.°   150
MACBETH. Give me your favor.° My dull brain was wrought
    With things forgotten. Kind gentlemen, your pains
    Are registered° where every day I turn
    The leaf to read them. Let us toward the king.
    [*To* BANQUO] Think upon what hath chanced, and, at more time,   155
    The interim having weighed it, let us speak
    Our free hearts each to other.
BANQUO.   Very gladly.
MACBETH. Till then, enough. Come, friends.   [*Exeunt.*

139. *Against . . . nature:* in such an unnatural way. 141–43. *My thought . . . surmise:* An act of
murder is as yet only imagined by Macbeth, but the thought of it shakes him, so that he cannot
act. 146–48. *New honors . . . use:* Macbeth wears his new honors like a new suit of clothes; as
yet, they don't seem to fit him. 150. *we stay upon your leisure:* we are waiting for you. 151. *Give me
your favor:* Pardon me. 153. *registered:* recorded (in his heart).

SCENE IV. *Forres. The Palace.*

[*Flourish.* * *Enter* DUNCAN, MALCOLM, DONALBAIN, LENNOX, *and* ATTENDANTS.]

DUNCAN. Is execution done on Cawdor? Are not
    Those in commission yet returned?
MALCOLM.   My liege,
    They are not yet come back. But I have spoke
    With one that saw him die; who did report
    That very frankly he confessed his treasons,   5
    Implored your highness' pardon and set forth

* *Flourish:* a trumpet fanfare.

A deep repentance. Nothing in his life
Became him like the leaving it; he died
As one that had been studied in his death
To throw away the dearest thing he owed,   10
As 'twere a careless trifle.

DUNCAN.   There's no art
To find the mind's construction in the face;°
He was a gentleman on whom I built
An absolute trust.

[*Enter* MACBETH, BANQUO, ROSS, *and* ANGUS.]

O worthiest cousin!
The sin of my ingratitude even now   15
Was heavy on me. Thou art so far before°
That swiftest wing of recompense is slow
To overtake thee. Would thou hadst less deserved,
That the proportion both of thanks and payment
Might have been mine! Only I have left to say,   20
More is thy due than more than all can pay.

MACBETH. The service and the loyalty I owe,
In doing it, pays itself. Your highness' part
Is to receive our duties; and our duties
Are to your throne and state, children and servants,   25
Which do but what they should, by doing everything
Safe toward° your love and honor.

DUNCAN.   Welcome hither;
I have begun to plant thee, and will labor
To make thee full of growing. Noble Banquo,
That hast no less deserved, nor must be known   30
No less to have done so, let me infold thee
And hold thee to my heart.

BANQUO.   There if I grow,
The harvest is your own.

DUNCAN.   My plenteous joys,
Wanton in fullness, seek to hide themselves
In drops of sorrow.° Sons, kinsmen, thanes,   35
And you whose places are the nearest, know
We° will establish our estate upon
Our eldest, Malcolm, whom we name hereafter
The Prince of Cumberland; which honor must
Not unaccompanied invest him only,   40
But signs of nobleness, like stars, shall shine
On all deservers.° From hence to Inverness,°

11–12. *There's . . . face:* There is no way to read a man's character from his face. 16. *before:* as used here, ahead. 27. *Safe toward:* with sure regard for. 33–35. *My . . . sorrow:* In other words, Duncan is so happy that he weeps for joy. 37. *We:* Duncan here, and elsewhere in the play, speaks of himself in the plural, as was the custom of kings. 35–42. In these lines Duncan establishes his son Malcolm as his successor but indicates that the others will receive suitable rewards for their services. In this period of Scottish history, lines of succession to the throne were not hereditary. Macbeth might have. succeeded Duncan legitimately, but Duncan's pronouncement now makes this impossible. 42. *Inverness:* Macbeth's castle, twenty-five miles away..

And bind us further to you.
MACBETH. The rest is labor, which is not used for you.°
    I'll be myself the harbinger and make joyful   45
    The hearing of my wife with your approach;
    So humbly take my leave.
DUNCAN.   My worthy Cawdor!
MACBETH. [*Aside*] The Prince of Cumberland! That is a step
    On which I must fall down, or else o'erleap,
    For in my way it lies. Stars, hide your fires;   50
    Let not light see my black and deep desires;
    The eye wink at the hand; yet let that be,
    Which the eye fears, when it is done, to see.   [*Exit.*
DUNCAN. True, worthy Banquo; he is full so valiant,
    And in his commendations I am fed;   55
    It is a banquet to me. Let's after him,
    Whose care is gone before to bid us welcome.
    It is a peerless kinsman.   [*Flourish. Exeunt.*

44. *The rest . . . for you:* Anything done for you is a pleasure; everything else is tedious (*labor*).

SCENE V. *Inverness.* MACBETH'S *castle.*

[*Enter* LADY MACBETH, *reading a letter.*]

LADY MACBETH. " They met me in the day of success; and I have learned by the
    perfectest report, they have more in them than mortal knowledge. When I
    burned in desire to question them further, they made themselves air, into
    which they vanished. Whiles I stood rapt in the wonder of it, came mis-
    sives° from the king, who all-hailed me ' Thane of Cawdor '; by which   5
    title, before, these weird sisters saluted me, and referred me to the coming
    on of time, with ' Hail, king that shalt be! ' This have I thought good to
    deliver thee, my dearest partner of greatness, that thou mightst not lose the
    dues of rejoicing, by being ignorant of what greatness is promised thee.
    Lay it to thy heart, and farewell."   10

Glamis thou art, and Cawdor; and shalt be
What thou art promised. Yet do I fear thy nature;
It is too full o' the milk of human kindness
To catch the nearest way. Thou wouldst be great;
Art not without ambition, but without   15
The illness° should attend it. What thou wouldst highly
That wouldst thou holily; wouldst not play false,
And yet wouldst wrongly win. Thou 'ldst have, great Glamis,
That which cries, " Thus thou must do, if thou have it ";
And that which rather thou dost fear to do   20
Than wishest should be undone.° Hie thee hither,
That I may pour my spirits in thine ear,

5. *missives:* messengers. 16. *illness:* as used here, wickedness. 18–21. *Thou 'ldst . . . undone:* The
thing that you want, great Glamis, requires doing certain things to obtain it, things you are afraid
to do, but, once done, you will not want undone.

And chastise with the valor of my tongue
All that impedes thee from the golden round,°
Which fate and metaphysical aid° doth seem   25
To have thee crowned withal.

[*Enter a* MESSENGER.]

What is your tidings?
MESSENGER. The king comes here tonight.
LADY MACBETH.   Thou 'rt mad to say it!
Is not thy master with him? who, were 't so,
Would have informed for preparation.
MESSENGER. So please you, it is true; our thane is coming.   30
One of my fellows had the speed of him,
Who, almost dead for breath, had scarcely more
Than would make up his message.
LADY MACBETH.   Give him tending;
He brings great news.   [*Exit* MESSENGER.
                    The raven himself is hoarse
That croaks the fatal entrance of Duncan   35
Under my battlements. Come, you spirits
That tend on mortal thoughts, unsex me here,
And fill me from the crown to the toe top-full
Of direst cruelty! make thick my blood;
Stop up the access and passage to remorse,   40
That no compunctious visitings of nature°
Shake my fell purpose, nor keep peace between
The effect and it! Come to my woman's breasts,
And take my milk for gall, you murdering ministers,°
Wherever in your sightless substances   45
You wait on nature's mischief! Come, thick night,
And pall thee in the dunnest smoke of hell,
That my keen knife see not the wound it makes,
Nor Heaven peep through the blanket of the dark,
To cry " Hold, hold! "

[*Enter* MACBETH.]

Great Glamis! worthy Cawdor!   50
Greater than both, by the all-hail hereafter!
Thy letters have transported me beyond
This ignorant present, and I feel now
The future in the instant.
MACBETH.   My dearest love,
Duncan comes here tonight.
LADY MACBETH.   And when goes hence?   55
MACBETH. Tomorrow, as he purposes.
LADY MACBETH.   O, never
Shall sun that morrow see!

24. *golden round:* crown. 25. *metaphysical aid:* the supernatural help implied by the witches'
prophecy. 41. *compunctious . . . nature:* natural feelings of pity. 44. *milk . . . ministers:* turn my
milk to bitterness (*gall*), you spirits of murder.

Your face, my thane, is as a book where men
May read strange matters. To beguile° the time,
Look like the time; bear welcome in your eye,   60
Your hand, your tongue; look like the innocent flower,
But be the serpent under 't. He that's coming
Must be provided for; and you shall put
This night's great business into my dispatch;
Which shall to all our nights and days to come   65
Give solely sovereign sway° and masterdom.
MACBETH. We will speak further.
LADY MACBETH.   Only look up clear;°
To alter favor° ever is to fear.
Leave all the rest to me.   [*Exeunt.*

59. *beguile:* deceive. 66. *solely sovereign sway:* absolute royal power. 67. *look up clear:* show a look
of innocence. 68. *alter favor:* change appearances; in other words, to look afraid.

SCENE VI. *Before* MACBETH'S *castle.*

[*Hautboys and torches.* Enter* DUNCAN, MALCOLM, DONALBAIN, BANQUO, LENNOX,
MACDUFF, ROSS, ANGUS, *and* ATTENDANTS.]

DUNCAN. This castle hath a pleasant seat;° the air
Nimbly and sweetly recommends itself
Unto our gentle senses.
BANQUO.   This guest of summer,
The temple-haunting martlet, does approve,
By his loved mansionry,° that the heaven's breath   5
Smells wooingly here; no jutty, frieze,
Buttress, nor coign of vantage, but this bird
Hath made his pendent bed and procreant cradle.°
Where they most breed and haunt, I have observed,
The air is delicate.

[*Enter* LADY MACBETH.]

DUNCAN.   See, see, our honored hostess!   10
The love that follows us sometime is our trouble,
Which still we thank as love. Herein I teach you
How you shall bid God 'ild° us for your pains,
And thank us for your trouble.
LADY MACBETH.   All our service
In every point twice done and then done double   15
Were poor and single business to contend
Against those honors deep and broad wherewith
Your majesty loads our house; for those of old,
And the late dignities heaped up to them,

* *Hautboys* (hō'boiz): oboes, used to announce the entrance of royalty; *torches* indicate that it is
night. 1. *seat:* location. 5. *mansionry:* building. 6–8. *no jutty . . . cradle:* The martlet (a bird like a
swallow) has made its nest and cradle for the young (*procreant cradle*) everywhere about the castle,
in every advantageous corner (*coign of vantage*). 13. *God 'ild:* God reward (us).

                        We rest your hermits.°
DUNCAN.   Where's the thane of Cawdor?   20
                        We coursed° him at the heels, and had a purpose
                        To be his purveyor;° but he rides well;
                        And his great love, sharp as his spur, hath holp him
                        To his home before us. Fair and noble hostess,
                        We are your guest tonight.
LADY MACBETH.   Your servants ever   25
                        Have theirs, themselves, and what is theirs in compt,°
                        To make their audit at your highness' pleasure,
                        Still° to return your own.
DUNCAN.   Give me your hand;
                        Conduct me to mine host. We love him highly,
                        And shall continue our graces toward him.   30
                        By your leave, hostess.   [Exeunt.

20. *We rest your hermits:* This means "We shall pray for you." Hermits were sometimes paid by a person or family to pray for the employer's soul. 21. *coursed:* chased. 22. *To be his purveyor:* to arrive ahead of him. 26. *compt:* readiness. 28. *Still:* always.

SCENE VII. MACBETH's *castle.*

[*Hautboys and torches. Enter a* SEWER,* *and divers* SERVANTS *with dishes and service, and pass over the stage. Then enter* MACBETH.]

MACBETH. If it were done when 'tis done, then 'twere well
                        It were done quickly. If the assassination
                        Could trammel up the consequence, and catch
                        With his surcease success;° that but this blow
                        Might be the be-all and the end-all here,   5
                        But° here, upon this bank and shoal of time,
                        We'ld jump° the life to come. But in these cases
                        We still have judgment here; that we but teach
                        Bloody instructions, which, being taught, return
                        To plague the inventor. This even-handed justice   10
                        Commends the ingredients of our poisoned chalice
                        To our own lips.° He's here in double trust;
                        First, as I am his kinsman and his subject,
                        Strong both against the deed; then, as his host,
                        Who should against his murderer shut the door,   15
                        Not bear the knife myself. Besides, this Duncan
                        Hath borne his faculties so meek, hath been
                        So clear in his great office, that his virtues
                        Will plead like angels, trumpet-tongued, against
                        The deep damnation of his taking-off;   20

* *Sewer:* a server, a servant whose duties are to arrange the table. 2–4. *If . . . success:* If only the murder would have no consequences, but be final and successful with Duncan's death (*surcease*). 6. *But:* even. 7. *jump:* risk. Macbeth would risk the consequences of murder in afterlife if he could be sure there would be no bad consequences in this life (*this bank and shoal of time*). 8–12. *that we . . . own lips:* If we practice murder, we teach others to murder us. This impartial (*even-handed*) justice offers (*commends*) the same fate to us that we propose for others.

And pity, like a naked newborn babe,
Striding the blast, or heaven's cherubin, horsed
Upon the sightless couriers° of the air,
Shall blow the horrid deed in every eye,
That tears shall drown the wind. I have no spur   25
To prick the sides of my intent, but only
Vaulting ambition, which o'erleaps itself
And falls on the other.°

[*Enter* LADY MACBETH.]

            How now! what news?
LADY MACBETH. He has almost supped. Why have you left the chamber?
MACBETH. Hath he asked for me?
LADY MACBETH.   Know you not he has?   30
MACBETH. We will proceed no further in this business.
    He hath honored me of late; and I have bought
    Golden opinions from all sorts of people,
    Which would be worn now in their newest gloss,
    Not cast aside so soon.
LADY MACBETH.   Was the hope drunk   35
    Wherein you dressed yourself? Hath it slept since?
    And wakes it now, to look so green and pale
    At what it did so freely? From this time
    Such I account thy love. Art thou afeard
    To be the same in thine own act and valor   40
    As thou art in desire? Wouldst thou have that
    Which thou esteem'st the ornament of life,°
    And live a coward in thine own esteem,
    Letting " I dare not " wait upon " I would,"
    Like the poor cat i' the adage?°
MACBETH.   Prithee, peace!   45
    I dare do all that may become a man;
    Who dares do more is none.
LADY MACBETH.   What beast was 't, then,
    That made you break this enterprise to me?°
    When you durst do it, then you were a man;
    And, to be more than what you were,° you would   50
    Be so much more the man. Nor time nor place
    Did then adhere,° and yet you would make both.
    They have made themselves, and that their° fitness now
    Does unmake you. I have given suck, and know
    How tender 'tis to love the babe that milks me;   55
    I would, while it was smiling in my face,
    Have plucked my nipple from his boneless gums,

---

23. *sightless couriers:* the winds. 28. *other:* i.e., the other side. 42. *ornament of life:* the crown.
45. *the poor cat i' the adage:* This refers to an old adage or proverb which goes "The cat would eat fish but would not wet her feet." 46–48. *I dare . . . to me:* Macbeth is defending himself. It isn't cowardice (as his wife suggests) that made him change his mind about killing Duncan; he'd dare anything that becomes a man. In that case, says Lady Macbeth, it must have been something other than a man (a *beast*) who started the whole business. 50. *to be more than what you were:* that is, to be king. 52. *Did then adhere:* was then appropriate. 53. *that their:* their very.

And dashed the brains out, had I so sworn as you
Have done to this.
MACBETH.   If we should fail?
LADY MACBETH.   We fail!
But screw your courage to the sticking-place   60
And we'll not fail. When Duncan is asleep —
Whereto the rather shall his day's hard journey
Soundly invite him — his two chamberlains
Will I with wine and wassail° so convince°
That memory, the warder of the brain,   65
Shall be a fume, and the receipt of reason
A limbeck only.° When in swinish sleep
Their drenchèd natures lie as in a death,
What cannot you and I perform upon
The unguarded Duncan? what not put upon   70
His spongy officers, who shall bear the guilt
Of our great quell?°
MACBETH.   Bring forth men children only;
For thy undaunted mettle should compose
Nothing but males. Will it not be received,
When we have marked with blood those sleepy two   75
Of his own chamber and used their very daggers,
That they have done 't?
LADY MACBETH.   Who dares receive it other,
As we shall make our griefs and clamor roar
Upon his death?
MACBETH.   I am settled, and bend up
Each corporal agent° to this terrible feat.   80
Away, and mock the time with fairest show;
False face must hide what the false heart doth know.   [*Exeunt.*

64. *wassail:* an intoxicating drink; *convince:* overcome. 66–67. *the receipt . . . only:* The mind
(*receipt of reason*) would become like a still (*limbeck*) which will distill only confused thoughts.
72. *quell:* murder. 80. *corporal agent:* bodily power.

ACT II

SCENE I. *Court of* MACBETH'S *castle.*

[*Enter* BANQUO, *and* FLEANCE* *bearing a torch before him.*]

BANQUO. How goes the night, boy?
FLEANCE. The moon is down; I have not heard the clock.
BANQUO. And she goes down at twelve.
FLEANCE.   I take 't, 'tis later, sir
BANQUO. Hold, take my sword. There's husbandry° in heaven;
Their candles are all out. Take thee that too.°   5

* *Fleance* (flē'ăns). 4. *husbandry:* economy. 5. *Take thee that too:* Apparently he gives Fleance his
sword belt as well as his sword.

A heavy summons° lies like lead upon me,
And yet I would not sleep. Merciful powers,
Restrain in me the cursèd thoughts that nature
Gives way to in repose!

[*Enter* MACBETH, *and a* SERVANT *with a torch.*]

Give me my sword.
Who's there?   10
MACBETH. A friend.
BANQUO. What, sir, not yet at rest? The king's abed.
He hath been in unusual pleasure, and
Sent forth great largess to your offices.°
This diamond he greets your wife withal,   15
By the name of most kind hostess; and shut up
In measureless content.°
MACBETH.   Being unprepared,
Our will became the servant to defect;
Which else should free have wrought.°
BANQUO.   All's well.
I dreamt last night of the three weird sisters: 20
To you they have showed some truth.
MACBETH.   I think not of them;
Yet, when we can entreat an hour to serve,
We would spend it in some words upon that business,
If you would grant the time.
BANQUO.   At your kind'st leisure.
MACBETH. If you shall cleave to my consent, when 'tis,   25
It shall make honor for you.
BANQUO.   So I lose none
In seeking to augment it, but still keep
My bosom franchised and allegiance clear,
I shall be counseled.°
MACBETH.   Good repose the while!
BANQUO. Thanks, sir; the like to you!   30

[*Exeunt* BANQUO *and* FLEANCE.

MACBETH. Go bid thy mistress, when my drink is ready,
She strike upon the bell. Get thee to bed.   [*Exit* SERVANT.
Is this a dagger which I see before me,
The handle toward my hand? Come, let me clutch thee.
I have thee not, and yet I see thee still.   35
Art thou not, fatal vision, sensible
To feeling as to sight?° or art thou but
A dagger of the mind, a false creation,

6. *heavy summons:* great weariness. 14. *largess to your offices:* gifts of money to the servant quarters. 16–17. *and shut up in measureless content:* The king has retired to his room, happy and well satisfied. 17–19. *Being . . . wrought:* Had Macbeth had more warning of the king's visit, his hospitality would have been more lavish. 25–29. *If you . . . counseled:* Macbeth promises to reward Banquo (*It shall make honor for you*) if he agrees to support Macbeth (*cleave to my consent*) when the time comes, and Banquo says that he will listen to Macbeth (*be counseled*) if he loses no honor in seeking to increase (*augment*) it and if he can keep his conscience free (*bosom franchised*) and retain his loyalty to the king (*allegiance clear*). 36–37. *sensible to feeling as to sight:* capable of being felt as well as seen.

Proceeding from the heat-oppressèd brain?
I see thee yet, in form as palpable°   40
As this which now I draw.
Thou marshal'st me the way that I was going;
And such an instrument I was to use.
Mine eyes are made the fools o' the other senses,
Or else worth all the rest; I see thee still,   45
And on thy blade and dudgeon° gouts of blood,
Which was not so before. There's no such thing.
It is the bloody business which informs°
Thus to mine eyes. Now o'er the one half-world
Nature seems dead, and wicked dreams abuse   50
The curtained sleep! witchcraft celebrates
Pale Hecate's offerings,° and withered murder,
Alarumed by his sentinel, the wolf,
Whose howl's his watch,° thus with his stealthy pace,
With Tarquin's ravishing strides, toward his design   55
Moves like a ghost. Thou sure and firm-set earth,
Hear not my steps, which way they walk, for fear
Thy very stones prate of my whereabout,
And take the present horror° from the time,
Which now suits with° it. Whiles I threat, he lives;   60
Words to the heat of deeds too cold breath gives.   [*A bell rings.*
I go, and it is done; the bell invites me.
Hear it not, Duncan; for it is a knell
That summons thee to heaven or to hell.   [*Exit.*

40. *palpable:* real, in the sense of being capable of being touched or felt. 46. *dudgeon:* handle. 48. *informs:* creates forms. 51–52. *witchcraft . . . offerings:* Witches pledged allegiance to Hecate (hĕk'át), goddess of the underworld and of witchcraft. 54. *howl's his watch:* tells time by howling. 59. *present horror:* the silence of midnight. 60. *suits with:* matches.

SCENE II. *The same.*

[*Enter* LADY MACBETH.]

LADY MACBETH. That which hath made them drunk hath made me bold;
    What hath quenched them hath given me fire. Hark! Peace!
    It was the owl that shrieked, the fatal bellman,°
    Which gives the stern'st good night. He is about it.
    The doors are open; and the surfeited grooms   5
    Do mock their charge with snores. I have drugged their possets,°
    That death and nature do contend about them,
    Whether they live or die.
MACBETH. [*Within*] Who's there? what, ho!
LADY MACBETH. Alack, I am afraid they have awaked,   10
    And 'tis not done. The attempt and not the deed
    Confounds° us. Hark! I laid their daggers ready;

3. *fatal bellman:* On the night before an execution, a bellman rang a hand bell outside the cell of the condemned, bidding him to repent his sins. 6. *possets:* bedtime drinks. 12. *Confounds:* ruins.

He could not miss 'em. Had he not resembled
My father as he slept, I had done 't.

[*Enter* MACBETH.]

My husband!

MACBETH. I have done the deed. Didst thou not hear a noise?   15

LADY MACBETH. I heard the owl scream and the crickets cry.
Did not you speak?

MACBETH.   When?

LADY MACBETH.   Now.

MACBETH.   As I descended?

LADY MACBETH. Ay.

MACBETH. Hark!
Who lies i' the second chamber?

LADY MACBETH.   Donalbain.   20

MACBETH. This is a sorry sight.   [*Looking on his hands.*

LADY MACBETH. A foolish thought, to say a sorry sight.

MACBETH. There's one did laugh in 's sleep, and one cried " Murder! "
That they did wake each other. I stood and heard them;
But they did say their prayers, and addressed them   25
Again to sleep.

LADY MACBETH. There are two lodged together.

MACBETH. One cried " God bless us! " and " Amen " the other,
As they had seen me with these hangman's hands.
Listening their fear, I could not say " Amen,"   30
When they did say " God bless us! "

LADY MACBETH.   Consider it not so deeply.

MACBETH. But wherefore could not I pronounce " Amen "?
I had most need of blessing, and " Amen "
Stuck in my throat.

LADY MACBETH.   These deeds must not be thought
After these ways; so, it will make us mad.   35

MACBETH. Methought I heard a voice cry " Sleep no more!
Macbeth does murder sleep," the innocent sleep,
Sleep that knits up the raveled sleave° of care,
The death of each day's life, sore labor's bath,
Balm of hurt minds, great nature's second course,   40
Chief nourisher in life's feast —

LADY MACBETH.   What do you mean?

MACBETH. Still it cried " Sleep no more! " to all the house;
" Glamis hath murdered sleep, and therefore Cawdor
Shall sleep no more; Macbeth shall sleep no more."

LADY MACBETH. Who was it that thus cried? Why, worthy thane,   45
You do unbend your noble strength, to think
So brainsickly of things. Go get some water,
And wash this filthy witness from your hand.
Why did you bring these daggers from the place?
They must lie there; go carry them; and smear   50
The sleepy grooms with blood.

38. *raveled sleave:* tangled skein.

MACBETH.   I'll go no more.
    I am afraid to think what I have done;
    Look on 't again I dare not.
LADY MACBETH.   Infirm of purpose!
    Give me the daggers. The sleeping and the dead
    Are but as pictures; 'tis the eye of childhood   55
    That fears a painted devil. If he do bleed,
    I'll gild the faces of the grooms withal;
    For it must seem their guilt.   [*Exit. Knocking within.*
MACBETH.   Whence is that knocking?
    How is 't with me, when every noise appalls me?
    What hands are here? Ha! they pluck out mine eyes.   60
    Will all great Neptune's ocean wash this blood
    Clean from my hand? No, this my hand will rather
    The multitudinous seas incarnadine,°
    Making the green one red.

[Re-enter LADY MACBETH.]

LADY MACBETH. My hands are of your color; but I shame   65
    To wear a heart so white. [*Knocking within.*] I hear a knocking
    At the south entry. Retire we to our chamber;
    A little water clears us of this deed.
    How easy is it, then! Your constancy°
    Hath left you unattended. [*Knocking within.*] Hark! more knocking.   70
    Get on your nightgown, lest occasion call us,
    And show us to be watchers. Be not lost
    So poorly in your thoughts.
MACBETH. To know my deed, 'twere best not know myself.   [*Knocking within.*
    Wake Duncan with thy knocking! I would thou couldst!   [*Exeunt.* 75

63. *incarnadine* (ĭn·kär′nà·dĭn): make red. 69. *constancy:* firmness of purpose.

SCENE III. *The same.*

[Knocking within. Enter a PORTER.]

PORTER.° Here' a knocking indeed! If a man were porter of hell gate, he should
have old turning the key. [*Knocking within.*] Knock, knock, knock! Who's
there, i' the name of Beelzebub? Here's a farmer, that hanged himself on
the expectation of plenty. Come in time; have napkins enow about you;
here you'll sweat for 't. [*Knocking within.*] Knock, knock! Who's there,   5
in the other devil's name? Faith, here's an equivocator, that could swear in

1. The speech that follows is said by a drunken porter (man who tends the gate) and is full of
puns and jests that refer to current happenings of Shakespeare's day. The porter, talking to himself, says that if a man were porter at *hell's gate*, he would grow old from letting so many damned
souls in (lines 1–2). He invokes the name of *Beelzebub* (bē·ĕl′zē·bŭb), Satan's assistant (line 3);
speaks of a farmer who hanged himself in profiteering on prices, a favorite object of satire in England
at this time (lines 3–4), and advises the farmer to bring plenty of towels with him; speaks of an
equivocator (liar) who could not lie himself into heaven (lines 6–8); and pretends to admit to hell
an *English tailor* whose goose — this word meant a tailor's iron — is to be cooked, or roasted because he has stolen a French fashion. The English critic DeQuincey praises this speech as an admirable way of relieving the great tension of the preceding scene.

both the scales against either scale; who committed treason enough for
God's sake, yet could not equivocate to heaven. O, come in, equivocator.
[*Knocking within.*] Knock, knock, knock! Who's there? Faith, here's an
English tailor come hither, for stealing out of a French hose. Come in,   10
tailor; here you may roast your goose. [*Knocking within.*] Knock, knock;
never at quiet! What are you? But this place is too cold for hell. I'll devil-
porter it no further; I had thought to have let in some of all professions
that go the primrose way to the everlasting bonfire. [*Knocking within.*]
Anon, anon! I pray you, remember the porter.   [*Opens the gate.*   15

[*Enter* MACDUFF *and* LENNOX.]

MACDUFF. Was it so late, friend, ere you went to bed,
    That you do lie so late?
PORTER. Faith, sir, we were carousing till the second cock;° and drink, sir, is a
    great provoker.
MACDUFF. I believe drink gave thee the lie last night.   20
PORTER. That it did, sir, i' the very throat on me. But I requited him for his lie;
    and, I think, being too strong for him, though he took up my legs some-
    time, yet I made a shift to cast him.
MACDUFF. Is thy master stirring?

[*Enter* MACBETH.]

    Our knocking has awaked him; here he comes.   25
LENNOX. Good morrow, noble sir.
MACBETH.   Good morrow, both.
MACDUFF. Is the king stirring, worthy thane?
MACBETH.   Not yet.
MACDUFF. He did command me to call timely on him.
    I have almost slipped the hour.
MACBETH.   I'll bring you to him.
MACDUFF. I know this is a joyful trouble to you;   30
    But yet 'tis one.°
MACBETH. The labor we delight in physics pain.°
    This is the door.
MACDUFF.   I'll make so bold to call,
    For 'tis my limited service.°   [*Exit.*
LENNOX. Goes the king hence today?
MACBETH.   He does — he did appoint so.   35
LENNOX. The night has been unruly: where we lay,
    Our chimneys were blown down; and, as they say,
    Lamentings heard i' the air; strange screams of death,
    And prophesying with accents terrible
    Of dire combustion and confused events   40
    New hatched to the woeful time. The obscure bird°
    Clamored the livelong night; some say, the earth
    Was feverous and did shake.

18. *second cock:* 3 A.M. 31. *one:* a trouble nevertheless. 32. *physics pain:* cures pain, or is pleasant.
34. *limited service:* assigned duty. 41. *obscure bird:* the owl.

MACBETH.   'Twas a rough night.
LENNOX. My young remembrance cannot parallel
    A fellow to it.   45

[*Re-enter* MACDUFF.]

MACDUFF. O horror, horror, horror! Tongue nor heart
    Cannot conceive nor name thee!
MACBETH ⎫
LENNOX ⎭   What's the matter?
MACDUFF. Confusion now hath made his masterpiece!
    Most sacrilegious murder hath broke ope
    The Lord's anointed temple,° and stole thence   50
    The life o' the building!
MACBETH.   What is 't you say? The life?
LENNOX. Mean you his majesty?
MACDUFF. Approach the chamber, and destroy your sight
    With a new Gorgon.° Do not bid me speak;
    See, and then speak yourselves.   [*Exeunt* MACBETH *and* LENNOX.
                   Awake, awake!   55
    Ring the alarum bell. Murder and treason!
    Banquo and Donalbain! Malcolm! awake!
    Shake off this downy sleep, death's counterfeit,
    And look on death itself! Up, up, and see
    The great doom's image!° Malcolm! Banquo!   60
    As from your graves rise up, and walk like sprites,°
    To countenance° this horror! Ring the bell.   [*Bell rings.*

[*Enter* LADY MACBETH.]

LADY MACBETH. What's the business,
    That such a hideous trumpet calls to parley
    The sleepers of the house? Speak, speak!
MACDUFF.   O gentle lady,   65
    'Tis not for you to hear what I can speak;
    The repetition, in a woman's ear,
    Would murder as it fell.

[*Enter* BANQUO.]

          O Banquo, Banquo,
    Our royal master's murdered!
LADY MACBETH.   Woe, alas!
    What, in our house?
BANQUO.   Too cruel anywhere.   70
    Dear Duff, I prithee, contradict thyself,
    And say it is not so.

---

50. *The Lord's anointed temple:* the body of the king. 54. *Gorgon:* a female monster (of Greek mythology) who turned to stone those who gazed upon her. 60. *The great doom's image:* Duncan's murder is compared to the end of the world. 61. *sprites:* ghosts. 62. *countenance:* be in keeping with.

[*Re-enter* MACBETH *and* LENNOX, *with* ROSS.]

MACBETH. Had I but died an hour before this chance,°
    I had lived a blessèd time; for, from this instant,
    There's nothing serious in mortality.   75
    All is but toys:° renown and grace is dead;
    The wine of life is drawn, and the mere lees
    Is left this vault° to brag of.

[*Enter* MALCOLM *and* DONALBAIN.]

DONALBAIN. What is amiss?
MACBETH.   You are, and do not know 't:
    The spring, the head, the fountain of your blood   80
    Is stopped; the very source of it is stopped.
MACDUFF. Your royal father's murdered.
MALCOLM.   O, by whom?
LENNOX. Those of his chamber, as it seemed, had done 't.
    Their hands and faces were all badged with blood;
    So were their daggers, which unwiped we found   85
    Upon their pillows.
    They stared, and were distracted; no man's life
    Was to be trusted with them.
MACBETH. O, yet I do repent me of my fury,
    That I did kill them.
MACDUFF.   Wherefore did you so?   90
MACBETH. Who can be wise, amazed, temperate and furious,
    Loyal and neutral, in a moment? No man.
    The expedition° of my violent love
    Outrun the pauser, reason. Here lay Duncan,
    His silver skin laced with his golden blood,   95
    And his gashed stabs looked like a breach in nature
    For ruin's wasteful entrance; there, the murderers,
    Steeped in the colors of their trade, their daggers
    Unmannerly breeched° with gore. Who could refrain,
    That had a heart to love, and in that heart   100
    Courage to make 's love known?
LADY MACBETH.   Help me hence, ho!
MACDUFF. Look to the lady.
MALCOLM. [*Aside to* DONALBAIN] Why do we hold our tongues,
    That most may claim this argument for ours?
DONALBAIN. [*Aside to* MALCOLM] What should be spoken here, where our fate, 105
    Hid in an auger hole, may rush, and seize us?°
    Let's away;
    Our tears are not yet brewed.

---

73. *chance:* occurrence. 76. *toys:* trifles. 78. *vault:* as used here, world. Macbeth is echoing Macduff's feeling that Duncan's murder spelled the end of the world. 93. *expedition:* hasty action. 99. *breeched:* completely covered. 105–106. *where our fate . . . seize us:* Malcolm and Donalbain sense there is danger for them in this murder; any small event (*auger hole*) may lead to their downfall.

MALCOLM.   [*Aside to* DONALBAIN] Nor our strong sorrow
    Upon the foot of motion.°
BANQUO.   Look to the lady: [LADY MACBETH *is carried out.*
    And when we have our naked frailties° hid,   110
    That suffer in exposure, let us meet,
    And question this most bloody piece of work,
    To know it further. Fears and scruples shake us.
    In the great hand of God I stand; and thence
    Against the undivulged pretense I fight   115
    Of treasonous malice.°
MACDUFF.   And so do I.
ALL.   So all.
MACBETH. Let's briefly put on manly readiness,
    And meet i' the hall together.
ALL.   Well contented.
        [*Exeunt all but* MALCOLM *and* DONALBAIN.
MALCOLM. What will you do? Let's not consort with them;
    To show an unfelt sorrow is an office   120
    Which the false man does easy. I'll to England.
DONALBAIN. To Ireland, I; our separated fortune
    Shall keep us both the safer. Where we are,
    There's daggers in men's smiles; the near in blood,
    The nearer bloody.°
MALCOLM.   This murderous shaft that's shot   125
    Hath not yet lighted,° and our safest way
    Is to avoid the aim. Therefore, to horse;
    And let us not be dainty of leave-taking,
    But shift away. There's warrant in that theft.
    Which steals itself, when there's no mercy left.   [*Exeunt.*   130

109. *Upon the foot of motion:* is not yet moving. 110. *naked frailties:* The guests of Macbeth were still in their nightclothes. 115–116. *Against . . . malice:* I fight against the as yet unrevealed treason which has committed this crime. 124–125. *the near in blood, the nearer bloody:* the closer the relationship (to Duncan) the more likely the danger of being murdered. 125–126. *This . . . lighted:* More murder may follow.

SCENE IV. *Outside* MACBETH'S *castle.*

[*Enter* ROSS *and an* OLD MAN.]

OLD MAN. Threescore and ten I can remember well;
    Within the volume of which time I have seen
    Hours dreadful and things strange; but this sore night
    Hath trifled former knowings.
ROSS.   Ah, good father,
    Thou seest, the heavens, as troubled with man's act,   5
    Threaten his bloody stage. By the clock, 'tis day,
    And yet dark night strangles the traveling lamp.°

7. *traveling lamp:* the sun.

Is 't night's predominance, or the day's shame,
That darkness does the face of earth entomb,
When living light should kiss it?
OLD MAN.   'Tis unnatural,   10
Even like the deed that's done. On Tuesday last,
A falcon, towering in her pride of place,
Was by a mousing owl hawked at and killed.
ROSS. And Duncan's horses — a thing most strange and certain —
Beauteous and swift, the minions of their race,   15
Turned wild in nature, broke their stalls, flung out,
Contending 'gainst obedience, as they would make
War with mankind.
OLD MAN.   'Tis said they eat each other.
ROSS. They did so, to the amazement of mine eyes
That looked upon 't. Here comes the good Macduff.   20

[*Enter* MACDUFF.]

How goes the world, sir, now?
MACDUFF.   Why, see you not?
ROSS. Is 't known who did this more than bloody deed?
MACDUFF. Those that Macbeth hath slain.
ROSS.   Alas, the day!
What good could they pretend?
MACDUFF.   They were suborned;°
Malcolm and Donalbain, the king's two sons,   25
Are stolen away and fled; which puts upon them
Suspicion of the deed.
ROSS.   'Gainst nature still!
Thriftless ambition, that wilt ravin up°
Thine own life's means! Then 'tis most like
The sovereignty will fall upon Macbeth.   30
MACDUFF. He is already named, and gone to Scone°
To be invested.
ROSS.   Where is Duncan's body?
MACDUFF. Carried to Colmekill,
The sacred storehouse° of his predecessors,
And guardian of their bones.
ROSS.   Will you to Scone?   35
MACDUFF. No, cousin, I'll to Fife.°
ROSS.   Well, I will thither.
MACDUFF. Well, may you see things well done there. Adieu!
Lest our old robes sit easier than our new!°
ROSS. Farewell, father.
OLD MAN. God's benison go with you; and with those   40
That would make good of bad, and friends of foes!   [*Exeunt.*

---

24. *suborned* (sŭb·ôrnd′): bribed. 28. *ravin up:* gobble up. 31. *Scone* (skōōn): the ancient place of coronation of Scottish kings. 34. *sacred storehouse:* tomb. 36. *Fife:* Macduff's castle. 38. *Lest . . . new:* Macduff here shows his misgivings about the future with Macbeth as king.

ACT III

[*Enter* BANQUO.]

BANQUO. Thou hast it now: king, Cawdor, Glamis, all,
    As the weird women promised, and, I fear,
    Thou play'dst most foully for 't; yet it was said
    It should not stand in thy posterity,
    But that myself should be the root and father   5
    Of many kings. If there come truth from them —
    As upon thee, Macbeth, their speeches shine —
    Why, by the verities° on thee made good,
    May they not be my oracles as well,
    And set me up in hope? But hush! no more.   10

[*Sennet* * *sounded. Enter* MACBETH, *as king,* LADY MACBETH, *as queen,* LENNOX,
ROSS, LORDS, LADIES, *and* ATTENDANTS.]

MACBETH. Here's our chief guest.
LADY MACBETH.   If he had been forgotten,
    It had been as a gap in our great feast,
    And all-thing° unbecoming.
MACBETH. Tonight we hold a solemn supper,° sir,
    And I'll request your presence.
BANQUO.   Let your highness   15
    Command upon me; to the which my duties
    Are with a most indissoluble tie
    For ever knit.°
MACBETH. Ride you this afternoon?
BANQUO. Ay, my good lord.   20
MACBETH. We should have else desired your good advice,
    Which still hath been both grave and prosperous,
    In this day's council; but we'll take tomorrow.
    Is 't far you ride?
BANQUO. As far, my lord, as will fill up the time   25
    'Twixt this and supper. Go not my horse the better,
    I must become a borrower of the night
    For a dark hour or twain.°
MACBETH.   Fail not our feast.
BANQUO. My lord, I will not.
MACBETH. We hear, our bloody cousins are bestowed   30
    In England and in Ireland, not confessing
    Their cruel parricide,° filling their hearers
    With strange invention. But of that tomorrow,
    When therewithal we shall have cause of state

---

8. *verities:* truths. * *Sennet:* sound of trumpets announcing entrance of a person of importance.
13. *all-thing:* altogether. 14. *solemn supper:* formal banquet. 16–18. *to the which . . . knit:* my duties
are inseparably bound to your commands. 26–28. *Go not . . . twain:* In other words, unless his horse
is swift he'll not be back before dark. 32. *parricide:* killing of a parent.

Craving us jointly.° Hie you to horse; adieu,   35
    Till you return at night. Goes Fleance with you?
BANQUO. Ay, my good lord. Our time does call upon 's.
MACBETH. I wish your horses swift and sure of foot;
    And so I do commend you to their backs.
    Farewell.   [*Exit* BANQUO.   40
    Let every man be master of his time
    Till seven at night. To make society
    The sweeter welcome, we will keep ourself
    Till suppertime alone; while° then, God be with you!
                    [*Exeunt all but* MACBETH *and an* ATTENDANT.
    Sirrah, a word with you: attend those men   45
    Our pleasure?
ATTENDANT. They are, my lord, without the palace gate.
MACBETH. Bring them before us.   [*Exit* ATTENDANT.
             To be thus is nothing;
    But to be safely thus.° — Our fears in Banquo
    Stick deep; and in his royalty of nature   50
    Reigns that which would be feared. 'Tis much he dares;
    And, to that dauntless temper of his mind,
    He hath a wisdom that doth guide his valor
    To act in safety. There is none but he
    Whose being I do fear; and, under him,   55
    My Genius is rebuked,° as, it is said,
    Mark Antony's was by Caesar. He chid the sisters
    When first they put the name of king upon me,
    And bade them speak to him; then prophetlike
    They hailed him father to a line of kings.   60
    Upon my head they placed a fruitless crown,
    And put a barren scepter in my gripe,
    Thence to be wrenched with an unlineal hand,
    No son of mine succeeding. If 't be so,
    For Banquo's issue have I filed° my mind;   65
    For them the gracious Duncan have I murdered;
    Put rancors in the vessel of my peace
    Only for them; and mine eternal jewel
    Given to the common enemy of man,
    To make them kings, the seed of Banquo kings!°   70
    Rather than so, come fate into the list,
    And champion me to the utterance!° Who's there?

    [*Re-enter* ATTENDANT, *with two* MURDERERS.]

    Now go to the door, and stay there till we call.   [*Exit* ATTENDANT.
    Was it not yesterday we spoke together?
FIRST MURDERER. It was, so please your highness.

35. *Craving us jointly:* demanding the attention of both of us. 44. *while:* until. 49. *But . . . thus:* unless we are safely thus. 56. *My Genius is rebuked:* Banquo stands in the way of Macbeth's realizing his ambition. 65. *filed:* defiled. 68–70. *and mine eternal jewel . . . the seed of Banquo kings:* Macbeth has sold his soul to the devil to make Banquo's descendants (rather than his own) kings. 72. *champion me to the utterance:* challenge me to fight to the finish.

MACBETH.   Well then, now   75
 Have you considered of my speeches? Know
 That it was he in the times past which held you
 So under fortune, which you thought had been
 Our innocent self. This I made good to you
 In our last conference, passed in probation with you,°   80
 How you were borne in hand,° how crossed, the instruments,
 Who wrought with them, and all things else that might
 To half a soul and to a notion crazed
 Say " Thus did Banquo."
FIRST MURDERER.   You made it known to us.
MACBETH. I did so, and went further, which is now   85
 Our point of second meeting. Do you find
 Your patience so predominant in your nature
 That you can let this go? Are you so gospeled
 To pray for this good man and for his issue,
 Whose heavy hand hath bowed you to the grave   90
 And beggared yours for ever?
FIRST MURDERER.   We are men, my liege.
MACBETH. Ay, in the catalogue ye go for men;
 As hounds and greyhounds, mongrels, spaniels, curs,
 Shoughs, water rugs, and demiwolves, are clept°
 All by the name of dogs; the valued file°   95
 Distinguishes the swift, the slow, the subtle,
 The housekeeper, the hunter, every one
 According to the gift which bounteous nature
 Hath in him closed, whereby he does receive
 Particular addition, from the bill   100
 That writes them all alike;° and so of men.
 Now, if you have a station in the file,
 Not i' the worst rank of manhood, say 't;
 And I will put that business in your bosoms,
 Whose execution takes your enemy off,   105
 Grapples you to the heart and love of us,
 Who wear our health but sickly in his life,
 Which in his death were perfect.°
SECOND MURDERER.   I am one, my liege,
 Whom the vile blows and buffets of the world
 Have so incensed that I am reckless what   110
 I do to spite the world.
FIRST MURDERER.   And I another
 So weary with disasters, tugged with fortune,°
 That I would set my life on any chance,
 To mend it, or be rid on 't.
MACBETH.   Both of you
 Know Banquo was your enemy.

79–80. *This . . . with you:* I gave you proof at our last meeting that Banquo was your enemy. 81. *borne in hand:* deceived. 94. *clept:* called. 95. *valued file:* list of those considered first class. 99–101. *whereby . . . alike:* i.e., every good dog has some special quality which makes him more than simply a "dog." 107–108. *Who wear . . . perfect:* In other words, Banquo's being alive is as an illness to Macbeth. 112. *tugged with fortune:* pulled about by bad luck.

BOTH MURDERERS.   True, my lord.   115
MACBETH. So is he mine; and in such bloody distance,
    That every minute of his being thrusts
    Against my near'st of life; and though I could
    With barefaced power sweep him from my sight
    And bid my will avouch° it, yet I must not,   120
    For° certain friends that are both his and mine,

120. *avouch:* justify. 121. *For:* because of.

" Both of you know Banquo was your enemy."

Whose loves I may not drop, but wail his fall°
Who I myself struck down; and thence it is,
That I to your assistance do make love,
Masking the business from the common eye   125
For sundry weighty reasons.
SECOND MURDERER.   We shall, my lord,
Perform what you command us.
FIRST MURDERER.   Though our lives —
MACBETH. Your spirits shine through you. Within this hour at most
I will advise you where to plant yourselves;
Acquaint you with the perfect spy o' the time,°   130
The moment on 't; for 't must be done tonight,
And something from° the palace; always thought
That I require a clearness;° and with him —
To leave no rubs nor botches in the work —
Fleance his son, that keeps him company,   135
Whose absence is no less material to me
Than is his father's, must embrace the fate
Of that dark hour. Resolve yourselves apart;°
I'll come to you anon.
BOTH MURDERERS.   We are resolved, my lord.
MACBETH. I'll call upon you straight; abide within.   140

                                        [*Exeunt* MURDERERS.

It is concluded. Banquo, thy soul's flight,
If it find heaven, must find it out tonight.   [*Exit.*

---

122. *but wail his fall:* To cover up, Macbeth must seem to bewail Banquo's death. 130. *the perfect spy o' the time:* the exact moment. 132. *something from:* some distance from. 132–133. *always . . . clearness:* It must always be remembered that I remain clear of this. 138. *Resolve yourselves apart:* Make your own decision.

SCENE II. *The palace.*

[*Enter* LADY MACBETH *and a* SERVANT.]

LADY MACBETH. Is Banquo gone from court?
SERVANT. Ay, madam, but returns again tonight.
LADY MACBETH. Say to the king, I would attend his leisure
For a few words.
SERVANT.   Madam, I will.   [*Exit.*
LADY MACBETH.   Naught's had, all's spent,
Where our desire is got without content.   5
'Tis safer to be that which we destroy
Than by destruction dwell in doubtful joy.

[*Enter* MACBETH.]

How now, my lord! why do you keep alone,
Of sorriest fancies your companions making,
Using those thoughts which should indeed have died   10
With them they think on? Things without all remedy

Should be without regard; what's done is done.

MACBETH. We have scotched° the snake, not killed it;
     She'll close and be herself, whilst our poor malice
     Remains in danger of her former tooth.   15
     But let the frame of things disjoint, both the worlds suffer,
     Ere we will eat our meal in fear,° and sleep
     In the affliction of these terrible dreams
     That shake us nightly. Better be with the dead,
     Whom we, to gain our peace, have sent to peace,   20
     Than on the torture of the mind to lie
     In restless ecstasy.° Duncan is in his grave;
     After life's fitful fever he sleeps well;
     Treason has done his worst; nor steel, nor poison,
     Malice domestic, foreign levy, nothing,   25
     Can touch him further.

LADY MACBETH.   Come on;
     Gentle my lord, sleek o'er your rugged looks;
     Be bright and jovial among your guests tonight.

MACBETH. So shall I, love; and so, I pray, be you.
     Let your remembrance apply to Banquo;   30
     Present him eminence,° both with eye and tongue;
     Unsafe the while, that we°
     Must lave our honors in these flattering streams,
     And make our faces vizards° to our hearts,
     Disguising what they are.

LADY MACBETH.   You must leave this.   35

MACBETH. O, full of scorpions is my mind, dear wife!
     Thou know'st that Banquo, and his Fleance, lives.

LADY MACBETH. But in them nature's copy 's not eterne.

MACBETH. There's comfort yet; they are assailable;
     Then be thou jocund; ere the bat hath flown   40
     His cloistered flight, ere to black Hecate's summons
     The shard-borne beetle° with his drowsy hums
     Hath rung night's yawning peal, there shall be done
     A deed of dreadful note.

LADY MACBETH.   What's to be done?

MACBETH. Be innocent of the knowledge, dearest chuck,   45
     Till thou applaud the deed. Come, seeling night,
     Scarf up the tender eye of pitiful day;°
     And with thy bloody and invisible hand
     Cancel and tear to pieces that great bond°
     Which keeps me pale! Light thickens, and the crow   50
     Makes wing to the rooky° wood;

---

13. *scotched:* wounded. 16–17. *But let . . . fear:* Let the universe fall apart and heaven and hell
perish (*both the worlds suffer*) before we let this murder unnerve us. 22. *ecstasy:* madness, mental
torment. 31. *Present him eminence:* Make much of him. 32. We are not safe as long as we. . . .
34. *vizards:* masks. 42. *shard-borne beetle:* the beetle borne aloft by its brittle wings. 46–47. *Come . . .
day:* This figure is drawn from falconry. Young falcons were trained by having their eyelids seeled
(sewn shut). 49. *great bond:* that which binds me; i.e., Banquo's life. 51. *rooky:* full of rooks, or crows.

Good things of day begin to droop and drowse;
Whiles night's black agents to their preys do rouse.
Thou marvel'st at my words; but hold thee still;
Things bad begun make strong themselves by ill.   55
So, prithee, go with me.   [*Exeunt.*

SCENE III. *A park near the palace.*

[*Enter three* MURDERERS.]

FIRST MURDERER. But who did bid thee join with us?
THIRD MURDERER.   Macbeth.
SECOND MURDERER. He needs not our mistrust, since he delivers
    Our offices° and what we have to do
    To the direction just.°
FIRST MURDERER.   Then stand with us.
    The west yet glimmers with some streaks of day;   5
    Now spurs the lated traveler apace
    To gain the timely inn; and near approaches
    The subject of our watch.
THIRD MURDERER.   Hark! I hear horses.
BANQUO. [*Within*] Give us a light there, ho!
SECOND MURDERER.   Then 'tis he; the rest
    That are within the note of expectation°   10
    Already are i' the court.
FIRST MURDERER.   His horses go about.
THIRD MURDERER. Almost a mile; but he does usually,
    So all men do, from hence to the palace gate
    Make it their walk.
SECOND MURDERER.   A light, a light!

[*Enter* BANQUO, *and* FLEANCE *with a torch.*]

THIRD MURDERER.   'Tis he.
FIRST MURDERER. Stand to 't.   15
BANQUO. It will be rain tonight.
FIRST MURDERER.   Let it come down.

[*They set upon* BANQUO.]

BANQUO. O treachery! Fly, good Fleance, fly, fly, fly!
    Thou mayst revenge. O slave!

[*Dies.* FLEANCE *escapes.*]

THIRD MURDERER. Who did strike out the light?
FIRST MURDERER.   Was 't not the way?
THIRD MURDERER. There's but one down; the son is fled.
SECOND MURDERER.   We have lost   20
    Best half of our affair.
FIRST MURDERER. Well, let's away, and say how much is done.   [*Exeunt.*

3. *offices:* duties. 4. *direction just:* exact detail. 10. *within . . . expectation:* among the invited guests.

SCENE IV. *The same. Hall in the palace.*

[*A banquet prepared. Enter* MACBETH, LADY MACBETH, ROSS, LENNOX, LORDS, *and* ATTENDANTS.]

MACBETH. You know your own degrees; sit down.° At first
    And last the hearty welcome.
LORDS.   Thanks to your majesty.
MACBETH. Ourself will mingle with society,°
    And play the humble host.
    Our hostess keeps her state, but in best time   5
    We will require her welcome.
LADY MACBETH. Pronounce it for me, sir, to all our friends;
    For my heart speaks they are welcome.

[*First* MURDERER *appears at the door.*]

MACBETH. See, they encounter thee with their hearts' thanks.
    Both sides are even; here I'll sit i' the midst;   10
    Be large in mirth; anon we'll drink a measure°
    The table round. [*Approaching the door.*] There's blood upon thy face.
MURDERER. 'Tis Banquo's then.
MACBETH. 'Tis better thee without than he within.°
    Is he dispatched?   15
MURDERER. My lord, his throat is cut; that I did for him.
MACBETH. Thou art the best o' the cutthroats: yet he's good
    That did the like for Fleance. If thou didst it,
    Thou art the nonpareil.°
MURDERER.   Most royal sir,
    Fleance is 'scaped.   20
MACBETH. Then comes my fit again. I had else been perfect,
    Whole as the marble, founded as the rock,
    As broad and general as the casing° air;
    But now I am cabined, cribbed, confined, bound in
    To saucy doubts and fears. But Banquo's safe?   25
MURDERER. Ay, my good lord; safe in a ditch he bides,
    With twenty trenchèd gashes on his head,
    The least a death to nature.
MACBETH.   Thanks for that;
    There the grown serpent lies; the worm° that's fled
    Hath nature that in time will venom breed,   30
    No teeth for the present. Get thee gone; tomorrow
    We'll hear ourselves again.°   [*Exit* MURDERER.
LADY MACBETH.   My royal lord,
    You do not give the cheer. The feast is sold

---

1. *You . . . down:* The lords and ladies were seated according to rank (or *degree*). 3. *Ourself will mingle with society:* Macbeth will come down from the special seat of honor accorded royalty and sit among his lords. 11. *measure:* toast. 14. *'Tis . . . within:* The blood is better outside you than inside him. 19. *the nonpareil* (nŏn'pá·rĕl'): something without equal. 23. *casing:* enclosing. 29. *worm:* little snake. 31–32. *tomorrow . . . again:* Tomorrow Macbeth will consider what's to be done about Fleance.

That is not often vouched, while 'tis amaking,
'Tis given with welcome.° To feed were best at home;   35
From thence the sauce to meat is ceremony;°
Meeting were bare without it.

MACBETH.   Sweet remembrancer!
Now, good digestion wait on appetite,
And health on both!

LENNOX.   May 't please your highness sit.

[*The* GHOST *of* BANQUO *enters, and sits in* MACBETH'S *place.*]

MACBETH. Here had we now our country's honor roofed,°   40
Were the graced person of our Banquo present;
Who may I rather challenge for unkindness
Than pity for mischance!°

ROSS.   His absence, sir,
Lays blame upon his promise. Please 't your highness
To grace us with your royal company.   45

MACBETH. The table's full.

LENNOX.   Here is a place reserved, sir.

MACBETH. Where?

LENNOX. Here, my good lord. What is 't that moves your highness?

MACBETH. Which of you have done this?

LORDS.   What, my good lord?

MACBETH. Thou canst not say I did it; never shake   50
Thy gory locks at me.

ROSS. Gentlemen, rise; his highness is not well.

LADY MACBETH. Sit, worthy friends; my lord is often thus,
And hath been from his youth. Pray you, keep seat;
The fit is momentary; upon a thought   55
He will again be well. If much you note him,
You shall offend him and extend his passion.
Feed, and regard him not. Are you a man?°

MACBETH. Ay, and a bold one, that dare look on that
Which might appall the devil.

LADY MACBETH.   O proper stuff!   60
This is the very painting of your fear;
This is the air-drawn dagger which, you said,
Led you to Duncan. O, these flaws and starts,
Impostors to true fear, would well become
A woman's story at a winter's fire,   65
Authorized° by her grandam. Shame itself!
Why do you make such faces? When all's done,
You look but on a stool.

MACBETH. Prithee, see there! behold! look! lo! how say you?
Why, what care I? If you canst nod, speak too.   70

33–35. *The feast . . . welcome:* The feast in which the host does not continually assure his guests
of their welcome is like a bought meal. 35–36. *To feed . . . ceremony:* Merely to eat, one had best
stay home; when dining out, politeness or ceremony adds a pleasant flavor to the meal. 40. *Here . . .
roofed:* We would have all the most honored men in the country under our roof. 42–43. *Who . . .
mischance:* Macbeth says he attributes Banquo's absence to discourtesy rather than to accident.
58. *Are you a man?:* This is addressed to Macbeth, out of the hearing of the guests. 66. *Authorized:*
vouched for.

If charnel houses° and our graves must send
Those that we bury back, our monuments
Shall be the maws of kites.°   [GHOST *vanishes.*
LADY MACBETH.   What, quite unmanned in folly?
MACBETH. If I stand here, I saw him.
LADY MACBETH.   Fie, for shame!
MACBETH. Blood hath been shed ere now, i' the olden time,   75
Ere humane statute purged the gentle weal;°
Ay, and since too, murders have been performed
Too terrible for the ear. The time has been,
That, when the brains were out, the man would die,
And there an end; but now they rise again,   80
With twenty mortal murders on their crowns,
And push us from our stools. This is more strange
Than such a murder is.
LADY MACBETH.   My worthy lord,
Your noble friends do lack you.
MACBETH.   I do forget.°
Do not muse at me, my most worthy friends;   85
I have a strange infirmity, which is nothing
To those that know me. Come, love and health to all;
Then I'll sit down. Give me some wine; fill full.
I drink to the general joy o' the whole table,
And to our dear friend Banquo, whom we miss;   90
Would he were here! to all, and him, we thirst,
And all to all.
LORDS.   Our duties, and the pledge.

[*Re-enter* GHOST.]

MACBETH. Avaunt! and quit my sight! let the earth hide thee!
Thy bones are marrowless, thy blood is cold;
Thou has no speculation° in those eyes   95
Which thou dost glare with!
LADY MACBETH.   Think of this, good peers,
But as a thing of custom; 'tis no other;
Only it spoils the pleasure of the time.
MACBETH. What man dare, I dare.
Approach thou like the rugged Russian bear,   100
The armed rhinoceros, or the Hyrcan° tiger;
Take any shape but that, and my firm nerves
Shall never tremble; or be alive again,
And dare me to the desert° with my sword;
If trembling I inhabit° then, protest me   105
The baby of a girl. Hence, horrible shadow!

71. *charnel houses:* burial vaults. 73. *maws of kites:* stomachs of vultures. In other words, it would
be better to let vultures devour the dead if they are going to break out from their tombs and come
back to haunt the living. 76. *Ere . . . weal:* before humane laws made the state civilized. Before
that time, lawless barbarism prevailed. 84. *I do forget:* At this point Macbeth turns back to address
the company. 95. *speculation:* intelligent expression; that is, the ghost's eyes were glassy. 101. *Hyr-*
can (hûr′kăn): from an ancient province of Asia, southeast of the Caspian Sea. 104. *desert:* a place
from which neither could escape. 105. *inhabit:* remain indoors.

Unreal mockery, hence!   [GHOST *vanishes.*
                                    Why, so; being gone
    I am a man again. Pray you, sit still.

LADY MACBETH. You have displaced the mirth, broke the good meeting,
    With most admired disorder.°

MACBETH.   Can such things be,   110
    And overcome us like a summer's cloud,
    Without our special wonder? You make me strange
    Even to the disposition that I owe,°
    When now I think you can behold such sights,
    And keep the natural ruby of your cheeks,   115
    When mine is blanched with fear.

ROSS.   What sights, my lord?

LADY MACBETH. I pray you, speak not; he grows worse and worse;
    Question enrages him. At once, good night.
    Stand not upon the order of your going,°
    But go at once.

LENNOX.   Good night; and better health   120
    Attend his majesty!

LADY MACBETH.   A kind good night to all!

                    [*Exeunt all but* MACBETH *and* LADY MACBETH.

MACBETH. It will have blood; they say, blood will have blood.
    Stones have been known to move and trees to speak;
    Augurs and understood relations have
    By maggot-pies and choughs and rooks brought forth   125
    The secret'st man of blood.° What is the night?

LADY MACBETH. Almost at odds with morning, which is which.

MACBETH. How say'st thou, that Macduff denies his person
    At our great bidding?

LADY MACBETH.   Did you send to him, sir?

MACBETH. I hear it by the way; but I will send.   130
    There's not a one of them but in his house
    I keep a servant fee'd.° I will tomorrow,
    And betimes I will, to the weird sisters.
    More shall they speak; for now I am bent to know,
    By the worst means, the worst. For mine own good,   135
    All causes shall give way. I am in blood
    Stepped in so far that, should I wade no more,
    Returning were as tedious as go o'er.
    Strange things I have in head, that will to hand;
    Which must be acted ere they may be scanned.   140

LADY MACBETH. You lack the season of all natures, sleep.

MACBETH. Come, we'll to sleep. My strange and self-abuse

---

110. *admired disorder:* as used here, amazing disorder; distraction. 112–113. *You . . . owe:* You
make me seem to behave unnaturally. *Owe* means *own* here. 119. *the order of your going:* Just as
the lords and ladies were seated according to rank, so they customarily departed according to rank.
124–126. *Augurs . . . blood:* Augurs, or fortunetellers, have been able by the flight of birds to discover even the most secret murders. 132. *fee'd:* in my pay as a spy.

Is the initiate fear° that wants hard use;
We are yet but young in deed.   [*Exeunt.*

143. *initiate fear:* fear of one who is just beginning.

SCENE V. *A heath.*

[*Thunder. Enter the three* WITCHES, *meeting* HECATE.]

FIRST WITCH. Why, how now, Hecate! you look angerly.
HECATE. Have I not reason, beldams° as you are,
    Saucy and overbold? How did you dare
    To trade and traffic with Macbeth
    In riddles and affairs of death;   5
    And I, the mistress of your charms,
    The close° contriver of all harms,
    Was never called to bear my part,
    Or show the glory of our art?
    And, which is worse, all you have done   10
    Hath been but for a wayward son,
    Spiteful and wrathful, who, as others do,
    Loves for his own ends, not for you.
    But make amends now; get you gone,
    And at the pit of Acheron°   15
    Meet me i' the morning; thither he
    Will come to know his destiny.
    Your vessels and your spells provide,
    Your charms and everything beside.
    I am for the air; this night I'll spend   20
    Unto a dismal and a fatal end;
    Great business must be wrought ere noon.
    Upon the corner of the moon
    There hangs a vaporous drop profound;
    I'll catch it ere it come to ground;   25
    And that distilled by magic sleights
    Shall raise such artificial sprites
    As by the strength of their illusion
    Shall draw him on to his confusion.
    He shall spurn fate, scorn death, and bear   30
    His hopes 'bove wisdom, grace, and fear;
    And you all know, security°
    Is mortals' chiefest enemy.
        [*Music and a song within:* " Come away, come away," etc.
    Hark! I am called; my little spirit, see,
    Sits in a foggy cloud, and stays for me.   [*Exit.*   35
FIRST WITCH. Come, let's make haste; she'll soon be back again.   [*Exeunt.*

2. *beldams:* hags. 7. *close:* secret. 15. *the pit of Acheron* (ăk′ĕr·ŏn): hell. In Greek mythology,
Acheron is the River of Woe leading to Hades. 32. *security:* false feeling of safety.

SCENE VI. *Forres. The palace.*

[Enter LENNOX *and another* LORD.]

LENNOX. My former speeches have but hit your thoughts,
    Which can interpret further;° only, I say,
    Things have been strangely borne.° The gracious Duncan
    Was pitied of Macbeth; marry, he was dead;
    And the right-valiant Banquo walked too late;   5
    Whom, you may say, if 't please you,° Fleance killed,
    For Fleance fled; men must not walk too late.
    Who cannot want° the thought how monstrous
    It was for Malcolm and for Donalbain
    To kill their gracious father? Damnèd fact!   10
    How it did grieve Macbeth! Did he not straight
    In pious rage the two delinquents tear,
    That were the slaves of drink and thralls of sleep?
    Was not that nobly done? Ay, and wisely too;
    For 'twould have angered any heart alive   15
    To hear the men deny 't. So that, I say,
    He has borne all things well; and I do think
    That had he Duncan's sons under his key —
    As, an 't please Heaven, he shall not — they should find
    What 'twere to kill a father; so should Fleance.   20
    But, peace! for from broad words° and 'cause he failed
    His presence at the tyrant's feast, I hear
    Macduff lives in disgrace. Sir, can you tell
    Where he bestows himself?

LORD.   The son of Duncan,
    From whom this tyrant holds the due of birth,°   25
    Lives in the English court, and is received
    Of the most pious Edward with such grace
    That the malevolence of fortune nothing
    Takes from his high respect.° Thither Macduff
    Is gone to pray the holy king, upon his aid   30
    To wake Northumberland and warlike Siward;
    That by the help of these — with Him above
    To ratify the work — we may again
    Give to our tables meat, sleep to our nights,°
    Free from our feasts and banquets bloody knives,   35
    Do faithful homage and receive free honors;
    All which we pine for now; and this report
    Hath so exasperate the king that he
    Prepares for some attempt of war.

2. *Which . . . further:* from which you can draw your own conclusions. 3. *borne:* managed.
6. Notice that from here on Lennox is using sarcasm. He is opposed to Macbeth and suspects his
treachery. 8. *want:* be without. 21. *broad words:* unguarded expressions. 25. *From whom . . . due
to birth:* Malcolm's claim to the throne is withheld by Macbeth. 28–29. *the malevolence . . . respect:*
In spite of his misfortunes his reputation is intact. 34. *Give . . . nights:* Normal life is impossible, in
other words, under Macbeth's tyranny.

LENNOX.   Sent he to Macduff?
LORD. He did; and with an absolute " Sir, not I,"   40
        The cloudy° messenger turns me his back,
        And hums, as who should say, " You'll rue the time
        That clogs me with this answer."°
LENNOX.   And that well might
        Advise him to a caution, to hold what distance
        His wisdom can provide. Some holy angel   45
        Fly to the court of England and unfold
        His message ere he come, that swift blessing
        May soon return to this our suffering country
        Under a hand accursed!
LORD.   I'll send my prayers with him.   [*Exeunt.*

41. *cloudy:* surly. 43. *clogs . . . answer:* makes me return reluctantly.

ACT IV

SCENE I. *A cavern. In the middle, a boiling caldron.*

[*Thunder. Enter the three* WITCHES.]

FIRST WITCH. Thrice the brinded° cat hath mewed.
SECOND WITCH. Thrice and once the hedge pig whined.
THIRD WITCH. Harpier° cries, " 'Tis time, 'tis time."
FIRST WITCH. Round about the caldron go;
        In the poisoned entrails throw.   5
        Toad, that under cold stone
        Days and nights has thirty-one
        Sweltered venom sleeping got,
        Boil thou first i' the charmèd pot.
ALL. Double, double toil and trouble;   10
        Fire burn, and caldron bubble.
SECOND WITCH. Fillet of a fenny snake,
        In the caldron boil and bake;
        Eye of newt and toe of frog,
        Wool of bat and tongue of dog,   15
        Adder's fork and blind worm's sting,
        Lizard's leg and howlet's wing,
        For a charm of powerful trouble,
        Like a hell broth boil and bubble.
ALL. Double, double toil and trouble;   20
        Fire burn, and caldron bubble.
THIRD WITCH. Scale of dragon, tooth of wolf,
        Witches' mummy, maw and gulf°

1. *brinded:* striped. 3. *Harpier:* one of the spirits attending the witches. 23. *maw and gulf:* stomach
and throat.

Of the ravined salt-sea shark,
Root of hemlock digged i' the dark,   25
Liver of blaspheming Jew,
Gall of goat, and slips of yew
Slivered in the moon's eclipse,
Nose of Turk and Tartar's lips,
Finger of birth-strangled babe   30
Ditch-delivered by a drab,
Make the gruel thick and slab;°
Add thereto a tiger's chaudron,°
For the ingredients of our caldron.
ALL. Double, double toil and trouble;   35
    Fire burn, and caldron bubble.
SECOND WITCH. Cool it with a baboon's blood,
    Then the charm is firm and good.

[*Enter* HECATE *to the other three* WITCHES.]

HECATE. O, well done! I commend your pains;
    And every one shall share i' the gains;   40
    And now about the caldron sing,
    Like elves and fairies in a ring,
    Enchanting all that you put in.

[*Music and a song:* " Black spirits," etc.
[HECATE *retires.*

SECOND WITCH. By the pricking of my thumbs,
    Something wicked this way comes.   45
        Open, locks,
        Whoever knocks!

[*Enter* MACBETH.]

MACBETH. How now, you secret, black, and midnight hags!
    What is 't you do?
ALL.   A deed without a name.
MACBETH. I conjure you, by that which you profess,   50
    Howe'er you come to know it, answer me;
    Though you untie the winds and let them fight
    Against the churches; though the yesty° waves
    Confound and swallow navigation up;
    Though bladed corn be lodged° and trees blown down; 55
    Though castles topple on their warders' heads;
    Though palaces and pyramids do slope
    Their heads to their foundations; though the treasure
    Of nature's germens° tumble all together,
    Even till destruction sicken; answer me   60
    To what I ask you.
FIRST WITCH.   Speak.
SECOND WITCH.   Demand.
THIRD WITCH.   We'll answer.

---

32. *slab:* like thick mud. 33. *chaudron:* entrails. 53. *yesty:* foaming. 55. *corn . . . lodged:* wheat laid flat by the wind before it can be harvested. 59. *nature's germens:* seeds of all living things.

FIRST WITCH. Say, if thou 'dst rather hear it from our mouths,
     Or from our masters'?
MACBETH.   Call 'em; let me see 'em.
FIRST WITCH. Pour in sow's blood, that hath eaten   65
     Her nine farrow; grease that's sweaten
     From the murderer's gibbet throw
     Into the flame.
ALL.   Come, high or low;
     Thyself and office° deftly show!

[Thunder. First Apparition: an armed HEAD.*]*

MACBETH. Tell me, thou unknown power —
FIRST WITCH.   He knows thy thought;
     Hear his speech, but say thou naught.   70
FIRST APPARITION. Macbeth! Macbeth! Macbeth! beware Macduff;
     Beware the thane of Fife. Dismiss me. Enough.   *[Descends.*
MACBETH. Whate'er thou art, for thy good caution, thanks;
     Thou hast harped° my fear aright: but one word more —
FIRST WITCH. He will not be commanded: here's another,   75
     More potent than the first.

[Thunder. Second Apparition: a bloody CHILD.†]*

SECOND APPARITION. Macbeth! Macbeth! Macbeth!
MACBETH. Had I three ears, I 'ld hear thee.
SECOND APPARITION. Be bloody, bold, and resolute; laugh to scorn
     The power of man, for none of woman born   80
     Shall harm Macbeth.   *[Descends.*
MACBETH. Then live, Macduff; what need I fear of thee?
     But yet I'll make assurance double sure,
     And take a bond of fate.° Thou shalt not live;
     That I may tell pale-hearted fear it lies,   85
     And sleep in spite of thunder.

[Thunder. Third Apparition: a CHILD *crowned,‡ with a tree in his hand.]*

               What is this
     That rises like the issue of a king,
     And wears upon his baby brow the round
     And top of sovereignty?
ALL.   Listen, but speak not to 't.
THIRD APPARITION. Be lion-mettled, proud; and take no care   90
     Who chafes, who frets, or where conspirers are.
     Macbeth shall never vanquished be until
     Great Birnam wood to high Dunsinane hill
     Shall come against him.   *[Descends.*
MACBETH.   That will never be.
     Who can impress the forest, bid the tree   95

---

68. *office:* thy function. * *an armed Head:* a symbol of Macduff. 74. *harped:* expressed. † *a bloody
Child:* Macduff at birth. 84. *take . . . fate:* To be sure the prophecy turns out, he will kill Macduff.
‡ *a Child crowned:* symbol of Malcolm.

Unfix his earth-bound root? Sweet bodements!° good!
Rebellion's head, rise never till the wood
Of Birnam rise, and our high-placed Macbeth
Shall live the lease of nature,° pay his breath
To time and mortal custom. Yet my heart   100
Throbs to know one thing: tell me, if your art
Can tell so much: shall Banquo's issue ever
Reign in this kingdom?

ALL.   Seek to know no more.

MACBETH. I will be satisfied; deny me this,
And an eternal curse fall on you! Let me know.   105
Why sinks that caldron? and what noise is this?   [*Hautboys.*

FIRST WITCH. Show!

SECOND WITCH. Show!

THIRD WITCH. Show!

ALL. Show his eyes, and grieve his heart;   110
Come like shadows, so depart!

[*A show of Eight* KINGS,* *the last with a glass* † *in his hand;* BANQUO'S GHOST *following.*]

MACBETH. Thou art too like the spirit of Banquo; down!
Thy crown doth sear mine eyeballs. And thy hair,
Thou other gold-bound brow, is like the first.
A third is like the former. Filthy hags!   115
Why do you show me this? A fourth! Start, eyes!
What, will the line stretch out to the crack of doom?
Another yet! A seventh! I'll see no more.
And yet the eighth appears, who bears a glass
Which shows me many more; and some I see   120
That twofold balls and treble scepters° carry.
Horrible sight! Now, I see, 'tis true;
For the blood-boltered° Banquo smiles upon me,
And points at them for his.° [APPARITIONS *vanish.*] What, is this so?

FIRST WITCH. Ay, sir, all this is so; but why   125
Stands Macbeth thus amazedly?
Come, sisters, cheer we up his sprites,
And show the best of our delights.
I'll charm the air to give a sound,
While you perform your antic round;°   130
That this great king may kindly say,
Our duties did his welcome pay.

[*Music. The* WITCHES *dance, and then vanish, with* HECATE.

MACBETH. Where are they? Gone? Let this pernicious hour
Stand aye accursèd in the calendar!
Come in, without there!

96. *bodements:* prophecies. 99. *lease of nature:* his allotted term of life; that is, he would die a
natural death. * *A show of Eight Kings:* a dumb show of figures passing across the stage silently,
representing the eight Stuart kings of Scotland. † *glass:* mirror. 121. *twofold balls and treble scepters:*
the insignia of James I, who united Scotland with England (1603) and later Ireland. 123. *blood-
boltered:* his hair wet with blood. 124. *points at them for his:* James I was traditionally considered a
descendant of Banquo. 130. *antic round:* fantastic dance.

[*Enter* LENNOX.]

LENNOX.   What's your grace's will?   135
MACBETH. Saw you the weird sisters?
LENNOX.   No, my lord.
MACBETH. Came they not by you?
LENNOX.   No, my lord.
MACBETH. Infected be the air whereon they ride;
    And damned all those that trust them! I did hear
    The galloping of horse: who was 't came by?   140
LENNOX. 'Tis two or three, my lord, that bring you word
    Macduff is fled to England.
MACBETH.   Fled to England!
LENNOX. Ay, my good lord.
MACBETH. Time, thou anticipatest my dread exploits;
    The flighty purpose never is o'ertook   145
    Unless the deed go with it. From this moment
    The very firstlings of my heart shall be
    The firstlings of my hand. And even now,
    To crown my thoughts with acts, be it thought and done.
    The castle of Macduff I will surprise;   150
    Seize upon Fife; give to the edge o' the sword
    His wife, and babes, and all unfortunate souls
    That trace him in his line. No boasting like a fool;
    This deed I'll do before this purpose cool.
    But no more sights! — Where are these gentlemen?   155
    Come, bring me where they are.   [*Exeunt.*

SCENE II. *Fife.* MACDUFF'S *castle.*

[*Enter* LADY MACDUFF, *her* SON, *and* ROSS.]

LADY MACDUFF. What had he done, to make him fly the land?
ROSS. You must have patience, madam.
LADY MACDUFF.   He had none;
    His flight was madness. When our actions do not,
    Our fears do make us traitors.
ROSS.   You know not
    Whether it was his wisdom or his fear.   5
LADY MACDUFF. Wisdom! to leave his wife, to leave his babes,
    His mansion and his titles in a place
    From whence himself does fly? He loves us not;
    He wants the natural touch; for the poor wren,
    The most diminutive of birds, will fight,   10
    Her young ones in her nest, against the owl.
    All is the fear and nothing is the love;°
    As little is the wisdom, where the flight
    So runs against all reason.

12. *All . . . love:* For Macduff, she says, fear is all-important and love means nothing.

ROSS.   My dearest coz,
    I pray you, school yourself; but for your husband,   15
    He is noble, wise, judicious, and best knows
    The fits o' the season.° I dare not speak much further;
    But cruel are the times, when we are traitors
    And do not know ourselves, when we hold rumor
    From what we fear, yet know not what we fear,   20
    But float upon a wild and violent sea
    Each way and move.° I take my leave of you;
    Shall not be long but I'll be here again.
    Things at the worst will cease, or else climb upward
    To what they were before. My pretty cousin,°   25
    Blessing upon you!
LADY MACDUFF. Fathered he is, and yet he's fatherless.
ROSS. I am so much a fool, should I stay longer,
    It would be my disgrace and your discomfort.
    I take my leave at once.   [*Exit.*   30
LADY MACDUFF. Sirrah, your father's dead;
    And what will you do now? How will you live?
SON. As birds do, mother.
LADY MACDUFF. What, with worms and flies?
SON. With what I get, I mean; and so do they.   35
LADY MACDUFF. Poor bird! thou 'ldst never fear the net nor lime,
    The pitfall nor the gin.°
SON. Why should I, mother? Poor birds they are not set for.
    My father is not dead, for all your saying.
LADY MACDUFF. Yes, he is dead. How wilt thou do for a father?   40
SON. Nay, how will you do for a husband?
LADY MACDUFF. Why, I can buy me twenty at any market.
SON. Then you'll buy 'em to sell again.
LADY MACDUFF. Thou speak'st with all thy wit; and yet, i' faith,
    With wit enough for thee.   45
SON. Was my father a traitor, mother?
LADY MACDUFF. Ay, that he was.
SON. What is a traitor?
LADY MACDUFF. Why, one that swears and lies.
SON. And be all traitors that do so?   50
LADY MACDUFF. Every one that does so is a traitor, and must be hanged.
SON. And must they all be hanged that swear and lie?
LADY MACDUFF. Every one.
SON. Who must hang them?
LADY MACDUFF. Why, the honest men.   55
SON. Then the liars and swearers are fools, for there are liars and swearers enow
    to beat the honest men and hang up them.
LADY MACDUFF. Now, God help thee, poor monkey! But how wilt thou do for a
    father?
SON. If he were dead, you 'ld weep for him; if you would not, it were a good   60
    sign that I should quickly have a new father.

17. *fits o' the season:* disorders of the times. 22. *Each way and move:* as a ship is tossed in a tempest
25. *My pretty cousin:* addressed to the boy, Macduff's son. 37. *gin:* trap.

LADY MACDUFF. Poor prattler, how thou talk'st!

[*Enter a* MESSENGER.]

MESSENGER. Bless you, fair dame! I am not to you known,
    Though in your state of honor I am perfect.°
    I doubt° some danger does approach you nearly.   65
    If you will take a homely° man's advice,
    Be not found here; hence, with your little ones.
    To fright you thus, methinks, I am too savage;
    To do worse to you were fell cruelty,
    Which is too nigh your person. Heaven preserve you!   70
    I dare abide no longer.   [*Exit.*
LADY MACDUFF.   Whither should I fly?
    I have done no harm. But I remember now
    I am in this earthly world; where to do harm
    Is often laudable, to do good sometime
    Accounted dangerous folly. Why then, alas,   75
    Do I put up that womanly defense,
    To say I have done no harm?

[*Enter* MURDERERS.]

        What are these faces?
FIRST MURDERER. Where is your husband?
LADY MACDUFF. I hope, in no place so unsanctified
    Where such as thou mayst find him.
FIRST MURDERER.   He's a traitor.   80
SON. Thou liest, thou shag-eared° villain!
FIRST MURDERER.   What, you egg!   [*Stabbing him.*
    Young fry of treachery!
SON.   He has killed me, mother:
    Run away, I pray you!   [*Dies.*
        [*Exit* LADY MACDUFF, *crying* " Murder! "
        [*Exeunt* MURDERERS, *following her.*

64. *perfect:* perfectly acquainted with. 65. *doubt:* suspect. 66. *homely:* plain. 81. *shag-eared:* hairy eared.

SCENE III. *England. Before the* KING'S *palace.*

[*Enter* MALCOLM *and* MACDUFF.]

MALCOLM. Let us seek out some desolate shade, and there
    Weep our sad bosoms empty.
MACDUFF.   Let us rather
    Hold fast the mortal° sword, and like good men
    Bestride our downfall'n birthdom.° Each new morn
    New widows howl, new orphans cry, new sorrows   5

3. *mortal:* deadly. 4. *birthdom:* native land.

Strike heaven on the face, that it resounds
As if it felt with Scotland and yelled out
Like syllable of dolor.°

MALCOLM.   What I believe, I'll wail,
What know, believe, and what I can redress,
As I shall find the time to friend, I will.   10
What you have spoke, it may be so perchance.
This tyrant, whose sole name blisters our tongues,
Was once thought honest; you have loved him well;
He hath not touched you yet. I am young; but something
You may deserve of him through me, the wisdom   15
To offer up a weak poor innocent lamb
To appease an angry god.°

MACDUFF. I am not treacherous.

MALCOLM.   But Macbeth is.
A good and virtuous nature may recoil
In an imperial charge.° But I shall crave your pardon;   20
That which you are my thoughts cannot transpose.
Angels are bright still, though the brightest fell.
Though all things foul would wear the brows of grace,
Yet grace must still look so.°

MACDUFF.   I have lost my hopes.

MALCOLM. Perchance even there where I did find my doubts.   25
Why in that rawness left you wife and child,
Those precious motives, those strong knots of love,
Without leave-taking? I pray you,
Let not my jealousies be your dishonors,
But mine own safeties.° You may be rightly just,   30
Whatever I shall think.

MACDUFF.   Bleed, bleed, poor country!
Great tyranny! lay thou thy basis sure,
For goodness dare not check thee; wear thou thy wrongs;
The title is affeered!° Fare thee well, lord;
I would not be the villain that thou think'st   35
For the whole space that's in the tyrant's grasp,
And the rich East to boot.

MALCOLM.   Be not offended;
I speak not as in absolute fear of you.
I think our country sinks beneath the yoke;
It weeps, it bleeds; and each new day a gash   40
Is added to her wounds. I think withal
There would be hands uplifted in my right;

6–8. *that . . . dolor:* The heavens resound as if they too felt Scotland's wrongs and echoed Scotland's lamentations. 14–17. *but something . . . god:* Malcolm fears that Macduff may be a tool of Macbeth seeking to betray him — Malcolm. 19–20. *A good . . . charge:* In other words, Macduff may not be his own master. His good and virtuous nature may be at the command of an evil king. 23–24. *Though . . . look so:* Goodness must still appear as goodness even though wickedness sometimes clothes itself in the same garb. In other words, Malcolm has no way of telling — so he says now, at least — whether Macduff is to be trusted or not. 29–30. *Let not . . . safeties:* I am suspicious not in order to dishonor you but to protect myself. 34. *affeered:* confirmed; that is, since goodness dares not oppose tyranny, tyranny's title or right to power is confirmed.

And here from gracious England have I offer
Of goodly thousands. But, for all this,
When I shall tread upon the tyrant's head,   45
Or wear it on my sword, yet my poor country
Shall have more vices than it had before,
More suffer and more sundry ways than ever,
By him that shall succeed.
MACDUFF.   What should he be?
MALCOLM. It is myself I mean; in whom I know   50
    All the particulars of vice so grafted
    That, when they shall be opened, black Macbeth
    Will seem as pure as snow, and the poor state
    Esteem him as a lamb, being compared
    With my confineless harms.
MACDUFF.   Not in the legions   55
    Of horrid hell can come a devil more damned
    In evils to top Macbeth.
MALCOLM.   I grant him bloody,
    Luxurious, avaricious, false, deceitful,
    Sudden, malicious, smacking of every sin
    That has a name; but there's no bottom, none,   60
    In my voluptuousness. Your wives, your daughters,
    Your matrons and your maids, could not fill up
    The cistern of my lust, and my desire
    All continent impediments° would o'erbear
    That did oppose my will. Better Macbeth   65
    Than such an one to reign.
MACDUFF.   Boundless intemperance
    In nature is a tyranny; it hath been
    The untimely emptying of the happy throne
    And fall of many kings. But fear not yet
    To take upon you what is yours. You may   70
    Convey your pleasures in a spacious plenty,
    And yet seem cold, the time you may so hoodwink.
    We have willing dames enough; there cannot be
    That vulture in you, to devour so many
    As will to greatness dedicate themselves,   75
    Finding it so inclined.
MALCOLM.   With this there grows
    In my most ill-composed affection such
    A staunchless avarice that, were I king,
    I should cut off the nobles for their lands,
    Desire his jewels and this other's house;   80
    And my more-having would be as a sauce
    To make me hunger more, that I should forge
    Quarrels unjust against the good and loyal,
    Destroying them for wealth.
MACDUFF.   This avarice
    Sticks deeper, grows with more pernicious root   85

64. *continent impediments:* restraints.

Than summer-seeming lust, and it hath been
The sword of° our slain kings. Yet do not fear;
Scotland hath foisons° to fill up your will,
Of your mere own.° All these are portable,°
With other graces weighed.   90
MALCOLM. But I have none. The king-becoming graces,
As justice, verity, temperance, stableness,
Bounty, perseverance, mercy, lowliness,
Devotion, patience, courage, fortitude,
I have no relish of them, but abound   95
In the division of each several crime,
Acting it many ways. Nay, had I power, I should
Pour the sweet milk of concord into hell,
Uproar the universal peace, confound
All unity on earth.
MACDUFF.   O Scotland, Scotland!   100
MALCOLM. If such a one be fit to govern, speak.
I am as I have spoken.
MACDUFF.   Fit to govern!
No, not to live. O nation miserable
With an untitled tyrant bloody-sceptered,
When shalt thou see thy wholesome days again,   105
Since that the truest issue of thy throne
By his own interdiction stands accursed,°
And does blaspheme his breed? Thy royal father
Was a most sainted king; the queen that bore thee,
Oftener upon her knees than on her feet,   110
Died every day she lived.° Fare thee well!
These evils thou repeat'st upon thyself
Have banished me from Scotland. O my breast,
Thy hope ends here!
MALCOLM.   Macduff, this noble passion,
Child of integrity, hath from my soul   115
Wiped the black scruples, reconciled my thoughts
To thy good truth and honor. Devilish Macbeth
By many of these trains hath sought to win me
Into his power, and modest wisdom plucks me
From overcredulous haste; but God above   120
Deal between thee and me! for even now
I put myself to thy direction, and
Unspeak mine own detraction,° here abjure
The taints and blames I laid upon myself,
For strangers to my nature. I am yet   125
Unknown to woman, never was forsworn,
Scarcely have coveted what was mine own,
At no time broke my faith, would not betray
The devil to his fellow, and delight

---

87. *The sword of:* that which has killed. 88. *foisons:* rich harvests. 89. *mere own:* own property; *portable:* endurable. 107. *By his . . . accursed:* Malcolm has accused himself of being unfit to govern. 110–111. *Oftener . . . lived:* The queen prepared in prayer for death. 123. *Unspeak mine own detraction:* take back the slander I uttered against myself.

No less in truth than life; my first false speaking   130
Was this upon myself. What I am truly,
Is thine and my poor country's to command;
Whither indeed, before thy here-approach,
Old Siward, with ten thousand warlike men,
Already at a point,° was setting forth.   135
Now we'll together; and the chance of goodness
Be like our warranted quarrel!° Why are you silent?

MACDUFF. Such welcome and unwelcome things at once
        'Tis hard to reconcile.

[*Enter a* DOCTOR.]

MALCOLM. Well; more anon. — Comes the king forth, I pray you?   140
DOCTOR. Ay, sir; there are a crew of wretched souls
        That stay his cure; their malady convinces
        The great assay of art; but at his touch —
        Such sanctity hath Heaven given his hand —
        They presently amend.
MALCOLM.   I thank you, Doctor.   [*Exit* DOCTOR.   145
MACDUFF. What's the disease he means?
MALCOLM.   'Tis called the evil;°
        A most miraculous work in this good king;
        Which often, since my here-remain in England,
        I have seen him do. How he solicits Heaven,
        Himself best knows; but strangely visited people,   150
        All swoln and ulcerous, pitiful to the eye,
        The mere despair of surgery, he cures,
        Hanging a golden stamp° about their necks,
        Put on with holy prayers; and 'tis spoken,
        To the succeeding royalty he leaves   155
        The healing benediction. With this strange virtue,
        He hath a heavenly gift of prophecy,
        And sundry blessings hang about his throne,
        That speak him full of grace.

[*Enter* ROSS.]

MACDUFF.   See, who comes here?
MALCOLM. My countryman; but yet I know him not.   160
MACDUFF. My ever-gentle cousin, welcome hither.
MALCOLM. I know him now. Good God, betimes remove
        The means that makes us strangers!°
ROSS.   Sir, amen.
MACDUFF. Stands Scotland where it did?
ROSS.   Alas, poor country!
        Almost afraid to know itself. It cannot   165

---

135. *at a point:* ready for action. 136–137. *the chance ... quarrel:* May our chance of success be
as good as the outcome of our argument. 146. *evil:* This speech refers to the king's supposed power
to cure scrofula, a dread skin disease, known at that time as the King's Evil. In Shakespeare's day,
King James I at first refused to continue the practice of touching sufferers but later consented.
This speech compliments him for his decision. 153. *stamp:* medal. 163. *The means ... strangers:*
Malcolm's exile has kept him out of touch with his countrymen.

Be called our mother, but our grave; where nothing,
But who knows nothing, is once seen to smile;
Where sighs and groans and shrieks that rend the air
Are made, not marked; where violent sorrow seems
A modern ecstasy.° The dead man's knell   170
Is there scarce asked for who;° and good men's lives
Expire before the flowers in their caps,
Dying or ere they sicken.

MACDUFF.   O, relation°
Too nice,° and yet too true!

MALCOLM.   What's the newest grief?

ROSS. That of an hour's age doth hiss the speaker;°   175
Each minute teems a new one.

MACDUFF.   How does my wife?

ROSS. Why, well.

MACDUFF.   And all my children?

ROSS.   Well too.

MACDUFF. The tyrant has not battered at their peace?

ROSS. No; they were well at peace when I did leave 'em.

MACDUFF. Be not a niggard of your speech; how goes 't?   180

ROSS. When I came hither to transport the tidings,
Which I have heavily borne, there ran a rumor
Of many worthy fellows that were out;°
Which was to my belief witnessed the rather,
For that I saw the tyrant's power afoot.   185
Now is the time of help; your eye in Scotland
Would create soldiers, make our women fight,
To doff their dire distresses.

MALCOLM.   Be 't their comfort
We are coming thither. Gracious England hath
Lent us good Siward and ten thousand men;   190
An older and a better soldier none
That Christendom gives out.

ROSS.   Would I could answer
This comfort with the like! But I have words
That would be howled out in the desert air,
Where hearing should not latch° them.

MACDUFF.   What concern they?   195
The general cause? or is it a fee grief°
Due to some single breast?

ROSS.   No mind that's honest
But in it shares some woe; though the main part
Pertains to you alone.

MACDUFF.   If it be mine,
Keep it not from me, quickly let me have it.   200

ROSS. Let not your ears despise my tongue for ever,

---

170. *modern ecstasy:* a slight mental disturbance. 170–171. *The dead . . . who:* People can no
longer keep track of Macbeth's victims. 173. *relation:* account. 174. *nice:* exact. 175. *That . . .
speaker:* Any grief an hour old is no longer news. 183. *out:* up in arms. 195. *latch:* catch. 196. *fee
grief:* private grief.

" All my pretty ones? Did you say all? "

          Which shall possess them with the heaviest sound
          That ever yet they heard.
MACDUFF.   Hum! I guess at it.
ROSS. Your castle is surprised; your wife and babes   205
          Savagely slaughtered: to relate the manner,
          Were, on the quarry of these murdered deer,
          To add the death of you.
MALCOLM.   Merciful Heaven!
          What, man! ne'er pull your hat upon your brows;
          Give sorrow words. The grief that does not speak
          Whispers the o'erfraught heart and bids it break.   210
MACDUFF. My children too?
ROSS.   Wife, children, servants, all
          That could be found.
MACDUFF.   And I must be from thence!
          My wife killed too?
ROSS.   I have said.
MALCOLM.   Be comforted.
          Let's make us medicines of our great revenge,
          To cure this deadly grief.   215
MACDUFF. He has no children. All my pretty ones?
          Did you say all? O hell kite! All?
          What, all my pretty chickens and their dam
          At one fell swoop?
MALCOLM. Dispute it° like a man.

  220. *Dispute it:* Resist your grief.

MACDUFF.   I shall do so; 220
But I must also feel it as a man.
I cannot but remember such things were,
That were most precious to me. Did Heaven look on,
And would not take their part? Sinful Macduff,
They were all struck for thee! naught that I am, 225
Not for their own demerits, but for mine,
Fell slaughter on their souls. Heaven rest them now!
MALCOLM. Be this the whetstone of your sword; let grief
Convert to anger; blunt not the heart, enrage it.
MACDUFF. O, I could play the woman with mine eyes 230
And braggart with my tongue! But, gentle heavens,
Cut short all intermission; front to front°
Bring thou this fiend to Scotland and myself;
Within my sword's length set him; if he 'scape,
Heaven forgive him too!
MALCOLM.   This tune goes manly. 235
Come, go we to the king; our power is ready;
Our lack is nothing but our leave. Macbeth
Is ripe for shaking, and the powers above
Put on their instruments.° Receive what cheer you may:
The night is long that never finds the day.   *[Exeunt.* 240

232. *front to front:* face to face. 238–239. *the powers . . . instruments:* The powers of heaven urge us, their agents, to battle.

ACT V

SCENE I. *Dunsinane. Anteroom in the castle.*

[Enter a DOCTOR OF PHYSIC *and a* WAITING-GENTLEWOMAN.]

DOCTOR. I have two nights watched with you, but can perceive no truth in your report. When was it she last walked?
GENTLEWOMAN. Since his majesty went into the field, I have seen her rise from her bed, throw her nightgown upon her, unlock her closet, take forth paper, fold it, write upon 't, read it, afterward seal it, and again return to bed; 5 yet all this while in a most fast sleep.
DOCTOR. A great perturbation in nature, to receive at once the benefit of sleep, and do the effects of watching! In this slumbery agitation, besides her walking and other actual performances, what, at any time, have you heard her say?
GENTLEWOMAN. That, sir, which I will not report after her. 10
DOCTOR. You may to me; and 'tis most meet you should.
GENTLEWOMAN. Neither to you nor any one; having no witness to confirm my speech.

[Enter LADY MACBETH, *with a taper.]*

Lo you, here she comes! This is her very guise; and, upon my life, fast asleep. Observe her; stand close. 15
DOCTOR. How came she by that light?

GENTLEWOMAN. Why, it stood by her; she has light by her continually; 'tis her command.

DOCTOR. You see, her eyes are open.

GENTLEWOMAN. Ay, but their sense is shut.   20

DOCTOR. What is it she does now? Look, how she rubs her hands.

GENTLEWOMAN. It is an accustomed action with her, to seem thus washing her
hands. I have known her continue in this a quarter of an hour.

LADY MACBETH. Yet here's a spot.

DOCTOR. Hark! she speaks. I will set down what comes from her, to satisfy my   25
remembrance the more strongly.

LADY MACBETH. Out, damned spot! out, I say! — One: two: why, then 'tis time to
do 't. — Hell is murky! — Fie, my lord, fie! a soldier, and afeard? What
need we fear who knows it, when none can call our power to account? —
Yet who would have thought the old man to have had so much blood in him?

DOCTOR. Do you mark that?   31

LADY MACBETH. The thane of Fife had a wife; where is she now? — What, will
these hands ne'er be clean? — No more o' that, my lord, no more o' that;
you mar all with this starting.

DOCTOR. Go to, go to; you have known what you should not.   35

GENTLEWOMAN. She has spoke what she should not, I am sure of that; Heaven
knows what she has known.

LADY MACBETH. Here's the smell of the blood still; all the perfumes of Arabia will
not sweeten this little hand. Oh, oh, oh!

DOCTOR. What a sigh is there! The heart is sorely charged.°   40

GENTLEWOMAN. I would not have such a heart in my bosom for the dignity of the
whole body.

DOCTOR. Well, well, well —

GENTLEWOMAN. Pray God it be, sir.

DOCTOR. This disease is beyond my practice; yet I have known those which   45
have walked in their sleep who have died holily in their beds.

LADY MACBETH. Wash your hands, put on your nightgown; look not so pale. — I
tell you yet again, Banquo's buried; he cannot come out on 's grave.

DOCTOR. Even so?

40. *charged:* burdened.

" What need we fear who knows it, when none can call our power to account? "

LADY MACBETH. To bed, to bed! There's knocking at the gate. Come, come, 50
　　come, come, give me your hand. What's done cannot be undone. — To bed,
　　to bed, to bed!　　　　　　　　　　　　　　　　　　　　　　　　*[Exit.*
DOCTOR. Will she go now to bed?
GENTLEWOMAN. Directly.
DOCTOR. Foul whisperings are abroad; unnatural deeds　　　　　　　55
　　Do breed unnatural troubles; infected minds
　　To their deaf pillows will discharge their secrets.
　　More needs she the divine than the physician.
　　God, God forgive us all! Look after her;
　　Remove from her the means of all annoyance,°　　　　　　　　60
　　And still keep eyes upon her. So, good night;
　　My mind she has mated,° and amazed my sight.
　　I think, but dare not speak.
GENTLEWOMAN.　　　　　　　　Good night, good doctor.　　　　*[Exeunt.*

60. *annoyance:* harm. 62. *mated:* overcome with amazement.

SCENE II. *The country near Dunsinane.*

[*Drum and colors.* Enter* MENTEITH,† CAITHNESS,‡ ANGUS, LENNOX, *and* SOL-
DIERS.]

MENTEITH. The English power is near, led on by Malcolm,
　　His uncle Siward and the good Macduff.
　　Revenges burn in them; for their dear causes
　　Would to the bleeding and the grim alarm°
　　Excite the mortified° man.
ANGUS.　　　　　　　　　　　Near Birnam wood　　　　　　　5
　　Shall we well meet them; that way are they coming.
CAITHNESS. Who knows if Donalbain be with his brother?
LENNOX. For certain, sir, he is not; I have a file
　　Of all the gentry. There is Siward's son,
　　And many unrough youths that even now　　　　　　　　　10
　　Protest their first of manhood.°
MENTEITH.　　　　　　　　　What does the tyrant?
CAITHNESS. Great Dunsinane he strongly fortifies.
　　Some say he's mad; others that lesser hate him
　　Do call it valiant fury; but, for certain,
　　He cannot buckle his distempered cause　　　　　　　　15
　　Within the belt of rule.°
ANGUS.　　　　　　　　　　　Now does he feel
　　His secret murders sticking on his hands;
　　Now minutely° revolts upbraid his faith breach;°
　　Those he commands move only in command,
　　Nothing in love. Now does he feel his title　　　　　　　20
　　Hang loose about him, like a giant's robe
　　Upon a dwarfish thief.

* *Drum and colors:* soldiers with a drum and a flag. † *Menteith* (mĕn·tēth′). ‡ *Caithness* (kāth′nĕs).
4. *alarm:* call to arms. 5. *mortified:* half dead. 11. *Protest . . . manhood:* have hardly reached manhood. 15–16. *He cannot . . . rule:* Macbeth cannot keep his evil cause under control. 18. *minutely:*
every minute; *faith breach:* disloyalty.

MENTEITH.   Who then shall blame
    His pestered senses to recoil and start,
    When all that is within him does condemn
    Itself for being there?
CAITHNESS.   Well, march we on,   25
    To give obedience where 'tis truly owed.
    Meet we the medicine of the sickly weal,°
    And with him pour we in our country's purge
    Each drop of us.
LENNOX.   Or so much as it needs,
    To dew the sovereign flower° and drown the weeds.°   30
    Make we our march toward Birnam.   [*Exeunt, marching.*

27. *the medicine of the sickly weal:* Malcolm and his army are the medicine which Scotland needs to heal the harassed commonwealth. 30. *sovereign flower:* Malcolm; *weeds:* Macbeth.

SCENE III. *Dunsinane. A room in the castle.*

[*Enter* MACBETH, DOCTOR, *and* ATTENDANTS.]

MACBETH. Bring me no more reports; let them fly all;°
    Till Birnam wood remove to Dunsinane,
    I cannot taint with fear. What's the boy Malcolm?
    Was he not born of woman? The spirits that know
    All mortal consequences have pronounced me thus: 5
    " Fear not, Macbeth; no man that's born of woman
    Shall e'er have power upon thee." Then fly, false thanes,
    And mingle with the English epicures!°
    The mind I sway by and the heart I bear
    Shall never sag with doubt nor shake with fear.   10

[*Enter a* SERVANT.]

    The devil damn thee black, thou cream-faced loon!
    Where got'st thou that goose look?
SERVANT. There is ten thousand —
MACBETH.   Geese, villain?
SERVANT.   Soldiers, sir.
MACBETH. Go, prick thy face, and over-red thy fear,
    Thou lily-livered boy. What soldiers, patch?°   15
    Death of thy soul! those linen cheeks of thine
    Are counselors to fear. What soldiers, whey-face?
SERVANT. The English force, so please you.
MACBETH. Take thy face hence.   [*Exit* SERVANT.
    Seyton!° — I am sick at heart,
    When I behold — Seyton, I say! — This push   20
    Will cheer me ever, or disseat me now.
    I have lived long enough. My way of life
    Is fall'n into the sear, the yellow leaf;
    And that which should accompany old age,

1. *let . . . all:* let them all desert me. 8. *epicures:* luxury seekers. 15. *patch:* fool. 19. *Seyton* (sē'tŏn).

As honor, love, obedience, troops of friends,   25
I must not look to have; but, in their stead,
Curses, not loud but deep, mouth honor, breath,
Which the poor heart would fain deny, and dare not.
Seyton!

[Enter SEYTON.*]*

SEYTON. What is your gracious pleasure?
MACBETH.   What news more?   30
SEYTON. All is confirmed, my lord, which was reported.
MACBETH. I'll fight till from my bones my flesh be hacked.
      Give me my armor.
SEYTON.   'Tis not needed yet.
MACBETH. I'll put it on.
      Send out moe° horses; skirr° the country round;   35
      Hang those that talk of fear. Give me mine armor.
      How does your patient, doctor?
DOCTOR.   Not so sick, my lord,
      As she is troubled with thick-coming fancies,
      That keep her from her rest.
MACBETH.   Cure her of that.
      Canst thou not minister to a mind diseased,   40
      Pluck from the memory a rooted sorrow,
      Raze out the written troubles of the brain
      And with some sweet oblivious antidote
      Cleanse the stuffed bosom of that perilous stuff
      Which weighs upon the heart?
DOCTOR.   Therein the patient   45
      Must minister to himself.
MACBETH. Throw physic° to the dogs; I'll none of it.
      Come, put mine armor on; give me my staff.
      Seyton, send out. Doctor, the thanes fly from me.
      Come, sir, dispatch. If thou couldst, doctor, cast°   50
      The water of my land, find her disease,
      And purge it to a sound and pristine° health,
      I would applaud thee to the very echo,
      That should applaud again. — Pull 't off, I say.° —
      What rhubarb, senna, or what purgative drug,   55
      Would scour these English hence? Hear'st thou of them?
DOCTOR. Ay, my good lord; your royal preparation
      Makes us hear something.
MACBETH.   Bring it after me.
      I will not be afraid of death and bane,
      Till Birnam forest come to Dunsinane.   60
DOCTOR. *[Aside]* Were I from Dunsinane away and clear,
      Profit again should hardly draw me here.   *[Exeunt.*

35. *moe:* more; *skirr:* scour. 47. *physic:* medicine. 50. *cast:* examine. 52. *pristine:* uncorrupted.
54. *Pull 't off, I say:* This sounds like an aside to Seyton, who has been told to pull off some pieces
of Macbeth's armor, put on wrong in his haste.

SCENE IV. *Country near Birnam wood.*

[*Drum and colors. Enter* MALCOLM, *old* SIWARD* *and his* SON, MACDUFF, MEN-
TEITH, CAITHNESS, ANGUS, LENNOX, ROSS, *and* SOLDIERS *marching.*]

MALCOLM. Cousins, I hope the days are near at hand
    That chambers will be safe.°
MENTEITH.   We doubt it nothing.
SIWARD. What wood is this before us?
MENTEITH.   The wood of Birnam.
MALCOLM. Let every soldier hew him down a bough
    And bear it before him; thereby shall we shadow   5
    The numbers of our host and make discovery
    Err in report of us.
SOLDIERS.   It shall be done.
SIWARD. We learn no other but the confident tyrant
    Keeps still in Dunsinane, and will endure
    Our setting down before 't.°
MALCOLM.   'Tis his main hope;   10
    For where there is advantage to be given,
    Both more or less have given him the revolt,°
    And none serve with him but constrainèd things
    Whose hearts are absent too.
MACDUFF.   Let our just censures
    Attend the true event, and put we on   15
    Industrious soldiership.°
SIWARD.   The time approaches
    That will with due decision make us know
    What we shall say we have and what we owe.
    Thoughts speculative their unsure hopes relate,
    But certain issue strokes must arbitrate;°   20
    Toward which advance the war.   [*Exeunt, marching.*

* *Siward* (sē'wärd). 1–2. *the days . . . safe:* Soon people will be able to sleep in peace. 8–10. *the
confident . . . before 't:* Macbeth has fortified himself at Dunsinane and will endure siege. 11–12. *where
. . . revolt:* Wherever there was opportunity (*advantage given*) both the higher and lower classes
(*more or less*) have deserted Macbeth. 14–16. *Let . . . soldiership:* We can pass final judgment after
we see what's happened. In the meantime, let's get on with the fighting. 16–20. *The time . . . arbitrate:*
We shall soon know what the situation is, and whether our speculations are true, but action alone
(*strokes*) will decide the issue for sure.

SCENE V. *Dunsinane. Within the castle.*

[*Enter* MACBETH, SEYTON, *and* SOLDIERS, *with drum and colors.*]

MACBETH. Hang out our banners on the outward walls;
    The cry is still " They come! " Our castle's strength
    Will laugh a siege to scorn; here let them lie
    Till famine and the ague eat them up.
    Were they not forced with those that should be ours,°   5
    We might have met them dareful, beard to beard,

5 *forced . . . ours:* reinforced with those who have deserted.

And beat them backward home.   [A cry of women within.
                        What is that noise?
SEYTON. It is the cry of women, my good lord.   [Exit.
MACBETH. I have almost forgot the taste of fears.
        The time has been, my senses would have cooled   10
        To hear a night-shriek; and my fell of hair°
        Would at a dismal treatise° rouse and stir
        As life were in 't. I have supped full with horrors;
        Direness, familiar to my slaughterous thoughts,
        Cannot once start me.

                [Re-enter SEYTON.]

                Wherefore was that cry?   15
SEYTON. The queen, my lord, is dead.
MACBETH. She should have died hereafter;°
        There would have been a time for such a word.
        Tomorrow, and tomorrow, and tomorrow,
        Creeps in this petty pace from day to day   20
        To the last syllable of recorded time,
        And all our yesterdays have lighted fools
        The way to dusty death. Out, out, brief candle!
        Life's but a walking shadow, a poor player
        That struts and frets his hour upon the stage   25
        And then is heard no more. It is a tale
        Told by an idiot, full of sound and fury,
        Signifying nothing.

             [Enter a MESSENGER.]

        Thou comest to use thy tongue; thy story quickly.
MESSENGER. Gracious my lord,   30
        I should report that which I say I saw,
        But know not how to do it.
MACBETH.   Well, say, sir.
MESSENGER. As I did stand my watch upon the hill,
        I looked toward Birnam, and anon, methought,
        The wood began to move.
MACBETH.   Liar and slave!   35
MESSENGER. Let me endure your wrath, if 't be not so.
        Within this three mile may you see it coming;
        I say, a moving grove.
MACBETH.   If thou speak'st false,
        Upon the next tree shalt thou hang alive,
        Till famine cling thee; if thy speech be sooth,°   40
        I care not if thou dost for me as much.
        I pull in resolution,° and begin
        To doubt the equivocation of the fiend
        That lies like truth: " Fear not, till Birnam wood

    11. *my fell of hair:* the hair on my scalp. 12. *dismal treatise:* gloomy story. 17. *She . . . hereafter:*
She was bound to die sometime. 40. *sooth:* truth. 42. *pull in resolution:* check courage; that is,
Macbeth will not struggle against fate.

Do come to Dunsinane." And now a wood   45
Comes toward Dunsinane. Arm, arm, and out!
If this which he avouches does appear,
There is nor flying hence nor tarrying here.
I 'gin to be aweary of the sun,
And wish the estate o' the world were now undone.   50
Ring the alarum bell! Blow, wind! come, wrack!
At least we'll die with harness on our back.   [*Exeunt.*

SCENE VI. *Dunsinane. Before the castle.*

[*Drums and colors. Enter* MALCOLM, *old* SIWARD, MACDUFF, *and their* ARMY, *with boughs.*]

MALCOLM. Now near enough; your leavy screens° throw down,
     And show like those you are. You, worthy uncle,
     Shall, with my cousin, your right noble son,
     Lead our first battle. Worthy Macduff and we
     Shall take upon 's else remains to do,   5
     According to our order.
SIWARD.   Fare you well.
     Do we but find the tyrant's power tonight,
     Let us be beaten, if we cannot fight.
MACDUFF. Make all our trumpets speak; give them all breath,
     Those clamorous harbingers° of blood and death.   [*Exeunt.*   10

1. *leavy screens:* the boughs used as camouflage. 10. *clamorous harbingers* (här′bĭn·jĕrz): noisy messengers.

SCENE VII. *Another part of the field.*

[*Alarums. Enter* MACBETH.]

MACBETH. They have tied me to a stake;° I cannot fly,
     But, bearlike, I must fight the course. What's he
     That was not born of woman? Such a one
     Am I to fear, or none.

[*Enter young* SIWARD.]

YOUNG SIWARD. What is thy name?
MACBETH.   Thou 'lt be afraid to hear it.   5
YOUNG SIWARD. No; though thou call'st thyself a hotter name
     Than any is in hell.
MACBETH.   My name's Macbeth.
YOUNG SIWARD. The devil himself could not pronounce a title
     More hateful to mine ear.
MACBETH.   No, nor more fearful.
YOUNG SIWARD. Thou liest, abhorrèd tyrant; with my sword   10
     I'll prove the lie thou speak'st.   [*They fight and young* SIWARD *is slain.*

1. *They have tied me to a stake:* a reference to bear-baiting, a popular Elizabethan sport. Bears were tied to a stake and set upon by dogs.

MACBETH.   Thou wast born of woman.
    But swords I smile at, weapons laugh to scorn,
    Brandished by man that's of a woman born.   [*Exit.*

[Alarums. Enter MACDUFF.]

MACDUFF. That way the noise is. Tyrant, show thy face!
    If thou be'st slain and with no stroke of mine,   15
    My wife and children's ghosts will haunt me still.
    I cannot strike at wretched kerns,° whose arms
    Are hired to bear their staves; either thou, Macbeth,
    Or else my sword with an unbattered edge
    I sheathe again undeeded. There thou shouldst be;   20
    By this great clatter, one of greatest note
    Seems bruited.° Let me find him, fortune!
    And more I beg not.   [*Exit. Alarums.*

[Enter MALCOLM and old SIWARD.]

SIWARD. This way, my lord; the castle's gently rendered:°
    The tyrant's people on both sides do fight;°   25
    The noble thanes do bravely in the war;
    The day almost itself professes yours,
    And little is to do.
MALCOLM.   We have met with foes
    That strike beside us.°
SIWARD.   Enter, sir, the castle.   [*Exeunt. Alarums.*

17. *kerns:* common foot soldiers hired as mercenaries. 22. *bruited:* reported. 24. *gently rendered:* surrendered without active defense. 25. *The tyrant's . . . fight:* Some of Macbeth's men are deserting him. 29. *beside us:* on our side.

SCENE VIII. Another part of the field.

[Enter MACBETH.]

MACBETH. Why should I play the Roman fool,° and die
    On mine own sword? Whiles I see lives, the gashes
    Do better upon them.

[Enter MACDUFF.]

MACDUFF.   Turn, hell-hound, turn!
MACBETH. Of all men else I have avoided thee.
    But get thee back; my soul is too much charged   5
    With blood of thine already.
MACDUFF.   I have no words;
    My voice is in my sword, thou bloodier villain
    Than terms can give thee out!   [*They fight.*
MACBETH.   Thou losest labor;
    As easy mayst thou the intrenchant air

1. *play the Roman fool:* Brutus and Cassius, ancient Romans who were also trapped, committed suicide.

With thy keen sword impress as make me bleed.   10
Let fall thy blade on vulnerable crests;°
I bear a charmèd life, which must not yield
To one of woman born.
MACDUFF.   Despair thy charm;
And let the angel whom thou still hast served
Tell thee, Macduff was from his mother's womb,   15
Untimely ripped.
MACBETH. Accursèd be that tongue that tells me so,
For it hath cowed my better part of man!
And be these juggling fiends no more believed,
That palter with us in a double sense;°   20
That keep the word of promise to our ear,
And break it to our hope. I'll not fight with thee.
MACDUFF. Then yield thee, coward,
And live to be the show and gaze o' the time.
We'll have thee, as our rarer monsters are,   25
Painted upon a pole,° and underwrit,
" Here may you see the tyrant."
MACBETH.   I will not yield,
To kiss the ground before young Malcolm's feet,
And to be baited with the rabble's curse.
Though Birnam wood be come to Dunsinane,   30
And thou opposed, being of no woman born,
Yet I will try the last. Before my body
I throw my warlike shield. Lay on, Macduff,
And damned be him that first cries " Hold, enough! "   [*Exeunt, fighting.*
                                                                    [*Alarums.*

[*Retreat. Flourish. Enter, with drum and colors,* MALCOLM, *old* SIWARD, ROSS, *the other* THANES, *and* SOLDIERS.]

MALCOLM. I would the friends we miss were safe arrived.   35
SIWARD. Some must go off;° and yet, by these I see,
So great a day as this is cheaply bought.
MALCOLM. Macduff is missing, and your noble son.
ROSS. Your son, my lord, has paid a soldier's debt.
He only lived but till he was a man;   40
The which no sooner had his prowess confirmed
In the unshrinking station where he fought,
But like a man he died.
SIWARD.   Then he is dead?
ROSS. Ay, and brought off the field. Your cause of sorrow
Must not be measured by his worth, for then   45
It hath no end.
SIWARD.   Had he his hurts before?°
ROSS. Ay, on the front.

11. *vulnerable crests:* heads that can be wounded. 20. *palter with us in a double sense:* deceive us by words that have a double meaning. 26. *Painted upon a pole:* that is, your picture painted on a placard fastened to a pole. 36. *Some must go off:* In a battle it is inevitable that some should lose their lives. 46. *Had he his hurts before?:* If young Siward's wounds were in the front, it would indicate to his father that he died fighting, not fleeing.

SIWARD.   Why then, God's soldier be he!
        Had I as many sons as I have hairs,   [*Flourish.*
        I would not wish them to a fairer death.
        And so, his knell is knolled.
MALCOLM.   He's worth more sorrow,   50
        And that I'll spend for him.
SIWARD.   He's worth no more.
        They say he parted well, and paid his score;
        And so, God be with him! Here comes newer comfort.

              [*Re-enter* MACDUFF, *with* MACBETH'S *head.*]

MACDUFF. Hail, king! for so thou art. Behold, where stands
        The usurper's cursèd head. The time is free.   55
        I see thee compassed with thy kingdom's pearl,°
        That speak my salutation in their minds;
        Whose voices I desire aloud with mine:
        Hail, King of Scotland!
ALL.   Hail, King of Scotland!   [*Flourish.*
MALCOLM. We° shall not spend a large expense of time   60
        Before we reckon with your several loves,
        And make us even with you. My thanes and kinsmen,
        Henceforth be earls, the first that ever Scotland
        In such an honor named. What's more to do,
        Which would be planted newly with the time,   65
        As calling home our exiled friends abroad
        That fled the snares of watchful tyranny;
        Producing forth the cruel ministers
        Of this dead butcher and his fiendlike queen,
        Who, as 'tis thought, by self and violent hands   70
        Took off her life; this, and what needful else
        That calls upon us, by the grace of Grace,
        We will perform in measure, time, and place;
        So, thanks to all at once and to each one,
        Whom we invite to see us crowned at Scone.   [*Flourish. Exeunt.*   75

    56. *thy kingdom's pearl:* the nobility of the kingdom; that is, the nobles. 60. *We:* Malcolm now
speaks of himself in the plural as befits a king.

READING DRAMA

The ideal approach to *Macbeth* or any other play is to see it performed on the stage. Since that is not possible for all of us, a second-best approach is to see a good movie or television version of it, or at least hear a phonographic recording of parts of the play.

Still, drama *is* literature and it can be read with great enjoyment. Especially with Shakespeare, you will find pleasure in re-reading and reflecting on passages of the play that are beautiful in expression or profound in meaning.

As you read *Macbeth,* you may find it helpful to consider four key questions that can be applied in reading almost all plays.

1. *What would this play look like and sound like on the stage?*

Take another look at the model of the Globe Theater on page 128. The Elizabethan stage is very different from our modern stage. Because there is no curtain in the Elizabethan theater, the action of the play is almost continuous. A scene is over when all the characters leave the stage; a new scene begins when another set of characters comes on. This flowing of one scene into another speeds up the action and makes a Shakespearean drama somewhat like our modern movies. The opening of the play was announced by a trumpet. Since there is no " curtain going up," Shakespeare usually begins his plays with a bit of arresting action to quiet his audience down. Does he follow this trick in *Macbeth?* How does Scene i establish the *atmosphere* of the play — that is, how does it suggest what the main tone or mood is likely to be?

Because the Elizabethan stage was almost entirely bare of sets and props, the playwright had to put descriptions of the setting into the mouths of the characters. What clues to stage " pictures " do you find in the dialogue? See, for example, Act I, Scene iii, line 77, and Scene vi, lines 1–10?

Remember that the Elizabethan theater had three main sections: the outer stage, the inner stage, and the upper stage or balcony. As you go through the play, point out scenes that would be acted on each of these stages. Which scenes require special properties and so would be done on the inner stage, where a small curtain could be drawn? (See Act III, Scene iv, for example.)

What scene in *Macbeth* would require apparitions — ghosts — to appear on the balcony? Why would this staging be effective? How would you stage Lady Macbeth's famous sleepwalking scene (Act V, Scene i)? How would you use right and left entrances for various scenes, as that of the drunken porter, Act II, Scene iii, or the battle in Act V?

In the Elizabethan theater there was no program or playbill passed out to the audience, listing the names and relationships of the characters. Cleverly, therefore, Shakespeare sometimes has the characters tell you *who* they are, as well as *where* they are. Try to find several instances of this self-identification in *Macbeth*.

It is important, too, to visualize the appearance of the characters. Perhaps you first pictured the witches in the garb of a typical Hallowe'en witch, but you will find that impression modified in Act I, Scene iii, lines 39–47. On the whole, however, there is little description of the way characters look, since the audience will actually see them. In Shakespeare's day, Elizabethan costumes were used for most plays, even if the setting was ancient Rome or eleventh-century Scotland. How would you dress the characters in *Macbeth?*

2. *Who are the main characters and what kinds of people are they?*

You know that Macbeth is the chief character of the play. He may serve here to illustrate how a playwright creates a character and makes him come alive in our minds. There are at least four distinct ways in which a character is developed in a play. Each of these may be illustrated by a passage from Act I concerning Macbeth (there are, of course, many such clues throughout the play).

a. Description of his actions by others (Sergeant, Scene ii, lines 16–41).

b. Description of his personality or character traits by others (Lady Macbeth, Scene v, lines 11–26).

c. His own thoughts in meditation (Scene iii, lines 129–44).

d. His talk and arguments with others (Scene vii, lines 28–82).

Review these passages and indicate what each tells you about Macbeth. Make a similar list of passages, from all five acts, that reveal the personalities or character traits of (*a*) Lady Macbeth, (*b*) Banquo, (*c*) Duncan, (*d*) Macduff, and (*e*) Malcolm.

Shakespeare is particularly clever at bringing out a character by contrast with other characters. What contrast did you notice between Duncan and Macbeth? What other pairs of characters can you contrast?

Shakespeare is a master of character development. Can you check in this play the various stages by which the gallant soldier Macbeth turns into a butcher? How does Macbeth's hopefulness gradually turn into despair? Why?

Note how Macbeth and Lady Macbeth

develop along different tracks. Both are ambitious, but Lady Macbeth takes the initiative at the start, and seems more bold and strong. How does this situation reverse itself during the play? Does Macbeth have more imagination or a more sensitive conscience than his wife?

3. What is the main plot of the drama?

A good plot is not just any story that comes along, but a story so arranged that it is an artistic whole. There are many speeches and actions that all fit, piece by piece, into the complete plot. Each action by Macbeth must result from what has preceded it and take Macbeth further on his downward career. To see how the plot develops, write a short summary of each act.

The suspense of the plot comes from your uncertainty as to its outcome. It lies in these questions: where will all these events lead Macbeth? will justice be done in the end? Somewhere along in the action is the turning point of the plot. Before this point in the play, Macbeth's crimes have brought him what he wanted; after this point, circumstances turn against him. Where exactly is this point in *Macbeth*?

The last act of a play should bring all the threads of the plot together in conclusion; it should decide the fate of the main character and solve all the problems that have arisen in the play. How is this illustrated in *Macbeth*?

4. What is the meaning of the play?

At the end of your first reading of the play, you are in a position to realize the point of the whole. In *Macbeth* it is evident that Shakespeare's purpose is to show the devastating effects of unrestrained ambition. How does this theme, or meaning, of the play affect you personally? Does it tell you something about the serious consequences of evil acts upon the persons who perform them? upon the persons who witness or are unwittingly involved in them? Does it make you realize the responsibility of a leader or ruler to the people under him? Does it sharpen your insight into human motives and desires?

The meaning of the play is found not only in its whole but also in its parts — in specific passages. How many powerful passages need to be clarified and thought over? What passages seem to you particularly significant in revealing Shakespeare's meaning?

STUDY OF THE PLAY BY ACTS

ACT I

1. Why is it important that Macbeth should *at first* be presented to us as a brave and honored soldier? How is he so presented?

2. In Scene iii, how did the witches' greeting affect Macbeth? What is the importance of Macbeth's sudden promotion to be thane of Cawdor?

3. The Elizabethan audience actually believed in witches; a modern audience does not. What difference would this make in the reaction of the two groups to the witches' prophecies?

4. Notice Banquo's speeches concerning the witches. Can the weird sisters *make* anything happen, or do they merely foresee the future? Are they put in the play as symbols of certain thoughts and emotions? Are they evil, mischievous, or neutral? Explain your answers by specific reference to the play.

5. In Scenes v–vii, how much evidence can you find that Macbeth is more frightened by the plan to kill Duncan than Lady Macbeth is? that they have previously considered doing so? Which of the two is the " brains " of the team? Analyze Macbeth's argument with himself at the beginning of Scene vii. What is he really afraid of? How does Lady Macbeth manage to stiffen his courage? Are her arguments logical? Are they just? What would Macbeth's future relations with his wife have been had he not followed her lead in their scheme?

ACT II

1. In the brief dialogue between Banquo and Macbeth at the beginning of the act, what do you learn about their regard for each other?

2. Analyze the " dagger speech," lines 33–64. In how many different ways does Macbeth see the dagger? What does the speech show of his mental state? Is he becoming stronger or weaker than he revealed himself in Act I?

3. How is the feeling of intense horror made impressive at the beginning of Scene ii? Do the knocking and the actions of the porter increase or destroy this horror? (A report by a student on De Quincey's essay " On the Knocking at the Gate in Macbeth " will throw some interesting light on its effect.)

4. Why did Macbeth kill the grooms? Was it a wise move? What reason did he give to the others?

ACT III

1. For what reason does Macbeth want Banquo murdered? What different reasons does he give the murderers? Why?

2. In this act how have Macbeth and his wife exchanged places since the murder of Duncan? Do Scenes i and ii taken together suggest that Macbeth has risen or fallen in a moral sense? Give reasons for your answer.

3. Scene iv is considered the turning point of the play. Look back on page 198 to the discussion of plot, and then explain how this scene may be considered a climax.

4. Why is Macbeth so upset by the escape of Fleance? What speeches of Macbeth seem to call forth the appearance of Banquo's ghost? What is ironic about this timing?

5. Considering all the circumstances of the two scenes, why does the illusion of the ghost show a more serious state of nerves than that of the dagger in Act II?

6. In this act what hints are given of the gathering forces of opposition to Macbeth?

ACT IV

1. Name all of the devices Shakespeare uses in creating a feeling of horror and impending doom at the beginning of this act. What effects do the witches' enchantments have upon Macbeth's morale? What is his final reaction to the witches? What further moral degeneration does he show at the end of the scene?

2. In Scene iii, why does Malcolm misrepresent his own character to Macduff? What events in this scene bring out the strong points in the characters of both these men?

ACT V

1. In Scene i, what words by Lady Macbeth show that she has been brooding over the past crimes? Untangle the confused mixture of words to show which crime she dwells on most frequently. What is the reason for this?

2. What lines foreshadow Lady Macbeth's death? What do we learn later of her death?

3. In the series of short scenes trace the final mental state of Macbeth through significant speeches. Where does he show false bravery, masking underlying fear? dependence on the witches' prophecies? sense of betrayal by the witches? realization of his misspent life?

4. Do you feel pity for Macbeth at any of these points? Do you think he was any less responsible for his acts because the witches' prophecies tempted him?

5. Is the outcome of the plot satisfying to you? What note of hope concludes the play.

CLASS ACTIVITIES

PANEL DISCUSSIONS
AND INFORMAL DEBATES

There are many points of possible argument in this play which can well be handled by special assignments to two or more students, with class discussion afterward.

1. Did Lady Macbeth really faint in Act II, Scene iii, or just pretend to do so?

2. What is the best way to stage the appearance of the ghost of Banquo in Act III: by a man? by illusions of mirrors and lights? by Macbeth's facial expressions only?

3. Which is the most dramatic moment of the play: the murder of Duncan with the knocking at the gate? the appearance of Banquo's ghost? the news of the murder of his family brought to Macduff? Lady Macbeth's sleepwalking scene?

DRAMATIZATION

Presenting a tragedy in class is more difficult than presenting a comedy, for unless the real spirit of the play is conveyed to the audience, it becomes farcical. Recommended scenes for you to dramatize are: Act I, Scenes i and iii (with brief interval of thunder or appropriate music); Act II, Scenes i, ii, and iii; Act III, Scene iv; Act IV, Scene i; Act V, Scenes i, iii, and v (consecutive with brief interval).

BEN JONSON 1573?–1637

Next to Shakespeare, Ben Jonson was the most important dramatist of the Elizabethan era. But unlike Shakespeare, he was a quarrelsome and overbearing person who led a colorful and often turbulent life. In his early youth he ran away to fight the Spaniards in Flanders because he had grown tired of laying bricks in London. In time, he returned, married, and became an actor and playwright. His quick temper got him into frequent trouble. One day he killed a fellow actor in a duel arising from a quarrel. He was thrown into prison and barely escaped hanging, but was branded on the left thumb in punishment. Another time, he almost had his nose and ears cut off when he confessed writing part of a comedy that offended the king.

Jonson was the first English dramatist to publish his plays. He was greatly loved and admired by his readers and by those who knew him personally. A group of young writers became his devoted followers and called themselves " Sons of Ben." He was made poet laureate, and today he lies buried in Westminster Abbey, where his tombstone bears these words: " O Rare Ben Jonson."

Jonson was a distinguished scholar, as his plays show. In them he attacks human gullibility, exposes social abuses, scores the follies of the day, and satirizes the baseness of human nature. He pokes fun at the absurd fashions of the times by means of exaggerated characters and situations in his plays. He is satirical rather than sympathetic. His best-known play, *Volpone,* has several times been revived in the present day. It tells of an old miser (his name means " The Fox ") who pretends to be dying in order to extract rich gifts from his greedy friends, who expect to be heirs. A less cynical side of Jonson is revealed in his poems, which are rich in appreciation of true beauty and nobility. " To Celia " is probably the only Elizabethan lyric well enough known to be sung by the general public today.

Title page, from an engraving, of the collected works of Ben Jonson, 1616.

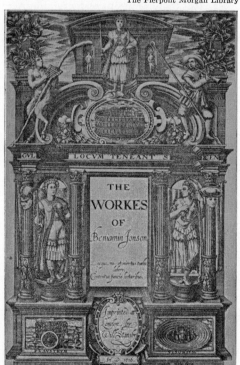

To Celia

Drink to me only with thine eyes,
    And I will pledge with mine;
Or leave a kiss but in the cup
    And I'll not look for wine.
The thirst that from the soul doth rise
    Doth ask a drink divine;   6
But might I of Jove's nectar° sup,
    I would not change for thine.

I sent thee late a rosy wreath,
    Not so much honoring thee   10
As giving it a hope that there
    It could not withered be;
But thou thereon didst only breathe
    And sent'st it back to me;
Since when it grows, and smells, I
    swear,   15
    Not of itself but thee!

7. *Jove's nectar:* the drink of the gods, a beverage of supernatural excellence.

The Noble Nature

It is not growing like a tree
In bulk, doth make Man better be;
Or standing long an oak, three hundred year,
To fall a log at last, dry, bald, and sere;
　　A lily of a day　　　　　　　　　　5
　　Is fairer far in May,
Although it fall and die that night —
It was the plant and flower of Light.
In small proportions we just beauties see;
And in short measures life may perfect be.　　10

To the Memory of My Beloved Master, William Shakespeare

To draw no envy, Shakespeare, on thy name,
Am I thus ample to thy book and fame;
While I confess thy writings to be such
As neither man nor muse can praise too much.
'Tis true, and all men's suffrage.° But these ways　　5
Were not the paths I meant unto thy praise;
For silliest° ignorance on these may light,
Which, when it sounds at best, but echoes right;
Or blind affection, which doth ne'er advance
The truth, but gropes, and urgeth all by chance;　　10
Or crafty malice might pretend this praise,
And think to ruin, where it seemed to raise. . . .
But thou art proof against them, and, indeed,
Above the ill fortune of them, or the need.
I therefore will begin. Soul of the age,　　15
The applause, delight, the wonder of our stage,
My Shakespeare, rise! I will not lodge thee by
Chaucer, or Spenser, or bid Beaumont lie
A little further, to make thee a room.
Thou art a monument without a tomb,　　20
And art alive still while thy book doth live,
And we have wits to read and praise to give. . . .

　　Several lines which are omitted here point out the superiority of Shakespeare to other dramatists of his day and compare him with a number of classical poets of antiquity. This passage contains the famous line: "He was not of an age, but for all time."

Or, for the laurel, he may gain a scorn;
For a good poet's made, as well as born.
And such wert thou; look how the father's face　　25
Lives in his issue, even so the race
Of Shakespeare's mind and manners brightly shines

5. *suffrage:* vote; decision. 7. *silliest:* simplest, most innocent. In Elizabethan times, the adjective *silly* meant simply "rustic" or "plain."

In his well turnèd and true filèd° lines,
In each of which he seems to shake a lance,°
As brandished at the eyes of ignorance.   30
Sweet Swan of Avon! what a sight it were
To see thee in our waters yet appear,
And make those flights upon the banks of Thames,
That so did take Eliza and our James!°
But stay, I see thee in the hemisphere   35
Advanced, and made a constellation there!
Shine forth, thou Star of poets, and with rage
Or influence chide or cheer the drooping stage,
Which, since thy flight from hence, hath mourned like night,
And despairs day, but for thy volume's light.   40

28. *filèd:* polished. 29. *shake a lance:* probably a pun on Shakespeare's name. 34. That so did please Queen Elizabeth and King James.

A POET OF MANY MOODS

1. You will enjoy hearing " To Celia " in a musical setting. Try to obtain a recording of it or encourage one of your group to sing it as a solo.

2. How would you describe in your own words the central thought of " The Noble Nature "? Look carefully at Jonson's choice of words. What picture is called to mind by line 4? What figure of speech did the poet use throughout the poem?

3. What is revealed about Jonson in his memorial tribute to Shakespeare? In what specific ways does he describe Shakespeare's greatness as a poet and dramatist?

FOR WRITING

These three poems by Jonson show different sides of his personality. Write a short essay on him as a person and a writer.

FRANCIS BACON 1561–1626

He was " the wisest, brightest, meanest of mankind," said the eighteenth-century poet Alexander Pope of Francis Bacon. Another picture of him is given by his contemporary, Ben Jonson: " He seemed to me ever, by his work, one of the greatest men, and most worthy of admiration that had been in many ages." All in all, Francis Bacon was a remarkable man, if a contradictory character. He was a scholar of tremendous learning and, as he said, took all knowledge for his province. He represents the first union in English literature of the man of letters and the man of science. He was, besides, an ambitious politician.

Until he was nineteen, Bacon had no financial worries. His father was Lord Keeper of the Seal to Queen Elizabeth, his mother a highborn lady known for her scholarship in Latin and Greek. When he was but twelve years old, Bacon went to Cambridge University; but he soon left, denouncing the educational system because it failed to challenge his mind. He then turned to travel, private study, and law. When his father died, Bacon found himself without funds. He resorted to moneylenders for help, and for the rest of his life he was hounded by creditors.

Bacon was not content to be a man of

Of Studies

FRANCIS BACON

letters and learning. He had political ambitions and sought to gain Queen Elizabeth's favor, without much success. When King James ascended to the throne, however, Bacon's star rose rapidly. He became Lord Chancellor and was titled a baron and viscount. But he had enemies in court and was soon convicted of accepting bribes, banished from Parliament, fined, and imprisoned. Although he remained in prison but two days, his political career was at an end. He devoted the remainder of his life to writing and to scientific experiment.

Francis Bacon is regarded as the first essayist in English literature. Much of his writing is philosophical, expressing his concern with men's understanding of themselves and the world they live in. One of his books, *The Advancement of Learning*, is a treatise about the divisions of knowledge. His essays cover a wide range of subjects, from such personal matters as " marriage and single life " to such abstractions as " truth." Bacon wrote more often in Latin than in English. His style in English, although sometimes difficult or obscure, is nevertheless full of grace and power.

STUDIES serve for delight, for ornament, and for ability. Their chief use for delight is in privateness and retiring; for ornament, is in discourse; and for ability, is in the judgment and disposition of business. For expert men [1] can execute, and perhaps judge of particulars, one by one; but the general counsels, and the plots and marshaling of affairs, come best from those that are learned. To spend too much time in studies is sloth; to use them too much for ornament is affectation; to make judgment wholly by their rules is the humor [2] of a scholar. They perfect nature, and are perfected by experience; for natural abilities are like natural plants, that need pruning by study; and studies themselves do give forth direction too much at large, except they be bounded in by experience. Crafty men [3] contemn studies, simple men admire them,[4] and wise men use them; for they teach not their own use; but that is a wisdom without them, and above them, won by observation. Read not to contradict and confute; nor to believe and take for granted; nor to find talk and discourse; but to weigh and consider. Some books are to be tasted, others to be swallowed, and some few to be chewed and digested; that is, some books are to be read only in parts; others to be read, but not curiously; [5] and

[1] *expert men:* men of practical skill and experience, as opposed to men of theoretical book learning.

[2] *humor:* in the Elizabethan sense, whim or disposition.

[3] *Crafty men:* men skilled in crafts, similar to "expert men."

[4] *simple men admire them:* unlettered men wonder at them.

[5] *curiously:* thoroughly and carefully; with great attention.

some few to be read wholly, and with diligence and attention. Some books also may be read by deputy, and extracts made of them by others; but that would be only in the less important arguments, and the meaner sort of books; else distilled books are like common distilled waters, flashy [1] things. Reading maketh a full man; conference a ready man; and writing an exact man. And therefore, if a man write little, he had need have a great memory; if he confer little, he had need have a present wit; and if he read little, he had need have much cunning, to seem to know that [2] he doth not. Histories make men wise; poets witty; the mathematics subtile; natural philosophy deep; moral grave; logic and rhetoric able to contend. *Abeunt studia in mores.*[3] Nay, there is no stond [4] or impediment in the wit but may be wrought out by fit studies; like as diseases of the body may have appropriate exercises. Bowling is good for the stone and reins; [5] shooting for the lungs and breast; gentle walking for the stomach; riding for the head; and the like. So if a man's wit be wandering, let him study the mathematics; for in demonstrations, if his wit be called away never so little, he must begin again. If his wit be not apt to distinguish or find differences, let him study the Schoolmen; [6] for they are *cymini sectores.* If he be not apt to beat over matters, and to call up one thing to prove and illustrate another, let him study the lawyers' cases. So every defect of the mind may have a special receipt.

[1] *flashy:* insipid.

[2] *that:* that which.

[3] *Abeunt . . . mores:* "Studies are turned into habits."

[4] *stond:* obstacle.

[5] *stone and reins:* "stone," the old name for a disease of the kidneys ("reins").

[6] *Schoolmen:* medieval scholars who were hairsplitters, or, as Bacon says in the Latin phrase following, splitters of cuminseeds in their prolonged arguments.

AN ELIZABETHAN STUDENT

1. In your own words give Bacon's definition of a scholar. Can you add to this definition? What does Bacon consider the main purposes of study? From your own experience, judging things in the light of the modern world, discuss Bacon's viewpoint pro and con. Do you agree with him that the study of a particular subject will have a specific effect on one's mind?

2. Name books that fall into each class of reading mentioned in Bacon's essay. Which type do you read most frequently? Can you add anything to the list Bacon gives of the *objectives* and *results* of reading?

SUGGESTION FOR WRITING

Try writing an essay of your own in Bacon's style — direct, concrete sentences marshaled one after another without particular attention to paragraphing or transitions. In 100 or 200 words take up a subject, such as athletics, schooling, or dating, about which you have personal opinions.

THE POWER OF WORDS

PREFIXES AND ROOTS

Bacon uses several words with the prefixes " con " and " contra " in talking about exchanging ideas. " Read not to contradict or confute," he says. In *contradict* the root is *dict,* to speak; the prefix is *contra,* against. When you contradict, you speak against another speaker. There is no suggestion in the word as to which view is the right one. But if you *confute* (prefix *con,* with or together; root *fute,* to make worthless), you prove that your side is right and the other is worthless.

Bacon says " conference maketh a ready man." We would probably express it, " Conversation makes a quick-witted man." Today *conference* is a more formal way of speaking together than Bacon probably meant. Look up its origin for an exact meaning of the word. How could you, during a *conference, contradict* another person or *confute* him by *refuting* his arguments? What is the difference between *confute* and *refute?*

The King James Bible

For many centuries the Bible was in Latin and was therefore unknown to the ordinary English people. During the Middle Ages they depended upon the miracle and mystery plays or upon the translation of the Bible by Wyclif (the first in English) for enlightenment. Then came William Tyndale (tǐn′dăl), fired with a desire to bring the Bible to everyone, even "the boy that driveth the plow." However, religious wars and conflicts cut short his work of translating and made a martyr of him. Miles Coverdale later issued a translation, based partly on Tyndale's; and he supervised the preparation of the Great Bible, which in 1540 was finally established in all the churches.

During the reign of King James I the need for a still better translation was recognized. Fifty-four scholars and churchmen assembled and worked for seven years to complete the King James Bible — perhaps the most familiar version among Protestants, although many other translations have since been made. The King James Version retains the vigor of the original Tyndale translation but is more poetic and colorful in language. Probably no other single book has had greater influence upon English literature than this translation of the Bible. Its literary value lies in its variety and wealth of material, written in a style that is stately and simple, direct and sometimes poetic.

The Prodigal Son

(*A Short Story*)

LUKE 15:11–32

A CERTAIN man had two sons. And the younger of them said to his father, "Father, give me the portion of goods that falleth to me." And he divided unto them his living.

And not many days after, the younger son gathered all together and took his journey into a far country, and there wasted his substance with riotous living. And when he had spent all, there arose a mighty famine in that land, and he began to be in want. And he went and joined himself to a citizen of that country, and he sent him into his fields to feed swine. And he would fain have filled his belly with the husks that the swine did eat, and no man gave unto him.

And when he came to himself, he said, "How many hired servants of my father's have bread enough and to spare, and I perish with hunger! I will arise and go to my father, and will say to him, 'Father, I have sinned against Heaven and before thee, and am no more worthy to be called thy son. Make me as one of thy hired servants.'"

And he arose and came to his father. But when he was yet a great way off, his father saw him and had compassion, and ran, and fell on his neck, and kissed him. And the son said unto him. "Father, I have sinned against Heaven and in thy sight and am no more worthy to be called thy son."

But the father said to his servants, "Bring forth the best robe and put it on him; and put a ring on his hand, and shoes on his feet; and bring hither the fatted calf, and kill it; and let us eat, and be merry. For this my son was dead and is alive again; he was lost, and is found." And they began to be merry.

Now his elder son was in the field; and as he came and drew nigh to the house, he heard music and dancing. And he called one of the servants and asked what these things meant. And he said unto him, "Thy brother is come, and thy father has killed the fatted calf, because he hath received him safe and sound."

And he was angry and would not go in; therefore came his father out and entreated him. And he answering said to his father, " Lo, these many years do I serve thee, neither transgressed I at any time thy commandment; and yet thou never gavest me a kid, that I might make merry with my friends. But as soon as this thy son was come, which hath devoured thy living, thou has killed for him the fatted calf."

And he said unto him, " Son, thou art ever with me, and all that I have is thine. It was meet that we should make merry and be glad, for this thy brother was dead, and is alive again; and was lost, and is found."

But the Greatest

of These Is Charity

(*An Essay*)

I CORINTHIANS 13

THOUGH I speak with the tongues of men and of angels and have not charity,[1] I am become as sounding brass or a tinkling cymbal. And though I have the gift of prophecy, and understand all mysteries, and all knowledge; and though I have all faith, so that I could remove mountains, and have not charity, I am nothing. And though I bestow all my goods to feed the poor, and though I give my body to be burned, and have not charity, it profiteth me nothing.

Charity suffereth long and is kind; charity envieth not; charity vaunteth not itself, is not puffed up; doth not behave itself unseemly, seeketh not her own, is not easily provoked, thinketh no

[1] *charity:* Throughout this essay, "charity" is used in the old sense of "love" rather than its more modern sense of "almsgiving." The modern revised versions usually substitute the word "love."

evil, rejoiceth not in iniquity, but rejoiceth in the truth; beareth all things, believeth all things, hopeth all things, endureth all things. Charity never faileth; but whether there be prophecies, they shall fail; whether there be tongues, they shall cease; whether there be knowledge, it shall vanish away. For we know in part,[2] and we prophesy in part.

But when that which is perfect is come, then that which is in part shall be done away. When I was a child, I spake as a child, I understood as a child, I thought as a child; but when I became a man I put away childish things. For now we see through a glass darkly, but then face to face; now I know in part, but then shall I know even as also I am known.

And now abideth faith, hope, charity, these three; but the greatest of these is charity.

The Ideal Wife

(*An Essay*)

PROVERBS 31

WHO CAN find a virtuous woman? For her price is far above rubies. The heart of her husband doth safely trust in her, so that he shall have no need of spoil. She will do him good and not evil all the days of her life. She seeketh wool, and flax, and worketh willingly with her hands. She is like the merchants' ships; she bringeth her food from afar. She riseth also while it is yet night, and giveth meat to her household, and a portion to her maidens. She considereth a field, and buyeth it; with the fruit of her hands she planteth a vineyard. She girdeth her loins with strength, and strengtheneth her arms. She perceiveth that her merchandise is good; her candle goeth

[2] *in part:* imperfectly.

not out by night. She layeth her hands to the spindle, and her hands hold the distaff. She stretcheth out her hand to the poor; yea, she reacheth forth her hands to the needy. She is not afraid of the snow for her household, for all her household are clothed with scarlet. She maketh herself coverings of tapestry; her clothing is silk and purple. Her husband is known in the gates, when he sitteth among the elders of the land. She maketh fine linen, and selleth it; and delivereth girdles unto the merchant. Strength and honor are her clothing, and she shall rejoice in time to come. She openeth her mouth with wisdom, and in her tongue is the law of kindness. She looketh well to the ways of her household, and eateth not the bread of idleness. Her children arise up, and call her blessed; her husband also, and he praiseth her. Many daughters have done virtuously, but thou excellest them all. Favor is deceitful, and beauty is vain, but a woman that feareth the Lord, she shall be praised. Give her of the fruit of her hands, and let her own works praise her in the gates.

Lyric Poems

The Bible is full of rich and beautiful lyric poetry, especially the Psalms. They do not *look* like poetry as the Bible is usually printed. Ancient Hebrew poetry did not have the rhyme or the regular patterns of accented and unaccented syllables of the poetry we read today. Its rhythm is based largely on questions and answers and on repetitions of an idea with slightly different phrasing. The translators of the King James Version were wise enough not to try to squeeze this poetry into an English style, but let it speak for itself in flowing rhythms.

The two psalms here given represent entirely different moods. The first expresses quiet confidence in the protection of God even in the midst of danger and trouble. The second is an exuberant hymn of praise to God, as the multitudes approach the great temple. It is possible to think of it as being sung by two great choruses, one asking the questions, the other answering. It seems to demand the magnificent accompaniment of cymbals and trumpets.

Psalm 121

I will lift up mine eyes unto the hills,
From whence cometh my help.
My help cometh from the Lord,
Which made heaven and earth.
He will not suffer thy foot to be moved;
He that keepeth thee will not slumber.
Behold, he that keepeth Israel
Shall neither slumber nor sleep.

The Lord is thy keeper;
The Lord is thy shade upon thy right hand.
The sun shall not smite thee by day,
Nor the moon by night.
The Lord shall preserve thee from all evil;
He shall preserve thy soul.
The Lord shall preserve thy going out and thy coming in
From this time forth, and even for evermore.

Psalm 24

The earth is the Lord's, and the fullness thereof;
The world, and they that dwell therein.
For he hath founded it upon the seas,
And established it upon the floods.
Who shall ascend into the hill of the Lord?   5
Or who shall stand in his holy place?
He that hath clean hands and a pure heart;
Who hath not lifted up his soul unto vanity, nor sworn deceitfully.
He shall receive the blessing from the Lord,
And righteousness from the God of his salvation.   10
This is the generation of them that seek him,
That seek thy face, O God of Jacob.

Lift up your heads, O ye gates;
And be ye lifted up, ye everlasting doors;
And the King of glory shall come in.   15
Who is the King of glory?
The Lord strong and mighty, the Lord mighty in battle.
Lift up your heads, O ye gates;
Even lift them up, ye everlasting doors;
And the King of glory shall come in.   20
Who is this King of glory?
The Lord of hosts, he is the King of glory.

FORM AND CONTENT

1. Why do you think the parable of "The Prodigal Son" is one of the best known and best loved in the New Testament? Just what is a parable? In what way was the father justified in acting as he did toward the two brothers? Do similar situations sometimes occur in modern families? What other famous parables do you know?

2. What is the importance of "charity" in a person's life? Which of the qualifications of charity as given in this essay are the hardest to live up to? What point does the author make about the place of childhood in life? What is the connection between this and charity? Is the word "charity" preferable to "love" in this selection? Why or why not?

3. Why are the Psalms poetry even though they lack regular meter and rhyme? For each Psalm, express in a sentence or two the main idea. Where do you find a striking use of contrast?

4. Read these selections in one or more of the revised versions of the Bible. Do you get a different understanding of any of them by so doing? Which versions do you like best?

SUGGESTIONS FOR WRITING

1. Write a dialogue between the Prodigal Son and the Elder Brother which might have taken place shortly after the former's return.

2. Write an essay on an ideal father, mother, teacher, or other type of person with whom you come in contact. Perhaps you may wish to give your style a Biblical touch; the style of "The Ideal Wife" is easy to imitate.

3. Choose some virtue other than "charity" and write a definition of its meaning and application to human life.

4. Write in free verse a short psalm of praise, petition, or mourning.

READING LIST FOR
THE ELIZABETHAN AGE

Anderson, Maxwell, *Elizabeth the Queen* and *Mary of Scotland*

These two plays about the famous cousins and rival queens are outstanding drama by a great American playwright.

Baker, Nina B., *Sir Walter Raleigh*

A biography with all the color and thrill of a novel, yet historically true throughout.

Barnes, Margaret C., *Brief Gaudy Hour* and *My Lady of Cleves*
Novels of two of Henry VIII's wives Ann Boleyn and Anne of Cleaves.

————, *Tudor Rose*
A sympathetic picture of Elizabeth, the Princess of York, who was married to the Lancastrian Henry VII to settle the Wars of the Roses. She was the grandmother of the first Queen Elizabeth.

Brady, Charles A., *Stage of Fools*
Sir Thomas More is pictured as a saint who suffers martyrdom for his beliefs. (Mature.)

Chidsey, Donald Barr, *Elizabeth I*
A short, briskly told story of Elizabeth as queen; the politics of her reign receives more attention than her personality. (Mature.)

Chute, Marchette, *Shakespeare's London*
Much research has made this not only an accurate book but also a readable one. Suppositions about Shakespeare are easily distinguished from proved facts.

Davis, William S., *Life in Elizabethan Days*
Excellent introduction to the period, showing a typical English community of the sixteenth century. (Mature.)

Delves-Broughton, Josephine, *The Heart of a Queen*
An excellent portrayal of Elizabeth, centering around her love for England, Dudley, and Essex.

Eyre, Katherine W., *Another Spring*
Pathetic story of Lady Jane Grey, who reigned for a few days on the English throne, and was beheaded for treason not of her own making.

Freemantle, Anne, *James and Joan*
Early life of James VI of Scotland before he became James I of England.

Goudge, Elizabeth, *Towers in the Mist*
Elizabeth and Lady Jane Grey before Elizabeth became queen.

Irwin, Margaret, series of four novels on different periods in the life of Queen Elizabeth:
Young Bess
Elizabeth, Captive Princess
The Gay Galliard
  Elizabeth and Mary of Scotland.
Elizabeth and the Prince of Spain
  Events leading up to the Spanish war.

Kingsley, Charles, *Westward Ho!*
An old favorite in which Raleigh, Drake, and other voyagers relive for you those exciting, often brutal, days on the high seas.

Letton, Jennette, and Letton, Francis, *Young Elizabeth*
Shows clearly all the conflicting forces around Elizabeth before she became queen.

Meadows, Denis, *Tudor Underground*
A stirring novel of the struggle of the Jesuits to restore Catholicism to Elizabethan England.

Michelson, Miriam, *Petticoat King*
How a woman monarch (Elizabeth) affected life in England.

Neale, J. E., *Queen Elizabeth*
Concise and readable biography.

Noyes, Alfred, " Forty Singing Seamen " and " Tales of the Mermaid Tavern " (both in his *Collected Poems*)
Narratives in verse told by famous persons of the period, the first by the voyagers, the second by the poets. (Mature.)

Scott, Sir Walter, *The Abbott*
About Mary Queen of Scots.

————, *Fortunes of Nigel*
When James I came to London he brought many Scottish followers who are graphically and humorously portrayed.

————, *Kenilworth*
Pictures vividly the Earl of Leicester's elaborate entertaining of Queen Elizabeth at Kenilworth castle, ending in a tragedy.

Shellabarger, Samuel, *The King's Cavalier*
Intrigue in the court of Henry VII.

Strachey, Lytton, *Elizabeth and Essex*
Excellent fictionalized biography showing Elizabeth's struggle between her determination to control her kingdom and her love for the Earl of Essex.

Twain, Mark, *The Prince and the Pauper*
Similarity of appearance causes the young prince Edward VI and a slum boy to exchange places. London conditions of that day are vividly pictured. (Easy reading.)

FOR LISTENING

The following selections have been recorded and are available on *Many Voices 6A:* " Who Is Silvia? " " Full Fathom Five," Shakespeare's sonnets 18, 73, 29, 55, and 116, *Macbeth:* Act I, Scene vii; Act V, Scene i; Act V, Scene v.

Parlament House   the Hall

THE SEVENTEENTH

CONTRASTED with Queen Elizabeth's reign, when feelings of national unity and patriotism prevailed, the seventeenth century was a period of turmoil. Before its end, Englishmen witnessed eight different " administrations " and four revolutions.

When Elizabeth, the last Tudor, died without a direct heir, the crown went to the son of Mary Queen of Scots, James I. Stuart monarchs ruled England for a little more than a century (1603–1714), except for the period of the Civil War and the Commonwealth (1642–1660). (The time of James' rule was included within the dates of the preceding Elizabethan period to avoid a break in the discussion of the careers of Shakespeare, Jonson, and Bacon.

In this turbulent era, men held partisan views that gave rise to open conflicts in politics, religion, and literature. The people experienced unrest and extreme disaster; at the same time they witnessed remarkable progress in art literature, and science. Let us look at some threads in the century's pattern

Westminster, now a part of London, is shown as it looked in 1647 from the opposite bank of Thames.

the Abby

CENTURY 1625-1700

POLITICAL TURMOIL

The arrogant and self-centered Charles I (1625–1649) clashed violently with his Parliament, made up of country squires and leading merchants. Charles tried to force the practices of the Church of England on the Scotch Presbyterians, and when Parliament countered his tyranny by refusing to vote him funds, he dismissed it and exacted heavy taxes in an illegal way. Discontent finally led to civil war in 1642.

Declaring allegiance to the king or to Oliver Cromwell's Parliamentary army was a difficult choice for many Englishmen. The tradition of the monarchy was strong; behind it stood the belief in the divine right of kings and the assumption that the king could do no wrong. Yet the Puritans, who had upheld the principle of freedom in religion, were now interested in civil freedom. They wanted a government more representative of the people — one that would be free from the willful tyrannies of a monarch. Many members of the old aristocracy and country landlords sided with the king's cause; they were called Royalists and Cavaliers. Cromwell's army of Roundheads (so

211

called because they cropped their hair short) claimed their support mainly from the middle classes and from the towns and cities.

Cromwell and his troops — called Ironsides because of their unyielding discipline — defeated the king's armies in 1646. Charles I was beheaded in 1649; the Commonwealth of England was set up; and Cromwell as Lord Protector ruled with relentless strictness until his death in 1658.

At Cromwell's death, his weak son Richard became ruler of the Commonwealth. The Stuart forces seized this opportunity to restore the monarchy, and Charles II was welcomed to the throne in 1660. His reign began the period called the Restoration, an elegant, flamboyant era in which the people, bored with serious-minded Puritan rule, turned to witty, frivolous pastimes.

In 1685, Charles was succeeded by his Catholic brother James II, whose attempts to force Catholicism on England ran counter to strong English prejudice. When rebellion broke out in 1688, Protestants petitioned James' daughter Mary and her Protestant husband William of Orange to come from Holland to take the throne. James fled to France, and William and Mary were made joint sovereigns of England. The Glorious Revolution of 1688 had ended without the loss of a single life.

This revolution resulted in more than an exchange of rulers. Parliament, before giving the crown to William and Mary, strengthened its position by drawing up a document comparable to the first ten amendments to our Constitution. This Bill of Rights safeguarded the rights of citizens by establishing a constitutional monarchy and by curbing the kingly power. England at last had achieved a stable government under law, a government which has never since been changed by violence.

THE LIFE OF THE TIME

While England's rulers were following one another in rapid succession, her ordinary citizens watched and participated in the excitement of the times. For a glimpse of life in those days, let us observe that memorable diarist, Mr. Samuel Pepys (1633–1703). Pepys seemed to know everyone and to go everywhere, and his diary gives us a lively, detailed account of the life of a Londoner during the early years of the Restoration.

Pepys was the fifth son of a tailor who, although his family had risen from yeoman farmers to the gentry, was unable to give his son much of a start in life. But Pepys was inquisitive and ambitious, and with help from scholarships, he worked his way through Cambridge. As a student he began to side with the Royalists. After 1660 his career prospered; he worked in the Navy office and finally became Secretary of the Admiralty. He observed shrewdly and relished to the utmost the gossip, the gaiety, and the frivolity of the court. He described the extravagant fashions in clothes, the many amusements of the day. He was devoted to music and the theater, and he was seriously interested in the work of scientific friends.

Political turmoil was not the only kind of disturbance that Pepys witnessed. A ravaging plague swept England in 1665, killing a quarter of the inhabitants of London. In the next year, the Great Fire of London occurred. That holocaust destroyed 13,000 inhabitants and many historic monuments, one of which was Saint Paul's Cathedral.

A CENTURY OF ADVANCE

One of the honors that Pepys enjoyed after his retirement was the presidency of the Royal Society. That body, founded in London in 1662, included both men of letters and brilliant scientists. One of the most notable of its members, Sir Isaac Newton, set forth the theory of gravity in his *Principia*. William Harvey discovered the secret of reproduction and the circulation of the blood. John Locke in his *Essay on the Human Understanding* established the modern principle that we form our ideas by reflecting on experience. What has become a great force in modern life was born: organized science.

Beginning with Francis Bacon, the seventeenth century was full of powerful intellects, many of whom devoted themselves to mathematics, philosophy, and literature. It was also an era of great music and great art. During the Restoration, the masque developed into the opera. Art helped to change the face of London. Sir Christopher Wren, England's greatest architect, started rebuilding Saint Paul's Cathedral. In addition, he built fifty-two beautiful churches in the growing city.

OLIVER CROMWELL

Metropolitan Museum of Art

RELIGIOUS CONFLICT

In religion, there was conflict first among Protestants themselves and later between Protestants and Catholics. Most of the king's supporters were members of the Church of England, or Anglicans. Opposed to them were the Puritans — a group of serious and independent Christians who wished to purify their religion of its worldly formality. The Puritans read their Bibles diligently, each making his own interpretation. They desired freedom to follow the dictates of conscience in the conduct of life and in the method of worship. Fundamentally Puritanism was a general attitude rather than a particular creed. Several modern Protestant denominations had their origins in this stern, ascetic way of life.

The power of the Puritans can hardly be overestimated: it led to the Pilgrims' settling in Massachusetts in 1620; it led to the overthrow of a government by regicide (king-killing). The Puritan spirit permeated literature, too; it inspired John Bunyan in prison, where he wrote *The Pilgrim's Progress,* a moving story of a man's journey toward salvation. John Milton, the greatest Puritan writer, was concerned with religious truth, politics, and freedom. He made the debate of the fallen angels in Hell into a kind of parliament in *Paradise Lost* and argued for freedom of the press in *Areopagitica.*

The Puritans split from the Anglicans, just as the Anglicans had separated from the Roman Catholics a century earlier; and the revolution of 1688 climaxed the current religious struggles.

LITERARY CURRENTS

In spite of controversy and civil war, men found time to write. The split of England into political camps was reflected in her literature. The lighthearted Cavalier poets illustrated in witty, graceful verse the devil-may-care attitudes of the court. Dramatists in the Stuart era guided the stage so far toward sensationalism that the theaters were closed after Cromwell came to power.

There were, however, serious writers, too. John Milton wrote in intricate, Latinized sentences about religion and philosophy; he also wrote some of the noblest poetry in our language. John Bunyan expressed the religious attitude of the working classes. Although Milton's *Paradise Lost* and Bunyan's *The Pilgrim's Progress* are considered the most important products of the Puritan spirit, they were both written after the fall of Cromwell's regime.

In a class by itself is Izaak Walton's famous book, *The Compleat Angler.* Walton seems to have taken some of his description of fishing technique from a recently discovered volume of the preceding century, but the bits of philosophy which make his book noteworthy are his own.

When Charles II set up his gay court, patterned after the French, the stern

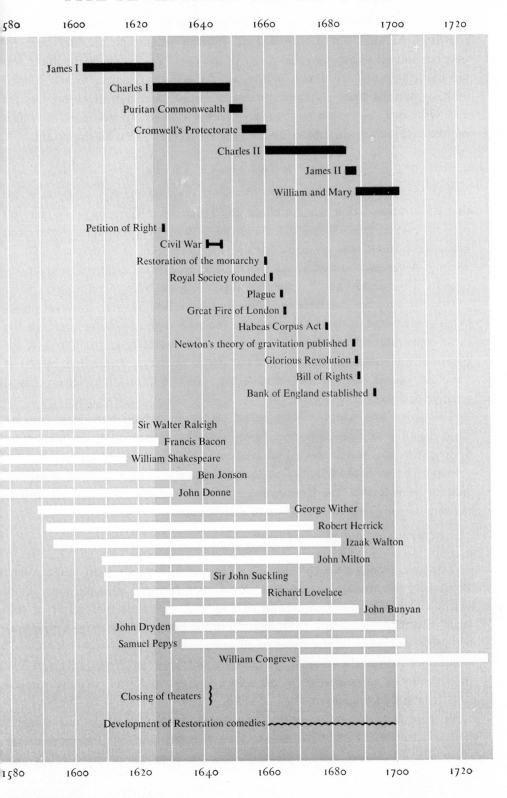

and gloomy Puritan regime seemed ended. In a funny, popular poem called *Hudibras,* Samuel Butler ridiculed all Puritan sects. The theaters were re-opened, and glittering comedies were all the rage. Their principal subject was the battle between the sexes, lightly, even cynically, treated. Grace seemed more important than goodness; manners outweighed morals. John Dryden and William Congreve helped to develop the comedy of manners, in which polished etiquette, witty dialogue, and the social code were all-important.

THE NEW PROSE STYLE

The period between 1660 and 1700 is often called the Age of Dryden, for that Restoration writer was, in effect, the father of modern prose. When you read his essays, you will see that he wrote with clarity, simplicity, order, and grace; he himself was proud of his age for developing a " correct " style of writing. A versatile writer, Dryden was a fine lyric poet, a satirist, a critic, an essayist, a translator, and a debater in verse on both politics and religion.

Other writers besides Dryden expressed themselves in clear, graceful prose. What contributed to the development of this new style of writing? Perhaps the most important influence was the growth of the scientific spirit. This was ap-parent in the writing of members of the Royal Society, all of whom aimed at " a close, naked, natural way of speaking; positive expressions, clear senses; a native easiness."

This spirit was fostered by a belief in reason, which had been growing since the time of Francis Bacon. Many remarkable men took an intellectual approach to life, and expressed themselves in clearly reasoned terms.

A third cause of the felicitous style of the age was delight in pleasing expres-sion for its own sake. The Restoration was interested in all forms of art, and its polished writing was an indication of this attitude.

SUMMARY

The seventeenth century was one of unrest and violence in many areas. Politically, the monarchy was overthrown, then restored after the stern inter-val of Cromwell's Commonwealth of England. An important result of this struggle was the constitutional limitation of the power of the king, with corre-sponding safeguards of the rights of citizens.

Religious turmoil — among Protestants and between Protestants and Ro-man Catholics — continued to stir men's feelings and was partially respon-sible for the Glorious Revolution of 1688.

In their daily life, ordinary Englishmen felt the impact of political and re-ligious struggles. Under Cromwell, they felt the serious, uncompromising spirit of the Puritans, only to be dazzled, a few years later, by the gaiety and extravagance of the Restoration. They were crushed, too, by the great disasters of plague and fire.

Music and the theater flourished; important advances in science were made. In literature, some of the greatest English writers appeared. Cavaliers, Puritans, and Restoration writers reflected the political temper of the times and expressed the intellectual curiosity of the age. A new prose style, lucid and graceful, foretold the trend of modern writing.

CAVALIER POETS

The lighter side of literature and life in the seventeenth century is reflected in the lyrics of the Cavalier poets. They sing of youth, love, happiness, and of beauty found in transient things; they take life as they find it — often with a mocking spirit.

ROBERT HERRICK (1591–1674) was probably the greatest of the Cavalier poets. He wrote more than fourteen hundred poems that reflect his sunny disposition, his gaiety of manner, and also his often cynical view of the world. Herrick loved people. As one of the company of wits and poets who called themselves "Sons of Ben," he spent carefree years in London. Then he took religious orders and became a vicar in Devonshire, where he found new enjoyment in the country festivals, feasts, and dances. Herrick was a strange clergyman, one whose love of nature and human pleasures was almost pagan. When the Commonwealth was established, Herrick lost his post, but with the restoration of Charles I in 1660, he returned to the vicarage to spend the rest of his life there.

GEORGE WITHER (1588–1667) was a curious combination of Cavalier and Puritan. Until the Civil War he apparently supported the Stuarts, and he wrote worldly poetry — love songs and pastoral lyrics. But he also wrote sharp social satires, and because of a poem attacking the government of Charles I, Wither was imprisoned for a long period. While in prison, he wrote an elaborate love poem containing the famous lyric "Shall I, Wasting in Despair."

On being released he became a serious-minded Puritan, serving in Cromwell's army as a major general. His later writings were rather uninspired hymns, psalms, and religious pamphlets.

SIR JOHN SUCKLING (1609–1642) was a dashing and gifted young man who was knighted at twenty-one and became a leader in the court of Charles I. After leaving Cambridge, Suckling led a furious life in London, gambling, joining other poets as a Son of Ben, and cutting an elegant figure as a cavalier to the king. At the age of thirty-three Suckling was forced to flee to France, where he died mysteriously. One story says he committed suicide on losing all his money; another suggests he was murdered by a revengeful servant. The most colorful of the Cavalier poets, Suckling portrays the superficial and flippant attitudes of Stuart court life.

RICHARD LOVELACE (1618–1658) was a gallant and handsome gentleman who spent his fortune and much of his time in prison for his king. He was born of a prominent and wealthy family and was educated at Oxford. For defending the deposed king, he was twice sent to prison, and while there composed a number of exquisite lyrics, including "To Althea, from Prison." Little is known of his last years, which were spent in poverty and obscurity. Lovelace's poetry and career are often paired with Suckling's. They were the perfect Cavaliers — brave soldiers, loyal courtiers, light of heart but sometimes satirical and mocking.

Counsel to Girls

ROBERT HERRICK

Gather ye rosebuds while ye may,
  Old Time is still° aflying:
And this same flower that smiles today,
  Tomorrow will be dying.

The glorious Lamp of Heaven, the Sun,
  The higher he's agetting   6
The sooner will his race be run,
  And nearer he's to setting.

That age is best which is the first,   9
  When youth and blood are warmer;
But being spent, the worse, and worst
  Times, still succeed the former.

Then be not coy, but use your time;
  And while ye may, go marry:
For having lost but once your prime,
  You may forever tarry.   16

2. *still:* always.

Shall I, Wasting in Despair

GEORGE WITHER

Shall I, wasting in despair,
Die, because a woman's fair?
Or make pale my cheeks with care,
'Cause another's rosy are?
Be she fairer than the day,
Or the flowery meads in May,
  If she be not so to me,
  What care I how fair she be?

Should my heart be grieved or pined,
'Cause I see a woman kind?   1
Or a well-disposèd nature
Joinèd with a lovely feature?
Be she meeker, kinder than
Turtle dove, or pelican,°
  If she be not so to me,   1
  What care I how kind she be?

Shall a woman's virtues move
Me to perish for her love?
Or her well-deserving known,
Make me quite forget mine own?   2
Be she with that goodness blest
Which may gain her name of best,
  If she be not such to me,
  What care I how good she be?

'Cause her fortune seems too high,   2
Shall I play the fool and die?
Those that bear a noble mind,
Where they want° of riches find,
Think, "What, with them, they would
  do
That, without them, dare to woo!"   3
  And unless that mind I see,
  What care I though great she be?

Great, or good, or kind, or fair,
I will ne'er the more despair!
If she love me (this believe!)   3
I will die, ere she shall grieve;
If she slight me when I woo,
I can scorn, and let her go;
  For if she be not for me,
  What care I for whom she be?   4

14. *pelican:* a bird which was believed to tea
open its breast in order to feed its offspring wit
its own blood. 28. *want:* lack.

The Constant Lover

SIR JOHN SUCKLING

Out upon it, I have loved
   Three whole days together!
And am like to love three more,
   If it prove fair weather.

Time shall molt away his wings   5
   Ere he shall discover
In the whole wide world again
   Such a constant lover.

But the spite on 't is, no praise
   Is due at all to me: 10
Love with me had made no stays,
   Had it any been but she.

Had it any been but she,
   And that very face,
There had been at least ere this   15
   A dozen dozen in her place.

Song FROM *Aglaura*°

SIR JOHN SUCKLING

Why so pale and wan, fond lover?
   Prithee, why so pale?
Will, when looking well can't move her,
   Looking ill prevail?
   Prithee, why so pale?   5

Why so dull and mute, young sinner?
   Prithee, why so mute?
Will, when speaking well can't win her,
   Saying nothing do 't?
   Prithee, why so mute?   10

Quit, quit for shame! This will not move;
   This cannot take her.
If of herself she will not love,
   Nothing can make her:
   The devil take her!   15

Title: *Aglaura* (à·glô'rá): a drama by Suckling, performed with great magnificence of scenery and costume at Blackfriars Theater.

To Althea,° from Prison

RICHARD LOVELACE

When Love with unconfinèd wings
   Hovers within my gates,
And my divine Althea brings
   To whisper at the grates;
When I lie tangled in her hair   5
   And fettered to her eye,
The birds that wanton° in the air
   Know no such liberty.

When flowing cups run swiftly round
   With no allaying Thames,°   10
Our careless heads with roses bound,
   Our hearts with loyal flames;
When thirsty grief in wine we steep,
   When healths and draughts go free —
Fishes that tipple in the deep   15
   Know no such liberty.

When, like committed linnets,° I
   With shriller throat shall sing
The sweetness, mercy, majesty,
   And glories of my king;°   20
When I shall voice aloud how good
   He is, how great should be,
Enlargèd° winds, that curl the flood,
   Know no such liberty.

Stone walls do not a prison make,   25
   Nor iron bars a cage;
Minds innocent and quiet take
   That for an hermitage;°
If I have freedom in my love
   And in my soul am free,   30
Angels alone, that soar above,
   Enjoy such liberty.

Title: *Althea* (ăl·thē'á). 7. *wanton* (wŏn'tŭn): play about. 9–10. *cups ... Thames:* wine undiluted with water (from the river Thames). 17. *committed linnets:* caged birds. 20. *my king:* Charles I, in whose service Lovelace was "committed" to prison. Notice that his punishment did not dampen his enthusiasm for the king. 23. *Enlargèd:* set free or released. 27–28 *Minds ... hermitage:* Even a prison may be suitable for quiet meditation.

To Lucasta,° on Going to the Wars

RICHARD LOVELACE

Tell me not, sweet, I am unkind,
   That from the nunnery
Of thy chaste breast and quiet mind
   To war and arms I fly.

True, a new mistress now I chase,   5
   The first foe in the field;
And with a stronger faith embrace
   A sword, a horse, a shield.

Yet this inconstancy is such
   As you, too, shall adore;   10
I could not love thee, dear, so much,
   Loved I not honor more.

Title: *Lucasta* (lū·kăs′tà).

LIGHT AND COURTLY LYRICS

1. How does Herrick's point of view in "Counsel to Girls" accord with what you learned about Herrick on page 217?

2. "The Constant Lover" professes a lighthearted, even cynical attitude toward love. Do you find any evidence that this outward cynicism actually conceals a genuine emotion?

3. In "To Althea," what three kinds of liberty are described? Note in the first three stanzas the comparison with something in nature. In what ways is the choice appropriate for each stanza? How does the fourth stanza form a climax to the three stanzas that precede it?

4. What subtle compliment does Lovelace pay Lucasta in the last stanza of the poem addressed to her? The last two lines summarize a Cavalier view of life. Why would this declaration be especially pleasing to a Cavalier lady?

5. Do you see any relation between the verse of Herrick and Lovelace and that of Ben Jonson? How would you compare and contrast the Elizabethan and Cavalier attitudes toward love, liberty, war, and duty? Is there a difference between the mood and the singing quality of lyrics in the two periods?

6. Do you notice a difference in spirit between Lovelace's poems and those of Wither and Suckling? Which poet is most sincere?

7. What conclusion about the times do you draw from the fact that four of the seventeenth century's best-known writers — Wither, Lovelace, Suckling, and John Bunyan — were imprisoned at various periods? What effect would such times have on the production of literature?

8. Find additional Cavalier lyrics by these and other poets in an anthology like Palgrave's *Golden Treasury* for reading aloud in class or for recording.

9. What modern writers of light satiric verse do you know?

JOHN DONNE 1573–1631

The Puritans were not the only religious writers of the seventeenth century. A group of Anglican poets, led by John Donne (dŭn), wrote intense poems that explore the intellectual and spiritual side of man. They were fond of writing an elaborate kind of verse, with farfetched and exaggerated figures of speech and an extravagant form of statement, called hyperbole (hī·pēr′bō·lē).

John Donne is more praised today than he was in any previous time. He is considered by some modern critics one of the great poets in English, although others complain that he twists both language and thought to an extreme. Donne was a nonconformist in literature. While the Elizabethans wrote of faithfulness in love, he praised inconstancy; while they celebrated beauty in life, Donne explored the dark paths of the mind; and while they depended on a fairly regular rhythm in verse, he varied lines, meter, and accent whenever he felt it necessary.

After attending Oxford, Donne led a gay, worldly life in London. He went on a military expedition to Spain and on his return was imprisoned for a time. Though he was born a Roman Catholic, later he was converted to the Church of England and became Dean of St. Paul's Cathedral, where he was famous as the most eloquent preacher of the day. His early poems are in the cynical, mundane vein of Cavalier writing; later he turned to metaphysical or philosophical themes.

Death Be Not Proud

Death be not proud, though some have called thee
Mighty and dreadful, for thou art not so;
For those whom thou think'st thou dost overthrow
Die not, poor Death; nor yet canst thou kill me.
From Rest and Sleep, which but thy picture be,   5
Much pleasure; then from thee much more must flow;
And soonest our best men with thee do go —
Rest of their bones and souls' delivery!

Thou 'rt slave to Fate, chance, kings, and desperate men,
And dost with poison, war, and sickness dwell;   10
And poppy° or charms can make us sleep as well
And better than thy stroke. Why swell'st° thou then?
One short sleep past, we wake eternally,
And Death shall be no more; Death, thou shalt die!

11. *poppy:* opium. 12. *swell'st:* that is, with pride.

A PHILOSOPHICAL POET

1. What reasons does Donne give for believing Death to be weak instead of powerful? How is Sleep a "picture" of Death? In what sense will Death "die"?

2. Can you describe the verse form of this poem? Compare it for rhyme scheme with one of Shakespeare's poems on pages 124–27.

"For whom the bell tolls" is a phrase that you know as the title of a novel by Ernest Hemingway; did you know that it is a quotation from Donne? Look up the beautiful prose statement from which it comes, Meditation 17 in Devotions upon Emergent Occasions, *and read it aloud.*

THE GROWTH OF THE ENGLISH LANGUAGE

The Seventeenth Century

During the seventeenth century the sovereigns of England were members of the Stuart family — and the Stuarts were always strongly influenced by the French. Mary Queen of Scots, from whom the Stuarts were descended, spent her girlhood days in France as the wife of the French dauphin, who died in 1560. France wielded a stronger influence on English language and literature during the seventeenth century than it had since the last part of the medieval period.

The Cavalier poets show simplicity of wording, neatness of pattern, and sophistication of tone, all of which are characteristic of the French manner of expression. Playwriting, too, illustrates a marked shift in style. Early in the century, before the Puritans closed the theaters in 1642, plays were closely akin to Elizabethan drama — extravagant and colorful. Ben Jonson, however, in his devotion to the classical unities of time, place, and action, foreshadowed the comedies which followed the reopening of the theaters in 1660. Restoration plays might violate the code of morals, but never the code that prescribed a closely woven plot, wit, and worldliness.

Not all poetry followed French models. John Milton, greatest poet of the century, was a belated Elizabethan. His earlier poems continued the pastoral tradition of Spenser's *Shepherd's Calendar*. If *Paradise Lost* (page 233) whirls us into great spaces beyond the stars, we recall that Spenser's Faerie Queene lived in a sort of never-never land.

Prose style also wore two faces. Milton's prose showed the results of intensive study of Latin. The modern reader can easily get lost in Milton's involved sentences, or weaken under his steady barrage of big words (Latin derivatives, of course). This ponderous style was not confined to Milton but was used by many theologians and scholars.

In the second half of the century we meet Dryden, who sensed that English speech was now quite different from what it had been a hundred years before. Many obsolete words and affectations had been trimmed off. Sentence structure had been greatly simplified. In his hands English became a precise instrument of thinking, more like French than like Latin. As he was practically a literary dictator in his day, Dryden's style was influential in forming the prose style of our own time, as well as that of the seventeenth century. His essay on page 256, except for a few archaic words, might well be a product of our own day.

A third style might be called Biblical prose because it resulted from the widespread reading of the King James Version of the Bible, published at the beginning of the century. This was the one book of distinctive style read by the common people, and, like Shakespeare's writings, it has enriched our speech by phrase after phrase. Here are some which you must have heard used entirely outside religious situations:

balm in Gilead
beat their swords into plowshares
sow the wind and reap the whirlwind
whited sepulchers full of dead men's bones
a house divided against itself

heap coals of fire on his head
thorn in the flesh
escaped with the skin of my teeth
the apple of his eye
a man after his own heart

The Bible added an element of dignity and beauty to the writing of many who had never darkened the doors of Oxford and Cambridge. The best example of this style in this volume is the selection from Bunyan's *The Pilgrim's Progress* (page 240). It is amazing that a totally uneducated tinker could produce a tale that has probably influenced more people than any other one book except the Bible. Bunyan used many of the older Saxon words, now on their way out, such as *befell, hubbub, runagate, cheapen* (to buy), *rabblement;* but side by side with them appear many Latin derivatives: *ignominy, commotion, heretic,* and *celestial.*

New words were flowing into the language from various sources. With colonists flocking to America in great numbers, the small trickle of Spanish and American Indian words, noted in the preceding chapter, had grown into a rapid stream. Englishmen learned the meanings of *maize, tepee, canoe, squaw, papoose, chipmunk,* and countless others. Little did the Londoner realize that these outlandish words were just the beginning of a significant cleavage between English and American vocabulary, spelling, punctuation, idiom, and slang. Separate dictionaries became necessary eventually, and books came to be written about the American language.

Commercial rivalry, too, made its mark on the language. Even in the Middle Ages the Low Countries had attained a place of importance in navigation and trade. You remember that Chaucer's Wife of Bath could weave as well as the women of Flanders — a great distinction, for weaving was a specialty of the Low Countries. Many terms used in weaving come to us from the Dutch language: *curl, spool, stripe, tuck.* When Charles I got England into an unpopular war with Holland, one result of the encounters on the sea was that we acquired *bowsprit, freight,* and *keel* from the Dutch. More recently we continued the list with *dock, yacht,* and *yawl.*

In contrast to the words needed for business dealings, came a whole new vocabulary in the realm of music. Toward the end of the century Italian music swept London off its feet. With Italian musical styles came musical terms which have never left our language and are familiar to all students and lovers of music today: *opera, aria, oratorio, soprano, contralto, allegro, piano, fortissimo, sonata, cantata.* Look up the derivation of some of them.

Largo came from the same Latin root as *large,* but the two words entered our language five hundred years apart. *Large* came through the Norman French and is first recorded in English in 1175; *largo* came through the Italian and is first mentioned in 1683. One could find many examples of these " word immigrants " to English, some of which " came over on the *Mayflower* " while others are newly arrived.

JOHN MILTON 1608–1674

Milton is known as the foremost Puritan in literature. But the word " Puritan " is often misleading, especially for Americans. Too often we think of the Puritans as black-frocked, joy-killing people who went about with gloomy thoughts and were given to witch hunting. Such a picture certainly does not fit John Milton, who took great pleasure in living and in art and who defended freedom for all.

When the *Mayflower* set sail for America in 1620, John Milton was twelve years old. He was reared in a well-to-do merchant's home, where the culture of the Renaissance was combined with the righteous life of the Puritans. His father was indulgent, allowing him time to read and study as he wished. John inherited from him the love for music that is reflected in his poetry. At Cambridge Milton won the esteem of his fellow students for his skill in fencing and

debating, and his last years there were happy ones.

Milton's life seems to revolve around three great decisions. At the university his first critical decision was to give up the idea of taking orders in the Anglican Church, as his family had planned. After taking his master's degree he lived quietly at his father's home in Horton, near London, writing some of his beautiful poems, including the elegy " Lycidas " and the masque *Comus*.

Then came two years of travel on the Continent, suddenly interrupted by news of trouble at home. He was forced to make a second important decision. With civil war threatening England, Milton felt he must return home to help the Puritan cause. He became a vigorous, hard-hitting pamphleteer. The times were rough and Milton used his literary weapons well, championing freedom and order in government and the personal rights of men.

A third decision had to be made when Milton found himself threatened by blindness. His early years of constant study had weakened his eyesight and now he was in danger of losing his sight entirely. Giving up his work might have saved him from this, but the call of duty was powerful. Charles I had been beheaded; Europe was aghast and even Englishmen themselves were terrified by the deed. Milton, as Cromwell's Latin Secretary, was left with the job of defending the course of the Commonwealth. While writing tracts, at the age of forty-four, he went completely blind.

The last ten years of Milton's life were marked by tragedy. The restoration of the Stuarts destroyed everything he had fought for; at the height of his literary powers he was blind and helpless; his family life was unsettled. Milton's first wife, with whom he had lived unhappily, died and left him with three small girls. For a time he attempted to bring them up alone, but presently he married again. His second wife died shortly after their marriage. Finally, a third wife, who long outlived him, brought him comfort and security.

L'Allegro AND Il Penseroso

All of us are creatures of moods that color our thinking and our responses to the passing world. There are times when we enjoy the amusing companionship of friends, the noise of holiday crowds, laughter, lively music, dancing, exciting stories — the lighter things of life. Other times we feel less active and want to be alone, quiet, thoughtful. At such times we need music or reading that harmonizes with our pensive mood.

" L'Allegro " and " Il Penseroso " are twin poems that capture and contrast the moods of the cheerful man and the thoughtful man, as the Italian titles indicate. In the first title you will recognize the musical term *allegro*, meaning " quick " or " lively "; and in the second, you may detect the root for the word " pensive." In the first poem the poet addresses Mirth as a gay, dancing nymph and asks her to accompany him in the sunlit fields of the country. In the second poem, he dismisses

" vain, deluding joys " and welcomes Melancholy, who is pictured as a nun, to be with him in the nightly solitude of his study. However, Milton does not speak of melancholy as a sorrowful thing but rather as a pleasantly reflective turn of mind. We can imagine that he himself enjoyed both moods at his country place at Horton, where he took part in the pastoral life, and where also he was able to shut himself up with his books.

It was the custom in Milton's day to introduce lyrics like these with a display of allusions to the classics. The opening lines of each poem, crammed with mythological references, have been omitted here.

L'Allegro

Haste thee, nymph, and bring with thee
Jest, and youthful Jollity,
Quips and cranks° and wanton wiles,°
Nods and becks and wreathèd smiles,
Such as hang on Hebe's° cheek,   5
And love to live in dimple sleek;
Sport that wrinkled Care derides,
And Laughter holding both his sides.
Come, and trip it as you go,
On the light fantastic toe;   10
And in thy right hand lead with thee
The mountain nymph, sweet Liberty;
And if I give thee honor due,
Mirth, admit me of thy crew,
To live with her, and live with thee,   15
In unreprovèd° pleasures free:

[COUNTRY SCENE AT MORN]

To hear the lark begin his flight,
And singing, startle the dull night,
From his watchtower in the skies,
Till the dappled dawn doth rise;   20
Then to come in spite of sorrow,
And at my window bid good morrow,
Through the sweetbrier or the vine,
Or the twisted eglantine;°

3. *cranks:* twists or turns in speech; *wanton wiles:* playful tricks. 5. *Hebe* (hē′bē): cupbearer to the Greek gods. 16. *unreprovèd:* not deserving of censure. 24. *eglantine* (ĕg′lăn·tīn): honeysuckle.

While the cock, with lively din,   25
Scatters the rear of darkness thin,
And to the stack, or the barn door,
Stoutly struts his dames before:
Oft listening how the hounds and horn°
Cheerly rouse the slumbering morn,   30
From the side of some hoar hill,
Through the high wood echoing shrill;
Sometime walking, not unseen,
By hedgerow elms,° on hillocks green,
Right against the eastern gate   35
Where the great sun begins his state,°
Robed in flames and amber light,
The clouds in thousand liveries dight;°
While the plowman, near at hand,
Whistles o'er the furrowed land,   40
And the milkmaid singeth blithe,
And the mower whets his scythe,
And every shepherd tells his tale°
Under the hawthorn° in the dale.
Straight mine eye hath caught new
          pleasures   45
Whilst the landskip° round it measures:
Russet lawns and fallows gray,
Where the nibbling flocks do stray;

Mountains on whose barren breast
The laboring clouds do often rest;   50
Meadows trim with daisies pied,°

29. *hounds and horn:* of hunters. 34. *hedgerow elms:* elm trees planted in rows for enclosure or separation of fields. 36. *state:* stately progress. 38. This line pictures the clouds dressed (*dight:* dīt) in colors from the sun, as servants are clothed in *liveries* by their master. 43. *tells his tale:* counts his sheep. 44. *hawthorn:* a tree or shrub with shiny leaves and white or pink fragrant flowers. 46. *landskip:* landscape. 51. *pied* (pīd): of two or more colors.

Shallow brooks and river wide;
Towers and battlements it sees
Bosomed high in tufted trees,
Where perhaps some beauty lies,   55
The cynosure° of neighboring eyes.

[PLEASURES OF THE COUNTRY]

Hard by, a cottage chimney smokes
From betwixt two agèd oaks,
Where Corydon and Thyrsis° met
Are at their savory dinner set   60
Of herbs and other country messes,°
Which the neat-handed Phyllis dresses;
And then in haste her bower° she leaves,
With Thestylis to bind the sheaves;
Or, if the earlier season lead,   65
To the tanned haycock in the mead.
Sometimes, with secure delight,
The upland hamlets will invite,
When the merry bells ring round,
And the jocund rebecks° sound   70
To many a youth and many a maid
Dancing in the checkered shade;
And young and old come forth to play
On a sunshine holiday,
Till the livelong daylight fail: 75
Then to the spicy nut-brown ale,
With stories told of many a feat,
How faery Mab° the junkets° eat.
She° was pinched and pulled, she said;
And he, by friar's lantern° led,   80
Tells how the drudging goblin° sweat
To earn his cream bowl duly set,

56. *cynosure* (sī'nṓ-shōor): the center of attention. 59. *Corydon* (kŏr'ĭ-dŏn) *and Thyrsis* (thûr'sĭs): conventional names for rustics or shepherds in pastoral poetry, as *Phyllis* and *Thestylis* (thĕs'tĭ-lĭs), in lines 62 and 64, are for country maidens. 61. *messes:* dishes. 63. *bower:* a rustic cottage or room. 70. *jocund rebecks* (jŏk'ŭnd rē'bĕks): merry violins. 78. *faery Mab:* probably a fairy of Welsh folklore. (A famous description of how she brings dreams is in *Romeo and Juliet,* Act I, Scene iv, lines 53–95); *junkets:* delicate sweetmeats, often made of curdled milk. 79. *She:* one of the rustic maids. 80. *friar's lantern:* sometimes called "will-o'-the-wisp" or "friar's rush"; a dancing light on marshy ground, supposed to lead travelers astray. 81. *drudging goblin:* Robin Goodfellow, who supposedly did chores at night to earn the food put out for him.

When in one night, ere glimpse of morn,
His shadowy flail hath threshed the corn
That ten day laborers could not end;   85
Then lies him down, the lubber fiend,°
And, stretched out all the chimney's
    length
Basks at the fire his hairy strength,
And crop-full out of doors he flings,
Ere the first cock his matin° rings.   90
Thus done the tales, to bed they creep,
By whispering winds soon lulled asleep.

[PLEASURES OF THE CITY]

Towered cities please us then,
And the busy hum of men,
Where throngs of knights and barons
    bold,   95
In weeds° of peace high triumphs°
    hold,
With store of ladies, whose bright eyes
Rain influence,° and judge the prize
Of wits or arms, while both contend
To win her grace whom all commend.
There let Hymen° oft appear   101
In saffron robe, with taper clear,
And pomp and feast and revelry,
With mask and antique pageantry;
Such sights as youthful poets dream   105
On summer eves by haunted stream.
Then to the well-trod stage anon,
If Jonson's learnèd sock° be on.
Or sweetest Shakespeare, Fancy's child,
Warble his native wood-notes° wild.
And ever, against eating cares,°   111

86. *lubber fiend:* awkward sprite. 90. *matin:* a morning song, or call to early prayers. 96. *weeds:* garments; *triumphs:* public shows or pageants. 97–98. *whose . . . influence:* The stars were once thought to affect human action; hence, the bright eyes of the ladies are compared to stars. 101. *Hymen* (hī'mĕn): Greek god of marriage. The smoking of his torch or taper was considered a bad omen; hence, *with taper clear* (line 102) would signify a happy marriage. 108. *sock:* symbolic of comedy, as the buskin or boot is of tragedy. 110. *native wood-notes:* implying that Shakespeare's verse is as natural as the singing of a bird, in contrast with the more "learned" poetry of Jonson. 111. *against eating cares:* as a protection against worries which eat up one's vitality.

Lap me in soft Lydian airs,°
Married to immortal verse,
Such as the meeting° soul may pierce,°
In notes with many a winding bout   115
Of linkèd sweetness long drawn out,
With wanton heed and giddy cunning,
The melting voice through mazes run-
    ning,
Untwisting all the chains that tie
The hidden soul of harmony;   120
That Orpheus'° self may heave his head
From golden slumber on a bed
Of heaped Elysian flowers, and hear
Such strains as would have won the ear
Of Pluto to have quite set free   125
His half-regained Eurydice.
    These delights if thou canst give,
    Mirth, with thee I mean to live.

112. *Lydian* (lĭd'ĭ-ăn) *airs:* soft melodies. Lydian is the name of one of the "modes" (varieties) of ancient Greek music. 114. *meeting:* responsive; *pierce:* comprehend. 121. *Orpheus* (ôr'fē-ŭs): the most famous musician of Greek mythology, who persuaded Pluto, king of the dead, to release his dead wife, *Eurydice* (ū·rĭd'-ĭ-sē). The condition was that Orpheus should not look back while leading her to the upper world; but he forgot himself at the last minute, and so lost her completely.

Il Penseroso

Come, pensive Nun, devout and pure,
Sober, steadfast, and demure,
All in a robe of darkest grain,°
Flowing with majestic train,
And sable stole of cypress lawn°   5
Over thy decent shoulders drawn.

3. *grain:* dye. 5. *sable . . . lawn:* black veil of crape.

Come, but keep thy wonted state,
With even step, and musing gait,
And looks commercing with the skies,
Thy rapt soul sitting in thine eyes: 10
There, held in holy passion still,
Forget thyself to marble,° till
With a sad leaden downward cast
Thou fix them on the earth as fast.
And join with thee calm Peace, and
    Quiet,   15
Spare° Fast, that oft with gods doth diet,
And hear the Muses in a ring
Aye round about Jove's altar sing;
And add to these retirèd Leisure,   19
That in trim gardens takes his pleasure;
But first, and chiefest, with thee bring
Him that yon soars on golden wing,
Guiding the fiery-wheelèd throne,
The cherub Contemplation.

[BEAUTIES OF A MOONLIT EVENING]

And the mute Silence hist along,   25
'Less Philomel° will deign a song,
In her sweetest, saddest plight,°
Smoothing the rugged brow of Night,
While Cynthia° checks her dragon yoke
Gently o'er the accustomed oak.   30
Sweet bird, that shunn'st the noise of
    folly,
Most musical, most melancholy!
Thee, chauntress, oft the woods among,
I woo, to hear thy evensong;
And, missing thee, I walk unseen   35
On the dry smooth-shaven green,
To behold the wandering moon
Riding near her highest noon,
Like one that had been led astray
Through the heaven's wide pathless
    way,   40
And oft, as if her head she bowed,
Stooping through a fleecy cloud.
Oft, on a plat of rising ground,
I hear the far-off curfew sound

Over some wide-watered shore,   45
Swinging slow with sullen roar.

[DELIGHTS OF THE FIRESIDE]

Or if the air will not permit,
Some still removèd place will fit,
Where glowing embers through the
    room
Teach light to counterfeit a gloom,   50
Far from all resort of mirth,
Save the cricket on the hearth,
Or the bellman's drowsy charm°
To bless the doors from nightly harm.

[PLEASURES OF READING]

Or let my lamp, at midnight hour,   55
Be seen in some high lonely tower
Where I may oft outwatch the Bear°
With thrice-great Hermes,° or unsphere
The spirit of Plato,° to unfold   59
What worlds or what vast regions hold

The immortal mind that hath forsook
Her mansion in this fleshly nook;
And of those demons° that are found
In fire, air, flood, or underground,
Whose power hath a true consent,°   65
With planet or with element.

12. *Forget thyself to marble:* become so completely engrossed in thought that you seem a marble statue. 16. *Spare:* an adjective, "lean." 26. *Philomel* (fĭl′ō·mĕl): the nightingale. 27. *plight:* mood. 29. *Cynthia* (sĭn′thĭ·à): or Diana, the moon goddess, whose chariot was drawn by dragons, and to whom the oak was sacred.

53. *bellman's drowsy charm:* night watchman's calling of the hours as he guarded the streets. 57. *outwatch the Bear:* to stay awake all night, for the constellation of the Bear never sets. 58, 59. *Hermes* (hûr′mēz): the Egyptian god of wisdom; *Plato* (plā′tō): a Greek philosopher who wrote on the immortality of the soul. 63. *demons:* According to Plato there were four elements: earth, water, air, fire. Later philosophers taught that each had its own presiding spirit, or "demon." 65. *consent:* harmony.

Sometime let gorgeous Tragedy
In sceptered pall° come sweeping by,
Presenting Thebes,° or Pelops'° line,
Or the tale of Troy° divine,   70
Or what (though rare) of later age
Ennobled hath the buskined stage.°
But, O sad Virgin! that thy power
Might raise Musaeus° from his bower;
Or bid the soul of Orpheus° sing   75
Such notes as, warbled to the string,
Drew iron tears down Pluto's cheek,
And made Hell grant what love did seek;
Or call up him that left half-told°
The story of Cambuscan bold,   80
Of Camball, and of Algarsife,
And who had Canace to wife
That owned the virtuous ring and glass,
And of the wondrous horse of brass,
On which the Tartar king did ride;   85
And if aught else great bards beside
In sage and solemn tunes have sung,
Of tourneys, and of trophies hung,
Of forests, and enchantments drear,
Where more is meant than meets the
    ear.   90

[BEAUTY OF A RAINY MORN]

Thus, Night, oft see me in thy pale ca-
    reer,
Till civil-suited° Morn appear,
Not tricked and frounced° as she was
    wont
With the Attic boy° to hunt,
But kerchiefed in a comely cloud,   95
While rocking winds are piping loud;

Or ushered with a shower still,
When the gust hath blown his fill,
Ending on the rustling leaves,   99
With minute drops from off the eaves.

[A SHADY WOOD]

And when the sun begins to fling
His flaring beams, me, Goddess, bring
To archèd walks of twilight groves,
And shadows brown, that Sylvan° loves,
Of pine, or monumental oak   105
Where the rude ax with heavèd stroke
Was never heard the nymphs to daunt,
Or fright them from their hallowed
    haunt.
There in close covert by some brook,
Where no profaner eye may look,   110

Hide me from day's garish eye,
While the bee, with honeyed thigh,
That at her flowery work doth sing,
And the waters murmuring,
With such consort as they keep,   115
Entice the dewy-feathered Sleep;
And let some strange mysterious dream
Wave at his wings in airy stream
Of lively portraiture displayed,
Softly on my eyelids laid;   120
And as I wake, sweet music breathe
Above, about, or underneath,
Sent by some spirit to mortals good,
Or the unseen Genius of the wood.°

68. *sceptered pall:* a kingly robe. 69, 70.
Thebes (thēbz), *Pelops'* (pē'lŏps) *line, Troy:*
all subjects of Greek tragedies. 72. *buskined
stage:* Buskins were high boots worn by ancient
actors to give dignity; hence, they are a symbol
of tragedy as the sock was of comedy. 74. *Mu-
saeus* (mū-zē'ŭs): a poet in mythology. 75. *soul
of Orpheus:* See note on Orpheus for line 121 of
"L'Allegro." 79. *him . . . half-told:* Chaucer
never finished the Squire's Tale, a romantic,
mysterious story described in the next few
lines. 92. *civil-suited:* in the sober garb of a
citizen. 93. *tricked and frounced:* dressed in gay
robes, probably with hair curled. 94. *Attic boy:*
Cephalus (sĕf'á·lŭs), a young huntsman of
Attica, beloved by Aurora, the dawn.

104. *Sylvan:* Sylvanus (sĭl·vā'nŭs), god of
the woodlands. 124. *Genius . . . wood:* The
ancient Greeks believed that a benign deity
dwelt in every grove.

[INSPIRATION WITHIN A CHURCH]

But let my due feet never fail   125
To walk the studious cloister's pale,°
And love the high embowèd roof,
With antique pillars massy proof,°
And storied windows richly dight,°
Casting a dim religious light.   130
There let the pealing organ blow
To the full-voiced quire below
In service high and anthems clear
As may with sweetness, through mine ear,
Dissolve me into ecstasies,   135
And bring all Heaven before mine eyes.

[SATISFACTIONS OF OLD AGE]

And may at last my weary age
Find out the peaceful hermitage,
The hairy gown and mossy cell,
Where I may sit and rightly spell°   140
Of every star that heaven doth shew,
And every herb that sips the dew,
Till old experience do attain
To something like prophetic strain.   144
　　These pleasures, Melancholy, give
　　And I with thee will choose to live.

126. *pale:* boundary. 128. *massy proof:* able to bear the weight they support. 129. *storied ... dight:* richly colored stained-glass windows telling Bible stories. 140. *spell:* learn the meaning by study.

POEMS OF CONTRASTED MOOD

1. Examine the structure of the two poems carefully. They are written flawlessly in the same meter; yet in one the words trip gaily, in the other they move in stately dignity. How does the poet achieve this effect? Point out how it is done by (*a*) choice of words, (*b*) characters, (*c*) scenes, (*d*) other devices.

2. Make two parallel columns and compare the resemblances and differences of the two poems on the following points: (*a*) time of day and a man's time of life covered; (*b*) companions chosen; (*c*) references to objects in nature — birds, heavenly bodies, sounds, others; (*d*) references to literature and music.

3. These poems are full of appeal to the senses, especially in their words of color and sound. Select some lines that seem especially rich in their pictures and sound effects. Did you find lines that you had heard quoted before you read the poem?

4. Analyze the characters of the cheerful man and the pensive man as Milton presents them. How are they different? Are they alike in any respect? Do you think they are young men or older men?

5. Would you consider these two poems examples of pastoral poetry? Why or why not? Are the country people treated romantically or realistically? Prove your points by details from the poems.

6. What lines or words in the poems tell you that Milton was a musician? List some pieces of music that you feel harmonize with the moods of the two poems. If possible, bring records to play to the class and follow with a class discussion. What does the music contribute to your appreciation of the poems?

SUGGESTIONS FOR WRITING

1. Write your own " L'Allegro " and " Il Penseroso," telling where you like to be and what you like to do when in these different moods.

2. Describe a country scene with which you are familiar, making it clearly American. Is there anything in the American scene that might correspond to the castle towers in the English landscape?

Short Poems

" On Shakespeare," the first short poem here, is to be found in the second edition of Shakespeare's plays and is the first of Milton's poems to be published. It is not likely that Milton ever saw Shakespeare (he was eight when Shakespeare died), and it may be that this tribute was inspired by Jonson's poem (see page 201), which ap-

peared in the first Shakespeare edition.

Like Shakespeare, Milton excelled in writing sonnets, though he did not produce as many or compose them in any sequence. " On His Having Arrived at the Age of Twenty-three " shows him as an earnest youth, on the threshold of his literary career. He wrote it at the time he was either writing or had just completed "L'Allegro" and "Il Penseroso." The second sonnet comes twenty years later, when Milton was forty-four and blind but ready to embark on his greatest works.

You will notice that the rhyme scheme is different from either Spenser's or Shake-speare's. This is the true Italian form — two quatrains (four-line stanzas) forming an octave (eight lines) always using the rhyme scheme *abba*. The concluding sestet (six lines) may have two or three rhymes and they may fall in any order the poet chooses.

On Shakespeare

What needs my Shakespeare for his honored bones
The labor of an age in pilèd stones?
Or that his hallowed relics should be hid
Under a star-ypointing pyramid?
Dear son of memory, great heir of fame,   5
What need'st thou such weak witness of thy name?
Thou in our wonder and astonishment
Hast built thyself a livelong monument.
For whilst, to the shame of slow-endeavoring art,
Thy easy numbers flow, and that each heart   10
Hath from the leaves of thy unvalued° book
Those Delphic° lines with deep impression took,
Then thou, our fancy of itself bereaving,
Dost make us marble° with too much conceiving,
And so sepulchred° in such pomp dost lie   15
That kings for such a tomb would wish to die.

11. *unvalued:* beyond any fixed value. 12. *Delphic* (dĕl'fĭk): prophetic or inspired; relating to the oracle at ancient Delphi. 14. *Dost . . . marble:* as still as marble through our thoughtful attention. Milton uses the same figure in "Il Penseroso," line 12. 15. *sepulchred* (here, sĕp·ŭl'kērd, but usually accented on the first syllable): put in a tomb.

On His Having Arrived at the Age of Twenty-three

How soon hath Time, the subtle thief of youth,
Stolen on his wing my three-and-twentieth year!
My hasting days fly on with full career,
But my late spring no bud or blossom shew'th.
Perhaps my semblance might deceive the truth   5
That I to manhood am arrived so near;
And inward ripeness doth much less appear,
That some more timely-happy spirits endu'th.°
Yet be it less or more, or soon or slow,
It shall be still in strictest measure even   10
To that same lot, however mean or high,
Toward which Time leads me, and the will of Heaven.
All is, if I have grace to use it so,
As ever in my great Taskmaster's eye.

8. *endu'th:* endows.

On His Blindness

Rhyme
scheme

When I consider how my light is spent ·   *a*
Ere half my days, in this dark world and wide,   *b*
And that one talent° which is death to hide   *b*
Lodged with me useless, though my soul more bent   *a*
5   To serve therewith my Maker, and present   *a*
My true account, lest He returning chide; · ·   *b*
" Doth God exact day labor, light denied? "   *b*
I fondly° ask. But Patience, to prevent   *a*
That murmur, soon replies, " God doth not need   *c*
10   Either man's work or his own gifts. Who best   *d*
Bear his mild yoke, they serve him best. His state   *e*
Is kingly: thousands at his bidding speed,   *c*
And post o'er land and ocean without rest; '   *d*
They also serve who only stand and wait."   *e*

3. *one talent:* see Matthew 25 : 14–30. 8. *fondly:* foolishly.

MILTON'S SHORT POEMS

1. Compare Milton's tribute to Shakespeare with Jonson's. Which poem reveals a better understanding of the dramatist? Which is more impressive? Why is this poem not a sonnet?

2. The two sonnets here offer an interesting study in contrast. What quality of the young man has been retained after twenty years? How has Milton kept his faith in God's direction of his talents? Apply these poems to your own experience.

Why is it a good habit to stop occasionally and take stock of your own personality and achievements?

3. In " On His Blindness " how does Milton apply the Biblical parable of the talents to himself? Describe in your own words the mental debate and final conclusion reached by Milton in this poem.

4. Reread a few Shakespearean sonnets for comparison with Milton's. How does the form differ? What difference in the division of thought within the sonnets do you notice?

Paradise Lost

Blindness is obviously a great handicap to a writer, yet curiously enough, it was a help toward Milton's completion of *Paradise Lost*. From his notebooks we know that Milton had for years planned a long poem that would tell the Biblical story of Creation. But not until he became blind was Milton relieved of the many tasks that had kept him from this work. *Paradise Lost*, which required seven years to write, is a literary epic, the greatest in the English language. Like a national or folk epic, such as *Beowulf*, a literary epic is a saga of grand and sweeping events. Milton followed *Paradise Lost* with two other works on a similar scale: *Paradise Regained*, which pictures the temptation of Christ in the wilderness; and *Samson Agonistes*, an adaptation of the Greek drama form in blank verse, which recounts the tragedy of Samson in his blindness, beset by enemies.

Paradise Lost tells in twelve books the

Biblical story of the temptation and fall of man at the hands of Satan. This much Milton took from the Book of Genesis, but to it he added pictures of Satan's expulsion from Heaven together with the rebel Angels. The scene of the epic is the world of space, shifting between Heaven and Hell and the World. The characters are ones we know well — Adam, Eve, Satan, Michael, Gabriel, and others from the Old Testament. Satan emerges as a fearless and determined leader, even though he leads in the wrong direction. The following passages are from Book I of *Paradise Lost*.

O f Man's first disobedience, and the fruit
Of that forbidden tree whose mortal taste
Brought death into the World, and all our woe,
With loss of Eden, till one greater Man°
Restore us, and regain the blissful seat,   5
Sing, Heavenly Muse° . . .
                    I thence
Invoke thy aid to my adventurous song,
That with no middle flight intends to soar
Above the Aonian mount,° while it pursues
Things unattempted yet in prose or rhyme.   10
And chiefly Thou, O Spirit,° that dost prefer
Before all temples the upright heart and pure,

The poet invokes the divine Spirit for inspiration to interpret God to man.

Instruct me, for Thou know'st; Thou from the first
Wast present, and, with mighty wings outspread,
Dovelike sat'st brooding on the vast Abyss,   15
And mad'st it pregnant: what in me is dark
Illumine, what is low raise and support;
That, to the height of this great argument,
I may assert Eternal Providence,
And justify the ways of God to men.   20
    Say first — for Heaven hides nothing from thy view,
Nor the deep tract of Hell — say first what cause

He searches for the cause of the fall of man

Moved our grand Parents, in that happy state,
Favored of Heaven so highly, to fall off
From their Creator, and transgress his will   25
For one restraint,° lords of the World besides.
Who first seduced them to that foul revolt?

It was Satan who deceived Eve, " the mother of mankind," in revenge after he with the rebel Angels was thrown from Heaven.

    The infernal Serpent; he it was whose guile,
Stirred up with envy and revenge, deceived
The mother of mankind, what time his pride   30
Had cast him out from Heaven, with all his host
Of rebel Angels, by whose aid, aspiring
To set himself in glory above his peers,
He trusted to have equaled the Most High,
If he opposed, and, with ambitious aim   35

4. *one greater Man:* Christ. 6. *Heavenly Muse:* not the pagan Muse, but the Spirit that inspired the men of the Bible. 9. *Aonian* (ā·ō'nĭ·ăn) *mount:* Helicon in Greece, supposed to be the home of the Muses. Milton means that he intends to write on a theme higher than Greek poetry had attempted. 11. *Spirit:* divine inspiration. 26. *one restraint:* that they should not eat of the fruit of the tree of knowledge.

Against the throne and monarchy of God,
Raised impious war in Heaven, and battle proud,
With vain attempt. Him the Almighty Power
Hurled headlong flaming from the ethereal sky,
With hideous ruin and combustion, down   40
To bottomless perdition; there to dwell
In adamantine° chains and penal fire,
Who durst defy the Omnipotent to arms.
   Nine times the space that measures day and night
To mortal men, he with his horrid crew   45
Lay vanquished, rolling in the fiery gulf,
Confounded, though immortal. But his doom
Reserved him to more wrath; for now the thought
Both of lost happiness and lasting pain
Torments him; round he throws his baleful eyes,   50
That witnessed° huge affliction and dismay,
Mixed with obdurate pride and steadfast hate.
At once, as far as Angel's ken,° he views
The dismal situation waste and wild.
A dungeon horrible, on all sides round,   55
As one great furnace flamed; yet from those flames
No light; but rather darkness visible
Served only to discover sights of woe,
Regions of sorrow, doleful shades, where peace   60

Satan and his followers find themselves in a horrible Hell. And rest can never dwell, hope never comes
That comes to all; but torture without end
Still urges,° and a fiery deluge, fed
With ever-burning sulfur unconsumed.
Such place Eternal Justice had prepared
For those rebellious; here their prison ordained   65
In utter darkness, and their portion set,
As far removed from God and light of Heaven
As from the center thrice to the utmost pole.°
Oh, how unlike the place from whence they fell!
There the companions of his fall, o'erwhelmed   70
With floods and whirlwinds of tempestuous fire,
He soon discerns; and, weltering by his side,
One next himself in power, and next in crime,
Long after known in Palestine, and named
Beelzebub.° To whom the Archenemy,   75
And thence in Heaven called Satan, with bold words
Breaking the horrid silence, thus began: —
   " If thou beest he — but, Oh, how fallen! how changed
From him! — who, in the happy realms of light,
Clothed with transcendent brightness, didst outshine   80

---

42. *adamantine* (ăd′*à*·mănt′ĭn): unbreakable, hard as a diamond. 51. *witnessed:* gave evidence of. 53. *ken:* sight. 62. *Still urges:* always presses. 68. *center . . . pole:* three times the distance from the earth (*center*) to the furthest point in the universe. 75. *Beelzebub* (bĕ·ĕl′zĕ·bŭb): In this poem the name is given to the fallen angel next in command to Satan, but in other connections it is often used as equivalent to Satan.

Myriads, though bright — if he whom mutual league,
United thoughts and counsels, equal hope
And hazard in the glorious enterprise,
Joined with me once, now misery hath joined
In equal ruin; into what pit thou seest   85
From what height fallen; so much the stronger proved
He with his thunder; and till then who knew
The force of those dire arms? Yet not for those,
Nor what the potent Victor in his rage
Can else inflict, do I repent, or change,   90
Though changed in outward luster, that fixed mind,
And high disdain from sense of injured merit,
That with the Mightiest raised me to contend,
And to the fierce contention brought along
Innumerable force of Spirits armed,   95
That durst dislike his reign, and, me preferring,
His utmost power with adverse power opposed
In dubious battle on the plains of Heaven,

236 THE SEVENTEENTH CENTURY

*Satan boldly says
"All is not lost"
and declares
eternal war on
Heaven with
"immortal hate."*

And shook his throne. What though the field be lost?
All is not lost; the unconquerable will,   100
And study of revenge, immortal hate,
And courage never to submit or yield:
And what is else not to be overcome?
That glory never shall his wrath or might
Extort from me. To bow and sue for grace   105
With suppliant knee, and deify his power
Who, from the terror of his arm, so late
Doubted° his empire — that were low indeed;
That were an ignominy and shame beneath
This downfall; since, by fate, the strength of gods,   110
And this empyreal° substance, cannot fail;
Since, through experience of this great event,
In arms not worse, in foresight much advanced,
We may with more successful hope resolve
To wage by force or guile eternal war,   115
Irreconcilable to our grand Foe,
Who now triumphs, and in the excess of joy
Sole reigning holds the tyranny of Heaven."
    So spake the apostate Angel, though in pain,
Vaunting aloud, but racked with deep despair;   120
And him thus answered soon his bold compeer:° —
    "O Prince, O Chief of many thronèd Powers
That led the embattled Seraphim° to war
Under thy conduct, and, in dreadful deeds
Fearless, endangered Heaven's perpetual King,   125
And put to proof his high supremacy,
Whether upheld by strength, or chance, or fate!
Too well I see and rue the dire event
That, with sad overthrow and foul defeat,
Hath lost us Heaven, and all this mighty host   130

*Beelzebub regrets
the loss of
Heaven and
would now serve
God as a slave
and obey his
will.*

In horrible destruction laid thus low,
As far as gods and heavenly essences
Can perish: for the mind and spirit remains
Invincible, and vigor soon returns,
Though all our glory extinct, and happy state   135
Here swallowed up in endless misery.
But what if He our Conqueror (whom I now
Of force believe almighty, since no less
Than such could have o'erpowered such force as ours)
Have left us this our spirit and strength entire,   140
Strongly to suffer and support our pains,
That we may so suffice his vengeful ire,
Or do him mightier service as his thralls
By right of war, whate'er his business be,
Here in the heart of Hell to work in fire,   145

108. *Doubted:* feared for. 111. *empyreal* (ĕm·pĭr'ē·ăl): belonging to the highest heaven. The fallen Angels still retain their immortality. 121. *compeer:* companion, equal. 123. *Seraphim* (sĕr'á·fĭm): Angels of the highest rank.

Or do his errands in the gloomy Deep?
What can it then avail though yet we feel
Strength undiminished, or eternal being
To undergo eternal punishment? "
    Whereto with speedy words the Archfiend replied: —   150
" Fallen Cherub, to be weak is miserable,
Doing or suffering:° but of this be sure —
To do aught good never will be our task,
But ever to do ill our sole delight,
As being the contrary to his high will   155
Whom we resist. If then his providence
Out of our evil seek to bring forth good,
Our labor must be to pervert that end,
And out of good still to find means of evil;
Which ofttimes may succeed so as perhaps   160
Shall grieve him, if I fail not, and disturb
His inmost counsels from their destined aim.
But see! the angry Victor hath recalled
His ministers of vengeance and pursuit

Satan denounces Back to the gates of Heaven: the sulfurous hail,   165
Beelzebub's Shot after us in storm, o'erblown hath laid
weakness and The fiery surge that from the precipice
makes plans to Of Heaven received us falling; and the thunder,
gather his forces Winged with red lightning and impetuous rage,
on a plain where Perhaps hath spent his shafts, and ceases now   170
they may consult To bellow through the vast and boundless Deep.
n how to " offend Let us not slip the occasion, whether scorn
our enemy." Or satiate° fury yield it from our Foe.
Seest thou yon dreary plain, forlorn and wild,
The seat of desolation, void of light,   175
Save what the glimmering of these livid flames
Casts pale and dreadful? Thither let us tend
From off the tossing of these fiery waves;
There rest, if any rest can harbor there;
And, reassembling our afflicted powers,   180
Consult how we may henceforth most offend
Our enemy, our own loss how repair,
How overcome this dire calamity,
What reinforcement we may gain from hope,
If not what resolution from despair."   185
    Thus Satan, talking to his nearest mate,
With head uplift above the wave, and eyes
That sparkling blazed; his other parts besides
Prone on the flood, extended long and large,
Lay floating many a rood.° . . .   190
So stretched out huge in length the Archfiend lay,
Chained on the burning lake; nor ever thence
Had risen, or heaved his head, but that the will

152. *Doing or suffering:* whether active or passive. 173. *satiate* (sā′shǐ·ăt): satisfied. 190. *rood:*
Milton conceived of the Angels as being enormous in size. A *rood* is equal to seven or eight yards.

Heaven permits Satan to carry out his evil plans and by so doing reap his own ruin and bring forth good for Man.
And high permission of all-ruling Heaven
Left him at large to his own dark designs,   195
That with reiterated crimes he might
Heap on himself damnation, while he sought
Evil to others, and enraged might see
How all his malice served but to bring forth
Infinite goodness, grace, and mercy, shown   200
On Man by him seduced, but on himself
Treble confusion, wrath, and vengeance poured.
      Forthwith upright he rears from off the pool
His mighty stature; on each hand the flames
Driven backward slope their pointing spires, and, rolled   205
In billows, leave i' the midst a horrid vale.
Then with expanded wings he steers his flight
Aloft, incumbent° on the dusky air,
That felt unusual weight; till on dry land
He lights — if it were land that ever burned   210
With solid, as the lake with liquid fire,
And such appeared in hue as when the force

Satan and Beelzebub exult in escaping from the burning lake and recovering their strength without the aid of Heaven.
Of subterranean wind transports a hill
Torn from Pelorus,° or the shattered side
Of thundering Etna, whose combustible   215
And fueled entrails, thence conceiving fire,
Sublimed° with mineral fury, aid the winds,
And leave a singèd bottom all involved°
With stench and smoke.° Such resting found the sole
Of unblest feet. Him followed his next mate;   220
Both glorying to have scaped the Stygian° flood
As gods, and by their own recovered strength,
Not by the sufferance of supernal° power.
      " Is this the region, this the soil, the clime,"
Said then the lost Archangel, " this the seat   225
That we must change for Heaven? — this mournful gloom
For that celestial light? Be it so, since he
Who now is sovereign can dispose and bid
What shall be right: farthest from him is best,

Satan accepts the horrors of damnation and announces himself the ruler of Hell.
Whom reason hath equaled, force hath made supreme   230
Above his equals. Farewell, happy fields,
Where joy forever dwells! Hail, horrors! hail,
Infernal World! and thou, profoundest Hell,
Receive thy new possessor — one who brings
A mind not to be changed by place or time.   235
The mind is its own place, and in itself
Can make a Heaven of Hell, a Hell of Heaven.

---

208. *incumbent:* lying. 214. *Pelorus* (pĕ·lōr′ŭs): a cape in Sicily, now Faro. 217. *Sublimed:* sublimated; i.e., turned into vapor by heat and solidified by cooling. 218. *involved:* enveloped 212–219. *as when . . . smoke:* An example of the extended simile which Milton frequently uses t strengthen his pictures. This comparison to Mount Etna will be especially vivid to those who hav seen moving pictures of volcanic eruptions. 221. *Stygian* (stĭj′ĭ·ăn): pertaining to the river Sty which in Greek mythology surrounded the abode of the dead. Satan and Beelzebub, because the are of immortal substance, cannot die. 223. *supernal:* heavenly.

What matter where, if I be still the same,
And what I should be, all but less than he
Whom thunder hath made greater? Here at least   240
We shall be free; the Almighty hath not built
Here for his envy, will not drive us hence:
Here we may reign secure; and, in my choice,
To reign is worth ambition, though in Hell:
Better to reign in Hell than serve in Heaven."   245

AN EPIC OF GOOD AND EVIL

1. Reread the story of the fall of man in the Old Testament and compare it with the account in Milton's poem. What has the poet added to the Biblical story? As a personification of evil, what attributes does Satan have? Wherein does his power lie?

2. What two beings carry on the dialogue in this selection? What differences are there in their attitudes?

3. Does Milton explain how Satan was able to continue in his evil deeds? What does he imply was the purpose of Heaven in so allowing him?

4. Select passages that appeal to you and read them aloud to the class. Show where Milton uses long words to obtain a sonorous, rolling effect.

5. Almost all literary epics open with an invocation to the Muse of Poetry to aid the poet in his task. Which of the opening lines comprise the invocation here? To whom are they addressed? What do the opening lines tell you about the poet's purpose?

6. Compare *Paradise Lost* with *Beowulf*. In what ways are they alike? different? Explain the difference between a literary epic and a folk or national epic.

THE POWER OF WORDS

PREFIXES AND MEANING

Milton, when picturing powerful forces of good and evil, uses powerful words — "the potent Victor," for example (line 89). *Potent* comes directly from the Latin word meaning powerful. Combined with *omni,* meaning *all,* it makes the exalted word for God in line 43, *Omnipotent* (ŏm·nĭp′ŏ·tĕnt), the all-powerful one. Two similar combinations are: *omnipresent* (ŏm′nĭ·prĕz′ĕnt), present everywhere, and *omniscient* (ŏm·nĭsh′ĕnt), knowing all. What other words do you know that have the prefix *omni?*

Another intensive prefix is *arch,* meaning *chief* or *great.* Satan is called the *Archenemy* (line 75), the *Archfiend* (lines 150 and 191) and the lost *Archangel* (line 225). Look up the word *archipelago* to see how this prefix figures in its meaning. The pronunciation of *arch* varies: When it is followed by a consonant it is pronounced *arch,* but followed by a vowel it is *ark.* There is an exception to this rule in the words mentioned above. Can you find it? How would you pronounce *archbishop, archduke, archangel,* and *architect?*

JOHN BUNYAN 1628–1688

While Milton voiced the Puritan ideals for the educated classes, John Bunyan spoke for the common people.

Because Bunyan was one of the first authors to write his autobiography, we know more of his inner life than of that of most of the early writers. He was a village tinker and for a while a common soldier in the Parliamentary army. The in-tense religious emotions prevalent at that time seized the imaginative Bunyan and caused him frightful pangs of conscience about his swearing, his Sunday sports on the green, and his failure to attend church. He visualized his mental struggles as the conflict between angels and devils. He longed to perform miracles, but was afraid to try lest he should fail and lose his faith.

He became a preacher and drew such crowds of laboring people to his outdoor services that his influence was greatly feared by the Royalists.

After the Restoration an act was passed to forbid meetings hostile to the established Church. Bunyan was brought to trial, and the judge urged him to give up his services. But, though he suffered agonies of spirit at the possibility of separation from his little blind daughter and the rest of his family, Bunyan would not yield his point. Consequently he spent almost twelve years in Bedford jail. He was, however, allowed considerable freedom to see his family and even to preach in the Baptist church. During these years his leisure enabled him to become a thorough student of two books — the only ones he had: the Bible and Fox's *Book of Martyrs.* Their influence is evident in his masterpiece, *The Pilgrim's Progress,* which, though probably written in jail, was not published until years after his release. The popularity of his book was truly remarkable. Today, next to the Bible, it has the largest number of translations into foreign languages of any book in the world.

The great allegory of *The Pilgrim's Progress* is told as if it were a dream. Christian, the hero, is seen as he leaves the City of Destruction to journey to the Celestial City. He carries a heavy burden of sin on his back and the Scriptures in his hand. One of his earliest difficulties is getting through the famous Slough of Despond, which proves too much for his companion, Pliable. But Christian, with the aid of Helpful, scrambles out and continues on his way. Further obstacles are encountered in the Hill of Difficulty, the Valley of Humili- ation, the Valley of the Shadow, and the imprisonment at Doubting Castle by the Giant Despair. Through the first few of these adventures Christian is accompanied by Faithful, who suffers martyrdom at Vanity Fair. After that, Hopeful joins Christian, and the two finally reach the Heavenly Gates, where they are greeted by the angels.

The following selection is one of the most significant passages in the book, partly because the term Vanity Fair has been so frequently used as a symbol of worldliness.

THEN I SAW in my dream, that when they were got out of the wilderness, they presently saw a town before them, and the name of that town is Vanity. And at the town there is a fair kept, called Vanity Fair; it is kept all the year long; it beareth the name of Vanity Fair, because the town where 'tis kept is lighter than vanity; and also because all that is there sold, or that cometh thither, is vanity. As is the saying of the wise, " All that cometh is Vanity."

This fair is no new-erected business, but a thing of ancient standing; I will show you the original of it.

Almost five thousand years agone, there were pilgrims walking to the Celestial City, as these two honest persons are; and Beelzebub, Apollyon,[1] and Legion, with their companions, perceiving by the path that the pilgrims made, that their way to the City lay through this town of Vanity, they contrived here to set up a fair; a fair wherein should be sold all sorts of vanity, and that it should last all the year long; therefore at this fair are all such merchandise sold, as houses, lands, trades, places, honors, preferments, titles, countries, kingdoms, pleasures, and delights of all sorts, as wives, husbands, children, masters, servants, lives, blood, bodies, souls, silver, gold, pearls, precious stones, and what not.

And moreover, at this fair there is at all times to be seen jugglings, cheats, games, plays, fools, apes, knaves, and rogues, and that of all sorts.

Here are to be seen too, and that for nothing, thefts, murders, false swearers, and that of a blood-red color.

[There follows a passage that identifies the streets and rows of Vanity Fair with the various nations of Europe, and tells how Beelzebub tried in vain to win Jesus to Vanity Fair. The commotion aroused by the Pilgrims Christian and Faithful is attributed to three causes: their strange clothing, their foreign language of Heaven, and their failure to be impressed by the wares at Vanity Fair.]

One chanced mockingly, beholding the carriages of the men, to say unto them, " What will ye buy? " But they, looking gravely upon him, answered, " We buy the Truth." At that there was an occasion taken to despise the men the more; some mocking, some taunting, some speaking reproachfully, and some calling upon others to smite them. At last things came to a hubbub and great stir in the fair, insomuch that all order was confounded.

Now was word presently brought to the Great One of the fair, who quickly came down and deputed some of his most trusty friends to take those men into examination, about whom the fair was almost overturned. So the men were brought to examination; and they that sat upon them, asked them whence they came, whither they went, and what they did there in such an unusual garb. The men told them that they were pilgrims and strangers in the world, and that they were going to their own country, which was the heavenly Jerusalem; and that they had given no occasion to the men of the town, nor yet to the merchandisers, thus to abuse them, and to let[2] them in their journey, except it was for that, when one asked them what they would buy, they said they would buy the Truth. But they that were appointed to examine them did not believe them to be any other than bedlams[3] and mad, or else such as came to put all things into a confusion in the fair. Therefore they took them and beat them, and besmeared them with dirt, and then put them into the cage, that they might be made a spectacle to all the men of the fair.

[1] *Beelzebub* (bē-ĕl'zē-bŭb): Satan; *Apollyon* (à-pŏl'yŭn): the angel of the bottomless pit.

[2] *let:* hinder.

[3] *bedlams:* insane men. The word is a contraction of Bethlehem, from the name of a famous hospital for the insane, St. Mary of Bethlehem.

There, therefore, they lay for some time, and were made the objects of any man's sport, or malice, or revenge, the Great One of the fair laughing still at all that befell them.

But the men being patient, and not rendering railing for railing, but contrariwise blessing, and giving good words for bad, and kindness for injuries done, some men in the fair that were more observing, and less prejudiced than the rest, began to check and blame the baser sort for their continual abuses done by them to the men; they, therefore, in angry manner let fly at them again, counting them as bad as the men in the cage, and telling them that they seemed confederates, and should be made partakers of their misfortunes. The others replied, that for aught they could see, the men were quiet, and sober, and intended nobody any harm; and that there were many that traded in their fair that were more worthy to be put into the cage, yea, and pillory too, than were the men that they had abused. Thus, after divers words had passed on both sides (the men behaving themselves all the while very wisely and soberly before them), they fell to some blows among themselves, and did harm one to another.

Then were these two poor men brought before their examiners again, and there charged as being guilty of the late hubbub that had been in the fair. So they beat them pitifully and hung irons upon them, and led them in chains up and down the fair, for an example and a terror to others, lest any should speak in their behalf, or join themselves unto them. But Christian and Faithful behaved themselves yet more wisely, and received the ignominy and shame that was cast upon them, with so much meekness and patience, that it won to their side (though but few in comparison of the rest) several of the men in the fair. This put the other party yet into a greater rage, insomuch that they concluded the death of these two men. Wherefore they threatened, that the cage nor irons should serve their turn, but that they should die, for the abuse they had done, and for deluding the men of the fair.

Then were they remanded to the cage again, until further order should be taken with them. So they put them in, and made their feet fast in the stocks.

Here also they called again to mind what they had heard from their faithful friend Evangelist, and were the more confirmed in their way and sufferings, by what he told them would happen to them. They also now comforted each other, that whose lot it was to suffer, even he should have the best on 't; therefore each man secretly wished that he might have that preferment: but committing themselves to the all-wise disposal of Him that ruleth all things, with much content they abode in the condition in which they were, until they should be otherwise disposed of.

Then a convenient time being appointed, they brought them forth to their trial, in order to their condemnation. When the time was come, they were brought before their enemies, and arraigned. The judge's name was Lord Hategood. Their indictment was one and the same in substance, though somewhat varying in form, the contents whereof was this:

" That they were enemies to and disturbers of their trade; that they had made commotions and divisions in the town, and had won a party to their own most dangerous opinions, in contempt of the law of their prince."

Then Faithful began to answer, that he had only set himself against that which had set itself against Him that is higher than the highest. And said he, " As for distubance, I make none, being myself a man of peace; the parties that were won to us, were won by beholding our truth and innocence, and they are only turned from the worse to the better. And as to the king you talk of, since he is Beelzebub, the enemy of our Lord, I defy him and all his angels."

Then proclamation was made, that

they that had aught to say for their Lord the King against the prisoner at the bar, should forthwith appear and give in their evidence. So there came in three witnesses, to wit, Envy, Superstition, and Pickthank.[1] They were then asked if they knew the prisoner at the bar; and what they had to say for their Lord the King against him.

Then stood forth Envy, and said to this effect: " My Lord, I have known this man a long time, and will attest upon my oath before this honorable Bench, that he is — "

Judge. " Hold! Give him his oath."

So they sware him. Then he said, " My Lord, this man, notwithstanding his plausible name, is one of the vilest men in our country. He neither regardeth prince nor people, law nor custom; but doth all that he can to possess all men with certain of his disloyal notions, which he in the general calls principles of faith and holiness. And in particular, I heard him once myself affirm that Christianity and the customs of our town of Vanity were diametrically opposite, and could not be reconciled. By which saying, my Lord, he doth at once not only condemn all our laudable doings, but us in the doing of them."

Then did the Judge say to him, " Hast thou any more to say? "

Envy. " My Lord, I could say much more, only I would not be tedious to the Court. Yet if need be, when the other gentlemen have given in their evidence, rather than anything shall be wanting that will dispatch him, I will enlarge my testimony against him." So he was bid stand by.

Then they called Superstition, and bid him look upon the prisoner. They also asked what he could say for their Lord the King against him? Then they sware him; so he began:

Superstition. " My Lord, I have no great acquaintance with this man, nor do I desire to have further knowledge of him; however, this I know, that he is a very pestilent fellow, from some discourse that the other day I had with him in this town; for then talking with him, I heard him say that our religion was naught, and such by which a man could by no means please God. Which sayings of his, my Lord, your Lordship very well knows what necessarily thence will follow, to wit, that we still do worship in vain, are yet in our sins, and finally shall be damned; and this is that which I have to say."

Then was Pickthank sworn, and bid say that he knew, in behalf of their Lord the King, against the prisoner at the bar.

Pickthank. " My Lord, and you gentlemen all: This fellow I have known of a long time, and have heard him speak things that ought not to be spoke; for he hath railed on our noble Prince Beelzebub, and hath spoken contemptibly of his honorable friends, with all the rest of our nobility; and he hath said, moreover, that if all men were of his mind, if possible, there is not one of these noblemen should have any longer a being in this town; besides, he hath not been afraid to rail on you, my Lord, who are now appointed to be his judge, calling you an ungodly villain, with many other such-like vilifying terms, with which he hath bespattered most of the gentry of our town."

When this Pickthank had told his tale, the Judge directed his speech to the prisoner at the bar, saying, " Thou runagate, heretic, and traitor, hast thou heard what these honest gentlemen have witnessed against thee? "

Faithful. " May I speak a few words in my own defense? "

Judge. " Sirrah, sirrah, thou deservest to live no longer, but to be slain immediately upon the place; yet that all men may see our gentleness toward thee, let us see what thou hast to say."

Faithful. " 1. I say then, in answer to what Mr. Envy hath spoken, I never said

[1] *Pickthank:* an archaic word meaning one who seeks favor by flattery or by talebearing.

ought but this, that what rule, or laws, or custom, or people, were flat against the Word of God, are diametrically opposite to Christianity. If I have said amiss in this, convince me of my error, and I am ready here before you to make my recantation.

" 2. As to the second, to wit, Mr. Superstition, and his charge against me, I said only this, that in the worship of God there is required a divine faith; but there can be no divine faith without a divine revelation of the will of God; therefore whatever is thrust into the worship of God that is not agreeable to divine revelation, cannot be done but by an human faith, which faith will not profit to eternal life.

" 3. As to what Mr. Pickthank hath said, I say (avoiding terms, as that I am said to rail, and the like) that the prince of this town, with all the rabblement his attendants, by this gentleman named, are more fit for a being in hell, than in this town and country; and so, the Lord have mercy upon me."

Then the Judge called to the jury (who all this while stood by, to hear and observe), " Gentlemen of the Jury, you see this man about whom so great an uproar hath been made in this town; you have also heard what these worthy gentlemen have witnessed against him; also you have heard his reply and confession. It lieth now in your breasts to hang him, or save his life; but yet I think meet to instruct you into our Law.

[The Judge then cites various laws enacted by kings of the Old Testament against the Israelites.]

" For that of Pharaoh,[1] his law was made upon a supposition, to prevent mischief, no crime being yet apparent; but here is a crime apparent. For the second and third, you see he disputeth against our religion; and for the treason he hath confessed, he deserveth to die the death."

Then went the jury out, whose names were, Mr. Blind-man, Mr. No-good, Mr. Malice, Mr. Love-lust, Mr. Live-loose, Mr. Heady, Mr. High-mind, Mr. Enmity, Mr. Liar, Mr. Cruelty, Mr. Hate-light, and Mr. Implacable; who every one gave in his private verdict against him among themselves, and afterwards unanimously concluded to bring him in guilty before the Judge. And first Mr. Blind-man the foreman, said, " I see clearly that this man is an heretic." Then said Mr. No-good, " Away with such a fellow from the earth." " Ay," said Mr. Malice, " for I hate the very looks of him." Then said Mr. Love-lust, " I could never endure him." " Nor I," said Mr. Live-loose, " for he would always be condemning my way." " Hang him, hang him," said Mr. Heady. " A sorry scrub," said Mr. High-mind. " My heart riseth against him," said Mr. Enmity. " He is a rogue," said Mr. Liar. " Hanging is too good for him," said Mr. Cruelty. " Let us dispatch him out of the way," said Mr. Hate-light. Then said Mr. Implacable, " Might I have all the world given me, I could not be reconciled to him; therefore let us forthwith bring him in guilty of death." And so they did; therefore he was presently condemned to be had from the place where he was, to the place from whence he came, and there to be put to the most cruel death that could be invented.

They therefore brought him out, to do with him according to their Law; and first they scourged him, then they buffeted him, then they lanced his flesh with knives; after that they stoned him with stones, then pricked him with their swords; and last of all they burned him to ashes at the stake.[2] Thus came Faithful to his end.

---

[1] *Pharaoh:* The story of Pharaoh's measures against the Israelites is told in Exodus 1.

[2] The description of Faithful's execution is no great exaggeration of the kind of torture common in Europe during religious persecutions.

PURITAN IDEALS

1. For what reasons do Christian and Faithful arouse the ire of the people at Vanity Fair? Which of these is probably the most serious cause of objection? Do the pilgrims have any sympathizers? If so, who are they?

2. Point out how the persons involved in the trial are particularly appropriate for Bunyan's purpose. Show how their words are in accordance with their names.

3. How does this selection reveal Bunyan's knowledge of the Bible? Do you know any men in the New Testament from whose experiences Bunyan may have derived some ideas for this experience of Christian and Faithful?

4. What teaching do you think Bunyan intended by the events at Vanity Fair? State his message as concisely as you can. Is it a message that is applicable to our own time? How do you account for the wide appeal of *The Pilgrim's Progress?*

SAMUEL PEPYS 1633–1703

Samuel Pepys (pēps) never considered himself a writer and, in fact, never intended to become one. Yet he wrote what is for the modern reader perhaps the most entertaining work of the seventeenth century. Throughout his life he was a busy man of affairs. His father was a poor tailor with ten other children to support, but Pepys managed to get to Cambridge with the aid of a relative and several scholarships. At twenty-two, with not a penny to start housekeeping, he married a girl of fifteen. With ambition and hard work he advanced quickly. He held an important position in the Navy Office and later became Secretary of the Admiralty. At fifty-five he retired into a pleasant and respected life, publishing a book about the Navy Office, receiving the honor of presidency of the Royal Society, and adding to his splendid library. This was, then, the career of a typical man of affairs, but with one important difference — Pepys kept a diary.

From the ages of twenty-seven to thirty-six, between 1660 and 1669, Samuel Pepys kept a diary which he wrote in a secret code or shorthand. Assured this security from prying eyes, he could be completely intimate and at ease in describing his personal life. More than a hundred years later, the Reverend John Smith discovered the six volumes of this diary among other books Pepys had bequeathed to Cambridge. It took him three years to decipher and transcribe it, and in 1825 the first edition of Pepys' *Diary,* which had never been intended for publication, appeared. Since then there have been many editions; it is the most famous diary in world literature.

Here we meet an extraordinary personality, Pepys himself, a small man with bright eyes, somewhat of a dandy in his dress, a great lover of music, a quick-tempered master, and an indefatigable worker who was often able to rise at four and work until midnight. Pepys recounts his vanities, his vexations, and his prejudices. Nothing is concealed in the *Diary.*

The Diary of
Samuel Pepys[1]

PERSONAL AFFAIRS

August 19, 1660. (Lord's Day.) This morning Sir W. Batten, Pen,[2] and myself, went to church to the churchwardens, to demand a pew, which at present could not be given us, but we are re-

[1] Abridged and modernized in spelling.
[2] *Sir W. Batten, Pen:* Sir William Batten and Sir William Pen (referred to in a later entry as "Sir Williams both") were members of the Navy Board of which Pepys was Clerk of the Acts.

solved to have one built. So we stayed and heard Mr. Mills, a very good minister. Home to dinner, where my wife had on her new petticoat that she bought yesterday, which indeed is a very fine cloth, and a fine lace, but that being of a light color, and the lace all silver, it makes no great show. Mr. Creed and my brother Tom dined with me. After they were gone I went up to put my papers in order and finding my wife's clothes lie carelessly laid up, I was angry with her, which I was troubled for. After that my wife and I went and walked in the garden, and so home to bed.

November 21, 1660. This morning my wife and I went to Paternoster Row, and there we bought some green watered moire for a morning waistcoat. And after that we went to Mr. Cade's to choose some pictures for our house. After that my wife went home, and I to Pope's Head and bought me an agate-hafted knife, which cost me 5s. So home to dinner, and so to the office all the afternoon, and at night to my violin (the first time that I have played on it since I came to this house) in my dining room, and afterward to my lute there, and I took much pleasure to have the neighbors come forth into the yard to hear me. So up to bed.

January 3, 1661. To the Theater: and here the first time that I ever saw women come upon the stage.[1]

March 27, 1661. To the Dolphin to a dinner of Mr. Harris's where Sir Williams both and my Lady Batten and her two daughters, and other company, where a great deal of mirth, and there stayed until 11 o'clock at night, and in our mirth I sang and sometimes fiddled. At last we fell to dancing, the first time that ever I did in my life, which I did wonder to see myself do.

May 31, 1661. I went to my father's,

[1] *women come upon the stage:* In Elizabethan times boys played the roles of women on the stage, and this custom continued until almost the end of the seventeenth century.

but to my great grief I found my father and mother in a great deal of discontent one with another, and indeed my mother is now grown so pettish that I know not how my father is able to bear with it. I did talk to her so as did not indeed become me, but I could not help it, she being so insufferably foolish and simple,

so that my father, poor man, is become a very unhappy man.

December 31, 1661. My wife and I this morning to the painter's, and there she sat [2] the last time. After supper, and my barber had trimmed me, I sat down to end my journal for this year, and my condition at this time, by God's blessing, is thus: my health is very good, and so my wife's in all respects: my servants, W. Hewer, Sarah, Nell, and Wayneman: my house at the Navy Office. I suppose myself to be worth about £500 clear in the world, and my goods of my house my own, and what is coming to me from Brampton when my father dies, which God defer. My chiefest thought is now to get a good wife for Tom, there being one offered by the Joyces, a cousin of

[2] *she sat:* She had been having her portrait painted.

theirs, worth £200 in ready money. But my greatest trouble is that I have for this last half year been a very great spendthrift in all manner of respects, that I am afeared to cast up my accounts, though I hope I am worth what I say above. But I will cast them up very shortly. I have newly taken a solemn oath about abstaining from plays and wine, which I am resolved to keep according to the letter of the oath which I keep by me.

June 8, 1662. (Lord's Day.) To my Lady's, and there supped with her; and merry among other things, with the parrot which my Lord hath brought from the sea, which speaks very well, and cries Poll so pleasantly that made my Lord give it to Lady Paulina; but my Lady her mother do not like it. Home and observe my man Will to walk with his cloak flung over his shoulder like a ruffian, which, whether it was that he might not be seen to walk along with the footboy I know not, but I was vexed at it; and coming home and after prayers, I did ask him where he learned that immodest garb, and he answered me that it was not immodest, or some such slight answer, at which I did give him two boxes on the ears, which I never did before, and so was after a little troubled at it.

THE EXECUTION OF A REGICIDE

October 13, 1660. I went out to Charing Cross, to see Major General Harrison [1] hanged, drawn, and quartered; which was done there, he looking as cheerful as any man could do in that condition. He was presently cut down, and his head and heart shown to the people, at which there was great shouts of joy. It is said that he said that he was sure to come shortly at the right hand of Christ to judge them that now had

judged him; and that his wife do expect his coming again. Thus it was my chance to see the King beheaded at Whitehall,[2] and to see the first blood shed in revenge for the blood of the King at Charing Cross. From thence to my Lord's, and took Captain Cuttance and Mr. Sheply to the Sun Tavern, and did give them some oysters. After that I went by water home, where I was angry with my wife for her things lying about, and in my passion kicked the little fine basket, which I bought her in Holland, and broke it, which troubled me after I had done it. Within all the afternoon setting up shelves in my study. At night to bed.

THE CORONATION OF CHARLES II

April 23, 1661. Coronation Day. About four I rose and got to the Abbey, where I followed Sir J. Denham,[3] the Surveyor, with some company that he was leading in. And with much ado, by the favor of Mr. Cooper, his man, did get up into a great scaffold across the north end of the Abbey, where with a great deal of patience I sat from past four till eleven before the King came in. And a great pleasure it was to see the Abbey raised in the middle, all covered with red, and a throne (that is a chair) and footstool on the top of it; and all the officers of all kinds, so much as the very fiddlers, in red vests.

At last comes in the Dean and Prebends [4] of Westminster, with the Bishops (many of them in cloth-of-gold copes), and after them the Nobility, all in their Parliament robes, which was a most magnificent sight. Then the Duke, and the King with a scepter (carried by my

---

[1] *Major General Harrison:* one of the signers of the death warrant of Charles I.

[2] King Charles I was beheaded in 1649, when Pepys was sixteen.

[3] *Sir J. Denham* was a popular poet as well as being in charge of government buildings.

[4] *Prebends* (prĕb'ĕndz): high officials in the church.

Lord Sandwich) and sword and mond [1] before him, and the crown too. The King in his robes, bare-headed, which was very fine. And after all had placed themselves, there was a sermon and the service; and then in the Choir at the high altar, the King passed through all the ceremonies of the Coronation, which to my great grief I and most in the Abbey could not see. The crown being put upon his head, a great shout began, and he came forth to the throne; and there passed more ceremonies: as taking the oath, and having things read to him by the Bishop; and his Lords (who put on their caps as soon as the King put on his crown) and bishops came, and kneeled before him. And three times the King at Arms [2] went to the three open places on the scaffold, and proclaimed, that if anyone could show any reason why Charles Stuart should not be King of England, that now he should come and speak. And a General Pardon also was read by the Lord Chancellor, and medals flung up and down by my Lord Cornwallis, of silver, but I could not come by any. But so great a noise that I could make but little of the music; and indeed, it was lost to everybody.

I went out a little while before the King had done all his ceremonies, and went round the Abbey to Westminster Hall, all the way within rails, and 10,000 people, with the ground covered with blue cloth; and scaffolds all the way. Into the Hall I got, where it was very fine with hangings and scaffolds one upon another full of brave ladies; and my wife in one little one, on the right hand. Here I stayed walking up and down, and at last, upon one of the side stalls, I stood and saw the King come in with all the persons (but the soldiers) that were yesterday in the cavalcade; and a most pleasant sight it was to see them in their several robes. And the King came in with his crown on, and his scepter in his hand, under a canopy borne up by six silver staves, carried by Barons of the Cinque Ports,[3] and little bells at every end.

And after a long time, he got up to the farther end, and all set themselves down at their several tables; and that was also a brave sight; and the King's first course carried up by the Knights of the Bath. And many fine ceremonies there was of the herald's leading up people before him, and bowing; and my Lord of Albemarle's going to the kitchen and eat a bit of the first dish that was to go to the King's table. But, above all, was these three Lords, Northumberland, and Suffolk, and the Duke of Ormond, coming before the courses on horseback, and staying so all dinnertime, and at last to bring up [4] [Dymock] the King's champion, all in armor on horseback, with his spear and target carried before him. And a herald proclaims, " That if any dare deny Charles Stuart to be lawful King of England, here was a champion that would fight with him "; and with these words, the champion flings down his gauntlet, and all this he do three times in his going up toward the King's table. At last when he is come, the King drinks to him, and then sends him the cup, which is of gold, and he drinks it off, and then rides back again with the cup in his hand. I went from table to table to see the bishops and all others at their dinner, and was infinitely pleased with it. And at the Lords' table, I met with William Howe, and he spoke to my Lord for me, and he did give me four rabbits and a pullet, and so I got it and Mr. Creed and I got Mr. Michell to give us some bread, and so we at a stall eat [5] it, as everybody

---

[1] *mond:* an orb of gold, with a cross set with precious stones.

[2] *King at Arms:* head of the heralds.

[3] *Cinque* (sĭngk) *Ports:* five ports on the English Channel: Hastings, Sandwich, Dover, Romney, and Hythe.

[4] The ceremony here described is no longer observed as part of the coronation. It was a holdover from the days of chivalry.

[5] *eat* (ĕt): Americans would say *ate.*

else did what they could get. I took a great deal of pleasure to go up and down, and look upon the ladies, and to hear the music of all sorts, but above all, the twenty-four violins.

THE LONDON FIRE

September 2, 1666. (Lord's Day.) Some of our maids sitting up late last night to get things ready against our feast today, Jane called us up about three in the morning, to tell us of a great fire they saw in the city. So I rose and slipped on my nightgown, and went to her window, and thought it to be on the back side of Mark Lane at the farthest; but, being unused to such fires as followed, I thought it far enough off; and so went to bed again and to sleep. About seven rose again to dress myself, and there looked out at the window, and saw the fire not so much as it was and farther off. So to my closet to set things to rights after yesterday's cleaning.

By and by Jane comes and tells me that she hears that above 300 houses have been burned down tonight by the fire we saw, and that it is now burning down all Fish Street, by London Bridge. So I made myself ready presently, and walked to the Tower,[1] and there got up upon one of the high places, Sir J. Robinson's little son going up with me; and there I did see the houses at that end of the bridge all on fire, and an infinite great fire on this and the other side the end of the bridge; which, among other people, did trouble me for poor little Michell and our Sarah on the bridge.[2] So down, with my heart full of trouble, to the Lieutenant of the Tower, who tells me that it begun this morning in the King's baker's house in Pudding Lane, and that it hath burned St. Magnus Church and most part of Fish Street already. So I

down to the waterside, and there got a boat and through bridge, and there saw a lamentable fire. Poor Michell's house, as far as the Old Swan, already burned that way, and the fire running farther, that in a very little time it got as far as the Steel Yard, while I was there. Everybody endeavoring to remove their goods, and flinging into the river or bringing them into lighters that lay off; poor people staying in their houses as long as till the very fire touched them, and then running into boats, or clambering from one pair of stairs by the waterside to another. And among other things, the poor pigeons, I perceive, were loath to leave their houses, but hovered about the windows and balconies till they were, some of them burned, their wings, and fell down. Having stayed, and in an hour's time seen the fire rage every way, and nobody, to my sight, endeavoring to quench it, but to

---

[1] *Tower:* the Tower of London.
[2] *on the bridge:* Old London Bridge was like a street with houses built on it.

remove their goods, and leave all to the fire, and having seen it get as far as the Steel Yard, and the wind mighty high and driving it into the City; [1] and everything, after so long a drought, proving combustible, even the very stones of churches. I to Whitehall, and there up to the King's closet in the Chapel, where people come about me, and I did give them an account dismayed them all, and word was carried in to the King. So I was called for, and did tell the King and Duke of York what I saw, and that unless his Majesty did command houses to be pulled down nothing could stop the fire. They seemed much troubled, and the King commanded me to go to my Lord Mayor from him, and command him to spare no houses, but to pull down before the fire every way. The Duke of York bid me tell him that if he would have any more soldiers he shall; and so did my Lord Arlington afterward, as a great secret. Here meeting with Captain Cocke, I in his coach, which he lent me, and Creed with me to Paul's, [2] and there walked along Watling Street, as well as I could, every creature coming away laden with goods to save, and here and there sick people carried away in beds. Extraordinary good goods carried in carts and on backs. At last met my Lord Mayor in Canning Street, like a man spent, with a handkerchief about his neck. To the King's message he cried, like a fainting woman, " Lord! what can I do? I am spent: people will not obey me. I have been pulling down houses; but the fire overtakes us faster than we can do it." That he needed no more soldiers and that, for himself, he must go and refresh himself, having been up all night.

So he left me, and I him, and walked home, seeing people all almost distracted, and no manner of means used to quench the fire. The houses, too,

so very thick thereabouts, and full of matter for burning, as pitch and tar, in Thames Street; and warehouses of oil, and wines, and brandy, and other things. Here I saw Mr. Issake Houblon, the handsome man, prettily dressed and dirty, at his door at Dowgate, receiving some of his brothers' things, whose houses were on fire; and, as he says, have been removed twice already; and he doubts (as it soon proved) that they must be in a little time removed from his house also, which was a sad consideration. And to see the churches all filling with goods by people who themselves should have been quietly there at this time.

By this time it was about twelve o'clock; and so home. Soon as dined, away, and walked through the city, the streets full of nothing but people and horses and carts laden with goods, ready to run over one another, and removing goods from one burned house to another. They now removing out of Canning Street (which received goods in the morning) into Lumbard Street, and farther; and among others I now saw my little goldsmith, Stokes, receiving some friend's goods, whose house itself was burned the day after. We parted at Paul's; he home, and I to Paul's Wharf, where I had appointed a boat to attend me, and took in Mr. Carcasse and his brother, whom I met in the street, and carried them below and above bridge, to and again to see the fire, which was now got farther, both below and above, and no likelihood of stopping it. Met with the King and Duke of York in their barge, and with them to Queenhithe, and there called Sir Richard Browne to them. Their order was only to pull down houses apace, and so below bridge at the waterside; but little was or could be done, the fire coming upon them so fast. Good hopes there was of stopping it at the Three Cranes above, and at Buttolph's Wharf below bridge, if care be used; but the wind carries it into the

[1] *City:* the area of the original city of London, now its commercial center.

[2] *Paul's:* St. Paul's Cathedral.

City, so as we know not by the waterside what it do there. River full of lighters and boats taking in goods, and good goods swimming in the water, and only observed that hardly one lighter or boat in three that had the goods of a house in, but there was a pair of virginals [1] in it.

Having seen as much as I could now, away to Whitehall by appointment and there walked to St. James's Park, and there met my wife and Creed and walked to my boat; and there upon the water again, and to the fire up and down, it still increasing, and the wind great. So near the fire as we could for smoke; and all over the Thames, with one's face in the wind, you were almost burned with a shower of firedrops. This is very true; so as houses were burned by these drops and flakes of fire, three or four, nay, five or six houses, one from another. When we could endure no more upon the water, we to a little alehouse on the Bankside, over against the Three Cranes, and there stayed till it was dark almost, and saw the fire grow; and, as it grew darker, appeared more and more, and in corners and upon steeples, and between churches and houses, as far as we could see up the hill of the City, in a most horrid malicious bloody flame, not like the fine flame of an ordinary fire. Barbary and her husband away before us. We stayed till, it being darkish, we saw the fire as only one entire arch of fire from this to the other side of the bridge and in a bow up the hill for an arch of above a mile long: it made me weep to see it. The churches, houses, and all on fire and flaming at once; and a horrid noise the flames made, and the crackling of houses at their ruin.

[1] *virginal:* a keyed musical instrument popular in the sixteenth and seventeenth centuries.

So home with a sad heart, and there find everybody discoursing and lamenting the fire; and poor Tom Hater come with some few of his goods saved out of his house, which is burned upon Fish Street Hill. I invited him to lie at my house, and did receive his goods, but was deceived in his lying there, the news coming every moment of the growth of the fire; so as we were forced to begin to pack up our own goods, and prepare for their removal; and did by moonshine (it being brave dry, and moonshine, and warm weather) carry much of my goods into the garden, and Mr. Hater and I did remove my money and iron chests into my cellar, as thinking that the safest place. And got my bags of gold into my office, ready to carry away, and my chief papers of accounts also there, and my tallies into a box by themselves. So great was our fear, as Sir W. Batten hath carts come out of the country to fetch away his goods this night. We did put Mr. Hater, poor man, to bed a little; but he got but very little rest, so much noise being in my house, taking down of goods.

3rd. About four o'clock in the morning, my Lady Batten sent me a cart to carry away all my money, and plate, and best things, to Sir W. Rider's at Bednall Green. Which I did, riding myself in my nightgown in the cart; and, Lord! to see how the streets and the highways are crowded with people running and riding, and getting of carts at any rate to fetch away things. I find Sir W. Rider tired with being called up all night, and receiving things from several friends. His house full of goods, and much of Sir W. Batten's and Sir W. Pen's. I am eased at my heart to have my treasure so well secured. Then home, with much ado to find a way, nor any sleep all this night to me nor my poor wife.

THE DIARY OF SAMUEL PEPYS

1. What does the *Diary* tell you about Pepys as a husband, a son, a brother, the master of a household, a social companion? What indications do you find that he was a "rising young man" in London?

2. What light does the *Diary* throw on life and customs of that day that differ from ours? What details of his description of public events stand out with special vividness in your mind? In modern life what events would attract the keen attention of a man like Pepys?

3. What, in your opinion, makes the *Diary* so interesting? Write down some rules for good reporting that you find illustrated in it. Students of journalism may discuss them in class.

SUGGESTIONS FOR WRITING

1. Write some diary entries of your own life, imitating Pepys' style as far as possible.

2. If you have witnessed a great fire, storm, accident, or other calamity, write an account of it, emphasizing details that will make the reader feel present himself.

3. Most people begin writing a diary sometime during their lives, but few keep it up. If you are one who has abandoned a diary, write an account of "My Troubles in Trying to Keep a Diary."

JOHN DRYDEN 1631–1700

Beginning with the seventeenth century, English writers became more close-knit as a group, more intimate with one another *as writers,* so that a figure like Ben Jonson in the early part of the century, or Dryden in the later part, could become the literary leader of a period. Today we often speak of the "Age of Dryden." Dryden was poet laureate, like Jonson before him. He wrote poetic plays, including the famous one about Antony and Cleopatra, *All for Love,* and many lyrics that established him as the first poet of his day. He wrote political satires, which were the outcome of the Puritan-Royalist controversies, and literary criticism. He has often been called "the father of English prose."

Dryden was born in a Puritan family and educated at Cambridge. His allegiances, political and religious, shifted with the times. In his early poetry he defended the Commonwealth, but after the Restoration he praised Charles II. He wrote first in support of the Church of England but again, when a Catholic king came to the throne, Dryden became a Catholic and wrote the noted poem "The Hind and the Panther," which represents the Catholic Church as a "milk-white Hind" beset by all sorts of animals representing the Protestant sects. When the Catholic James II was driven from the throne in 1688, Dryden remained constant in his faith, thereby losing all his political advantages. He spent his last years mainly in writing translations of the classics. When he died, he was buried with honor at the side of Chaucer in Westminster Abbey.

Alexander's Feast, or the Power of Music

The first choral society was formed in London in 1683. Every November 22 this society gave a concert in honor of St. Cecilia, the patron saint of music. The following ode is one of two Dryden wrote for these occasions. St. Cecilia was an early Christian martyr who, legend says, invented an arrangement of musical pipes, the forerunner of the organ, on which she played such exquisite music that an angel came down from heaven to listen.

In his tribute to music, Dryden chose as his central character Alexander the Great (356–323 B.C.), the powerful conqueror of the known world of his day. The scene is ancient Persia on a feast day. With the lovely young Thais (thā'ĭs) as companion,

Alexander listens to his musician Timotheus (tǐ·mŏth′ê·ŭs) play the lyre. He is
moved to pride, pity, love, anger; he is, in
fact, overcome by the power of the music.

But, Dryden concludes, although Timotheus conquered a conqueror, Cecilia performed an equal or greater feat: she called
an angel down from heaven.

Twas at the royal feast for Persia won
      By Philip's warlike son —
    Aloft in awful state
    The godlike hero sate
      On his imperial throne;   5
  His valiant peers were placed around,
Their brows with roses and with myrtles bound,
(So should desert in arms be crowned);
The lovely Thais by his side
Sate like a blooming Eastern bride   10
In flower of youth and beauty's pride:
    Happy, happy, happy pair!
      None but the brave,
      None but the brave,
      None but the brave deserves the fair!   15

    Timotheus placed on high
      Amid the tuneful quire°
With flying fingers touched the lyre;
    The trembling notes ascend the sky
      And heavenly joys inspire.   20
The song began from Jove,°
Who left his blissful seats above —
Such is the power of mighty love!
A dragon's fiery form belied the god;°
Sublime on radiant spires he rode   25
When he to fair Olympia° pressed,
And while he sought her snowy breast,
Then round her slender waist he curled,
And stamped an image of himself, a sovereign
    of the world.
— The listening crowd admire the lofty sound.   30
A present deity! they shout around;
A present deity! the vaulted roofs rebound;
        With ravished ears
        The monarch hears,
        Assumes the god;   35
        Affects to nod
    And seems to shake the spheres.

17. *quire:* an old spelling of "choir." 21. Timotheus began by
singing about Jove, the chief of the gods, who was supposed to
be Alexander's father. In ancient days popular belief often acclaimed a ruler as a descendant of a god. In Dryden's own day
the "divine right of kings" was a parallel superstition clung to
by the Royalists. 24. *A dragon's . . . god:* Jove assumed the shape
of a dragon. 26. *Olympia* (ō·lǐm′pǐ·à): The name of Alexander's
mother was Olympias.

The praise of Bacchus° then the sweet musician sung,
    Of Bacchus ever fair and ever young;
        The jolly god in triumph comes;   40
        Sound the trumpets, beat the drums!
            Flushed with a purple grace
            He shows his honest face
Now give the hautboys breath; he comes, he comes!
        Bacchus, ever fair and young,   45
           Drinking joys did first ordain;
        Bacchus' blessings are a treasure,
        Drinking is the soldier's pleasure;
            Rich the treasure,
            Sweet the pleasure,   50
        Sweet is pleasure after pain.

Soothed with the sound, the king grew vain;
    Fought all his battles o'er again,
And thrice he routed all his foes, and thrice he slew the slain!
    The master saw the madness rise,   55
    His glowing cheeks, his ardent eyes;
    And while he Heaven and Earth defied
    Changed his hand and checked his pride.
        He chose a mournful Muse
        Soft pity to infuse;   60
        He sung Darius° great and good,
          By too severe a fate
        Fallen, fallen, fallen, fallen,
          Fallen from his high estate,
         And weltering in his blood;   65
        Deserted at his utmost need
        By those his former bounty fed;
        On the bare earth exposed he lies
        With not a friend to close his eyes.
        With downcast looks the joyless victor sate,   70
            Revolving in his altered soul
                The various turns of Chance below;
            And now and then a sigh he stole,
                And tears began to flow.

        The mighty master smiled to see   75
        That love was in the next degree;
        'Twas but a kindred sound to move,
        For pity melts the mind to love.
          Softly sweet, in Lydian° measures
          Soon he soothed his soul to pleasures.   80
        War, he sung, is toil and trouble,

38. *Bacchus* (băk′ŭs): the god of wine. 61. *Darius* (dȧ·rī′ŭs):
the Persian king whom Alexander had just defeated. 79. *Lydian:*
The music of Lydia, a province of Asia Minor, was of light and
delicate quality.

    Honor but an empty bubble;
        Never ending, still beginning,
    Fighting still, and still destroying;
        If the world be worth thy winning,   85
    Think, O think, it worth enjoying;
        Lovely Thais sits beside thee,
        Take the good the gods provide thee!
— The many rend the skies with loud applause;
So Love was crowned, but Music won the cause.   90
    The prince, unable to conceal his pain,
            Gazed on the fair
            Who caused his care,
    And sighed and looked, sighed and looked,
    Sighed and looked, and sighed again;   95
At length with love and wine at once oppressed
The vanquished victor sunk upon her breast.

    Now strike the golden lyre again:
    A louder yet, and yet a louder strain!
    Break his bands of sleep asunder   100
    And rouse him like a rattling peal of thunder.
        Hark, hark! the horrid sound
            Has raised up his head;
            As awaked from the dead
        And amazed he stares around.   105
    Revenge, revenge, Timotheus cries,
        See the Furies° arise!
        See the snakes that they rear,
        How they hiss in their hair,
    And the sparkles that flash from their eyes!   110
        Behold a ghastly band,
        Each a torch in his hand!
Those are Grecian ghosts, that in battle were slain,
        And unburied remain°
        Inglorious on the plain.   115
        Give the vengeance due
        To the valiant crew!
Behold how they toss their torches on high,
    How they point to the Persian abodes
And glittering temples of their hostile gods.   120
— The princes applaud with a furious joy;
And the King seized a flambeau° with zeal to destroy;

107. *Furies:* the Greek avengers of crime, who were represented
as furious creatures with snaky hair. 114. *unburied remain:* The
Greeks believed that the soul of an unburied person could not
cross the river Styx into the realms of the dead, but must wander
piteously on the nearer shore until burial. This belief gives
special force to the vengeance of the next lines. 122. *flambeau:*
a flaming torch.

Thais led the way
    To light him to his prey,
And, like another Helen,° fired another Troy!   125

     — Thus, long ago,
  Ere heaving bellows learned to blow,
    While organs yet were mute,
    Timotheus, to his breathing flute
      And sounding lyre   130
Could swell the soul to rage, or kindle soft desire.
  At last divine Cecilia came,
  Inventress of the vocal frame;°
The sweet enthusiast from her sacred store
  Enlarged the former narrow bounds,   135
  And added length to solemn sounds,
With Nature's mother wit, and arts unknown before.
  — Let old Timotheus yield the prize
    Or both divide the crown;
  He raised a mortal to the skies;   140
    She drew an angel down!

125. *Helen:* the wife of the Greek king Menelaus who, by eloping to Troy with Paris, brought on the Trojan War, which resulted in the burning of Troy. 133. *vocal frame:* the organ.

An Essay on Dramatic Poesy

Before Dryden's time there was little of what we today call *literary criticism* — discussions of the importance or merits or interesting features of literature. Dryden's *Essay on Dramatic Poesy* is perhaps the first important work in English literary criticism. In the excerpt given here, he considers the ancients versus the moderns — always a favorite topic with critics. He discusses writers close to his own times, and he contrasts Shakespeare, who followed none of the old classical rules of writing drama, with Jonson, who wrote along the principles of the ancient Greek and Roman dramatists. You will notice that Dryden sees value in both schools of thought.

To BEGIN, then, with Shakespeare. He was the man who of all modern, and perhaps ancient poets, had the largest and most comprehensive soul. All the images of Nature were still present in him, and he drew them, not laboriously, but luckily; when he describes anything, you more than see it, you feel it too. Those who accuse him to have wanted [1] learning give him the greater commendation: he was naturally learned. He needed not the spectacles of books to read Nature; he looked inwards, and found her there. I cannot say he is everywhere alike; were he so, I should do him injury to compare him with the greatest of mankind. He is many times flat, insipid; his comic wit degenerating into clenches,[2] his serious swelling into bombast. But he is always great when some great occasion is presented to him; no man can say he ever had a fit subject for his wit [3] and did not raise himself as high above the rest of poets,

Quantum lenta solent inter viburna cupressi.[4]

The consideration of this made Mr. Hales of Eton say, that there is no subject of which any poet ever writ, but he would produce it much better done in Shakespeare; and however others are now more generally preferred before him, yet the age wherein he lived, which had contemporaries with him Fletcher and Jonson, never equalled them to him in their esteem: and in the last King's

court, when Ben's reputation was at highest, Sir John Suckling, and with him the greater part of the courtiers, set our Shakespeare far above him.

Beaumont and Fletcher,[5] of whom I am next to speak, had, with the advantage of Shakespeare's wit, which was their precedent, great natural gifts, improved by study. . . . The first play that brought Fletcher and him in esteem was their *Philaster:* for, before that, they had written two or three very unsuccessfully, as the like is reported of Ben Jonson, before he writ *Every Man in His Humor.* Their plots were generally more regular than Shakespeare's, especially those that were made before Beaumont's death; and they understood and imitated the conversation of gentlemen much better; whose wild debaucheries, and quickness of wit in repartees, no poet before them could paint as they have done. Humor, which Ben Jonson derived from particular persons, they made it their business not to describe: they represented all the passions very lively, but above all, love. I am apt to believe the English language in them arrived to its highest perfection: what words have since been taken in are rather superfluous than ornamental. Their plays are now the most pleasant and frequent entertainments of the stage; two of theirs being acted through the year for one of Shakespeare's or Jonson's: the reason is, because there is a certain gaiety in their comedies, and pathos in their more serious plays, which suit generally with all men's humors. Shakespeare's language is likewise a little obsolete, and Ben Jonson's wit comes short of theirs.

As for Jonson, to whose character I am now arrived, if we look upon him while he was himself (for his last plays were but his dotages [6]), I think him the

---

[1] *wanted:* lacked.

[2] *clenches:* puns; this meaning is now obsolete.

[3] *wit:* Throughout, Dryden uses the word "wit" to mean "imaginative and inventive mind," rather than just "humor," as we tend today to define it.

[4] *Quantum . . . cupressi:* as cypresses are accustomed to rise above bending shrubs.

[5] *Beaumont and Fletcher:* English dramatists of the Elizabethan era who were joint authors of many plays.

[6] *dotages* (dō'tĭj·ĕz): products of a feeble old age.

Dryden's prose style is often considered a model of grace and clarity. His influence on the English language was such that Dr. Samuel Johnson said of him: " He found it brick and he left it marble."

most learned and judicious writer which any theater ever had. He was a most severe judge of himself, as well as others. One cannot say he wanted wit, but rather that he was frugal of it. In his works you find little to retrench or alter. Wit, and language, and humor also in some measure we had before him; but something of art was wanting to the drama till he came. He managed his strength to more advantage than any who preceded him. You seldom find him making love in any of his scenes, or endeavoring to move the passions; his genius was too sullen and saturnine [1] to do it gracefully, especially when he knew he came after those who had performed both to such a height. Humor was his proper sphere; and in that he delighted most to represent mechanic people.[2] He was deeply conversant in the ancients, both Greek and Latin, and he borrowed boldly from them: there is scarcely a poet or historian among the Roman authors of those times whom he has not translated in *Sejanus* and *Catiline*.[3] But he has done his robberies so openly, that one may see he fears not to be taxed by any law. He invades authors like a monarch; and what would be theft in other poets is only victory in him. With the spoils of these writers he so represents old Rome to us, in its rites, ceremonies, and customs, that if one of their poets had written either of his tragedies, we had seen less of it than in him. If there was any fault in his language, 'twas that he weaved it too closely and laboriously, in

---

[1] *saturnine* (săt′ĕr·nĭn): gloomy, dull.
[2] *mechanic people:* people of the artisan class.
[3] *Sejanus* (sē·jā′nŭs) and *Catiline* (kăt′ĭ·lĭn): plays by Jonson.

his comedies especially: perhaps, too, he did a little too much to Romanize our tongue, leaving the words which he translated almost as much Latin as when he found them: wherein, though he learnedly followed their language, he did not enough comply with the idiom of ours. If I would compare him with Shakespeare, I must acknowledge him the more correct poet, but Shakespeare the greater wit. Shakespeare was the Homer,[4] or father of our dramatic poets; Jonson was the Virgil,[5] the pattern of elaborate writing; I admire him, but I love Shakespeare. To conclude of him; as he has given us the most correct plays, so in the precepts which he has laid down in his *Discoveries,* we have as many and profitable rules for perfecting the stage, as any wherewith the French can furnish us. . . .

---

[4] *Homer:* the author of the *Iliad* and perhaps the *Odyssey*, the greatest of ancient epic poems.
[5] *Virgil:* Roman author of the epic, the *Aeneid*.

DRYDEN AS POET AND CRITIC

1. Give a brief picture of the setting of " Alexander's Feast " as you imagine it. What point does Dryden make about music? How is his poem a compliment to St. Cecilia?

2. The following musical selections will provide a good background for the poem:

Lines 21–37: " Ode to Joy " Beethoven's *Ninth Symphony,* last movement
Lines 38–51: " Soldier's Chorus " from Gounod's *Faust*
Lines 52–74: " The Death of Ase " by Grieg
Lines 75–97: " Serenade " by Schubert
Lines 98–115: *1812 Overture* by Tchaikovsky
Lines 126–41: *Largo* by Handel

What other music are you reminded of by the different moods of the poem?

3. In the *Essay on Dramatic Poesy* what differences do you find between Dryden's appraisal of Shakespeare and that of Ben Jonson in his poem on page 201? Why does one feel more confidence in a critic's judg-

ment when he makes both favorable and unfavorable criticisms? Can you find in *Macbeth* or other plays some examples of Shakespeare's puns and bombast mentioned by Dryden? Wherein does he think Shakespeare's excellence lies?

4. According to Dryden, what are Jonson's strong and weak points? Does he condemn Jonson for borrowing from the ancients? Discuss " borrowing " in the present dramatic world.

READING LIST FOR
THE SEVENTEENTH CENTURY

Barnes, Margaret, *With All My Heart*
Romantic story of Restoration times, based on the life of Catherine, wife of Charles II.

Bentley, Phyllis E., *The Power and the Glory*
A tale of English weavers during the troubled years of the mid-seventeenth century. Charles I and Cromwell both appear in the story.

Blackmore, R. D., *Lorna Doone*
Classic romance of a sturdy yeoman and the child of an outlaw family, set in southwestern England. Ruthless Judge Jeffreys is a vividly drawn historical character.

Brittain, Vera M., *Valiant Pilgrim, The Story of John Bunyan and Puritan England*
A vividly written biography of a unique Puritan whose " dreams " influenced the world.

Bryher, Winnifred, *The Player's Boy*
Not much plot, but a beautifully written story of the days following Queen Elizabeth.

Buchan, John, *Oliver Cromwell*
Excellent biography, clarifying some of the seeming contradictions in Cromwell's character. (Mature.)

Cannon, Le Grand, *Come Home at Even*
Seeking religious freedom, an Englishman and his wife go to America, but return to England when the wife becomes homesick for the old country.

Costain, Thomas, *For My Great Folly*
English pirates during the reign of James I.

Doyle, A. Conan, *Micah Clarke*
Doyle makes the stirring events of Monmouth's Rebellion in 1685 as exciting as his Sherlock Holmes stories.

Fuller, Edmund, *John Milton*
Emphasis on Milton as a seventeenth-century man.

Hawes, C. B., *Dark Frigate*
Thrilling adventures of an English runaway lad on the high seas. Excellent picture of seventeenth-century ships and sailing hazards. (Easy reading.)

Irwin, Margaret, *Strange Prince*
The decisive battle of Marston Moor, in which Prince Rupert, in command of Royalist forces, was first victor, then vanquished.

John, Ivan, *Crippled Splendor*
The life of James Stuart.

Mills, Dorothy, *Renaissance and Reformation*
Clarifies many confusing points in these two great ages.

Neill, Robert, *Rebel Heiress*
A romantic tale of the Restoration, with emphasis on differences in religion and politics.

Quiller-Couch, Arthur, *The Splendid Spur*
The Western campaign of Charles I during the Civil War.

Sabatini, Raphael, *Fortune's Fool*
A novel about Monmouth's Rebellion, and the events preceding the Glorious Revolution, including an account of the Plague.

Scott, Sir Walter, *Old Mortality*
A story about the Covenanters and Cavaliers of Scotland, as told by an eccentric cleaner of gravestones.

——, *Woodstock*
Many historical characters, such as Ben Jonson and Milton, enter into this tale of the disguises and escapes of Charles II during the Commonwealth.

Sutcliff, Rosemary, *Simon*
How a personal friendship between a Cavalier and a Roundhead is affected by the English Civil War. The author knows her scenes first hand. (Easy reading.)

FOR LISTENING

The following poems have been recorded and are available on *Many Voices 6A:* " Death Be Not Proud," " Counsel to Girls," " The Constant Lover," " To Althea, from Prison," " Shall I, Wasting in Despair," " On His Blindness."

THE EIGHTEENTH

COMPLACENCY — a satisfaction with the achievements of the past century — marked the beginning of the eighteenth century. The upper classes, in complete control, wanted no religious enthusiasts, no reformers, no revolutionaries. Men of the time accepted the idea of a stable social order, handed down from one age to another. They believed in reason, and their watchword was Common Sense.

The century closed, however, with revolutions exploding in the American colonies and in France. The aristocrats tried to maintain their wealth and political power, but the middle classes were exerting their force and becoming more powerful as the century ended. As always, these great movements in history are reflected in the literature of the times.

EXPANDING EMPIRE

Common sense began at home in government. Rival factions, learning to live together without bloodshed or revolution, united as a family against threats from the outside. Rivalry and war with France helped as much as

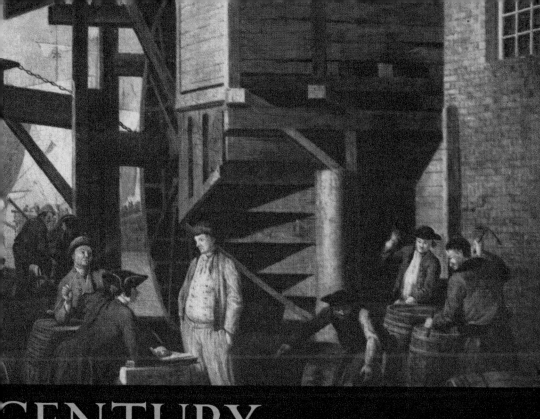

CENTURY 1700-1800

anything to keep Englishmen together. Off and on for more than a hundred years — from 1689 until Napoleon lost the Battle of Waterloo in 1815 — England and France were at war. Just as Spain had been the huge expanding power that menaced the Elizabethans, now France had become the great threat. Yet France did not make good her threat, and the English Georges emerged at the end of the century with a vastly expanded empire, despite the loss of the American colonies.

In this century England acquired Gibraltar (which gave her control of the Mediterranean), Canada, and some of the West Indies, as well as trading posts in Africa and parts of India. Most of these territories were won as a result of wars. The campaigns were fought always on foreign soil with small professional armies, including paid foreign soldiers — like the Hessians that made up more than half of the British forces in the American campaigns.

England was becoming more and more involved in world affairs as she gradually built up her territories. As far as the ordinary Londoner was concerned, however, war affected only his morning news and his trade ledger, for he paid heavy taxes on such things as linen, silk, sugar, tea, and coffee. Englishmen followed each season's campaign with about as much interest, and as much danger to themselves, as we have in following a World Series in baseball. The effect of these wars, however, changed the face of the world by increasing the power, confidence, and extent of the British empire.

"RULE, BRITANNIA"

The eighteenth century produced the words for the British national anthem, " God Save the King," and both the words and music of another patriotic song, " Rule, Britannia." England ruled the waves and was mistress of the seas. She liked to think of herself as the worthy successor of the great Roman Empire. The first half of the century was often called the Augustan Age, after the first Roman Emperor, Augustus. Never in modern times, Englishmen believed, had civilization come so close to the peak of polite perfection as in their own country and their own age.

Because so many people agreed in thinking that the age was perfecting and expanding civilization, the polish and glitter and confidence of the upper classes was inevitable. England seemed to be the center of the seven seas. It was easy for an Englishman to assume that by a flick of the pen in London, the fur trade of Hudson's Bay Company, a stamp tax in the American colonies, or an edict governing the lives of millions in India could be decided.

Toward the end of the century, a new trend became evident. Advances in farming and industrial methods came about with the invention of a drill for sowing seed, a threshing machine, a pumping machine for mines. From the spinning jenny there evolved a new loom, patented by Arkwright in 1768. James Watt obtained the first patent for his steam engine a year later. These and other inventions ushered in the Industrial Revolution, whose profound effects were felt throughout all of English life and literature.

LONDON, THE HUB OF LIFE

All roads led to London. The kind of city life familiar to us today was then beginning. Its outstanding institution was the coffeehouse, the meeting place in which to hear the news of the day. Each group had its special coffeehouse: the clergy, Childs; the politicians, St. James; the stockholders, Jonathans; men of fashion, Whites; the literati, Wills and Buttons.

It was a fashionable city, but it was also a city of opportunity. To make their fortunes, young men took the highroads to London — from Lichfield (Johnson and Garrick), from Scotland (James Boswell), from Ireland (Oliver Goldsmith). The city was crowded and exciting. " A man who is tired of London," said Johnson, " is tired of life."

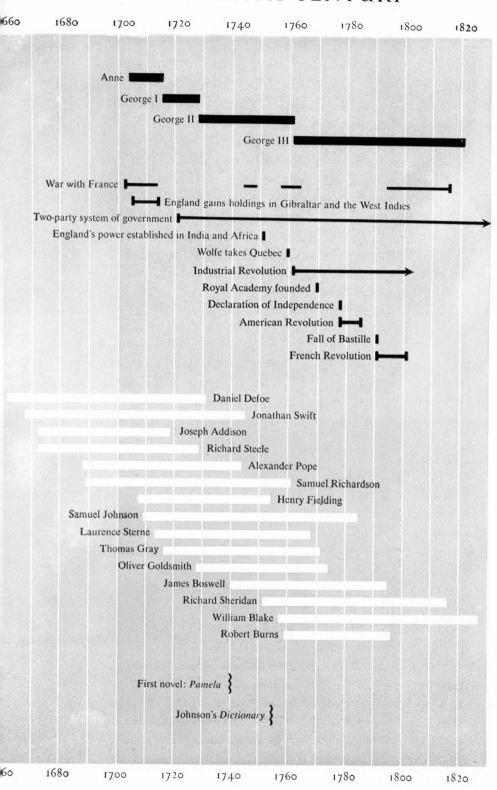

660   1680   1700   1720   1740   1760   1780   1800   1820

Anne

George I

George II

George III

War with France

England gains holdings in Gibraltar and the West Indies

Two-party system of government

England's power established in India and Africa

Wolfe takes Quebec

Industrial Revolution

Royal Academy founded

Declaration of Independence

American Revolution

Fall of Bastille

French Revolution

Daniel Defoe

Jonathan Swift

Joseph Addison

Richard Steele

Alexander Pope

Samuel Richardson

Henry Fielding

Samuel Johnson

Laurence Sterne

Thomas Gray

Oliver Goldsmith

James Boswell

Richard Sheridan

William Blake

Robert Burns

First novel: *Pamela* }

Johnson's *Dictionary* }

60   1680   1700   1720   1740   1760   1780   1800   1820

THE FIRST THREE GEORGES

England, having had enough of headstrong monarchs in the seventeenth century, was content to put up with a set of rather dull monarchs in the eighteenth. After William and Mary came Queen Anne (1702–1714), Mary's sister and the last of the Stuarts. Though her reign produced a brilliant literature and society, she herself was somewhat mouselike and commonplace, and unlucky enough to have none of her many children live to succeed her. When she died, her cousin from the small German kingdom of Hanover was brought in to rule England as George I (1714–1727). He could speak no English and took little interest in his adopted country. His son George II (1727–1760) was different rather than better. It was said that " a dapper and strutting German has stepped into the shoes of a boorish and surly one." George II had a long reign, but his grandson George III (1760–1820) had the longest reign of them all, though his last years were clouded by insanity. George III had enough of his ancestors' dense stubbornness to lose the American colonies even while his empire was expanding on other fronts.

TWO-PARTY POLITICS

Because the Hanoverian kings possessed little appeal and were not fluent in the language of the country they ruled, the government fell increasingly into the hands of party leaders. Their contests established the two-party system, which has continued to operate in both England and the United States ever since. The Tory or conservative party defended the kingship, the old traditions, and the noble country families. The Whig or liberal party, allied with the city aristocrats and merchants, sought to increase the powers of Parliament and to advance commerce, education, and human brotherhood. Between them, the two parties controlled the cabinet of the king's ministers. One of the Whig ministers, Robert Walpole, held such power from 1721 to 1742 that he practically created the office of Prime Minister.

To nearly every Englishman, money and power in government seemed important. Political pamphlets did then the work now done by radio, television, newspapers, billboards, and campaign speeches. Each party prized good writers, and literary men were eager to offer their services in shaping the government. Alexander Pope was a friend of brilliant statesmen. Jonathan Swift wrote many powerful tracts for the Tories, and he became embittered when they brought him no preferment. Joseph Addison had some amusing as well as wise things to say about " party feeling " (see page 297). Daniel Defoe, more widely known to the men of his time for his political pamphlets than for *Robinson Crusoe,* might be called a political profiteer, for he sold the services of his pen to both sides.

BRITAIN
1700-1837

SCOTLAND

Edinburgh [1]

Auchinleck [3]

Ayr [2]

R. Doon

R. Afton

R. Tweed

Abbotsford [4]

LAKE
DISTRICT

Grasmere [5]

YORKSHIRE
MOORS

Haworth [8]

IRELAND

Lissoy [6]

Dublin [7]

Newstead Abbey [9]

WALES

ENGLAND

Lichfield [10]

Birmingham

Cambridge

Tintern Abbey [11]

Oxford

Stoke Poges [12]

London [13]

Twickenham [14]

1 Boswell was born here; so was Sir Walter Scott, whose novel *The Heart of Midlothian* is set here. 2 Home of Robert Burns. 3 Family seat of the Boswells. 4 Scott's home. 5 Wordsworth and his sister lived in Dove Cottage here. 6 Oliver Goldsmith lived here and perhaps modeled his *Deserted Village* on Lissoy. 7 Birthplace and home of Jonathan Swift. 8 The Brontës lived here. 9 Family seat of Lord Byron. 10 Birthplace of Joseph Addison and Samuel Johnson. 11 Wordsworth wrote his famous ode overlooking this ruin. 12 Thought to be the scene of Gray's "Elegy Written in a Country Churchyard." 13 Coffeehouses flourished in London. Johnson worked on his dictionary in Grub Street; *The Tatler* and *The Spectator* were published here, as was Defoe's early newspaper *The Review*. Boswell recorded his life in London in his *Journal*. Lamb lived and worked in London, and Keats was born here. 14 Alexander Pope's home and, later, Horace Walpole's residence were here.

In the early eighteenth century, then, literature and politics were closely connected. In that Age of Reason the government depended upon arguments and ideas rather than force. The pen seemed mightier than the sword.

ELEGANCE IN ARCHITECTURE

Cultivated formality demanded attractive surroundings. The city of London took on a new kind of beauty — in its parks and esplanades, in Buckingham Palace, and in the churches rebuilt after the Great Fire of 1666. All of these new buildings had Greek and Roman architectural features. The public buildings — for example, the rotunda in the gardens at Ranelagh and the Pantheon in Oxford Street — were spectacular and splendid. In the parks and in the formal gardens of Vauxhall (*vox hall*), the people promenaded and marveled at the overpowering classical columns and domes.

The domestic architecture was in the good taste of the age. In America today there are many so-called Georgian houses, with the same fine brick façades, white Grecian columns, balance, and pleasing proportions that characterized English architecture at the time. The four Adam brothers used Greek models for their elegant interior decoration, while furniture by Chippendale, Hepplewhite, and Sheraton was original and beautiful in design. In this century the Wedgwood potteries began their long history of making fine china, and many of our most popular designs in silverware today are the products of eighteenth-century silversmiths.

The sedan chair was a common means of transportation for English gentlemen in the eighteenth century. The elegance of the period was reflected in clothing, even that of

ELEGANCE IN MANNERS AND DRESS

The literature of the time reflects the interest in manners. In *Gulliver's Travels*, Swift set a very high standard for conduct, largely by demonstrating that much actual behavior was trivial or ridiculous. Pope, in *The Rape of the Lock*, showed how a smooth-running and cultivated society depends upon proportion and good sense and good humor. Addison and Steele in their *Tatler* and *Spectator* essays persuasively pictured well-bred behavior and correct manners — in church, at the theater, playing politics, or making love.

Swift, Pope, and Addison were all critics of manners, but only Swift was savage in his satire. The other two were sympathetic with the very society they were smiling at. Addison admired his characters, even while he found the coquette's heart amusing, or pointed out the foibles of Sir Roger de Coverley, his goodhearted country gentleman.

The upper-class Englishman was as proud and careful of his dress as he was of his manners. Illustrations of this period show ladies wearing full, exquisite costumes, with elaborate powdered headdresses. The men also went in for color and fine materials, for gold braid and lace, snuff-boxes, knee breeches, and silver buckles. In his own home the eighteenth-century gentleman might wear a turban to keep off the chill air, but in formal society, he powdered his hair or wore a curled wig. Even Doctor Johnson, who was careless of his appearance, was forced by his friends to wear wigs, one of which was singed as he nearsightedly peered at books held close to the candle.

children, and in household furnishings like the delicate Chippendale settee and the formal Wedgwood pottery.

DOCTOR JOHNSON'S CIRCLE

Doctor Johnson had his wig trouble (and his Whig trouble, for he was a staunch Tory) only after he was a famous and rather terrifying old man. Against the new currents of thought, Samuel Johnson's influence was powerful. Since he and his friends still maintained conservative ideas, the Age of Johnson followed without much change after the Age of Pope, as the preceding decades are sometimes labeled. The Great Bear, as Johnson was called, knew all the celebrities of his day, and even had a private interview with King George III. One of his best friends was Sir Joshua Reynolds, the painter who was the first president of the Royal Academy, founded in 1768 to promote the fine arts. David Garrick, the best actor of the century, was first Johnson's pupil and later his close friend. Johnson knew Edward Gibbon, who wrote *The Decline and Fall of the Roman Empire* in six volumes of perfectly flowing prose. He knew Oliver Goldsmith and Richard Sheridan, who were making the stage brilliant once again with their comedies *She Stoops to Conquer* and *The School for Scandal*. The statesman and orator Edmund Burke and Doctor Johnson had the greatest respect for each other. Johnson's own massive style in his essays, coupled with the reputation he acquired by compiling his famous *Dictionary* in 1755, made him the literary dictator of London. Young James Boswell came down from Scotland particularly to meet the great lexicographer, and luckily for Johnson and for the world, Boswell became Johnson's friend and biographer.

THE GROWING BROTHERHOOD OF MAN

The old aristocratic society gradually changed. A new spirit was creeping in — a new sense of independence among the underprivileged classes, a new feeling of brotherhood, a new sympathy and warmth. During the last fifty years of the century, people witnessed the American and the French revolutions; they heard the watchwords of liberty, fraternity, and equality. Emotions ran high and the times were restless; yet many believed that a great and better age was beginning.

Englishmen were learning sympathy for others. In the early years of the century, people took trips through the London insane asylum of St. Mary of Bethlehem in order to laugh at the roaring bedlamites. In contrast, the paintings and engravings of William Hogarth, such as " Gin Lane " and " The Rake's Progress " portray the poor with pity and the slums of London with indignation. Reynolds and Gainsborough painted fine ladies and gentlemen in the grand style; but Hogarth in his grotesque, satiric engravings made England aware that all over the country things were wrong and should be changed.

The new literary form — the novel — also widened the social awareness of Englishmen. Defoe wrote of adventurers and rogues and women of loose morals. Richardson made a heroine of Pamela, a virtuous, middle-class maid-servant. Fielding wrote of country squires and roving parsons, imprisoned debtors and ordinary young men. Smollett revealed the seamy and swash-buckling sides of life. Literature, particularly the novel, was portraying life in the lower and middle classes, not the polite society of aristocrats alone. In subject matter and style, writers were becoming more warmly human.

In poetry as well as in the novel, new tones of tenderness and sentiment were heard. Warm emotion began to replace the earlier laughing wit. " The short and simple annals of the poor " were beginning to arouse interest and sympathy. People shed tears over the neglected geniuses that Gray celebrated in the country churchyard at Stoke Poges, or rejoiced with him that such simple country folk had lived " far from the madding crowd's ignoble strife." They were touched by the pictures of perfect rural life that Goldsmith gave in *The Deserted Village*.

Englishmen came to feel that genius was quite different from education or good family. Anyone might be born with original genius. If genius touched an obscure or humble person, so much the better. At one time there was brief public acclaim for a poet who was a thresher and another who was a milkmaid. When the poetic genius Robert Burns, a poor Scots plowman, came along, Edinburgh and London welcomed him with open arms.

FORERUNNERS OF THE ROMANTIC AGE

In Robert Burns, a warmhearted, simple poet, we note the beginnings of a new spirit in men. Burns is the greatest of the forerunners of the romantic spirit in literature, which was to dominate the first half of the next century. In Burns' poetry, and to a lesser extent in Gray's and Blake's, we find the traits and attitudes that mark the change from classicism to romanticism. These have already been pointed out briefly as (1) a sturdy and plainly expressed belief in the brotherhood of man; (2) a deep sympathy with humble lives, human and animal alike; (3) a sense of the independent spirit of man and his natural right to freedom.

Such attitudes are evident on a grand scale in the American Revolution. We must not forget that the battle against tyrannical government was fought not only by Americans but also by English patriots, many of whom opposed George III, Lord North, and other ministers. In a sense, the freedom that the thirteen colonies had won by 1783 had been won also by liberty-loving English-men at home. England had profited from her own mistakes. Her government was firm enough, her people tolerant enough to make possible the enormous expansion that lay ahead.

SUMMARY

In the eighteenth century great changes occurred in England. The nation, expanding from an island to an empire, developed commerce, encouraged industry, increased its wealth, and enriched the arts. At the end of the century, England ruled the seas.

It was a great age of political factions. The Tory party represented the conservative ideals of the country nobility; the Whigs stood for extending the powers of Parliament and for advancing commerce, education, and liberal ideals.

The arts of living flourished in architecture, painting, and literature. Even in graceful furniture, attractive pottery, and fine silverware, English craftsmen excelled.

The elegant society of the early eighteenth century flowered in the writings of Pope, Swift, Addison, and Johnson. However, a reaction to the classical style spurred the first revival of the romantic spirit of earlier days. Literature began portraying the life of the lower and middle classes. A new spirit is evident in Burns, Gray, and Blake — the forerunners of Romanticism.

ALEXANDER POPE 1688–1744

Alexander Pope was a little, wizened, hunchbacked man, but the mind in his puny body was more than a match for the brilliant minds of a brilliant age. He was *the* poet of his day. Nowadays we don't think of Pope's writing as being highly poetic in an imaginative sense or in emotional appeal. Styles have changed. In Pope's day poetry was clipped, terse, and satiric. It had to be " correct " in form, which meant it had to be written in rhymed couplets, each of the two lines in iambic pentameter. No one has surpassed Pope in this kind of verse.

In the eighteenth century quarrels were often started — and settled — in satiric verse. There were times when Pope used his poems like weapons against his political foes and literary rivals. His famous *Dunciad,* or epic of dunces, is a witty and often savage cataloguing of the weaknesses and pretensions of scores of London's writers of the time.

Though his quarrelsomeness and his physical deformity made life hard for Pope, he was unusually fortunate in other ways.

Educated at home as a child, Pope was a prodigy. He began writing polished verses at eleven, and later said he had written his *Essay on Man* at the age of twelve. Because he was a Catholic, he was denied entrance into Oxford or Cambridge and was unable to obtain the political preferment given to other writers. Yet fame came to him early, and he made literature his means of livelihood.

He wrote " Pastorals " at sixteen; at twenty-three he published *An Essay on Criticism,* a didactic poem hailed for its clear, concise reasoning. *The Rape of the Lock* gave him wide reputation at twenty-four; by thirty-two he had made a fortune through his translation from the Greek of *The Iliad.* Because of his health, he then retired from hectic London life to a beautiful villa at Twickenham on the Thames, where he could entertain his few congenial friends in the formal garden and avoid his literary enemies — except in print.

Pope's age was primarily an age of prose, and he wrote only poetry; yet his influence over other writers was so great, both in his own day and later, that we speak today of the Age of Pope.

The Rape of the Lock

Though Pope was often quarrelsome, he had many friends to whom he showed the kindly side of his nature. On one notable occasion he attempted unsuccessfully to act as peacemaker. The result was a unique poem. A certain foppish young baron named Lord Petre had cut off a curl from the hair of Miss Arabella Fermor and refused to give it up. Out of this trivial incident there arose between the two families a quarrel which threatened to become a feud. A friend of Pope's named Caryll suggested that the author write a poem to show the absurdity of all this to-do. Pope, therefore, wrote a " mock heroic " poem. By treating his subject in the grand style of the old epic poems about the Greek heroes, he made it appear particularly ridiculous.

Here you will recognize some of the characteristics of *The Iliad* or *The Odyssey:* These old epics open with a statement of the theme of the poem, followed by an invocation to the Muse to inspire the writer. (You will remember that Milton opens *Paradise Lost* in this same way.) The lives of human beings are influenced throughout by the gods and goddesses, who protect their favorites by warning them in dreams of impending danger; they hover over them in battle and often enter directly into the fray in disguise. After a battle there are songs of triumph by the victors and great lamentations from the vanquished. In the end, mortals are often raised to the rank of gods. Notice how Pope applies these heroic devices to the trivialities of court life.

The poem is in five cantos; but because of its great length, only a part of it is given here. Canto I opens with a formal statement of the theme — " what mighty contests rise from trivial things " — and invokes the Muse to inspire the poet. Then Belinda, heroine of the story, while sleeping late in the morning is visited by the sylph Ariel, who explains that fair ladies are guarded by sylphs and other supernatural creatures who were once living women. Ariel then warns her that some dread fate is hanging over her head, and closes:

" Beware of all, but most beware of man! "

Belinda, awakened by her lap dog, forgets all about the dream while reading a love letter and performing her morning worship before the dressing table, where she adores the heavenly image appearing in the mirror.

In Canto II, Belinda is seen in a pleasure boat on the Thames, being conducted with a group of other young fashionables to the palace of Hampton Court. An adventurous baron admires two curls of Belinda's hair lying upon her neck and determines to obtain them. Belinda's protecting sylph Ariel, greatly agitated at the danger, exhorts the other airy beings hovering about to protect her in every way. The closing lines of the canto are full of suspense:

" With beating hearts the dire event they
    wait,
Anxious and trembling for the birth of
    fate."

CANTO III

Close by those meads, forever crowned with flowers,
Where Thames with pride surveys his rising towers,
There stands a structure of majestic frame,°
Which from the neighboring Hampton takes its name.
Here Britain's statesmen oft the fall foredoom   5
Of foreign tyrants and of nymphs at home;
Here thou, great Anna! whom three realms obey,°
Dost sometimes counsel take — and sometimes tea.°
  Hither the heroes and the nymphs resort,
To taste awhile the pleasures of a court;   10

A gay party of young gentlemen and ladies go up the Thames to Hampton Court.

In various talk th' instructive hours they passed,
Who gave the ball, or paid the visit last;
One speaks the glory of the British Queen,
And one describes a charming Indian screen;
A third interprets motions, looks, and eyes;   15
At every word a reputation dies.
Snuff, or the fan,° supply each pause of chat,
With singing, laughing, ogling, and all that.
  Meanwhile, declining from the noon of day,
The sun obliquely shoots his burning ray;   20
The hungry judges soon the sentence sign,
And wretches hang that jurymen may dine;
The merchant from th' Exchange° returns in peace,
And the long labors° of the toilet cease.

In the afternoon Belinda and two lords engage in a three-handed game of cards.

Belinda now, whom thirst of fame invites,   25
Burns to encounter two adventurous knights,
At omber singly to decide their doom;
And swells her breast with conquests yet to come.
Straight the three bands prepare in arms to join,

3. *structure . . . frame:* Hampton Court, a handsome royal residence near London. 7. Queen Anne was ruler of England, Scotland, and Ireland. 8. *tea:* pronounced tā. 17. *Snuff, or the fan:* Snuff taking in the eighteenth century was almost as widespread among gentlemen as cigarette smoking is today. A lady was seldom without her fan to occupy her hands and often to help her flirtations. 23. *Exchange:* a place where merchants, brokers, and bankers met to transact business. 24. *long labors:* Because of the elaborate, towering headdresses of that time, ladies often spent most of the day at their dressing tables preparing for a ball in the evening.

Each band the number of the sacred nine.°   30
Soon as she spreads her hand, th' aerial guard
Descend, and sit on each important card:
First, Ariel perched upon a Matador,°
Then each, according to the rank they bore;
For sylphs, yet mindful of their ancient race,   35
Are, as when women, wondrous fond of place.
   Behold, four kings in majesty revered,
With hoary whiskers and a forky beard;
And four fair queens whose hands sustain a flower,

The game is
compared to a   The expressive emblem of their softer power;   40
great battle   Four knaves in garbs succinct,° a trusty band,
among kings.   Caps on their heads, and halberts° in their hand;
And particolored troops, a shining train,
Draw forth to combat on the velvet plain.
   The skillful nymph reviews her force with care: 45
Let spades be trumps! she said, and trumps they were.
   Now move to war her sable Matadors,
In show like leaders of the swarthy Moors.
Spadillio° first, unconquerable lord!
Led off two captive trumps and swept the board.   50
As many more Manillio° forced to yield
And marched a victor from the verdant field.°
Him Basto° followed, but his fate more hard
Gained but one trump and one plebeian card.
With his broad saber next, a chief in years,   55
The hoary majesty of spades appears,
Puts forth one manly leg, to sight revealed,
The rest his many-colored robe concealed.
The rebel knave, who dares his prince engage,
Proves the just victim of his royal rage.   60
E'en mighty Pam,° that kings and queens o'erthrew,
And mowed down armies in the fights of Loo,
Sad chance of war! now destitute of aid,
Falls undistinguished by the victor spade!
   Thus far both armies to Belinda yield;
Now to the baron fate inclines the field.
His warlike Amazon her host invades,
The imperial consort of the crown of spades;
The club's black tyrant first her victim died,
Spite of his haughty mien, and barbarous pride.   70
What boots° the regal circle on his head,
His giant limbs, in state unwieldy spread;

---

30. *the sacred nine:* The nine cards in each player's hand are compared to the nine Muses of the
Greeks. 33. *Matador:* a card that had power to take a trick, derived from the Spanish word for bull-
fighter. 41. *succinct* (sŭk·sĭngkt'): belted. 42. *halberts* (hăl'bĕrts): long-handled weapons with metal
heads. 49. *Spadillio:* the ace of spades. 51. *Manillio:* another trump card. 52. *verdant field:* The omber
table was covered with green cloth. 53. *Basto:* the ace of clubs. 61. *Pam:* In a card game called *Loo,*
the knave of clubs, Pam, was the highest card and therefore "o'erthrew kings and queens" and
"mowed down armies." In omber, the game now being played, the knave was less powerful. 71. *What
boots:* of what benefit is.

Belinda's luck changes. The baron's queen of spades takes her king of clubs; his run of diamonds takes several tricks.

That long behind he trails his pompous robe,
And, of all monarchs, only grasps the globe?
   The baron now his diamonds pours apace;   75
Th' embroidered king who shows but half his face,
And his refulgent° queen, with powers combined,
Of broken troops an easy conquest find.
Clubs, diamonds, hearts, in wild disorder seen,
With throngs promiscuous° strew the level green.   80
Thus when dispersed a routed army runs,
Of Asia's troops, and Afric's sable sons,
With like confusion different nations fly,
Of various habit, and of various dye,
The pierced battalions disunited fall,   85
In heaps on heaps; one fate o'erwhelms them all.
   The knave of diamonds tries his wily arts,
And wins (oh, shameful chance!) the queen of hearts.
At this the blood the virgin's cheek forsook,
A livid paleness spreads o'er all her look;   90
She sees, and trembles at the approaching ill,
Just in the jaws of ruin, and codille.°
And now (as oft in some distempered state)
On one nice trick depends the general fate.
An ace of hearts steps forth; the king unseen   95

Belinda wins when her king of hearts takes the baron's ace of hearts.

Lurked in her hand, and mourned his captive queen:
He springs to vengeance with an eager pace,
And falls like thunder on the prostrate ace.
The nymph exulting fills with shouts the sky;
The walls, the woods, and long canals reply.   100
   O thoughtless mortals; ever blind to fate,
Too soon dejected, and too soon elate.
Sudden, these honors shall be snatched away,
And cursed forever this victorious day.
   For lo! the board with cups and spoons is crowned,   105
The berries crackle, and the mill turns round;°

The card game ended, coffee is served in a "rich repast."

On shining altars of Japan° they raise
The silver lamp; the fiery spirits blaze;
From silver spouts the grateful liquors glide,
While China's earth° receives the smoking tide.   110
At once they gratify their scent and taste,
And frequent cups prolong the rich repast.
Straight hover round the fair her airy band;
Some, as she sipped, the fuming liquor fanned,
Some o'er her lap their careful plumes displayed,   115
Trembling, and conscious of the rich brocade.
Coffee (which makes the politician wise,
And see through all things with his half-shut eyes)

---

77. *refulgent:* radiant, resplendent. 80. *promiscuous:* mixed. 92. *codille:* a term meaning the defeat of the lone hand. 106. *The berries . . . round:* Prepared coffee could not be bought in those days, but the coffee berries were ground in a small hand mill at the table. 107. *altars of Japan:* Imported lacquered tables were popular at this time. 110. *China's earth:* The cups were earthenware imported from China.

Sent up in vapors to the baron's brain
New stratagems the radiant locks to gain.   120
Ah, cease, rash youth! desist ere 'tis too late,
Fear the just gods, and think of Scylla's fate!°
Changed to a bird, and sent to flit in air,
She dearly pays for Nisus' injured hair!
    But when to mischief mortals bend their will,
How soon they find fit instruments of ill!
Just then Clarissa drew with tempting grace
A two-edged weapon from her shining case:
So ladies in romance assist their knight,
Present the spear, and arm him for the fight.
He takes the gift with reverence, and extends
The little engine on his fingers' ends;

Clarissa, one of This just behind Belinda's neck he spread,
the ladies, helps As o'er the fragrant steams she bends her head.
the baron's plan Swift to the lock a thousand sprites repair,   135
by handing him A thousand wings, by turns, blow back the hair;
her scissors. The And thrice they twitched the diamond in her ear;
sprites scurry to Thrice she looked back, and thrice the foe drew near.
protect Belinda. Just in that instant, anxious Ariel sought
The close recesses of the virgin's thought;   140
As on the nosegay in her breast reclined,
He watched th' ideas rising in her mind,
Sudden he viewed, in spite of all her art,
An earthly lover lurking at her heart.
Amazed, confused, he found his power expired,   145
Resigned to fate, and with a sigh retired.
    The peer now spreads the glittering *forfex*° wide,
T' inclose the lock; now joins it, to divide.
Belinda's curl is E'en then, before the fatal engine closed,
severed — the A wretched sylph too fondly interposed: 150
rape of the lock! Fate urged the shears, and cut the sylph in twain,
(But airy substance soon unites again).
The meeting points the sacred hair dissever
From the fair head, forever, and forever!
    Then flashed the living lightning from her eyes,   155
And screams of horror rend th' affrighted skies.
Not louder shrieks to pitying Heaven are cast,
When husbands, or when lap dogs breathe their last;
Or when rich China vessels, fallen from high,
In glittering dust and painted fragments lie!   160
    "Let wreaths of triumph now my temples twine,"
The victor cried; "the glorious prize is mine!
While fish in streams, or birds delight in air,
Or in a coach and six the British fair,
As long as *Atalantis*° shall be read,   165
Or the small pillow grace a lady's bed,

---

122. *Scylla's* (sĭl'ăz) *fate:* Scylla betrayed her father, King Nisus, by sending the enemy a lock of his hair. 147. *forfex* (fôr'fĕks): Latin for *shears.* 165. *Atalantis:* a popular book of scandalous gossip.

The baron exults
over the
permanent fame
he has won by
his conquest.

While visits shall be paid on solemn days,
When numerous wax lights in bright order blaze,
While nymphs take treats, or assignations give,
So long my honor, name, and praise shall live!   170
What Time would spare, from steel receives its date,°
And monuments, like men, submit to fate!
Steel could the labor of the gods destroy,
And strike to dust th' imperial towers of Troy;
Steel could the works of mortal pride confound,   175
And hew triumphal arches to the ground.
What wonder then, fair nymph! thy hairs should feel,
The conquering force of unresisted steel? "

171. *receives its date:* is destroyed.

CANTO V

In Canto IV, Umbriel, a melancholy sprite, brings a bag (similar
to the bag of winds once held by Ulysses) in which are contained
" the force of female lungs, sighs, sobs, and passions, and the war
of tongues." These he empties over the head of Belinda, who immediately bursts into loud lamentations on the loss of her lock. She
then calls upon Sir Plume to aid her in regaining her lock. This ineffectual fop swears the favorite oaths of the time — " Zounds!
Plague on 't! Prithee, pox! " — but fails to move the baron, who
maintains that he will keep the lock forever.
      Then, in Canto V — the last one — Clarissa, a more serious-
minded young lady than the others, urges good sense and good
humor, but in vain. The story concludes with a mighty battle between the belles and the beaux.

" To arms, to arms! " the fierce virago cries,
And swift as lightning to the combat flies.
All side in parties, and begin th' attack;
Fans clap, silks rustle, and tough whalebones crack;
Heroes' and heroines' shouts confus'dly rise,   5
And bass and treble voices strike the skies.
No common weapons in their hands are found,
Like gods they fight, nor dread a mortal wound.°

The lords and
ladies engage in
a battle — of
words and looks
— equal to those
described by
Homer in The
Iliad.

      So when bold Homer makes the gods engage,
And heavenly breasts with human passions rage;   10
'Gainst Pallas, Mars, Latona, Hermes° arms;
And all Olympus° rings with loud alarms:
Jove's thunder roars, Heaven trembles all around,
Blue Neptune storms, the bellowing deeps resound;
Earth shakes her nodding towers, the ground gives way,   15
And the pale ghosts start at the flash of day!
      Triumphant Umbriel on a sconce's° height
Clapped his glad wings, and sat to view the fight;

8. The gods, being immortal, did not have to fear death in battle. 11. *Pallas, Mars, Latona,*
Hermes: all gods who directed the Trojan War. The first and fourth were on the side of the Greeks,
the second and third on the Trojan side. 12. *Olympus:* the mountain in northern Greece on which
the gods supposedly lived. 17. *sconce's:* A sconce is a candle holder attached to the wall.

Propped on their bodkin spears,° the sprites survey
The growing combat, or assist the fray.   20
    While through the press enraged Thalestris flies,
And scatters death around from both her eyes,
A beau and witling° perished in the throng,
One died in metaphor, and one in song.
" O cruel nymph! a living death I bear,"   25
Cried Dapperwit,° and sunk beside his chair.
A mournful glance Sir Fopling° upward cast,
" Those eyes are made so killing " — was his last.
Thus on Mæander's° flowery margin lies
Th' expiring swan, and as he sings he dies.   30
    When bold Sir Plume had drawn Clarissa down,
Chloe stepped in and killed him with a frown;
She smiled to see the doughty hero slain,
But, at her smile, the beau revived again.

The lock of hair   Now Jove suspends his golden scales in air,   35
is found to be   Weighs the men's wits against the lady's hair;
heavier than the
intelligence of   The doubtful beam long nods from side to side;
the young lords.   At length the wits mount up, the hairs subside.
    See, fierce Belinda on the Baron flies,
With more than usual lightning in her eyes;   40
Nor feared the chief th' unequal fight to try,
Who sought no more than on his foe to die.
But this bold lord with manly strength endued,
She with one finger and a thumb subdued:
Just where the breath of life his nostrils drew,   45
A charge of snuff the wily virgin threw;
The gnomes direct, to every atom just,
The pungent grains of titillating dust.
Sudden, with starting tears each eye o'erflows,
And the high dome re-echoes to his nose.   50
    " Now meet thy fate," incensed Belinda cried,
And drew a deadly bodkin from her side. . . .
    " Boast not my fall," he cried, " insulting foe!
Thou by some other shalt be laid as low;
Nor think to die dejects my lofty mind;   55
All that I dread is leaving you behind!
Rather than so, ah, let me still survive,
And burn in Cupid's flames — but burn alive."
    " Restore the lock! " she cries; and all around
" Restore the lock! " the vaulted roofs rebound.   60
Not fierce Othello in so loud a strain
Roared for the handkerchief that caused his pain.°

---

19. *bodkin spears:* large needles. 23. *witling:* a gentleman with empty pretensions to high intelligence. 26. *Dapperwit* and *Sir Fopling* (line 27) were names of humorous characters in sophisticated
comedies of the time. 29. *Mæander's:* The Mæander was a winding river in Asia, often mentioned
in classical poetry. 61–62. In Shakespeare's tragedy *Othello*, the hero is convinced of his wife's
faithlessness when she cannot find a handkerchief which he had given her. The handkerchief had
actually been stolen by an enemy to be used as evidence against her. The scene in which Othello
demands the handkerchief of Desdemona is highly dramatic.

But see how oft ambitious aims are crossed,
And chiefs contend till all the prize is lost!
The lock, obtained with guilt, and kept with pain,   65
In every place is sought, but sought in vain.
With such a prize no mortal must be blessed,
So Heav'n decrees! with Heav'n who can contest?
    Some thought it mounted to the lunar sphere,
Since all things lost on earth are treasured there.   70
There heroes' wits are kept in ponderous vases,
And beaux' in snuffboxes and tweezer cases;
There broken vows and deathbed alms are found,
And lovers' hearts with ends of riband bound. . . .
    But trust the Muse — she saw it upward rise,   75
Though marked by none but quick, poetic eyes. . . .

Belinda's lost lock A sudden star, it shot through liquid air,
becomes a star And drew behind a radiant trail of hair. . . .
in the sky; and   Then cease, bright nymph! to mourn thy ravished hair,
the poet calls on Which adds new glory to the shining sphere!   80
Belinda to cease Not all the tresses that fair head can boast,
mourning, for Shall draw such envy as the lock you lost.
the Muse of For, after all the murders of your eye,
poetry will make When, after millions slain, yourself shall die;
the lock immortal. When those fair suns shall set, as set they must,   85

And all those tresses shall be laid in dust:
This lock, the Muse shall consecrate to fame,
And 'midst the stars inscribe Belinda's name.

Pope's Epigrams

No authors except Shakespeare and Milton have given to
our language so many quotable lines and phrases as Pope.
His neat couplets are easy to remember, and his comments
on life and learning are usually brief, clever, and exact.
As their names suggest, these poems are essays in verse.

1. Hope springs eternal in the human breast:
   Man never is but always to be blest.
   An Essay on Man, Epistle I, lines 95–96.

2. All nature is but art, unknown to thee;
   All chance, direction, which thou canst not see;
   All discord, harmony not understood;
   All partial evil, universal good;
   And spite of pride, in erring reason's spite,
   One truth is clear, Whatever is, is right.
   Ibid., lines 289–94.

3. Honor and shame from no condition rise;
   Act well your part, there all the honor lies.
   Ibid., Epistle IV, lines 193–94.

4. A wit's a feather, and a chief a rod;
An honest man's the noblest work of God.
Ibid., lines 247–48.

5. 'Tis education forms the common mind:
Just as the twig is bent the tree's inclined.
Moral Essays, Epistle I, lines 149–50.

6. A little learning is a dangerous thing;
Drink deep, or taste not the Pierian [1] spring:
There shallow drafts intoxicate the brain,
And drinking largely [2] sobers us again.
An Essay on Criticism, Part II, lines 15–18.

7. True ease in writing comes from art, not chance,
As those move easiest who have learned to dance.
'Tis not enough no harshness gives offense —
The sound must seem an echo to the sense.
Ibid., lines 162–65.

8. To err is human, to forgive divine.
Ibid., line 325.

9. For fools rush in where angels fear to tread.
Ibid., Part III, line 66.

[1] *Pierian* (pī·ẹr'ĭ·ăn): Pieria was the region where the Muses were first worshiped; hence, the spring represents the understanding of the arts and sciences. [2] *largely:* deeply.

THE WIT OF TWICKENHAM

THE RAPE OF THE LOCK

1. Select several passages to show how Pope makes unimportant incidents of social life sound like world-shaking events. What effect does he produce by linking something serious with something trivial?

2. In the description of the card game, what is the extended metaphor that is used? Is it an effective comparison? Do any of the details of behavior of the gentlemen and ladies remind you of behavior of young people today?

3. How is the battle between the beaux and belles made to appear ridiculous? What details suggest the fashions of the day?

4. Point out lines and passages where Pope is imitating the old heroic poems. For what kind of verse is the heroic couplet (the form Pope uses) appropriate?

EPIGRAMS

1. Do you agree with Pope's ideas in all of these sayings? From your experience, can you support or attack these ideas?

2. Which quotation expresses one of Pope's standards for literature? Is this standard still considered important by poets today?

THE POWER OF WORDS

UNUSUAL COLOR WORDS

The description of the card game gives Pope an opportunity to introduce some color words. Beginning with line 38 of Canto III we see the four kings each with *hoary* (silvery white) whiskers. *Hoary* (from the Old English for *frost*) suggests both color and age and is usually applied to hair, not to skin or to garments. In contrast to the white beards there are the *sable Matadors* and *swarthy Moors.* Look up the derivations of these words.

The card table is called the *verdant* field. *Verdant* goes back through French to Latin, where it means *green.* Card tables in the eighteenth century were likely to be covered with a green cloth, which gave the resemblance to the grassy battlefield.

THE GROWTH OF THE ENGLISH LANGUAGE

The Eighteenth Century

In the early part of the eighteenth century there were two cross-currents at work in the stream of the English language. One was a continuation of the growth that had occurred during the Elizabethan age and the Restoration. The other force sought to confine language within neat limitations. The non-critical members of the population, careless of technical niceties of grammar and spelling, were eager to bring in new and exhilarating words. But many literary men believed that the time had come to give the language shape and stability, even at the cost of expansion and liveliness.

We have seen what Dryden did at the end of the seventeenth century to trim the language into an admirable prose style. Of the same mind, but with more specific proposals for attaining the end, were Defoe, Swift, and Addison. They all bemoaned the indifference and often scorn of the court for *correctness* (a word that was not heard of before their time). Defoe ridiculed the misspelling that was characteristic of the nobility, citing the example of a lord who described the accidental drowning of a servant as " a mollinkolli accidence be happen'd in our house."

Swift wrote a scathing paper for *The Tatler* on the state of the language, which Addison followed up in his milder manner by occasional comments in *The Spectator*. But Swift's most famous dictum on language came in a letter addressed to the Lord Treasurer containing a Proposal for Correcting, Improving, and Ascertaining [limiting] the English Tongue. Here he said that the language reached its highest point from Queen Elizabeth's day to the beginning of the Restoration, and that it had been degenerating ever since in the mouths of the fashionable figures of court and town, and in the writing of stupid poets. He blamed the poets for the contraction of words to suit their meter, as in such forms as *drudg'd, disturb'd, fledg'd,* in which the *ed* was originally pronounced as a separate syllable. (Note that modern English keeps both the clipped pronunciation and the *e* instead of an apostrophe, to show the eye that *ed* is the past or participial ending.) Swift condemned the new idea that we ought to spell as we speak, on the ground that so many styles of pronunciation in different classes, different localities, and different times would make any printed standards impossible. He predicted that without some definite regulation of present tendencies, two hundred years hence (which would be 1912) the world would be unable to read the writings of the eighteenth century. To avoid this sad outcome Swift proposed that an Academy of suitable persons be appointed to " ascertain and fix " our language forever. Such an unrealistic proposal, had it been followed, would have created a literary " dictatorship " whose function would be to prohibit all future life and growth in the language.

Swift's idea was approved by the Lord Treasurer and a sum of money was appropriated for it, but no Academy ever materialized. The nobility continued to misspell, the town and college wits continued to coin new words and abbreviate old ones, the criminal classes still slyly introduced their cant phrases into the best society.

The word *slang,* which then applied only to the special vocabularies of the underworld, has now come to be a general term for all words and phrases not yet admitted into formal usage. But today such words are not looked upon askance as often as they were by older purists, for we realize that if a new word fills a real need it will soon become a part of the language. To show the folly of totally condemning all new or strangely formed words, we need only look back to the eighteenth century when the following words were frowned upon in polite usage: *mob* (abbreviation of the Latin *mobile vulgus*), *enthusiasm, extra, fun, gambling, humbug, nervous, shabby, fop.* There were many others.

At the end of the seventeenth century came the first suggestion that English literature would be better than Latin declamations for study in schools. In the eighteenth century, the old grammar schools, teaching Greek and Latin only, were gradually superseded by charity schools and private schools where the study of English was introduced. This innovation raised the standard of English used by both the aristocratic and the humble classes.

The period became a great age for the appearance of dictionaries. In the fifteenth and sixteenth centuries there had been two-language dictionaries, but it was not till the very end of the sixteenth that we find one with explanations of words in the mother tongue. The seventeenth century introduced a new type of vernacular dictionary containing two separate lists: choice words and vulgar words.

In the eighteenth century a rash of dictionaries broke out. The greatest in attempt, in accomplishment, and in influence was the one written by Dr. Samuel Johnson, of whom you will read more in the following pages. He intended to make a complete list of words in English, give definitions, and show how the words had been used by quotations from literature. He did not try to indicate pronunciation except for accent. When in doubt about accepting a word as good English, he often decided on the basis of the word's ancestry. Thus *sherbet,* traceable through Arabic to Persian, was admitted; but *punch,* apparently without a family tree, was branded as a cant word.

Later the whole matter of acceptability of words was more successfully solved by Dr. George Campbell, a Scottish schoolmaster, who established three tests for standard English, still generally accepted: *national* (not only local), *reputable* (used by reputable people), and *present* (not fallen into disuse). Campbell, however, was scornful of words " betraying some frivolous humor in the formation of them," such as *bamboozle, topsy-turvy, helter-skelter,* and *hurly-burly.* He was somewhat lacking in a sense of humor.

Fewer borrowings from foreign languages appeared in the eighteenth century than earlier, but there were some. The emphasis on classical architecture accounted for the addition of words from the Greek: *porch* and *attic* (from the state Attica), for example. With the advent of George I to the throne, French became the court language. But French words came in more through the New World than the court; *prairie, crevasse, shanty,* and *bayou* became familiar.

It was during the eighteenth century that the real deviation between English and American usage and pronunciation began to be evident, especially after American independence reduced communication across the Atlantic. The influx into the middle states of German and Scandinavian colonists brought into American English words and sounds that never became accepted in the old country. Then too, America was still a frontier land and new words had to be devised for phenomena not to be seen in England. Thus came into being *landslide, snowplow, basswood, catbird, mudhen, bobolink, ground hog, rattlesnake.*

JONATHAN SWIFT 1667–1745

Swift and Pope were congenial as friends and writers. Both had sharp tongues and sharper pens; both hated dullness and sentimentality. Swift was born in Dublin, of English parents, aristocratic but poor. After his father's death, Swift became dependent upon an uncle for his education at Dublin University, and later upon Sir William Temple, a relative in England who employed him as a private secretary. The proud, independent young man found this position hard to bear. He passed several years, at two different times, at the beck and call of his employer, whom he thought pretentious, and he suffered such indignities as being forced to eat in the servants' hall. Finally, he struck out for himself by taking religious orders in the Church of England and entering politics as a writer. Because of his brilliant party writings, Swift rose rapidly and gained great influence among the Tories, then ruling England. In 1713 he was appointed dean of St. Patrick's in Dublin. He had hoped to become a bishop, but when the Tories lost power, his chances were ruined, and he remained in Dublin as dean for thirty-two years.

Swift was a moody, self-tortured, and often despondent man. While at Sir William's estate in Surrey he developed his friendship with Esther Johnson, who was considerably younger than he was. His numerous letters to her were published under the title *Journal to Stella* (*Esther* is the Hebrew for *star, Stella* is the Latin). He loved her deeply but somewhat hopelessly; whether they married is one of the unsolved mysteries in English literary history. Late in life Swift grew increasingly despondent until he finally suffered a mental disorder.

Swift is best known for his satires; he was the most versatile of English satirists. *The Battle of the Books* (between ancient and modern writers) was written as part of a literary controversy. *A Modest Proposal* — in which Swift suggests that English absentee landlords might fatten the Irish children to serve on their dinner tables as a new luxury — represents his political defense of the Irish and reflects his deep hatred of human cruelty and exploitation. *Gulliver's Travels,* his masterpiece, is a satire on humanity in general and shows the truth of Swift's observation about himself: that he hated mankind but loved men as individuals.

Gulliver's Travels

It is ironic that a book written to satirize everything from the king to all mankind should today be looked on by most people as a book for young readers. Because Swift made use of pygmies and giants, the first part of the book is an entertaining fairy tale for children, who like it for its strange adventure. Actually, Swift cleverly used an interesting tale to poke fun at human vanities, and *Gulliver's Travels* can thus be read on two levels, one of storytelling interest and one of underlying, symbolic meaning.

The book was published anonymously, purporting to be the true adventures of one Lemuel Gulliver. The opening chapter contributes to the illusion of reality by its details of Gulliver's past life and the circumstances of the voyage and shipwreck, all told in the most matter-of-fact way. Then Gulliver suddenly finds himself in the land of the Lilliputians (lĭl·ĭ·pū′shănz), creatures only six inches tall; but again the narrative moves with such directness and simplicity and with such careful attention to mathematical proportions that it becomes almost plausible in its absurdity.

THE VOYAGE TO LILLIPUT [1]

In the first two chapters Gulliver is discovered in his sleep by the Lilliputians. He is transported with great difficulty to

[1] *Lilliput* (lĭl′ĭ·pŭt).

their capital, where he is housed in a deserted temple. He wins favor with the emperor, is taught their language, but is deprived of his sword and pistols. The satire in this adventure becomes more evident in Chapter III, where the pretensions of English politicians and the royal court are made ridiculous by reduction to a tiny scale.

Mʏ GENTLENESS and good behavior had gained so far on the emperor and his court, and indeed upon the army and people in general, that I began to conceive hopes of getting my liberty in a short time. I took all possible methods to cultivate this favorable disposition. The natives came by degrees to be less apprehensive of any danger from me. I would sometimes lie down and let five or six of them dance on my hand; and at last the boys and girls would venture to come and play at hide-and-seek in my hair. I had now made a good progress in understanding and speaking their language.

The emperor had a mind, one day, to entertain me with several of the country shows, wherein they exceed all nations I have known, both for dexterity and magnificence. I was diverted with none so much as that of the rope dancers, performed upon a slender white thread, extended about two feet and twelve inches from the ground. Upon which I shall desire liberty, with the reader's patience, to enlarge a little.

This diversion is only practiced by those persons who are candidates for great employments and high favor at court. They are trained in this art from their youth, and are not always of noble birth or liberal education. When a great office is vacant, either by death or disgrace (which often happens), five or six of those candidates petition the emperor to entertain his majesty and the court with a dance on the rope; and whoever jumps the highest, without falling, succeeds in the office. Very often the chief ministers themselves are com-

manded to show their skill, and to convince the emperor that they have not lost their faculty. Flimnap,[1] the treasurer, is allowed to cut a caper on the strait rope at least an inch higher than any other lord in the whole empire. I have seen him do the somersault several times together upon a trencher,[2] fixed on a rope, which is no thicker than a common packthread in England. My friend Reldresal, principal secretary for private affairs, is, in my opinion, if I am not partial, the second after the treasurer; the rest of the great officers are much upon a par.

These diversions are often attended by fatal accidents, whereof great numbers are on record. I myself have seen two or three candidates break a limb. But the danger is much greater when the ministers themselves are commanded to show their dexterity! for, by contending to excel themselves and their fellows, they strain so far that there is hardly one of them who hath not received a fall,[3] and some of them two or three. I was assured that a year or two before my arrival, Flimnap would have infallibly broke his neck if one of the king's cushions, that accidentally lay on the ground, had not weakened the force of his fall.

There is likewise another diversion, which is only shown before the emperor and empress and first minister, upon particular occasions. The emperor lays on the table three fine silken threads,[4] of six inches long; one is blue, the other

[1] *Flimnap:* probably meant to be Sir Robert Walpole, a famous eighteenth-century Whig statesman.
[2] *trencher:* a wooden platter.
[3] *a fall:* that is, a loss of office. At this time there was considerable shifting of power between Whigs and Tories. Walpole had been deprived of his office previous to the publication of this book. The "cushion" referred to, a few lines down, is a reference to the intervention by the king on behalf of one of his favorites.
[4] *three . . . threads:* a suggestion of the badges of the Orders of the Garter, Bath, and Thistle, which were often given as political awards.

red, and the third green. These threads are proposed as prizes for those persons whom the emperor hath a mind to distinguish by a peculiar mark of his favor. The ceremony is performed in his majesty's great chamber of state, where the candidates are to undergo a trial of dexterity very different from the former, and such as I have not observed the least resemblance of in any other country of the old or the new world.

The emperor holds a stick in his hands, both ends parallel to the horizon, while the candidates, advancing one by one, sometimes leap over the stick, sometimes creep under it backward and forward several times, according as the stick is advanced or depressed. Sometimes the emperor holds one end of the stick, and his first minister the other; sometimes the minister has it entirely to himself. Whoever performs his part with most agility, and holds out the longest in leaping and creeping, is rewarded with the blue colored silk; the red is given to the next, and the green to the third, which they all wear girt twice round about the middle; and you see few great persons about this court who are not adorned with one of these girdles.

The horses of the army, and those of the royal stables, having been daily led before me, were no longer shy, but would come up to my very feet without starting. The riders would leap them over my hand as I held it on the ground; and one of the emperor's huntsmen, upon a large courser, took my foot, shoe and all, which was indeed a prodigious leap.

I had the good fortune to divert the emperor one day after a very extraordinary manner. I desired he would order several sticks of two feet high, and the thickness of an ordinary cane, to be brought me; whereupon his majesty commanded the master of his woods to give directions accordingly; and the next morning six woodmen arrived with

as many carriages, drawn by eight horses to each.

I took nine of these sticks, and fixing them firmly in the ground in a quadrangular figure, two feet and a half square, I took four other sticks and tied them parallel at each corner, about two feet from the ground; then I fastened my handkerchief to the nine sticks that stood erect, and extended it on all sides, till it was as tight as the top of a drum; and the four parallel sticks, rising about five inches higher than the handkerchief, served as ledges on each side.

When I had finished my work, I desired the emperor to let a troop of his best horse, twenty-four in number, come and exercise upon this plain. His majesty approved of the proposal, and I took them up one by one in my hands, ready mounted and armed, with the proper officers to exercise them. As soon as they got into order, they divided into two parties, performed mock skirmishes, discharged blunt arrows, drew their swords, fled and pursued, attacked and retired, and, in short, discovered the best military discipline I ever beheld. The parallel sticks secured them and their horses from falling over the stage; and the emperor was so much delighted that he ordered this entertainment to be repeated several days, and once was pleased to be lifted up and give the word of command; and, with great difficulty, persuaded even the empress herself to let me hold her in her close chair within two yards of the stage, from whence she was able to take a full view of the whole performance.

It was my good fortune that no ill accident happened in these entertainments; only once a fiery horse, that belonged to one of the captains, pawing with his hoof, struck a hole in my handkerchief, and his foot slipping, he overthrew his rider and himself; but I immediately relieved them both, and covering the hole with one hand, I set down the troop with the other, in the same manner as I took them up. The horse that fell was strained in the left shoulder, but the rider got no hurt, and I repaired my handkerchief as well as I could; however, I would not trust to the strength of it any more in such dangerous enterprises.

About two or three days before I was set at liberty, as I was entertaining the court with these kinds of feats, there arrived an express to inform his majesty that some of his subjects riding near the place where I was first taken up had seen a great black substance lying on the ground, very oddly shaped, extending its edges round as wide as his majesty's bedchamber, and rising up in the middle as high as a man; that it was no living creature, as they at first apprehended, for it lay on the grass without motion; and some of them had walked round it several times; that, by mounting upon each other's shoulders, they had got to the top, which was flat and even, and, stamping upon it, they found it was hollow within; that they humbly conceived it might be something belonging to the man-mountain; and if his majesty pleased, they would undertake to bring it with only five horses.

I presently knew what they meant, and was glad at heart to receive this intelligence.[1] It seems, upon my first reaching the shore after our shipwreck, I was in such confusion that, before I came to the place where I went to sleep, my hat, which I had fastened with a string to my head while I was rowing, and had stuck on all the time I was swimming, fell off after I came to land; the string, as I conjecture, breaking by some accident which I never observed, but thought my hat had been lost at sea. I entreated his imperial majesty to give orders it might be brought to me as soon as possible, describing to him the use and nature of it; and the next day the wagoners arrived with it, but not in a very good condition; they had bored two holes in the brim, within an inch and a half of the edge, and fastened two hooks in the holes; these hooks were tied by a long cord to the harness, and thus my hat was dragged along for above half an English mile; but the ground in that country being extremely smooth and level, it received less damage than I expected.

Two days after this adventure, the emperor, having ordered that part of the army which quarters in and about his metropolis to be in readiness, took a fancy of diverting himself in a very singular manner. He desired I would stand like a colossus,[2] with my legs as far asunder as I conveniently could. He then commanded his general (who was an old, experienced leader and a great patron of mine) to draw up the troops in close order and march them under me; the foot by twenty-four in a breast and the horse by sixteen, with drums beating, colors flying, and pikes advanced. This body consisted of three thousand foot and a thousand horse. . . .

I had sent so many memorials and petitions for my liberty that his majesty at length mentioned the matter, first in the cabinet, and then in a full council; where it was opposed by none, except Skyresh Bolgolam who was pleased, without any provocation, to be my mortal enemy. But it was carried against him by the whole board, and confirmed by the emperor. That minister was *galbet*, or admiral of the realm, very much in his master's confidence, and a person well versed in affairs, but of a morose and sour complexion.[3] However, he was at length persuaded to comply; but prevailed that the articles and conditions upon which I should be set free, and to which I must swear, should be drawn up by himself.

[1] *intelligence:* news, information.

[2] *colossus:* an enormous statue.

[3] *complexion:* In the eighteenth century this word often referred to temperament rather than to the coloring and texture of the face.

These articles were brought to me by Skyresh Bolgolam in person, attended by two undersecretaries, and several persons of distinction. After they were read, I was demanded to swear to the performance of them, first in the manner of my own country, and afterward in the method prescribed by their laws; which was, to hold my right foot in my left hand, and to place the middle finger of my right hand on the crown of my head, and my thumb on the tip of my right ear.

But because the reader may be curious to have some idea of the style and manner of expression peculiar to that people, as well as to know the articles upon which I recovered my liberty, I have made a translation of the whole instrument, word for word, as near as I was able, which I here offer to the public.

" *Golbasto Momaren Evlame Gurdilo Shefin Mully Ully Gue,* most mighty Emperor of Lilliput, delight and terror of the universe, whose dominions extend five thousand *blustrugs* (about twelve miles in circumference) to the extremities of the globe; monarch of all monarchs, taller than the sons of men; whose feet press down to the center, and whose head strikes against the sun; at whose nod the princes of the earth shake their knees; pleasant as the spring, comfortable as the summer, fruitful as autumn, dreadful as winter. His most sublime Majesty proposeth to the man-mountain, lately arrived to our celestial dominions, the following articles, which by a solemn oath he shall be obliged to perform.

" 1. The man-mountain shall not depart from our dominions without our li-cense under our great seal.

" 2. He shall not presume to come into our metropolis without our express order; at which time the inhabitants shall have two hours' warning to keep within their doors.

" 3. The said man-mountain shall

He desired I would stand like a colossus . . .

confine his walks to our principal high roads, and not offer to walk or lie down in a meadow or field of corn.

" 4. As he walks the said roads, he shall take the utmost care not to trample upon the bodies of any of our loving subjects, their horses or carriages, nor take any of our said subjects into his hands without their own consent.

" 5. If an express requires extraordinary dispatch, the man-mountain shall be obliged to carry in his pocket the messenger and horse a six days' journey once in every moon, and return the said messenger back (if so required) safe to our imperial presence.

" 6. He shall be our ally against our enemies in the island of Blefuscu, and do his utmost to destroy their fleet, which is now preparing to invade us.

" 7. That the said man-mountain shall at his times of leisure be aiding and assisting to our workmen, in helping to raise certain great stones toward covering the wall of the principal park, and other our royal buildings.

" 8. That the said man-mountain shall, in two moons' time, deliver in an exact survey of the circumference of our dominions, by a computation of his own paces round the coast.

" 9. That upon his solemn oath to observe all the above articles, the said man-mountain shall have a daily allowance of meat and drink sufficient for the support of 1,728 of our subjects, with free access to our royal person, and other marks of our favor. Given at our palace at Belfaborac the twelfth day of the ninety-first moon of our reign."

I swore and subscribed to these articles with great cheerfulness and content, although some of them were not so honorable as I could have wished; which proceeded wholly from the malice of Skyresh Bolgolam the high admiral; whereupon my chains were immediately unlocked, and I was at full liberty; the emperor himself in person did me the honor to be by at the whole ceremony. I made my acknowledgments by prostrating myself at his majesty's feet; but he commanded me to rise; and after many gracious expressions, which to avoid the censure of vanity, I shall not repeat, he added that he hoped I should prove a useful servant, and well deserve all the favors he had already conferred upon me, or might do for the future.

The reader may please to observe that in the last article for the recovery of my liberty the emperor stipulates to allow me a quantity of meat and drink sufficient for the support of 1,728 Lilliputians. Sometime after, asking a friend at court how they came to fix on that determined number, he told me that his majesty's mathematicians having taken the height of my body by the help of a quadrant, and finding it to exceed theirs in the proportion of twelve to one, they concluded, from the similarity of their bodies, that mine must contain at least 1,728 of theirs, and consequently would require as much food as was necessary to support that number of Lilliputians. By which the reader may conceive an idea of the ingenuity of that people, as well as the prudent and exact economy of so great a prince.

[Gulliver's greatest service to Lilliput is his capture of the fleet of the enemy country, Blefuscu. By cutting the anchor ropes with his knife and attaching fifty ships to a central cable, he is able to drag them after him as he wades across the channel between the two countries.

The jealousy of Skyresh Bolgolam, mentioned in Chapter III, finally results in the proposed impeachment of Gulliver, of which he is warned in time to escape to Blefuscu. Here he is kindly received in spite of his previous treatment of this nation. (This is a satire on the impeachment and escape to France of Bolingbroke, a leader of the Tory party and an intimate friend of Swift.) Soon after, Gulliver discovers a derelict lifeboat. He manages to get away in the lifeboat, and he carries home in his pocket some cattle and sheep as proof that his strange experiences actually did happen.]

SUMMARIES OF SUCCEEDING VOYAGES

VOYAGE TO BROBDINGNAG [1]

Gulliver's second voyage takes him to the land of the giants, where the situation of the previous trip is exactly reversed. The inhabitants are twelve times as tall as Gulliver, instead of one-twelfth his height. Here again the king's court is satirized, partly through the contempt the giant king feels for England as described by Gulliver. Man is also made ridiculous through the misadventures of Gulliver, who is almost devoured by the baby, torn to pieces by the rats, drowned in the cream pitcher by the queen's jealous dwarf, and dropped from the roof of the gigantic palace by a playful monkey. Finally his little cagelike house is carried away by a great eagle, and he is dropped in the ocean, rescued by a passing vessel, and returned to his native country. Back home again, he has great difficulty in readjusting himself to the fact that people are of his own size.

VOYAGE TO LAPUTA [2] AND BALNIBARBI [3]

The third voyage is a satire on learned people. Gulliver is drawn up into a flying island, Laputa, inhabited by musicians, mathematicians, and philosophers. They are so absent-minded that they must be attended by servants who dutifully recall their masters' attention to practical affairs. Later Gulliver is lowered to the mainland, Balnibarbi, where he visits the academy at Lagado, the metropolis. Here the satire is on scientific experimentation, with which Swift was not in sympathy.

THE COUNTRY OF THE HOUYHNHNMS [4]

The account of Gulliver's last voyage is the most biting satire of all. He finds a land governed by horses of the highest intelligence and uprightness. Their name and the occasional words of their language quoted by Gulliver are intended to represent the whinnying of horses. After learning this language Gulliver is able to converse with the king, but in describing the affairs of Europe he discovers that the horse-people have no words for many evils of personal character or government. Gulliver's account of a European war so horrifies the noble Houyhnhnm that he condemns Gulliver's countrymen as worse than the repulsive Yahoos, creatures in the shape of men who serve the horses, without pretense of intelligence. Gulliver pictures the land of the horses as one where peace and contentment are never marred by disease, bribery, flattery, fraud, politics, courtiers, lords, fiddlers, judges, or dancing masters. In short, the land of the horses is an ideal state.

THE MEANING OF GULLIVER'S TRAVELS

1. To what individuals and groups did Swift direct his satire?

2. Make a list of the different aspects of life satirized by Swift in these selections. How many of them might still be criticized today? Which of them no longer exist?

3. How did the Lilliputians arrive at the figure they gave as the necessary amount of food for Gulliver?

4. Does Swift go beyond limits of reason in condemning his country? What can you find in his life which made him bitter toward the government and the Church?

WRITING AND REPORTING

1. Try writing about a journey to an imaginary country through which you satirize practices of your own school or of modern life. For example, you might satirize automobile touring, Christmas shopping, motion pictures, high-pressure salesmanship, radio or television fans, politics, or the dominance of athletics.

2. Plan a series of oral reports after reading other parts of *Gulliver's Travels*. Be sure to bring out the point of Swift's criticism in the various incidents.

THE POWER OF WORDS

PRECISION

In describing the skills of the Lilliputians, Swift says the candidates for honors in the court undergo a trial of *dexterity* in leaping

---

[1] *Brobdingnag* (brŏb'dĭng·năg): The inhabitants were Brobdingnagians (brŏb·dĭng·năg'ĭ·ănz).

[2] *Laputa* (là·pūt'à).

[3] *Balnibarbi* (băl·nĭ·bär'bĭ).

[4] *Houyhnhnms* (hōō·ĭn'ŭmz).

over or creeping under a stick held by the emperor, and that the one showing the greatest *agility* is given the highest award. Though both *dexterity* and *agility* describe speed and skill of action, there is a difference in their precise meanings. *Agility* applies specifically to the suppleness of the limbs. *Dexter* is the Latin word for *right hand;* therefore *dexterity* is especially appropriate for hand skills. A related word is *ambidextrous.* Why do you suppose the root *dexter* appears in this word meaning " using both hands with equal ease "? (For a further insight into the significance of right-handedness, look up the derivation of *sinister.*)

Swift speaks of the *ingenuity* of the Lilliputians in calculating the amount of food needed by Gulliver. *Ingenuity* is mental agility — quickness to find solutions for new problems or to contrive new devices. Do you recognize other common words derived from the same root?

Make a list of several acts or situations that need dexterity, agility, and ingenuity. See how many synonyms you can find for these words, and discuss distinctions in their precise use.

DANIEL DEFOE 1661?–1731

Defoe, the first important English journalist, had a curious and colorful career. The brain of this middle-class Whig teemed with projects and reforms, many of which were far beyond the ideas of his day.

The son of a London butcher, he married, traveled on the Continent, and served in the army before he began to write. For nine years he ran almost singlehandedly the *Review* (1704), one of the early London newspapers, and he turned out political pamphlets by the score. In *The Shortest Way with Dissenters,* Defoe made the seemingly savage suggestion that death or violent penalties be meted out to members of dissenting churches, to one of which

he himself belonged. Supporters of the Church of England accepted this as a serious solution but soon discovered that they had been tricked and ridiculed. When they had Defoe put in the pillory, he immediately composed a satiric " Hymn to the Pillory," which his friends sang in the streets while pelting him with flowers.

Defoe's talent as a reporter led him from newspapers and pamphlets to writing fictitious history like *The Journal of the Plague Year.* In *Robinson Crusoe,* his best-known book, he describes the adventures of a shipwrecked sailor cast away on a desert island as if he were reporting a series of actual facts.

The Journal of the Plague Year

This book is an example of Defoe's ability to persuade readers that fiction is literal truth, by his direct style and careful reporting of details. With the accuracy of a historian and the graphic detail of an imaginative writer, he pictures London in the grip of a horrible epidemic.

The *Journal* purports to be the diary of a Londoner who lived through the Great Plague of 1665, when thousands upon thousands of city dwellers were struck down by the rampant disease. Defoe was

only about four years old at the time, so he drew entirely on records and conversations for his information. The narrative tells of the writer's indecision about leaving London for the safety of the country. Because he feels an obligation to look after his servants and his business, and because he finds consolation in the Bible (" Surely he shall deliver thee . . . from the noisome pestilence "), the writer decides to stay. Thus he is able to describe the day-by-day horrors of the epidemic.

1665. It pleased God that I was still spared, and very hearty and sound in health, but very impatient of being pent up within doors without air, as I had been for fourteen days, or thereabouts; and I could not restrain myself, but I would go to carry a letter for my brother to the Posthouse. Then it was, indeed, that I observed a profound silence in the streets. When I came to the Posthouse, as I went to put in my letter, I saw a man stand in one corner of the yard, and talking to another at a window, and a third had opened a door belonging to the office. In the middle of the yard lay a small leather purse, with two keys hanging at it, and money in it, but nobody would meddle with it. I asked how long it had lain there; the man at the window said it had lain almost an hour, but they had not meddled with it, because they did not know but the person who dropped it might come back to look for it. I had no such need of money, nor was the sum so big that I had any inclination to meddle with it to get the money at the hazard it might be attended with; so I seemed to go away, when the man who had opened the door said he would take it up; but so that if the right owner came for it, he should be sure to have it. So he went in and fetched a pail of water, and set it down hard by the purse, then went again and fetched some gunpowder and cast a good deal of powder upon the purse, and then made a train from that which he had thrown loose upon the purse; the train reached about two yards. After this he goes in a third time, and fetches out a pair of tongs red hot, and which he had prepared, I suppose, on purpose; and first setting fire to the train of powder, that singed the purse, and also smoked the air sufficiently. But he was not content with that; but he then takes up the purse with the tongs, holding it so long till the tongs burnt through the purse, and then he shook the money out into the pail of water, so he carried it in. The money, as I re-member, was about thirteen shillings, and some smooth groats, and brass farthings.

There might, perhaps, have been several poor people, as I have observed above, that would have been hardy enough to have ventured for the sake of the money; but you may easily see, by what I have observed, that the few people who were spared were very careful of themselves at that time when the distress was so exceeding great. . . .

It would pierce the hearts of all that came by to hear the piteous cries of those infected people, who being thus out of their understandings by the violence of their pain, or the heat of their blood, were either shut in, or perhaps tied in their beds and chairs, to prevent their doing themselves hurt, and who would make a dreadful outcry at their being confined, and at their not being permitted to " die at large," as they called it, and as they would have done before.

This running of distempered people about the streets was very dismal, and the Magistrates did their utmost to prevent it; but as it was generally in the night and always sudden, when such attempts were made, the officers could not be at hand to prevent it, and even when they got out in the day, the officers appointed did not care to meddle with them, because, as they were all grievously infected, to be sure, when they were come to that height, so they were more than ordinarily infectious, and it was one of the most dangerous things that could be to touch them. On the other hand, they generally ran on, not knowing what they did, till they dropped down stark dead, or till they had exhausted their spirits so as that they would fall, and then die in perhaps half an hour or an hour; and what was most piteous to hear, they were sure to come to themselves entirely in that half-hour or hour, and then to make most grievous and piercing cries and lamentations in the deep afflicting sense of the condition they were in. This was much of it before the order for shutting up of houses was strictly put in execution, for at first the watchmen were not so rigorous and severe, as they were afterward, in the keeping the people in; that is to say, before they were, I mean some of them, severely punished for their neglect, failing in their duty, and letting people who were under their care slip away, or conniving at their going abroad, whether sick or well. But after they saw the officers appointed to examine into their conduct were resolved to have them do their duty, or be punished for the omission, they were more exact, and the people were strictly restrained; which was a thing they took so ill, and bore so impatiently, that their discontents can hardly be described; but there was an absolute necessity for it, that must be confessed, unless some other measures had been timely entered upon, and it was too late for that.

Had not this particular of the sick being restrained as above, been our case at that time,[1] London would have been the most dreadful place that ever was in the world; there would, for aught I know, have as many people died in the streets as died in their houses; for when the Distemper was at its height, it generally made them raving and delirious, and when they were so, they would never be persuaded to keep in their beds but by force; and many, who were not tied, threw themselves out of windows, when they found they could not get leave to go out of their doors.

It was for want of people conversing one with another, in this time of calamity, that it was impossible any particular person could come at the knowledge of all the extraordinary cases that occurred in different families; and particularly I believe it was never known to this day how many people in their deliriums drowned themselves in the Thames, and in the river which runs from the marshes by Hackney, which we generally called Ware River, or Hackney River. As to those which were set down in the weekly bill,[2] they were indeed few; nor could it be known of any of those, whether they drowned themselves by accident or not. But I believe, I might reckon up more, who, within the compass of my knowledge or observation really drowned themselves in that year than are put down in the bill of all put together, for many of the bodies were never found, who yet were known to be so lost: and the like, in other methods of self-destruction. There was also one man, in or about Whitecross Street, who burnt himself to death in his bed; some said it was done by himself, others that it was by the treachery of the nurse that attended him; but that he had the Plague upon him was agreed by all. . . .

We that were Examiners[3] were often not able to come at the knowledge of the Infection being entered into a house till it was too late to shut it up; and sometimes not till the people that were left were all dead. In Petticoat Lane two houses together were infected, and several people sick; but the Distemper was so well concealed that the Examiner, who was my neighbor, got no knowledge of it, till notice was sent him that the people were all dead, and that the carts[4] should call there to fetch them away. The two heads of the families concerted their measures, and so ordered their matters, as that when the Examiner was in the neighborhood, they appeared generally at a time, and answered, that is, lied for one another; or got some of the neighborhood to say

[1] *Had not . . . time:* if we had not restrained the sick people in the manner described above.

[2] *bill:* a list of the dead in each parish and the cause of death.

[3] *Examiners:* men whose job it was to determine which houses had been infected by the plague.

[4] *carts:* The dead bodies were collected at night in carts and taken to a common burial ground, since the churchyards would not hold them all.

they were all in health, and, perhaps, knew no better, till death making it impossible to keep it any longer as a secret, the Dead carts were called in the night to both houses, and so it became public; but when the Examiner ordered the constable to shut up the houses, there was nobody left in them but three people, two in one house, and one in the other, just dying, and a nurse in each house, who acknowledged that they had buried five before, that the houses had been infected nine or ten days, and that for all the rest of the two families, which were many, they were gone, some sick, some well, or whether sick or well, could not be known.

In like manner, at another house in the same lane, a man, having his family infected, but very unwilling to be shut up, when he could conceal it no longer, shut up himself; that is to say, he set the great Red Cross upon his door, with the words — " Lord have Mercy upon Us "; and so deluded the Examiner, who supposed it had been done by the constable by order of the other Examiner, for there were two Examiners to every district or precinct; by this means he had free egress and regress [1] into his house again, and out of it, as he pleased, notwithstanding it was infected; till at length his stratagem was found out, and then he, with the sound part of his servants and family, made off, and escaped; so they were not shut up at all. . . .

It is here, however, to be observed, that after the funerals became so many that people could not toll the bell, mourn, or weep, or wear black for one another, as they did before; no, nor so much as make coffins for those that died; so after a while the fury of the Infection appeared to be so increased, that in short, they shut up no houses at all. It seemed enough that all the remedies of that kind had been used till they were found fruitless, and that the Plague

spread itself with an irresistible fury; so that as the Fire, the succeeding year, spread itself, and burnt with such violence, that the citizens, in despair, gave over [2] their endeavors to extinguish it, so in the Plague, it came at last to such violence that the people sat still, looking at one another, and seemed quite abandoned to despair. Whole streets seemed to be desolated, and not to be shut up only, but to be emptied of their inhabitants; doors were left open, and windows stood shattering with the wind in empty houses for want of people to shut them. In a word, people began to give up themselves to their fears, and to think that all regulations and methods were in vain, and that there was nothing to be hoped for, but an universal Desolation; and it was even in the height of this general despair that it pleased God to stay his hand, and to slacken the fury of the Contagion, in such a manner as was even surprising (like its beginning), and demonstrated it to be his own particular Hand, and that above, if not without, the Agency of Means, as I shall take notice of in its proper place.

[2] *over:* up.

AN EARLY JOURNALIST

1. What evidence does Defoe give to show that London was in a state of panic during the plague? What attempts were made to maintain order? How successful were they? What examples are given of the orders being evaded during the plague?

2. In what way does this journal reveal that Defoe could move easily from fact to fiction? How does he create an atmosphere of horror?

3. Defoe's description should be compared with Pepys' account of the Great Fire. Which do you consider more graphic, more realistic in impression? Why? In what way does Defoe's description remind you of present-day newspaper reporting?

4. Small groups of students may do some library research on the great plagues of the fourteenth and seventeenth centuries. What were their effects in England?

[1] *egress and regress:* exit and entrance.

JOSEPH ADDISON 1672–1719

and

RICHARD STEELE 1672–1729

JOSEPH ADDISON

RICHARD STEELE

The names of Addison and Steele are inevitably linked together, because they were not only intimate friends but literary partners in one of the most significant enterprises in English literature: *The Spectator*. This modest little paper was the ancestor of our magazines and the feature articles in today's newspapers. It established a new style of writing in English literature, that of the familiar essay.

Though noticeably unlike in disposition, the two men were close friends from childhood. A year before Addison's death they quarreled over politics, which strangely enough had helped keep them together over the years. Both were Whigs and therefore opposite to Pope and Swift, who as Tories led a different literary group.

Joseph Addison and Richard Steele first met at the Charterhouse School in London, though Addison was born in England and Steele in Ireland. They continued together through Oxford, where Addison was an accomplished scholar and where Steele already began to show his lively but sometimes extravagant personality. Steele was good-natured, eloquent, versatile in moods, and inefficient. For a time he was captain of the Coldstream Guards, the manager of a theater for which he wrote several sentimental comedies, and official gazetteer for the Whig party, a job that Addison secured for him. Later he turned to still more ventures as magazine publisher, poet, reformer, and Member of Parliament. Always impulsive, sometimes without funds, Steele cut a dashing figure in London. Though he was not as great a literary figure as Addison, he is remembered as a vigorous and original one.

Addison was quite a different person in many ways: elegant, quiet, and dignified. He was kindly, though shy and somewhat withdrawn. It is said that when he arose in Parliament to make his first speech, he was so embarrassed that he sat down without saying a word and never tried again to make a speech there. His triumphs were in literature instead. Though his enduring fame is as an essayist and stylist of English prose (Samuel Johnson once advised students of English to give their "days and nights" to reading Addison), he had one great success in the drama. His tragedy *Cato* was received with great acclaim, largely because the audience could read in its Roman scenes subtle suggestions of the political issues of the day. Three years before his death Addison married the Countess of Warwick and was appointed Secretary of State.

In 1709 Steele started a paper called *The Tatler,* and stated that his purpose was to enliven mere news with gossip of the coffeehouses. Later Addison contributed a few pieces and the two friends renewed their association.

When *The Tatler* was discontinued because of political difficulties, they decided to found together *The Spectator,* which would be devoted to literature, manners, and morals. Steele had written two-thirds of *The Tatler,* but Addison wrote more than half the essays in the new journal. (All the essays from *The Spectator* included here are by Addison.) The essays are signed by the "Spectator," who is presented as a man of good sense, good breeding, and good nature, going quietly about London, saying little but seeing much. It might well serve as a picture of Addison himself.

The Tatler
(1709–1711)

When Steele launched his new paper, *The Tatler,* he used the pen name of Isaac Bickerstaff. This name alone was enough to sell the paper because of a practical joke played the year before by Jonathan Swift. A quack astrologer and almanac maker named Partridge had been making a great deal of money out of gullible people by his predictions. To expose the faker, Swift had issued a rival almanac by an imaginary Isaac Bickerstaff, predicting "by the unerring stars" the death of Partridge on March 30. On that day the newspapers carried detailed accounts of the funeral of Partridge and an elegy on him. When Partridge protested that he was not dead,

Bickerstaff retorted that his own stars had proved him so, and that these statements came from an impostor. When, therefore, this new periodical appeared under the name of Bickerstaff, the town was naturally alert for further entertainment. It was clever advertising on Steele's part.

The following Prospectus gives the general plan of *The Tatler* and shows the importance of the coffeehouses as a gathering place for the social, political, and literary life of that day.

PROSPECTUS

No. 1. Tuesday, 12 April, 1709.

*Quicquid agunt homines —
nostri est farrago libelli.*[1]

Juvenal's *Satires,* I, 85–86.

THOUGH the other papers, which are published for the use of the good people of England, have certainly very wholesome effects, and are laudable in their particular kinds, they do not seem to come up to the main design of such narrations, which, I humbly presume, should be principally intended for the use of politic persons, who are so public-spirited as to neglect their own affairs to look into transactions of state. Now these gentlemen, for the most part, being persons of strong zeal, and weak intellects, it is both a charitable and necessary work to offer something, whereby such worthy and well-affected members of the commonwealth may be instructed, after their reading, what to think; which shall be the end and purpose of this my paper, wherein I shall, from time to time, report and consider all matters of what kind soever that shall occur to me, and publish such my advices and reflections every Tuesday, Thursday, and Saturday in the week, for the convenience of the post. I resolve to

[1] Pope's embellished translation of this Latin motto is:
"Whate'er men do, or say, or think, or dream, Our motley paper seizes for its theme."

have something which may be of entertainment to the fair sex, in honor of whom I have invented the title of this paper. I therefore earnestly desire all persons, without distinction, to take it in for the present *gratis,*[1] and hereafter at the price of one penny, forbidding all hawkers to take more for it at their peril. And I desire all persons to consider that I am at a very great charge [2] for proper materials for this work, as well as that, before I resolved upon it, I had settled a correspondence in all parts of the known and knowing world. And forasmuch as this globe is not trodden upon by mere drudges of business only, but that men of spirit and genius are justly to be esteemed as considerable agents in it, we shall not, upon a dearth of news, present you with musty foreign edicts, and dull proclamations, but shall divide our relation of the passages which occur in action or discourse throughout this town, as well as elsewhere, under such dates of places as may prepare you for the matter you are to expect in the following manner.

All accounts of gallantry, pleasure, and entertainment shall be under the article of White's Chocolate House; poetry under that of Will's Coffeehouse; learning, under the title of Grecian; foreign and domestic news, you will have from St. James's Coffeehouse; and what else I have to offer on any other subject shall be dated from my own Apartment.

I once more desire my reader to consider, that as I cannot keep an ingenious man to go daily to Will's under twopence each day, merely for his charges;[3] to White's under sixpence; nor to the Grecian, without allowing him some plain Spanish,[4] to be as able as others at the learned table; and that a good observer cannot speak with even Kid-

ney [5] at St. James's without clean linen; I say, these considerations will, I hope, make all persons willing to comply with my humble request (when my *gratis* stock is exhausted) of a penny apiece; especially since they are sure of some proper amusement, and that it is impossible for me to want means to entertain them, having, besides the force of my own parts,[6] the power of divination, and that I can, by casting a figure, tell you all that will happen before it comes to pass.

But this last faculty I shall use very sparingly, and speak but of few things until they are passed, for fear of divulging matters which may offend our superiors.

[5] *Kidney:* name of a waiter.
[6] *force . . . parts:* the power of my own abilities.

The Spectator (1711–1712)

Two months after the appearance of the last number of *The Tatler,* the first number of *The Spectator* was issued. Its avowed purpose was " to enliven morality with wit, and to temper wit with morality." The extravagances and absurdities of the fashionable life of the day were gently yet pointedly satirized. The popularity of the little periodical was tremendous. From about three thousand, the circulation increased until as many as twenty thousand of certain issues were printed. Considering the size of London at that time and the limited number of possible readers, this was an astounding circulation.

Like our newspapers, this little paper appeared daily on the breakfast table, and contained its " classified ads " of Wanted, Lost or Stolen, Amusements, and Merchandise, many of which offer amusing reading today. But it was written in a more finished literary style and was more limited in its scope than a newspaper, having only one main article to an issue. It lasted through five hundred and fifty-five numbers.

To Steele is given credit for originating

[1] *gratis:* given without charge.
[2] *charge:* pains.
[3] *charges:* expenses. The twopence would buy him some coffee, presumably.
[4] *Spanish:* wine.

the club to which the Spectator was supposed to belong, consisting of a lawyer, a merchant, an ex-army captain, an elderly gallant, and a country baronet. The last of these appealed to Addison's imagination especially, and some of the most famous essays of *The Spectator* were devoted to this country gentleman, Sir Roger de Coverley. When printed together they form a running narrative, which is, in effect, a predecessor of the novel.

SIR ROGER AT CHURCH

No. 112. Monday, July 9, 1711.

First, in obedience to thy country's rites,
Worship th' immortal gods.[1]

I AM ALWAYS very well pleased with a country Sunday, and think, if keeping holy the seventh day were only a human institution, it would be the best method that could have been thought of for the polishing and civilizing of mankind. It is certain the country people would soon degenerate into a kind of savages and barbarians, were there not such frequent returns of a stated time, in which the whole village meet together with their best faces, and in their cleanliest habits, to converse with one another upon indifferent subjects, hear their duties explained to them, and join together in adoration of the Supreme Being. Sunday clears away the rust of the whole week, not only as it refreshes in their minds the notions of religion, but as it puts both the sexes upon appearing in their most agreeable forms, and exerting all such qualities as are apt to give them a figure in the eye of the village. A country fellow distinguishes himself as much in the churchyard as a citizen does upon the 'Change,[2]

the whole parish politics being generally discussed in that place either after sermon or before the bell rings.

My friend Sir Roger, being a good churchman, has beautified the inside of his church with several texts of his own choosing. He has likewise given a handsome pulpit cloth, and railed in the communion table at his own expense. He has often told me that at his coming to his estate he found his parishioners very irregular; and that in order to make them kneel and join in the responses, he gave every one of them a hassock and a common prayer book; and at the same time employed an itinerant singing master, who goes about the country for that purpose, to instruct them rightly in the tunes of the psalms; upon which they now very much value themselves, and indeed outdo most of the country churches that I have ever heard.

As Sir Roger is landlord to the whole congregation; he keeps them in very good order, and will suffer nobody to sleep in it besides himself; for if by chance he has been surprised into a short nap at sermon, upon recovering out of it he stands up and looks about him, and if he sees anybody else nodding, either wakes them himself, or sends his servant to them. Several other of the old knight's peculiarities break out upon these occasions. Sometimes he will be lengthening out a verse in the singing psalms, half a minute after the rest of the congregation have done with it; sometimes when he is pleased with the matter of his devotion, he pronounces Amen three or four times to the same prayer; and sometimes stands up when everybody else is upon their knees, to count the congregation, or see if any of his tenants are missing.

I was yesterday very much surprised to hear my old friend in the midst of the service calling out to one John Matthews to mind what he was about, and not disturb the congregation. This John Matthews it seems is remarkable for being an idle fellow, and at that time was

---

[1] The motto is from Pythagoras, a Greek philosopher of the sixth century B.C.
[2] *'Change:* Exchange, a place where business was transacted among merchants, brokers, etc.

kicking his heels for his diversion. This authority of the knight, though exerted in that odd manner which accompanies him in all circumstances of life, has a very good effect upon the parish, who are not polite [1] enough to see anything ridiculous in his behavior; besides that the general good sense and worthiness of his character makes his friends observe these little singularities as foils that rather set off than blemish his good qualities.

As soon as the sermon is finished, nobody presumes to stir till Sir Roger is gone out of the church. The knight walks down from his seat in the chancel between a double row of his tenants, that stand bowing to him on each side; and every now and then inquires how such a one's wife, or mother, or son, or father do, whom he does not see at church; which is understood as a secret reprimand to the person that is absent.

The chaplain has often told me that upon a catechizing day, when Sir Roger has been pleased with a boy that answers well, he has ordered a Bible to be given him next day for his encouragement; and sometimes accompanies it with a flitch of bacon to his mother. Sir Roger has likewise added five pounds a year to the clerk's [2] place; and, that he may encourage the young fellows to make themselves perfect in the church service, has promised upon the death of the present incumbent, who is very old, to bestow it according to merit.

The fair understanding between Sir Roger and his chaplain, and their mutual concurrence in doing good, is the more remarkable, because the very next village is famous for the differences and contentions that rise between the parson and the squire, who live in a perpetual state of war. The parson is always preaching at the squire; and the squire, to be revenged on the parson, never comes to church. The squire has made all his tenants atheists and tithe stealers,[3] while the parson instructs them every Sunday in the dignity of his order, and insinuates to them almost in every sermon that he is a better man than his patron. In short, matters are come to such an extremity that the squire has not said his prayers either in public or private this half year; and that the parson threatens him, if he does not mend his manners, to pray for him in the face of the whole congregation.

Feuds of this nature, though too frequent in the country, are very fatal to the ordinary people; who are so used to be dazzled with riches that they pay as much deference to the understanding of a man of an estate as of a man of learning; and are very hardly brought to regard any truth, how important soever it may be, that is preached to them, when they know there are several men of five hundred a year [4] who do not believe it.

PARTY FEELING

No. 125. Tuesday, July 24, 1711.

Ne, pueri, ne tanta animis assuescite bella;
Neu patriae validas in viscera vertite vires.[5]

Virgil.

[1.] [6] My worthy friend, Sir Roger, when we are talking of the malice of

---

[3] *tithe stealers:* persons who neglect to pay their church tax.

[4] *five . . . year:* with a yearly income of five hundred pounds.

[5] "Do not, my children, make such wars familiar to your minds; nor turn your mighty strength against the life of your country."

[6] The numbers at the beginning of each paragraph are not in the original, but are put in to clarify references in the special study of the essay on page 304.

---

[1] *polite:* versed in etiquette.

[2] *clerk's:* refers to the parish clerk, a lay church official who assists in the services.

parties, very frequently tells us an accident that happened to him when he was a high school boy, which was at a time when feuds ran high between Roundheads [1] and Cavaliers. This worthy knight, being then but a stripling, had occasion to inquire which was the way to St. Anne's Lane, upon which the person whom he spoke to, instead of answering his question, called him a young popish cur and asked him who had made Anne a saint. The boy, being in some confusion, inquired of the next he met, which was the way to Anne's Lane; but was called a prick-eared cur for his pains and, instead of being shown the way, was told that she had been a saint before he was born, and would be one after he was hanged. " Upon this," says Sir Roger, " I did not think fit to repeat the former question but, going into every lane of the neighborhood, asked what they called the name of that lane." By which ingenious artifice he found the place he inquired after, without giving offense to any party. Sir Roger generally closes this narrative with reflections on the mischief that parties do in the country: how they spoil good neighborhood and make honest gentlemen hate one another; besides, that they manifestly tend to the prejudice of the land tax and the destruction of the game.

[2.] There cannot a greater judgment befall a country than such a dreadful spirit of division as rends a government into two distinct people and makes them greater strangers and more averse to one another than if they were actually two different nations. The effects of such a division are pernicious to the last degree, with regard not only to those advantages which they give the common enemy, but to those private evils which they produce in the heart of almost every particular person. This influence is very fatal to both men's morals and their understandings; it sinks the virtue of a nation — and not only so, but destroys even common sense.

[3.] A furious party spirit, when it rages in its full violence, exerts itself in civil war and bloodshed; and, when it is under its greatest restraints, naturally breaks out in falsehood, detraction, calumny, and a partial administration of justice. In a word, it fills a nation with spleen [2] and rancor and extinguishes all the seeds of good nature, compassion, and humanity.

[4.] Plutarch [3] says, very finely, that a man should not allow himself to hate even his enemies, because, says he, if you indulge this passion in some occasions it will rise of itself in others; if you hate your enemies you will contract such a vicious habit of mind as by degrees will break out upon those who are your friends, or those who are indifferent to you. I might here observe how admirably this precept of morality (which derives the malignity of hatred from the passion itself, and not from its object) answers to that great rule which was dictated to the world about a hundred years before this philosopher wrote; [4] but, instead of that, I shall only take notice, with a real grief of heart, that the minds of many good men among us appear soured with party principles, and alienated from one another in such a manner as seems to me altogether inconsistent with the dictates of either reason or religion. Zeal for a public cause is apt to breed passions in the hearts of virtuous persons to which the regard of their own private interest would never have betrayed them.

[5.] If this party spirit has so ill an ef-

---

[1] *Roundheads:* nickname for the short-haired Puritans. The anecdote which follows illustrates the religious differences in the English Civil War (see pages 211–12). The Royalists (or Cavaliers) kept to the Episcopal belief, which recognized saints; the Puritans, however, rejected the whole idea of sainthood.

[2] *spleen:* anger, spite.

[3] *Plutarch* (plōō′tärk): writer of biographies of famous Greeks and Romans (46?–120).

[4] The rule referred to is Jesus' command, "Love your enemies . . ." (Matthew 5:44).

William Hogarth's " Canvassing for Votes " shows two agents for rival candidates offering bribes for the votes of a farmer — and the farmer accepting both bribes. This picture, rich in detail, is an example of Hogarth's realism and satire.

fect on our morals, it has likewise a very great one on our judgments. We often hear a poor insipid paper or pamphlet cried up, and sometimes a noble piece depreciated, by those who are of a different principle from the author. One who is actuated by this spirit is almost under an incapacity of discerning either real blemishes or beauties. A man of merit in a different principle is like an object seen in two different mediums — that appears crooked or broken, however straight or entire it may be in itself. For this reason there is scarce a person of any figure in England who does not go by two contrary characters, as opposite to one another as light and darkness. Knowledge and learning suffer in a particular manner from this strange prejudice, which at present prevails amongst all ranks and degrees in the British nation. As men formerly be-

came eminent in learned societies by their parts and acquisitions, they now distinguish themselves by the warmth and violence with which they espouse their respective parties. Books are valued upon the like considerations: an abusive, scurrilous style passes for satire, and a dull scheme of party notions is called fine writing.

[6.] There is one piece of sophistry practiced by both sides, and that is the taking any scandalous story that has ever been whispered or invented of a private man, for a known, undoubted truth, and raising suitable speculations upon it. Calumnies that have never been proved, or have been often refuted, are the ordinary postulatums [1] of these infamous scribblers — upon which they proceed as upon first principles granted

[1] *postulatums* (pŏs′tṫ·lā′tŭmz): things assumed without proof.

by all men, though in their hearts they know they are false or at best very doubtful. When they have laid these foundations of scurrility, it is no wonder that their superstructure is every way answerable to them. If this shameless practice of the present age endures much longer, praise and reproach will cease to be motives of action in good men.

[7.] There are certain periods of time in all governments when this inhuman spirit prevails. Italy was long torn in pieces by the Guelphs and Ghibellines,[1] and France by those who were for and against the league;[2] but it is very unhappy for a man to be born in such a stormy and tempestuous season. It is the restless ambition of artful men that thus breaks a people into factions, and draws several well-meaning persons to their interest by a specious concern for their country. How many honest minds are filled with uncharitable and barbarous notions, out of zeal for the public good! What cruelties and outrages would they not commit against men of an adverse party, whom they would honor and esteem if, instead of considering them as they are represented, they knew them as they are! Thus are persons of the greatest probity seduced into shameful errors and prejudices, and made bad men even by that noblest of principles — the love of their country. I cannot here forbear mentioning the famous Spanish proverb, " If there were neither fools nor knaves in the world, all people would be of one mind."

[8.] For my own part I could heartily wish that all honest men would enter into an association for the support of one another against the endeavors of those whom they ought to look upon as their common enemies, whatsoever side they may belong to. Were there such an honest body of neutral forces we should never see the worst of men in the great figures of life, because they are useful to a party; nor the best unregarded, because they are above practicing those methods which would be grateful to their faction. We should then single every criminal out of the herd and hunt him down, however formidable and overgrown he might appear. On the contrary we should shelter distressed innocence and defend virtue, however beset with contempt or ridicule, envy or defamation. In short, we should not any longer regard our fellow subjects as Whigs or Tories, but should make the man of merit our friend and the villain our enemy.

THE COQUETTE'S HEART

No. 281. Tuesday, January 22, 1712.

Pectoribus inhians spirantia consulit exta.[3]

Virgil.

HAVING already given an account of the dissection of a beau's head,[4] with the several discoveries made on that occasion, I shall here, according to my promise, enter upon the dissection of a coquette's heart, and communicate to the public such particularities as we observed in that curious piece of anatomy.

I should perhaps have waived this undertaking, had not I been put in mind of my promise by several of my unknown correspondents, who are very im-

---

[1] *Guelphs* (gwĕlfs) *and Ghibellines* (gĭb'ĕ-lĭnz): Italian parties during the latter part of the Middle Ages. At first they had opposing principles of government, but they later fought largely over personal power.

[2] *league:* probably a reference to the Holy, or Catholic, League, a successful alliance formed in 1576 by the Pope and leaders in Spain and France to prevent the Huguenots from gaining the French throne.

[3] " Anxious, the reeking entrails he consults." This is a reference to the ancient practice of divination by examining the entrails of sacrificial animals.

[4] In an earlier essay the Spectator analyzed a young man of fashion.

portunate with me to make an example of the coquette, as I have already done of the beau. It is therefore in compliance with the request of friends that I have looked over the minutes of my former dream, in order to give the public an exact relation of it, which I shall enter upon without further preface.

Our operator, before he engaged in this visionary dissection, told us that there was nothing in his art more difficult than to lay open the heart of a coquette, by reason of the many labyrinths and recesses which are to be found in it, and which do not appear in the heart of any other animal.

He desired us first of all to observe the pericardium, or outward case of the heart, which we did very attentively; and by the help of our glasses discerned in it millions of little scars, which seemed to have been occasioned by the points of innumerable darts and arrows, that from time to time had glanced upon the outward coat; though we could not discover the smallest orifice [1] by which any of them had entered and pierced the inward substance.

Every smatterer in anatomy knows that this pericardium, or case of the heart, contains in it a thin reddish liquor, supposed to be bred from the vapors which exhale out of the heart and, being stopped here, are condensed into this watery substance. Upon examining this liquor, we found that it had in it all the qualities of that spirit which is made use of in the thermometer to show the change of weather.

Nor must I here omit an experiment one of the company assured us he himself had made with this liquor, which he found in great quantity about the heart of a coquette whom he had formerly dissected. He affirmed to us that he had actually inclosed it in a small tube made after the manner of a weatherglass; but that, instead of acquainting him with the variations of the atmos-

phere, it showed him the qualities of those persons who entered the room where it stood. He affirmed also that it rose at the approach of a plume of feathers, an embroidered coat, or a pair of fringed gloves; and that it fell as soon as an ill-shaped periwig, a clumsy pair of shoes, or an unfashionable coat came into his house. Nay, he proceeded so far as to assure us that upon his laughing aloud when he stood by it, the liquor mounted very sensibly, and immediately sank again upon his looking serious. In short, he told us that he knew very well by this invention whenever he had a man of sense or a coxcomb in his room.

Having cleared away the pericardium, or the case, and liquor above mentioned, we came to the heart itself. The outward surface of it was extremely slippery, and the mucro, or point, so very cold withal that upon endeavoring to take hold of it, it glided through the fingers like a smooth piece of ice.

The fibers were turned and twisted in a more intricate and perplexed manner than they are usually found in other hearts; insomuch that the whole heart was wound up together like a Gordian knot,[2] and must have had very irregular and unequal motions, while it was employed in its vital function.

One thing we thought very observable, namely, that upon examining all the vessels which came into it, or issued out of it, we could not discover any communication that it had with the tongue.

We could not but take notice likewise that several of those little nerves in the heart which are affected by the sentiments of love, hatred, and other passions, did not descend to this before us from the brain, but from the muscles which lie about the eye.

Upon weighing the heart in my hand,

[2] *Gordian knot:* a famous intricate knot in ancient history. The legend was that whoever could undo it would reign over the entire East. Alexander the Great, on hearing this, cut it in two with his sword.

[1] *orifice* (ŏr′ĭ·fĭs): opening.

I found it to be extremely light, and consequently very hollow, which I did not wonder at, when, upon looking into the inside of it, I saw multitudes of cells and cavities running one within another, as our historians describe the apartments of Rosamond's bower.[1] Several of these little hollows were stuffed with innumerable sorts of trifles, which I shall forbear giving any particular account of, and shall, therefore, only take notice of what lay first and uppermost, which, upon our unfolding it, and applying our microscopes to it, appeared to be a flame-colored hood.

We are informed that the lady of this heart, when living, received the addresses of several who made love to her, and did not only give each of them encouragement, but made everyone she conversed with believe that she regarded him with an eye of kindness; for which reason we expected to have seen the impression of multitudes of faces among the several plaits and foldings of the heart; but to our great surprise not a single print of this nature discovered itself till we came into the very core and center of it. We there observed a little figure, which, upon applying our glasses to it, appeared dressed in a very fantastic manner. The more I looked

upon it, the more I thought I had seen the face before, but could not possibly recollect either the place or time; when at length one of the company, who had examined this figure more nicely [2] than the rest, showed us plainly by the make of its face, and the several turns of its features, that the little idol which was thus lodged in the very middle of the heart was the deceased beau, whose head I gave some account of in my last Tuesday's paper.

As soon as we had finished our dissection, we resolved to make an experiment of the heart, not being able to determine among ourselves the nature of its substance, which differed in so many particulars from that in the heart of other females. Accordingly, we laid it into a pan of burning coals, when we observed in it a certain salamandrine [3] quality that made it capable of living in the midst of fire and flame, without being consumed or so much as singed.

As we were admiring this strange phenomenon, and standing round the heart in a circle, it gave a most prodigious sigh, or rather crack, and dispersed all at once in smoke and vapor. This imaginary noise, which methought was louder than the burst of a cannon, produced such a violent shake in my brain, that it dissipated the fumes of sleep, and left me in an instant broad awake.

[2] *nicely:* carefully.
[3] *salamandrine* (săl'á·măn'drĭn): like the salamander, a little lizard supposedly able to live in fire.

TATLER AND SPECTATOR ESSAYS

1. What information is given in the "Prospectus" of *The Tatler* as to its purpose, frequency, price, the type of readers to whom it will appeal, and its subject matter?

2. How did *The Spectator* differ from *The Tatler?* How do these papers resemble a modern newspaper? a magazine?

3. Give a picture of Sir Roger from

[1] *Rosamond's bower:* a labyrinth or maze which Henry II built for the fair Rosamond in order to hide her from his jealous wife.

these essays. Which of his traits make you like him? Which are amusing? Do you know any person who resembles him?

4. How does the coquette compare with the young ladies in *The Rape of the Lock?* Which do you consider the more enjoyable satire, Pope's or Addison's?

5. Select passages from " The Coquette's Heart " which are particularly clever in suggesting the light-mindedness of the girl. How does Addison make the physical details of the heart illustrate the coquette's behavior? If you were to look up the manners of the Age of Elegance — as the eighteenth century is sometimes called — you would find how fashionable coquetry was. To what extent does Addison's criticism of the coquette apply to modern youth?

WRITING AND DISCUSSION

1. In imitation of *The Spectator,* write a prospectus for a small paper to circulate in your school or neighborhood. Prepare character sketches of class members or town figures, in the manner of the Sir Roger papers. Or write a satire on school life, such as " A Freshman's Head " or " A Senior's Heart."

2. Organize a panel to answer the following question: Who had the greatest influence on public manners — Pope, Swift, Steele, or Addison? Supplement your reading of these four authors with some research in histories and encyclopedias on the manners of the eighteenth century. You will also want to find out more about each writer's influence on his readers.

Hymn

This majestic hymn by Addison expresses the eighteenth-century belief in the perfect order of the universe. It is based on the opening of the Nineteenth Psalm and is still sung in churches to the familiar tune adapted from Haydn's oratorio *Creation.* Read the psalm and compare it with the hymn, noting how Addison has rephrased the thought.

The spacious firmament on high,
With all the blue ethereal sky,
And spangled heavens, a shining frame,
Their great Original proclaim.
Th' unwearied Sun from day to day 5
Does his Creator's power display;
And publishes to every land
The work of an Almighty hand.

Soon as the evening shades prevail,
The Moon takes up the wondrous tale;
And nightly to the listening Earth 11
Repeats the story of her birth:
Whilst all the stars that round her burn,
And all the planets in their turn,
Confirm the tidings as they roll, 15
And spread the truth from pole to pole.

What though in solemn silence all
Move round the dark terrestrial ball;
What though no real voice nor sound
Amidst their radiant orbs be found?
In Reason's ear they all rejoice, 21
And utter forth a glorious voice;
Forever singing as they shine,
" The Hand that made us is divine."

READING THE ESSAY

So far in this book you have read several essays. You will recognize that this term specifies a short prose piece, often gracefully informal, that is unified in theme or subject.

Historically, the French writer Michel de Montaigne originated this literary form in the sixteenth century. He named it from the word *essai*, which means " trial " or " attempt," for his writing represented a modest endeavor to express his beliefs and meditations on some subject. Later, some of Bacon's writing took the same form.

You will find that the essay has two extremes. One is the loose personal essay (such as Charles Lamb's " Dream Children " on page 394), in which the author's innermost private thoughts are expressed in an easy confidential style. The other is an essay more formal in style and organization (for example, Huxley's " A Liberal Education " on page 473), which logically covers a complete argument. An essay may fall at any point between these two poles of formality and informality.

Let us take a closer look at " Party Feeling " by Addison. There are many different ways of looking at an essay, but almost any examination is bound to consider three elements: idea, structure, and mood.

IDEA

It is hard to miss Addison's main point, even on a quick reading. He believes that fanatical party politics are bad, since they injure men's morals and judgment and degrade the spirit of a nation. He presents this idea clearly, and develops it through a logical consideration of relevant details. We know that this is an essay written to appeal to the intellect — a rational discussion of the subject of partisan political feeling.

STRUCTURE

Your enjoyment of any good essay is increased by seeing how it is put together. An analysis of " Party Feeling " in outline form will be enlightening. Such an outline is started here, with each numbered main topic representing a paragraph.

1. A particular anecdote may show the kind of mischief that party politics do in the country.
2. Partisan division is pernicious, since —
    a. It aids the enemy, and
    b. It harms each citizen in
        (1) his morals, and
        (2) his understanding or common sense.
3. Carried to an extreme, it can extinguish all good emotions in a nation and bring on civil war and bloodshed.
4. Morally, hatred or fanaticism against one's enemies harms a man because the hatred, springing from " the passion itself and not from its object," soon pervades his character.

Now, go ahead and complete the outline for the remaining four paragraphs.

This, then, is the argument. You can see that Addison writes forcefully and does not waste words. In a good essay the ideas follow in a logical development; all are relevant to one another and to the main thought. Is this true of " Party Feeling "? Could any part of this essay be omitted without weakening it?

In the last paragraph, Addison makes a proposal for avoiding the ill effects of party feeling. What else does he accomplish in this paragraph? How is it an effective conclusion to his argument?

MOOD AND TONE

Not all essays are logical arguments; many are significant not so much for *what* they say as for *how* the author expresses himself. In any personal essay, the writer's mood, or the tone that is apparent in his writing, is an important element.

Addison's tone here is intelligent, gentle, and sometimes humorous. It is hard to establish this light mood in an essay like " Party Feeling," which has a serious purpose throughout. But the introduction and conclusion get us into and out of the argument by smooth gradations. The first paragraph begins quite informally with the Spectator's reminiscence about his worthy friend, Sir Roger de Coverley. This catches our interest and is funny in itself. Even here, Addison does not lose the thread of his thought, for he speaks of the " malice of parties " as his theme in the opening sentence.

Cleverest of all is the last phrase in the first paragraph, where we learn indirectly that Sir Roger, even when he is talking against party feeling, cannot help showing it himself: as a country gentleman he is against higher land taxes and against anything that might interfere with his hunting.

What indications of Addison's personal feeling do you find in the following paragraphs? What is the effect of his manner on the reader?

The last paragraph also lightens the argument, for it begins with the phrase " For my own part," and the Spectator once more steps in with a hearty wish in his own person.

SAMUEL JOHNSON 1709–1784

and

JAMES BOSWELL 1740–1795

Doctor Samuel Johnson was the literary dictator of the last half of the eighteenth century. A picturesque figure — huge, rambling, scarred of face, thunderous of voice, and slovenly of dress — Johnson drew about him the most talented men of his age. He was the oracle of the famous Literary Club which included David Garrick, the actor; Sir Joshua Reynolds, the painter; Oliver Goldsmith, the poet and novelist; Richard Sheridan, the dramatist; Edmund Burke, the statesman and defender of America — and James Boswell, his biographer. Today we know Johnson best through Boswell's biography. In fact, Boswell is far more widely read than Johnson himself, whose importance resided mainly in his personal influence. He could talk fluently and learnedly on practically any subject. He molded the taste of his age with his conversation, and to this day we prize his critical judgments on men of letters.

Samuel Johnson in his early career waged a constant struggle against poverty. He was brought up in the country town of Lichfield, where his father was a bookseller, poor in money but rich in reading lore. Sam was a proud young man. At Oxford he once threw away a much-needed pair of shoes given to him by a fellow student because he could not take charity. As a schoolteacher at Lichfield he

DR. SAMUEL JOHNSON

Portrait by Sir Joshua Reynolds

was impatient to leave. He finally journeyed a hundred miles to London, sharing a horse with his pupil, David Garrick.

In London Johnson was unsuccessful in selling his writings, which included poetry, biography, and essays, and he took to hack writing. Slowly he gained recognition, mainly from his famous *Dictionary,* his paper *The Rambler,* and his *Lives of the English Poets.* Yet he remained poor, and his one novel, *Rasselas,* was written in four days to pay the expense of his mother's funeral. At fifty-three he was relieved, finally, by a pension from George III.

From Boswell's *The Life of Samuel Johnson* we get a rounded picture of Johnson: he was a gruff and stern man but a kindly one. He supported in his house a number of poor and unfortunate people, including Miss Williams, his old, half-blind housekeeper, who is reputed to have used her thumb to judge whether the guests' tea-cups needed refilling! All in all, he deserved to have the age named for him, and to have James Boswell at his side to record his life and times for posterity.

James Boswell is recognized as one of the greatest biographers in English literature. A Scotsman of wealthy family who came to London to get a commission in the army, Boswell was ambitious, impulsive, and often lacking in judgment. Yet he had a true gift for writing and the rare insight to recognize his life work on meeting Samuel Johnson. For years, whenever the two men met, Boswell recorded Johnson's conversation, his habits, his peculiarities: the biographer submerged his own personality in that of his subject. But Boswell was a personality in his own right. His journals, not discovered until the twentieth century, reveal him as a vain, sometimes ridiculous youth, yet in many ways an appealing one. He was a delightful writer with a keen sense of observation and a lively humor that never failed him.

Letter to Lord Chesterfield

The significance of this letter is in its relation to the system of patronage prevalent in England in Johnson's time. Since the reading public was small, the only way a man could obtain any substantial financial return from writing was by securing a patron among the wealthy nobility. It was understood that the author would dedicate his work to the patron, who in return saw to the author's welfare. When the *Dictionary* was first contemplated, Johnson requested the support of Lord Chesterfield, the most elegant gentleman of his day. The result is told in the following letter. Johnson showed his native independence of spirit and is said to have hereby sounded the death knell of the whole patronage system. In connection with this, you should read the selection "The Dictionary" from Boswell's *Life* on page 308.

February 7, 1755.

To the Right Honorable the Earl of Chesterfield.

My Lord:

I have been lately informed by the proprietor of the *World* [1] that two papers, in which my Dictionary is recommended to the public, were written by your Lordship. To be so distinguished is an honor which, being very little accustomed to favors from the great, I know not well how to receive, or in what terms to acknowledge.

When, upon some slight encouragement, I first visited your Lordship, I was overpowered, like the rest of mankind, by the enchantment of your address, and could not forbear to wish that I might boast myself *Le vainqueur du vainqueur de la terre* [2] — that I might obtain that regard for which I saw the world contending; but I found my attendance so little encouraged that neither pride nor modesty would suffer me to continue it. When I had once addressed your Lordship in public, I had exhausted all the art of pleasing which a retired and uncourtly scholar can possess. I had done all that I could; and no man is well pleased to have his all neglected, be it ever so little.

Seven years, my Lord, have now

[1] *the World:* a newspaper run by Edward Moore, a friend of Johnson's.
[2] "The conqueror of the conqueror of the world."

passed since I waited in your outward rooms, or was repulsed from your door; during which time I have been pushing on my work through difficulties, of which it is useless to complain, and have brought it, at last, to the verge of publication without one act of assistance, one word of encouragement, or one smile of favor. Such treatment I did not expect, for I never had a Patron before.

The shepherd in Virgil grew at last acquainted with Love, and found him a native of the rocks.[1]

Is not a Patron, my Lord, one who looks with unconcern on a man struggling for life in the water, and when he has reached ground, encumbers him with help? The notice which you have been pleased to take of my labors, had

[1] *The shepherd . . . rocks:* a reference to a passage in Virgil's eighth Eclogue (a pastoral poem in which shepherds converse on the cruelty and inhumanity of love).

it been early, had been kind; but it has been delayed till I am indifferent, and cannot enjoy it; till I am solitary, and cannot impart it; till I am known, and do not want it. I hope it is no very cynical asperity not to confess obligations where no benefit has been received, or to be unwilling that the Public should consider me as owing that to a Patron which Providence has enabled me to do for myself.

Having carried on my work thus far with so little obligation to any favorer of learning, I shall not be disappointed though I should conclude it, if less be possible, with less; for I have been long wakened from that dream of hope, in which I once boasted myself with so much exultation.

My Lord,
Your Lordship's most humble,
Most obedient servant,
Sam: Johnson.

Definitions from Johnson's Dictionary

Some of Johnson's definitions are famous for showing his prejudices, his errors, his use of big words to define a fairly simple term, and, at times, his humor.

Excise duty: a hateful tax levied by wretches hired by those to whom excise is paid.

Oats: a grain which in England is generally given to horses, but in Scotland supports the people.

Pension: an allowance made to anyone without an equivalent.[2] In England it is generally understood to mean pay given to a state hireling for treason to his country.

Pensioner: a slave of state hired by a stipend to obey his master. [Later, when Johnson himself became a pensioner, he replied to the critics who reminded

[2] *equivalent* (ê·kwĭv′à·lĕnt): service of equal value.

him of this definition: " I wish my pension were twice as large that they might make twice as much noise."]

Tory: one who adheres to the ancient constitution of the State and the apostolical hierarchy of the Church of England; opposed to a Whig.

Whig: the name of a faction.

Lexicographer: a writer of dictionaries, a harmless drudge.

Grub Street: the name of a street in London, much inhabited by writers of small histories, dictionaries, and temporary poems: whence any mean production is called *Grub Street.*

Pastern: the knee of a horse. [On being asked by a lady why he defined it thus, he said, " Ignorance, madam, pure ignorance."]

Network: anything reticulated or decussated at equal distances with interstices between the intersections.

The Life of Samuel Johnson

JAMES BOSWELL

[THE DICTIONARY]

This selection is from the first part of the biography, covering the period before Boswell became acquainted with Johnson.

HOW LONG this immense undertaking had been the object of his contemplation, I do not know. I once asked him by what means he had attained to that astonishing knowledge of our language by which he was enabled to realize a design of such extent and accumulated difficulty. He told me that " it was not the effect of particular study; but that it had grown up in his mind insensibly." . . .

That he was fully aware of the arduous nature of the undertaking, he acknowledges; and shows himself perfectly sensible of it in the conclusion of his " Plan "; but he had a noble consciousness of his own abilities, which enabled him to go on with undaunted spirit.

Dr. Adams found him one day busy at his Dictionary, when the following dialogue ensued:

Adams: " This is a great work, Sir. How are you to get all the etymologies? " [1]

Johnson: " Why, Sir, here is a shelf with Junius, and Skinner,[2] and others; and there is a Welsh gentleman who has published a collection of Welsh proverbs, who will help me with the Welsh."

Adams: " But, Sir, how can you do this in three years? "

Johnson: " Sir, I have no doubt that I can do it in three years."

Adams: " But the French Academy, which consists of forty members, took forty years to compile their Dictionary."

Johnson: " Sir, thus it is. This is the proportion. Let me see: forty times forty is sixteen hundred. As three to sixteen hundred so is the proportion of an Englishman to a Frenchman."

With so much ease and pleasantry could he talk of that prodigious labor which he had undertaken to execute.

While the Dictionary was going forward, Johnson lived part of the time in Holborn, part in Gough Square, Fleet Street; and he had an upper room fitted up like a countinghouse for the purpose, in which he gave to the copyists their several tasks. The words, partly taken from other Dictionaries, and partly supplied by himself, having been first written down with spaces left between them, he delivered in writing their etymologies, definitions, and various significations. The authorities were copied from the books themselves, in which he had marked the passages with a black-lead pencil, the traces of which could be easily effaced. I have seen several of them in which that trouble had not been taken; so that they were just as when used by the copyists. It is remarkable that he was so attentive in the choice of the passages in which words were authorized that one may read page after page of his Dictionary with improvement and pleasure; and it should not pass unobserved that he has quoted no author whose writings had a tendency to hurt sound religion and morality.

The necessary expense of preparing a work of such magnitude for the press must have been a considerable deduction from the price stipulated to be paid for the copyright.[3] I understand that nothing was allowed by the booksellers on that account; and I remember his telling me that a large portion of it having, by mistake, been written upon both sides of the paper, so as to be incon-

---

[1] *etymologies* (ĕt'ǐ·mŏl'ō·jǐz): origins and derivations of words.

[2] *Junius and Skinner:* seventeenth-century English scholars, both of whom wrote books on etymology. Skinner was also a physician.

[3] The price was £1,575.

venient for the compositor, it cost him twenty pounds to have it transcribed upon one side only.

[BOSWELL'S FIRST MEETING WITH DR. JOHNSON]

Mr. Thomas Davies, the actor, who then kept a bookseller's shop in Russell Street, Covent Garden, told me that Johnson was very much his friend, and came frequently to his house, where he more than once invited me to meet him: but by some unlucky accident or other he was prevented from coming to us. . . .

At last, on Monday the 16th of May, when I was sitting in Mr. Davies' back parlor, after having drunk tea with him and Mrs. Davies, Johnson unexpectedly came into the shop; and Mr. Davies having perceived him through the glass door in the room in which we were sitting, advancing toward us — he announced his awful approach to me, somewhat in the manner of an actor in the part of Horatio, when he addresses Hamlet on the appearance of his father's ghost, " Look, my Lord, it comes." I found that I had a very perfect idea of Johnson's figure, from the portrait of him painted by Sir Joshua Reynolds soon after he had published his Dictionary, in the attitude of sitting in his easy chair in deep meditation; which was the first picture his friend did for him, which Sir Joshua very kindly presented to me, and from which an engraving has been made for this work. Mr. Davies mentioned my name, and respectfully introduced me to him. I was much agitated; and recollecting his prejudice against the Scotch, of which I had heard much, I said to Davies, " Don't tell him where I come from."

" From Scotland," cried Davies, roguishly.

" Mr. Johnson (said I), I do indeed come from Scotland, but I cannot help it."

I am willing to flatter myself that I meant this as light pleasantry to soothe and conciliate him, and not as an hu-

JAMES BOSWELL

miliating abasement at the expense of my country. But however that might be, this speech was somewhat unlucky; for with that quickness of wit for which he was so remarkable, he seized the expression " come from Scotland," which I used in the sense of being of that country; and, as if I had said that I had come away from it, or left it, retorted, " That, Sir, I find, is what a very great many of your countrymen cannot help."

This stroke stunned me a good deal; and when we had sat down, I felt myself not a little embarrassed, and apprehensive of what might come next.

He then addressed himself to Davies: " What do you think of Garrick? He has refused me an order for the play for Miss Williams, because he knows the house will be full, and that an order would be worth three shillings."

Eager to take any opening to get into conversation with him, I ventured to say, " O, Sir, I cannot think Mr. Garrick would grudge such a trifle to you."

" Sir (said he, with a stern look), I have known David Garrick longer than you have done; and I know no right you have to talk to me on the subject."

Perhaps I deserved this check; for it was rather presumptuous in me, an entire stranger, to express any doubt of the justice of his animadversion [1] upon his old acquaintance and pupil. I now felt myself much mortified, and began to think that the hope which I had long indulged of obtaining his acquaintance was blasted. And, in truth, had not my ardor been uncommonly strong, and my resolution uncommonly persevering, so rough a reception might have deterred me forever from making any further attempts. Fortunately, however, I remained upon the field not wholly discomfited; and was soon rewarded by hearing some of his conversation. . . .

A few days afterward I called on Davies, and asked him if he thought I might take the liberty of waiting on Mr. Johnson at his Chambers in the Temple.[2] He said I certainly might, and that Mr. Johnson would take it as a compliment. So on Tuesday the 24th of May, after having been enlivened by the witty sallies of Messieurs Thornton, Wilkes, Churchill, and Lloyd,[3] with whom I had passed the morning, I boldly repaired to Johnson. His Chambers were on the first floor of No. 1, Inner Temple-lane, and I entered them with an impression given me by the Reverend Dr. Blair, of Edinburgh, who had been introduced to him not long before, and described his having " found the Giant in his den "; an expression which, when I came to be pretty well acquainted with Johnson, I repeated to him, and he was diverted at this picturesque account of himself.

He received me very courteously: but it must be confessed that his apartment, and furniture, and morning dress were sufficiently uncouth. His brown suit of clothes looked very rusty: he had on a little old shriveled unpowdered wig, which was too small for his head; his shirt neck and knees of his breeches were loose; his black worsted stockings ill drawn up; and he had a pair of unbuckled shoes by way of slippers. But all these slovenly particularities were forgotten the moment that he began to talk. Some gentlemen, whom I do not recollect, were sitting with him; and when they went away, I also rose; but he said to me, " Nay, don't go."

" Sir (said I), I am afraid that I intrude upon you. It is benevolent to allow me to sit and hear you."

He seemed pleased with this compliment, which I sincerely paid him, and answered, " Sir, I am obliged to any man who visits me." . . .

When I rose a second time, he again pressed me to stay, which I did.

He told me that he generally went abroad at four in the afternoon and seldom came home till two in the morning. I took the liberty to ask if he did not think it was wrong to live thus, and not make more use of his great talents. He owned it was a bad habit. On reviewing, at the distance of many years, my journal of this period, I wonder how, at my first visit, I ventured to talk to him so freely, and that he bore it with so much indulgence.

Before we departed, he was so good as to promise to favor me with his company one evening at my lodgings; and, as I took my leave, shook me cordially by the hand. It is almost needless to add that I felt no little elation at having now so happily established an acquaintance of which I had been so long ambitious.

My readers will, I trust, excuse me for being thus minutely circumstantial, when it is considered that the acquaintance of Dr. Johnson was to me a most valuable acquisition, and laid the foundation of whatever instruction and entertainment they may receive from my collections concerning the great subject

---

[1] *animadversion* (ăn′i·măd·vûr′shŭn): criticism, usually adverse.

[2] *Temple:* an area of London in which lawyers lived and where law courts are located.

[3] *Thornton . . . Lloyd:* literary wits and friends of Boswell.

This satirical engraving by Rowlandson shows Johnson clutching Boswell as they stroll up High Street in a fog so thick that if he let go they might lose each other!

of the work which they are now perusing.

[DR. JOHNSON'S PECULIARITIES]

He had another particularity,[1] of which none of his friends even ventured to ask an explanation. It appeared to me some superstitious habit, which he had contracted early, and from which he had never called upon his reason to disentangle him. This was his anxious care to go out or in at a door or passage by a certain number of steps from a certain point, or at least so as that either his right or his left foot (I am not certain which) should constantly make the first actual movement when he came close to the door or passage. Thus I conjecture: for I have, upon innumerable occasions, observed him suddenly stop, and then seem to count his steps with a deep earnestness; and when he had neglected or gone wrong in this sort of magical movement, I have seen him go back again, put himself in a proper posture to begin the ceremony, and, having gone through it, break from his abstraction, walk briskly on, and join his companion. Sir Joshua Reynolds has observed him to go a good way about, rather than cross a particular alley in Leicester [2] Fields; but this Sir Joshua imputed to his having had some disagreeable recollections associated with it.

[1] *another particularity:* The first one described was his habit of talking to himself.

[2] *Leicester* (lĕs′tēr).

That the most minute singularities which belonged to him, and made very observable parts of his appearance and manner, may not be omitted, it is requisite to mention that while talking or even musing as he sat in his chair, he commonly held his head to one side toward his right shoulder, and shook it in a tremulous manner, moving his body backward and forward, and rubbing his left knee in the same direction, with the palm of his hand. In the intervals of articulating he made various sounds with his mouth; sometimes giving a half whistle, sometimes as if ruminating, or what is called chewing the cud, sometimes making his tongue play backward from the roof of his mouth, as if clucking like a hen, and sometimes protruding it against his upper gums in front, as if pronouncing quickly under his breath, too, too, too: all this accompanied sometimes with a thoughtful look, but more frequently with a smile. Generally when he had concluded a period,[1] in the course of a dispute, by which time he was a good deal exhausted by violence and vociferation, he used to blow out his breath like a whale. This I suppose was a relief to his lungs; and seemed in him to be a contemptuous mode of expression, as if he had made the arguments of his opponents fly like chaff before the wind.

[JOHNSON AND GOLDSMITH]

The following incident takes place at dinner at the home of two booksellers, where about a dozen gentlemen, including Johnson, Boswell, and Goldsmith, are assembled. A long conversation is first reported.

During this argument, Goldsmith sat in restless agitation, from a wish to get in and shine. Finding himself excluded, he had taken his hat to go away, but remained for some time with it in his hand, like a gamester, who, at the close of a long night, lingers for a little while, to see if he can have a favorable open-

[1] *concluded a period:* ended a sentence.

ing to finish with success. Once when he was beginning to speak, he found himself overpowered by the loud voice of Johnson, who was at the opposite end of the table, and did not perceive Goldsmith's attempt. Thus disappointed of his wish to obtain the attention of the company, Goldsmith in a passion threw down his hat, looking angrily at Johnson, and exclaimed in a bitter tone, " Take it." When Toplady was going to speak, Johnson uttered some sound, which led Goldsmith to think that he was beginning again, and taking the words from Toplady. Upon which, he seized this opportunity of venting his own envy and spleen, under the pretext of supporting another person: " Sir (said he to Johnson), the gentleman has heard you patiently for an hour: pray allow us now to hear him."

Johnson (sternly): " Sir, I was not interrupting the gentleman. I was only giving him a signal of my attention. Sir, you are impertinent." Goldsmith made no reply, but continued in the company for some time.

He and Mr. Langton and I went together to the Club, where we found Mr. Burke, Mr. Garrick, and some other members, and among them our friend Goldsmith, who sat silently brooding over Johnson's reprimand to him after dinner. Johnson perceived this, and said aside to some of us, " I'll make Goldsmith forgive me "; and then called to him in a loud voice, " Dr. Goldsmith — something passed today where you and I dined: I ask your pardon." Goldsmith answered placidly, " It must be much from you, Sir, that I take ill." And so at once the difference was over, and they were on as easy terms as ever, and Goldsmith rattled away as usual.

In our way to the Club tonight, when I regretted that Goldsmith would, upon every occasion, endeavor to shine, by which he often exposed himself, Mr. Langton observed that he was not like Addison, who was content with the fame of his writings, and did not aim also at excellency in conversation, for which he found himself unfit: and that he said to a lady who complained of his having talked little in company, " Madam, I have but ninepence in ready money, but I can draw for a thousand pounds." I observed that Goldsmith had a great deal of gold in his cabinet, but not content with that, was always taking out his purse. Johnson: " Yes, Sir, and that so often an empty purse! "

Goldsmith's incessant desire of being conspicuous in company was the occasion of his sometimes appearing to such disadvantage as one should hardly have supposed possible in a man of his genius. When his literary reputation had risen deservedly high, and his society was much courted, he became very jealous of the extraordinary attention which was everywhere paid to Johnson. One evening, in a circle of wits, he found fault with me for talking of Johnson as entitled to the honor of unquestionable superiority. " Sir (said he), you are for making a monarchy of what should be a republic."

He was still more mortified, when talking in a company with fluent vivacity, and, as he flattered himself, to the admiration of all who were present; a German who sat next him, and perceived Johnson rolling himself as if about to speak, suddenly stopped him, saying, " Stay, stay — Toctor Shonson is going to say something." This was, no doubt, very provoking, especially to one so irritable as Goldsmith, who frequently mentioned it with strong expressions of indignation.

It may also be observed that Goldsmith was sometimes content to be treated with an easy familiarity, but upon occasions would be consequential and important. An instance of this occurred in a small particular. Johnson had a way of contracting the names of his friends: as Beauclerk, Beau; Boswell, Bozzy; Langton, Lanky; Murphy, Mur; Sheridan, Sherry. I remember one day, when Tom Davies was telling that Dr. Johnson said, " We are all in labor for a name to Goldy's play," Goldsmith seemed displeased that such a liberty should be taken with his name, and said, " I have often desired him not to call me Goldy." Tom was remarkably attentive to the most minute circumstance about Johnson. I recollect his telling me once, on my arrival in London, " Sir, our great friend has made an improvement on his appellation of old Mr. Sheridan. He calls him now Sherry derry."

Boswell's London Journal, 1762–1763

Boswell's journal, secreted or neglected by the Boswell family over the centuries, finally found its way to Yale University. The first of many projected volumes was published in 1950. Its detailed account of the life of a young eighteenth-century man-about-town — alternately naïve and sophisticated, fun-loving and earnest — delighted readers. Boswell's journal became a literary sensation and a best seller. The journal throws further light not only upon Boswell himself, but also upon his unusual friendship with Johnson. The following selections show how Boswell sought Johnson's advice in the affairs of his private life, and in what kindly spirit Johnson replied. The first entry here quoted also illustrates Boswell's habit of jotting down unconnected sentences he remembered from conversations with his friend.

From *Boswell's London Journal, 1762–1763*, edited by Frederick A. Pottle, published by McGraw-Hill Book Company. Copyright, 1950, by Yale University.

Saturday 25 June [1763] . . . I told him all my story. " Sir," said he, " your father has been wanting to make the man of you at twenty which you will be at thirty. Sir, let me tell you that to be a Scotch landlord,[1] where you have a number of families dependent upon and attached to you, is perhaps as high a situation as humanity can arrive at. A merchant upon 'Change with a hundred thousand pounds is nothing. The Duke of Bedford with all his immense fortune is but a little man in reality. He has no tenants who consider themselves as under his patriarchal care.

" Sir, a father and a son should part at a certain time of life. I never believed what my father said. I always thought

[1] Boswell's father was Laird of Auchinleck (ô'kĭn·lĕk'), a Scotch landowner and jurist. Boswell, the eldest son, was due to inherit his father's lands and responsibilities.

that he spoke ex officio,[2] as a priest does.

" Sir, I am a friend to subordination. It is most conducive to the happiness of society. There is a reciprocal pleasure in governing and being governed.

" Sir, I think your breaking off idle connections by going abroad is a matter of importance. I would go where there are courts and learned men."

I then complained to him how little I knew, and mentioned study. " Sir," said he, " don't talk of study just now. I will put you upon a plan. It will require some time to talk of that." I put out my hand. " Will you really take a charge of me? It is very good in you, Mr. Johnson, to allow me to sit with you thus. Had I but thought some years ago that I should pass an evening with the Author of *The Rambler!*" These expressions were all from the heart, and he perceived that they were; and he was very complacent and said, " Sir, I am glad we have met. I hope we shall pass many evenings and mornings too together."

Thursday 14 July. Mr. Johnson and I met at the Mitre by ourselves. He was in most excellent humor, though the night was very rainy. I said it was good for the vegetable part of the creation. " Ay, Sir," said he, " and for the animals who eat those vegetables, and for the animals who eat those animals." We had a good supper, which made us very comfortable.

I said, " You and I, Sir, are very good companions, but my father and I are not so. Now what can occasion this? For you are as old a man as my father, and you are certainly as learned and as knowing." " Sir," said he, " I am a man of the world. I live in the world, and I take in some measure the color of the world as it moves along. But your father is a judge in a remote part of the country, and all his notions are taken from the old world. Besides, there must always be a struggle between a father

[2] *ex officio* (ĕks ŏ·fĭsh'ĭ·ō): because of his office (here as a father).

Five lively volumes of "The Private Papers of James Boswell" have resulted from the long-hidden manuscript of Boswell's journal. They are:

Boswell's London Journal, 1762–1763

Boswell in Holland, 1763–1764

Boswell on the Grand Tour: Germany and Switzerland, 1764

Boswell on the Grand Tour: Italy, Corsica, and France, 1765–1766

Boswell in Search of a Wife, 1766–1769

and son, while the one aims at power and the other at independency." I told him that I was afraid of my father's forcing me to be a lawyer. " Why, Sir," said he, " you need not be afraid of his forcing you to be a laborious practicing lawyer. That is not in his power. For, as the proverb says, ' One man may lead a horse to the water, but twenty cannot make him drink.' He may be displeased, but it will not go far. If he only insists on your having as much law as is necessary for a man of property, and endeavors to get you into Parliament, he is quite in the right."

Saturday 16 July . . . He advised me to keep a journal of my life, fair and undisguised. He said it would be a very good exercise, and would yield me infinite satisfaction when the ideas were faded from my remembrance. I told him that I had done so ever since I left Scotland. He said he was very happy that I pursued so good a plan. And now, O my journal! art thou not highly dignified? Shalt thou not flourish tenfold? No former solicitations or censures could tempt me to lay thee aside; and now is there any argument which can outweigh the sanction of Mr. Samuel Johnson? He said indeed that I should keep it private, and that I might surely have a friend who would burn it in case of my death. For my own part, I have at present such an affection for this my journal that it shocks me to think of burning it. I rather encourage the idea of having it

carefully laid up among the archives of Auchinleck. However, I cannot judge fairly of it now. Some years hence I may. I told Mr. Johnson that I put down all sorts of little incidents in it. " Sir," said he, " there is nothing too little for so little a creature as man. It is by studying little things that we attain the great knowledge of having as little misery and as much happiness as possible."

A UNIQUE LITERARY PAIR

1. What light is thrown on Johnson's character by his conduct toward Lord Chesterfield?

2. Compare with others your impressions of Johnson's personality and attitude toward people. Is your impression favorable or unfavorable? Why was he so much admired in spite of his peculiarities?

3. Contrast Johnson and Goldsmith. Which of the two appeals to you more? Do you think Boswell gives an objective picture of Goldsmith? Why or why not?

4. Boswell submerged himself in the personality of Dr. Johnson, a man thirty years older than he was. Does he seem to you to be impartial or partial as a biographer? Why? Specifically, what do you notice in his biography that you do not find in most biographies?

5. On what basis did Johnson gain such great influence over his age? How does he typify the eighteenth century? Do we have literary dictators today? What do literary dictators have in common with political dictators?

6. How would you describe the friendship of Boswell and Johnson as it is shown in Boswell's journal? What was Johnson's attitude toward Boswell? Was there mutual admiration and respect between these two men?

CLASS ACTIVITIES

1. Write and enact a short play or dramatized conversation of the Literary Club for presentation before the class.

2. Plan brief oral reports on the following members of the Literary Club: Sir Joshua Reynolds, David Garrick, Edmund Burke, Oliver Goldsmith.

OLIVER GOLDSMITH 1728–1774

Johnson's friend "Goldy" was an irresponsible, lovable, witty Irishman whose life presents a combination of pathos and absurdity. His boyhood in the little Irish village of Lissoy is accurately pictured in *The Deserted Village*. At school the awkward, pock-marked boy was regarded as a dunce, and at Trinity College, Dublin, he came out at the foot of his class. Money given him by relatives so that he could study law or emigrate to America he lost in gambling or in mysterious ways, and then he turned up as smiling as ever. For a time he studied medicine at Edinburgh and later on the Continent. Returning to England, he tried acting, working in a chemist's shop, teaching in a boys' school, and even begging, before finally taking up literature.

Here at last he found something he could do superbly. Goldsmith has the unique distinction among eighteenth-century writers of having produced a poem (*The Deserted Village*), a comedy (*She Stoops to Conquer*), and a novel (*The Vicar of Wakefield*) that are still read and enjoyed today. The story goes that when Goldsmith was about to be imprisoned for not paying his rent, Johnson rescued him by selling the manuscript of *The Vicar of Wakefield* to a bookseller for sixty pounds. Goldsmith made a better income from his hack writing. He turned out textbooks of

history with astounding rapidity and inaccuracy. Some of the statements in his *Animated Nature* justify the remark made by one of his friends that he didn't know one fowl from another until it appeared cooked on the table.

With greater prosperity, Goldsmith spent most of his time with the members of the famous Literary Club. There he was usually the butt of the jokes. On one occasion when he was late as usual, they all wrote epitaphs on him. Garrick's ran thus:

" Here lies Nolly Goldsmith, for shortness
     called ' Noll,'
   Who wrote like an angel and talked like
     poor Poll."

However, Goldsmith had a certain sly wit in conversation, too. Once when he and Johnson were looking at the tombs in Westminster Abbey, Johnson quoted a Latin sentence that meant, " Perhaps our names also will be mingled with these." On the way home they passed Temple Bar, where heads of criminals used to be exposed. Goldsmith thereupon repeated in Latin with different emphasis: " Perhaps our names also will be mingled with *these*." Fortunately it was the first rather than the second prophecy that came true. Johnson wrote the inscription for the memorial to Goldsmith in the Abbey: " He touched nothing that he did not adorn."

The Deserted Village

Three well-known poems of the eighteenth century portray the life of the common people — *The Deserted Village,* Gray's " Elegy Written in a Country Churchyard," Burns' " The Cotter's Saturday Night." Curiously enough, each represents a different country of the British Isles. Gray depicts England, Burns Scotland, while Goldsmith writes of Auburn, a fictitious name for an Irish village, probably similar to Lissoy. All three of them express the

growing interest in humble lives, in contrast to the strict and sophisticated writing of Pope and Johnson. The style of Goldsmith's poem is not markedly different from earlier eighteenth-century writers, but the subject matter and sentiment of *The Deserted Village* pointed forward to the new romantic movement.

The last part of the poem, a prolonged lamentation over the woes of the peasants, has been omitted here.

Sweet Auburn! loveliest village of the plain,
Where health and plenty cheered the laboring swain,
Where smiling spring its earliest visit paid,
And parting summer's lingering blooms delayed;
Dear lovely bowers of innocence and ease,   5
Seats of my youth, when every sport could please,
How often have I loitered o'er thy green,°
Where humble happiness endeared each scene!
How often have I paused on every charm,
The sheltered cot,° the cultivated farm,   10
The never-failing brook, the busy mill,
The decent church that topped the neighboring hill,
The hawthorn bush, with seats beneath the shade
For talking age and whispering lovers made!
How often have I blest the coming day,   15
When toil remitting lent its turn to play,
And all the village train, from labor free,
Led up their sports beneath the spreading tree,
While many a pastime circled in the shade,
The young contending as the old surveyed;   20
And many a gambol frolicked o'er the ground,
And sleights of art° and feats of strength went round.
And still, as each repeated pleasure tired,
Succeeding sports the mirthful band inspired;
The dancing pair that simply sought renown   25
By holding out to tire each other down;
The swain mistrustless° of his smutted face,
While secret laughter tittered round the place;
The bashful virgin's sidelong looks of love,
The matron's glance that would those looks reprove.   30
These were thy charms, sweet village! sports like these,
With sweet succession, taught even toil to please;
These round thy bowers their cheerful influence shed;
These were thy charms — but all these charms are fled.

Sweet smiling village, loveliest of the lawn,   35
Thy sports are fled, and all thy charms withdrawn;
Amidst thy bowers the tyrant's hand is seen,
And desolation saddens all thy green;
One only master grasps the whole domain,°
And half a tillage stints thy smiling plain.   40
No more thy glassy brook reflects the day,
But, choked with sedges, works its weedy way;

---

7. *green:* an open lawn in the middle of a village, a center for recreation. 10. *cot:* cottage.
22. *sleights of art:* skillful turns. We still use the word in *sleight of hand.* 27. *mistrustless:* unaware.
39. This line refers to the process known as "enclosure," whereby the common grazing lands of
villages were taken over by wealthy landowners.

Along the glades, a solitary guest,
The hollow sounding bittern guards its nest;
Amidst thy desert walks the lapwing flies,   45
And tires their echoes with unvaried cries.
Sunk are thy bowers in shapeless ruin all,
And the long grass o'ertops the moldering wall;
And trembling, shrinking from the spoiler's hand,
Far, far away thy children leave the land.   50

Ill fares the land, to hastening ills a prey,
Where wealth accumulates, and men decay.
Princes and lords may flourish, or may fade;
A breath can make them, as a breath has made;
But a bold peasantry, their country's pride,   55
When once destroyed, can never be supplied.

A time there was, ere England's griefs began,
When every rood° of ground maintained its man;
For him light labor spread her wholesome store,
Just gave what life required, but gave no more;   60
His best companions, innocence and health;
And his best riches, ignorance of wealth.

But times are altered; trade's unfeeling train
Usurp the land and dispossess the swain;°
Along the lawn, where scattered hamlets rose,   65
Unwieldy wealth and cumbrous pomp repose,
And every want to opulence allied,
And every pang that folly pays to pride.
These gentle hours that plenty bade to bloom,
Those calm desires that asked but little room,   70
Those healthful sports that graced the peaceful scene,
Lived in each look, and brightened all the green;
These, far departing, seek a kinder shore,
And rural mirth and manners are no more.

Sweet Auburn! parent of the blissful hour,   75
Thy glades forlorn confess the tyrant's power.
Here, as I take my solitary rounds
Amidst thy tangling walks and ruined grounds,
And, many a year elapsed, return to view
Where once the cottage stood, the hawthorne grew,   80
Remembrance wakes with all her busy train,
Swells at my breast, and turns the past to pain.

In all my wanderings round this world of care,
In all my griefs — and God has given my share —
I still had hopes, my latest° hours to crown,   85
Amidst these humble bowers to lay me down;

58. *rood:* one-fourth of an acre. 63–64. *trade's . . . swain:* a reference to the effects of the Industrial Revolution on village life. 85. *latest:* last.

To husband out life's taper at the close,
And keep the flame from wasting by repose;
I still had hopes, for pride attends us still,
Amidst the swains to show my book-learned skill,   90
Around my fire an evening group to draw,
And tell of all I felt, and all I saw;
And, as a hare whom hounds and horns pursue
Pants to the place from whence at first she flew,
I still had hopes, my long vexations past,   95
Here to return — and die at home at last.

O blest retirement, friend to life's decline,
Retreats from care, that never must be mine,
How happy he who crowns in shades like these
A youth of labor with an age of ease;   100
Who quits a world where strong temptations try,
And, since 'tis hard to combat, learns to fly!
For him no wretches, born to work and weep,
Explore the mine, or tempt the dangerous deep;
No surly porter stands in guilty state,   105
To spurn imploring famine from the gate;
But on he moves to meet his latter end,
Angels around befriending virtue's friend;
Bends to the grave with unperceived decay,
While resignation gently slopes the way;   110
And, all his prospects brightening to the last,
His heaven commences ere the world be past!

Sweet was the sound, when oft at evening's close
Up yonder hill the village murmur rose;
There, as I passed with careless steps and slow,   115
The mingling notes came softened from below;
The swain responsive as the milkmaid sung,
The sober herd that lowed to meet their young,
The noisy geese that gabbled o'er the pool,
The playful children just let loose from school,   120
The watchdog's voice that bayed the whispering wind,
And the loud laugh that spoke the vacant mind —
These all in sweet confusion sought the shade,
And filled each pause the nightingale had made.
But now the sounds of population fail,   125
No cheerful murmurs fluctuate in the gale,
No busy steps the grass-grown footway tread,
For all the bloomy flush of life is fled.
All but yon widowed, solitary thing,
That feebly bends beside the plashy° spring;   130
She, wretched matron, forced in age, for bread,
To strip the brook with mantling cresses° spread,
To pick her wintry faggot from the thorn,

---

130. *plashy* (plăsh′ĭ): marshy. 132. *mantling cresses:* plants spreading over a surface.

To seek her nightly shed, and weep till morn;
She only left of all the harmless train,   135
The sad historian of the pensive plain.

Near yonder copse, where once the garden smiled,
And still where many a garden flower grows wild;
There, where a few torn shrubs the place disclose,
The village preacher's° modest mansion rose.   140
A man he was to all the country dear,
And passing rich with forty pounds a year;°
Remote from towns he ran his godly race,
Nor e'er had changed, nor wished to change his place;
Unpracticed he to fawn, or seek for power,   145
By doctrines fashioned to the varying hour;
Far other aims his heart had learned to prize,
More skilled to raise the wretched than to rise.
His house was known to all the vagrant train;
He chid their wanderings but relieved their pain.   150
The long-remembered beggar was his guest,
Whose beard descending swept his aged breast;
The ruined spendthrift, now no longer proud,
Claimed kindred there, and had his claims allowed;

The broken soldier, kindly bade to stay,   155
Sat by the fire, and talked the night away,
Wept o'er his wounds or, tales of sorrow done,
Shouldered his crutch and showed how fields were won.
Pleased with his guests, the good man learned to glow,
And quite forgot their vices in their woe;   160
Careless their merits or their faults to scan,
His pity gave ere charity began.

Thus to relieve the wretched was his pride,
And e'en his failings leaned to virtue's side;
But in his duty prompt at every call,   165
He watched and wept, he prayed and felt for all;
And, as a bird each fond endearment tries
To tempt its new-fledged offspring to the skies,
He tried each art, reproved each dull delay,
Allured to brighter worlds, and led the way.   170

Beside the bed where parting life was laid,
And sorrow, guilt, and pain by turns dismayed,
The reverend champion stood. At his control
Despair and anguish fled the struggling soul;
Comfort came down the trembling wretch to raise,   175
And his last faltering accents whispered praise.

140. *village preacher:* The following portrait is perhaps a composite portrait of Goldsmith's
father and brother, both of whom were preachers. 142. This comment on the preacher's income
suggests the economic conditions of that day and place. See the table on page 811.

At church, with meek and unaffected grace,
His looks adorned the venerable place;
Truth from his lips prevailed with double sway,
And fools, who came to scoff, remained to pray.   180
The service past, around the pious man,
With steady zeal, each honest rustic ran;
Even children followed with endearing wile,
And plucked his gown to share the good man's smile.
His ready smile a parent's warmth expressed;   185
Their welfare pleased him, and their cares distressed;
To them his heart, his love, his griefs were given,
But all his serious thoughts had rest in heaven.
As some tall cliff that lifts its awful form,
Swells from the vale, and midway leaves the storm,   190
Though round its breast the rolling clouds are spread,
Eternal sunshine settles on its head.

Beside yon straggling fence that skirts the way,
With blossomed furze unprofitably gay,
There, in his noisy mansion, skilled to rule,   195
The village master° taught his little school.
A man severe he was, and stern to view;
I knew him well, and every truant knew;
Well had the boding tremblers learned to trace
The day's disasters in his morning face;   200
Full well they laughed with counterfeited glee
At all his jokes, for many a joke had he;
Full well the busy whisper circling round
Conveyed the dismal tidings when he frowned.
Yet he was kind, or, if severe in aught,   205
The love he bore to learning was in fault;
The village all declared how much he knew;
'Twas certain he could write, and cipher too;
Lands he could measure, terms and tides presage,°
And even the story ran that he could gauge;°   210
In arguing, too, the parson owned his skill,
For, even though vanquished, he could argue still;
While words of learned length and thundering sound
Amazed the gazing rustics ranged around;
And still they gazed, and still the wonder grew,   215
That one small head could carry all he knew.
But past is all his fame. The very spot
Where many a time he triumphed is forgot.

Near yonder thorn that lifts its head on high,
Where once the signpost caught the passing eye,   220
Low lies that house where nut-brown draughts° inspired,

---

196. *The village master:* thought to be a portrait of Goldsmith's own schoolmaster. 209. *terms and tides presage:* figure out in advance the time for law sessions and church festivals, such as Easter. 210. *gauge:* measure the capacity of casks. 221. *nut-brown draughts:* drinks of ale.

Where graybeard mirth and smiling toil retired,
Where village statesmen talked with looks profound,
And news much older than their ale went round.
Imagination fondly stoops to trace   225
The parlor splendors of that festive place:
The whitewashed wall, the nicely sanded floor,
The varnished clock that clicked behind the door;
The chest contrived a double debt to pay,
A bed by night, a chest of drawers by day;   230
The pictures placed for ornament and use,
The twelve good rules,° the royal game of goose;°
The hearth, except when winter chilled the day,
With aspen boughs and flowers and fennel° gay;
While broken teacups, wisely kept for show,   235
Ranged o'er the chimney, glistened in a row.

Vain transitory splendors! could not all
Reprieve the tottering mansion from its fall?
Obscure it sinks, nor shall it more impart
An hour's importance to the poor man's heart.   240
Thither no more the peasant shall repair
To sweet oblivion of his daily care;
No more the farmer's news, the barber's tale,
No more the woodman's ballad shall prevail;
No more the smith his dusky brow shall clear,   245
Relax his ponderous strength, and lean to hear;
The host himself no longer shall be found
Careful to see the mantling bliss° go round;
Nor the coy maid, half willing to be pressed,
Shall kiss the cup to pass it to the rest.   250

Yes! let the rich deride, the proud disdain,
These simple blessings of the lowly train;
To me more dear, congenial to my heart,
One native charm, than all the gloss of art.
Spontaneous joys, where nature has its play,   255
The soul adopts, and owns their first-born sway;
Lightly they frolic o'er the vacant mind,
Unenvied, unmolested, unconfined.
But the long pomp, the midnight masquerade,
With all the freaks° of wanton wealth arrayed —   260
In these, ere trifles half their wish obtain,
The toiling pleasure sickens into pain;
And, even while fashion's brightest arts decoy,
The heart distrusting asks if this be joy.

---

232. *twelve good rules:* brief rules such as "Reveal no secrets" and "Pick no quarrels" which
were attributed to Charles I and often hung up in inns; *goose:* a game played with checkers and dice,
somewhat like parchesi. 234. *fennel:* a garden herb. 248. *mantling bliss:* foaming ale. Compare with
the use of *mantling* in line 132. 260. *freaks:* whims.

GOLDSMITH'S VILLAGE FOLK

1. How does Goldsmith idealize plain country folk? How realistic is his picture, do you think? What passages express a new attitude toward people of humble position? Point out the specific passages which show that Goldsmith also had characteristics of the classical school of Pope.

2. How do subject matter and sentiment in the poem point to the Romantic movement?

3. Which scenes and persons in *The Deserted Village* stand out in your mind most vividly? Compare the pictures of the parson and schoolmaster with some of Chaucer's characters. Which author's descriptions seem more realistic? Which do you prefer?

CLASS ACTIVITIES

1. Read a complete version of *The Deserted Village* and sum up — in a panel discussion — Goldsmith's opinions on Irish farm conditions, on the value of farmers to a nation and to city life, on Irish immigration, and on living conditions in America. Judge his opinions in the light of subsequent history.

2. Goldsmith's lively play *She Stoops to Conquer* contains some good scenes for class dramatization.

3. Short skits could be written from some of the scenes in the novel *The Vicar of Wakefield*.

4. Compare the vicar in that novel with the parson in *The Deserted Village*. Which seems more credible to you?

Elegy on the Death of a Mad Dog

It would be too bad to leave the poetry of merry Oliver Goldsmith on such a melancholy note as that struck in *The Deserted Village*. Here is a neat absurdity as a contrast. You will find it quite different from other elegies!

Good people all, of every sort,
  Give ear unto my song;
And if you find it wondrous short,
  It cannot hold you long.

In Islington there was a man   5
  Of whom the world might say
That still a godly race° he ran,
  Whene'er he went to pray.

A kind and gentle heart he had,
  To comfort friend and foes;   10
The naked every day he clad,
  When he put on his clothes.

And in that town a dog was found,
  As many dogs there be,
Both mongrel, puppy, whelp, and
  hound   15
  And cur of low degree.

This dog and man at first were friends;
  But when a pique began,
The dog to gain his private ends,
  Went mad and bit the man.   20

Around from all the neighboring streets
  The wondering people ran,
And swore the dog had lost his wits,
  To bite so good a man.

The wound it seemed both sore and sad
  To every Christian eye;   26
And while they swore the dog was mad,
  They swore the man would die.

But soon a wonder came to light,
  That showed the rogues they lied;   30
The man recovered of the bite;
  The dog it was that died.

7. *godly race:* Compare with line 143 of *The Deserted Village*.

FORERUNNERS OF THE ROMANTIC AGE

THOMAS GRAY 1716–1771

In his day, Thomas Gray was recognized as the foremost English poet; he was offered (but declined to accept) the position of poet laureate. Today he is remembered chiefly as the author of one of the best-known poems in the English language, "Elegy Written in a Country Churchyard."

By keeping a shop, Gray's mother earned enough money to send her son to fashionable Eton and later to Cambridge, where he steeped himself in classical literature. With his former schoolmate Horace Walpole, Gray spent three years on a tour of the Continent. It was an adventurous experience, and both he and Walpole have left a vivid record of it in letters. Thereafter, Gray, who never married, lived the quiet life of a Cambridge professor. He was an enthusiastic student of Anglo-Saxon and Welsh folklore; in this respect he foreshadows the great interest that the nineteenth-century Romantic poets took in old English and Scottish ballads. Gray's poems are few in number but were painstakingly composed and polished. His "Elegy Written in a Country Churchyard" was nine years in the writing!

Gray represents the transition from classical to romantic literature in England — from the strictly patterned verse and sophisticated ideas of Pope and Johnson to the simpler, freer verse forms and the depiction of nature and common life found in later Romantic poets like Wordsworth. Gray's verse form is only slightly varied from Pope's, but his poetry reveals a romantic spirit in its personal tone and in its emotional expressions on nature and death. Dr. Johnson thought Gray a dull poet, but General Wolfe, who won Quebec from the French in 1763, said of the "Elegy Written in a Country Churchyard" before entering the great battle: "I would rather be the author of those lines than take Quebec."

Elegy Written in a Country Churchyard

The curfew tolls the knell of parting day,
    The lowing herd wind slowly o'er the lea,
The plowman homeward plods his weary way,
    And leaves the world to darkness and to me.

Now fades the glimmering landscape on the sight,   5
    And all the air a solemn stillness holds,
Save where the beetle wheels his droning flight,
    And drowsy tinklings lull the distant folds;

Save that from yonder ivy-mantled tower
    The moping owl does to the moon complain   10
Of such, as wandering near her secret bower,
    Molest her ancient solitary reign.

Beneath those rugged elms, that yew tree's shade,
　　Where heaves the turf in many a moldering heap,
Each in his narrow cell forever laid,   15
　　The rude forefathers of the hamlet sleep.

The breezy call of incense-breathing morn,
　　The swallow twittering from the straw-built shed,
The cock's shrill clarion, or the echoing horn,°
　　No more shall rouse them from their lowly bed.   20

For them no more the blazing hearth shall burn,
　　Or busy housewife ply her evening care:
No children run to lisp their sire's return,
　　Or climb his knee the envied kiss to share.

Oft did the harvest to their sickle yield,   25
　　Their furrow oft the stubborn glebe° has broke;
How jocund did they drive their team afield!
　　How bowed the woods beneath their sturdy stroke!

Let not ambition mock their useful toil,
　　Their homely joys, and destiny obscure;   30
Nor grandeur hear with a disdainful smile,
　　The short and simple annals of the poor.

The boast of heraldry,° the pomp of power,
　　And all that beauty, all that wealth e'er gave,
Awaits alike the inevitable hour.°   35
　　The paths of glory lead but to the grave.

Nor you, ye proud, impute to these the fault,
　　If memory o'er their tomb no trophies raise,
Where through the long-drawn aisle and fretted vault°
　　The pealing anthem swells the note of praise.   40

Can storied urn° or animated° bust
　　Back to its mansion call the fleeting breath?
Can honor's voice provoke° the silent dust,
　　Or flatt'ry soothe the dull cold ear of Death?

Perhaps in this neglected spot is laid   45
　　Some heart once pregnant with celestial fire;
Hands,° that the rod of empire might have swayed,
　　Or waked to ecstasy the living lyre.

---

19. *horn:* the horn of a hunter. 26. *glebe:* ground. 33. *The boast of heraldry:* Heraldry is the study
of family coats of arms; hence, this phrase means the pride of having a great family. 35. *hour:* the
subject of the verb *awaits.* The hour of death lies in wait for all the things (lines 33–34) that are
causes of earthly pride. 39. *fretted vault:* church roof ornamented by elaborate design. 41. *storied urn:*
an urn inscribed with pictures that tell the story of the deceased; *animated:* lifelike. 43. *provoke:*
arouse. 47. *Hands:* subject of *might have swayed.*

But knowledge to their eyes her ample page
    Rich with the spoils of time did ne'er unroll;   50
Chill penury repressed their noble rage,
    And froze the genial° current of the soul.

Full many a gem of purest ray serene,
    The dark unfathomed caves of ocean bear;
Full many a flower is born to blush unseen,   55
    And waste its sweetness on the desert air.

Some village Hampden° that with dauntless breast
    The little tyrant of his fields withstood,
Some mute inglorious Milton here may rest,
    Some Cromwell guiltless of his country's blood.   60

The applause of listening senates to command,
    The threats of pain and ruin to despise,
To scatter plenty o'er a smiling land,
    And read their history in a nation's eyes,°

Their lot forbade: nor circumscribed alone   65
    Their growing virtues, but their crimes confined;
Forbade to wade through slaughter to a throne,
    And shut the gates of mercy on mankind,

The struggling pangs of conscious truth to hide,
    To quench the blushes of ingenuous shame,   70
Or heap the shrine of luxury and pride
    With incense kindled at the Muse's flame.

Far from the madding° crowd's ignoble strife,
    Their sober wishes never learned to stray;
Along the cool sequestered vale of life   75
    They kept the noiseless tenor° of their way.

Yet ev'n these bones from insult to protect,
    Some frail memorial still erected nigh,

52. *genial:* warm or living. 57. *Hampden:* a landowner who resisted one of the tax assessments of Charles I, and thus made the matter of unjust taxes a public issue. 61–64. This whole stanza is the object of *forbade* in the first line of the next stanza. 73. *madding:* wild, furious. 76. *tenor* (tĕn′ẽr): even course.

With uncouth rhymes and shapeless sculpture decked,
   Implores the passing tribute of a sigh.   80

Their name, their years, spelt by the unlettered Muse,
   The place of fame and elegy supply;
And many a holy text around she strews,
   That teach the rustic moralist to die.

For who to dumb forgetfulness a prey,   85
   This pleasing anxious being e'er resigned,
Left the warm precincts of the cheerful day,
   Nor cast one longing lingering look behind?

On some fond breast the parting soul relies,
   Some pious drops the closing eye requires;   90
Ev'n from the tomb the voice of nature cries,
   Ev'n in our ashes live their wonted fires.

For thee,° who mindful of the unhonored dead
   Dost in these lines their artless tale relate;
If chance, by lonely contemplation led,   95
   Some kindred spirit shall inquire thy fate,

Haply some hoary-headed swain may say,
   " Oft have we seen him at the peep of dawn
Brushing with hasty steps the dews away,
   To meet the sun upon the upland lawn.   100

" There at the foot of yonder nodding beech
   That wreathes its old fantastic roots so high,
His listless length at noontide would he stretch,
   And pore upon the brook that babbles by.

" Hard by yon wood, now smiling as in scorn,   105
   Muttering his wayward fancies he would rove,
Now drooping, woeful wan, like one forlorn,
   Or crazed with care, or crossed in hopeless love.

   93. *thee:* Gray himself.

" One morn I missed him on the customed hill,
   Along the heath and near his favorite tree,   110
Another came; nor yet beside the rill,
   Nor up the lawn, nor at the wood was he;

" The next, with dirges due in sad array
   Slow through the church-way path we saw him borne.
Approach and read (for thou canst read)° the lay,   115
   Graved on the stone beneath yon aged thorn."°

THE EPITAPH

Here rests his head upon the lap of earth
   A youth to fortune and to fame unknown.
Fair science frowned not on his humble birth,°
   And melancholy marked him for her own.   120

Large was his bounty, and his soul sincere,
   Heaven did a recompense as largely send;
He gave to misery all he had, a tear;
   He gained from Heaven ('twas all he wished) a friend.

No farther seek his merits to disclose,   125
   Or draw his frailties from their dread abode,
(There they alike in trembling hope repose)
   The bosom of his Father and his God.

115. *thou canst read:* In the eighteenth century, a large proportion of the country people were unable to read. 116. *thorn:* hawthorn. 119. His humble birth had not prevented his having a good education.

Bonham

GRAY'S "ELEGY"

1. By what details does Gray put the reader in a thoughtful mood at the opening of the poem?

2. The "Elegy" falls into clear-cut divisions of thought. What stanzas would you include in each of these three beginning divisions: (*a*) the setting, (*b*) the imagined life of the villagers, (*c*) death, the common end of all classes, rich and poor? The remainder of the poem can be divided into four sections. How would you divide the stanzas and what descriptions would you give to each division?

3. With what details does he represent happiness in the life of the country folk?

4. Line 47 suggests a possible statesman or ruler. What other hidden potentialities in the lives of the common people does Gray suggest? Why were these potentialities not fulfilled?

5. What picture of himself does Gray paint from line 98 on? Does it correspond with what you know of Gray's life?

6. Find phrases, pictures, and ideas that recall "Il Penseroso" (page 227) and *The Deserted Village* (page 316).

7. How does Gray's verse form — rhyme scheme and stanza division — differ from that of Pope? What elements of the new romantic trend in literature do you find in this poem?

THE POWER OF WORDS

WORDS EASILY CONFUSED

In line 70 Gray uses the word *ingenuous* (ĭn·jĕn'ū·ŭs), which is easily confused with *ingenious* (ĭn·jēn'yŭs). An *ingenuous* person may be one of high character, noble and honest. The word is also used to suggest candor, frankness, and naïveté. Which quality does Gray probably have in mind when he says that the villagers' humble lot kept them from quenching "the blushes of ingenuous shame"? How would you reexpress this line?

How does *ingenuous* differ from *ingenious*? List several fictitious or actual characters you have encountered in this book that you would consider ingenuous, and several that were ingenious.

WILLIAM BLAKE 1757–1827

William Blake, a unique figure in English literature, was the complete opposite of writers of the classical school. He was a religious mystic in an age of reason. Born of a poor family, he received practically no formal education, though he struggled to attend a drawing school. At fourteen he was apprenticed to an engraver, and that trade became an important means of livelihood, for his pictures and his poetry were not widely accepted during his lifetime. He employed his talent for sketching by producing some powerful drawings to illustrate not only his own poems but also Milton's *Paradise Lost,* Dante's *Divine Comedy,* and the Book of Job from the Bible. All his life Blake devoted himself to expressing his mystical faith and his visions of a heavenly world. He was encouraged by his handsome, uneducated wife, who learned to draw and paint so that she could help him in his work. On one occasion Mrs. Blake is reported to have said, "I have very little of Mr. Blake's company. He is always in Paradise."

Although readers in his own day were confused by the symbolism and hidden meanings in his prophetic books like *The Marriage of Heaven and Hell,* the delicate images and fancifulness of his earlier *Songs of Innocence* and *Songs of Experience* appealed to the later romantic poets. Blake's intensity and beauty of language are more appreciated today than ever before, as are his exceptional qualities as both artist and poet.

Blake engraved his poems on metal plates and decorated them with his own designs. Both illustrations and text reveal how his imagination soared to tropical jungles (which he had never seen) and to the abode of God and angels. He was a unique creator who ignored the strict poetic rules of the classicist to follow his own original style. Reading the *Songs* with their attendant designs adds to one's understanding of them. Of the three that follow, " The Lamb " is from *Songs of Innocence;* " The Tiger " and " The Clod and the Pebble " from *Songs of Experience.* Readers who delight in imaginative power will enjoy their delicate and subtle magic.

This engraving is one of twenty-one Blake illustrations for the Book of Job. Its mystic and other worldly quality is found in most of Blake's work. He felt that there is a basic harmony in the universe, and he struggled as poet and artist to express this feeling.

The Lamb

Little Lamb, who made thee?
Dost thou know who made thee?
Gave thee life, and bid thee feed,
By the stream and o'er the mead;
Gave thee clothing of delight,   5
Softest clothing, woolly, bright;
Gave thee such a tender voice,
Making all the vales rejoice?
   Little Lamb, who made thee?
   Dost thou know who made thee?   10

   Little Lamb, I'll tell thee,
   Little Lamb, I'll tell thee:
He is callèd by thy name,
For He calls Himself a Lamb,
He is meek, and He is mild;   15
He became a little child.
I a child, and thou a lamb,
We are callèd by His name.
   Little Lamb, God bless thee!
   Little Lamb, God bless thee!   20

The Tiger

Tiger, tiger, burning bright
In the forest of the night,
What immortal hand or eye
Could frame thy fearful symmetry?

In what distant deeps or skies   5
Burnt the fire of thine eyes?
On what wings dare he aspire?
What the hand dare seize the fire?

And what shoulder, and what art,
Could twist the sinews of thy heart?
When thy heart began to beat,   11
What dread hand forged thy dread feet?

What the hammer? What the chain?
In what furnace was thy brain?
What the anvil? What dread grasp   15
Dared its deadly terrors clasp?

When the stars threw down their spears,
And watered heaven with their tears,
Did He smile his work to see?
Did He who made the lamb make thee?

Tiger, tiger, burning bright   21
In the forest of the night,
What immortal hand or eye
Dare frame thy fearful symmetry?

The Clod and the Pebble

" Love seeketh not itself to please,
    Nor for itself hath any care,
But for another gives its ease,
    And builds a Heaven in Hell's despair."

So sung a little Clod of Clay,   5
    Trodden with the cattle's feet,
But a Pebble of the brook
    Warbled out these meters meet:

" Love seeketh only Self to please,
    To bind another to Its delight,   10
Joys in another's loss of ease,
    And builds a Hell in Heaven's despite."

BLAKE — ARTIST AND POET

1. What do you think the lamb in Blake's poem symbolizes? What is the spirit of this poem?

2. State in your own words the central thought in " The Tiger." Blake wrote " The Tiger " after " The Lamb." Can you point out a relationship between the poems?

3. In " The Clod and the Pebble " Blake suggests that love varies in its nature. Do you agree? In what human relationships might you find the two kinds of love?

ROBERT BURNS 1759–1796

Burns might be called the national poet of Scotland. Among the many writers that that country has produced, no name sets afire the loyalty and pride of Scots as " Bobbie Burns " does. Their own idiom of speech is made musical in his lyrics. The hard lives and poverty of some of their people is glorified through the laurels won by a peasant boy. Their essentially independent spirit is proclaimed to the world in the ringing lines of " A man's a man for a' that."

Burns was born in a two-room clay cot-

tage built by his father near Ayr in southwestern Scotland. Poverty pursued the family from one stony farm to another. The father gave his sons the best education available to peasants, but it was meager. Robert supplemented his schooling by ardently reading the Bible, *The Spectator*, Pope's poems, and a book of lyrics that first inspired him to write songs.

As the plowboy developed into a lively, handsome young man, he was often in scrapes, resulting from too much drinking, satires on the ministers, and numerous romances. Finally, the father of his sweetheart Jean Armour made life so miserable for him that he decided to sail for Jamaica. To raise money for his passage he published his first volume, *Poems: Chiefly in Scottish Dialect,* in 1786. It won immediate success. Instead of going to Jamaica, Burns went to Edinburgh in triumph. Edinburgh society lionized him but after a time turned away from the young poet because he remained the earthy peasant — friendly, genial, but not given to polite ways. Back he went to the farm, married Jean Armour, and wrote some of his finest poetry. But his health — never strong because of his poor early life — weakened. He increas-

ingly took to drink; and poverty, as always, plagued him and his family. Burns died at thirty-seven.

No sooner had he breathed his last than the whole country united to honor him. Ten thousand persons are said to have followed him to his grave at Dumfries. Contributions poured in for his destitute family. Two handsome marble monuments were eventually erected, one at Dumfries and the other at Ayr, not far from the banks of the bonnie Doon. But cold marble is a poor memorial for warmhearted, impulsive, generous Robert Burns. His real monument is his poetry, which keeps ever alive his best self.

Songs

Scotland gave to English literature a great song writer in Robert Burns. No one else has combined quite the same lilting melody and warm human emotion. In the following songs he sings of exuberance, sorrow, faithful affection, patriotism, and sturdy independence. Some are sung in his own person; some are dramatically put into the mouths of imaginary or historical characters; in others, the poet makes shrewd observations on his fellow humans. Many of them were set to old Scotch airs already in existence; some have since been set to music.

Sweet Afton

Flow gently, sweet Afton! among thy green braes,°
Flow gently, I'll sing thee a song in thy praise;
My Mary's asleep by thy murmuring stream,
Flow gently, sweet Afton, disturb not her dream.

Thou stock dove whose echo resounds through the glen,   5
Ye wild whistling blackbirds in yon thorny den,
Thou green-crested lapwing, thy screaming forbear,
I charge you, disturb not my slumbering Fair.

How lofty, sweet Afton, thy neighboring hills,
Far marked with the courses of clear, winding rills;   10
There daily I wander as noon rises high,
My flocks and my Mary's sweet cot in my eye.

How pleasant thy banks and green valleys below,
Where, wild in the woodlands, the primroses blow;
There oft, as mild ev'ning weeps over the lea,   15
The sweet-scented birk° shades my Mary and me.

1. *braes* (brāz): hillsides. 16. *birk:* birch.

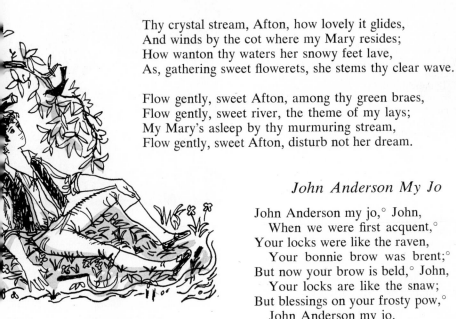

Thy crystal stream, Afton, how lovely it glides,
And winds by the cot where my Mary resides;
How wanton thy waters her snowy feet lave,
As, gathering sweet flowerets, she stems thy clear wave.   20

Flow gently, sweet Afton, among thy green braes,
Flow gently, sweet river, the theme of my lays;
My Mary's asleep by thy murmuring stream,
Flow gently, sweet Afton, disturb not her dream.

The Banks o' Doon

Ye flowery banks o' bonnie Doon,
   How can ye blume sae fair!
How can ye chant, ye little birds,
   And I sae fu' o' care!

Thou'lt break my heart, thou bonnie
   bird,   5
   That sings upon the bough;
Thou minds me o' the happy days,
   When my fause° luve was true.

Thou'lt break my heart, thou bonnie
   bird,
   That sings beside thy mate;   10
For sae I sat, and sae I sang,
   And wist na° o' my fate.

Aft hae I roved by bonnie Doon
   To see the woodbine twine,
And ilka° bird sang o' its luve,   15
   And sae did I o' mine.

Wi' lightsome heart I pu'd° a rose,
   Frae aff its thorny tree;
And my fause luver staw° my rose
   But left the thorn wi' me.   20

8. *fause:* false. 12. *wist na:* knew not. 15. *ilka:*
every. 17. *pu'd:* pulled. 19. *staw:* stole.

John Anderson My Jo

John Anderson my jo,° John,
   When we were first acquent,°
Your locks were like the raven,
   Your bonnie brow was brent;°
But now your brow is beld,° John,   5
   Your locks are like the snaw;
But blessings on your frosty pow,°
   John Anderson my jo.

John Anderson my jo, John,
   We clamb the hill thegither;   10
And mony a canty° day, John,
   We've had wi' ane anither.
Now we maun° totter down, John,
   And hand in hand we'll go,
And sleep thegither at the foot,   15
   John Anderson my jo.

1. *jo:* joy, sweetheart. 2. *acquent:* acquainted.
4. *brent:* smooth. 5. *beld:* bald. 7. *pow:* head.
11. *canty:* cheerful. 13. *maun:* must.

Bannockburn

Robert the Bruce carried on the work begun
by Wallace of freeing Scotland from English
domination in the days of Edward I. The battle of Bannockburn (băn′ŭk·bûrn), fought in
1314 in central Scotland, was a critical engagement. The English far outnumbered the
Scots; but Bruce, by digging pits in the plain
and covering them with leaves, caused the
English cavalry to be overcome by panic, and
thus won the day. The occasion is looked on
by Scots as one of the great milestones in their
history. This poem is supposed to be Bruce's
address to his army before the battle. Through
the Scottish leader, Burns voices a characteristic desire for freedom. It is said that he composed the poem while galloping over a moor
in a thunderstorm.

Scots, wha hae° wi' Wallace bled,
Scots, wham Bruce has aften led;
Welcome to your gory bed,
    Or to victory!

Now's the day, and now's the hour; 5
See the front o' battle lour;°
See approach proud Edward's power —
    Chains and slavery!

Wha will be a traitor knave?
Wha can fill a coward's grave? 10
Wha sae base as be a slave?
    Let him turn and flee!

Wha for Scotland's king and law
Freedom's sword will strongly draw,
Freeman stand, or Freeman fa', 15
    Let him follow me!

By oppression's woes and pains!
By your sons in servile chains!
We will drain our dearest veins,
    But they shall be free! 20

Lay the proud usurpers low!
Tyrants fall in every foe!
Liberty's in every blow! —
    Let us do or die!°

1. *wha hae:* who have. 6. *lour:* lower, threaten.
24. *die:* Scottish pronunciation is dē.

A Man's a Man for A' That

Here speaks a prophetic voice for the coming
acceptance of the brotherhood of man. As the
first clear note of democracy, this poem is one
of the most significant written in the eighteenth century.

Is there, for honest poverty,
    That hings his head, an' a' that?
The coward slave, we pass him by,
    We dare be poor for a' that!
        For a' that, an' a' that, 5
          Our toils obscure, an' a' that;
        The rank is but the guinea's stamp;°
        The man's the gowd° for a' that.

What tho' on hamely fare we dine,
    Wear hodden-gray,° an' a' that; 10
Gie fools their silks, and knaves their
      wine,
    A man's a man for a' that.
        For a' that, an' a' that,
          Their tinsel show, an' a' that;
        The honest man, though e'er sae
          poor, 15
        Is king o' men for a' that.

Ye see yon birkie,° ca'd a lord,
    Wha struts, an' stares, an' a' that;
Tho' hundreds worship at his word,
    He's but a coof° for a' that. 20

7. *guinea's stamp:* mold for stamping out
gold coins. 8. *gowd:* gold. 10. *hodden-gray:*
coarse cloth. 17. *birkie:* fellow. 20. *coof:* fool.

For a' that, an' a' that,
  His riband, star,° an' a' that,
The man o' independent mind,
  He looks and laughs at a' that.

A prince can mak' a belted knight,   25
  A marquis, duke, an' a' that;
But an honest man's aboon° his might,
  Guid faith he mauna fa' that!°
    For a' that, an' a' that,
      Their dignities, an' a' that,   30
    The pith o' sense, an' pride o' worth,
    Are higher rank than a' that.

Then let us pray that come it may,
  As come it will for a' that,
That sense and worth, o'er a' the earth,
  May bear the gree,° an' a' that.   36
    For a' that, an' a' that,
      It's coming yet, for a' that,
    That man to man, the warld o'er,
    Shall brothers be for a' that.   40

22. *riband, star:* insignia of titles and honors.
27. *aboon:* above. 28. *he . . . that:* he can't make
that. 36. *bear the gree:* take the prize.

To a Mouse

ON TURNING HER UP IN HER NEST
WITH THE PLOW, NOVEMBER, 1785

This and the following poem form an interesting pair in several respects: they have unusual meter, unconventional subjects, and frequently quoted lines. Their moods are in
strong contrast: on the one hand, the despair
of thwarted ambition; on the other, the rollicking humor of an irrepressible wag.

Wee, sleekit,° cowrin', tim'rous beastie,
O, what a panic's in thy breastie!
Thou need na start awa sae hasty
  Wi' bickering brattle!°

1. *sleekit:* sleek. 4. *bickering brattle:* hasty
scamper.

I wad be laith° to rin an' chase thee   5
  Wi' murd'rin pattle!°

I'm truly sorry man's dominion
Has broken nature's social union,
And justifies that ill opinion
  Which makes thee startle   10
At me, thy poor, earthborn companion,
  An' fellow mortal!

I doubt na, whyles,° but thou may
  thieve;
What then? poor beastie, thou maun
  live!
A daimen icker in a thrave°   15
  'S a sma' request;
I'll get a blessin' wi' the lave,°
  An' never miss 't!

Thy wee bit housie, too, in ruin!   19
It's silly wa's° the win's are strewin'!
An' naething, now, to big a new ane,°
  O' foggage° green!
An' bleak December's winds ensuin',
  Baith snell° an' keen!

Thou saw the fields laid bare and waste,
An' weary winter comin' fast,   26
An' cozie here, beneath the blast,
  Thou thought to dwell,
Till crash! the cruel coulter° passed
  Out through thy cell.   30

That wee bit heap o' leaves an' stibble
Has cost thee mony a weary nibble!
Now thou's turn'd out, for a' thy trouble,
  But house or hald,°
To thole° the winter's sleety dribble
  An' cranreuch° cauld!   36

5. *laith* (lāth): loath, reluctant. 6. *pattle:*
plowstaff. 13. *whyles:* at times. 15. *A daimen
. . . thrave:* an occasional head of grain in a
shock. 17. *lave:* rest. 20. *silly wa's:* weak walls.
21. *big . . . ane:* build a new one. 22. *foggage:*
herbage. 24. *snell:* sharp. 29. *coulter* (kōl'tĕr):
plow. 34. *But house or hald:* without a dwelling
place. 35. *thole:* endure. 36. *cranreuch* (krăn'-
rŭk): hoarfrost.

But, Mousie, thou art no thy lane°
In proving foresight may be vain;
The best laid schemes o' mice an' men
    Gang aft agley,°   40
An' lea'e us nought but grief an' pain,
    For promis'd joy.

Still thou art blest, compared wi' me,
The present only toucheth thee;
But och! I backward cast my e'e   45
    On prospects drear!
An' forward, though I canna see,
    I guess an' fear!

37. *no thy lane:* not alone. 40. *Gang aft agley*
(*à·glē′*): oft go astray.

To a Louse

ON SEEING ONE ON
A LADY'S BONNET AT CHURCH

Ha! wh' are ye gaun, ye crowlin' ferlie!°
Your impudence protects you sairly;°
I canna say but ye strunt° rarely,
    Owre gauze and lace;
Though faith! I fear ye dine but sparely
    On sic a place.   6

Ye ugly, creepin', blastit wonner,°
Detested, shunned by saunt an' sinner!
How dare ye set your fit° upon her,
    Sae fine a lady?   10
Gae somewhere else, and seek your din-
    ner
    On some poor body.

Swith, in some beggar's haffet squattle;°
There ye may creep, and sprawl, and
    sprattle°
Wi' ither kindred jumping cattle,   15
    In shoals and nations;
Where horn nor bane° ne'er dare un-
    settle
    Your thick plantations.

1. *crowlin' ferlie* (fĕr′lĭ): crawling wonder.
2. *sairly:* greatly. 3. *strunt:* strut. 7. *blastit
wonner:* blasted wonder. 9. *fit:* foot. 13. *Swith
. . . squattle:* Be off with you! Sprawl in some
beggar's temple. 14. *sprattle:* struggle. 17. *horn
nor bane:* comb nor poison.

Now haud ye there,° ye're out o' sight,
Below the fatt'rels,° snug an' tight;   20
Na, faith ye yet! ye'll no be right
    Till ye've got on it,
The very tapmost tow'ring height
    O' Miss's bonnet.

My sooth! right bauld ye set your nose
    out,   25
As plump and gray as onie grozet;°
O for some rank mercurial rozet,°
    Or fell red smeddum!°
I'd gie you sic a hearty dose o't,
    Wad dress your droddum!°   30

I wad na been surprised to spy
You on an auld wife's flannen toy;°
Or aiblins some bit duddie boy,°
    On's wyliecoat;°
But Miss's fine Lunardi!° fie,   35
    How daur ye do 't?

O Jenny, dinna toss your head,
An' set your beauties a' abroad!°
Ye little ken what cursèd speed
    The blastie's makin'!   40
Thae winks and finger ends, I dread,
    Are notice takin'!

O wad some Pow'r the giftie gie us
To see oursels as ithers see us!
It wad frae mony a blunder free us,   45
    And foolish notion:
What airs in dress an' gait wad lea'e us,
    And e'en devotion!

19. *haud ye there:* stay where you are.
20. *fatt'rels:* ribbon ends. 26. *onie grozet*
(grŏz′ĭt): any gooseberry. 27. *rozet:* rosin.
28. *smeddum:* powder. 30. *Wad . . . droddum:*
would put an end to you. 32. *flannen toy:*
flannel headdress. 33. *Or . . . boy:* or perhaps
on some little ragged boy. 34. *wyliecoat* (wī′lĭ-
kōt′): flannel vest. 35. *Lunardi:* a bonnet named
for an aeronaut of that day, probably with
winglike ribbons. 38. *abread:* abroad.

The Cotter's Saturday Night

This well-known poem, which takes us back in spirit to " Elegy Written in a Country Churchyard " and *The Deserted Village,* was published in Burns' first volume. An interesting comment comes from Robert's brother Gilbert: " Robert had frequently remarked to me that he thought there was something peculiarly venerable in the phrase, ' Let us worship God,' used by a decent, sober head of a family, introducing family worship. To this sentiment of the author the world is indebted for ' The Cotter's Saturday Night.' The cotter is an exact copy of my father, in his manners, his family devotion, and exhortations. . . ."

INSCRIBED TO ROBERT AIKEN, ESQ.°

Let not ambition mock their useful toil,
Their homely joys, and destiny obscure;
Nor grandeur hear, with a disdainful smile,
The short and simple annals of the poor.
                              Gray.

My loved, my honored, much respected friend!
No mercenary bard this homage pays;°
With honest pride, I scorn each selfish end,
My dearest meed, a friend's esteem and praise;
To you I sing, in simple Scottish lays,   5
The lowly train in life's sequestered scene,
The native feelings strong, the guileless ways,
What Aiken in a cottage would have been;
Ah! though his worth unknown, far happier there, I ween!

November chill blaws loud wi' angry sugh;°   10
The shortening winter day is near a close;
The miry beasts retreating frae the pleugh;°
The blackening trains o' craws to their repose:
The toilworn Cotter° frae his labor goes, —
This night his weekly moil° is at an end, —   15
Collects his spades, his mattocks, and his hoes,
Hoping the morn in ease and rest to spend,
And weary, o'er the moor, his course does hameward bend.

At length his lonely cot appears in view,
Beneath the shelter of an aged tree;   20
The expectant wee things, toddlin', stacher° through
To meet their dad, wi' flichterin' noise an' glee.

Inscription *Robert Aiken:* a warm friend of Burns in Ayr, who had helped to make his poems known. 2. Burns says he is not dedicating his poem to Aiken for hope of reward. See note on Johnson's letter to Chesterfield (page 306) for explanation of the patronage system. 10. *sugh* (sōōĸ; the Scotch *gh* represents a blowing out of breath between an *h* and a *k*): sough; moan. 12. *pleugh* (plūĸ): plow. 14. *Cotter:* cottager. 15. *moil:* labor. 21. *stacher* (stăĸ'ĕr): stagger.

His wee bit ingle,° blinkin' bonnilie,°
His clean hearthstane, his thrifty wifie's smile,
The lisping infant prattling on his knee,   25
Does a' his weary kiaugh° and care beguile,
An' makes him quite forget his labor an' his toil.

Belyve,° the elder bairns° come drappin' in,
At service out, amang the farmers roun',
Some ca' the pleugh,° some herd, some tentie rin   30
A cannie errand° to a neibor town.
Their eldest hope, their Jenny, woman-grown,
In youthfu' bloom, love sparkling in her e'e,
Comes hame, perhaps to shew a braw° new gown,
Or deposit her sair-won penny fee,   35
To help her parents dear, if they in hardship be.

With joy unfeigned, brothers and sisters meet,
And each for other's weelfare kindly spiers.°
The social hours, swift-winged, unnoticed fleet;
Each tells the uncos° that he sees or hears.   40
The parents, partial, eye their hopeful years;
Anticipation forward points the view;
The mother, wi' her needle an' her shears,
Gars° auld claes look amaist as weel's the new;
The father mixes a' wi' admonition due.   45

Their master's an' their mistress's command
The yonkers a' are warnèd to obey;
An' mind their labors wi' an eydent° hand,
An' ne'er, though out o' sight, to jauk° or play;
" An' O! be sure to fear the Lord alway,   50
An' mind your duty, duly, morn an' night;
Lest in temptation's path ye gang astray,
Implore His counsel and assisting might;
They never sought in vain that sought the Lord aright! "

But hark! a rap comes gently to the door;   55
Jenny, wha kens the meaning o' the same,
Tells how a neibor lad cam o'er the moor,
To do some errands, and convoy her hame.
The wily mother sees the conscious flame
Sparkle in Jenny's e'e, and flush her cheek;   60
Wi' heart-struck, anxious care, inquires his name,
While Jenny hafflins° is afraid to speak;
Weel pleased the mother hears it's nae wild worthless rake.

---

23. *ingle:* fire, fireplace; *bonnilie:* prettily. 26. *kiaugh* (kyäh): trouble, anxiety. 28. *Belyve:* by
and by; *bairns:* children. 30. *ca' the pleugh:* drive the plow. 30–31. *tentie . . . errand:* heedfully run
a careful errand. 34. *braw:* handsome. 38. *spiers* (spērz): inquires. 40. *uncos:* strange things; news.
44. *Gars:* makes. This line means: makes old clothes look almost as good as new. 48. *eydent* (ī'děnt):
industrious. 49. *jauk* (jäk): waste time. 62. *hafflins:* partly.

Wi' kindly welcome Jenny brings him ben,°
A strappin' youth; he takes the mother's eye;   65
Blythe Jenny sees the visit's no ill taen;
The father cracks° of horses, pleughs, and kye,°
The youngster's artless heart o'erflows wi' joy,
But blate and laithfu',° scarce can weel behave;
The mother, wi' a woman's wiles, can spy   70
What makes the youth sae bashfu' and sae grave,
Weel pleased to think her bairn's respected like the lave.°

O happy love! where love like this is found!
O heartfelt raptures! bliss beyond compare!
I've pacèd much this weary, mortal round,
And sage experience bids me this declare —
" If Heaven a draft of heavenly pleasure spare,
One cordial in this melancholy vale,
'Tis when a youthful, loving, modest pair
In other's arm breathe out the tender tale,
Beneath the milk-white thorn that scents the evening gale."

Is there, in human form, that bears a heart,
A wretch! a villain! lost to love and truth!
That can, with studied, sly, ensnaring art,
Betray sweet Jenny's unsuspecting youth?   85
Curse on his perjured arts! dissembling smooth!
Are honor, virtue, conscience, all exiled?
Is there no pity, no relenting ruth,
Points to the parents fondling o'er their child;
Then paints the ruined maid, and their distraction wild?   90

But now the supper crowns their simple board,
The halesome parritch,° chief of Scotia's food;
The sowpe° their only hawkie° does afford,
That yont the hallam° snugly chows her cood.
The dame brings forth, in complimental mood,   95
To grace the lad, her weel-hained kebbuck fell;°
An' aft he's prest, an' aft he ca's it guid.
The frugal wifie, garrulous, will tell
How 'twas a towmond auld, sin' lint was i' the bell.°

The cheerfu' supper done, wi' serious face,   100
They round the ingle form a circle wide;
The sire turns o'er with patriarchal grace
The big ha' Bible,° ance his father's pride.

<hr />

64. *ben:* into the parlor. The Scotch peasant's house had two rooms called *but an' ben,* kitchen and parlor. 67. *cracks:* talks. Compare our use in the slang "wisecracks"; *kye:* cows. 69. *blate and laithfu':* shy and bashful. 72. *lave:* rest. 92. *halesome parritch:* wholesome porridge, i.e., oatmeal. 93. *sowpe:* sup of milk; *hawkie:* cow. 94. *yont the hallam:* beyond the partition, in the same house. 96. *weel-hained kebbuck fell:* well-kept sharp cheese. 99. *a . . . bell:* a year old since flax was in flower. 103. *ha' Bible:* hall or family Bible.

His bonnet reverently is laid aside,
His lyart haffets° wearing thin and bare;   105
Those strains that once did sweet in Zion glide,
He wales° a portion with judicious care;
And " Let us worship God! " he says with solemn air.

.   .   .   .

From scenes like these old Scotia's grandeur springs,
That makes her loved at home, revered abroad: 110
Princes and lords are but the breath of kings,
" An honest man's the noblest work of God ";°
And certes, in fair Virtue's heavenly road,
The cottage leaves the palace far behind.
What is a lordling's pomp? a cumbrous load,   115
Disguising oft the wretch of human kind,
Studied in arts of hell, in wickedness refined!

O Scotia! my dear, my native soil!
For whom my warmest wish to Heaven is sent,
Long may thy hardy sons of rustic toil   120
Be blest with health, and peace, and sweet content!
And oh! may Heaven their simple lives prevent
From luxury's contagion, weak and vile!
Then, howe'er crowns and coronets be rent,
A virtuous populace may rise the while,   125
And stand a wall of fire around their much-loved isle.

O Thou! who poured the patriotic tide
That streamed through Wallace's undaunted heart,
Who dared to nobly stem tyrannic pride,
Or nobly die, the second glorious part — °   130
(The patriot's God peculiarly thou art,
His friend, inspirer, guardian, and reward!)
O never, never Scotia's realm desert,
But still the patriot, and the patriot-bard,
In bright succession raise, her ornament and guard! 135

105. *lyart haffets:* gray temples. 107. *wales:* selects. 112. This line is quoted from Pope's *Essay on Man.* 130. *part:* alternative.

SCOTLAND'S SPOKESMAN

THE SONGS

1. For each of these lyrics, decide what is the prevalent emotion — love, sorrow, joy, patriotism? State the situation and the point of each. Practice reading these songs aloud to bring out the rhythmic quality.

THREE LONGER POEMS

1. How does " A Man's a Man for A' That " reveal the new democratic spirit that was emerging in the eighteenth century? What ideas and customs does Burns challenge? What is the significance of the poem in Burns' own life?

2. What points of similarity do you find in " To a Mouse " and " To a Louse "? What marked contrast in mood? What Scottish words give the humorous touch in " To a Louse "? Show how the point made at the end of each poem is a natural outgrowth of the situation. What frequently quoted lines come at the close of each?

3. How do the subject matter and meter of these three poems show that Burns was far removed from the classical school of Pope? Compare Burns with Pope, Goldsmith, and Gray. What characteristics of the Romantic school does Burns display?

THE COTTER'S SATURDAY NIGHT

1. What similarity can you find between the opening description in the second and third stanzas and the opening of Gray's " Elegy "? What are some differences?

2. Describe the different members of the family. What were the Saturday night pleasures of the family? What lines show respect of members of the family for one another? Why was Saturday night probably the happiest time for this family? What characteristics attributed to the Scotch as a nation are evident in the description of this home?

3. What are Burns' own comments on this Scotch peasant life? How do his ideas compare with those of Goldsmith on the Irish peasants in *The Deserted Village?* What change do you note in his language when he begins to philosophize?

SUGGESTIONS FOR WRITING

1. Write your prescription for happiness in a family group.

2. Try writing some lyrics based on those emotions to which Burns gives expression: joy, sorrow, love, patriotism.

READING LIST FOR THE EIGHTEENTH CENTURY

Ashton, Helen, *Footman in Powder*

Jem Wyett, a royal servant who begins as a pantry boy, is happy because he was born with the soul of a lackey.

Balderston, John L., *Berkeley Square*

A three-act play about an American in eighteenth-century London.

Clifford, James L., *Young Sam Johnson*

A readable biography of Sam Johnson's early years in Lichfield to his life in London in 1749, after he had completed his *Dictionary.*

Defoe, Daniel, *Robinson Crusoe*

A strange and fascinating tale of a shipwrecked mariner who lives on a desert island off the east coast of South America.

De La Torre-Bueno, Lillian, *Dr. Sam Johnson*

A series of mysterious episodes, original and imaginative, in the career of the great lexicographer Dr. Johnson.

Falkner, John M., *Moonfleet*

A tale of smugglers in which orphaned John Trenchard follows the lure of a valuable diamond along a path of violence.

Forester, Cecil S., *Lord Hornblower*

Horatio leaves Lady Barbara, concludes his private war with Napoleon, quiets a mutiny, and is made a peer by his grateful sovereign.

Frye, Pearl, *Game for Empires*

A superior biographical novel of Nelson, from his command of the *Agamemnon* to the French defeat in the Battle of the Nile.

Goldsmith, Oliver, *She Stoops to Conquer*

A comedy of love in disguise. A bashful young man mistakes a squire's home for an inn.

———, *The Vicar of Wakefield*

The unworldly Dr. Primrose and his family are the subject of this delightful story of English country life.

Nordhoff, Charles B., and Hall, James Norman, *Mutiny on the Bounty*

Rebellion aboard the *Bounty* from England to the South Seas in 1787, a famous trial, and what became of the mutineers. For a continuation of the story see *Men Against the Sea* and *Pitcairn's Island.*

Norman, Charles, *The Pundit and the Player*

The life stories of two outstanding personalities are interwoven: David Garrick and Samuel Johnson.

Orczy, Baroness Emmuska, *The Scarlet Pimpernel*

A titled Englishman calling himself the " Scarlet Pimpernel " assists condemned or suspected Frenchmen to escape from France during the Reign of Terror.

Sabatini, Raphael, *Scaramouche*

A colorful and romantic story of intrigue in the early days of the French Revolution.

Scott, Sir Walter, *Guy Mannering*

Gypsy life and smuggling as it was practiced in the late eighteenth century.

———, *Waverly*

During the rebellion of 1745–46, exiled

Prince Charles Edward and his followers, the Jacobites, try to gain the English throne.

Shellabarger, Samuel, *Lord Chesterfield and His World*

Portrait of an extraordinary man, a representative of eighteenth-century England at its worst and at its best.

Sheridan, Richard B., *The Rivals* and *The School for Scandal*

Two famous satirical plays on eighteenth-century society, still popular on the stage.

Stevenson, Robert L., *Kidnapped*

Many exciting adventures take place in the highlands of Scotland during the Jacobite rebellion.

Tarkington, Booth, *Monsieur Beaucaire*

At Bath, an English resort, a French nobleman masquerades as a barber and falls in love with an English girl.

Thackeray, William M., *Henry Esmond*

A biographic story of a Cavalier and Jacobite at the time of Queen Anne. Addison, Steele, and others are introduced.

FOR LISTENING

Burns' "A Man's a Man for A' That" and "To a Mouse" have been recorded and are available on *Many Voices 6A.*

THE ENGLISH NOVEL

STORYTELLING in literature takes many forms; two of its oldest forms are the epic poem and the drama. In this book there are examples of both: *Beowulf* and *Paradise Lost* are epic poems; *Macbeth* is drama. A third long form of narrative is the novel. No novel is included in this book because of space limitations, but the reading lists suggest enough good fiction for your reading for many years.

A NEW FORM OF LITERATURE

Compared with poetry and drama, the novel is a newcomer in literature — only about two hundred years old. Until its appearance, man's storytelling instinct found outlet most often in long poems or in drama. Even before books were available, poets recited long tales — epics like *The Odyssey* in Greece or *Beowulf* in England — and actors presented them on the stage. The kind of story that we know today as the novel — a long work of prose fiction — did not exist until the eighteenth century.

FORMS OF PROSE FICTION

It is difficult to define the novel exactly; not all imaginary stories told in prose can be called novels in our present-day use of the term. Malory's *Morte d'Arthur* is ordinarily called a prose *romance* — a long, loose story of heroic adventures. Romances satisfy people's craving for action and for black-or-white characters: incredibly vile villains who are eventually overthrown by impossibly courageous heroes who win ravishingly beautiful heroines. Such stories do not usually have a tight-knit plot, nor do they attempt to show life as it is. You can observe elements of the romance in many movies and comic strips today.

Another form of prose fiction is the *fantasy*. Here the imagination is allowed free rein. Unusual situations are developed to extremes in order to prove some point, and sometimes great ingenuity is exercised. Swift's *Gulliver's Travels* is a fantasy, filled with miniature men, giants, islands floating in the air, and talking horses. Many stories about Utopias, or ideal societies, fall into the category of fantasy, including the sixteenth-century *Utopia* by Thomas More and the twentieth-century *Brave New World* by Aldous Huxley. So too George Orwell has written the fantasies *Animal Farm* and *1984,* which exaggerate the traits of a totalitarian government in order to show its inherent evil. Science fiction — for example, the exciting tales by H. G. Wells — may also fall into this class.

The straight *adventure story* has always been a popular form of prose fiction. Here, as in romances, action and hairbreadth escapes are the important things. However, characters and background may be portrayed convincingly, as in Defoe's *Robinson Crusoe*. In the seventeenth century the adventure story was so popular as to develop a special form: the picaresque novel, a story about a " rogue " (*picaro* in Spanish) and his cunning escapades. The most popular novels of the twentieth century are often adventure stories — look at the best-seller list in any current newspaper. The detective " whodunit," the melodramatic " dime novel " of the early twentieth century, and the tale of violence are all forms of the adventure story.

All of these branches of prose fiction — the romance, the fantasy, the adventure story — have one thing in common: they are willing to twist the experiences of the actual world, shape imaginary events, and exaggerate grotesquely in order to prove a point or hold our interest in fast action.

On the other side, always, is the world as it is, with real people in contact with other real people. And this is the subject matter for the realistic novel. *A true novel is a long story organized toward a significant conclusion and dealing with convincing, though imagined, people in their relations with one another*. Ideally the novel must be artistically constructed; it must induce belief; and it must give a picture of the social world as we might know it.

EARLY NOVELISTS

The novel sprang into full flower in the eighteenth century with the writings of Samuel Richardson, Henry Fielding, and Laurence Sterne. Conditions at that time were favorable for this new form of literature. Printing presses improved so that they could turn out thousands of copies rapidly. More people could read, as education spread to the middle classes, and more people had money to pay the booksellers in return for amusement. They were curious and inquisitive. A professional inventor of tall tales like Daniel Defoe could earn a living by selling stories of adventure like *Robinson Crusoe,* or lurid accounts of shady characters like Captain Singleton, Colonel Jack, and the female rogue, Moll Flanders.

But the reading public also wanted stories about people like themselves, ordinary middle-class citizens. SAMUEL RICHARDSON satisfied this need in 1740 with his immensely popular novel *Pamela,* and later with *Clarissa Harlowe* and *Sir Charles Grandison. Pamela* is often called the first English novel because of its psychological insight into personality and its slow building up of real characters in fully developed situations. Told in the form of letters written by the heroine to her parents, it recounts how a serving girl, because of her virtuous character, changes the passion of her master into true love, and finally becomes his wife. For modern tastes, the moral of the story is over-emphasized (its subtitle is " Virtue Rewarded "), but Richardson's subtle knowledge of human nature is still impressive today.

HENRY FIELDING began writing by satirizing Richardson's sentiment. Fielding's *Joseph Andrews* is supposedly Pamela's brother, whose virtue also is under attack. But Fielding soon abandoned the idea of parody, for his own ability to create full-blooded, warm-hearted, and reckless individuals was apparent. His great work is *Tom Jones.* If you want to live in eighteenth-century England, seeing its country squires and gamekeepers, its city society and London jails, read this novel. It is funny and fast paced, and Fielding has made a hero out of an impulsive, well-meaning, very ordinary young man.

The third of these early English novelists, LAURENCE STERNE, is particularly interesting today because he invented a new manner of telling a story: letting one subject suggest another as it does in our daydreams, with no conformance to time sequence or logic. Whereas Richardson and Fielding controlled tight plots, Sterne picks up little incidents wherever he finds them. In his long masterpiece, *The Life and Opinions of Tristram Shandy,* he finds so many things to interest him that he even has trouble in getting his hero born! But through the delightfully grotesque figures of Tristram's father and " my Uncle Toby " and Corporal Trim, Sterne introduces something new into English literature, mixing satire and sentiment with many a whim and quirk. In Sterne, the laugh is never far from the tear.

THE GOTHIC ROMANCE AND LATER DETECTIVE FICTION

The present-day romantic interest in mysterious adventures and faraway places was anticipated in the late eighteenth century by the Gothic romance of which Horace Walpole's *The Castle of Otranto* is a good example. Using gloomy castles, strange and ominous happenings, and a variety of romantic characters, writers like Mrs. Ann Radcliffe in her *The Mysteries of Udolpho* alternately puzzled and chilled readers. In the next century the Gothic romance gave way to more realistic novels that depended less on supernatural events and vague, remote medieval settings, yet kept the element of suspense and a puzzling plot. Wilkie Collins's *The Moonstone* (1868) is not only the first detective novel in English but one of the best. Try it, or Conan Doyle's *Hound of the Baskervilles,* if you like the formula: " Thrill the nerves, chill the heart, spill the blood, and kill the villain."

NINETEENTH-CENTURY NOVELISTS

Such nineteenth-century writers as Scott, Jane Austen, Charlotte and Emily Brontë, Dickens, Thackeray, George Eliot, and Trollope made the novel the most widely read and influential form of English literature.

Almost singlehandedly, SIR WALTER SCOTT opened the eyes of Englishmen and Europeans to their own past history with his historical romances. *Ivanhoe* and *Kenilworth,* for example, are im-

Jane Austen   Sir Walter Scott   Charlotte Brontë

aginative reconstructions of the Middle Ages and the Renaissance. Many readers, however, think that Scott is at his best in his handling of native Scottish stories (*The Heart of Midlothian, The Bride of Lammermoor*). Later writers followed his brilliant example in writing historical romances — notably Dickens with *A Tale of Two Cities* and Thackeray with *Henry Esmond*. Today historical romances are a popular kind of fiction; witness the large number of American novels that deal with our own past.

In contrast, JANE AUSTEN never departed from the world immediately about her. In *Pride and Prejudice* and *Sense and Sensibility* she tells beautifully constructed stories of quiet, well-bred life in provincial towns and countrysides. Her usual theme is a girl's slow making up of her mind about whom to marry. Jane Austen is subtle, witty, and balanced. If you want to test the qualities of a typical novel against the definition given on page 343, take one of Jane Austen's as a standard.

Up in Yorkshire in the north of England, the Brontë family (father, son, and three daughters) was developing unexpected genius. The three Brontë sisters wrote with intense passion. CHAR-

LOTTE BRONTË in *Jane Eyre* tells the story of a governess who loved a gloomy, stormy hero. EMILY BRONTË in *Wuthering Heights* uses the bleak, windswept, northern moors as a setting for a tragic story of a love that was stronger than hate and death.

CHARLES DICKENS we all know, for he is one of the most popular and prolific of novelists. He ranged from the bubbling spirits of *The Pickwick Papers* to the flowing tears of Little Nell's death in *The Old Curiosity Shop*. His great gift was his vitality. He created whole worlds of characters, exaggerated but unforgettable. His sympathy with the oppressed, his indignation against social injustice, made him a significant voice in the Victorian Age. You will walk the streets of London and the lanes of England when you read *David Copperfield, Oliver Twist,* and *Bleak House.*

WILLIAM MAKEPEACE THACKERAY showed surpassing skill in revealing a complete panorama of society. Sometimes he proceeded by organizing it around a single hero, as in *Pendennis;* sometimes by contrasting two heroines, like Becky Sharp and Amelia Sedley in *Vanity Fair;* sometimes by taking a

Charles Dickens   George Eliot   Wm. Makepeace Thackeray

whole group of characters, as in *The Virginians*. Unlike Dickens, Thackeray was concerned with the upper classes of English society. He writes in an urbane manner about the foibles and vanities of the country gentlefolk and the sophisticated sets of London. His novels reflect the atmosphere of the latter society, being a trifle weary and cynical in tone.

GEORGE ELIOT also had the power to create complete social groups. She added to this power a moral fervor of her own and an ability to devise plots that almost equals Jane Austen's. Her real name was Mary Ann Evans, but her masculine pen name concealed her sex from the public for many years. Her *Mill on the Floss* is a poignant story of Maggie Tulliver growing up, and her *Middlemarch*, a study of provincial life, is one of the spacious and solid English novels.

ANTHONY TROLLOPE is being rediscovered today. Like the three Victorians last mentioned, he was a tireless writer. In more than fifty novels he created the imaginary county of Barsetshire, and filled it with clergymen, farmers, politicians, sweet young women, and fierce older ones. Trollope does not have the passion and tension of the Brontës or of Dickens; he is more relaxed, like Jane Austen. But for a good-tempered story of believable people in fully realized surroundings, read *Barchester Towers* or *The Small House at Allington*.

THREE GREAT LATER NOVELISTS

Bridging the nineteenth and twentieth centuries, new writers kept the English novel powerful and varied.

GEORGE MEREDITH wrote in an artificial style that exploded in epigrams like fireworks. In spite of his mannered writing, he conveys to the reader his delight in nature and in active social life. In *The Ordeal of Richard Feverel* he tells a passionate and piercing story of young love.

THOMAS HARDY, on the contrary, is tragic in his view of life. Many of his characters are doomed by fate and by inescapable accident. Hardy is a master at creating a natural background so haunting that it seems to take part as a character in the story — Egdon Heath in *The Return of the Native* or *The Mayor of Casterbridge* are examples.

JOSEPH CONRAD shares this power to summon up actual places, though his settings range over the whole world — Africa, South America, the Pacific Islands, and the seven seas. His heroes solve their moral problems against the great backgrounds of the sea and sky. If you read Conrad's *Typhoon, Heart of Darkness, Victory,* or *Lord Jim,* you will share his spirit of calm nobility, of a spectator looking at the miracle of the earth and the waters.

THE MODERN ENGLISH NOVEL

The early twentieth century, like the nineteenth, is rich in novel writing, and again its variety can only be touched upon briefly. Bennett, Galsworthy, and Wells form a representative trio. ARNOLD BENNETT is as realistic as a good reporter in writing about his industrial " Five Towns " and his middle-class characters. JOHN GALSWORTHY puts together the history of a large money-making family and all their relatives by marriage through successive generations, in three novels that compose *The Forsyte Saga*. H. G. WELLS writes not only of the life about him, but boldly imagines what life in future generations may be like. He was the prophet of modern science in many of his novels.

You may sample the style of many of these novelists through their short stories included in this book. Far places are still brought to England's doorstep — India by Rudyard Kipling, South America by W. H. Hudson, Scotland by James M. Barrie, the sea by W. W. Jacobs, the imaginary Asian Shangri-La by James Hilton in *Lost Horizon,* Europe and the Far East by Somerset Maugham.

EXPERIMENTING IN NEW FORMS

The twentieth century has seen many experiments in ways of writing the novel. Some of these you would find difficult in manner, but you should know something about the pioneers.

E. M. FORSTER takes as his characters quiet, harmless, provincial people, but he usually introduces some mysterious force — a hidden instinct, a weird or unexplained or supernatural phenomenon — that causes us to re-examine the basis of human life. His great novel, *A Passage to India,* is full of disturbing conflicts highlighted by the contrast between East and West.

ALDOUS HUXLEY is essentially a philosopher and writer of essays; his novels attack social problems by means of scintillating conversations that are more like debates than the dialogue of the usual novel.

VIRGINIA WOOLF is extremely perceptive of fine shades of feeling and of all the sensations of living. Her novels (*Mrs. Dalloway, To the Lighthouse*) record the flow of her heroines' thoughts. She was the leading novelist in the " stream-of-consciousness " technique made popular after World War I.

JAMES JOYCE is a giant figure of controversy. His early *Portrait of the Artist as a Young Man* is not hard reading, but in *Ulysses* and *Finnegan's Wake* he twists language to express dream states until the words seem at first unrecognizable. His mastery of expression is notable, and his influence on other writers has been profound.

Other contemporary writers, such as Joyce Cary, Evelyn Waugh, Liam O'Flaherty, Seán O'Faoláin, and Graham Greene, have given new shapes and patterns to the novel and have many admirers.

The voices of the novelists throughout the British Commonwealth reflect ties of common interest and good will. Alan Paton and Nadine Gordimer (South Africa), Hugh MacLennan and Morley Callaghan (Canada), Judith Wright and James McAuley (Australia) have made the world aware of the diversity of novels written in English.

Some Notable English Novels

1700

1719	Defoe's *Robinson Crusoe*
1740	Richardson's *Pamela*
1749	Fielding's *Tom Jones*
1760	Sterne's *Tristram Shandy*
1766	Goldsmith's *The Vicar of Wakefield*

1800

1813	Jane Austen's *Pride and Prejudice*
1819	Scott's *Ivanhoe*
1847	Charlotte Brontë's *Jane Eyre*
1847	Thackeray's *Vanity Fair*
1847	Emily Brontë's *Wuthering Heights*
1849	Dickens' *David Copperfield*
1857	Trollope's *Barchester Towers*
1859	Meredith's *The Ordeal of Richard Feverel*
1861	George Eliot's *Silas Marner*
1878	Hardy's *The Return of the Native*
1883	Stevenson's *Treasure Island*

1900

1900	Conrad's *Lord Jim*
1901	Kipling's *Kim*
1904	Hudson's *Green Mansions*
1908	Bennett's *Old Wives' Tale*
1915	Maugham's *Of Human Bondage*
1922	Galsworthy's *The Forsyte Saga*
1924	Forster's *A Passage to India*
1927	Virginia Woolf's *To the Lighthouse*
1932	Huxley's *Brave New World*
1934	Hilton's *Good-bye, Mr. Chips*
1945	Waugh's *Brideshead Revisited*
1950	O'Flaherty's *Insurrection*
1951	Cary's *The Horse's Mouth*
1953	Hartley's *The Go-Between*
1955	Elizabeth Bowen's *A World of Love*
1956	Rebecca West's *The Fountain Overflows*

THE ROMANTIC

ROMANTICISM — the predominant literary mode of the first third of the nineteenth century — was expressed almost entirely in poetry. However, the attitudes of the literary romanticists were not typical of those of most Englishmen: these writers were either far ahead of the times or rebels against current beliefs and customs. The government of the day was not " romantic "; neither were economic conditions " romantic." To understand this, we must first get a clear notion of what is meant by Romanticism.

WHAT DOES "ROMANTICISM" MEAN?

As a way of thinking and as an approach to literature, Romanticism is associated with *vitality, powerful emotion, limitless and dreamlike ideas.* Classicism, by contrast, is associated with *order, common sense, controlled reason.* We have seen these influences in the Age of Pope.

As a historical period in English literature, the Age of Romanticism extends roughly from 1798, when Wordsworth and Coleridge published their *Lyrical Ballads,* to the 1830's, when Queen Victoria came to the throne and

all of the important romantic poets except Wordsworth were dead. During this period, the ideas behind the revolutions in America and France increasingly occupied the thoughts of Englishmen, too. People were looking at the world in new and striking ways; literature reflected this revolt against outworn traditions and attitudes.

Many of the poets of the time shared, in varying degrees, these special qualities of Romanticism:

1. A strong sense of the beauty of the world around them
2. A deep sympathy with obscure, humble, underprivileged people
3. A vivid imagination capable of constructing fantastic dream worlds
4. A feeling of rebellion against tyrannical authority, based on a belief in liberty for the individual
5. An interest in ancient legends and traditions
6. A sense of melancholy or loneliness

They took materials from the past — legends, myths, folktales — and reshaped them into vivid and beautiful expressions of new ideas and feelings.

349

DELIGHT IN NATURE

The Romantic poets worshiped natural beauty. William Wordsworth, who is perhaps the greatest poet of the period, is particularly remembered for his delight in nature. In contrast with the " citified " eighteenth-century writers, Wordsworth, Coleridge, and Southey lived close to nature among the lakes and mountains of northern England. As a group they are known as the Lake Poets. Wordsworth observed natural scenes closely, meditated on them deeply, and from his earliest boyhood drew from nature a sense of exaltation that was almost religious. He sensed a living spirit in the natural world " whose dwelling is the light of setting suns." Matthew Arnold speaks of Wordsworth's " healing power," for he felt that Wordsworth " laid us, as we were at birth, on the cool flowery lap of earth."

SYMPATHY WITH THE HUMBLE

Wordsworth felt that men were at their best when living a simple life close to nature. He believed that the real feelings of the heart flourished best in a " humble and rustic life." He wished to write for ordinary people in simple words drawn from " the very language of men." Like Burns and Gray before him, Wordsworth reflected the growing belief in democracy, a faith in the common man who plows the fields, who watches the changing seasons, who may be buried obscurely in a country churchyard. A flower, a little child, an old shepherd could give Wordsworth thoughts " too deep for tears."

THE WORLD OF IMAGINATION

Coleridge also wrote poems about nature and simple country living, but his special interest lay in the mysterious world of imagination. When he and Wordsworth published their famous book *Lyrical Ballads,* they divided their task. Wordsworth took subjects from ordinary life and made them seem unusually beautiful, full of an important wonder. Coleridge took wondrous or supernatural happenings and made them seem actual. Wordsworth found glory in the commonplace; Coleridge found reality in the unearthly.

Turning away from the crisp wit of the eighteenth century, the new Romantic poets were finding undiscovered countries in their own imaginations. With Coleridge you can sail the enchanted Antarctic and equatorial seas in the company of his ancient mariner, or enter " caverns measureless to man " in the realm of Kubla Khan. Keats, hypnotized by gazing at a Grecian urn or hearing a nightingale, can give you glimpses through

> " Magic casements, opening on the foam
> Of perilous seas, in faery lands forlorn."

REBELLION AGAINST SOCIETY

The first generation of Romantics — such men as Wordsworth, Coleridge, and Southey — wrote poems about nature, about common country folk, about supernatural dreams. They were trying to find a substitute for the ugly industrial life that worked such hardships on certain classes. Like Shelley and Byron in the next generation of Romantic poets, they were revolutionists in their desire for liberty for the individual.

Of course, the belief in liberty was not a new idea. The Anglo-Saxons had felt it; the Elizabethans had felt it; Milton had felt it. The forerunners of Romanticism — eighteenth-century writers like Gray, Goldsmith, and Burns — had felt it. But each age has its distinctive way of looking at persisting concepts, and the Romantics had a fresh view of the meaning of liberty. Their eager expression of this view took the form of some of the most vital and beautiful literature in all English history.

During the early years of the French Revolution, Wordsworth, a young man traveling through France, was attracted by this great new experiment in government. The French Revolution breathed hope into human hearts, a hope that wars and politics and industrial unrest and tortoise-slow social changes could not entirely kill.

Coleridge and his friend Southey planned an ideal community made up of free men of good will, gladly sharing their property; but like so many of the Romantics' projects, their plans never worked out. Byron opposed tyranny in his poetry and in his life. Shelley called upon the people to —

> " Rise like lions after slumber
> In unvanquishable number!
> Shake your chains to earth, like dew
> Which in sleep had fallen on you —
> Ye are many, they are few! "

Wherever it could be found, the idea of liberty roused the Romantic poets. In *Hellas* (1821), Shelley expressed the thought that the attempt of the Greeks to free themselves from the Turks might mean that

> " The world's great age begins anew."

In the cause of Greek freedom, Byron made his last journey; he died of a fever among the Greek insurgents at Missolonghi in 1824.

INTEREST IN THE PAST

Two kinds of hope were felt by the Romantics: they wished to improve life in the present, but they also sought an ideal life apart from " here and now."

Each of the Romantics tried in his own way to find an ideal country. Byron's way was to fight for Greece. Shelley and Keats not only created beautiful imagined landscapes, but also traveled to Italy. Charles Lamb, whose essays you will read, remained in London as a clerk in the India House, but spent his spare time reading the Elizabethan dramatists and writing essays full of wistful memories and fanciful dreams. Many of the Romantics found stimulation in actual travel, but they knew as well that travel in one's imagination to far centuries and far places can make life varied and interesting and valuable.

Particularly in the chivalry and high adventure of the Middle Ages did the Romantic spirit move easily. The great example is Walter Scott, with his historical novels, such as *Ivanhoe* and *The Talisman,* and his popular long narrative poems, such as *The Lady of the Lake.* Scott enthusiastically collected and published volumes of old Scottish ballads. Coleridge and Keats not only chose old stories and far-off ages, but they also wrote at times in the form of the medieval ballad.

From the actual world, Romantic writers turned to the past or to imaginary worlds, where there were no boundaries to confine them.

MELANCHOLY AND LONELINESS

To the Romantics, poetry was the hope of the world. Shelley wrote that poets were the prophets of the future; they were the unacknowledged legislators of mankind. He wished for the fierce energy of the west wind, so that his thoughts might be blown over the whole world to create new life. Keats sought steadily for perfect beauty and perfect truth, expressed in perfect poetry.

Such high hopes of ideal attainment could hardly be realized. The resulting disappointment led to a kind of melancholy that underlies much Romantic poetry. Unable to attain their best aspirations or to hold their ecstasy for any length of time at a high pitch, the poets left many of their most ambitious poems unfinished. Byron turned to cynicism and flippancy; Coleridge turned to philosophy; Wordsworth turned to dry lecturing in verse. Shelley knew that " Our sweetest songs are those that tell of saddest thoughts." Keats also learned that melancholy springs from knowing that beauty must die, and that " The fancy cannot cheat so well as she is famed to do." Because they aimed so high, the Romantics were often in anguish at falling short of their aim.

ENGLAND AND FRANCE

It was a dangerous period. In England, political passions and fervent ideals clashed with powerful forces that were determined to prevent any changes. Edmund Burke, who had defended the American colonies, attacked the French Revolution as dangerous; he preferred slow changes based on a re-

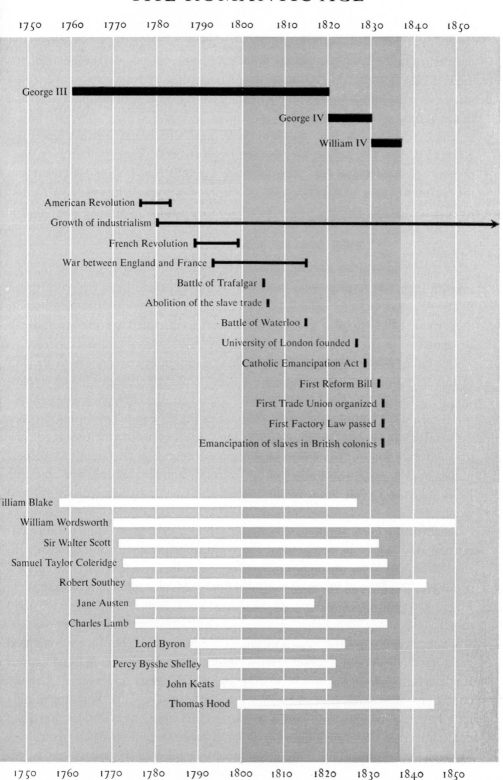

1750 1760 1770 1780 1790 1800 1810 1820 1830 1840 1850

George III

George IV

William IV

American Revolution
Growth of industrialism
French Revolution
War between England and France
Battle of Trafalgar
Abolition of the slave trade
Battle of Waterloo
University of London founded
Catholic Emancipation Act
First Reform Bill
First Trade Union organized
First Factory Law passed
Emancipation of slaves in British colonies

William Blake
William Wordsworth
Sir Walter Scott
Samuel Taylor Coleridge
Robert Southey
Jane Austen
Charles Lamb
Lord Byron
Percy Bysshe Shelley
John Keats
Thomas Hood

spect for tradition. As the average Englishman watched France, he came to believe that a militaristic state was developing under Napoleon. Napoleon had decided that if all people should have privileges, all people should fight for them. Consequently the enormous peoples' armies of Napoleon transformed war from a game for professionals into a mass movement overrunning Europe in campaigns of conquest and expansion.

There was danger that England itself, a secure island fortress since the Norman Conquest, might be invaded by Napoleon. Finally, however, Napoleon was defeated at the Battle of Waterloo in 1815. England, Russia, and the German states, at the Congress of Vienna, set up a " Holy Alliance " that for the rest of the century discouraged liberal reforms as well as revolutions.

THE INDUSTRIAL REVOLUTION

At home as well as abroad, changes came about slowly. On the surface, English men and women were much as they always had been: they were still fighting France in great wars; they were still debating new laws in Parliament; they were still following the latest fashions as dictated by the sleek Beau Brummell.

But underneath, England was becoming a different country. With the fall of the Napoleonic Empire, England had no close competitors in her expansion over the globe. Her increasing trade was paralleled by increasing industry. There were innumerable new discoveries in this age of invention, already well started in the eighteenth century. The use of coal for smelting made the iron industry boom. The steam engine gave England great factories and permitted heavy, rapid transportation by railroads and steamships. The spinning jenny and the power loom revolutionized the weaving of linen, cotton, and wool.

Surprisingly fast, England was turning into a manufacturing nation: importing raw materials in her own ships, transporting them on her own railroads, running them through the factories, and finally exporting the finished products. The face of the world was changing. Machines were replacing men. Manpower and horsepower were used less; coal, iron, and steam were used more.

Changes increased the wealth of the nation as a whole, but they also caused great hardships among certain groups. International competition handicapped English farmers. In the mushrooming industrial towns and factories, living conditions were atrocious. The mines and the mills, with their appallingly long hours, poor pay, and sordid working conditions, were little better than penitentiaries. When machines threw hand laborers and small craftsmen out of work, the competition among the unemployed was so severe that wages dropped shamefully low. Abuses were widespread; the need for reform was desperate, but reform came slowly.

SLOW CHANGES IN GOVERNMENT

The government remained conservative. With the rise of industry, the rich commercial classes began to share power with the old aristocrats. But the barons of industry, as conservative as the aristocrats, were even less interested in improving the lot of workers. The poor had few who could help them. Government regulation of industry hardly existed in England. Furthermore, Adam Smith, a Scotsman, had founded the new science of economics with his book *The Wealth of Nations* (published in 1776), and the current theory was to let things work themselves out according to the laws of supply and demand. Economic ideas were coldly impersonal and utilitarian rather than humanitarian.

Nevertheless, reforms were begun. Laws were enacted against child labor. Prison sentences were softened (in the eighteenth century a man could be thrown into jail for debt, deported or hanged for stealing a small sum). Freedom of the press was broadened; education was bettered. Restrictions against Roman Catholics were eased; an improved poor law was feebly attempted. The slave trade was peacefully abolished in the first half of the century; Robert Owen, a self-made businessman, helped to organize a Trades Union in 1834, though the government dissolved it.

The spirit of liberty spread slowly but steadily. In 1832, after bitter debate and opposition, the important Reform Bill was passed. This bill gave governmental control to the now powerful middle class, largely by increasing the number of those eligible to vote and by correcting inequalities in representation in Parliament. Little by little, Englishmen were becoming more nearly free and equal. There remained, of course, great masses of underprivileged people — whole classes who had no voice in determining their government.

SUMMARY

The Romanticism of the early nineteenth century was a reaction against the formality of the Age of Pope. New ideas were expressed: emphasis on human emotions, sympathy with the humble classes and desire for social justice, appreciation of the individual, love for the romantic past, and eagerness to blaze new trails. The mood of Romanticism prepared the country for a literary outburst. Wordsworth and Coleridge opened new subjects for poetry. Byron, Shelley, and Keats produced poetry excelling in lyric beauty. Prose was somewhat overshadowed, but the essay was further developed by Lamb and others, and the novel was rapidly becoming an influential literary form.

During the first part of the ninetenth century, England was increasingly involved in French affairs. The struggle with Napoleon eventually resulted in victory for the English and their allies. Meanwhile problems were developing in England. With increased trade and the invention of new machinery, factories mushroomed in the Industrial Revolution; great industrial centers drew workers from the countryside. The poorer classes suffered atrocious conditions, but gradually reforms were made in the poor laws; the slave trade was abolished; education and labor conditions were improved. In the Reform Bill of 1832, the government, although basically conservative, made some progress toward a more representative democracy.

WILLIAM WORDSWORTH

1770–1850

To understand Wordsworth, it is important to know something of the natural surroundings among which he lived. In a section of northwestern England known as the Lake District, nature has been lavish not only with lakes, but with mountains, streams, and waterfalls over which the shifting lights and shades and seasonal colors play with ever-varying effect. Here Wordsworth spent the greater part of his long life.

In part of his long poem *The Prelude*, Wordsworth has left a full account of his boyhood in the Cumberland hills. It is significant that, more than any other English poet up to his day, he studied the thoughts, feelings, and reactions of children, and traced the part played by childhood in the total development of a person's life. "The child is father of the man," is one of his most famous lines. His love of outdoor life as a boy deepened and matured until he became the great interpreter of nature in poetry. He sensed a divine spirit within all forms of nature. Even birds and flowers, he believed, were aware of pleasure in being alive. To Wordsworth, nature was mankind's best moral teacher. Nature was, in fact, his religion, and he has been called "nature's high priest."

At Cambridge another dominant interest came into Wordsworth's life. The world was seething with new political ideas. The Americans had recently won their independence; now the French masses were rising against the tyranny of the aristocrats. While on a trip across the Channel in 1791, young Wordsworth enthusiastically adopted the side of the French revolutionists, but when his family cut off his allowance at the end of a year, he returned to England. Later, he turned against the radical democratic ideas of the time and became conservative, much to the distaste of some of his admirers. Robert Browning reproachfully called him a "lost leader."

A close companionship with his sister Dorothy was one of the abiding influences of Wordsworth's life. Another was his long friendship with Coleridge. The two men had met in their twenties, when Wordsworth and Dorothy were living in southern England. The three young people found an immediate bond in their ardent discussions of poetry while on long hikes through the Somerset hills. Out of this association came *Lyrical Ballads,* the book which marks the beginning of the Romantic movement. The single, musical lyrics in this volume, so different from the polished, formal verse of the eighteenth century, were unfavorably received at first, but later their profound importance was recognized.

For fifty years Wordsworth lived near Grasmere in the Lake District, with his wife, his devoted sister, and a circle of congenial literary friends. Sir Walter Scott and Ralph Waldo Emerson were among his famous visitors. Wordsworth's last thirty years were largely unproductive poetically, but his fame and greatness were already established. At the age of seventy-three he was made poet laureate. He was buried in the little churchyard at Grasmere.

Lines Written in Early Spring

This poem and "The Tables Turned" give the core of Wordsworth's attitude toward nature as expressed in *Lyrical Ballads*. In the first he voices his belief that the creatures of nature share human feelings, but, in contrast to man, they experience only harmony and joy. In the second poem the poet shows that nature is also a great moral teacher who tells us more of truth than the books of the sages.

I heard a thousand blended notes,
While in a grove I sate reclined,
In that sweet mood when pleasant thoughts
Bring sad thoughts to the mind.

To her fair works did Nature link   5
The human soul that through me ran;
And much it grieved my heart to think
What man has made of man.

Through primrose tufts, in that green bower,
The periwinkle trailed its wreaths;   10
And 'tis my faith that every flower
Enjoys the air it breathes.

The birds around me hopped and played,
Their thoughts I cannot measure;
But the least motion which they made,
It seemed a thrill of pleasure.   16

The budding twigs spread out their fan,
To catch the breezy air;
And I must think, do all I can,
That there was pleasure there.   20

If this belief from heaven be sent,
If such be Nature's holy plan,
Have I not reason to lament
What man has made of man?

The Tables Turned

Up! up! my Friend, and quit your books;
Or surely you'll grow double.
Up! up! my Friend, and clear your
    looks;
Why all this toil and trouble?

The sun, above the mountain's head,   5
A freshening luster mellow
Through all the long green fields has
    spread,
His first sweet evening yellow.

Books! 'tis a dull and endless strife;
Come, hear the woodland linnet,   10
How sweet his music! on my life,
There's more of wisdom in it.

And hark! how blithe the throstle sings!
He, too, is no mean preacher;
Come forth into the light of things;   15
Let Nature be your teacher.

She has a world of ready wealth,
Our minds and hearts to bless —
Spontaneous   wisdom   breathed   by
    health,
Truth breathed by cheerfulness.   20

One impulse from a vernal° wood
May teach you more of man,
Of moral evil and of good,
Than all the sages can.

Sweet is the lore that Nature brings;   25
Our meddling intellect
Misshapes   the   beauteous   forms   of
    things —
We murder to dissect.

Enough of Science and of Art;
Close up those barren leaves;   30
Come forth, and bring with you a heart
That watches and receives.

21. *vernal:* springlike.

She Was a Phantom of Delight

This lyric characterizes the poet's wife, Mary Hutchinson. Each of the stanzas represents a progressive stage in his acquaintance with her.

She was a phantom of delight
When first she gleamed upon my
  sight;
A lovely apparition, sent
To be a moment's ornament;
Her eyes as stars of twilight fair;   5
Like twilight's, too, her dusky hair;
But all things else about her drawn
From Maytime and the cheerful dawn;
A dancing shape, an image gay,
To haunt, to startle, and waylay.   10

I saw her upon nearer view,
A spirit, yet a woman too!
Her household motions light and free,
And steps of virgin liberty;
A countenance in which did meet   15

Sweet records, promises as sweet;
A creature not too bright or good
For human nature's daily food;
For transient sorrows, simple wiles,
Praise, blame, love, kisses, tears, and
  smiles.   20

And now I see with eye serene
The very pulse of the machine;
A being breathing thoughtful breath,
A traveler between life and death;
The reason firm, the temperate will,   25
Endurance, foresight, strength and skill;
A perfect woman, nobly planned,
To warn, to comfort, and command;
And yet a spirit still, and bright
With something of angelic light.   30

She Dwelt among the Untrodden Ways

This is one of five "Lucy Poems" centering around an imaginary girl of the English countryside. They are lyrics through which the poet expresses praise of the influence of nature on a young girl and describes his emotion at her death.

She dwelt among the untrodden ways
  Beside the springs of Dove;°
A maid whom there were none to praise,
  And very few to love.

A violet by a mossy stone   5
  Half-hidden from the eye!
— Fair as a star, when only one
  Is shining in the sky.

She lived unknown, and few could know
  When Lucy ceased to be;   10
But she is in her grave, and, oh,
  The difference to me!

2. *Dove:* a river in the Midlands of England.

To a Skylark (1805)

Up with me! up with me into the clouds!
    For thy song, Lark, is strong;
Up with me! up with me into the clouds!
    Singing, singing,
With clouds and sky about thee ringing,   5
    Lift me, guide me till I find
That spot which seems so to thy mind!°

I have walked through wildernesses dreary
And today my heart is weary;
Had I now the wings of a Faery,   10
Up to thee would I fly.
There is madness about thee, and joy divine
In that song of thine;
Lift me, guide me high and high
To thy banqueting place in the sky.   15

    Joyous as morning
Thou art laughing and scorning;
Thou hast a nest for thy love and thy rest.
And, though little troubled with sloth,
Drunken Lark!° thou would'st be loath   20
To be such a traveler as I.
Happy, happy Liver,
With a soul as strong as a mountain river
Pouring out praise to the Almighty Giver,
    Joy and jollity be with us both!   25

Alas! my journey, rugged and uneven,
Through prickly moors or dusty ways must wind;
But hearing thee, or others of thy kind,
As full of gladness and as free of heaven,
I, with my fate contented, will plod on,   30
And hope for higher raptures, when life's day is done.

7. *so to thy mind:* so much to your liking. 20. *Drunken Lark!:* i.e., with joy and song.

To a Skylark (1825)

Ethereal minstrel! pilgrim of the sky!
    Dost thou despise the earth where cares abound?
Or, while the wings aspire, are heart and eye
    Both with thy nest upon the dewy ground?
Thy nest which thou canst drop into at will,   5
Those quivering wings composed, that music still!
Leave to the nightingale her shady wood;
    A privacy of glorious light is thine;
Whence thou dost pour upon the world a flood
    Of harmony, with instinct more divine;   10
Type of the wise who soar, but never roam;
True to the kindred points of heaven and home!

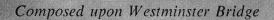

Composed upon Westminster Bridge

Earth has not anything to show more fair:
Dull would he be of soul who could pass by
A sight so touching in its majesty:
This city now doth, like a garment, wear
The beauty of the morning; silent bare,
Ships, towers, domes, theaters, and temples lie
Open unto the fields, and to the sky;
All bright and glittering in the smokeless air.
Never did sun more beautifully steep
In his first splendor, valley, rock, or hill;
Ne'er saw I, never felt, a calm so deep!
The river glideth at his own sweet will:
Dear God! the very houses seem asleep;
And all that mighty heart is lying still!

London, 1802

Although this sonnet is named for the place and time of its writing, its theme is really liberty. It was composed on the poet's return from France, where he had seen the results of Napoleon's rule. He invokes the spirit of Milton to arouse the English people from their indifference in the crisis faced by their neighbors.

Milton! thou should'st be living at this hour;
England hath need of thee; she is a fen°
Of stagnant waters; altar, sword, and pen,
Fireside, the heroic wealth of hall and bower,°
Have forfeited their ancient English dower　　　　5
Of inward happiness. We are selfish men;
Oh! raise us up, return to us again;
And give us manners, virtue, freedom, power.
Thy soul was like a Star, and dwelt apart;
Thou hadst a voice whose sound was like the sea;　　　10
Pure as the naked heavens, majestic, free,
So didst thou travel on life's common way,
In cheerful godliness; and yet thy heart
The lowliest duties on herself did lay.

2. *fen:* a bog. 4. *hall and bower:* a reference to Anglo-Saxon times when the hall and bower were the main rooms in the large houses of various tribes.

The World Is Too Much with Us

Wordsworth felt that man was losing the power to see the Divine in nature. This sonnet is a criticism of the new industrial civilization that was developing.

The world is too much with us; late and soon,
Getting and spending, we lay waste our powers;
Little we see in Nature that is ours;
We have given our hearts away, a sordid boon!
This sea that bares her bosom to the moon;　　　　5
The winds that will be howling at all hours,
And are upgathered now like sleeping flowers;
For this, for everything, we are out of tune;
It moves us not. — Great God! I'd rather be
A Pagan suckled in a creed outworn;　　　　10
So might I, standing on this pleasant lea,
Have glimpses that would make me less forlorn;
Have sight of Proteus° rising from the sea;
Or hear old Triton blow his wreathèd horn.

13. *Proteus* (prō′tūs) and *Triton* (trī′tŏn; line 14) were sea gods in Greek mythology.

Lines Composed a Few Miles above Tintern Abbey

The finest expression of Wordsworth's philosophy is reached in this poem and the "Ode on Intimations of Immortality" which follows. Here he meditates on what nature has meant to him over a period of years. He marks the change in his feelings from youth to manhood (he was twenty-eight when he wrote the poem) and looks forward to the future blessing and consolation that nature can bring to one's entire life. The immediate occasion of his writing the poem was a return visit to the Wye River in Monmouthshire, Wales. Tintern Abbey itself, a picturesque ruin, does not enter into the poem at all.

The decorations with this poem are nineteenth-century type ornaments, appropriate to Wordsworth's musings about nature.

Five years have passed; five summers, with the length
Of five long winters! and again I hear
These waters, rolling from their mountain springs
With a soft inland murmur. — Once again
Do I behold these steep and lofty cliffs, 5
That on a wild secluded scene impress
Thoughts of more deep seclusion; and connect
The landscape with the quiet of the sky.
The day is come when I again repose

After five years, Here, under this dark sycamore, and view 10
the poet returns These plots of cottage ground, these orchard tufts,
to the fertile Which at this season, with their unripe fruits,
river valley and Are clad in one green hue, and lose themselves
from a cliff over 'Mid groves and copses. Once again I see
the valley once These hedgerows, hardly hedgerows, little lines
again views Of sportive wood run wild: these pastoral farms,
the scene. Green to the very door; and wreaths of smoke
Sent up, in silence, from among the trees!
With some uncertain notice, as might seem
Of vagrant dwellers in the houseless woods, 20
Or of some hermit's cave, where by his fire
The hermit sits alone.

             These beauteous forms,
Through a long absence, have not been to me
As is a landscape to a blind man's eye;

The beauty of But oft, in lonely rooms, and 'mid the din 25
this scene had Of towns and cities, I have owed to them
remained with the In hours of weariness, sensations sweet,
poet during his Felt in the blood, and felt along the heart;
absence; its And passing even into my purer mind,
memory has With tranquil restoration: — feelings, too, 30
influenced him to Of unremembered pleasure: such, perhaps,
acts of kindness As have no slight or trivial influence
and love and On that best portion of a good man's life,
given to him the His little, nameless, unremembered acts
serene mood that Of kindness and of love. Nor less, I trust, 35
brings the
deepest
understanding
of life.

To them I may have owed another gift,
Of aspect more sublime; that blessed mood
In which the burthen of the mystery,
In which the heavy and the weary weight
Of all this unintelligible world,   40
Is lightened — that serene and blessed mood,
In which the affections gently lead us on,
Until, the breath of this corporeal frame°
And even the motion of our human blood
Almost suspended, we are laid asleep   45
In body, and become a living soul;
While with an eye made quiet by the power
Of harmony, and the deep power of joy,
We see into the life of things.
                                        If this
Be but a vain belief, yet, oh! how oft —   50
In darkness and amid the many shapes
Of joyless daylight; when the fretful stir
Unprofitable, and the fever of the world,

In the past he Have hung upon the beatings of my heart —
had often How oft, in spirit, have I turned to thee,   55
returned in spirit O sylvan° Wye! thou wanderer through the woods,
to the Wye, and How often has my spirit turned to thee!
he now rejoices
that this moment   And now, with gleams of half-extinguished thought,
will give him With many recognitions dim and faint,
pleasure in And somewhat of a sad perplexity,   60
future years. The picture of the mind revives again;
While here I stand, not only with the sense
Of present pleasure, but with pleasing thoughts
That in this moment there is life and food
For future years. And so I dare to hope,   65
Though changed, no doubt, from what I was when first
I came among these hills; when like a roe
I bounded o'er the mountains, by the sides
Of the deep rivers, and the lonely streams,
Wherever nature led — more like a man   70

When first he Flying from something that he dreads, than one
came here as a Who sought the thing he loved. For nature then
young man, (The coarser pleasures of my boyish days,
whatever And their glad animal movements all gone by)
appealed to his To me was all in all. — I cannot paint   75
senses enraptured What then I was. The sounding cataract
him without Haunted me like a passion; the tall rock,
stirring him to The mountain, and the deep and gloomy wood,
meditation. Their colors and their forms, were then to me
An appetite; a feeling and a love,   80
That had no need of a remoter charm,°
By thought supplied, nor any interest

---

43. *corporeal* (kôr·pō′rē·ăl) *frame:* the body. 56. *sylvan:* wooded. 81. *remoter charm:* an attraction
apart from the scene itself.

Unborrowed from the eye. That time is past,
And all its aching joys are now no more,
And all its dizzy raptures. Not for this   85
Faint I, nor mourn nor murmur; other gifts
Have followed; for such loss, I would believe,
Abundant recompense. For I have learned
To look on nature, not as in the hour
Of thoughtless youth; but hearing oftentimes   90
The still, sad music of humanity,
Nor harsh nor grating, though of ample power
To chasten and subdue. And I have felt
A presence that disturbs me with the joy

Now the poet has Of elevated thoughts; a sense sublime   95
found a divine Of something far more deeply interfused,
spirit in nature, Whose dwelling is the light of setting suns,
a spirit that he And the round ocean and the living air,
recognizes as a And the blue sky, and in the mind of man;
part of his A motion and a spirit, that impels   100
own soul.
All thinking things, all objects of all thought,
And rolls through all things. Therefore am I still
A lover of the meadows and the woods
And mountains; and of all that we behold
From this green earth; of all the mighty world   105
Of eye, and ear — both what they half create,
And what perceive; well pleased to recognize
In nature and the language of the sense,
The anchor of my purest thoughts, the nurse,
The guide, the guardian of my heart, and soul   110
Of all my moral being.
                    Nor perchance,
If I were not thus taught, should I the more
Suffer my genial° spirits to decay;
For thou art with me here upon the banks
Of this fair river; thou my dearest Friend,   115
My dear, dear Friend;° and in thy voice I catch
The language of my former heart, and read
My former pleasures in the shooting lights
Of thy wild eyes. Oh! yet a little while
May I behold in thee what I was once,   120

In his sister, he My dear, dear Sister! and this prayer I make,
sees his own Knowing that Nature never did betray
former joy in The heart that loved her; 'tis her privilege,
nature for its Through all the years of this our life, to lead
outward beauty. From joy to joy; for she can so inform   125
He trusts that The mind that is within us, so impress
she will learn a With quietness and beauty, and so feed
deeper faith in With lofty thoughts, that neither evil tongues,
nature and will Rash judgments, nor the sneers of selfish men,
be comforted by
it all her life.

113. *genial:* cheerful. 116. *dear, dear Friend:* his sister, Dorothy Wordsworth, his close companion
during his youth and for many years after his marriage. Her journals give an illuminating picture
of their life at Grasmere, their long walking tours, and their conversations with friends and visitors.

Nor greetings where no kindness is, nor all 130
The dreary intercourse of daily life,
Shall e'er prevail against us, or disturb
Our cheerful faith, that all which we behold
Is full of blessings. Therefore let the moon
Shine on thee in thy solitary walk; 135
And let the misty mountain winds be free
To blow against thee: and, in after years,
When these wild ecstasies shall be matured
Into a sober pleasure; when thy mind
Shall be a mansion for all lovely forms, 140
Thy memory be as a dwelling place
For all sweet sounds and harmonies; oh! then,
If solitude, or fear, or pain, or grief,
Should be thy portion, with what healing thoughts
Of tender joy wilt thou remember me, 145
And these my exhortations! Nor, perchance —
If I should be where I no more can hear
Thy voice, nor catch from thy wild eyes these gleams
Of past existence — wilt thou then forget
That on the banks of this delightful stream 150
We stood together; and that I, so long
A worshiper of Nature, hither came
Unwearied in that service: rather say
With warmer love — oh! with far deeper zeal
Of holier love. Nor wilt thou then forget, 155
That after many wanderings, many years
Of absence, these steep woods and lofty cliffs,
And this green pastoral landscape, were to me
More dear, both for themselves and for thy sake!

My Heart Leaps Up

Possibly Wordsworth would never have become a poet if he
had grown up in London, for he received more inspiration from
nature's beauty than from books or people. This short lyric
serves as an appropriate introduction to the ode that follows.
What wish is the poet expressing? How can a *child* be *father*
of a man?

My heart leaps up when I behold
   A rainbow in the sky.
So was it when my life began;
So is it now I am a man,
So be it when I shall grow old, 5
   Or let me die!
The child is father of the man;
And I could wish my days to be
Bound each to each by natural piety.°

9. *natural piety:* an inherent reverence for the
spirit of God that pervades all nature.

Intimations of Immortality

Emerson called this ode the greatest poem of the nineteenth century. Since the whole poem is long and difficult, only the core of it is given here. The complete title Wordsworth gave the poem helps to explain it: " Ode. Intimations of Immortality from Recollections of Early Childhood."

Wordsworth's idea of immortality implies timelessness. If a person believes in immortality, he feels not only that he will never really die but that in a sense he has always been alive — that he had an existence before his present life on this earth. Wordsworth does not " know " this existence through any scholarly or logical reasoning, but through experience, through instinct, through hints, suggestions — " intimations." The great sense of vitality, of new mysterious life, which he has observed in young children leads him to suggest that at birth our souls have come from some far, glorious place.

In the section of the poem included here, you will find this idea of immortality stated, as well as the related thought that the world soon changes our early innocence and makes us forget our divine beginning.

Our birth is but a sleep and a forgetting;
The soul that rises with us, our life's star,
   Hath had elsewhere its setting,
     And cometh from afar;
   Not in entire forgetfulness,   5
   And not in utter nakedness,
But trailing clouds of glory do we come
     From God, who is our home.
Heaven lies about us in our infancy!
Shades of the prison house° begin to close   10
     Upon the growing boy,
But he beholds the light, and whence it flows.
     He sees it in his joy;
The youth, who daily farther from the east°
   Must travel, still is Nature's priest,°   15
     And by the vision splendid
     Is on his way attended;
At length the man perceives it die away,
And fade into the light of common day.

Earth fills her lap with pleasures of her own;   20
Yearnings she hath in her own natural kind,
And, even with something of a mother's mind,
     And no unworthy aim,
   The homely nurse doth all she can
To make her foster child, her inmate man,   25
     Forget the glories he hath known,
And that imperial palace whence he came.

Behold the child among his newborn blisses,
   A six years' darling of a pygmy size!

10. *prison house:* worldly existence. 14. *east:* the beginning of his existence, as the beginning of the sun's daily journey. 15. *Nature's priest:* one who feels a spiritual unity with nature.

See, where 'mid work of his own hand he lies,   30
Fretted by sallies of his mother's kisses,
With light upon him from his father's eyes!
See, at his feet, some little plan or chart,
Some fragment from his dream of human life,
Shaped by himself with newly learnèd art;   35
    A wedding or a festival,
    A mourning or a funeral;
       And this hath now his heart,
    And unto this he frames his song;
       Then will he fit his tongue   40
To dialogues of business, love, or strife;
      But it will not be long
      Ere this be thrown aside,
      And with new joy and pride
The little actor cons another part;   45
Filling from time to time his " humorous stage "°
With all the persons, down to palsied age,
That life brings with her in her equipage;°
      As if his whole vocation
      Were endless imitation.   50

Thou little child, yet glorious in the might
Of heaven-born freedom on thy being's height,
Why with such earnest pains dost thou provoke°
The years to bring the inevitable yoke,
Thus blindly with thy blessedness at strife?   55
Full soon thy soul shall have her earthly freight,
And custom lie upon thee with a weight,
Heavy as frost, and deep almost as life!

46. *humorous stage:* a reference to a famous speech in Shakespeare's *As You Like It*, in which
life is compared to a stage and men to actors who, as their lives progress, play various parts. *Humorous* here means moody, variable. 48. *equipage:* literally, a carriage with attendants. 53. *provoke.*
to call forth (the root meaning of the word).

" NATURE'S HIGH PRIEST "

LYRICS AND SONNETS

1. From these poems select lines and phrases that bring out (1) Wordsworth's attitude toward nature, (2) his ideas about the nature of birds and flowers, and (3) his regard for human society. Is nature always as harmonious as Wordsworth pictures it? From your own knowledge, give instances of warring elements and cruelty in nature. Do you agree with Wordsworth that we can learn more from nature than from pages of the past or knowledge collected in books, as he says in " The Tables Turned "?

2. In " She Was a Phantom of Delight," show what stage of acquaintance is represented by each stanza. Tell in your own words what type of woman Mrs. Wordsworth is shown to be. What does the poet consider are the characteristics of a perfect wife?

3. The skylark has always been a favorite bird with English poets. Reread earlier poems and passages on the skylark by Shakespeare (pages 121 and 125) and Milton (page 225). What habits of the bird are emphasized in all of these passages? What situations and emotions in human life are suggested by these habits?

4. At what time of day and in what kind of weather did Wordsworth observe London in " Composed upon Westminster Bridge "? What aspects of the city especially impressed him?

5. In " London, 1802," why does Wordsworth think England needs Milton? Does he emphasize Milton's characteristics as a man or as a poet? What particular experiences in Milton's life do you think he had in mind? Are the conditions mentioned in this sonnet true of our own time and nation?

6. In " The World Is Too Much with Us," what does Wordsworth think has put us out of tune with nature? Why would he rather be an ancient pagan?

7. Study the rhyme scheme of each of Wordsworth's sonnets. Are they similar or varied? Are they like Shakespeare's or Milton's sonnets?

LINES COMPOSED A FEW MILES ABOVE TINTERN ABBEY

1. Picture the scene as it appears to Wordsworth from the high cliff on the Wye. What is the season of the year?

2. This poem shows three stages in the poet's growth. What are these stages? Find the lines that show these divisions of thought.

3. In what way can love of nature safeguard and protect one's future? Find lines that would be good to memorize as showing this feeling of security in nature.

4. What does the introduction of Dorothy Wordsworth add to the poem? What wishes and hopes does the poet express for his sister?

INTIMATIONS OF IMMORTALITY

1. Find lines that reflect Wordsworth's observation of children. How does Wordsworth's idea of the influences around the child at the beginning of his life contrast with the religious doctrine that man is sinful from birth?

2. In the last part of the " Ode " (not included here), Wordsworth discusses how man can gain strength from his mature experiences and yet retain some of the joy of his early life. How does this idea relate to the philosophy in " Tintern Abbey "?

SUGGESTIONS FOR WRITING

In connection with your study of Wordsworth, choose one of these suggestions for writing:

1. A description of some place of natural beauty with which you are familiar

2. A comparison of outdoor life with that of cities

3. A consideration of the attention given to nature by modern Americans

4. A description of your feelings on revisiting some scene after a long interval

If you feel inclined to express your ideas in poetry, so much the better.

THE GROWTH OF THE ENGLISH LANGUAGE

The Romantic Age

Have you ever read a book that was actually *printed* before the nineteenth century? If so, you have probably been aware of certain peculiarities which may have hindered your understanding. For instance, the letter *s* used to have a long line somewhat resembling the letter *f* today: the word *wise* looks like *wife*. The modern reader frequently finds himself caught with a wrong interpretation of a sentence until he learns to recognize that *s*. Then too, the paragraphs and sentences are much longer than we are accustomed to, and are sprinkled with colons and semicolons. The last word of each page is repeated at the top of the next page. Spelling is different, though Dr. Johnson's *Dictionary* so stabilized spelling that variations in the last part of the eighteenth century are not so noticeable as in books printed earlier, and capital letters are used with a freer hand than nowadays. During the late eighteenth century and first half of the nineteenth century these peculiarities were gradually abandoned and the present style definitely established.

The period covered by this chapter shows in many ways the results of attempts by previous writers and grammarians to standardize the language. Grammars were published in greater numbers than ever before and reached the public through increasing numbers of schools. The ambition to speak " correctly " took hold of the middle classes as the reading public rapidly increased.

One of the most interesting language developments of this period came in America, which now, as a free country, asserted its linguistic independence.

Certain words and phrases, originating in the United States, became known as Americanisms. Englishmen who respected their mother tongue did not use these American expressions, which they considered to be uncouth. Ironically, in America there persisted among rural people many of the pronunciations and constructions which had characterized the speech of the upper classes in England in the seventeenth century. A telling example of this is James Russell Lowell's *Biglow Papers,* in which the Yankee Horatio Biglow uses many a pronunciation which scholars have attributed to the casual colloquial style of the Restoration aristocrats.

Chief advocate of a standardized American style was Noah Webster, whose first spelling book, appearing in 1783, was quite radical in some of its suggested changes. But he became more conservative as time went on. His great work, the first real American dictionary (1828) was eclipsed by that of William Worcester (Wooster) in 1831; but later Webster's dictionary won a place that has been maintained by groups of linguists who have carried on his work long after his death.

Three innovations by Webster are noteworthy. He used American authors such as Franklin and Irving for his examples of usage, instead of confining himself to British authors. He gave preference to American cultivated pronunciation where it deviated from British, and was more lenient in allowing alternate pronunciations. He advocated certain simpler forms of spelling, some of which have become nationally accepted:

-or instead of *-our* (as in *honor*), *-er* for *-re* (as in *theater*), and no doubling of final consonants retained where there is no change of accent (as in *traveling*). The original forms prevail in England.

Meanwhile, across the sea the English purists, with their grammars based largely on Latin grammar, were wielding more and more influence. One British " authority " on language said he would use no words not used by Dryden. A curious grammar of 1823 intended for " Use of Schools and of Young Persons in General, but more especially for the Use of Soldiers, Sailors, Apprentices, and Ploughboys " must have been a comfort to all such persons, for it disapproved of irregular verbs and advocated such regular forms as *blowed, springed, sweeped,* and *throwed!*

Let us turn to the effects of Romanticism on the English language. In the first place, the Romantics believed in being guided by instincts and emotions, rather than by rules; thus they were not language purists. They believed in writing new kinds of literature, in seeking new verse forms, in finding new language to express their thoughts. Sometimes their interest in coining words led to ridiculous extremes. Southey concocted *critickasting, fuzzgig,* and *evangelizationeer!* De Quincey, far from recognizing the authority of grammarians, thought the best examples of the use of the mother tongue were to be heard by listening to mothers and young children (and he was not intending a pun). Wordsworth wanted to get away from so-called poetic language and use " the very language of men," meaning that of humble men, not pedants. He believed, however, in " purifying " that language.

Much of this was reaction against the formal style of conversation at that time. To realize the difference a hundred years can make in the ordinary daily talk of human beings, one need only read the novels of Jane Austen, who faithfully reproduced the speech of the early nineteenth century.

We are greatly indebted to the English novel for the light it throws on English speech in general. Before the rise of the novel in the eighteenth century, there were only plays and poetry to reveal to modern linguists the ordinary speech habits of bygone days. Neither of these presented a wholly natural mode of communication.

Scott's novels made an additional contribution. They served to add to the interest in Scottish dialect which Burns' poems had aroused in the late eighteenth century. The Northern dialect now attained a place in literature which it had not held since medieval times. Indeed the whole Romantic movement brought the distant past back to life, and some of the language of the past came with it. Scott made the terms of chivalry understood by the man on the street. To smaller groups of readers Gray had already introduced the old Welsh and Norse legends, and Keats echoed the overtones of Spenser. Coleridge's criticism stimulated new interest in Shakespeare. In " The Rime of the Ancient Mariner " Coleridge also uses some obsolete Old English words, as *wot* and *ween*. While such words never returned to active use, they at least returned to the reader's understanding, and have often appeared since to create an archaic atmosphere.

In general, the Romantics were a fortunate foil to the purists, for they brought back something of the freedom and vitality of Elizabethan days.

SAMUEL TAYLOR COLERIDGE
1772–1834

Everyone who knew Coleridge was fascinated by his brilliant conversation. Wordsworth once said, " The only wonderful man I ever knew was Coleridge." But good talk vanishes, and therefore much of his genius is lost to us today. However, we have abundant evidence of the man's wide-ranging mind from his lectures, critical articles, and literary remembrances. We know that in his criticism he opened a new and appreciative point of view toward Shakespeare. In poetry his reputation stands on a small group of poems, some of them only fragments, and on his masterpiece of imagination, " The Rime of the Ancient Mariner." If he had left us nothing else, this poem alone would fix his stature as a great poet.

Coleridge was the thirteenth child of a Devonshire clergyman. When his father died, he was sent at the age of ten to Christ's Hospital, a famous free school in London. Here the lonely boy withdrew into the realms of the imagination, which served him so well in his later poetry. Here, too, began his lifelong friendship with Charles Lamb, who was later to tell of how Coleridge, slovenly dressed and with an abstracted air, would " lecture " brilliantly to their schoolmates. A second great friendship was formed during college days with the poet Robert Southey, who shared Coleridge's plan of forming an ideal colony on the Susquehanna River in America. (They chose this site because the name was poetic!) This dream never came true, but the lives of the two men were inevitably bound together, for they married sisters. A third and especially stimulating friendship was with Wordsworth. The association of these two men was remarkable: each produced his best poetry during the years that they were intimate friends. Together they published *Lyrical Ballads,* that notable collection of the early poems of each.

Coleridge's weakness was lack of sustained effort. He never fulfilled the promise of his early poetry, and writing became a painful task for him. He was hampered further by his unsuccessful attempts to conquer the opium habit which he had formed while suffering from rheumatism.

Often at odds with his wife, he roamed about the Continent, while his family found a home with Southey in the Lake District. He studied German philosophy and tried journalism for a time, founding a short-lived paper called *The Watchman.* Because of his political views he was once arrested at Napoleon's orders, but he escaped disguised as a steward on an American vessel. Toward the end of his life his health weakened greatly, and during his last eighteen years he lived with a London physician. As a famed lecturer and literary lion of London, he enjoyed the homage of many younger literary men, among them Ralph Waldo Emerson.

The Rime of the Ancient Mariner

This poem is unique in the history of ballad writing. The eerie incidents of the story, the spell of the supernatural, and the sustained archaic style all contribute to make it an unforgettable poem, popular alike with young and old. The marginal gloss was written, not by the editors, but by the poet himself.

PART I

An ancient Mariner meeteth three Gallants bidden to a wedding feast and detaineth one.

It is an ancient Mariner,
And he stoppeth one of three.
" By thy long gray beard and glittering eye,
Now wherefore stopp'st thou me?

" The Bridegroom's doors are opened wide,   5
And I am next of kin;
The guests are met, the feast is set;
May'st hear the merry din."

He holds him with his skinny hand;
" There was a ship," quoth he.   10
" Hold off! unhand me, graybeard loon! "
Eftsoons° his hand dropped he.

He holds him with his glittering eye —
The Wedding Guest stood still,

The Wedding Guest is spellbound by the eye of the old seafaring man and constrained to hear his tale.

And listens like a three years' child;   15
The Mariner hath his will.

The Wedding Guest sat on a stone;
He cannot choose but hear;
And thus spake on that ancient man,
The bright-eyed Mariner.   20

12. *Eftsoons:* quickly.

" The ship was cheered, the harbor cleared,
Merrily did we drop
Below the kirk,° below the hill,
Below the lighthouse top.

The Mariner tells how the ship sailed southward with a good wind and fair weather, till it reached the Line.°

" The sun came up upon the left,   25
Out of the sea came he —
And he shone bright, and on the right
Went down into the sea.

" Higher and higher every day,
Till over the mast at noon — "   30
The Wedding Guest here beat his breast,
For he heard the loud bassoon.

The Wedding Guest heareth the bridal music; but the Mariner continueth his tale.

The bride hath paced into the hall,
Red as a rose is she;
Nodding their heads before her goes   35
The merry minstrelsy.

The Wedding Guest he beat his breast,
Yet he cannot choose but hear;
And thus spake on that ancient man,
The bright-eyed Mariner.   40

The ship driven by a storm toward the South Pole.

" And now the Storm blast came, and he
Was tyrannous and strong.
He struck with his o'ertaking wings,
And chased us south along.

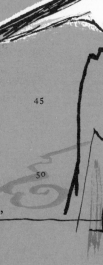

" With sloping masts and dipping prow,   45
As who pursued with yell and blow
Still treads the shadow of his foe,
And forward bends his head,
The ship drove fast, loud roared the blast,
And southward aye we fled.   50

" And now there came both mist and snow,
And it grew wondrous cold;
And ice, mast-high, came floating by,
As green as emerald.

The land of ice, and of fearful sounds, where no living thing was to be seen.

" And through the drifts° the snowy clifts°   55
Did send a dismal sheen;
Nor shapes of men nor beasts we ken° —
The ice was all between.

23. *kirk:* church. Marginal gloss: *Line:* the equator.
55. *drifts:* mist; *clifts:* icebergs. 57. *ken:* see.

" The ice was here, the ice was there,
The ice was all around;   60
It cracked and growled, and roared and howled
Like noises in a swound!°

ill a great sea
ird, called the
lbatross, came
ough the snow
fog, and was
received with
great joy and
hospitality.

" At length did cross an Albatross,
Thorough° the fog it came;
As if it had been a Christian soul,   65
We hailed it in God's name.

" It ate the food it ne'er had eat,°
And round and round it flew.
The ice did split with a thunder fit;
The helmsman steered us through!   70

And lo! the
atross proveth
a bird of good
omen, and
oweth the ship
as it returned
northward
rough fog and
floating ice.

" And a good south wind sprung up behind;
The albatross did follow,
And every day, for food or play,
Came to the mariners' hollo!

" In mist or cloud, on mast or shroud,°   75
It perched for vespers° nine;
Whiles all the night, through fog-smoke white,
Glimmered the white moonshine."

The ancient
Mariner
inhospitably
leth the pious
bird of good
omen.

" God save thee, ancient Mariner!
From the fiends, that plague thee thus! —
Why look'st thou so? "° — " With my crossbow 80
I shot the Albatross!

62. *swound:* swoon or dream. 64. *Thorough:* through.
67. *eat:* pronounced ĕt, old form of eaten. 75. *shroud:*
rope of the rigging. 76. *vespers:* evenings. 79–81. The
wedding guest says this.

PART II

" The Sun now rose upon the right,
Out of the sea came he,
Still hid in mist, and on the left   85
Went down into the sea.

" And the good south wind still blew behind,
But no sweet bird did follow,
Nor any day for food or play
Came to the mariners' hollo!   90

" And I had done a hellish thing,
And it would work 'em woe;
For all averred, I had killed the bird
That made the breeze to blow.
Ah wretch! said they, the bird to slay,   95
That made the breeze to blow!

" Nor dim nor red, like God's own head,
The glorious Sun uprist;°
Then all averred, I had killed the bird
That brought the fog and mist.   100
'Twas right, said they, such birds to slay,
That bring the fog and mist.

" The fair breeze blew, the white foam flew,
The furrow° followed free;
We were the first that ever burst   105
Into that silent sea.

" Down dropped the breeze, the sails dropped down,
'Twas sad as sad could be;
And we did speak only to break
The silence of the sea!   110

" All in a hot and copper sky,
The bloody Sun, at noon,

98. *uprist:* arose. 104. *furrow:* wake of the ship.

Right up above the mast did stand,
No bigger than the Moon.

" Day after day, day after day,   115
We stuck, nor breath nor motion;
As idle as a painted ship
Upon a painted ocean.

And the
Albatross begins
to be avenged.
" Water, water, everywhere,
And all the boards did shrink;   120
Water, water, everywhere,
Nor any drop to drink.

" The very deep did rot; O Christ!
That ever this should be!
Yea, slimy things did crawl with legs   125
Upon the slimy sea.

A spirit had
followed them:
one of the
invisible
inhabitants of
this planet,
neither departed
souls nor angels.
They are very
numerous, and
there is no
climate or element
without one or
more.
" About, about, in reel and rout°
The death fires danced at night;
The water, like a witch's oils,
Burnt green and blue and white.   130

" And some in dreams assurèd were
Of the Spirit that plagued us so;
Nine fathom deep he had followed us
From the land of mist and snow.

The shipmates,
in their sore
distress, would
fain throw the
whole guilt on
the ancient
Mariner, in sign
whereof they
hang the dead
sea bird round
his neck.
" And every tongue, through utter drought,   135
Was withered at the root;
We could not speak, no more than if
We had been choked with soot.

" Ah! welladay! what evil looks
Had I from old and young!
Instead of the cross, the Albatross
About my neck was hung.

127. *rout:* tumultuous crowd.

PART III

" There passed a weary time. Each throat
Was parched, and glazed each eye.
A weary time! a weary time!

The ancient   How glazed each weary eye,
Mariner   When looking westward, I beheld
beholdeth a sign
in the element   A something in the sky.
afar off.

" At first it seemed a little speck,
And then it seemed a mist;
It moved and moved, and took at last
A certain shape, I wist.°

" A speck, a mist, a shape, I wist!
And still it neared and neared;
As if it dodged a water sprite,
It plunged and tacked and veered.

At its nearer   " With throats unslaked, with black lips baked,
approach, it   We could nor laugh nor wail;
seemeth him to
be a ship, and at   Through utter drought all dumb we stood!
a dear ransom he   I bit my arm, I sucked the blood,   160
freeth his speech
from the bonds   And cried, A sail! A sail!
of thirst.

" With throats unslaked, with black lips baked,
Agape they heard me call;
Gramercy!° they for joy did grin,
A flash of joy.   And all at once their breath drew in,   165
As they were drinking all.

And horror   " See! see! (I cried) she tacks no more!
follows. For can   Hither to work us weal;°
it be a ship that
comes onward   Without a breeze, without a tide,
without wind or   She steadies with upright keel!   170
tide?

" The western wave was all aflame.
The day was well-nigh done!
Almost upon the western wave
Rested the broad bright Sun;
When that strange shape drove suddenly   175
Betwixt us and the Sun.

It seemeth him   " And straight the Sun was flecked with bars,
but the skeleton   (Heaven's Mother send us grace!)
of a ship.
As if through a dungeon grate he peered
With broad and burning face.   180

" Alas! (thought I, and my heart beat loud)
How fast she nears and nears!

152. *wist:* knew. 164. *Gramercy* (grá·mûr′sĭ): great thanks.
168. *work us weal:* help us.

Are those her sails that glance in the Sun,
Like restless gossameres?°

And its ribs are seen as bars on the face of the setting Sun. The Specter-Woman and her Death mate, and no other on board the skeleton ship.

" Are those her ribs through which the Sun
Did peer, as through a grate?
And is that Woman all her crew?
Is that a Death? and are there two?
Is Death that woman's mate?

Like vessel, like crew!

" Her lips were red, her looks were free,°   190
Her locks were yellow as gold.
Her skin was as white as leprosy,
The Nightmare Life-in-Death was she,
Who thicks man's blood with cold.

Death and Life-in-Death have diced for the ship's crew, and she (the latter) winneth the ancient Mariner.

" The naked hulk alongside came,   195
And the twain were casting dice;
' The game is done! I've won! I've won! '
Quoth she, and whistles thrice.

No twilight within the courts of the Sun.

" The Sun's rim dips; the stars rush out;
At one stride comes the dark;   200
With far-heard whisper, o'er the sea,
Off shot the specter bark.

At the rising of the Moon,

" We listened and looked sideways up!
Fear at my heart, as at a cup,
My lifeblood seemed to sip!   205
The stars were dim, and thick the night,
The steersman's face by his lamp gleamed white;
From the sails the dew did drip —
Till clomb° above the eastern bar
The hornèd Moon, with one bright star   210
Within the nether tip.

One after another,

" One after one, by the star-dogged Moon,
Too quick for groan or sigh,
Each turned his face with a ghastly pang,
And cursed me with his eye,   215

His shipmates drop down dead.

" Four times fifty living men,
(And I heard nor sigh nor groan)
With heavy thump, a lifeless lump,
They dropped down one by one.

But Life-in-Death begins her work on the ancient Mariner.

" The souls did from their bodies fly —   220
They fled to bliss or woe!
And every soul, it passed me by,
Like the whizz of my crossbow! "

184. *gossameres:* floating webs. Coleridge changed the spelling of *gossamers* to rhyme with *nears.* 190. *free:* wild.
209. *clomb:* climbed.

PART IV

" I fear thee, ancient Mariner!
I fear thy skinny hand!   225
And thou art long, and lank, and brown,
As is the ribbed sea sand.

" I fear thee and thy glittering eye,
And thy skinny hand, so brown." —
" Fear not, fear not, thou Wedding Guest!   230
This body dropped not down.

" Alone, alone, all, all alone,
Alone on a wide, wide sea!
And never a saint took pity on
My soul in agony.   235

" The many men, so beautiful!
And they all dead did lie;
And a thousand thousand slimy things
Lived on! and so did I.

" I looked upon the rotting sea,
And drew my eyes away;
I looked upon the rotting deck,
And there the dead men lay.

" I looked to heaven, and tried to pray;
But or° ever a prayer had gushed,   245
A wicked whisper came, and made
My heart as dry as dust.

" I closed my lids, and kept them close,
And the balls like pulses beat;
For the sky and the sea, and the sea and the sky   250
Lay like a load on my weary eye,
And the dead were at my feet.

" The cold sweat melted from their limbs,
Nor rot nor reek did they;
The look with which they looked on me   255
Had never passed away.

245. *or:* before.

In his loneliness and fixedness he yearneth toward the journeying Moon, and the stars that still sojourn, yet still move onward; and everywhere the blue sky belongs to them, and is their appointed rest, and their native country and their own natural homes — which they enter unannounced, as lords that are certainly expected; and yet there is a silent joy at their arrival.

" An orphan's curse would drag to hell
A spirit from on high;
But oh! more horrible than that
Is a curse in a dead man's eye!   260
Seven days, seven nights, I saw that curse,
And yet I could not die.

" The moving Moon went up the sky,
And nowhere did abide;
Softly she was going up,   265
And a star or two beside —

" Her beams bemocked the sultry main,°
Like April hoarfrost spread;
But where the ship's huge shadow lay,
The charmèd water burnt alway   270
A still and awful red.

" Beyond the shadow of the ship,
I watched the water snakes.
They moved in tracks of shining white,
And when they reared, the elfish light   275
Fell off in hoary flakes.

By the light of the Moon he beholdeth God's creatures of the great calm.

" Within the shadow of the ship
I watched their rich attire;
Blue, glossy green, and velvet black,
They coiled and swam, and every track   280
Was a flash of golden fire.

" Oh happy living things! no tongue
Their beauty might declare.
A spring of love gushed from my heart,
And I blessed them unaware;
Sure my kind saint took pity on me,
And I blessed them unaware.

Their beauty and their happiness.

He blesseth them in his heart.

" The selfsame moment I could pray;
And from my neck so free
The Albatross fell off, and sank
Like lead into the sea.

The spell begins to break.

267. *main:* sea.

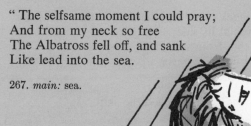

PART V

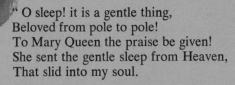

" O sleep! it is a gentle thing,
Beloved from pole to pole!
To Mary Queen the praise be given!
She sent the gentle sleep from Heaven, 295
That slid into my soul.

By grace of the
holy Mother the
ancient Mariner
is refreshed with
rain.

" The silly° buckets on the deck,
That had so long remained,
I dreamt that they were filled with dew;
And when I awoke, it rained. 300

" My lips were wet, my throat was cold,
My garments all were dank;
Sure I had drunken in my dreams,
And still my body drank.

" I moved, and could not feel my limbs; 305
I was so light — almost
I thought that I had died in sleep,
And was a blessèd ghost.

He heareth
sounds and seeth
strange sights
and commotions
in the sky and
the elements.

" And soon I heard a roaring wind.
It did not come anear; 310
But with its sound it shook the sails,
That were so thin and sere.°

" The upper air burst into life!
And a hundred fire flags sheen,°
To and fro they were hurried about! 315
And to and fro, and in and out,
The wan stars danced between.

" And the coming wind did roar more loud,
And the sails did sigh like sedge;°
And the rain poured down from one black cloud;
The Moon was at its edge. 321

" The thick black cloud was cleft, and still
The Moon was at its side;
Like waters shot from some high crag,
The lightning fell with never a jag, 325
A river steep and wide.

The bodies of
the ship's crew
are inspired, and
the ship
moves on.

" The loud wind never reached the ship,
Yet now the ship moved on!
Beneath the lightning and the Moon
The dead men gave a groan. 330

297. *silly:* empty; useless. 312. *sere:* dried up.
314. *fire flags sheen:* bright lightning flashes.
319. *sedge:* tall rushes.

" They groaned, they stirred, they all uprose,
Nor spake, nor moved their eyes;
It had been strange, even in a dream,
To have seen those dead men rise.

" The helmsman steered, the ship moved on;   335
Yet never a breeze upblew;
The mariners all 'gan work the ropes,
Where they were wont° to do;
They raised their limbs like lifeless tools —
We were a ghastly crew.   340

" The body of my brother's son
Stood by me, knee to knee:
The body and I pulled at one rope,
But he said nought to me."

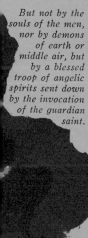

*But not by the
souls of the men,
nor by demons
of earth or
middle air, but
by a blessed
troop of angelic
spirits sent down
by the invocation
of the guardian
saint.*

" I fear thee, ancient Mariner! "   345
" Be calm, thou Wedding Guest!
'Twas not those souls that fled in pain,
Which to their corses° came again,
But a troop of spirits blest;

" For when it dawned — they dropped their arms,
And clustered round the mast;   351
Sweet sounds rose slowly through their mouths,
And from their bodies passed.

" Around, around, flew each sweet sound,
Then darted to the Sun;   355
Slowly the sounds came back again,
Now mixed, now one by one.

" Sometimes adropping from the sky
I heard the skylark sing;
Sometimes all little birds that are,   360
How they seemed to fill the sea and air
With their sweet jargoning!°

" And now 'twas like all instruments,
Now like a lonely flute;
And now it is an angel's song,   365
That makes the heavens be mute.

" It ceased; yet still the sails made on
A pleasant noise till noon,
A noise like of a hidden brook
In the leafy month of June,   370
That to the sleeping woods all night
Singeth a quiet tune.

338. *wont:* accustomed. 348. *corses:* corpses.
362. *jargoning:* confused sound.

" Till noon we quietly sailed on,
Yet never a breeze did breathe;
Slowly and smoothly went the ship,   375
Moved onward from beneath.

The lonesome
Spirit from the
South Pole
carries on the
ship as far as
the Line, in
obedience to the
angelic troop,
but still requireth
vengeance.

" Under the keel nine fathom deep,
From the land of mist and snow,
The Spirit slid; and it was he
That made the ship to go.   380
The sails at noon left off their tune,
And the ship stood still also.

" The Sun, right up above the mast,
Had fixed her to the ocean;
But in a minute she 'gan stir,   385
With a short uneasy motion —
Backward and forward half her length
With a short uneasy motion.

" Then like a pawing horse let go,
She made a sudden bound;   390
It flung the blood into my head,
And I fell down in a swound.

The Polar Spirit's
fellow demons,
the invisible
inhabitants of
the element, take
part in his
wrong; and two
of them relate,
one to the other,
that penance
long and heavy
for the ancient
Mariner hath
been accorded to
the Polar Spirit,
who returneth
southward.

" How long in that same fit I lay,
I have not to declare;
But ere my living life returned,   395
I heard, and in my soul discerned,
Two voices in the air.

" ' Is it he? ' quoth one, ' Is this the man?
By him who died on cross,
With his cruel bow he laid full low   400
The harmless Albatross.

" ' The Spirit who bideth by himself
In the land of mist and snow,
He loved the bird that loved the man
Who shot him with his bow.'   405

" The other was a softer voice,
As soft as honeydew;
Quoth he, ' The man hath penance done,
And penance more will do.'

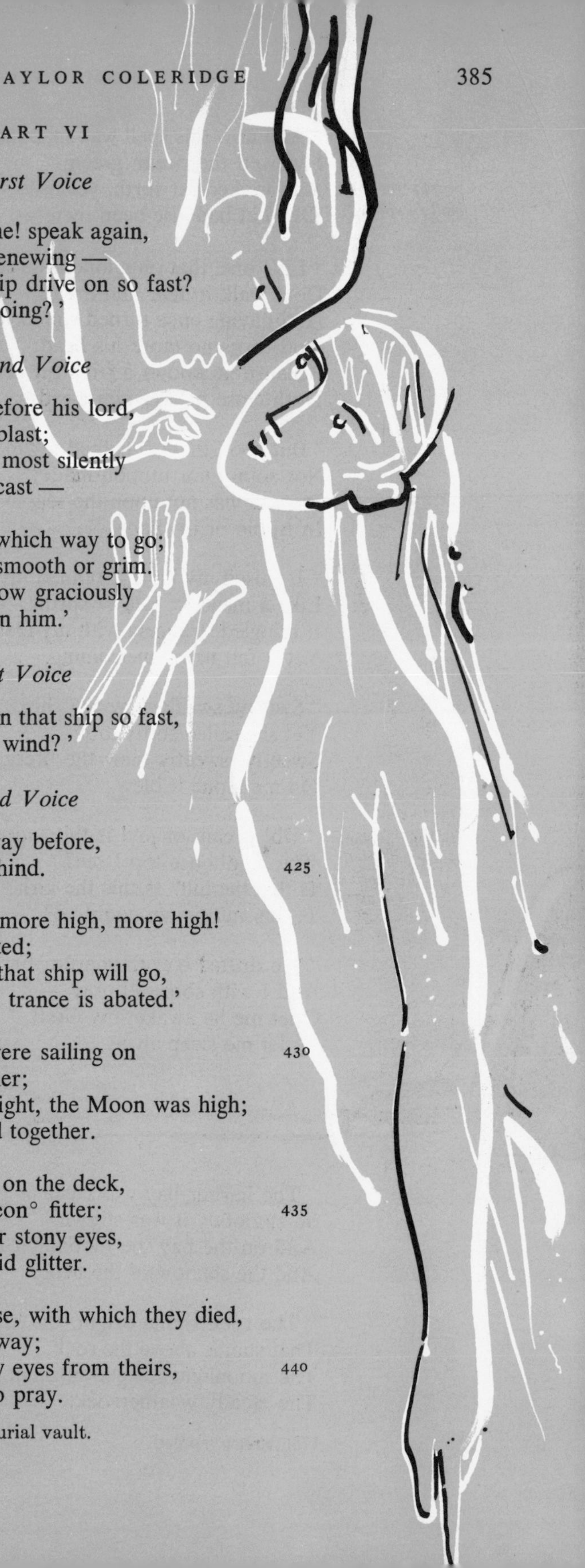

PART VI

First Voice

" ' But tell me, tell me! speak again,
Thy soft response renewing —
What makes that ship drive on so fast?
What is the ocean doing? '

Second Voice

" ' Still as a slave before his lord,
The ocean hath no blast;
His great bright eye most silently
Up to the Moon is cast —

" ' If he may know which way to go;
For she guides him smooth or grim.
See, brother, see! how graciously
She looketh down on him.'

*The Mariner
hath been cast
into a trance, for
the angelic
power causeth
the vessel to
drive northward
faster than
human life could
endure.*

First Voice

" ' But why drives on that ship so fast,
Without or wave or wind? '

Second Voice

" ' The air is cut away before,
And closes from behind.   425

" ' Fly, brother, fly! more high, more high!
Or we shall be belated;
For slow and slow that ship will go,
When the Mariner's trance is abated.'

*The supernatural
motion is
retarded ; the
Mariner awakes,
and his penance
begins anew.*

" I woke, and we were sailing on   430
As in a gentle weather;
'Twas night, calm night, the Moon was high;
The dead men stood together.

" All stood together on the deck,
For a charnel dungeon° fitter;   435
All fixed on me their stony eyes,
That in the Moon did glitter.

" The pang, the curse, with which they died,
Had never passed away;
I could not draw my eyes from theirs,   440
Nor turn them up to pray.

435. *charnel dungeon:* burial vault.

"And now this spell was snapped; once more
I viewed the ocean green,
And looked far forth, yet little saw
Of what had else been seen —   445

*The curse is
finally expiated.*

"Like one, that on a lonesome road
Doth walk in fear and dread,
And having once turned round, walks on,
And turns no more his head;
Because he knows a frightful fiend   450
Doth close behind him tread.

"But soon there breathed a wind on me,
Nor sound nor motion made;
Its path was not upon the sea,
In ripple or in shade.   455

"It raised my hair, it fanned my cheek
Like a meadow gale of spring —
It mingled strangely with my fears,
Yet it felt like a welcoming.

"Swiftly, swiftly flew the ship,   460
Yet she sailed softly too;
Sweetly, sweetly blew the breeze —
On me alone it blew.

*And the ancient
Mariner beholdeth
his native
country.*

"Oh! dream of joy! is this indeed
The lighthouse top I see?   465
Is this the hill? Is this the kirk?
Is this mine own countree?

"We drifted o'er the harbor bar,
And I with sobs did pray —
O let me be awake, my God!
Or let me sleep alway.

"The harbor bay was clear as glass,
So smoothly it was strewn!°
And on the bay the moonlight lay,
And the shadow of the Moon.   475

"The rock shone bright, the kirk no less,
That stands above the rock;
The moonlight steeped in silentness
The steady weathercock.

473. *strewn:* spread.

" And the bay was white with silent light
Till, rising from the same,
Full many shapes, that shadows were,
In crimson colors came.

*The angelic
spirits leave the
dead bodies*

" A little distance from the prow
Those crimson shadows were;   485
I turned my eyes upon the deck —
Oh, Christ, what saw I there!

" Each corse lay flat, lifeless and flat,
And, by the holy rood!°
A man all light, a seraph°-man,   490
On every corse there stood.

*And appear in
their own forms
of light.*

" This seraph band, each waved his hand;
It was a heavenly sight!
They stood as signals to the land,
Each one a lovely light;   495

" This seraph band, each waved his hand;
No voice did they impart —
No voice; but oh! the silence sank
Like music on my heart.

" But soon I heard the dash of oars,   500
I heard the Pilot's cheer;
My head was turned perforce away,
And I saw a boat appear.

" The Pilot and the Pilot's boy,
I heard them coming fast;   505
Dear Lord in Heaven! it was a joy
The dead men could not blast.

" I saw a third — I heard his voice;
It is the Hermit good!
He singeth loud his godly hymns   510
That he makes in the wood.
He'll shrieve° my soul, he'll wash away
The Albatross's blood.

489. *rood:* cross.
490. *seraph:* angel.
512. *shrieve* (shrēv): absolve from sin.

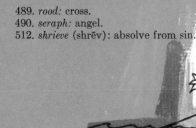

PART VII

The Hermit of the wood

" This Hermit good lives in that wood
Which slopes down to the sea.   515
How loudly his sweet voice he rears!
He loves to talk with mariners
That come from a far countree.

" He kneels at morn, and noon, and eve —
He hath a cushion plump;
It is the moss that wholly hides
The rotted old oak stump.

" The skiff boat neared; I heard them talk,
' Why, this is strange, I trow!°
Where are those lights so many and fair,   525
That signal made but now? '

" ' Strange, by my faith! ' the Hermit said —

Approacheth the ship with wonder.

' And they answered not our cheer!°
The planks looked warped! and see those sails,
How thin they are and sere!   530
I never saw aught like to them,
Unless perchance it were

" ' Brown skeletons of leaves that lag
My forest brook along,
When the ivy tod° is heavy with snow,   535
And the owlet whoops to the wolf below,
That eats the she-wolf's young.'

" ' Dear Lord! it hath a fiendish look ' —
(The Pilot made reply)
' I am afeared ' — ' Push on, push on! '   540
Said the Hermit cheerily.

" The boat came closer to the ship,
But I nor spake nor stirred;
The boat came close beneath the ship,
And straight° a sound was heard.

The ship suddenly sinketh.

" Under the water it rumbled on,
Still louder and more dread;
It reached the ship, it split the bay;
The ship went down like lead.

524. *trow* (trō): think. The rhyme suggests
that Coleridge pronounced it *trou.*
528. *cheer:* call, hail.
535. *ivy tod:* ivy bush.
545. *straight:* immediately.

*The ancient
Mariner is
saved in the
Pilot's boat.*

" Stunned by that loud and dreadful sound,   550
Which sky and ocean smote,
Like one that hath been seven days drowned
My body lay afloat;
But swift as dreams, myself I found
Within the Pilot's boat.   555

" Upon the whirl, where sank the ship,
The boat spun round and round;
And all was still, save that the hill
Was telling of the sound.

" I moved my lips — the Pilot shrieked
And fell down in a fit;
The holy Hermit raised his eyes,
And prayed where he did sit.

" I took the oars; the Pilot's boy,
Who now doth crazy go,
Laughed loud and long, and all the while
His eyes went to and fro.
' Ha! ha! ' quoth he, ' full plain I see,
The Devil knows how to row.'

" And now, all in my own countree,   570
I stood on the firm land!
The Hermit stepped forth from the boat,
And scarcely he could stand.

*The ancient
Mariner earnestly
entreateth the
Hermit to shrieve
him, and the
penance of life
falls on him.*

" ' O shrieve me, shrieve me, holy man! '
The Hermit crossed his brow.   575
' Say quick,' quoth he, ' I bid thee say —
What manner of man art thou? '

" Forthwith this frame of mine was wrenched
With a woeful agony,
Which forced me to begin my tales;   580
And then it left me free.

*And ever and
anon throughout
his future life an
agony constraineth
him to travel
from land
to land*

" Since then, at an uncertain hour,
That agony returns;
And till my ghastly tale is told,
This heart within me burns.   585

" I pass, like night, from land to land;
I have strange power of speech;
That moment that his face I see
I know the man that must hear me;
To him my tale I teach.

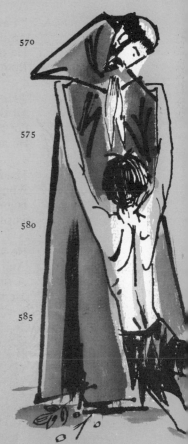

" What loud uproar bursts from that door!
The wedding guests are there;
But in the garden bower the bride
And bridemaids singing are;
And hark the little vesper bell,   595
Which biddeth me to prayer!

" O Wedding Guest! this soul hath been
Alone on a wide, wide sea;
So lonely 'twas, that God himself
Scarce seemèd there to be.   600

" O sweeter than the marriage feast,
'Tis sweeter far to me,
To walk together to the kirk
With a goodly company! —

" To walk together to the kirk,   605
And all together pray,
While each to his great Father bends,
Old men, and babes, and loving friends,
And youths and maidens gay!

And to teach by
his own example
love and reverence
to all things that
God made and
loveth.

" Farewell, farewell; but this I tell   610
To thee, thou Wedding Guest!
He prayeth well, who loveth well
Both man and bird and beast.

" He prayeth best, who loveth best
All things both great and small;   615
For the dear God who loveth us,
He made and loveth all."

The Mariner, whose eye is bright,
Whose beard with age is hoar,
Is gone; and now the Wedding Guest   620
Turned from the bridegroom's door.

He went like one that hath been stunned,
And is of sense forlorn;
A sadder and a wiser man,
He rose the morrow morn.

Kubla Khan°

This poem is but a fragment of a gorgeous oriental dream picture. In the summer of 1797, while the poet was reading in Purchas' *Pilgrimage* a description of the palace of Kubla Khan, he fell asleep and dreamed the scene described here. The fantastic quality of his dream was probably due in part to the opium which Coleridge had begun taking during the previous year. On awakening he wrote hastily until he was interrupted by a visitor; then he found that the rest was forgotten. While the main features came from the book he had been reading, the incomparable imagery and music are his.

In Xanadu° did Kubla Khan
A stately pleasure dome decree,
Where Alph,° the sacred river, ran
Through caverns measureless to man
    Down to a sunless sea.   5
So twice five miles of fertile ground
With walls and towers were girdled round;
And here were gardens bright with sinuous° rills,
Where blossomed many an incense-bearing tree;
And here were forests ancient as the hills,   10
Enfolding sunny spots of greenery.

But oh! that deep romantic chasm which slanted
Down the green hill athwart a cedarn cover!°
A savage place! as holy and enchanted
As e'er beneath a waning moon was haunted   15
By woman wailing for her demon lover!
And from this chasm, with ceaseless turmoil seething,
As if this earth in fast thick pants were breathing,
A mighty fountain momently was forced,
Amid whose swift half-intermitted burst   20
Huge fragments vaulted like rebounding hail,
Or chaffy grain beneath the thresher's flail;
And mid these dancing rocks at once and ever
It flung up momently the sacred river.
Five miles meandering with a mazy motion   25
Through wood and dale the sacred river ran,
Then reached the caverns measureless to man,
And sank in tumult to a lifeless ocean;
And mid this tumult Kubla heard from far
Ancestral voices prophesying war!   30

Title: *Kubla Khan* (kōōb′lá kän): a thirteenth-century ruler, founder of the Mongol dynasty of China. "Khan," or "cham," is equivalent to "King." The proper names in the poem, whether of real places or imaginary, help to create an atmosphere of mystery and romance. 1. *Xanadu* (zăn′á·dōō): a region of Tartary, an indefinite area in Asia and Europe. 3. *Alph:* Perhaps this name is taken from Alpheus, in classical mythology a river god who loved and pursued Arethusa until Diana changed her into a stream. Their waters united in a fountain in Sicily. 8. *sinuous* (sĭn′ū·ŭs): winding. 13. *athwart a cedarn cover:* across a thick covering of cedar trees.

The shadow of the dome of pleasure
Floated midway on the waves;
Where was heard the mingled measure
From the fountain and the caves.
It was a miracle of rare device,   35
A sunny pleasure dome with caves of ice!

A damsel with a dulcimer°
In a vision once I saw;
It was an Abyssinian maid,
And on her dulcimer she played,   40
Singing of Mount Abora.°
Could I revive within me
Her symphony and song,
To such a deep delight 'twould win me,
That with music loud and long,   45
I would build that dome in air,
That sunny dome! those caves of ice!
And all who heard should see them there,
And all should cry, Beware! Beware!
His flashing eyes, his floating hair!   50
Weave a circle round him thrice,
And close your eyes with holy dread,
For he on honeydew hath fed,
And drunk the milk of Paradise.

37. *dulcimer* (dŭl'sĭ·mēr): a musical instrument having metallic wires played with light hammers. The word means "sweet song," a phrase that well describes its light, delicate tone. 41. *Mount Abora:* not positively identified; probably Amara, a mountain in Abyssinia. On it, according to tradition, was an earthly paradise like Kubla Khan's.

IMAGINATIVE MASTERPIECES

THE RIME OF THE ANCIENT MARINER

1. You should read this poem aloud and visualize its strange scenes to appreciate fully the melodic, imaginative power of Coleridge. Point out passages in which sound, rhythm, and pictorial details support the sense.

2. Notice how abruptly the Mariner tells of the shooting of the Albatross. Is this fact significant? What explanation can you give for the Mariner's act? Why was it a "hellish" thing? Was the attitude of the Mariner's shipmates basically different from his? Find a passage to support your answer.

3. What had to die within the Mariner before he could be saved? Which lines show his clinging to evil ways — his turning to hate instead of love. Why couldn't he pray?

4. What is the significance of the word *unaware* in line 285? What does it tell you about the Mariner's salvation?

5. What supernatural elements in the story make the lesson a *fearful* one? Do you think fear is an appropriate emotion for this tale to arouse? Why?

6. What lines sum up the theme of the poem? What part does the Wedding Guest play in the poem?

7. Compare *The Rime of the Ancient Mariner* with ancient ballads.

8. Do the illustrations which accompany this poem add to its impact? Discuss them with your classmates.

KUBLA KHAN

1. In what ways is this poem like a dream? Is there any connection between lines 37–54 and the preceding ones?

2. What lines are notable for imagery and music? What effects are gained by variations in length of line? By variations in rhyme?

SUGGESTIONS FOR WRITING

Describe a dream of your own, or write a supernatural tale with a serious theme.

THE POWER OF WORDS

ARCHAIC WORDS

With the revived interest in ancient ballads, Romantic poets turned to archaic forms of language. An example is *wist* (*The Ancient Mariner*, line 152), past tense of the verb *wit*, meaning *to know*. We still have the noun *wit* in active use, but the verb remains only in a few odd forms such as the legal term *to wit* in the sense of *namely*. How does the word's meaning figure in the present-day term *unwittingly?*

Another old verb form is *I trow* (trō) meaning *I think* or *believe*. This survived into Elizabethan days and is found occasionally in Shakespeare.

Silly (line 297) has an interesting history. The original Anglo-Saxon word *saelig* meant *good* or *happy*. It came to be used as a term of endearment for frail or weak persons or children, and the meaning of the word shifted to *weak,* then to *weak-minded* or *empty-headed.* In *The Ancient Mariner* the idea of emptiness is transferred from the head to the buckets. How does our use of *silly* today show traces of all these meanings?

CHARLES LAMB 1775–1834

Unlike his friends Wordsworth and Coleridge, Charles Lamb was a product and admirer of the city. Once when he visited the Lake Poets in their beautiful countryside he confessed that he missed the chimney pots of London and was eager to return to the crowded, bustling streets.

For thirty-three years Lamb worked as an accountant in the East India House. When someone asked him once what he had written, he pointed to the long row of ledgers about his desk, and jokingly added that they were all manuscript copies of his works. This whimsical outlook on life made Lamb a great conversationalist, a choice letter writer, and a friend to be cherished. His personality lent itself perfectly to the writing of familiar essays, which were assembled at various times under the title *Essays of Elia* (ē'lĭ·à). Through these he won his immortality. Many of them are autobiographical, with fictitious names supplied for his family and friends: Elia is Lamb himself, and Cousin Bridget is his sister Mary.

Between the lines of these essays we can read some of the privations and sorrows of Lamb's life, but his difficulties never rise to the surface in the form of bitterness or complaint. Poverty sent him to the charity school of Christ's Hospital, where he met Coleridge. The recurring mental illness of his sister Mary brought real tragedy into the family. When Lamb was only twenty-one, Mary, while out of her mind, stabbed her mother to death. Under ordinary circumstances Mary would have been sent to an asylum, but because of the solemn promise of Charles to guard her she was committed to his care. For forty years his brotherly care continued, interrupted several times when Mary's malady returned and she was forced to enter an institution. In her lucid periods Mary was a charming companion, and added to the pleasure of the weekly gatherings of congenial friends around the Lamb fireplace. Together the brother and sister wrote *Tales from Shakespeare,* Charles retelling in prose for young readers the tragedies and Mary the comedies. Charles himself never married, because he feared insanity was hereditary in his family.

After Lamb received a pension from the East India House at the age of fifty, he lived in retirement for nine years. In one of his essays called "The Superannuated Man" he tells of his strange feeling, after his release from the office, that every day was Sunday. The two essays which follow are among his most famous — the first for delicate and restrained pathos, the second for its gentle philosophy about poverty and wealth, youth and age.

Dream Children

CHILDREN love to listen to stories about their elders, when *they* were children; to stretch their imagination to the conception of a traditionary great-uncle, or grandame, whom they never saw. It was in this spirit that my little ones crept about me the other evening to hear about their great-grandmother Field,[1] who lived in a great house in Norfolk (a hundred times bigger than that in which they and papa lived) which had been the scene (so at least it was generally believed in that part of the country) of the tragic incidents which they had lately become familiar with from the ballad of the " Children in the Wood." Certain it is that the whole story of the children and their cruel uncle was to be seen fairly carved out in wood upon the chimney piece of the great hall, the whole story down to the Robin Redbreasts;[2] till a foolish rich person pulled it down to set up a marble one of modern invention in its stead, with no story upon it. Here Alice put out one of her dear mother's looks, too tender to be called upbraiding.

Then I went on to say how religious and how good their great-grandmother Field was, how beloved and respected by everybody, though she was not indeed the mistress of this great house, but had only the charge of it (and yet in some respects she might be said to be the mistress of it too) committed to her by the owner, who preferred living in a newer and more fashionable mansion which he had purchased somewhere in the adjoining county; but still she lived in it in a manner as if it had been her own, and kept up the dignity of the great house in a sort while she lived, which afterward came to decay, and was nearly pulled down, and all its old ornaments stripped and carried away to the owner's other house, where they were set up, and looked as awkward as if someone were to carry away the old tombs they had seen lately at the Abbey, and stick them up in Lady C.'s tawdry gilt drawing room. Here John smiled, as much as to say, " that would be foolish indeed."

And then I told how, when she came to die, her funeral was attended by a concourse of all the poor, and some of the gentry too, of the neighborhood for many miles round, to show their respect for her memory, because she had been such a good and religious woman; so good indeed that she knew all the Psaltery[3] by heart, ay, and a great part of the Testament besides. Here little Alice spread her hands.

Then I told what a tall, upright, graceful person their great-grandmother Field once was; and how in her youth she was esteemed the best dancer — here Alice's little right foot played an involuntary movement, till, upon my looking grave, it desisted — the best dancer, I was saying, in the county, till a cruel disease, called a cancer, came, and bowed her down with pain; but it could never bend her good spirits, or make them stoop, but they were still upright, because she was so good and religious.

Then I told how she was used to sleep by herself in a lone chamber of the great lone house; and how she believed that an apparition of two infants was to be seen at midnight gliding up and down the great staircase near where she slept, but she said, " those innocents would do her no harm "; and how frightened I used to be, though in those days I had my maid to sleep with me,

[1] *great-grandmother Field:* a reference to Mary Field, Lamb's grandmother, a housekeeper at a country home in Hertfordshire.
[2] *Robin Redbreasts:* At the end of the ballad, the robins cover the bodies of the children with leaves.
[3] *Psaltery:* Psalms of David, as used in the Book of Common Prayer.

because I was never half so good or religious as she; and yet I never saw the infants. Here John expanded all his eyebrows and tried to look courageous.

Then I told how good she was to all her grandchildren, having us to the great house in the holidays, where I in particular used to spend many hours by myself, in gazing upon the old busts of the Twelve Caesars, that had been Emperors of Rome, till the old marble heads would seem to live again, or I to be turned into marble with them; how I never could be tired with roaming about that huge mansion, with its vast empty rooms, with their worn-out hangings, fluttering tapestry, and carved oaken panels, with the gilding almost rubbed out — sometimes in the spacious old-fashioned gardens, which I had almost to myself, unless when now and then a solitary gardening man would cross me — and how the nectarines and peaches hung upon the walls, without my ever offering to pluck them, because they were forbidden fruit, unless now and then — and because I had more pleasure in strolling about among the old melancholy-looking yew trees, or the firs, and picking up the red berries, and the fir apples,[1] which were good for nothing but to look at — or in lying about upon the fresh grass with all the fine garden smells around me — or basking in the orangery, till I could almost fancy myself ripening too along with the oranges and the limes in that grateful warmth — or in watching the dace that darted to and fro in the fishpond, at the bottom of the garden, with here and there a great sulky pike hanging midway down the water in silent state, as if it mocked at their impertinent friskings — I had more pleasure in these busy-idle diversions than in all the sweet flavors of peaches, nectarines, oranges, and suchlike common baits for children. Here John slyly deposited back upon the plate a bunch of grapes,

which, not unobserved by Alice, he had meditated dividing with her, and both seemed willing to relinquish them for the present as irrelevant.

Then, in somewhat a more heightened tone, I told how, though their great-grandmother Field loved all her grandchildren, yet in an especial manner she might be said to love their uncle, John L———,[2] because he was so handsome and spirited a youth, and a king to the rest of us; and, instead of moping about in solitary corners, like some of us, he would mount the most mettlesome horse he could get, when but an imp no bigger than themselves, and make it carry him half over the county in a morning, and join the hunters when there were any out — and yet he loved the old great house and gardens too, but had too much spirit to be always pent up within their boundaries — and how their uncle grew up to man's estate as brave as he was handsome, to the admiration of everybody, but of their great-grandmother Field most especially; and how he used to carry me upon his back when I was a lame-footed boy — for he was a good bit older than me — many a mile when I could not walk for pain; and how in after life he became lame-footed too, and I did not always (I fear) make allowances enough for him when he was impatient and in pain, nor remember sufficiently how considerate he had been to me when I was lame-footed; and how when he died, though he had not been dead an hour, it seemed as if he had died a great while ago, such a distance there is betwixt life and death; and how I bore his death as I thought pretty well at first, but afterward it haunted and haunted me; and though I did not cry or take it to heart as some do, and as I think he would have done if I had died, yet I missed him all day long, and

---

[1] *fir apples:* fir cones.

[2] *John L———:* John Lamb, Charles Lamb's elder brother who died shortly before this essay was written. His lameness (mentioned later) was due to an injury.

knew not till then how much I had loved him. I missed his kindness, and I missed his crossness, and wished him to be alive again, to be quarreling with him (for we quarreled sometimes) rather than not have him again, and was as uneasy without him as he, their poor uncle, must have been when the doctor took off his limb.[1] Here the children fell a-crying, and asked if their little mourning which they had on was not for uncle John, and they looked up, and prayed me not to go on about their uncle, but to tell them some stories about their pretty dead mother.

Then I told how for seven long years, in hope sometimes, sometimes in despair, yet persisting ever, I courted the fair Alice W———n;[2] and, as much as children could understand, I explained to them what coyness, and difficulty, and denial, meant in maidens — when suddenly, turning to Alice, the soul of the first Alice looked out at her eyes with such a reality of representment,[3] that I became in doubt which of them stood there before me, or whose that bright hair was; and while I stood gazing, both the children gradually grew fainter to my view, receding, and still receding, till nothing at last but two mournful features were seen in the uttermost distance, which, without speech, strangely impressed upon me the effects of speech: " We are not of Alice, nor of thee, nor are we children at all. The children of Alice call Bartrum father. We are nothing; less than nothing, and dreams. We are only what might have been, and must wait upon the tedious shores of Lethe[4] millions of ages before we have existence and a name " — and immediately awaking, I found myself quietly seated in my bachelor armchair, where I had fallen asleep, with the faithful Bridget unchanged by my side — but John L. (or James Elia) was gone forever.

Old China

In a simple, conversational style, Lamb gives free rein to his feelings in " Old China." In his love of old literature and old things and in his attitudes toward life, Lamb is a Romantic. This essay not only provides a glimpse into his life, but it also reveals a delineation of the blessings of poverty.

I HAVE an almost feminine partiality for old china. When I go to see any great house, I inquire for the china-closet, and next for the picture gallery. I cannot defend the order of preference, but by saying, that we have all some taste or other, of too ancient a date to admit of our remembering distinctly that it was an acquired one. I can call to mind the first play, and the first exhibition, that I was taken to; but I am not conscious of a time when china jars and saucers were introduced into my imagination.

I had no repugnance then — why should I now have? — to those little, lawless, azure-tinctured grotesques, that under the motion of men and women, float about, uncircumscribed by any element, in that world before perspective — a china tea-cup.

I like to see my old friends — whom distance cannot diminish — figuring up in the air (so they appear to our optics), yet on *terra firma* still — for so we must in courtesy interpret that speck of deeper blue, which the decorous artist, to prevent absurdity, had made to spring up beneath their sandals.

I love the men with women's faces, and the women, if possible, with still more womanish expressions.

---

[1] *doctor . . . limb:* an imaginary detail.

[2] *Alice W———n:* Alice Winterton, probably Ann Simmons, whom Lamb loved when he was a young man. She married a Mr. Bartrum.

[3] *representment:* portrayal, picturing.

[4] *Lethe* (lē'thē): in Greek mythology, the river of forgetfulness.

Here is a young and courtly Mandarin, handing tea to a lady from a salver — two miles off. See how distance seems to set off respect! And here the same lady, or another — for likeness is identity on tea-cups — is stepping into a little fairy boat, moored on the hither side of this calm garden river, with a dainty mincing foot, which in a right angle of incidence (as angles go in our world) must infallibly land her in the midst of a flowery mead — a furlong off on the other side of the same strange stream!

Farther on — if far or near can be predicated of their world — see horses, trees, pagodas, dancing the hays.[1]

Here — a cow and rabbit couchant, and coextensive — so objects show, seen through the lucid atmosphere of fine Cathay.[2]

I was pointing out to my cousin last evening, over our Hyson [3] (which we are old fashioned enough to drink unmixed still of an afternoon), some of these *speciosa miracula* [4] upon a set of extraordinary old blue china (a recent purchase) which we were now for the first time using; and could not help remarking how favorable circumstances had been to us of late years, that we could afford to please the eye sometimes with trifles of this sort — when a passing sentiment seemed to over-shade the brows of my companion. I am quick at detecting these summer clouds in Bridget.

" I wish the good old times would come again," she said, " when we were not quite so rich. I do not mean that I want to be poor; but there was a middle state " — so she was pleased to ramble on — " in which I am sure we were a great deal happier. A purchase is but a purchase, now that you have money enough to spare. Formerly it used to be

[1] *hays:* country dances.
[2] *Cathay:* the old name for China.
[3] *Hyson:* a kind of tea.
[4] *speciosa miracula:* Latin for "shining wonders."

a triumph. When we coveted a cheap luxury (and, O! how much ado I had to get you to consent in those times!) we were used to have a debate two or three days before, and to weigh the *for* and *against,* and think what we might spare it out of, and what saving we could hit upon, that should be an equivalent. A thing was worth buying then, when we felt the money that we paid for it.

" Do you remember the brown suit, which you made to hang upon you till all your friends cried shame upon you, it grew so threadbare — and all because of that folio Beaumont and Fletcher,[5] which you dragged home late at night from Barker's in Covent Garden? Do you remember how we eyed it for weeks before we could make up our minds to the purchase, and had not come to a determination till it was near ten o'clock of the Saturday night, when you set off from Islington, fearing you should be too late — and when the old bookseller with some grumbling opened his shop, and by the twinkling taper (for he was setting bedwards) lighted out the relic from his dusty treasures — and when

[5] *folio Beaumont and Fletcher:* the plays of Beaumont and Fletcher, Elizabethan dramatists, bound in a large book.

you lugged it home, wishing it were twice as cumbersome — and when you presented it to me — and when we were exploring the perfectness of it (*collating,* you called it) — and while I was repairing some of the loose leaves with paste, which your impatience would not suffer to be left till daybreak — was there no pleasure in being a poor man? Or can those neat black clothes which you wear now, and are so careful to keep brushed, since we have become rich and finical — give you half the honest vanity with which you flaunted it about in that over-worn suit — your old corbeau [1] — for four or five weeks longer than you should have done, to pacify your conscience for the mighty sum of fifteen — or sixteen shillings was it? — a great affair we thought it then — which you had lavished on the old folio? Now you can afford to buy any book that pleases you, but I do not see that you ever bring me home any nice old purchases now.

" When you came home with twenty apologies for laying out a less number of shilling upon that print after Lionardo, which we christened the ' Lady Blanch '; when you looked at the purchase, and thought of the money — and thought of the money, and looked again at the picture — was there no pleasure in being a poor man? Now, you have nothing to do but to walk into Colnaghi's, and buy a wilderness of Lionardos. Yet do you?

" Then, do you remember our pleasant walks to Enfield, and Potter's Bar, and Waltham, when we had a holyday — holydays and all other fun are gone now we are rich — and the little handbasket in which I used to deposit our day's fare of savory cold lamb and salad — and how you would pry about at noon-tide for some decent house, where we might go in, and produce our store — only paying for the ale that you must call for — and speculate upon the looks of the landlady, and whether she was likely to allow us a table-cloth — and wish for such another honest hostess as Izaak Walton has described many a one on the pleasant banks of the Lea, when he went a-fishing — and sometimes they would prove obliging enough, and sometimes they would look grudgingly upon us — but we had cheerful looks still for one another, and would eat our plain food savorily, scarcely grudging Piscator [2] his Trout Hall? Now — when we go out a day's pleasuring, which is seldom moreover, we *ride* part of the way — and go into a fine inn, and order the best of dinners, never debating the expense — which, after all, never has half the relish of those chance country snaps, when we were at the mercy of uncertain usage, and a precarious welcome.

" You are too proud to see a play anywhere now but in the pit. Do you remember where it was we used to sit, when we saw the battle of Hexham, and the Surrender of Calais, and Bannister and Mrs. Bland in the Children in the Wood — when we squeezed out our shillings a-piece to sit three or four times in a season in the one-shilling gallery — where you felt all the time that you ought not to have brought me — and more strongly I felt obligation to you for having brought me — and the pleasure was the better for a little shame — and when the curtain drew up, what cared we for our place in the house, or what mattered it where we were sitting, when our thoughts were with Rosalind in Arden, or with Viola at the Court of Illyria? [3] You used to say, that the gallery was the best place of all for enjoying a play socially — that the relish of such exhibitions must be in proportion to the infrequency of going — that the company we met there, not being in general readers of plays, were obliged to at-

---

[1] *corbeau:* dark greenish-black color.

[2] *Piscator:* a character in Walton's *Compleat Angler.*

[3] *Rosalind . . . Illyria:* characters and scenes in *As You Like It* and *Twelfth Night,* respectively.

tend the more, and did attend to what was going on, on the stage — because a word lost would have been a chasm, which it was impossible for them to fill up. With such reflections we consoled our pride then — and I appeal to you whether, as a woman, I met generally with less attention and accommodation than I have done since in more expensive situations in the house? The getting in indeed, and the crowding up those inconvenient staircases, was bad enough — but there was still a law of civility to woman recognized to quite as great an extent as we ever found in the other passages — and how a little difficulty overcome heightened the snug seat and the play, afterwards! Now we can only pay our money and walk in. You cannot see, you say, in the galleries now. I am sure we saw, and heard too, well enough then — but sight, and all, I think, is gone with our poverty.

" There was pleasure in eating strawberries, before they became quite common — in the first dish of peas, while they were yet dear — to have them for a nice supper, a treat. What treat can we have now? If we were to treat ourselves now — that is, to have dainties a little above our means, it would be selfish and wicked. It is the very little more that we allow ourselves beyond what the actual poor can get at, that makes what I call a treat — when two people, living together, as we have done, now and then indulge themselves in a cheap luxury, which both like; while each apologizes, and is willing to take both halves of the blame to his single share. I see no harm in people making much of themselves in that sense of the word. It may give them a hint how to make much of others. But now — what I mean by the word — we never do make much of ourselves. None but the poor can do it. I do not mean the veriest poor of all, but persons as we were, just above poverty.

" I know what you were going to say, that it is mighty pleasant at the end of the year to make all meet — and much ado we used to have every Thirty-first Night of December to account for our exceedings — many a long face did you make over your puzzled accounts, and in contriving to make out how we had spent so much — or that we had not spent so much — or that it was impossible that we should spend so much next year — and still we found our slender capital decreasing — but then, betwixt ways, and projects, and compromises of one sort or another, and talk of curtailing this charge, and doing without that for the future — and the hope that youth brings, and laughing spirits (in which you were never poor till now) we pocketed up our loss, and in conclusion, with ' lusty brimmers ' (as you used to quote it out of *hearty cheerful Mr. Cotton,* as you called him), we used to welcome in the ' coming guest.' Now we have no reckoning at all at the end of the old year — no flattering promises about the new year doing better for us."

Bridget is so sparing of her speech on most occasions, that when she gets into a rhetorical vein, I am careful how I interrupt it. I could not help, however, smiling at the phantom of wealth which her dear imagination had conjured up out of a clear income of poor —— hundred pounds a year. " It is true we were happier when we were poorer, but we were also younger, my cousin. I am afraid we must put up with the excess, for if we were to shake the superflux into the sea, we should not much mend ourselves. That we had much to struggle with, as we grew up together, we have reason to be most thankful. It strengthened, and knit our compact closer. We could never have been what we have been to each other, if we had always had the sufficiency which you now complain of. The resisting power — those natural dilations of the youthful spirit, which circumstances cannot straiten — with us are long since passed away. Competence to age is supplementary youth, a sorry supplement indeed, but I fear the best that is to be had. We must ride where we formerly walked: live better, and lie softer — and shall be wise to do so — than we had means to do in those good old days you speak of. Yet could those days return — could you and I once more walk our thirty miles a day — could Bannister and Mrs. Bland again be young, and you and I be young to see them — could the good old one-shilling gallery days return — they are dreams, my cousin, now — but could you and I at this moment, instead of this quiet argument, by our well-carpeted fireside, sitting on this luxurious sofa — be once more about, and squeezed, and elbowed by the poorest rabble of poor gallery scramblers — could I once more hear those anxious shrieks of yours — and the delicious *Thank God, we are safe,* which always followed when the topmost stair, conquered, let in the first light of the whole cheerful theater down beneath us — I know not the fathom line that ever touched a descent so deep as I would be willing to bury more wealth in than Croesus had, or the great R —— is supposed to have, to purchase it. And now do just look at that merry little Chinese waiter holding an umbrella, big enough for a bed-tester, over the head of that pretty insipid half-Madonnaish chit of a lady in that very blue summer-house."

FAMILIAR ESSAYS

DREAM CHILDREN

1. Which parts of this essay give actual facts of Lamb's life? Which are fictitious? Where does Lamb show restraint in suggesting but not bewailing some of the misfortunes of his life? How does this affect your feeling toward Lamb?

2. What details make John and Alice seem like real children?

3. What is the general tone and style of this essay? Notice how the repeated phrase, "Then I told" gives a certain rhythmic quality to the style.

4. Do you think Lamb wanted you to recognize the essay as a dream at the beginning or to be surprised when it was shown to be only a dream? Compare this essay with another famous dream, "Kubla Khan." Which seems to you to resemble more nearly an actual dream? Why?

OLD CHINA

1. Was Lamb an accurate observer?

2. What were some of the blessings of being poor, in Lamb's view? What part did youth play in their pleasures when they were poorer? In your opinion, when is poverty more intensely felt — in youth or in old age?

SUGGESTION FOR WRITING

Imitating in part Lamb's method, write an original familiar essay on conversations with dream characters, book characters, or other imaginary persons.

SIR WALTER SCOTT 1771–1832

As a boy Walter Scott was fascinated by the tales of Scotland's past told him by his mother and grandfather. In accordance with his father's wishes, young Scott studied law at the University of Edinburgh and practiced it for a time. But his interest in writing grew, and at the age of thirty-one he published a collection of old Scottish folk ballads. In the next few years this book was followed by three long original narrative poems, of which *The Lady of the Lake* is the most famous. The supposed scene of the story, Loch Katrine, with its little Ellen's Isle, the home of the heroine, marks the center of the "Scott country" to which tourists flock today.

For a time Scott was the most popular poet in England. Then he turned to prose and produced the long series of Waverley novels, the authorship of which he kept secret for several years. Many of these popular, romantic novels are widely read today. They are remarkable for their high level of excellence and for their re-creation of the past with vigor and great richness of colorful detail.

With the fortune that he reaped from these books, Scott bought Abbotsford, a handsome manor house on the Tweed River south of Edinburgh. He was made a baronet, and at Abbotsford he enjoyed the life of a medieval Scots " laird," with his faithful retainers, hunting preserves, and hearty hospitality. But the publishing house

that was to support all this grandeur failed, and Scott and his partners were confronted with a debt of more than $600,000. In this crisis he undertook to pay off the entire debt himself by writing still more novels. Though handicapped by failing health, at times writing in extreme pain, he paid over half the amount. So highly esteemed was Scott that the government sent a naval vessel to take him to the Mediterranean away from the rigors of a winter in Scotland. After cruising for about a year, he felt that death was approaching and returned to his beloved Abbotsford, where he died, in the heart of the Lowlands he had described so well.

My Native Land

The love of homeland inspired Scott to write these stirring lines in *The Lay of the Last Minstrel,* Canto VI, Stanza I.

Breathes there the man, with soul so
    dead,
Who never to himself hath said,
  This is my own, my native land!
Whose heart hath ne'er within him
    burned,   4
As home his footsteps he hath turned,
  From wandering on a foreign strand!
If such there breathe, go, mark him well;
For him no Minstrel raptures swell;
High though his titles, proud his name,
Boundless his wealth as wish can claim;
Despite those titles, power, and pelf,   11
The wretch, concentered all in self,
Living, shall forfeit fair renown,
And, doubly dying, shall go down
To the vile dust, from whence he sprung,
Unwept, unhonored, and unsung.   16

Proud Maisie

Scott, like Shakespeare, often scattered little bursts of song throughout his longer writings. This song is from the novel *The Heart of Midlothian,* Chapter XL. Observe the skill with which the little tragedy is developed in brief space. The second stanza gives the hint, the third the direct statement, the fourth interprets in a different way the lights and the singing which would normally be part of a wedding.

Proud Maisie is in the wood,
  Walking so early;
Sweet Robin sits on the bush,
  Singing so rarely.

" Tell me, thou bonny bird,   5
  When shall I marry me? "
" When six braw° gentlemen
  Kirkward° shall carry ye."

" Who makes the bridal bed,
  Birdie, say truly? "   10
" The gray-headed sexton
  That delves the grave duly.

" The glowworm o'er grave and stone
  Shall light thee steady.
The owl from the steeple sing,   15
  ' Welcome, proud lady.' "

7. *braw:* fine; smartly dressed. 8. *Kirkward:* churchward; toward the church.

Jock o' Hazeldean

" Why weep ye by the tide, ladie?
   Why weep ye by the tide?
I'll wed ye to my youngest son,
   And ye sall be his bride.
And ye sall be his bride, ladie,   5
   Sae comely to be seen " —
But aye she loot the tears down fa'°
   For Jock o' Hazeldean.

" Now let this willfu' grief be done,
   And dry that cheek so pale;   10
Young Frank is chief of Errington,
   And lord of Langley dale;
His step is first in peaceful ha',°
   His sword in battle keen " —

7. *aye . . . fa':* ever she continued to weep.
13. *ha':* hall.

But aye she loot the tears down fa'   15
   For Jock o' Hazeldean.

" A chain of gold ye sall not lack,
   Nor braid to bind your hair;
Nor mettled hound,° nor managed
   hawk,°
   Nor palfrey° fresh and fair;   20
And you, the foremost o' them a',
   Shall ride our forest queen " —
But aye she loot the tears down fa'
   For Jock o' Hazeldean.

The kirk was decked at morningtide,   25
   The tapers glimmered fair;
The priest and bridegroom wait the
   bride,
   And dame and knight are there.
They sought her baith by bower and
   ha' —
   The ladie was not seen!   30
She's o'er the Border,° and awa'
   Wi' Jock o' Hazeldean.

19. *mettled hound:* a spirited hunting dog;
managed hawk: a hawk trained for hunting.
20. *palfrey:* a horse trained for ladies. 31. *Border:* the boundary between Scotland and England. She has fled to escape pursuit.

A LOYAL SCOTSMAN

1. In " My Native Land " what is Scott's attitude toward his homeland? What question is the poet asking in the first six lines? How does he answer it?

2. Explain " doubly dying " in line 14. What is the effect of the three words in the last line?

3. In " Proud Maisie " what is the prophecy of the bird? Who are the " six braw gentlemen "? Compare this passage with the famous ninth stanza of Gray's " Elegy " (see page 325).

4. What ballad characteristics mark " Jock o' Hazeldean "? Who is the speaker in the first three stanzas? What effect is gained through the refrain?

WRITING A BALLAD

You have read and sung many ballads, old and new. Now try writing a ballad with a modern setting.

GEORGE GORDON, LORD BYRON 1788–1824

The most dashing figure among the Romantic poets, Byron was a titled lord — handsome, athletic, and courageous. Endowed with literary genius, he was acclaimed throughout Europe as the leading English poet of his day. He had a stormy, proud, sensitive disposition, and a love of personal liberty that led him to defy most of the conventions of society. His whole life was " tempest-tossed."

To understand Byron, we must consider his upbringing. His father, a spendthrift army captain, called " Mad Jack " Byron, died when the boy was three years old. His mother was emotional, unstable, and tyrannical. She resented their poverty but prized their noble ancestry. At times she overindulged her son, but she also railed at him and taunted him for his clubfoot, his one physical blemish. At the age of ten, he inherited his great-uncle's estate, Newstead Abbey. Afterward he had a good education, and at twenty-one was by birthright seated in the House of Lords.

Byron's literary career began at eighteen while he was at Cambridge. His first volume of verse was attacked and ridiculed by the influential literary quarterly *Edinburgh Review*. The indignant poet retaliated with a biting satire, " English Bards and Scotch Reviewers." His next literary venture made his name.

After two years of touring on the Continent, he produced an astounding travelogue, *Childe Harold's Pilgrimage,* written in the difficult Spenserian stanza. After its publication Byron said, " I awoke one morning to find myself famous." Later he wrote many long poems or poetic dramas with lonely, romantic, mysterious heroes, subtly suggesting portraits of himself. He was now at the height of his popularity, eclipsing even Walter Scott.

But after a few years the attitude of the public changed. Whispers of his love affairs and his unconventional behavior were increasing; his wife left him suddenly after a year of marriage. Angered by the public's censure, and unsettled as always, he left England forever. He wandered from one place to another on the Continent, and for a time joined Shelley's little group in Italy. His restless life ended with a generous and noble act. Greece was fighting to gain independence from Turkey. This conflict aroused all Byron's instincts to champion the oppressed, and he gave both his money and his entire effort to the cause. Soon after becoming an officer in the Greek army, he fell ill in a little Greek town and died of a fever at the age of thirty-six.

Byron's vigorous, colorful poems with their romantic pictures of castles and prisons, mountains and sea, make their appeal to all readers, but especially to young people. His narrative verse — the greatest since Milton — and his poetic satires like *Don Juan* make him stand out among the Romantics. Generations of readers have recognized him as a poet of energy and magnificence.

She Walks in Beauty

This lyric, which has been set to music, was inspired by the poet's first meeting with his cousin by marriage, Mrs. Wilmot. The occasion of their meeting was an evening party at which Mrs. Wilmot appeared in a black dress with spangles.

She walks in beauty, like the night
   Of cloudless climes and starry skies;
And all that's best of dark and bright
   Meet in her aspect° and her eyes:
Thus mellowed to that tender light   5
   Which heaven to gaudy day denies.

One shade the more, one ray the less,
   Had half impaired the nameless grace
Which waves in every raven tress,
   Or softly lightens o'er her face;   10
Where thoughts serenely sweet express
   How pure, how dear their dwelling place.

And on that cheek, and o'er that brow,
   So soft, so calm, so eloquent,
The smiles that win, the tints that glow,   15
   But tell of days in goodness spent,
A mind at peace with all below,
   A heart whose love is innocent!

4. *aspect:* countenance.

The Destruction of Sennacherib

Sennacherib,[1] king of Assyria in the seventh century B.C., led his army into Judea and besieged Jerusalem. According to the Bible story in II Kings 19:35–37, an angel of the Lord smote the Assyrians in camp during the night. With a mere remnant of his forces Sennacherib retreated in haste to his own country. Jerusalem was saved. Byron's portrayal of this event is both stirring and beautiful.

[1] *Sennacherib* (sĕ·năk′ĕr·ĭb) is also called the Assyrian. It was a custom in early times to identify the king by the name of the country he ruled.

The Assyrian came down like the wolf on the fold,
And his cohorts were gleaming in purple and gold;
And the sheen of their spears was like stars on the sea,
When the blue wave rolls nightly on deep Galilee.

Like the leaves of the forest when Summer is green,   5
That host with their banners at sunset were seen;
Like the leaves of the forest when Autumn hath blown,
That host on the morrow lay withered and strown.°

For the Angel of Death spread his wings on the blast,
And breathed in the face of the foe as he passed;   10
And the eyes of the sleepers waxed deadly and chill,
And their hearts but once heaved, and for ever grew still!

And there lay the steed with his nostril all wide,
But through it there rolled not the breath of his pride;
And the foam of his gasping lay white on the turf,   15
And cold as the spray of the rock-beating surf.

And there lay the rider distorted and pale,
With the dew on his brow, and the rust on his mail;
And the tents were all silent, the banners alone,
The lances unlifted, the trumpet unblown.   20

And the widows of Ashur° are loud in their wail,
And the idols are broke in the temple of Baal;°
And the might of the Gentile,° unsmote by the sword,
Hath melted like snow in the glance of the Lord!

8. *strown:* strewn, scattered. 21. *Ashur:* Assyria. 22. *Baal* (bā′ǎl): one of the Assyrian gods.
23. *Gentile:* Sennacherib; so called because he was a stranger to the Hebrew beliefs.

Stanzas Written on the Road Between Florence and Pisa°

In this poem one can almost hear the hoofbeats of the horse
Byron was riding. This meter was one of Byron's favorites, for
it conveyed the vigor and exuberance which contributed to his
great popularity as a poet.

Oh, talk not to me of a name great in story —
The days of our youth are the days of our glory;
And the myrtle and ivy of sweet two-and-twenty
Are worth all your laurels, though ever so plenty.

What are garlands and crowns to the brow that is wrinkled?   5
'Tis but a dead flower with May dew besprinkled:
Then away with all such from a head that is hoary!
What care I for the wreaths that can *only* give glory?

Title: *Pisa* (pē′zà).

Oh Fame! — if I e'er took delight in thy praises,
'Twas less for the sake of thy high-sounding phrases　　　10
Than to see the bright eyes of the dear one discover
She thought that I was not unworthy to love her.

There chiefly I sought thee, *there* only I found thee;
Her glance was the best of the rays that surround thee;
When it sparkled o'er aught that was bright in my story,　　　15
I knew it was love, and I felt it was glory.

The Prisoner of Chillon

In Switzerland in June 1816, Byron visited the castle of Chillon (shē·yôN'), where during the sixteenth century François Bonnivard, a Swiss patriot and reformer who wished to make Geneva a republic, was held as a prisoner for six years. This castle is built on a rock just off the northeastern shore of Lake Leman (now commonly called Lake Geneva), with the great peaks of the Alps towering behind it. Byron was impressed by the picturesque surroundings, the massive walls, and the underground dungeon with its romance of long-dead prisoners.

This long poem Byron wrote in two days, when he was detained in the neighborhood by a storm. Although his descriptions of the settings are exact, he did not adhere strictly to historical fact, for Bonnivard had no brothers imprisoned with him.

Byron's intense sympathy with the cause of liberty is reflected here. To him Bonnivard is not merely a single prisoner; he represents all martyrs in the onward march of freedom throughout the ages.

My hair is gray, but not with years,
　　　　Nor grew it white
　　　　In a single night,
As men's have grown from sudden fears;
My limbs are bowed, though not with toil,　　　5
　　But rusted with a vile repose,
For they have been a dungeon's spoil,
　　And mine has been the fate of those
To whom the goodly earth and air
Are banned, and barred — forbidden fare;　　　10
But this was for my father's faith
I suffered chains and courted death;
That father perished at the stake
For tenets he would not forsake;
And for the same his lineal race°　　　15
In darkness found a dwelling-place;
We were seven — who now are one,
　　Six in youth, and one in age,
Finished as they had begun,
　　Proud of Persecution's rage;　　　20

15. *lineal race:* children.

One in fire, and two in field
Their belief with blood have sealed,
Dying as their father died,
For the God their foes denied;
Three were in a dungeon cast,   25
Of whom this wreck is left the last.

There are seven pillars of Gothic° mold,
In Chillon's dungeons deep and old,
There are seven columns, massy and
    gray,
Dim with a dull imprisoned ray,   30
A sunbeam which hath lost its way
And through the crevice and the cleft
Of the thick wall is fallen and left;
Creeping o'er the floor so damp,
Like a marsh's meteor lamp.°   35
And in each pillar there is a ring,
    And in each ring there is a chain;
That iron is a cankering thing,
    For in these limbs its teeth remain,
With marks that will not wear away,   40
Till I have done with this new day,
Which now is painful to these eyes,
Which have not seen the sun to rise
For years — I cannot count them o'er,
I lost their long and heavy score   45
When my last brother drooped and died,
And I lay living by his side.

They chained us each to a column stone,
And we were three — yet, each alone.
We could not move a single pace,   50
We could not see each other's face,
But with that pale and livid light
That made us strangers in our sight.
And thus together — yet apart,
Fettered in hand, but joined in heart,   55
'Twas still some solace, in the dearth
Of the pure elements of earth,
To hearken to each other's speech,
And each turn comforter to each
With some new hope, or legend old,   60
Or song heroically bold;

27. *Gothic:* a medieval form of architecture.
Byron's description of this dungeon is exact;
the rings that attached the prisoners' chains
to the column and their footprints on the pavement are still to be seen. Byron carved his name
on one of the pillars. 35. *marsh's meteor lamp:*
the will-o'-the-wisp.

But even these at length grew cold.
Our voices took a dreary tone,
An echo of the dungeon stone,
    A grating sound, not full and free,   65
    As they of yore were wont to be;
    It might be fancy, but to me
They never sounded like our own.

I was the eldest of the three,
    And to uphold and cheer the rest   70
    I ought to do — and did my best —
And each did well in his degree.
    The youngest, whom my father loved,
Because our mother's brow was given
To him, with eyes as blue as heaven —
    For him my soul was sorely moved;
And truly might it be distressed   77
To see such bird in such a nest;
For he was beautiful as day —
    When day was beautiful to me   80
    As to young eagles, being free —
    A polar day, which will not see
A sunset till its summer's gone,°
    Its sleepless summer of long light,
The snow-clad offspring of the sun;   85
    And thus he was as pure and bright,
And in his natural spirit gay,
With tears for naught but others' ills,
And then they flowed like mountain rills,
Unless he could assuage the woe   90
Which he abhorred to view below. .

The other was as pure of mind,
But formed to combat with his kind;
Strong in his frame, and of a mood
Which 'gainst the world in war had
    stood   95
And perished in the foremost rank
    With joy° — but not in chains to pine;
His spirit withered with their clank;
    I saw it silently decline —
    And so perchance in sooth° did mine;
But yet I forced it on to cheer   101
Those relics of a home so dear.
He was a hunter of the hills,
    Had followed there the deer and wolf;

82–83. Near the poles the day lasts the
whole season. 95–97. *had stood . . . joy:* would
have stood and would have perished with joy.
100. *sooth:* truth.

To him this dungeon was a gulf,   105
And fettered feet the worst of ills.

Lake Leman lies by Chillon's walls;
A thousand feet in depth below
Its massy° waters meet and flow;
Thus much the fathom line was sent   110
From Chillon's snow-white battlement,
    Which round about the wave en-
        thralls;°
A double dungeon wall and wave
Have made — and like a living grave,
Below the surface of the lake   115
The dark vault lies wherein we lay;
We heard it ripple night and day;
    Sounding o'er our heads it knocked;
And I have felt the winter's spray
Wash through the bars when winds were
        high   120
And wanton in the happy sky;
    And then the very rock hath rocked,
    And I have felt it shake, unshocked,
Because I could have smiled to see
The death that would have set me free.

I said my nearer brother pined,   126
I said his mighty heart declined,
He loathed and put away his food;
It was not that 'twas coarse and rude,
For we were used to hunter's fare,   130
And for the like had little care.
The milk drawn from the mountain goat
Was changed for water from the moat;
Our bread was such as captives' tears
Have moistened many a thousand years,
Since man first pent his fellow men 136
Like brutes within an iron den;
But what were these to us or him?
These wasted not his heart or limb;
My brother's soul was of that mold   140
Which in a palace had grown cold,
Had his free breathing been denied
The range of the steep mountain's side;
But why delay the truth? — he died.
I saw, and could not hold his head, 145
Nor reach his dying hand — nor dead —
Though hard I strove, but strove in vain
To rend and gnash my bonds in twain.

109. *massy:* massive or heavy. 112. *enthralls:*
holds captive.

He died, and they unlocked his chain,
And scooped for him a shallow grave
Even from the cold earth of our cave.
I begged them as a boon to lay   152
His corse in dust whereon the day
Might shine — it was a foolish thought,
But then within my brain it wrought,
That even in death his free-born breast
In such a dungeon could not rest.   157
I might have spared my idle prayer —
They coldly laughed, and laid him there,
The flat and turfless earth above   160
The being we so much did love;
His empty chain above it leant,
Such murder's fitting monument!

But he, the favorite and the flower,
Most cherished since his natal hour,
His mother's image in fair face,   166
The infant love of all his race,
His martyred father's dearest thought,
My latest° care, for whom I sought
To hoard my life, that his might be 170
Less wretched now, and one day free;
He, too, who yet had held untired
A spirit natural or inspired —
He, too, was struck, and day by day
Was withered on the stalk away.   175
Oh, God! it is a fearful thing
To see the human soul take wing
In any shape, in any mood;
I've seen it rushing forth in blood;
I've seen it on the breaking ocean   180
Strive with a swol'n convulsive motion,
I've seen the sick and ghastly bed
Of sin, delirious with its dread;
But these were horrors — this was woe
Unmixed with such — but sure and slow.
He faded, and so calm and meek,   186
So softly worn, so sweetly weak,
So tearless, yet so tender — kind
And grieved for those he left behind;
With all the while a cheek whose
        bloom   190
Was as a mockery of the tomb,
Whose tints as gently sunk away
As a departing rainbow's ray;
An eye of most transparent light,
That almost made the dungeon bright;

169. *latest:* last.

And not a word of murmur, not   196
A groan o'er his untimely lot —
A little talk of better days,
A little hope my own to raise,
For I was sunk in silence — lost   200
In this last loss, of all the most;
And then the sighs he would suppress
Of fainting nature's feebleness,
More slowly drawn, grew less and less;
I listened, but I could not hear;   205
I called, for I was wild with fear;
I knew 'twas hopeless, but my dread
Would not be thus admonishèd;
I called, and thought I heard a sound —
I burst my chain with one strong bound,
And rushed to him — I found him not,
I only stirred in this black spot,   212
I only lived, *I* only drew
The accursèd breath of dungeon dew;
The last, the sole, the dearest link   215
Between me and the eternal brink,°
Which bound me to my failing race,
Was broken in this fatal place.
One on the earth, and one beneath —
My   brothers — both   had   ceased   to
      breathe.   220
I took that hand which lay so still,
Alas! my own was full as chill;
I had not strength to stir, or strive,
But felt that I was still alive —
A frantic feeling, when we know   225
That what we love shall ne'er be so.
            I know not why
            I could not die,
I had no earthly hope — but faith,
And that forbade a selfish° death.   230

What next befell me then and there
      I know not well — I never knew —
First came the loss of light, and air,
      And then of darkness too.
I had no thought, no feeling — none —
Among the stones I stood a stone,   236
And was scarce conscious what I wist,
As shrubless crags within the mist;
For all was blank, and bleak, and gray;
It was not night, it was not day;   240

216. *eternal brink:* death. 230. *selfish:* self-
inflicted. His religion forbade taking his own
life.

In connection with this poem, you should read Byron's moving " Sonnet on Chillon," which expresses in beautiful form his passionate devotion to liberty — the " Eternal Spirit of the chainless Mind." Swinburne regarded that sonnet as one of Byron's " noblest and completest poems."

It was not even in the dungeon light,
So hateful to my heavy sight,
But vacancy absorbing space,
And fixedness without a place;
There were no stars, no earth, no time,
No check,° no change, no good, no
   crime,   246
But silence, and a stirless breath
Which neither was of life nor death;
A sea of stagnant idleness,
Blind, boundless, mute, and motionless!

A light broke in upon my brain —   251
   It was the carol of a bird;
It ceased, and then it came again,
   The sweetest song ear ever heard,
And mine was thankful till my eyes   255
Ran over with the glad surprise,
And they that moment could not see
I was the mate of misery;
But then by dull degrees came back
My senses to their wonted track;   260
I saw the dungeon walls and floor
Close slowly round me as before,
I saw the glimmer of the sun
Creeping as it before had done,
But through the crevice where it came
That bird was perched, as fond and
   tame,   266
   And tamer than upon the tree;
A lovely bird, with azure wings,
And song that said a thousand things,
   And seemed to say them all for me!
I never saw its like before,   271
I ne'er shall see its likeness more;°
It seemed like me to want a mate,
But was not half so desolate,
And it was come to love me when   275

246. *No check:* no stopping or halting.
272. *more:* again.

None lived to love me so again,
And cheering from my dungeon's brink,
Had brought me back to feel and think.
I know not if it late were free,
   Or broke its cage to perch on mine,
But knowing well captivity,   281
   Sweet bird; I could not wish for thine!
Or if it were, in wingèd guise,
A visitant from Paradise;
For — Heaven forgive that thought! the
   while   285
Which made me both to weep and
   smile —
I sometimes deemed that it might be
My brother's soul come down to me;
But then at last away it flew,
And then 'twas mortal well I knew,   290
For he would never thus have flown,
And left me twice so doubly lone,
Lone as the corse within its shroud,
Lone as a solitary cloud —
   A single cloud on a sunny day,   295
While all the rest of heaven is clear,
A frown upon the atmosphere,
That hath no business to appear
   When skies are blue, and earth is gay.

A kind of change came in my fate;   300
My keepers grew compassionate;
I know not what had made them so,
They were inured to sights of woe,
But so it was — my broken chain
With links unfastened did remain,   305
And it was liberty to stride
Along my cell from side to side,
And up and down, and then athwart,
And tread it over every part;
And round the pillars one by one,   310
Returning where my walk begun,
Avoiding only, as I trod,
My brothers' graves without a sod;
For if I thought with heedless tread
My step profaned their lowly bed,   315
My breath came gaspingly and thick,
And my crushed heart fell blind and
   sick.

I made a footing in the wall,
   It was not therefrom to escape,
For I had buried one and all   320

Who loved me in a human shape;
And the whole earth would henceforth
    be
A wider prison unto me.
No child, no sire, no kin had I,
No partner in my misery;   325
I thought of this, and I was glad,
For thought of them had made me mad;
But I was curious to ascend
To my barred windows, and to bend
Once more, upon the mountains high,
The quiet of a loving eye.   331

I saw them, and they were the same,
They were not changed like me in frame;
I saw their thousand years of snow
On high — their wide long lake below,
And the blue Rhone in fullest flow;   336
I heard the torrents leap and gush
O'er channeled rock and broken bush;
I saw the white-walled distant town,
And whiter sails go skimming down;
And then there was a little isle,   341
Which in my very face did smile,
    The only one in view;
A small green isle; it seemed no more,
Scarce broader than my dungeon floor,
But in it there were three tall trees,   346
And o'er it blew the mountain breeze,
And by it there were waters flowing,
And on it there were young flowers
      growing,
    Of gentle breath and hue.   350
The fish swam by the castle wall,
And they seemed joyous each and all;
The eagle rode the rising blast,
Methought he never flew so fast
As then to me he seemed to fly;   355
And then new tears came in my eye,
And I felt troubled — and would fain°
I had not left my recent chain;
And when I did descend again,
The darkness of my dim abode   360
Fell on me as a heavy load;
It was as is a new-dug grave,
Closing o'er one we sought to save —
And yet my glance, too much op-
      pressed°
Had almost need of such a rest.   365

357. *would fain:* wished. 364. *oppressed:* that
is, with the unaccustomed sights.

It might be months, or years, or days;
    I kept no count, I took no note,
I had no hope my eyes to raise,
    And clear them of their dreary mote;
At last men came to set me free;   370
    I asked not why, and recked° not
      where;
It was at length the same to me,
Fettered or fetterless to be,
    I learned to love despair.
And thus when they appeared at last,
And all my bonds aside were cast,   376
These heavy walls to me had grown
A hermitage — and all my own,
And half I felt as they were come
To tear me from a second home;   380
With spiders I had friendship made,
And watched them in their sullen trade,
Had seen the mice by moonlight play,
And why should I feel less than they?
We were all inmates of one place,   385
And I, the monarch of each race,
Had power to kill — yet, strange to tell!
In quiet we had learned to dwell.
My very chains and I grew friends,
So much a long communion tends   390
To make us what we are — even I
Regained my freedom with a sigh.

371. *recked:* cared.

These stanzas (178–84 of Canto IV of *Childe Harold's Pilgrimage*), considered among Byron's most sublime lines, are a worthy tribute not only to the time-defying ocean but to its effects on the empires which border it. Byron observes that great empires of the past, once centers of art, religion, and law, are now ruins washed by the ever-changing yet changeless sea.

Characteristically, Byron delighted in the grand aspects of nature, such as mountain ranges and the turbulent ocean. His enduring love of the sea can be paralleled with that of both earlier and later English writers.

There is a pleasure in the pathless woods,
There is a rapture on the lonely shore,
There is society, where none intrudes,
By the deep sea, and music in its roar;
I love not man the less, but nature more,　　　5
From these our interviews, in which I steal
From all I may be, or have been before,
To mingle with the universe, and feel
What I can ne'er express, yet cannot all conceal.

Roll on, thou deep and dark blue Ocean — roll!　　　10
Ten thousand fleets sweep over thee in vain;
Man marks the earth with ruin — his control
Stops with the shore — upon the watery plain
The wrecks are all thy deed, nor doth remain
A shadow of man's ravage, save his own,°　　　15
When for a moment, like a drop of rain,
He sinks into thy depths with bubbling groan —
Without a grave, unknelled, uncoffined, and unknown.

His steps are not upon thy path — thy fields
Are not a spoil for him — thou dost arise　　　20
And shake him from thee; the vile strength he wields
For earth's destruction thou dost all despise,
Spurning him from thy bosom to the skies,
And send'st him, shivering in thy playful spray
And howling, to his gods, where haply° lies　　　25
His petty hope in some near port or bay,
And dashest him again to earth; there let him lay.°

15. *save his own:* except his own destruction (*ravage*). 25. *haply:* perhaps. 27. *lay:* Byron's note on his galley proof suggests that he made this grammatical error purposely, for the sake of the rhyme.

The armaments which thunderstrike the walls
Of rock-built cities, bidding nations quake
And monarchs tremble in their capitals,   30
The oak leviathans,° whose huge ribs make
Their clay creator° the vain title take
Of lord of thee, and arbiter of war —
These are thy toys, and as the snowy flake,
They melt into thy yeast of waves, which mar   35
Alike the Armada's° pride, or spoils of Trafalgar.°

Thy shores are empires, changed in all save thee —
Assyria, Greece, Rome, Carthage, what are they?
Thy waters washed them power while they were free,
And many a tyrant since;° their shores obey   40
The stranger, slave, or savage; their decay
Has dried up realms to deserts — not so thou,
Unchangeable save to thy wild waves' play.
Time writes no wrinkle on thine azure brow;
Such as creation's dawn beheld, thou rollest now.   45

Thou glorious mirror, where the Almighty's form
Glasses itself in tempest; in all time,
Calm or convulsed — in breeze, or gale, or storm,
Icing the pole, or in the torrid clime
Dark-heaving — boundless, endless, and sublime;   50
The image of eternity, the throne
Of the Invisible; even from out thy slime
The monsters of the deep are made; each zone
Obeys thee; thou goest forth, dread, fathomless, alone.

And I have loved thee, Ocean! and my joy   55
Of youthful sports was on thy breast to be
Borne, like thy bubbles, onward; from a boy
I wantoned with thy breakers° — they to me
Were a delight; and if the freshening sea
Made them a terror — 'twas a pleasing fear,   60
For I was as it were a child of thee,
And trusted to thy billows far and near,
And laid my hand upon thy mane — as I do here.

31. *leviathans* (lĕ·vī′à·thănz): monstrous sea animals, described
several times in the Old Testament. Here the word means huge
ships. 32. *clay creator:* man. 36. *Armada* (är·mä′dà): refers to the
defeat of the Spanish Armada in 1588. *Trafalgar* (trà·făl′gẽr,
but here must be accented on the first syllable for the meter):
Nelson's memorable victory over the French and Spanish fleets
in 1805. 39–40. The ocean brought power to these empires, and,
when they had fallen, it brought tyrants to rule them. 58. Byron
was a famous swimmer. He succeeded in swimming across the
Hellespont (now called the Dardanelles) to verify the possibility
of the Greek myth that Leander had done so to meet Hero.

POEMS OF A "GLORIOUS APOLLO"

SHORT POEMS

1. Compare "She Walks in Beauty" with "She Was a Phantom of Delight" (page 359) as to both the physical and the spiritual qualities of the women described. In the mind of each poet what constitutes a woman's chief beauty?

2. In "The Destruction of Sennacherib" note the swift panorama of pictures. How many distinct pictures can you find? What sharp contrasts are there? Read the Bible story on which the poem is based.

3. In "Stanzas Written on the Road Between Florence and Pisa," what does Byron mean by the word "glory"?

THE PRISONER OF CHILLON

1. Recount the persecution of the Bonnivard family as given in stanza one. How does this make you feel toward the prisoner at the outset? What details of the imprisonment increase this feeling?

2. Differentiate the personalities of the three brothers. Compare the speaker's emotions on the death of each brother. What lines show the climax of his despair?

3. How does Byron create a strong impression of the lapse of years? How does the bird affect the prisoner's mental state? What other creatures are in the prison?

4. What changes come about in the prisoner's condition? Can you account for the change in the keepers?

5. How does the prisoner feel when released? Do you regard this as natural or unnatural under the circumstances?

APOSTROPHE TO THE OCEAN

1. What theme unifies these stanzas into a complete poem? Compare Byron's view of nature with Wordsworth's.

2. Compare this poem with "The Seafarer" (page 36). Which gives the better picture of the sea? the stronger personal reaction? Which lines identify Byron as a romantic writer?

PERCY BYSSHE SHELLEY

1792–1822

"Tameless, and swift, and proud" wrote Shelley, describing himself as resembling the west wind. Indeed he spent much of his life struggling rebelliously against conventions of the society in which he was born. His conflict began at Eton, where the older boys goaded this gentle-looking, imaginative boy by chasing him with mud balls and branding him " Mad Shelley." It continued at Oxford, where he was expelled for writing a pamphlet " On the Necessity of Atheism." He antagonized his wealthy father by eloping at nineteen with a sixteen-year-old girl, Harriet Westbrook. A few years later he fell in love with the beautiful and talented Mary Godwin, daughter of William Godwin, whose home was a center for the political radicals and free thinkers of London. Harriet, then only twenty-one, drowned herself in despair. Shelley and Mary were then married.

Two years later they moved to Italy. Byron joined them for a time, and other English friends formed a small, congenial colony. Here in the short space of four years Shelley produced his best poetry. Not long before his thirtieth birthday, while he and two companions were crossing the Gulf of Leghorn in a small yacht, a raging storm arose and the men were drowned. When their bodies were later washed ashore, Shelley's friends burned his body on a great funeral pyre on the beach, in the manner of the ancient Greeks. Byron swam far out to sea to watch the flames that marked the end of his fellow exile.

Shelley had an innate gentleness and sweetness of disposition. He was a generous and loyal friend, an idealist who never lost faith in the power of love and good will. He was passionately devoted to the idea of personal freedom and unconcerned with the individual's responsibilities to society. He maintained that human conduct would always be good if based on sincere convictions and not bound by laws and social conventions.

Shelley was a prolific writer. His long poems — *Adonais* (an elegy on the death of Keats) and *Prometheus Unbound* — are intense pleas for freeing the human spirit from the conditions of life that enchain it. His shorter lyrics have a rhythmic beauty and ethereal quality of spirit that lift Shelley to a high pinnacle in the realm of English lyric poetry.

To Night

Swiftly walk o'er the western wave,
    Spirit of Night!
Out of the misty eastern cave,
Where, all the long and lone daylight,
Thou wovest dreams of joy and fear,   5
Which make thee terrible and dear —
    Swift be thy flight!

Wrap thy form in a mantle gray,
    Star-inwrought!°
Blind with thine hair the eyes of Day;
Kiss her until she be wearied out;   11
Then wander o'er city and sea and land,
Touching all with thine opiate wand° —
    Come, long-sought!

When I arose and saw the dawn,   15
    I sighed for thee;

When light rode high, and the dew was
    gone,
And noon lay heavy on flower and tree,
And the weary Day turned to his rest,
Lingering like an unloved guest,   20
    I sighed for thee.

Thy brother Death came, and cried,
    " Wouldst thou me? "
Thy sweet child Sleep, the filmy-eyed,
Murmured like a noontide bee,   25
" Shall I nestle near thy side?
Wouldst thou me? " — And I replied,
    " No, not thee! "

Death will come when thou art dead,
    Soon, too soon —   30
Sleep will come when thou art fled;
Of neither would I ask the boon
I ask of thee, belovèd Night —
Swift be thine approaching flight,
    Come soon, soon!   35

9. *Star-inwrought:* with stars woven into it.
13. *opiate wand:* sleep-producing power.

The Cloud

"The poet," writes Mary Godwin Shelley, "marked the cloud as it sped across the heavens, while he floated in his boat on the Thames." The cloud, personified, is speaking throughout the poem; therefore Shelley's personal emotions are not in evidence as in the poems addressed to the skylark and the west wind which follow it. These three are often grouped as Shelley's great trilogy. In all of them we feel the lift and rush of flight in an element purer than air.

I bring fresh showers for the thirsting flowers,
    From the seas and the streams;
I bear light shade for the leaves when laid
    In their noonday dreams.
From my wings are shaken the dews that waken   5
    The sweet buds every one,
When rocked to rest on their mother's breast,
    As she dances about the sun.
I wield the flail of the lashing hail,
    And whiten the green plains under,   10
And then again I dissolve it in rain,
    And laugh as I pass in thunder.

I sift the snow on the mountains below,
    And their great pines groan aghast;
And all the night 'tis my pillow white,   15
    While I sleep in the arms of the blast.
Sublime on the towers of my skyey° bowers
    Lightning my pilot sits;
In a cavern under is fettered the thunder,
    It struggles and howls at fits;   20
Over earth and ocean, with gentle motion,
    This pilot is guiding me,
Lured by the love of the genii that move
    In the depths of the purple sea;
Over the rills, and the crags, and the hills,   25
    Over the lakes and the plains,
Wherever he dream, under mountain or stream,
    The Spirit he loves remains;
And I all the while bask in Heaven's blue smile,
    Whilst he is dissolving in rains.   30

The sanguine° Sunrise, with his meteor eyes,
    And his burning plumes outspread,
Leaps on the back of my sailing rack,°
    When the morning star shines dead;
As on the jag of a mountain crag,   35
    Which an earthquake rocks and swings,
An eagle alit one moment may sit
    In the light of its golden wings.

17. *skyey* (skī′ĭ): of the sky. 31. *sanguine:* blood-red (the root meaning of the word). 33. *sailing rack:* broken clouds, floating through the air.

And when Sunset may breathe, from the lit sea beneath,
   Its ardors of rest and of love,   40
And the crimson pall of eve may fall
   From the depth of Heaven above,
With wings folded I rest, on mine airy nest,
   As still as a brooding dove.
That orbèd maiden with white fire laden,   45
   Whom mortals call the Moon,
Glides glimmering o'er my fleecelike floor,
   By the midnight breezes strewn;
And wherever the beat of her unseen feet,
   Which only the angels hear,   50
May have broken the woof of my tent's thin roof,
   The stars peep behind her and peer;
And I laugh to see them whirl and flee,
   Like a swarm of golden bees,
When I widen the rent in my wind-built tent,   55
   Till the calm rivers, lakes, and seas,
Like strips of the sky fallen through me on high,
   Are each paved with the moon and these.

I bind the Sun's throne with a burning zone,°
   And the Moon's with a girdle of pearl;   60
The volcanoes are dim, and the stars reel and swim
   When the whirlwinds my banner unfurl.
From cape to cape, with a bridgelike shape,
   Over a torrent sea,
Sunbeam-proof, I hang like a roof —   65
   The mountains its columns be.
The triumphal arch through which I march
   With hurricane, fire, and snow,
When the Powers of the air are chained to my chair,
   Is the million-colored bow;   70
The sphere fire° above its soft colors wove,
   While the moist Earth was laughing below.

I am the daughter of Earth and Water,
   And the nursling of the Sky;
I pass through the pores of the ocean and shores,   75
   I change, but I cannot die.
For after the rain when with never a stain
   The pavilion of Heaven is bare,
And the winds and sunbeams with their convex gleams
   Build up the blue dome of air,   80
I silently laugh at my own cenotaph,°
   And out of the caverns of rain,
Like a child from the womb, like a ghost from the tomb,
   I arise and unbuild it again.

59. *zone:* girdle, belt. 71. *sphere fire:* the light of the heavens.
81. *cenotaph:* a monument erected in honor of the dead buried
elsewhere; here, the cloud's cenotaph is the "blue dome of air."

To a Skylark

Of the origin of this poem, Mrs. Shelley wrote: " It was a
beautiful summer evening, while wandering along the lanes
whose myrtle hedges were the bowers of the fireflies, that
we heard the caroling of the skylark which inspired one of
the most beautiful of his poems." Notice how the verse
form suggests the motion of the bird. The first four short
lines represent the swift upward dart of the bird; the fifth
long line corresponds to the long, steady, graceful sweep
of the soaring bird.

Hail to thee, blithe spirit!
   Bird thou never wert,
That from heaven, or near it,
   Pourest thy full heart
In profuse strains of unpremeditated art.

Higher still and higher
   From the earth thou springest
Like a cloud of fire;
   The blue deep thou wingest,
And singing still dost soar, and soaring ever singest.   10

In the golden lightning
   Of the sunken sun,
O'er which clouds are bright'ning,
   Thou dost float and run;
Like an unbodied joy whose race is just begun.   15

The pale purple even°
   Melts around thy flight;
Like a star of heaven
   In the broad daylight
Thou art unseen, but yet I hear thy shrill delight,   20

Keen as are the arrows
   Of that silver sphere,°
Whose intense lamp narrows

16. *even:* evening. 22. *silver sphere:* the morning star.

In the white dawn clear,
Until we hardly see, we feel that it is there.   25

All the earth and air
    With thy voice is loud,
As, when night is bare,
    From one lonely cloud
The moon rains out her beams, and heaven is overflowed.   30

What thou art we know not;
    What is most like thee?
From rainbow clouds there flow not
    Drops so bright to see,
As from thy presence showers a rain of melody.   35

Like a poet hidden
    In the light of thought,
Singing hymns unbidden,
    Till the world is wrought
To sympathy with hopes and fears it heeded not;   40

Like a high-born maiden
    In a palace tower,
Soothing her love-laden
    Soul in secret hour
With music sweet as love, which overflows her bower;   45

Like a glowworm golden
    In a dell of dew,
Scattering unbeholden
    Its aerial hue
Among the flowers and grass, which screen it from the view;   50

Like a rose embowered
    In its own green leaves,
By warm winds deflowered,
    Till the scent it gives
Makes faint with too much sweet those heavy-wingèd thieves;   55

Sound of vernal showers
    On the twinkling grass,
Rain-awakened flowers,
    All that ever was
Joyous, and clear, and fresh, thy music doth surpass.   60

Teach us, sprite or bird,
    What sweet thoughts are thine;
I have never heard
    Praise of love or wine
That panted forth a flood of rapture so divine.

Chorus Hymeneal,°
   Or triumphal chant,
Matched with thine, would be all
   But an empty vaunt,
A thing wherein we feel there is some hidden want.   70

What objects are the fountains°
   Of thy happy strain?
What fields, or waves, or mountains?
   What shapes of sky or plain?
What love of thine own kind? what ignorance of pain?   75

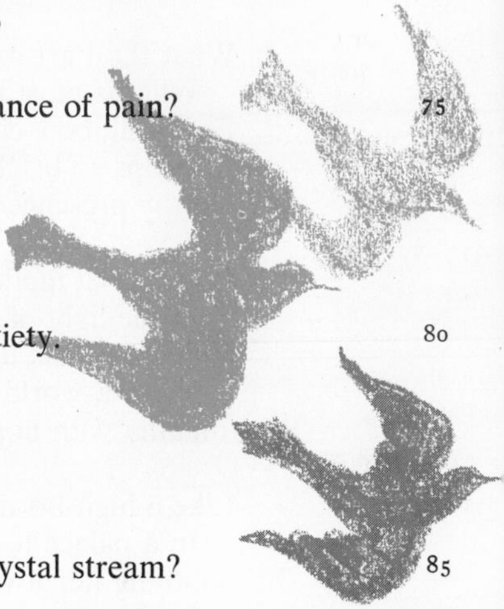

With thy clear keen joyance
   Languor cannot be;
Shadow of annoyance
   Never came near thee;
Thou lovest, but ne'er knew love's sad satiety.   80

Waking or asleep,
   Thou of death must deem°
Things more true and deep
   Than we mortals dream,
Or how could thy notes flow in such a crystal stream?   85

We look before and after,
   And pine for what is not;
Our sincerest laughter
   With some pain is fraught;
Our sweetest songs are those that tell of saddest thought.   90

Yet if° we could scorn
   Hate, and pride, and fear;
If we were things born
   Not to shed a tear,
I know not how thy joy we ever should come near.   95

Better than all measures
   Of delightful sound
Better than all treasures
   That in books are found,
Thy skill to poet were,° thou scorner of the ground!   100

Teach me half the gladness
   That thy brain must know,
Such harmonious madness
   From my lips would flow,
The world should listen then, as I am listening now.   105

66. *Chorus Hymeneal* (hī′mĕ·nē′ăl): marriage chant. Hymen was the Greek god of marriage.
71. *fountains:* sources, or inspiration. 82. *deem:* know. 91. *if:* even if. 100. *were:* would be.

Ode to the West Wind

The construction of this poem is beautifully precise. Each of the first three parts invokes the powerful west wind, which in the first part is shown driving the leaves, in the second the clouds, and in the third the waves. In the fourth part the poet imagines himself as each of these three playthings of the wind and calls for inspiration in his personal despondency. In the fifth, he prays that his ideas be given the power of the wind, and spread throughout the world. The oft-quoted last line is an expression of hope.

I

O wild West Wind, thou breath of Autumn's being,
Thou, from whose unseen presence the leaves dead
Are driven, like ghosts from an enchanter fleeing,

Yellow, and black, and pale, and hectic red,
Pestilence-stricken multitudes: O thou,   5
Who chariotest to their dark wintry bed

The wingèd seeds, where they lie cold and low,
Each like a corpse within its grave, until
Thine azure sister of the Spring° shall blow

Her clarion° o'er the dreaming earth, and fill   10
(Driving sweet buds like flocks to feed in air)
With living hues and odors plain and hill;

Wild Spirit, which art moving everywhere;
Destroyer and preserver; hear, Oh, hear!

II

Thou on whose stream, 'mid the steep sky's commotion,
Loose clouds like earth's decaying leaves are shed,   16
Shook from the tangled boughs of Heaven and Ocean,

Angels° of rain and lightning; there are spread
On the blue surface of thine airy surge,
Like the bright hair uplifted from the head   20

Of some fierce Maenad,° even from the dim verge
Of the horizon to the zenith's° height,
The locks of the approaching storm. Thou dirge

9. *sister of the Spring:* south wind. 10. *clarion:* a trumpet with a pure, clear tone. 18. *Angels:* messengers (from the Greek *angelos*). 21. *Maenad* (mē'năd): a priestess of Bacchus, *fierce* because she engaged in wild and frenzied ceremonies in honor of the god. 22. *zenith:* the point in the heavens directly overhead.

Of the dying year, to which this closing night
Will be the dome of a vast sepulcher,   25
Vaulted with all thy congregated might

Of vapors, from whose solid atmosphere
Black rain, and fire, and hail will burst: Oh, hear!

III

Thou who didst waken from his summer dreams
The blue Mediterranean, where he lay,   30
Lulled by the coil of his crystalline streams,

Beside a pumice° isle in Baiae's bay,°
And saw in sleep old palaces and towers
Quivering within the wave's intenser day,

All overgrown with azure moss and flowers   35
So sweet, the sense faints picturing them! Thou
For whose path the Atlantic's level powers°

Cleave themselves into chasms, while far below
The sea blooms and the oozy woods which wear
The sapless foliage of the ocean, know   40

Thy voice and suddenly grow gray with fear,
And tremble and despoil themselves: Oh, hear!

IV

If I were a dead leaf thou mightest bear;
If I were a swift cloud to fly with thee;
A wave to pant beneath thy power, and share   45

The impulse of thy strength, only less free
Than thou, O uncontrollable! If even
I were as in my boyhood, and could be

The comrade of thy wanderings over heaven,
As then, when to outstrip thy skyey speed   50
Scarce seemed a vision;° I would ne'er have striven

As thus with thee in prayer in my sore need.
Oh, lift me as a wave, a leaf, a cloud!
I fall upon the thorns of life! I bleed!

A heavy weight of hours has chained and bowed   55
One too like thee: tameless, and swift, and proud.

32. *pumice:* formed from lava; *Baiae's* (bä′yäz) *bay,* near Naples,
is close to nearly extinct volcanoes which still rumble and erupt
occasionally. The area was famous as a resort of the ancient
Romans. 37. *level powers:* surfaces. 51. *vision:* that is, something
impossible to attain.

V

Make me thy lyre, even as the forest is;
What if my leaves are falling like its own!
The tumult of thy mighty harmonies

Will take from both a deep, autumnal tone,   60
Sweet though in sadness. Be thou, spirit fierce,
My spirit! Be thou me, impetuous one!

Drive my dead thoughts over the universe
Like withered leaves to quicken a new birth!
And, by the incantation of this verse,   65

Scatter, as from an unextinguished hearth
Ashes and sparks, my words among mankind!
Be through my lips to unawakened earth

The trumpet of a prophecy! O wind,
If Winter comes, can Spring be far behind?   70

Ozymandias°

In reading an ancient Greek historian, Shelley had learned
of the gigantic statue described here. In this poem, he expresses two ideas that occur frequently in his verse — the
vainglory of kings and the inconstancy of life.

I met a traveler from an antique land
Who said: " Two vast and trunkless legs of stone
Stand in the desert. . . . Near them, on the sand,
Half sunk, a shattered visage lies, whose frown,
And wrinkled lip, and sneer of cold command   5
Tell that its sculptor well those passions read
Which yet survive, stamped on these lifeless things,
The hand that mocked them, and the heart that fed;°
And on the pedestal these words appear;
' My name is Ozymandias, king of kings;   10
Look on my works, ye Mighty, and despair! '
Nothing beside remains. Round the decay
Of that colossal wreck, boundless and bare
The lone and level sands stretch far away."

Title: *Ozymandias* (ŏz′ĭ·măn′dĭ·ăs): a corruption of a name of Rameses II (1324?–1258? B.C.),
a famous Egyptian king, a great builder of palaces and temples. Many statues of him are found in
Egypt; the one referred to here is probably near Thebes. 6–8. These lines mean that the passions
of the king, as shown on his face by the sculptor, have survived both the hand of the sculptor himself, who imitated ("mocked") them, and the heart of the king, which caused ("fed") those passions.

A Lament

This poem and the one that follows were written in the last two years of Shelley's life and published in *Posthumous Poems* (1824), two years after his death. Both of them suggest the troubled and tempestuous spirit of Shelley's last days. He seems even to have had a premonition of his early tragic death.

O world! O life! O time!
On whose last steps° I climb,
  Trembling at that where I had stood before;
When will return the glory of your prime?°
No more — oh, nevermore!   5
Out of the day and night
A joy has taken flight;
  Fresh spring, and summer, and winter hoar,
Move my faint heart with grief, but with delight
No more — oh, nevermore!   10

2. *last steps:* The poet compares life to a stairway, whose end he is nearing. 4. *prime:* the beginning of life.

A Dirge

Rough wind, that moanest loud
  Grief too sad for song;
Wild wind, when sullen cloud
  Knells all the night long;
Sad storm, whose tears are vain,   5
Bare woods, whose branches strain,
Deep caves and dreary main,
  Wail, for the world's wrong!

SHELLEY'S POETRY

TO A SKYLARK

1. The thought divisions of this poem are indicated by the following outline: (1) lines 1–30, where and when the bird's song is heard; (2) lines 31–60, description of the bird's song by a series of comparisons; (3) lines 61–75, the sources and nature of its song; (4) lines 76–105, the disparity between the lark's joy and man's troubled state. What does each stanza contribute to these main ideas?

2. To what different things is the skylark compared? What quality do all these things have in common with the bird? Why are they less lovely to the poet than the bird is?

3. Compare this poem with Wordsworth's poems on the skylark (page 360) for similar words used to describe the effect of the bird's song on the hearer. What is the effect which each poet emphasizes? In what way is Shelley's reaction to the skylark's song different from that of Shakespeare, of Milton, and of Wordsworth?

4. Is it true that " our sweetest songs are those that tell of saddest thought "? Give some examples in both music and poetry. Are the greatest works of literature tragedies?

ODE TO THE WEST WIND

1. See the last paragraph in the section *Reading Lyric Poetry* on page 427.

2. How well did Shelley understand his own nature? What incidents in his life illustrate the adjectives by which he describes himself in this poem?

3. Study carefully the interlocking rhyme scheme. Interlocking means that the middle rhyme of each triplet becomes the first and third rhyme of the next triplet: a-b-a, b-c-b, c-d-c, d-e-d, e-e. This is an old form called *terza rima,* derived from Italian poetry. Chaucer also used it. The couplet at the end of each part is Shelley's addition to the old form.

4. You may recall that an ode is a lyric poem characterized by noble feeling and dignity of style. What distinguishes this ode in tone and form from Wordsworth's " Intimations of Immortality "?

SONNET AND LYRICS

1. Compare Shelley's " To Night " with Longfellow's " Hymn to the Night," written several years later. What mood is common to both poems?

2. What in the situation of the statue of Ozymandias would especially appeal to a man of Shelley's temperament? Wherein lies the irony of the inscription?

3. Write out the rhyme scheme of the sonnet to discover how unusual it is. Even in this restricted form Shelley showed his love of freedom.

4. Which of the two posthumous lyrics seems to you the more despairing? Why? What lines seem to foretell Shelley's death?

THE POWER OF WORDS

SIMILES

In the "Ode to the West Wind" Shelley's rich imagination weaves simile after simile into an intricate pattern of figurative language. In the first stanza, the autumn wind is compared to an enchanter and the dried leaves to ghosts which he drives before him. (Aside from its importance to the meter, why is *ghosts* a more suitable word here than any of its synonyms?) Two lines down, the leaves are called *pestilence-stricken multitudes*. Then the seeds driven into the ground are called *corpses*. So far, everything contributes to the idea of death. But with the coming of spring the whole metaphor shifts its emphasis to new life. What may be the purpose of a clarion? Why are buds likened to flocks?

Make a similar analysis of the rest of the poem to show how the figures interlock and reinforce the alternately despondent and hopeful mood of the poet. What else in nature besides the West Wind is personified (given human attributes or form)?

READING LYRIC POETRY

This is not the first time you have read lyric poetry. In fact, you have been hearing, reading, and singing lyric poems all your life. Children have a keen sense of rhythm, and for them simple verses are a natural form of expression. As man matures and becomes more complex in personality, the lyric poetry through which he speaks (or sings) also becomes more complex — more subtly imaginative in its content, more varied in its rhythms, more intricate in its language. The Romantic Age brought English lyric poetry to a climax of richness and beauty. In its highest forms, however, lyric poetry may sometimes baffle the reader by its difficulties, so it may be well to consider here some of the ways to approach a lyric poem.

APPROACHING THE LYRIC

You already know, of course, that a lyric poem does not tell a story about people as a narrative or dramatic poem does. We are not, then, looking for a sequence of events or analyzing character. We are dealing entirely with more intangible things — thoughts, emotions, fine shades of meaning. One of the first requisites in approaching a lyric poem is to open our minds willingly to the thoughts of another person, and be ready to identify ourselves as far as possible with that person's experience. A striking example of this "identification" can be found in "The Cloud." In reading this poem you must for a moment cease to be a mortal on earth looking *up* at a cloud. You must, instead, become that cloud, free in the heavens, looking *down* on the earth. Then only can you appreciate the cloud's song as Shelley sings it. Similarly, you may recall that Robert Burns' lyrics offer many good examples of how a poet utters the thoughts of different kinds of people — an old wife, a gentle lover, Bruce addressing his army. A good lyric poem gives the reader an idea of the type of person speaking or the circumstances that called forth the poem. Sometimes these may not be obvious on first reading, but usually they become clear on a careful rereading.

Another requisite for gaining the full value of a lyric poem is first to hear or read it as a whole. Detailed study — by looking up words in a dictionary or by trying to understand each sentence fully before continuing — should come *after* the first reading. Let the poem have a chance to make a total first impression on you. Don't reject a poem or become disturbed if you do not completely understand it on the first reading. A good poem must often be lived with for a while before its meaning is fully revealed to you.

METER AND ALLITERATION

The *sound* of any poem, of course, should never be overlooked. In a lyric poem the metrical form is especially important, because it contributes greatly to the total effect, matching both mood and meaning. Reading lyric poetry with the eye alone is almost like trying to read sheet music with the eye alone. A favorable approach, then, is to read aloud. In " The Cloud " consider the unusual meter and the internal rhymes in alternate lines. What swing and gusto these give to the constantly shifting life of the cloud! The whole poem moves with the speed of racing clouds on a windy day:

" The triumphal arch through which I march
    With hurricane, fire, and snow,
When the Powers of the air are chained to my chair,
    Is the million-colored bow . . ."

In the next Shelley poem, " To a Skylark," an entirely different tempo is given by the meter. How do the first four lines suggest the swift upward flight of the bird? How does the fifth line suggest a different kind of motion?

Lyric poetry is a broad term including everything from deeply thoughtful philosophic poems like Wordsworth's odes to flippant little songs like those of the Cavalier poets. It is fortunate that English poetry has such varied meters to voice these different moods. The dignified blank verse of " Tintern Abbey " establishes a mood of serious meditation. Not all lyrics create definite musical effects, yet some employ a pronounced rhythmic meter. The " feet " of " The Destruction of Sennacherib " gallop; those of " Flow Gently, Sweet Afton " tiptoe.

The Romantic poets were eagerly searching for new meters to produce new emotional effects. The nineteenth century is therefore the best period in which to study different verse forms. The eighteenth century was bound by the classical convention of the rhymed couplet, while the twentieth tends to break away into free verse. You have now had enough experience in meters to build up your own list of metrical forms with illustrations from the poetry in this volume. Such a project would be valuable to continue through the rest of this year's study.

Other devices besides meter add to the sound-value of a poem. One of the oldest in English poetry is alliteration, harking back to Anglo-Saxon days. In " The Cloud " not a stanza is without this effec-tive repetition of initial sounds. To see how alliteration adds to the smoothness and swiftness of a line, try substituting non-alliterative words for those with a common consonant in these lines:

" I sift the snow on the mountains below,
    And their great pines groan aghast "

or

" The stars peep behind her and peer . . ."

IMAGERY

Probably the most important single element in reading a lyric poem is to grasp its imaginative quality, which, along with meter, distinguishes a poem from a piece of prose that might express the same thought. The imagination takes fire largely from the imagery of a poem. In " The Cloud " notice how much the word *flail* accomplishes toward an instantaneous picture in the line " I wield the flail of the lashing hail." How superbly the cloud is personified in the phrase, " And laugh as I pass in thunder." Again, we have a sense of great height in " Sublime on the towers of my skyey bowers, Lightning my pilot sits," or an impression of calm beauty in the following lines:

" That orbèd maiden with white fire laden,
    Whom mortals call the Moon,
Glides glimmering o'er my fleecelike floor,
    By the midnight breezes strewn."

Imagery results from not only personification (assigning human feelings or actions to inanimate things) but also metaphor, or comparisons. The cloud's surface is called a " tent's thin roof "; the stars are said to move " like a swarm of golden bees." Look at the poem closely to discover how many other examples of personification and metaphor you can find. The lyric poet often wishes to convey abstract emotions and thoughts; to do this, he uses concrete images.

DESIGN OF THE POEM

There remains one more point to consider — the general design of the poem. A poet does not just string together a series of imaginative lines in a chosen meter; he writes a poem to express something. You may not associate anything as prosaic as an outline with lyric poetry, but you may be sure that a good poet has in mind something like an outline — a definite progression of ideas to a conclusion. This is evident in the three stanzas of Wordsworth's " She Was a Phantom of Delight " (page 359). A sonnet may show its design in a clear division between octave and sestet.

How does the design of thoughts work out in " The Cloud "? First we see the action of the cloud under various weather conditions — the light summer storms, the more menacing mountain storms, at sunrise, at sunset, in the moonlight. Then a stanza summarizes the force and magnificence of the cloud as it relates to all the elements of the heavens. Finally the last stanza analyzes the very nature of the cloud

and explains its immortality. You can easily see how the design would be weakened by changing the order of these topics.

One of the most carefully designed lyric poems in literature is Shelley's " Ode to the West Wind." It will repay thorough study on all the points touched upon in this discussion — identifying yourself with the speaker and grasping the thought or emotion he expresses, reading the poem as a whole before studying its details, examining its unusual meter, looking for other devices which enhance its musical sound, letting your imagination be stirred by its figurative language, and appreciating how its design combines all elements into a perfect whole.

JOHN KEATS 1795–1821

It may truly be said of Keats that one overpowering idea shaped his work. For he was a man preoccupied with beauty; in beauty he perceived love, power, truth. He gave expression to this philosophy in some of the most beautiful lyric poetry in English.

In contrast to the aristocratic Byron and Shelley, Keats was of humble origin. His father kept a stable in London, and Keats was born in the family quarters in the same

building. He had some schooling before he was left an orphan at the age of fifteen. During the seven years that he studied to become a surgeon, he eagerly read the Greek myths and Spenser's *The Faerie Queene*. With the encouragement of newfound literary friends he forsook medicine to devote himself to poetry. Between the ages of twenty-two and twenty-five he published three volumes, the total output on which his fame rests. Though he was a vigorous youth, he developed a bad case of tuberculosis and was forced to seek the warmer climate of Italy. Less than five months later, at the age of twenty-five, he died in Rome. Little did he know that his poetry would eventually receive world recognition, for during his life the critics had given his volumes scathing reviews. There is pathos in the epitaph he wrote for himself: " Here lies one whose name was writ in water."

Besides his literary disappointment, Keats had other anxieties. His younger brother Tom, to whom he was devoted, died of tuberculosis, a disease which hovered like a shadow over Keats' whole family. Then Keats fell in love with a young neighbor, Fanny Brawne, whom he characterized on first meeting as " beautiful and elegant, graceful, silly, fashionable, and strange." She proved to be an unsympathetic and self-centered girl, who throughout their engagement brought as much distress as happiness to her lover.

The names of Shelley and Keats are often linked, partly because of a certain exquisite quality they have in common, partly because Shelley wrote one of the most famous of all elegies, *Adonais,* on the death of Keats. In disposition, however, the two men were quite different. Although few of Keats' published poems reveal that he had a jovial, whimsical side, more like Lamb than Shelley, this fact comes out in his letters, especially those written to his sister Fanny, eight years his junior. Nor did he share Shelley's ideas of the evils of society and religion. If life proved hard, he could always find solace in the world of literature and art where —

A thing of beauty is a joy forever:
Its loveliness increases; it will never
Pass into nothingness; but still will keep
A bower quiet for us, and a sleep
Full of sweet dreams, and health, and
    quiet breathing.   — *Endymion*

On First Looking into Chapman's Homer

Although Keats knew no Greek, he loved Greek mythology. When he was about twenty-one he borrowed a translation of Homer by George Chapman, an Elizabethan poet. He and a lifelong friend, Charles C. Clarke, sat up till daylight reading it — " Keats shouting with delight as some passage of special energy struck his imagination." The next morning his friend found this sonnet on his breakfast table:

Much have I traveled in the realms of gold,°
And many goodly states and kingdoms seen;
Round many western islands have I been
Which bards in fealty to Apollo° hold.
Oft of one wide expanse had I been told   5
That deep-browed Homer ruled as his demesne;°
Yet did I never breathe its pure serene°
Till I heard Chapman speak out loud and bold.
Then felt I like some watcher of the skies
When a new planet swims into his ken;   10
Or like stout Cortez° when with eagle eyes
He stared at the Pacific — and all his men
Looked at each other with a wild surmise —
Silent, upon a peak in Darien.°

1. The terms *realms of gold, goodly states and kingdoms* (line 2), and *western islands* (line 3) are here used metaphorically to represent the range of literature in which Keats had read. 4. *Apollo:* the Greek god of poetry and music. 6. *demesne* (dĕ·mān′, but here dĕ·mēn′): domain; land over which one rules. 7. *serene:* air. 11. *Cortez* (kôr′tĕz): It was Balboa, not Cortez, who discovered the Pacific Ocean from a mountain in Central America. 14. *Darien* (dâr′ĭ·ĕn′): the eastern part of the Isthmus of Panama.

Bright Star! Would I Were Steadfast As Thou Art

The autumn before his death Keats sailed for Italy with a companion, Joseph Severn. Becalmed off the coast of England, the poet watched the evening star — pure, radiant, alone. It awakened in him the grief and yearning expressed in these lines.

Bright star! would I were steadfast as thou art —
   Not in lone splendor hung aloft the night
And watching, with eternal lids apart,
   Like nature's patient, sleepless Eremite,°
The moving waters at their priestlike task   5
   Of pure ablution round earth's human shores,
Or gazing on the new soft-fallen mask
   Of snow upon the mountains and the moors —
No — yet still steadfast, still unchangeable,
   Pillowed upon my fair love's ripening breast,   10
To feel forever its soft fall and swell,
   Awake forever in a sweet unrest,
Still, still to hear her tender-taken breath,
And so live ever — or else swoon to death.

4. *Eremite* (ĕr′ĕ·mīt): a religious recluse; a hermit.

Ode on a Grecian Urn

In the British Museum, Keats had studied the fine collection of Greek marbles with figures cut in relief. Though there are several large vases among them, no one of these could have served as an exact model for his poem. In fact, much scholarly research has failed to uncover any vase with just such scenes as he describes. His picture is a composite one, put together from typical Greek carvings he had seen. He shows us a clear picture of one side of the urn in the first three stanzas and of the other side in the fourth stanza. Two moments of ancient times have thus been given immortality.

Thou still unravished bride of quietness,
  Thou foster child of silence and slow time,
Sylvan historian, who canst thus express
  A flowery tale more sweetly than our rhyme:
What leaf-fringed legend haunts about thy shape   5
  Of deities or mortals, or of both,
    In Tempe° or the dales of Arcady?°
What men or gods are these? What maidens loath?
  What mad pursuit? What struggle to escape?
    What pipes and timbrels?° What wild ecstasy?   10

Heard melodies are sweet, but those unheard
  Are sweeter; therefore, ye soft pipes, play on;
Not to the sensual ear, but, more endeared,
  Pipe to the spirit ditties of no tone.
Fair youth, beneath the trees, thou canst not leave   15
  Thy song, nor ever can those trees be bare;
    Bold Lover, never, never canst thou kiss,
Though winning near the goal — yet, do not grieve;
  She cannot fade, though thou hast not thy bliss,
    Forever wilt thou love, and she be fair!   20

Ah, happy, happy boughs! that cannot shed
  Your leaves, nor ever bid the Spring adieu;
And, happy melodist, unwearièd,
  Forever piping songs forever new;
More happy love! more happy, happy love!   25
  Forever warm and still to be enjoyed,
    Forever panting, and forever young;
All breathing human passion far above,
  That leaves a heart high-sorrowful and cloyed,
    A burning forehead, and a parching tongue.   30

7. *Tempe:* a lovely valley in Thessaly, Greece; *Arcady* (är′kå·dĭ): a picturesque region of Greece, characterized by its beauty and by the contentment of those who dwelt there. 10. *timbrels:* tambourines.

Who are these coming to the sacrifice?
　　To what green altar, O mysterious priest,
Lead'st thou that heifer lowing at the skies,
　　And all her silken flanks with garlands dressed?
What little town by river or sea shore,   35
　　Or mountain-built with peaceful citadel,
　　　Is emptied of this folk, this pious morn?
And, little town, thy streets for evermore
　　Will silent be; and not a soul to tell
　　　Why thou art desolate, can e'er return.   40

O Attic° shape! Fair attitude! with brede°
　　Of marble men and maidens overwrought,
With forest branches and the trodden weed;
　　Thou, silent form, dost tease us out of thought
As doth eternity. Cold Pastoral!°   45
　　When old age shall this generation waste,
　　　Thou shalt remain, in midst of other woe
Than ours, a friend to man, to whom thou say'st,
　　" Beauty is truth, truth beauty " — that is all
　　　Ye know on earth, and all ye need to know.   50

41. *Attic:* pertaining to Attica, a kingdom of ancient Greece; *brede:* embroidery. 45. *Cold Pastoral:*
Keats compares the urn to a pastoral poem (a poem that deals with shepherds and the countryside),
which was a favorite verse form of the ancient Greeks.

When I Have Fears

Written in 1817, toward the beginning of his literary career,
this sonnet shows how long Keats dreaded the disease that
afflicted his family.

　　　When I have fears that I may cease to be
　　　Before my pen has gleaned my teeming brain,
　　　Before high-pilèd books, in charactery,°
　　　Hold like rich garners the full ripened grain;
　　　When I behold, upon the night's starred face,   5
　　　Huge cloudy symbols of a high romance,
　　　And think that I may never live to trace
　　　Their shadows, with the magic hand of chance;°
　　　And when I feel, fair creature of an hour,°
　　　That I shall never look upon thee more,   10
　　　Never have relish in the fairy power
　　　Of unreflecting love — then on the shore
　　　Of the wide world I stand alone, and think
　　　Till love and fame to nothingness do sink.

3. *charactery:* letters. 8. *chance:* inspiration. 9. *fair creature of an hour:* perhaps, idealized woman. This sonnet was written before Keats had met Fanny Brawne.

Ode to a Nightingale

In the spring of 1819 a nightingale built its nest next to the
house where Keats was living. The poet took great pleasure
in the song of the bird and composed this poem at that
time. He repeated it to one of his friends during an evening walk, before he actually wrote it out. The death of
Keats' younger brother Tom, which had occurred the
previous December, is referred to in the third stanza.

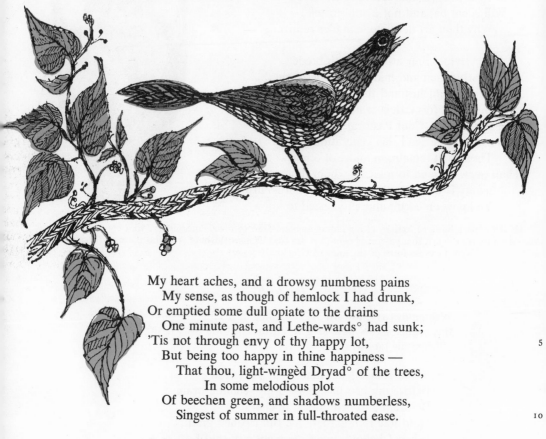

My heart aches, and a drowsy numbness pains
  My sense, as though of hemlock I had drunk,
Or emptied some dull opiate to the drains
  One minute past, and Lethe-wards° had sunk;
'Tis not through envy of thy happy lot,   5
  But being too happy in thine happiness —
    That thou, light-wingèd Dryad° of the trees,
      In some melodious plot
Of beechen green, and shadows numberless,
    Singest of summer in full-throated ease.   10

O for a draught of vintage! that hath been
  Cooled a long age in the deep-delved earth,
Tasting of Flora° and the country green,
  Dance, and Provençal° song, and sunburnt mirth!
O for a beaker full of the warm South,   15
  Full of the true, the blushful Hippocrene,°
    With beaded bubbles winking at the brim,
      And purple-stainèd mouth;

4. *Lethe-wards:* toward the Greek river of forgetfulness, whose waters prepared the good to ent[er]
the bliss of the Elysian Fields. 7. *Dryad:* a wood nymph. 13. *Flora:* goddess of flowers. 14. *Provenç*[al]
(prŏv'ĕn·säl'; in this line, however, the meter requires an accent on the second syllable.): pertainin[g]
to Provence in southern France, home of the medieval troubadours. 16. *Hippocrene* (hĭp'ō·krēn[)]
a fountain on Mount Helicon, sacred to the Muses.

That I might drink, and leave the world unseen,
  And with thee fade away into the forest dim;   20

Fade far away, dissolve, and quite forget
  What thou among the leaves hast never known,
The weariness, the fever, and the fret
  Here, where men sit and hear each other groan;
Where palsy shakes a few, sad, last gray hairs;   25
  Where youth grows pale and specter-thin, and dies;
    Where but to think is to be full of sorrow
      And leaden-eyed despairs;
  Where Beauty cannot keep her lustrous eyes
    Or new Love pine at them beyond tomorrow.   30

Away! away! for I will fly to thee,
  Not charioted by Bacchus and his pards,°
But on the viewless° wings of Poesy,
  Though the dull brain perplexes and retards:
Already with thee! tender is the night,   35
  And haply the Queen Moon is on her throne,
    Clustered around by all her starry Fays;°
      But here there is no light,
  Save what from heaven is with the breezes blown
    Through verdurous glooms and winding mossy ways.   40

I cannot see what flowers are at my feet,
  Nor what soft incense hangs upon the boughs,
But, in embalmèd° darkness, guess each sweet
  Wherewith the seasonable month endows
The grass, the thicket, and the fruit tree wild;   45
  White hawthorn, and the pastoral eglantine;
    Fast fading violets covered up in leaves;
      And mid-May's eldest child,
  The coming musk rose, full of dewy wine,
    The murmurous haunt of flies on summer eves.   50

Darkling° I listen; and, for many a time
  I have been half in love with easeful Death,
Called him soft names in many a musèd rhyme,
  To take into the air my quiet breath;
Now more than ever seems it rich to die,   55
  To cease upon the midnight with no pain,
    While thou art pouring forth thy soul abroad
      In such an ecstasy!
  Still wouldst thou sing, and I have ears in vain —
    To thy high requiem become a sod.   60

32. *Bacchus and his pards:* The god of wine rode in a chariot drawn by leopards. 33. *viewless:* invisible. 37. *Fays:* fairies. The moon is here identified with the queen of the fairies. 43. *embalmèd:* balmy. 51. *Darkling:* in the dark.

Thou wast not born for death, immortal Bird!
No hungry generations tread thee down;
The voice I hear this passing night was heard
In ancient days by emperor and clown;
Perhaps the selfsame song that found a path   65
Through the sad heart of Ruth,° when, sick for home,
She stood in tears amid the alien corn;
The same that ofttimes hath
Charmed magic casements, opening on the foam
Of perilous seas, in fairylands forlorn.   70

Forlorn! the very word is like a bell
To toll me back from thee to my sole self!
Adieu! the fancy cannot cheat so well
As she is famed° to do, deceiving elf.
Adieu! adieu! thy plaintive anthem fades   75
Past the near meadows, over the still stream,
Up the hillside; and now 'tis buried deep
In the next valley glades.
Was it a vision, or a waking dream?
Fled is that music — Do I wake or sleep?   80

66. *Ruth:* heroine of the Book of Ruth in the Bible. For this part of her story, see the second chapter. 74. *famed:* reported.

Poetry is either something that lives like fire inside of you . . . or else it is nothing, an empty, formalized bore around which pedants can endlessly drone their notes and explanations. " The Grecian Urn " is unbearably beautiful with every syllable as inevitable as the notes in Beethoven's Ninth Symphony, *or it's just something you don't understand. It is what it is because an extraordinary genius passed at that point in history and touched it. I suppose I've read it a hundred times. About the tenth time I began to know what it is about, and caught the chime in it and the exquisite inner mechanics. Likewise with the " Nightingale " which I can never read through without tears in my eyes; likewise the " Pot of Basil " with its great stanzas about the two brothers; and " The Eve of Saint Agnes " which*

has the richest, most sensuous imagery in English, not excepting Shakespeare. And finally his three or four great sonnets, " Bright Star " and the others.

Knowing those things young and granted an ear, one can scarcely ever afterwards be unable to distinguish between gold and dross in what one reads. In themselves those eight poems are a scale of workmanship for anybody who wants to know truly about words, their most utter value for evocation, persuasion, or charm. For a while after you quit Keats all other poetry seems to be only whistling or humming.

F. Scott Fitzgerald

From a letter quoted in the Princeton Alumni Weekly, *March 9, 1956. Used by permission of Frances Scott Fitzgerald Lanahan.*

The Eve of St. Agnes

In this metrical romance the poet uses as his setting a castle in medieval Italy. The chapel with its stone images of lords and ladies, the great hall, and the chamber of Madeline with its triple-arched casement are pictured in vivid detail. The medieval characters of beadsman (an old man supported by a family in return for his regular prayers), nurse, warrior guests, and romantic lovers combine with archaic language to weave a spell of rare, unearthly beauty. The theme, like that of *Romeo and Juliet,* is the flowering of young love against a background of age, death, and human intolerance.

St. Agnes was an early Christian martyr who, after her death, appeared to her parents in a vision with a lamb. Thereafter the white lamb, symbol of purity, was sacred to her. The legend on which this story is based is that a maiden, by observing certain rites on St. Agnes' Eve, which occurs on January 20, may have a glimpse of her future husband.

St. Agnes' Eve — Ah, bitter chill it was!
The owl, for all his feathers, was acold;
The hare limped trembling through the frozen grass,
And silent was the flock in wooly fold;
Numb were the Beadsman's fingers, while he told   5
His rosary, and while his frosted breath,
Like pious incense from a censer old,
Seemed taking flight for heaven, without a death,
Past the sweet Virgin's picture, while his prayer he saith.

His prayer he saith, this patient, holy man;   10
Then takes his lamp, and riseth from his knees,
And back returneth, meager, barefoot, wan,
Along the chapel aisle by slow degrees;
The sculptured dead, on each side, seem to freeze,
Imprisoned in black, purgatorial rails;°   15
Knights, ladies, praying in dumb orat'ries,°
He passeth by; and his weak spirit fails
To think how they may ache in icy hoods and mails.°

Northward he turneth through a little door,
And scarce three steps, ere Music's golden tongue   20
Flattered to tears this aged man and poor;
But no — already had his deathbell rung;
The joys of all his life were said and sung;
His was harsh penance on St. Agnes' Eve;
Another way he went, and soon among   25
Rough ashes sat he for his soul's reprieve,
And all night kept awake, for sinners' sake to grieve.

That ancient Beadsman heard the prelude soft;
And so it chanced, for many a door was wide,
From hurry to and fro. Soon, up aloft,   30

15. *purgatorial rails:* burial robes. 16. *orat'ries:* oratories, small chapels for private prayers. 18. *mails:* coats of armor.

The silver, snarling trumpets 'gan to chide;
The level chambers, ready with their pride,
Were glowing to receive a thousand guests;
The carvèd angels, ever eager-eyed,
· Stared, where upon their heads the cornice rests,   35
With hair blown back, and wings put crosswise on their breasts.

At length burst in the argent revelry,°
With plume, tiara, and all rich array,
Numerous as shadows, haunting fairily
The brain, new stuffed, in youth, with triumphs gay   40
Of old romance. These let us wish away,
And turn, sole-thoughted, to one Lady there,
Whose heart had brooded, all that wintry day,
On love, and winged St. Agnes' saintly care,
As she had heard old dames full many times declare.   45

They told her how, upon St. Agnes' Eve,
Young virgins might have visions of delight,
And soft adorings from their loves receive
Upon the honeyed middle of the night,
If ceremonies due they did aright;   50
As, supperless to bed they must retire,
And couch supine° their beauties, lily white;
Nor look behind, nor sideways, but require
Of Heaven with upward eyes for all that they desire.

Full of this whim was thoughtful Madeline;   55
The music, yearning like a god in pain,
She scarcely heard; her maiden eyes divine,
Fixed on the floor, saw many a sweeping train
Pass by — she heeded not at all; in vain
Came many a tiptoe, amorous cavalier,   60
And back retired; not cooled by high disdain,
But she saw not; her heart was otherwhere;
She sighed for Agnes' dreams, the sweetest of the year.

37. *argent revelry:* shining group of revelers. 52. *couch supine* (sū·pīn′): lay flat.

She danced along with vague, regardless eyes,
Anxious her lips, her breathing quick and short;   65
The hallowed hour was near at hand; she sighs
Amid the timbrels, and the thronged resort
Of whisperers in anger, or in sport;
'Mid looks of love, defiance, hate, and scorn,
Hoodwinked with fairy fancy; all amort,°   70
Save to St. Agnes and her lambs unshorn,°
And all the bliss to be before tomorrow morn.

So, purposing each moment to retire,
She lingered still. Meantime, across the moors,
Had come young Porphyro,° with heart on fire   75
For Madeline. Beside the portal doors,
Buttressed from moonlight,° stands he, and implores
All saints to give him sight of Madeline,
But for one moment in the tedious hours,
That he might gaze and worship all unseen;   80
Perchance speak, kneel, touch, kiss — in sooth such things have been.

He ventures in; let no buzzed whisper tell;
All eyes be muffled, or a hundred swords
Will storm his heart, Love's feverous citadel;
For him, those chambers held barbarian hordes,   85
Hyena foemen, and hot-blooded lords,
Whose very dogs would execrations howl
Against his lineage; not one breast affords
Him any mercy, in that mansion foul,
Save one old beldame,° weak in body and in soul.   90

Ah, happy chance! the aged creature came,
Shuffling along with ivory-headed wand,
To where he stood, hid from the torch's flame,
Behind a broad hall pillar, far beyond
The sound of merriment and chorus bland.   95
He startled her; but soon she knew his face,
And grasped his fingers in her palsied hand,
Saying, " Mercy, Porphyro! hie thee from this place;
They are all here tonight, the whole bloodthirsty race!

" Get hence; get hence! there's dwarfish Hildebrand;   100
He had a fever late, and in the fit
He cursèd thee and thine, both house and land;
Then there's that old Lord Maurice, not a whit
More tame for his gray hairs — Alas me! flit!

70. *amort:* as if dead. 71. *lambs unshorn:* In honor of St. Agnes, the symbol of youth and innocence,
two lambs were sacrificed annually in the church on her eve. The wool was later spun and woven
by the nuns into garments for the poor. 75. *Porphyro* (pôr′fĭ·rō). 77. *Buttressed from moonlight:*
He is standing in the shadow of one of the buttresses which supported the walls of the castle.
90. *beldame* (bĕl′dăm): an old woman.

Flit like a ghost away." — " Ah, Gossip° dear,   105
We're safe enough; here in this armchair sit
And tell me how " — " Good Saints! not here, not here;
Follow me, child, or else these stones will be thy bier."

He followed through a lowly archèd way,
Brushing the cobwebs with his lofty plume;   110
And as she muttered, " Wella — welladay! "
He found him in a little moonlight room,
Pale, latticed, chill, and silent as a tomb.
" Now tell me where is Madeline," said he,
" O tell me, Angela, by the holy loom   115
Which none but secret sisterhood may see,
When they St. Agnes' wool are weaving piously."

" St. Agnes! Ah! it is St. Agnes' Eve —
Yet men will murder upon holy days.
Thou must hold water in a witch's sieve,°   120
And be liege lord of all the Elves and Fays,
To venture so: it fills me with amaze
To see thee, Porphyro! — St. Agnes' Eve!
God's help! my lady fair the conjurer plays
This very night; good angels her deceive!   125
But let me laugh awhile, I've mickle° time to grieve."

Feebly she laugheth in the languid moon,
While Porphyro upon her face doth look,
Like puzzled urchin on an aged crone
Who keepeth closed a wondrous riddle book,   130
As spectacled she sits in chimney nook.
But soon his eyes grew brilliant, when she told
His lady's purpose; and he scarce could brook
Tears, at the thought of those enchantments cold,
And Madeline asleep in lap of legends old.   135

Sudden a thought came like a fullblown rose,
Flushing his brow, and in his painèd heart
Made purple riot; then doth he propose
A stratagem, that makes the beldame start.
" A cruel man and impious thou art.   140
Sweet lady, let her pray, and sleep, and dream
Alone with her good angels, far apart
From wicked men like thee. Go, go! — I deem
Thou canst not surely be the same that thou didst seem."°

" I will not harm her, by all saints I swear,"   145
Quoth Porphyro: " O may I ne'er find grace
When my weak voice shall whisper its last prayer,

---

105. *Gossip:* godmother. 120. *hold . . . sieve:* have supernatural powers. 126. *mickle:* much (a Scottish expression). 144. You cannot be as honorable as I thought you were.

If one of her soft ringlets I displace,
Or look with ruffian passion in her face.
Good Angela, believe me by these tears;   150
Or, I will, even in a moment's space,
Awake, with horrid shout, my foemen's ears,
And beard them, though they be more fanged than wolves and bears."

" Ah! why wilt thou affright a feeble soul?
A poor, weak, palsy-stricken churchyard thing,   155
Whose passing bell may ere the midnight toll;
Whose prayers for thee, each morn and evening,
Were never missed." Thus plaining,° doth she bring
A gentler speech from burning Porphyro;
So woeful, and of such deep sorrowing,   160
That Angela gives promise she will do
Whatever he shall wish, betide her weal or woe.°

Which was, to lead him, in close secrecy,
Even to Madeline's chamber, and there hide
Him in a closet, of such privacy   165
That he might see her beauty unespied,
And win perhaps that night a peerless bride,
While legioned fairies paced the coverlet,
And pale enchantment held her sleepy-eyed.
Never on such a night have lovers met,   170
Since Merlin° paid his Demon all the monstrous debt.

" It shall be as thou wishest," said the Dame;
" All cates° and dainties shall be storèd there
Quickly on this feast night; by the tambour frame°
Her own lute thou wilt see; no time to spare,   175
For I am slow and feeble, and scarce dare
On such a catering trust my dizzy head.
Wait here, my child, with patience; kneel in prayer
The while. Ah! thou must needs the lady wed,
Or may I never leave my grave among the dead."   180

So saying, she hobbled off with busy fear.
The lover's endless minutes slowly passed;
The dame returned, and whispered in his ear
To follow her; with aged eyes aghast
From fright of dim espial. Safe at last,   185
Through many a dusky gallery, they gain
The maiden's chamber, silken, hushed, and chaste;
Where Porphyro took covert, pleased amain.°
His poor guide hurried back with agues° in her brain.

158. *plaining*: complaining. 162. *betide . . . woe*: whether good or evil come of it. 171. *Merlin*: a magician, the offspring of demons, who was at last overpowered by means of one of his own spells reversed. 173. *cates*: dainty, choice food. 174. *tambour frame*: embroidery hoops, shaped like a tambour or drum. 188. *amain*: greatly. 189. *agues* (ā′gūz): An ague causes one to shake from either fever or cold; in other words, she was frightened.

Her faltering hand upon the balustrade,   190
Old Angela was feeling for the stair,
When Madeline, St. Agnes' charmèd maid,
Rose, like a missioned spirit, unaware:
With silver taper's light, and pious care,
She turned, and down the aged gossip led   195
To a safe level matting. Now prepare,
Young Porphyro, for gazing on that bed;
She comes, she comes again, like ringdove frayed° and fled.

Out went the taper as she hurried in;
Its little smoke, in pallid moonshine, died;   200
She closed the door, she panted, all akin
To spirits of the air, and visions wide;
No uttered syllable or woe betide!
But to her heart, her heart was voluble,
Paining with eloquence her balmy side;   205
As though a tongueless nightingale should swell
Her throat in vain, and die, heart-stifled, in her dell.

A casement high and triple-arched there was,
All garlanded with carven imageries
Of fruits, and flowers, and bunches of knotgrass,   210
And diamonded with panes of quaint device,
Innumerable of stains and splendid dyes,
As are the tiger moth's deep-damasked° wings;
And in the midst, 'mong thousand heraldries,
And twilight saints, and dim emblazonings,   215
A shielded scutcheon blushed with blood of queens and kings.°

Full on this casement shone the wintry moon,
And threw warm gules° on Madeline's fair breast,
As down she knelt for heaven's grace and boon;

198. *frayed:* frightened. 213. *deep-damasked:* patterned. 216. A coat of arms shaped like a shield
was colored red to indicate a royal family. 218. *gules* (gūlz): red, represented in heraldry by parallel
lines.

Rose bloom fell on her hands, together pressed,   220
And on her silver cross soft amethyst,
And on her hair a glory, like a saint:
She seemed a splendid angel, newly dressed,
Save wings, for heaven; Porphyro grew faint;
She knelt, so pure a thing, so free from mortal taint.   225

Anon his heart revives; her vespers done,
Of all its wreathèd pearls her hair she frees;
Unclasped her warmèd jewels one by one;
Loosens her fragrant bodice; by degrees
Her rich attire creeps rustling to her knees;   230
Half-hidden, like a mermaid in seaweed,
Pensive awhile she dreams awake, and sees,
In fancy, fair St. Agnes in her bed,
But dares not look behind, or all the charm is fled.

Soon, trembling in her soft and chilly nest,   235
In sort of wakeful swoon, perplexed she lay,
Until the poppied° warmth of sleep oppressed
Her soothèd limbs, and soul fatigued away;
Flown, like a thought, until the morrow day;
Blissfully havened both from joy and pain;   240
Clasped like a missal° where swart Paynims° pray;
Blinded alike from sunshine and from rain,
As though a rose should shut, and be a bud again.

Stolen to this paradise, and so entranced,
Porphyro gazed upon her empty dress,   245
And listened to her breathing, if it chanced
To wake into a slumberous tenderness;
Which when he heard, that minute did he bless,
And breathed himself; then from the closet crept,
Noiseless as fear in a wide wilderness,   250
And over the hushed carpet, silent, stepped,
And 'tween the curtains peeped, where, lo! how fast she slept.

Then by the bedside, where the faded moon
Made a dim, silver twilight, soft he set
A table, and half-anguished, threw thereon   255
A cloth of woven crimson, gold, and jet —
O for some drowsy Morphean amulet!°
The boisterous, midnight, festive clarion,
The kettledrum, and far-heard clarinet,
Affray° his ears, though but in dying tone —   260
The hall door shuts again, and all the noise is gone.

237. *poppied:* druglike. 241. *missal:* Mass book; *Paynims:* pagans. Her eyes were as tightly closed in sleep as a prayer book would be in pagan lands. 257. *Morphean amulet:* a charm pertaining to the god of dreams; that is, one to keep her asleep. 260. *Affray:* frighten.

And still she slept an azure-lidded sleep,
In blanchèd linen, smooth, and lavendered,°
While he from forth the closet brought a heap
Of candied apple, quince, and plum, and gourd;   265
With jellies soother° than the creamy curd,
And lucent° sirups, tinct° with cinnamon;
Manna and dates, in argosy transferred
From Fez;° and spicèd dainties, every one,
From silken Samarkand° to cedared Lebanon.°   270

These delicates he heaped with glowing hand
On golden dishes and in baskets bright
Of wreathèd silver; sumptuous they stand
In the retirèd quiet of the night,
Filling the chilly room with perfume light. —   275
" And now, my love, my seraph fair, awake!
Thou art my heaven, and I thine eremite;
Open thine eyes, for meek St. Agnes' sake,
Or I shall drowse beside thee, so my soul doth ache."

Thus whispering, his warm, unnervèd arm   280
Sank in her pillow. Shaded was her dream
By the dusk curtains — 'twas a midnight charm
Impossible to melt as icèd stream;
The lustrous salvers in the moonlight gleam;
Broad golden fringe upon the carpet lies;   285
It seemed he never, never could redeem
From such a steadfast spell his lady's eyes;
So mused awhile, entoiled in woofèd° phantasies.

Awakening up, he took her hollow lute —
Tumultuous — and, in chords that tenderest be,   290
He played an ancient ditty, long since mute,
In Provence called " La belle dame sans merci ";°
Close to her ear touching the melody;
Wherewith disturbed, she uttered a soft moan;
He ceased — she panted quick — and suddenly   295
Her blue affrayèd eyes wide open shone;
Upon his knees he sank, pale as smooth-sculptured stone.

Her eyes were open, but she still beheld,
Now wide awake, the vision of her sleep;
There was a painful change, that night expelled   300
The blisses of her dream so pure and deep,
At which fair Madeline began to weep,

---

263. *lavendered:* perfumed with lavender. 266. *soother:* smoother. 267. *lucent* (lū′sĕnt): clear; *tinct:* delicately flavored. 269. *Fez:* a city in Morocco. 270. *Samarkand:* a city of Turkestan, famous for its manufacture of silk; *Lebanon:* a country at the eastern end of the Mediterranean. From it came the timbers of cedar which were used in Solomon's temple. 288. *woofèd:* intertwined, as the threads are in weaving. 292. *"La belle dame sans merci":* the beautiful lady without mercy.

And moan forth witless words with many a sigh;
While still her gaze on Porphyro would keep;
Who knelt, with joinèd hands and piteous eyes,   305
Fearing to move or speak, she looked so dreamingly.

" Ah, Porphyro! " said she, " but even now
Thy voice was at sweet tremble in mine ear,
Made tunable with every sweetest vow;
And those sad eyes were spiritual and clear;   310
How changed thou art! how pallid, chill, and drear!
Give me that voice again, my Porphyro,
Those looks immortal, those complainings dear!
Oh, leave me not in this eternal woe,
For if thou diest, my Love, I know not where to go."   315

Beyond a mortal man impassioned far
At these voluptuous accents, he arose,
Ethereal, flushed, and like a throbbing star
Seen mid the sapphire heaven's deep repose;
Into her dream he melted, as the rose   320
Blendeth its odor with the violet —
Solution sweet; meantime the frost wind blows
Like Love's alarum pattering the sharp sleet
Against the windowpanes; St. Agnes' moon hath set.

'Tis dark; quick pattereth the flaw-blown° sleet;   325
" This is no dream, my bride, my Madeline! "
'Tis dark; the icèd gusts still rave and beat.
" No dream, alas! alas! and woe is mine!
Porphyro will leave me here to fade and pine. —
Cruel! what traitor could thee thither bring?   330
I curse not, for my heart is lost in thine,
Though thou forsakest a deceivèd thing —
A dove forlorn and lost with sick unprunèd wing."

" My Madeline; sweet dreamer! lovely bride!
Say, may I be for aye thy vassal° blest?   335
Thy beauty's shield, heart-shaped and vermeil-dyed?°
Ah, silver shrine, here will I take my rest
After so many hours of toil and quest,
A famished pilgrim — saved by miracle.
Though I have found, I will not rob thy nest   340
Saving of thy sweet self; if thou think'st well
To trust, fair Madeline, to no rude infidel.

" Hark! 'tis an elfin storm from fairyland,
Of haggard seeming,° but a boon indeed.

325. *flaw-blown:* squall-blown. 335. *vassal:* in feudal times, a knight who pledged allegiance to
his overlord. 336. *vermeil-dyed* (vûr'mĭl): vermilion, bright red. 344. *haggard seeming:* wild in aspect.

Arise — arise! the morning is at hand —   345
The bloated wassailers will never heed —
Let us away, my love, with happy speed;
There are no ears to hear, or eyes to see —
Drowned all in Rhenish° and the sleepy mead.°
Awake! arise! my love, and fearless be,   350
For o'er the southern moors I have a home for thee."

She hurried at his words, beset with fears,
For there were sleeping dragons all around,
At glaring watch, perhaps, with ready spears —
Down the wide stairs a darkling way they found —   355
In all the house was heard no human sound.
A chain-drooped lamp° was flickering by each door;
The arras,° rich with horseman, hawk, and hound,
Fluttered in the besieging wind's uproar;
And the long carpets rose along the gusty floor.   360

They glide, like phantoms, into the wide hall;
Like phantoms, to the iron porch, they glide;
Where lay the porter, in uneasy sprawl,
With a huge empty flagon by his side.
The wakeful bloodhound rose, and shook his hide,   365
But his sagacious eye an inmate owns;°
By one and one, the bolts full easy slide —
The chains lie silent on the footworn stones —
The key turns, and the door upon its hinges groans.

And they are gone; ay, ages long ago   370
These lovers fled away into the storm.
That night the Baron dreamt of many a woe,
And all his warrior guests, with shade and form
Of witch, and demon, and large coffin worm,
Were long benightmared. Angela the old   375
Died palsy-twitched, with meager face deform;
The Beadsman, after thousand aves told,
For aye unsought-for slept among his ashes cold.

349. *Rhenish* (rĕn′ĭsh): wine made near the Rhine River; *mead:* a drink made of fermented honey. 357. *chain-drooped lamp:* lamp hanging on a chain. 358. *arras* (ăr′ăs): tapestry hanging on the wall to keep out drafts. 366. *owns:* recognizes.

POEMS FROM " REALMS OF GOLD "

SONNETS

1. In " On First Looking into Chapman's Homer " point out how Keats compares geographical discovery with discovery in literature. What feeling is shown in the last lines? What books have given you the same feeling?

2. In " Bright Star " how does Keats wish to resemble the star? How would he differ from it?

3. In " When I Have Fears " what two great longings are expressed? What metaphor does the poet use to describe creative writing?

ODE ON A GRECIAN URN

1. Explain the significance of the various names Keats gives the urn in the first three lines. In your own words give a clear picture of the two scenes on the urn, showing what is happening at the moment the artist has caught and preserved the action.

2. What in Keats' own life helps us to grasp his emotion in the third stanza?

3. In giving the urn's message at the end, Keats uses both *thou* and *ye*. To what different persons or things do they refer? Discuss whether you think the poet means to apply this message to all of life. Do you agree with him? Give some examples to support your opinion.

ODE TO A NIGHTINGALE

1. What emotions are aroused in the poet by the song of the nightingale? What similarities and what differences do you find between Keats' response in this poem and Shelley's in " To a Skylark "?

2. What line refers to the death of Keats' brother Tom? What lines may refer to his feeling for Fanny Brawne, whom he met at about this time?

3. Discuss the contrast made in this poem between the world of reality and the world of fancy. How does the word *forlorn* in line 71 bring him back to reality?

4. How does the seventh stanza recall the " Ode on a Grecian Urn "?

THE EVE OF ST. AGNES

1. How many details can you discover which give a medieval flavor to the story, setting it apart from modern times?

2. At the end of the story, what becomes of the lovers, the beadsman, the nurse, the baron, and the guests? How is a veil of mystery thrown over the conclusion? Does this add to the romantic appeal of the poem, in your opinion?

3. How does Keats' handling of an elopement story differ from Scott's in " Jock o' Hazeldean "? In what way is this difference characteristic of the two poets?

4. What stanza form does Keats use in this poem? What other poems that you have read in this book are written in this form?

THE POWER OF WORDS

SENSUOUS IMAGERY

Keats is one of the masters of language that appeals to the senses. Two pairs of contrasting stanzas from " The Eve of St. Agnes " clearly illustrate his skill.

In the opening stanza of the poem the reader cannot escape the dominant note of cold. Many lines have at least one word to add to the sensation: *bitter chill, acold, limped trembling, frozen, silent, numb, frosted*. The crowning simile suggests a striking image by likening the Beadsman's frosted breath to the cloud of incense from an old censer rising toward heaven.

The cold of the outside world is contrasted to the richness and beauty of the scene in Madeline's chamber. The two stanzas from lines 253 to 270 appeal to every one of the five senses:

sight: a dim silver twilight; a cloth of woven crimson, gold, and jet; azure-lidded sleep; blanchèd linen, smooth; all the foods in lines 265–69; silken Samarkand and cedared Lebanon.

sound: the musical instruments " affray his ears," then are silent.

smell and taste: the fruits, jellies, and sirups mentioned appeal to *three* senses, smell, taste, and sight; lavendered linen; spiced dainties.

touch: smooth linen (to the hands); jellies smoother than the creamy curd (to the tongue).

List images in the next three stanzas that appeal to the senses.

ROBERT SOUTHEY 1774–1843

The Battle of Blenheim

Robert Southey, the third of the trio of Lake Poets, was a popular poet laureate of his time. His verse lacks the genius of Wordsworth's and Coleridge's, but the vigorous ballad style of his many narrative and descriptive poems is highly readable.

Southey's treatment of the battle of Blenheim (blĕn′ĭm) is an early expression against the cruelty and futility of war. That battle, fought in 1704 in a town in Bavaria, was a decisive victory for the English and Austrians over the French and Bavarians. The war grew out of the rivalries and jealousies of several ruling families of Europe. In the poem Kaspar stands for the older generation that took war for granted. The children voice questions about the famous battle of 1704 — which Addison once glorified in a poem — that serve to reveal the futility of war.

It was a summer evening,
　Old Kaspar's work was done,
And he before his cottage door
　Was sitting in the sun;
And by him sported on the green　　　5
His little grandchild Wilhelmine.

She saw her brother Peterkin
　Roll something large and round
Which he beside the rivulet
　In playing there had found;　　　10
He came to ask what he had found
That was so large and smooth and
　　round.

Old Kaspar took it from the boy
　Who stood expectant by;
And then the old man shook his head,
　And with a natural sigh　　　16
" 'Tis some poor fellow's skull," said he,
" Who fell in the great victory.

" I find them in the garden,
　For there's many here about;　　　20
And often when I go to plow
　The plowshare turns them out.
For many thousand men," said he,
" Were slain in that great victory."

" Now tell us what 'twas all about,"　　25
　Young Peterkin he cries;
And little Wilhelmine looks up
　With wonder-waiting eyes;
" Now tell us all about the war,　　　29
And what they fought each other for."

" It was the English," Kaspar cried,
　" Who put the French to rout;
But what they fought each other for
　I could not well make out.
But everybody said," quoth he,　　　35
" That 'twas a famous victory.

" My father lived at Blenheim then,
　Yon little stream hard by;
They burnt his dwelling to the ground,
　And he was forced to fly;　　　40
So with his wife and child he fled,
Nor had he where to rest his head.

" With fire and sword the country round
　Was wasted far and wide,
And many a childing mother then　　　45
　And newborn baby died;
But things like that, you know, must be
At every famous victory.

" They say it was a shocking sight
　After the field was won;　　　50
For many thousand bodies here
　Lay rotting in the sun;
But things like that, you know, must be
After a famous victory.

" Great praise the Duke of Marlbro'°
   won   55
  And our good Prince Eugene ";°
" Why, 'twas a very wicked thing! "

55. *Duke of Marlbro':* The Duke of Marlborough was the commander of the British
forces. 56. *Prince Eugene:* commander of the
Austrian forces. Notice that Kaspar bore him
no ill will though he was on the side that burned
Kaspar's father's home. This attitude shows
that there were no issues in the campaign which
were clear to the country people.

Said little Wilhelmine.
" Nay — nay — my little girl," quoth he,
" It was a famous victory.   60

" And everybody praised the Duke
  Who this great fight did win."
" But what good came of it at last? "
  Quoth little Peterkin.
" Why that I cannot tell," said he,   65
" But 'twas a famous victory."

THOMAS HOOD 1799–1845

The Song of the Shirt

Thomas Hood experienced such poverty
and sickness himself that he had great
sympathy with the suffering of others. A
Londoner, he edited several magazines, and
was acquainted with Lamb and other literary men. He is remembered for his humorous poetry, as well as serious poems like
" The Song of the Shirt." Like " The Battle
of Blenheim," this poem expresses the
growing humanitarian spirit of the times.
The origin of " The Song of the Shirt " was
a newspaper account concerning a woman
on trial for pawning articles that belonged
to her employer. Evidence presented at the
trial showed that she had received only
seven shillings a week for making trousers
at home. On this sum (see the monetary
table on page 811) she was supporting herself and her family. The timely appearance
of this poem had a decided effect in improving labor legislation.

With fingers weary and worn,
  With eyelids heavy and red,
A woman sat, in unwomanly rags,
  Plying her needle and thread —
Stitch! stitch! stitch!   5
  In poverty, hunger, and dirt,
And still with a voice of dolorous pitch
  She sang the " Song of the Shirt."

" Work! work! work!
  While the cock is crowing aloof!   10
And work — work — work,
  Till the stars shine through the roof!
It's Oh! to be a slave
  Along with the barbarous Turk,
Where woman has never a soul to save,°
  If this is Christian work!   16

" Work — work — work,
  Till the brain begins to swim;
Work — work — work,
  Till the eyes are heavy and dim!   20
Seam, and gusset,° and band,
  Band, and gusset, and seam,
Till over the buttons I fall asleep,
  And sew them on in a dream!

" O, Men, with Sisters dear!   25
  Oh, Men, with Mothers and Wives!
It is not linen you're wearing out,
  But human creatures' lives!
Stitch — stitch — stitch,
  In poverty, hunger, and dirt,   30

15. *woman . . . save:* refers to a Moslem
belief. 21. *gusset:* an extra strip inserted to
strengthen or widen a garment.

Sewing at once, with a double thread,
  A shroud° as well as a Shirt.

" But why do I talk of Death?
  That Phantom of grisly bone,
I hardly fear its terrible shape,   35
  It seems so like my own —
It seems so like my own,
  Because of the fasts I keep;
Oh, God! that bread should be so dear
  And flesh and blood so cheap! 40

" Work — work — work!
  My labor never flags;
And what are its wages? A bed of straw,
  A crust of bread — and rags.
That shattered roof — this naked floor —
  A table — a broken chair — 46
And a wall so blank, my shadow I thank
  For sometimes falling there!

" Work — work — work!
  From weary chime to chime, 50
Work — work — work,
  As prisoners work for crime!
Band, and gusset, and seam,
  Seam, and gusset, and band,
Till the heart is sick, and the brain be-
    numbed, 55
  As well as the weary hand.

" Work — work — work,
  In the dull December light,
And work — work — work,
  When the weather is warm and
    bright — 60
While underneath the eaves
  The brooding swallows cling
As if to show me their sunny backs
  And twit me with the spring.

" Oh, but to breathe the breath 65
  Of the cowslip and primrose sweet —
With the sky above my head,
  And the grass beneath my feet;
For only one short hour
  To feel as I used to feel, 70

32. *shroud:* a garment in which to wrap
the dead. In other words, this cruel situation
will cause the seamstress' death.

Before I knew the woes of want
  And the walk that costs a meal.

" Oh! but for one short hour!
  A respite however brief!
No blessèd leisure for Love or Hope, 75
  But only time for Grief!
A little weeping would ease my heart,
  But in their briny bed
My tears must stop, for every drop
  Hinders needle and thread! " 80

With fingers weary and worn,
  With eyelids heavy and red,
A woman sat, in unwomanly rags,
  Plying her needle and thread —
Stitch! stitch! stitch! 85
  In poverty, hunger, and dirt,
And still with a voice of dolorous
    pitch, —
Would that its tone could reach the
    Rich! —
  She sang this " Song of the Shirt! "

TWO HUMANITARIANS

1. Robert Southey's poem is a study in contrasts. What contrasts can you find between persons, between attitudes, between ideas about war? What other poems have you read that show the cruelty and futility of war?

2. Through what channel did Hood hope that he might " reach the Rich "? Why did the seamstress continue to sing? " The Song of the Shirt " has been translated into several foreign languages; do you understand its wide appeal?

RESEARCH AND REPORTS

1. Compare " The Song of the Shirt " with Mrs. Browning's " The Cry of the Children," Edwin Markham's " The Man with the Hoe," and Margaret Widdemer's " Factories."

2. Look up working conditions for women and children in England in the early nineteenth century and the reforms which followed. Compare conditions of that time with present working conditions in England and the United States.

READING LIST FOR THE ROMANTIC AGE

Austen, Jane, *Pride and Prejudice*
A mother tries to find husbands for her five daughters among the quiet country gentlefolk.

——, *Sense and Sensibility*
A satire directed against commonplace foolishness. Two sisters of different temperaments are contrasted.

Barrington, E. Beck, *Glorious Apollo*
Lord Byron's love affairs, his ill-fated marriage, and his tragic death are explored.

Becker, May L., *Presenting Miss Jane Austen*
An authentic, thorough study of the life and times of Jane Austen, with emphasis on exciting moments.

Brighouse, Harold, *The Night of " Mr. H."*
A one-act play showing Charles Lamb's bravery when his play *Mr. H.* was a failure at the Drury Lane Theater in London.

Brontë, Charlotte, *Shirley*
Capital and labor and the emancipation of women are issues in this moorland story.

Brown, Alice, *Charles Lamb*
A vivid five-act dramatization of the lives of Charles Lamb, his sister Mary, Lamb's sweetheart, and the man she married.

Carr, John D., *Bride of Newgate*
Continuous suspense in the story of Darwent's marriage one hour before he is to die, his escape, and his life afterward.

Collins, Norman, *Black Ivory*
In 1829 off the African coast, a fourteen-year-old boy encounters highjacking, mutiny, and violence.

Farnol, Jeffrey, *The Amateur Gentleman*
The son of an ex-prizefighter, after inheriting a fortune, goes to London to become a gentleman.

Fitch, Clyde, *Beau Brummel*
A four-act play about the famous dandy who was favored at court, loved a commoner, and finally died in poverty.

Forester, C. S., *Hornblower and the Atropos*
Young Captain Hornblower journeys across England, takes part in Nelson's funeral, and recovers a huge treasure in an English sunken ship.

Gaskell, Elizabeth, *Cranford*
A pleasing story of small-community life in Cranford where spinsters live in a genteel manner on inherited money.

Goudge, Elizabeth, *Gentian Hill*
An irresistible romance, based on an old Devonshire legend, in which a princess living in a peasant's home falls in love with a young midshipman in Lord Nelson's fleet.

Hardy, Thomas, *Trumpet Major*
Suspense prevails in this story of family life and love during the Napoleonic terror.

Lamb, Charles, *Essays of Elia* and *Last Essays of Elia*
Essays written purely for fun and entertainment. Read " A Chapter on Ears " and " The Praise of Chimney Sweeps " in the first volume, and " The Superannuated Man " and " Poor Relations " in the second.

——, *Tales from Shakespeare*
Twenty plays of Shakespeare transposed into prose — the comedies by Mary Lamb and the tragedies by Charles Lamb.

Pearson, Hesketh, *Sir Walter Scott*
Follows Scott through his lameness, his struggle against monetary problems, his happiness in marriage, and his literary successes.

Stevenson, Robert L., *St. Ives*
A tale of the daring adventures of a French prisoner who escapes from Edinburgh castle.

Thackeray, William M., *Vanity Fair*
In this satire, Becky Sharp, an ambitious young girl, uses every trick she knows to get ahead in society.

Trollope, Anthony, *The Eustace Diamonds*
A mystery story about the unscrupulous Lady Eustace and her diamonds.

Winwar, Frances, *The Romantic Rebels*
Excellent biographical studies of Byron, Shelley, and Keats.

FOR LISTENING

The following poems have been recorded and are available on *Many Voices 6A:* " The Rime of the Ancient Mariner " (Part I), " She Dwelt among the Untrodden Ways," " Composed upon Westminster Bridge," " The World Is Too Much with Us." These selections are on *Many Voices 6B:* " Apostrophe to the Ocean," " Ode to the West Wind," " Ode on a Grecian Urn," " On First Looking into Chapman's Homer."

THE VICTORIAN

Eighteen-year-old Victoria succeeded to the throne in 1837, and for the third time gave a queen's name to a period of cultural achievement. The British people were delighted to have as their ruler a gracious, serious young girl with the look of a queen; she was the embodiment of the romantic ideals of the preceding half century. Sixty years later, at her Diamond Jubilee in 1897, her subjects were still intensely loyal to her. Although the queen lived until 1901, the first year of the twentieth century is an appropriate time to ring down the curtain on the Victorian Age. If we think of the literary output, however, 1892 is perhaps a more suitable date, for it marked the death of Tennyson, the most representative voice of all the great Victorian writers.

England traveled a path of progress and prosperity in this complex period. It was a time of vigor and variety, of stability and power.

VICTORIAN SERIOUSNESS

After reading the pieces that follow in this section, see if you agree that the dominant note of the Victorian Age was its *moral seriousness*. The Victorians

AGE 1837-1900

have been called " earnest " and " eminent." This does not mean that they lacked humor: people who could produce the *Pickwick Papers, Alice in Wonderland,* and *H.M.S. Pinafore* knew how to laugh. Instead, it means that they felt that life was worth living; they were confident and hopeful enough to believe that they could make it better. This moral seriousness explains their energy and enthusiasm in attempting to increase knowledge and improve mankind's lot. They did not live their lives in compartments, but as a part of a vast complex world. In their pursuits, some Victorians did achieve positions of great power and eminence. The many details described below can, for the most part, be traced to a central characteristic: the Victorians' constant concern with propriety and virtue.

ONE YEAR AS A CROSS SECTION

To understand this complex age, let us turn a magnifying glass on a single year: 1850.

We feel that we are standing at the crossroads of many different worlds.

Under the direction of Prince Albert, Victoria's husband, preparations are going on in London to build the Crystal Palace, an enormous glass building, designed for the International Exposition to be held the next year — the first of the great world's fairs that bring together the most remarkable products of all nations.

What is happening in literature in 1850? The last of the Romantics, William Wordsworth, dies at the age of eighty. Robert Louis Stevenson, who will write stories and essays, poems and novels, is born. Robert Browning and his no-less-famous wife Elizabeth Barrett are publishing books of poems. (Hers is *Sonnets from the Portuguese,* celebrating their love.) Novels are being written by a brilliant trio: Charles Dickens, Thackeray, and George Eliot. At this time, the current Dickens novel happens to be *David Copperfield,* which millions of English and American youngsters for years will read or see dramatized. With George Eliot, who will soon become the greatest of the Victorian woman novelists, a new element enters into literary tradition: women writers begin to gain recognition. (It was some time before women were wholeheartedly accepted as authors, however; witness the masculine pseudonyms adopted by George Eliot and the Brontë sisters.)

Many ideas are fermenting in this year of 1850. In his newest work, *Latter-Day Pamphlets,* the famous Scotsman Thomas Carlyle thunders against popular government and the "dismal science" of economics. Here is a book called *Social Statics* by Herbert Spencer, who during his long life is to become the great popular explainer of science and evolution. And here are copies of a little magazine called *The Germ* (with poems by Christina and Dante Gabriel Rossetti), which was indeed the germ or first seed of the Pre-Raphaelite Movement, about which we shall hear later.

If one year can bring forth such various literary productions, what can be said of the age? We have touched on only a few of the most important names, but we have come out with a representative group: Stevenson, Browning, Elizabeth Barrett, Dickens, Thackeray, Eliot, Carlyle, Spencer, and the two Rossettis. Great Britain was a mental powerhouse of good writers, and ordinary people were taking pleasure in buying their books and reading them.

ONE MAN'S VIEW

Let us consider a man who possessed, in balanced proportions, all the elements of the Victorian Age. Alfred Tennyson was a typical Victorian: dignified, serious, handsome, respected, hard-working at his craft. For Tennyson, 1850 was a banner year. Not only did he publish his greatest poem, *In Memoriam* (on which he had worked for seventeen years), but he was also appointed poet laureate to succeed Wordsworth.

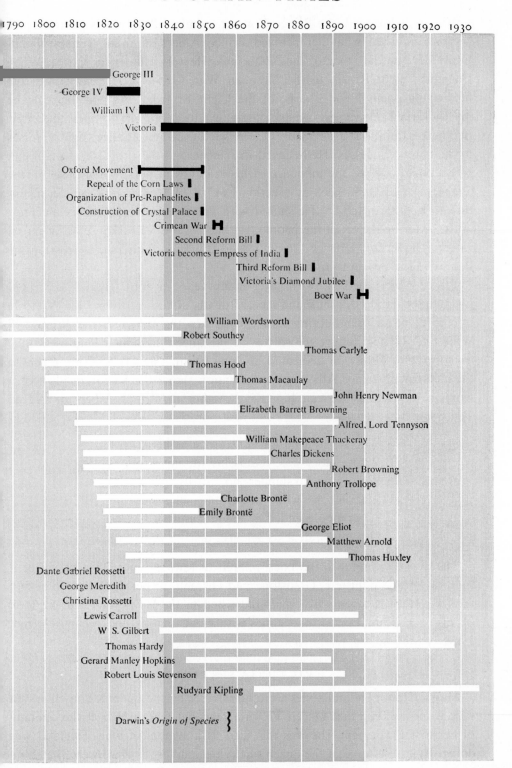

1790 1800 1810 1820 1830 1840 1850 1860 1870 1880 1890 1900 1910 1920 1930

George III
George IV
William IV
Victoria

Oxford Movement
Repeal of the Corn Laws
Organization of Pre-Raphaelites
Construction of Crystal Palace
Crimean War
Second Reform Bill
Victoria becomes Empress of India
Third Reform Bill
Victoria's Diamond Jubilee
Boer War

William Wordsworth
Robert Southey
Thomas Carlyle
Thomas Hood
Thomas Macaulay
John Henry Newman
Elizabeth Barrett Browning
Alfred, Lord Tennyson
William Makepeace Thackeray
Charles Dickens
Robert Browning
Anthony Trollope
Charlotte Brontë
Emily Brontë
George Eliot
Matthew Arnold
Thomas Huxley
Dante Gabriel Rossetti
George Meredith
Christina Rossetti
Lewis Carroll
W. S. Gilbert
Thomas Hardy
Gerard Manley Hopkins
Robert Louis Stevenson
Rudyard Kipling

Darwin's *Origin of Species* }

1790 1800 1810 1820 1830 1840 1850 1860 1870 1880 1890 1900 1910 1920 1930

Victoria's husband, the Prince Consort, admired Tennyson's poetry. Since Victoria admired what her beloved Prince Albert admired, Tennyson naturally became the voice of the Victorians. He was a devoted patriot. When England fought Russia in the Crimean War (1854–56), Tennyson wrote his ringing poem " The Charge of the Light Brigade." As poet laureate he loyally turned out verses to mark official events — an ode to open the International Exhibition, a poem on Queen Victoria's first Jubilee, lighter verses to the royal princesses. He believed in science and the progress of mankind. In his poems we see the influence of his readings in botany (" Flower in the Crannied Wall "), in geology (section LIV of *In Memoriam*), and in invention (" Locksley Hall "). He shared with Prince Albert and others an interest in bettering the lot of the people. He had a good Victorian sense of moral values (shown in " Ulysses ") and a deep Christian faith (see " Crossing the Bar " and the Proem to *In Memoriam*).

Prince Albert died in 1861, after many years of conscientious service to his adopted land. Her husband's early death, a terrible blow, led Victoria into forty years of mourning and earned her the title of " the Widow of Windsor." To help relieve the sorrow of the queen, now his friend as well as his sovereign, Tennyson dedicated his long poem, *The Idylls of the King,* to the memory of Prince Albert. The dedication shows the Victorian ideal of a gentleman, whether we call him King Arthur or Prince Albert or Alfred Tennyson himself:

> Who reverenced his conscience as his king;
> Whose glory was, redressing human wrong;
> Who spoke no slander, no, nor listened to it;
> Wearing the white flower of a blameless life.
> Sweet nature gilded by the gracious gleam
> Of Letters, dear to Science, dear to Art.

The queen, grateful to the poet, offered to reward him with a title. But it took two prime ministers, Gladstone and Disraeli, to persuade him to accept the title. He was seventy-five years old when in the House of Lords he took off his cocked hat, bowed three times with great dignity, and became Alfred, Lord Tennyson.

VICTORIA'S REIGN

Manners, morals, and styles were largely set by the queen's household. In fact, from the time that Queen Victoria read her first speech at the opening of her first Parliament, she was regarded as a symbol of what England was doing. By listing some of the queen's activities, almost as if we were sketching a diary for her, we can trace the course of the whole Victorian Age:

1842. She made her first railway journey. *The age of steam, of mechanical power, of invention, was approaching*. This was the period that introduced safety matches, photography, painless operations under ether and chloroform, antiseptic surgery, advances in sanitation, the X ray, the telegraph, and the telephone.

1843. She visited the French king. It was the first time since Henry VIII that an English sovereign had visited a French sovereign. *International alliances were becoming important*. England tried for peace and for

QUEEN VICTORIA

a "balance of power" among European nations. After Prussia defeated France in 1870, two great alliances were taking shape — Germany, Austria, and Italy on one side, and later, England, France, and Russia on the other. These alliances eventually determined the opposing sides in World War I.

1844. Victoria opened the new buildings of the Royal Exchange, a center for commercial transactions. *England was becoming the financial center of the world*. All over the globe she was investing her newly acquired wealth from trade. Through such insurance houses as Lloyd's of London, through the Bank of England (which came to be called the " Old Lady of Threadneedle Street "), England was quietly dominating the farthest colonies through the power of money.

1846. Victoria consented to the repeal of the Corn Laws. (" Corn " is the English term for wheat or grain.) The Corn Laws, by placing high import taxes on wheat for the benefit of English farming interests, made bread expensive. The poor of England were close to starvation. In Ireland, a quarter of the population died within two years during the " Black Famine " when the potato crop failed. The repeal of the Corn Laws indicates that *the British began to encourage free trade,* without government protection of favored classes by means of taxes or trade barriers. England needed the markets of the world to give life blood to her Empire.

1857. The queen herself conferred the Victoria Cross on the heroes of the Crimean War. This war against Russia was fought largely to keep the waterway between the Mediterranean and the Black Sea open; thus *England protected her interests abroad.* By 1876 Victoria had become " Empress of India," an achievement that was engineered by her brilliant prime minister, Benjamin Disraeli, leader of the Conservatives (and also a novelist). To bind the British Empire together, he also acquired for his country a new waterway to the East — the Suez Canal between the Mediterranean and the Red Sea.

1861. Following her husband's guidance, Victoria persuaded her ministers to refrain from helping the South in the American War Between the States. *England was divided in its feeling, but public sentiment favored the North.* English aid to the Confederacy might have split the United States permanently; yet England remained neutral, even though her neutrality worked great hardships on the English mills and workers that depended on Southern cotton.

1885. Victoria supported the Third Reform Bill. All men could now vote. Under a constitutional sovereign, *England had become a democracy* — that is, the people through their votes had become the final authority in government. This bill was largely the work of William Gladstone — leader of the Liberal party, champion of freedom, and prime minister during the greater part of Queen Victoria's later reign. Throughout the period, conditions of the working classes slowly improved. For instance, it now became possible for a lower-class child to get at least an elementary education.

1900. In her eighties, Victoria went to Ireland to encourage the recruiting of her soldiers, now fighting the Boer War in South Africa. *England had her problems in holding the Empire together.* Even the Irish were unrelenting in trying to free the Irish Church from government ties and to get Home Rule.

1901. Victoria died, and her funeral train was driven through London to Windsor with military honors. An age had closed. Its queen had seen the advances of science and commerce, the power politics that grouped nations in perilous balance, the expansion of industry and of finance, the progress of democracy, the concern for the underprivileged, the defense of the Empire by force of arms — all these and more.

WRITERS AS TEACHERS

Believing optimistically in progress, the typical Victorian writer set about improving his readers by increasing their knowledge and clarifying their moral standards.

BRITAIN
1837-1900

SCOTLAND

● Edinburgh [1]

● Ecclefechan [2]

IRELAND

ARAN
ISLANDS

● Dublin [3]

WALES

ENGLAND

● Rugby [5]

● Cambridge

● Lake
Killarney [4]

Oxford [6] ●

Windsor ●   ● London [7]

● Canterbury

Dover [8] ●

Isle of
Wight [9]

1 R. L. Stevenson was born here. **2** Carlyle's birthplace. **3** Cardinal Newman was rector at Dublin University, and Gerard Manley Hopkins taught Greek there. **4** Setting for Tennyson's "Bugle Song." **5** Matthew Arnold attended the famous school at Rugby and later returned to teach. **6** Hopkins studied and Lewis Carroll taught mathematics at Oxford University. **7** Much of England's literary life centered in London. Macaulay knew the city well and described it in his history. The Rossettis wrote and painted here. Robert Browning courted Elizabeth Barrett at her home in Wimpole Street. Dickens lived in the city and wrote about it with warmth and color. Gilbert and Sullivan's operettas were first seen in London. **8** Scene of Matthew Arnold's "Dover Beach." **9** Tennyson had a home here.

Scientists are best represented by Charles Darwin. His *The Origin of Species,* published in 1859, is a landmark in the history of thought, though its general ideas had been fermenting for many years. Darwin's theory of evolution maintains that life changes slowly from one form to another, and that nature selects the fittest to survive. His description is of a process that is impersonal but hopeful, suggesting human progress and rewarding those who make an effort to overcome obstacles. Tennyson in *In Memoriam* struggled with the conflict between old religious doctrines and the new interpretations, which biology and geology had introduced, of the place of man in this world. In their essays and lectures, Thomas Huxley and Herbert Spencer presented to the public the ideas of the new science.

Historians such as Macaulay wrote long and detailed studies of England. Carlyle wrote on everything from the Middle Ages to the French Revolution, from Cromwell to Frederick the Great of Prussia, in his attempt to show that civilizations advance by obedience to great heroes and leaders.

Educators may be exemplified by Matthew Arnold, whose father was a famous headmaster of Rugby School, and who himself was an inspector of schools. Over and over again in his effectively simple style, Arnold laughed at, argued with, and cajoled the English people, trying to overcome their smugness, intolerance, and ignorance. He defined culture as the best that has been thought and said. In his own poetry and criticism, he taught the English to seek for the best.

Religious writers are well represented by John Henry Newman, one of the great stylists in English prose. In the 1830's and 1840's, the Oxford Movement in the Church of England developed as a reaction against materialism and spiritual indifference. Newman, after much soul-searching, left the Anglican Church for the Roman Catholic Church, in which he finally became a cardinal. Newman's painful struggle between different faiths, as well as the impact of the new science upon religion, compelled men to look closely at their beliefs.

Novelists reached an enormous audience, and gave to the Victorians their favorite form of literature. Charles Dickens wrote melodramatic plots about the poor and the oppressed so convincingly that he made the English conscious of the need for reform in their systems of law, education, and wealth. William Makepeace Thackeray encompassed whole societies in his colorful portrayal of English life. George Eliot presented deeply earnest stories dealing persuasively with the Victorian ideals of duty and self-sacrifice. Many other writers wrote effectively in this form, but Dickens, Thackeray, and Eliot remain the Big Three among the novelists.

Poets also had their Big Three — Tennyson, Browning, and Arnold. They too were teachers: Tennyson, of a belief in the future strong enough to overcome his native melancholy; Browning, of an unquenchable optimism and interest in all individuals; Arnold, of a philosophy of endurance and of perfecting one's own best nature.

TRENDS IN POETRY AND PAINTING

Shortly after 1850 another group of poets, whom we might call the Little Three, came into prominence: Dante Gabriel Rossetti, William Morris, and Algernon Swinburne. Their interest in other arts was supported at first by the influential art critic John Ruskin, whose theory is typically Victorian: great art is produced for use and can only be produced by good men. The Romantic influence was reawakening, and Ruskin turned men back toward the Middle Ages, as Coleridge and Keats had done earlier. This romantic revival, embodied in the works of a group called the Pre-Raphaelite Brotherhood, included Rossetti and Morris and several prominent painters. They wished to get away from the conventionality and correctness of the Renaissance artist Raphael; they preferred the childlike directness of earlier, medieval painters.

Rossetti himself was skillful in the use of color and design. William Morris not only invented the comfortable Morris chair, but returned also to medieval ideas of making beautiful objects by hand instead of by machinery. He published superb books on his own Kelmscott Press and introduced his ideas of lightness, color, and design into the interior decoration of the average British home.

NEW CURRENTS IN THE LATER DECADES

Near the end of the century, England grew restless under the prevailing seriousness and decorum. Many people talked scornfully of " Victorian compromise " — that unfailing reconciliation of opposite points of view. People who distrusted the goodness of human nature spoke of Victorian " hypocrisy." Influenced by foreign literatures, a new generation of late Victorian writers started defiant little movements and magazines in London, bringing in the " gay Nineties." A different spirit entered the age. Oscar Wilde wrote crackling comedies and made unforgettable epigrams; Aubrey Beardsley created daringly different drawings that shocked the public. " The sickness of the century " led so many gifted writers to sad ends that William Butler Yeats called the young writers of the Nineties who were his friends the " tragic generation."

Another current of thought and manners in the latter part of the century carried forward the healthier spirit of Dickens and the earlier literature. There was, for example, gaiety in the Gilbert and Sullivan operas and in Lewis Carroll's poems and his *Alice in Wonderland*. There were Robert Louis Stevenson's graceful essays, short stories of adventure, and tender or child-like poems.

Deeper down flowed an undercurrent of grim responsibility, even of pessimism. Thomas Hardy — novelist, short-story writer, poet — held this view powerfully and consistently throughout his work. Rudyard Kipling, the poet and short-story writer of the whole Empire, believed that his Indian officials and British soldiers and explorers and sailors were carrying the " white man's burden." Kipling could not forget that the Empire that comprised a quarter of the world, if it were not to melt away like all the empires of the past, had to rest, not upon guns and ships, but upon " an humble and a contrite heart."

SUMMARY

The Victorians, living in a vast and complex world, were able to achieve peace, prosperity, and progress.

By winning campaigns in India, Egypt, and South Africa, the Victorians brought order and strength into their Empire. In trying for a " balance of power " among European nations, England remained an important force in world politics.

Under a constitutional sovereign, the basis for democracy was broadened by the Reform Bills. Conditions of the working classes improved; public education was introduced; and more men were permitted to vote.

It was a period of advance in many areas: invention, science, commerce, industry, finance, education, religion, and art. The problems created by these advances occupied the deepest thought of Victorian writers. In poetry, in the serious essay, and particularly in the novel, the Victorians excelled. In the midst of astounding variety, the dominating force is toward a better world through co-operation, intelligence, and a moral seriousness.

THOMAS CARLYLE 1795–1881

Thomas Carlyle, like his fellow Scotsman Robert Burns, had a hard struggle against poverty. His father, a stonemason with nine children, was determined that his brilliant son should study for the ministry at Edinburgh University. Thomas, then fifteen years old, walked the hundred miles from his birthplace, Ecclefechan (ĕk"l·fĕk'-ăn), to Edinburgh. Of his five years of painful economy there, he writes: " I was without friends, experience, or connection in the sphere of human business, was of sly humor, proud enough and to spare, and had begun my long curriculum of dyspepsia." This nagging and persistent illness contributed to his irritable temperament, for which he was known and feared all his life. Influenced by his study of German philosophy, Carlyle developed a marked pessimism about mankind. He was a reformer, but history rather than religion became his teacher.

While tutoring in London he married Jane Welsh, a beautiful Scottish girl, who fortunately had a farm in southern Scotland where they could live at little expense. Her letters to her friends describing their none-too-easy life were written in delightful style, and have since been published in several editions. In 1834 the Carlyles moved to London, and their house in Cheyne Row became a center for the gathering of literary people, as Lamb's home had been earlier. (Lamb died the year the Carlyles moved to London.) In spite of his gruff and thorny exterior, Carlyle had the power to make warm friends among those who recognized his sincerity and his genius. Dickens, Thackeray, and Tennyson greatly admired him, and when Emerson first went to Europe, his most earnest desire was to meet Carlyle. Their thirty-year friendship won for each a reading public in the other's country.

The Fall of the Bastille

A tragic circumstance was connected with the writing of Carlyle's famous history *The French Revolution.* Carlyle had given his manuscript to his friend, the economist John Stuart Mill, to read, and Mill's servant accidentally used the sheets to build a fire one morning. Carlyle had kept no notes and at first could not recall any of his writing. He spent a week reading novels to calm his mind; then he laboriously rewrote the whole book.

The following selection shows Carlyle's highly individual style, with its broken, exclamatory sentences. He gives the reader the feeling of being actually present and experiencing the excitement and suspense of the scene.

The gloomy Bastille (băs·tēl') prison, surrounded by a moat, had stood since the fourteenth century at one of the gates of Paris. With its long history of unjust imprisonments and forgotten prisoners, it had become a symbol of the oppressions of the French monarchy. The day of its destruction, July 14, 1789, became the date for the annual celebration of national independence, just as July 4 is Independence Day in America.

THE BASTILLE is besieged! On, then, all Frenchmen that have hearts in your bodies! Roar with all your throats of cartilage and metal, ye sons of liberty; stir spasmodically whatsoever of utmost faculty is in you, soul, body, or spirit, for it is the hour! Smite thou, Louis Tournay, cartwright of the Marais,[1] old soldier of the Régiment Dauphiné;[2] smite at that outer drawbridge chain, though the fiery hail whistles around thee! Never, over nave[3] or felloe,[4] did thy ax strike such a stroke. Down with it, man; down with it to Orcus;[5] let the whole accursed edifice sink thither, and tyranny be swallowed up forever! Mounted, some say, on the roof of the guard room, some " on bayonets stuck into joints of the wall," Louis Tournay smites, brave Aubin Bonnemère[6] (also an old soldier) seconding him. The chain yields, breaks; the huge drawbridge slams down, thundering. Glorious! and yet, alas! it is still but the outworks. The eight grim towers with their invalide[7] musketry, their paving stones and cannon mouths, still soar

---

[1] *Marais* (mä·rā'): a manufacturing quarter of Paris.

[2] *Régiment Dauphiné* (rā·zhē·mäɴ' dō·fē·nā'): regiment of the Dauphin, or king's son.

[3] *nave:* the hub of a wheel.

[4] *felloe:* a segment of the rim of a wooden wheel.

[5] *Orcus:* in Roman mythology, the home of the dead; the underworld.

[6] *Bonnemère* (bŏn·mĕr').

[7] *invalide* (àn·vȧ·lēd'): veteran (originally, wounded soldier).

aloft intact; ditch yawning impassable, stonefaced; the inner drawbridge with its *back* toward us; the Bastille is still to take! . . .

Paris, wholly, has got to the acme of its frenzy, whirled all ways by panic madness. At every street barricade there whirls, simmering, a minor whirlpool, strengthening the barricade, since God knows what is coming; and all minor whirlpools play distractedly into that grand fire maelstrom [1] which is lashing round the Bastille.

And so it lashes and roars. Cholat,[2] the wine merchant, has become an impromptu cannoneer. See Georget,[3] of the marine service, fresh from Brest,[4] play the King of Siam's cannon. Singular (if we were not used to the like). Georget lay last night taking his ease at his inn; the King of Siam's cannon also lay, knowing nothing of *him* for a hundred years; yet now, at the right instant, they have got together, and discourse eloquent music; for, hearing what was toward, Georget sprang from the Brest diligence,[5] and ran. Gardes Françaises,[6] also, will be here with real artillery. Were not the walls so thick! Upward from the esplanade, horizontally from all neighboring roofs and windows, flashes one irregular deluge of musketry, without effect. The invalides lie flat, firing comparatively at their ease from behind stone; hardly through portholes show the tip of a nose. We fall, shot, and make no impression!

Let conflagration rage of whatsoever is combustible! Guardrooms are burnt, invalides messrooms. A distracted " peruke maker with two fiery torches " is for burning " the saltpeters of the arsenal," had not a woman run screaming, had not a patriot, with some tincture of natural philosophy, instantly struck the wind out of him (butt of musket on pit of stomach), overturned barrels, and stayed the devouring element. A young, beautiful lady seized, escaping, in these outer courts, and thought, falsely, to be De Launay's [7] daughter, shall be burnt in De Launay's sight; she lies, swooned, on a paillasse; [8] but, again, a patriot — it is brave Aubin Bonnemère, the old soldier — dashes in, and rescues her. Straw is burnt; three cartloads of it, hauled hither, go up in white smoke, almost to the choking of patriotism itself; so that Elie had, with singed brows, to drag back one cart, and Réole, the " gigantic haberdasher," another. Smoke as of Tophet,[9] confusion as of Babel,[10] noise as of the crack of doom!

Blood flows, the aliment of new madness. The wounded are carried into

[1] *maelstrom* (māl'strŏm): a whirlpool off the northwest coast of Norway; used figuratively, any turmoil of resistless movement or influence.

[2] *Cholat* (shō·lä').

[3] *Georget* (zhôr·zhĕ').

[4] *Brest:* a naval station in northwest France.

[5] *diligence* (dē·lē·zhäns'): stagecoach.

[6] *Gardes Françaises* (gärd frän·sĕz'): French guards.

[7] *De Launay* (dĕ lō·nā'): governor of the Bastille; slain after its capture.

[8] *paillasse* (păl·yäs'): a straw mattress.

[9] *Tophet* (tō'fĕt): a place near Jerusalem used for burning sacrifices and, later, refuse.

[10] *Babel* (bā'bĕl): a confusion of many voices; from the Tower of Babel (Genesis 11:9).

houses of the Rue Cerisaie;[1] the dying leave their last mandate not to yield till the accursed stronghold fall. And yet, alas! how fall? The walls are so thick! Deputations, three in number, arrive from the Hôtel-de-Ville.[2] . . . These wave their town flag in the arched gateway, and stand, rolling their drum, but to no purpose. In such crack of doom De Launay cannot hear them, dare not believe them; they return, with justified rage, the whew of lead still singing in their ears. What to do? The firemen are here, squirting with their fire pumps on the invalides' cannon to wet the touchholes; they unfortunately cannot squirt so high, but produce only clouds of spray. Individuals of classical knowledge propose *catapults*. Santerre, the sonorous brewer of the suburb Saint-Antoine, advises rather that the place be fired by " a mixture of phosphorus and oil of turpentine spouted up through forcing pumps." O Spinola-Santerre,[3] has thou the mixture *ready?* Every man his own engineer! And still the fire deluge abates not; even women are firing, and Turks — at least one woman (with her sweetheart) and one Turk. Gardes Françaises have come; real cannon, real cannoneers. Usher Maillard is busy; half-pay Elie, half-pay Hulin, rage in the midst of thousands.

How the great Bastille clock ticks (inaudible) in its inner court, there, at its ease, hour after hour; as if nothing special, for it or the world, were passing! It tolled one when the firing began, and is now pointing toward five, and still the firing slakes not. Far down in their vaults, the seven prisoners hear muffled din as of earthquakes; their turnkeys answer vaguely.

Woe to thee, De Launay, with thy poor hundred invalides! . . .

What shall De Launay do? One thing only De Launay could have done — what he said he would do. Fancy him sitting, from the first, with lighted taper, within arm's length of the powder magazine; motionless, like an old Roman senator, or bronze lamp holder; coldly apprising all manner of men, by a slight motion of his eye, what his resolution was. Harmless he sat there, while unharmed; but the king's fortress, meanwhile, could, might, would, or should in nowise be surrendered, save to the king's messengers; one old man's life is worthless, so it be lost with honor; but think, ye brawling *canaille*,[4] how will it be when a whole Bastille springs skyward? In such statuesque, taper-holding attitude, one fancies De Launay might have left Thuriot, the red clerks of the Basoche, curé[5] of St. Stephen, and all the tagrag and bobtail of the world, to work their will.

And yet, withal, he could not do it. . . . Distracted he hovers between two — hopes in the middle of despair; surrenders not his fortress; declares that he will blow it up, seizes torches to blow it up, and does not blow it. Unhappy old De Launay, it is the death agony of the Bastille and thee! Jail, jailoring, and jailor, all three, such as they may have been, must finish.

For four hours now has the world bedlam roared; call it the world chimera[6] blowing fire! The poor invalides have sunk under their battlements, or rise only with reversed muskets; they have made a white flag of napkins, go beating the chamade,[7] or seeming to beat, for one can hear nothing. The very Swiss at the portcullis[8] look weary of

---

[1] *Rue Cerisaie* (rū sĕr·ē·sā'): a street in Paris.

[2] *Hôtel-de-Ville* (ō·tĕl d'vēl'): City Hall.

[3] *Spinola-Santerre* (spĭ·nō'là-sàn·târ'): San-terre, a leader of the Parisian Revolutionary mob, is likened to General Spinola, who captured a fortress in Holland in 1625.

[4] *canaille* (kå'nä'y'): the vulgar multitude; the mob.

[5] *curé* (kū·rā'): parish priest.

[6] *chimera* (kĭ·mēr'å): a mythical fire-breathing animal.

[7] *chamade* (shå·mäd'): a drum or trumpet signal for a parley.

[8] *Swiss at the portcullis:* The French hired Swiss mercenaries as guards. The portcullis was an iron grating at the entrance.

firing, disheartened in the fire deluge; a porthole at the drawbridge is opened, as by one that would speak. See Huissier Maillard, the shifty man! On his plank, swinging over the abyss of that stoned ditch, plank resting on parapet, balanced by weight of patriots, he hovers perilous — such a dove toward such an ark! Deftly, thou shifty usher; one man already fell and lies smashed, far down there against the masonry! Usher Maillard falls not; deftly, unerringly, he walks, with outspread palm. The Swiss holds a paper through the porthole; the shifty usher snatches it and returns. Terms of surrender: Pardon, immunity to all! Are they accepted? " Foi d'officier (on the word of an officer)," answers half-pay Hulin, or half-pay Elie — for men do not agree on it — " they are! " Sinks the drawbridge, Usher Maillard bolting it when down; rushes in the living deluge; the Bastille is fallen! *Victoire! La Bastille est prise!* [1]

CARLYLE'S HISTORY

1. Describe in your own words the outer appearance of the Bastille, and just what happened to cause it to surrender. What descriptive touches make the scene vivid and dramatic?

2. What is the attitude of the mob toward the aristocrats? What do you learn about mob psychology? Does Carlyle show sympathy with either side? Support your answer with specific references.

3. Some class members should read Dickens' account of the fall of the Bastille in *A Tale of Two Cities* (Book II, Chapter 21), and tell the class what likenesses and what differences they find in the two versions. Dickens based his narrative largely on Carlyle's.

[1] Victory! The Bastille is taken!

THOMAS BABINGTON MACAULAY 1800–1859

Carlyle and Macaulay are often coupled as the greatest writers of history and essay during the Victorian Age. Yet how unlike are their lives and their talents! Carlyle was a rough-hewn, gloomy, often secluded man who scolded against the times; Macaulay was a bland, confident, earnest public figure, whose writings were extremely popular.

Macaulay embarked on his literary career with an essay on Milton. Later he entered Parliament, where he spoke brilliantly in behalf of the Reform Bill to extend suffrage and championed the cause of Negro slaves in the West Indies. During these active years of public service, young Macaulay was constantly writing prose, and he even ventured into the field of poetry with *Lays of Ancient Rome,* which are still popular narrative poems. At thirty-nine he began his *History of England,* a work that has since become standard. (It brought him more than $150,000 in royalties, but twice that amount was lost to him by the inadequate copyright laws of the day, which prevented his receiving royalties from sales in America.) At fifty-seven he was made Lord Macaulay. Two years later he died and was buried in Westminster Abbey.

Such a career points to the sturdy qualities of honesty, industry, perseverance, and devotion to public welfare. Macaulay was sometimes criticized for his lack of deep insight into human problems, his prejudice, and his apparent inability to see all sides of a question. " I wish," said one of his contemporaries in government, " that I could be as sure of anything as Lord Macaulay is of everything."

London Streets

In contrast to Carlyle's jagged sentences and headlong style is the smooth, direct style of Macaulay. Both use graphic details to hold the attention of the reader, but the effect produced is entirely different. As a result of the detail in which Macaulay pictured the bygone ages, he covered in five volumes of his *History of England* only sixteen years, from James II to Queen Anne. London as here described was much the same throughout the late seventeenth and eighteenth centuries.

THE POSITION of London, relatively to the other towns of the empire, was, in the time of Charles II, far higher than at present. For at present the population of London is little more than six times the population of Manchester or of Liverpool. In the days of Charles II the population of London was more than seventeen times the population of Bristol or of Norwich. It may be doubted whether any other instance can be mentioned of a great kingdom in which the first city was more than seventeen times as large as the second. There is reason to believe that in 1685 London had been, during about half a century, the most populous capital in Europe. The inhabitants, who are now at least nineteen hundred thousand, were then probably little more than half a million. . . .

We should greatly err if we were to suppose that any of the streets and squares then bore the same aspect as at present. The great majority of the houses, indeed, have, since that time, been wholly, or in great part, rebuilt. If the most fashionable parts of the capital could be placed before us, such as they then were, we should be disgusted by their squalid appearance, and poisoned by their noisome atmosphere. In Covent Garden a filthy and noisy market was held close to the dwellings of the great. Fruit women screamed, cart-

ers fought, cabbage stalks and rotten apples accumulated in heaps at the thresholds of the Countess of Berkshire and of the Bishop of Durham.

The center of Lincoln's Inn Fields [1] was an open space where the rabble congregated every evening, within a few yards of Cardigan House and Winchester House, to hear mountebanks harangue, to see bears dance, and to set dogs at oxen. Rubbish was shot in every part of the area. Horses were exercised there. The beggars were as noisy and importunate as in the worst-governed cities of the Continent. A Lincoln's Inn mumper [2] was a proverb. The whole fraternity knew the arms and liveries of every charitably disposed grandee in the neighborhood, and, as soon as his lordship's coach and six appeared, came hopping and crawling in crowds to persecute him. These disorders lasted, in spite of many accidents, and of some legal proceedings, till, in the reign of George II, Sir Joseph Jekyll, Master of the Rolls, was knocked down and nearly killed in the middle of the square. Then at length palisades were set up, and a pleasant garden laid out.

Saint James' Square [3] was a receptacle for all the offal and cinders, for all the dead cats and dead dogs of Westminster.[4] At one time a cudgel player [5] kept the ring there. At another time an impudent squatter settled himself there, and built a shed for rubbish under the windows of the gilded saloons in which the first magnates of the realm, Norfolk, Ormond, Kent, and Pembroke, gave banquets and balls. It was not till these nuisances had lasted through a whole generation, and till much had been writ-

---

[1] *Lincoln's Inn Fields:* the largest square in London, surrounded by lawyers' offices and old mansions.

[2] *mumper:* a beggar and impostor.

[3] *Saint James' Square:* later a fashionable district.

[4] *Westminster:* the section of London where the government houses are located.

[5] *cudgel player:* a man skilled in defending himself with cudgel or staff.

Macaulay was a child prodigy. He could read at the age of three; at four he could repeat long passages from memory. When he was eight, he wrote a Compendium of Universal Knowledge! *At Cambridge he took top honors in all his subjects except mathematics.*

ten about them, that the inhabitants applied to Parliament for permission to put up rails, and to plant trees.

When such was the state of the region inhabited by the most luxurious portion of society, we may easily believe that the great body of the population suffered what would now be considered as insupportable grievances. The pavement was detestable; all foreigners cried shame upon it. The drainage was so bad that in rainy weather the gutters soon became torrents. Several facetious poets have commemorated the fury with which these black rivulets roared down Snow Hill and Ludgate Hill, bearing to Fleet Ditch a vast tribute of animal and vegetable filth from the stalls of butchers and greengrocers. This flood was profusely thrown to right and left by coaches and carts. To keep as far from the carriage road as possible was therefore the wish of every pedestrian. The mild and timid gave the wall. The bold and athletic took it. If two roisterers met, they cocked their hats in each other's faces, and pushed each other about till the weaker was shoved toward the kennel.[1] If he was a mere bully he sneaked off, muttering that he should find a time. If he was pugnacious, the encounter probably ended in a duel behind Montague House.[2]

The houses were not numbered. There would indeed have been little advantage in numbering them; for of the coachmen, chairmen,[3] porters, and errand boys of London, a very small pro-

portion could read. It was necessary to use marks which the most ignorant could understand. The shops were therefore distinguished by painted or sculptured signs, which gave a gay and grotesque aspect to the streets. The walk from Charing Cross to Whitechapel lay through an endless succession of Saracens' Heads, Royal Oaks, Blue Bears, and Golden Lambs, which disappeared when they were no longer required for the direction of the common people.

When the evening closed in, the difficulty and danger of walking about London became serious indeed. The garret windows were opened, and pails were emptied, with little regard to those who were passing below. Falls, bruises, and broken bones were of constant occurrence. For, till the last year of the reign of Charles II, most of the streets were left in profound darkness. Thieves and robbers plied their trade with impunity; yet they were hardly so terrible to peaceable citizens as another class of ruffians. It was a favorite amusement of dissolute young gentlemen to swagger by night about the town, breaking windows, upsetting sedans, beating quiet men, and offering rude caresses to pretty women. Several dynasties of these tyrants had, since the Restoration, domineered over the streets. The Muns and Tityre Tus had given place to the Hectors, and the Hectors had been recently succeeded by the Scourers. At a later period rose the Nicker, the Hawcubite, and the yet more dreaded name of Mohawk. The machinery for keeping the peace was utterly contemptible. There was an act of Common Council which provided that more than a thousand watchmen should be constantly on the alert in the city, from sunset to sunrise, and that every inhabitant should take his turn of duty. But this act was negligently executed. Few of those who were summoned left their homes; and those few generally found it more agreeable to tipple in alehouses than to pace the streets. . . .

---

[1] *kennel:* street gutter.

[2] *Montague* (mŏn′tȧ·gū) *House:* a government building in Whitehall.

[3] *chairmen:* men who carried the sedan chairs.

London Coffeehouses

The coffeehouse must not be dismissed with a cursory mention. It might indeed at that time have been not improperly called a most important political institution. No Parliament had sat for years. The municipal council of the city had ceased to speak the sense of the citizens. Public meetings, harangues, resolutions, and the rest of the modern machinery of agitation had not yet come into fashion. Nothing resembling the modern newspaper existed. In such circumstances the coffeehouses were the chief organs through which the public opinion of the metropolis vented itself.

The first of these establishments had been set up, in the time of the Commonwealth, by a Turkey merchant, who had acquired among the Mohammedans a taste for their favorite beverage. The convenience of being able to make appointments in any part of the town, and of being able to pass evenings socially at a very small charge, was so great that the fashion spread fast. Every man of the upper or middle class went daily to his coffeehouse to learn the news and to discuss it. Every coffeehouse had one or more orators to whose eloquence the crowd listened with admiration, and who soon became what the journalists of our own time have been called, a fourth Estate of the realm. The court had long seen with uneasiness the growth of this new power in the state. An attempt had been made, during Danby's [1] administration, to close the coffeehouses. But men of all parties missed their usual places of resort so much that there was an universal outcry. The government did not venture, in opposition to a feeling so strong and general, to enforce a regulation of which the legality might well be questioned. Since that time ten years had elapsed, and during those years the number and influence of the coffeehouses had been constantly increasing. Foreigners remarked that the coffeehouse was that which especially distinguished London from all other cities; that the coffeehouse was the Londoner's home, and that those who wished to find a gentleman commonly asked, not whether he lived in Fleet Street or Chancery Lane, but whether he frequented the Grecian or the Rainbow. Nobody was excluded from these places who laid down his penny at the bar. Yet every rank and profession, and every shade of religious and political opinion, had its own headquarters. There were houses near Saint James' Park where fops congregated, their heads and shoulders covered with black or flaxen wigs, not less ample than those which are now worn by the Chancellor and by the Speaker of the House of Commons. The wig came from Paris; and so did the rest of the fine gentleman's ornaments, his embroidered coat, his fringed gloves, and the tassel which upheld his pantaloons. The conversation was in that dialect which, long after it had ceased to be spoken in fashionable circles, continued, in the mouth of Lord Foppington,[2] to excite the mirth of theaters. The atmosphere was like that of a perfumer's shop. Tobacco in any other form than that of richly scented snuff was held in abomination. If any clown, ignorant of the usages of the house, called for a pipe, the sneers of the whole assembly and the short answers of the waiters soon convinced him that he had better go somewhere else. Nor, indeed, would he have had far to go. For, in general, the coffee-rooms reeked with tobacco like a guard-room; and strangers sometimes expressed their surprise that so many people should leave their own firesides to sit in the midst of eternal fog and stench.

Nowhere was the smoking more constant than at Will's. That celebrated

---

[1] *Danby:* Thomas Osborn, Lord Danby; Lord Treasurer under Charles II.

[2] *Foppington:* a character in *The Relapse*, by Vanbrugh; he pronounced "Lord" as "Lard."

A lively scene in an eighteenth-century coffeehouse.

house, situated between Covent Garden and Bow Street, was sacred to polite letters. There the talk was about poetical justice and the unities of place and time. There was a faction for Perrault [1] and the moderns, a faction for Boileau [2] and the ancients. One group debated whether *Paradise Lost* ought not to have been in rhyme. To another an envious poetaster demonstrated that *Venice Preserved* [3] ought to have been hooted from the stage. Under no roof was a greater variety of figures to be seen. There were earls in stars and garters, clergymen in cassocks and bands, pert Templars,[4] sheepish lads from the universities, translators and index makers in ragged coats of frieze. The great press was to get near the chair where John Dryden sat. In winter that chair was always in the warmest nook by the fire; in summer it stood in the balcony.

[1] *Perrault* (pĕ′rō′): French writer (1628–1703); member of the French Academy.
[2] *Boileau* (bwȧ′lō′): French satirist and critic (1636–1711); member of the French Academy. The two disputed the merits of ancient and modern literature.
[3] *Venice Preserved:* a play by Thomas Otway (1652–1685). It was produced in London in 1953.
[4] *Templars:* lawyers and law students, who resided in the Temple.

To bow to the Laureate, and to hear his opinion of Racine's [5] last tragedy or of Bossu's [6] treatise on epic poetry, was thought a privilege. A pinch from his snuffbox was an honor sufficient to turn the head of a young enthusiast. There were coffeehouses where the first medical men might be consulted. Doctor John Radcliffe, who, in the year 1685, rose to the largest practice in London, came daily, at the hour when the Exchange was full, from his house in Bow Street, then a fashionable part of the capital, to Garaway's, and was to be found, surrounded by surgeons and apothecaries, at a particular table. There were Puritan coffeehouses where no oath was heard, and where lank-haired men discussed election and reprobation through their noses; Jew coffeehouses where dark-eyed money-changers from Venice and from Amsterdam greeted each other; and Popish coffeehouses where, as good Protestants believed, Jesuits planned, over their cups, another great fire, and cast silver bullets to shoot the King.

These gregarious habits had no small share in forming the character of the Londoner of that age. He was, indeed, a different being from the rustic Englishman. There was not then the intercourse which now exists between the two classes. Only very great men were in the habit of dividing the year between town and country. Few esquires came to the capital thrice in their lives. Nor was it yet the practice of all citizens in easy circumstances to breathe the fresh air of the fields and woods during some weeks of every summer. A cockney, in a rural village, was stared at as much as if he had intruded into a kraal [7] of Hottentots. On the other hand, when the Lord of a Lincolnshire or Shropshire manor appeared in Fleet Street, he was as easily distinguished from the

[5] *Racine* (rȧ′sēn′): French poet (1639–1699).
[6] *Bossu* (bô′sü′): French critic (1631–1680).
[7] *kraal* (kräl): a stockaded village of South African natives.

resident population as a Turk or a lascar.[1] His dress, his gait, his accent, the manner in which he stared at the shops, stumbled into the gutters, ran against the porters, and stood under the waterspouts, marked him out as an excellent subject for the operations of swindlers and banterers. Bullies jostled him into the kennel. Hackney coachmen splashed him from head to foot. Thieves explored with perfect security the huge pockets of his horseman's coat, while he stood entranced by the splendor of the Lord Mayor's show. Money droppers, sore from the cart's tail,[2] introduced themselves to him, and appeared to him the most honest, friendly gentlemen that he had ever seen. Painted women, the refuse of Lewkner Lane and Whetstone Park, passed themselves on him for countesses and maids of honor. If he asked his way to Saint James', his informants sent him to Mile End.[3] If he went into a shop, he was instantly discerned to be a fit purchaser of everything that nobody else would buy, of secondhand embroidery, copper rings, and watches that would not go. If he rambled into any fashionable coffeehouse, he became a mark for the insolent derision of fops and the grave waggery of Templars. Enraged and mortified, he soon returned to his mansion, and there, in the homage of his tenants, and the conversation of his boon companions, found consolation for the vexations and humiliations which he had undergone. There he was once more a great man, and saw nothing above himself except when at the assizes [4] he took his seat on the bench, near the Judge, or when at the muster of the militia he saluted the Lord Lieutenant.

---

[1] *lascar:* East Indian sailor.
[2] *Money droppers . . . tail:* cheats, who had been tied to a cart and whipped through the streets.
[3] *Mile End:* a poor district in the east end of London.
[4] *assizes* (ă·sīz′ĕz): sessions of the county court.

MACAULAY'S HISTORY

1. Explain briefly conditions in London in the late seventeenth century, as to street cleanliness, identification of shops, the troubles of pedestrians (especially those who came from the country). What different groups were to be found in the coffeehouses?

2. Judging Carlyle and Macaulay by the selections in this book, what differences do you observe in their style (sentence structure, choice of words, use of detail, etc.)? How do these selections differ from the historical writing familiar to you?

CLASS ACTIVITIES

1. In a panel, discuss the great improvements in city conditions that have been made since the time this history describes. Would you have enjoyed living in the London of those days? Why, or why not? In a modern city what various institutions take care of those needs and interests to which the coffeehouses once catered?

2. Some students might read and report to the class the interesting passage on travel conditions in Chapter III of Volume 1 of Macaulay's *History of England.* If possible, illustrate your talk with pictures of old coaches.

THE POWER OF WORDS

EXPRESSIVE ADJECTIVES

Macaulay uses three adjectives which are good ones to add to your vocabulary: *facetious* (fȧ·sē′shŭs), *pugnacious* (pŭg-nā′shŭs), and *gregarious* (grē·gâr′ĭ·ŭs). Macaulay says that several facetious poets have written about the bad drainage system of old London. If you did not know the word, the context might lead you to think that they wrote indignantly, but no, they wrote with intent to make the reader laugh. This intent is always important in the word *facetious.* A person may be unconsciously funny, or naturally witty, or mildly humorous, but if he is purposely taking a light attitude about some serious matter, he is being facetious. What poems have you read in this book to which the word *facetious* might be applied?

Though the poets might treat the drainage system lightly, the pedestrians did not always do so. If one of two persons who tried to get next to the wall at the same moment happened to be *pugnacious,* there might be a duel. You will find in this case that the origin of this word clearly explains its meaning. Look it up.

Gregarious is a pleasanter word. The Londoners of the coffee shops had gregarious habits; that is, they liked to mingle with groups of people. The original root meant a *flock* or *herd.* How does this apply to the meaning of the word? Among the authors about whom you have read in this book, name one or two who were typically gregarious, one or two who were the opposite. Could you apply the adjective to either Macaulay or Carlyle?

JOHN HENRY NEWMAN
1801–1890

and THOMAS HENRY HUXLEY
1825–1895

Newman and Huxley, leading essayists of the period, reflect the Victorians' absorbing interest in two fields: religion and science. With typical earnestness, writers and thinkers of the time were examining both the spiritual and the natural realms of life. Often their religious beliefs and their scientific beliefs clashed, but just as often they sought to reconcile them in a broad view of education. For the Victorians were above all energetic teachers and learners; both Newman and Huxley were not only essayists but educators.

John Henry Newman typified the personal earnestness of the Victorians. He found his answers the hard way, through much soul searching and a marked break with his past. The first half of his life was spent chiefly at Oxford, as a student to begin with, later as a teacher and clergyman. Early in his career as rector of St. Mary's Church he met differences of opinion which led him to resign and to go to the Continent for a while.

During the next dozen years he became closely associated with the Oxford Movement (not to be confused with the religious group of a similar name in our own day). His many sermons and tracts in behalf of this movement pleaded for firmer belief in the early doctrines of the Christian church. In 1845, the halfway point in his life, he left the Anglican Church for the Roman Catholic Church. As the prime minister said, "England reeled under the shock." In answer to much criticism, Newman wrote an autobiography, *Apologia pro Vita Sua,* to explain and justify this step. Late in life he was made a cardinal.

In 1854 Newman was sent to Dublin as rector of a newly established Catholic university. During his few years there, he prepared a series of lectures, *The Idea of a University Defined,* from which the following essays are taken. The thoughtful style and noble standards of these two famous definitions show why Newman was able to win back those whom he had previously antagonized. Today his memory is honored by both Roman Catholics and Protestants.

Thomas Henry Huxley reflects the tremendous growth of interest in science during the Victorian Age. Today it is hard to realize that only a hundred years ago universities almost ignored science in favor of classical languages and literatures. Had Huxley gone to Oxford or Cambridge, his career might have been quite different. But the meager income of his parents forbade higher education, and he was placed on the naval vessel *Rattlesnake* to learn medicine from the ship's surgeon. Four years later he left the navy to become a Fellow of the Royal Society. Thereafter his life was spent as an essayist, lecturer, and experimenter in such varied fields as physiology, biology, paleontology (the study of fossils), and comparative anatomy.

With a fine gift for wit, clear organization, and simple, direct style, Huxley did great service in making science understandable to the masses. At a time when England was split into two camps over the theory of evolution, Huxley became the great defender and popularizer of Darwin's *The Origin of Species*. Against the attackers of Darwin who feared that the new discoveries of science would undermine religion, Huxley argued for greater freedom of research and education so that truth could be known.

The Educated Man

JOHN HENRY NEWMAN

A UNIVERSITY is not a birthplace of poets or of immortal authors, of founders of schools, leaders of colonies, or conquerors of nations. It does not promise a generation of Aristotles or Newtons, of Napoleons or Washingtons, of Raphaels or Shakespeares, though such miracles of nature it has before now contained within its precincts. Nor is it content on the other hand with forming the critic or the experimentalist, the economist or the engineer, though such too it includes within its scope. But a university training is the great ordinary means to a great but ordinary end; it aims at raising the intellectual tone of society, at cultivating the public mind, at purifying the national taste, at supplying true principles to popular enthusiasm and fixed aims to popular aspiration, at giving enlargement and sobriety to the ideas of the age, at facilitating the exercise of political power, and refining the intercourse of private life. It is the education which gives a man a clear conscious view of his own opinions and judgments, a truth in developing them, an eloquence in expressing them, and a force in urging them. It teaches him to see things as they are, to get right to the point, to disentangle a skein of thought, to detect what is sophistical, and to discard what is irrelevant. It prepares him to fill any post with credit, and to master any subject with facility. It shows him how to accommodate himself to others, how to throw himself into their state of mind, how to bring before them his own, how to influence them, how to come to an understanding with them, how to bear with them. He is at home in any society, he has common ground with every class; he knows when to speak and when to be silent; he is able to converse, he is able to listen; he can ask a question pertinently, and gain a lesson seasonably, when he has nothing to impart himself; he is ever ready, yet never in the way; he is a pleasant companion, and a comrade you can depend upon; he knows when to be serious and when to trifle, and he has a sure tact which enables him to trifle with gracefulness and to be serious with effect. He has the repose of mind which lives in itself, while it lives in the world, and which has resources for its happiness at home when it cannot go abroad. He has a gift which serves him in public, and supports him in retirement, without which good fortune is but vulgar, and with which failure and disappointment have a charm.

The Gentleman

IT IS almost a definition of a gentleman to say he is one who never inflicts pain. This description is both refined and, as far as it goes, accurate. He is mainly occupied in merely removing the obstacles which hinder the free and unembarrassed action of those about him, and he concurs with their movements rather than takes the initiative himself. His benefits may be considered as parallel to what are called comforts or conveniences in arrangements of a personal nature; like an easy chair or a good fire, which do their part in dispelling cold and fatigue, though nature provides both means of rest and animal heat without them. (The true gentleman in like manner carefully avoids whatever may cause a jar or a jolt in the minds of those with whom he is cast — all clashing of opinion, or collision of feeling, all restraint, or suspicion, or gloom, or resentment; his great concern being to make everyone at their ease and at home.) He has his eyes on all his company; he is tender toward the bashful, gentle toward the distant, and merciful toward the absurd; he can recollect to whom he is speaking; he guards against unreasonable allusions, or topics which may irritate; he is seldom prominent in conversation, and never wearisome. He makes light of favors while he does them, and seems to be receiving when he is conferring. He never speaks of himself except when compelled, never defends himself by a mere retort, he has no ears for slander or gossip, is scrupulous in imputing motives to those who interfere with him, and interprets everything for the best. He is never mean or little in his disputes, never takes unfair advantage, never mistakes personalities or sharp sayings for arguments, or insinuates evil which he dare not say out. From a long-sighted prudence, he observes the maxim of the ancient sage, that we should ever conduct ourselves toward our enemy as if he were one day to be our friend. He has too much good sense to be affronted at insults, he is too well employed to remember injuries, and too indolent to bear malice. He is patient, forbearing, and resigned, on philosophical principles; he submits to pain because it is inevitable, to bereavement because it is irreparable, and to death because it is his destiny. If he engages in controversy of any kind, his disciplined intellect preserves him from the blundering discourtesy of better, perhaps, but less educated minds, who, like blunt weapons, tear and hack, instead of cutting clean, who mistake the point in argument, waste their strength on trifles, misconceive their adversary, and leave the question more involved than they find it. He may be right or wrong in his opinion, but he is too clearheaded to be unjust; he is as simple as he is forcible, and as brief as he is decisive. Nowhere shall we find greater candor, consideration, indulgence; he throws himself into the minds of his opponents; he accounts for their mistakes. He knows the weakness of human reason as well as its strength, its province and its limits. If he be an unbeliever, he will be too profound and large-minded to ridicule religion or to act against it; he is too wise to be a dogmatist or fanatic in his infidelity. He respects piety and devotion; he even supports institutions as venerable, beautiful, or useful, to which he does not assent; he honors the ministers of religion, and it contents him to decline its mysteries without assailing or denouncing them. He is a friend of religious toleration, and that not only because his philosophy has taught him to look on all forms of faith with an impartial eye, but also from the gentleness and effeminacy of feeling which is the attendant on civilization.

Lead, Kindly Light

In richly figurative poetry, this hymn expresses the serene faith
that Newman found in religion. It was written before his conversion, as he was returning to England from Sicily.

Lead, kindly Light, amid the encircling gloom,
    Lead thou me on;
The night is dark, and I am far from home,
    Lead thou me on.
Keep thou my feet; I do not ask to see   5
The distant scene; one step enough for me.

I was not ever thus, nor prayed that thou
    Should'st lead me on;
I loved to choose and see my path, but now
    Lead thou me on.   10
I loved the garish day; and spite of fears,
Pride ruled my will; remember not past years.

So long thy power has blessed me, sure it still
    Will lead me on,
O'er moor and fen, o'er crag and torrent, till   15
    The night is gone,
And with the morn those angel faces smile,
Which I have loved long since, and lost awhile.

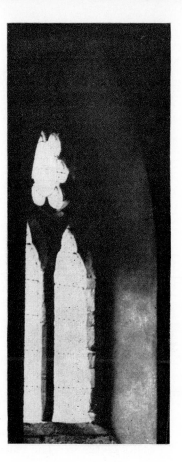

A Liberal Education

THOMAS HENRY HUXLEY

Huxley was not a scientist in a narrow
sense only; he believed in applying the
laws of science to the whole of life. The
following statement of his views is part of
a long address delivered to the South London Working Men's College in 1868. This
college, founded in 1854, was one evidence of the growing interest in popular
education during the Victorian Age. Compulsory education was not yet established,
but it was on its way. In the first part of
this address Huxley says: " I believe we
should have compulsory education in the
course of [the] next session [of Parliament]
if there were the least probability that half
a dozen leading statesmen of different parties would agree what that education
should be." He then goes on to show what
he believes to be the purpose and scope of
a liberal education.

SUPPOSE it were perfectly certain
that the life and fortune of every one
of us would, one day or other, depend
upon his winning or losing a game of
chess. Don't you think that we should
all consider it to be a primary duty to
learn at least the names and the moves
of the pieces; to have a notion of a
gambit, and a keen eye for all the means
of giving and getting out of check? Do
you not think that we should look with

a disapprobation amounting to scorn upon the father who allowed his son, or the state which allowed its members, to grow up without knowing a pawn from a knight?

Yet it is a very plain and elementary truth, that the life, the fortune, and the happiness of every one of us, and, more or less, of those who  are connected with us, do depend upon our knowing something of the rules of a game infinitely more difficult and complicated than chess. It is a game which has been played for untold ages, every man and woman of us being one of the two players in a game of his or her own. The chessboard is the world, the pieces are the phenomena of the universe, the rules of the game are what we call the laws of Nature. The player on the other side is hidden from us. We know that his play is always fair, just, and patient. But also we know, to our cost, that he never overlooks a mistake, or makes the smallest allowance for ignorance. To the man who plays well, the highest stakes are paid, with that sort of overflowing generosity with which the strong shows delight in strength. And one who plays ill is checkmated — without haste, but without remorse.

My metaphor will remind some of you of the famous picture in which Retzsch has depicted Satan playing at chess with man for his soul. Substitute for the mocking fiend in that picture, a calm, strong angel who is playing for love, as we say, and would rather lose than win — and I should accept it as an image of human life.

Well, what I mean by Education is learning the rules of this mighty game. In other words, education is the instruction of the intellect in the laws of Na-

ture, under which name I include not merely things and their forces but men and their ways; and the fashioning of the affections and of the will into an earnest and loving desire to move in harmony with those laws. For me education means neither more nor less than this. Anything which professes to call itself education must be tried by this standard, and if it fails to stand the test, I will not call it education, whatever may be the force of authority, or of numbers, upon the other side.

It is important to remember that, in strictness, there is no such thing as an uneducated man. Take an extreme case. Suppose that an adult man, in the full vigor of his faculties, could be suddenly placed in the world, as Adam is said to have been, and then left to do as he best might. How long would he be left uneducated? Not five minutes. Nature would begin to teach him, through the eye, the ear, the touch, the properties of objects. Pain and pleasure would be at his elbow telling him to do this and avoid that; and by slow degrees the man would receive an education, which, if narrow, would be thorough, real, and adequate to his circumstances, though there would be no extras and very few accomplishments.

And if to this solitary man entered a second Adam, or better still, an Eve, a new and greater world, that of social and moral phenomena, would be revealed. Joys and woes, compared with which all others might seem but faint shadows, would spring from the new relations. Happiness and sorrow would take the place of the coarser monitors, pleasure and pain; but conduct would still be shaped by the observation of the natural consequences of actions; or, in other words, by the laws of the nature of man.

To every one of us the world was once as fresh and new as to Adam. And then, long before we were susceptible of any other mode of instruction, Nature took us in hand, and every minute of waking life brought its educational influence, shaping our actions into rough accordance with Nature's laws, so that we might not be ended untimely by too gross disobedience. Nor should I speak of this process of education as past for anyone, be he as old as he may. For every man the world is as fresh as it was at the first day, and as full of untold novelties for him who has the eyes to see them. And Nature is still continuing her patient education of us in that great university, the universe, of which we are all members — Nature having no Test-Acts.[1]

Those who take honors in Nature's university, who learn the laws which govern men and things and obey them, are the really great and successful men in this world. The great mass of mankind are the " Poll," [2] who pick up just enough to get through without much discredit. Those who won't learn at all are plucked; [3] and then you can't come up again. Nature's pluck means extermination.

Thus the question of compulsory education is settled so far as Nature is concerned. Her bill on that question was framed and passed long ago. But, like all compulsory legislation, that of Nature is harsh and wasteful in its operation. Ignorance is visited as sharply as willful disobedience — incapacity meets with the same punishment as crime. Nature's discipline is not even a word and a blow, and the blow first; but the blow without the word. It is left to you to find out why your ears are boxed.

The object of what we commonly call education — that education in which man intervenes and which I shall distinguish as artificial education — is to make good these defects in Nature's methods; to prepare the child to receive Nature's education, neither incapably nor ignorantly, nor with willful disobedience; and to understand the preliminary symptoms of her displeasure, without waiting for the box on the ear. In short, all artificial education ought to be an anticipation of natural education. And a liberal education is an artificial education, which has not only prepared a man to escape the great evils of disobedience to natural laws, but has trained him to appreciate and to seize upon the rewards, which Nature scatters with as free a hand as her penalties.

That man, I think, has had a liberal education, who has been so trained in youth that his body is the ready servant of his will, and does with ease and pleasure all the work that, as a mechanism, it is capable of; whose intellect is a clear, cold, logic engine, with all its parts of equal strength, and in smooth working order; ready, like a steam engine, to be turned to any kind of work, and spin the gossamers as well as forge the anchors of the mind; whose mind is stored with a knowledge of the great and fundamental truths of Nature and of the laws of her operations; one who, no stunted ascetic, is full of life and fire, but whose passions are trained to come to heel by a vigorous will, the servant of a tender conscience; who has learned to love all beauty, whether of Nature or of art, to hate all vileness, and to respect others as himself.

Such an one and no other, I conceive, has had a liberal education; for he is, as completely as a man can be, in harmony with Nature. He will make the best of her, and she of him. They will get on together rarely; she as his ever beneficent mother; he as her mouthpiece, her conscious self, her minister and interpreter.

---

[1] *Test-Acts:* acts which at that time excluded from English universities all those who did not profess the established religion.

[2] *"Poll":* The poll degree at Cambridge was the common degree, without honors. The term was derived from a Greek word, οἱ πολλοί, (hoi polloi) meaning "the many." We still use this term today to mean "the common people."

[3] *plucked:* English college slang, same as "flunked" in America.

VICTORIAN ESSAYISTS

1. What are the chief characteristics of a gentleman according to Newman's definition? Can a person be a great man and still not be a gentleman? Conversely, can a person be a gentleman and not be a great man? Are gentlemen in Newman's sense of the word common or uncommon among your acquaintances?

2. What characteristics of Newman's gentleman would also fit a lady? What requirements would you add?

3. What does Huxley say about an uneducated man? Would Newman agree with him on this, do you think? How would you relate the idea of a self-made man, so often mentioned in America, to Huxley's ideas on this subject?

4. What are Huxley's standards for a liberal education? What does he consider to be the reward of such an education?

5. Study each author's method of presenting an argument. How does each gain the reader's interest? How does he arrive at conclusions? Compare Huxley and Newman as stylists. Which do you prefer?

CLASS ACTIVITIES

1. For a panel discussion, use the theme " Education for Living." Let one student present Newman's ideas, another present Huxley's, a third describe what experiences your own school gives toward this end, a fourth discuss what is lacking in your present school experience.

2. Write your own definitions of " The Born Leader," " The True Teacher," " The Best Parent," or " A Real Friend."

3. If you are interested in science, report on Huxley's " A Piece of Chalk."

ALFRED, LORD TENNYSON
1809–1892

Born into a large family, Tennyson grew up in Somersby, Lincolnshire, where his father was rector. Most of his early education was received directly from his scholarly father, who recognized and encouraged the boy's precosity. Alfred and his brother Charles wrote and published a volume, *Poems of Two Brothers,* the year before they entered Cambridge together.

In college the shy, reserved Alfred found a close friend in brilliant, vivacious Arthur Hallam, thought to be the most promising youth of the class. A few years after leaving college Hallam died suddenly. Tennyson was stunned by the cruel fate that had taken one so young, so talented, and so beloved; and in his sorrow, he began to have personal and religious doubts. In a series of poems which, during seventeen years, recorded the stages of his grief, doubt, resignation, and finally, faith, Tennyson wrote his masterpiece, published in 1850 as *In Memoriam.* The immediate success of this work and his award of a pension and appointment as poet laureate in the same year made it financially possible for Tennyson to marry a woman to whom he had been engaged fourteen years earlier. Afterward, his long poems, like *The Idylls of the King,* were eagerly awaited.

Assured financially, Tennyson and his wife occupied successively two beautiful homes — one on the Isle of Wight, the other in Surrey. Tennyson lived almost in seclusion. Even as an old man he was a striking figure — " a great black, shaggy man " — who looked the part of a poet.

Flower in the Crannied Wall

This miniature poem and the one which
follows reveal two important aspects of Tennyson's poetry: his responsiveness to the
scientific thinking of his day, and his close
observation of nature.

Flower in the crannied wall,
I pluck you out of the crannies,
I hold you here, root and all, in my
    hand,
Little flower — but *if* I could understand
What you are, root and all, and all in
    all,   5
I should know what God and man is.

The Eagle

He clasps the crag with crooked hands,
Close to the sun in lonely lands,
Ringed with the azure world, he stands.

The wrinkled sea beneath him crawls,
He watches from his mountain walls,
And like a thunderbolt he falls.   6

Songs from *The Princess*

Tennyson wrote a long narrative poem,
The Princess, to defend higher education
for women, an idea much challenged in the
middle of his century. Between the cantos
of this poem he later inserted lyrics.

"Tears, Idle Tears" was written on a
visit to Tintern Abbey when, he writes,
"the woods were all yellowing with
autumn, seen through the ruined windows. . . . It is distance that charms the
past." The melancholy mood of this poem

in recalling vanished days shows Tennyson to have been a true follower of the
romantic tradition.

"The Bugle Song," written the year of
Tennyson's marriage, is said to have been
suggested to him while he and his bride
were visiting beautiful Lake Killarney in
Ireland. The dying echoes of a bugle
blown at sunset are effectively contrasted
with the living echoes sent from one soul
to another.

Tears, Idle Tears

Tears, idle tears, I know not what they mean,
Tears from the depth of some divine despair
Rise in the heart, and gather to the eyes,
In looking on the happy autumn fields,
And thinking of the days that are no more.   5

Fresh as the first beam glittering on a sail,
That brings our friends up from the underworld,°
Sad as the last which reddens over one
That sinks with all we love below the verge;
So sad, so fresh, the days that are no more.   10

Ah, sad and strange as in dark summer dawns
The earliest pipe of half-awakened birds
To dying ears, when unto dying eyes
The casement slowly grows a glimmering square;
So sad, so strange, the days that are no more.   15

7. *underworld:* the other side of the globe.

Dear as remembered kisses after death,
And sweet as those by hopeless fancy feigned
On lips that are for others; deep as love,
Deep as first love, and wild with all regret;
O Death in Life, the days that are no more.   20

The Bugle Song

The splendor falls on castle walls
    And snowy summits old in story;
The long light shakes across the lakes,
    And the wild cataract leaps in glory.
Blow, bugle, blow, set the wild echoes flying,   5
Blow, bugle; answer, echoes, dying, dying, dying.

Oh, hark, oh, hear! how thin and clear,
    And thinner, clearer, farther going!
Oh, sweet and far from cliff and scar°
    The horns of Elfland faintly blowing!   10
Blow, let us hear the purple glens replying;
Blow, bugle; answer, echoes, dying, dying, dying.

O love, they die in yon rich sky,
    They faint on hill or field or river;
Our echoes roll from soul to soul,   15
    And grow forever and forever.
Blow, bugle, blow, set the wild echoes flying,
And answer, echoes, answer, dying, dying, dying.

9. *scar:* bare rock.

The Lady of Shalott

In his boyhood Tennyson was fascinated by the stories of King Arthur's knights, and it was natural for him to turn to them later as subjects for poetry. The twelve metrical tales included in *The Idylls of the King* were composed over a period of twenty-six years (1859–1885). But long before that time the poet had written this legend of the Lady of Shalott (1832). The melodious and magic quality of this version is often preferred to the more elaborate story of Elaine and Lancelot, one of the knights of the Round Table, in the *Idylls*.

Tennyson explains the symbolism of the Lady thus: " The newborn love for something, for someone in the wide world from which she has been so long excluded takes her out of the region of shadows into that of realities."

PART I

On either side the river lie
Long fields of barley and of rye,
That clothe the wold° and meet the sky;
And through the field the road runs by
    To many-towered Camelot;°   5
And up and down the people go,
Gazing where the lilies blow
Round an island there below,
    The island of Shallot.

3. *wold:* an open stretch of rising ground.
5. *Camelot:* a mysterious city where King Arthur and his knights held court in medieval romances.

Willows whiten,° aspens quiver,   10
Little breezes dusk and shiver
Through the wave that runs forever
By the island in the river
    Flowing down to Camelot.
Four gray walls, and four gray towers,
Overlook a space of flowers,   16
And the silent isle embowers
    The Lady of Shalott.

By the margin, willow-veiled,
Slide the heavy barges° trailed   20
By slow horses; and unhailed
The shallop° flitteth silken-sailed
    Skimming down to Camelot.
But who hath seen her wave her hand?
Or at the casement seen her stand?   25
Or is she known in all the land,
    The Lady of Shalott?

Only reapers, reaping early
In among the bearded barley,
Hear a song that echoes cheerly   30
From the river winding clearly
    Down to towered Camelot:
And by the moon the reaper weary,
Piling sheaves in uplands airy,
Listening, whispers, " 'Tis the fairy   35
    Lady of Shalott."

PART II

There she weaves by night and day
A magic web with colors gay.
She has heard a whisper say,
A curse is on her if she stay   40
    To look down to Camelot.
She knows not what the curse may be,
And so she weaveth steadily,
And little other care hath she,
    The Lady of Shalott.   45

And moving through a mirror clear
That hangs before her all the year,
Shadows of the world appear.

10. *whiten:* Leaves turned by the breeze
show their underside, which is white. 20. *barges:*
roomy, flat-bottomed freight boats; here drawn
by horses along the river banks. 22. *shallop:* a
light pleasure boat.

There she sees the highway near
    Winding down to Camelot: 50
There the river eddy whirls,
And there the surly village churls,°
And the red cloaks of market girls,
    Pass onward from Shalott.

Sometimes a troop of damsels glad,   55
An abbot on an ambling pad,°
Sometimes a curly shepherd lad,
Or long-haired page in crimson clad,
    Goes by to towered Camelot:
And sometimes through the mirror blue
The knights come riding two and two:
She hath no loyal knight and true,   62
    The Lady of Shalott.

But in her web she still delights
To weave the mirror's magic sights,   65
For often through the silent nights
A funeral, with plumes and lights
    And music, went to Camelot:
Or when the moon was overhead,
Came two young lovers lately wed;   70
" I am half sick of shadows," said
    The Lady of Shalott.

52. *churls:* country folk. 56. *pad:* an easy-
paced riding horse.

PART III

A bow-shot from her bower eaves,
He rode between the barley sheaves,
The sun came dazzling through the
    leaves,   75
And flamed upon the brazen greaves°
  Of bold Sir Lancelot.
A red-cross knight° forever kneeled
To a lady in his shield,
That sparkled on the yellow field,   80
  Beside remote Shalott.

The gemmy° bridle glittered free,
Like to some branch of stars we see
Hung in the golden Galaxy.°
The bridle bells rang merrily   85
  As he rode down to Camelot:
And from his blazoned baldric° slung,
A mighty silver bugle hung,
And as he rode his armor rung,
  Beside remote Shalott.   90

All in the blue unclouded weather
Thick-jeweled shone the saddle leather,
The helmet and the helmet feather
Burned like one burning flame together
  As he rode down to Camelot.   95
As often through the purple night,
Below the starry clusters bright,
Some bearded meteor, trailing light,
  Moves over still Shalott.

His broad clear brow in sunlight
    glowed;   100
On burnished hoofs his war horse trode;
From underneath his helmet flowed
His coal-black curls as on he rode,
  As he rode down to Camelot.
From the bank and from the river   105
He flashed into the crystal mirror,
" Tirra lirra," by the river
  Sang Sir Lancelot.

76. *greaves:* armor for the legs below the knees.
78. *red-cross knight:* a symbol of St. George, patron saint of England. He slew the dragon, and
thus saved a maiden from sacrifice. 82. *gemmy:*
studded with jewels. 84. *Galaxy:* the Milky
Way, a pathway of myriad stars stretching
across the middle heavens. 87. *blazoned baldric:*
a decorated belt worn diagonally across the
chest.

She left the web, she left the loom,
She made three paces through the room,
She saw the water lily bloom,   111
She saw the helmet and the plume,
  She looked down to Camelot.
Out flew the web and floated wide;
The mirror cracked from side to side;
" The curse is come upon me," cried
  The Lady of Shalott.   117

PART IV

In the stormy east wind straining,
The pale yellow woods were waning,
The broad stream in his banks com-
    plaining,   120
Heavily the low sky raining
  Over towered Camelot;
Down she came and found a boat
Beneath a willow left afloat,
And round about the prow she wrote
  The Lady of Shalott.   126

And down the river's dim expanse —
Like some bold seër in a trance,
Seeing all his own mischance —
With a glassy countenance   130
  Did she look to Camelot.
And at the closing of the day
She loosed the chain, and down she lay;
The broad stream bore her far away,
  The Lady of Shalott.   135

Lying, robed in snowy white
That loosely flew to left and right —
The leaves upon her falling light —
Through the noises of the night
  She floated down to Camelot: 140
And as the boathead wound along
The willowy hills and fields among,
They heard her singing her last song,
  The Lady of Shalott.

Heard a carol, mournful, holy,   145
Chanted loudly, chanted lowly,
Till her blood was frozen slowly,
And her eyes were darkened wholly,
  Turned to towered Camelot.
For ere she reached upon the tide   150
The first house by the waterside,
Singing in her song she died,
  The Lady of Shalott.

Under tower and balcony,
By garden wall and gallery,   155
A gleaming shape she floated by,
Dead-pale between the houses high,
   Silent into Camelot.
Out upon the wharves they came   159
Knight and burgher,° lord and dame,
And round the prow they read her name,
   The Lady of Shalott.

160. *burgher:* citizen.

Who is this? and what is here?
And in the lighted palace near
Died the sound of royal cheer;   165
And   they   crossed   themselves   for
   fear,
   All the knights at Camelot:
But Lancelot mused a little space;
He said, " She has a lovely face;
God in his mercy lend her grace,   170
   The Lady of Shalott."

Ulysses°

In this poem Tennyson draws his subject from ancient Greek sources. Ulysses, the famous hero of many adventures in *The Odyssey,* is pictured years after the time described in that epic. Here the old man expresses his urge to go out again into the world to accomplish something worth-while, rather than to rust away in a life of ease at home. To Tennyson's generation this poem symbolized the constant striving onward and upward of civilized man. It is said that " Ulysses " was the deciding factor in the government's choice of Tennyson to receive a pension.

     It little profits that an idle king,
     By this still hearth, among these barren crags,
     Matched with an aged wife, I mete and dole°
     Unequal laws° unto a savage race,
     That hoard, and sleep, and feed, and know not me.   5
     I cannot rest from travel; I will drink
     Life to the lees. All times I have enjoyed
     Greatly, have suffered greatly, both with those
     That loved me, and alone; on shore, and when

Title: *Ulysses* (û·lĭs′ēz). 3. *mete and dole:* measure and give out. 4. *Unequal laws:* unfair laws. The people were not civilized enough to be governed by the kind of laws Ulysses approved.

Through scudding drifts the rainy Hyades°   10
Vexed the dim sea. I am become a name;
For always roaming with a hungry heart
Much have I seen and known — cities of men
And manners, climates, councils, governments,
Myself not least, but honored of them all —   15
And drunk delight of battle with my peers,
Far on the ringing plains of windy Troy.
I am a part of all that I have met;
Yet all experience is an arch wherethrough
Gleams that untraveled world whose margin fades   20
Forever and forever when I move.°
How dull it is to pause, to make an end,
To rust unburnished, not to shine in use!
As though to breathe were life! Life piled on life
Were all too little, and of one to me   25
Little remains; but every hour is saved
From that eternal silence, something more,
A bringer of new things; and vile it were
For some three suns to store and hoard myself,
And this gray spirit yearning in desire   30
To follow knowledge like a sinking star,
Beyond the utmost bound of human thought.

     This is my son, mine own Telemachus,
To whom I leave the scepter and the isle° —
Well-loved of me, discerning to fulfill   35
This labor, by slow prudence to make mild
A rugged people, and through soft degrees
Subdue them to the useful and the good.
Most blameless is he, centered in the sphere
Of common duties, decent not to fail   40
In offices of tenderness, and pay
Meet adoration to my household gods,
When I am gone. He works his work, I mine.

     There lies the port; the vessel puffs her sail;
There gloom the dark, broad seas. My mariners,   45
Souls that have toiled, and wrought, and thought with me —
That ever with a frolic welcome took
The thunder and the sunshine, and opposed
Free hearts, free foreheads — you and I are old;
Old age hath yet his honor and his toil.   50
Death closes all; but something ere the end,
Some work of noble note, may yet be done,
Not unbecoming men that strove with Gods.
The lights begin to twinkle from the rocks;

10. *Hyades* (hī′á·dēz): stars in the constellation Taurus, supposed to bring rain. 19–21. All experience beckons me on to more experiences lying beyond. 34. *isle:* Ulysses' kingdom was Ithaca, an island off the west coast of Greece. Telemachus (tĕ·lĕm′á·kŭs) a youth in *The Odyssey*, is now a mature man, well suited to rule the kingdom.

The long day wanes; the slow moon climbs; the deep   55
Moans round with many voices. Come, my friends,
'Tis not too late to seek a newer world.
Push off, and sitting well in order smite
The sounding furrows; for my purpose holds
To sail beyond the sunset, and the baths   60
Of all the western stars, until I die.
It may be that the gulfs will wash us down;
It may be we shall touch the Happy Isles,°
And see the great Achilles,° whom we knew.
Though much is taken, much abides; and though   65
We are not now that strength which in old days
Moved earth and heaven, that which we are, we are —
One equal temper of heroic hearts,
Made weak by time and fate, but strong in will
To strive, to seek, to find, and not to yield.   70

63. *Happy Isles:* the place where heroes went after death. 64. *Achilles* (á·kĭl′ēz): the strongest hero of the Trojan War, in which Ulysses had taken part before his long series of adventures on the return journey.

Locksley Hall

A Prophecy

"Locksley Hall" is a monologue spoken by a rejected lover who seeks to drown his private sorrows by active participation in public affairs. This famous prophetic passage is remarkable because the poem was published in 1842, long before man had succeeded in the first steps of conquering the air (except by simple balloons). Within a century two great world wars have fulfilled the prophecy of the "airy navies." Tennyson's other prophecy, "the federation of the world," brings to mind the establishment of the United Nations.

For I dipped into the future, far as human eye could see,
Saw the vision of the world, and all the wonder that would be;

Saw the heavens fill with commerce, argosies° of magic sails,
Pilots of the purple twilight, dropping down with costly bales;

Saw the heavens fill with shouting, and there rained a ghastly dew,   5
From the nations' airy navies grappling in the central blue;

Far along the world-wide whisper of the south wind rushing warm,
With the standards of the peoples plunging through the thunderstorm;

Till the war drum throbbed no longer, and the battle flags were furled
In the parliament of man, the federation of the world.   10

There the common sense of most shall hold a fretful realm in awe,
And the kindly earth shall slumber, lapped in universal law.

3. *argosies:* fleets of ships laden with vast riches.

In Memoriam

Common consent has named the three greatest elegies (poems of mourning for the dead) in English literature: Milton's " Lycidas," on Edward King, a college friend drowned before the completion of his studies; Shelley's *Adonais,* on John Keats; Tennyson's *In Memoriam,* on Arthur Hallam. The similarity in the situations that called forth these elegies is apparent. Each poem mourns a young man of great talent cut off before he is able to fulfill the promise of his youth. However, *In Memoriam* differs from the others in two respects. The personal tie between Tennyson and Hallam was the strongest friendship of the three. Besides being warm college friends, they had traveled together, and Hallam was engaged to Tennyson's sister. *In Memoriam* is a series of one hundred and thirty-one short meditations on the meaning of life and death, written through seventeen years of thought and spiritual struggle. It represents Tennyson's most mature poetry.

The Proem, which always appears first in the printed editions, was the last part to be composed. It is a prayer asking for greater faith in divine love and immortal life though we are confronted with confusion and change.

Section XXVII presents the idea that it is better for a man to bear sorrow and loss than to exist with a complete lack of sensitiveness and feeling.

Section LIV declares that good can eventually come out of ill even though we are confused by seeming injustice at the moment, for there is a divine plan to be accepted with faith.

Section CVI, a complete song in itself, shows the New Year's bells as a symbol of the progress from old outworn practices and evils to the new era of peace and goodness based on the example of Christ.

Break, Break, Break

Just as the stories of King Arthur come into Tennyson's poetry again and again, so also he finds a constantly recurring theme in another Arthur, his college friend Hallam (see page 476). The four poems that follow already reveal Tennyson's change of attitude toward this tragic loss over a period of years. The first published expression (1842) is this poignant lyric " Break, Break, Break." The poet hears sad sounds played by the breakers as he stands upon the shore.

Break, break, break,
  On thy cold gray stones, O Sea!
And I would that my tongue could utter
  The thoughts that arise in me.

Oh, well for the fisherman's boy,   5
  That he shouts with his sister at play!
Oh, well for the sailor lad,
  That he sings in his boat on the bay!

And the stately ships go on
  To their haven under the hill;   10
But oh, for the touch of a vanished
    hand,
  And the sound of a voice that is still!

Break, break, break,
  At the foot of thy crags, O Sea!
But the tender grace of a day that is
    dead   15
  Will never come back to me.

PROEM

Strong Son of God, immortal Love,
  Whom we, that have not seen thy
    face,
  By faith, and faith alone, embrace,
Believing where we cannot prove;   4

Thine are these orbs of light and shade;
    Thou madest Life in man and brute;
    Thou madest Death; and lo, thy foot
Is on the skull which thou hast made.°

Thou wilt not leave us in the dust;
    Thou madest man, he knows not why,
    He thinks he was not made to die;   11
And thou hast made him; thou art just.°

Thou seemest human and divine,
    The highest, holiest manhood, thou;
    Our wills are ours, we know not how;
Our wills are ours, to make them thine.

Our little systems have their day;   17
    They have their day and cease to be;
    They are but broken lights° of thee,
And thou, O Lord, art more than they.

We have but faith; we cannot know;   21
    For knowledge is of things we see;
    And yet we trust it comes from thee,
A beam in darkness;° let it grow.

Let knowledge grow from more to
    more,   25
    But more of reverence in us dwell;
    That mind and soul, according well,
May make one music as before,

But vaster. We are fools and slight;
    We mock thee when we do not fear;
    But help thy foolish ones to bear;   31
Help thy vain worlds to bear thy light.°

Forgive what seemed my sin° in me;
    What seemed my worth° since I be-
        gan;
    For merit lives from man to man,   35
And not from man, O Lord, to thee.

6–8. Thou dost control life and death.
9–12. Death cannot be the end of everything,
or thou (God) art just. 19. *broken lights:*
colored or prismatic lights; the partial truth
obtainable in this world. 24. *A beam in darkness:*
Knowledge that comes from God is like a beam
of light in the midst of darkness. 32. *light:* the
perfect truth. 33. *sin:* mourning for the dead.
34. *worth:* devotion to the memory of Hallam.
Tennyson asks forgiveness for both his grief
and his devotion.

Forgive my grief for one removed,
    Thy creature, whom I found so fair.
    I trust he lives in thee, and there
I find him worthier to be loved.   40

Forgive these wild and wandering cries,
    Confusions of a wasted youth;
    Forgive them where they fail in truth,
And in thy wisdom make me wise.

XXVII

I envy not in any moods
    The captive void of noble rage,
    The linnet born within the cage,
That never knew the summer woods;

I envy not the beast that takes   5
    His license in the field of time,
    Unfettered by the sense of crime,
To whom a conscience never wakes;

Nor, what may count itself as blest,   9
    The heart that never plighted troth
    But stagnates in the weeds of sloth;
Nor any want-begotten rest.°

I hold it true, whate'er befall;
    I feel it, when I sorrow most;
    'Tis better to have loved and lost   15
Than never to have loved at all.

9–12. (I envy not) the kind of rest or peace
that comes from absence (want) of human ties
or affections.

LIV

Oh, yet we trust that somehow good
    Will be the final goal of ill,
    To pangs of nature, sins of will,
Defects of doubt, and taints of blood;°

That nothing walks with aimless feet;
    That not one life shall be destroyed,
    Or cast as rubbish to the void,   7
When God hath made the pile com-
    plete;

3–4. Four kinds of ills are specified: physical, moral, spiritual, and inherited.

That not a worm is cloven in vain;
    That not a moth with vain desire   10
    Is shriveled in a fruitless fire,
Or but subserves another's gain.

Behold, we know not anything;
    I can but trust that good shall fall
    At last — far off — at last, to all,   15
And every winter change to spring.

So runs my dream; but what am I?
    An infant crying in the night;
    An infant crying for the light;
And with no language but a cry.°   20

17–20. Man is as helpless as an infant in the presence of mysteries he does not understand.

CVI

Ring out, wild bells, to the wild sky,
    The flying cloud, the frosty light;
    The year is dying in the night;
Ring out, wild bells, and let him die.

Ring out the old, ring in the new,   5
    Ring, happy bells, across the snow;
    The year is going, let him go;
Ring out the false, ring in the true.

Ring out the grief that saps the mind,
    For those that here we see no more;
    Ring out the feud of rich and poor,
Ring in redress to all mankind.   12

Ring out a slowly dying cause,
    And ancient forms of party strife;
    Ring in the nobler modes of life,   15
With sweeter manners, purer laws.

Ring out the want, the care, the sin,
    The faithless coldness of the times;
    Ring out, ring out my mournful rhymes,
But ring the fuller minstrel in.   20

Ring out false pride in place and blood,
    The civic slander and the spite;
    Ring in the love of truth and right,
Ring in the common love of good.

Ring out old shapes of foul disease;   25
    Ring out the narrowing lust of gold;
    Ring out the thousand wars of old,
Ring in the thousand years of peace.

Ring in the valiant man and free,
    The larger heart, the kindlier hand;
    Ring out the darkness of the land,   31
Ring in the Christ that is to be.

In the Valley of Cauteretz

Eleven years after the publication of *In Memoriam*, Tennyson wrote this poem on his second visit to the beautiful valley of Cauteretz in the Pyrenees, where he had traveled with Arthur Hallam thirty-two years before. The memory of his friend is here brought back to him with renewed vividness.

All along the valley, stream that flashest white,
Deepening thy voice with the deepening of the night,
All along the valley, where thy waters flow,
I walked with one I loved two and thirty years ago.
All along the valley, while I walked today,   5
The two and thirty years were a mist that rolls away;
For all along the valley, down thy rocky bed,
Thy living voice to me was as the voice of the dead,
And all along the valley, by rock and cave and tree,
The voice of the dead was a living voice to me.   10

Crossing the Bar

Tennyson tells us that this lyric, written in his eighty-first year, "came in a moment." That evening, when the poet read it aloud, his son said enthusiastically, "It is the crown of your life's work." A few days before his death Tennyson said to his son, "Mind you put 'Crossing the Bar' at the end of my poems." The request has always been observed in the many editions of Tennyson's poetry.

Sunset and evening star,
  And one clear call for me!
And may there be no moaning° of the
    bar,
  When I put out to sea,

But such a tide as moving seems asleep,
  Too full for sound and foam,   6

3. *moaning:* It is a popular belief that the ebbing tide moans when a death has occurred.

When that which drew from out the
    boundless deep
  Turns again home.

Twilight and evening bell,
  And after that the dark!   10
And may there be no sadness of fare-
    well,
  When I embark;

For though from out our bourne° of
    Time and Place
  The flood may bear me far,
I hope to see my Pilot face to face   15
  When I have crossed the bar.

13. *bourne:* bounded territory, referring here to earthly life. Compare with "the boundless deep" (of Eternity), line 7.

THOUGHTFUL AND MELODIOUS POEMS

THE SHORT LYRICS

1. For each of the short lyrics, indicate in a sentence the main idea expressed, or Tennyson's prevailing mood. What words or details in the poem convey the mood?

2. In "Tears, Idle Tears" show how the difference in the refrain at the end of each stanza grows out of the thought of that stanza. Why are these tears "idle"?

3. In "The Bugle Song" show how each stanza represents a stage in the life of an echo. Which single word in each of the last two stanzas recalls the sunset glory of the first one?

THE LADY OF SHALOTT

1. The Lady is a symbol of someone who has experienced life indirectly only. To what extent is this possible? What does her final end symbolize, in your opinion? Can you think of other possible situations the Lady might represent?

2. Why is so much stress laid on the splendor of Lancelot and his equipment? How has the Lady's reaction toward him been prepared for in Part II? Wherein lies the special pathos of his words at the end of the poem?

ULYSSES

1. Review the chief incidents in the career of Ulysses after the Trojan War was over. What was the name of his " aged wife "?

2. Discuss in what way the spirit of Ulysses represents all civilization.

3. Select the lines in the poem which best bring out these main ideas:

a. Life is a series of experiences, each one of which leaves its mark.

b. Life's possibilities are endless.

c. No individual lives long enough to experience all that life has to offer.

d. Life must be activity, not mere being. It must be met, in spite of its sorrows, with hope and courage.

IN MEMORIAM

In Memoriam is a thoughtful analysis of one of life's greatest problems. Use this outline to help you follow the beliefs expressed in the Proem.

Lines 1–8. God in wisdom has made all things, including death.

Lines 9–12. He will not let the soul perish.

Lines 13–16. Human beings have the will to do right.

Lines 17–20. Our systems and organizations are but imperfect reflections of God's spirit.

Lines 21–32. Greater knowledge will bring greater reverence for life's mysteries.

Line 33–44. The poet prays for greater faith and for divine mercy.

1. In section XXVII why does the poet not envy the captive bird and the beast without a conscience, even though they are spared his distress? Do you agree that it is better to have had painful experiences than no deeply moving experiences at all?

2. What in section LIV suggests that Tennyson was troubled by the new scientific doctrines derived from evolutionary theories, such as the " struggle for existence " and " survival of the fittest "? Is his conclusion on the matter hopeful or despairing?

3. In section CVI what evils does the poet wish to disappear? What good things does he want to come in? In what way is the mood of this section different from that of earlier sections?

CROSSING THE BAR

1. Of " Crossing the Bar," Professor R. M. Alden wrote: " It is a pure lyrical allegory, in which every word has a double meaning, substance, and shadow, each contributing to and taking nothing from the other." Find examples of this double meaning in the details of setting out to sea.

2. Compare Tennyson's attitude toward approaching death in " Crossing the Bar " with that of other well-known poets, such as Keats in " When I Have Fears " and Shelley in " A Lament " and " A Dirge."

THE POWER OF WORDS

WORDS AND IMAGES

In Part III of " The Lady of Shalott " there is a fine example of Tennyson's skill in using words to produce a desired effect. Sir Lancelot is the center of the picture. As in an actual painting, the central figure holds our eye by the intensity of light that is concentrated upon it. Tennyson uses two kinds of words. There are the direct words full of the vitality of light: *dazzling, flamed, sparkled, glittered, shone, burned, burning, flame, glowed, flashed* — ten within the space of thirty lines. Then there are the *indirect* words which add to the effect because our experience tells us what sunlight does to certain colors, metals, and jewels. So we find the colors: *red, yellow, golden, blue, purple,* with a dash of *coal-black* for contrast. The reflecting surfaces are seen in *brazen* greaves, *gemmy* bridle, *blazoned* baldric, *silver* bugle, *thick-jeweled* saddle leather.

Trace in Part IV words that directly state an emotion of grief and those that contribute indirectly to the mood through color, sound, or condition of nature.

ELIZABETH BARRETT BROWNING 1806–1861

and ROBERT BROWNING 1812–1889

The Brownings are perhaps the most famous couple in English literature. Robert Browning is now recognized as the greater poet of the two, but before Elizabeth and Robert met, she was better known than he.

During her girlhood Elizabeth Barrett showed a marked bent toward classical studies and wrote several ambitious poems. Then at sixteen, while tightening the girth on her saddle horse, she suffered a back injury which caused her to be bedridden. Now deprived of the world at large, she retreated to the refuge of her studies and her writing.

In the meantime Robert Browning, six years younger, was growing up in Camberwell, a suburb of London. He was fortunate in his home background, for his father combined business success with scholarly tastes, while his mother was a woman of high ideals and considerable musical talent. Robert, an only son, was given every possible advantage — private tutoring, travel, and a workshop of his own where he assembled a small menagerie and began the close study of nature so evident in his writing. Recognition of his talent came slowly. His early poems were hard to understand, and the public seemed to prefer the simple, melodious verses of Tennyson.

Then came the dramatic meeting of the two poets, their intense love affair, and their elopement to Italy. Their fifteen years of married life, spent mostly in Florence, brought health to Elizabeth, and to both of them the happiness of congenial interests and creative work together.

After Elizabeth's death Browning returned to England with their only child. The poet was an energetic, handsome man who enjoyed the pleasures of society, but he continued regular hours of writing as well. He wrote a number of poetic dramas for Macready, the famous actor, but these were not successful on the stage.

Browning's poetry won increasing favor with the public during the latter part of his life. He was lionized in London; indeed, Browning Societies which met to interpret the obscurities of many of his poems became an intellectual fad of the day. The poet died in Italy, a land he associated with his love of his wife, and was buried in the Poet's Corner of Westminster Abbey.

Sonnets from the Portuguese

ELIZABETH BARRETT BROWNING

Elizabeth Barrett Browning's *Sonnets from the Portuguese* are the best example of a true sonnet sequence since Elizabethan times. She wrote these forty-four sonnets during Browning's courtship of her, but did not show them to him until after their marriage. One day she slipped them into his pocket and told him to destroy them if he did not like them. Later he said, " I dared not reserve to myself the finest sonnets in any language since Shakespeare."

Mrs. Browning's admiration for one of the classic poets of Portugal had led her husband to nickname her " the little Portugee." This suggested the title chosen for the sequence.

Sonnet 1

I thought once how Theocritus° had sung
Of the sweet years, the dear and wished-for years,
Who each one in a gracious hand appears
To bear a gift for mortals, old or young;
And, as I mused it in his antique tongue,   5
I saw, in gradual vision through my tears,
The sweet, sad years, the melancholy years,
Those of my own life, who by turns° had flung
A shadow across me. Straightway I was 'ware,
So weeping, how a mystic Shape° did move   10
Behind me, and drew me backward by the hair;
And a voice said in mastery, while I strove —
" Guess now who holds thee? " — " Death," I said. But, there,
The silver answer rang — " Not Death, but Love."

1. *Theocritus* (thē'ŏk'rĭ·tŭs): a Sicilian poet of the third century B.C.; the first writer of pastoral idyls. 8. *by turns:* This phrase refers to the loss of her mother and the tragic death of her brother by drowning. 10. *Shape:* Destiny or Fate.

Sonnet 6

Go from me. Yet I feel that I shall stand
Henceforth in thy shadow. Nevermore
Alone upon the threshold of my door
Of individual life, I shall command
The uses of my soul, nor lift my hand   5
Serenely in the sunshine as before,
Without the sense of that which I forebore . . .
Thy touch upon the palm. The widest land
Doom takes to part us, leaves thy heart in mine
With pulses that beat double. What I do   10
And what I dream include thee, as the wine
Must taste of its own grapes. And when I sue
God for myself, He hears that name of thine,
And sees within my eyes the tears of two.

Sonnet 14

If thou must love me, let it be for nought
Except for love's sake only. Do not say,
" I love her for her smile — her look — her way
Of speaking gently — for a trick of thought
That falls in well with mine, and certes° brought   5
A sense of pleasant ease on such a day " —
For these things in themselves, Belovèd, may
Be changed, or change for thee — and love, so wrought,
May be unwrought so. Neither love me for
Thine own dear pity's wiping my cheeks dry —   10
A creature might forget to weep, who bore
Thy comfort long, and lose thy love thereby!
But love me for love's sake, that evermore
Thou may'st love on, through love's eternity.

5. *certes:* certainly.

Sonnet 43

How do I love thee? Let me count the ways.
I love thee to the depth and breadth and height
My soul can reach, when feeling out of sight
For the ends of Being and ideal Grace.
I love thee to the level of every day's   5
Most quiet need, by sun and candlelight.
I love thee freely, as men strive for Right;
I love thee purely, as they turn from Praise.
I love thee with the passion put to use
In my old griefs, and with my childhood's faith.   10
I love thee with a love I seemed to lose
With my lost saints — I love thee with the breath,
Smiles, tears, of all my life! — and, if God choose,
I shall but love thee better after death.

Poems by Robert Browning

Browning's poetical genius flowered in many directions. He could write delicate lyrics as well as rousing marching songs. Perhaps he was most successful with his dramatic lyrics. They are usually in the form of a monologue, in which a single speaker supplies through the delicate play of his emotions the whole background of a dramatic situation, and even suggests the presence and dialogue of other characters. The short monologues, such as " My Last Duchess," are most often read today, but his masterpiece is a combina-tion of dramatic monologues into one unified poem, *The Ring and the Book.* In this long poem the story of a horrible murder is told through the monologues of twelve different persons, a perfect illustration of how point of view affects the telling of a story.

The first two poems which follow are reminiscent of Cavalier times. From your study of the seventeenth century, you know the contrasting traits of the Round-heads and Cavaliers. Browning here conveys typical moods of the Cavaliers.

Give a Rouse

King Charles, and who'll do him right now?
King Charles, and who's ripe for fight now?
Give a rouse;° here's, in hell's despite° now,
King Charles!
Who gave me the goods that went since?   5
Who raised me the house that sank once?
Who helped me to gold I spent since?
Who found me in wine you drank once?

CHORUS:
King Charles, and who'll do him right now?
King Charles, and who's ripe for fight now?   10
Give a rouse; here's, in hell's despite now,
King Charles!

To whom used my boy George quaff else,
By the old fool's side that begot him?°
For whom did he cheer and laugh else,   15
While Noll's° damned troopers shot him?

CHORUS:
King Charles, and who'll do him right now?
King Charles, and who's ripe for fight now?
Give a rouse; here's, in hell's despite now,
King Charles!   20

3. *rouse:* a cheer, a signal for the toast to the King; *in hell's despite:* in defiance of hell. 13–14. To whom else was my son George accustomed to drink a toast as he stood by my side? 16. *Noll:* an abbreviation for Oliver, a term of contempt for Oliver Cromwell. Meter: Notice the rough meter produced by the almost exclusive use of monosyllables, and the coming together at the end of each line of two accented syllables: *right now, went since, quaff else,* etc. This is important to the effective oral reading of the poem.

Boot and Saddle

Boot, saddle, to horse, and away!
Rescue my castle before the hot day
Brightens to blue from its silvery gray,
CHORUS: *Boot, saddle, to horse, and away!*

Ride past the suburbs, asleep as you'd say;   5
Many's the friend there, will listen and pray,
" God's luck to gallants that strike up the lay —
CHORUS: *Boot, saddle, to horse, and away!* "

Forty miles off, like a roebuck at bay,
Flouts Castle Brancepeth the Roundheads' array;°   10
Who laughs, " Good fellows ere this, by my fay,°
CHORUS: *Boot, saddle, to horse, and away!* "

10. Castle Brancepeth mocks at the attacking forces of the Roundheads. This castle is in Northumberland. 11. *fay:* faith.

Who? My wife Gertrude; that, honest and gay,
Laughs when you talk of surrendering, " Nay!
I've better counselors; what counsel they?   15
CHORUS: *Boot, saddle, to horse, and away!* "

Song FROM *Pippa Passes*

This lyric, perhaps Browning's most perfect, is one of four
songs of Pippa, a young worker in the silk mills at Asolo,
Italy. On her one holiday in the year she passes around the
town singing, and, unknown to herself, her songs — at morning, noon, evening, and night — help four important people of
her city at a crisis in each of their lives. This short song gives
the philosophy of the whole poem, which it introduces.

The year's at the spring
And day's at the morn;
Morning's at seven;
The hillside's dew-pearled;

The lark's on the wing;   5
The snail's on the thorn;
God's in his heaven —
All's right with the world!

Home Thoughts, from the Sea

Browning made his first voyage to Italy in 1838. While passing along the coast of Portugal and Spain, he was filled with gratitude toward England for her past struggles for freedom and longed to repay her in some way. Three places caught his eye as he mused: *Cape Saint Vincent* (line 1): a promontory on the southwest coast of Portugal; *Cadiz* (here kā′dĭz) *Bay* (line 2): a gulf southeast of Cape Saint Vincent, where the Spanish fleets that threatened England were defeated by Drake in 1587, and again by Essex and Raleigh in 1596; *Trafalgar* (tră-făl′ger) (line 3): a point on the southwest coast of Spain where Nelson defeated the French and Spanish navies in 1805.

Nobly, nobly Cape Saint Vincent to the Northwest died away;
Sunset ran, one glorious blood-red, reeking into Cadiz Bay;
Bluish 'mid the burning water, full in face Trafalgar lay;
In the dimmest Northeast distance dawned Gibraltar grand and gray;
" Here and here did England help me: how can I help England? " — say,   5
Whoso turns as I, this evening, turns to God to praise and pray,
While Jove's planet° rises yonder, silent over Africa.

7. *Jove's planet:* Jupiter, an evening star.

Home Thoughts, from Abroad

The poet, now in Italy, longs for the beauty of early spring in England.

Oh, to be in England
Now that April's there,
And whoever wakes in England
Sees, some morning, unaware,
That the lowest boughs and the brushwood sheaf   5
Round the elm tree bole° are in tiny leaf,
While the chaffinch° sings on the orchard bough
In England — now!

And after April, when May follows,
And the whitethroat° builds, and all the swallows!   10
Hark, where my blossomed pear tree in the hedge
Leans to the field and scatters on the clover
Blossoms and dewdrops — at the bent spray's edge —
That's the wise thrush! he sings each song twice over,
Lest you should think he never could recapture   15
The first fine careless rapture!
And though the fields look rough with hoary dew,
All will be gay when noontide wakes anew
The buttercups, the little children's dower
— Far brighter than this gaudy melon flower!   20

6. *bole:* tree trunk. 7. *chaffinch:* a common European songbird. 10. *whitethroat:* a European warbler.

My Last Duchess

This poem is perhaps the most popular of Browning's dramatic monologues. The term *dramatic monologue* means a piece in which there is only one speaker, not soliloquizing, but directly addressing another person or group, whose responses or gestures are often suggested by the words of the speaker.

The scene is in the castle of the Duke of Ferrara, an arrogant Italian nobleman of the Renaissance period. The duke is showing a painting of his first wife to an envoy who has been sent to arrange the details of a second marriage. With keen dramatic skill, wherein every detail is significant, Browning shows us the true character of the duke, revealed through his discussion of his artless young wife. Browning's skill at portraying character — rare in lyric poets — is clearly exhibited.

That's my last Duchess painted on the wall,
Looking as if she were alive; I call
That piece a wonder, now; Fra Pandolf's° hands
Worked busily a day, and there she stands.
5 Will 't please you sit and look at her? I said
" Fra Pandolf " by design, for never read
Strangers like you that pictured countenance,
The depth and passion of its earnest glance,
But to myself they turned (since none puts by

3. *Fra Pandolf:* an imaginary monk and painter of the Italian Renaissance period. "Fra" means "Brother."

₁₀ The curtain I have drawn for you, but I)
And seemed as they would ask me, if they durst,
How such a glance came there; so, not the first
Are you to turn and ask thus. Sir, 'twas not
Her husband's presence only, called that spot
₁₅ Of joy into the Duchess' cheek: perhaps
Fra Pandolf chanced to say, " Her mantle laps
Over my lady's wrist too much," or, " Paint
Must never hope to reproduce the faint
Half flush that dies along her throat "; such stuff
₂₀ Was courtesy, she thought, and cause enough
For calling up that spot of joy. She had
A heart . . . how shall I say? . . . too soon made glad,
Too easily impressed; she liked whate'er
She looked on, and her looks went everywhere.
₂₅ Sir, 'twas all one! My favor at her breast,
The dropping of the daylight in the West,
The bough of cherries some officious fool
Broke in the orchard for her, the white mule
She rode with round the terrace — all and each
₃₀ Would draw from her alike the approving speech,
Or blush, at least. She thanked men — good; but thanked
Somehow . . . I know not how . . . as if she ranked
My gift of a nine-hundred-year-old name
With anybody's gift. Who'd stoop to blame
₃₅ This sort of trifling? Even had you skill
In speech — which I have not — to make your will
Quite clear to such an one, and say, " Just this
Or that in you disgusts me; here you miss
Or there exceed the mark " — and if she let
₄₀ Herself be lessoned so, nor plainly set
Her wits to yours, forsooth, and made excuse
— E'en then would be some stooping, and I choose
Never to stoop. Oh, sir, she smiled, no doubt,
Whene'er I passed her; but who passed without
₄₅ Much the same smile? This grew; I gave commands;
Then all smiles stopped together. There she stands
As if alive. Will 't please you rise? We'll meet
The company below, then. I repeat,
The Count your Master's known munificence
₅₀ Is ample warrant that no just pretense
Of mine for dowry will be disallowed;
Though his fair daughter's self, as I avowed
At starting, is my object. Nay, we'll go
Together down,° sir! Notice Neptune,° though,
₅₅ Taming a sea horse, thought a rarity,
Which Claus of Innsbruck° cast in bronze for me.

53–54. *we'll go together down:* The envoy, out of respect, has dropped behind the duke, who calls him forward to a position of equality. 54. *Neptune:* the Greek god of the sea. 56. *Claus of Innsbruck:* an imaginary sculptor.

Love among the Ruins

The scene of this monologue is the Roman Campagna (kắm·pän′yả), the open country surrounding the capital city. The speaker is a shepherd who eagerly anticipates his return to his young wife. Their home is a ruined turret, on the spot where, in ancient days, stood a loftier tower from which the Roman emperor watched the chariot races.

In the first four stanzas the quiet campagna is contrasted with the tumult of the ancient city. The last three stanzas contrast the temporary nature of all earthly things with the realization that " love is best."

Where the quiet-colored end of evening smiles
    Miles and miles
On the solitary pastures where our sheep
    Half-asleep
Tinkle homeward through the twilight, stray or stop   5
    As they crop —
Was the site once of a city great and gay
    (So they say),°
Of our country's very capital, its prince
    Ages since   10
Held his court in, gathered councils, wielding far
    Peace or war.

Now — the country does not even boast a tree,
    As you see,
To distinguish slopes of verdure, certain rills   15
    From the hills
Intersect and give a name to (else they run
    Into one),
Where the domed and daring palace shot its spires
    Up like fires   20
O'er the hundred-gated circuit of a wall
    Bounding all,
Made of marble, men might march on nor be pressed,
    Twelve abreast.

And such plenty and perfection, see, of grass   25
    Never was!
Such a carpet as, this summertime, o'erspreads
    And embeds
Every vestige of the city, guessed alone,°
    Stock or stone —   30
Where a multitude of men breathed joy and woe
    Long ago;
Lust of glory pricked their hearts up, dread of shame
    Struck them tame;
And that glory and that shame alike, the gold   35
    Bought and sold.

8. *they say:* The archæologists alone can determine this fact; so the shepherd takes his data from them. 29. *guessed alone:* Now one can only guess where the city was because the site is covered by grass.

Now — the single little turret that remains
    On the plains,
By the caper° overrooted, by the gourd
    Overscored,°   40
While the patching houseleek's° head of blossom winks
    Through the chinks —
Marks the basement whence a tower in ancient time
    Sprang sublime,
And a burning ring, all round, the chariots traced   45
    As they raced,
And the monarch and his minions° and his dames
    Viewed the games.

And I know — while thus the quiet-colored eve
    Smiles to leave   50
To their folding, all our many tinkling fleece
    In such peace,
And the slopes and rills in undistinguished gray
    Melt away —
That a girl with eager eyes and yellow hair   55
    Waits me there
In the turret whence the charioteers caught soul
    For the goal,
When the king looked, where she looks now, breathless, dumb
    Till I come.   60

But he looked upon the city, every side,
    Far and wide,
All the mountains topped with temples, all the glades'
    Colonnades,°
All the causeys,° bridges, aqueducts — and then,   65
    All the men!
When I do come, she will speak not, she will stand,
    Either hand
On my shoulder, give her eyes the first embrace
    Of my face,   70
Ere we rush, ere we extinguish sight and speech
    Each on each.

In one year they sent a million fighters forth
    South and North,
And they built their gods a brazen pillar high   75
    As the sky,

39. *caper:* a Mediterranean shrub, abundant on old walls and rocks. Its flower buds are often used as a seasoning. 39–40. *gourd overscored:* The climbing vine, overrunning the turret, has marked or scored it as if with lines. 41. *houseleek:* a common plant with thick, fleshy leaves and yellow or purple flowers, frequently found on old walls and roofs. 47. *minions:* attendants; more strictly, favorites. 63–64. *glades' Colonnades:* The open spaces in the woods are enclosed by trees, just as a large building is often enclosed by a series of columns. 65. *causeys:* Ruins of old causeways, or raised sidewalks, and aqueducts may still be seen in the Roman Campagna.

Yet reserved a thousand chariots in full force —
　　Gold, of course.
O heart! O blood that freezes, blood that burns!
　　Earth's returns°　　　　　　　　　　　　　　　　80
For whole centuries of folly, noise and sin!
　　Shut them in,
With their triumphs and their glories and the rest!
　　Love is best.

80. *Earth's returns:* the rewards of temporal or earthly efforts.

Prospice°

These lines were written in 1861, seven months after the death
of Mrs. Browning. They express Browning's undaunted spirit
in the face of death and his firm belief in eventual reunion
with his beloved wife. As he had faced the joyous contest of
living, so he would meet the final struggle with death.

Fear death? — to feel the fog in my throat,
　　The mist in my face,
When the snows begin, and the blasts denote
　　I am nearing the place,
The power of the night, the press of the storm,　　　5
　　The post of the foe;
Where he stands, the Arch Fear in a visible form,
　　Yet the strong man must go;
For the journey is done and the summit attained,
　　And the barriers fall,　　　　　　　　　　　　10
Though a battle's to fight ere the guerdon be gained
　　The reward of it all.
I was ever a fighter, so — one fight more,
　　The best and the last!
I would hate that death bandaged my eyes, and forbore,　15
　　And bade me creep past.
No! let me taste the whole of it, fare like my peers,
　　The heroes of old,
Bear the brunt, in a minute pay glad life's arrears°
　　Of pain, darkness, and cold.　　　　　　　　20
For sudden the worst turns the best to the brave,
　　The black minute's at end,
And the elements' rage, the fiend-voices° that rave,
　　Shall dwindle, shall blend,
Shall change, shall become first a peace out of pain,　　25
　　Then a light, then thy breast,
O thou soul of my soul! I shall clasp thee again,
　　And with God be the rest!

Title: *Prospice* (prō·spĭk′ĭ): look forward (Latin). 17–20. His life had been so happy that he
had avoided pain, darkness, and cold — the common lot of man. He would pay these debts
(*arrears*) all at once in the moment of dying. 23. *fiend-voices:* This term refers to a legend that
fiends try to snatch the soul away from the powers of light as it leaves the body.

THE BROWNINGS' POETRY

SONNETS FROM THE PORTUGUESE

1. From evidence within the sonnets show (a) that they were written by a woman, (b) that their author was familiar with Greek literature, (c) that they represent a definite series of steps in a courtship, (d) that the one courted had been ill or an invalid.

2. How does Elizabeth Browning's concept of love compare with that revealed in Shakespeare's sonnets? in the Raleigh and Marlowe poems?

BROWNING'S SHORT POEMS

1. What differences in the meter of the two Cavalier lyrics produce the effect of cheering in the first and of riding in the second? What characteristics of the Cavaliers are emphasized in these lyrics?

2. In Pippa's song, how do lines 4–6 contrast, yet relate, to the first three lines? Contrast the last line with that of Shelley's " Dirge " (page 424). How is each typical of the general attitude of its author?

3. What mood is common to the two " Home Thoughts " poems? What happened at Trafalgar that would especially stir the heart of an Englishman of Browning's day? What details of an English spring differ from spring as you have experienced it? Where does the last line of " Home Thoughts, from Abroad " suggest that Browning is at the time of writing? Pick out vivid bits of local color in this poem. When you are homesick, for what sights and sounds do you long?

MY LAST DUCHESS

1. Contrast the characters of the husband and wife as Browning discloses both. What was it in his wife that annoyed the duke?

2. What possible interpretations might be given to lines 45 and 46: " I gave commands; Then all smiles stopped together "? What happened to the duchess?

3. What do you think was the purpose of the duke's interview? What impression do you suppose the duke made on the envoy? Why does the duke prize the painting of his wife?

4. Contrast Browning's use of the heroic couplet with Pope's in " The Rape of the Lock."

LOVE AMONG THE RUINS

1. How is the contrast between the past grandeur and the present bareness emphasized and made effective?

2. How do the motives behind the sports, buildings, and wars of the vanished civilization compare with the emotions of the two young people, in value? in permanence?

PROSPICE

1. How is this title in harmony with Browning's philosophy, as judged from his poetry? How does the poem reveal his whole personality?

2. Compare this poem on death in movement, imagery, climax, and spirit with Tennyson's " Crossing the Bar " (page 487) and with the other poems mentioned for comparison on page 488. How does Browning differ from all the others in what he most eagerly anticipates in immortality?

THE POWER OF WORDS

MONOSYLLABLES

In contrast to the smoothness of Tennyson's writing, Browning's style often seems abrupt and harsh. He achieves tremendous power and drive by his use of monosyllables. In " Give a Rouse " you will find only three or four words of two syllables and none of more than two. How is this style appropriate to the situation and to the singers in the poem? (A poem like this one could probably not be written in Italian or Spanish, but the short Anglo-Saxon words in English make it relatively easy to use monosyllables alone.) Not only are the words short, but the very construction of the sentences is awkward and rough. Is it possible to read smoothly a line like " To whom used my boy George quaff else? " Could Tennyson have used this style for a poem like " The Lady of Shalott "? Why not? Where else in the Browning poems do you find this style?

Try writing a few sentences describing some exciting climax such as a fire, an accident, or the end of a close football game, in which you use as many monosyllables and as few long words as possible. Do you like the effect you have produced, or would you prefer the passage with some longer words interspersed? Why?

THE GROWTH OF THE ENGLISH LANGUAGE

The Victorian Age

The Victorian Age continued and accentuated the tendencies we have already noted in the Romantic Age. There were still two schools of thought on language usage: on the one hand were the conservatives — grammarians, schoolmasters, the newly rich middle class who were not sure of their " correctness," the ambitious merchants who wished to mingle easily with the upper classes. On the other hand were the writers who, with the heritage of the Romantic tradition, were unafraid of innovations, and the aristocracy who spoke as they heard the language used in their own class, without regard for formal rules of grammar.

New styles in pronunciation came in largely through this second group, but new styles in punctuation and spelling came in chiefly through the printers. Many authors were indifferent to such matters. It is said that Dickens left his punctuation entirely to the printer, but some writers who had had more schooling kept a watchful eye on the " points." Gradually the colon and semicolon, which had been all too obvious in earlier printing, thinned out. The system of modern punctuation slowly evolved in the Victorian era.

In the earlier part of the nineteenth century the wide study of English grammar (influenced by Latin forms) tended to result in long, formal sentences, in which every part fitted perfectly with every other part, and a neat diagram could be made of the whole. Macaulay's writings illustrate the perfection of sentence structure which made him the idol of the schoolmaster; yet he was astute enough to realize the value of the contrasting short sentence for relief. On the other hand, Carlyle's sentences have no rhyme or reason. They change direction, break off suddenly, and defy analysis. Carlyle, too, was a great coiner of words, and for his whole unique style it was necessary to coin another new word — Carlylese.

In general, the style of mid-Victorian conversation revealed by the novels of the day was heavy and formal. Husbands and wives used the titles Mr. and Mrs. in addressing each other. Proposals of marriage were oratorical masterpieces. Lofty sentiments abounded on all occasions. It is hard for us today to believe that people ever talked in that way, but they undoubtedly did on some occasions at least.

Of course, revolt was bound to follow such extremes. In the last two or three decades of the century even the language of literature began to limber up. Stevenson and Kipling came in like a breath of fresh air. Gilbert and Sullivan made people laugh at their own follies. The young George Bernard Shaw began to shock the public out of its complacency.

Meanwhile the English language had been growing rapidly all through the century. The opening up of trade with the Orient brought in words like *pongee* from China, *bamboo* from Malaya, *kimono* from Japan. The extension of the British Empire familiarized Britons with words pertaining to the life of distant people. India, with the help of Kipling's genius, supplied the largest number (*rajah* and *pundit,* for example). Australia and New Zealand sent a trickle of strange terms (*boomerang*). The Boer War flooded London with words from

Africa, many of which were originally Dutch (*veldt*). And of course, Americanisms poured in with every boatload of visitors from the New World.

Then there were new words, not names of anything, but strange adjectives or other parts of speech that came from no one knows where. These caused great distress to particular people. Macaulay objected to *talented, influential,* and *gentlemanly.* Other much-criticized newcomers were *reliable* and *environment. Lengthy* fought a long battle for admittance and is still to be found on some taboo lists. (*Taboo* itself came from the Samoan.) It is enlightening to read lists of objectionable neologisms (new terms) compiled fifty years ago and find how large a proportion of them are now unquestionably accepted.

Some new developments on the American side of the ocean should be pointed out. In the years preceding the War Between the States, the United States received great numbers of immigrants from Germany, Switzerland, Scandinavia, Scotland, and Ireland, most of whom settled in the vast midland plains and gradually made their way west. It is interesting to note that the borrowings from Germany and the Scandinavian countries often pertained to food (*wieners, frankfurters, smorgasbord*).

This mixture of nationalities west of the Alleghenies tended to produce a speech somewhat different from that of New England and the south Atlantic coast — areas more exclusively influenced by England. But surprisingly enough, there developed over the width of a continent a uniformity of language greater than England has in her much smaller territory. An Englishman traveling in this country expressed his amazement at finding he could understand and be understood in all parts of the United States more easily than in many counties of his own Great Britain. This speaks well both for the universal public education in the United States and for the high development of swift communications. Of course, differences of pronunciation can be easily detected in different localities, but they add interest to conversation rather than detracting from our comprehension.

We must also recognize the contributions of science and invention to the language — they were far greater than in any previous century. Medicine, physics, chemistry, biology, mathematics, transportation, new machines for the factory and the home were adding new words all the time. The purists balked at many of these, especially if a Greek root was combined with a word from another language. They also objected to the suffix *-ize* being added to all kinds of nouns and verbs to identify the many new processes. Even proper names were so treated as in " to *macadamize* roads." But this concern with linguistic origins made no difference to the general public, and if a word was needed it stuck.

Viewed as a whole, the Victorian Age witnessed great expansion, and at the same time standardization, of the English language.

CHARLES DICKENS 1812–1870

Charles Dickens was primarily a novelist (as such he is discussed on page 345), but he also made a contribution to short fiction. Short stories as a form of writing developed more rapidly in America than in England. Yet at the same time that Hawthorne and Poe were writing beautifully constructed stories on this side of the Atlantic, Dickens as a young newspaper reporter was trying his hand with a series called *Sketches by Boz.* Soon afterward he became the most popular fiction writer of his day through another series of rambling adventures, *Pickwick Papers,* published serially in a magazine. In both books there is more of the short story than of the sustained narrative; in both, the tales are only loosely connected by featuring the same characters. Then, too, one of Dickens' best known writings, *A Christmas Carol,* is a comparatively short piece of fiction, and his book *Christmas Stories* is a collection of short stories.

Pickwick Papers, with its illustrations by " Phiz " (who would correspond to a popular cartoonist of our day), took London by storm. Everyone waited breathlessly for the next monthly installment which would relate the adventures of the kindly, naïve Mr. Pickwick and his three friends who formed the Pickwick Club. These three absurd gentlemen — Tupman, Snodgrass, and Winkle — accompany their leader on a tour of " scientific " investigation and discovery through England. With Mr. Pickwick is his servant, Sam Weller, whose broad Cockney dialect produces much of the humor in the stories. In the course of their travels the Pickwickians become acquainted with Mr. Wardle, a hospitable country squire who invites them to spend Christmas with him at Manor Farm, where they are in the following account. Each of the Pickwickians has his particular pride — and folly. Mr. Winkle, for instance, has boasted of his athletic prowess.

Mr. Pickwick on the Ice

OLD WARDLE led the way to a pretty large sheet of ice; and the fat boy and Mr. Weller having shoveled and swept away the snow which had fallen on it during the night, Mr. Bob Sawyer adjusted his skates with a dexterity which to Mr. Winkle was perfectly marvelous, and described circles with his left leg, and cut figures of eight, and inscribed upon the ice, without once stopping for breath, a great many other pleasant and astonishing devices, to the excessive satisfaction of Mr. Pickwick, Mr. Tupman, and the ladies, which reached a pitch of positive enthusiasm when old Wardle and Benjamin Allen, assisted by the aforesaid Bob Sawyer, performed some mystic evolutions which they called a reel.

All this time Mr. Winkle, with his face and hands blue with the cold, had been forcing a gimlet into the soles of his feet, and putting his skates on with the points behind, and getting the straps into a very complicated and entangled state, with the assistance of Mr. Snodgrass, who knew rather less about skates than a Hindu. At length, however, with the assistance of Mr. Weller, the unfortunate skates were firmly screwed and buckled on, and Mr. Winkle was raised to his feet.

" Now, then, sir," said Sam, in an encouraging tone; " off with you, and show 'em how to do it."

" Stop, Sam, stop! " said Mr. Winkle, trembling violently, and clutching hold of Sam's arms with the grasp of a drowning man. " How slippery it is, Sam! "

" Not an uncommon thing upon ice, sir," replied Mr. Weller. " Hold up, sir! "

This last observation of Mr. Weller's

bore reference to a demonstration Mr. Winkle made, at the instant, of a frantic desire to throw his feet in the air and dash the back of his head on the ice.

" These — these — are very awkward skates; ain't they, Sam? " inquired Mr. Winkle, staggering.

" I'm afeerd there's a orkard gen'l'm'n in 'em, sir," replied Sam.

" Now, Winkle," cried Mr. Pickwick, quite unconscious that there was anything the matter. " Come; the ladies are all anxiety."

" Yes, yes," replied Mr. Winkle, with a ghastly smile; " I'm coming."

" Just agoin' to begin," said Sam, endeavoring to disengage himself. " Now, sir, start off! "

" Stop an instant, Sam," gasped Mr. Winkle, clinging most affectionately to Mr. Weller. " I find I've got a couple of coats at home that I don't want, Sam. You may have them, Sam."

" Thank'ee, sir," replied Mr. Weller.

" Never mind touching your hat, Sam," said Mr. Winkle, hastily; " you needn't take your hand away to do that. I meant to have given you five shillings this morning for a Christmas box, Sam. I'll give it you this afternoon, Sam."

" You're wery good, sir," replied Mr. Weller.

" Just hold me at first, Sam; will you? " said Mr. Winkle. " There — that's right. I shall soon get in the way of it, Sam. Not too fast, Sam; not too fast."

Mr. Winkle, stooping forward with his body half doubled up, was being assisted over the ice by Mr. Weller, in a very singular and unswanlike manner, when Mr. Pickwick most innocently shouted from the opposite bank, —

" Sam! "

" Sir? " said Mr. Weller.

" Here. I want you."

" Let go, sir," said Sam. " Don't you hear the governor acallin'? Let go, sir."

With a violent effort, Mr. Weller disengaged himself from the grasp of the agonized Pickwickian, and in so doing administered a considerable impetus to the unhappy Mr. Winkle. With an accuracy which no degree of dexterity or practice could have insured, that unfortunate gentleman bore swiftly down into the center of the reel, at the very moment when Mr. Bob Sawyer was performing a flourish of unparalleled beauty. Mr. Winkle struck wildly against him, and with a loud crash they both fell heavily down. Mr. Pickwick ran to the spot. Bob Sawyer had risen to his feet, but Mr. Winkle was far too wise to do anything of the kind in skates. He was seated on the ice making spasmodic efforts to smile; but anguish was depicted on every lineament of his countenance.

" Are you hurt? " inquired Mr. Benjamin Allen, with great anxiety.

" Not much," said Mr. Winkle, rubbing his back very hard.

" I wish you'd let me bleed [1] you," said Mr. Benjamin, with great eagerness.

" No, thank you," replied Mr. Winkle, hurriedly.

" I really think you had better," said Allen.

" Thank you," replied Mr. Winkle, " I'd rather not."

" What do you think, Mr. Pickwick? " inquired Bob Sawyer.

Mr. Pickwick was excited and indignant. He beckoned to Mr. Weller and said, in a stern voice, " Take his skates off."

" No; but really I had scarcely begun," remonstrated Mr. Winkle.

" Take his skates off," repeated Mr. Pickwick, firmly.

The command was not to be resisted. Mr. Winkle allowed Sam to obey it in silence.

" Lift him up," said Mr. Pickwick. Sam assisted him to rise.

Mr. Pickwick retired a few paces apart from the bystanders, and beckoning his friend to approach, fixed a

[1] *bleed:* a common treatment by doctors in those days. Benjamin Allen and Bob Sawyer were young medical students.

searching look upon him, and uttered, in a low but distinct and emphatic tone, these remarkable words —

" You're a humbug, sir."

" A what? " said Mr. Winkle, starting.

" A humbug, sir. I will speak plainer, if you wish it. An impostor, sir."

With these words Mr. Pickwick turned slowly on his heel, and rejoined his friends.

While Mr. Pickwick was delivering himself of the sentiment just recorded, Mr. Weller and the fat boy, having by their joint endeavors cut out a slide, were exercising themselves thereupon in a very masterly and brilliant manner. Sam Weller, in particular, was displaying that beautiful feat of fancy sliding which is currently denominated " knocking at the cobbler's door," and which is achieved by skimming over the ice on one foot, and occasionally giving a two-penny postman's knock upon it with the other. It was a good long slide, and there was something in the motion which Mr. Pickwick, who was very cold with standing still, could not help envying.

" It looks a nice, warm exercise that, doesn't it? " he inquired of Wardle, when that gentleman was thoroughly out of breath by reason of the indefatigable manner in which he had converted his legs into a pair of compasses, and drawn complicated problems on the ice.

" Ah, it does indeed," replied Wardle. " Do you slide? "

" I used to do so, on the gutters, when I was a boy," replied Mr. Pickwick.

" Try it now," said Wardle.

" Oh, do, please, Mr. Pickwick! " cried all the ladies.

" I should be very happy to afford you any amusement," replied Mr. Pickwick, " but I haven't done such a thing these thirty years."

" Pooh, pooh! Nonsense! " said Wardle, dragging off his skates with the impetuosity which characterized all his proceedings. " Here; I'll keep you company. Come along! " And away went the good-tempered old fellow down the slide with a rapidity which came very close upon Mr. Weller, and beat the fat boy all to nothing.

Mr. Pickwick skating at Manor Farm — a drawing by Phiz from the first edition of Pickwick Papers. *Most of Dickens' fiction was illustrated by Phiz's clever pen.*

Mr. Pickwick paused, considered, pulled off his gloves and put them in his hat; took two or three short runs, balked himself as often, and at last took another run, and went slowly and gravely down the slide, with his feet about a yard and a quarter apart, amidst the gratified shouts of all the spectators.

" Keep the pot abilin', sir! " said Sam; and down went Wardle again, and then Mr. Pickwick, and then Sam, and then Mr. Winkle, and then Mr. Bob Sawyer, and then the fat boy, and then Mr. Snodgrass, following closely upon each other's heels, and running after each other with as much eagerness as if all their future prospects in life depended on their expedition.

It was the most intensely interesting thing to observe the manner in which Mr. Pickwick performed his share in the ceremony: to watch the torture of anxiety with which he viewed the person behind, gaining upon him at the imminent hazard of tripping him up; to see him gradually expend the painful force which he had put on at first, and turn slowly round on the slide, with his face toward the point from which he had started; to contemplate the playful smile which mantled on his face when he had accomplished the distance, and the eagerness with which he turned round when he had done so and ran after his predecessor — his black gaiters tripping pleasantly through the snow, and his eyes beaming cheerfulness and gladness through his spectacles. And when he was knocked down (which happened upon the average every third round), it was the most invigorating sight that can possibly be imagined to behold him gather up his hat, gloves, and handkerchief with a glowing countenance, and resume his station in the rank with an ardor and enthusiasm that nothing could abate.

The sport was at its height, the sliding was at the quickest, the laughter was at the loudest, when a sharp, smart crack was heard. There was a quick rush toward the bank, a wild scream from the ladies, and a shout from Mr. Tupman. A large mass of ice disappeared; the water bubbled up over it; Mr. Pickwick's hat, gloves, and handkerchief were floating on the surface; and this was all of Mr. Pickwick that anybody could see.

Dismay and anguish were depicted on every countenance; the males turned pale, and the females fainted; Mr. Snodgrass and Mr. Winkle grasped each other by the hand, and gazed at the spot where their leader had gone down, with frenzied eagerness; while Mr. Tupman, by way of rendering the promptest assistance, and at the same time conveying to any persons who might be within hearing the clearest possible notion of the catastrophe, ran off across the country at his utmost speed, screaming " Fire! " with all his might.

It was at this very moment, when old Wardle and Sam Weller were approaching the hole with cautious steps, and Mr. Benjamin Allen was holding a hurried consultation with Mr. Bob Sawyer on the advisability of bleeding the company generally, as an improving little bit of professional practice — it was at this very moment that a face, head, and shoulders emerged from beneath the water, and disclosed the features and spectacles of Mr. Pickwick.

" Keep yourself up for an instant — for only one instant! " bawled Mr. Snodgrass.

" Yes, do; let me implore you — for my sake! " roared Mr. Winkle, deeply affected. The adjuration was rather unnecessary — the probability being that if Mr. Pickwick had declined to keep himself up for anybody else's sake, it would have occurred to him that he might as well do so for his own.

" Do you feel the bottom there, old fellow? " said Wardle.

" Yes, certainly," replied Mr. Pickwick, wringing the water from his head and face, and gasping for breath. " I fell upon my back. I couldn't get on my feet at first."

The clay upon so much of Mr. Pickwick's coat as was yet visible bore testimony to the accuracy of this statement; and as the fears of the spectators were still further relieved by the fat boy's suddenly recollecting that the water was nowhere more than five feet deep, prodigies of valor were performed to get him out. After a vast quantity of splashing, and cracking, and struggling, Mr. Pickwick was at length fairly extricated from his unpleasant position, and once more stood on dry land.

" Oh, he'll catch his death of cold," said Emily.

" Dear old thing! " said Arabella. " Let me wrap this shawl round you, Mr. Pickwick."

" Ah, that's the best thing you can do," said Wardle; " and when you've got it on, run home as fast as your legs can carry you, and jump into bed directly."

A dozen shawls were offered on the instant. Three or four of the thickest having been selected, Mr. Pickwick was wrapped up, and started off, under the guidance of Mr. Weller — presenting the singular phenomenon of an elderly gentleman, dripping wet, and without a hat, with his arms bound down to his sides, skimming over the ground without any clearly defined purpose, at the rate of six good English miles an hour.

But Mr. Pickwick cared not for appearances in such an extreme case, and urged on by Sam Weller, he kept at the very top of his speed until he reached the door of Manor Farm, where Mr. Tupman had arrived some five minutes before, and had frightened the old lady into palpitations of the heart by impressing her with the unalterable conviction that the kitchen chimney was on fire — a calamity which always presented itself in glowing colors to the old lady's mind when anybody about her evinced the smallest agitation.

Mr. Pickwick paused not an instant until he was snug in bed. Sam Weller lighted a blazing fire in the room, and took up his dinner; a bowl of punch was carried up afterward, and a grand carouse held in honor of his safety. Old Wardle would not hear of his rising, so they made the bed the chair, and Mr. Pickwick presided. A second and a third bowl were ordered in. And when Mr. Pickwick awoke next morning there was not a symptom of rheumatism about him; which proves, as Mr. Bob Sawyer very justly observed, that there is nothing like hot punch in such cases; and that if ever hot punch did fail to act as a preventative, it was merely because the patient fell into the vulgar error of not taking enough of it.

THE PICKWICKIANS

Characterize Mr. Pickwick, Mr. Winkle, Bob Sawyer, and Sam Weller. How do their personalities add to the humor of the situations?

REPORTS AND WRITING

1. To give the class a more complete picture of the Pickwick Club's adventures, some students might describe other amusing adventures from *Pickwick Papers*.

2. Write a narrative showing yourself or someone else in an absurd predicament.

THE POWER OF WORDS

EXAGGERATION FOR EFFECT

Dickens frequently uses big words to enhance the humor of his tale. They give a mock-heroic touch to the simple incidents. For example, *catastrophe* and *calamity*, usually reserved for train wrecks, earthquakes, and the like, are here applied to Mr. Pickwick's breaking through the ice, and to an old lady's belief that the chimney was on fire. Mr. Winkle roared an *adjuration* to his supposedly drowning friend. The word denotes a serious appeal to someone; Winkle's appeal is of course ridiculous.

Find other examples of humor created by the use of big words. Write a short description of some simple school or household " calamity " in this style.

MATTHEW ARNOLD 1822–1888

The meaning and content of a good education were the concern of many Victorian writers. You have already noted the ideas of Newman and Huxley. Through his novels Dickens brought about reforms in the treatment of young pupils in boarding schools. But Arnold was the only one of the major writers who was also a professional educator. For thirty-five years he led a busy life as government inspector of schools. He came by this interest naturally, for his father, Dr. Thomas Arnold, was headmaster of Rugby, one of the most famous boys' schools of England. Matthew started his teaching career at Rugby.

In literature, Arnold's first interest was poetry, but after his first two volumes were coldly received, he turned to the writing of essays. Later he received a pension from the government and toured the United States giving lectures. A versatile and learned man, Arnold was an earnest critic of his age. In *Essays in Criticism* he wrote: "Culture is the study of perfection, and looks beyond machinery and coal; hates hatred and all sham; has one great passion, the passion for sweetness and light."

Much of Arnold's poetry is tinged with sadness and pessimism, traceable often to the conflict in the thinking of his day between science and religion. Yet there is always a clear and simple beauty in his lines, reminiscent of the Greek poetry in which he was widely read. In "Dover Beach," one of his best-loved poems, both these elements are strongly marked.

Dover Beach

The sea is calm tonight.
The tide is full, the moon lies fair
Upon the Straits° — on the French coast, the light
Gleams, and is gone; the cliffs of England stand,
Glimmering and vast, out in the tranquil bay.   5
Come to the window, sweet is the night air!
Only, from the long line of spray
Where the sea meets the moon-blanched sand,
Listen! you hear the grating roar
Of pebbles which the waves suck back, and fling,   10
At their return, up the high strand,
Begin, and cease, and then again begin,
With tremulous cadence slow, and bring
The eternal note of sadness in.

Sophocles° long ago   15
Heard it on the Aegean,° and it brought
Into his mind the turbid ebb and flow
Of human misery; we
Find also in the sound a thought,
Hearing it by this distant northern sea.   20

3. *Straits:* the Strait of Dover, the shortest distance between England and the Continent.
15. *Sophocles* (sŏf'ō·klēz): an Athenian writer of tragedy (496?–406 B.C.), one of the three greatest in the golden age of Greek drama. 16. *Aegean* (ē·jē'ăn): an arm of the Mediterranean Sea, between Greece and Asia Minor.

The sea of faith
Was once, too, at the full, and round earth's shore
Lay like the folds of a bright girdle furled;
But now I only hear
Its melancholy, long, withdrawing roar,   25
Retreating to the breath
Of the night wind down the vast edges drear
And naked shingles° of the world.

Ah, love, let us be true
To one another! for the world, which seems   30
To lie before us like a land of dreams,
So various, so beautiful, so new,
Hath really neither joy, nor love, nor light,
Nor certitude, nor peace, nor help for pain;
And we are here as on a darkling plain   35
Swept with confused alarms of struggle and flight,
Where ignorant armies clash by night.

28. *shingles:* pebbly shores, common in England.

ARNOLD'S PESSIMISM

1. State in your own words the problem, or doubt, in the poet's mind. How might this poem illustrate the conflict between science and religion in Victorian times? Into what two main divisions of thought does the poem fall? What subdivisions are there in the second half?

2. What link does the poet feel between himself and Sophocles? In what way are the troubled thoughts of the two poets like the sea? What consolation does he find in the midst of a confused world? Is the last stanza descriptive of our situation today?

DANTE GABRIEL ROSSETTI

1828–1882

and CHRISTINA ROSSETTI

1830–1894

Love of poetry was a natural inheritance in the Rossetti family. The father was an exiled Italian who, besides teaching his native language in Kings College, London, wrote commentaries on the great Italian poet Dante, for whom he named his son. All of his four children did some writing, and Dante and Christina earned a secure place in the roll of English poets.

Dante Gabriel Rossetti thought of himself more as a painter than a poet, and practiced the two arts throughout his life. In both he expressed his love of rich color and his desire to " encourage the simplicity of nature in all things." He was an influential member of the Pre-Raphaelite Brotherhood of painters and writers (see page 459). In some of his early paintings we see the face of Christina. Later, the central figure was usually his wife, the beautiful Elizabeth Siddal. After only two years of marriage, Elizabeth, who was tubercular, tragically died. Rossetti, in despair, buried all his unpublished poems beside her, but several years later his friends induced the poet to allow them to recover the poems for publication. The success of this volume encouraged him to continue writing during the last twenty secluded years of his life. His sonnet sequence of 101 poems, called *The House of Life,* is among the greatest in English literature. In addition, Rossetti wrote ballads and lyrics, all stamped with his strongly pictorial quality. Notice this quality in " Silent Noon " and " The Woodspurge," one poem symbolizing the great love, the other the great grief, of his life.

Christina Rossetti, one of the masters of the English sonnet, led a life of self-sacrifice. A devout Anglican, she refused to marry two suitors because of religious differences. The first of these love affairs caused her intense grief, as some of her poems show. After devoting much of her life to the care of her mother and two elderly aunts, she herself became almost an invalid for her last twenty years. She found consolation in her poetry, and in prose writings of a religious nature. It has been said that all we know of her is that she was a great saint and a great poet.

Silent Noon

DANTE GABRIEL ROSSETTI

Your hands lie open in the long fresh grass,
The finger points look through like rosy blooms;
Your eyes smile peace. The pasture gleams and glooms
'Neath billowing skies that scatter and amass.
All round our nest, far as the eye can pass,   5
Are golden kingcup fields with silver edge
Where the cow parsley skirts the hawthorn hedge.
'Tis visible silence, still as the hourglass.
Deep in the sun-searched growths the dragonfly
Hangs like a blue thread loosened from the sky —   10
So this winged hour is dropped to us from above.
Oh! clasp we to our hearts, for deathless dower,
This close-companioned inarticulate hour
When twofold silence was the song of love.

Spring

DANTE GABRIEL ROSSETTI

Soft-littered is the new year's lambing fold,
And in the hollowed haystack at its side
The shepherd lies o' nights now, wakeful-eyed
At the ewes' travailing call through the dark cold.
The young rooks cheep 'mid the thick caw o' the old: 5
And near unpeopled streamsides, on the ground,
By her spring-cry the moor hen's nest is found,
Where the drained floodlands flaunt their marigold.
Chill are the gusts to which the pastures cower,
And chill the current where the young reeds stand   10
As green and close as the young wheat on land:
Yet here the cuckoo and the cuckoo flower
Plight to the heart Spring's perfect imminent hour
Whose breath shall soothe you like your dear one's hand.

The Woodspurge

DANTE GABRIEL ROSSETTI

In a moment of intense despair, some irrelevant image may be strongly impressed in one's memory, to be associated ever afterward with the grief it accompanied. This characteristic of the human mind is the subject of this poem. The woodspurge is a flowering plant with a three-part blossom.

The wind flapped loose, the wind was
    still,
Shaken out dead from tree and hill;
I had walked on at the wind's will —
I sat now, for the wind was still.

Between my knees my forehead was —
My lips, drawn in, said not Alas!   6
My hair was over in the grass,
My naked ears heard the day pass.

My eyes, wide open, had the run
Of some ten weeds to fix upon;   10
Among those few, out of the sun,
The woodspurge flowered, three cups in
    one.

From perfect grief there need not be
Wisdom or even memory:
One thing then learned remains to me,
The woodspurge has a cup of three.   16

A Birthday

CHRISTINA ROSSETTI

My heart is like a singing bird
    Whose nest is in a watered shoot;
My heart is like an apple tree
    Whose boughs are bent with thickset
    fruit;
My heart is like a rainbow shell   5
    That paddles in a halcyon sea;°
My heart is gladder than all these
    Because my love is come to me.

Raise me a dais of silk and down;   9
    Hang it with vair° and purple dyes;
Carve it in doves, and pomegranates,
    And peacocks with a hundred eyes;
Work it in gold and silver grapes
    In leaves, and silver fleurs-de-lys;
Because the birthday of my life   15
    Is come, my love is come to me.

6. *halcyon* (hăl′sĭ·ŭn) *sea:* calm, peaceful sea, which is supposed to exist for fourteen days each winter when the kingfisher, or halcyon, nests on the waves. 10. *vair:* a kind of fur used in the Middle Ages.

Remember

CHRISTINA ROSSETTI

Remember me when I am gone away,
Gone far away into the silent land;
When you can no more hold me by the hand,
Nor I half turn to go, yet turning stay.
Remember me when no more, day by day,   5
You tell me of our future that you planned;
Only remember me; you understand
It will be late to counsel then or pray.
Yet if you should forget me for a while
And afterward remember, do not grieve;   10
For if the darkness and corruption leave
A vestige of the thoughts that once I had,
Better by far you should forget and smile
Than that you should remember and be sad.

THE ROSSETTIS

DANTE GABRIEL

1. Find evidence from Rossetti's poems that he was a painter with a trained eye for color and design. Show also that sound — and the suggestion of silence — are important elements in these poems.

2. By what details does the poet suggest utter despair in " The Woodspurge "? Can you think of an instance when some trivial detail impressed itself on your mind during an important or moving experience?

CHRISTINA

1. In what sense is the word " birthday " used in the first poem? Contrast the pictures of natural beauty in the first stanza with the details of oriental splendor and luxury in the second.

2. How is the mood of " Remember " different from that of " A Birthday "? What do the two together suggest of the author's experience?

SUGGESTIONS FOR REPORTS

Choose one of these special topics:

1. Rossetti as an artist. If possible show prints of his paintings in class and point out the faces of his sister and wife in them.

2. The Pre-Raphaelite Brotherhood. Present a report on who they were and what they stood for.

LEWIS CARROLL 1832–1898

Lewis Carroll is a name known to all children who have delighted in the story of *Alice in Wonderland* and its sequel *Through the Looking Glass*. Few of them have guessed that hiding behind this pen name was a learned professor of mathematics at Oxford, the Reverend Charles Lutwidge Dodgson. While he was teaching there and writing books on mathematics, for a quarter of a century, Dodgson found expression for the other side of his nature in writing nonsense verse and gay fanciful stories for children. There is more meaning back of the strange characters in that distorted world of the Alice books than first appears. Adults find that the upside-down world of Alice reflects almost uncannily the true nature of life.

" A Sea Dirge " (not from the Alice books) is in marked contrast to many other poems on the sea which run through English literature. With characteristic drollery Lewis Carroll denounces the sea as his " pet peeve."

A Sea Dirge

There are certain things — as, a spider, a ghost,
    The income tax, gout, an umbrella for three —
That I hate, but the thing that I hate the most
    Is a thing they call the Sea.

Pour some salt water over the floor —   5
    Ugly I'm sure you'll allow it to be;
Suppose it extended a mile or more,
    That's very like the Sea.

Beat a dog till he howls outright —
    Cruel, but all very well for a spree;   10
Suppose that he did so day and night,
    That would be like the Sea.

I had a vision of nurserymaids;
    Tens of thousands passed by me —
All leading children with wooden spades,   15
    And this was by the Sea.

Who invented those spades of wood?
    Who was it cut them out of the tree?
None, I think, but an idiot could —
    Or one that loved the Sea.   20

It is pleasant and dreamy, no doubt, to float
    With " thoughts as boundless, and souls as free ";
But, suppose you are very unwell in the boat —
    How do you like the Sea?

There is an insect that people avoid   25
    (Whence is derived the verb " to flee ").
Where have you been by it most annoyed?
    In lodgings by the Sea.

If you like your coffee with sand for dregs,
    A decided hint of salt in your tea,   30
And a fishy taste in the very eggs —
    By all means choose the Sea.

And if, with these dainties to drink and eat,
    You prefer not a vestige of grass or tree,
And a chronic state of wet in your feet,   35
    Then — I recommend the Sea.

For *I* have friends who dwell by the coast —
    Pleasant friends they are to me!
It is when I am with them I wonder most
    That anyone likes the Sea.   40

They take me a walk; though tired and stiff,
  To climb the heights I madly agree;
And, after a tumble or so from the cliff,
  They kindly suggest the Sea.

I try the rocks, and I think it cool   45
  That they laugh with such an excess of glee,
As I heavily slip into every pool
  That skirts the cold, cold Sea.

A DIFFERENT SEA POEM

1. In " A Sea Dirge " what various aspects of the sea arouse Carroll's distaste? Which comparisons are most amusing to you? What are your own reactions to the sea? Are they based on firsthand experience or on what you have heard and read about the sea?

2. Contrast the moods created in the following poems on the sea: " The Seafarer " (page 36), " The Rime of the Ancient Mariner " (page 373), " Apostrophe to the Ocean " (page 412), " Break, Break, Break " (page 484), " Crossing the Bar " (page 487), " Home Thoughts, from the Sea " (page 493). What can you conclude from this variety of poetry on the sea?

W. S. GILBERT 1836–1911

William Schwenck Gilbert is rarely spoken of alone; his name is invariably made part of the pair Gilbert and Sullivan. But before meeting Sullivan he had made a name as the witty author of satirical verses in *Bab Ballads*. Gilbert wrote the librettos and Sullivan the music for a series of light operas which are still as popular as they were back in the seventies and eighties. Today high school students continue to stage *H.M.S. Pinafore, The Mikado*, and others. Traveling professional companies specializing in Gilbert and Sullivan still go up and down the land. The most famous of these companies is the D'Oyly Carte, which was organized by Richard D'Oyly Carte, an astute theater producer who brought Gilbert and Sullivan together and first produced their works.

Much of Gilbert's humor lies in his unexpected rhymes and many-syllabled words that ripple along. His lines read almost as well as they sing. He was a master of satire. He knew how to ridicule the army, the navy, and the government without offending the public.

On page 673 you will find a chapter from Hesketh Pearson's *Gilbert and Sullivan,* which points out some of Gilbert's personal peculiarities, and tells of the beginnings of *H.M.S. Pinafore*. Two songs from that operetta are given here.

He Is an Englishman

BOATSWAIN: He is an Englishman!
             For he himself has said it,
             And it's greatly to his credit
             That he is an Englishman!
CHORUS: *That he is an Englishman!*
BOATSWAIN: For he might have been a
             Roosian,   6
             A French or Turk or Proosian,
             Or perhaps Italian!
CHORUS: *Or perhaps Italian!*
BOATSWAIN: But in spite of all temptations   10
             To belong to other nations,
             He remains an Englishman!
             He remains an Englishman!
Chorus repeats last four lines.

When I Was a Lad

When I was a lad I served a term
As office boy to an attorney's firm.
I cleaned the windows and I swept the floor,
And I polished up the handle of the big front door.
CHORUS: *He polished up the handle of the big front door.*   5

I polished up the handle so carefullee
That now I am the ruler of the Queen's Navee!
CHORUS: *He polished up the handle so carefullee*
         That now he is the ruler of the Queen's Navee!

[For each stanza the chorus repeats three lines, as shown in the first stanza.]

As office boy I made such a mark   10
That they gave me the post of a junior clerk.°
I served the writs with a smile so bland,
And I copied all the letters in a big round hand.

I copied all the letters in a hand so free
That now I am the ruler of the Queen's Navee!   15

In serving writs I made such a name
That an articled clerk I soon became;
I wore clean collars and a brand-new suit
For the pass examination at the Institute.

That pass examination did so well for me   20
That now I am the ruler of the Queen's Navee!

Of legal knowledge I acquired such a grip
That they took me into the partnership.
And that junior partnership, I ween,
Was the only ship that I ever had seen.   25

But that kind of ship so suited me
That now I am the ruler of the Queen's Navee!

I grew so rich that I was sent
By a pocket borough° into Parliament.
I always voted at my party's call,   30
And I never thought of thinking for myself at all.

I thought so little they rewarded me
By making me the ruler of the Queen's Navee!

11. *clerk:* The British pronounce this to rhyme with *mark*. 29. *pocket borough:* Before the election reforms of the nineteenth century, certain boroughs had become so reduced in population that they could be easily controlled or "put in the pocket" by a wealthy or powerful candidate.

Now landsmen all, whoever you may be,
If you want to rise to the top of the tree, 35
If your soul isn't fettered to an office stool,
Be careful to be guided by this golden rule,

Stick close to your desks and never go to sea,
And you all may be rulers of the Queen's Navee!

VICTORIANS RIDICULED

1. In "He Is an Englishman" Gilbert is poking fun at exaggerated national pride. In the selection on page 677 about *H.M.S. Pinafore*, you will find an amusing parody on this song, proposed as an adaptation of the idea to America.

2. In "When I Was a Lad" Gilbert satirizes two different things: the "self-made man" type of biography, and the British Navy. Give specific lines which most clearly ridicule each of these. Show why both these songs from *H.M.S. Pinafore* would arouse laughter instead of resentment.

ROBERT LOUIS STEVENSON

1850—1894

You probably come upon Robert Louis Stevenson as an old friend. Nearly every teen-age boy and girl reads *Treasure Island*, and many have seen a motion-picture version of it. Probably when you were even younger you read (or listened to) *A Child's Garden of Verses*. Stevenson has something to interest every age. Now you are ready for his essays and psychological stories, which make their appeal to mature people.

Stevenson's whole life was a struggle against disease, yet his literary output was large and vigorous, enriched by some of these adverse conditions. He was nursed through a sickly childhood by a devoted Scottish nurse, to whom he dedicated *A Child's Garden of Verses*. His walking tours in Scotland gave him background for the descriptions of bleak moors and lonely hills in *Kidnapped* and other romances. A similar journey through southern France, taken for his health, resulted in *Travels with a Donkey* and other books of essays. In France he met a charming American, Mrs. Fanny Osbourne, whom he later married in California, after her divorce. The long trip across an ocean and a continent to join her played havoc with his weak constitution, but his wife's nursing saved his life. After a number of years spent in various parts of the United States and Europe, the Stevensons moved, again for his health, to Vailima, Samoa. His " Vailima Letters " to his many friends show him as a master of the art of letter writing.

The variety of Stevenson's work has been indicated by the mention so far of novels, poetry, essays, and letters. One other type is necessary to complete the picture — the short story. Stevenson's contribution to this literary form is of the greatest importance. Up to his time the short story had not been developed in England as it had in America. You will notice that " Markheim " is the first short story in the modern manner to appear in this book. It strikes a new note in its emphasis on the psychological approach to character and to the personal problem of right and wrong.

Stevenson is remembered and loved for his personality as well as for his books. The kindliness, the humor, and the sheer pluck of the man in his long fight against disease gave all who knew him a feeling of close friendship to him. Even in remote Samoa, where he spent his last years, he won the friendship of the natives. They named him " Tusitala " (teller of tales) and revered him as a chieftain. On his death, to do him signal honor, sixty of them cut a path through heavy underbrush to the top of Mount Vailima, where they buried him. When Mrs. Stevenson died,

she was buried beside him. On the monument are two bronze tablets: Stevenson's bearing the epitaph " Requiem," which he wrote for himself; and hers, the closing stanza of " My Wife," his affectionate tribute to her.

My Wife

Trusty, dusky, vivid, true,
With eyes of gold and bramble-dew,
　　Steel-true and blade-straight,
The great Artificer
　　Made my mate.　　　　　　　　　5

Honor, anger, valor, fire;
A love that life could never tire,
　　Death quench, or evil stir,
The mighty Master
　　Gave to her.　　　　　　　　　10

Teacher, tender,° comrade, wife,
A fellow farer true through life,
　　Heart-whole and soul-free,
The august Father
　　Gave to me.　　　　　　　　　15

11. *tender:* an attendant or nurse.

Requiem

Under the wide and starry sky
Dig the grave and let me lie.
Glad did I live and gladly die,
　　And I laid me down with a will.

This be the verse you grave for me:　　5
Here he lies where he longed to be;
Home is the sailor, home from sea,
　　And the hunter home from the hill.

El Dorado

Stevenson's buoyant, courageous nature speaks through this essay from his collection *Virginibus Puerisque* (For Girls and Boys). " El Dorado " means " The Golden," a name originally given to a fabulous king in a wealthy city, supposedly in South

America. Later the name came to mean any visionary quest.

The central theme of the essay is that satisfaction and joy lie in the effort toward a goal rather than the final attainment of it.

IT SEEMS as if a great deal were attainable in a world where there are so many marriages and decisive battles, and where we all, at certain hours of the day, and with great gusto and dispatch, stow a portion of victuals finally and irretrievably into the bag which contains us. And it would seem also, on a hasty view, that the attainment of as much as possible was the one goal of man's contentious life. And yet, as regards the spirit, this is but a semblance. We live in an ascending scale when we live happily, one thing leading to another in an endless series. There is always a new horizon for onward-looking men, and although we dwell on a small planet, immersed in petty business and not enduring beyond a brief period of years, we are so constituted that our hopes are inaccessible, like stars, and the term of hoping is prolonged until the term of life. To be truly happy is a question of how we begin and not of how we end, of what we want and not of what we have. An aspiration is a joy forever, a possession as solid as a landed estate, a fortune which we can never exhaust and which gives us year by year a revenue of pleasurable activity. To have many of these is to be spiritually rich. Life is only a very dull and ill-directed theater unless we have some interests in the piece; and to those who have neither art nor science, the world is a mere arrangement of colors, or a rough footway where they may very well break their shins. It is in virtue of his own desires and curiosities that any man continues to exist with even patience, that he is charmed by the look of things and people, and that he wakens every morning with a renewed appetite for work and pleasure. Desire and curiosity are the two eyes through which he sees the world in the most enchanted colors; it is they that make women beautiful or fossils interesting; and the man may squander his estate and come to beggary, but if he keeps these two amulets he is still rich in the possibilities of pleasure. Suppose he could take one meal so compact and comprehensive that he should never hunger any more; suppose him, at a glance, to take in all the features of the world and allay the desire for knowledge; suppose him to do the like in any province of experience — would not that man be in a poor way for amusement ever after?

One who goes touring on foot with a single volume in his knapsack reads with circumspection, pausing often to reflect, and often laying the book down to contemplate the landscape or the prints in the inn parlor; for he fears to come to an end of his entertainment, and be left companionless on the last stages of his journey. A young fellow recently finished the works of Thomas Carlyle, winding up, if we remember aright, with the ten notebooks upon Frederick the Great. "What!" cried the young fellow, in consternation, " is there no more Carlyle? Am I left to the daily papers? " A more celebrated instance is that of Alexander, who wept bitterly because he had no more worlds to subdue. And when Gibbon had finished the *Decline and Fall*,[1] he had only a few moments of joy; and it was with a " sober melancholy " that he parted from his labors.

Happily we all shoot at the moon with ineffectual arrows; our hopes are set on inaccessible El Dorado; we come to an end of nothing here below. Interests are only plucked up to sow themselves again, like mustard. You would think, when the child was born, there would be an end to trouble; and yet it is only the beginning of fresh anxieties; and when you have seen it through its teething and its education, and at last its marriage, alas! it is only to have new fears, new quivering sensibilities, with every day; and the health of your chil-

---

[1] *Decline and Fall:* This work on the Roman Empire occupied Gibbon twenty-four years.

dren's children grows as touching a concern as that of your own. Again, when you have married your wife, you would think you were got upon a hilltop, and might begin to go downward by an easy slope. But you have only ended courting to begin marriage. Falling in love and winning love are often difficult tasks to overbearing and rebellious spirits; but to keep in love is also a business of some importance, to which both man and wife must bring kindness and good will. The true love story commences at the altar, when there lies before the married pair a most beautiful contest of wisdom and generosity, and a lifelong struggle toward an unattainable ideal. Unattainable? Ay, surely unattainable, from the very fact that they are two instead of one.

" Of making books there is no end," complained the Preacher; [1] and did not perceive how highly he was praising letters as an occupation. There is no end, indeed, to making books or experiments, or to travel, or to gathering wealth. Problem gives rise to problem. We may study forever, and we are never as learned as we would. We have never made a statue worthy of our dreams. And when we have discovered a continent, or crossed a chain of mountains, it is only to find another ocean or another plain upon the further side. In the infinite universe there is room for our swiftest diligence and to spare. It

[1] *Preacher:* Ecclesiastes 12:12.

is not like the works of Carlyle, which can be read to an end. Even in a corner of it, in a private park, or in the neighborhood of a single hamlet, the weather and the seasons keep so deftly changing that although we walk there for a lifetime there will be always something new to startle and delight us.

There is only one wish realizable on the earth; only one thing that can be perfectly attained: Death. And from a variety of circumstances we have no one to tell us whether it be worth attaining.

A strange picture we make on our way to our chimeras,[2] ceaselessly marching, grudging ourselves the time for rest; indefatigable, adventurous pioneers. It is true that we shall never reach the goal; it is even more than probable that there is no such place; and if we lived for centuries and were endowed with the powers of a god, we should find ourselves not much nearer what we wanted at the end. O toiling hands of mortals! O unwearied feet, traveling ye know not whither! Soon, soon, it seems to you, you must come forth on some conspicuous hilltop, and but a little way further, against the setting sun, descry the spires of El Dorado. Little do ye know your own blessedness; for to travel hopefully is a better thing than to arrive, and the true success is to labor.

[2] *chimeras* (kĭ·mē'raz): The word *chimera* originally meant an imaginary monster, but it has come to mean a vain or foolish fancy.

Markheim

In the eighteen-eighties, short stories in the modern manner began to appear in England. Writers were following Poe's definition of the short story as an art form. In a short space, Poe said, a story should make a single clear-cut impression without deviations and side plots, and it should maintain a dominant mood from the first word to the last. " Markheim " was one of

the most successful of early stories in this manner. It was printed along with others, some of them considerably longer, in Stevenson's volume, *The Merry Men* (1887). It still holds its place as one of the great short stories of the nineteenth century. Its emphasis on the psychological aspect of crime gave new treatment to an old subject. In the same volume appeared the longer tale " Dr. Jekyll and Mr. Hyde," which personified the dual nature of man so dramatically that these names have passed into common speech as representing the good and bad sides of an individual. Stevenson was tapping new sources of story interest of which twentieth-century writers have since made wide use.

Y E S," said the dealer, " our windfalls are of various kinds. Some customers are ignorant, and then I touch a dividend on my superior knowledge. Some are dishonest," and here he held up the candle, so that the light fell strongly on his visitor, " and in that case," he continued, " I profit by my virtue."

Markheim had but just entered from the daylight streets, and his eyes had not yet grown familiar with the mingled shine and darkness in the shop. At these pointed words, and before the near presence of the flame, he blinked painfully and looked aside.

The dealer chuckled. " You come to me on Christmas Day," he resumed, " when you know that I am alone in my house, put up my shutters, and make a point of refusing business. Well, you will have to pay for that; you will have to pay for my loss of time, when I should be balancing my books; you will have to pay, besides, for a kind of manner that I remark in you today very strongly. I am the essence of discretion, and ask no awkward questions; but when a customer cannot look me in the eye, he has to pay for it." The dealer once more chuckled; and then, changing to his usual business voice, though still with a note of irony, " You can give, as usual, a clear account of how you came into the possession of the object? " he continued. " Still your uncle's cabinet? A remarkable collector, sir! "

And the little pale, round-shouldered dealer stood almost on tiptoe, looking over the top of his gold spectacles, and nodding his head with every mark of disbelief. Markheim returned his gaze with one of infinite pity, and a touch of horror.

" This time," said he, " you are in error. I have not come to sell, but to buy. I have no curios to dispose of; my uncle's cabinet is bare to the wainscot; even were it still intact, I have done well on the Stock Exchange, and should more likely add to it than otherwise, and my errand today is simplicity itself. I seek a Christmas present for a lady," he continued, waxing more fluent as he struck into the speech he had prepared; " and certainly I owe you every excuse for thus disturbing you upon so small a matter. But the thing was neglected yesterday; I must produce my little compliment at dinner; and, as you very well know, a rich marriage is not a thing to be neglected."

There followed a pause, during which the dealer seemed to weigh this statement incredulously. The ticking of many clocks among the curious lumber of the shop, and the faint rushing of the cabs in a near thoroughfare, filled up the interval of silence.

" Well, sir," said the dealer, " be it so. You are an old customer after all; and if, as you say, you have the chance of a good marriage, far be it from me to be an obstacle. Here is a nice thing for a lady, now," he went on, " this hand glass — fifteenth-century, warranted; comes from a good collection, too; but I reserve the name, in the interests of my customer, who was just like yourself, my dear sir, the nephew and sole heir of a remarkable collector."

The dealer, while he thus ran on in his dry and biting voice, had stooped to take the object from its place; and, as he had done so, a shock had passed through Markheim, a start both of hand and foot, a sudden leap of many tumultuous passions to the face. It passed as swiftly as it came, and left no trace beyond a certain trembling of the hand that now received the glass.

" A glass," he said hoarsely, and then paused, and repeated it more clearly. " A glass? For Christmas? Surely not."

" And why not? " cried the dealer. " Why not a glass? "

Markheim was looking upon him with an indefinable expression. " You ask me why not? " he said. " Why, look here — look in it — look at yourself! Do you like to see it? No! nor I — nor any man."

The little man had jumped back when Markheim had so suddenly confronted him with the mirror; but now, perceiving there was nothing worse on hand, he chuckled. " Your future lady, sir, must be pretty hard-favored," said he.

" I ask you," said Markheim, " for a Christmas present, and you give me this — this damned reminder of years and sins and follies — this hand conscience! Did you mean it? Had you a thought in your mind? Tell me. It will be better for you if you do. Come, tell me about yourself. I hazard a guess now, that you are in secret a very charitable man? "

The dealer looked closely at his companion. It was very odd, Markheim did not appear to be laughing; there was something in his face like an eager sparkle of hope, but nothing of mirth.

" What are you driving at? " the dealer asked.

" Not charitable? " returned the other, gloomily. " Not charitable; not pious; not scrupulous; unloving; unbeloved; a hand to get money, a safe to keep it. Is that all? Dear God, man, is that all? "

" I will tell you what it is," began the dealer, with some sharpness, and then broke off again with a chuckle. " But I see this is a love match of yours, and you have been drinking the lady's health."

" Ah! " cried Markheim, with a strange curiosity. " Ah, have you been in love? Tell me about that."

" I! " cried the dealer. " I in love! I never had the time, nor have I the time today for all this nonsense. Will you take the glass? "

" Where is the hurry? " returned Markheim. " It is very pleasant to stand here talking; and life is so short and insecure that I would not hurry away from any pleasure — no, not even from so mild a one as this. We should rather cling, cling to what little we can get, like a man at a cliff's edge. Every second is a cliff, if you think upon it — a cliff a mile high — high enough, if we fall, to dash us out of every feature of humanity. Hence it is best to talk pleasantly. Let us talk of each other; why should we wear this mask? Let us be confidential. Who knows, we might become friends? "

" I have just one word to say to you," said the dealer. " Either make your purchase, or walk out of my shop."

" True, true," said Markheim. " Enough fooling. To business. Show me something else."

The dealer stooped once more, this time to replace the glass upon the shelf, his thin blond hair falling over his eyes as he did so. Markheim moved a little nearer, with one hand in the pocket of his greatcoat; he drew himself up and filled his lungs; at the same time many different emotions were depicted together on his face — terror, horror, and resolve, fascination, and a physical repulsion; and through a haggard lift of his upper lip, his teeth looked out.

" This, perhaps, may suit," observed the dealer; and then, as he began to rearise, Markheim bounded from behind upon his victim. The long, skewerlike dagger flashed and fell. The dealer struggled like a hen, striking his temple on the shelf, and then tumbled on the floor in a heap.

Time had some score of small voices in that shop, some stately and slow as was becoming to their great age, others garrulous and hurried. All these told out the seconds in an intricate chorus of tickings. Then the passage of a lad's feet, heavily running on the pavement, broke in upon these smaller voices and startled Markheim into the consciousness of his surroundings. He looked about him awfully. The candle stood on the counter, its flame solemnly wagging in a draft; and by that inconsiderable movement, the whole room was filled with noiseless bustle and kept heaving like a sea: the tall shadows nodding, the gross blots of darkness swelling and dwindling as with respiration, the faces of the portraits and the china gods changing and wavering like images in water. The inner door stood ajar, and peered into that leaguer of shadows with a long slit of daylight like a pointing finger.

From these fear-stricken rovings, Markheim's eyes returned to the body of his victim, where it lay both humped and sprawling, incredibly small and strangely meaner than in life. In these poor, miserly clothes, in that ungainly attitude, the dealer lay like so much sawdust. Markheim had feared to see it, and, lo! it was nothing. And yet, as he gazed, this bundle of old clothes and pool of blood began to find eloquent voices. There it must lie; there was none to work the cunning hinges or direct the miracle of locomotion — there it must lie till it was found. Found! ay, and then? Then would this dead fish lift up a cry that would ring over England, and fill the world with the echoes of pursuit. Ay, dead or not, this was still the enemy. " Time was that when the brains were out," [1] he thought; and the first word struck into his mind. Time, now that the deed was accomplished — time, which had closed for the victim, had become instant and momentous for the slayer.

The thought was yet in his mind, when, first one and then another, with every variety of pace and voice — one deep as the bell from a cathedral turret, another ringing on its treble notes the prelude of a waltz — the clocks began to strike the hour of three in the afternoon.

[1] See *Macbeth*, Act III, Scene 4, lines 78–79.

The sudden outbreak of so many tongues in that dumb chamber staggered him. He began to bestir himself, going to and fro with the candle, beleaguered by moving shadows, and startled to the soul by chance reflections. In many rich mirrors, some of home designs, some from Venice or Amsterdam, he saw his face repeated and repeated, as it were an army of spies; his own eyes met and detected him; and the sound of his own steps, lightly as they fell, vexed the surrounding quiet. And still as he continued to fill his pockets, his mind accused him, with a sickening iteration, of the thousand faults of his design. He should have chosen a more quiet hour; he should have prepared an alibi; he should not have used a knife; he should have been more cautious, and only bound and gagged the dealer, and not killed him; he should have been more bold, and killed the servant also; he should have done all things otherwise; poignant regrets, weary, incessant toiling of the mind to change what was unchangeable, to plan what was now useless, to be the architect of the irrevo-

In many rich mirrors he saw his face . . .

cable past. Meanwhile, and behind all this activity, brute terrors, like the scurrying of rats in a deserted attic, filled the more remote chambers of his brain with riot; the hand of the constable would fall heavy on his shoulder, and his nerves would jerk like a hooked fish; or he beheld, in galloping defile, the dock, the prison, the gallows, and the black coffin. Terror of the people in the street sat down before his mind like a besieging army. It was impossible, he thought, but that some rumor of the struggle must have reached their ears and set on edge their curiosity; and now, in all the neighboring houses, he divined them sitting motionless and with uplifted ear — solitary people, condemned to spend Christmas dwelling alone on memories of the past, and now startlingly recalled from that tender exercise; happy family parties, struck into silence round the table, the mother still with raised finger: every degree and age and humor, but all, by their own hearths, prying and hearkening and weaving the rope that was to hang him. Sometimes it seemed to him he could not move too softly; the clink of the tall Bohemian goblets rang out loudly like a bell; and alarmed by the bigness of the ticking, he was tempted to stop the clocks. And then, again, with a swift transition of his terrors, the very silence of the place appeared a source of peril, and a thing to strike and freeze the passer-by; and he would step more boldly, and bustle aloud among the contents of the shop, and imitate, with elaborate bravado, the movements of a busy man at ease in his own house.

But he was now so pulled about by different alarms that, while one portion of his mind was still alert and cunning, another trembled on the brink of lunacy. One hallucination in particular took a strong hold on his credulity. The neighbor hearkening with white face beside his window, the passer-by arrested by a horrible surmise on the pavement — these could at worst suspect,

they could not know; through the brick walls and shuttered windows only sounds could penetrate. But here, within the house, was he alone? He knew he was; he had watched the servant set forth sweethearting, in her poor best, " out for the day " written in every ribbon and smile. Yes, he was alone, of course; and yet, in the bulk of empty house about him, he could surely hear a stir of delicate footing — he was surely conscious, inexplicably conscious, of some presence. Ay, surely; to every room and corner of the house his imagination followed it; and now it was a faceless thing, and yet had eyes to see with; and again it was a shadow of himself! and yet again behold the image of the dead dealer, reinspired with cunning and hatred.

At times, with a strong effort, he would glance at the open door which still seemed to repel his eyes. The house was tall, the skylight small and dirty, the day blind with fog; and the light that filtered down to the ground story was exceedingly faint, and showed dimly on the threshold of the shop. And yet, in that strip of doubtful brightness, did there not hang wavering a shadow?

Suddenly, from the street outside, a very jovial gentleman began to beat with a staff on the shop door, accompanying his blows with shouts and railleries in which the dealer was continually called upon by name. Markheim, smitten into ice, glanced at the dead man. But no! he lay quiet still; he was fled away far beyond earshot of these blows and shoutings; he was sunk beneath seas of silence; and his name, which would once have caught his notice above the howling of a storm, had become an empty sound. And presently the jovial gentleman desisted from his knocking and departed.

Here was a broad hint to hurry what remained to be done, to get forth from this accusing neighborhood, to plunge into a bath of London multitudes, and to reach, on the other side of day, that haven of safety and apparent innocence — his bed. One visitor had come; at any moment another might follow and be more obstinate. To have done the deed, and yet not to reap the profit, would be too abhorrent a failure. The money, that was now Markheim's concern; and as a means to that, the keys.

He glanced over his shoulder at the open door, where the shadow was still lingering and shivering; and with no conscious repugnance of the mind, yet with a tremor of the belly, he drew near the body of his victim. The human character had quite departed. Like a suit half-stuffed with bran, the limbs lay scattered, the trunk doubled, on the floor; and yet the thing repelled him. Although so dingy and inconsiderable to the eye, he feared it might have more significance to the touch. He took the body by the shoulders, and turned it on its back. It was strangely light and supple, and the limbs, as if they had been broken, fell into the oddest postures. The face was robbed of all expression; but it was as pale as wax, and shockingly smeared with blood about one temple. That was, for Markheim, the one displeasing circumstance. It carried him back, upon the instant, to a certain fair day in a fishers' village: a gray day, a piping wind, a crowd upon the street, the blare of brasses, the booming of drums, the nasal voice of a ballad singer; and a boy going to and fro, buried over head in the crowd and divided between interest and fear, until, coming out upon the chief place of concourse, he beheld a booth and a great screen with pictures, dismally designed, garishly colored: Brownrigg with her apprentice; the Mannings with their murdered guest; Weare in the death grip of Thurtell; [1] and a score besides of fa-

[1] *Brownrigg, Mannings, Thurtell:* Elizabeth Brownrigg was a murderess of the eighteenth century; the Mannings and Thurtell were murderers of a later date. The pictures were probably to advertise waxworks of notorious criminals, which were formerly a popular form of side show at country fairs.

mous crimes. The thing was as clear as an illusion; he was once again that little boy; he was looking once again, and with the same sense of physical revolt, at these vile pictures; he was still stunned by the thumping of the drums. A bar of that day's music returned upon his memory; and at that, for the first time, a qualm came over him, a breath of nausea, a sudden weakness of the joints, which he must instantly resist and conquer.

He judged it more prudent to confront than to flee from these considerations; looking the more hardily in the dead face, bending his mind to realize the nature and greatness of his crime. So little a while ago that face had moved with every change of sentiment, that pale mouth had spoken, that body had been all on fire with governable energies; and now, and by his act, that piece of life had been arrested, as the horologist, with interjected finger, arrests the beating of the clock. So he reasoned in vain; he could rise to no more remorseful consciousness; the same heart which had shuddered before the painted effigies of crime, looked on its reality unmoved. At best, he felt a gleam of pity for one who had been endowed in vain with all those faculties that can make the world a garden of enchantment, one who had never lived and who was now dead. But of penitence, no, not a tremor.

With that, shaking himself clear of these considerations, he found the keys and advanced toward the open door of the shop. Outside, it had begun to rain smartly; and the sound of the shower upon the roof had banished silence. Like some dripping cavern, the chambers of the house were haunted by an incessant echoing, which filled the ear and mingled with the ticking of the clocks. And, as Markheim approached the door, he seemed to hear, in answer to his own cautious tread, the steps of another foot withdrawing up the stair. The shadow still palpitated loosely on the threshold. He threw a ton's weight of resolve upon his muscles, and drew back the door.

The faint, foggy daylight glimmered dimly on the bare floor and stairs; on the bright suit of armor posted, halbert in hand, upon the landing; and on the dark wood carvings and framed pictures that hung against the yellow panels of the wainscot. So loud was the beating of the rain through all the house that, in Markheim's ears, it began to be distinguished into many different sounds. Footsteps and sighs, the tread of regiments marching in the distance, the chink of money in the counting, and the creaking of doors held stealthily ajar, appeared to mingle with the patter of the drops upon the cupola and the gushing of the water in the pipes. The sense that he was not alone grew upon him to the verge of madness. On every side he was haunted and begirt by presences. He heard them moving in the upper chambers; from the shop, he heard the dead man getting to his legs; and as he began with a great effort to mount the stairs, feet fled quietly before him and followed stealthily behind. If he were but deaf, he thought, how tranquilly he would possess his soul! And then again, and hearkening with ever fresh attention, he blessed himself for that unresting sense which held the outposts and stood a trusty sentinel upon his life. His head turned continually on his neck; his eyes, which seemed starting from their orbits, scouted on every side, and on every side were half rewarded as with the tail of something nameless vanishing. The four and twenty steps to the first floor were four and twenty agonies.

On that first story the doors stood ajar, three of them like three ambushes, shaking his nerves like the throats of cannon. He could never again, he felt, be sufficiently immured and fortified from men's observing eyes; he longed to be home, girt in by walls, buried among bedclothes, and invisible to all but God. And at that thought he wondered a little, recollecting tales of other murderers and the fear they were said to entertain of heavenly avengers. It was not so, at least, with him. He feared the laws of nature, lest, in their callous and immutable procedure, they should preserve some damning evidence of his crime. He feared tenfold more, with a slavish, superstitious terror, some scission in the continuity of man's experience, some willful illegality of nature. He played a game of skill, depending on the rules, calculating consequence from cause; and what if nature, as the defeated tyrant overthrew the chessboard, should break the mold of their succession? The like had befallen Napoleon (so writers said) when the winter changed the time of its appearance. The like might befall Markheim: the solid walls might become transparent and reveal his doings like those of bees in a glass hive; the stout planks might yield under his foot like quicksands and detain him in their clutch; ay, and there were soberer accidents that might destroy him: if, for instance, the house should fall and imprison him beside the body of his victim; or the house next door should fly on fire, and the firemen invade him from all sides. These things he feared; and, in a sense, these things might be called the hands of God reached forth against sin. But about God himself he was at ease; his act was doubtless exceptional, but so were his excuses, which God knew; it was there, and not among men, that he felt sure of justice.

When he got safe into the drawing room, and shut the door behind him, he was aware of a respite from alarms. The room was quite dismantled, uncarpeted besides, and strewn with packing cases and incongruous furniture; several great pier glasses, in which he beheld himself at various angles, like an actor on a stage; many pictures, framed and unframed, standing, with their faces to the wall; a fine Sheraton [1] sideboard, a cabinet of marquetry, and a great old bed, with tapestry hangings. The windows opened to the floor; but by great good fortune the lower part of the shutters had been closed, and this concealed him from the neighbors. Here, then, Markheim drew in a packing case before the cabinet, and began to search among the keys. It was a long business, for there were many; and it was irksome, besides; for, after all, there might be nothing in the cabinet, and time was on the wing. But the closeness of the occupation sobered him. With the tail of his eye he saw the door — even glanced at it from time to time directly, like a besieged commander pleased to verify the good estate of his defenses. But in truth he was at peace. The rain falling in the street sounded natural and pleasant. Presently, on the other side, the notes of a piano were wakened to the music of a hymn, and the voices of many children took up the air and words. How stately, how comfortable was the melody! How fresh the youthful voices! Markheim gave ear to it smilingly, as he sorted out the keys; and his mind was thronged with answerable ideas and images; churchgoing children and the pealing of the high organ; children afield, bathers by the brookside, ramblers on the brambly common, kitefliers in the windy and cloud-navigated sky; and then, at another cadence of the hymn, back again to church, and the somnolence of summer Sundays, and the high, genteel voice of the parson (which he smiled a little to recall), and the painted Jacobean [2] tombs, and the dim lettering of the Ten Commandments in the chancel.

[1] *Sheraton:* Thomas Sheraton (1751–1806), a famous English furniture maker.
[2] *Jacobean* (jăk'ō·bē'ăn): pertaining to the reign of the English kings named James in the seventeenth century.

And as he sat thus, at once busy and absent, he was startled to his feet. A flash of ice, a flash of fire, a bursting gush of blood, went over him, and then he stood transfixed and thrilling. A step mounted the stair slowly and steadily, and presently a hand was laid upon the knob, and the lock clicked, and the door opened. Fear held Markheim in a vise. What to expect he knew not, whether the dead man walking, or the official ministers of human justice, or some chance witness blindly stumbling in to consign him to the gallows. But when a face was thrust into the aperture, glanced round the room, looked at him, nodded and smiled as if in friendly recognition, and then withdrew again, and the door closed behind it, his fear broke loose from his control in a hoarse cry. At the sound of this the visitant returned.

" Did you call me? " he asked pleasantly, and with that he entered the room and closed the door behind him.

Markheim stood and gazed at him with all his eyes. Perhaps there was a film upon his sight, but the outlines of the newcomer seemed to change and waver like those of the idols in the wavering candlelight of the shop; and at times he thought he knew him; and at times he thought he bore a likeness to himself; and always, like a lump of living terror, there lay in his bosom the conviction that this thing was not of the earth and not of God.

And yet the creature had a strange air of the commonplace, as he stood looking on Markheim with a smile; and when he added: " You are looking for the money, I believe? " it was in the tones of everyday politeness.

Markheim made no answer.

" I should warn you," resumed the other, " that the maid has left her sweetheart earlier than usual and will soon be here. If Mr. Markheim be found in this house I need not describe to him the consequences."

" You know me? " cried the murderer.

The visitor smiled. " You have long been a favorite of mine," he said; " and I have long observed and often sought to help you."

" What are you? " cried Markheim: " the devil? "

" What I may be," returned the other, " cannot affect the service I propose to render you."

" It can," cried Markheim; " it does! Be helped by you? No, never; not by you! You do not know me yet; thank God, you do not know me! "

" I know you," replied the visitant, with a sort of kind severity or rather firmness. " I know you to the soul."

" Know me! " cried Markheim. " Who can do so? My life is but a travesty and slander on myself. I have lived to belie my nature. All men do; all men are better than this disguise that grows about and stifles them. You see each dragged away by life, like one whom bravos have seized and muffled in a cloak. If they had their own control — if you could see their faces, they would be altogether different, they would shine out for heroes and saints! I am worse than most; my self is more overlaid; my excuse is known to me and God. But, had I the time, I could disclose myself."

" To me? " inquired the visitant.

" To you before all," returned the murderer. " I supposed you were intelligent. I thought — since you exist — you would prove a reader of the heart. And yet you would propose to judge me by my acts! Think of it; my acts! I was born and I have lived in a land of giants; giants have dragged me by the wrists since I was born out of my mother — the giants of circumstance. And you would judge me by my acts! But can you not look within? Can you not understand that evil is hateful to me? Can you not see within me the clear writing of conscience, never blurred by any willful sophistry although too often disregarded? Can you not read me for a thing that surely must be common as humanity — the unwilling sinner? "

" All this is very feelingly expressed," was the reply, " but it regards me not. These points of consistency are beyond my province, and I care not in the least by what compulsion you may have been dragged away, so as you are but carried in the right direction. But time flies; the servant delays, looking in the faces of the crowd and at the pictures on the hoardings, but still she keeps moving nearer; and remember, it is as if the gallows itself were striding toward you through the Christmas streets! Shall I help you — I, who know all? Shall I tell you where to find the money? "

" For what price? " asked Markheim.

" I offer you the service for a Christmas gift," returned the other.

Markheim could not refrain from smiling with a kind of bitter triumph. " No," said he, " I will take nothing at your hands; if I were dying of thirst, and it was your hand that put the pitcher to my lips, I should find the courage to refuse. I may be credulous, but I will do nothing to commit myself to evil."

" I have no objection to a deathbed repentance," observed the visitant.

" Because you disbelieve their efficacy! " Markheim cried.

" I do not say so," returned the other; " but I look on these things from a different side, and when the life is done my interest falls. The man has lived to serve me, to spread black looks under color of religion, or to sow tares in the wheat field, as you do, in a course of weak compliance with desire. Now that he draws so near to his deliverance, he can add but one act of service — to repent, to die smiling, and thus to build up in confidence and hope the more timorous of my surviving followers. I am not so hard a master. Try me. Accept my help. Please yourself in life as you have done hitherto; please yourself more amply, spread your elbows at the board; and when the night begins to fall and the curtains to be drawn, I tell you, for your greater comfort, that you will find it even easy to compound your quarrel with your conscience, and to make a truckling peace with God. I came but now from such a deathbed, and the room was full of sincere mourners, listening to the man's last words; and when I looked into that face, which had been set as a flint against mercy, I found it smiling with hope."

"And do you, then, suppose me such a creature?" asked Markheim. "Do you think I have no more generous aspirations than to sin, and sin, and sin, and, at last, sneak into heaven? My heart rises at the thought. Is this, then, your experience of mankind? or is it because you find me with red hands that you presume such baseness? and is this crime of murder indeed so impious as to dry up the very springs of good?"

"Murder is to me no special category," replied the other. "All sins are murder, even as all life is war. I behold your race, like starving mariners on a raft, plucking crusts out of the hands of famine and feeding on each other's lives. I follow sins beyond the moment of their acting; I find in all that the last consequence is death; and to my eyes, the pretty maid who thwarts her mother with such taking graces on a question of a ball, drips no less visibly with human gore than such a murderer as yourself. Do I say that I follow sins? I follow virtues also; they differ not by the thickness of a nail, they are both scythes for the reaping angel of Death. Evil, for which I live, consists not in action but in character. The bad man is dear to me; not the bad act, whose fruits, if we could follow them far enough down the hurtling cataract of the ages, might yet be found more blessed than those of the rarest virtues. And it is not because you have killed a dealer, but because you are Markheim, that I offered to forward your escape."

"You know me?" cried the murderer.

" I will lay my heart open to you," answered Markheim. " This crime on which you find me is my last. On my way to it I have learned many lessons; itself is a lesson, a momentous lesson. Hitherto I have been driven with revolt to what I would not; I was a bond-slave to poverty, driven and scourged. There are robust virtues that can stand in these temptations; mine was not so: I had a thirst of pleasure. But today, and out of this deed, I pluck both warning and riches — both the power and a fresh resolve to be myself. I become in all things a free actor in the world; I begin to see myself all changed, these hands the agents of good, this heart at peace. Something comes over me out of the past; something of what I have dreamed on Sabbath evenings to the sound of the church organ, of what I forecast when I shed tears over noble books, or talked, an innocent child, with my mother. There lies my life; I have wandered a few years, but now I see once more my city of destination."

" You are to use this money on the Stock Exchange, I think? " remarked the visitor; " and there, if I mistake not, you have already lost some thousands? "

" Ah," said Markheim, " but this time I have a sure thing."

" This time, again you will lose," replied the visitor, quietly.

" Ah, but I keep back the half! " cried Markheim.

" That also you will lose," said the other.

The sweat started upon Markheim's brow. " Well, then, what matter? " he exclaimed. " Say it be lost, say I am plunged again in poverty, shall one part of me, and that the worse, continue until the end to override the better? Evil and good run strong in me, haling me both ways. I do not love the one thing, I love all. I can conceive great deeds, renunciations, martyrdoms; and though I be fallen to such a crime as murder, pity is no stranger to my thoughts. I pity the poor; who knows their trials better than myself? I pity and help them; I prize love, I love honest laughter; there is no good thing nor true thing on earth but I love it from my heart. And are my vices only to direct my life, and my virtues to lie without effect, like some passive lumber of the mind? Not so; good, also, is a spring of acts."

But the visitant raised his finger. " For six and thirty years that you have been in this world," said he, " through many changes of fortune and varieties of humor, I have watched you steadily fall. Fifteen years ago you would have started at a theft. Three years back you would have blenched at the name of murder. Is there any crime, is there any cruelty or meanness, from which you still recoil? — five years from now I shall detect you in the fact! Downward, downward lies your way; nor can anything but death avail to stop you."

" It is true," Markheim said huskily, " I have in some degree complied with evil. But it is so with all: the very saints, in the mere exercise of living, grow less dainty, and take on the tone of their surroundings."

" I will propound to you one simple question," said the other; " and as you answer, I shall read to you your moral horoscope. You have grown in many things more lax; possibly you do right to be so; and at any account, it is the same with all men. But granting that, are you in any one particular, however trifling, more difficult to please with your own conduct, or do you go in all things with a looser rein? "

" In any one? " repeated Markheim, with an anguish of consideration. " No," he added, with despair, " in none! I have gone down in all."

" Then," said the visitor, " content yourself with what you are, for you will never change; and the words of your part on this stage are irrevocably written down."

Markheim stood for a long while silent, and indeed it was the visitor who first broke the silence. " That being so," he said, " shall I show you the money? "

" And grace? " cried Markheim.

" Have you not tried it? " returned the other. " Two or three years ago, did I not see you on the platform of revival meetings, and was not your voice the loudest in the hymn? "

" It is true," said Markheim; " and I see clearly what remains for me by way of duty. I thank you for these lessons from my soul; my eyes are opened, and I behold myself at last for what I am."

At this moment, the sharp note of the doorbell rang through the house; and the visitant, as though this were some concerted signal for which he had been waiting, changed at once in his demeanor.

" The maid! " he cried. " She has returned, as I forewarned you, and there is now before you one more difficult passage. Her master, you must say, is ill; you must let her in, with an assured but rather serious countenance — no smiles, no overacting, and I promise you success! Once the girl within, and the door closed, the same dexterity that has already rid you of the dealer will relieve you of this last danger in your path. Thenceforward you have the whole evening — the whole night, if needful — to ransack the treasures of the house and to make good your safety. This is help that comes to you with the mask of danger. Up! " he cried: " up, friend; your life hangs trembling in the scales: up, and act! "

Markheim steadily regarded his counselor. " If I be condemned to evil acts," he said, " there is still one door of freedom open — I can cease from action. If my life be an ill thing, I can lay it down. Though I be, as you say truly, at the beck of every small temptation, I can yet, by one decisive gesture, place myself beyond the reach of all. My love of good is damned to barrenness; it may,

and let it be! But I have still my hatred of evil; and from that, to your galling disappointment, you shall see that I can draw both energy and courage."

The features of the visitor began to undergo a wonderful and lovely change: they brightened and softened with a tender triumph; and, even as they brightened, faded and dislimned. But Markheim did not pause to watch or understand the transformation. He opened the door and went downstairs very slowly, thinking to himself. His past went soberly before him; he beheld it as it was, ugly and strenuous like a dream, random as chance medley — a scene of defeat. Life, as he thus reviewed it, tempted him no longer; but on the farther side he perceived a quiet haven for his bark. He paused in the passage, and looked into the shop, where the candle still burned by the dead body. It was strangely silent. Thoughts of the dealer swarmed into his mind, as he stood gazing. And then the bell once more broke out into impatient clamor.

He confronted the maid upon the threshold with something like a smile.

" You had better go for the police," said he: " I have killed your master."

POET AND TELLER OF TALES

POEMS

1. Compare Stevenson's poem to his wife with Wordsworth's " She Was a Phantom of Delight " (page 359). Which seems to you the finer tribute?

2. How did Stevenson achieve a happy outlook on life in spite of his handicaps?

EL DORADO

1. How does the title of the essay relate to its theme? Where is the main idea stated? What illustrations does Stevenson use to prove his point?

2. From your own experience give examples that cause you to agree or disagree with Stevenson's theory of the real satisfactions in life.

MARKHEIM

1. What details does the author use early in the story to build up the two characters? Why is a secondhand shop a particularly appropriate place to create the atmosphere desired in this story? Which element — setting, character, action — has Stevenson made most important?

2. Where and how is the idea of conscience first introduced? At what point does the working of conscience become the main part of the story?

3. Discuss the various thoughts that pass through Markheim's mind while he is alone in the shop. What kind of man do they show him to be?

4. How do you explain the presence of the stranger? What purpose does he serve in the story?

5. Notice carefully the conversation between Markheim and the stranger. The stranger submits him to a series of temptations to further evil. What are they? How does Markheim react toward each? Why does the stranger's face undergo a change at the very end? In what ways is Markheim's final act a solution to the problem?

6. Compare this story with Poe's "The Tell-tale Heart," in which a murderer also gives himself up to the police. What noticeable differences are there in the situation?

GERARD MANLEY HOPKINS

1844–1889

Among the Victorians, Hopkins seems like a modern poet. His sparkling images, his condensed thought, his skillful innovations in rhythm are the marks of a fresh and original talent. Hopkins' highly individual way of expression reveals a mind that darts rapidly from image to image, sometimes leaving the reader to ponder, more slowly, on the idea behind the words. His influence on twentieth-century poets has been considerable.

Hopkins' poetry was long hidden from the world; Robert Bridges, then poet laureate of England, was responsible for its first publication in 1918. He had been a friend of Hopkins at Oxford, where the latter studied and later preached. Converted to Catholicism at the age of 22, Hopkins was received into the church by Cardinal Newman; later he became a Jesuit priest. From 1884 he taught Greek at the Royal University of Ireland in Dublin.

Pied Beauty

Glory be to God for dappled things —
    For skies of couple-color as a brinded cow;
      For rose-moles all in stipple upon trout that swim;
Fresh-firecoal chestnut-falls; finches' wings;
    Landscape plotted and pieced — fold, fallow, and plow;   5
    And all trades, their gear and tackle and trim.

All things counter, original, spare, strange;
    Whatever is fickle, freckled (who knows how?)
      With swift, slow; sweet, sour; adazzle, dim;
He fathers-forth whose beauty is past change: 10
        Praise him.

Heaven-Haven

A nun takes the veil

I have desired to go
Where springs not fail,
To fields where flies no sharp and sided hail
And a few lilies blow.

And I have asked to be   5
Where no storms come,
Where the green swell is in the havens dumb,
And out of the swing of the sea.

IMAGERY AND IDEA

1. What does the title " Pied Beauty " mean? What are the " dappled things " that attract the poet? Describe the mood of this poem. Does it seem to you an appropriate expression of deep religious feeling?

2. Hopkins compares the active outside world with the sequestered world of a nunnery in " Heaven-Haven." Pick out the several ways in which he makes the comparison. From what realm do his images come?

3. Both of these poems illustrate Hopkins' original style of expression. Notice the sharply breaking sounds, and the unusual position of words, as in " Where the green swell is in the havens dumb," and " For rose-moles all in stipple upon trout that swim." What is the effect of this style? Point out rarely used or archaic words, and examples of alliterative language.

THOMAS HARDY 1840–1928

Though he was born before the mid-point of the nineteenth century, Hardy seems almost a modern writer. More than any other author, he is a link between the Victorian era and modern times. Hardy's writing career falls into two distinct parts — fiction and poetry — divided almost at the turn of the century. He wrote the last of a series of notable novels, including *The Return of the Native* and *Far from the Madding Crowd,* in 1896. At that time he and George Meredith were undoubtedly the greatest living English novelists.

From 1904 to 1908 Hardy published various parts of a long dramatic poem, *The Dynasts.* Though it was written apparently to show England's part in the Napoleonic wars, it is actually a great study of man's whole destiny, representing the thinking of the modern world, as Milton's *Paradise Lost* represented that of the seventeenth century. Hardy's reputation as a poet was at once established.

The setting of both Hardy's fiction and poetry is " Wessex," a name he used to characterize the six southwest counties of England, including his own home, Dorset. Here he worked as a young church architect before turning to writing, and here he spent his honored last years. Hardy's death was an occasion for national mourning. His ashes were buried in Westminster Abbey, but in accordance with his last wish his heart was returned to his own parish churchyard in the little Dorsetshire village of Stinsford.

Hardy's short stories, like his novels and poems, are repeatedly concerned with the part that fate plays in the lives of people, and they often depict characters who are defeated by circumstance. " Tony Kytes," though it is far lighter in mood than most of Hardy's stories, introduces an element of coincidence or chance. It also reveals Hardy's distinctive view of women, which holds them to be charming but often un-dependable in character. The speaker in the story is a native of Wessex who is bringing a former resident up to date on the recent happenings of the village.

Tony Kytes, the Archdeceiver

I SHALL never forget Tony's face. 'Twas a little, round, firm, tight face, with a seam here and there left by the smallpox, but not enough to hurt his looks in a woman's eye, though he'd had it badish when he was a boy. So very serious-looking and unsmiling 'e was, that young man, that it really seemed as if he couldn't laugh at all without great pain to his conscience. He looked very hard at a small speck in your eye when talking to 'ee. And there was no more sign of a whisker or beard on Tony Kytes's face than on the palm of my hand. He used to sing ' The Tailor's Breeches' with a religious manner, as if it were a hymn. He was quite the women's favorite, and in return for their likings he loved 'em in shoals.

" But in course of time Tony got fixed down to one in particular, Milly Richards — a nice, light, small, tender little thing; and it was soon said that they were engaged to be married. One Saturday he had been to market to do business for his father, and was driving home the wagon in the afternoon. When he reached the foot of the very hill we shall be going over in ten minutes, who should he see waiting for him at the top but Unity Sallet, a handsome girl, one of the young women he'd been very tender toward before he'd got engaged to Milly.

" As soon as Tony came up to her she said, ' My dear Tony, will you give me a lift home? '

" ' That I will, darling,' said Tony. ' You don't suppose I could refuse 'ee? '

" She smiled a smile, and up she hopped, and on drove Tony.

" ' Tony,' she says, in a sort of tender chide, ' why did ye desert me for that other one? In what is she better than I? I should have made 'ee a finer wife, and a more loving one, too. 'Tisn't girls that are so easily won at first that are the best. Think how long we've known each other — ever since we were children almost — now haven't we, Tony? '

" ' Yes, that we have,' says Tony, astruck with the truth o't.

" ' And you've never seen anything in me to complain of, have ye, Tony? Now tell the truth to me.'

" ' I never have, upon my life,' says Tony.

" ' And — can you say I'm not pretty, Tony? Now look at me! '

" He let his eyes light upon her for a long while. ' I really can't,' says he. ' In fact, I never knowed you was so pretty before! '

" ' Prettier than she? '

" What Tony would have said to that nobody knows, for before he could speak, what should he see ahead, over the hedge past the turning, but a feather he knew well — the feather in Milly's hat — she to whom he had been thinking of putting the question as to giving out the banns that very week.

" ' Unity,' says he, as mild as he could, ' here's Milly coming. Now I shall catch it mightily if she sees 'ee riding here with me; and if you get down she'll be turning the corner in a moment, and, seeing 'ee in the road, she'll know we've been coming on together. Now, dearest Unity, will ye, to avoid all

"Tony Kytes, the Archdeceiver" from *Life's Little Ironies* by Thomas Hardy, reprinted by permission of Macmillan and Company Limited and the Trustees of the Hardy Estate.

unpleasantness, which I know ye can't bear any more than I, will ye lie down in the back part of the wagon, and let me cover you over with the tarpaulin till Milly has passed? It will all be done in a minute. Do! — and I'll think over what we've said; and perhaps I shall put a loving question to you after all, instead of to Milly. 'Tisn't true that it is all settled between her and me.'

"Well, Unity Sallet agreed, and lay down at the back end of the wagon, and Tony covered her over, so that the wagon seemed to be empty but for the loose tarpaulin; and then he drove on to meet Milly.

"'My dear Tony!' cries Milly, looking up with a little pout at him as he came near. 'How long you've been coming home! Just as if I didn't live at Upper Longpuddle at all! And I've come to meet you as you asked me to do, and to ride back with you, and talk over our future home — since you asked me, and I promised. But I shouldn't have come else, Mr. Tony!'

"'Ay, my dear, I did ask ye — to be sure I did, now I think of it — but I had quite forgot it. To ride back with me, did you say, dear Milly?'

"'Well, of course! What can I do else? Surely you don't want me to walk, now I've come all this way?'

"'Oh, no, no! I was thinking you might be going on to town to meet your mother. I saw her there — and she looked as if she might be expecting 'ee.'

"'Oh, no; she's just home. She came across the fields, and so got back before you.'

"'Ah! I didn't know that,' says Tony. And there was no help for it but to take her up beside him.

"They talked on very pleasantly, and looked at the trees and beasts and birds and insects, and at the plowmen at work in the fields, till presently who should they see looking out of the upper window of a house that stood beside the road they were following but Hannah Jolliver, another young beauty of the place at that time, and the very first woman that Tony had fallen in love with — before Milly and before Unity, in fact — the one that he had almost arranged to marry instead of Milly. She was a much more dashing girl than Milly Richards, though he'd not thought much of her of late. The house Hannah was looking from was her aunt's.

"'My dear Milly — my coming wife, as I may call 'ee,' says Tony in his modest way, and not so loud that Unity could overhear, 'I see a young woman looking out of window who I think may accost me. The fact is, Milly, she had a notion that I was wishing to marry her, and since she's discovered I've promised another, and prettier than she, I'm rather afeared of her temper if she sees us together. Now, Milly, would you do me a favor — my coming wife, as I may say?'

"'Certainly, dearest Tony,' says she.

"'Then would ye creep under the tarpaulin just here in the front of the wagon, and hide there out of sight till

"Would you do me a favor?"

we've passed the house? She hasn't seen us yet. You see, we ought to live in peace and good will since 'tis almost Christmas, and 'twill prevent angry passions rising, which we always should do.'

" ' I don't mind, to oblige you, Tony,' Milly said; and though she didn't care much about doing it, she crept under, and crouched down just behind the seat, Unity being snug at the other end. So they drove on till they got near the roadside cottage. Hannah had soon seen him coming, and waited at the window, looking down upon him. She tossed her head a little disdainful and smiled offhand.

" ' Well, aren't you going to be civil enough to ask me to ride home with you? ' she says, seeing that he was for driving past with a nod and a smile.

" ' Ah, to be sure! What was I thinking of? ' said Tony, in a flutter. ' But you seem as if you was staying at your aunt's? '

" ' No, I am not,' she said. ' Don't you see I have my bonnet and jacket on? I have only called to see her on my way home. How can you be so stupid, Tony? '

" ' In that case — ah — of course you must come along wi' me,' says Tony, feeling a dim sort of sweat rising up inside his clothes. And he reined in the horse, and waited till she'd come downstairs, and then helped her up beside him. He drove on again, his face as long as a face that was a round one by nature well could be.

" Hannah looked round sideways into his eyes. ' This is nice, isn't it, Tony? ' she says. ' I like riding with you.'

" Tony looked back into her eyes. ' And I with you,' he said, after a while. In short, having considered her, he warmed up, and the more he looked at her the more he liked her, till he couldn't for the life of him think why he had ever said a word about marriage to Milly or Unity while Hannah Jolliver was in question. So they sat a little clos-

er and closer, their feet upon the footboard and their shoulders touching, and Tony thought over and over again how handsome Hannah was. He spoke tenderer and tenderer, and called her ' dear Hannah ' in a whisper at last.

" ' You've settled it with Milly by this time, I suppose,' said she.

" ' N — no, not exactly.'

" ' What? How low you talk, Tony.'

" ' Yes — I've a kind of hoarseness. I said, not exactly.'

" ' I suppose you mean to? '

" ' Well, as to that — ' His eyes rested on her face, and hers on his. He wondered how he could have been such a fool as not to follow up Hannah. ' My sweet Hannah! ' he bursts out, taking her hand, not being really able to help it, and forgetting Milly and Unity and all the world besides. ' Settled it? I don't think I have! '

" ' Hark! ' says Hannah.

" ' What? ' says Tony, letting go her hand.

" ' Surely I heard a sort of little screaming squeak under that tar cloth? Why, you've been carrying corn, and there's mice in this wagon, I declare! ' She began to haul up the tails of her gown.

" ' Oh, no; 'tis the axle,' said Tony, in an assuring way. ' It do go like that sometimes in dry weather.'

" ' Perhaps it was. . . . Well, now, to be quite honest, dear Tony, do you like her better than me? Because — because, although I've held off so independent, I'll own at last that I do like 'ee, Tony, to tell the truth; and I wouldn't say no if you asked me — you know what.'

" Tony was so won over by this pretty offering mood of a girl who had been quite the reverse (Hannah had a backward way with her at times, if you can mind) that he just glanced behind, and then whispered very soft, ' I haven't quite promised her, and I think I can get out of it, and ask you that question you speak of.'

" ' Throw over Milly? — all to marry

me! How delightful!' broke out Hannah, quite loud, clapping her hands.

"At this there was a real squeak — an angry, spiteful squeak, and afterward a long moan, as if something had broke its heart, and a movement of the wagon cloth.

"'Something's there!' said Hannah, starting up.

"'It's nothing, really,' says Tony, in a soothing voice, and praying inwardly for a way out of this. 'I wouldn't tell 'ee at first, because I wouldn't frighten 'ee. But, Hannah, I've really a couple of ferrets in a bag under there, for rabbiting, and they quarrel sometimes. I don't wish it knowed, as 'twould be called poaching. Oh, they can't get out, bless ye! — you are quite safe. And — and — what a fine day it is, isn't it, Hannah, for this time of year? Be you going to market next Saturday? How is your aunt now?' And so on, says Tony, to keep her from talking any more about love in Milly's hearing.

"But he found his work cut out for him, and wondering again how he should get out of this ticklish business, he looked about for a chance. Nearing home he saw his father in a field not far off, holding up his hands as if he wished to speak to Tony.

"'Would you mind taking the reins a moment, Hannah,' he said, much relieved, 'while I go and find out what Father wants?'

"She consented, and away he hastened into the field, only too glad to get breathing time. He found that his father was looking at him with rather a stern eye.

"'Come, come, Tony,' says old Mr. Kytes, as soon as his son was alongside him, 'this won't do, you know.'

"'What?' says Tony.

"'Why, if you mean to marry Milly Richards, do it, and there's an end o't. But don't go driving about the country with Jolliver's daughter and making a scandal. I won't have such things done.'

"'I only asked her — that is, she asked me — to ride home.'

"'She? Why, now, if it had been Milly, 'twould have been quite proper; but you and Hannah Jolliver going about by yourselves —'

"'Milly's there, too, Father.'

"'Milly? Where?'

"'Under the tarpaulin! Yes; the truth is, Father, I've got rather into a nunny-watch,[1] I'm afeard! Unity Sallet is there, too — yes, under the other end of the tarpaulin. All three are in that wagon, and what to do with 'em I know no more than the dead. The best plan is, as I'm thinking, to speak out loud and plain to one of 'em before the rest, and that will settle it; not but what 'twill cause 'em to kick up a bit of a miff, for certain. Now, which would you marry, Father, if you was in my place?'

"'Whichever of 'em did *not* ask to ride with thee.'

"'That was Milly, I'm bound to say, as she only mounted by my invitation. But Milly —'

"'Then stick to Milly, she's the best — But look at that!'

"His father pointed toward the wagon. 'She can't hold that horse in. You shouldn't have left the reins in her hands. Run on and take the horse's head, or there'll be some accident to them maids!'

"Tony's horse, in fact, in spite of Hannah's tugging at the reins, had started on his way at a brisk walking pace, being very anxious to get back to the stable, for he had had a long day out. Without another word, Tony rushed away from his father to overtake the horse.

"Now, of all things that could have happened to wean him from Milly, there was nothing so powerful as his father's recommending her. No; it could not be Milly, after all. Hannah must be the one, since he could not marry all three. This he thought while running after the wagon. But queer things were happening inside it.

[1] *nunny-watch:* embarrassing situation.

" It was, of course, Milly who had screamed under the tarpaulin, being obliged to let off her bitter rage and shame in that way at what Tony was saying, and never daring to show, for very pride and dread o' being laughed at, that she was in hiding. She became more and more restless, and in twisting herself about, what did she see but another woman's foot and white stocking close to her head. It quite frightened her, not knowing that Unity Sallet was in the wagon likewise. But after the fright was over she determined to get to the bottom of all this, and she crept and crept along the bed of the wagon, under the cloth, like a snake, when lo and behold, she came face to face with Unity.

" ' Well, if this isn't disgraceful! ' says Milly, in a raging whisper, to Unity.

" ' 'Tis,' says Unity, ' to see you hiding in a young man's wagon like this, and no great character belonging to either of ye! '

" ' Mind what you are saying! ' replied Milly, getting louder. ' I am engaged to be married to him, and haven't

Out rolled the three maidens . . .

I a right to be here? What right have you, I should like to know? What has he been promising you? A pretty lot of nonsense, I expect! But what Tony says to other women is all mere wind, and no concern to me! '

" ' Don't you be too sure! ' says Unity. ' He's going to have Hannah, and not you, nor me either; I could hear that.'

" Now, at these strange voices sounding from under the cloth Hannah was thunderstruck a'most into a swound; and it was just at this time that the horse moved on. Hannah tugged away wildly, not knowing what she was doing; and as the quarrel rose louder and louder Hannah got so horrified that she let go the reins altogether. The horse went on at his own pace, and coming to the corner where we turn round to drop down the hill to Lower Longpuddle he turned too quick, the off-wheels went up the bank, the wagon rose sideways till it was quite on edge upon the near axles, and out rolled the three maidens into the road in a heap.

" When Tony came up, frightened and breathless, he was relieved enough to see that neither of his darlings was

hurt, beyond a few scratches from the brambles of the hedge. But he was rather alarmed when he heard how they were going on at one another.

" 'Don't ye quarrel, my dears — don't ye!' says he, taking off his hat out of respect to 'em. And then he would have kissed them all round, as fair and square as a man could, but they were in too much of a talking to let him, and screeched and sobbed till they was quite spent.

" 'Now, I'll speak out honest, because I ought to,' says Tony, as soon as he could get heard. 'And this is the truth,' says he: 'I've asked Hannah to be mine, and she is willing, and we are going to put up the banns next —'

" Tony had not noticed that Hannah's father was coming up behind, nor had he noticed that Hannah's face was beginning to bleed from the scratch of a bramble. Hannah had seen her father, and had run to him, crying worse than ever.

" 'My daughter is *not* willing, sir,' says Mr. Jolliver, hot and strong. 'Be you willing, Hannah? I ask ye to have spirit enough to refuse him.'

" 'I have spirit, and I do refuse him!' says Hannah, partly because her father was there, and partly, too, in a tantrum because of the discovery and the scratch on her face. 'Little did I think when I was so soft with him just now that I was talking to such a false deceiver!'

" 'What, you won't have me, Hannah?' says Tony, his jaw hanging down like a dead man's.

" 'Never; I would sooner marry no — nobody at all!' she gasped out, though with her heart in her throat, for she would not have refused Tony if he had asked her quietly, and her father had not been there, and her face had not been scratched by the bramble. And having said that, away she walked upon her father's arm, thinking and hoping he would ask her again.

" Tony didn't know what to say next. Milly was sobbing her heart out; but as his father had strongly recommended her he couldn't feel inclined that way. So he turned to Unity.

" 'Well, will you, Unity dear, be mine?' he says.

" 'Take her leavings? Not I!' says Unity. 'I'd scorn it!' And away walks Unity Sallet likewise, though she looked back when she'd gone some way, to see if he was following her.

" So there at last were left Milly and Tony by themselves, she crying in watery streams, and Tony looking like a tree struck by lightning.

" 'Well, Milly,' he says at last, going up to her, 'it do seem as if fate had ordained that it should be you and I, or nobody. And what must be must be, I suppose. Hey, Milly?'

" 'If you like, Tony. You didn't really mean what you said to them?'

" 'Not a word of it,' declares Tony, bringing down his fist upon his palm.

" And then he kissed her, and put the wagon to rights, and they mounted together; and their banns were put up the very next Sunday."

Weathers

This is the weather the cuckoo likes,
    And so do I;
When showers betumble the chestnut spikes,
    And nestlings fly;
And the little brown nightingale bills his best,   5
And they sit outside the Traveler's Rest,
And maids come forth sprig muslin dressed,
And citizens dream of the South and West,
    And so do I.

This is the weather the shepherd shuns,   10
    And so do I;
When beeches drip in browns and duns,
    And thresh, and ply;
And hill-hid tides throb, throe on throe,
And meadow rivulets overflow,   15
And drops on gate bars hang in a row,
And rooks in families homeward go,
    And so do I.

Afterward

When the Present has latched its postern behind my tremulous stay,
    And the May month flaps its glad green leaves like wings,
Delicate-filmed as new-spun silk, will the neighbors say,
    " He was a man who used to notice such things "?

If it be in the dusk when, like an eyelid's soundless blink,   5
    The dewfall hawk comes crossing the shades to alight
Upon the wind-warped upland thorn, a gazer may think,
    " To him this must have been a familiar sight."

If I pass during some nocturnal blackness, mothy and warm,
    When the hedgehog travels furtively over the lawn,   10
One may say, " He strove that such innocent creatures should come to no harm,
    But he could do little for them; and now he is gone."

If, when hearing that I have been stilled at last, they stand at the door,
    Watching the full-starred heavens that winter sees,
Will this thought rise on those who will meet my face no more,   15
    " He was one who had an eye for such mysteries "?

And will any say when my bell of quittance is heard in the gloom,
    And a crossing breeze cuts a pause in its outrollings,
Till they rise again, as they were a new bell's boom,
    " He hears it not now, but used to notice such things "?   20

"Weathers" and "Afterward" from *Collected Poems* by Thomas Hardy, reprinted by permission of Macmillan and Company Limited and the Trustees of the Hardy Estate.

The Darkling Thrush

I leant upon a coppice gate
  When Frost was specter-gray,
And Winter's dregs made desolate
  The weakening eye of day.
The tangled vine-stems scored the sky 5
  Like strings of broken lyres,
And all mankind that haunted nigh
  Had sought their household fires.

The land's sharp features seemed to be
  The Century's corpse outleant,   10
His crypt the cloudy canopy,
  The wind his death lament.
The ancient pulse of germ and birth
  Was shrunken hard and dry,
And every spirit upon earth   15
  Seemed fervorless as I.

At once a voice arose among
  The bleak twigs overhead
In a fullhearted evensong
  Of joy illimited;   20
An aged thrush, frail, gaunt, and small,
  In blast-beruffled plume,
Had chosen thus to fling his soul
  Upon the growing gloom.

So little cause for carolings   25
  Of such ecstatic sound
Was written on terrestrial things
  Afar or nigh around,
That I could think there trembled
    through
  His happy good-night air   30
Some blessèd Hope, whereof he knew
  And I was unaware.

In Time of
" The Breaking of Nations "

Only a man harrowing clods
  In a slow silent walk,
With an old horse that stumbles and
    nods
  Half asleep as they stalk.

Only thin smoke without flame   5
  From the heaps of couch grass:
Yet this will go onward the same
  Though dynasties pass.

Yonder a maid and her wight°
  Come whispering by;   10
War's annals will fade into night
  Ere their story die.

9. *wight:* an archaic or jocose word for *man.*

HARDY'S PROSE AND POETRY

TONY KYTES, THE ARCHDECEIVER

1. What details of the opening paragraphs establish the setting and the mood of the story? What evidences of " Wessex " local color can you find throughout the story?

2. Show in what ways the story illustrates two of the characteristics of Hardy mentioned in the introduction. In what way does the story fit the title of the collection in which it first appeared: *Life's Little Ironies?*

3. Compare the humor of this story with that of " Mr. Pickwick on the Ice " (page 502) as to the type of incident involved and the characterization.

POEMS

1. Which seasons does Hardy depict in " Weathers "? How do you feel about these two kinds of weather?

2. In " Afterward " note the different phrases used to describe the coming of death. By what characteristic does the poet wish to be remembered after death?

3. What is the tone of " The Darkling Thrush " and by what details does the poet establish it? What is the significance of the thrush in the development of the mood of the poem? How does this poem compare in its outlook on life with " Dover Beach " (page 507)?

4. Look up the Biblical passage from which the title " In Time of ' The Breaking of Nations ' " is derived (Jeremiah 51:20). In this poem, what universal experiences of men are contrasted with war? What is the poet's purpose in making the contrast?

˧RUDYARD KIPLING 1865–1936

Like Hardy, Kipling belongs to both the Victorian and the modern age. His life was at mid-point at the turn of the century, and while his reputation was definitely established during the eighties and nineties, he was probably the most widely read British author in the first decades of the twentieth century. In both verse and fiction Kipling has been a favorite storyteller of millions. Children treasure the animal stories of India told in *The Jungle Book,* and later they thrill to the excitement of *Kim,* his best-known novel. Readers of all ages enjoy the quick sketching of his army ballads such as " Danny Deever " and " Gunga Din." But his fame rests most securely on his numerous volumes of short stories, filled with the hilarious antics and sometimes strange fates of the British soldier.

Kipling was born in Bombay, and he is always associated with India, though he was educated and lived in England for most of his life. At seventeen he became editor of a newspaper at Lahore, and for the next nine years he gathered material for many of his later books — exotic Indian backgrounds of dusty villages and colonial military posts, of lush jungles and remote mountain passes. Kipling married an American girl from Vermont and spent five years there. One of his novels, *Captains Courageous,* has a New England setting. Travel was one of Kipling's delights; there are few places " east and west " he did not visit and write about.

Kipling was out of favor with officialdom in his own day, and with critics of later days. Though he was the most eligible of poets, Queen Victoria kept him from becoming poet laureate because of satiric descriptions (he called her the " Widow of Windsor " in *Barrack-Room Ballads*). However, Kipling won the Nobel Prize in Literature in 1907. Afterward, he was criticized as a defender of British imperialism. But that issue, at least since India has been granted independence, has passed, and readers continue to enjoy Kipling as the master storyteller.

Miss Youghal's *Sais*°

This story from *Plain Tales from the Hills* illustrates in small space several points about Kipling's stories. It deals with British official and army life in India. It suggests that Kipling himself must have been, like Strickland, capable of " going native " so completely that he was lost in the crowd. At the end of this story of the *sais,* we find a typical mannerism of the author. Because his brain was overflowing with so many stories, he seldom concluded one tale without hinting that he had another good story up his sleeve. He often ends — " But that is another story."

" Miss Youghal's *Sais* " is preceded by a motto:

Title: *Youghal* (youl); *sais* (sīs): a sais is a servant in charge of horses.

"Miss Youghal's *Sais*" from *Plain Tales from the Hills* by Rudyard Kipling. Reprinted by permission of A. P. Watt and Son, Macmillan and Company of Canada, and Mrs. George Bambridge.

When Man and Woman are agreed, what can the Kazi do? — *Mohammedan Proverb*

SOME people say that there is no romance in India. Those people are wrong. Our lives hold quite as much romance as is good for us. Sometimes more.

Strickland was in the police, and people did not understand him; so they said he was a doubtful sort of man and passed by on the other side. Strickland had himself to thank for this. He held the extraordinary theory that a policeman in India should try to know as much about the natives as the natives themselves. Now, in the whole of upper India, there is only *one* man who can pass for Hindu or Mohammedan, *chamar*[1] or *faquir*,[2] as he pleases. He is feared and respected by the natives from the Ghor Kathri to the Jamma Musjid; and he is supposed to have the gift of invisibility and executive control over many devils. But what good has this done him with the government? None in the world. He has never got Simla[3] for his charge; and his name is almost unknown to Englishmen.

Strickland was foolish enough to take that man for his model; and, following out his absurd theory, dabbled in unsavory places no respectable man would think of exploring — all among the native riffraff. He educated himself in this peculiar way for seven years, and people could not appreciate it. He was perpetually " going Fantee " among natives, which, of course, no man with any sense believes in. He was initiated into the *Sat Bhai* at Allahabad[4] once, when he was on leave; he knew the Lizard

[1] *chamar* (shà·mär′): skin dresser.
[2] *faquir* (fä·kēr′): priest.
[3] *Simla:* the summer capital of India; situated in the Himalayas.
[4] *Allahabad* (ăl′à·hä·bäd′): an important city on the Ganges at the foot of the Himalayas. The other places mentioned in this paragraph are in northern India.

Song of the Sansis, and the *Hálli-Hukk* dance, which is a religious cancan of a startling kind. When a man knows who dances the *Hálli-Hukk,* and how, and when, and where, he knows something to be proud of. He has gone deeper than the skin. But Strickland was not proud, though he had helped once, at Jagadhri, at the Painting of the Death Bull, which no Englishman must even look upon; had mastered the thieves' patter of the *chángars;* had taken a Eusufzai horse thief alone near Attock; and had stood under the *mimbar* board[5] of a Border mosque and conducted service in the manner of a Sunni Mollah.

His crowning achievement was spending eleven days as a *faquir* in the gardens of Baba Atal at Amritsar,[6] and there picking up the threads of the great Nasiban murder case. But people said, justly enough, " Why on earth can't Strickland sit in his office and write up his diary, and recruit, and keep quiet, instead of showing up the incapacity of his seniors? " So the Nasiban murder case did him no good departmentally; but, after his first feeling of wrath, he returned to his outlandish custom of prying into native life. By the way, when a man once acquires a taste for this particular amusement, it abides with him all his days. It is the most fascinating thing in the world; Love not excepted. Where other men took ten days to the Hills, Strickland took leave for what he called *shikar,*[7] put on the disguise that appealed to him at the time, stepped down into the brown crowd, and was swallowed up for a while. He was a quiet, dark young fellow — spare; black eyes — and, when he was not thinking of something else, a very interesting companion. Strickland on Native Progress as he had seen it was worth hearing. Natives hated Strick-

[5] *mimbar board:* sounding board, a structure over a pulpit.
[6] *Amritsar* (ŭm·rĭt′sēr): a city in the Punjab, the Northwest Province of India.
[7] *shikar* (shē·kär′): hunting.

land; but they were afraid of him. He knew too much.

When the Youghals came into the station, Strickland — very gravely, as he did everything — fell in love with Miss Youghal; and she, after a while, fell in love with him because she could not understand him. Then Strickland told the parents; but Mrs. Youghal said she was not going to throw her daughter into the worst-paid department in the Empire, and old Youghal said, in so many words, that he mistrusted Strickland's ways and works, and would thank him not to speak or write to his daughter any more. "Very well," said Strickland, for he did not wish to make his ladylove's life a burden. After one long talk with Miss Youghal he dropped the business entirely.

The Youghals went up to Simla in April.

In July Strickland secured three months' leave on "urgent private affairs." He locked up his house — though not a native in the province would wittingly have touched "Estreek-in Sahib's" gear for the world — and went down to see a friend of his, an old dyer, at Tarn Taran.

Here all trace of him was lost, until a *sais* met me on the Simla Mall with this extraordinary note:

DEAR OLD MAN,
    Please give bearer a box of cheroots — Supers, No. 1, for preference. They are freshest at the Club. I'll repay when I reappear; but at present I'm out of society.
                    Yours,
                        E. STRICKLAND.

I ordered two boxes, and handed them over to the *sais* with my love. That *sais* was Strickland, and he was in old Youghal's employ, attached to Miss Youghal's Arab. The poor fellow was suffering for an English smoke, and knew that, whatever happened, I should hold my tongue till the business was over.

Later on, Mrs. Youghal, who was wrapped up in her servants, began talking at houses where she called of her paragon among *saises* — the man who was never too busy to get up in the morning and pick flowers for the breakfast table, and who blacked — actually *blacked* — the hoofs of his horse like a London coachman! The turnout of Miss Youghal's Arab was a wonder and a delight. Strickland — Dulloo, I mean — found his reward in the pretty things that Miss Youghal said to him when she went out riding. Her parents were pleased to find she had forgotten all her foolishness for young Strickland and said she was a good girl.

Strickland vows that the two months of his service were the most rigid mental discipline he has ever gone through. Quite apart from the little fact that the wife of one of his fellow *saises* fell in love with him and then tried to poison him with arsenic because he would have nothing to do with her, he had to school himself into keeping quiet when Miss Youghal went out riding with some man who tried to flirt with her, and he was forced to trot behind, carrying the blanket and hearing every word! Also, he had to keep his temper when he was slanged in Benmore porch [1] by a policeman — especially once when he was abused by a Naik he had himself recruited from Isser Jang village — or, worse still, when a young subaltern called him a pig for not making way quickly enough.

But the life had its compensations. He obtained great insight into the ways and thefts of *saises* — enough, he says, to have summarily convicted half the *chamar* population of the Punjab if he had been on business. He became one of the leading players at knucklebones, which all *jampanis* [2] and many *saises* play while they are waiting outside the Government House or the Gaiety Theater of nights; he learned to smoke to-

[1] *Benmore porch:* entrance to the recreation center.

[2] *jampanis* (jăm·pá·nēz'): bearers of a jampan — like a sedan chair.

bacco that was three-fourths cow-dung; and he heard the wisdom of the grizzled *Jemadar* [1] of the Government House *saises,* whose words are valuable. He saw many things which amused him; and he states, on honor, that no man can appreciate Simla properly till he has seen it from the *sais's* point of view. He also says that if he chose to write all he saw, his head would be broken in several places.

Strickland's account of the agony he endured on wet nights, hearing the music and seeing the lights in " Benmore," with his toes tingling for a waltz and his head in a horse blanket, is rather amusing. One of these days, Strickland is going to write a little book on his experiences. That book will be worth buying; and even more worth suppressing.

Thus, he served faithfully as Jacob served for Rachel; [2] and his leave was nearly at an end when the explosion came. He had really done his best to keep his temper in the hearing of the

[1] *Jemadar* (jĕm·à·där′): a native sergeant.
[2] The story of Jacob and Rachel is in Genesis 29 : 15–30.

flirtations I have mentioned; but he broke down at last. An old and very distinguished general took Miss Youghal for a ride, and began that specially offensive " you're-only-a-little-girl " sort of flirtation — most difficult for a woman to turn aside deftly, and most maddening to listen to. Miss Youghal was shaking with fear at the things he said in the hearing of her *sais.* Dulloo — Strickland — stood it as long as he could. Then he caught hold of the general's bridle, and, in most fluent English, invited him to step off and be heaved over the cliff. Next minute Miss Youghal began crying; and Strickland saw that he had hopelessly given himself away, and everything was over.

The general nearly had a fit, while Miss Youghal was sobbing out the story of the disguise and the engagement that was not recognized by the parents. Strickland was furiously angry with himself, and more angry with the general for forcing his hand; so he said nothing, but held the horse's head and prepared to thrash the general as some sort of satisfaction. But when the general had

Miss Youghal was sobbing, but the general laughed.

thoroughly grasped the story, and knew who Strickland was, he began to puff and blow in the saddle, and nearly rolled off with laughing. He said Strickland deserved a V. C.,[1] if it were only for putting on a *sais's* blanket. Then he called himself names, and vowed that he deserved a thrashing, but he was too old to take it from Strickland. Then he complimented Miss Youghal on her lover. The scandal of the business never struck him; for he was a nice old man, with a weakness for flirtations. Then he laughed again, and said that old Youghal was a fool. Strickland let go of the cob's head, and suggested that the general had better help them, if that was his opinion. Strickland knew Youghal's weakness for men with titles and letters after their names and high official position. " It's rather like a forty-minute farce," said the general, " but, begad, I *will* help, if it's only to escape that tremendous thrashing I deserve. Go along to your home, my *sais*-policeman, and change into decent kit, and I'll attack Mr. Youghal. Miss Youghal, may I ask you to canter home and wait? "

About seven minutes later, there was a wild hurroosh at the club. A *sais,* with blanket and headrobe, was asking all the men he knew: " For Heaven's sake lend me decent clothes! " As the men did not recognize him, there were some peculiar scenes before Strickland could get a hot bath, with soda in it, in one room, a shirt here, a collar there, a pair of trousers elsewhere, and so on. He galloped off, with half the club wardrobe on his back, and an utter stranger's pony under him, to the house of old Youghal. The general, arrayed in purple and fine linen, was before him. What the general had said Strickland never knew, but Youghal received Strickland with moderate civility; and Mrs. Youghal, touched by the devotion

[1] *V. C.:* Victoria Cross, the highest crown award for military valor.

of the transformed Dulloo, was almost kind. The general beamed and chuckled, and Miss Youghal came in, and almost before old Youghal knew where he was, the parental consent had been wrenched out, and Strickland had departed with Miss Youghal to the telegraph office to wire for his kit. The final embarrassment was when a stranger attacked him on the Mall and asked for the stolen pony.

So, in the end, Strickland and Miss Youghal were married, on the strict understanding that Strickland should drop his old ways, and stick to departmental routine, which pays best and leads to Simla. Strickland was far too fond of his wife, just then, to break his word, but it was a sore trial to him; for the streets and the bazaars, and the sounds in them, were full of meaning to Strickland, and these called to him to come back and take up his wanderings and his discoveries. Someday I will tell you how he broke his promise to help a friend. That was long since, and he has, by this time, been nearly spoiled for what he would call *shikar*. He is forgetting the slang, and the beggar's cant, and the marks, and the signs, and the drift of the undercurrents, which, if a man would master, he must always continue to learn.

But he fills in his departmental returns beautifully.

✓ *Recessional*

This hymn was written to celebrate the Diamond Jubilee of Queen Victoria, June 22, 1897, which marked the sixtieth anniversary of her ascension to the throne. A " recessional " is a hymn sung as the choir and clergy leave the chancel after the service.

God of our fathers, known of old,
  Lord of our far-flung battle line,
Beneath whose awful Hand we hold
  Dominion over palm and pine —
Lord God of Hosts, be with us yet,   5
Lest we forget — lest we forget!

" Recessional " from *The Five Nations* by Rudyard Kipling. Reprinted by permission of A. P. Watt and Son, Macmillan and Company of Canada, and Mrs. George Bambridge.

The tumult and the shouting dies;
  The captains and the kings depart;
Still stands Thine ancient sacrifice,
  An humble and a contrite heart.   10
Lord God of Hosts, be with us yet,
Lest we forget — lest we forget!

Far-called, our navies melt away;
  On dune and headland sinks the fire;°
Lo, all our pomp of yesterday   15
  Is one with Nineveh and Tyre!°
Judge of the nations, spare us yet,
Lest we forget — lest we forget!

14. As a part of the opening ceremonies of the Jubilee, bonfires "on dune and headland" were lighted one by one on signal until the island of Great Britain was encircled with a wall of protecting fire, which the poet now sees fading away. 16. *Nineveh and Tyre:* ancient cities, long since destroyed.

If drunk with sight of power, we loose
  Wild tongues that have not Thee in
    awe,   20
Such boasting as the Gentiles° use,
  Or lesser breeds without the Law —
Lord God of Hosts, be with us yet,
Lest we forget — lest we forget!

For heathen heart that puts her trust
  In reeking tube° and iron shard,° 26
All valiant dust that builds on dust,
  And guarding calls not Thee to guard,
For frantic boast and foolish word —
Thy mercy on Thy people, Lord!   30

21. *Gentiles:* here used in the Biblical sense — not belonging to the chosen people of God. 26. *tube:* the barrel of a gun; *shard:* destructive fragments of the bombshell.

Tommy

From his years of residence in India and his journalistic work on the *Military Gazette,* Kipling knew the Anglo-Indian soldier intimately. In Kipling's day the professional soldier was often regarded as an undesirable character. In this characteristic poem from *Barrack-Room Ballads,* written long before World War I, a typical " Tommy Atkins " speaks his mind and presents the grievances of his lot.

I went into a public 'ouse° to get a pint o' beer,
The publican° 'e up an' sez, " We serve no redcoats here."
The girls be'ind the bar they laugh an' giggled fit to die,
I outs into the street again an' to myself sez I:
    Oh, it's Tommy this, an' Tommy that, an' " Tommy, go away ";   5
    But it's " Thank you, Mister Atkins," when the band begins to play —
    The band begins to play, my boys, the band begins to play,
    Oh, it's ". Thank you, Mister Atkins," when the band begins to play.

I went into a theater as sober as could be,
They gave a drunk civilian room, but 'adn't none for me;   10
They sent me to the gallery or round the music 'alls,
But when it comes to fightin', Lord! they'll shove me in the stalls!°
    For it's Tommy this, an' Tommy that, an' " Tommy, wait outside ";
    But it's " Special train for Atkins " when the trooper's on the tide —
    The troopship's on the tide, my boys, the troopship's on the tide,   15
    Oh, it's " Special train for Atkins " when the trooper's on the tide.

1. *public 'ouse:* a tavern. 2. *publican:* the innkeeper. 12. *stalls:* the best seats in English theaters.

"Tommy" from *Barrack-Room Ballads* by Rudyard Kipling. Reprinted by permission of A. P. Watt and Son, Macmillan and Company of Canada, and Mrs. George Bambridge.

Yes, makin' mock o' uniforms that guard you while you sleep
Is cheaper than them uniforms, an' they're starvation cheap;
An' hustlin' drunken soldiers when they're goin' large a bit
Is five times better business than paradin' in full kit.°   20
    Then it's Tommy this, an' Tommy that, an' " Tommy, 'ow's yer soul? "
But it's " Thin red line of 'eroes " when the drums begin to roll —
The drums begin to roll, my boys, the drums begin to roll,
Oh, it's " Thin red line of 'eroes " when the drums begin to roll.

We aren't no thin red 'eroes, nor we aren't no blackguards too,   25
But single men in barricks, most remarkable like you;
An' if sometimes our conduck isn't all your fancy paints,
Why, single men in barricks don't grow into plaster saints;
    While it's Tommy this, an' Tommy that, an' " Tommy, fall be'ind,"
But it's " Please to walk in front, sir," when there's trouble in the wind —   30
There's trouble in the wind, my boys, there's trouble in the wind,
Oh, it's " Please to walk in front, sir," when there's trouble in the wind.

You talk o' better food for us, an' schools, an' fires, an' all;
We'll wait for extry rations if you treat us rational.
Don't mess about the cookroom slops, but prove it to our face   35
The Widow's uniform is not the soldier-man's disgrace.
    For it's Tommy this, an' Tommy that, an' " Chuck him out, the brute! "
But, it's " Savior of 'is country " when the guns begin to shoot;
An' it's Tommy this, an' Tommy that, an' anything you please;
An' Tommy ain't a bloomin' fool — you bet that Tommy sees!   40

20. *paradin' in full kit:* marching with the heavy load of the infantryman.

L'Envoi°

When Earth's last picture is painted, and the tubes are twisted and dried,
When the oldest colors have faded, and the youngest critic has died,
We shall rest, and, faith, we shall need it — lie down for an aeon or two,
Till the Master of All Good Workmen shall put us to work anew.

And those that were good shall be happy: they shall sit in a golden chair;   5
They shall splash at a ten-league canvas with brushes of comets' hair.
They shall find real saints to draw from — Magdalene, Peter, and Paul;
They shall work for an age at a sitting and never be tired at all!

And only the Master shall praise us, and only the Master shall blame;
And no one shall work for money and no one shall work for fame,   10
But each for the joy of the working, and each, in his separate star,
Shall draw the Thing as he sees It for the God of Things as They are!

Title: *L'Envoi:* a postscript to a poem, book, or essay. Kipling wrote this poem to close his book *The Seven Seas.*

"L'Envoi" from *The Seven Seas* by Rudyard Kipling. Reprinted by permission of A. P. Watt and Son, Macmillan and Company of Canada, and Mrs. George Bambridge.

The Ballad of East and West

This virile ballad recounts the meeting of two young heroes — the Englishman, representative of Western civilization, and the Afghan, representing the Eastern civilization.
The setting is the northwest frontier of India, where the
British troops in the border forts were constantly fighting
against the depredations of the native outlaws. Published
in 1890, this poem with its swinging meter, vivid imagery,
and powerful diction brought Kipling immediate acclaim.

Oh, East is East, and West is West, and never the twain shall meet,
Till Earth and Sky stand presently at God's great Judgment Seat;
But there is neither East nor West, Border, nor Breed, nor Birth,
When two strong men stand face to face, though they come from the ends of the
earth!

Kamal° is out with twenty men to raise the Border side,   5
And he has lifted the Colonel's mare that is the Colonel's pride.
He has lifted her out of the stable-door between the dawn and the day,
And turned the calkins° upon her feet, and ridden her far away.
Then up and spoke the Colonel's son that led a troop of the Guides:°
" Is there never a man of all my men can say where Kamal hides? "   10
Then up and spoke Mohammed Khan, the son of the Ressaldar:°
" If ye know the track of the morning mist, ye know where his pickets are.
At dusk he harries the Abazai° — at dawn he is into Bonair,°
But he must go by Fort Bukloh to his own place to fare.
So if ye gallop to Fort Bukloh as fast as a bird can fly,   15
By the favor of God ye may cut him off ere he win the Tongue of Jagai.
But if he be past the Tongue of Jagai, right swiftly turn ye then,
For the length and the breadth of that grisly plain is sown with Kamal's men.
There is rock to the left, and rock to the right, and low lean thorn between,
And ye may hear a breech-bolt snick where never a man is seen."   20
The Colonel's son has taken horse, and a raw rough dun was he,
With the mouth of a bell and the heart of Hell and the head of a gallows-tree.
The Colonel's son to the Fort has won, they bid him stay to eat —
Who rides at the tail of a Border thief, he sits not long at his meat.
He's up and away from Fort Bukloh as fast as he can fly,   25
Till he was aware of his father's mare in the gut of the Tongue of Jagai,
Till he was aware of his father's mare with Kamal upon her back,
And when he could spy the white of her eye, he made the pistol crack.
He has fired once, he has fired twice, but the whistling ball went wide.
" Ye shoot like a soldier," Kamal said. " Show now if ye can ride! "   30
It's up and over the Tongue of Jagai, as blown dust-devils go,
The dun he fled like a stag of ten, but the mare like a barren doe.

5. *Kamal* (kä′mȧl): the leader of the Afghans. 8. *calkins* (kôk′ĭnz): bent metal pieces on a
horseshoe to prevent slipping. 9. *Guides:* trusted native troops, who served with the English
as guides and interpreters. 11. *Ressaldar* (rĕs-ȧl-där′): a native Indian commander of a troop of
cavalry. 13. *Abazai* (ȧ-bȧ-zī′), *Bonair* (bō-nâr′): settlements about forty miles apart on the frontier
of the Punjab district.

"The Ballad of East and West" from *Barrack-Room Ballads* by Rudyard Kipling. Reprinted by permission of A. P. Watt and
Son, Macmillan and Company of Canada, and Mrs. George Bambridge.

The dun he leaned against the bit and slugged his head above,
But the red mare played with the snaffle bars,° as a maiden plays with a glove.
There was rock to the left and rock to the right, and low lean thorn between,   35
And thrice he heard a breech-bolt snick tho' never a man was seen.
They have ridden the low moon out of the sky, their hoofs drum up the dawn,
The dun he went like a wounded bull, but the mare like a new-roused fawn.
The dun he fell at a watercourse — in a woeful heap fell he,
And Kamal has turned the red mare back, and pulled the rider free.   40
He has knocked the pistol out of his hand — small room was there to strive,
" 'Twas only by favor of mine," quoth he, " ye rode so long alive:
There was not a rock for twenty mile, there was not a clump of tree,
But covered a man of my own men with his rifle cocked on his knee.
If I had raised my bridle hand, as I have held it low,   45
The little jackals that flee so fast were feasting all in a row.
If I had bowed my head on my breast, as I have held it high,
The kite that whistles above us now were gorged till she could not fly."
Lightly answered the Colonel's son: " Do good to bird and beast,
But count who come for the broken meats before thou makest a feast.   50
If there should follow a thousand swords to carry my bones away,
Belike the price of jackal's meal were more than a thief could pay.
They will feed their horse on the standing crop, their men on the garnered grain.
The thatch of the byres° will serve their fires when all the cattle are slain.
But if thou thinkest the price be fair, — thy brethren wait to sup,   55
The hound is kin to the jackal-spawn — howl, dog, and call them up!
And if thou thinkest the price be high, in steer and gear and stack,
Give me my father's mare again, and I'll fight my own way back! "
Kamal has gripped him by the hand and set him upon his feet.
" No talk shall be of dogs," said he, " when wolf and gray wolf meet.   60
May I eat dirt if thou hast hurt of me in deed or breath;
What dam of lances brought thee forth to jest at the dawn with Death? "

34. *snaffle bars:* jointed bridles without curbs. 54. *byres:* cow barns.

Lightly answered the Colonel's son: " I hold by the blood of my clan:
Take up the mare for my father's gift — by God, she has carried a man! "
The red mare ran to the Colonel's son, and nuzzled against his breast;   65
" We be two strong men," said Kamal then, " but she loveth the younger best.
So she shall go with a lifter's dower, my turquoise-studded rein,
My 'broidered saddle and saddlecloth, and silver stirrups twain."
The Colonel's son a pistol drew, and held it muzzle end,
" Ye have taken the one from a foe," said he. " Will ye take the mate from a
    friend? "   70
" A gift for a gift," said Kamal straight; " a limb for the risk of a limb.
Thy father has sent his son to me, I'll send my son to him! "
With that he whistled his only son, that dropped from a mountain crest —
He trod the ling° like a buck in spring, and he looked like a lance in rest.
" Now here is thy master," Kamal said, " who leads a troop of the Guides,   75
And thou must ride at his left side as shield on shoulder rides.
Till Death or I cut loose the tie, at camp and board and bed,
Thy life is his — thy fate it is to guard him with thy head.
So, thou must eat the White Queen's meat, and all her foes are thine,
And thou must harry thy father's hold for the peace of the Border-line.   80
And thou must make a trooper tough and hack thy way to power —
Belike they will raise thee to Ressaldar when I am hanged in Peshawur! "°

They have looked each other between the eyes, and there have found no fault.
They have taken the Oath of the Brother-in-Blood on leavened bread and salt;
They have taken the Oath of the Brother-in-Blood on fire and fresh-cut sod,   85
On the hilt and the haft of the Khyber knife,° and the Wondrous Names of God.°

74. *ling:* heather. 82. *Peshawur* (pĕ·shä′wȧr): the seat of the British government in Northwest
Frontier Province. 86. *Khyber* (kī′bĕr) *knife:* a knife used in Khyber Pass, a narrow road between
India and Afghanistan; *Wondrous Names of God:* one hundred Mohammedan names given to
God, one revealed only to the priests, the others given in the Koran.

The Colonel's son he rides the mare and Kamal's boy the dun,
And two have come back to Fort Bukloh where there went forth but one.
And when they drew to the Quarter-Guard, full twenty swords flew clear —
There was not a man but carried his feud with the blood of the mountaineer.   90
" Ha' done! ha' done! " said the Colonel's son. " Put up the steel at your sides!
Last night ye had struck at a Border thief — tonight 'tis a man of the Guides! "

Oh, East is East, and West is West, and never the twain shall meet,
Till Earth and Sky stand presently at God's great Judgment Seat;
But there is neither East nor West, Border, nor Breed, nor Birth,   95
When two strong men stand face to face, though they come from the ends of the
    earth!

A WRITER OF THE EMPIRE

MISS YOUGHAL'S SAIS

1. In what kind of predicament did Strickland find himself? What personal qualities and past experience enabled him to carry out his plan? Did his conduct in any way differ from that of a native *sais?*

2. What do you learn of Indian life and customs from this story? Does the life of the English colony sound pleasant or unpleasant as described? What traits of the English in India during the time of the Empire do you observe?

POETRY

1. What great fear and what fervent prayer are expressed in " Recessional "? In your own words restate the moral Kipling draws in this hymn. Why are the title and the warning appropriate for the occasion (Victoria's Diamond Jubilee)? How may the life of a nation be compared to that of an individual?

2. In " Tommy " does the soldier have a legitimate complaint to make or not? Discuss the public attitude toward soldiers during peace time, with particular reference to our own country.

3. In " L'Envoi " how does Kipling picture heaven? What ideals of art, work, and life are realized in this heaven? Can they ever be realized on earth?

4. The theme of " The Ballad of East and West " is clearly stated at the beginning. Recount briefly what happens in the story that carries out the theme. How do present world conditions have bearing on this theme?

SUGGESTIONS FOR WRITING

1. Adapt " Miss Youghal's *Sais* " for radio or television. Present it to the class with proper sound effects.

2. Describe a predicament that you were able to get out of because of an earlier experience.

READING LIST FOR THE VICTORIAN AGE

Bellasis, Margaret, *Mrs. Betsey*
    A complicated and romantic plot of a young widow as housekeeper in a run-down country house in Kent.

Bennett, Arnold, *The Old Wives' Tale*
    Life in a small English industrial town, and in Paris, described with sympathy and humor.

Besier, Rudolph, *The Barretts of Wimpole Street*
    A three-act play about Elizabeth Barrett's life before her marriage, her courtship by Browning, and their elopement.

Bonnet, Theodore, *The Mudlark*
    A ragamuffin from the London streets eludes the guards and gains admittance to Windsor Castle to see Queen Victoria.

Braithwaite, William S., *The Bewitched Parsonage*
    An exciting introduction to the Brontë family, written with literary skill.

Brontë, Charlotte, *Jane Eyre*
    Jane falls in love with her employer — a strange but fascinating man — and many surprises await the reader.

Brontë, Emily, *Wuthering Heights*

A wild tale of love and hate among the rough people of the Yorkshire moors.

Burnett, Constance, *The Silver Answer*

Re-creation of Elizabeth Barrett's life in the home of her strict and possessive father, her courtship, marriage to Robert Browning, and their life together.

De La Roche, Mazo, *Mary Wakefield*

A turbulent love story set in a Canadian locale of the 1890's.

Dickens, Charles, *David Copperfield*

Many of Dickens' best-known characters are in this story based on his own life.

————, *Oliver Twist*

After a boy from an English workhouse is trained to be a pickpocket, he struggles against severe obstacles to escape from an environment of crime.

Du Maurier, Daphne, *My Cousin Rachel*

Philip Ashley meets his uncle's widow, succumbs to her charms, but learns what may be the truth about his uncle's death.

Eliot, George, *Adam Bede*

A man of high character finds himself in many perplexing situations.

————, *Mill on the Floss*

In a tragic story of affection and antipathy between a sister and brother, some humor is provided by three comic aunts.

Field, Isobel, *This Life I've Loved*

Robert Louis Stevenson seen through the eyes of his stepdaughter.

Galsworthy, John, *The Forsyte Saga*

Younger and older generations are contrasted in this chronicle of the Forsyte family from Victorian times into the twentieth century.

Hardy, Thomas, *The Return of the Native*

Fatal misunderstandings between relatives and a subtle yielding to temptation lead a strong person to a tragic death.

Hinkley, Laura L., *The Stevensons: Louis and Fanny*

A biography of Stevenson's childhood in Scotland, Fanny's early life in Indianapolis, their marriage in San Francisco, and their travels around the world.

Housman, Laurence, *Victoria Regina*

A brilliant play of outstanding episodes in Queen Victoria's life from girlhood to her Diamond Jubilee.

Hudson, William H., *Green Mansions*

A beautifully written fantasy of the love of an Englishman for Rima, a birdlike creature, in a South American forest.

Jarden, Mary Louise, *The Young Brontës*

"This tale, as I have told it, has been of the childhood and growing up days of the four Brontë geniuses."

Kipling, Rudyard, *Kim*

An orphaned son of an Irish soldier "goes native" in India and reveals a side of Indian life that few Europeans ever see.

Leonowens, Anna, *The English Governess at the Siamese Court*

A story, a film, and a musical have been made from this account of teaching the king's children in Siam (Thailand) in the 1860's.

Maugham, W. S., *Maugham's Choice of Kipling's Best*

Sixteen Kipling stories and an introductory essay by Maugham.

Pearson, Hesketh, *Dizzy*

A colorful picture of an outstanding Prime Minister, a true Englishman and a great friend to Queen Victoria.

Stern, Gladys B., *Robert Louis Stevenson*

A vigorous personality is presented in an informal style in this brief, straightforward biography.

Stevenson, Robert L., *Dr. Jekyll and Mr. Hyde*

The supernatural change of personality symbolizes the conflict between the good and evil in man.

Waite, Helen E., *How Do I Love Thee?*

The moving story of Elizabeth Barrett, whose courage and love have thrilled generations and whose marriage stirred the Victorian world.

Woodham-Smith, Cecil, *Lonely Crusader*

Exciting, inspiring, informative, is this shortened version of an earlier biography of Florence Nightingale.

Woolf, Virginia, *Flush*

The romance of Elizabeth Barrett and Robert Browning is told as if by Elizabeth's cocker spaniel.

FOR LISTENING

The following poems have been recorded and are available on *Many Voices 6B:* "My Last Duchess," "Bugle Song," "Remember," "How Do I Love Thee?"

THE MODERN

LITERATURE is a major outlet for the stream of ideas born of this modern age. In an era of high-speed presses and millions of educated readers, writers of all kinds have multiplied. Life in the modern world is complex, exciting, and challenging; the literature of this age is rich, varied, and poignant. To read the literature of twentieth-century England is to grow in an understanding of the age which this writing both influences and reflects.

A CENTURY OF GREAT CHANGES

Until her death in 1901, Queen Victoria seemed to be the fixed center of an enormous world state. Rulers from many countries had attended her Diamond Jubilee in 1897 and had witnessed the pomp and power of the British Empire. The sun never set upon that empire; it girdled the globe and controlled the seas as well as a quarter of the earth's land.

The Festival of Britain, a glorious spectacle of that nation without austerity, dazzled Britons and their visitors in 1951. Shown above is the great exposition in London, displaying technological and artistic works.

AGE 1900-

Little more than half a century has changed all that. Two world wars, depressions, general strikes, and government crises have altered the living conditions and the social and political thinking of Englishmen.

The key to the whole period might be phrased in a short sentence: the twentieth century is the century of the common citizen. Whatever has happened in government, in war, in science, in economics, has required his participation, or worked for his safety and betterment, or depended upon his numbers. His imagination has been fired in making plans for a different future.

CHANGES IN SOCIAL CONDITIONS

As England's wealth and power have declined, so have its wealthy and privileged classes. The English aristocracy, both of birth and of money, is diminishing rapidly. Great estates are being broken up or made into public monuments to the nation's long and glorious past. If it could be said that the battle of Waterloo was won on the playing fields of Eton (an exclusive, aristocratic school), it can be said today that England's struggle for peace and security has been won in the ordinary schoolrooms, where equal rights prevail and where young citizens are taught to act for the good of all.

Changes are apparent in the life of the ordinary, middle-class people, too. If they live in London, they are in the midst of an enormous, bustling metropolis. The extensive damage from wartime bombing has been repaired; modern buildings have replaced old, historic ones in many places. Away from the city, a typical English family may live in a " semi-detached villa " or a " ribbon development," where the houses have adjoining side walls in order to cut down the cost of heating and to save space. You may be sure that they will have a garden, too, no matter how small.

Listening to the programs of the government-controlled British Broadcasting Corporation on the radio, the Englishman may hear the best in music and literature and drama. The Independent Television Authority introduced commercial television to the British people in 1955. Children are given an education in elementary and secondary schools; and boys and girls, on the basis of their ability, may win scholarships at Oxford or Cambridge, or the numerous city universities that have developed rapidly during the twentieth century. Educational opportunity has greatly expanded for Englishmen.

England has built up a vast and complex system of social security for the common citizen. His tax money has in part been spent to provide him with insurance against personal misfortune. If he is ill, if he needs glasses or new teeth or an operation, the government provides a national health service; if he is out of a job, he gets unemployment relief; if he is old, he is entitled to a pension.

CHANGES IN GOVERNMENT

Britain's program for social and material welfare is costly. The common citizen must pay for what he gets, and the government taxes severely. What he spends costs him a great deal extra in hidden taxes on all business and manufacture. With not enough to go around, the modern state is learning to distribute what it has more fairly, more nearly equally to all. This requires a

All Englishmen, from workmen to schoolboys, have felt the changes resulting from

complicated system of law, government control, price fixing, rationing, and socialized industries.

Political parties have learned to stand together in times of crises. During World War I, the coalition government was led by David Lloyd George, the head of the Liberal party. During the economic upheavals and unemployment problems of the world between wars, Ramsay MacDonald was the first prime minister from the Labor party. In World War II, England was united under Winston Churchill, the indomitable leader of the Conservatives. In 1945 the Labor party with Clement Attlee as prime minister instituted a program of social legislation, but by 1951 Winston Churchill was again back in power. Finally in 1955 Churchill handed over the leadership of the Conservative party to Anthony Eden, who was followed by Harold Macmillan in 1957.

Through all such shifts in power, the English monarchs have held the allegiance of their subjects. They have become the symbols of England, in part by accepting the will of the people and in part by representing that will. Edward VII succeeded Victoria, and in spite of his pleasure-loving ways cemented the bonds between England, France, and Russia that held so well during World War I against Germany. The salty, sea-loving George V kept England steady during that war. The dashing Prince of Wales, as Edward VIII, gave up the throne rather than divide England into factions over his marriage to an American divorcee. His brother George VI succeeded him, and with Queen Elizabeth and their daughters, Princess Elizabeth and Princess Margaret, endured the dangers and privations of World War II. Queen Elizabeth II, Victoria's great-great-granddaughter, succeeded to the throne in 1952. To all Englishmen her coronation in 1953 symbolized hope for another great Elizabethan Age.

CHANGES IN EMPIRE

After the war many Englishmen realized that the Empire could no longer be maintained in its old form. In the last decade England has learned to command the loyalty of many of its subjects through freedom, and a restless em-

twentieth-century wars and important social legislation.

pire is being transformed into a friendly commonwealth. Since 1945 England has poured billions into African development. Within a few years after the war, India was given her freedom; that country is now an independent republic within the Commonweath. All of Ireland except the six northern counties had won its status as a free state in the period between the wars. For decades the great nations of Canada, South Africa, Australia, and New Zealand have been independent. They are held to the mother country by ties of common interest and good will as well as by the organization of the Commonwealth.

England and the United States have learned the same lesson in the modern age: that the only lasting agreements are those that are freely made. In a sense, therefore, the British Empire has not dissolved, but a closer union in common thought and beliefs has developed.

THE WORLD OF ENGLISH WRITERS

The English language is like a great country where no passports or translators or interpreters are needed; here a man is judged by what he has to tell us. Boundaries of class or race or nation scarcely exist.

One of the significant characteristics of the writing of the new age is a lessening of the differences that once set English literature apart from American literature. Writers of both countries today are not only closer together in subject matter and in style, but are occasionally at home in both countries. T. S. Eliot, the poet who is perhaps the most influential writer in England, was born in St. Louis, Missouri, and educated at Harvard; he is now a British subject. Contrasted to Eliot is W. H. Auden, one of the leading poets in America, who was born in England, educated at Oxford, and is now an American citizen. The ideas that find expression in the poetry of Sidney Keyes, Henry Reed, and Dylan Thomas are also apparent in recent American poetry.

You will read three modern plays: one about Englishmen, one about Irishmen, and one whose main character is a Scot. Each of these plays has been produced many times on both sides of the Atlantic; some of Shaw's plays have been staged all over Europe as well.

The great republic of letters accepts as its citizens all those who write and think well: George Orwell, born in India, was a traveled, cosmopolitan individual with a searching mind; Alan Paton's novel of Africa, *Cry, the Beloved Country,* was a best seller in England and the United States; Katherine Mansfield, born in New Zealand, interpreted life in that country and England; Joseph Conrad was a Pole who learned to write English professionally only as a grown man; James Barrie, a great dramatist and storyteller, was a Scot, and James Joyce, the most original and most difficult novelist, was an Irishman. In literature, the English-speaking world is One World.

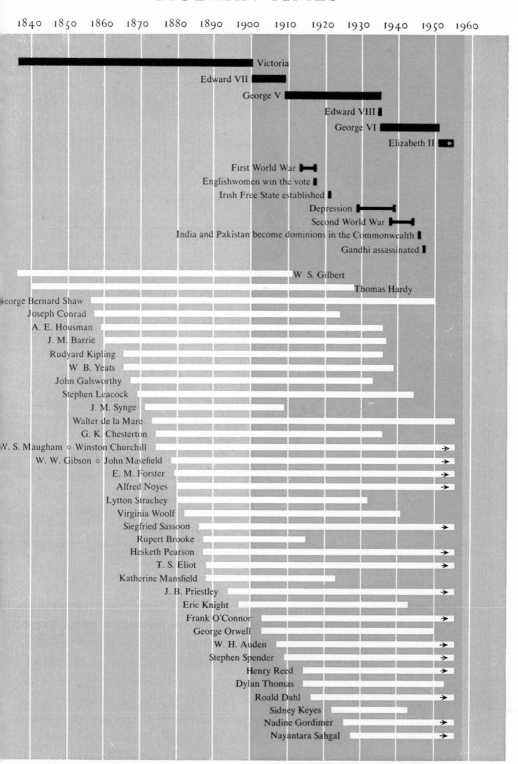

1840 1850 1860 1870 1880 1890 1900 1910 1920 1930 1940 1950 1960

Victoria
Edward VII
George V
Edward VIII
George VI
Elizabeth II

First World War
Englishwomen win the vote
Irish Free State established
Depression
Second World War
India and Pakistan become dominions in the Commonwealth
Gandhi assassinated

W. S. Gilbert
Thomas Hardy
George Bernard Shaw
Joseph Conrad
A. E. Housman
J. M. Barrie
Rudyard Kipling
W. B. Yeats
John Galsworthy
Stephen Leacock
J. M. Synge
Walter de la Mare
G. K. Chesterton
W. S. Maugham ○ Winston Churchill
W. W. Gibson ○ John Masefield
E. M. Forster
Alfred Noyes
Lytton Strachey
Virginia Woolf
Siegfried Sassoon
Rupert Brooke
Hesketh Pearson
T. S. Eliot
Katherine Mansfield
J. B. Priestley
Eric Knight
Frank O'Connor
George Orwell
W. H. Auden
Stephen Spender
Henry Reed
Dylan Thomas
Roald Dahl
Sidney Keyes
Nadine Gordimer
Nayantara Sahgal

1840 1850 1860 1870 1880 1890 1900 1910 1920 1930 1940 1950 1960

IDEAS IN MODERN ENGLISH LITERATURE

Literature, dealing with human personality and relationships, does much toward keeping men aware of themselves, toward making us steadily conscious of the importance of each individual. It will be hard for you to find a story or poem or essay in the following pages of which this is not true. In the modern age this has been especially important. Modern writers seem to be asserting the dignity of the individual against the great impersonal forces of war, of science, of economic systems in today's world.

Here again, and in great variety, appear the mixed threads that make up the English character — the action and bravery and endurance of the Anglo-Saxon, the humor and imagination of the Celt, the gaiety and culture of the Norman Frenchman, the boldness of the Elizabethan, the urge for freedom of the seventeenth-century Englishman, the love of order and graceful living of the eighteenth-century gentleman, the deep emotion of the Romantics, the moral earnestness of the Victorians, the sense of the rights of the common citizen that is characteristic of the modern man. It is all English literature combined that makes us realize our capacities in the free play and fair play of the mind.

The voices of many writers seem to blend into a single voice that says: let every man have his chance to be himself; help us to realize the almost infinite varieties which human nature can assume; give us the power, through the experiences of twelve centuries of literature, to understand ourselves.

SUMMARY

With the death of Queen Victoria, an age of great changes was ushered in. During half a century England has lost its pre-eminent position in world trade and politics, yielding to both West and East. The twentieth century has been the century of the common citizen whose government, whether Labor or Conservative, insures him his health, employment, and care in old age, as well as providing for his education.

Great changes have occurred in English society with the decline of the moneyed and aristocratic classes. Coalition cabinets have held the nation together through wartime and economic crises. With the freeing of India and Ireland, voluntary compacts based on mutual ties and interests have replaced former imperial power. In literature and art the English language has become a republic of letters in which peoples of many cultures meet. English literature draws on the threads of the past — on the diverse races and societies that made modern Britain — and stands forth in an age threatened by mass movements as a tribute to and a defender of the individual's conscience and the individual's creativeness.

MODERN SHORT STORIES

IN THIS BOOK you already have read short stories by Charles Dickens, Robert Louis Stevenson, Thomas Hardy, and Rudyard Kipling. Dickens' tales are not really comparable to the short story as we know it today. Stevenson, with his emphasis on the psychological aspect of human behavior, approached the short story in the modern manner. Hardy and Kipling belong as much to the twentieth century as to the nineteenth. The short story, defined and mastered by Poe and Hawthorne, is largely an American development in literature; however, in the modern age, English writers as well can claim distinction in this field.

Almost everyone enjoys a short story. It tells a narrative neatly and quickly; it concentrates action in a small space. If skillfully written, there is a sense of anticipation or suspense to hold a reader. But it would be a mistake to assume that short stories are cut to a pattern, or that, being brief, they are limited in subject matter. If we look over the range of English short stories from Stevenson's time to the present, we see a tremendous variety of style and much inventiveness.

The short story usually is limited to a single series of events; it introduces only one main character, or at most two; it establishes a dominant mood immediately which it holds throughout. This might be called the " classic " style of the short story. No one has performed more brilliantly in this style than the Englishman Somerset Maugham. Maugham hangs his story on a strong thread of *plot,* but at the same time he concentrates on *character* portrayal. He is a storyteller of the highest rank, and his narratives are told with skill and craftsmanship. In the section that follows " The Verger," you will have a chance to analyze Maugham's method of building a story.

But not all short stories follow this style. Joseph Conrad wrote stories that, while they are not as long as novels, are not as restricted in form as most short stories. Conrad emphasizes *setting* in his stories, as you will notice in reading " The Lagoon." He takes care to create the actual physical location of his narrative and to suggest its influence on the characters. Katherine Mansfield shows a writer's skill in controlling the reader's *emotional response.* What we customarily call action, or plot, is hardly recognizable as such in her stories. Instead, there will often be a fleeting glimpse into the inner spirit of a person — as dramatic as the most melodramatic plot.

Principal experimenters in both the modern English novel and the short story have tried to work out true and precise answers to such questions as these: How many different personalities exist in each one of us? How can we describe the unconscious mind and hidden instincts that control so much of human life? What is time really, and how can we understand it? What ways of writing will help to convey new psychological discoveries? Many writers today are experimenting with stories that do not follow the traditional form of plot development, leading to a climax — stories that are, instead, concerned with incidents or situations that are developed but not brought to a conclusive ending. The impact of such stories comes from the fact that they mirror life situations realistically. Since they have no " end " in the usual sense, the reader may continue to develop the situation in his imagination. As usually happens, considerable time must elapse before such experiments are accepted as standard English literature, along with the older forms.

Not only in technique, but also in subject matter, the English short story has roamed far afield. Kipling's stories of India have been, in a later time, paralleled by those of E. M. Forster and Rumer Godden. Conrad's tours of the South Seas as a master of merchant vessels lent plots and color to the stories he wrote later. Somerset Maugham has set his many tales East and West — in America, China, Africa, India, and France. Nadine Gordimer, a young writer from Johannesburg, has become a fresh interpreter of the South African scene.

Frank O'Connor has chosen the Irish as his special province. In a story, he prefers to give a brief glimpse of life — maybe only a conversation between two people — and his Irishman is always presented realistically. Roald Dahl, in writing of the unusual, the improbable,

and the bizarre, reveals insights into certain kinds of human motivation. Eric Knight's stories of the Yorkshire countrymen are local color fiction that reveal the simplicity and good humor of ordinary people in present-day England.

And always, like other types of modern literature, the English short story has attempted to picture life realistically and honestly. What it has sometimes lacked in humor or in sheer storytelling skill, it has made up in a sincere portrayal of people and situations. Like contemporary novelists, short story writers deal with the social and economic and moral problems that confront individuals in our complex civilization. Galsworthy has created what amounts to a social record of the age; H. G. Wells has used fiction to promote his ideas about society. All in all, British writers have made modern fiction a mirror of what we know and think in our time.

The Verger

W. SOMERSET MAUGHAM 1874–

The early life of W. Somerset Maugham (môm) was unhappy. He was born in France of English parents who both died when he was still a boy. He went to England to live in the cold, stern atmosphere of his uncle's home. This setting appears in Maugham's novel *Cakes and Ale*, in which he describes a boy like himself: shy, uncertain, afflicted with a stammer, but also imaginative and responsive. Maugham studied in English schools and at the University of Heidelberg. He wanted to be a writer but instead studied medicine at the insistence of his uncle. After a year's internship in the Lambeth slums of London, he suffered an attack of tuberculosis and soon left to travel on the Continent, where he began writing. He worked steadily for

years; success did not come easily. In his most famous novel, *Of Human Bondage,* he tells the moving story of a young medical student much like himself.

Somerset Maugham has become perhaps the most accomplished storyteller of our time. He has traveled the world over and gathered tales along the way — stories and novels and plays with strange incidents, odd characters, often exotic settings. Possibly one secret of his popularity lies in his stated purpose in writing — entertainment. " Pleasure," he says, " is in itself good." Yet Maugham writes of neither the pleasant nor the pretty. While he does not make a special pleading for the poor and underprivileged, he depicts the upper classes with an irony that is often malicious.

THERE HAD BEEN a christening that afternoon at St. Peter's, Neville Square, and Albert Edward Foreman still wore his verger's [1] gown. He kept his new one, its folds as full and stiff as though it were made not of alpaca but of perennial bronze, for funerals and weddings (St. Peter's, Neville Square, was a church much favored by the fashionable for these ceremonies), and now he wore only his second best. He wore it with complacence; for it was the dignified symbol of his office, and without it (when he took it off to go home) he had the disconcerting sensation of being somewhat insufficiently clad. He took pains with it; he pressed it and ironed it himself. During the sixteen years he had been verger of this church he had had a succession of such gowns; but he had never been able to throw them away when they were worn out, and the complete series, neatly wrapped up in brown paper, lay in the bottom drawer of the wardrobe in his bedroom.

The verger busied himself quietly, replacing the painted wooden cover on the marble font, taking away a chair that had been brought for an infirm old lady, and waited for the vicar to have finished in the vestry so that he could tidy up in there and go home. Presently he saw him walk across the chancel, genuflect in front of the high altar, and come down the aisle; but he still wore his cassock.

"What's he 'anging about for?" the verger said to himself. "Don't 'e know I want my tea?"

The vicar had been but recently appointed, a red-faced, energetic man in his early forties, and Albert Edward still regretted his predecessor, a clergyman of the old school who preached leisurely sermons in a silvery voice and dined out a great deal with his more aristocratic

parishioners. He liked things in church to be just so, but he never fussed; he was not like this new man who wanted to have his finger in every pie. But Albert Edward was tolerant. St. Peter's was in a very good neighborhood and the parishioners were a very nice class of people. The new vicar had come from the East End, and he couldn't be expected to fall in all at once with the discreet ways of his fashionable congregation.

"All this 'ustle," said Albert Edward. "But give 'im time; he'll learn."

When the vicar had walked down the aisle so far that he could address the verger without raising his voice more than was becoming in a place of worship, he stopped.

"Foreman, will you come into the vestry for a minute? I have something to say to you."

"Very good, sir."

The vicar waited for him to come up and they walked up the church together.

"A very nice christening, I thought, sir. Funny 'ow the baby stopped cryin' the moment you took him."

"I've noticed they very often do," said the vicar, with a little smile. "After all, I've had a good deal of practice with them."

It was a source of subdued pride to him that he could nearly always quiet a whimpering infant by the manner in which he held it, and he was not unconscious of the amused admiration with which mothers and nurses watched him settle the baby in the crook of his surpliced arm. The verger knew that it pleased him to be complimented on his talent.

The vicar preceded Albert Edward into the vestry. Albert Edward was a trifle surprised to find the two churchwardens there. He had not seen them come in. They gave him pleasant nods.

"Good afternoon, my lord. Good afternoon, sir," he said to one after the other.

They were elderly men, both of them,

[1] verger: an employee, or official, who takes care of the interior of a church building and exhibits it to visitors.

and they had been churchwardens almost as long as Albert Edward had been verger. They were sitting now at a handsome refectory table that the old vicar had brought many years before from Italy, and the vicar sat down in the vacant chair between them. Albert Edward faced them, the table between him and them, and wondered with slight uneasiness what was the matter. He remembered still the occasion on which the organist had got into trouble and the bother they had had to hush things up. In a church like St. Peter's, Neville Square, they couldn't afford a scandal. On the vicar's red face was a look of resolute benignity, but the others bore an expression that was slightly troubled.

"He's been naggin' them, he 'as," said the verger to himself. "He's jockeyed them into doin' something, but they don't 'alf like it. That's what it is; you mark my words."

But his thoughts did not appear on Albert Edward's clean-cut and distinguished features. He stood in a respectful but not obsequious attitude. He had been in service before he was appointed to his ecclesiastical office, but only in very good houses, and his deportment was irreproachable. Starting as a page boy in the household of a merchant prince, he had risen by due degrees from the position of fourth to first footman; for a year he had been singlehanded butler to a widowed peeress and, till the vacancy occurred at St. Peter's, butler with two men under him in the house of a retired ambassador. He was tall, spare, grave, and dignified. He looked, if not like a duke, at least like an actor of the old school who specialized in dukes' parts. He had tact, firmness, and self-assurance. His character was unimpeachable.

The vicar began briskly.

"Foreman, we've got something rather unpleasant to say to you. You've been here a great many years, and I think his lordship and the general agree with me that you've fulfilled the duties of your office to the satisfaction of everybody concerned."

The two churchwardens nodded.

"But a most extraordinary circumstance came to my knowledge the other day and I felt it my duty to impart it to the churchwardens. I discovered to my astonishment that you could neither read nor write."

The verger's face betrayed no sign of embarrassment.

"The last vicar knew that, sir," he replied. "He said it didn't make no difference. He always said there was a great deal too much education in the world for 'is taste."

"It's the most amazing thing I ever heard," cried the general. "Do you mean to say that you've been verger of this church for sixteen years and never learned to read or write?"

"I went into service when I was twelve, sir. The cook in the first place tried to teach me once; but I didn't seem to 'ave the knack for it, and then what with one thing and another I never seemed to 'ave the time. I've never really found the want of it. I think a lot of these young fellows waste a lot of time readin' when they might be doin' something useful."

"But don't you want to know the news?" said the other churchwarden. "Don't you ever want to write a letter?"

"No, me lord, I seem to manage very well without. And of late years, now they've all these pictures in the papers, I get to know what's goin' on pretty well. Me wife's quite a scholar, and if I want to write a letter she writes it for me. It's not as if I was a bettin' man."

The two churchwardens gave the vicar a troubled glance and then looked down at the table.

"Well, Foreman, I've talked the matter over with these gentlemen and they quite agree with me that the situation is impossible. At a church like St. Peter's, Neville Square, we cannot have a verger who can neither read nor write."

Albert Edward's thin, sallow face reddened and he moved uneasily on his feet, but he made no reply.

"Understand me, Foreman, I have no complaint to make against you. You do your work quite satisfactorily. I have the highest opinion both of your character and of your capacity, but we haven't the right to take the risk of some accident that might happen owing to your lamentable ignorance. It's a matter of prudence as well as of principle."

"But couldn't you learn, Foreman?" asked the general.

"No, sir, I'm afraid I couldn't — not now. You see, I'm not as young as I was, and, if I couldn't seem able to get the letters in me 'ead when I was a nipper,[1] I don't think there's much chance of it now."

"We don't want to be harsh with you, Foreman," said the vicar. "But the churchwardens and I have quite made up our minds. We'll give you three months, and if at the end of that time you cannot read and write I'm afraid you'll have to go."

Albert Edward had never liked the new vicar. He'd said from the beginning that they'd made a mistake when they gave him St. Peter's. He wasn't the type of man they wanted with a classy congregation like that. And now he straightened himself a little. He knew his value and he wasn't going to allow himself to be put upon.

"I'm very sorry, sir; I'm afraid it's no good. I'm too old a dog to learn new tricks. I've lived a good many years without knowin' 'ow to read and write, and without wishin' to praise myself — self-praise is no recommendation — I don't mind sayin' I've done my duty in that state of life in which it 'as pleased a merciful providence to place me, and if I *could* learn now I don't know as I'd want to."

"In that case, Foreman, I'm afraid you must go."

He walked slowly back to the vestry and hung up his verger's gown.

"Yes, sir, I quite understand. I shall be 'appy to 'and in my resignation as soon as you've found somebody to take my place."

But when Albert Edward, with his usual politeness, had closed the church door behind the vicar and the two churchwardens, he could not sustain the air of unruffled dignity with which he had borne the blow inflicted upon him, and his lips quivered. He walked slowly back to the vestry and hung up on its proper peg his verger's gown. He sighed as he thought of all the grand funerals and smart weddings it had seen. He tidied everything up, put on his coat, and hat in hand walked down the aisle. He locked the church door behind him. He strolled across the square; but, deep in his sad thoughts, he did not take the street that led him home, where a nice strong cup of tea awaited him — he took the wrong turning.

He walked slowly along. His heart was heavy. He did not know what he

[1] *nipper:* English slang for small boy.

"The Verger" is one of Maugham's best-known stories; it has been filmed with two more under the title Trio. *Four other stories make up a film entitled* Quartet. *Maugham's stories have also been presented on television, where they have been introduced by the author himself. A conscious artist who is interested in the sources as well as the forms of storytelling, Maugham has told much about his modes of working in* A Writer's Notebook, *begun when he was eighteen and published when he was seventy-five.*

should do with himself. He did not fancy the notion of going back to domestic service; after being his own master for so many years — for the vicar and churchwardens could say what they liked; it was he that had run St. Peter's, Neville Square — he could scarcely demean himself by accepting a situation. He had saved a tidy sum, but not enough to live on without doing something; and life seemed to cost more every year. He had never thought to be troubled with such questions. The vergers of St. Peter's, like the popes of Rome, were there for life. He had often thought of the pleasant reference the vicar would make, in his sermon at evensong the first Sunday after his death, to the long and faithful service and the exemplary character of their late verger Albert Edward Foreman.

He sighed deeply. Albert Edward was a nonsmoker and a total abstainer, but with a certain latitude; that is to say, he liked a glass of beer with his dinner and when he was tired he enjoyed a cigarette. It occurred to him now that one would comfort him and, since he did not carry them, he looked about him for a shop where he could buy a packet of

Gold Flakes. He did not at once see one and walked on a little. It was a long street, with all sorts of shops in it; but there was not a single one where you could buy cigarettes.

" That's strange," said Albert Edward.

To make sure, he walked right up the street again. No, there was no doubt about it. He stopped and looked reflectively up and down.

" I can't be the only man as walks along this street and wants a fag," he said. " I shouldn't wonder but what a fellow might do very well with a little shop here. Tobacco and sweets, you know."

He gave a sudden start.

" That's an idea," he said. " Strange 'ow things come to you when you least expect it."

He turned, walked home, and had his tea.

" You're very silent this afternoon, Albert," his wife remarked.

" I'm thinkin'," he said.

He considered the matter from every point of view, and next day he went along the street and by good luck found a little shop to let that looked as though it would exactly suit him. Twenty-four hours later he had taken it and, when a month after that he left St. Peter's, Neville Square, forever, Albert Edward Foreman set up in business as a tobacconist and newsagent. His wife said it was a dreadful comedown after being verger of St. Peter's; but he answered that you had to move with the times, the church wasn't what it was, and 'enceforward he was going to render unto Caesar [1] what was Caesar's. Albert Edward did very well. He did so well that in a year or so it struck him that he might take a second shop and put a manager in. He looked for another long street that hadn't got a tobacconist in it and when he found it, and a shop to let, took it and stocked it. This was a success too. Then it occurred to him

[1] *render unto Caesar:* see Matthew 22:21.

that if he could run two he could run half a dozen; so he began walking about London, and whenever he found a long street that had no tobacconist, and a shop to let, he took it. In the course of ten years he had acquired no less than ten shops and he was making money hand over fist. He went round to all of them himself every Monday, collected the week's takings and took them to the bank.

One morning when he was there, paying in a bundle of notes and a heavy bag of silver, the cashier told him that the manager would like to see him. He was shown into an office and the manager shook hands with him.

"Mr. Foreman, I wanted to have a talk to you about the money you've got on deposit with us. D'you know exactly how much it is?"

"Not within a pound or two, sir; but I've got a pretty rough idea."

"Apart from what you paid in this morning, it's a little over thirty thousand pounds. That's a very large sum to have on deposit and I should have thought you'd do better to invest it."

"I wouldn't want to take no risk, sir. I know it's safe in the bank."

"You needn't have the least anxiety. We'll make you out a list of absolutely gilt-edged securities. They'll bring you in a better rate of interest than we can possibly afford to give you."

A troubled look settled on Mr. Foreman's distinguished face.

"I've never 'ad anything to do with stocks and shares and I'd 'ave to leave it all in your 'ands," he said.

The manager smiled.

"We'll do everything. All you'll have to do next time you come in is just to sign the transfers."

"I could do that all right," said Albert uncertainly. "But 'ow should I know what I was signin'?"

"I suppose you can read," said the manager a trifle sharply.

Mr. Foreman gave him a disarming smile.

"Well, sir, that's just it. I can't. I know it sounds funny like, but there it is! I can't read or write — only me name, an' I only learned to do that when I went into business."

The manager was so surprised that he jumped up from his chair.

"That's the most extraordinary thing I ever heard."

"You see, it's like this, sir — I never 'ad the opportunity until it was too late, and then some'ow I wouldn't. I got obstinate like."

The manager stared at him as though he were a prehistoric monster.

"And do you mean to say that you've built up this important business and amassed a fortune of thirty thousand pounds without being able to read or write? Good God, man, what would you be now if you had been able to?"

"I can tell you that, sir," said Mr. Foreman, a little smile on his still aristocratic features. "I'd be verger of St. Peter's, Neville Square."

READING THE SHORT STORY

What should we watch for in reading a short story? Most readers want to discover satisfactory answers to two questions: *Why* was this short story written? *How* does it achieve its effects? Let us try to answer these questions by examining Somerset Maugham's "The Verger."

THE PURPOSE OF THE STORY

Maugham's plot is simple: the caretaker of a church in London, forced to resign because he cannot read and write, makes a fortune of £ 30,000 by setting up tobacco shops.

What is the idea back of the story? Does it purport to show that lack of schooling helps in business? Is it an attack on the church and a defense of business, or is it the other way around? Is the story a tragedy because the verger must resign, or a comedy because he becomes successful? Is the author deliberately turning ordinarily accepted values upside down? To answer such questions we must go beyond the mere outline, or plot, of the story and look at its structure, its characters, its general mood.

STRUCTURE

More than half of " The Verger " is told in two scenes: one, the conversation of the principal character with the vicar and the two churchwardens; the other (much shorter), the talk between the principal character and the bank manager. Try dividing the story into the following sections: (1) *introduction* (what is introduced here?); (2) *transition,* conversation between verger and vicar as they walk into the vestry; (3) *big scene* (why is it the main scene?); (4) *transition,* verger leaving the church and walking across London; (5) *brief scene,* at tea with his wife; (6) *straight narrative,* the happenings of ten years condensed into a single paragraph; (7) *final scene.*

Now look back over the story and see how each transition is handled. If you were filming this story, how much time out of a total of thirty minutes would you give to each section of it? Why is Foreman's wife kept in the background? When do you get a flashback that tells of the verger's earlier life? When do you learn about his lifetime's savings as verger? About his smoking and drinking habits? How does each of these pieces of information fit into the *sequence of events* in the story?

CHARACTERS

There are several ways to suggest character; Maugham uses many of them here. Character may be revealed by *conversation* and *action.* Notice everything that Foreman says. Why does Maugham make Foreman talk to himself in a lower-class dialect? In how many places through the story does Maugham indicate what is going on in someone's mind by describing what they are doing? Here is one example: " Albert Edward's thin, sallow face reddened and

he moved uneasily on his feet, but he made no reply."

One of the hero's two principal actions is his decision *not* to meet the conditions imposed by his superiors. What is his other principal decision, and how do both decisions show his independence as well as his confidence in his own worth?

Character may be presented, of course, in *direct description.* Find as many short descriptions — phrases or words — as you can that build up your picture of Foreman. Can you find a single statement in the story which might serve to sum up Foreman's character? Finally, character may often be revealed by showing the *interaction between two persons.* What is the effect of the contrast between the verger and the bank manager? Watching the verger and the manager together, what conclusions can you draw about the extent to which they understand each other?

GENERAL MOOD

We have dug down deep enough into the story by now so that we can say definitely that the mood is comic, not tragic. The whole story is built up like a good joke; and like a good joke it ends with a quip which is at the same time inevitable and surprising. His comic spirit does not mean that Maugham is without a serious purpose. What is that purpose?

How does the story suggest these larger questions: Is there any necessary connection between learning and virtue? Can an education be used for harmful ends as well as for good? The topsy-turvy standards of this story make us look again at all our accepted beliefs. *Why* do we respect a vicar more than a verger, or for that matter, a bank president more than a janitor? Why should we respect our superiors in our work or social groups?

READING OTHER STORIES

No two stories, of course, are absolutely alike in purpose or approach. Each has its own center and its own emphasis. But if you ask the questions " Why was the story written? " and " How can I understand its purpose by looking closely at its structure, its characters, and its general tone or mood? " you will be well on the way to doubling your enjoyment of stories.

The Lagoon

JOSEPH CONRAD 1857–1924

Joseph Conrad was the pen name of a Polish youth who became one of the most remarkable figures in twentieth-century English literature. Until he was twenty-one, he could speak no English. He did not begin his writing career until he was thirty, yet he became one of England's great novelists. His real name was Teodor Józef Konrad Korzeniowski. He was born in the Ukraine, where his parents were political exiles, but was educated at Cracow, Poland, under the guidance of an uncle. He liked to read and was fortunate to find in his father's library translations of Shakespeare, Cervantes, Hugo, and other classics.

From early youth, Conrad yearned for a life at sea, and when he was seventeen he left home to become a sailor. Within a short time he was a seaman, mate, and then master of French and British merchant vessels. He said later that he picked up English from the sailors and from newspapers. Though he never studied grammar in his life, at twenty-three he passed an examination to show that he had " mastered " English. Joseph Conrad also wanted to *write* in English. While on shipboard he began his first novel, *Almayer's Folly*. Later, retiring from the Merchant Marine, he began to write steadily. He was constantly goaded by debt, the need to support his family, and a relentless desire to succeed.

The sea is never far away in a Conrad story. Like Herman Melville in American literature, Conrad is the great storyteller of the sea in English fiction. In novels (*Victory, Lord Jim,* and others), in long stories (*The Secret Sharer, Youth, Typhoon*), and in short stories like " The Lagoon," the sounds and moods of the sea run through his writing. But Conrad stories are not travelogues. Vigorously and with keen psychological insight, he is always probing into the hidden motives and problems of men. The grandeur of the sea and the mystery of tropic shores or shady riverbanks are backdrops for memorable character studies.

THE WHITE MAN, leaning with both arms over the roof of the little house in the stern of the boat, said to the steersman:

" We will pass the night in Arsat's clearing. It is late."

The Malay only grunted, and went on looking fixedly at the river. The white man rested his chin on his crossed arms and gazed at the wake of the boat. At the end of the straight avenue of forests cut by the intense glitter of the river, the sun appeared unclouded and dazzling, poised low over the water that shone smoothly like a band of metal. The forests, somber and dull, stood motionless and silent on each side of the broad stream. At the foot of big, towering trees, trunkless nipa palms rose from the mud of the bank, in bunches of leaves enormous and heavy, that hung unstirring over the brown swirl of eddies. In the stillness of the air every tree, every leaf, every bough, every tendril of creeper and every petal of minute blossoms seemed to have been bewitched into an immobility perfect and final. Nothing moved on the river but the eight paddles that rose flashing regularly, dipped together with a single splash, while the steersman swept right and left with a periodic and sudden flourish of his blade describing a glinting semicircle above his head. The churned-up water frothed alongside with a confused murmur. And the white man's canoe, advancing upstream in the short-lived disturbance of its own making, seemed to enter the portals of a land from which the very memory of motion had forever departed.

The white man, turning his back upon

the setting sun, looked along the empty and broad expanse of the sea reach. For the last three miles of its course the wandering, hesitating river, as if enticed irresistibly by the freedom of an open horizon, flows straight into the sea, flows straight to the east — to the east that harbors both light and darkness. Astern of the boat the repeated call of some bird, a cry discordant and feeble, skipped along over the smooth water and lost itself, before it could reach the other shore, in the breathless silence of the world.

The steersman dug his paddle into the stream, and held hard with stiffened arms, his body thrown forward. The water gurgled aloud; and suddenly the long straight reach seemed to pivot on its center, the forests swung in a semicircle, and the slanting beams of sunset touched the broadside of the canoe with a fiery glow, throwing the slender and distorted shadows of its crew upon the streaked glitter of the river. The white man turned to look ahead. The course of the boat had been altered at right angles to the stream, and the carved dragonhead on its prow was pointing now at a gap in the fringing bushes of the bank. It glided through, brushing the overhanging twigs, and disappeared from the river like some slim and amphibious creature leaving the water for its lair in the forests.

The narrow creek was like a ditch: tortuous, fabulously deep; filled with gloom under the thin strip of pure and shining blue of the heaven. Immense trees soared up, invisible behind the festooned draperies of creepers. Here and there, near the glistening blackness of the water, a twisted root of some tall tree showed among the tracery of small ferns, black and dull, writhing and motionless, like an arrested snake. The short words of the paddlers reverberated loudly between the thick and somber walls of vegetation. Darkness oozed out from between the trees, through the

The carved dragonhead on the prow of the boat was pointing at a gap in the fringing bushes of the bank.

tangled maze of the creepers, from behind the great fantastic and unstirring leaves; the darkness, mysterious and invincible; the darkness scented and poisonous of impenetrable forests.

The men poled in the shoaling water. The creek broadened, opening out into a wide sweep of a stagnant lagoon. The forests receded from the marshy bank, leaving a level strip of bright green, reedy grass to frame the reflected blueness of the sky. A fleecy pink cloud drifted high above, trailing the delicate coloring of its image under the floating leaves and the silvery blossoms of the lotus. A little house, perched on high piles, appeared black in the distance. Near it, two tall nibong palms, that seemed to have come out of the forests in the background, leaned slightly over the ragged roof, with a suggestion of sad tenderness and care in the droop of their leafy and soaring heads.

The steersman, pointing with his paddle, said, " Arsat is there. I see his canoe fast between the piles."

The polers ran along the sides of the boat glancing over their shoulders at the end of the day's journey. They would have preferred to spend the night somewhere else than on this lagoon of weird aspect and ghostly reputation. Moreover, they disliked Arsat, first as a stranger, and also because he who repairs a ruined house, and dwells in it, proclaims that he is not afraid to live amongst the spirits that haunt the places abandoned by mankind. Such a man can disturb the course of fate by glances or words; while his familiar ghosts are not easy to propitiate by casual wayfarers upon whom they long to wreak the malice of their human master. White men care not for such things, being unbelievers and in league with the Father of Evil, who leads them unharmed through the invisible dangers of this world. To the warnings of the righteous they oppose an offensive pretense of disbelief. What is there to be done?

So they thought, throwing their weight on the end of their long poles. The big canoe glided on swiftly, noiselessly, and smoothly, toward Arsat's clearing, till, in a great rattling of poles thrown down, and the loud murmurs of " Allah be praised! " it came with a gentle knock against the crooked piles below the house.

The boatmen with uplifted faces shouted discordantly, " Arsat! O Arsat! " Nobody came. The white man began to climb the rude ladder giving access to the bamboo platform before the house. The juragan [1] of the boat said sulkily, " We will cook in the sampan,[2] and sleep on the water."

" Pass my blankets and the basket," said the white man, curtly.

He knelt on the edge of the platform to receive the bundle. Then the boat shoved off, and the white man, standing up, confronted Arsat, who had come out through the low door of his hut. He was a man young, powerful, with broad chest and muscular arms. He had nothing on but his sarong.[3] His head was bare. His big, soft eyes stared eagerly at the white man, but his voice and demeanor were composed as he asked, without any words of greeting:

" Have you medicine, Tuan? " [4]

" No," said the visitor in a startled tone. " No. Why? Is there sickness in the house? "

" Enter and see," replied Arsat, in the same calm manner, and turning short round, passed again through the small doorway. The white man, dropping his bundles, followed.

In the dim light of the dwelling he made out on a couch of bamboos a woman stretched on her back under a broad sheet of red cotton cloth. She lay still, as if dead; but her big eyes, wide

[1] *juragan:* native leader or captain.

[2] *sampan:* flat-bottomed boat, used in river and harbor traffic.

[3] *sarong:* skirt or kilt worn by both sexes in the Malay Peninsula.

[4] *Tuan:* term of respect, like Sir, used by natives to white men.

" Will she die? " Arsat asked.

open, glittered in the gloom, staring upward at the slender rafters, motionless and unseeing. She was in a high fever, and evidently unconscious. Her cheeks were sunk slightly, her lips were partly open, and on the young face there was the ominous and fixed expression — the absorbed, contemplating expression of the unconscious who are going to die. The two men stood looking down at her in silence.

" Has she been long ill? " asked the traveler.

" I have not slept for five nights," answered the Malay, in a deliberate tone. " At first she heard voices calling her from the water and struggled against me who held her. But since the sun of today rose she hears nothing — she hears not me. She sees nothing. She sees not me — me! "

He remained silent for a minute, then asked softly:

" Tuan, will she die? "

" I fear so," said the white man, sorrowfully. He had known Arsat years ago, in a far country in times of trouble and danger, when no friendship is to be despised. And since his Malay friend had come unexpectedly to dwell in the hut on the lagoon with a strange woman, he had slept many times there, in his journeys up and down the river. He liked the man who knew how to keep faith in council and how to fight without fear by the side of his white friend. He liked him — not so much perhaps as a man likes his favorite dog — but still he liked him well enough to help and ask no questions, to think sometimes vaguely and hazily in the midst of his own pursuits, about the lonely man and the long-haired woman with audacious face and triumphant eyes, who lived together hidden by the forests — alone and feared.

The white man came out of the hut in time to see the enormous conflagration of sunset put out by the swift and stealthy shadows that, rising like a black and impalpable vapor above the tree-tops, spread over the heaven, extinguishing the crimson glow of floating clouds and the red brilliance of departing daylight. In a few moments all the stars came out above the intense blackness of the earth and the great lagoon gleaming suddenly with reflected lights resembled an oval patch of night sky flung down into the hopeless and abysmal night of the wilderness. The white man had some supper out of the basket, then collecting a few sticks that lay about the platform, made up a small fire, not for warmth, but for the sake of the smoke, which would keep off the mosquitoes. He wrapped himself in the blankets and sat with his back against the reed wall of the house, smoking thoughtfully.

Arsat came through the doorway with noiseless steps and squatted down by the fire. The white man moved his outstretched legs a little.

" She breathes," said Arsat in a low voice, anticipating the expected question. " She breathes and burns as if with a great fire. She speaks not; she hears not — and burns! "

He paused for a moment, then asked in a quiet, incurious tone:

" Tuan . . . will she die? "

The white man moved his shoulders uneasily and uttered in a hesitating manner:

" If such is her fate."

" No, Tuan," said Arsat, calmly. " If such is my fate. I hear, I see, I wait. I remember . . . Tuan, do you remember the old days? Do you remember my brother? "

" Yes," said the white man. The Malay rose suddenly and went in. The other, sitting still outside, could hear the voice in the hut. Arsat said: " Hear me! Speak! " His words were succeeded by a complete silence. " O Diamelen! " he cried, suddenly. After that cry there was a deep sigh. Arsat came out and sank down again in his old place.

They sat in silence before the fire. There was no sound within the house, there was no sound near them; but far away on the lagoon they could hear the voices of the boatmen ringing fitful and distinct on the calm water. The fire in the bow of the sampan shone faintly in the distance with a hazy red glow. Then it died out. The voices ceased. The land and the water slept invisible, unstirring, and mute. It was as though there had been nothing left in the world but the glitter of stars streaming, ceaseless and vain, through the black stillness of the night.

The white man gazed straight before him into the darkness with wide-open eyes. The fear and fascination, the inspiration and the wonder of death — of death near, unavoidable, and unseen, soothed the unrest of his race and stirred the most indistinct, the most intimate of his thoughts. The ever-ready suspicion of evil, the gnawing suspicion that lurks in our hearts, flowed out into the stillness round him — into the stillness profound and dumb, and made it appear untrustworthy and infamous, like the placid and impenetrable mask of an unjustifiable violence. In that fleeting and powerful disturbance of his being, the earth, enfolded in the starlight peace, became a shadowy country of inhuman strife, a battlefield of phantoms terrible and charming, august or ignoble, struggling ardently for the possession of our helpless hearts. An unquiet and mysterious country of inextinguishable desires and fears.

A plaintive murmur rose in the night; a murmur saddening and startling, as if the great solitudes of surrounding woods had tried to whisper into his ear the wisdom of their immense and lofty indifference. Sounds hesitating and vague floated in the air round him, shaped themselves slowly into words; and at last flowed on gently in a murmuring stream of soft and monotonous sentences. He stirred like a man waking up and changed his position slightly. Arsat, motionless and shadowy, sitting with bowed head under the stars, was speaking in a low and dreamy tone:

". . . for where can we lay down the heaviness of our trouble but in a friend's heart? A man must speak of war and of love. You, Tuan, know what war is, and you have seen me in time of danger seek death as other men seek life! A writing may be lost; a lie may be written; but what the eye has seen is truth and remains in the mind! "

" I remember," said the white man, quietly. Arsat went on with mournful composure:

" Therefore I shall speak to you of love. Speak in the night. Speak before both night and love are gone — and the eye of day looks upon my sorrow and my shame; upon my blackened face; upon my burnt-up heart."

A sigh, short and faint, marked an almost imperceptible pause, and then his words flowed on, without a stir, without a gesture.

" After the time of trouble and war was over and you went away from my country in the pursuit of your desires, which we, men of the islands, cannot understand, I and my brother became again, as we had been before, the sword-bearers of the Ruler. You know we were men of family, belonging to a ruling race, and more fit than any to carry on our right shoulder the emblem of power. And in the time of prosperity Si Dendring showed us favor, as we, in time of sorrow, had showed to him the faithfulness of our courage. It was a time of peace. A time of deer hunts and cock-fights; of idle talks and foolish squabbles between men whose bellies are full and weapons are rusty. But the sower watched the young rice shoots grow up without fear, and the traders came and went, departed lean and returned fat into the river of peace. They brought news, too. Brought lies and truth mixed together, so that no man knew when to rejoice and when to be sorry. We heard from them about you also. They had seen you here and had seen you there. And I was glad to hear, for I remembered the stirring times, and I always remembered you, Tuan, till the time came when my eyes could see nothing in the past, because they had looked upon the one who is dying there — in the house."

He stopped to exclaim in an intense whisper, " O Mara bahia! O Calamity! " then went on speaking a little louder:

" There's no worse enemy and no better friend than a brother, Tuan, for one brother knows another, and in perfect knowledge is strength for good or evil. I loved my brother. I went to him and told him that I could see nothing but one face, hear nothing but one voice. He told me: ' Open your heart so that she can see what is in it — and wait. Patience is wisdom. Inchi Midah may die or our Ruler may throw off his fear of a woman! ' . . . I waited — . . . You remember the lady with the veiled face, Tuan, and the fear of our Ruler before her cunning and temper. And if she wanted her servant, what could I do? But I fed the hunger of my heart on short glances and stealthy words. I loitered on the path to the bathhouses in the daytime, and when the sun had fallen behind the forest I crept along the jasmine hedges of the women's court-yard. Unseeing, we spoke to one another through the scent of flowers, through the veil of leaves, through the blades of long grass that stood still before our lips; so great was our prudence, so faint was the murmur of our great longing. The time passed swiftly . . . and there were whispers among women — and our enemies watched — my brother was gloomy, and I began to think of killing and of a fierce death. . . . We are of a people who take what they want — like you whites. There is a time when a man should forget loyalty and respect. Might and authority are given to rulers, but to all men is given love and strength and courage. My brother said, ' You shall take her from their midst. We are two who are like one.' And I answered, ' Let it be soon, for I find no warmth in sunlight that does not shine upon her.' Our time came when the Ruler and all the great people went to the mouth of the river to fish by torchlight. There were hundreds of boats, and on the white sand, between the water and the forests, dwellings of leaves were built for the households of the Rajahs. The smoke of cooking fires was like a blue mist of the evening, and many voices rang in it joyfully. While they were making the boats ready to beat up the fish, my brother came to me and said, ' Tonight! ' I looked to my weapons, and when the time came our canoe took its place in the circle of boats carrying the torches. The lights blazed on the water, but behind the boats there was darkness. When the shouting began and the excitement made them like mad we dropped out. The water swallowed our fire, and we floated back to the shore that was dark with only here and there the glimmer of embers. We could hear the talk of slave girls among the sheds. Then we found a place deserted and silent. We waited there. She came. She came running along the shore, rapid and leaving no trace, like a leaf driven by the wind into the sea. My brother said gloomily, ' Go and take her; carry her into our boat.' I lifted her in my arms. She panted. Her heart was beating against my breast. I said, ' I take you from those people. You came to the cry of my heart, but my arms take you into my boat against the will of the great! ' ' It is right,' said my brother. ' We are men who take what we want and can hold it against many. We should have taken her in daylight.' I said, ' Let us be off '; for since she was in my boat I began to think of our Ruler's many men. ' Yes. Let us be off,' said my brother. ' We are cast out and this boat is our country now — and the sea is our refuge.' He lingered with his foot on the shore, and I entreated him to hasten, for I remembered the strokes of her heart against my breast and thought that two men cannot withstand a hundred. We left, paddling downstream close to the bank; and as we passed by the creek where they were fishing, the great shouting had ceased, but the murmur of voices was loud like the humming of insects flying at noonday. The boats floated, clustered together, in the red light of torches, under a black roof of smoke; and men talked of their sport. Men that boasted, and praised, and jeered — men that would have been our friends in the morning, but on that night were already our enemies. We paddled swiftly past. We had no more friends in the country of our birth. She sat in the middle of the canoe with covered face; silent as she is now; unseeing as she is now — and I had no regret at what I was leaving because I could hear her breathing close to me — as I can hear her now."

He paused, listened with his ear turned to the doorway, then shook his head and went on:

" My brother wanted to shout the cry of challenge — one cry only — to let the people know we were freeborn robbers who trusted our arms and the great sea. And again I begged him in the name of our love to be silent. Could I not hear her breathing close to me? I knew the pursuit would come quick enough. My brother loved me. He dipped his paddle without a splash. He only said, ' There is a half a man in you now — the other half is in that woman. I can wait. When you are a whole man again, you will come back with me here to shout defiance. We are sons of the same mother.' I made no answer. All my strength and all my spirit were in my hands that held the paddle — for I longed to be with her in a safe place beyond the reach of men's anger and of women's spite. My love was so great, that I thought it could guide me to a country where death was unknown, if I could only escape from Inchi Midah's fury and from our Ruler's sword. We paddled with haste, breathing through our teeth. The blades bit deep into the smooth water. We passed out of the river; we flew in clear channels among the shallows. We skirted the black coast; we skirted the sand beaches where the sea speaks in whispers to the land; and the gleam of white sand flashed back past our boat, so swiftly she ran upon the water. We spoke not. Only once I said, ' Sleep, Diamelen, for soon you may want all your strength.' I heard the sweetness of her voice, but I never turned my head. The sun rose and still we went on. Water fell from my face like rain from a cloud. We flew in the light and heat. I never looked back, but I knew that my brother's eyes, behind me, were looking steadily ahead, for the boat went as straight as a bushman's dart, when it leaves the end of the sumpitan.[1] There was no better paddler, no better steersman than my brother. Many times, together, we had won races in that canoe. But we never had put out our strength as we did then — then, when for the last time we paddled together! There was no braver or stronger man in our country than my brother. I

---

[1] *sumpitan:* a kind of blowgun for discharging a dart, used by natives of Borneo and adjacent islands.

could not spare the strength to turn my head and look at him, but every moment I heard the hiss of his breath getting louder behind me. Still he did not speak. The sun was high. The heat clung to my back like a flame of fire. My ribs were ready to burst, but I could no longer get enough air into my chest. And then I felt I must cry out with my last breath, ' Let us rest! ' . . . ' Good! " he answered; and his voice was firm. He was strong. He was brave. He knew not fear and no fatigue. . . . My brother! "

A murmur powerful and gentle, a murmur vast and faint; the murmur of trembling leaves, of stirring boughs, ran through the tangled depths of the forests, ran over the starry smoothness of the lagoon, and the water between the piles lapped the slimy timber once with a sudden splash. A breath of warm air touched the two men's faces and passed on with a mournful sound — a breath loud and short like an uneasy sigh of the dreaming earth.

Arsat went on in an even, low voice.

" We ran our canoe on the white beach of a little bay close to a long tongue of land that seemed to bar our road; a long wooded cape going far into the sea. My brother knew that place. Beyond the cape a river has its entrance, and through the jungle of that land there is a narrow path. We made a fire and cooked rice. Then we lay down to sleep on the soft sand in the shade of our canoe, while she watched. No sooner had I closed my eyes than I heard her cry of alarm. We leaped up. The sun was halfway down the sky already, and coming in sight in the opening of the bay we saw a prau[1] manned by many paddlers. We knew it at once; it was one of our Rajah's praus. They were watching the shore, and saw us. They beat the gong, and turned the head of the prau into the bay. I felt my heart become weak within my breast. Diamelen sat on the sand and covered her face. There was no escape by sea.

[1] *prau:* swift Malayan vessel with sharp prow and stern, sailing equally well in either direction.

My brother laughed. He had the gun you had given him, Tuan, before you went away, but there was only a handful of powder. He spoke to me quickly: ' Run with her along the path. I shall keep them back, for they have no fire-arms, and landing in the face of a man with a gun is certain death for some. Run with her. On the other side of that wood there is a fisherman's house — and a canoe. When I have fired all the shots I will follow. I am a great runner, and before they can come up we shall be gone. I will hold out as long as I can, for she is but a woman — that can neither run nor fight, but she has your heart in her weak hands.' He dropped behind the canoe. The prau was coming. She and I ran, and as we rushed along the path I heard shots. My brother fired — once — twice — and the booming of the gong ceased. There was silence behind us. That neck of land is narrow. Before I heard my brother fire the third shot I saw the shelving shore, and I saw the water again; the mouth of a broad river. We crossed a grassy glade. We ran down to the water. I saw a low hut above the black mud, and a small canoe hauled up. I heard another shot behind me. I thought, ' That is his last charge.' We rushed down to the canoe; a man came running from the hut, but I leaped on him, and we rolled together in the mud. Then I got up, and he lay still at my feet. I don't know whether I had killed him or not. I and Diamelen pushed the canoe afloat. I heard yells behind me, and I saw my brother run across the glade. Many men were bounding after him. I took her in my arms and threw her into the boat, then leaped in myself. When I looked back I saw that my brother had fallen. He fell and was up again, but the men were closing round him. He shouted, ' I am coming! ' The men were close to him. I looked. Many men. Then I looked at her. Tuan, I pushed the canoe! I pushed it into deep water. She was kneeling forward looking at me, and I said, ' Take your pad-

" I heard yells behind me, then I pushed the canoe into deep water."

dle,' while I struck the water with mine. Tuan, I heard him cry. I heard him cry my name twice; and I heard voices shouting, ' Kill! Strike! ' I never turned back. I heard him calling my name again with a great shriek, as when life is going out together with the voice — and I never turned my head. My own name! . . . My brother! Three times he called — but I was not afraid of life. Was she not there in that canoe? And could I not with her find a country where death is forgotten — where death is unknown! "

The white man sat up. Arsat rose and stood, an indistinct and silent figure above the dying embers of the fire. Over the lagoon a mist drifting and low had crept, erasing slowly the glittering images of the stars. And now a great expanse of white vapor covered the land: it flowed cold and gray in the darkness, eddied in noiseless whirls round the tree trunks and about the platform of the house, which seemed to float upon a restless and impalpable illusion of a sea. Only far away the tops of the trees stood outlined on the twinkle of heaven, like a somber and forbidding shore — a coast deceptive, pitiless and black.

Arsat's voice vibrated loudly in the profound peace.

" I had her there! I had her! To get her I would have faced all mankind. But I had her — and — "

His words went out ringing into the empty distances. He paused, and seemed to listen to them dying away very far — beyond help and beyond recall. Then he said quietly:

" Tuan, I loved my brother."

A breath of wind made him shiver. High above his head, high above the silent sea of mist the drooping leaves of the palms rattled together with a mournful and expiring sound. The white man stretched his legs. His chin rested on his chest, and he murmured sadly without lifting his head:

" We all love our brothers."

Arsat burst out with an intense whispering violence —

" What did I care who died? I wanted peace in my own heart."

He seemed to hear a stir in the house — listened — then stepped in noiselessly. The white man stood up. A breeze was coming in fitful puffs. The stars shone paler as if they had retreated into the frozen depths of immense space. After a chill gust of wind there were a few seconds of perfect calm and absolute silence. Then from behind the black and wavy line of the forests a column of golden light shot up into the heavens and spread over the semicircle of the eastern horizon. The sun had risen. The mist lifted, broke into drifting patches, vanished into thin flying wreaths; and the unveiled lagoon lay, polished and black, in the heavy shadows at the foot of the wall of trees. A white eagle rose over it with a slanting and ponderous flight, reached the clear sunshine and appeared dazzlingly brilliant for a moment, then soaring higher, became a dark and motionless speck before it vanished into the blue as if it had left the earth forever. The white man, standing gazing upward before the doorway, heard in the hut a confused and broken murmur of distracted words ending with a loud groan. Suddenly Arsat stumbled out with outstretched hands, shivered, and stood still for some time with fixed eyes. Then he said:

" She burns no more."

Before his face the sun showed its edge above the treetops rising steadily. The breeze freshened; a great brilliance burst upon the lagoon, sparkled on the rippling water. The forests came out of the clear shadows of the morning, became distinct, as if they had rushed nearer — to stop short in a great stir of leaves, of nodding boughs, of swaying branches. In the merciless sunshine the whisper of unconscious life grew louder, speaking in an incomprehensible voice round the dumb darkness of that human sorrow. Arsat's eyes wandered slowly, then stared at the rising sun.

" I can see nothing," he said half aloud to himself.

" There is nothing," said the white man, moving to the edge of the platform and waving his hand to his boat. A shout came faintly over the lagoon and the sampan began to glide toward the abode of the friend of ghosts.

" If you want to come with me, I will wait all the morning," said the white man, looking away upon the water.

" No, Tuan," said Arsat, softly. " I shall not eat or sleep in this house, but I must first see my road. Now I can see nothing — see nothing! There is no light and no peace in the world; but there is death — death for many. We are sons of the same mother — and I left him in the midst of enemies; but I am going back now."

He drew a long breath and went on in a dreamy tone:

" In a little while I shall see clear enough to strike — to strike. But she has died, and . . . now . . . darkness."

He flung his arms wide open, let them fall along his body, then stood still with unmoved face and stony eyes, staring at the sun. The white man got down into his canoe. The polers ran smartly along the sides of the boat, looking over their shoulders at the beginning of a weary journey. High in the stern, his head muffled up in white rags, the juragan sat moody, letting his paddle trail in the water. The white man, leaning with both arms over the grass roof of the little cabin, looked at the shining ripple of the boat's wake. Before the sampan passed out of the lagoon into the creek he lifted his eyes. Arsat had not moved. He stood lonely in the searching sunshine; and he looked beyond the great light of a cloudless day into the darkness of a world of illusions.

A STORY POWERFUL AND EXOTIC

1. What specifically appeals to you in this story? Would you consider the main element of the story its plot, its characters, its setting, or its general mood? Try to analyze it in the manner in which " The Verger " was analyzed on pages 565–66.

2. Is Arsat a simple or complex character? How do the two men regard each other? What are Arsat's values or standards of behavior? What conflict does he face in the situation he describes? Discuss whether you agree with the decision he makes.

3. What does the story tell you about the primitive Malayans, their customs, beliefs, standards of conduct, and attitudes? What is Conrad's attitude toward the natives, as far as you can judge from the story?

4. As a point of departure in reading more Conrad, compare the description of the country around this lagoon with the settings in *Youth* and *Typhoon*. Or compare the portrayal of native character here with that in *The Nigger of the Narcissus*.

THE POWER OF WORDS

POETIC LANGUAGE

Conrad is one of the most poetic of modern short story writers. His descriptions of remote waters and forests are superb, not only in giving the reader clear pictures, but also in creating a mood that haunts the reader and wraps him in a magic spell. In the opening of " The Lagoon " Conrad wants us to feel a sense of awe caused by the deep silence and the beauty of the scene. Select words and passages that contribute to this effect. Look also for sections that describe water to discover how Conrad creates impressions of sounds and sights accurately, yet poetically. Make a list of metaphors that seem effective to you.

Acme

JOHN GALSWORTHY 1867–1933

The year before his death John Galsworthy was awarded the Nobel Prize for Literature. It was a well-deserved honor, for Galsworthy had been writing distinguished fiction and drama for a third of a century.

In his person, Galsworthy represented the best tradition of England — descent from a cultivated family of Surrey, education at Harrow and Oxford, and training in the law. Though he did not practice his profession, his legal turn of mind emerges in his writings. Concerned with the problems his characters must face, he is always the unbiased judge, not the prosecuting attorney. No other modern writer gives quite the same impression of sane and balanced judgment of his characters. He shows so clearly why people act as they do that the reader can scarcely condemn even the most unpleasant of them. His great social dramas suggest the nature of their conflicts by the titles: *Justice* — the irony of how the process of law wrecks the life of a weak character; *Strife* — the devastating results of capital-labor troubles; *Escape* — the emotional experiences of an escaped convict; *Loyalties* — the cross-purposes of allegiances when a crime is involved.

In the novel Galsworthy created the Forsyte family and followed their fortunes through several generations, beginning with the Victorians. Three of his novels were combined into *The Forsyte Saga*, one of the truly great works of our century. A later volume, *A Modern Comedy*, brings the younger Forsytes through World War I.

Galsworthy was always keenly aware of the tastes of his time. He was one of the first playwrights to use natural, colloquial speech in his plays rather than the stilted style prevalent in earlier drama. The little story "Acme," though in a lighter, more satirical vein than most of his work, shows that he maintained his interest in the theater right into the days when the movies were competing with serious drama.

IN THESE DAYS no man of genius need starve. The following story of my friend Bruce may be taken as proof of this assertion. Nearly sixty when I first knew him, he must have written already some fifteen books, which had earned him the reputation of " a genius " with the few who know. He used to live in York Street, Adelphi, where he had two rooms up the very shaky staircase of a house chiefly remarkable for the fact that its front door seemed always open. I suppose there never was a writer more indifferent to what people thought of him. He profoundly neglected the press — not with one of those neglects which grow on writers from reading reviews of their own works; he seemed never to read criticism — but with the basic neglect of " an original," a nomadic spirit, a stranger in modern civilization, who would leave his attic for long months of wandering and come back there to hibernate and write a book. He was a tall, thin man, with a face rather like Mark Twain's, black eyebrows which bristled and shot up, a bitten, drooping, gray mustache, and fuzzy gray hair; but his eyes were like owl's eyes, piercing, melancholy, dark brown, and gave to his rugged face the extraordinary expression of a spirit remote from the flesh which had captured it. He was a bachelor, who seemed to avoid women; perhaps they had taught him that, for he must have been very attractive to them.

The year of which I write had been to my friend Bruce the devil, monetarily speaking. With his passion for writing that for which his age had no taste — what could he expect? His last book had been a complete frost. He had undergone, too, an operation which had cost him much money and left him very weak. When I went to see him that October I found him stretched out on two chairs, smoking the Brazilian cigarettes which he affected — and which always affected me, so black and strong they were, in their yellow maize-leaf coverings. He had a writing pad on his knee, and sheets of paper scattered all around. The room had a very meager look. I had not seen him for a year and more, but he looked up at me as if I'd been in yesterday.

" Hello! " he said. " I went into a thing they call a cinema [1] last night. Have you ever been? "

" Ever been? Do you know how long the cinema has been going? Since about 1900."

" Well! What a *thing!* I'm writing a skit on it! "

" How — a skit? "

" Parody — wildest yarn you ever read."

He took up a sheet of paper and began chuckling to himself.

" My heroine," he said, " is an octoroon. Her eyes swim, and her lovely bosom heaves. Everybody wants her, and she's more virtuous than words can say. The situations she doesn't succumb to would freeze your blood; they'll roast your marrow. She has a perfect devil of a brother with whom she was brought up, and who knows her deep dark secret and wants to trade her off to a millionaire who also has a deep dark secret. All together, there are four deep dark secrets in my yarn. It's a corker."

" What a waste of your time! " I said.

" My time! " he answered fiercely. " What's the use of my time? Nobody buys my books."

" Who's attending you? "

" Doctors! They take your money, that's all. I've got no money. Don't talk

about me! " Again he took up a sheet of manuscript, and chuckled.

" Last night — at that place — they had — good heavens! — a race between a train and a motorcar. Well, I've got one between a train, a motorcar, a flying machine, and a horse."

I sat up.

" May I have a look at your skit," I said, " when you've finished it? "

" It *is* finished. Wrote it straight off. D'you think I could stop and then go on again with a thing like that? " He gathered the sheets and held them out to me. " Take the thing — it's amused me to do it. The heroine's secret is that she isn't an octoroon at all; she's a De La Casse — purest Creole [2] blood of the South; and her villainous brother isn't her brother; and the bad millionaire isn't a millionaire; and her penniless lover is. It's rich, I tell you! "

" Thanks," I said dryly, and took the sheets.

I went away concerned about my friend, his illness and his poverty, especially his poverty, for I saw no end to it.

After dinner that evening I began languidly to read his skit. I had not read two pages of the thirty-five before I started up, sat down again, and feverishly read on. Skit! By George! He had written a perfect scenario — or, rather,

[2] *Creole* (krē′ōl): a person of mixed Spanish and French descent, usually in the Southern states, particularly Louisiana, settled originally by those nationalities.

[1] *cinema* (sĭn′ē·má): British term for the moving picture house as well as the picture itself.

that which wanted the merest professional touching-up to be perfect. I was excited. It was a little gold mine if properly handled. Any good film company, I felt convinced, would catch at it. Yes! But how to handle it? Bruce was such an unaccountable creature, such a wild old bird. Imagine his having only just realized the cinema! If I told him his skit was a serious film, he would say: "Good heavens!" and put it in the fire, priceless though it was. And yet, how could I market it without *carte blanche,*[1] and how get *carte blanche* without giving my discovery away? I was deathly keen on getting some money for him; and this thing, properly

worked, might almost make him independent. I felt as if I had a priceless museum piece which a single stumble might shatter to fragments. The tone of his voice when he spoke of the cinema — "What a *thing!*" — kept coming back to me. He was prickly proud, too — very difficult about money. Could I work it without telling him anything? I knew he never looked at a newspaper. But should I be justified in taking advantage of that — in getting the thing accepted and produced without his knowing? I revolved the question for hours, and went to see him again next day.

[1] *carte blanche* (kärt' bläɴsh'): French expression for complete authority.

He was reading.

"Hello! You again? What do you think of this theory — that the Egyptians derive from a Saharan civilization?"

"I don't think," I said.

"It's nonsense. This fellow —"

I interrupted him.

"Do you want that skit back, or can I keep it?"

"Skit? What skit?"

"The thing you gave me yesterday."

"That! Light your fire with it. This fellow —"

"Yes," I said; "I'll light a fire with it. I see you're busy."

"Oh, no! I'm not," he said. "I've nothing to do. What's the good of my writing? I earn less and less with every book that comes out. I'm dying of poverty."

"That's because you won't consider the public."

"How can I consider the public when I don't know what they want?"

"Because you won't take the trouble to find out. If I suggested a way to you of pleasing the public and making money, you'd kick me out of the room."

And the words: "For instance, I've got a little gold mine of yours in my pocket," were on the tip of my tongue, but I choked them back. "Daren't risk it!" I thought. "He's given you the thing. *Carte blanche — cartes serrées!* "[1]

I took the gold mine away and promptly rough-shaped it for the film. It was perfectly easy, without any alteration of the story. Then I was faced with the temptation to put his name to it. The point was this: If I took it to a film company as an authorless scenario, I should get only authorless terms; whereas, if I put his name to it, with a little talking I could double the terms at least. The film public didn't know his name, of course, but the inner literary public did, and it's wonderful how you can impress the market with the word "genius" judiciously used. It was too dangerous, however; and at last I hit on a middle course. I would take it to them with no name attached, but tell them it was by "a genius" and suggest that they could make capital out of the incognito. I knew they would feel it *was* by a genius.

I took it to an excellent company next day with a covering note saying: "The author, a man of recognized literary genius, for certain reasons prefers to remain unknown." They took a fortnight in which to rise, but they rose. They had to. The thing was too good in itself. For a week I played them over terms. Twice I delivered an ultimatum — twice they surrendered; they knew too well what they had got. I could have made a contract with two thousand pounds down which would have brought at least another two thousand pounds before the contract term closed; but I compounded for one that gave me three thousand pounds down as likely to lead to less difficulty with Bruce. The terms were not a whit too good for what was really the "acme" of scenarios. If I could have been quite open I could certainly have done better. Finally, however, I signed the contract, delivered the manuscript, and received a check for the price. I was

elated, and at the same time knew that my troubles were just beginning. With Bruce's feeling about the film, how the deuce should I get him to take the money? Could I go to his publishers and conspire with them to trickle it out to him gradually as if it came from his books? That meant letting them into the secret; besides, he was too used to receiving practically nothing from his books; it would lead him to make inquiry, and the secret was bound to come out. Could I get a lawyer to spring an inheritance on him? That would mean no end of lying and elaboration, even if a lawyer would consent. Should I send him the money in Bank of England notes with the words: "From a lifelong admirer of your genius"? I was afraid he would suspect a trick, or stolen notes, and go to the police to trace them. Or should I just go, put the check on the table, and tell him the truth?

The question worried me terribly, for I didn't feel entitled to consult others who knew him. It was the sort of thing that, if talked over, would certainly leak out. It was not desirable, however, to delay cashing a big check like that. Besides, they had started on the production. It happened to be a slack time, with a dearth of good films, so that they were rushing it on. And in the meantime there was Bruce — starved of everything he wanted, unable to get away for want of money, depressed about his health and his future. And yet so completely had he always seemed to me different, strange, superior to this civilization of ours, that the idea of going to him and saying simply: "This is yours, for the film you wrote," scared me. I could hear his: "I? Write for the cinema? What do you mean?"

When I came to think of it, I had surely taken an extravagant liberty in marketing the thing without consulting him. I felt he would never forgive that, and my feeling toward him was so affectionate, even reverential, that I simply hated the idea of being wiped out of his

---

[1] *Carte blanche — cartes serrées:* French expression interpreted broadly to mean, "Since you are free to do as you wish in the matter, go ahead, do something about it."

good books. At last I hit on a way that by introducing my own interest might break my fall. I cashed the check, lodged the money at my bank, drew my own check on it for the full amount, and, armed with that and the contract, went to see him.

He was lying on two chairs smoking his Brazilians and playing with a stray cat which had attached itself to him. He seemed rather less prickly than usual, and, after beating about the bushes of his health and other matters, I began:

" I've got a confession to make, Bruce."

" Confession! " he said. " What confession? "

" You remember that skit on the film you wrote and gave me about six weeks ago? "

" No."

" Yes, you do — about an octoroon."
He chuckled. " Oh! ah! That! "

I took a deep breath, and went on:
" Well, I sold it; and the price of course belongs to you."

" What? Who'd print a thing like that? "

" It isn't printed. It's been made into a film — superfilm, they call it."

His hand came to a pause on the cat's back, and he glared at me. I hastened on:

" I ought to have told you what I was doing, but you're so prickly, and you've got such confounded superior notions. I thought if I did you'd be biting off your nose to spite your own face. The fact is it made a marvelous scenario. Here's the contract, and here's a check on my bank for the price — three thousand pounds. If you like to treat me as your agent, you owe me three hundred pounds. I don't expect it, but I'm not proud like you, and I shan't sneeze."

" Good heavens! " he said.

" Yes, I know. But it's all nonsense, Bruce. You can carry scruples to altogether too great length. Tainted source! Everything's tainted, if you come to that. The film's a quite justified expression of modern civilization — a natural outcome of the age. It gives amusement; it affords pleasure. It may be vulgar, it may be cheap, but we *are* vulgar, and we *are* cheap, and it's no use pretending we're not — not you, of course, Bruce, but people at large. A vulgar age wants vulgar amusement, and if we can give it that amusement we ought to; life's not too cheery, anyway."

The glare in his eyes was almost paralyzing me, but I managed to stammer on:

" You live out of the world — you don't realize what humdrum people want; something to balance the grayness, the — the banality of their lives. They want blood, thrill, sensation of all sorts. You didn't mean to give it them, but you have, you've done them a benefit, whether you wish to or not, and the money's yours and you've got to take it."

The cat suddenly jumped down. I waited for the storm to burst.

" I know," I dashed on, " that you hate and despise the film — "

Suddenly his voice boomed out:

" Bosh! What are you talking about? Film! I go there every other night."

It was my turn to say: " Good heavens! " And ramming contract and check into his empty hand, I bolted, closely followed by the cat.

A SERIOUS WRITER IN A LIGHT MOOD

1. From this story what do you gather as to Galsworthy's attitude toward the movies? What do you think of Bruce's scenario? Is the author lightly satirical or bitterly hostile toward the type of plot popular in the movies?

2. Where does the author come nearest to serious criticism of the public taste of his age? Do you agree with his opinion?

3. Where in the story do you find evidence of Galsworthy's legal mind?

4. Are you surprised at the outcome? Was the outcome prepared for in any way?

5. Galsworthy is an author you will want to know, and there is no better way than to start with his plays. *Strife* and *Justice* will make you see society in a new light.

THE POWER OF WORDS

SYNONYMS DISCRIMINATED

The word *acme* has a wealth of synonyms, all referring to the top or highest point. Some may be used for material high points, as the *summit* or *peak* of a mountain. *Acme,* however, cannot be so applied, for it relates to the highest point in values or ideas, always suggesting an approach to perfection. Likewise *climax* and *culmination* refer to top points in emotion, effort, or ambition. By appropriate phrases or sentences show how each of the following words may apply both to the physical world and to the realm of ideas: *pinnacle, apex, meridian, zenith, summit,* and *peak.* Why is *acme* the best word out of all these synonyms to serve as the title of Galsworthy's story?

The Garden Party

KATHERINE MANSFIELD 1888–1923

In spite of ill-health and a tragically short life, Katherine Mansfield wrote short stories that won her a secure place in modern English literature. Her real name was Kathleen Beauchamp; she was born of a wealthy family in Wellington, New Zealand. She attended Queen's College, London, as a young girl. Her urge to write was great, and on returning to New Zealand she was restless and unhappy. After many conflicts with her domineering father, she returned to London. At first she lived recklessly. Impetuously she married her music teacher and left him almost immediately. An attack of tuberculosis forced her to go to Germany to recuperate, and here she began to write stories. In England once again, she married the editor and critic J. Middleton Murry and began to be known as a literary reviewer and story writer. But appreciation of her work came too late for her to enjoy. She died at the age of thirty-five while living in France.

In some of her stories Katherine Mansfield illuminates the whole lifetime of a character in the flash of a single episode. She reveals people as they really are, and her sympathy extends to all kinds of characters. Charwomen or upper-class ladies, they are to her people with highly individual personalities. In the following story you will see young people and adults in a carefree mood enjoying a party, and then in a serious mood as they are touched by a nearby accident. You will find here much truth about people.

AND AFTER ALL the weather was ideal. They could not have had a more perfect day for a garden party if they had ordered it. Windless, warm, the sky without a cloud. Only the blue was veiled with a haze of light gold, as it is sometimes in early summer. The gardener had been up since dawn, mowing the lawns and sweeping them, until the grass and the dark flat rosettes, where the daisy plants had been, seemed to shine. As for the roses, you could not help feeling they understood that roses are the only flowers that impress people at garden parties; the only flowers that everybody is certain of knowing. Hundreds, yes, literally hundreds, had come out in a single night; the green bushes bowed down as though they had been visited by archangels.

Breakfast was not yet over before the men came to put up the marquee.[1]

"Where do you want the marquee put, Mother?"

"My dear child, it's no use asking me. I'm determined to leave everything to you children this year. Forget I am your mother. Treat me as an honored guest."

But Meg could not possibly go and supervise the men. She had washed her hair before breakfast, and she sat drinking her coffee in a green turban, with a dark wet curl stamped on each cheek. Jose, the butterfly, always came down in a silk petticoat and a kimono jacket.

"You'll have to go, Laura; you're the artistic one."

Away Laura flew, still holding her piece of bread-and-butter. It's so delicious to have an excuse for eating out of doors, and besides, she loved having to arrange things; she always felt she could do it so much better than anybody else.

Four men in their shirt sleeves stood grouped together on the garden path. They carried staves covered with rolls of canvas, and they had big tool bags slung on their backs. They looked impressive. Laura wished now that she had not got the bread-and-butter, but there was nowhere to put it, and she couldn't possibly throw it away. She blushed and tried to look severe and even a little bit short-sighted as she came up to them.

"Good morning," she said, copying her mother's voice. But that sounded so fearfully affected that she was ashamed, and stammered like a little girl. "Oh — er — have you come — is it about the marquee?"

"That's right, miss," said the tallest of the men, a lanky, freckled fellow, and he shifted his tool bag, knocked back his straw hat and smiled down at her. "That's about it."

His smile was so easy, so friendly that Laura recovered. What nice eyes he had, small, but such a dark blue! And now she looked at the others. They were smiling too. "Cheer up, we won't bite," their smile seemed to say. How very nice workmen were! And what a beautiful morning! She mustn't mention the morning; she must be businesslike. The marquee.

"Well, what about the lily lawn? Would that do?"

And she pointed to the lily lawn with the hand that didn't hold the bread-and-butter. They turned; they stared in the direction. A little fat chap thrust out his underlip, and the tall fellow frowned.

"I don't fancy it," said he. "Not conspicuous enough. You see, with a thing like a marquee," and he turned to Laura in his easy way, "you want to put it somewhere where it'll give you a bang slap in the eye, if you follow me."

Laura's upbringing made her wonder for a moment whether it was quite respectful of a workman to talk to her of bangs slap in the eye. But she did quite follow him.

"A corner of the tennis court," she suggested. "But the band's going to be in one corner."

---

[1] marquee (mär·kē'): a canopy or a tent without walls.

" That's the place, miss. Against those trees. That'll do fine."

"H'm, going to have a band, are you? " said another of the workmen. He was pale. He had a haggard look as his dark eyes scanned the tennis court. What was he thinking?

"Only a very small band," said Laura gently. Perhaps he wouldn't mind so much if the band was quite small. But the tall fellow interrupted.

"Look here, miss, that's the place. Against those trees. Over there. That'll do fine."

Against the karakas.[1] Then the karaka trees would be hidden. And they were so lovely, with their broad, gleaming leaves, and their clusters of yellow fruit. They were like trees you imagined growing on a desert island, proud, solitary, lifting their leaves and fruits to the sun in a kind of silent splendor. Must they be hidden by the marquee?

They must. Already the men had shouldered their staves and were mak-

[1] *karakas* (kä·rä′käz).

ing for the place. Only the tall fellow was left. He bent down, pinched a sprig of lavender, put his thumb and forefinger to his nose, and snuffed up the smell. When Laura saw that gesture she forgot all about the karakas in her wonder at him caring for things like that — caring for the smell of lavender. How many men that she knew would have done such a thing? Oh, how extraordinarily nice workmen were, she thought. Why couldn't she have workmen for friends rather than the silly boys she danced with and who came to Sunday night supper? She would get on much better with men like these.

It's all the fault, she decided, as the tall fellow drew something on the back of an envelope, something that was to be looped up or left to hang, of these absurd class distinctions. Well, for her part, she didn't feel them. Not a bit, not an atom. . . . And now there came the chock-chock of wooden hammers. Someone whistled, someone sang out, " Are you right there, matey? " " Matey! " The friendliness of it, the — the — Just to prove how happy she was, just to show the tall fellow how at home she felt, and how she despised stupid conventions, Laura took a big bite of her bread-and-butter as she stared at the little drawing. She felt just like a work-girl.

" Laura, Laura, where are you? Telephone, Laura! " a voice cried from the house.

" Coming! " Away she skimmed, over the lawn, up the path, up the steps, across the veranda, and into the porch. In the hall her father and Laurie were brushing their hats ready to go to the office.

" I say, Laura," said Laurie very fast, " you might just give a squiz at my coat before this afternoon. See if it wants pressing."

" I will," said she. Suddenly she couldn't stop herself. She ran at Laurie and gave him a small, quick squeeze. " Oh, I do love parties, don't you? " gasped Laura.

" Ra-ther," said Laurie's warm, boyish voice, and he squeezed his sister too, and gave her a gentle push. " Dash off to the telephone, old girl."

The telephone. " Yes, yes; oh yes. Kitty? Good morning dear. Come to lunch. Do, dear. Delighted, of course. It will only be a very scratch meal — just the sandwich crusts and broken meringue shells and what's left over. Yes, isn't it a perfect morning? Your white? Oh, I certainly should. One moment — hold the line. Mother's calling." And Laura sat back. " What, Mother? Can't hear."

Mrs. Sheridan's voice floated down the stairs. " Tell her to wear that sweet hat she had on last Sunday."

" Mother says you're to wear that *sweet* hat you had on last Sunday. Good. One o'clock. Bye-bye."

Laura put back the receiver, flung her arms over her head, took a deep breath, stretched and let them fall. " Huh," she sighed, and the moment after the sigh she sat up quickly. She was still listening. All the doors in the house seemed to be open. The house was alive with soft, quick steps and running voices. The green baize door that led to the kitchen regions swung open and shut with a muffled thud. And now there came a long, chuckling absurd sound. It was the heavy piano being moved on its stiff castors. But the air! If you stopped to notice, was the air always like this? Little faint winds were playing chase, in at the tops of the windows, out at the doors. And there were two tiny spots of sun, one on the inkpot, one on a silver photograph frame, playing too. Darling little spots. Especially the one on the inkpot lid. It was quite warm. A warm little silver star. She could have kissed it.

The front door bell pealed, and there sounded the rustle of Sadie's print skirt on the stairs. A man's voice murmured; Sadie answered, careless, " I'm sure I don't know. Wait. I'll ask Mrs. Sheridan."

" What is it, Sadie? " Laura came into the hall.

" It's the florist, Miss Laura."

It was, indeed. There, just inside the door, stood a wide, shallow tray full of pots of pink lilies. No other kind. Nothing but lilies — canna lilies, big pink flowers, wide open, radiant, almost frighteningly alive on bright crimson stems.

" O-oh, Sadie! " said Laura, and the sound was like a little moan. She crouched down as if to warm herself at that blaze of lilies; she felt they were in her fingers, on her lips, growing in her breast.

" It's some mistake," she said faintly. " Nobody ever ordered so many. Sadie, go and find mother."

But at that moment Mrs. Sheridan joined them.

" It's quite right," she said calmly. " Yes, I ordered them. Aren't they lovely? " She pressed Laura's arm. " I was passing the shop yesterday, and I saw them in the window. And I suddenly thought for once in my life I shall have enough canna lilies. The garden party will be a good excuse."

" But I thought you said you didn't mean to interfere," said Laura. Sadie had gone. The florist's man was still outside at his van. She put her arm around her mother's neck and gently, very gently, she bit her mother's ear.

" My darling child, you wouldn't like a logical mother, would you? Don't do that. Here's the man."

He carried more lilies still, another whole tray.

" Bank them up, just inside the door, on both sides of the porch, please," said Mrs. Sheridan. " Don't you agree, Laura? "

" Oh, I *do,* Mother."

In the drawing room Meg, Jose and good little Hans had at last succeeded in moving the piano.

" Now, if we put this chesterfield [1] against the wall and move everything out of the room except the chairs, don't you think? "

" Quite."

" Hans, move these tables into the smoking room, and bring a sweeper to take these marks off the carpet and — one moment, Hans — " Jose loved giving orders to the servants, and they loved obeying her. She always made them feel they were taking part in some drama. " Tell mother and Miss Laura to come here at once."

" Very good, Miss Jose."

She turned to Meg. " I want to hear what the piano sounds like, just in case I'm asked to sing this afternoon. Let's try over ' This Life Is Weary.' "

Pom! Ta-ta-ta *Tee*-ta! The piano burst out so passionately that Jose's face changed. She clasped her hands. She looked mournfully and enigmatically at her mother and Laura as they came in.

[1] *chesterfield:* a kind of overstuffed sofa.

This Life is *Wee*-ary,
A Tear — a Sigh.
A Love that *Chan*-ges,
    This Life is *Wee*-ary,
A Tear — a Sigh.
A Love that *Chan*-ges,
And then . . . Good-by!

But at the word " Good-by," and although the piano sounded more desperate than ever, her face broke into a brilliant, dreadfully unsympathetic smile.

" Aren't I in good voice, Mummy? " she beamed.

This Life is *Wee*-ary,
Hope comes to Die
A Dream — a *Wa*-kening.

But now Sadie interrupted them. " What is it, Sadie? "

" If you please, m'm, cook says have you got the flags for the sandwiches? "

" The flags for the sandwiches, Sadie? " echoed Mrs. Sheridan dreamily. And the children knew by her face that she hadn't got them. " Let me see." And she said to Sadie firmly, " Tell cook I'll let her have them in ten minutes."

Sadie went.

" Now, Laura," said her mother quickly. " Come with me into the smoking room. I've got the names somewhere on the back of an envelope. You'll have to write them out for me. Meg, go upstairs this minute and take that wet thing off your head. Jose, run and finish dressing this instant. Do you hear me, children, or shall I have to tell your father when he comes home tonight? And — and, Jose, pacify cook if you do go into the kitchen, will you? I'm terrified of her this morning."

The envelope was found at last behind the dining room clock, though how it had got there Mrs. Sheridan could not imagine.

" One of you children must have stolen it out of my bag, because I remember vividly — cream cheese and lemon curd. Have you done that? "

" Yes."

" Egg and — " Mrs. Sheridan held the envelope away from her. " It looks like mice. It can't be mice, can it? "

" Olive, pet," said Laura, looking over her shoulder.

" Yes, of course, olive. What a horrible combination it sounds. Egg and olive."

They were finished at last, and Laura took them off to the kitchen. She found Jose there pacifying the cook, who did not look at all terrifying.

" I have never seen such exquisite sandwiches," said Jose's rapturous voice. " How many kinds did you say there were, cook? Fifteen? "

" Fifteen, Miss Jose."

" Well, cook, I congratulate you."

Cook swept up crusts with the long sandwich knife, and smiled broadly.

" Godber's has come," announced Sadie, issuing out of the pantry. She had seen the man pass the window.

That meant the cream puffs had come. Godber's were famous for their cream puffs. Nobody ever thought of making them at home.

" Bring them in and put them on the table, my girl," ordered cook.

Sadie brought them in and went back to the door. Of course Laura and Jose were far too grown-up to really care about such things. All the same, they couldn't help agreeing that the puffs looked very attractive. Very. Cook began arranging them, shaking off the extra icing sugar.

" Don't they carry one back to all one's parties? " said Laura.

" I suppose they do," said practical Jose, who never liked to be carried back. " They look beautifully light and feathery, I must say."

" Have one each, my dears," said cook in her comfortable voice. " Yer ma won't know."

Oh, impossible. Fancy cream puffs so soon after breakfast. The very idea made one shudder. All the same, two minutes later Jose and Laura were licking their fingers with that absorbed inward look that only comes from whipped cream.

" Let's go into the garden, out by the back way," suggested Laura. " I want to see how the men are getting on with the marquee. They're such awfully nice men."

But the back door was blocked by cook, Sadie, Godber's man, and Hans.

Something had happened.

" Tuk-tuk-tuk," clucked cook like an agitated hen. Sadie had her hand clapped to her cheek as though she had toothache. Hans' face was screwed up in the effort to understand. Only Godber's man seemed to be enjoying himself; it was his story.

" What's the matter? What's happened? "

" There's been a horrible accident," said cook. " A man killed."

" A man killed! Where? How? When? "

But Godber's man wasn't going to have his story snatched from under his very nose.

" Know those little cottages just below here, miss? " Know them? Of course, she knew them. " Well, there's a young chap living there, name of Scott, a carter. His horse shied at a traction engine, corner of Hawke Street this morning, and he was thrown out on the back of his head. Killed."

" Dead! " Laura stared at Godber's man.

" Dead when they picked him up," said Godber's man with relish. " They were taking the body home as I came up here." And he said to the cook, " He's left a wife and five little ones."

" Jose, come here." Laura caught hold of her sister's sleeve and dragged her through the kitchen to the other side of the green baize door. There she paused and leaned against it. " Jose! " she said, horrified, " however are we going to stop everything? "

" Stop everything, Laura! " cried Jose in astonishment. " What do you mean? "

" Stop the garden party, of course."
Why did Jose pretend?

But Jose was still more amazed.
" Stop the garden party? My dear Laura,
don't be so absurd. Of course we can't
do anything of the kind. Nobody ex-
pects us to. Don't be so extravagant."

" But we can't possibly have a garden
party with a man dead just outside the
front gate."

That really was extravagant, for the
little cottages were in a lane to themselves at the very bottom of a steep rise
that led up to the house. A broad road
ran between. True, they were far too
near. They were the greatest possible
eyesore, and they had no right to be in
that neighborhood at all. They were little mean dwellings painted a chocolate
brown. In the garden patches there was
nothing but cabbage stalks, sick hens,
and tomato cans. The very smoke coming out of their chimneys was poverty-
stricken. Little rags and shreds of
smoke, so unlike the great silvery
plumes that uncurled from the Sheridans' chimneys. Washerwomen lived in
the lane and sweeps and a cobbler, and
a man whose house-front was studded
all over with minute bird cages. Children
swarmed. When the Sheridans were little they were forbidden to set foot there
because of the revolting language and
of what they might catch. But since they
were grown-up, Laura and Laurie on
their prowls sometimes walked through.
It was disgusting and sordid. They came
out with a shudder. But still one must
go everywhere; one must see everything.
So through they went.

" And just think of what the band
would sound like to that poor woman,"
said Laura.

" Oh, Laura! " Jose began to be seriously annoyed. " If you're going to stop
a band playing every time someone has
an accident, you'll lead a very strenuous
life. I'm every bit as sorry about it as
you. I feel just as sympathetic." Her
eyes hardened. She looked at her sister
just as she used to when they were little

and fighting together. " You won't bring
a drunken workman back to life by being sentimental," she said softly.

" Drunk! Who said he was drunk? "
Laura turned furiously on Jose. She
said, just as they had used to say on
those occasions, " I'm going straight up
to tell Mother."

" Do, dear," cooed Jose.

" Mother, can I come into your
room? " Laura turned the big glass
doorknob.

" Of course, child. Why, what's the
matter? What's given you such a color? "
And Mrs. Sheridan turned round from
her dressing table. She was trying on a
new hat.

" Mother, a man's been killed," began Laura.

" *Not* in the garden? " interrupted
her mother.

" No, no! "

" Oh, what a fright you gave me! "
Mrs. Sheridan sighed with relief, and
took off the big hat and held it on her
knees.

" But listen, Mother," said Laura.
Breathless, half choking, she told the
dreadful story. " Of course, we can't
have our party, can we? " she pleaded.
" The band and everybody arriving.
They'd hear us, Mother; they're nearly
neighbors! "

To Laura's astonishment her mother
behaved just like Jose; it was harder to
bear because she seemed amused. She
refused to take Laura seriously.

" But, my dear child, use your common sense. It's only by accident we've
heard of it. If someone had died there
normally — and I can't understand how
they keep alive in those poky little holes
— we should still be having our party,
shouldn't we? "

Laura had to say " yes " to that, but
she felt it was all wrong. She sat down
on her mother's sofa and pinched the
cushion frill.

" Mother, isn't it really terribly heartless of us? " she asked.

" Darling! " Mrs. Sheridan got up and

came over to her, carrying the hat. Before Laura could stop her she had popped it on. " My child! " said her mother, " the hat is yours. It's made for you. It's much too young for me. I have never seen you look such a picture. Look at yourself." And she held up her hand mirror.

" But, Mother," Laura began again. She couldn't look at herself; she turned aside.

This time Mrs. Sheridan lost patience just as Jose had done.

" You are being very absurd, Laura," she said coldly. " People like that don't expect sacrifices from us. And it's not very sympathetic to spoil everybody's enjoyment as you're doing now."

" I don't understand," said Laura, and she walked quickly out of the room into her own bedroom. There, quite by chance, the first thing she saw was this charming girl in the mirror, in her black hat trimmed with gold daisies, and a long black velvet ribbon. Never had she imagined she could look like that. Is Mother right? she thought. And now she hoped her mother was right. Am I being extravagant? Perhaps it was extravagant. Just for a moment she had another glimpse of that poor woman and those little children, and the body being carried into the house. But it all seemed blurred, unreal, like a picture in the newspaper. I'll remember it again after the party's over, she decided. And somehow that seemed quite the best plan. . . .

Lunch was over by half-past one. By half-past two they were all ready for the fray. The green-coated band had arrived and was established in a corner of the tennis court.

" My dear! " trilled Kitty Maitland, " aren't they too like frogs for words? You ought to have arranged them round the pond with the conductor in the middle on a leaf."

Laurie arrived and hailed them on his way to dress. At the sight of him Laura remembered the accident again. She wanted to tell him. If Laurie agreed with the others, then it was bound to be all right. And she followed him into the hall.

" Laurie! "

" Hallo! " He was halfway upstairs, but when he turned round and saw Laura he suddenly puffed out his cheeks and goggled his eyes at her. " My word, Laura! You do look stunning," said Laurie. " What an absolutely topping hat! "

Laura said faintly " Is it? " and smiled up at Laurie, and didn't tell him after all.

Soon after that people began coming in streams. The band struck up; the hired waiters ran from the house to the marquee. Wherever you looked there were couples strolling, bending to the flowers, greeting, moving on over the lawn. They were like bright birds that had alighted in the Sheridans' garden for this one afternoon, on their way to — where? Ah, what happiness it is to be with people who all are happy, to press hands, press cheeks, smile into eyes.

" Laura, how well you look! "

" What a becoming hat, child! "

" Laura, you look quite Spanish. I've never seen you look so striking."

And Laura, glowing, answered softly, " Have you had tea? Won't you have an ice? The passion-fruit ices really are rather special." She ran to her father and begged him. " Daddy darling, can't the band have something to drink? "

And the perfect afternoon slowly ripened, slowly faded, slowly its petals closed.

" Never a more delightful garden party . . ." " The greatest success. . . ." " Quite the most . . ."

Laura helped her mother with the good-bys. They stood side by side in the porch till it was all over.

" All over, all over, thank heaven," said Mrs. Sheridan. " Round up the others, Laura. Let's go and have some fresh coffee. I'm exhausted. Yes, it's been very successful. But oh, these parties, these parties! Why will you children insist on giving parties! " And they all of them sat in the deserted marquee.

" Have a sandwich, Daddy dear. I wrote the flag."

" Thanks." Mr. Sheridan took a bite and the sandwich was gone. He took another. " I suppose you didn't hear of a beastly accident that happened today? " he said.

" My dear," said Mrs. Sheridan, holding up her hand, " we did. It nearly ruined the party. Laura insisted we should put it off."

" Oh, Mother! " Laura didn't want to be teased about it.

" It was a horrible affair all the same," said Mr. Sheridan. " The chap was married, too. Lived just below in the lane, and leaves a wife and half a dozen kiddies, so they say."

An awkward little silence fell. Mrs. Sheridan fidgeted with her cup. Really, it was very tactless of father. . . .

Suddenly she looked up. There on the table were all those sandwiches, cakes, puffs, all uneaten, all going to be wasted. She had one of her brilliant ideas.

" I know," she said. " Let's make up a basket. Let's send that poor creature some of this perfectly good food. At any rate, it will be the greatest treat for the children. Don't you agree? And she's sure to have neighbors calling in and so on. What a point to have it all ready prepared. Laura! " She jumped up. " Get me the big basket out of the stairs cupboard."

" But, Mother, do you really think it's a good idea? " said Laura.

Again, how curious, she seemed to be different from them all. To take scraps from their party. Would the poor woman really like that?

" Of course! What's the matter with you today? An hour or two ago you were insisting on us being sympathetic, and now — "

Oh, well! Laura ran for the basket. It was filled, it was heaped by her mother.

" Take it yourself, darling," said she. " Run down just as you are. No, wait, take the arum lilies too. People of that class are so impressed by arum lilies."

" The stems will ruin her lace frock," said practical Jose.

So they would. Just in time. Only the basket, then. " And, Laura! " — her mother followed her out of the marquee — " don't on any account — "

" What, Mother? "

No, better not put such ideas into the child's head! " Nothing! Run along."

It was just growing dusky as Laura shut their garden gates. A big dog ran by like a shadow. The road gleamed white, and down below in the hollow the little cottages were in deep shade. How quiet it seemed after the afternoon. Here she was going down the hill to somewhere where a man lay dead, and she couldn't realize it. Why couldn't she? She stopped a minute. And it seemed to her that kisses, voices, tinkling spoons, laughter, the smell of crushed grass were somehow inside her. She had no room for anything else. How strange! She looked up at the pale sky, and all she thought was, " Yes, it was the most successful party."

Now the broad road was crossed. The lane began, smoky and dark. Women in shawls and men's tweed caps hurried by. Men hung over the palings; the children played in the doorways. A low hum came from the mean little cottages. In some of them there was a flicker of light, and a shadow, crablike, moved across the window. Laura bent her head and hurried on. She wished now she had put on a coat. How her frock shone! And the big hat with the velvet streamer — if only it was another hat! Were the people looking at her! They must be. It was a mistake to have come; she knew all along it was a mistake. Should she go back even now?

No, too late. This was the house. It must be. A dark knot of people stood outside. Beside the gate an old, old woman with a crutch sat in a chair,

"Step this way, please, miss," she said in an oily voice, and Laura followed her into the kitchen.

watching. She had her feet on a newspaper. The voices stopped as Laura drew near. The group parted. It was as though they had known she was coming here.

Laura was terribly nervous. Tossing the velvet ribbon over her shoulder, she said to a woman standing by, "Is this Mrs. Scott's house?" and the woman, smiling queerly said, "It is, my lass."

Oh, to be away from this! She actually said, "Help me, God!" as she walked up the tiny path and knocked. To be away from those staring eyes, or to be covered up in anything, one of those women's shawls, even. I'll just leave the basket and go, she decided. I shan't even wait for it to be emptied.

Then the door opened. A little woman in black showed in the gloom.

Laura said, "Are you Mrs. Scott?" But to her horror the woman answered, "Walk in please, miss," and she was shut in the passage.

"No," said Laura, "I don't want to come in. I only want to leave this bas-

ket. Mother sent — "

The little woman in the gloomy passage seemed not to have heard her. "Step this way, please, miss," she said in an oily voice, and Laura followed her.

She found herself in a wretched little low kitchen, lighted by a smoky lamp. There was a woman sitting before the fire.

"Em," said the little creature who had let her in. "Em! It's a young lady." She turned to Laura. She said meaningly, "I'm 'er sister, miss. You'll excuse 'er, won't you?"

"Oh, but of course!" said Laura. "Please, please don't disturb her. I — I only want to leave — "

But at that moment the woman at the fire turned around. Her face, puffed up, red, with swollen eyes and swollen lips, looked terrible. She seemed as though she couldn't understand why Laura was there. What did it mean? Why was this stranger standing in the kitchen with a basket? What was it all about? And the poor face puckered up again.

" All right, my dear," said the other. " I'll thenk the young lady."

And again she began, " You'll excuse her, miss, I'm sure," and her face, swollen too, tried an oily smile.

Laura only wanted to get out, to get away. She was back in the passage. The door opened. She walked straight through into the bedroom, where the dead man was lying.

" You'd like a look at 'im, wouldn't you? " said Em's sister, and she brushed past Laura over to the bed. " Don't be afraid, my lass, — " and now her voice sounded fond and sly, and fondly she drew down the sheet — " 'e looks a picture. There's nothing to show. Come along, my dear."

Laura came.

There lay a young man, fast asleep — sleeping so soundly, so deeply, that he was far, far away from them both. Oh, so remote, so peaceful. He was dreaming. Never wake him up again. His head was sunk in the pillow, his eyes were closed; they were blind under the closed eyelids. He was given up to his dream. What did garden parties and baskets and lace frocks matter to him? He was far from all those things. He was wonderful, beautiful. While they were laughing and while the band was playing, this marvel had come to the lane. Happy . . . happy . . . All is well, said that sleeping face. This is just as it should be. I am content.

But all the same you had to cry, and she couldn't go out of the room without saying something to him. Laura gave a loud childish sob.

" Forgive my hat," she said.

And this time she didn't wait for Em's sister. She found her way out of the door; down the path, past all those dark people. At the corner of the lane she met Laurie.

He stepped out of the shadow. " Is that you, Laura? "

" Yes."

" Mother was getting anxious. Was it all right? "

" Yes, quite. Oh, Laurie! " She took his arm, she pressed up against him.

" I say, you're not crying, are you? " asked her brother.

Laura shook her head. She was.

Laurie put his arm around her shoulder. " Don't cry," he said in his warm, loving voice. " Was it awful? "

" No," sobbed Laura. " It was simply marvelous. But, Laurie — " She stopped, she looked at her brother. " Isn't life," she stammered, " isn't life — " But what life was she couldn't explain. No matter. He quite understood.

" *Isn't it,* darling? " said Laurie.

A DELICATE, POIGNANT STORY

1. What is Laura's reaction to the workmen with the marquee? How does this prepare you for the rest of the story? Does Laura really supervise the workmen? Who was to take charge of the party? What is the significance of Mrs. Sheridan's ordering the lilies?

2. Katherine Mansfield is known for her ability to reveal character. Point out those incidents which you feel are the best in revealing the characters of Laura, Mrs. Sheridan, and Jose. How does each character react to the news of the accident? Do you think the author understands young people?

3. Describe Laura's feelings when she takes the food to Mrs. Scott. Do you think that she is changed by this experience? At the end of the story, what is she trying to express to Laurie? Can you put her feeling into words?

SUGGESTION FOR WRITING

Were you aware of the change in mood from lightheartedness to sadness in this story? Write of a personal incident in which you experienced a change in contrasting moods. You might use happiness and sorrow, love and hate, or anticipation and disappointment. Be sure to show what brought about the change in mood.

All Yankees Are Liars

ERIC KNIGHT 1897–1943

Few modern English authors have lived a more varied life than Eric Knight. He was a man of two cultures — an Anglo-American; for him, going across the Atlantic was almost like going across the street. Knight was born in Yorkshire, in the north of England, but he married an American and lived in this country intermittently. His experiences here and abroad provided a broad background for a writer of fiction: art student in New York, factory worker in Manchester, screen writer in Hollywood, critic for the Philadelphia *Ledger,* major in the United States Army, soldier in a Canadian regiment in World War I. During World War II he was killed in an airplane crash.

Eric Knight's stories reflect his sympathetic understanding of the lives of ordinary people. His *Song on Your Bugles* and his last novel, *This Above All,* are moving stories about the common workers of England; and *The Flying Yorkshireman,* while a delightful fantasy, is also a shrewd appraisal of the foibles and strengths of his countrymen. The following story illustrates Knight's ability to weave " local color " into fiction. Its setting is his native Yorkshire, the characters are village folk, and their dialect and mannerisms are those with which the author was fondly familiar. But the influence of America is also apparent in the story. Knight knew America, and he proves in humorous fashion that " all Yankees are liars."

> *You can always tell the Irish,*
> *You can always tell the Dutch.*
> *You can always tell a Yankee;*
> *But you cannot tell him much.*

MR. SMITH was pleased with The Spread Eagle. He was pleased with Polkingthorpe Brig. The village was off the beaten track — the truly rural sort of English village the American always wants to see.

The inn was low and rambling, with great sloping roofs. Over the door swung the sign — a darksome bird in a weatherbeaten setting.

Everything justified his decision to take this bicycle trip up into the north — the mullioned [1] windows, the roaring fire, the Yorkshire accents of the men who shuffled over the sanded stone floor of the low-ceilinged room as they played darts. Mr. Smith was almost beginning to understand what they were talking about. During his excellent high tea he had sorted out the four men playing darts. One was Saw Cooper, a farmer; a small old man was referred to as Sam; a young, bright-faced lad who played darts left-handed was Gollicker Pearson; and the fourth, a huge man, was just called Ian.

Mr. Smith watched them play, listening to the endless thwock of the darts in the cork board as he finished his meal. The barmaid, plump, corn-haired, came toward him, her apron rustling stiffly.

" Would there be owt else? "

" No. It was a very good meal." Mr. Smith smiled. He wanted to make the girl talk some more. " Er — what do they do for fun in this place of an evening? "

" Foon? " she repeated. " Well, they sit here — or o' Sat'day neights lots o' fowk goa ovver to Wuxley to t' pictures." She waited. " They gate Boock D'Arcy i' T' Singing Cowboy," she added suggestively.

Mr. Smith had already become acquainted with British cinemas in small towns. Also, he was a Southern Californian, and had that familiarity with

---

[1] *mullioned* (mŭl'yŭnd): windows whose panes are divided by slender vertical bars.

movies that belongs to all Southern Californians. He had no inclination to go four miles to see a last year's Class B Western. " No. I think I'll have another ale and sit here," he said.

" If tha'll sit ovver by t' fire, Ah'll bring it to thee theer. Then Ah can clean oop here."

Mr. Smith sat on the bench by the generous fire and nursed his ale. The dart game came to an end with Saw Cooper losing and paying for the round. The men brought their mugs to the fire. Mr. Smith shifted politely. The men, in the presence of a stranger, grew quiet. Mr. Smith decided to put them at ease.

" Pretty chilly for an October evening, isn't it? "

The men considered the remark, as if looking at both sides of it. Finally Saw Cooper spoke.

" Aye," he said.

The others nodded. There was silence, and the five regarded the fire. Then, suddenly, young Gollicker smiled.

" Tha shouldn't heed t' cowd, being a Yankee," he said.

" Ah, but I'm not a Yankee," Mr. Smith said.

They stared at him in disbelief.

" Yankees," explained Mr. Smith, " come from New England."

They looked from Mr. Smith to one another. The big man named Ian took a deep breath.

" Yankees," he said, " coom fro' t' United States."

" Well, yes. New England is a part of the United States," Mr. Smith said. " But it's thousands of miles away from where I live. In fact, believe it or not, I should think you're closer to the Yankees than I am. You see, the United States is a big country. In the part where the Yankees come from, it gets very cold in the winter. Where I am — in Southern California — it never snows. Why, I've never known it to snow there in all my life."

" No snow? " Gollicker breathed.

Mr. Smith smiled. For, after all, he was a Southern Californian — and they were discussing climate. " No snow," he said. " In wintertime we have a bit of a rainy season, but after February it clears, and then it doesn't even rain for nine months — not a drop."

" Noa rain for a nine month — noan at all? " Saw Cooper asked.

" Not a drop. Day after day, the sun comes out, clear skies, never a drop of rain for nine months. Never! "

" Whet do ye graw theer, lad? " Saw asked slyly.

" Lots of things. Truck vegetables, oranges — all kinds of things."

There was a silence again. Big Ian took a breath.

" Orinjis," he said, and then took another breath, " graw i' Spain."

He looked at Mr. Smith so emphatically that Mr. Smith nodded.

" Oh, yes," he said. " They grow in Spain, too, I understand."

" Orinjis," Ian repeated, " graw i' Spain."

That seemed to settle the question. They all looked in the fire in silence. Saw Cooper sniffed.

" Whet else graws theer? "

" Well, I have a ranch there; we grow alfalfa."

" Whet's that off to be? "

" Alfalfa? We use it for hay. It's a desert plant originally, but it thrives in California. We get eight cuttings a year."

" Eight cuttings o' hay a year? "

" Eight cuttings a year."

The little man, Sam, spoke for the first time: " Mister, if it doan't rain for a nine month, how can ye get eight cuttings o' hay a year? "

" Oh, that's easy," Mr. Smith said. " We irrigate the land." He went into a short but conclusive description of irrigating.

" Heh," Saw Cooper said. " Wheer's this here watter coom fro'? "

" In the San Fernando Valley we buy it from the water company, just like you do in your homes."

" Wheer do they get it? "

" From reservoirs."

" If it doan't rain, where's t' reservoys get t' watter? "

" Oh, we pipe it down from five hundred miles north. It rains a lot up there."

" And ye sprinkle t' farming land out o' t' watter tap. How mony acres hesta? "

" It isn't like sprinkling from the tap, of course. I used that to illustrate. The pipes are large — we have fourteen-inch valves on our pipes. We flood the land — cover it right over with water."

Saw looked in the fire. " Does corn graw theer? "

" Well, generally our land is too valuable to put into corn. But it will grow corn fourteen feet high."

They made noises in their throats and shifted their feet.

" Fohteen foot," Saw breathed. " Eigh, ba gum! "

" Mister," Sam said, " once Ah were oop to see t' Firth o' Forth brig. Ah suppose they hev bigger brigs i' Yankee-land? "

Mr. Smith should have touched on the new Oakland bridge, but then, he was a *Southern* Californian.

" We have bridges, but they're building vehicular tunnels under the rivers now."

" Whet for? "

" Well, there's so much motor traffic."

" How mony moatorcars goa through 'em? "

Mr. Smith lit his pipe happily. They seemed quite interested in America.

" I couldn't say. The way they turn 'em out, I should say there's hundreds of thousands."

" How fast do they turn 'em out? " Gollicker asked.

" I don't know. I think they roll out finished at the rate of one every couple of minutes."

" And they goa i' tunnels, not i' brigs? " Sam commented.

" Oh, we have some bridges."

" Big uns, Ah suppose."

" Well," Mr. Smith said modestly, thinking of the Pulaski Skyway coming into New York, " we have some that go right over entire towns. You're practically on one bridge for miles."

Saw Cooper spat in the fire. " How mony fowk is there in all America? "

Mr. Smith didn't know, but he felt expansive. And after all, there was South America, too.

" A quarter of a billion, I should say," he hazarded.

" A quarter of a billion," they repeated. Then they stared at Mr. Smith,

" We have some bridges," Mr. Smith said modestly, " that go right over entire towns."

and he became aware of their disbelief.

"Wait a moment," he said. "I think a billion is different in America from here. It's a thousand million in America and a million million here, isn't it?"

"A billion," said Ian slowly, "is a billion."

The others nodded, and then Ian stood. The others rose, too.

"Oh — er — wait a minute. Won't you all have a drink with me?" Mr. Smith invited.

"Us is off to play darts for a round — us four," Ian said meaningly.

The other three laughed.

"Ah knew them theer brigs o' thine'd hev to be big," Saw Cooper said as a parting shot as he swung over the bench. "That's so's they'd be able to goa ovver wheat what graws fohteen foot high when ye sprinkle it fro' t' watter tap."

He grinned at the others in victory.

"I didn't say wheat; I said corn," Mr. Smith protested.

"Same thing," Saw snapped.

"It isn't. Wheat grows in an ear. Corn grows on a cob; it has broad long leaves."

"Heh! That's maize," Saw said.

Big Ian stepped between Saw Cooper and Mr. Smith.

"Now, lad," he said flatly, "tha said corn, and Ah heeard thee. Thee and thy orinjis, and farming out o' t' watter tap, and brigs ovver cities, and it nivver rains, and denying th' art a Yankee, and a billion is a billion and yet it ain't. Tha's tripped thysen oop a dozen times, it seems to me. Now, hesta owt to say?"

Mr. Smith looked at Big Ian, standing belligerently with legs widespread and his thumbs in the waistband of his corduroy trousers. He looked round and saw everyone in the inn waiting, silent.

Then a curious thing happened. In that minute the smell of soft-coal smoke and pig-twist tobacco and ale was gone, and instead Mr. Smith was smelling the mixed odor of sun-baked land and citrus blossom and jasmine and eucalyptus trees, just as you smell it in the cool darkness coming across the San Fernando Valley. And he was homesick. Suddenly it felt unreal that he should be so far from home, sitting in an English inn with these men about him. He looked up at the faces, forbidding in their expression of disapproval. And he began to laugh.

It was all so unreal that he laughed until he cried. Every time he looked up he saw the faces, now even more comical in their bewilderment than they had been in their disapproval. They stared at him, and then Big Ian began to laugh.

"Eigh, Ah'll be jiggered!" he roared. "Drat ma buttons if Ah won't!"

It was Mr. Smith's turn to be puzzled now.

Big Ian roared, and suddenly slapped Mr. Smith on the back so heartily that his chin flew up in the air and then banged back on his chest. The others looked on in amazement.

"Why, whet's oop, Ian?" Saw asked.

"Why, ye gowks!" Ian roared. "He's laughing at ye! He's been heving us on! Sitting theer for an hour, keeping his mug straight and telling us the tale! And us swallering it, thinking he was serious!"

"But," Mr. Smith said — "but you don't ———"

"Nay, now no moar on it!" Ian roared. "Ye've codded us for fair, and done it champion! Lewk at owd Sam's face!"

The others regarded Ian and scratched their heads and grinned sheepishly, and finally looked at Mr. Smith in admiration.

"But — " Mr. Smith began again.

"Nay, now, ye copped us napping," Ian said, "and here's ma hand on it. Soa we'll hev noa moar — onless ye'd like to tell us whet Yankeeland's rightly like."

Mr. Smith drew a deep breath. "Well, what would you like to hear about?"

"About cowboys," young Gollicker breathed. "Werta ivver a cowboy?"

For a moment Mr. Smith stood on a

brink, and then an imp pushed him over.

"Of course I've been a cowboy — naturally," Mr. Smith said. "What would you like to hear about it?"

"Wait a minute," Gollicker said. They all adjusted themselves on the bench. "Now," he went on, "tell us about a roundup — tha knaws, 'Ah'm yeading for t' last roundup,' like Bing Crosby sings."

Mr. Smith held his mental breath and plunged.

"Ah," he said. "A roundup and the life of a cowboy. Up at the crack of dawn, mates, and down to the corral. There you rope your horse —— "

"A mustang?" Gollicker asked.

"A mustang," Mr. Smith agreed.

"A wild one off'n the prairies, happen?"

"Indeed a wild one from off the prairies," Mr. Smith agreed. "I see you know America yourself."

Gollicker grinned modestly. "Doan't let me interrupt, measter," he apologized.

Mr. Smith drew another breath. He saw he was up against at least one expert, so he made it very good. Inwardly he thanked fate for what he had hitherto regarded as two entirely misspent weeks on a Nevada dude ranch. He gave them, in more senses than one, a moving picture of the cowboy's life.

When he was done, Gollicker sighed and Big Ian nodded.

"Now," Sam said, "how about them bloody buffalo?"

"Ah, the buffalo," Mr. Smith said. "The thundering herd! The bison! For a while there was danger — or thought to be — that the herds were dying out. But now, I am glad to say — and no doubt you are just as glad to hear — the herds are increasing, and ere long, again the crack of a rifle will bring down a bull in full gallop."

"But how about them bloody Indians?" Saw put in.

Mr. Smith considered the Indians at the station in Santa Fe. They didn't seem at all satisfactory. But he was inspired. He drew himself up.

"You will pardon me if I do not speak of that," he said. "We have not too much love for the paleface who stole our lands. I say 'we,' for my mother was Yellow Blanket, a princess of the Blackfoot tribe. Therefore, let us not speak of the white man and the red man."

He stared into the fire — majestically, he hoped.

"Now, see what tha's done?" Ian said to Saw. "Happen it'll learn thee to keep thy yapper shut once in a while. . . . Tha maun excuse him, measter. Tell us about gangsters instead. Didta ivver run into any gangsters?"

"Run into them? Why, how could you help it?" Mr. Smith asked.

Swiftly and graphically he painted for them an America in which here was the town where the bullets of the gangs cracked day and night. Here was the last street, and on it the last house, and beyond that was the trackless prairie where the buffalo thundered, the cowboy rode and the Indian ever lurked.

As he finished, he looked up. Everyone in the inn was listening. Men had gathered behind him silently. At the bar, the maid leaned on her elbows, entranced.

"Ah, I talk too much," Mr. Smith said.

"Nay, goa on, lad," they said. "Goa on."

"Well, it's dry work. How about a drink?"

"Champion," said Saw.

"Owd on," Big Ian said. "Us'll play darts for a round."

"Now, Ian, if the lad wants to buy —— "

"Ah said," Ian repeated, "us'll play darts — onybody that wishes to be in on t' round. And t' loser will pay."

Mr. Smith paid anyhow, for the dart game was trickier than he had thought, and they all seemed to be experts.

He was getting very much better when the barmaid called: " Time, gentlemen, please."

Mr. Smith was sorry. It had been a good evening. They all said good night cheerfully. Big Ian shook him by the hand.

" Well, soa long, lad. We had a champion time. But Ah just want to say, tha didn't fool me when tha were kidding us at first. Tha sees, for one thing, us goas to t' pictures and so us knaws whet America's really like. And then Ah'd allus heeard tell that all Yankees were liars."

" Yes," Mr. Smith said, regarding his conscience, " I did tell some lies."

" Aye, but Ah suppose it's a way ye Yankees hev," Ian said. " But it's all right as long as tha told us t' trewth finally."

YANKEES AND YORKSHIREMEN

1. How does the four-line jingle at the beginning fit the story? What does the name " Yankee " mean as Mr. Smith uses it? How do the Yorkshiremen use the term?

2. What is the central idea of the story? When do the Yorkshiremen begin to disbelieve Mr. Smith? How does Mr. Smith finally win their favor? In what ways do the Yorkshiremen remind you of people in general?

3. In what part of England is Yorkshire? This story is full of what is usually called " local color " — descriptions of setting and characters, and use of dialect that build up an impression of a particular place. Find several examples of local color.

4. How would you describe Eric Knight's humor? Select passages that particularly amused you. How do the characters contribute to the humor?

The Majesty of the Law

FRANK O'CONNOR 1903–

Frank O'Connor, whose nonliterary name is Michael O'Donovan, took an active part in the long Civil War in Ireland. Although he had little formal schooling, he has become a scholar, critic, linguist, and one of the best-known Irish writers. His Ireland is the Ireland of the small shopkeeper, the teacher, and the clerk, against the background of the Irish Catholic Church.

Today he spends much of his time revising and selecting those stories for which he wants to be remembered. He has published several collections; in 1954 *More Stories,* a selection of twenty-nine short tales, appeared. He has written a great many stories, and they are surprisingly varied and original. They follow no single pattern, and seem almost to tell themselves. Most of his tales have a moral or a theme that the reader recognizes as the author's purpose in writing — but O'Connor seems always to make his point indirectly.

OLD DAN BRIDE was breaking brosna [1] for the fire when he heard a step up the path. He paused, a bundle of saplings on his knee.

Dan had looked after his mother while the spark of life was in her, and after her death no other woman had crossed the threshold. Signs on it, his house had that look. Almost everything in it he had made with his own hands in his own way. The seats of the chairs were only slices of log, rough and round and thick as the saw had left them, and with the rings still plainly visible through the grime and polish that coarse trouser bottoms had in the course of long years imparted. Into these Dan had rammed stout knotted-ash boughs, which served alike for legs and back. The deal table,

[1] *brosna:* a bundle of twigs.

bought in a shop, was an inheritance from his mother, and a great pride and joy to him, though it rocked forward and back whenever he touched it. On the wall, unglazed and fly spotted, hung in mysterious isolation a Marcus Stone [1] print, and beside the door was a calendar representing a race horse. Over the door hung a gun, old but good and in excellent condition, and before the fire was stretched an old setter who raised his head expectantly whenever Dan rose or even stirred.

He raised it now as the steps came nearer, and when Dan, laying down the bundle of saplings, cleaned his hands thoughtfully on the seat of his trousers, he gave a loud bark, but this expressed no more than a desire to display his own watchfulness. He was half human and knew that people thought he was old and past his prime.

A man's shadow fell across the oblong of dusty light thrown over the half door before Dan looked round.

"Are you alone, Dan?" asked an apologetic voice.

"Oh, come in, come in, sergeant, come in and welcome," exclaimed the old man, hurrying on rather uncertain feet to the door, which the tall policeman opened and pushed in. He stood there, half in sunlight, half in shadow, and seeing him so, you would have realized how dark was the interior of Dan's house. One side of his red face was turned so as to catch the light, and behind it an ash tree raised its boughs of airy green against the sky. Green fields, broken here and there by clumps of red-brown rock, flowed downhill, and beyond them, stretched all across the horizon, was the sea, flooded and almost transparent with light. The sergeant's face was fat and fresh, the old man's face, emerging from the twilight of the kitchen, had the color of wind and sun, while the features had been so shaped

by the struggle with time and the elements that they might as easily have been found impressed upon the surface of a rock.

"Begor, Dan," said the sergeant, "'tis younger you're getting."

"Middling I am, sergeant, middling," agreed the old man in a voice which seemed to accept the remark as a compliment of which politeness would not allow him to take too much advantage. "No complaints."

"Faith, and 'tis as well. No wan but a born idiot would believe them. And th' ould dog don't look a day older."

The dog gave a low growl as though to show the sergeant that he would remember this unmannerly reference to his age, but indeed he growled every time he was mentioned, under the impression that people could have nothing but ill to say of him.

"And how's yourself, sergeant?"

"Well, now, like that in the story, Dan, neither on the pig's back or at the horse's tail. We have our own little worries, but, thanks be to God, we have our compensations."

"And the wife and care?"

"Good, glory and praise be to God, good. They were away from me with a month, the lot of them, at the mother-in-law's place in Clare." [2]

"Ah, do you tell me so?"

"I had a fine, quiet time."

The old man looked about him, and then retired to the nearby bedroom from which he emerged a moment later with an old shirt. With this he solemnly wiped the seat and back of the log chair nearest the fire.

"Take your ease, now, take your ease. 'Tis tired you must be after the journey. How did you come?"

"Teigue Leary it was that gave me a lift. Wisha, now Dan, don't you be putting yourself about. I won't be stopping. I promised them I'd be back inside an hour."

"What hurry is on you?" asked the

[1] *Marcus Stone* (1840–1921): an English painter whose sentimental scenes were widely known through engravings.

[2] *Clare:* a county in Ireland.

old man. " Look now, your foot was on the path when I rose from putting kindling on the fire."

" Now! Now! You're not making tea for me."

" I am not then, but for myself, and very bad I'll take it if you won't join me."

" Dan, Dan, that I mightn't stir, but 'tisn't an hour since I had a cup at the barracks."

" Ah, *Dhe,* whisht, now! Whisht, will you! I have something that'll put an appetite on you."

The old man swung the heavy kettle on to the chain over the open fire, and the dog sat up, shaking his ears with an expression of the deepest interest. The policeman unbuttoned his tunic, opened his belt, took a pipe and a plug of tobacco from his breast pocket, and, crossing his legs in easy posture, began to cut the tobacco slowly and carefully with his pocketknife. The old man went to the dresser, and took down two handsomely decorated cups, the only cups he had, which, though chipped and handleless, were used at all only on very rare occasions: for himself, he preferred tea from a basin. Happening to glance into them, he noticed that they bore the trace of disuse and had collected a substantial share of the fine white dust which was constantly circulating within the little smoky cottage. Again he thought of the shirt, and, rolling up his sleeves with a stately gesture, he wiped them inside and out till they shone. Then he bent and opened the cupboard. Inside was a quart bottle of pale liquid, obviously untouched. He removed the cork and smelled the contents, pausing for a moment in the act as though to recollect where exactly he had noticed that particular smoky odor before. Then, reassured, he rose and poured out with a liberal hand.

" Try that now, sergeant," he said.

The sergeant, concealing whatever qualms he might have felt at the thought of imbibing illegal whisky, looked carefully into the cup, sniffed, and glanced up at old Dan.

" It looks good," he commented.

" It should be."

" It tastes good, too," he added.

" Ah, sha," said Dan, clearly not wishing to praise his own hospitality in his own house, " 'tis of no great excellence."

" You're a good judge, I'd say," said the sergeant without irony.

" Ever since things became what they are," said Dan, carefully guarding himself from a too direct reference to the peculiarities of the law administered by his guest, " liquor is not what it used to be."

" I have heard that remark made before now," said the sergeant thoughtfully. " I have often heard it said by men of wide experience that liquor used to be better in the old days."

" Liquor," said the old man, " is a thing that takes time. There was never a good job done in a hurry."

" 'Tis an art in itself."

" Just so."

" And an art takes time."

" And knowledge," added Dan with emphasis. " Every art has its secrets, and the secrets of distilling are being lost the way the old songs were lost. When I was a boy there wasn't a man in the barony [1] but had a hundred songs in his head, but with people running here, there, and everywhere, the songs were lost. . . . Ever since things became what they are," he repeated on the same guarded note, " there's so much running about the secrets are lost."

" There must have been a power of them."

" There was. Ask any man today that makes liquor do he know how to make it of heather."

" And was it made of heather? " asked the policeman.

" It was."

---

[1] *barony* (băr'ō·nĭ): Irish county division.

" Did you ever drink it yourself? "

" I did not; but I knew men that drank it. And a purer, sweeter, wholesomer drink never tickled a man's gullet. Babies they used to give it to and growing children."

" Musha,[1] Dan, I think sometimes 'twas a great mistake of the law to set its hand against it."

Dan shook his head. His eyes answered for him, but it was not in nature that in his own house a man should criticize the occupation of his guest.

" Maybe so, maybe not," he said in a noncommittal tone.

" But sure, what else have the poor people? "

" Them that makes the laws have their own good reasons."

" All the same, Dan, all the same, 'tis a hard law."

The sergeant would not be outdone in generosity. Politeness required him not to yield to the old man's defense of his superiors and their mysterious ways.

" It is the secrets I would be sorry for," said Dan, summing up. " Men die, and men are born, and where one man drained another will plow, but a secret lost is lost for ever."

" True," said the sergeant mournfully. " Lost for ever."

Dan took the policeman's cup, rinsed it in a bucket of clear water beside the door and cleaned it anew with the aid of the shirt. Then he placed it carefully at the sergeant's elbow. From the dresser he took a jug of milk and a blue bag containing sugar: this he followed up with a slab of country butter and — a sign that his visitor was not altogether unexpected — a round cake of homemade bread, fresh and uncut. The kettle sang and spat, and the dog, shaking his ears, barked at it angrily.

" Go 'way, you brute! " growled Dan, kicking him out of his way.

He made the tea and filled the two cups. The sergeant cut himself a large slice of bread and buttered it thickly.

" It is just like medicines," said the old man, resuming his theme with the imperturbability of age. " Every secret there was is lost. And leave no one tell me a doctor is the measure of one that has secrets from old times."

" How could he? " asked the sergeant with his mouth full.

" The proof of that was seen when there were doctors and wise people there together."

" It wasn't to the doctors the people went, I'll engage."

" It was not. And why? " . . . With a sweeping gesture the old man took in the whole world outside his cabin. " Out there on the hillsides is the sure cure for every disease. Because it is written " — he tapped the table with his thumb — " it is written by the poets ' an galar'san leigheas go bhfaghair le ceile ' (wherever you find the disease you will find the cure). But people walk up the hills and down the hills and all they see is flowers. Flowers! As if God Almighty — honor and praise to Him — had nothing better to do with His time than be making ould flowers! "

" Things no doctor could cure the wise people cured."

" Ah musha, 'tis I know it," said Dan bitterly, " 'tis I know it, not in my mind but in my own four bones."

" Do you tell me the rheumatics do be at you always? "

" They do. . . . Ah, if you were living, Kitty O'Harra, or you, Nora Malley of the Glen, 'tisn't I would be dreading the mountain wind or the sea wind; 'tisn't I'd be creeping down with me misfortunate red ticket[2] for the blue and pink and yellow dribble-drabble of their ignorant dispensary! "

" Why then, indeed," said the sergeant with sudden determination, " I'll get you a bottle for that."

---

[1] *Musha:* indeed.

[2] *misfortunate red ticket:* a slip for free medicine.

" Ah, there's no bottle ever made will cure me! "

" There is, there is. Don't talk now till you try it. My own mother's brother, it cured him when he was that bad he wanted the carpenter to cut the two legs off him with a hand saw."

" I'd give fifty pounds to be rid of it," said Dan. " I would and five hundred! "

The sergeant finished his tea in a gulp, blessed himself and struck a match, which he then allowed to go out as he answered some question of the old man's. He did the same with a second and third, as though titillating [1] his appetite with delay. At last he succeeded in getting it alight, and then the two men pulled round their chairs, placed their toes side by side in the ashes, and in deep puffs, lively bursts of conversation and long, long silences, enjoyed their pipes.

" I hope I'm not keeping you," said the sergeant, as though struck by the length of his visit.

" Erra, what keep? "

" Tell me if I am. The last thing I'd like to do is to waste a man's time."

" Och, I'd ask nothing better than to have you here all night."

" I like a little talk myself," admitted the policeman.

And again they became lost in conversation. The light grew thick and colored, and wheeling about the kitchen before it disappeared became tinged with gold; the kitchen itself sank into a cool grayness with cold light upon the cups and the basins and plates upon the dresser. From the ash tree a thrush began to sing. The open hearth gathered brightness till its light was a warm, even splash of crimson in the twilight.

Twilight was also descending without when the sergeant rose to go. He fastened his belt and tunic and carefully brushed his clothes. Then he put on his cap, tilted a little to side and back.

[1] *titillating* (tĭt′ĭ·lāt′ĭng): stimulating.

" Well," he said, " that was a great talk."

" It's a pleasure," said Dan, " a real pleasure, that's what it is."

" And I won't forget the bottle."

" Heavy handling from God to you! "

" Good-by now, Dan."

" Good-by and good luck."

Dan did not offer to accompany the sergeant beyond the door. Then he sat down in his old place by the fire. He took out his pipe once more, blew through it thoughtfully, and just as he leaned forward for a twig to kindle it he heard steps returning to the house. It was the sergeant. He put his head a little way over the half door.

" Oh, Dan," he called softly.

" Ay, sergeant," replied Dan, looking round, but with one hand still reaching for the twig. He could not see the sergeant's face, only hear his voice.

" I suppose you're not thinking of paying that little fine, Dan? "

There was a brief silence. Dan pulled out the lighted twig, rose slowly and shambled toward the door, stuffing it down into the almost empty bowl of the pipe. He leaned over the half door, while the sergeant with hands in the pockets of his trousers gazed rather in the direction of the laneway, yet taking in a considerable portion of the sea line.

" The way it is with me, sergeant," replied Dan unemotionally, " I am not."

" I was thinking that, Dan. I was thinking you wouldn't."

There was a long silence during which the voice of the thrush grew shriller and merrier. The sunken sun lit up islands of purple cloud moored high above the wind.

" In a way," said the sergeant, " that was what brought me."

" I was just thinking so, sergeant, it struck me and you going out the door."

" If 'twas only the money, I'm sure there's many would be glad to oblige you."

" I know that, sergeant. No, 'tisn't the money so much as giving that fellow the satisfaction of paying. Because he angered me, sergeant."

The sergeant made no comment upon this, and another long silence ensued.

" They gave me the warrant,"[1] he said at last in a tone which dissociated him from all connection with the document.

" Ay, begod! " said Dan, without interest.

" So whenever 'twould be convenient to you — "

" Well, now you mention it," said Dan, by way of throwing out a suggestion for debate, " I could go with you now."

" Oh, tut, tut! " protested the sergeant with a wave of his hand, dismissing the idea as the tone required.

" Or I could go tomorrow," added Dan, warming up to the issue.

" Just as you like now," replied the sergeant, scaling up his voice accordingly.

" But as a matter of fact," said the old man emphatically, " the day that would be most convenient to me would be Friday after dinner, seeing that I have some messages to do in town, and I wouldn't have me jaunt for nothing."

" Friday will do grand," said the sergeant, with relief that this delicate matter was now practically disposed of. " You could just walk in yourself and tell them I told you."

" I'd rather have yourself, if 'twould be no inconvenience, sergeant. As it is, I'd feel a bit shy."

" You needn't then. There's a man from my own parish there, a warder;[2] one Whelan. You could say you wanted him, and I'll guarantee when he knows you're a friend of mine he'll make you as comfortable as if you were at home by your own fire."

" I'd like that fine," said Dan with satisfaction.

" Well, good-by again now, Dan. I'll have to hurry."

" Wait now, wait, till I see you to the road! "

Together the two men strolled down the laneway while Dan explained how it was that he, a respectable old man, had had the grave misfortune to open the head of another old man in such a way as to necessitate his being removed to the hospital, and why it was that he could not give the old man in question the satisfaction of paying in cash for an injury brought about through the victim's own unmannerly method of argument.

" You see, sergeant," he said, " the way it is, he's there now, and he's looking at us as sure as there's a glimmer of sight in his wake, wandering, wathery eyes, and nothing would give him more gratification than for me to pay. But I'll punish him. I'll lie on bare boards for him. I'll suffer for him, sergeant, till he won't be able to rise his head, nor any of his children after him, for the suffering he put on me."

On the following Friday he made ready his donkey and butt[3] and set out. On his way he collected a number of neighbors who wished to bid him farewell. At the top of the hill he stopped to send them back. An old man, sitting in the sunlight, hastily made his way within doors, and a moment later the door of his cottage was quietly closed.

Having shaken all his friends by the hand, Dan lashed the old donkey, shouted " Hup, there! " and set out alone along the road to prison.

TWO IRISHMEN

1. What does the title " The Majesty of the Law " mean to you after finishing the story? What is the idea that O'Connor is mainly concerned with? How does he suggest it through the characters' actions and

---

[1] *warrant:* an order issued by a court to take someone in custody, to arrest.

[2] *warder:* a prison guard.

[3] *butt:* a kind of heavy cart.

their relationship? How does the setting contribute to the main idea of the story?

2. How do you know that the sergeant's serving the warrant was not an afterthought? Why did the sergeant not mention it earlier? Why was Dan being served the warrant? Why does he prefer to go to prison rather than pay costs or a fine?

3. O'Connor knows Ireland to the roots, and in all his stories he conveys the atmosphere of the country and the personality of its people. What Irish customs did you note? What characteristics of the Irish people are revealed?

Poison

ROALD DAHL 1916–

Like some earlier English writers, Roald Dahl substituted travel for a university degree. At eighteen he left his home in South Wales to join the Shell Oil Company in London and later to work in Tanganyika. When war came in 1939, he enlisted in the RAF; with his fighter squadron he served in the Libyan desert, Greece, and Syria. After recovering from war injuries, he came to Washington in 1942 as Assistant Air Attaché to the British Embassy. Here he began to write short stories. When he was discharged at the end of the war with the rank of Wing Commander, Dahl began to travel back and forth between England and America, and at present he lives in this country.

His first twelve stories — all about flying — were published as *Over to You* in 1946. Most of the eighteen stories in the later *Someone Like You* have appeared in such magazines as the *New Yorker, Harper's,* and *Collier's.* In 1955 his play *The Honeys,* a spine-tingling thriller, was performed on Broadway. Dahl is a craftsman who knows how to make the improbable seem probable. He has been called the British O. Henry for his anecdotal tricks and surprise endings; but his stories have an additional bizarre quality that is unique. " Poison " is one of his most unusual stories: short on character, long on suspense.

I T M U S T have been around midnight when I drove home, and as I approached the gates of the bungalow I switched off the head lamps of the car so the beam wouldn't swing in through the window of the side bedroom and wake Harry Pope. But I needn't have bothered. Coming up the drive I noticed his light was still on, so he was awake anyway — unless perhaps he'd dropped off while reading.

I parked the car and went up the five steps to the balcony, counting each step carefully in the dark so I wouldn't take an extra one which wasn't there when I got to the top. I crossed the balcony, pushed through the screen doors into the house itself and switched on the light in the hall. I went across to the door of Harry's room, opened it quietly, and looked in.

He was lying on the bed and I could see he was awake. But he didn't move. He didn't even turn his head toward me, but I heard him say, " Timber, Timber, come here."

He spoke slowly, whispering each word carefully, separately, and I pushed the door right open and started to go quickly across the room.

" Stop. Wait a moment, Timber." I could hardly hear what he was saying. He seemed to be straining enormously to get the words out.

" What's the matter, Harry? "

" Sshhh! " he whispered. " Sshhh . . . don't make a noise. Take your shoes off before you come nearer. *Please* do as I say, Timber."

The way he was speaking reminded me of George Barling after he got shot in the stomach when he stood leaning against a crate containing a spare airplane engine, holding both hands on his stomach and saying things about the German pilot in just the same hoarse straining half whisper Harry was using now.

"Quickly, Timber, but take your shoes off first."

I couldn't understand about taking off the shoes but I figured that if he was as ill as he sounded I'd better humor him, so I bent down and removed the shoes and left them in the middle of the floor. Then I went over to his bed.

"Don't touch the bed! For heaven's sake don't touch the bed!" He was still speaking like he'd been shot in the stomach and I could see him lying there on his back with a single sheet covering three-quarters of his body. He was wearing a pair of pajamas with blue, brown, and white stripes, and he was sweating terribly. It was a hot night and I was sweating a little myself, but not like Harry. His whole face was wet and the pillow around his head was sodden with moisture. It looked like a bad go of malaria to me.

"What is it, Harry?"

"A krait,"[1] he said.

"A *krait!* Oh, oh! Where'd it bite you? How long ago?"

"Shut up," he whispered.

"Listen, Harry," I said, and leaned forward and touched his shoulder. "We've got to be quick. Come on now, quickly, tell me where it bit you." He was lying there very still and tense as though he was holding on to himself hard because of sharp pain.

"I haven't been bitten," he whispered. "Not yet. It's on my stomach. Lying there asleep."

I took a quick pace backward; I couldn't help it, and I stared at his stomach or rather at the sheet that covered it. The sheet was rumpled in several places, and it was impossible to tell if there was anything underneath.

"You don't really mean there's a krait lying on your stomach now?"

"I swear it."

"How did it get there?" I shouldn't have asked the question because it was easy to see he wasn't fooling. I should have told him to keep quiet.

"I was reading," Harry said, and he spoke very slowly, taking each word in turn and speaking it carefully so as not to move the muscles of his stomach. "Lying on my back reading and I felt something on my chest, behind the book. Sort of tickling. Then out of the corner of my eye saw this little krait sliding over my pajamas. Small, about ten inches. Knew I mustn't move. Couldn't have anyway. Lay there watching it. Thought it would go over top of the sheet." Harry paused and was silent for a few moments. His eyes looked down along his body toward the place where the sheet covered his stomach, and I could see he was watching to make sure his whispering wasn't disturbing the thing that lay there.

"There was a fold in the sheet," he said, speaking more slowly than ever now and so softly I had to lean close to hear him. "See it, it's still there. It went under that. I could feel it through my pajamas, moving on my stomach. Then it stopped moving and now it's lying there in the warmth. Probably asleep. I've been waiting for you." He raised his eyes and looked at me.

"How long ago?"

"Hours," he whispered. "Hours and bloody hours and hours. I can't keep still much longer. I've been wanting to cough."

There was not much doubt about the truth of Harry's story. As a matter of fact it wasn't a surprising thing for a krait to do. They hang around people's houses and they go for the warm places.

[1] *krait* (krīt): a venomous snake of India, allied to the cobra; causes more deaths than any other snake.

The surprising thing was that Harry hadn't been bitten. The bite is quite deadly, except sometimes when you catch it at once; and they kill a fair number of people each year in Bengal, mostly in the villages.

"All right, Harry," I said, and now I was whispering too. "Don't move and don't talk any more unless you have to. You know it won't bite unless it's frightened. We'll fix it in no time."

I went softly out of the room in my stocking feet and fetched a small sharp knife from the kitchen. I put it in my trouser pocket ready to use instantly in case something went wrong while we were still thinking out a plan. If Harry coughed or moved or did something to frighten the krait and get bitten, I was going to be ready to cut the bitten place and try to suck the venom out. I came back to the bedroom and Harry was still lying there very quiet and sweating all over his face. His eyes followed me as I moved across the room to his bed and I could see he was wondering what I'd been up to. I stood beside him, trying to think of the best thing to do.

"Harry," I said, and now when I spoke I put my mouth almost on his ear so I wouldn't have to raise my voice above the softest whisper, "I think the best thing to do is for me to draw the sheet back very, very gently. Then we could have a look first. I think I could do that without disturbing it."

"Don't be a damn' fool." There was no expression in his voice. He spoke each word too slowly, too carefully, and too softly for that. The expression was in the eyes and around the corners of the mouth.

"Why not?"

"The light would frighten him. It's dark under there now."

"Then how about whipping the sheet back quick and brushing it off before it has time to strike?"

"Why don't you get a doctor?" Harry said. The way he looked at me told me I should have thought of that

myself in the first place.

"A doctor. Of course. That's it. I'll get Ganderbai."

I tiptoed out to the hall, looked up Ganderbai's number in the book, lifted the phone and told the operator to hurry.

"Doctor Ganderbai," I said. "This is Timber Woods."

"Hello, Mr. Woods. You not in bed yet?"

"Look, could you come round at once? And bring serum — for a krait bite."

"Who's been bitten?" The question came so sharply it was like a small explosion in my ear.

"No one. No one yet. But Harry Pope's in bed and he's got one lying on his stomach — asleep under the sheet on his stomach."

For about three seconds there was silence on the line. Then speaking slowly, not like an explosion now but slowly, precisely, Ganderbai said, "Tell him to keep quite still. He is not to move or to talk. Do you understand?"

"Of course."

"I'll come at once!" He rang off and I went back to the bedroom. Harry's eyes watched me as I walked across to his bed.

"Ganderbai's coming. He said for you to lie still."

"What does he think I'm doing!"

"Look, Harry, he said no talking. Absolutely no talking. Either of us."

"Why don't you shut up then?" When he said this, one side of his mouth started twitching with rapid little downward movements that continued for a while after he finished speaking. I took out my handkerchief and very gently I wiped the sweat off his face and neck, and I could feel the slight twitching of the muscle — the one he used for smiling — as my fingers passed over it with the handkerchief.

I slipped out to the kitchen, got some ice from the icebox, rolled it up in a napkin, and began to crush it small.

stood there, frowning, nibbling his lip.

" You see," he said at last. " There is a way to do this. You know what we must do — we must administer an anesthetic to the creature where it lies."

It was a splendid idea.

" It is not safe," he continued, " because a snake is cold-blooded and anesthetic does not work so well or so quick with such animals, but it is better than any other thing to do. We could use ether . . . chloroform . . ." He was speaking slowly and trying to think the thing out while he talked.

"Which shall we use? "

" Chloroform," he said suddenly. " Ordinary chloroform. That is best. Now quick! " He took my arm and pulled me toward the balcony. " Drive to my house! By the time you get there I will have waked up my boy on the telephone and he will show you my poisons cupboard. Here is the key of the cupboard. Take a bottle of chloroform. It has an orange label and the name is printed on it. I stay here in case anything happens. Be quick now, hurry! No, no, you don't need your shoes! "

I drove fast and in about fifteen minutes I was back with the bottle of chloroform. Ganderbai came out of Harry's room and met me in the hall. " You got it? " he said. " Good, good. I just been telling him what we are going to do. But now we must hurry. It is not easy for him in there like that all this time. I am afraid he might move."

He went back to the bedroom and I followed, carrying the bottle carefully with both hands. Harry was lying on the bed in precisely the same position as before with the sweat pouring down his cheeks. His face was white and wet. He turned his eyes toward me and I smiled at him and nodded confidently. He continued to look at me. I raised my thumb, giving him the okay signal. He closed his eyes. Ganderbai was squatting down by the bed, and on the floor beside him was the hollow rubber tube that he had previously used as a tourniquet, and

he'd got a small paper funnel fitted into one end of the tube.

He began to pull a little piece of the sheet out from under the mattress. He was working directly in line with Harry's stomach, about eighteen inches from it, and I watched his fingers as they tugged gently at the edge of the sheet. He worked so slowly it was almost impossible to discern any movement either in his fingers or in the sheet that was being pulled.

Finally he succeeded in making an opening under the sheet and he took the rubber tube and inserted one end of it in the opening so that it would slide under the sheet along the mattress toward Harry's body. I do not know how long it took him to slide that tube in a few inches. It may have been twenty minutes, it may have been forty. I never once saw the tube move. I knew it was going in because the visible part of it grew gradually shorter, but I doubted that the krait could have felt even the faintest vibration. Ganderbai himself was sweating now, large pearls of sweat standing out all over his forehead and along his upper lip. But his hands were steady, and I noticed that his eyes were watching, not the tube in his hands, but the area of crumpled sheet above Harry's stomach.

Without looking up, he held out a hand to me for the chloroform. I twisted out the ground-glass stopper and put the bottle right into his hand, not letting go till I was sure he had a good hold on it. Then he jerked his head for me to come closer and he whispered, " Tell him I'm going to soak the mattress and that it will be very cold under his body. He must be ready for that and he must not move. Tell him now."

I bent over Harry and passed on the message.

" Why doesn't he get on with it? " Harry said.

" He's going to now, Harry. But it'll feel very cold, so be ready for it."

" Oh, blast, get on, get on! " For the

first time he raised his voice, and Ganderbai glanced up sharply, watched him for a few seconds, then went back to his business.

Ganderbai poured a few drops of chloroform into the paper funnel and waited while it ran down the tube. Then he poured some more. Then he waited again, and the heavy sickening smell of chloroform spread out over the room bringing with it faint unpleasant memories of white-coated nurses and white surgeons standing in a white room around a long white table. Ganderbai was pouring steadily now and I could see the heavy vapor of the chloroform swirling slowly like smoke above the paper funnel. He paused, held the bottle up to the light, poured one more funnelful and handed the bottle back to me. Slowly he drew out the rubber tube from under the sheet; then he stood up.

The strain of inserting the tube and pouring the chloroform must have been great, and I recollect that when Ganderbai turned and whispered to me, his voice was small and tired. " We'll give it fifteen minutes. Just to be safe."

I leaned over to tell Harry. " We're going to give it fifteen minutes, just to be safe. But it's probably done for already."

" Then why don't you look and see! " Again he spoke loudly and Ganderbai sprang round, his small brown face suddenly very angry. He had almost pure black eyes and he stared at Harry and Harry's smiling muscle started to twitch. I took my handkerchief and wiped his wet face, trying to stroke his forehead a little for comfort as I did so.

Then we stood and waited beside the bed, Ganderbai watching Harry's face all the time in a curious intense manner. The little Indian was concentrating all his will power on keeping Harry quiet. He never once took his eyes from the patient and although he made no sound, he seemed somehow to be shouting at him all the time, saying: Now listen, you've got to listen, you're not going to go spoiling this now, d'you hear me; and Harry lay there twitching his mouth, sweating, closing his eyes, opening them, looking at me, at the sheet, at the ceiling, at me again, but never at Ganderbai. Yet somehow Ganderbai was holding him. The smell of chloroform was oppressive and it made me feel sick, but I couldn't leave the room now. I had the feeling someone was blowing up a huge balloon and I could see it was going to burst but I couldn't look away.

At length Ganderbai turned and nodded and I knew he was ready to proceed. " You go over to the other side of the bed," he said. " We will each take one side of the sheet and draw it back together, but very slowly please, and very quietly."

" Keep still now, Harry," I said and I went around to the other side of the bed and took hold of the sheet. Ganderbai stood opposite me, and together we began to draw back the sheet, lifting it up clear of Harry's body, taking it back very slowly, both of us standing well away but at the same time bending forward, trying to peer underneath it. The smell of chloroform was awful. I remember trying to hold my breath and when I couldn't do that any longer I tried to breathe shallow so the stuff wouldn't get into my lungs.

The whole of Harry's chest was visible now, or rather the striped pajama top which covered it, and then I saw the white cord of his pajama trousers, neatly tied in a bow. A little farther and I saw a button, a mother-of-pearl button, and that was something I had never had on my pajamas, a fly button, let alone a mother-of-pearl one. This Harry, I thought, he is very refined. It is odd how one sometimes has frivolous thoughts at exciting moments, and I distinctly remember thinking about Harry being very refined when I saw that button.

Apart from the button there was nothing on his stomach.

We pulled the sheet back faster then,

and when we had uncovered his legs and feet we let the sheet drop over the end of the bed onto the floor.

" Don't move," Ganderbai said, " don't move, Mr. Pope "; and he began to peer around along the side of Harry's body and under his legs.

" We must be careful," he said. " It may be anywhere. It could be up the leg of his pajamas."

When Ganderbai said this, Harry quickly raised his head from the pillow and looked down at his legs. It was the first time he had moved. Then suddenly he jumped up, stood on his bed and shook his legs one after the other violently in the air. At that moment we both thought he had been bitten and Ganderbai was already reaching down into his bag for a scalpel and a tourniquet when Harry ceased his caperings and stood still and looked at the mattress he was standing on and shouted, " It's not there! "

Ganderbai straightened up and for a moment he too looked at the mattress; then he looked up at Harry. Harry was all right. He hadn't been bitten and now he wasn't going to get bitten and he wasn't going to be killed and everything was fine. But that didn't seem to make anyone feel any better.

" Mr. Pope, you are of course *quite* sure you saw it in the first place? " There was a note of sarcasm in Ganderbai's voice that he would never have employed in ordinary circumstances. " You don't think you might possibly have been dreaming, do you, Mr. Pope? " The way Ganderbai was looking at Harry, I realized that the sarcasm was not seriously intended. He was only easing up a bit after the strain.

Harry stood on his bed in his striped pajamas, glaring at Ganderbai, and the color began to spread out over his cheeks.

" Are you telling me I'm a liar? " he shouted.

Ganderbai remained absolutely still, watching Harry. Harry took a pace forward on the bed and there was a shining look in his eyes.

" Why, you dirty little Hindu sewer rat! "

" Shut up, Harry! " I said.

" You dirty . . ."

" Harry! " I called. " Shut up, Harry! " It was terrible, the things he was saying.

Ganderbai went out of the room as though neither of us was there, and I followed him and put my arm around his shoulder as he walked across the hall and out onto the balcony.

" Don't you listen to Harry," I said. " This thing's made him so he doesn't know what he's saying."

We went down the steps from the balcony to the drive and across the drive in the darkness to where his old Morris car was parked. He opened the door and got in.

" You did a wonderful job," I said. " Thank you so very much for coming."

" All he needs is a good holiday," he said quietly, without looking at me, then he started the engine and drove off.

A TENSE AND SUBTLE DRAMA

1. What does the title " Poison " mean to you after reading the story? In what way is this story ironic? Although the main action is based on a supposition that proves to be false, something very real occurs in this story; what is it? What response does the last remark, made by Dr. Ganderbai, arouse in you? Can you think of an ending quite different from the one here? What does the story reveal to you about the author's insight into the attitudes and standards of individuals?

2. We often judge a story on its plausibility, the likelihood of the happenings. Defend or attack the plausibility of this story. What do you learn from " Poison " about the way to end a story?

3. To what extent does the author reveal the personalities of Harry, Timber, and Dr. Ganderbai? In what ways are they alike and different?

4. If you enjoyed this story, read others in his collection *Someone Like You*.

The Train from Rhodesia

NADINE GORDIMER 1925–

Talent was recognized early in Nadine Gordimer, a young interpreter of South Africa. This Englishwoman began writing at the age of nine; at the age of fifteen she was writing for magazines in her home city of Johannesburg, about the people of that city and the small mining towns. She graduated from the University of Witwatersrand in Johannesburg, and she has continued to make that city her home. Writing as a teenager and now as a mature woman, she has shown unusual talent.

Nadine Gordimer gained attention with the publication of *The Soft Voice of the Serpent* (1952), a collection of stories, some of which were first published in *Harper's, The Yale Review,* and the *New Yorker. The Lying Days* (1953), her first novel, is filled with echoes of autobiography.

Miss Gordimer is concerned not so much with South African landscape as with situations, valid and accurate. She presents with deep feeling the problems of her native land. Her writing has been compared to that of Virginia Woolf — " crystalline and gentle." But she does not ignore hard and glaring realities: race riots, murder, and the grim aspects of life in a South African mining town.

Craftsmanship and a perception of the happiness and disappointments of daily living are evident in " The Train from Rhodesia." This is a story in which much of the meaning is hidden beneath the surface. You must read carefully in order to appreciate the author's subtle communication of tensions.

THE TRAIN came out of the red horizon and bore down toward them over the single straight track.

The stationmaster came out of his little brick station with its pointed chalet roof, feeling the creases in his serge uniform in his legs as well. A stir of preparedness rippled through the squatting native vendors waiting in the dust; the face of a carved wooden animal, eternally surprised, stuck out of a sack. The stationmaster's barefoot children wandered over. From the gray mud huts with the untidy heads that stood within a decorated mud wall, chickens, and dogs with their skin stretched like parchment over their bones, followed the piccanins [1] down to the track. The flushed and perspiring west cast a reflection, faint, without heat, upon the station, upon the tin shed marked " Goods," upon the walled kraal, [2] upon the gray tin house of the stationmaster and upon the sand, that lapped all around, from sky to sky, cast little rhythmical cups of shadow, so that the sand became the sea, and closed over the children's black feet softly and without imprint.

The stationmaster's wife sat behind the mesh of her verandah. Above her hand the hunk of a sheep's carcass moved slightly, dangling in a current of air.

They waited.

The train called out, along the sky; but there was no answer; and the cry hung on: I'm coming . . . I'm coming . . .

The engine flared out now, big, whisking a dwindling body behind it; the track flared out to let it in.

Creaking, jerking, jostling, gasping, the train filled the station.

Here, let me see that one — the young woman curved her body further out of the corridor window. Missus? smiled the

[1] *piccanins* (pĭk′à·nĭnz): native children.
[2] *kraal* (kräl): a village of South African natives.

old boy, looking at the creatures he held in his hand. From a piece of string on his gray finger hung a tiny woven basket; he lifted it, questioning. No, no, she urged, leaning down toward him, across the height of the train, toward the man in the piece of old rug; that one, that one, her hand commanded. It was a lion, carved out of soft dry wood that looked like spongecake; heraldic, black and white, with impressionistic detail burnt in. The old man held it up to her still smiling, not from the heart, but at the customer. Between its Vandyke [1] teeth, in the mouth opened in an endless roar too terrible to be heard, it had a black tongue. Look, said the young husband, if you don't mind! And round the neck of the thing, a piece of fur (rat? rabbit? meerkat?); a real mane, majestic, telling you somehow that the artist had delight in the lion.

All up and down the length of the train in the dust the artists sprang, walking bent, like performing animals, the better to exhibit the fantasy held toward the faces on the train. Buck, startled and stiff, staring with round black and white eyes. More lions, standing erect, grappling with strange, thin, elongated warriors who clutched spears and showed no fear in their slits of eyes. How much, they asked from the train, how much?

Give me penny, said the little ones with nothing to sell. The dogs went and sat, quite still, under the dining car, where the train breathed out the smell of meat cooking with onion.

A man passed beneath the arch of reaching arms meeting gray-black and white in the exchange of money for the staring wooden eyes, the stiff wooden legs sticking up in the air; went along under the voices and the bargaining, interrogating the wheels. Past the dogs; glancing up at the dining car where he could stare at the faces, behind glass, drinking beer, two by two, on either side

of a uniform railway vase with its pale dead flower. Right to the end, to the guard's van, where the stationmaster's children had just collected their mother's two loaves of bread; to the engine itself, where the stationmaster and the driver stood talking against the steaming complaint of the resting beast.

The man called out to them, something loud and joking. They turned to laugh, in a twirl of steam. The two children careered over the sand, clutching the bread, and burst through the iron gate and up the path through the garden in which nothing grew.

Passengers drew themselves in at the corridor windows and turned into compartments to fetch money, to call someone to look. Those sitting inside looked up: suddenly different, caged faces, boxed in, cut off, after the contact of outside. There was an orange a piccanin would like. . . . What about that chocolate? It wasn't very nice. . . .

A young girl had collected a handful of the hard kind, that no one liked, out of the chocolate box, and was throwing them to the dogs, over at the dining car. But the hens darted in, and swallowed the chocolates, incredibly quick and accurate, before they had even dropped in the dust, and the dogs, a little bewildered, looked up with their brown eyes, not expecting anything.

— No, leave it, said the girl, don't take it. . . .

Too expensive, too much, she shook her head and raised her voice to the old boy, giving up the lion. He held it up where she had handed it to him. No, she said, shaking her head. Three-and-six? [2] insisted her husband, loudly. Yes baas! laughed the boy. *Three-and-six?* — the young man was incredulous. Oh leave it — she said. The young man stopped. Don't you want it? he said, keeping his face closed to the boy. No, never mind, she said, leave it. The old native kept

---

[1] *Vandyke:* pointed. Usually a pointed beard, such as those seen in pictures by Van Dyck.

[2] *Three-and-six:* three shillings and six pence. See the table on page 811 for the value of this amount.

his head on one side, looking at them sideways, holding the lion. Three-and-six, he murmured, as old people repeat things to themselves.

The young woman drew her head in. She went into the coupé and sat down. Out of the window, on the other side, there was nothing; sand and bush; a thorn tree. Back through the open doorway, past the figure of her husband in the corridor, there was the station, the voices, wooden animals waving, running feet. Her eye followed the funny little valance of scrolled wood that outlined the chalet roof of the station; she thought of the lion and smiled. That bit of fur round the neck. But the wooden buck, the hippos, the elephants, the baskets that already bulked out of their brown paper under the seat and on the luggage rack! How will they look at home? Where will you put them? What will they mean away from the places you found them? Away from the unreality of the last few weeks? The man outside. But he is not part of the unreality; he is for good now. Odd . . . somewhere there was an idea that he, that living with him, was part of the holiday, the strange places.

Outside, a bell rang. The stationmaster was leaning against the end of the train, green flag rolled in readiness. A few men who had got down to stretch their legs sprang on to the train, clinging to the observation platforms, or perhaps merely standing on the iron step, holding the rail; but on the train, safe from the one dusty platform, the one tin house, the empty sand.

There was a grunt. The train jerked. Through the glass the beer drinkers looked out, as if they could not see beyond it. Behind the fly-screen, the stationmaster's wife sat facing back at them beneath the darkening hunk of meat.

There was a shout. The flag drooped out. Joints not yet co-ordinated, the segmented body of the train heaved and bumped back against itself. It began to move; slowly the scrolled chalet moved past it, the yells of the natives, running alongside, jetted up into the air, fell back at different levels. Staring wooden faces waved drunkenly, there, then gone, questioning for the last time at the windows. Here, one-and-six baas! — As one automatically opens a hand to catch a thrown ball, a man fumbled wildly down his pocket, brought up the shilling and sixpence and threw them out; the old native, gasping, his skinny toes splaying the sand, flung the lion.

The piccanins were waving, the dogs stood, tails uncertain, watching the train go: past the mud huts, where a woman turned to look, up from the smoke of

The old native, gasping, flung the lion.

the fire, her hand pausing on her hip.

The stationmaster went slowly in under the chalet.

The old native stood, breath blowing out the skin between his ribs, feet tense, balanced in the sand, smiling and shaking his head. In his opened palm, held in the attitude of receiving, was the retrieved shilling and sixpence.

The blind end of the train was being pulled helplessly out of the station.

The young man swung in from the corridor, breathless. He was shaking his head with laughter and triumph. Here! he said. And waggled the lion at her. One-and-six!

What? she said.

He laughed. I was arguing with him for fun, bargaining — when the train had pulled out already, he came tearing after. . . . One-and-six baas! So there's your lion.

She was holding it away from her, the head with the open jaws, the pointed teeth, the black tongue, the wonderful ruff of fur facing her. She was looking at it with an expression of not seeing, of seeing something different. Her face was drawn up, wryly, like the face of a discomforted child. Her mouth lifted nervously at the corner. Very slowly, cautious, she lifted her finger and touched the mane, where it was joined to the wood.

But how could you, she said. He was shocked by the dismay of her face.

Good Lord, he said, what's the matter?

If you wanted the thing, she said, her voice rising and breaking with the shrill impotence [1] of anger, why didn't you buy it in the first place? If you wanted it, why didn't you pay for it? Why didn't you take it decently, when he offered it? Why did you have to wait for him to run after the train with it, and give him one-and-six? One-and-six!

She was pushing it at him, trying to

force him to take it. He stood astonished, his hands hanging at his sides.

But you wanted it! You liked it so much?

— It's a beautiful piece of work, she said fiercely, as if to protect it from him.

You liked it so much! You said yourself it was too expensive —

Oh *you* — she said, hopeless and furious. *You.* . . . She threw the lion on to the seat.

He stood looking at her.

She sat down again in the corner and, her face slumped in her hand, stared out of the window. Everything was turning round inside her. One-and-six. One-and-six. One-and-six for the wood and the carving and the sinews of the legs and the switch of the tail. The mouth open like that and the teeth. The black tongue, rolling, like a wave. The mane round the neck. To give one-and-six for that. The heat of shame mounted through her legs and body and sounded in her ears like the sound of sand pouring. Pouring, pouring. She sat there, sick. A weariness, a tastelessness, the discovery of a void made her hands slacken their grip, atrophy emptily, as if the hour was not worth their grasp. She was feeling like this again. She had thought it was something to do with singleness, with being alone and belonging too much to oneself.

She sat there not wanting to move or speak, or to look at anything, even; so that the mood should be associated with nothing, no object, word or sight that might recur and so recall the feeling again. . . . Smuts [2] blew in grittily, settled on her hands. Her back remained at exactly the same angle, turned against the young man sitting with his hands drooping between his sprawled legs, and the lion, fallen on its side in the corner.

The train had cast the station like a skin. It called out to the sky, I'm coming, I'm coming; and again, there was no answer.

[1] *impotence* (ĭm′pŏ·tĕns): weakness.

[2] *Smuts:* soot, coal dust.

CONTRASTS — EXPLICIT
AND IMPLICIT

1. Two ways of life are contrasted in this story. Describe them. How does Nadine Gordimer show greater sympathy toward one way? Does she succeed in making your sympathy lie with the same group?

2. In what ways does the treatment of setting determine this story's theme? Why is South Africa a particularly suitable background for the idea in this story? Find passages that describe the setting well.

3. This is not a story with much action or suspense, yet within the first few pages you are made aware of two problems which must be solved, or at least developed, in some way before the story can end. One, a relatively trivial conflict, contrasts with the other, a matter of a personal relationship. What are the problems? What happens in connection with each?

4. How is the girl's attitude toward her husband affected by his purchase of the lion? What does she feel about him? Do you think her feeling was *caused* by the incident on the train, or did it have deeper roots? What did the lion represent to the girl? What did it represent to her husband?

5. How does this story differ from other stories that you have read in this book? What is the significance of the train being mentioned at the beginning and at the end of the story? What do you notice about the dialogue that is different from the dialogue in most stories?

SUGGESTION FOR WRITING

If the story had its setting in America or in another country with which you are familiar, how might it be told? Using the same theme, create a setting, plot, and characters for a story of your own.

READING LIST FOR
MODERN FICTION

SHORT STORIES

Chesterton, G. K., *Father Brown Omnibus*
Fifty stories in which a priest-detective, Father Brown, solves mystery after mystery.

Dahl, Roald, *Someone Like You*
Weird and imaginative stories that will not be forgotten.

Doyle, A. Conan, *The Adventures of Sherlock Holmes*
Some of the best mystery and detective stories by a world favorite.

Galsworthy, John, *Caravan*
Here are the outstanding stories by a master craftsman.

Garrity, Devin A. (editor), *Forty-four Irish Short Stories*
An anthology, from Yeats to Frank O'Connor.

Goodman, Jack (editor), *Fireside Book of Dog Stories*
A dog fancier will enjoy especially the stories by Galsworthy, Kipling, D. H. Lawrence, and Eric Knight.

Irwin, Margaret E., *Bloodstock, and Other Stories*
Stories from Ireland, unusual and ghostly stories, and a pathetic story titled *Mrs. Oliver Cromwell.*

Kneale, Nigel, *Tomato Cain and Other Stories*
Stories of familiar emotions and events; tales that are uncanny and unfathomable.

Kuebler, Harold (editor), *The Treasury of Science Fiction Classics*
Huxley, Priestley, and H. G. Wells are some of the authors of these stories of adventure in the worlds of the future.

O'Connor, Frank, *Traveller's Samples* and *More Stories*
Winning stories that present the charm and tragedy of everyday life.

O'Faoláin, Seán, *The Man Who Invented Sin*
Essence of Ireland with very real Irishmen transmitted in fifteen stories.

Priestley, J. B., *The Other Place and Other Stories of the Same Sort*
How the supernatural seems to play a part in everyday life is found in all nine stories.

Sansom, William, *Something Terrible, Something Lovely*
Several stories vivid and tense, others clever and brittle, by a young writer.

Schweikert, Harry C. (editor), *Short Stories*
Jacobs, Hardy, Conrad, Kipling, Bennett, Barrie, Galsworthy, and Katherine Mansfield are represented with a story and biographical sketch.

NOVELS

Abse, Dannie, *Ash on a Young Man's Sleeve*

With humor and pathos, a youth in South Wales becomes aware of the forces engulfing the world in a second world war.

Bagnold, Enid, *National Velvet*

Velvet, a young English girl, rides her piebald in the Grand National race.

Barrie, Sir James M., *The Little Minister*

The love affair of the Auld Licht minister and Lady Babbie, who pretends to be a gypsy.

Beaty, David, *The Four Winds*

Fascinating scenes of men who operate the Mid-Atlantic Line of British Empire Airways and the heroism of the pilots.

Bentley, Phyllis, *Noble in Reason*

Christopher Jarmayne is pictured first as an ill-adjusted child in Yorkshire and then as an old man, successful as a novelist and as a family man.

Bowen, Elizabeth, *A World of Love*

Each member of an impoverished family is touched by finding letters written by a man killed in World War I.

Cary, Joyce, *Except the Lord*

The son of a stableman and member of a devoted family in the west country shows a man and a career in the making.

Conrad, Joseph, *Lord Jim*

Psychological study of a young Englishman losing his honor, settling in a Malay village, and finally regaining his courage.

Cronin, Archibald J., *The Citadel*

A young doctor struggles against mediocrity, forgets honor and ideals, and is brought to his senses by a tragic error.

Dane, Clemence, *The Flower Girls*

Colorful first family of the English theater discovered by Jacy Florister in a setting ranging from Covent Garden to Hollywood.

Du Maurier, Daphne, *The King's General*

Sir Richard Grenville shares the tumultuous life of Honor Harris during the stress and strife of England's civil wars.

Forster, Edward M., *A Passage to India*

A potent story that reveals, with subtlety and power, the character of Moslems and Hindus as well as Englishmen.

Gallico, Paul W., *Love of Seven Dolls*

An engaging bit of whimsey about a French waif and seven exceedingly human puppets.

Godden, Rumer, *An Episode of Sparrows*

Lovejoy Mason, deserted by her mother and left to fend for herself in London's back streets, struggles to create beauty out of drabness.

Gordimer, Nadine, *The Lying Days*

First twenty-four years of a girl brought up by conventional parents in a mining suburb of Johannesburg, South Africa.

Hammond-Innes, Ralph, *Naked Land*

Action in the rugged territory between the Sahara Desert and the high Atlas Mountains is volatile from two causes: landslides and Berber nationalism.

Hilton, James, *Good-bye, Mr. Chips*

A moving story of an English schoolmaster and his associations with boys of three generations.

Llewellyn, Richard, *How Green Was My Valley*

An old man, recalling the green valley of his youth, depicts alternately the tragedy and comedy of a Welsh mining village.

Maugham, W. Somerset, *Mr. Maugham Himself*

Short pieces and his great story *Of Human Bondage,* the search of a young man for a way of life, his struggles against a physical handicap, and his tangled emotions.

Paton, Alan, *Cry, the Beloved Country*

After the murder of his son, a white man works with a Zulu parson, the father of the murderer, to bring new understanding to the South African scene.

Priestley, J. B., *The Magicians*

Faced with retirement and no private interests, a middle-aged man discovers that life has just begun.

Snow, Charles P., *New Men*

Exciting descriptions of atomic scientists at work and conflicts created between scientist and bureaucrat, personified by two brothers.

Thirkell, Angela, *What Did It Mean?*

The enthusiastic preparation of loyal subjects in Barsetshire for the coronation of Queen Elizabeth II.

Waugh, Evelyn, *Officers and Gentlemen*

In this sequel to *Men at Arms,* Guy Crouchback gets assigned to the Commandos and finds himself in combat in Crete.

Wells, H. G., *Seven Famous Novels*

A package of reading matter by a creator of illusions that excite and entertain.

THE GROWTH OF THE ENGLISH LANGUAGE

The Modern Age

You who have spent your entire lives in the twentieth century have probably accepted our language as you hear and see it without much thought as to how it grew and became what it now is. The chapters running through this book have, we hope, given you a new outlook on language — an understanding that it is not a static thing, but a living, changing organism just as a human body is. Just what English will be one or two hundred years from now we cannot certainly say, but we are quite sure that our language will still be understandable, even if it is dubbed " quaint " or " archaic."

The first half of the twentieth century has brought some interesting developments. During the decade of peace before there was such a thing as a world war, there was a miniature war over Simplified Spelling. The movement was started toward the end of the nineteenth century by a group of people who deplored the unphonetic spelling of English and thought that the time had come for drastic action. In 1906, President Theodore Roosevelt directed the Government Printing Office to use three hundred simplified forms. This edict brought on a minor crisis. Protesting letters flooded the White House and storms of disapproval shook the editorial columns of newspapers and magazines. The President retracted his order. Though the Simplified Spelling Board continued to issue new lists from time to time, it never regained the prestige it had lost. Such an experience shows the impossibility of performing a major operation on language. It must change slowly by natural forces which neither man nor reason can completely control.

George Bernard Shaw continued to make his caustic thrusts at our illogical language. In the Preface to *Pygmalion* he says: " The English have no respect for their language, and will not teach their children to speak it. They spell it so abominably that no man can teach himself what it sounds like. It is impossible for an Englishman to open his mouth without making some other Englishman hate or despise him. German and Spanish are accessible to foreigners; English is not accessible even to the Englishman. The reformer England needs today is an energetic phonetic enthusiast. That is why I have made such a one the hero of a popular play." This is the play you will soon be reading (pages 718–68).

The British tend to pronounce their words even less according to the spelling than we do. For instance, we give value to every syllable of *dictionary* and *millinery,* while the British slur the unaccented syllables until the words sound like *diction'ry* and *millin'ry.* This disparity between spelling and pronunciation is especially true of place names, which frequently catch up the American tourist to his embarrassment. Some of the most striking examples are Harwich (Hăr'idge), Greenwich (Grĕn'ich), Leicester (Lĕs'ter), Cirencester (Sĭs'-eter), and Featherstonehaugh (feest''n-hay). We also have to watch out for family names, for Beauchamp is pronounced Bee'cham, and Cholmondeley sounds like Chŭm'ly. Sometimes the difference between British and American pronunciation is merely a matter of accent, as when the Englishman says *muni'ci'pal* and *labor'atory.*

English spelling shows deviation from American in such words as: *storey* (of a house), *pyjama, kerb, tyre* (of a wheel), *gaol* (jail).

Americans abroad encounter different names for many ordinary objects. The Englishman's car wears a bonnet instead of a hood. He takes a tram instead of a streetcar; drives a lorry instead of a truck. He goes to the cinema instead of the movies. He enjoys a spot of tea in the afternoon. At dinner he uses a serviette instead of a napkin. When his wife wants a spool of thread, she asks for a reel of cotton. But misunderstandings because of such terminology are growing less as the interchange between the two countries increases.

World events have given us hundreds of new words. What first appeared as servicemen's slang has often proved useful enough to be accepted in good standing. The new world of the air has produced an entire vocabulary unknown a hundred years ago. Interest in medicine and psychiatry has put new scientific terms in everyone's mouth. The inventions of the last fifty years have required new terms to describe them. Who can measure the possible effect of broadcasting on unifying speech? Already the British Broadcasting Corporation has appointed a board of six men to endeavor to arrive at a standard of speech. (The background of these six is rather surprising — one Scottish, two Welsh, one Irish, one American by birth, leaving only one who is thoroughly English.) It is possible that movies, radio, and television may have an effect upon speech comparable to that of printing upon spelling.

On the whole, the style of expression of the twentieth century has been much less formal and ornate than that of the nineteenth. Simplified spelling may have failed, but simplified style has succeeded. Credit for this may be given to the influence of journalism, certain authors like Hemingway who have a large following, and the increased tempo of life which can no longer tolerate verbosity and complicated structure. There has been great reaction against the teaching of formal grammar; some schools do not teach it at all. Those that do have eliminated many of the terms and constructions that were derived from Latin and have made it follow more closely the natural form of English.

What about English as a world language? It is now the mother tongue of two continents, North America and Australia, besides other widely scattered parts of the British Commonwealth. It is the chief secondary language of most of Western Europe, India, Japan, the Pacific Islands, and some parts of China. Its lack of complicated inflections and involved grammar make it an easy language to learn, even though the discrepancies between spelling and pronunciation are a stumbling block to foreigners.

Thus we see that the English language, which started as a mere rivulet, has grown into a mighty river. What its social and cultural future may be we can only guess, but we can ourselves participate in its linguistic future as sensitive users of English words.

MODERN POETRY

THE POETRY of the twentieth century, like its life, is diverse and complex. Our time, when horizons are widening in many directions, is one of a bewildering variety of stimuli, challenges, frustrations, and rewards. In many periods of the past poets sought to escape from the confusions of life about them by withdrawing into a realm of their own, sometimes distant in time and place, sometimes purely imaginary. They even had a language of their own. Certain subjects and forms of expression were " poetic," others were considered unsuitable to a poem. But the twentieth century's dominant mood in every type of literature has been one of realism. Nothing that the poet sees about him is regarded as too commonplace or too prosaic for a poem. He may see hidden meaning or underlying beauty anywhere. For instance, in the nineteenth century many condemned the railroad as destructive of the natural beauty of the countryside, but Stephen Spender finds in an express train unique harmonies unknown to nature (see page 657).

The twentieth century has produced some new attitudes toward life and toward human beings. Auden scoffs at some of these in his poems on page 655. Many discoveries have been made about the human mind, particularly about the unconscious mind, which is not controlled by reason or the will. Modern poets sometimes write in terms of half-realized desires, hidden realities, or a " stream of consciousness," depending on the reader to provide the associations that will make the poem meaningful. Writers as different as Yeats and Eliot, De la Mare and Auden are pioneers in applying psychological insights to poetry.

Modern poetry can often be identified by its marked difference of expression from that of the past. This was first evident in the discarding of the more formal or flowery phrases of some earlier poetry in favor of specific and colloquial language, which added vigor to the verse. Then followed experimentation with free rhythms that often broke away completely from standard meters. Other poets introduced powerful symbols to suggest their meaning. Such experimentation is exciting; it may also be puzzling. But when the reader becomes accustomed to new sounds, and, by thoughtful rereading, grasps the idea, he is repaid many times in enjoyment.

These are the chief *new* offerings that modern poetry has for us. Because the life of our century is the culmination of life in preceding ages, its poetry has also developed from what has gone before. Many poems in this section are characterized by the beauty of language, the regularity of rhythm, the love of nature, and the universal meaning that have always been associated with good poetry.

At the beginning of the twentieth century the poets were, on the whole, simple, cheerful, positive, and pleased with themselves. Perhaps they were a bit sentimental — that is, they responded with too much emotion to actual life, weeping or cheering a bit too easily.

The first group of poets that rebelled against this simple cheerfulness formed the Imagist Movement, which flourished from 1912 to 1917. The Imagists believed that a poem should be cool, unimpassioned, short. It should follow a natural and free rhythm of its own, instead of fitting into artificial and sometimes padded regular stanzas. The Imagist influence is still apparent in the irregular rhythms of today's poets, and in their distrust of rhetoric and of obvious teaching in poetry.

World War I developed a group of young soldier poets torn by pity at the bloodshed they witnessed, but filled with hope that a better world might quickly emerge from the conflict. Siegfried Sassoon, whom you will meet in the following pages, was one of these. In the 1920's there was a reaction against such optimism. Young men and women talked of themselves as the Lost Generation, and the poets of the Twenties spent their energies in describing chaos, in reflecting in their poems the puzzles that they found in the world, and in reacting against evils by writing brilliant satires.

In the 1930's there was another reaction, this time against the mocking cynicism of the Twenties. A new group of young poets championed extreme, radical political opinions — W. H. Auden, Stephen Spender, and others. Their poems tended to criticize existing society, to show sympathy with the underprivileged and the outcasts, and to predict a better world to come. The seriousness of their opinions is best shown in the Spanish Civil War of the late 1930's, when many of them, by their participation, actively supported the Loyalists.

Literature is always striking a balance. If a strong trend in one direction upsets the balance, the next generation or decade tends to initiate a counter trend. Since much of the earlier poetry was quite difficult, many poets of the 1940's and 1950's try to make a poem simple. World War II produced a large number of poets who, because they had been brought face to face with grim situations, wished to make their poems and their lives count for something.

There is enough variety of the old and the new so that anyone ought to be able to find favorite friends. Modern poetry has many voices. Some of them, you will find as you listen to them, voice your own ideas and impulses. For we can ask of a poet, in the words of W. H. Auden —

> Follow, poet, follow right
> To the bottom of the night,
> With your unconstraining voice
> Still persuade us to rejoice . . .
>
> In the deserts of the heart
> Let the healing fountain start,
> In the prison of his days
> Teach the free man how to praise.

From "In Memory of W. B. Yeats" from *Another Time* by W. H. Auden, copyright, 1940, by W. H. Auden. Reprinted by permission of Random House, Inc., and Faber and Faber Limited.

A. E. HOUSMAN 1859–1936

Alfred Edward Housman's reputation as a poet rests on the high quality of his comparatively few poems. In 1896 he published *A Shropshire Lad,* containing sixty-three simple lyrics. They were the meditations of a farm boy, many of them tinged with a wistful, ironic, or pessimistic tone, but others filled with the joyousness of springtime in the country. So distinctive was the flavor of these poems that Housman was immediately established as a leader among the new poets of the twentieth century. He did not publish again for twenty-six years. Then it was an even smaller volume called *Last Poems.* A third volume was published after his death.

Writing poetry was not the main occupation of Housman's life, for he was a gifted classical scholar. After leaving Oxford, he worked for ten years in the government patent office, and for the rest of his life was a professor of Latin.

To an Athlete Dying Young

The time you won your town the race
We chaired you through the market-
   place;
Man and boy stood cheering by,
And home we brought you shoulder-
   high.

Today, the road all runners come,   5
Shoulder-high we bring you home,
And set you at your threshold down,
Townsman of a stiller town.

Smart lad, to slip betimes away
From fields where glory does not stay,
And early though the laurel grows,   11
It withers quicker than the rose.

Eyes the shady night has shut
Cannot see the record cut,
And silence sounds no worse than
   cheers   15
After earth has stopped the ears:

Now you will not swell the rout
Of lads that wore their honors out,
Runners whom renown outran
And the name died before the man.   20

So set, before its echoes fade,
The fleet foot on the sill of shade,
And hold to the low lintel up
The still-defended challenge-cup.

And round that early-laureled head   25
Will flock to gaze the strengthless dead,
And find unwithered on its curls
The garland briefer than a girl's.

*"Standing Youth" by Wilhelm Lehmbruck
(about 1911).*

Museum of Modern Art

"To an Athlete Dying Young" from *Collected Poems of A. E. Housman*. Copyright, 1940, by Henry Holt and Company, Inc. Reprinted by permission of the publishers, The Society of Authors as the Literary Representative of the Trustees of the Estate of the late A. E. Housman, and Messrs. Jonathan Cape Limited, publishers of A. E. Housman's *Collected Poems*.

Loveliest of Trees

Loveliest of trees, the cherry now
Is hung with bloom along the bough,
And stands about the woodland ride°
Wearing white for Eastertide.

Now, of my three score years and ten,   5
Twenty will not come again,
And take from seventy springs a score,
It only leaves me fifty more.

And since to look at things in bloom
Fifty springs are little room,   10
About the woodlands I will go
To see the cherry hung with snow.

3. *ride:* a road intended for horseback travel.

Far in a Western Brookland

Far in a western brookland
  That bred me long ago
The poplars stand and tremble
  By pools I used to know.

"Loveliest of Trees" by A. E. Housman. Reprinted by permission of The Society of Authors and Jonathan Cape Limited.
"Far in a Western Brookland" from *A Shropshire Lad* by A. E. Housman. Reprinted by permission of Henry Holt and Company, Inc., and The Society of Authors as the Literary Representative of the Trustees of the Estate of the late A. E. Housman, and Messrs. Jonathan Cape Limited, publishers of A. E. Housman's *Collected Poems*.

There, in the windless nighttime,   5
  The wanderer, marveling why,
Halts on the bridge to hearken
  How soft the poplars sigh.

He hears: no more remembered
  In fields where I was known,   10
Here I lie down in London
  And turn to rest alone.

There, by the starlit fences,
  The wanderer halts and hears
My soul that lingers sighing   15
  About the glimmering weirs.

LYRICS FROM SHROPSHIRE

1. Each of the lyrics expresses a different mood. For each one, state the mood briefly and write a sentence expressing the central thought of the poem.

2. Where in these poems do you find sharp contrasts, sometimes wistful, sometimes ironical?

3. Notice that Housman uses a ballad measure. Are these poems ballads? How do they illustrate almost perfectly the usual definition of a lyric poem?

WILLIAM BUTLER YEATS 1865–1939

In contrast to the meager output of Housman, the total amount of Yeats' (yāts) writing is tremendous. This is partly due to patriotic as well as poetic fervor, for Yeats took an active part in the Celtic Renaissance, and he was a senator in the newly established Irish Free State. He was born in Dublin and educated in London, but during his early years he lived with his grandparents in the Irish coastal town of Sligo (slī'gō).

One of the founders of the Irish National Theater in Dublin, Yeats' special interest was poetic drama; but when the policy of the theater turned to realistic prose plays, Yeats proved that he could write effectively in either medium. *The Land of Heart's Desire* is an example of his richly symbolical verse dramas; *The Pot of Broth*, of a successful prose play. Today Yeats is as well known for his early lyrics, richly embroidered with metaphors and symbols. In 1923 the Nobel Prize for Literature was conferred upon him for " his consistently emotional poetry, which in the strictest artistic form expresses a people's spirit."

The Wild Swans at Coole°

The trees are in their autumn beauty,
The woodland paths are dry,
Under the October twilight the water
Mirrors a still sky;
Upon the brimming water among the stones   5
Are nine-and-fifty swans.

The nineteenth autumn has come upon me
Since I first made my count;
I saw, before I had well finished,
All suddenly mount   10
And scatter wheeling in great broken rings
Upon their clamorous wings.

I have looked upon those brilliant creatures,
And now my heart is sore.
All's changed since I, hearing at twilight,   15
The first time on this shore,
The bell-beat of their wings above my head,
Trod with a lighter tread.

Unwearied still, lover by lover,
They paddle in the cold   20
Companionable streams or climb the air;
Their hearts have not grown old;
Passion or conquest, wander where they will,
Attend upon them still.

But now they drift on the still water   25
Mysterious, beautiful;
Among what rushes will they build,
By what lake's edge or pool
Delight men's eyes when I awake some day
To find they have flown away?   30

Title: *Coole* (kōo′lĭ): the estate of Yeats' friend and fellow dramatist Lady Gregory.

Drawing by Henri Matisse for Poésies de Mallarmé (*1932*).

The Lake Isle of Innisfree

The Celtic spirit, with its yearning for the remote, the beautiful, the ideal, is melodiously caught in this poem. Of its origin
the author says: "I had still the ambition, formed . . . in my
teens, of living in imitation of Thoreau on Innisfree [a little
island in Lough Gill, Ireland] . . . and when walking through
Fleet Street [London], very homesick, I heard a little tinkle of
water and saw a fountain in a shopwindow . . . and began to
remember lake water. From the sudden remembrance came
my poem, 'Innisfree.'"

I will arise and go now, and go to Innisfree,
   And a small cabin build there, of clay and wattles° made;
Nine bean rows will I have there, a hive for the honeybee,
   And live alone in the bee-loud glade.

And I shall have some peace there, for peace comes dropping slow,   5
   Dropping from the veils of the morning to where the cricket sings;
There midnight's all aglimmer, and noon a purple glow,
   And evening full of the linnet's wings.

I will arise and go now, for always night and day
   I hear lake water lapping with low sounds by the shore;   10
While I stand on the roadway, or on the pavements gray,
   I hear it in the deep heart's core.

   2. *wattles:* twigs and pliable rods woven together.

The Fiddler of Dooney

From the earliest days of singers and storytellers, the Irish have
held their musicians and poets in high esteem. Although this
ballad has a light tone, underneath is the fiddler's strong belief
in the sacredness of his important calling.

When I play on my fiddle in Dooney,°   When we come to the end of time,
Folk dance like the wave of the sea;   To Peter° sitting in state,   10
My cousin is priest in Kilvarnet,°   He will smile on the three old spirits,
My brother in Moharabuiee.°   But call me first through the gate;

I passed by brother and cousin;   5   For the good are always the merry,
They read in their books of prayer;   Save by an evil chance,
I read in my book of songs   And the merry love the fiddle,   15
I bought at the Sligo fair.   And the merry love to dance;

   And when the folk there spy me,
   They will all come up to me,
   With "Here is the fiddler of Dooney!"
   And dance like a wave of the sea.   20

   1, 3, 4. *Dooney, Kilvarnet, Moharabuiee* (mō·hä·rä·bū·ē'): hamlets on the west coast of Ireland.
10. *Peter:* Saint Peter, keeper of the gates of Heaven.

"The Lake Isle of Innisfree" from *Early Poems and Stories* and "The Fiddler of Dooney" from *Later Poems* by William Butler
Yeats. Both reprinted by permission of The Macmillan Company, New York; Macmillan Company of Canada, Ltd.; and A. P.
Watt and Son.

YEATS' POEMS

1. In "The Wild Swans at Coole" at what season of the year and what time of day does the poet describe the swans? What contrast does he feel between himself and the swans after nineteen years? While watching birds fly south, have you ever asked yourself the same question as that in the last stanza?

2. What details in "The Lake Isle of Innisfree" suggest the peace of spirit to be found there? To which poem of Housman's does it have some resemblance in mood?

3. Why does the fiddler of Dooney mention the occupation of his two relatives? Why does he think he will be given preference on entering Heaven? Do you agree with the philosophy in the fourth stanza?

4. What traits and ideas do you notice in these poems that might be called Irish or Celtic?

WALTER DE LA MARE 1873–1956

"Walter de la Mare's *Collected Poems* would be my first choice," said a critic once, "if I were to make a present to a child, or a sweetheart, or an old gentleman, or in general, to any happily constituted person. From the first page to the last, one is in the land of poetry, in the atmosphere of genuine folklore, in the age of creative faith."

One would scarcely suspect that the subject of this tribute spent twenty years in the London office of the Anglo-American Oil Company. A grant from the Crown enabled him to withdraw from this prosaic work in 1908 and give free rein to that rare imaginative gift which he displayed in his prose work as well as in his poetry. His *The Memoirs of a Midget* shows a distorted world as seen from the position of a midget — like Gulliver among the giants, only with pathetic rather than satirical effect. His poems for and about children have taken their place as classics beside Stevenson's *A Child's Garden of Verses*. "The Listeners" and "Silver" are De la Mare's most-quoted poems; both take us into a magical world.

The Listeners

"Is there anybody there?" said the Traveler,
　　Knocking on the moonlit door;
And his horse in the silence champed the grasses
　　Of the forest's ferny floor;
And a bird flew up out of the turret,　　　　　　　　　5
　　Above the Traveler's head;
And he smote upon the door again a second time;
　　"Is there anybody there?" he said.
But no one descended to the Traveler;
　　No head from the leaf-fringed sill　　　　　　　　10
Leaned over and looked into his gray eyes,

"The Listeners" from *Collected Poems* by Walter de la Mare. Reprinted by permission of Henry Holt and Company, Inc.

Where he stood perplexed and still.
But only a host of phantom listeners
   That dwelt in the lone house then
Stood listening in the quiet of the moonlight   15
   To that voice from the world of men;
Stood thronging the faint moonbeams on the dark stair,
   That goes down to the empty hall,
Hearkening in an air stirred and shaken
   By the lonely Traveler's call.   20
And he felt in his heart their strangeness,
   Their stillness answering his cry,
While his horse moved, cropping the dark turf,
   'Neath the starred and leafy sky;
For he suddenly smote on the door, even   25
   Louder, and lifted his head —
" Tell them I came, and no one answered,
   That I kept my word," he said.
Never the least stir made the listeners,
   Though every word he spake   30
Fell echoing through the shadowiness of the still house
   From the one man left awake.
Ay, they heard his foot upon the stirrup,
   And the sound of iron on stone,
And how the silence surged softly backward,   35
   When the plunging hoofs were gone.

Sam

When Sam goes back in memory,
   It is to where the sea
Breaks on the shingle, emerald-green,
   In white foam, endlessly;
He says — with small brown eye on
     mine —   5
   " I used to keep awake,
And lean from my window in the moon,
   Watching those billows break.
And half a million tiny hands,
   And eyes, like sparks of frost,   10
Would dance and come tumbling into
     the moon,
   On every breaker tossed.
And all across from star to star,
   I've seen the watery sea,
With not a single ship in sight,   15
   Just ocean there, and me;
And heard my father snore. And once,
   As sure as I'm alive,

Out of those wallowing, moon-flecked
     waves
   I saw a mermaid dive;   20
Head and shoulders above the wave,
   Plain as I now see you,
Combing her hair, now back, now front,
   Her two eyes peeping through;
Calling me, ' Sam! ' — quietlike —
   ' Sam–' . . .   25
   But me . . . I never went,
Making believe I kind of thought
   'Twas someone else she meant . . .
Wonderful lovely there she sat,
   Singing the night away,   30
All in the solitudinous sea
   Of that there lonely bay.
P'raps," he'd smooth his hairless mouth,
   " P'raps, if 'twere now, my son,
P'raps, if I heard a voice say, ' Sam! '
   Morning would find me gone."   36

Silver

Slowly, silently, now the moon
Walks the night in her silver shoon;
This way, and that, she peers, and sees
Silver fruit upon silver trees;
One by one the casements catch   5
Her beams beneath the silvery thatch;
Couched in his kennel, like a log,
With paws of silver sleeps the dog;
From their shadowy cote the white
   breasts peep
Of doves in a silver-feathered sleep;   10
A harvest mouse goes scampering by,
With silver claws and a silver eye;
And moveless fish in the water gleam,
By silver reeds in a silver stream.

"Silver" from *Collected Poems* by Walter de la Mare. Reprinted by permission of Henry Holt and Company, Inc.

SCENES AND STORIES

1. What is your interpretation of the story which the poet suggests in " The Listeners "? By what details of sight, sound, and silence is the atmosphere created?

What is unusual about its rhythm? Contrast the meter of the odd and even lines.

2. How old do you think Sam is? How old would you say the supposed narrator of the poem is? In what kind of speech does Sam talk? Does he use any definitely " poetic " or " unpoetic " words?

3. " Silver " presents an unusual picture. How many times is the word *silver* used?

THE POWER OF WORDS

BUILDING AN EFFECT

In " The Listeners," beginning with line 13 we find the following words, about one to a line: *phantom, lone, quiet, faint, dark, lonely, strangeness, stillness, leafy, echoing, shadowless* — all leading up to that magnificent climax in the last two lines.

In " Silver " De la Mare has created an effect of intense moonlight by repeating the same word *silver* over and over. Which of the two methods, variety or intensity, do you think is more effective? Can you find other poems which employ one or the other of these methods?

WILFRID WILSON GIBSON 1878–

Gibson, in contrast to De la Mare, writes of the world of grim realities. He was brought up in the bleak Northumbrian hills, peopled, as someone once said, by shepherds, sheep dogs, and sheep. The environment of workingmen and poor villagers sets the tone for his later poetry. Whether he treats of World War I or the lives of industrial workers, he is mainly concerned with tragedy and death. Man is at the mercy of great forces outside his will. This underlying theme is shown in " The Stone," a poem whose tragic situation and sharply chiseled lines are unforgettable. " The Ice Cart," in a lighter vein, takes us momentarily into the world of fancy, but in the end we are rudely awakened in " that intolerable street." Realism prevails.

The Stone

" And will you cut a stone for him,
To set above his head?
And will you cut a stone for him —
A stone for him? " she said.

Three days before, a splintered rock   5
Had struck her lover dead —
Had struck him in the quarry dead,
Where, careless of the warning call,

"The Stone" from *Collected Poems* by Wilfrid Wilson Gibson. Reprinted by permission of the author and The Macmillan Company.

He loitered, while the shot was fired —
A lively stripling, brave and tall,   10
And sure of all his heart desired —
A flash, a shock,
A rumbling fall —
And, broken 'neath the broken rock,
A lifeless heap, with face of clay,   15
And still as any stone he lay,
With eyes that saw the end of all.

I went to break the news to her;
And I could hear my own heart beat
With dread of what my lips might say;
But some poor fool had sped before;   21
And flinging wide her father's door,
Had blurted out the news to her,
Had struck her lover dead for her,
Had struck the girl's heart dead in her,
Had struck life lifeless, at a word,   26
And dropped it at her feet;
Then hurried on his witless way,
Scarce knowing she had heard.
And when I came she stood alone —   30
A woman, turned to stone;
And though no word at all she said,
I knew that all was known.

Because her heart was dead,
She did not sigh nor moan.   35
Her mother wept;
She could not weep.
Her lover slept;
She could not sleep.
Three days, three nights,   40
She did not stir.
Three days, three nights
Were one to her,
Who never closed her eyes
From sunset to sunrise,   45
From dawn to evenfall —
Her tearless, staring eyes,
That seeing nought, saw all.

The fourth night when I came from
     work,
I found her at my door.   50
" And will you cut a stone for him? "
She said, and spoke no more,
But followed me, as I went in,
And sank upon a chair;

And fixed her gray eyes on my face   55
With still, unseeing stare.
And, as she waited patiently,
I could not bear to feel
Those still, gray eyes that followed me,
Those eyes that plucked the heart from
     me,   60
Those eyes that sucked the breath from
     me
And curdled the warm blood in me,
Those eyes that cut me to the bone,
And pierced my marrow like cold steel.

And so I rose, and sought a stone,   65
And cut it, smooth and square;
And, as I worked, she sat and watched,
Beside me, in her chair.
Night after night, by candlelight,
I cut her lover's name.   70
Night after night, so still and white,
And like a ghost she came;
And sat beside me, in her chair,
And watched with eyes aflame.
She eyed each stroke,   75
And hardly stirred;
She never spoke
A single word;
And not a sound or murmur broke
The quiet, save the mallet stroke.   80

With still eyes ever on my hands,
With eyes that seemed to burn my
     hands,
My wincing, overwearied hands,
She watched, with bloodless lips apart,
And silent, indrawn breath;   85
And every stroke my chisel cut,
Death cut still deeper in her heart;
The two of us were chiseling,
Together, I and death.

And when at length the job was done,
And I had laid the mallet by,   91
As if, at last, her peace were won,
She breathed his name; and, with a sigh,
Passed slowly through the open door —
And never crossed my threshold more.

Next night I labored late, alone,   96
To cut her name upon the stone.

The Ice Cart

Perched on my city office-stool,
I watched with envy, while a cool
And lucky carter handled ice. . . .
And I was wandering in a trice,
Far from the gray and grimy heat   5
Of that intolerable street,
O'er sapphire berg and emerald floe,
Beneath the still, cold ruby glow
Of everlasting Polar night,
Bewildered by the queer half-light,   10
Until I stumbled, unawares,
Upon a creek where big white bears
Plunged headlong down with flourished
     heels,
And floundered after shining seals
Through shivering seas of blinding blue.
And as I watched them, ere I knew,   16
I'd stripped, and I was swimming, too,
Among the seal-pack, young and hale,
And thrusting on with threshing tail,
With twist and twirl and sudden leap   20
Through crackling ice and salty deep —
Diving and doubling with my kind,
Until at last, we left behind
Those big white, blundering hulks of
     death,
And lay, at length, with panting breath
Upon a far untraveled floe,   26
Beneath a gentle drift of snow —
Snow drifting gently, fine and white,

Out of the endless Polar night,
Falling and falling evermore   30
Upon that far untraveled shore,
Till I was buried fathoms deep
Beneath that cold, white drifting
     sleep —
Sleep drifting deep,
Deep drifting sleep. . . .   35

The carter cracked a sudden whip:
I clutched my stool with startled grip,
Awakening to the grimy heat
Of that intolerable street.

IMAGINATION AND REALISM

1. In what way does " The Stone " resemble an old ballad? a modern dramatic monologue? Three kinds of stone enter into this tragic story. Can you identify them? The girl's fate is told by inference in two simple lines. Is this more effective than a long account would be?

2. In " The Ice Cart " do you think that the speaker is describing an actual dream while dozing at his desk, or just a flight of his imagination while awake? Give your reasons. Select words that give a feeling of cold, and that convey strange lighting effects.

3. What characteristics of these two poems mark Gibson as a realistic writer? Find evidence of his powerful imagination.

"The Ice Cart" from *Collected Poems* by Wilfrid Wilson Gibson. Reprinted by permission of the author, Macmillan & Co., Ltd., and Macmillan Company of Canada, Ltd.

G. K. CHESTERTON 1874–1936

The versatile Gilbert Keith Chesterton had many sides, only one of which is represented here. Besides poetry he wrote essays and a series of detective stories.

In some ways Chesterton resembled Dr. Samuel Johnson. He was large in frame, indifferent to his personal appearance, agile in conversation, prolific in essay writing, and keenly analytic in his lives of literary men, such as Robert Browning and G. B. Shaw. One tendency of Chesterton's prose style is his use of the paradox, an apparent contradiction of terms that nevertheless throws new light on the truth. In " The World State " he expresses one of the world's problems by means of a paradox.

Lepanto

Out of a sixteenth-century battle Chesterton created one of the finest of modern chants. Banging, clanging, colorful, its music beats until we feel in our own pulses the marching song of the mighty host of warriors. This battle was fought in the Gulf of Lepanto (between central and southern Greece), on October 7, 1571. Because the capture of Cyprus by the Turks threatened the end of Venetian trade and even the stability of Spain, Pope Pius V had called for the gathering of a fleet from all the Christian nations. Don John of Austria, a brilliant strategist, was in command of the two hundred and eight vessels of the Christian powers which opposed two hundred and seventy-three small and more poorly equipped Turkish vessels. Both sides depended on galleys manned by prisoners. (This was the last important historical engagement in which galleys were used.) Through their heavier vessels and superior discipline the Christians won the battle, only a few of the Turkish vessels escaping capture or destruction. The Christians lost some eight thousand men; the Turks, more than twenty thousand. Moreover, the Turkish naval power was so broken that it never again threatened the peace of Christian Europe. These historical details are enlivened and glorified by the virile lines of this poem.

White founts falling in the Courts of the Sun,
And the Soldan of Byzantium° is smiling as they run;
There is laughter like the fountains in that face of all men feared,
It stirs the forest darkness, the darkness of his beard;
It curls the blood-red crescent, the crescent of his lips;   5
For the inmost sea° of all the earth is shaken with his ships.
They have dared the white republics on the capes of Italy,
They have dashed the Adriatic round the Lion of the Sea,°
And the Pope has cast his arms abroad for agony and loss,
And called the kings of Christendom for swords about the Cross.   10
The cold queen° of England is looking in the glass;
The shadow of the Valois° is yawning at the Mass;
From evening isles fantastical rings faint the Spanish gun,
And the Lord upon the Golden Horn° is laughing in the sun.

Dim drums throbbing, in the hills half heard,   15
Where only on a nameless throne a crownless prince° has stirred,
Where, risen from a doubtful seat and half-attainted stall,
The last knight of Europe takes weapons from the wall,
The last and lingering troubadour to whom the bird has sung,
That once went singing southward when all the world was young.   20
In that enormous silence, tiny and unafraid,
Comes up along a winding road the noise of the Crusade.
Strong gongs groaning as the guns boom far,
Don John of Austria is going to the war;

2. *Soldan of Byzantium* (sŏl'dăn . . . bĭ·zăn'shĭ·ŭm): Sultan of Constantinople. 6. *inmost sea:* the Mediterranean. 8. *Lion of the Sea:* The winged lion of St. Mark is the emblem of Venice. 11. *cold queen:* Elizabeth of England did not take part in this expedition. 12. *shadow of the Valois* (vá'lwä'): Charles IX was nominally King of France, but actually he was in the power of Catherine de' Medici, the Duchess of Valois. 14. *Lord upon the Golden Horn:* The Sultan's palace in Constantinople overlooks an arm of the Bosporus called the Golden Horn. 16. *crownless prince:* Don John of Austria.

Stiff flags straining in the night blasts cold   25
In the gloom black-purple, in the glint old-gold,
Torchlight crimson on the copper kettledrums,
Then the tuckets,° then the trumpets, then the cannon, and he comes.
Don John laughing in the brave beard curled,
Spurning of his stirrups like the thrones of all the world,   30
Holding his head up for a flag of all the free.
Love light of Spain — hurrah!
Death light of Africa!
Don John of Austria
Is riding to the sea.   35

Mahound° is in his paradise above the evening star;
(*Don John of Austria is going to the war.*)
He moves a mighty turban on the timeless houri's° knees,
His turban that is woven of the sunsets and the seas.
He shakes the peacock gardens as he rises from his ease,   40
And he strides among the treetops and is taller than the trees;
And his voice through all the garden is a thunder sent to bring
Black Azrael° and Ariel° and Ammon° on the wing.
Giants and the Genii,
Multiplex of wing and eye,   45
Whose strong obedience broke the sky
When Solomon° was king.

They rush in red and purple from the red clouds of the morn,
From the temples where the yellow gods shut up their eyes in scorn;
They rise in green robes roaring from the green hells of the sea   50
Where fallen skies and evil hues and eyeless creatures be,
On them the sea valves cluster and the gray sea forests curl,
Splashed with a splendid sickness, the sickness of the pearl;
They swell in sapphire smoke out of the blue cracks of the ground —
They gather and they wonder and give worship to Mahound.   55
And he saith, " Break up the mountains where the hermitfolk can hide,
And sift the red and silver sands lest bone of saint abide,
And chase the Giaours° flying night and day, not giving rest,
For that which was our trouble comes again out of the west.
We have set the seal of Solomon on all things under sun,   60
Of knowledge and of sorrow and endurance of things done.
But a noise is in the mountains, in the mountains, and I know
The voice that shook our palaces — four hundred years ago:°
It is he that saith not ' Kismet ';° it is he that knows not Fate;
It is Richard,° it is Raymond,° it is Godfrey° at the gate!   65
It is he whose loss is laughter when he counts the wager worth,
Put down your feet upon him, that our peace be on the earth."

28. *tuckets:* a flourish of trumpets. 36. *Mahound* (má·hound′): Mohammed. 38. *timeless houri* (hoō′rï): In the Mohammedan paradise, the faithful were rewarded with the companionship of beautiful women (*houris*) throughout eternity. 43. *Azrael* (ăz′rā·ĕl): the angel of death; *Ariel:* the spirit of the air; *Ammon:* the highest god of the Egyptians. 47. *Solomon:* According to Mohammedan legend, Solomon had a ring inscribed with the name of God which gave him control over demons and genii of the underworld. 58. *Giaours* (jourz): unbelievers; an insulting name used by Mohammedans for anyone not of their faith. 63. *four hundred years ago:* at the time of the early Crusades. 64. *Kismet:* Fate. 65. *Richard, Raymond, Godfrey:* leaders in early Crusades.

For he heard drums groaning and he heard guns jar,
(*Don John of Austria is going to the war.*)
Sudden and still — hurrah!   70
Bolt from Iberia!°
Don John of Austria
Is gone by Alcalar.

St. Michael's on his Mountain° in the sea roads of the north
(*Don John of Austria is girt and going forth.*)   75
Where the gray seas glitter and the sharp tides shift
And the seafolk labor and the red sails lift.
He shakes his lance of iron and he claps his wings of stone;
The noise is gone through Normandy; the noise is gone alone;
The North is full of tangled things and texts and aching eyes,   80
And dead is all the innocence of anger and surprise,
And Christian killeth Christian in a narrow dusty room,
And Christian dreadeth Christ that hath a newer face of doom,
And Christian hateth Mary that God kissed in Galilee —
But Don John of Austria is riding to the sea.   85
Don John calling through the blast and the eclipse
Crying with the trumpet, with the trumpet of his lips,
Trumpet that sayeth *ha!*
    Domino gloria!°
Don John of Austria   90
Is shouting to the ships.

The Pope was in his chapel before day or battle broke,
(*Don John of Austria is hidden in the smoke.*)
The hidden room in man's house where God sits all the year,
The secret window whence the world looks small and very dear.   95
He sees as in a mirror on the monstrous twilight sea
The crescent of his cruel ships whose name is mystery;
They fling great shadows foe-wards, making Cross and Castle° dark;
They veil the plumèd lions on the galleys of St. Mark;°
And above the ships are palaces of brown, black-bearded chiefs,   100
And below the ships are prisons, where with multitudinous griefs,
Christian captives° sick and sunless, all a laboring race repines
Like a race in sunken cities, like a nation in the mines.
They are lost like slaves that swat,° and in the skies of morning hung
The stairways of the tallest gods when tyranny was young.   105
They are countless, voiceless, hopeless as those fallen or fleeing on
Before the high Kings' horses in the granite of Babylon.
And many a one grows witless in his quiet room in hell
Where a yellow face looks inward through the lattice of his cell,
And he finds his God forgotten, and he seeks no more a sign —   110
(*But Don John of Austria has burst the battle line!*)

71. *Iberia:* Spain. 74. *St. Michael's on his Mountain:* Mont St. Michel, a rocky islet off the coast
of France, sacred to St. Michael. 89. *Domino gloria* (dō′mĭ·nō glō′rĭ·à): Glory be to God! 98. *Cross
and Castle:* the arms of Aragon and of Castile. 99. *galleys of St. Mark:* the Venetian ships.
102. *Christian captives:* galley slaves in the Turkish fleet. 104. *swat:* obsolete form of *sweated.*

Don John pounding from the slaughter-painted poop,
Purpling all the ocean like a bloody pirate's sloop,
Scarlet running over on the silvers and the golds,
Breaking of the hatches up and bursting of the holds,   115
Thronging of the thousands up that labor under sea
White for bliss and blind for sun and stunned for liberty.
Vivat Hispania!°
Domino gloria!
Don John of Austria   120
Has set his people free!

Cervantes° on his galley sets the sword back in the sheath
(*Don John of Austria rides homeward with a wreath.*)
And he sees across a weary land a straggling road in Spain,
Up which a lean and foolish knight° forever rides in vain,   125
And he smiles, but not as Sultans smile, and settles back the blade. . . .
(*But Don John of Austria rides home from the Crusade.*)

118. *Vivat Hispania:* Long live Spain! 122. *Cervantes* (sĕr·văn′tēz): Miguel de Cervantes (1547–1616), the author of *Don Quixote* (dŏn kwĭk′sŏt), Spain's great satirical classic. 125. *a lean and foolish knight:* Don Quixote.

The World State

Oh, how I love Humanity,
    With love so pure and pringlish,°
And how I hate the horrid French,
    Who never will be English!

The International Idea,   5
    The largest and the clearest,
Is welding all the nations now,
    Except the one that's nearest.

This compromise has long been known,
    This scheme of partial pardons,   10
In ethical societies
    And small suburban gardens —

The villas and the chapels where
    I learned with little labor
The way to love my fellow man   15
    And hate my next-door neighbor.

2. *pringlish:* a pure invention. What does the word suggest to you?

CHESTERTON'S POETRY

1. The very dash and surge of "Lepanto" tend to obscure the orderly progress of the thought, which might be analyzed as follows:
    a. The Soldan's arrogant laughter;
    b. Rumors of the gathering of the Christian hosts;
    c. Mohammed's summons to his helpers;
    d. Their arrival and Mohammed's orders to them;
    e. The rally of the Christians, forgetful of internal strifes, to the call;
    f. The Pope's scrutiny of the battle of the galleys;
    g. The thoughts of one combatant — Cervantes.
Complete each picture for color and detail.

2. Report on the battle of Lepanto as described in a history book. How closely does Chesterton follow actual occurrences?

3. "The World State" shows that it is easier to talk about brotherly love than to practice it. Can you illustrate Chesterton's point from affairs in today's world? in the United States? in your own community?

JOHN MASEFIELD 1878—

John Masefield has been England's poet laureate since 1930. Interested in common people and everyday concerns, he is a down-to-earth and robust writer.

Orphaned as a child, Masefield was at fourteen apprenticed as a cabin boy on a merchant ship. Between voyages he tramped about in various countries and for several months worked in a New York barroom. Then a reading of Chaucer reawakened in him a childhood love of poetry. He determined to return to England and devote his life to literature. His *Salt-Water Ballads* (1902) and his later book-length poem *Dauber* struck the keynote of his writing. The tang and terror of the sea, as well as its beauty, were there. His reputation was established with a long poem, *The Everlasting Mercy,* in which a brutal boxer tells of his religious conversion. This poem shocked the public by its frank language, and at the same time fascinated readers by its powerful narrative.

During a long life of active writing, Masefield has produced novels, boys' adventure stories, plays, essays, biographies, and accounts of his own war experiences at Gallipoli; but his poetry tops them all in importance.

In his younger years, Masefield lectured and read his poems in America, and was often seen among the literary people of London. At present he leads a retired life at Penbury, Gloucestershire. In person he is gentle, modest, and somewhat shy — quite different from the rough and rugged characters in his poems.

A Consecration

In this poem, the introduction to *Salt-Water Ballads,* the poet consecrates himself and his poetic efforts to the toilers and sufferers of the world.

Not of the princes and prelates with periwigged charioteers
Riding triumphantly laureled to lap the fat of the years —
Rather the scorned — the rejected — the men hemmed in with the spears;

The men of the tattered battalion which fights till it dies,
Dazed with the dust of the battle, the din, and the cries,   5
The men with the broken heads and the blood running into their eyes.

Not the bemedaled Commander, beloved of the throne,
Riding cockhorse to parade when the bugles are blown,
But the lads who carried the koppie° and cannot be known.

Not the ruler for me, but the ranker, the tramp of the road,   10
The slave with the sack on his shoulders pricked on with the goad,
The man with too weighty a burden, too weary a load.

9. *koppie:* from *kopje,* a hill; a term used by the British during the Boer War in South Africa.

"The Foundling" by Ernst Barlach (1922).

The sailor, the stoker of steamers, the man with the clout,°
The chanteyman° bent at the halliards putting a tune to the shout,
The drowsy man at the wheel and the tired lookout.   15

Others may sing of the wine and the wealth and the mirth,
The portly presence of potentates goodly in girth —
Mine be the dirt and the dross, the dust and scum of the earth!

Theirs be the music, the color, the glory, the gold;
Mine be a handful of ashes, a mouthful of mold.   20
Of the maimed, of the halt and the blind in the rain and the cold —
Of these shall my songs be fashioned, my tales be told.

   13. *clout:* a rag or cloth, here used for cleaning. 14. *chanteyman:* the sailor who leads in a song
called a chantey, used to lighten the labor at the *halliards* (ropes for hoisting).

Laugh and Be Merry

Laugh and be merry; remember, better the world with a song,
Better the world with a blow in the teeth of a wrong.
Laugh, for the time is brief, a thread the length of a span,
Laugh and be proud to belong to the old proud pageant of man.

Laugh and be merry; remember, in olden time,   5
God made heaven and earth, for joy He took in a rime,
Made them, and filled them full with the strong red wine of His mirth,
The splendid joy of the stars, the joy of the earth.

So we must laugh and drink from the deep blue cup of the sky,
Join the jubilant song of the great stars sweeping by,   10
Laugh, and battle, and work, and drink of the wine outpoured
In the dear green earth, the sign of the joy of the Lord.

Laugh and be merry together, like brothers akin,
Guesting awhile in the rooms of a beautiful inn,
Glad till the dancing stops, and the life of the music ends.   15
Laugh till the game is played; and be you merry, my friends.

The West Wind

It's a warm wind, the west wind, full of birds' cries;
I never hear the west wind but tears are in my eyes.
For it comes from the west lands, the old brown hills,
And April's in the west wind, and daffodils.

It's a fine land, the west land, for hearts as tired as mine,   5
Apple orchards blossom there, and the air's like wine.
There is cool green grass there, where men may lie at rest,
And the thrushes are in song there, fluting from the nest.

" Will ye not come home, brother? ye have been long away,
It's April, and blossom time, and white is the spray;   10
And bright is the sun, brother, and warm is the rain, —
Will ye not come home, brother, home to us again?

" The young corn is green, brother, where the rabbits run,
It's blue sky, and white clouds, and warm rain and sun.
It's song to a man's soul, brother, fire to a man's brain,   15
To hear the wild bees and see the merry spring again.

" Larks are singing in the west, brother, above the green wheat,
So will ye not come home, brother, and rest your tired feet?
I've a balm for bruised hearts, brother, sleep for aching eyes,"
Says the warm wind, the west wind, full of birds' cries.   20

"Laugh and Be Merry" and "The West Wind" from *Collected Poems* by John Masefield. Both reprinted by permission of The Macmillan Company, publishers.

It's the white road westwards is the road I must tread
To the green grass, the cool grass, and rest for heart and head,
To the violets and the warm hearts and the thrushes' song,
In the fine land, the west land, the land where I belong.

ENGLAND'S POET LAUREATE

1. What types of people inspire the poet in " A Consecration "? How does this poem (written at the beginning of the twentieth century) suggest the new trend in all forms of writing that makes the literature of our century different from that which preceded it? How does the rhyme scheme of this poem resemble that of Shelley's " Ode to the West Wind " (page 421)?

2. From the short lyrics, what do you discover as to the poet's special interests, disposition, and philosophy of life? Be specific in your answer.

ALFRED NOYES 1880—

" England's Ambassador to America " was one description of Alfred Noyes. Perhaps more than any other modern English poet, he has come to know the United States through residence, teaching, and lecturing here. Educated at Oxford, the tall, lithe Noyes was a natural athlete. He rowed on the winning crew and took part in other sports at college; and these interests later added to his appeal for American college and high school audiences before whom he lectured. For a time he was visiting professor of modern poetry at Princeton University. World War I took him to the Baltic Sea on a mine destroyer. Between the wars his home was on the Isle of Wight, where Tennyson once lived. During World War II Noyes moved to California and taught at the University of California. Many of his later poems have American settings.

Noyes' major poetic work harks back to the past. Robin Hood is the hero of his poetic drama *Sherwood;* the Elizabethan Age is reflected in his epic *Drake* and in *Tales of the Mermaid Tavern,* which pictures Shakespeare's contemporaries. Such subjects are admirably rendered by Noyes' free-swinging, rollicking ballad style. You will enjoy this vigorous style in the following poem, which is, however, set in modern London.

The Barrel Organ

There's a barrel organ caroling across a golden street
  In the City° as the sun sinks low;
And the music's not immortal; but the world has made it sweet

2. *City:* When capitalized, this word means a particular part of London — the old original center, once enclosed by walls, now the banking and business district.

And fulfilled it with the sunset glow;
And it pulses through the pleasures of the City and the pain   5
   That surround the singing organ like a large eternal light;
And they've given it a glory and a part to play again
   In the Symphony° that rules the day and night.

And now it's marching onward through the realms of old romance,
   And trolling out a fond familiar tune,   10
And now it's roaring cannon down to fight the King of France,
   And now it's prattling softly to the moon.
And all around the organ there's a sea without a shore
   Of human joys and wonders and regrets;
To remember and to recompense the music evermore   15
   For what the cold machinery forgets. . . .

         Yes; as the music changes,
            Like a prismatic glass,°
         It takes the light and ranges
            Through all the moods that pass;   20
         Dissects the common carnival
            Of passions and regrets,
         And gives the world a glimpse of all
            The colors it forgets.

         And there *La Traviata*° sighs   25
            Another sadder song;
         And there *Il Trovatore*° cries
            A tale of deeper wrong;
         And bolder knights to battle go
            With sword and shield and lance,   30
         Than ever here on earth below
            Have whirled into — *a dance!* —

Go down to Kew° in lilac time, in lilac time, in lilac time;
   Go down to Kew in lilac time (it isn't far from London!)
And you shall wander hand in hand with love in summer's wonderland;   35
   Go down to Kew in lilac time (it isn't far from London!)

The cherry trees are seas of bloom and soft perfume and sweet perfume,
   The cherry trees are seas of bloom (and oh, so near to London!)
And there they say, when dawn is high and all the world's a blaze of sky
   The cuckoo, though he's very shy, will sing a song for London.   40

The Dorian° nightingale is rare, and yet they say you'll hear him there
   At Kew, at Kew in lilac time (and oh, so near to London!)

8. *Symphony:* the rhythm of life. 18. Like the changes in light refracted by a glass prism.
25, 27. *La Traviata, Il Trovatore* (lä trä·vyä′tä, ĕl trō′vä·tö′rä): tragic operas by Verdi, containing many well-known airs. 33. *Kew:* a suburb of London, famous for its botanical gardens.
41. *Dorian:* pertaining to Doris, a district in ancient Greece.

The linnet and the throstle, too, and after dark the long halloo
   And golden-eyed *tu-whit, tu-whoo* of owls that ogle London.

For Noah hardly knew a bird of any kind that isn't heard   45
   At Kew, at Kew in lilac time (and oh, so near to London!)
And when the rose begins to pout and all the chestnut spires are out
   You'll hear the rest, without a doubt, all chorusing for London:

Come down to Kew in lilac time, in lilac time, in lilac time;
   Come down to Kew in lilac time (it isn't far from London!)   50
And you shall wander hand in hand with love in summer's wonderland;
   Come down to Kew in lilac time (it isn't far from London!)

And then the troubadour begins to thrill the golden street,
   In the City as the sun sinks low;
And in all the gaudy busses there are scores of weary feet   55
Marking time, sweet time, with a dull mechanic beat,
And a thousand hearts are plunging to a love they'll never meet.
Through the meadows of the sunset, through the poppies and the wheat,
   In the land where the dead dreams go.

. . . .

      So it's Jeremiah, Jeremiah,   60
         What have you to say
      When you meet the garland girls
         Tripping on their way?

      All around my gala hat
         I wear a wreath of roses   65
      (A long and lonely year it is
         I've waited for the May!)
      If anyone should ask you,
         The reason why I wear it is —
      My own love, my true love is coming home today.   70

And it's buy a bunch of violets for the lady
   (*It's lilac time in London; it's lilac time in London!*)
Buy a bunch of violets for the lady;
   While the sky burns blue above;

On the other side the street you'll find it shady   75
   (*It's lilac time in London; it's lilac time in London!*)
But buy a bunch of violets for the lady,
   And tell her she's your own true love.

There's a barrel organ caroling across a golden street
   In the City as the sun sinks glittering and slow;   80
And the music's not immortal; but the world has made it sweet
And enriched it with the harmonies that make a song complete
In the deeper heavens of music where the night and morning meet,
   As it dies into the sunset glow;

And it pulses through the pleasures of the City and the pain   85
    That surround the singing organ like a large eternal light,
And they've given it a glory and a part to play again
    In the Symphony that rules the day and night.

              And there, as the music changes,
                  The song runs round again;   90
              Once more it turns and ranges
                  Through all its joy and pain,
              Dissects the common carnival
                  Of passions and regrets;
              And the wheeling world remembers all   95
                  The wheeling song forgets.

              Once more *La Traviata* sighs
                  Another sadder song;
              Once more *Il Trovatore* cries
                  A tale of deeper wrong;   100
              Once more the knights to battle go
                  With sword and shield and lance
              Till once, once more, the shattered foe
                  Has whirled into — *a dance!*

Come down to Kew in lilac time, in lilac time, in lilac time;   105
    Come down to Kew in lilac time (it isn't far from London!)
And you shall wander hand in hand with love in summer's wonderland,
    Come down to Kew in lilac time (it isn't far from London!)

CITY MOODS AND MUSIC

1. What is the central idea of " The Barrel Organ "? What is the purpose of the sudden changes of meter in the course of the poem?

2. The barrel organ, which used to be a common sight in large cities, is now practically extinct. Have you ever heard one? What kinds of music are now heard in the street?

3. Compare this poem with " Alexander's Feast " (page 253). Which one seems to you more effective in showing the power of music over human emotion? Give your reasons. List some pieces of music which have a strong emotional effect on you, and tell what the effect is.

DOROTHEA MACKELLAR

From 1788 when the first British colony was founded in Australia until 1901 when it became a united commonwealth in the British Empire, this continent of the South Seas developed so rapidly that Australians had little leisure or inclination for purely literary production. With the twentieth century, however, came a quickening of the creative impulse which has increasingly brought Australia into the stream of English literature.

Typical of the poetry called forth by the patriotic fervor
of the Australians is the following poem by Dorothea Mackellar. She was born in New South Wales toward the end
of the nineteenth century, the daughter of Sir Charles Mackellar, a prominent man in the affairs of the commonwealth. In 1911, while still in her twenties, Dorothea published a book of poems, *The Closed Door,* containing " My
Country." The appeal of the poem was immediate, and it
has remained a loved and much-quoted expression of Australian devotion. Miss Mackellar has since published three
volumes of verse and three novels.

My Country

The love of field and coppice,
Of green and shaded lanes,
Of ordered woods and gardens
Is running in your veins.
Strong love of gray-blue distance,   5
Brown streams and soft, dim skies —
I know, but cannot share it,
My love is otherwise.

I love a sunburnt country,
A land of sweeping plains,   10
Of ragged mountain ranges,
Of droughts and flooding rains.
I love her far horizons,
I love her jewel-sea,
Her beauty and her terror —   15
The wide brown land for me!

The stark white ring-barked forests,
All tragic to the moon,
The sapphire-misted mountains,
The hot gold hush of noon,   20
Green tangle of the brushes
Where lithe lianas° coil,
And orchids deck the tree-tops,
And ferns the warm dark soil.

Core of my heart, my country!   25
Her pitiless blue sky,
When sick at heart, around us
We see the cattle die —

But then the gray clouds gather,
And we can bless again   30
The drumming of an army,
The steady soaking rain.

Core of my heart, my country!
Land of the rainbow gold,
For flood and fire and famine   35
She pays us back threefold.
Over the thirsty paddocks,
Watch after many days,
The filmy veil of greenness
That thickens as we gaze . . .   40

An opal-hearted country,
A willful, lavish land —
All you who have not loved her,
You will not understand —
Though Earth holds many splendors,   45
Wherever I may die,
I know to what brown country,
My homing thoughts will fly.

AUSTRALIAN LANDSCAPE

1. To whom is the first stanza apparently addressed? What marked contrast is
there between that country and the poet's
native land?

2. What hardships and unpleasant conditions does she emphasize? Does this diminish or increase the effect of her love
for her country? Why?

3. What similarities can you see between the scenery of " My Country " and
that of certain parts of the United States?

22. *lianas* (lê-ä′näz): climbing plants that
have roots in the ground. Woody lianas are
characteristic of tropical rain forests.

" My Country " by Dorothea Mackellar from *Book of New Zealand and Australian Verse,* 1945 and 1949 Editions. Reprinted by
permission of the author.

RUPERT BROOKE

1887–1915

Rupert Brooke was outstanding among several young poets who died in World War I. " A golden young Apollo," as a friend called him, he started out life with everything in his favor: good looks, a keen mind, athletic prowess, and fine family background (his father was assistant headmaster of Rugby school). After college he traveled extensively throughout Europe, America, and the South Seas. Soon after he enlisted in the war, he was sent to the Dardanelles, but he never reached this destination. Death by blood poisoning overtook him on the way. The little island of Skyros in the Aegean Sea is the " corner of a foreign field that is forever England " that Brooke mentions in his sonnet " The Soldier." The manuscript of this sonnet is kept in the British Museum as a symbol and memorial of a whole generation of young men.

Brooke managed to live intensely during his few years, as is shown by the following poem, which lists all the simple things of our common life which gave him especial joy. Through perpetuating them in this much-prized poem he did indeed " cheat drowsy Death."

The Great Lover

I have been so great a lover: filled my days
So proudly with the splendor of Love's praise,
The pain, the calm, the astonishment,
Desire illimitable, and still content,
And all dear names men use, to cheat despair,   5
For the perplexed and viewless streams that bear
Our hearts at random down the dark of life.
Now, ere the unthinking silence on that strife
Steals down, I would cheat drowsy Death so far,
My night shall be remembered for a star   10
That outshone all the suns of all men's days.
Shall I not crown them with immortal praise
Whom I have loved, who have given me, dared with me
High secrets, and in darkness knelt to see
The inenarrable° godhead of delight?   15
Love is a flame — we have beaconed the world's night;
A city — and we have built it, these and I;
An emperor — we have taught the world to die.
So, for their sakes I loved, ere I go hence,

15. *inenarrable* (ĭn′ē·năr′ȧ·b'l): unspeakable; indescribable.

And the high cause of Love's magnificence,   20
And to keep loyalties young, I'll write those names
Golden forever, eagles, crying flames,
And set them as a banner, that men may know,
To dare the generations, burn, and blow
Out on the wind of Time, shining and streaming.   25

These I have loved:
                    White plates and cups, clean-gleaming,
Ringed with blue lines; and feathery, fairy dust;
Wet roofs, beneath the lamplight; the strong crust
Of friendly bread; and many-tasting food;
Rainbows; and the blue bitter smoke of wood;   30
And radiant raindrops couching in cool flowers;
And flowers themselves, that sway through sunny hours,
Dreaming of moths that drink them under the moon;
Then, the cool kindliness of sheets, that soon
Smooth away trouble; and the rough male kiss   35
Of blankets; grainy wood; live hair that is
Shining and free; blue-massing clouds; the keen
Unpassioned beauty of a great machine;
The benison of hot water; furs to touch;
The good smell of old clothes; and other such —   40
The comfortable smell of friendly fingers,
Hair's fragrance, and the musty reek that lingers
About dead leaves and last year's ferns —
                                        Dear names,
And thousand others throng to me! Royal flames;
Sweet water's dimpling laugh from tap or spring;   45
Holes in the ground; and voices that do sing —
Voices in laughter, too; and body's pain,
Soon turned to peace; and the deep-panting train;
Firm sands; the little dulling edge of foam
That browns and dwindles as the wave goes home;   50
And washen stones, gay for an hour; the cold
Graveness of iron; moist black earthen mold;
Sleep; and high places; footprints in the dew;
And oaks; and brown horse chestnuts, glossy-new;
And new-peeled sticks; and shining pools on grass —   55
All these have been my loves. And these shall pass.
Whatever passes not, in the great hour,
Nor all my passion, all my prayers, have power
To hold them with me through the gate of Death.
They'll play deserter, turn with the traitor breath,   60
Break the high bond we made, and sell Love's trust
And sacramental covenant to the dust.
— Oh, never a doubt but, somewhere, I shall wake,
And give what's left of love again, and make
New friends, new strangers —
                            But the best I've known,   65

Stays here, and changes, breaks, grows old, is blown
About the winds of the world, and fades from brains
Of living men, and dies.
                Nothing remains.

O dear my loves, O faithless, once again
This one last gift I give: that after men   70
Shall know, and later lovers, far-removed,
Praise you, " All these were lovely "; say, " He loved."

The Soldier

If I should die, think only this of me:
    That there's some corner of a foreign field
That is forever England. There shall be
    In that rich earth a richer dust concealed;
A dust whom England bore, shaped, made aware,   5
    Gave, once, her flowers to love, her ways to roam,
A body of England's, breathing English air,
    Washed by the rivers, blest by suns of home.

And think, this heart, all evil shed away,
    A pulse in the eternal mind, no less   10
        Gives somewhere back the thought by England given;
Her sights and sounds; dreams happy as her day;
    And laughter, learnt of friends; and gentleness,
        In hearts at peace, under an English heaven.

LIFE AND IMMORTALITY

1. Note in " The Great Lover " the keen awareness and the vigorous enthusiasm that the poet brought to the everyday experiences of living. How many of the things listed in the poem would you choose for your personal list of " loves "? What other things would you include?

2. Look through the list to discover some original metaphors, such as the " cool kindliness " of sheets and raindrops " couching " in cool flowers.

3. In " The Soldier " how is the poet's idea of immortality linked with his ideal of patriotism? Why do you think this poem is especially prized? In what way can it be said to have universal appeal, even though the feeling expressed is toward England?

4. In both of these poems Brooke has touched in some way on immortality. Compare his ideas on the subject with those expressed in Tennyson's *In Memoriam* (page 484) and Wordsworth's " Ode on Immortality " (page 367). Whose ideas seem most convincing?

SUGGESTIONS FOR WRITING

1. Write a description of familiar objects or scenes in your life that you would consider your " loves." (If you prefer to try poetry, go ahead.) Try to use some fresh and striking metaphors as Brooke does, to give the reader a quick picture or a sympathetic reaction to the thing described.

2. The converse of this theme also makes for natural expression — things you hate. A sample of this theme is Carroll's " A Sea Dirge " (page 512). Which subject — your likes or your dislikes — lends itself best to humorous treatment?

SIEGFRIED SASSOON 1886—

The terrible toll that World War I took of young poets was
not only in the loss of promising young lives but also in
the bitterness it left with the survivors. " Let no one from
henceforth," said Siegfried Sassoon, " say one word coun-
tenancing war." Sassoon was a young man of wealthy family, an Oxford graduate who wrote poetry, and loved hunting and music. His life was abruptly changed by military
service — as were the lives of hundreds of men. He was
made a captain, and was later awarded the Military Cross
for bravery. His experiences convinced him of the fundamental baseness and futility of war, and his poems painted
it with uncompromising realism. Much of Sassoon's writing
in the Twenties and Thirties was milder in tone, but he will
probably be best remembered for his invectives against war.

Dreamers

Soldiers are citizens of death's gray land,
   Drawing no dividend from time's tomorrows.
In the great hour of destiny they stand,
   Each with his feuds, and jealousies, and sorrows.
Soldiers are sworn to action; they must win   5
   Some flaming, fatal climax with their lives.
Soldiers are dreamers; when the guns begin
   They think of firelit homes, clean beds, and wives.

I see them in foul dug-outs, gnawed by rats,
   And in the ruined trenches, lashed with rain.   10
Dreaming of things they did with balls and bats,
   And mocked by hopeless longing to regain
Bank-holidays, and picture shows, and spats,
   And going to the office in the train.

Everyone Sang

The armistice of World War I came on November 11, 1918.
Imagine how the sudden news affected soldiers who had gone
through four hard years of fighting!

Everyone suddenly burst out singing;
And I was filled with such delight ——
As prisoned birds must find in freedom
Winging wildly across the white ——
Orchards and dark green fields; on; on; and out of sight.   5

Everyone's voice was suddenly lifted,
And beauty came like the setting sun.
My heart was shaken with tears, and horror
Drifted away. . . . O, but everyone
Was a bird; and the song was wordless; the singing will never be done.   10

A SOLDIER'S POEMS

1. How does Sassoon show his feeling toward war in " Dreamers "? What does the second line mean? (In the business world, what are dividends?) In what sense do we, in times of peace, draw dividends from the future?

2. How do the dreams of these soldiers suggest the difference between the fighters of the two great world wars of the twen-

tieth century and those of earlier wars? What references in the poem point toward World War I rather than World War II?

3. Is this poem a sonnet? Prove your answer. What do you notice that is unusual about the rhyme scheme?

4. In " Everyone Sang " why is Sassoon's comparison of a soldier with a free-winging bird so appropriate? Why was the song " wordless "? In what way will the singing " never be done "?

T. S. ELIOT 1888—

Thomas Stearns Eliot's literary career is a marked example of the changes a man's thinking may undergo with the shifting experiences of life. By birth he was a Middle Western American from St. Louis, Missouri. Moving eastward, he attended Harvard, then the Sorbonne in Paris, then Oxford as a Rhodes scholar. The English way of life so appealed to him that he continued to live abroad and in 1927 became a naturalized British subject.

In his early poems Eliot revolted against the cheerfulness, smoothness, and obviousness of preceding poets. He wrote poetry that was hard and brittle. In design, these poems are zigzags of classical allusions, wit, obscure symbols, and cryptic phrases. In mood, they convey the impression that life is futile — hardly worth the effort of drawing breath. Note the titles of his most famous early poems — *The Waste Land* and *The Hollow Men*.

But his next long poem, *Ash Wednesday* (1930) showed a change in Eliot's attitude. The note of despair is gradually replaced by one of religious faith. From that time on, Eliot's work takes on a different tone. In *Murder in the Cathedral* he dramatized the death of Thomas à Becket, a Christian martyr of the time of Henry II. This beautiful and significant verse play has often been produced by professional and religious groups. In recent years Eliot has produced two more successful plays in verse, *The Cocktail Party* (1950) and *The Confidential Clerk* (1953). The dialogue in his plays is patterned in a loose metrical form somewhat like *Beowulf*. All his writing — drama, poetry, and prose — has subtle underlying meanings which are not apparent from a superficial reading. His work repays thoughtful study.

The Hollow Men

Mistah Kurtz — he dead.
*A penny for the Old Guy.**

"Interior of Helmet"
by Henry Moore (1940).

I

We are the hollow men
We are the stuffed men
Leaning together
Headpiece filled with straw. Alas!
Our dried voices, when   5
We whisper together
Are quiet and meaningless
As wind in dry grass
Or rats' feet over broken glass
In our dry cellar   10

    Shape without form, shade without
      color,
Paralyzed force, gesture without mo-
    tion;°

    Those who have crossed
With direct eyes, to death's other King-
    dom°
Remember us — if at all — not as lost
Violent souls, but only   16
As the hollow men
The stuffed men.

II

Eyes I dare not meet in dreams
In death's dream kingdom   20
These do not appear:
There, the eyes are
Sunlight on a broken column
There, is a tree swinging
And voices are   25
In the wind's singing

* *Mistah Kurtz:* a character in Joseph Conrad's novel *Heart of Darkness*, a cultivated
philosopher who dies unremembered in the
African jungle. *A penny for the Old Guy:* This is
a cry used by children on Guy Fawkes Day in
England to obtain handouts, much as is done
in America on Halloween. 12. These are descriptions, or suggestions, of modern man's lack
of power and usefulness. 13–14. The dead, who
stare (*with direct eyes*); *death's other Kingdom*
implies that this life is a kind of death also.

More distant and more solemn
Than a fading star.

Let me be no nearer
In death's dream kingdom   30
Let me also wear
Such deliberate disguises
Rat's coat, crowskin, crossed staves
In a field
Behaving as the wind behaves   35
No nearer —

Not that final meeting
In the twilight kingdom

III

This is the dead land
This is cactus land   40
Here the stone images
Are raised, here they receive
The supplication of a dead man's hand°
Under the twinkle of a fading star.

Is it like this   45
In death's other kingdom
Waking alone
At the hour when we are
Trembling with tenderness
Lips that would kiss   50
Form prayers to broken stone.

IV

The eyes are not here
There are no eyes here
In this valley of dying stars
In this hollow valley   55
This broken jaw of our lost kingdoms

In this last of meeting places
We grope together
And avoid speech
Gathered on this beach of the tumid
river   60

Sightless, unless
The eyes reappear

43. Men pray (*supplication*) to outworn tradition (*stone images*). In the next stanza the
poet says that men desire the vigor and warmth
of life (*would kiss*) but can only pray fearfully,
because of their lack of faith.

As the perpetual star°
Multifoliate rose
Of death's twilight kingdom   65
The hope only
Of empty men.

V

*Here we go round the prickly pear
Prickly pear prickly pear
Here we go round the prickly pear   70
At five o'clock in the morning.°*

Between the idea
And the reality
Between the motion
And the act   75
Falls the Shadow°
      For Thine is the Kingdom

Between the conception
And the creation
Between the emotion   80
And the response
Falls the Shadow
            Life is very long

Between the desire
And the spasm   85
Between the potency
And the existence
Between the essence
And the descent
Falls the Shadow   90
      For Thine is the Kingdom

63. That is, men will be ineffectual (*sightless*)
unless they regain their faith (*eyes reappear as
the perpetual star*). 71. This is, of course, a familiar nursery rhyme. *Prickly pear* is desert
cactus and thus is appropriately substituted
for the usual "mulberry bush." Contrasted
with the Lord's Prayer line that follows (*For
Thine is the Kingdom*), the nursery rhyme suggests the meaninglessness of modern life.
76. Once again the poet indicates man's lack
of power and usefulness. This stanza and the
two that follow say that man has lost the power
to achieve, to accomplish, to build; always the
Shadow of lost faith and failure falls between
what he seeks and what he obtains.

For Thine is
Life is
For Thine is the

  This is the way the world ends   95
This is the way the world ends
This is the way the world ends
Not with a bang but a whimper.

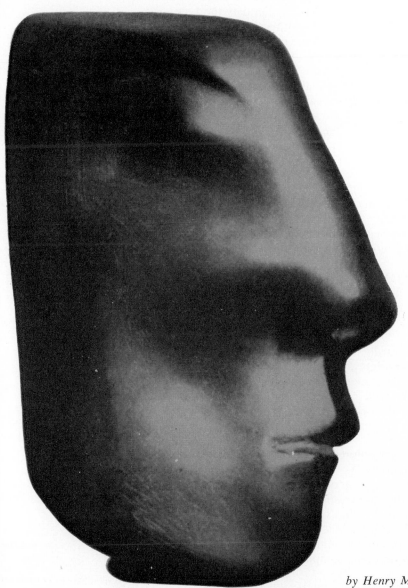

"Mask"
by Henry Moore (1930).

Macavity: the Mystery Cat

"Macavity" illustrates Eliot's sense of humor and witty interplay of words. It is from a book of fourteen short poems about cats, *Old Possum's Book of Practical Cats,* which begins with the theory that all cats have three names: the one they are known by, an individual name that describes them alone, and their secret name that they apparently meditate upon for long periods. The individual names given by the poet to various types of cat are indeed masterpieces. In the following poem, Macavity suggests a *cavity* — nothing there. See how appropriate it is to the animal's nature.

Macavity's a Mystery Cat: he's called the Hidden Paw —
For he's the master criminal who can defy the Law.
He's the bafflement of Scotland Yard, the Flying Squad's despair:
For when they reach the scene of crime — *Macavity's not there!*

Macavity, Macavity, there's no one like Macavity, 5
He's broken every human law, he breaks the law of gravity.
His powers of levitation would make a fakir stare,
And when you reach the scene of crime — *Macavity's not there!*
You may seek him in the basement, you may look up in the air —
But I tell you once and once again, *Macavity's not there!* 10

Macavity's a ginger cat, he's very tall and thin;
You would know him if you saw him, for his eyes are sunken in.
His brow is deeply lined with thought, his head is highly domed;
His coat is dusty from neglect, his whiskers are uncombed.
He sways his head from side to side, with movements like a snake; 15
And when you think he's half asleep, he's always wide awake.

Macavity, Macavity, there's no one like Macavity,
For he's a fiend in feline shape, a monster of depravity.
You may meet him in a by-street, you may see him in the square —
But when a crime's discovered, then *Macavity's not there!* 20

He's outwardly respectable. (They say he cheats at cards.)
And his footprints are not found in any file of Scotland Yard's.
And when the larder's looted or the jewel case is rifled,
Or when the milk is missing or another Peke's been stifled,
Or the greenhouse glass is broken, and the trellis past repair — 25
Ay, there's the wonder of the thing! *Macavity's not there!*

And when the Foreign Office finds a Treaty's gone astray,
Or the Admiralty lose some plans and drawings by the way,
There may be a scrap of paper in the hall or on the stair —
But it's useless to investigate — *Macavity's not there!* 30
And when the loss has been disclosed, the Secret Service say:
"It *must* have been Macavity!" — but he's a mile away.
You'll be sure to find him resting, or a-licking of his thumbs,
Or engaged in doing complicated long division sums.

Macavity, Macavity, there's no one like Macavity,   35
There never was a cat of such deceitfulness and suavity.
He always has an alibi and one or two to spare:
At whatever time the deed took place — MACAVITY WASN'T THERE!
And they say that all the cats whose wicked deeds are widely known
(I might mention Mungojerrie, I might mention Griddlebone)   40
Are nothing more than agents for the Cat who all the time
Just controls their operations: the Napoleon of Crime!

TWO SIDES OF ELIOT

1. Try to state in simple direct words the thought of each section of "The Hollow Men." Besides the symbols explained in the footnotes look for other symbols which you can interpret yourself. Compare expressions like "a headpiece filled with straw" with the slang phrase "a stuffed shirt." Do these phrases describe the same or different types of men?

2. What prominent men of today would you class as "hollow men"? Which are the opposite, full of character and purpose?

3. Compare "The Hollow Men" with Shakespeare's famous lines in *Macbeth*, "Out, out, brief candle" (page 192, lines 23–28). Which poet better conveys to you the idea that life is meaningless? Eliot arrives at this conclusion at the beginning of his life, Macbeth at the end. What differences do you see in the causes that made each arrive at this opinion?

4. In "Macavity," point out various attributes of a human criminal given to Macavity. How is the atmosphere of a detective story maintained? Would this poem be equally pertinent if written about a dog? Why or why not? Have you ever known a cat like Macavity?

W. H. AUDEN 1907–

Wystan Hugh Auden's life falls into two parts. His first thirty-two years were spent mostly in England. He was born in York, educated at Oxford, and for a while was a schoolmaster. The year 1937 was an important one for him. Like many other young writers of both England and America, he went to the help of the Loyalists in the Spanish Civil War, by driving an ambulance. In that same year he married the daughter of Thomas Mann, the famous German novelist, and was also awarded the King's Poetry medal.

A new phase of Auden's life began in 1939 when he came to the United States to take up permanent residence. While living in Brooklyn, he wrote an opera about the American folk hero Paul Bunyan. He frequently reads and lectures in American colleges.

Auden has written plays and critical articles, sometimes in collaboration with other writers. His main interest, however, is poetry, and he has been called the most versatile living poet. His early work shows the influence of Gerard Manley Hopkins in its obscurity and its rather strange, crowded figures of speech. His friend Stephen Spender once said that Auden's poetry has a "vitality, an explosive violence that leaves his contemporaries dazed."

Musée des Beaux Arts°

About suffering they were never wrong,
The Old Masters: how well they understood
Its human position; how it takes place
While someone else is eating or opening a window or just walking dully along;
How, when the aged are reverently, passionately waiting   5
For the miraculous birth, there always must be
Children who did not specially want it to happen, skating
On a pond at the edge of the wood:
They never forgot
That even the dreadful martyrdom must run its course   10
Anyhow in a corner, some untidy spot
Where the dogs go on with their doggy life and the torturer's horse
Scratches its innocent behind on a tree.

In Brueghel's *Icarus,*° for instance: how everything turns away
Quite leisurely from the disaster; the ploughman may   15
Have heard the splash, the forsaken cry,
But for him it was not an important failure; the sun shone
As it had to on the white legs disappearing into the green
Water; and the expensive delicate ship that must have seen
Something amazing, a boy falling out of the sky,   20
Had somewhere to get to and sailed calmly on.

Title: *Musée des Beaux Arts* (mü'·zā' dă bōz är): Museum of Fine Arts. 14. *Icarus* (ĭk'·à·rŭs): a
painting by Pieter Brueghel (brû'gĕl) (1564?–1638?) in the Royal Museum in Brussels. In a Greek
legend, Icarus attempted to fly with a pair of wings made of feathers held together by wax. They
melted when he got too near the sun, and he fell into the sea and was drowned.

Who's Who

This sonnet contrasts a man's active public life — as reflected
by the kind of facts recorded in *Who's Who* — with a facet of
his intimate private life. The poet makes no comment but lets
the reader judge for himself which of the two sides of his life
is more important.

A shilling life° will give you all the facts:
How Father beat him, how he ran away,
What were the struggles of his youth, what acts
Made him the greatest figure of his day:
Of how he fought, fished, hunted, worked all night,   5
Though giddy, climbed new mountains; named a sea:
Some of the last researchers even write
Love made him weep his pints like you and me.
With all his honors on, he sighed for one
Who, say astonished critics, lived at home;   10
Did little jobs about the house with skill
And nothing else; could whistle; would sit still
Or potter round the garden; answered some
Of his long marvelous letters but kept none.

1. *shilling life:* a biography in a popular edition (bought for a shilling).

The Unknown Citizen

(To JS/07/M/378*

THIS MARBLE MONUMENT IS
ERECTED BY THE STATE)

He was found by the Bureau of Statistics to be
One against whom there was no official complaint,
And all the reports on his conduct agree
That, in the modern sense of an old-fashioned word, he was a saint,
For in everything he did he served the Greater Community.
Except for the war till the day he retired
He worked in the factory and never got fired,
But satisfied his employers, Fudge Motors Inc.
Yet he wasn't a scab or odd in his views,
For his Union reports that he paid his dues,   10
(Our report on his Union shows it was sound)
And our Social Psychology workers found
That he was popular with his mates and liked a drink.
The Press are convinced that he bought a paper every day
And that his reactions to advertisements were normal in every way. 15
Policies taken out in his name prove that he was fully insured,
And his Health Card shows he was once in hospital but left it cured.

* *JS/07/M/378:* the unknown citizen's file number.

Both Producers Research and High-Grade Living declare
He was fully sensible to the advantages of the Installment Plan
And had everything necessary to the Modern Man,   20
A phonograph, a radio, a car, and a frigidaire.
Our researchers into Public Opinion are content
That he held the proper opinions for the time of year.
When there was peace, he was for peace; when there was war, he went.
He was married and added five children to the population,   25
Which our Eugenists say was the right number for a parent of his generation,
And our teachers report that he never interfered with their education.
Was he free? Was he happy? The question is absurd:
Had anything been wrong, we certainly should have heard.

A POET WHO QUESTIONS

1. In "Musée des Beaux Arts" what does Auden mean by the "human position" of suffering? How does he see suffering portrayed in the painting of Icarus? State in a sentence the main idea of the poem. Does this point of view seem hard-hearted to you?

2. In "Who's Who" what is the marked contrast between the man's public life and his private life? Is the "one" he loved the kind of person you would expect him to choose? Why or why not? What does the last line show you about this person?

3. In what ways is the individual pictured in "The Unknown Citizen" typical of our times? What method widely used by business, social, and government organizations is held up to scorn here? Comment on the last two lines of the poem. What is their significance? What light do they throw on the attitude of the poet toward our civilization?

STEPHEN SPENDER

1909—

At seventeen Stephen Spender had his own printing press and was earning money by printing labels. Later he put the press to good use in printing his own poems. He did not need to depend on it for an income, however, for his father, a journalist and lecturer at Oxford, was well-to-do. Spender was able to devote himself to poetry, and later to literary magazines. At Oxford he associated with a small group of poets of the "new school," of which Auden was the leader.

Just before World War II, Spender traveled and studied in Germany, where his blue eyes, golden hair, and fair skin brought him the compliment of being a specimen of the "pure Nordic type." He was secretly both amused and irritated by this description, for the Nazis, not knowing that his mother was partly Jewish, at once made apparent their false ideas on race.

Spender is not so satirical as some of the other poets of his generation, nor does he seek poetry as an escape. He thinks that poetry should say to the reader, "This is what life is like. It is even realer, less to be evaded than you thought. But I offer you an example of acceptance and understanding. Now, go back and live!"

The Express

After the first powerful plain manifesto
The black statement of pistons, without more fuss
But gliding like a queen, she leaves the station.
Without bowing and with restrained unconcern
She passes the houses which humbly crowd outside,   5
The gasworks and at last the heavy page
Of death, printed by gravestones in the cemetery.
Beyond the town there lies the open country
Where, gathering speed, she acquires mystery,
The luminous self-possession of ships on ocean.   10
It is now she begins to sing — at first quite low,
Then loud, and at last with a jazzy madness —
The song of her whistle screaming at curves,
Of deafening tunnels, brakes, innumerable bolts.
And always light, aerial, underneath   15
Goes the elate meter of her wheels.
Steaming through metal landscape on her lines,
She plunges new eras of wild happiness
Where speed throws up strange shapes, broad curves,
And parallels clean like the steel of guns.   20
At last, further than Edinburgh or Rome,
Beyond the crest of the world, she reaches night
Where only a low streamline brightness
Of phosphorus on the tossing hills is white.
Ah, like a comet through flame, she moves entranced   25
Wrapt in her music no bird song, no, nor bough
Breaking with honey buds, shall ever equal.

Moving Through
the Silent Crowd

Moving through the silent crowd
Who stand behind dull cigarettes
These men who idle in the road
I have the sense of falling light.

They lounge at corners of the street   5
And greet friends with a shrug of
    shoulder
And turn their empty pockets out,
The cynical gestures of the poor.

Now they've no work, like better men
Who sit at desks and take much pay.   10
They sleep long nights and rise at ten
To watch the hours that drain away.

I'm jealous of the weeping hours
They stare through with such hungry
    eyes.
I'm haunted by these images,   15
I'm haunted by their emptiness.

Word

The word bites like a fish.
Shall I throw it back free
Arrowing to that sea
Where thoughts lash tail and fin?
Or shall I pull it in   5
To rhyme upon a dish?

AN OBSERVER OF MODERN LIFE

1. Is the poem " The Express " purely pictorial or does it offer comments on modern living as well? Older poets, like Wordsworth, for example, looked on the railroad as an ugly intrusion on the beauties of nature. What do you think is Spender's view on this matter?

2. " Moving Through the Silent Crowd " pictures the period of depression in the Thirties. What conditions have changed since then that make this situation less common? What details in the poem may still be true under certain conditions? What are the conditions? Have you ever watched a crowd similar to this one? When? Where? What psychological effects of idleness are here suggested?

3. In " Word " what is the point of having most of the poem in the form of questions? Compare this poem with an equally brief one by Emily Dickinson, " A Word," and with Elinor Wylie's " Pretty Words."

DYLAN THOMAS

1914—1953

A lecturer at Cambridge said of Dylan (dĭl′ăn) Thomas, " He was the most poetical poet of our time. He talked and dressed and behaved and lived like a poet; he was reckless, flamboyant, irreverent, innocent, and bibulous. And his verse, too, had a romantic wildness about it that even the readers who could make nothing of it recognized as ' poetic.' " Thomas' poetry is rich with symbolism and original images. A poet who often demands much of his readers, he has been hailed as the most original and refreshing lyric genius of our time.

Thomas was born in South Wales. He lived with his wife and children in the seacoast village of Laugharne. Thomas was still a young man when he died suddenly in New York City while on an American reading tour. Not long before his death he published his *Collected Poems 1934–53*. He left a number of unpublished poems which will undoubtedly appear posthumously. Thomas also wrote prose essays, poetic drama, and documentary film scripts.

Do Not Go Gentle into That Good Night

Do not go gentle into that good night,
Old age should burn and rave at close of day;
Rage, rage against the dying of the light.

Though wise men at their end know dark is right,
Because their words had forked no lightning they   5
Do not go gentle into that good night.

Good men, the last wave by, crying how bright
Their frail deeds might have danced in a green bay,
Rage, rage against the dying of the light.

Wild men who caught and sang the sun in flight,   10
And learn, too late, they grieved it on its way,
Do not go gentle into that good night.

Grave men, near death, who see with blinding sight
Blind eyes could blaze like meteors and be gay,
Rage, rage against the dying of the light.   15

And you, my father, there on the sad height,
Curse, bless, me now with your fierce tears, I pray.
Do not go gentle into that good night.
Rage, rage against the dying of the light.

Fern Hill

Now as I was young and easy under the apple boughs
About the lilting house and happy as the grass was green,
　　The night above the dingle° starry,
　　　　Time let me hail and climb
　　Golden in the heydays of his eyes,   5
And honored among wagons I was prince of the apple towns
And once below a time I lordly had the trees and leaves
　　　　Trail with daisies and barley
　　Down the rivers of the windfall light.

And as I was green and carefree, famous among the barns 10
About the happy yard and singing as the farm was home,
　　In the sun that is young once only,
　　　　Time let me play and be
　　Golden in the mercy of his means,
And green and golden I was huntsman and herdsman, the calves 15
Sang to my horn, the foxes on the hills barked clear and cold,
　　　　And the sabbath rang slowly
　　In the pebbles of the holy streams.

　　3. *dingle:* little valley.

Woodcut by Frans Masereel for Die Geschichte von Til Ulenspiegel.

All the sun long it was running, it was lovely, the hay
Fields high as the house, the tunes from the chimneys, it was air 20
   And playing, lovely and watery
     And fire green as grass.
   And nightly under the simple stars
As I rode to sleep the owls were bearing the farm away,
All the moon long I heard, blessed among stables, the night-jars° 25
   Flying with the ricks,° and the horses
     Flashing into the dark.

And then to awake, and the farm, like a wanderer white
With the dew, come back, the cock on his shoulder: it was all
   Shining, it was Adam and maiden, 30
     The sky gathered again
   And the sun grew round that very day.
So it must have been after the birth of the simple light
In the first, spinning place, the spellbound horses walking warm
   Out of the whinnying green stable 35
     On to the fields of praise.

And honored among foxes and pheasants by the gay house
Under the new made clouds and happy as the heart was long,
   In the sun born over and over,
     I ran my heedless ways, 40
   My wishes raced through the house high hay
And nothing I cared, at my sky blue trades, that time allows
In all his tuneful turning so few and such morning songs
   Before the children green and golden
     Follow him out of grace, 45

Nothing I cared, in the lamb white days, that time would take me
Up to the swallow thronged loft by the shadow of my hand,
   In the moon that is always rising,
     Nor that riding to sleep
   I should hear him fly with the high fields 50
And wake to the farm forever fled from the childless land.
Oh as I was young and easy in the mercy of his means,
     Time held me green and dying
   Though I sang in my chains like the sea.

25. *night-jars:* a kind of night bird.   26. *ricks:* haystacks.

POEMS OF VIGOR AND SUBTLETY

1. What is the poet's central thought in "Do Not Go Gentle into That Good Night"? To whom is he speaking? What do "good night" and "the dying of the light" symbolize? What other symbols in the poem can you interpret? Do you think this poem could have been written by an old man? Explain your reasoning.

2. What is the setting of "Fern Hill"? What specific scenes and activities does the poet mention?

3. "Fern Hill" is full of striking images and of sounds that are particularly memorable. Select phrases or lines that you like — why are they effective? How does the poet create the mood of exhilaration and joy? What is the thought in the last stanza that changes the mood?

HENRY REED 1914–
and SIDNEY KEYES 1922–1943

Of the several gifted young poets that have appeared in England in recent years, perhaps two are particularly important.

Henry Reed was educated in Edward VI school, and Birmingham University. He served in the army during 1941–42, and in the Foreign Office after that. In the past ten years he had been engaged in journalism, broadcasting, and writing radio scripts. One of his most interesting contributions in the latter field was a radio version of Melville's *Moby Dick*. In 1946 Reed published a volume of verse, *A Map of Verona*.

Sidney Keyes, who died in World War II at twenty-one, left a remarkable legacy of poems which had appeared in various magazines. Ninety-seven of these were collected in a memorial volume; thirty others were not considered worthy of inclusion; the verse he wrote in Africa was lost. Between the ages of sixteen and twenty-one he must have written almost one hundred and fifty short poems, many of which show merit beyond what is expected of so young a writer. Keyes entered Oxford in 1940, joined the army in 1942, and after only two weeks of active service was taken prisoner and died " from unknown causes " while in the enemy's camp.

Lives

HENRY REED

You cannot cage a field.
You cannot wire it, as you wire a summer's roses
To sell in towns; you cannot cage it
Or kill it utterly. All you can do is to force
Year after year from the stream to the cold woods   5
The heavy glitter of wheat, till its body tires
And the yield grows weaker and dies. But the field never dies,
Though you built on it, burn it black, or domicile
A thousand prisoners upon its empty features.
You cannot kill a field. A field will reach   10
Right under the streams to touch the limbs of its brothers.

But you can cage the woods.
You can throw up fences, as round a recalcitrant heart
Spring up remonstrances. You can always cage the woods,

Hold them completely. Confine them to hill or valley, 15
You can alter their face, their shape; uprooting their outer saplings
You can even alter their wants, and their smallest longings
Press to your own desires. The woods succumb
To the paths made through their life, withdraw the trees,
Betake themselves where you tell them, and acquiesce. 20
The woods retreat; their protest of leaves whirls
Pitifully to the cooling heavens, like dead or dying prayers.

But what can you do with a stream?
You can widen it here, or deepen it there, but even
If you alter its course entirely it gives the impression 25
That this is what it always wanted. Moor hens return
To nest or hide in the reeds which quickly grow up there,
The fishes breed in it, stone settles on to stone.
The stream announces its places where the water will bubble
Daily and unconcerned, contentedly ruffling and scuffling 30
With the drifting sky or the leaf. Whatever you do,
A stream has rights, for a stream is always water;
To cross it you have to bridge it; and it will not flow uphill.

Greenwich Observatory

SIDNEY KEYES

This onion-dome holds all intricacies
Of intellect and star-struck wisdom; so
Like Coleridge's head with multitudinous
Passages riddled, full of strange instruments
Unbalanced by a touch, this organism 5
From wires and dials spins introverted life.
It never looks, squat on its concrete shoulders,
Down at the river's swarming life, nor sees
Cranes' groping insect-like activity
Nor slow procession of funnels past the docks. 10
Turning its inner wheels, absorbed in problems
Of space and time, it never hears
Birds singing in the park or children's laughter.
Alive, but in another way, it broods
On this its Highgate,° hypnotized 15
In lunar reverie and calculation.
Yet night awakes it; blind lids open
Leaden to look upon the moon:
A single goggling telescopic eye
Enfolds the spheric wonder of the sky. 20

April 1940.

15. *Highgate:* a London suburb, where Coleridge lived. The high gate of a walled city was the chief exit to the outside world; so the observatory may represent an opening to the heavens.

"Greenwich Observatory" from *Collected Poems* by Sidney Keyes. Reprinted by permission of Routledge & Kegan Paul Ltd.

TWO YOUNGER POETS

1. In " Lives " what three differences are brought out between field, woods, and stream? Had you ever thought of these differences before, or do the ideas come to you with a sense of novelty? Could you make any comparison with three types of human beings?

2. Why does Keyes refer to Greenwich Observatory as an " onion-dome "? What is particularly interesting in his comparison to Coleridge's head? In what other ways is the Observatory made to resemble a human being?

READING LIST FOR MODERN POETRY

Collections of the poetry of all the writers you have just read are available and thus are not listed here. Some of these anthologies contain American as well as English verse.

Auden, W. H. (editor), *The Oxford Book of Light Verse*

Cunliffe, J. W. (editor), *Poems of the Great War*
Poetry of World War I.

Garrity, D. A. (editor), *New Irish Poets*

Gillis, Adolph, and Benét, W. R. (editors), *Poems for Modern Youth*
Easily understood poems.

Ledward, P., and Strang, C. (editors), *Poems of This War*
The poems of World War II.

Le Gallienne, Richard (editor), *A Modern Book of English Verse*

Stephens, James, *Collected Poems*
Poems by an Irishman with a sharp wit and a gay fancy.

Untermeyer, Louis (editor), *Modern British Poetry*
Editions of this comprehensive anthology have been coming out since 1920. Excellent biographical and critical materials are included.

Yeats, W. B. (editor), *The Oxford Book of Modern Verse*

FOR LISTENING

The following poems have been recorded and are available on *Many Voices 6B:* " The Hollow Men," " Do Not Go Gentle into That Good Night."

The reproductions of the works of art that appear with the poems in this section have been selected for their appropriateness to a setting in which modern poetry is being read, discussed, and thought about. The artists are all contemporaries of the poets; they have in common a depth of insight and intensity of feeling about the plight of modern man.

Wilhelm Lehmbruck (p. 622): born in Germany, 1881; studied in Düsseldorf; died in Berlin, 1919. He was the first modern master of expressionism in sculpture. His work, though strong and direct, shows extreme sensitivity.

Henri Matisse (p. 625): born in France, 1869; died, 1954. One of the greatest of modern artists, Matisse excelled in painting, sculpture, etching, and drawing. Breaking with tradition, he became a leader of the fauves (French for " wild beasts ") and produced masterpieces.

Ernest Barlach (p. 637): born in Prussia, 1870; died in Germany, 1938. Known mainly as a sculptor, he was also a master lithographer and woodcut artist. His bold, massive forms reflect rugged strength. Most of his sculptures were destroyed by the Nazis, but much of his art has been saved for the world in American museums and private collections.

Henry Moore (pp. 649, 651): born in Yorkshire, England, 1898; now living in Hertfordshire. Among the foremost sculptors of our day, he has made a profound contribution to abstract and nonobjective sculpture.

Frans Masereel (p. 660): born in Belgium, 1889; now living in Paris. A painter and graphic artist, he is well known for his books that tell stories in pictures only (without words). He created his own stories, cut the woodblocks, and printed the books on his own press.

MODERN BIOGRAPHY

WITH BUT a few exceptions there were not many distinguished biographies written in England before the twentieth century. Boswell's *The Life of Samuel Johnson* is, of course, the great exception. Most of the earlier biographies were either dry factual records of famous lives or obviously biased accounts designed to pay tribute to greatness. Few readers turned to biography for enjoyment. Today, however, biography is one of the most popular types of reading matter, largely because of recent changes in its purpose and style. Biographies and autobiographies have now become strong competitors of fiction for the favor of the reading public.

Nowadays the writer tries to present his subject as a human being, not a statue in the hall of fame. Rapid advances in the study of psychology have thrown new light on how to analyze and judge human beings. More than ever we enjoy studying the *whole* personality. We want to estimate a person in the full light of both his virtues and his weaknesses, his successes and his failures. We see significance in his family history, in his childhood experiences, and in the extent and nature of his early education. We consider his acts and achievements against the background of the society of his day. Facts as mere information in chronological order have given place to the use of facts to identify, define, interpret, and illuminate character.

Along with this new approach in selecting material for a biography came a change in the style of presenting the material. Some of the art of the novelist has been adopted by the biographer, and he freely employs the fiction devices of incident, conversation, suspense, and climax. In fact, the praiseworthy desire to make his characters come alive sometimes leads the writer into temptation. He may tell what his main character was thinking at a given moment or under certain circumstances. If such thoughts are documented by letters, diaries, or other materials, he will be using sound methods of accurate biography. But if few intimate records are available, the introduction of private conversations and inner thoughts becomes pure fiction. If not expertly handled, this method may give a distorted view of the subject. Used carefully and skillfully, however, it can add to the interest and vividness of the whole book.

Thus we have a new form — fictionalized biography. This modern invention is a cross between a completely documented biography and a biographical or historical novel (such as Sir Walter Scott popularized). In it the author boldly departs from proved fact about actual people although he is writing about real events.

The autobiography has been a highly popular form in our century and has given a new outlet of expression for young people. War has brought such unusual experiences to many of them that they have sought to perpetuate their lives in print. The reading public, increasingly concerned with all ages and types of humanity, has eagerly read these firsthand accounts.

In the process of enlivening and humanizing English biography, Lytton Strachey was perhaps the most important of the pioneers. Significantly, he gave his entire attention to biography. Many authors write lives of famous people as a side line, but not Lytton Strachey. He was an artist as well as a recorder. He and others have succeeded in giving new life to biographical writing.

Queen Victoria's Accession

LYTTON STRACHEY 1880–1932

Like a breath of fresh air, Lytton Strachey (lĭt''n strā'chĭ) blew the dust off the dull shelves of biography. " It is perhaps as difficult to write a good life as to live one," he said. " To preserve in a becoming brevity which excludes everything that is redundant, and nothing that is significant — that surely is the first duty of a biographer. The second, no less surely, is to maintain his own freedom of speech." These two duties he followed consistently.

Strachey was a member of a distinguished family; his father, Sir Richard Strachey, was an Indian administrator, and his cousin John is a writer and a leader in England's Labor party. After his Cambridge days Lytton became a writer of reviews and magazine articles, but his name was little known in 1918 when he published *Eminent Victorians*. Here he " maintained his freedom of speech " by frank appraisals of four nineteenth-century figures who had become objects of hero worship. This book may be said to have launched the new type of biography, for it brought forth many imitators. Strachey's reputation was firmly established by *Elizabeth and Essex*, a full-length biography about the queen and her ill-fated lover. His best-known work is *Queen Victoria*, from which the following selection is taken.

T HE NEW QUEEN was almost entirely unknown to her subjects. In her public appearances her mother had invariably dominated the scene. Her private life had been that of a novice in a convent: hardly a human being from the outside world had ever spoken to her; and no human being at all, except her mother and the Baroness Lehzen,[1]

[1] *Baroness Lehzen* (lā'tzĕn): Victoria's governess, a clergyman's daughter from Hanover, Germany.

had ever been alone with her in a room. Thus it was not only the public at large that was in ignorance of everything concerning her; the inner circles of statesmen and officials and highborn ladies were equally in the dark. When she suddenly emerged from this deep obscurity, the impression that she created was immediate and profound. Her bearing at her first Council filled the whole gathering with astonishment and admiration; the Duke of Wellington, Sir Robert Peel, even the savage Croker, even the cold and caustic Greville [2] — all were completely carried away. Everything that was reported of her subsequent proceedings seemed to be of no less happy augury. Her perceptions were quick, her decisions were sensible, her language was discreet; she performed her royal duties with extraordinary facility. Among the outside public there was a great wave of enthusiasm. Sentiment and romance were coming into fashion; and the spectacle of the little girl-queen, innocent, modest, with fair hair and pink cheeks, driving through her capital, filled the hearts of the beholders with raptures of affectionate loyalty. What, above all, struck everybody with overwhelming force was the contrast between Queen

[2] *Duke of Wellington* (1769–1852): victor over Napoleon at the battle of Waterloo, and an important leader of the Conservative party. *Sir Robert Peel* (1788–1850): a leader of the Conservative party and later Prime Minister (1841–46). *Croker:* John Wilson Croker (1780–1857), at this time retired secretary of the Admiralty, prominent member of the Conservative party, and a literary critic. *Greville* (grĕv'ĭl): Charles C. F. Greville (1794–1865), clerk of the council, writer of a famous diary published after his death.

Victoria and her uncles.[1] The nasty old men, debauched and selfish, pigheaded and ridiculous, with their perpetual burden of debts, confusions, and disreputabilities — they had vanished like the snows of winter, and here at last, crowned and radiant was the spring. Lord John Russell,[2] in an elaborate oration, gave voice to the general sentiment. He hoped that Victoria might prove an Elizabeth without her tyranny, an Anne without her weakness. He asked England to pray that the illustrious Princess who had just ascended the throne with the purest intentions and the justest desires might see slavery abolished, crime diminished, and education improved. He trusted that her people would henceforward derive their strength, their conduct, and their loyalty from enlightened religious and moral principles, and that, so fortified, the reign of Victoria might prove celebrated to posterity and to all the nations of the earth.

Very soon, however, there were signs that the future might turn out to be not quite so simple and roseate as a delighted public dreamed. The "illustrious Princess" might perhaps, after all, have something within her which squared ill with the easy vision of a well-conducted heroine in an edifying storybook. The purest intentions and the justest desires? No doubt; but was that all? To those who watched closely, for instance, there might be something ominous in the curious contour of that little mouth. When, after her first Council, she crossed the anteroom and found her mother waiting for her, she said, "And now, Mamma, am I really and truly Queen?" "You see, my dear, that it is so." "Then, dear

THE DUCHESS OF KENT AND VICTORIA

Mamma, I hope you will grant me the first request I make to you, as Queen. Let me be by myself for an hour." For an hour she remained in solitude. Then she reappeared, and gave a significant order: her bed was to be moved out of her mother's room. It was the doom of the Duchess of Kent. The long years of waiting were over at last; the moment of a lifetime had come; her daughter was Queen of England; and that very moment brought her own annihilation. She found herself, absolutely and irretrievably, shut off from every vestige of influence, of confidence, of power. She was surrounded, indeed, by all the outward signs of respect and consideration; but that only made the inward truth of her position the more intolerable. Through the mingled formalities of court etiquette and filial duty she could never penetrate to Victoria. She was unable to conceal her disappointment and rage. *"Il n'y a plus d'avenir pour moi,"* she exclaimed to Madame de Lieven; *"je ne suis plus rien."* [3] For eighteen years, she said, this child had been the sole object of her existence, of her thoughts, her hopes, and now — no! she would not be comforted, she had lost everything, she was to the last degree unhappy. Sailing, so gallantly and so pertinaciously, through the buffeting storms of life, the stately vessel, with

[1] *her uncles:* Victoria's father, who died when she was less than a year old, was the Duke of Kent, one of the four sons of George III. Two of these sons became kings as George IV and William IV. When William died in 1837, Victoria was heir to the throne.

[2] *Lord John Russell* (1792–1878): a leader of the Liberal party.

[3] *il . . . rien:* "There is no more future for me. I am no longer anything."

sails still swelling and pennons flying, had put into harbor at last; to find nothing — a land of bleak desolation.

Within a month of the accession the realities of the new situation assumed a visible shape. The whole royal household moved from Kensington to Buckingham Palace, and, in the new abode, the Duchess of Kent was given a suite of apartments entirely separate from the Queen's. By Victoria herself the change was welcomed, though, at the moment of departure, she could afford to be sentimental. " Though I rejoice to go into B. P. for many reasons," she wrote in her diary, " it is not without feeling of regret that I shall bid adieu forever to this my birthplace, where I have been born and bred, and to which I am really attached! " Her memory lingered for a moment over visions of the past: her sister's wedding, pleasant balls and delicious concerts . . . and there were other recollections. "I have gone through painful and disagreeable scenes here, 'tis true," she concluded, " but still I am fond of the poor old palace."

[Here follows a long discussion of two of the Queen's advisers, Baroness Lehzen and Baron Stockmar, a German doctor who had proved his sagacity as adviser to Victoria's Uncle Leopold, brother of Victoria's mother and king of Belgium.]

With Lehzen to supervise every detail of her conduct, with Stockmar in the next room, so full of wisdom and experience of affairs, with her Uncle Leopold's letters, too, pouring out so constantly their stream of encouragements, general reflections, and highly valuable tips, Victoria, even had she been without other guidance, would have stood in no lack of private counselors. But other guidance she had; for all these influences paled before a new star, of the first magnitude, which, rising suddenly upon her horizon, immediately dominated her life.

William Lamb, Viscount Melbourne, was fifty-eight years of age, and had been for the last three years Prime Minister of England. In every outward respect he was one of the most fortunate of mankind. He had been born into the midst of riches, brilliance, and power. Nature had given him beauty and brains; the unexpected death of an elder brother brought him wealth, a peerage, and the possibility of high advancement. Bound

MELBOURNE

to succeed, and to succeed easily, he was gifted with so fine a nature that his success became him. His mind, at once supple and copious, his temperament, at once calm and sensitive, enabled him not merely to work, but to live with perfect facility and with the grace of strength. In society he was a notable talker, a captivating companion, a charming man. If one looked deeper, one saw at once that he was not ordinary, that the piquancies of his conversation and his manner — his free-and-easy vaguenesses, his abrupt questions, his lollings and loungings, his innumerable oaths — were something more than an amusing ornament, were the outward manifestations of an individuality that was fundamental. . . .

And now, with old age upon him, his life took a sudden, new, extraordinary turn. He became, in the twinkling of an eye, the intimate adviser and the daily companion of a young girl who had stepped all at once from a nursery to a throne. . . . However, he was used to delicacies, and he met the situation with consummate success. His behavior was from the first moment impeccable. His manner toward the young Queen mingled, with perfect facility, the watchfulness and the respect of a statesman and a courtier with the tender solicitude of a parent. He was at once reverential and affectionate, at once the servant and the guide. At the same time the habits of his life underwent a surprising change. His comfortable, unpunctual days became subject to the unaltering routine of a palace; no longer did he sprawl on sofas; not a single " damn " escaped his lips. The man of the world who had been the friend of Byron and the Regent, the talker whose paradoxes had held Holland House enthralled, the cynic whose ribaldries had enlivened so many deep potations, the lover whose soft words had captivated such beauty and such passion and such wit, might now be seen, evening after evening, talking with infinite politeness to a schoolgirl, bolt upright, amid the silence and the rigidity of court etiquette.

On her side Victoria was instantaneously fascinated by Lord Melbourne. The good report of Stockmar had no doubt prepared the way; Lehzen was wisely propitiated; and the first highly favorable impression was never afterward belied. She found him perfect; and perfect in her sight he remained. Her absolute and unconcealed adoration was very natural; what innocent young creature could have resisted, in any circumstances, the charm and the devotion of such a man? But, in her situation, there was a special influence which gave a peculiar glow to all she felt. After years of emptiness and dullness and suppression she had come suddenly, in the heyday of youth, into freedom and power. She was mistress of herself, of great domains and palaces; she was Queen of England. Responsibilities and difficulties she might have, no doubt, and in heavy measure; but one

feeling dominated and absorbed all others — the feeling of joy. Everything pleased her. She was in high spirits from morning till night. Mr. Creevey,[1] grown old now, and very near his end, catching a glimpse of her at Brighton, was much amused, in his sharp fashion, by the ingenuous gaiety of " little Vic." — " A more homely [2] little being you never beheld, when she is at her ease, and she is evidently dying to be always more so. She laughs in real earnest, opening her mouth as wide as it can go, showing not very pretty gums. . . . She eats quite as heartily as she laughs, I think I may say she gobbles. . . . She blushes and laughs every instant in so natural a way as to disarm anybody." But it was not merely when she was laughing or gobbling that she enjoyed herself; the performance of her official duties gave her intense satisfaction. " I really have immensely to do," she wrote in her *Journal* a few days after her accession; " I receive so many communications from my Ministers, but I like it very much." And again, a week later, " I repeat what I said before that I have so many communications from the Ministers, and from me to them, and I get so many papers to sign every day, that I have always a very great deal to do. I delight in this work." Through the girl's immaturity the vigorous predestined tastes of the woman were pushing themselves into existence with eager velocity, with delicious force.

One detail of her happy situation deserves particular mention. Apart from the splendor of her social position and the momentousness of her political one, she was a person of great wealth. As soon as Parliament met, an annuity of £385,000 was settled upon her. When the expenses of her household had been

---

[1] *Mr. Creevey:* Thomas Creevey (1764–1838), well-known London Whig (earlier name for Liberal). His journals give a valuable picture of the late Georgian era.

[2] *homely:* In English usage, this word means informal or unaffected in manners.

discharged, she was left with £68,000 a year of her own. She enjoyed, besides, the revenues of the Duchy of Lancaster, which amounted annually to over £27,000. The first use to which she put her money was characteristic: she paid off her father's debts. In money matters, no less than in other matters, she was determined to be correct. She had the instincts of a man of business; and she never could have borne to be in a position that was financially unsound.

With youth and happiness gilding every hour, the days passed merrily enough. And each day hinged upon Lord Melbourne. Her diary shows us, with undiminished clarity, the life of the young sovereign during the early months of her reign — a life satisfactorily regular, full of delightful business, a life of simple pleasures, mostly physical — riding, eating, dancing — a quick, easy, highly unsophisticated life, sufficient unto itself. The light of the morning is upon it; and, in the rosy radiance, the figure of " Lord M." emerges, glorified and supreme. If she is the heroine of the story, he is the hero; but indeed they are more than hero and heroine, for there are no other characters at all. Lehzen, the Baron, Uncle Leopold, are unsubstantial shadows — the incidental supers of the piece. Her paradise was peopled by two persons, and surely that was enough. One sees them together still, a curious couple, strangely united in those artless pages, under the magical illumination of that dawn of eighty years ago; the polished high fine gentleman with the whitening hair and the whiskers and the thick dark eyebrows and the mobile lips and the big expressive eyes; and beside him the tiny Queen — fair, slim, elegant, active, in her plain girl's dress and little tippet, looking up at him earnestly, adoringly, with eyes blue and projecting, and half-open mouth. So they appear upon every page of the *Journal;* upon every page Lord M. is present, Lord M. is speaking, Lord M. is being amusing, in-

structive, delightful, and affectionate at once, while Victoria drinks in the honeyed words, laughs till she shows her gums, tries hard to remember, and runs off, as soon as she is left alone, to put it all down. Their long conversations touched upon a multitude of topics. Lord M. would criticize books, throw out a remark or two on the British Constitution, make some passing reflections on human life, and tell story after story of the great people of the eighteenth century. Then there would be business — a dispatch perhaps from Lord Durham in Canada, which Lord M. would read. But first he must explain a little. " He said that I must know that Canada originally belonged to the French, and was only ceded to the English in 1760, when it was taken in an expedition under Wolfe: ' a very daring enterprise,' he said. Canada was then entirely French, and the British only came afterward. . . . Lord M. explained this very clearly (and much better than I have done) and said a good deal more about it. He then read me Durham's dispatch, which is a very long one and took him more than ½ an hour to read. Lord M. read it beautifully with that fine soft voice of his, and with so much expression, so that it is needless to say I was much interested by it." And then the talk would take a more personal turn. Lord M. would describe his boyhood, and she would learn that " he wore his hair long, as all boys then did, till he was 17 (how handsome he must have looked!)." Or she would find out about his queer tastes and habits — how he never carried a watch, which seemed quite extraordinary. " ' I always ask the servant what o'clock it is, and then he tells me what he likes,' said Lord M." Or, as the rooks wheeled about round the trees, " in a manner which indicated rain," he would say that he could sit looking at them for an hour, and " was quite surprised at my disliking them. . . . Lord M. said, ' The rooks are my delight.' "

The day's routine, whether in London or at Windsor, was almost invariable. The morning was devoted to business and Lord M. In the afternoon the whole court went out riding. The Queen, in her velvet riding habit, and a top hat with a veil draped about the brim, headed the cavalcade; and Lord M. rode beside her. The lively troupe went fast and far, to the extreme exhilaration of Her Majesty. Back in the palace again, there was still time for a little more fun before dinner — a game of battledore and shuttlecock, perhaps, or a romp along the galleries with some children. Dinner came, and the ceremonial decidedly tightened. The gentleman of highest rank sat on the right hand of the Queen; on her left — it soon became an established rule — sat Lord Melbourne. After the ladies had left the dining room, the gentlemen were not permitted to remain behind for very long; indeed, the short time allowed them for their wine drinking formed the subject — so it was rumored — of one of the very few disputes between the Queen and her Prime Minister; but her determination carried the day, and from that moment after-dinner drunkenness began to go out of fashion. When the company was reassembled in the drawing room the etiquette was stiff. For a few moments the Queen spoke in turn to each one of her guests; and during these short uneasy colloquies the aridity of royalty was likely to become painfully evident. One night, Mr. Greville, the Clerk of the Privy Council, was present; his turn soon came; the middle-aged, hard-faced *viveur* [1] was addressed by his young hostess. " Have you been riding today, Mr. Greville? " asked the Queen. " No, Madam, I have not," replied Mr. Greville. " It was a fine day," continued the Queen. " Yes, Madam, a very fine day," said Mr. Greville. " It was rather cold, though," said the

[1] *viveur* (vē·vûr′): one who lives at a fast and reckless pace.

Queen. " It was rather cold, Madam," said Mr. Greville. " Your sister, Lady Frances Egerton, rides, I think, doesn't she? " said the Queen. " She does ride sometimes, Madam," said Mr. Greville.

GREVILLE

There was a pause, after which Mr. Greville ventured to take the lead, though he did not venture to change the subject. " Has your Majesty been riding today? " asked Mr. Greville. " Oh, yes, a very long ride," answered the Queen with animation. " Has your Majesty got a nice horse? " said Mr. Greville. " Oh, a very nice horse," said the Queen. It was over. Her Majesty gave a smile and an inclination of the head, Mr. Greville a profound bow, and the next conversation began with the next gentleman. When all the guests had been disposed of, the Duchess of Kent sat down to her whist, while everybody else was ranged about the round table. Lord Melbourne sat beside the Queen, and talked pertinaciously — very often apropos to the contents of one of the large albums of engravings with which the round table was covered — until it was half-past eleven and time to go to bed.

Occasionally, there were little diversions: the evening might be spent at the opera or at the play. Next morning the royal critic was careful to note down her impressions. " It was Shakespeare's tragedy of *Hamlet,* and we came in at the beginning of it. Mr. Charles Kean (son of old Kean) acted the part of Hamlet, and I must say beautifully. His conception of this very difficult, and I may almost say incomprehensible, character is admirable; his delivery of all the fine long speeches quite beautiful; he is excessively graceful and all his actions and attitudes are good, though not at all good-looking in face. . . . I came away just as *Hamlet* was over." Later on, she went to see Macready in *King Lear.* The story was new to her; she knew nothing about it, and at first she took very little interest in what was passing on the stage; she preferred to chatter and laugh with the Lord Chamberlain. But, as the play went on, her mood changed; her attention was fixed, and then she laughed no more. Yet she was puzzled; it seemed a strange, a horrible business. What did Lord M. think? Lord M. thought it was a very fine play, but to be sure, "a rough, coarse play, written for those times, with exaggerated characters." "I'm glad you've seen it," he added. But, undoubtedly, the evenings which she enjoyed most were those on which there was dancing. She was always ready enough to seize any excuse — the arrival of cousins — a birthday — a gathering of young people — to give the command for that. Then, when the band played, and the figures of the dancers swayed to the music, and she felt her own figure swaying too, with youthful spirits so close on every side — then her happiness reached its height, her eyes sparkled, she must go on and on into the small hours of the morning. For a moment Lord M. himself was forgotten.

The months flew past. The summer was over: "the pleasantest summer I ever passed in my life, and I shall never forget this first summer of my reign." With surprising rapidity, another summer was upon her. The coronation came and went — a curious dream. The antique, intricate, endless ceremonial worked itself out as best it could, like some machine of gigantic complexity which was a little out of order. The small central figure went through her gyrations. She sat; she walked; she prayed; she carried about an orb that was almost too heavy to hold; the Archbishop of Canterbury came and crushed a ring upon the wrong finger, so that she was ready to cry out with the pain; old Lord Rolle tripped up in his mantle and fell down the steps as he was doing homage; she was taken into a side chapel, where the altar was covered with a tablecloth, sandwiches, and bottles of wine; she perceived Lehzen in an upper box and exchanged a smile with her as she sat, robed and crowned, on the Confessor's throne.[1] "I shall ever remember this day as the proudest of my life," she noted. But the pride was soon merged once more in youth and simplicity. When she returned to Buckingham Palace at last she was not tired; she ran up to her private rooms, doffed her splendors, and gave her dog Dash its evening bath.

Life flowed on again with its accustomed smoothness — though, of course, the smoothness was occasionally disturbed.

[1] *the Confessor's throne:* the coronation throne of Edward the Confessor, next to the last of the Saxon kings before the Norman Conquest.

A YOUNG QUEEN

1. What does Victoria's relationship with her mother, as briefly described here, suggest to you about her character? About the demands of being a country's ruler?

2. Summarize your impression of Victoria and Lord Melbourne together. Why did Melbourne appeal to her so greatly? As she grew older, do you think she would become critical of him? Why or why not?

3. In what ways did Victoria show the common sense of a mature woman? In what ways, the lively disposition of a young girl? Can you point out examples of Strachey's use of irony in describing her?

4. What do you think of the usual eve-

ning activities at the palace? What qualities that we think of as characteristically " Victorian " did they have?

5. How does Strachey's account of Victoria's coronation compare with Pepys' description of that of Charles II (see page 247)? What very human touch comes at the end of Victoria's coronation day?

6. The interest of the whole world was centered on the coronation of Elizabeth II of England in June, 1953. What reasons can you give for the interest of other nations in this event? How did this coronation differ from that of all preceding monarchs? What parts of the coronation ritual mentioned by Strachey were observed in 1953?

The Launching of *H.M.S. Pinafore*

HESKETH PEARSON 1887–

After finishing Bedford Grammar School, Pearson " wasted " (as he said) two years as a clerk in a London shipping office. In 1911 he went on the stage, where he remained for many years, except for the brief interval of World War I. His theatrical experience brought him in touch with many of the leading producers of the time, and it was natural that several subjects of his biographies should have been persons connected with the stage.

In 1931 Pearson gave up acting for writing. In twenty-five years he has produced an imposing array of books, mainly biographies, but also some essays of travel and criticism. Among his best-known books are *Tom Paine*, *G.B.S.: A Full Length Portrait* (George Bernard Shaw), and biographies of Benjamin Disraeli (entitled *Dizzy*) and Sir Walter Scott.

You have already met W. S. Gilbert on page 513, and read two of the famous songs from that perennial favorite, *H.M.S. Pinafore*. In earlier chapters of his double biography *Gilbert and Sullivan*, Pearson brings out the difference in background of these partners: Gilbert, of the comfortable middle class, with opportunities for attending Oxford and studying law — Sullivan, the son of a poorly paid clarinet player in a theater orchestra. Their particular talents were evident early in life. Gilbert had written fifteen plays by the time he was twenty-five. Sullivan entered the choir of Chapel Royal at twelve years of age, and composed madrigals in bed after lights were out. Through scholarships he was able to attend the Royal Academy of Music and the Conservatory at Leipzig, where he began seriously to compose music.

In disposition the two men were quite different. Gilbert had a sharp tongue and often " carried a chip on his shoulder." The rehearsals of his plays were sometimes punctuated by his outbursts of temper. On the other hand, the handsome, sweet-tempered Sullivan charmed everyone who met him, and was constantly being helped to new opportunities by his friends. Later he was a great favorite of the royal family and was knighted.

Gilbert and Sullivan began their collaboration at the suggestion of Richard D'Oyly Carte, a theater manager, in 1870. *Trial by Jury* was the first of their famous light operas. *H.M.S. Pinafore* was launched in 1877.

JUST BEFORE the end of the year Sullivan received the scenario *H.M.S. Pinafore* from Gilbert, who said: " I have little doubt whatever but that you will be pleased with it." Sullivan was so much pleased with it that, returning home, he began to work on it at once, in spite of the most violent attacks of illness. Throughout the entire period of composition he was racked with pain, and only managed to complete the work between paroxysms of agony which almost left him insensible.

"The Launching of *H.M.S. Pinafore*," from *Gilbert and Sullivan* by Hesketh Pearson, published by Hamish Hamilton Ltd. Reprinted by permission of the author.

Paroxysms of a different kind were taking place on the stage during rehearsals. Gilbert was already enforcing those methods of production which were to make his name a byword in the profession and revolutionize the art of dramatic presentation. He had learned from Robertson that, in drama, the whole was greater than the part, and he was busy subordinating his actors to the play. He regarded each of his librettos as a composer regards a symphony, which can be wrecked by the playing of a single false note, and he determined from the outset to achieve perfect harmony from his orchestra of actors. Every word had to be said with a certain inflection. Every movement had to be made in a certain manner, every position had to be judged to a square inch, every piece of " business " had to be considered in its relation to the scene. The actors were not allowed, as in the old days, to emerge for an instant from the frame of the picture he was trying to create. They were like chessmen on a board, to be moved at the discretion of the player-producer; they were like marionettes, whose motions were governed by the master; they were the members of a team, under the strict discipline of its captain.

For this reason he preferred his actors to be novices, who could be taught by himself and would not resent the teaching. For this reason, too, he arrived at the first rehearsal with a fairly complete mental picture of all the moves, all the inflections, all the " business," and all the positions of all the actors at every moment of the play. For hour after hour before the commencement of rehearsals he would sit at his desk with replicas of the scenes on a scale of half an inch to a foot, with blocks of wood three inches high representing the males, two and a half inches high representing the females, and work out every detail of the production. It was not likely therefore that he was going to stand any nonsense

from an actor who was solely concerned with his part and who did not mind what happened to the play so long as he made a personal success. At the rehearsals of *Pinafore* a player of the older school refused to repeat for perhaps the fiftieth time a piece of " business " which Gilbert was patiently instructing him to do.

" No, sir, I object," said the actor warmly. " I have been on the stage quite long enough."

" Quite," agreed Gilbert, and dismissed him on the spot.

Gilbert could never see eye-to-eye with people who considered that their proper place was in the center of the stage, and when a lady who was rehearsing the part of Josephine in *Pinafore* pointed out that she had always occupied that position in Italian opera, he remarked:

" Unfortunately this is not Italian opera, but only a low burlesque of the worst possible kind."

The lady continued her career in Italian opera.

Another well-known actress who was cast for a part in *Pinafore* walked out of the theater when she heard that a newcomer with no experience named Jessie Bond was to play in her scenes. Though upsetting at the time, it turned out luckily for Gilbert and Sullivan, as Jessie Bond became one of the most popular Savoy favorites.

Explosions between producer and actors were frequent in the early days, though when Gilbert had gained the complete ascendancy over his actors that had always been his aim, their occurrence was rare. His anger only flashed out when anyone questioned his authority, and his wit was usually confined to such harmless squibs as that recorded by Barrington:

" Cross left on that speech, I think, Barrington, and sit on the skylight over the saloon, pensively," advised Gilbert at a rehearsal of *Pinafore*.

The actor did so, but the stage car-

One of Gilbert's own witty sketches for H.M.S. Pinafore — *"But in spite of all temptations to belong to other nations, he remains an Englishman!"*

penter had sewn the skylight with pack-thread and it collapsed under Barrington's fourteen stone.[1]

"That's expensively," remarked Gilbert.

H.M.S. Pinafore was produced on May 25th, 1878, and, its merits apart, caused something of a sensation because of the caricature of W. H. Smith, the publisher, who had recently been appointed First Lord of the Admiralty by Disraeli. For some of the lyrics Gilbert had drawn on the *Bab Ballads,*[2] one of which he adapted for his present purpose. This cutting ridicule of the political game, together with the satire on blatant patriotism in the same opera, reveals a vital aspect of Gilbert's character and explains why he had to wait so long for a knighthood.

It must be repeated that the qualities

[1] *fourteen stone:* 196 pounds. The British use the unit *stone* (14 pounds) for heavy weights.

[2] *Bab Ballads:* verses written and illustrated by Gilbert for *Fun* magazine in 1869. Cleverly written, they satirize amiably the violence and crime so evident in London at that time. The collection made Gilbert famous as a literary figure.

of wariness and daring were mixed in his nature in about equal proportions; and also, it may be added, stupidity and insight. He was a typical Briton with a streak of genius, possibly the only known example. He could see through a thing, but he could not see around it. He was visited with sudden flashes of reality, but he was not gifted with a steady vision. He had acute perceptions, but no guiding philosophy. He was a respectable man who made fun of respectability, a sentimentalist who laughed at sentiment, a patriot who ridiculed patriotism. Again and again, at the bidding of some powerful intuition, he exposed a social or national absurdity, but as often as not he failed to see the point of his exposure and fell back upon a piece of conventional claptrap which was equally typical of him. His sudden exhibitions of daring and insight, coupled with his native caution and conventionality, made his work uneven and incalculable, and it was Sullivan's music that rendered it wholly palatable to the Victorians. The Englishman is perhaps the only man in the world who can laugh at himself; add music to the satire and he brings the house down, for music removes the sting of reality. Nevertheless, the chief powers in the land never quite got over the "contempt of court" shown in *Trial by Jury,* the contempt in *Pinafore,* and the continuous digs at authority in the rest of the operas, culminating with the contempt of the Royal Court in *Utopia;* and they took their only possible revenge. The average Englishman laughed, applauded, and whistled the delectable tunes; the important Englishman watched, smiled wryly, and sometimes writhed inwardly.

Owing to the fact that London was visited by a heat wave that summer, the audiences at the Opera Comique varied in size and the directors had periodical fits of panic. They announced the withdrawal of the piece about once a fortnight and canceled the announcement whenever the receipts went up. D'Oyly Carte calmed them to the best of his ability, but both he and the company were kept on tenterhooks for months owing to the nervous condition of his codirectors. Then two things happened to give the show a fillip. Sullivan, who was conducting the Promenade Concerts at Covent Garden, included an arrangement of the *Pinafore* music in one evening's program. It was liked so much that crowds of concertgoers visited the opera, which was running to good houses by the end of August. Next came the news that *Pinafore* had taken New York by storm and was playing to enormous business at no less than eight theaters; and since England was just beginning to model her taste on that of America, and America was just beginning to accept everything English as a model of taste, *Pinafore* soon became the rage in both countries.

Of course it was pirated in America. There was no copyright agreement between the two countries; and unless the author of a play could produce it on the spot, before anyone else could steal it and produce it first, he could whistle for his royalties. American publishers and

theatrical managers made fortunes out of *Pinafore* while Gilbert and Sullivan gnashed their teeth in impotence. Adding insult to injury, the Americans put in a number of local "gags," songs about "pants" (which they have an incurable habit of rhyming with "dance") [1] and suchlike unsuitable sallies. Gilbert, Sullivan, and Carte decided that something had to be done about it, and the latter sailed for America to take stock of the situation.

In the summer of that year a long report from Carte persuaded Gilbert and Sullivan to visit America in order to give their authorized version of *Pinafore* in New York. Before leaving, Sullivan underwent an operation for crushing the stone in the kidney, and received felicitations upon its success from the Prince of Wales and the Duke of Edinburgh. Gilbert was suffering from a different complaint. " I will not have another libretto of mine produced if the Americans are going to steal it," he declared, " not that I need the money so much, but it upsets my digestion."

Reporters swooped down upon them the instant their boat reached New York, and the American public, through the medium of its press, was quickly introduced to the two famous visitors: the librettist, a tall military-looking gentleman, with fair hair, rosy complexion, bright blue eyes and high massive forehead, who spoke quickly and jerkily in a deep hearty voice; the composer, a short, plump, daintily-clad person, with a thick neck, dark hair and eyes, olive-tinted mobile face, sensuous lips, and tender expression, whose voice was wistful and full of feeling. They were interviewed so thoroughly that Sullivan wondered " Where do all these Americans end? " and Gilbert ceased to wonder. Each of them took pains to make it known that he had done far better work than *Pinafore* unaided by the other.

[1] *pants:* The British used only the word *trousers,* and pronounced *dance* as *däns,* so that *pants* (pănts) and *dance* (däns) seemed crude.

Gilbert said it was a little mortifying to find that a trifle like *Pinafore* should so far exceed in success the plays he held in more serious estimation. Sullivan regretted that his oratorios and other compositions of a more classical and ambitious style had not received the popular approval accorded to *Pinafore*. Neither of them felt unduly flattered when some judge, in an after-dinner speech, hoped they would be brought before him on the charge of being drunk and disorderly, so that he might repay the pleasure *Pinafore* had given him by letting them off. Nor was Gilbert altogether pleased when an American impresario had the bright idea that they might heap up a pile of dollars if only they would prepare an American version of the piece.

"Say now, Mr. Gilbert," said this gentleman, "all you've got to do is to change H.M.S. to U.S.S., pull down the British ensign, hoist the stars and stripes, and anchor your ship off Jersey beach. Then, in place of your First Lord of the Admiralty, introduce our navy boss. All the rewriting you'd want would be some new words to Bill Bobstay's song — just let him remain an American instead of an Englishman. Now ain't that a cute notion, sir?"

"Well, yes," replied Gilbert thoughtfully, "perhaps your suggestion is a good one, but I see some difficulties in carrying it out. In the first place I'm afraid I'm not sufficiently versed in your vernacular to translate my original English words. The best I could do would be something like this:

He is Ameri-can!
  Though he himself has said it,
  'Tis not much to his credit,
That he is Ameri-can!
For he might have been a Dutchman,
An Irish, Scotch, or such a man,
Or perhaps an Englishman!
  But in spite of hanky-panky,
  He remains a true-born Yankee,
A cute Ameri-can." [1]

[1] See the original version on page 513.

The impresario was delighted; he swore it would save the situation and set New York ablaze. After a few moments' reflection Gilbert gravely abandoned the notion, on the ground that such words might impair the friendly relations between the two countries.

While Gilbert and Sullivan were rehearsing their opera and being entertained and interviewed until their heads swam, the barrel organs of New York were churning out the tunes of *Pinafore*, the music shops were flooded with its scores, most of the theaters were playing it, and such was the demand for it throughout the States that one paper announced: "At present there are forty-two companies playing *Pinafore* about the country. Companies formed after six p.m. yesterday are not included." The authorized edition of the work appeared on December 1st at the Fifth Avenue Theater and received an ovation. Everyone in the audience was of course already familiar with the airs, but the orchestration, with which the numerous American bands had not troubled their heads, was a revelation. It was greeted as a comparatively new work and it looked as if a ninth company were about to coin money in the city. Gilbert, in his speech before the curtain after the first performance, said: "It has been our purpose to produce something that should be innocent but not imbecile." That was the slogan of the collaborators: clean but clever fun.

FAMOUS COLLABORATORS

1. What differences between Gilbert and Sullivan in appearance and disposition are brought out here? Is it surprising that these two men worked so well together? Discuss.

2. Would you have liked being an actor under Gilbert's direction? If you have had any experience in amateur dramatics, discuss whether actors should be allowed to have some part in the stage direction.

3. Show how the two songs from *Pinafore* on pages 513–14 illustrate Gilbert's ridicule of the English ruling classes. What

would this have to do with Gilbert's having to " wait so long for a knighthood "? If you have seen other Gilbert and Sullivan operettas discuss wherein the ridicule lies.

4. What do you think of the proposed American version of *Pinafore?* How do you suppose Americans would have reacted to the words suggested for " He is an Englishman "? Pearson says the English are the only people who can laugh at themselves. If you think Americans also have this faculty, give some examples to prove it.

THE POWER OF WORDS

WORD DISCRIMINATION

Pearson uses five words descriptive of various kinds of humor. A *caricature* is an exaggerated picture in writing or in drawing. It most commonly applies to a person,

as, the caricature of the First Lord of the Admiralty in *Pinafore. Ridicule* is a more general word. It may be applied to a specific person, an idea, or a whole social system, as in " ridicule of the political game." *Satire* is a special kind of ridicule, employing subtlety and cleverness. This word is also used to describe a type of literature. *Absurdity* applies to the innate quality in something that lays it open to ridicule. (Gilbert exposed national absurdities.) *Sally* applies to a particular passage or remark made in a witty, humorous vein.

Of these five words, which can be used as verbs? Which have adjectives based on the same root?

Point out the distinctions among the following words which pertain to humor with a sharp edge: *derision, mockery, sarcasm, irony, raillery.*

The Death of Gandhi

NAYANTARA SAHGAL 1927–

Lyric poets are to be expected among young people, but a biographer who is very young is a phenomenon. The author of the following selection wrote it in her twenties. She is unusual in another way. She is a Hindu from Delhi, India, who in 1947 was graduated from Wellesley College, and returned

to India at a significant point in its history. She represents, therefore, the widening of the stream of English literature not only to other parts of the world, but to other races.

Nayantara Sahgal (nī·an·tä'rà su̇·gäl') is unusual in a third respect — her family connections. Out of the rich experiences of her short life she has written a vivid and highly enjoyable autobiography. She is the daughter of Madame Pandit, once president of the United Nations assembly, and later India's foreign minister to London. Her uncle is Jawaharlal Nehru (ja·wä'har-läl nā'rōō), Prime Minister of India. While Nayantara was in America her father died in prison, where he was carrying out the nonresistance principles of his friend, Mahatma Gandhi (mà·hät'mà gän'dĭ).

Through the eyes of this young author we see a personal side of Gandhi, his humor and his gentle affection for the three young girls of the Pandit family.

The odd title of Mrs. Sahgal's autobiography — *Prison and Chocolate Cake* — is explained by her association of her father's going to prison with the chocolate cake they had for dinner that night. It may also be said to represent the great contrasts between the rich background of this young aristocrat and the sacrifices made by older members of her family for principles they believed in.

W E W E N T to a room at the end of a corridor, where he was seated on a mat on the floor, with a number of people around him. I took my shoes off at the door, and on entering touched Bapu's [1] feet. I felt a smart slap on my cheek as he pulled me down beside him, and I heard his chuckle, so infectious that it brought smiles to the faces of the others in the room, as grown-ups smile at a child's spontaneous peal of laughter.

" So! " he said in Hindi, his eyes twinkling. " You have come home! What are you going to do now? Not too grown up to talk to me about it, I hope."

Gandhiji had recently seen his countrymen engaged in bitter fighting against one another, ignoring the lesson of non-violence he had sought to teach them, for the Partition [2] had brought much tragedy and bloodshed in its wake. Yet in spite of his profound hurt and disappointment, he had not forgotten the little girl who had gone away to America. Despite the many demands made daily on him for guidance, he showed an interest in her future.

" I want to talk to you, Bapu," I said earnestly, " when you are not too busy."

" Busy? I am never too busy. Let me know when you are coming."

[1] *Bapu* (băp'ōō): an intimate name for Gandhi used by the Pandit family, who were his close friends. Another affectionate form they used was *Gandhiji* (gän·dē'jĭ). With their long formal names, Hindus often use abbreviated pet names within their intimate circles.

[2] *Partition:* The separation of India (Hindu) and Pakistan (Moslem) took place during 1947 just before the author's return to India. By a long walking tour in the danger zones, Gandhi had exerted considerable influence in restraining riots between the two factions.

In the clamor that was Delhi in 1947 Bapu remained a sanctuary of calm thought. During the riots that had broken out in some parts of India both before and after the Partition, he had, whenever he could, gone fearlessly among the rioters exhorting them to give up their madness. Yet though he had been in the turmoil and danger, he had somehow remained unperturbed by it. Now he was back in Delhi, holding prayer meetings in the garden of Birla House every evening. As before, *bhajans* [3] and hymns were sung at these gatherings and passages were read from the *Bhagavad-Gita*,[4] followed by talks by him.

To those who listened, they were unlike any talks they had heard before, for Bapu thought out loud rather than spoke with the desire to have any effect on his audience. Gandhiji was not a politician. He was not afraid to change his mind or to contradict himself if he believed he had made a mistake. He was not ashamed to proclaim that his religion was his guide. And, as always, his concern was with the suffering of his fellow men and how he could best alleviate it. Independence had come to India, but no one in India could have been less impressed by it than the man who had made its achievement possible for his country. It had never been his chief concern. His preoccupation had been with morality. So while Indian statesmen drew up elaborate plans for the country's development and welfare, Bapu's quiet voice was content to preach his moral code: that right means must be employed to attain right ends, that nothing great and good can be built up on a soiled foundation.

A number of foreign visitors used to attend those prayer meetings, and I wondered what they thought of the un-impressive-looking, sparsely clad little

[3] *bhajans* (bä'jänz): religious songs of the Hindus.
[4] *Bhagavad-Gita* (bŭg'a·văd·gē'tä): the supreme devotional scripture of India.

Mohandas Gandhi

1869–1948

No character more amazing than Mohandas Gandhi has appeared in the twentieth century. Born in India, he was educated in London and showed great ability as a lawyer. While living for some years in South Africa he engaged in efforts to free Indians there from unfair legal restrictions. During this period he developed the method of " passive resistance " for which his name is famous. Later, back in India, he won many converts, who joined him in protesting against government measures they thought unjust by going to prison, staging hunger strikes, boycotting English goods, and even lying down in front of railroad trains. Gandhi's influence grew, and he became known the world over as a leader whose power lay in the force of his personality and his ideals. His followers gave him the title of Mahatma, meaning Great Soul. Finally, after many years of " non-violent non-co-operation," Gandhi's goal of Indian independence was reached in 1946. Then, at the age of seventy-nine, he undertook to quiet the hostility between Hindu and Moslem by a long walking tour through the villages of the danger zone. These efforts brought about his death by the bullet of a resentful young Hindu.

man who seemed to charm such adoration out of the people around him. Did they treat what they saw as an interesting phenomenon but one that could not possibly happen in England, or America, or Holland, or wherever they happened to hail from? What did it all mean to them, I wondered. My own reaction was awe mingled with reverence. Could it be true that a man could talk of love and truth and goodness, and apply these religious terms to politics, and not be laughed at? Could it be true that such sentiments could actually guide a nation's policy? Yet in India all these things were true. I felt wonderfully elated that I was an Indian and that to be an Indian in Gandhi's India would forever be associated with this eminently sane way of thinking. . . .

Will anyone ever understand the reason why Gandhiji was shot, or, for that matter, Christ crucified or Socrates condemned to death? Can madness of this sort have been dictated by sanity? Can it have had any meaning except to make those who lived after them bitterly repent the crimes of their fellow human beings? Who stood to gain by Gandhiji's death? Not the assassin, because he was caught, tried, and eventually hanged. Not the enemies of Gandhiji's teachings, because his death threw the searchlight on his message more powerfully than ever before. In his lifetime he had been called a saint. His martyrdom crowned him with an even more glorious immortality. To ask the reason why he was killed is to probe a mystery that has no beginning. The whys of history are seldom answered.

Indi [1] and I were having tea at home on the evening of January 30, 1948, when we were summoned to Birla House by an urgent telephone call saying that Gandhiji had been shot on his way to a prayer meeting. Shock numbed us to all sensation as we got into the car and hurried to him; the others, his

[1] *Indi:* familiar name for her cousin Indira Nehru.

relatives and followers gathered around his body in his room at Birla House, seemed to be affected the same way. There was silence in the room as Gandhiji breathed his last.

Mamu [1] received the news at a meeting and arrived at the scene soon after us. I do not think that as he strode into the room, tense with anxiety at the news he had been given, he realized that Gandhiji had passed away. I do not think he believed that Gandhiji could die so suddenly, so wordlessly, leaving him alone at the time when he needed advice and help more than ever before. The group of people in the room who had stood aside to let Mamu stride in watched without a sound as he knelt beside the beloved body and forgot himself in his grief for a brief moment. But what had happened was too colossal a phenomenon to permit the luxury of grief. When Mamu rose to his feet, he had regained complete self-control, and through the ordeal of loneliness and personal loss which was to follow in the days to come he was never again to show a vestige of it. Those who could bear to look at his face during those days saw a strained white mask through which only the eyes revealed stark anguish.

Word of the assassination had leaped through Delhi like a flame fanned by wind, for soon dumb, stricken hordes of men and women had collected like sentinels around Birla House, and out of every window one could see a brown blur of faces. They did not make a sound, and an unnatural silence reigned. It was as if the earth and time stood still for those few minutes. That was in the beginning, when they were too stunned to speak. Later they clamored wildly, shouting, crying, and jostling one another in a stampede to break into the house. They became a little calmer when it was announced that they would

be allowed to file past Gandhiji's body and see it before the funeral on the following day. Some officials were in favor of embalming the body so that it would be preserved for at least a few days and people from all over India might have the opportunity to pay their last respects to it before it was cremated. But Gandhiji, foreseeing the possibility of some such occurrence, had always said that he did not wish his body to be preserved after his death for any reason at all.

It is significant that when one is faced with the shock of a loved one's death, one's first question is not: " Where has he gone? What has become of him? " This thought dawns later with the pain. But first one whimpers: " What will become of me now that he has left me? " This was surely the question uppermost in the hearts of the mourning multitudes, for their expressions were those of lost children. It was the question in many of our hearts as we sat, still shocked, still unbelieving, listening to Mamu's broadcast telling the people of India that their Bapu was no more.

Into that climate of fear and uncertainty Mrs. Naidu came the next morning from the U.P.,[2] where she was Governor. Her face was haggard and her eyes glassy with unshed tears, but her spirit was as indomitable as ever.

" What is all the sniveling about? " she demanded harshly. " Would you rather he had died of decrepit old age or indigestion? This was the only death great enough for him."

Gandhiji's funeral was to take place the day after his death, and hours in advance people lined the route his procession was to follow, for it had been announced over the radio by Mamu. It was a route that would require innumerable arrangements, and Mamu and others had sat up nearly all night to make them. In the morning we were told that there would be a few convey-

---

[1] *Mamu* (mä'mōō): familiar name for the author's uncle, Jawaharlal Nehru.

[2] *U.P.*: United Provinces, two large provinces of northwest India.

ances for those among us who felt they could not walk the entire distance.

Padmasi [1] spoke for us all when she said simply: " We will walk. It is the last time we shall be walking with Bapu."

It was an agonizing walk. For all the thousands who silently watched the procession go by, many thousands more frantically besieged the open truck carrying the flower-wreathed body, weeping bitterly, trying once again to touch Bapu's feet. It was impossible to take even a short step forward without being crushed from all sides. The procession left Birla House in the morning. It was evening when it reached the cremation ground, a distance of about three miles.

I realized as we inched our way along with difficulty that I was in the midst of something more than a grieving multitude. This was more even than the funeral procession of India's most beloved leader. I was among human beings for whom walking with Bapu had had a profound significance, for they had walked with him over the rough and smooth of much of India's recent history. They could not now resign themselves to the fact that he who had led them over many arduous paths was never going to walk with them again. Bapu's slight figure had walked, staff in hand, over a large part of India. To walk is to make slow progress. It is to think with clarity and to notice with heightened awareness all that is around you, from the small insects that cross your path to the horizon in the distance. To walk is the way of the pilgrim, and for Bapu every walk had been a pilgrimage, the dedication of the body in preparation for the spirit's sacrifice. It was no accident that he had chosen to walk. To walk, moreover, was often the only way open to the average Indian. It required no vehicle but his own body

and cost him nothing but his energy. Gandhiji took this simple necessity and sublimated it, as he took so much that was obvious and commonplace and translated it into a joyful effort.

As the flames of the funeral pyre consumed Bapu's body, we sat around it at some distance on the ground. Members of the diplomatic corps were there, and in front of them all the Earl and Countess Mountbatten,[2] seated cross-legged on the ground like the rest of us. Gandhiji had inspired heartfelt homage from the people whose Government had so often made a prisoner of him.

Some days after the funeral a special train took Gandhiji's ashes to Allahabad,[3] where in accordance with Hindu practice, they were to be immersed in the Ganges. Mamu and other members of the family, together with the Mountbattens, were to fly to Allahabad to receive the train, and I was among those privileged to travel on it. The compartment containing the ashes was flower-decked and fragrant. The people in it, Gandhiji's relatives and the close followers who had served him all his life, sang *bhajans* most of the way. There was no weeping any more, for his presence seemed to be among them amid the flowers, the songs, and the verses from the *Gita* which he had loved best. At every station huge lamenting crowds filled the platform and at times tried to storm the compartment containing the urn of ashes. And so, amid song and prayer and the homage of millions of his countrymen, the train reached Allahabad. It was a city that had seen the performance of the last rites of many members of my family; it seemed fitting that Bapu's ashes, too, should be brought here, for he had ruled their lives.

[2] *Mountbatten:* Lord Louis Mountbatten was the first Governor General of the Dominion of India after the separation. He is an uncle of the Duke of Edinburgh, husband of Queen Elizabeth II.

[3] *Allahabad* (ăl´*a*·hä·bäd´): ancient holy city of India on the *Ganges* (găn´jēz), a sacred river.

[1] *Padmasi* (păd·mä´sĭ): daughter of Mrs. Naidu, mentioned earlier.

The ashes were immersed in the Ganges, where a mammoth crowd had gathered on the bank, and afterwards we all went back to Delhi. From that time onward it seemed to me that Mamu's devotion to his work was almost religious in nature, though he did not like the word " religion " and did not consider that it could ever apply to him. His face took on a spiritual transparency, like that of a monk. So must an apostle of Jesus have looked after his Master's crucifixion, and so must he have taken upon himself the burden of the cross.

Back in Delhi I felt at sea. It was true that I had not worked with Gandhiji, gone to prison at his call, or made any sacrifice for my country's sake. That had been the work of a different generation. My sisters and I, and other young people like me, had been merely onlookers. But still I felt at sea, and I think the reason was that my feeling of loss went deeper than consciousness. It was as if the continuity of a long process begun before my birth had suddenly snapped like a dry twig, leaving me entirely without a sense of direction. I had grown up within a magic circle, which now had melted away, leaving me unprotected.

With an effort I roused myself from my imaginings. Was I, after all, going to relegate my childhood and all that it represented to the realm of a dream I had dreamed? Were my values so fragile — had Bapu lived and died for nothing? — that I could so easily lose courage when he was no longer there? Millions of people would have been ordinary folk, living their humdrum lives unperturbed, but for him. He had come to disturb them profoundly, to jolt them out of indifference, to awaken them to one another's suffering, and in so doing to make them reach for the stars. Those stars still beckoned luminously. Bapu's ashes had been scattered over the Ganges, but what if he had gone? We were still there, young, strong, and proud, to bear his banner before us. Who among us dared lose heart when there was this work to be done? The curtain had rung down over a great drama, but another one was about to begin. Gandhi was dead, but his India would live on in his children.

A GREAT LEADER OF OUR CENTURY

1. What unusual characteristics of Gandhi does the author bring out at the beginning of this chapter? How does he differ in appearance and personality from most leaders who have worked for national independence?

2. How was the news of Gandhi's fatal injury received by his relatives and friends? by Nehru? by the people of Delhi? by Mrs. Naidu? What questions about the meaning of such martyrdom are brought out here?

3. Describe the unusual funeral procession. What deeper significance did " walking with Bapu " have? How did the villagers along the route show their grief?

4. At the end of the chapter how is a sense of dedication to the memory of Gandhi brought out?

READING LIST FOR MODERN BIOGRAPHY

Barrie, James M., *Margaret Ogilvy*
This fine tribute to his mother also gives considerable insight into Scottish life and character.

Brickhill, Paul, *Reach for the Sky*
A thrilling account of Douglas Bader, the legless air ace of the Battle of Britain, who was shot down and escaped from German prisons.

Cecil, Lord David, *Melbourne*
Queen Victoria's first prime minister, to whom Strachey has already introduced you; one of the best-written biographies of our century. (Mature.)

Conrad, Joseph, *Personal Record*
Of special interest in this autobiography is Conrad's account of how he came to write some of his stories.

Crawford, Marion, *The Little Princesses*
A vivid picture of Queen Elizabeth II and Princess Margaret in their growing years, as told by their governess.

Hudson, William H., *Far Away and Long Ago*

The South American boyhood of an Englishman who not only studied nature but could also paint it in colorful words.

Lavine, Sigmund A., *Wandering Minstrels We*

A recent and very full account of the famous pair — Gilbert and Sullivan.

Masefield, John, *In the Mill*

England's poet laureate tells of his early struggles to make a living in America, and of the reading he did there which most influenced him.

Pearson, Hesketh, *Sir Walter Scott, His Life and Personality*

The romantic life of one of Scotland's greatest poets and novelists, by a major modern biographer.

Pippett, Aileen, *The Moth and the Star*

An admirer of Virginia Woolf assesses her life and art.

Raverat, Gwen, *Period Piece*

A granddaughter of Charles Darwin, gifted with a lively style, describes the life of English young people in the early days of this century, and sketches in her famous relatives.

Tuckerman, Arthur, *The Old School Tie*

If you want to see the difference between English and American secondary schools, you will enjoy this man's account of his youth, especially his vacations on the continent with his father.

Woodham-Smith, Cecil, *Lonely Crusader*

A full, scholarly life of Florence Nightingale which convinces you of the greatness of this pioneer in nursing. (Mature.)

MODERN ESSAYS

EARLIER in this book you have read essays written in the past three centuries. Taken together, they show the evolution of this form of writing.

In the seventeenth century, Bacon wrote compact, clear statements of his ideas on a variety of subjects. Dryden inaugurated a kind of literary criticism that is still familiar to us today.

In the eighteenth century, Addison and Steele, writing for periodicals, produced short essays designed to entertain and influence the thinking of the public.

In the nineteenth century, Lamb and Stevenson expressed personal viewpoints in their graceful familiar essays. Carlyle, Macaulay, Newman, and Huxley wrote essays that were serious discussions of important subjects like science, education, and history.

With the twentieth century comes a still more complex development of the essay. Periodicals — and people with enough education to read them — have multiplied in the English-speaking world to an amazing degree. For the general public the term *article* has almost taken the place of the word *essay*. In newspapers and magazines the trend is toward factual, informative prose pieces that keep us up to date with a fast-moving world. The result is that essays are now sometimes regarded as rather formal, " literary " efforts. However, the term *essay* may still be used to designate a relatively short, unified prose composition on any subject, in any style.

Perhaps what most distinguishes the essay from reporting is that the personality of the writer always shines through it. Essayists are stimulating people whose interests cover a broad range. Whether they are discussing war, letter writing, or picnics, their writing is colored by personal attitudes. The essays you will read in this section are both serious and light, personal and social, concerned with large issues and with small ones. Some tell a story, some discuss a topic; all express an individual point of view in artistic form.

Delight

J. B. PRIESTLEY 1894–

John Boynton Priestley is already known to you as the author of the introduction to this book. One of the most versatile literary figures in England today, he has written successful novels, such as *The Good Companions* and *Festival* (a story using the 1951 Festival of Britain as a setting), and has had many of his plays produced on Broadway as well as in England. Many people think, however, that Priestley is at his best as an essayist. Americans have especially enjoyed his *Midnight on the Desert* because it gives the reactions of an understanding Englishman to many aspects of American life. For a vivid picture of modern English life in his native Midlands, his *English Journey* is unexcelled.

One of Priestley's books, *Delight,* might be called a pocket piece for busy readers. This small volume contains a collection of brief personal comments — some scarcely long enough to be called essays — that record the many things that have given the author delight. Priestley says that he is in part making amends for all the grumbling he has done in the past. The following selections from *Delight* should provide you with a pleasant reading experience.

Cooking Picnics

L IKE MOST men and unlike nearly all women, those atavistic [1] creatures, I detest picnics. One reason is that I am usually very hungry out in the open and I dislike the kind of food provided by picnics. Thus, there are few things to eat better than a properly dressed salad in a fine big salad bowl, but there are few things less appetizing than an undressed salad out of a paper bag or cardboard box. Then, except for thick slices of ham between thin slices of bread, I have a growing distaste for the whole sandwich family, especially paste, egg, or cheese sandwiches. Again, anything with jam in it or on it is a curse on a summer's day. Finally, there is a peculiarly hard, green, sour little apple that must be grown specially for picnic boxes. Nevertheless, I have delighted in my time — and am not yet past it — in one kind of picnic, namely, the cooking picnic. This is for great souls. The instrumental basis of it is the frying pan.

Sausages will do, though steak of course is better. Fried potatoes are essential, and persons whose stomachs shrink from a greasy chip rather underdone should stay at home and nibble health foods. Coffee, which stands up to wood smoke better than tea, is the beverage. The cooking picnic is, I will admit, a smoky job, at least in this damp climate of ours. I have superintended cooking picnics — and I am a natural superintendent on all these occasions — with inflamed and streaming eyes and every sinus wrecked, spluttering and cough-

[1] *atavistic* (ăt′á·vĭst′ĭk): showing characteristics of remote or primitive ancestors.

ing and choking, damning and blasting, glaring at would-be helpful children until they ran away and howled. I have stoked, and fried and stewed and dished out portions until there was nothing left for me but a few bits of greasy muck and a half a cup of coffee grounds. And even my pipe has tasted all wrong in the inferno of wood smoke. Yet I would not have missed a moment of it for a five-pound lunch in a private room on somebody else's expense sheet. Somewhere among the damp obstinate sticks, the dwindling sausages, the vanishing fat, the potatoes that would not brown and the water that would not boil, the billowing smoke on the hillside, the monstrous appetites of the company, there has been delight like a crumb of gold.

No School Report

WE FATHERS of families have one secret little source of delight that is closed to other men. As we read the school reports upon our children, we realize with a sense of relief that can rise to delight that — thank Heaven — nobody is reporting in this fashion upon us. What a nightmare it would be if our personalities were put through this mincing machine! [1] I can imagine my own report: *" Height and weight at beginning of term* — 5 feet, 9 inches: 13 stone, 10 pounds. At end of term — 5 feet, 8 inches: 14 stone, 2 pounds. Note: Through greed and lack of exercise, J.B. is putting on weight and is sagging. He must get out more and eat and drink less. *Conduct* — Not satisfactory. J.B. is increasingly irritable, inconsiderate, and unco-operative. He is inclined to blame others for faults in himself. He complains of lack of sleep but persists in remaining awake to finish rubbishy detective stories. He smokes far too much, and on several occasions has been discovered smoking in bed. There is no real harm in him but at the present time he tends to be self-indulgent, lazy, vain, and touchy. He should be encouraged to spend some weeks this summer with the Sea Scouts or at a Harvest Camp. *English Language and Literature:* Fair but inclined to be careless. *French:* A disappointing term. *History:* Has not made the progress here that we expected of him. Should read more. *Mathematics:* Very poor. *Art:* Has made some attempts both at oils and water color but shows little aptitude. Has been slack in his Appreciation and did not attend Miss Mulberry's excellent talks on the Italian Primitives.[2] *Music:* Fair, but will not practice. *Natural History:* Still professes an interest but finds it impossible to remember names of birds, butterflies, flowers. Has not joined in the Rambles this term. *Chemistry:* Clearly has no interest in this subject. *Physics:* Poor, though occasionally shows interest. Fails to comprehend basic laws. *Physical Culture:* Sergeant Beefer reports that J.B. has been frequently absent and is obviously far from keen. A bad term. *General Report:* J.B. is not the bright and helpful member of our little community that he once promised to be. He lacks self-discipline and does not try to cultivate a cheery outlook. There are times when he still exerts himself — e.g., he made a useful contribution to the end of term production of *A Comedy of Errors* — but he tends to be lazy and egoistical. His housemaster has had a talk with him, but I suggest that stronger parental guidance would be helpful, and is indeed necessary." And then I would be asked to see my father, and would find him staring and frowning

---

[1] *mincing machine:* British for *meat grinder.*

[2] *Italian Primitives:* early Italian painters.

at this report, and then he would stare and frown at me and would begin asking me, in his deep and rather frightening voice, what on earth was the matter with me. But it can't happen, not this side of the grave. I am knee-deep in the soggy world of graying hair and rotting teeth, of monstrous taxes and overdrafts, of vanishing friends and fading sight; but at least, I can tell myself delightedly, nobody is writing a school report upon me.

Women and Clothes

WOMEN who say they are indifferent to clothes, like men who say they do not mind what they eat, should be distrusted; there is something wrong. And men who sneer at woman's passionate concern about dress should be banished to the woods. For my part I delight in women when they go into a conference huddle over new clothes. They seem to me then most themselves and the furthest removed from my sex. They are at such times completely in their own world. They are half children, half witches. Note their attitude during these clothes conferences. For example, their absolutely clear-sighted realism about themselves. We chaps always peer at ourselves through a haze of good will. We never believe we are as fat or as thin and bony as other people say we are. The ladies are free of all such illusions. (Notice the direct level glances they give each other on these occasions.) So in their clothes conference, unlike all masculine conferences, there is no clash of illusions. All of them meet on the firm ground of fact. What is known is immediately taken into account: Kate's left shoulder is higher than her right; Meg is very broad across the hips; Phyllis has very short legs. The conference line — and very sensible too — is that we are all imperfect creatures, so how do we make the best of ourselves? (If politicians and their senior officials tried the same line at international conferences, they could change the whole world in a week.) Yet the whole clothes huddle is not simply so much grim realism. There is one grand illusion that they all share and never dream of challenging. It is the belief that out of these clothes, with necessary swaps and alterations, beauty and witchery can emerge, that somewhere here is the beginning of an enchanted life. And I for one find this altogether delightful.

DELIGHTS AND OPINIONS

1. Do you agree with Priestley on the relative merits of basket picnics and cooking picnics? Justify your position. Account for the increased popularity of cooking picnics. Why will some men who would never want to cook on the kitchen stove be delighted to cook on an outdoor grill? Explain some changes in family life, habits, and house planning during the twentieth century that encourage outdoor cooking.

2. One important ingredient of a sense of humor is the ability to laugh at oneself. How is Priestley's sense of humor demonstrated in " No School Report "? Try this essay on your father and see how he reacts toward it. How does the form of this school report resemble or differ from the reports sent out by your school? What type of school do you judge Priestley's son attended? Give evidence for your answers from the report.

3. Is Priestley's attitude toward women's clothes typical of that of most men? What does he admire in women's conferences about clothes?

SUGGESTIONS FOR WRITING

Write an essay or series of brief comments on some of your own " delights," using, as Priestley does, a light touch with some underlying serious purpose.

Shooting an Elephant

GEORGE ORWELL 1903–1950

England lost one of her most original writers in the untimely death of George Orwell. His last book, *1984,* caused a sensation on both sides of the Atlantic. Always a provocative writer, with a keen insight into social and political situations, Orwell was a skillful and entertaining novelist as well as an essayist. A contemporary called him " the conscience of his age."

Orwell was born in India, but at an early age was sent to boarding school in England. After finishing his education at Eton, he had a short experience with the Imperial Police in Burma. The following essay narrates an exciting incident of his service there, and shows how his thinking on world problems was beginning to develop. He decided to become a writer, and went to Paris, where he lived through several years of extreme poverty. When at last his books succeeded, his health failed him. He said of *1984,* " It wouldn't have been so gloomy if I hadn't been so ill."

IN MOULMEIN, in lower Burma, I was hated by large numbers of people — the only time in my life that I have been important enough for this to happen to me. I was subdivisional police officer of the town, and in an aimless, petty kind of way an anti-European feeling was very bitter. No one had the guts to raise a riot, but if a European woman went through the bazaars alone somebody would probably spit betel juice over her dress. As a police officer I was an obvious target and was baited whenever it seemed safe to do so. When a nimble Burman tripped me up on the football field and the referee (another Burman) looked the other way, the crowd yelled with hideous laughter. This happened more than once. In the end the sneering yellow faces of young men that met me everywhere, the insults hooted after me when I was at a safe distance, got badly on my nerves. The young Buddhist priests were the worst of all. There were several thousands of them in the town and none of them seemed to have anything to do except stand on street corners and jeer at Europeans.

All this was perplexing and upsetting. For at that time I had already made up my mind that imperialism was an evil thing and the sooner I chucked up my job and got out of it the better. Theoretically — and secretly, of course — I was all for the Burmese and all against their oppressors, the British. As for the job I was doing, I hated it more bitterly than I can perhaps make clear. In a job like that you see the dirty work of Empire at close quarters. The wretched prisoners huddling in the stinking cages of the lockups, the gray, cowed faces of the long-term convicts, the scarred buttocks of men who had been flogged with bamboos — all these oppressed me with an intolerable sense of guilt. But I could get nothing into perspective. I was young and ill-educated and I had to think out my problems in the utter silence that is imposed on every Englishman in the East. I did not know that the British Empire is dying, still less did I know that it is a great deal better than the younger empires that are going to supplant it. All I knew was that I was stuck between my hatred of the empire I served and my rage against the

evil-spirited little beasts who tried to make my job impossible. With one part of my mind I thought of the British Raj as an unbreakable tryanny, as something clamped down, in *saecula saeculorum*,[1] upon the will of prostrate peoples; with another part I thought that the greatest joy in the world would be to drive a bayonet into a Buddhist priest's guts. Feelings like these are the normal by-product of imperialism; ask any Anglo-Indian official, if you can catch him off duty.

One day something happened which in a roundabout way was enlightening. It was a tiny incident in itself, but it gave me a better glimpse than I had had before of the real nature of imperialism — the real motives for which despotic governments act. Early one morning the subinspector at a police station the other end of the town rang me up on the phone and said that an elephant was ravaging the bazaar. Would I please come and do something about it? I did not know what I could do, but I wanted to see what was happening and I got onto a pony and started out. I took my rifle, an old .44 Winchester and much too small to kill an elephant, but I thought the noise might be useful *in terrorem.*[2] Various Burmans stopped me on the way and told me about the elephant's doings. It was not, of course, a wild elephant, but a tame one which had gone " must." [3] It had been chained up, as tame elephants always are when their attack of " must " is due, but on the previous night it had broken its chain and escaped. Its mahout,[4] the only person who could manage it when it was in that state, had set out in pursuit, but had taken the wrong direction and was now twelve hours' journey away, and in the morning the elephant had suddenly

[1] *saecula* (sĕk′û·lá) *saeculorum:* forever and ever.

[2] *in terrorem:* in case of fright.

[3] " *must* ": a condition of dangerous frenzy.

[4] *mahout* (má·hout′): the keeper and driver of an elephant.

reappeared in the town. The Burmese population had no weapons and were quite helpless against it. It had already destroyed somebody's bamboo hut, killed a cow and raided some fruit stalls and devoured the stock; also it had met the municipal rubbish van and, when the driver jumped out and took to his heels, had turned the van over and inflicted violences upon it.

The Burmese subinspector and some Indian constables were waiting for me in the quarter where the elephant had been seen. It was a very poor quarter, a labyrinth of squalid huts, thatched with palm leaf, winding all over a steep hillside. I remember it was a cloudy, stuffy morning at the beginning of the rains. We began questioning the people where the elephant had gone and, as usual, failed to get any definite information. That is invariably the case in the East; a story always sounds clear enough at a distance, but the nearer you get to the scene of events the vaguer it becomes. Some of the people said that the elephant had gone in one direction, some said that it had gone in another, some professed not even to have heard of any elephant. I had made up my mind that the whole story was a pack of lies, when I heard yells a little distance way. There was a loud, scandalized cry of " Go away, child! Go away this instant! " and an old woman with a switch in her hand came round the corner of a hut, violently shooing away a crowd of naked children. Some more women followed, clicking their tongues and exclaiming; evidently there was something the children ought not to have seen. I rounded the hut and saw a man's dead body sprawling in the mud. He was an Indian, a black Dravidian [1] coolie, almost naked, and he could not have been dead many minutes. The people said that the elephant had come suddenly upon him round the corner of the hut, caught

him with its trunk, put its foot on his back, and ground him into the earth. This was the rainy season and the ground was soft, and his face had scored a trench a foot deep and a couple of yards long. He was lying on his belly with arms crucified and head sharply twisted to one side. His face was coated with mud, the eyes wide open, the teeth bared and grinning with an unendurable agony. (Never tell me, by the way, that the dead look peaceful. Most of the corpses I have seen looked devilish.) The friction of the great beast's foot had stripped the skin from his back as neatly as one skins a rabbit. As soon as I saw the dead man I sent an orderly to a friend's house nearby to borrow an elephant rifle. I had already sent back the pony, not wanting it to go mad with fright and throw me if it smelt the elephant.

The orderly came back in a few minutes with a rifle and five cartridges, and meanwhile some Burmans had arrived and told us that the elephant was in the paddy fields [2] below, only a few hundred yards away. As I started forward practically the whole white population of the quarter flocked out of the houses and followed me. They had seen the rifle and were all shouting excitedly that I was going to shoot the elephant. They had not shown much interest in the elephant when he was merely ravaging their homes, but it was different now that he was going to be shot. It was a bit of fun to them, as it would be to an English crowd; besides they wanted the meat. It made me vaguely uneasy. I had no intention of shooting the elephant — I had merely sent for the rifle to defend myself if necessary — and it is always unnerving to have a crowd following you. I marched down the hill, looking and feeling a fool, with the rifle over my shoulder and an ever growing army of people jostling at my heels. At the bottom, when you got away from the

[1] *Dravidian* (drȧ·vĭd′ĭ-ăn): belonging to an ancient race of India, numerous in the south.

[2] *paddy fields:* rice fields.

American Museum of Natural History

At that distance, the elephant looked no more dangerous than a cow.

huts, there was a metaled road and beyond that a miry waste of paddy fields a thousand yards across, not yet plowed but soggy from the first rains and dotted with coarse grass. The elephant was standing eight yards from the road, his left side toward us. He took not the slightest notice of the crowd's approach. He was tearing up bunches of grass, beating them against his knees to clean them, and stuffing them into his mouth.

I had halted on the road. As soon as I saw the elephant I knew with perfect certainty that I ought not to shoot him. It is a serious matter to shoot a working elephant — it is comparable to destroying a huge and costly piece of machinery — and obviously one ought not to do it if it can possibly be avoided. And at that distance, peacefully eating, the elephant looked no more dangerous than a cow. I thought then and I think now that his attack of " must " was already passing off; in which case he would merely wander harmlessly about until the mahout came back and caught him. Moreover, I did not want in the least to shoot him. I decided that I

would watch him a little while to make sure that he did not turn savage again, and then go home.

But at that moment I glanced round at the crowd that had followed me. It was an immense crowd, two thousand at the least and growing every minute. It blocked the road for a long distance on either side. I looked at the sea of yellow faces above the garish clothes — faces all happy and excited over this bit of fun, all certain that the elephant was going to be shot. They were watching me as they would watch a conjurer about to perform a trick. They did not like me, but with the magical rifle in my hand I was momentarily worth watching. And suddenly I realized that I would have to shoot the elephant after all. The people expected it of me and I had got to do it; I could feel their two thousand wills pressing me forward irresistibly. And it was at this moment, as I stood there with the rifle in my hands, that I first grasped the hollowness, the futility of the white man's dominion in the East. Here was I, the white man with his gun, standing in

Many of Orwell's books appeal to young people. These are some of his best:

Animal Farm: *a satire on life in a dictatorship.*

1984: *a grimly realistic picture of the suppressed, robotlike lives of Londoners under a dictatorial superstate in the year 1984. Its concepts of "Big Brother," who saw everything, and "Thought Police" created a new kind of horror story.*

Such, Such Were the Joys: *essays, including a scathing account of Orwell's unhappy school days.*

Dickens, Dali, and Others: *more essays, some literary, showing the great range of Orwell's interests and intelligence.*

front of the unarmed crowd — seemingly the leading actor of the piece; but in reality I was only an absurd puppet pushed to and fro by the will of those yellow faces behind. I perceived in this moment that when the white man turns tyrant it is his own freedom that he destroys. He becomes a sort of hollow, posing dummy, the conventionalized figure of a sahib.[1] For it is the condition of his rule that he shall spend his life in trying to "impress the natives," and so in every crisis he has got to do what the "natives" expect of him. He wears a mask, and his face grows to fit it. I had got to shoot the elephant. I had committed myself to doing it when I sent for the rifle. A sahib has got to act like a sahib; he has got to appear resolute, to know his own mind and do definite things. To come all that way, rifle in hand, with two thousand people marching at my heels, and then to trail feebly away, having done nothing — no, that was impossible. The crowd would laugh at me. And my whole life, every white man's in the East, was one long struggle not to be laughed at.

But I did not want to shoot the ele-

[1] *sahib* (sä′ĭb): native term for a European gentleman.

phant. I watched him beating his bunch of grass against his knees, with that preoccupied grandmotherly air that elephants have. It seemed to me that it would be murder to shoot him. At that age I was not squeamish about killing animals, but I had never shot an elephant and never wanted to. (Somehow it always seems worse to kill a large animal.) Besides, there was the beast's owner to be considered. Alive, the elephant was worth at least a hundred pounds; dead, he would only be worth the value of his tusks, five pounds, possibly. But I had got to act quickly. I turned to the experienced-looking Burmans who had been there when we arrived, and asked them how the elephant had been behaving. They all said the same thing; he took no notice of you if you left him alone, but he might charge if you went too close to him.

It was perfectly clear to me what I ought to do. I ought to walk up to within, say, twenty-five yards of the elephant and test his behavior. If he charged, I could shoot; if he took no notice of me, it would be safe to leave him until the mahout came back. But I also knew that I was going to do no such thing. I was a poor shot with a rifle and the ground was soft mud into which one would sink at every step. If the elephant charged and I missed him, I should have about as much chance as a toad under a steam roller. But even then I was not thinking particularly of my own skin, only of the watchful yellow faces behind. For at that moment, with the crowd watching me, I was not afraid in the ordinary sense, as I would have been if I had been alone. A white man mustn't be frightened in front of "natives"; and so, in general, he isn't frightened. The thought in my mind was that if anything went wrong those two thousand Burmans would see me pursued, caught, trampled on, and reduced to a grinning corpse like that Indian up the hill. And if that happened it was quite probable that some of them would laugh.

That would never do. There was only one alternative. I shoved the cartridges into the magazine and lay down on the road to get a better aim.

The crowd grew very still, and a deep, low, happy sigh, as of people who see the theater curtain go up at last, breathed from innumerable throats. They were going to have their bit of fun after all. The rifle was a beautiful German thing with cross-hair sights. I did not know then that in shooting an elephant one would shoot to cut an imaginary bar running from earhole to earhole. I ought, therefore, as the elephant was sideways on, to have aimed straight at his earhole; actually I aimed several inches in front of this, thinking the brain would be further forward.

When I pulled the trigger I did not hear the bang or feel the kick — one never does when a shot goes home — but I heard the devilish roar of glee that went up from the crowd. In that instant, in too short a time, one would have thought, even for the bullet to get there, a mysterious, terrible change had come over the elephant. He neither stirred nor fell, but every line of his body had altered. He looked suddenly stricken, shrunken, immensely old, as though the frightful impact of the bullet had paralyzed him without knocking him down. At last, after what seemed a long time — it might have been five seconds, I dare say — he sagged flabbily to his knees. His mouth slobbered. An enormous senility seemed to have settled upon him. One could have imagined him thousands of years old. I fired again into the same spot. At the second shot he did not collapse but climbed with desperate slowness to his feet and stood weakly erect, with legs sagging and head drooping. I fired a third time. That was the shot that did for him. You could see the agony of it jolt his whole body and knock the last remnant of strength from his legs. But in falling he seemed for a moment to rise, for as his hind legs collapsed beneath him he seemed to tower upward like a huge rock toppling, his trunk reaching skywards like a tree. He trumpeted for the first and only time. And then down he came, his belly toward me, with a crash that seemed to shake the ground even where I lay.

I got up. The Burmans were already racing past me across the mud. It was obvious that the elephant would never rise again, but he was not dead. He was breathing very rhythmically with long rattling gasps, his great mound of a side painfully rising and falling. His mouth was wide open — I could see far down into caverns of pink throat. I waited a long time for him to die, but his breathing did not weaken. Finally I fired my two remaining shots into the spot where I thought his heart must be. The thick blood welled out of him like red velvet, but still he did not die. His body did not even jerk when the shots hit him, the tortured breathing continued without a pause. He was dying, very slowly and in great agony, but in some world remote from me where not even a bullet could damage him further. I felt that I had got to put an end to that dreadful noise. It seemed dreadful to see the great beast lying there, powerless to move and yet powerless to die, and not even to be able to finish him. I sent back for my small rifle and poured shot after shot into his heart and down his throat. They seemed to make no impression. The tortured gasps continued as steadily as the ticking of a clock.

In the end I could not stand it any longer and went away. I heard later that it took him half an hour to die. Burmans were bringing dahs [1] and baskets even before I left, and I was told they had stripped his body almost to the bones by afternoon.

Afterwards, of course, there were endless discussions about the shooting of the elephant. The owner was furious, but he was only an Indian and could do

[1] *dahs* (däz): bowls.

nothing. Besides, legally I had done the right thing, for a mad elephant has to be killed, like a mad dog, if its owner fails to control it. Among the Europeans, opinion was divided. The older men said I was right, the younger men said it was a shame to shoot an elephant for killing a coolie, because an elephant was worth more than any Coringhee [1] coolie. And afterwards I was very glad that the coolie had been killed; it put me legally in the right and gave me a sufficient pretext for shooting the elephant. I often wondered whether any of the others grasped that I had done it solely to avoid looking a fool.

[1] *Coringhee* (kô·rĭn′gē).

BRITISH OFFICER IN THE EAST

1. Why was Orwell hated by many people in Burma? In what little ways was this hatred shown? Summarize his ideas on what the Burmese attitudes indicate about imperialism.

2. What characteristics common to human nature everywhere are shown by the Burmese on hearing that an elephant is to be shot?

3. What made Orwell think that he should not shoot the elephant? Why did he feel he must do it? What did this paradox show him of the weakness of imperialism?

4. What different opinions were expressed by various people as to whether he should have shot the elephant? How do you feel about this matter?

Modern Letters

VIRGINIA WOOLF 1882–1941

Virginia Woolf was the daughter of Sir Leslie Stephen, a distinguished scholar, critic, and biographer. Throughout her childhood her natural talents were stimulated by association with poets, artists, musicians, and novelists who were friends of her father. After her marriage to Leonard Woolf, a London editor, in 1912, the two set up a hand press for publishing limited editions of modern literature, which later developed into the full-fledged publishing house, The Hogarth Press. At their home in the Bloomsbury section of London, the Woolfs were part of the remarkable intellectual circle called the "Bloomsbury Group," which included Lytton Strachey, E. M. Forster, and others.

It is difficult to say whether Virginia Woolf was more distinguished as a novelist or as an essayist and critic. In fiction she blazed new trails in technique, being one of the early advocates of "stream of consciousness" stories. Her novels, such as *To the Lighthouse* and *The Years,* emphasize the psychology of the characters rather than plot. Using some of the methods of the novel, she also wrote a unique biography, *Flush,* the story of Elizabeth Barrett's cocker spaniel, in which is given a " dog's-eye view " of the famous Browning courtship.

In the essay, Virginia Woolf showed her talent for literary criticism. She was an enthusiastic reader whose interests ranged from medieval to modern literature, and though she could be as scholarly and as discriminating as the best of critics, she preferred to think of herself as the " common reader." Two of her volumes of essays are so entitled. " Modern Letters " reflects some of the social changes that have come about since the eighteenth century when letter writing was in its heyday.

AMONG the commonplaces, this one takes a prominent place — that the art of letter writing is dead; that it flourished in the days of the frank,[1] dwindled under the penny post, and was dealt its death blow by the telephone — now it lies feebly expiring. Once in a way it might be well to look into this truism, to examine the day's post, to compare the flimsy sheets of today, rapidly written over in such various hands with those statelier compositions that were a week, or perhaps a month, on the road, and were, therefore, written in much better hands upon paper that still lies crisp between thumb and finger.

There, of course, lie some of the chief distinctions between the old letters and the new — more care, more time went to their composition. But need we take it for granted that care and time are wholly to the good? A letter then was written to be read and not by one person only. It was a composition that did its best to deserve the expense it cost. The arrival of the post was an occasion.

The sheets were not for the waste-paper basket in five minutes, but for handing round, and reading aloud and then for deposit in some family casket as a record. These undoubtedly were inducements to careful composition, to the finishing of sentences, the artful disposition of trifles, the polish of phrases, the elaboration of arguments and the arts of the writing master. But whether Sir William Temple,[2] who wished to know if Dorothy was well and happy and to be assured that she loved him, enjoyed her letters as much as we enjoy them is perhaps doubtful. Sir Horace Mann or West or Gray did not, one guesses, break the seals of Walpole's [3] thick packets in a hurry. One can imagine that they waited for a good fire, and a bottle of wine, and a group of friends and then read the witty and delightful pages aloud, in perfect confidence that nothing was going to be said that was too private for another ear — indeed, the very opposite was the case — such wit, such polish, such a budget of news was too good for a single person and demanded to be shared with others. Often, more often than not, the great letter writers were suppressed novelists, frustrated essayists born before their time. In our day, Dorothy Osborne would have been an admirable biographer, and Walpole one of our most distinguished and prolific journalists — whether to the profit or loss of the world it is impossible to say. Indisputably they practiced to perfection a peculiar art, born of special

---

[1] *frank:* free transmission of letters. A penny post was established for London alone in 1680. Mail coaches first began to deliver letters elsewhere in 1784. Charges varied with the distance until a uniform penny post rate was established in 1840.

[2] *Sir William Temple* (1628–1699): statesman and author. The Dorothy referred to below was Dorothy Osborne, who later became his wife. For Temple's connection with Jonathan Swift, see page 282.

[3] *Walpole:* Horace Walpole (1717–1797), the novelist and man of letters. At Eton he formed a "Quadruple Alliance" with three other students, two of whom are referred to above, Richard West and Thomas Gray, the poet. Sir Horace Mann, the British envoy to Tuscany, with whom Walpole spent a year in Florence, carried on a long correspondence with Walpole, for they never met again after that year.

The Bloomsbury Group is the name given to a number of remarkable people whose association was an important feature of London's literary life. Virginia Woolf, E. M. Forster, and Lytton Strachey were the most famous members of the group; others were John Maynard Keynes, the eminent and witty economist, Clive Bell, an art critic and Mrs. Woolf's brother-in-law, and Roger Fry, a painter and art critic whose biography Mrs. Woolf wrote later. These friends lived and worked in the Bloomsbury section of London — a quiet neighborhood near the British Museum — and they met often for lively conversation about art and life. Virginia Woolf was then, according to an observer, " a shy, aloof young woman, intensely receptive to any experience new to her." And Strachey has been described thus: " Silent, hunched in a corner, all beard and spectacles, not even appearing to listen, he would wait his opportunity and pounce." Nevertheless, these gifted people had gay times as well as serious ones, and the stimulation that they provided for one another is reflected in their art.

circumstances, but to go on, as we in our rash condemnatory mood so often do, to say that their art was the art of letter writing and that we have lost it, and that our art, because it differs from theirs, is no art at all, seems an unnecessary act of pessimism and self-depreciation.

Here, of course, there should be laid down once and for all the principles of letter writing. But since Aristotle [1] never got so far and since the art has always been an anonymous and hand-to-mouth practice, whose chief adepts would have been scandalized had they been convicted of design or intention, it will be more convenient to leave those principles obscure. Let us turn, therefore, without a yard measure to examine the morning's post, and those posts of other mornings that have been thrust pell-

mell into old drawers more from laziness than from any desire to preserve a record for posterity. These pages came by post, were addressed by one person to one person, fell into the letter box, and were laid on the breakfast table — that is all. In the first place, they are very badly written. Whether the invention of the fountain pen is to blame, certainly a well-formed handwriting is now the rarest of happy discoveries. Moreover, no common style of writing prevails. Here it slants, here it bends back; it is rapid, and running in almost every case. The paper too is of all sizes, and colored blue, green, and yellow; much of it is shoddy enough, and coated with some smooth glaze which will no doubt turn traitor before fifty years are passed. This haphazard harum-scarum individuality is reflected in the style. There is none at first showing — each writer makes his own. Urgent need is the begetter of most of these pages. The writers have forgotten, or want to know, or wish to be sure, or must remind one. A sentence about the weather may be thrown in as makeweight; an initial is scrawled, the stamp stuck on upside down, and so off it goes. The whole affair is purely utilitarian.

Besides these, however, though not so common, are letters written mostly from abroad, with the old wish to get into touch with a friend, to give news, to communicate in short what would be said in a private conversation. A friend marooned in a Spanish inn, one traveling in Italy, one who has taken up his residence in India, these are now the nearest representatives of Cowper [2] at Olney writing to Lady Hesketh at Bath. But with what a difference! In the first place nobody would be so rash as to read a modern letter, even from Rangoon, in mixed company. One does not know what is coming next. Modern let-

[1] *Aristotle* (ăr'ĭs·tŏt''l): Greek philosopher (384-322 B.C.) who analyzed the principles of good writing.

[2] *Cowper* (kōō'pĕr): William Cowper (1731-1800), English poet. He carried on a lifelong correspondence with Lady Hesketh, who was his cousin.

ter writers are highly indiscreet. Almost certainly there is some phrase that will cause pain. Very careful editing is needed before a letter can be read aloud to friends. And then our conventions allow of so much freedom of speech — language is so colloquial, slap dash, and unpruned that the presence of someone of another generation would be a grave deterrent. What is sincerity might be mistaken for coarseness. Further, the modern letter writer is so casual, and so careless of the forms and ceremonies of literature, that the pages do not stand the ordeal of reading aloud well. But then, on the other hand, the privacy, the intimacy of these letters make them far more immediately interesting and exciting than the old letters. There is no news for the whole world in them, because newspapers have made that unneeded. Only one person is written to, and the writer had some reason for wishing to write to him or her in particular. Its meaning is private, its news intimate. For these reasons it is a rash incriminating document and the proper place for it is not between the pages of the family Bible but in a drawer with a key.

There then, pell-mell, with all their imperfections thick upon them, they are stuffed — today's post on top of yesterday's post and so on, undocketed, unsorted, as they came. And as the years pass, so they accumulate. The drawers are almost bursting with letters; some of the writers are dead, others have vanished; others write no more. What is to be done with them? Let us look quickly through them and see whether the time has not come to burn them. But once begin dipping and diving, reading this and reading that, and what to do with them is completely forgotten. Page after page is turned. Here are invitations to parties ten years old. Here are postcards demanding the return of lost umbrellas. Here are childish sheets thanking for boxes of water-color paints. Here are calculations about the cost of building a house. Here are long, wild, profuse

letters, all about somebody who did not want, it seems, to marry somebody else. The effect is indescribable. One could swear one heard certain voices, smelt certain flowers, was in Italy, was in Spain, was horribly bored, terribly unhappy, tremendously excited all over again. If the art of letter writing consists in exciting the emotions, in bringing back the past, in reviving a day, a moment, nay a very second of past time, then these obscure correspondents, with their hasty haphazard ways, their gibes and flings, their irreverence and mockery, their careful totting [1] up of days and dates, their general absorption in the moment and entire carelessness what posterity will think of them, beat Cowper, Walpole, and Edward FitzGerald [2] hollow. Yes, but what to do with them? The question remains, for as one reads it becomes perfectly plain that the art of letter writing has now reached a stage, thanks to the penny post and telephone, where it is not dead — that is the last word to apply to it — but so much alive as to be quite unprintable. The best letters of our time are precisely those that can never be published.

[1] *totting* (tŏt′ĭng): colloquial abbreviation of *totaling*.
[2] *Edward FitzGerald* (1809–1883): English poet, famous for his translation of the *Rubáiyát* of Omar Khayyám.

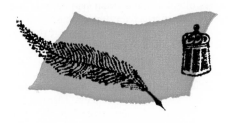

LETTERS — OLD AND NEW

1. What changed circumstances of life does the author think account for the letters of our century and earlier ones? Do

you agree with her? Can you think of any other causes for changes? Has the typewriter affected personal letters in any way?

2. Does her description of modern letters fit those that you or your family receive? How or how not? Do you agree with her comment that two different generations may not feel the same about the freedom of speech in a modern letter? Why does she think modern letters may be more interesting to the recipient than the older letters were?

3. How do you keep letters you have received, or do you throw them away? What situations of modern living make the keeping of letters difficult? Have you had the experience of the author in rereading old letters after a lapse of time? What did they seem like to you?

4. What other famous letter writers can you name besides those mentioned in this essay? How many of the authors you have studied in this volume could be put in that class? Read some of their letters and comment on them.

SUGGESTION FOR WRITING

Write a long newsy letter to a friend or relative that would be suitable to read aloud to the class. A recent trip would make an especially appropriate subject.

Tolerance

E. M. FORSTER 1879–

Edward Morgan Forster has won his literary laurels through the high quality of his work, not by a large output of books. By 1908 he had published four novels with only moderate success. Then there was a lapse of sixteen years before his masterpiece appeared. This novel, *A Passage to India,* based on his own experience in that country, was truly a distinguished piece of fiction. It has served to tie Forster's name inevitably to India, though a comparatively short portion of his life was spent there. It is not a "local color" novel like Kipling's *Kim,* but rather a penetrating study of the effects different backgrounds and attitudes of mind have upon people who are thrown together by circumstances.

The following essay is from Forster's collection *Two Cheers for Democracy,* a title that the author explains thus: "So Two Cheers for Democracy: one because it admits variety and two because it permits criticism. Two cheers are quite enough: there is no occasion to give three. Only Love the Beloved Republic deserves that."

Written in 1941, during what were for England the darkest days of the war, "Tolerance" expresses a viewpoint that is pertinent today.

EVERYBODY is talking about reconstruction. Our enemies have their schemes for a new order in Europe, maintained by their secret police, and we on our side talk of rebuilding London or England, or western civilization, and we make plans how this is to be done. Which is all very well, but when I hear such talk, and see the architects sharpening their pencils and the contractors getting out their estimates, and the statesmen marking out their spheres of influence, and everyone getting down to the job, a very famous text occurs to me: "Except the Lord build the house, they labor in vain who build it." Beneath the poetic imagery of these words lies a hard scientific truth, namely, unless you have a sound attitude of mind, a right psychology, you cannot construct or reconstruct anything that will endure. The text is true, not only for religious people, but for workers whatever their outlook, and it is significant that one of our historians, Dr. Arnold Toynbee, should have chosen it to preface his great study of the growth and decay of civilizations. Surely the only sound foundation for a civilization is a sound state of mind. Architects, contractors, international commissioners, marketing boards, broadcasting corporations will never, by themselves, build a new world. They must be inspired by the proper spirit, and there must be the proper spirit in the people for whom they are working. For instance, we shall never have a beautiful new London until people refuse to live in ugly houses. At present, they don't mind; they demand comfort, but are indifferent to civic beauty; indeed they have no taste. I live myself in a hideous block of flats, but I can't say it worries me, and until we are worried, all schemes for reconstructing London beautifully must automatically fail.

What though is the proper spirit? We agree that the basic problem is psychological, that the Lord must build if the work is to stand, that there must be a sound state of mind before diplomacy or economics or trade conferences can function. But what state of mind is sound? Here we may differ. Most people, when asked what spiritual quality is needed to rebuild civilization, will reply "Love." Men must love one another, they say; nations must do likewise, and then the series of cataclysms which is threatening to destroy us will be checked.

Respectfully but firmly, I disagree. Love is a great force in private life; it is indeed the greatest of all things; but love in public affairs does not work. It has been tried again and again: by the Christian civilizations of the Middle Ages, and also by the French Revolution, a secular movement which reasserted the Brotherhood of Man. And it has always failed. The idea that nations should love one another, or that business concerns or marketing boards should love one another, or that a man in Portugal should love a man in Peru of whom he has never heard — it is absurd, unreal, dangerous. It leads us into perilous and vague sentimentalism. "Love is what is needed," we chant, and then sit back and the world goes on as before. The fact is we can only love what we know personally. And we cannot know much. In public affairs, in the rebuilding of civilization, something much less dramatic and emotional is needed, namely, tolerance. Tolerance is a very dull virtue. It is boring. Unlike love, it has always had a bad press. It is negative. It merely means putting up with people, being able to stand things. No one has ever written an ode to tolerance, or raised a statue to her. Yet this is the quality which will be most needed after the war. This is the sound state of mind which we are looking for. This is the only force which will enable different races and classes and interests to settle down together to the work of reconstruction.

The world is very full of people — appallingly full; it has never been so full before, and they are all tumbling over each other. Most of these people one doesn't know and some of them one doesn't like; doesn't like the color of their skins, say, or the shapes of their noses, or the way they blow them or don't blow them, or the way they talk, or their smell, or their clothes, or their fondness for jazz or their dislike of jazz, and so on. Well, what is one to do? There are two solutions. One of them is the Nazi solution. If you don't like people, kill them, banish them, segregate them, and then strut up and down proclaiming that you are the salt of the earth. The other way is much less thrilling, but it is on the whole the way of the democracies, and I prefer it. If you don't like people, put up with them as well as you can. Don't try to love them: you can't, you'll only strain yourself. But try to tolerate them. On the basis of that tolerance a civilized future may be built. Certainly I can see no other foundation for the postwar world.

For what it will most need is the negative virtues: not being huffy, touchy, irritable, revengeful. I have lost all faith in positive militant ideals; they can so seldom be carried out without thousands of human beings getting maimed or imprisoned. Phrases like " I will purge this nation," " I will clean up this city," terrify and disgust me. They might not have mattered when the world was emptier: they are horrifying now, when one nation is mixed up with another, when one city cannot be organically separated from its neighbors. And, another point: reconstruction is unlikely to be rapid. I do not believe that we are psychologically fit for it, plan the architects never so wisely. In the long run, yes, perhaps: the history of our race justifies that hope. But civilization has its mysterious regressions, and it seems to me that we are fated now to be in one of them, and must recognize this and behave accordingly. Tolerance, I believe, will be imperative after the establishment of peace. It's always useful to take a concrete instance: and I have been asking myself how I should behave if, after peace was signed, I met Germans who had been fighting against us. I shouldn't try to love them: I shouldn't feel inclined. They have broken a window in my little ugly flat for one thing. But I shall try to tolerate them, because it is common sense, because in the postwar world we shall have to live with Germans. We can't exterminate them, any more than they have succeeded in exterminating the Jews. We shall have to put up with them, not for any lofty reason, but because it is the next thing that will have to be done.

I don't then regard tolerance as a great eternally established divine principle, though I might perhaps quote " In My Father's House are many mansions " in support of such a view. It is just a makeshift, suitable for an overcrowded and overheated planet. It carries on when love gives out, and love generally gives out as soon as we move away from our home and our friends, and stand among strangers in a queue for potatoes. Tolerance is wanted in the queue; otherwise we think, " Why will people be so slow? "; it is wanted in the tube,[1] or " Why will people be so fat? "; it is wanted at the telephone, or " Why are they so deaf? " or conversely, " Why do they mumble? " It is wanted in the street, in the office, at the factory, and it is wanted above all between classes, races, and nations. It's dull. And yet it entails imagination. For you have all the time to be putting yourself in someone else's place. Which is a desirable spiritual exercise.

This ceaseless effort to put up with other people seems tame, almost ignoble, so that it sometimes repels generous natures, and I don't recall many great men who have recommended tolerance. St. Paul certainly did not. Nor did Dante. However, a few names occur. Going back over two thousand years, and to India, there is the great Buddhist Emperor Asoka, who set up inscriptions recording not his own exploits but the need for mercy and mutual understanding and peace. Going back about four hundred years, to Holland, there is the Dutch scholar Erasmus, who stood apart from the religious fanaticism of the Reformation and was abused by both parties in consequence. In the same century there was the Frenchman Montaigne, subtle, intelligent, witty, who lived in his quiet country house and wrote essays which still delight and confirm the civilized. And England: there was John Locke, the philosopher; there was Sydney Smith, the Liberal and liberalizing divine; there was Lowes Dickinson, writer of *A Modern Symposium,* which might be called the Bible of Tolerance. And Germany — yes, Germany: there was Goethe. All these men testify to the creed which I have been trying to express: a negative creed, but necessary for the salvation of this crowded jostling modern world.

tube: subway.

Two more remarks. First, it is very easy to see fanaticism in other people, but difficult to spot in oneself. Take the evil of racial prejudice. We can easily detect it in the Nazis; their conduct has been infamous ever since they rose to power. But we ourselves — are we guiltless? We are far less guilty than they are. Yet is there no racial prejudice in the British Empire? Is there no color question? I ask you to consider that, those of you to whom tolerance is more than a pious word. My other remark is to forestall a criticism. Tolerance is not the same as weakness. Putting up with people does not mean giving in to them. This complicates the problem. But the rebuilding of civilization is bound to be complicated. I only feel certain that unless the Lord builds the house, they will labor in vain who build it. Perhaps, when the house is completed, love will enter it, and the greatest force in our private lives will also rule in public life.

THOUGHTS ON BUILDING A NEW WORLD

1. What Bible text does Forster say should guide the thinking of those who would build a better world? How does he interpret this text in modern, nonreligious terms? How does he differ from many others in his choice of a key word for the necessary attitude between nations? Explain the difference between the two words he considers. Give reasons for his preference.

2. Why has the author lost faith in militant ideals? What attitude does he expect to have toward the Germans after the war? Cite some of the everyday experiences in which he thinks this attitude is needed.

3. Though the world situation has changed since Forster wrote this essay in 1941, how do his arguments apply to the problems of today? Do you agree or disagree with his ideas? If you do not agree entirely, how would you go about finding solutions to some of the problems that concern him?

A Churchill Sampler

SIR WINSTON CHURCHILL 1874–

We need not await the verdict of history to place Sir Winston Churchill among England's greatest men. His leadership carried England through the darkest period of her entire history — from the summer of 1940 to the fall of 1941. Then England stood alone, with a formidable enemy massed across the English Channel ready to attack. Who was this man who was to lead England through her hour of greatest peril?

The famous Duke of Marlborough was his ancestor; his father was Lord Randolph Churchill; his mother, a brilliant and beautiful American, was the former Jennie Jerome. Churchill's early career included army service in India, Egypt, and South Africa, and a brief period as a war correspondent. In 1900 he entered the House of Commons as a member of the Conservative party. He was in government service almost continuously from that time until he retired in 1955. At the outbreak of World War II he became First Lord of the Admiralty (the equivalent of our Secretary of the Navy), and in 1940 he was made Prime Minister. Here his magnificent qualities of mind and spirit inspired the English people with the unparalleled courage to fight alongside their allies to victory.

In 1953 Churchill received two notable honors. Queen Elizabeth made him Knight of the Garter, and he is now Sir Winston. Later in the year he was given the Nobel Prize for Literature. All his life, in the midst of a busy public career, he has been a writer. A collection of his speeches, *Blood,*

Sweat, and Tears, took its title from a sentence in his first speech as Prime Minister, just as Hitler was approaching through Holland: " I have nothing to offer but blood, toil, tears, and sweat." After World War II came his notable series of five memoirs covering the entire conflict: *The Gathering Storm, Their Finest Hour, The Grand Alliance, The Hinge of Fate,* and *Triumph and Tragedy.* He is now at work on the long-contemplated *History of the English-Speaking Peoples.* Two volumes have already appeared: *The Birth of Britain* (to 1485) and *The New World* (1485–1688).

Churchill is a master of prose. His incisive expression and ready wit lift his style far above that of most men in public life.

The Nature of Modern War

In *The Gathering Storm,* Churchill reviews some of his earlier impressions of world tensions which had been far from settled by World War I. This passage (written in 1928) on the meaning of war in our century is significant in the light of what followed. It is still pertinent for readers today in our far-from-peaceful world.

I T W A S N O T until the dawn of the twentieth century of the Christian Era that war began to enter into its kingdom as the potential destroyer of the human race. The organization of mankind into great states and empires, and the rise of nations to full collective consciousness, enabled enterprises of slaughter to be planned and executed upon a scale and with a perseverance never before imagined. All the noblest virtues of individuals were gathered together to strengthen the destructive capacity of the mass. Good finances, the resources of world-wide credit and trade, the accumulation of large capital reserves made it possible to divert for considerable periods the energies of whole peoples to the task of devastation. Democratic institutions gave expression to the

will power of millions. Education not only brought the course of the conflict within the comprehension of everyone, but rendered each person serviceable in a high degree for the purpose in hand. The press afforded a means of unification and of mutual stimulation. Religion, having discreetly avoided conflict on the fundamental issues, offered its encouragements and consolations, through all its forms, impartially to all the combatants. Lastly, Science unfolded her treasures and her secrets to the desperate demands of men, and placed in their hand agencies and apparatus almost decisive in their character.

In consequence many novel features presented themselves. Instead of fortified towns being starved, whole nations were methodically subjected, or sought to be subjected, to the process of reduction by famine. The entire population in one capacity or another took part in the war; all were equally the object of attack. The air opened paths along which death and terror could be carried far behind the lines of the actual armies, to women, children, the aged, the sick, who in earlier struggles would perforce have been left untouched. Marvelous organization of railroads, steamships, and motor vehicles placed and maintained tens of millions of men continuously in action. Healing and surgery in their exquisite developments returned them again and again to the shambles. Nothing was wasted that could contribute to the process of waste. The last dying kick was brought into military utility.

But all that happened in the four years of the Great War was only a prelude to what was preparing for the fifth year. The campaign of the year 1919 would have witnessed an immense accession to the powers of destruction. Had the Germans retained the morale to make good their retreat to the Rhine, they would have been assaulted in the summer of 1919 with forces and by methods incomparably more prodigious than any yet employed. Thousands of airplanes would have shattered their cities. Scores of thousands of cannon would have blasted their front. Arrangements were being made to carry simultaneously a quarter of a million men, together with all their requirements, continuously forward across country in mechanical vehicles moving ten or fifteen miles each day. Poison gases of incredible malignity, against which only a secret mask (which the Germans could not obtain in time) was proof, would have stifled all resistance and paralyzed all life on the hostile front subjected to attack. No doubt the Germans too had their plans. But the hour of wrath had passed. The signal of relief was given, and the horrors of 1919 remained buried in the archives of the great antagonists.

The war stopped as suddenly and as universally as it had begun. The world lifted its head, surveyed the scene of ruin, and victors and vanquished alike drew breath. In a hundred laboratories, in a thousand arsenals, factories and bureaus, men pulled themselves up with a jerk, and turned from the task in which they had been absorbed. Their projects were put aside unfinished, unexecuted; but their knowledge was preserved; their data, calculations, and discoveries were hastily bundled together and docketed " for future reference " by the War Offices in every country. The campaign of 1919 was never fought; but its ideas go marching along. In every army they are being explored, elaborated, refined, under the surface of peace, and should war come again to the world, it is not with the weapons and agencies prepared for 1919 that it will be fought, but with developments and extensions of these which will be incomparably more formidable and fatal.

It is in these circumstances that we entered upon that period of exhaustion which has been described as Peace. It gives us at any rate an opportunity to consider the general situation. Certain somber facts emerge, solid, inexorable, like the shapes of mountains from drifting mist. It is established that henceforward whole populations will take part in war, all doing their utmost, all subjected to the fury of the enemy. It is established that nations who believe their life is at stake will not be restrained from using any means to secure their existence. It is probable — nay, certain — that among the means which will next time be at their disposal will be agencies and processes of destruction wholesale, unlimited, and perhaps, once launched, uncontrollable.

Mankind has never been in this position before. Without having improved appreciably in virtue or enjoying wiser guidance, it has got into its hands for the first time the tools by which it can unfailingly accomplish its own extermination. That is the point in human destinies to which all the glories and toils of men have at last led them. They would do well to pause and ponder upon their new responsibilities. Death stands at attention, obedient, expectant, ready to serve, ready to shear away the peoples en masse; ready, if called on, to pulverize, without hope of repair, what is left of civilization. He awaits only the word of command. He awaits it from a frail, bewildered being, long his victim, now — for one occasion only — his Master.

The Miracle of Dunkirk

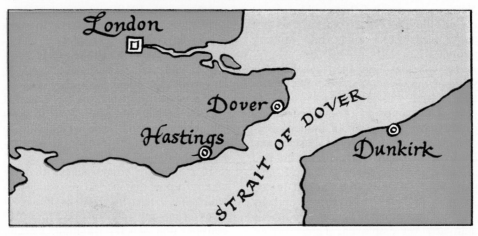

On June 4, 1940, Winston Churchill, Prime Minister of Great Britain, stood before the House of Commons to deliver this account of the successful evacuation of some three hundred thousand men of the British Expeditionary Forces. The position of the British Army, trapped on the beaches of northern France with its back to the English Channel, appeared hopeless and tragic. The Belgian Army had already surrendered; the French Army had ceased to be a fighting organization. For the British the choice seemed to be suicidal defense or humiliating surrender. A plan for rescue was hastily conceived. It demanded the concerted effort of all branches of the British armed services, aided by hundreds of volunteers manning small boats of every type. The achievement at Dunkirk has already taken its place among the heroic episodes of history.

THE GERMAN eruption swept like a sharp scythe around the right and rear of the Armies of the north. Eight or nine armored divisions, each of about four hundred armored vehicles of different kinds, but carefully assorted to be complementary and divisible into small self-contained units, cut off all communications between us and the main French Armies. It severed our own communications for food and ammunition, which ran first to Amiens and afterward through Abbeville, and it shoved its way up the coast to Boulogne and Calais and almost to Dunkirk. Behind this armored and mechanized onslaught came a number of German divisions in lorries, and behind them again there plodded comparatively slowly the dull brute mass of the ordinary German Army and German people, always so ready to be led to the trampling down in other lands of liberties and comforts which they have never known in their own land.

I have said this armored scythe-stroke almost reached Dunkirk — almost but not quite. Boulogne and Calais were the scenes of desperate fighting. The Guards defended Boulogne for a while and were then withdrawn by orders from this country. The Rifle Brigade, the 60th Rifles, and the Queen Victoria's Rifles, with a battalion of British tanks and one thousand Frenchmen, in all about four thousand strong, defended Calais to the last. The British Brigadier was given an hour to surrender. He spurned the offer, and four days of intense street fighting passed before silence reigned over Calais, which marked the end of a memorable resistance. Only thirty unwounded survivors were brought off by the Navy, and we do not know the fate of their comrades. Their sacrifice, however, was not in vain. At least two armored divisions, which otherwise would have been turned against the British Expeditionary Force, had to be sent to overcome them. They have added another page to the glories of the light divisions, and the time gained enabled the Gravelines water lines to be flooded and to be held by the French troops.

Thus it was that the port of Dunkirk was kept open. When it was found impossible for the Armies of the north to reopen their communications to Amiens with the main French Armies, only one choice remained. It seemed, indeed, forlorn. The Belgian, British, and French Armies were almost surrounded. Their sole line of retreat was to a single port and to its neighboring beaches. They were pressed on every side by heavy attacks and far outnumbered in the air.

When, a week ago today, I asked the House to fix this afternoon as the occasion for a statement, I feared it would be my hard lot to announce the greatest military disaster in our long history. I thought — and some good judges agreed with me — that perhaps twenty thousand or thirty thousand men might be re-embarked. But it certainly seemed that the whole of the French First Army and the whole of the British Expeditionary Force north of the Amiens-Abbeville gap would be broken up in the open field or else would have to capitulate for lack of food and ammunition. These were the hard and heavy tidings for which I called upon the House and the nation to prepare themselves a week ago. The whole root and core and brain of the British Army, on which and around which we were to build, and are

to build, the great British Armies in the later years of the war, seemed about to perish upon the field or to be led into an ignominious and starving captivity. . . .

The enemy attacked on all sides with great strength and fierceness, and their main power, the power of their far more numerous Air Force, was thrown into the battle or else concentrated upon Dunkirk and the beaches. Pressing in upon their narrow exit, both from the east and from the west, the enemy began to fire with cannon upon the beaches by which alone the shipping could approach or depart. They sowed magnetic mines in the channels and seas; they sent repeated waves of hostile aircraft, sometimes more than a hundred strong in one formation, to cast their bombs upon the single pier that remained, and upon the sand dunes upon which the troops had their eyes for shelter. Their U-boats, one of which was sunk, and their motor launches took their toll of the vast traffic which now began. For four days or five days an intense struggle reigned. All their armored divisions — or what was left of them — together with great masses of infantry and artillery, hurled themselves in vain upon the ever-narrowing, ever-contracting appendix within which the British and French Armies fought.

Meanwhile the Royal Navy, with the willing help of countless merchant seamen, strained every nerve to embark the British and Allied troops; 220 light warships and 650 other vessels were engaged. They had to operate upon the difficult coast, often in adverse weather, under an almost ceaseless hail of bombs and an increasing concentration of artillery fire. Nor were the seas, as I have said, themselves free from mines and torpedoes. It was in conditions such as these that our men carried on, with little or no rest, for days and nights on end, making trip after trip across the dangerous waters, bringing with them always men whom they had rescued.

The numbers they have brought back are the measure of their devotion and their courage. The hospital ships, which brought off many thousands of British and French wounded, being so plainly marked, were a special target for Nazi bombs; but the men and women on board them never faltered in their duty.

The Royal Air Force, which had already been intervening in the battle, so far as its range would allow, from home bases, now used part of its main metropolitan fighter strength and struck at the German bombers and at the fighters which in large numbers protected them. This struggle was protracted and fierce. Suddenly the scene was cleared; the crash and thunder has for the moment — but only for the moment — died away. A miracle of deliverance, achieved by valor, by perseverance, by perfect discipline, by faultless service, by resource, by skill, by unconquerable fidelity, is manifest to us all. The enemy was hurled back by the retreating British and French troops. He was so roughly handled that he did not hurry their departure seriously. The Royal Air Force engaged the main strength of the German Air Force, and inflicted upon them losses of at least four to one; and the Navy, using nearly one thousand ships of all kinds, carried over three hundred and thirty-five thousand men, French and British, out of the jaws of death and shame, to their native land and to the tasks which lie immediately ahead. We must be very careful not to assign to this deliverance the attributes of a victory. Wars are not won by evacuations. But there was a victory inside this deliverance, which should be noted. It was gained by the Air Force. Many of our soldiers coming back have not seen the Air Force at work; they saw only the bombers which escaped its protective attacks. They underrate its achievements. I have heard much talk of this; that is why I go out of my way to say this. I will tell you about it.

This was a great trial of strength between the British and German Air Forces. Can you conceive a greater objective for the Germans in the air than to make evacuation from these beaches impossible and to sink all these ships which were displayed, almost to the extent of thousands? Could there have been an objective of greater military importance and significance for the whole purpose of the war than this? They tried hard, and they were beaten back; they were frustrated in their task. We got the Army away and they have paid fourfold for any losses which they have inflicted. Very large formations of German airplanes — and we know that they are a very brave race — have turned on several occasions from the attack of one-quarter of their number of the Royal Air Force, and have dispersed in different directions. Twelve airplanes have been hunted by two. One airplane was driven into the water and cast away by the mere charge of a British airplane, which had no more ammunition. All of our types — the Hurricane, the Spitfire, and the new Defiant — and all our pilots have been vindicated as superior to what they have at present to face.

When we consider how much greater would be our advantage in defending the air above this island against an overseas attack, I must say that I find in these facts a sure basis upon which practical and reassuring thoughts may rest. I will pay my tribute to these young airmen. The great French Army was very largely, for the time being, cast back and disturbed by the onrush of a few thousands of armored vehicles. May it not also be that the cause of civilization itself will be defended by the skill and devotion of a few thousand airmen? There never has been, I suppose, in all the world, in all the history of war, such an opportunity for youth. The Knights of the Round Table, the Crusaders, all fall back into the past — not only distant but prosaic; these young men, going forth every morn to guard their native land and all that we stand for, holding in their hands these instruments of colossal and shattering power, of whom it may be said that

Every morn brought forth a noble chance
And every chance brought forth a noble
  knight

deserve our gratitude, as do all of the brave men who, in so many ways and on so many occasions, are ready, and continue ready, to give life and all for their native land.

I return to the Army. In the long series of very fierce battles, now on this front, now on that, fighting on three fronts at once, battles fought by two or three divisions against an equal or somewhat larger number of the enemy, and fought fiercely on some of the old grounds that so many of us knew so well — in these battles our losses in men have exceeded thirty thousand killed, wounded, and missing. I take occasion to express the sympathy of the House to all who have suffered bereavement or who are still anxious. The President of the Board of Trade is not here today. His son has been killed, and many in the House have felt the pangs of affliction in the sharpest form. But I will say this about the missing: we have had a large number of wounded come home safely to this country, but I would say about the missing that there may be very many reported missing who will come back home, someday, in one way or another. In the confusion of this fight it is inevitable that many have been left in positions where honor required no further resistance from them.

Against this loss of over thirty thousand men, we can set a far heavier loss certainly inflicted upon the enemy. But our losses in material are enormous. We have perhaps lost one-third of the men we lost in the opening days of the battle of 21st March, 1918, but we have lost nearly as many guns — nearly one thousand — and all our transport, all the armored vehicles that were with the Army in the north. This loss will impose a further delay on the expansion of our military strength. That expansion had not been proceeding as fast as we had hoped. The best of all we had to give had gone to the British Expeditionary Force; and although they had not the numbers of tanks and some articles of equipment which were desirable, they were a very well and finely equipped Army. They had the first fruits of all that our industry had to give, and that is gone. And now here is this further delay. How long it will be, how long it will last, depends upon the exertions which we make in this island. An effort the like of which has never been seen in our records is now being made. Work is proceeding everywhere, night and day, Sundays and weekdays. Capital and Labor have cast aside their interests, rights, and customs and put them into the common stock. Already the flow of munitions has leaped forward. There is no reason why we should not in a few months overtake the sudden and serious loss that has come upon us, without retarding the development of our general program.

Nevertheless, our thankfulness at the escape of our Army and so many men, whose loved ones have passed through an agonizing week, must not blind us to the fact that what has happened in France and Belgium is a colossal military disaster. The French Army has been weakened; the Belgian Army has been lost; a large part of those fortified lines upon which so much faith had been reposed is gone; many valuable mining districts and factories have passed into the enemy's possession; the whole of the Channel ports are in his hands, with all the tragic consequences that follow from that, and we must expect another blow to be struck almost immediately at us or at France. We are told that Herr Hitler has a plan for invading the British Isles. This has often been thought of before. When Napoleon lay at Boulogne for a year with his flat-bottomed boats and his Grand Army, he was told by someone, " There are bitter weeds in England." There are certainly a great many more of them since the British Expeditionary Force returned.

I would observe that there has never been a period in all these long centuries of which we boast when an absolute

Churchill on War and Peace

What General Weygand has called the Battle of France is over. The Battle of Britain is about to begin. Upon this battle depends the survival of Christian civilization. Upon it depends our own British life and the long continuity of our institutions and our empire. The whole fury and might of the enemy must very soon be turned on us. Hitler knows that he will have to break us in this island or lose the war. If we can stand up to him, all Europe may be free, and the life of the world may move forward into broad sunlit uplands. But if we fail, then the whole world, including the United States, including all that we have known and cared for, will sink into the abyss of a new dark age, made more sinister and perhaps more protracted by the light of perverted science. Let us therefore brace ourselves to our duty and so bear ourselves that if the British Empire and its Commonwealth last for a thousand years, men will still say " This was their finest hour."

(Speech in the House, June 18, 1940 —
the day of the French capitulation.)

The problems of victory are more agreeable than those of defeat, but they are no less difficult.

(Speech in the House,
November 1942.)

guarantee against invasion, still less against serious raids, could have been given to our people. In the days of Napoleon the same wind which would have carried his transports across the Channel might have driven away the blockading fleet. There was always the chance, and it is that chance which has excited and befooled the imaginations of many Continental tyrants. Many are the tales that are told. We are assured that novel methods will be adopted, and when we see the originality of malice, the ingenuity of aggression, which our enemy displays, we may certainly prepare ourselves for every kind of novel stratagem and every kind of brutal and treacherous maneuver. I think that no idea is so outlandish that it should not be considered and viewed with a searching, but at the same time, I hope, with a steady eye. We must never forget the solid assurances of sea power and those which belong to air power if it can be locally exercised.

I have, myself, full confidence that if all do their duty, if nothing is neglected, and if the best arrangements are made, as they are being made, we shall prove ourselves once again able to defend our island home, to ride out the storm of war, and to outlive the menace of tyranny, if necessary for years, if necessary alone. At any rate, that is what we are going to try to do. That is the resolve of His Majesty's Government — every man of them. That is the will of Parliament and the nation. The British Empire and the French Republic, linked together in their cause and in their need, will defend to the death their native soil, aiding each other like good comrades to the utmost of their strength. Even though large tracts of Europe and many old and famous states have fallen or may fall into the grip of the Gestapo and all the odious apparatus of Nazi rule, we shall not flag or fail. We shall go on to the end: we shall fight in France; we shall fight on the seas and oceans; we shall fight with growing confidence and growing strength in the air; we shall defend our island, whatever the cost may be — we shall fight on the beaches; we shall fight on the landing grounds, we shall fight in the fields and in the streets; we shall fight in the hills. We shall never surrender, and even if, which I do not for a moment believe, this island or a large part of it were subjugated and starving, then our Empire beyond the seas, armed and guarded by the British Fleet, would carry on the struggle until, in God's good time, the New World with all its power and might, steps forth to the rescue and the liberation of the old.

THE VOICE OF A LEADER

1. Outline the major points which, according to Churchill, distinguish twentieth-century warfare from that of earlier times. Give some specific illustrations of methods used in World War I which were quite unlike those in nineteenth-century wars.

2. The author foresaw great changes in methods of later wars. Give examples of the fulfillment of his prophecy in World War II. What new weapons may be used in a future world war? Should high school students consider such subjects? Why or why not?

3. In " The Miracle of Dunkirk " how did the circumstances under which the speech was delivered affect the nature of Churchill's account of what had happened? How did they add to the effect of the emotional climax?

4. With a map to help you, study the progress of events so that you can give a clear account of (a) the position of the opposing forces, (b) the effect of the British delaying action at Calais, (c) the battle of Dunkirk, (d) the co-operative participation of the Royal Navy and the Royal Air Force.

5. Was the prophecy of the closing lines fulfilled?

6. Study the qualities of Churchill's style by noting (a) the directness and clearness of his sentences, (b) his use of repetition for emphasis, (c) his use of parallel construction and balanced sentences, (d) his emotional appeal.

A Salutation from Across the Sea

STEPHEN BUTLER LEACOCK 1869–1944

Stephen Leacock was born in England and moved to Canada with his family at the age of six. He graduated from the University of Toronto and took his Ph.D. at Chicago. In 1901 he began his career of thirty-five years at McGill University in Montreal, where he was head of the department of political economy.

In his writings, Stephen Leacock, like Lewis Carroll, led a double life. Learned people respected him for his books on political science and social justice; the public at large loved him for the rich vein of humor which was revealed in volume after volume of merriment for more than thirty years. He was a master of parody, as shown in *Nonsense Novels, Frenzied Fiction*, and

Winsome Winnie, where he ridicules trite, melodramatic novels. Other titles that are suggestive of laughs between the covers are *Arcadian Adventures with the Idle Rich, Moonbeams from the Larger Lunacy, The Garden of Folly,* and *Too Much College.*

Leacock was in great demand as a speaker at public banquets. His humor seemed entirely unforced, a natural overflow of his genial nature without bitterness or unkindness of any sort. So much did his books and his speeches make him part of American life that many persons never thought of him as a national of another country. Thus he was, like Canada itself, a bridge between Great Britain and the

United States. In "A Salutation from Across the Sea," he combines the New World's point of view with loyalty to those "Odd People" across the sea.

THE BRITISH Are an Odd People. They have their own ways and they stick to them; and I like every one of them.

They have their own way of talking. When an Englishman has anything surprising to tell he never exaggerates it, never overstates it — in fact he makes as little of it as possible. And a Scotchman doesn't even mention it. An Englishman can speak of a play of Shakespeare as "rather good," and of grand opera as "not half bad." He can call Haile Selassie[1] a "rather decent little chap," and the President of the United States a "thoroughly good sort."

Sometimes this modesty of speech is perhaps carried a little too far. An Englishman when he has to talk about himself, doesn't refer to himself as "I," but calls himself "one." In my club the other day a newly arrived Englishman said, "One finds Canada simply wonderful; of course one had seen India and all that, but here one finds everything so different." What could I expect to say — that one was terribly glad to know that one liked Canada, that if one would take a drink with one, one would push the bell. Yet I like that way of talking. It's better than the everlasting "I — I — I." Only I think that next time I'll call myself "two."

A Scotchman of course doesn't use "one." He simply calls himself "a body." He's not referring to his soul, before strangers.

But this modest British way of talking without making things sound too big

has the advantage that it keeps the world in its right focus. On our side of the water we get so filled up with admiration, with such a sense of the bigness of potentates and magnates, that we feel small ourselves. We wouldn't know how to behave if we met the Negris of Abyssinia or the Magnum[2] of Magnesia. They're all one to the Britisher — Rajahs, and Rams and Sams, he calls them all "Jimmy."

The British Are an Odd People; even in their recreation. They have their own games, and they carry them all round the world with them. When other nations go among natives they bring a whole collection of decrees and ordinances. The Englishman just brings a briar-root pipe and a cricket bag. He opens it and he says: "Now this is cricket and I'll show you johnnies how to play. Ali Baba, you just roll out that coconut matting and, Ibn Swot, you stick in these wickets." Two seasons later Ali Baba is taken "home" to play for Hants against Bucks,[3] or Potts against Crooks — anyway, another quarter million square miles is annexed.

The British Are an Odd People. They are people of high character; and yet they don't have any particular moral code to guide them. They just go by whether anything is "the thing." If it is, you do it; if it's not you don't. Strangers often wonder, for example, why the Opposition in Parliament doesn't make a row about this or that. But the answer is that it would hardly be "the thing." The whole of British government is carried on in that way. A member rises in the House and asks a question on which seems to hang the whole life of the nation. The Parliamentary Under-Secretary for Horticulture answers that min-

---

[1] *Haile Selassie* (hī′lĕ sĕ·làs′ĭ) (1890–   ): emperor of Ethiopia, important in world affairs when Italy invaded his country in 1935 and he appealed to the League of Nations for help. The failure of the League to prevent this invasion was one of the causes of its downfall.

[2] *Negris . . . Magnum:* imaginary humorous titles. Negus of Abyssinia is one of the actual titles of the Emperor of Ethiopia.

[3] *Hants . . . Bucks:* familiar abbreviations of the counties Hampshire and Buckinghamshire in southern England. Potts and Crooks are humorous parodies on these names.

isters know it but won't say it. Then it's not " the thing " to ask any more. In the United States they need a whole constitution of thousands and thousands of words, and they get tangled up in the clauses. The British constitution is just " the thing." Of course, there are no rules to guide private morals. I mean to say one learnt one's catechism when one was young, but as a matter of fact it is rather the thing to forget it.

Yes, The British Are an Odd People: they have their own ways in eating and drinking. And I like them. Take their afternoon tea. They have it at the South Pole, and they serve it half way through a naval engagement. And what, after all, more charming than the tea tray with its white cloth, the silver teapot, the delicate cups and the thin bread and butter; and what better excuse for slipping in a real drink, just after? Sometimes I think that's what it's for. Only you must be careful not to get absent-minded, and when your hostess asks, " How do you take yours? " you mustn't answer, " Off the shelf," or " Plenty of soda, please." Or no — it wouldn't matter. She'd understand and give it to you.

Oh, Yes, The British Are an Odd People — and I like all their odd ways. Well, after all, why not? I mean to say, one was born in Hampshire, Eh, what.

FRIENDLY FUN

1. This is an easy essay to outline. Identify the main divisions which Leacock uses to show the peculiarities of the British, and under each put his specific examples as subtopics.

2. Leacock's typical method of humor is to begin with true facts from which he goes to ridiculous exaggeration. In this essay, separate the true facts from the exaggerations. Do you find these differences easy to distinguish, or is there difference of opinion in the class?

3. In what spirit does Leacock poke fun at the British? Do you think they could be offended by any of his remarks?

READING AND WRITING

1. You would enjoy dipping into Leacock's collections of humor at almost any point. Try some of them and select an essay to read aloud in class.

2. Following Leacock's general plan, write a humorous comment on any of the types of people with whom you have had experience, such as parents, brothers and sisters, teachers, freshmen, etc.

READING LIST FOR MODERN ESSAYS

Browsing through the collections of essays in your library is a good way to find entertaining essays. Such books may include both English and American writers; often there are biographical notes that give the writer's nationality if you do not know it.

Archbold, W. A. J., *Nineteen Modern Essays*
Galsworthy, Wells, Belloc, Chesterton, and others are to be found in this book.

Buchan, John, *Pilgrim's Way*
Read " My Country," expressing warm appreciation by a Scotch-Canadian.

Cooke, Alistair, *One Man's America*
A newspaperman, formerly English but now American, takes an inquiring look at our country.

Fairbrother, Nan, *An English Year*
There is real British flavor in these delightful reflections around the calendar.

Highet, Gilbert, *People, Places, and Books*
Mr. Highet, a Scotsman, has recorded his radio talks on the subjects of the title.

Jameson, Robert U. (editor), *Essays Old and New,* 3rd edition
This collection includes Forster, Leacock, Churchill, Stevenson, and others.

Macaulay, Rose, *Personal Pleasures*
Akin to the mood of Priestley's *Delight.*

Struther, Jan, *A Pocketful of Pebbles*
The tradition of the informal, personal essay is perpetuated in this " Pocketful," written by the author of *Mrs. Miniver.*

FOR LISTENING

A portion of Churchill's speech of June 18, 1940, quoted on page 708, has been recorded and is available on *Many Voices 6B.*

MODERN DRAMA

IN ELIZABETHAN times the drama flowered as never before or after in any of the world's literatures. Shakespeare, Marlowe, and Ben Jonson made English drama pre-eminent. Yet, curiously, it was nearly three hundred years before another period of great plays enriched the English stage. Between Shakespeare and George Bernard Shaw there were but a handful of distinguished playwrights, and drama became almost a submerged art.

ENGLISH DRAMA AFTER THE ELIZABETHANS

Of course plays were being written during this interval. Except for the twenty years during the seventeenth century when playhouses were closed by the Puritans, the theater was always a popular form of entertainment. But each of these three centuries had its own great weakness to prevent its becoming a really creative age of drama. In the remnant of the seventeenth century, after playhouses were reopened in 1660, the chief enemy of permanently living drama was the flippancy and indecency characteristic of the Restoration. In the eighteenth century, slavishness to French and ancient classical models produced stilted, high-flown tragedies and comedies. In the middle of the century, however, Oliver Goldsmith and Richard B. Sheridan broke the spell with their witty and original comedies. Goldsmith's *She Stoops to Conquer* and Sheridan's *The School for Scandal* still hold the stage in competition with modern comedy. Nineteenth-century drama suffered from two circumstances: the novel was a new, exciting form of writing that drew talent away from the drama; and when literary men did attempt plays, they tended to ignore the liveliness and suspense of what we call "good theater." Instead they wrote plays based on weighty, dusty historical plots and used poetic language that had little appeal for the general public.

It is significant that both Tennyson and Browning, the two greatest poets of the period, tried writing drama without much success. Evidently, the Victorian manner of writing did not carry well across the footlights.

THE BEGINNINGS OF MODERN DRAMA

In the last years of the nineteenth century the first dawn of a brilliant new age of drama was seen to the east of England. Henrik Ibsen, the great Norwegian playwright, was creating a different type of drama, serious in content, simple and conversational in style, and, above all, realistic in portraying ordinary people and the problems they face in life. Important new dramatists with fresh, vital messages appeared all over Europe — Strindberg in Sweden, Maeterlinck in Belgium, Pirandello in Italy — and their influence spread to England and America. The modern dramatic age began to awaken.

Ibsen was first brought to the attention of the English by a young drama critic, George Bernard Shaw. Soon he began to write plays himself, comedies instead of tragedies, but resembling Ibsen's plays in their sharp comments on the social injustices and moral weaknesses of our civilization. Shaw was the dominant figure in the twentieth-century drama of England. His long life, which ended in 1950, and his tremendous output of notable plays, produced throughout the English-speaking world, enabled him to outstrip any other claimant to the distinction. His pre-eminence has not diminished since his death.

THE IRISH NATIONAL THEATER

A significant center of drama at the beginning of the century was the Irish National Theater. It grew out of a nationalistic trend, known as the Celtic Renaissance, which sought to arouse patriotic interest in Ireland's folklore and the ancient writings in Celtic. The Irish who campaigned and agitated for independence from England (won finally in 1922) were allied with the literary movement; William Butler Yeats, the most prolific and able writer of Irish poetic drama, significantly became a senator in the new Irish Free State.

The National Theater, housed in the Abbey Theater of Dublin, not only stimulated the writing and production of plays among its own members, but also inspired similar groups elsewhere in England and America. The amateur " little theater " movement and the one-act play, which reached their height of popularity in the United States in the first quarter of the twentieth century, were largely influenced by Ireland's Abbey Players.

Riders to the Sea (pages 770–77) by Synge (sĭng) is one of the crowning productions of the Irish theater and an outstanding example of condensed tragedy. Sean (shôn) O'Casey, who moved to England after the unpopular reception of his realistic, sometimes bitter plays about poverty-stricken Irishmen, is probably Britain's greatest living dramatist. On the comic side, Lady Gregory's one-act character plays of Irish peasants are always popular, as are Lord Dunsany's strange little dramas marked by fantastic situations and ironic humor.

GALSWORTHY AND BARRIE

On the London stage, two men besides Shaw were outstanding playwrights during the first part of the century. In the section of modern short stories you have met John Galsworthy, whose skill in both fiction and drama places him high among modern writers. Galsworthy wrote seven important plays, mostly tragic, before World War I. In the twenties appeared his greatest play, *Loyalties,* and his last one of importance, *Escape,* in which he experimented with a series of scenes somewhat in the manner of the moving picture. This was considered a marked innovation in 1926, but has since come to be an accepted technique. Following the main trend of much twentieth-century literature, Galsworthy wrote realistic plays dealing with important social problems. The titles of his plays *Strife* and *Justice* suggest this.

The third important name of the early century was James M. Barrie, who is probably best remembered for his charming fantasy, *Peter Pan.* You will read a perennial favorite by Barrie, *The Old Lady Shows Her Medals* (pages 778–800). Barrie's sentimental and whimsical comedies are in decided contrast to Shaw's satirical comedies and Galsworthy's tragedies. Within his own field it would be hard to find his equal.

PRESENT–DAY ENGLISH DRAMA

Following World War I some of the energy and inventiveness in modern drama seemed to leave England as it entered America. In the first quarter of the century British dramatists easily outclassed Americans; in the second quarter the situation was reversed. Yet there is a constant exchange of plays across the Atlantic, and many playwrights are equally well known on both continents. For example, the popular English playwright Terence Rattigan is also known to Broadway audiences. Margaret Sullavan (an American) and Vivien Leigh (an Englishwoman) have both appeared in his play *The Deep Blue Sea.* J. B. Priestley, the author of plays depicting middle-class English life, has lived in the United States and written about it in several books. Somerset Maugham, the novelist and short-story writer who made his early reputation with polished, satiric comedies, has lived and written here. Recently he dramatized some of his stories for American television. Noel Coward, the witty author of sophisticated plays, including musical comedies, has acted in American movies and television, and his plays have been produced on Broadway. Indeed, it is usually safe to assume that one season's hit in London will draw packed houses the next year on Broadway.

A significant development in modern drama is apparent in the writings of T. S. Eliot and Christopher Fry: a revival of poetic drama in England. An American poet who is now a naturalized English citizen, Eliot combined a medieval subject with the style of ancient Greek drama (having a chorus comment on the significance of the action) in *Murder in the Cathedral* (1935). One of his later plays, *The Cocktail Party* (1949), is a psychological drama in which modern conversation is skillfully put into the rhythms of a verse form adapted from Old English. Fry, a brilliant poet, writes in a style more nearly Elizabethan, rich with imagery and musical, swinging blank verse. His *A Phoenix Too Frequent* and *The Lady's Not for Burning* have awakened hopes that English drama may yet recapture the poetic glory of Shakespeare's day.

Eliot's *The Confidential Clerk*, Fry's *The Dark Is Light Enough*, and Rattigan's *Separate Tables* are recent examples of the great variety in British drama. England has not one kind but many kinds of theater.

Lyrics on pages 715–17 quoted with permission of Coward-McCann, Inc., publishers, *My Fair Lady* by Alan Jay Lerner and Frederick Loewe, copyright 1956 by Alan Jay Lerner and Frederick Loewe Photographs by Leo Friedman.

MY FAIR LADY is Broadway's sparkling musical version of *Pygmalion*. This American adaptation of George Bernard Shaw's play about the transformation of an uneducated Cockney girl combines songs and dances with some definite points of view about the English language. As the curtain rises, Professor Higgins is holding forth:

can't the English learn to speak!

" An Englishman's way of speaking absolutely classifies him;
The moment he talks he makes some other Englishman despise him.
One common language I'm afraid we'll never get.
Oh, why can't the English learn to set
A good example to people whose English is painful to your ears?
The Scotch and the Irish leave you close to tears.
There even are places where English completely disappears.
In America, they haven't used it for years! "

715

Eliza, the flower girl whose speech betrays her class, presents
a challenge to Higgins and Pickering, both students of dialects.
In three months, Higgins suggests, he could pass her off as
a duchess at an ambassador's garden party. Her education begins.

" If you spoke as she does, sir,
instead of the way you do,
why, you might be
selling flowers, too."

" In 'ertford, 'ereford and 'ampshire,
'urricanes 'ardly hever 'appen! "

By George, she's got it!

Professor Higgins and Colonel Pickering break into
a dance when Eliza at last masters the pronunciation
of "The rain in Spain stays mainly in the plain."

Pygmalion

GEORGE BERNARD SHAW 1856–1950

George Bernard Shaw became a legend in his own lifetime, and his death on November 2, 1950, marked the end of the early pioneers in modern literature. His life spanned almost a century, and he was actively writing drama of a vigorous and original kind almost to the end of his days. Although his sharp tongue and satiric attitude toward conventional thinking made him many enemies, he was generally acknowledged during his last quarter century to be England's greatest living writer.

Shaw was born in Dublin of Irish gentry whom he described as " revolving impecuniously in a sort of vague second cousinship round a baronetcy." His mother — a woman of forceful character — drew her children to her after separation from Shaw's father, an intemperate man who was unsuccessful both as a businessman and head of a household. Shaw followed his mother and sisters to London, and here he devoted himself to self-improvement. His first nine years in that city were ones of struggle and hardship; he earned only thirty dollars by his pen in that time. He became one of the first socialists in England, wrote pamphlets for the Fabian Society, and expounded his ideas from the free-for-all platforms in Hyde Park.

During the eighties and nineties, Shaw became a journalist, writing criticism of music, drama, books, and art for various newspapers. Thus he became known to the literary world. Journalistic criticism fascinated him because it gave him the opportunity to express his ideas to a wide public.

Because he grew disgusted with the poor quality of plays being presented, Shaw began writing plays himself. He interested Ellen Terry, the leading romantic actress of the time, in modern drama; she was the inspiration for several of his plays and a lifelong friend and correspondent as well. Discarding the accepted rules of drama, he wrote as he pleased. Some of his plays were lacking in action, and they included a great deal of talk, but it was never dull talk. Shaw used the stage as a forum for his ideas on politics, religion, race, and universal betterment. He always stirred people to think for themselves.

Shaw wrote some fifty plays during a half century of active drama composition. Some of them were historical plays: *Caesar and Cleopatra* (ancient Rome and Egypt), *The Devil's Disciple* (the American Revolution), *Androcles and the Lion* (early Christian martyrs in Rome), *Saint Joan* (Joan of Arc). He did not write merely to picture history, however — rather to upset it and give some new point of view on the characters themselves, or some new interpretation of historical records.

Shaw carried on the Irish tradition of light comedy with brilliant dialogue in *Arms and the Man* (from which *The Chocolate Soldier*, a widely popular musical comedy, was drawn), *Candida*, and *Pygmalion*. These are among his comedies best liked by young people.

Like Dr. Samuel Johnson, Shaw was

known for the peculiarities of his personality as well as his literary ability. His active mind was full of theories: he was, for instance, a staunch vegetarian and a great attacker of standard English spelling, leaving, at his death, a large fortune to promote its " reform." But his reputation rests securely on the enduring qualities of his writing, which transcend personal idiosyncrasies. In 1925 he was awarded the Nobel Prize for Literature, and several decades later he remains one of the most widely read and admired modern English writers.

Pygmalion, written in 1912, has been a successful play on stage, screen, and television. Shaw took its title from a Greek myth, in which the sculptor Pygmalion carved an ivory statue of a maiden and then fell in love with it. He entreated the goddess Aphrodite for a wife resembling the statue, and she brought the statue to life. Shaw's Pygmalion is Professor Higgins, a phonetician who makes a business as well as a hobby of recording and studying various dialects. Higgins changes the cockney speech of an illiterate, bedraggled flower girl of the London streets into English that is acceptable to the upper classes.

But more than that, through the strong influence of her new environment upon her character, a sensitive woman emerges from what had been a " squashed cabbage leaf." You will find that *Pygmalion* is a satire in Shaw's most amusing manner.

In the first act what happens is more important than who the main characters are. Most of these are not even identified by name during the early part of this act. As these persons become increasingly important to the play, however, you will learn to identify them as:

Miss Eynsford Hill, the daughter Clara
Mrs. Eynsford Hill, the mother
Mr. Eynsford Hill, the son Freddy
Eliza Doolittle, the flower girl
Professor Henry Higgins, the note taker and teacher of phonetics
Colonel Pickering, the gentleman and student of Indian dialects.

In the second act, two new characters are introduced:
Mrs. Pearce, Henry Higgins' housekeeper
Alfred Doolittle, Eliza's father.

In the third act, you will meet:
Mrs. Higgins, Henry Higgins' mother.

ACT I

Covent Garden [1] *at 11:15* P.M. *Torrents of heavy summer rain. Cab whistles blowing frantically in all directions. Pedestrians running for shelter into the market and under the portico* [2] *of St. Paul's Church, where there are already several people, among them a lady and her daughter in evening dress. They are all peering out gloomily at the rain, except one man with his back turned to the rest, who seems wholly preoccupied with a notebook in which he is writing busily.*

[1] *Covent Garden:* a site north of the Strand, London, occupied by the principal fruit, flower, and vegetable market. Covent Garden Theater is the most important place for grand opera in London.

[2] *portico* (pōr'tǐ·kō): a platform with a protecting roof.

The church clock strikes the first quarter.

THE DAUGHTER (*in the space between the central pillars, close to the one on her left*). I'm getting chilled to the bone. What can Freddy be doing all this time? He's been gone twenty minutes.

THE MOTHER (*on her daughter's right*). Not so long. But he ought to have got us a cab by this.

A BYSTANDER (*on the lady's right*). He won't get no cab not until half-past eleven, missus, when they come back after dropping their theater fares.

THE MOTHER. But we must have a cab. We can't stand here until half-past eleven. It's too bad.

THE BYSTANDER. Well, it ain't my fault, missus.

THE DAUGHTER. If Freddy had a bit of gumption, he would have got one at the theater door.

THE MOTHER. What could he have done, poor boy?

THE DAUGHTER. Other people got cabs. Why couldn't he?

[FREDDY *rushes in out of the rain from the Southampton Street side, and comes between them closing a dripping umbrella. He is a young man of twenty, in evening dress, very wet round the ankles.*]

THE DAUGHTER. Well, haven't you got a cab?

FREDDY. There's not one to be had for love or money.

THE MOTHER. Oh, Freddy, there must be one. You can't have tried.

THE DAUGHTER. It's too tiresome. Do you expect us to go and get one ourselves?

FREDDY. I tell you they're all engaged. The rain was so sudden: nobody was prepared; and everybody had to take a cab. I've been to Charing Cross one way and nearly to Ludgate Circus the other; and they were all engaged.

THE MOTHER. Did you try Trafalgar Square?

FREDDY. There wasn't one at Trafalgar Square.

THE DAUGHTER. Did you try?

FREDDY. I tried as far as Charing Cross Station. Did you expect me to walk to Hammersmith?

THE DAUGHTER. You haven't tried at all.

THE MOTHER. You really are very helpless, Freddy. Go again; and don't come back until you have found a cab.

FREDDY. I shall simply get soaked for nothing.

THE DAUGHTER. And what about us? Are we to stay here all night in this draught, with next to nothing on? You selfish pig —

FREDDY. Oh, very well! I'll go, I'll go.

[*He opens his umbrella and dashes off Strandwards, but comes into collision with a flower girl, who is hurrying in for shelter, knocking her basket out of her hands. A blinding flash of lightning, followed instantly by a rattling peal of thunder, orchestrates the incident.*]

THE FLOWER GIRL. Nah then, Freddy, look wh' y' gowin, deah.

FREDDY. Sorry. (*He rushes off.*)

THE FLOWER GIRL (*picking up her scattered flowers and replacing them in the basket*). There's menners f' yer! Te-oo banches o' voylets trod into the mad.[1] (*She sits down on the plinth [2] of the column, sorting her flowers, on the lady's right. She is not at all an attractive person. She is perhaps eighteen, perhaps twenty, hardly older. She wears a little sailor hat of black straw that has long been exposed to the dust and soot of London and has seldom if ever been brushed. Her hair needs washing rather badly: its mousy color can hardly be natural. She wears a shoddy black coat that reaches nearly to her knees and is shaped to her waist. She has a brown skirt with a coarse apron. Her boots are much the worse for wear. She is no doubt as clean as she can afford to be; but compared to the ladies she is very dirty. Her features are no worse than theirs; but their condition leaves something to be desired; and she needs the services of a dentist.*)

THE MOTHER. How do you know that my son's name is Freddy, pray?

THE FLOWER GIRL. Ow, eez ye-ooa san, is e? Wal, fewd dan y' de-ooty bawmz a mather should, eed now bettern to spawl a pore gel's flahrzn than ran away athaht pyin. Will ye-oo py me

---

[1] "There is manners for you! Two bunches of violets trod in the mud." The girl speaks with a cockney accent.

[2] *plinth* (plĭnth): lowest member of the base of a column.

f'them? [1] (*Here, with apologies, this desperate attempt to represent her dialect without a phonetic alphabet must be abandoned as unintelligible outside London.*)

THE DAUGHTER. Do nothing of the sort, Mother. The idea!

THE MOTHER. Please allow me, Clara. Have you any pennies?

THE DAUGHTER. No. I've nothing smaller than sixpence.

THE FLOWER GIRL (*hopefully*). I can give you change for a tanner,[2] kind lady.

THE MOTHER (*to Clara*). Give it to me. (*Clara parts reluctantly.*) Now (*to the girl*) this is for your flowers.

THE FLOWER GIRL. Thank you kindly, lady.

THE DAUGHTER. Make her give you the change. These things are only a penny a bunch.

THE MOTHER. Do hold your tongue, Clara. (*To the girl*) You can keep the change.

THE FLOWER GIRL. Oh, thank you, lady.

THE MOTHER. Now tell me how you know that young gentleman's name.

THE FLOWER GIRL. I didn't.

THE MOTHER. I heard you call him by it. Don't try to deceive me.

THE FLOWER GIRL (*protesting*). Who's trying to deceive you? I called him Freddy or Charlie same as you might yourself if you was talking to a stranger and wished to be pleasant. (*She sits down beside her basket.*)

THE DAUGHTER. Sixpence thrown away! Really, Mamma, you might have spared Freddy *that*. (*She retreats in disgust behind the pillar.*)

[*An elderly gentleman of the amiable military type rushes into the shelter, and closes a dripping umbrella. He is in the same plight as* FREDDY, *very wet about the ankles. He is in evening dress, with a light overcoat. He takes the place left vacant by the* DAUGHTER'S *retirement.*]

THE GENTLEMAN. Phew!

THE MOTHER (*to the* GENTLEMAN). Oh, sir, is there any sign of its stopping?

THE GENTLEMAN. I'm afraid not. It started worse than ever about two minutes ago. (*He goes to the plinth beside the* FLOWER GIRL; *puts up his foot on it; and stoops to turn down his trouser end.*)

THE MOTHER. Oh dear! (*She retires sadly and joins her daughter.*)

THE FLOWER GIRL (*taking advantage of the military gentleman's proximity to establish friendly relations with him*). If it's worse, it's a sign it's nearly over. So cheer up, Captain; and buy a flower off a poor girl.

THE GENTLEMAN. I'm sorry. I haven't any change.

THE FLOWER GIRL. I can give you change, Captain.

THE GENTLEMAN. For a sovereign? I've nothing less.

THE FLOWER GIRL. Garn![3] Oh do buy a flower off me, Captain. I can change half-a-crown. Take this for tuppence.

THE GENTLEMAN. Now don't be troublesome: there's a good girl. (*Trying his pockets*) I really haven't any change — Stop! Here's three hapence, if that's any use to you. (*He retreats to the other pillar.*)

THE FLOWER GIRL (*disappointed, but thinking three halfpence better than nothing*). Thank you, sir.

THE BYSTANDER (*to the girl*). You be careful; give him a flower for it. There's a bloke [4] here behind taking down every blessed word you're saying. (*All turn to the man who is taking notes.*)

[1] "Oh, he is your son, is he? Well, if you had done your duty by him as a mother should, he would know better than to spoil a poor girl's flowers and then run away without paying. Will you pay me for them?"

[2] *tanner:* English slang for a sixpence. (For the value of this coin and other pieces of English money, see page 811.)

[3] *Garn:* expression of disappointment and anger.

[4] *bloke:* slang name for a person.

THE FLOWER GIRL (*springing up terrified*). I ain't done nothing wrong by speaking to the gentleman. I've a right to sell flowers if I keep off the curb. (*Hysterically*) I'm a respectable girl. So help me, I never spoke to him except to ask him to buy a flower off me. (*General hubbub, mostly sympathetic to the* FLOWER GIRL *but deprecating* [1] *her excessive sensibility. Cries of* Don't start hollerin. Who's hurting you? Nobody's going to touch you. What's the good of fussing? Steady on. Easy easy, etc., *come from the elderly staid spectators, who pat her comfortingly. Less patient ones bid her shut her head, or ask her roughly what is wrong with her. A remoter group, not knowing what the matter is, crowd in and increase the noise with question and answer:* What's the row? What's he do? Where is he? A tec [2] taking her down. What! him? Yes! Him over there. Took money off the gentleman, etc. *The* FLOWER GIRL, *distraught and mobbed, breaks through them to the* GENTLEMAN, *crying wildly*) Oh, sir, don't let him charge me. You dunno what it means to me. They'll take away my character and drive me on the streets for speaking to gentlemen. They —

THE NOTE TAKER (*coming forward on her right, the rest crowding after him*). There, there, there, there! Who's hurting you, you silly girl? What do you take me for?

THE BYSTANDER. It's all right; he's a gentleman. Look at his boots. (*Explaining to the* NOTE TAKER) She thought you was a copper's nark, sir.

THE NOTE TAKER (*with quick interest*). What's a copper's nark?

THE BYSTANDER (*inapt at definition*). It's a — well, it's a copper's nark, as you might say. What else would you call it? A sort of informer.

THE FLOWER GIRL (*still hysterical*).

---

[1] *deprecating* (dĕp′rē·kā′tĭng): deploring; disapproving.
[2] *tec:* detective.

I take my Bible oath I never said a word —

THE NOTE TAKER (*overbearing but good-humored*). Oh, shut up, shut up. Do I look like a policeman?

THE FLOWER GIRL (*far from reassured*). Then what did you take down my words for? How do I know whether you took me down right? You just show me what you've wrote about me. (*The* NOTE TAKER *opens his book and holds it steadily under her nose, though the pressure of the mob trying to read it over his shoulders would upset a weaker man.*) What's that? That ain't proper writing. I can't read that.

THE NOTE TAKER. I can. (*Reads, reproducing her pronunciation exactly*) " Cheer ap, Keptin; n' baw ya flahr orf a pore gel."

THE FLOWER GIRL (*much distressed*). It's because I called him Captain. I meant no harm. (*To the* GENTLEMAN) Oh, sir, don't let him lay a charge agen me for a word like that. You —

THE GENTLEMAN. Charge! I make no charge. (*To the* NOTE TAKER) Really, sir, if you are a detective, you need not begin protecting me against molestation by young women until I ask you. Anybody could see that the girl meant no harm.

THE BYSTANDERS GENERALLY (*demonstrating against police espionage*). Course they could. What business is it of yours? You mind your own affairs. He wants promotion, he does. Taking down people's words! Girl never said a word to him. What harm if she did? Nice thing a girl can't shelter from the rain without being insulted, etc., etc., etc. (*She is conducted by the more sympathetic demonstrators back to her plinth, where she resumes her seat and struggles with her emotion.*)

THE BYSTANDER. He ain't a tec. He's a blooming busybody: that's what he is. I tell you, look at his boots.

THE NOTE TAKER (*turning on him genially*). And how are all your people down at Selsey?

THE BYSTANDER (*suspiciously*). Who told you my people come from Selsey?

THE NOTE TAKER. Never you mind. They did. (*To the girl*) How do you come to be up so far east? You were born in Lisson Grove.

THE FLOWER GIRL (*appalled*). Oh, what harm is there in my leaving Lisson Grove? It wasn't fit for a pig to live in; and I had to pay four-and-six a week. (*In tears*) Oh, boo — hoo — oo —

THE NOTE TAKER. Live where you like; but stop that noise.

THE GENTLEMAN (*to the girl*). Come, come! he can't touch you: you have a right to live where you please.

A SARCASTIC BYSTANDER (*thrusting himself between the* NOTE TAKER *and the* GENTLEMAN). Park Lane, for instance. I'd like to go into the Housing Question with you, I would.

THE FLOWER GIRL (*subsiding into a brooding melancholy over her basket, and talking very low-spiritedly to herself*). I'm a good girl, I am.

THE SARCASTIC BYSTANDER (*not attending to her*). Do you know where *I* come from?

THE NOTE TAKER (*promptly*). Hoxton.

[*Titterings. Popular interest in the* NOTE TAKER'S *performance increases.*]

THE SARCASTIC ONE (*amazed*). Well, who said I didn't? Bly me! You know everything, you do.

THE FLOWER GIRL (*still nursing her sense of injury*). Ain't no call to meddle with me, he ain't.

THE BYSTANDER (*to her*). Of course he ain't. Don't you stand it from him. (*To the* NOTE TAKER) See here! What call have you to know about people what never offered to meddle with you? Where's your warrant?

SEVERAL BYSTANDERS (*encouraged by this seeming point of law*). Yes, where's your warrant?

THE FLOWER GIRL. Let him say what he likes. I don't want to have no truck with him.

THE BYSTANDER. You take us for dirt under your feet, don't you? Catch you taking liberties with a gentleman!

THE SARCASTIC BYSTANDER. Yes, tell *him* where he come from if you want to go fortune-telling.

THE NOTE TAKER. Cheltenham, Harrow, Cambridge, and India.

THE GENTLEMAN. Quite right. (*Great laughter. Reaction in the* NOTE TAKER'S *favor. Exclamations of* He knows all about it. Told him proper. Hear him tell the toff[1] where he come from? *etc.*) May I ask, sir, do you do this for your living at a music hall?

THE NOTE TAKER. I've thought of that. Perhaps I shall some day.

[*The rain has stopped; and the persons on the outside of the crowd begin to drop off.*]

THE FLOWER GIRL (*resenting the reaction*). He's no gentleman, he ain't, to interfere with a poor girl.

THE DAUGHTER (*out of patience, pushing her way rudely to the front and displacing the* GENTLEMAN, *who politely retires to the other side of the pillar*). What on earth is Freddy doing? I shall get pneumonia if I stay in this draught any longer.

THE NOTE TAKER (*to himself, hastily making a note of her pronunciation of "monia"*). Earl's Court.

THE DAUGHTER (*violently*). Will you please keep your impertinent remarks to yourself.

THE NOTE TAKER. Did I say that out loud? I didn't mean to. I beg your pardon. Your mother's Epsom, unmistakably.

THE MOTHER (*advancing between her daughter and the* NOTE TAKER). How very curious! I was brought up in Large-lady Park, near Epsom.

THE NOTE TAKER (*uproariously amused*). Ha! ha! What a devil of a

---

[1] *toff* (tŏf): slang for a dandy.

name! Excuse me. (*To the* DAUGHTER) You want a cab, do you?

THE DAUGHTER. Don't dare speak to me.

THE MOTHER. Oh please, please, Clara. (*Her daughter repudiates her with an angry shrug and retires haughtily.*) We should be so grateful to you, sir, if you found us a cab. (*The* NOTE TAKER *produces a whistle.*) Oh, thank you. (*She joins her daughter.*)

[*The* NOTE TAKER *blows a piercing blast.*]

THE SARCASTIC BYSTANDER. There! I knowed he was a plain-clothes copper.

THE BYSTANDER. That ain't a police whistle. That's a sporting whistle.

THE FLOWER GIRL (*still preoccupied with her wounded feelings*). He's no right to take away my character. My character is the same to me as any lady's.

THE NOTE TAKER. I don't know whether you've noticed it, but the rain stopped about two minutes ago.

THE BYSTANDER. So it has. Why didn't you say so before? And us losing our time listening to your silliness! (*He walks off toward the Strand.*)

THE SARCASTIC BYSTANDER. I can tell where *you* come from. You come from Anwell. Go back there.

THE NOTE TAKER (*helpfully*). Hanwell.[1]

THE SARCASTIC BYSTANDER (*affecting great distinction of speech*). Thenk you, teacher. Haw haw! So long. (*He touches his hat with mock respect and strolls off.*)

THE FLOWER GIRL. Frightening people like that! How would he like it himself?

THE MOTHER. It's quite fine now, Clara. We can walk to a motor bus. Come. (*She gathers her skirts above her ankles and hurries off toward the Strand.*)

THE DAUGHTER. But the cab — (*her mother is out of hearing*). Oh, how tiresome! (*She follows angrily.*)

[*All the rest have gone except the* NOTE TAKER, *the* GENTLEMAN, *and the* FLOWER GIRL, *who sits arranging her basket and still pitying herself in murmurs.*]

THE FLOWER GIRL. Poor girl! Hard enough for her to live without being worried and chivied.[2]

THE GENTLEMAN (*returning to his former place on the* NOTE TAKER'S *left*). How do you do it, if I may ask?

THE NOTE TAKER. Simply phonetics. The science of speech. That's my profession: also my hobby. Happy is the man who can make a living by his hobby! You can spot an Irishman or a Yorkshireman by his brogue. *I* can place any man within six miles. I can place him within two miles in London. Sometimes within two streets.

THE FLOWER GIRL. Ought to be ashamed of himself, unmanly coward!

THE GENTLEMAN. But is there a living in that?

THE NOTE TAKER. Oh yes. Quite a fat one. This is an age of upstarts. Men begin in Kentish Town with £80 a year, and end in Park Lane with a hundred thousand. They want to drop Kentish Town; but they give themselves away every time they open their mouths. Now I can teach them —

THE FLOWER GIRL. Let him mind his own business and leave a poor girl —

THE NOTE TAKER (*explosively*). Woman! Cease this detestable boohooing instantly, or else seek the shelter of some other place of worship.

THE FLOWER GIRL (*with feeble defiance*). I've a right to be here if I like, same as you.

THE NOTE TAKER. A woman who utters such depressing and disgusting sounds has no right to be anywhere — no right to live. Remember that you are

---

[1] *Hanwell:* location of a mental hospital.

[2] *worried and chivied:* a cockney expression, meaning worried and tormented.

a human being with a soul and the divine gift of articulate speech — that your native language is the language of Shakespeare and Milton and the Bible — and don't sit there crooning like a bilious pigeon.

THE FLOWER GIRL (*quite over-whelmed, looking up at him in mingled wonder and deprecation without daring to raise her head*). Ah-ah-ah-ow-ow-ow-oo!

THE NOTE TAKER (*whipping out his book*). Heavens! what a sound! (*He writes; then holds out the book and reads, reproducing her vowels exactly.*) Ah-ah-ah-ow-ow-ow-oo!

THE FLOWER GIRL (*tickled by the performance, and laughing in spite of herself*). Garn!

THE NOTE TAKER. You see this creature with her curbstone English: the English that will keep her in the gutter to the end of her days. Well, sir, in three months I could pass that girl off as a duchess at an ambassador's garden party. I could even get her a place as lady's maid or shop assistant, which requires better English. That's the sort of thing I do for commercial millionaires. And on the profits of it I do genuine scientific work in phonetics, and a little as a poet on Miltonic lines.

THE GENTLEMAN. I am myself a student of Indian dialects; and —

THE NOTE TAKER (*eagerly*). Are you? Do you know Colonel Pickering, the author of *Spoken Sanscrit?* [1]

THE GENTLEMAN. I *am* Colonel Pickering. Who are you?

THE NOTE TAKER. Henry Higgins, author of *Higgins' Universal Alphabet.* [2]

PICKERING (*with enthusiasm*). I came from India to meet you.

HIGGINS. I was going to India to meet you.

PICKERING. Where do you live?

HIGGINS. 27A Wimpole Street. Come and see me tomorrow.

PICKERING. I'm at the Carlton. Come with me now and let's have a jaw over some supper.

HIGGINS. Right you are.

THE FLOWER GIRL (*to* PICKERING, *as he passes her*). Buy a flower, kind gentleman. I'm short for my lodging.

PICKERING. I really haven't any change. I'm sorry. (*He goes away.*)

HIGGINS (*shocked at the girl's mendacity* [3]). Liar. You said you could change half-a-crown.

THE FLOWER GIRL (*rising in desperation*). You ought to be stuffed with nails, you ought. (*Flinging the basket at his feet*) Take the whole blooming basket for sixpence.

[*The church clock strikes the second quarter.*]

HIGGINS (*hearing in it the voice of God, rebuking him for his Pharisaic* [4] *want of charity to the poor girl*). A reminder. (*He raises his hat solemnly; then throws a handful of money into the basket and follows* PICKERING.)

THE FLOWER GIRL (*picking up a half-crown*). Ah-ow-ooh! (*Picking up a couple of florins*) Aaah-ow-ooh! (*Picking up several coins*) Aaaaaah-ow-ooh! (*Picking up a half-sovereign*) Aaaaaaa-aaaaah-ow-ooh!!!

FREDDY (*springing out of a taxicab*). Got one at last. Hallo! (*To the girl*) Where are the two ladies that were here?

THE FLOWER GIRL. They walked to the bus when the rain stopped.

FREDDY. And left me with a cab on my hands! Damnation!

THE FLOWER GIRL (*with grandeur*). Never mind, young man. I'm going home in a taxi. (*She sails off to the cab. The driver puts his hand behind him*

[1] *Sanscrit* (săn′skrĭt): ancient language of the Hindus of India.

[2] *Universal Alphabet:* Shaw is speaking here. He felt that a universal alphabet would help to solve many problems.

[3] *mendacity* (mĕn·dăs′ĭ·tĭ): lying.

[4] *Pharisaic* (făr′ĭ·sā′ĭk): The Pharisees were a group among the ancient Jews known for their formality and strictness. Higgins realizes his strictness of thought and lack of charity toward the flower girl.

and holds the door firmly shut against her. Quite understanding his mistrust, she shows him her handful of money.) Eightpence ain't no object to me, Charlie. (*He grins and opens the door.*) Angel Court, Drury Lane, round the corner of Micklejohn's oil shop. Let's see how fast you can make her hop it. (*She gets in and pulls the door to with a slam as the taxicab starts.*)

FREDDY. Well, I'm dashed!

MEETING THE CHARACTERS

1. Major characters of a play generally are identified by name when they first appear. Why are the characters not identified in the opening of Act I? Notice what types of people are represented in this act. How would you describe them? How do the mother and her daughter differ in character? What kind of man is Freddy?

2. Why does the crowd stir up a dispute between the flower girl and the note taker? Whose side does the group take? Why? What do you learn about the flower girl that helps you to understand what kind of a person she is? How does she react to the sudden possession of money?

3. The flower girl speaks a cockney dialect. Look up "cockney" to determine what kind of a dialect it is and what people speak it. Why do you think Shaw includes some speeches written in cockney? What reason does he give for not continuing to write the cockney dialect?

4. Why is the note taker referred to as a detective? What is his profession? What kind of people does he teach? Can you tell what his feelings are toward his pupils? What is his attitude toward the flower girl?

5. What do Higgins, the note taker, and Colonel Pickering, the gentleman, have in common? At this point in the play, try to formulate some idea of the kind of men Higgins and Pickering are. Are they both gentlemen? Give reasons for your answers.

ACT II

Next day at 11 A.M. HIGGINS' laboratory in Wimpole Street. It is a room on the first floor, looking on the street, and was meant for the drawing room. The double doors are in the middle of the back wall; and persons entering find in the corner to their right two tall file cabinets at right angles to one another against the walls. In this corner stands a flat writing table, on which are a phonograph, a laryngoscope,[1] a row of tiny organ pipes with bellows, a set of lamp chimneys for singing flames with burners attached to a gas plug in the wall by an indiarubber tube, several tuning forks of different sizes, a life-size image of half a human head, showing in section the vocal organs, and a box containing a supply of wax cylinders for the phonograph.

Further down the room, on the same side, is a fireplace, with a comfortable leather-covered easy chair at the side of the hearth nearest the door, and a coal scuttle. There is a clock on the mantelpiece. Between the fireplace and the phonograph table is a stand for newspapers.

On the other side of the central door, to the left of the visitor, is a cabinet of shallow drawers. On it is a telephone and the telephone directory. The corner beyond, and most of the side wall, is occupied by a grand piano, with the keyboard at the end furthest from the door, and a bench for the player extending the full length of the keyboard. On the piano is a dessert dish heaped with fruit and sweets, mostly chocolates.

The middle of the room is clear. Besides the easy chair, the piano bench, and two chairs at the phonograph table, there is one stray chair. It stands near

---

[1] *laryngoscope* (lă·rĭng′gō·skōp): an instrument for examining the voice.

the fireplace. On the walls, engravings: mostly Piranesis [1] *and mezzotint portraits. No paintings.*

PICKERING *is seated at the table, putting down some cards and a tuning fork which he has been using.* HIGGINS *is standing up near him, closing two or three file drawers which are hanging out. He appears in the morning light as a robust, vital, appetizing sort of man of forty or thereabouts, dressed in a professional-looking black frock coat with a white linen collar and black silk tie. He is of the energetic, scientific type, heartily, even violently interested in everything that can be studied as a scientific subject, and careless about himself and other people, including their feelings. He is, in fact, but for his years and size, rather like a very impetuous baby " taking notice " eagerly and loudly, and requiring almost as much watching to keep him out of unintended mischief. His manner varies from genial bullying when he is in a good humor to stormy petulance when anything goes wrong; but he is so entirely frank and void of malice that he remains likable even in his least reasonable moments.*

HIGGINS (*as he shuts the last drawer*). Well, I think that's the whole show.

PICKERING. It's really amazing. I haven't taken half of it in, you know.

HIGGINS. Would you like to go over any of it again?

PICKERING (*rising and coming to the fireplace, where he plants himself with his back to the fire*). No, thank you; not now. I'm quite done up for this morning.

HIGGINS (*following him, and standing beside him on his left*). Tired of listening to sounds?

PICKERING. Yes. It's a fearful strain. I rather fancied myself because I can pronounce twenty-four distinct vowel sounds, but your hundred and thirty

[1] *Piranesi:* Italian engraver of the eighteenth century.

beat me. I can't hear a bit of difference between most of them.

HIGGINS (*chuckling, and going over to the piano to eat sweets*). Oh, that comes with practice. You hear no difference at first; but you keep on listening, and presently you find they're all as different as A from B. (MRS. PEARCE *looks in; she is* HIGGINS' *housekeeper.*) What's the matter?

MRS. PEARCE (*hesitating, evidently perplexed*). A young woman wants to see you, sir.

HIGGINS. A young woman! What does she want?

MRS. PEARCE. Well, sir, she says you'll be glad to see her when you know what she's come about. She's quite a common girl, sir. Very common indeed. I should have sent her away, only I thought perhaps you wanted her to talk into your machines. I hope I've not done wrong, but really you see such queer people sometimes — you'll excuse me, I'm sure, sir —

HIGGINS. Oh, that's all right, Mrs. Pearce. Has she an interesting accent?

MRS. PEARCE. Oh, something dreadful, sir, really. I don't know how you can take an interest in it.

HIGGINS (to PICKERING). Let's have her up. Show her up, Mrs. Pearce. (*He rushes across to his working table and picks out a cylinder to use on the phonograph.*)

MRS. PEARCE (*only half resigned to it*). Very well, sir. It's for you to say. (*She goes downstairs.*)

HIGGINS. This is rather a bit of luck. I'll show you how I make records. We'll set her talking; and I'll take it down first in Bell's Visible Speech; then in broad Romic; and then we'll get her on the phonograph so that you can turn her on as often as you like with the written transcript before you.

MRS. PEARCE (*returning*). This is the young woman, sir.

[*The FLOWER GIRL enters in state. She has a hat with three ostrich feathers — orange, sky-blue, and red. She has a nearly clean apron, and the shoddy coat has been tidied a little. The pathos of this deplorable figure, with its innocent vanity and consequential air, touches PICKERING, who has already straightened himself in the presence of MRS. PEARCE. But as to HIGGINS, the only distinction he makes between men and women is that when he is neither bullying nor exclaiming to the heavens against some featherweight cross, he coaxes women as a child coaxes its nurse when it wants to get anything out of her.*]

HIGGINS (*brusquely,*[1] *recognizing her with unconcealed disappointment, and at once, babylike, making an intolerable grievance of it*). Why, this is the girl I jotted down last night. She's no use: I've got all the records I want of the

Lisson Grove lingo [2]; and I'm not going to waste another cylinder on it. (*To the girl*) Be off with you: I don't want you.

THE FLOWER GIRL. Don't you be so saucy. You ain't heard what I come for yet. (*To MRS. PEARCE, who is waiting at the door for further instructions*) Did you tell him I come in a taxi?

MRS. PEARCE. Nonsense, girl! What do you think a gentleman like Mr. Higgins cares what you came in?

THE FLOWER GIRL. Oh, we *are* proud! He ain't above giving lessons, not him. I heard him say so. Well, I ain't come here to ask for any compliment; and if my money's not good enough I can go elsewhere.

HIGGINS. Good enough for what?

THE FLOWER GIRL. Good enough for ye-oo. Now you know, don't you? I'm come to have lessons, I am. And to pay for 'em too; make no mistake.

HIGGINS (*stupified*). Well!!! (*Recovering his breath with a gasp*) What do you expect me to say to you?

THE FLOWER GIRL. Well, if you was a gentleman, you might ask me to sit down, I think. Don't I tell you I'm bringing you business?

HIGGINS. Pickering, shall we ask this baggage to sit down, or shall we throw her out of the window?

THE FLOWER GIRL (*running away in terror to the piano, where she turns at bay*). Ah-ah-oh-ow-ow-ow-oo! (*Wounded and whimpering*) I won't be called a baggage when I've offered to pay like any lady.

[*Motionless, the two men stare at her from the other side of the room, amazed.*]

PICKERING (*gently*). What is it you want, my girl?

THE FLOWER GIRL. I want to be a lady in a flower shop 'stead of selling at the corner of Tottenham [3] Court Road.

---

[1] *brusquely* (brŭsk'lĭ): abruptly.

[2] *lingo* (lĭng'gō): dialect.

[3] *Tottenham* (tŏt'năm).

But they won't take me unless I can talk more genteel. He said he could teach me. Well, here I am ready to pay him — not asking any favor — and he treats me as if I was dirt.

MRS. PEARCE. How can you be such a foolish ignorant girl as to think you could afford to pay Mr. Higgins?

THE FLOWER GIRL. Why shouldn't I? I know what lessons cost as well as you do, and I'm ready to pay.

HIGGINS. How much?

THE FLOWER GIRL (*coming back to him, triumphant*). Now you're talking! I thought you'd come off it when you saw a chance of getting back a bit of what you chucked at me last night. (*Confidentially*) You'd had a drop in, hadn't you?

HIGGINS (*peremptorily*). Sit down.

THE FLOWER GIRL. Oh, if you're going to make a compliment of it —

HIGGINS (*thundering at her*). Sit down.

MRS. PEARCE (*severely*). Sit down, girl. Do as you're told. (*She places the stray chair near the hearthrug between* HIGGINS *and* PICKERING, *and stands behind it waiting for the girl to sit down.*)

THE FLOWER GIRL. Ah-ah-ah-ow-ow-oo! (*She stands, half rebellious, half bewildered.*)

PICKERING (*very courteous*). Won't you sit down?

LIZA (*coyly*). Don't mind if I do. (*She sits down.* PICKERING *returns to the hearthrug.*)

HIGGINS. What's your name?

THE FLOWER GIRL. Liza Doolittle.

HIGGINS (*declaiming gravely*).
Eliza, Elizabeth, Betsy and Bess,
They went to the woods to get a bird's
    nes':

PICKERING. They found a nest with four eggs in it:

HIGGINS. They took one apiece, and left three in it.

[*They laugh heartily at their own wit.*]

LIZA. Oh, don't be silly.

MRS. PEARCE. You mustn't speak to the gentleman like that.

LIZA. Well, why won't he speak sensible to me?

HIGGINS. Come back to business. How much do you propose to pay me for the lessons?

LIZA. Oh, I know what's right. A lady friend of mine gets French lessons for eighteenpence an hour from a real French gentleman. Well, you wouldn't have the face to ask me the same for teaching me my own language as you would for French; so I won't give more than a shilling. Take it or leave it.

HIGGINS (*walking up and down the room, rattling his keys and his cash in his pockets*). You know, Pickering, if you consider a shilling, not as a simple shilling, but as a percentage of this girl's income, it works out as fully equivalent to sixty or seventy guineas from a millionaire.

PICKERING. How so?

HIGGINS. Figure it out. A millionaire has about £150 a day. She earns about half-a-crown.

LIZA (*haughtily*). Who told you I only —

HIGGINS (*continuing*). She offers me two-fifths of her day's income for a lesson. Two-fifths of a millionaire's income for a day would be somewhere about £60. It's handsome. By George, it's enormous! It's the biggest offer I ever had.

LIZA (*rising, terrified*). Sixty pounds! What are you talking about? I never offered you sixty pounds. Where would I get —

HIGGINS. Hold your tongue.

LIZA (*weeping*). But I ain't got sixty pounds. Oh —

MRS. PEARCE. Don't cry, you silly girl. Sit down. Nobody is going to touch your money.

HIGGINS. Somebody is going to touch you, with a broomstick, if you don't stop sniveling. Sit down.

LIZA (*obeying slowly*). Ah-ah-ah-ow-oo-o! One would think you was my father.

HIGGINS. If I decide to teach you, I'll be worse than two fathers to you. Here! (*He offers her his silk handkerchief.*)

LIZA. What's this for?

HIGGINS. To wipe your eyes. To wipe any part of your face that feels moist. Remember: that's your handkerchief; and that's your sleeve. Don't mistake the one for the other if you wish to become a lady in a shop.

[LIZA, *utterly bewildered, stares helplessly at him.*]

MRS. PEARCE. It's no use talking to her like that, Mr. Higgins. She doesn't understand you. Besides, you're quite wrong. She doesn't do it that way at all. (*She takes the handkerchief.*)

LIZA (*snatching it*). Here! You give me that handkerchief. He give it to me, not to you.

PICKERING (*laughing*). He did. I think it must be regarded as her property, Mrs. Pearce.

MRS. PEARCE (*resigning herself*). Serve you right, Mr. Higgins.

PICKERING. Higgins, I'm interested. What about the ambassador's garden party? I'll say you're the greatest teacher alive if you make that good. I'll bet you all the expenses of the experiment you can't do it. And I'll pay for the lessons.

LIZA. Oh, you are real good. Thank you, Captain.

HIGGINS (*tempted, looking at her*). It's almost irresistible. She's so deliciously low — so horribly dirty —

LIZA (*protesting extremely*). Ah-ah-ah-ah-ow-ow-oo-oo!!! I ain't dirty: I washed my face and hands afore I come, I did.

PICKERING. You're certainly not going to turn her head with flattery, Higgins.

MRS. PEARCE (*uneasy*). Oh, don't say that, sir. There's more ways than one of turning a girl's head; and nobody can do it better than Mr. Higgins, though he may not always mean it. I do hope, sir, you won't encourage him to do anything foolish.

HIGGINS (*becoming excited as the idea grows on him*). What is life but a series of inspired follies? The difficulty is to find them to do. Never lose a chance. It doesn't come every day. I shall make a duchess of this draggletailed guttersnipe.

LIZA (*strongly deprecating this view of her*). Ah-ah-ah-ow-ow-oo!

HIGGINS (*carried away*). Yes, in six months — in three if she has a good ear and a quick tongue — I'll take her anywhere and pass her off as anything. We'll start today! now! this moment! Take her away and clean her, Mrs. Pearce. Monkey Brand, if it won't come off any other way. Is there a good fire in the kitchen?

MRS. PEARCE (*protesting*). Yes, but —

HIGGINS (*storming on*). Take all her clothes off and burn them. Ring up Whiteley or somebody for new ones. Wrap her up in brown paper 'til they come.

LIZA. You're no gentleman, you're not, to talk of such things. I'm a good girl, I am; and I know what the like of you are, I do.

HIGGINS. We want none of your Lisson Grove prudery[1] here, young woman. You've got to learn to behave like a duchess. Take her away, Mrs. Pearce. If she gives you any trouble, wallop her.

LIZA (*springing up and running between* PICKERING *and* MRS. PEARCE *for protection*). No! I'll call the police, I will.

MRS. PEARCE. But I've no place to put her.

HIGGINS. Put her in the dustbin.

LIZA. Ah-ah-ah-ow-ow-oo!

PICKERING. Oh come, Higgins! Be reasonable.

MRS. PEARCE (*resolutely*). You *must* be reasonable, Mr. Higgins. Really you must. You can't walk over everybody like this.

[1] *prudery* (proōd'ĕr·ĭ): excessive modesty in speech, behavior, or dress.

[HIGGINS, *thus scolded, subsides. The hurricane is succeeded by a zephyr of amiable surprise.*]

HIGGINS (*with professional exquisiteness of modulation*). I walk over everybody! My dear Mrs. Pearce, my dear Pickering, I never had the slightest intention of walking over anyone. All I propose is that we should be kind to this poor girl. We must help her to prepare and fit herself for her new station in life. If I did not express myself clearly it was because I did not wish to hurt her delicacy, or yours.

[LIZA, *reassured, steals back to her chair.*]

MRS. PEARCE (*to* PICKERING). Well, did you ever hear anything like that, sir?

PICKERING (*laughing heartily*). Never, Mrs. Pearce. Never.

HIGGINS (*patiently*). What's the matter?

MRS. PEARCE. Well, the matter is, sir, that you can't take a girl up like that as if you were picking up a pebble on the beach.

HIGGINS. Why not?

MRS. PEARCE. Why not! But you don't know anything about her. What about her parents? She may be married.

LIZA. Garn!

HIGGINS. There! As the girl very properly says, Garn! Married indeed! Don't you know that a woman of that class looks a worn-out drudge of fifty a year after she's married?

LIZA. Who'd marry me?

HIGGINS (*suddenly resorting to the most thrillingly beautiful low tones in his best elocutionary [1] style*). By George, Eliza, the streets will be strewn with the bodies of men shooting themselves for your sake before I've done with you.

MRS. PEARCE. Nonsense, sir. You mustn't talk like that to her.

LIZA (*rising and squaring herself determinedly*). I'm going away. He's off his chump, he is. I don't want no balmies teaching me.

HIGGINS (*wounded in his tenderest point by her insensibility to his elocution*). Oh, indeed! I'm mad, am I? Very well, Mrs. Pearce, you needn't order the new clothes for her. Throw her out.

LIZA (*whimpering*). Nah-ow. You got no right to touch me.

MRS. PEARCE. You see now what comes of being saucy. (*Indicating the door*) This way, please.

LIZA (*almost in tears*). I didn't want no clothes. I wouldn't have taken them. (*She throws away the handkerchief.*) I can buy my own clothes.

HIGGINS (*deftly retrieving the handkerchief and intercepting her on her reluctant way to the door*). You're an ungrateful wicked girl. This is my return for offering to take you out of the gutter and dress you beautifully and make a lady of you.

MRS. PEARCE. Stop, Mr. Higgins. I won't allow it. It's you that are wicked. Go home to your parents, girl; and tell them to take better care of you.

LIZA. I ain't got no parents. They told me I was big enough to earn my own living and turned me out.

MRS. PEARCE. Where's your mother?

LIZA. I ain't got no mother. Her that turned me out was my sixth stepmother. But I done without them. And I'm a good girl, I am.

HIGGINS. Very well, then, what on earth is all this fuss about? The girl doesn't belong to anybody — is no use to anybody but me. (*He goes to* MRS. PEARCE *and begins coaxing.*) You can adopt her, Mrs. Pearce. I'm sure a daughter would be a great amusement to you. Now don't make any more fuss. Take her downstairs, and —

MRS. PEARCE. But what's to become of her? Is she to be paid anything? Do be sensible, sir.

HIGGINS. Oh, pay her whatever is

---

[1] *elocutionary* (ĕl'ō·kū'shŭn·ĕr·ĭ): pertaining to the art of public speaking.

necessary. Put it down in the house-keeping book. (*Impatiently*) What on earth will she want with money? She'll have her food and her clothes. She'll only drink if you give her money.

LIZA (*turning on him*). Oh you *are* a brute. It's a lie! Nobody ever saw the sign of liquor on me. (*She goes back to her chair and plants herself there defiantly.*)

PICKERING (*in good-humored remonstrance*). Does it occur to you, Higgins, that the girl has some feelings?

HIGGINS (*looking critically at her*). Oh no, I don't think so. Not any feelings that we need bother about. (*Cheerily*) Have you, Eliza?

LIZA. I got my feelings same as anyone else.

HIGGINS (*to* PICKERING, *reflectively*). You see the difficulty?

PICKERING. Eh? What difficulty?

HIGGINS. To get her to talk grammar. The mere pronunciation is easy enough.

LIZA. I don't want to talk grammar. I want to talk like a lady.

MRS. PEARCE. Will you please keep to the point, Mr. Higgins? I want to know on what terms the girl is to be here. Is she to have any wages? And what is to become of her when you've finished your teaching? You must look ahead a little.

HIGGINS (*impatiently*). What's to become of her if I leave her in the gutter? Tell me that, Mrs. Pearce.

MRS. PEARCE. That's her own business, not yours, Mr. Higgins.

HIGGINS. Well, when I've done with her, we can throw her back into the gutter; and then it will be her own business again; so that's all right.

LIZA. Oh, you've no feeling heart in you: you don't care for nothing but yourself. (*She rises and takes the floor resolutely.*) Here! I've had enough of this. I'm going (*making for the door*). You ought to be ashamed of yourself, you ought.

HIGGINS (*snatching a chocolate cream from the piano, his eyes suddenly beginning to twinkle with mischief*). Have some chocolates, Eliza.

LIZA (*halting, tempted*). How do I know what might be in them? I've heard of girls being drugged by the like of you.

[HIGGINS *whips out his penknife; cuts a chocolate in two; puts one half into his mouth and bolts it; and offers her the other half.*]

HIGGINS. Pledge of good faith, Eliza. I eat one half; you eat the other. (LIZA *opens her mouth to retort; he pops the half chocolate into it.*) You shall have boxes of them, barrels of them, every day. You shall live on them. Eh?

LIZA (*who has disposed of the chocolate after being nearly choked by it*). I wouldn't have ate it, only I'm too lady-like to take it out of my mouth.

HIGGINS. Listen, Eliza. I think you said you came in a taxi.

LIZA. Well, what if I did? I've as good a right to take a taxi as anyone else.

HIGGINS. You have, Eliza; and in future you shall have as many taxis as you want. You shall go up and down and round the town in a taxi every day. Think of that, Eliza.

MRS. PEARCE. Mr. Higgins, you're tempting the girl. It's not right. She should think of the future.

HIGGINS. At her age! Nonsense! Time enough to think of the future when you haven't any future to think of. No, Eliza. Do as this lady does: think of other people's futures; but never think of your own. Think of chocolates, and taxis, and gold, and diamonds.

LIZA. No, I don't want no gold and no diamonds. I'm a good girl, I am. (*She sits down again, with an attempt at dignity.*)

HIGGINS. You shall remain so, Eliza, under the care of Mrs. Pearce. And you shall marry an officer in the Guards, with a beautiful moustache: the son of a marquis, who will disinherit him for marrying you, but will relent when he sees your beauty and goodness —

PICKERING. Excuse me, Higgins; but I really must interfere. Mrs. Pearce is quite right. If this girl is to put herself in your hands for six months for an experiment in teaching, she must understand thoroughly what she's doing.

HIGGINS. How can she? She's incapable of understanding anything. Besides, do any of us understand what we are doing? If we did, would we ever do it?

PICKERING. Very clever, Higgins; but not sound sense. (*To* ELIZA) Miss Doolittle —

LIZA (*overwhelmed*). Ah-ah-ow-oo!

HIGGINS. There! That's all you'll get out of Eliza. Ah-ah-ow-oo! No use explaining. As a military man you ought to know that. Give her her orders; that's what she wants. Eliza, you are to live here for the next six months, learning how to speak beautifully, like a lady in a florist's shop. If you're good and do whatever you're told, you shall sleep in a proper bedroom, and have lots to eat, and money to buy chocolates and take rides in taxis. If you're naughty and idle you will sleep in the back kitchen among the black beetles, and be walloped by Mrs. Pearce with a broomstick. At the end of six months you shall go to Buckingham Palace in a carriage, beautifully dressed. If the King finds out you're not a lady, you will be taken by the police to the Tower of London, where your head will be cut off as a warning to other presumptuous flower girls. If you are not found out, you shall have a present of seven-and-sixpence to start life with as a lady in a shop. If you refuse this offer you will be a most ungrateful and wicked girl; and the angels will weep for you. (*To* PICKERING) Now are you satisfied, Pickering? (*To* MRS. PEARCE) Can I put it more plainly and fairly, Mrs. Pearce?

MRS. PEARCE (*patiently*). I think you'd better let me speak to the girl properly in private. I don't know that I can take charge of her or consent to the arrangement at all. Of course I know you don't mean her any harm; but

when you get what you call interested in people's accents, you never think or care what may happen to them or you. Come with me, Eliza.

HIGGINS. That's all right. Thank you, Mrs. Pearce. Bundle her off to the bathroom.

LIZA (*rising reluctantly and suspiciously*). You're a great bully, you are. I won't stay here if I don't like. I won't let nobody wallop me. I never asked to go to Bucknam Palace, I didn't. I was never in trouble with the police, not me. I'm a good girl —

MRS. PEARCE. Don't answer back, girl. You don't understand the gentleman. Come with me. (*She leads the way to the door, and holds it open for* ELIZA.)

LIZA (*as she goes out*). Well, what I say is right. I won't go near the King, not if I'm going to have my head cut off. If I'd known what I was letting myself in for, I wouldn't have come here. I always been a good girl; and I never offered to say a word to him; and I don't owe him nothing; and I don't care; and I won't be put upon; and I have my feelings the same as anyone else —

[MRS. PEARCE *shuts the door; and* ELIZA'S *plaints* [1] *are no longer audible.* PICKERING *comes from the hearth to the chair and sits astride it with his arms on the back.*]

PICKERING. Excuse the straight question, Higgins. Are you a man of good character where women are concerned?

HIGGINS (*moodily*). Have you ever met a man of good character where women are concerned?

PICKERING. Yes, very frequently.

HIGGINS (*dogmatically, lifting himself on his hands to the level of the piano, and sitting on it with a bounce*). Well, I haven't. I find that the moment I let a a woman make friends with me, she becomes jealous, exacting, suspicious, and

---

[1] *plaints:* complaints.

a damned nuisance. I find that the moment I let myself make friends with a woman, I become selfish and tyrannical. Women upset everything. When you let them into your life, you find that the woman is driving at one thing and you're driving at another.

PICKERING. At what, for example?

HIGGINS (*coming off the piano restlessly*). Oh, Lord knows! I suppose the woman wants to live her own life, and the man wants to live his; and each tries to drag the other on to the wrong track. One wants to go north and the other south; and the result is that both have to go east, though they both hate the east wind. (*He sits down on the bench at the keyboard.*) So here I am, a confirmed old bachelor, and likely to remain so.

PICKERING (*rising and standing over him gravely*). Come, Higgins! You know what I mean. If I'm to be in this business I shall feel responsible for that girl. I hope it's understood that no advantage is to be taken of her position.

HIGGINS. What! That thing! Sacred, I assure you. (*Rising to explain*) You see, she'll be a pupil; and teaching would be impossible unless pupils were sacred. I've taught scores of American millionairesses how to speak English — the best-looking women in the world. I'm seasoned. They might as well be blocks of wood. I might as well be a block of wood. It's —

[MRS. PEARCE *opens the door. She has* ELIZA'S *hat in her hand.* PICKERING *retires to the easy chair at the hearth and sits down.*]

HIGGINS (*eagerly*). Well, Mrs. Pearce, is it all right?

MRS. PEARCE (*at the door*). I just wish to trouble you with a word, if I may, Mr. Higgins.

HIGGINS. Yes, certainly. Come in. (*She comes forward.*) Don't burn that, Mrs. Pearce. I'll keep it as a curiosity. (*He takes the hat.*)

MRS. PEARCE. Handle it carefully, sir, *please.* I had to promise her not to burn it; but I had better put it in the oven for a while.

HIGGINS (*putting it down hastily on the piano*). Oh! thank you. Well, what have you to say to me?

PICKERING. Am I in the way?

MRS. PEARCE. Not at all, sir. Mr. Higgins, will you please be very particular what you say before the girl?

HIGGINS (*sternly*). Of course. I'm always particular about what I say. Why do you say this to me?

MRS. PEARCE (*unmoved*). No, sir, you're not at all particular when you've mislaid anything or when you get a little impatient. Now it doesn't matter before me. I'm used to it. But you really must not swear before the girl.

HIGGINS (*indignantly*). *I* swear! (*Most emphatically*) I never swear. I detest the habit. What the devil do you mean?

MRS. PEARCE (*stolidly*). That's what I mean, sir. You swear a great deal too much. I don't mind your damning and blasting, and *what* the devil and *where* the devil and *who* the devil —

HIGGINS. Mrs. Pearce, this language from your lips! Really!

MRS. PEARCE (*not to be put off*). — but there is a certain word I must ask you not to use. The girl has just used it herself because the bath was too hot. It begins with the same letter as bath. She knows no better: she learnt it at her mother's knee. But she must not hear it from your lips.

HIGGINS (*loftily*). I cannot charge myself with having ever uttered it, Mrs. Pearce. (*She looks at him steadfastly. He adds, hiding an uneasy conscience with a judicial air*) Except perhaps in a moment of extreme and justifiable excitement.

MRS. PEARCE. Only this morning, sir, you applied it to your boots, to the butter, and to the brown bread.

HIGGINS. Oh, that! Mere alliteration, Mrs. Pearce, natural to a poet.

MRS. PEARCE. Well, sir, whatever you choose to call it, I beg you not to let the girl hear you repeat it.

PICKERING. Oh, *please,* Higgins. I'm west country myself. (*To* DOOLITTLE) How did you know the girl was here if you didn't send her?

DOOLITTLE. It was like this, Governor. The girl took a boy in the taxi to give him a jaunt. Son of her landlady, he is. He hung about on the chance of her giving him another ride home. Well, she sent him back for her luggage when she heard you was willing for her to stop here. I met the boy at the corner of Long Acre and Endell Street.

HIGGINS. Public house. Yes?

DOOLITTLE. The poor man's club, Governor. Why shouldn't I?

PICKERING. Do let him tell his story, Higgins.

DOOLITTLE. He told me what was up. And I ask you, what was my feelings and my duty as a father? I says to the boy, "You bring me the luggage," I says —

PICKERING. Why didn't you go for it yourself?

DOOLITTLE. Landlady wouldn't have trusted me with it, Governor. She's that kind of woman, you know. I had to give the boy a penny afore he trusted me with it, the little swine. I brought it to her just to oblige you like, and make myself agreeable. That's all.

HIGGINS. How much luggage?

DOOLITTLE. Musical instrument, Governor. A few pictures, a trifle of jewelry, and a bird-cage. She said she didn't want no clothes. What was I to think from that, Governor? I ask you as a parent what was I to think?

HIGGINS. So you came to rescue her from worse than death, eh?

DOOLITTLE (*appreciatively: relieved at being so well understood*). Just so, Governor. That's right.

PICKERING. But why did you bring her luggage if you intended to take her away?

DOOLITTLE. Have I said a word about taking her away? Have I now?

HIGGINS (*determinedly*). You're go-

ing to take her away, double quick. (*He crosses to the hearth and rings the bell.*)

DOOLITTLE (*rising*). No, Governor. Don't say that. I'm not the man to stand in my girl's light. Here's a career opening for her, as you might say; and —

[MRS. PEARCE *opens the door and awaits orders.*]

HIGGINS. Mrs. Pearce, this is Eliza's father. He has come to take her away. Give her to him. (*He goes back to the piano, with an air of washing his hands of the whole affair.*)

DOOLITTLE. No. This is a misunderstanding. Listen here —

MRS. PEARCE. He can't take her away, Mr. Higgins. How can he? You told me to burn her clothes.

DOOLITTLE. That's right. I can't carry the girl through the streets like a blooming monkey, can I? I put it to you.

HIGGINS. You have put it to me that you want your daughter. Take your daughter. If she has no clothes, go out and buy her some.

DOOLITTLE (*desperate*). Where's the clothes she come in? Did I burn them or did your missus here?

MRS. PEARCE. I am the housekeeper, if you please. I have sent for some clothes for your girl. When they come you can take her away. You can wait in the kitchen. This way, please.

[DOOLITTLE, *much troubled, accompanies her to the door; then hesitates; finally turns confidentially to HIGGINS.*]

DOOLITTLE. Listen here, Governor. You and me is men of the world, ain't we?

HIGGINS. Oh! Men of the world, are we? You'd better go, Mrs. Pearce.

MRS. PEARCE. I think so, indeed, sir. (*She goes, with dignity.*)

PICKERING. The floor is yours, Mr. Doolittle.

DOOLITTLE (*to* PICKERING). I thank you, Governor. (*To* HIGGINS, *who takes refuge on the piano bench, a little overwhelmed by the proximity of his visitor; for* DOOLITTLE *has a professional flavor of dust about him*) Well, the truth is, I've taken a sort of fancy to you, Governor; and if you want the girl, I'm not so set on having her back home again but what I might be open to an arrangement. Regarded in the light of a young woman, she's a fine handsome girl. As a daughter she's not worth her keep; and so I tell you straight. All I ask is my rights as a father; and you're the last man alive to expect me to let her go for nothing; for I can see you're one of the straight sort, Governor. Well, what's a five-pound note to you? And what's Eliza to me? (*He returns to his chair and sits down judicially.*)

PICKERING. I think you ought to know, Doolittle, that Mr. Higgins's intentions are entirely honorable.

DOOLITTLE. Course they are, Governor. If I thought they wasn't, I'd ask fifty.

HIGGINS (*revolted*). Do you mean to say, you callous rascal, that you would sell your daughter for £50?

DOOLITTLE. Not in a general way I wouldn't; but to oblige a gentleman like you I'd do a good deal, I do assure you.

PICKERING. Have you no morals, man?

DOOLITTLE (*unabashed*). Can't afford them, Governor. Neither could you if you was as poor as me. Not that I mean any harm, you know. But if Liza is going to have a bit out of this, why not me too?

HIGGINS (*troubled*). I don't know what to do, Pickering. There can be no question that as a matter of morals it's a positive crime to give this chap a farthing. And yet I feel a sort of rough justice in his claim.

DOOLITTLE. That's it, Governor. That's all I say. A father's heart, as it were.

PICKERING. Well, I know the feeling; but really it seems hardly right —

DOOLITTLE. Don't say that, Governor. Don't look at it that way. What am I, Governors both? I ask you, what am I? I'm one of the undeserving poor, that's what I am. Think of what that means to a man. It means that he's up agen middle class morality all the time. If there's anything going, and I put in for a bit of it, it's always the same story: " You're undeserving; so you can't have it." But my needs is as great as the most deserving widow's that ever got money out of six different charities in one week for the death of the same husband. I don't need less than a deserving man; I need more. I don't eat less hearty than him; and I drink a lot more. I want a bit of amusement, cause I'm a thinking man. I want cheerfulness and a song and a band when I feel low. Well, they charge me just the same for everything as they charge the deserving. What is middle class morality? Just an excuse for never giving me anything. Therefore, I ask you, as two gentlemen, not to play that game on me. I'm playing straight with you. I ain't pretending to be deserving. I'm undeserving; and I mean to go on being undeserving. I like it; and that's the truth. Will you take advantage of a man's nature to do him out of the price of his own daughter what he's brought up and fed and clothed by the sweat of his brow until she's growed big enough to be interesting to you two gentlemen? Is five pounds unreasonable? I put it to you; and I leave it to you.

HIGGINS (*rising, and going over to* PICKERING). Pickering, if we were to take this man in hand for three months, he could choose between a seat in the Cabinet and a popular pulpit in Wales.

PICKERING. What do you say to that, Doolittle?

DOOLITTLE. Not me, Governor, thank you kindly. I've heard all the preachers and all the prime ministers — for I'm a thinking man and game for politics or religion or social reform same as all the other amusements — and I tell you it's a dog's life any way you look at it. Undeserving poverty is my line. Taking one station in society with another, it's — it's — well, it's the only one that has any ginger in it, to my taste.

HIGGINS. I suppose we must give him a fiver.

PICKERING. He'll make a bad use of it, I'm afraid.

DOOLITTLE. Not me, Governor, so help me I won't. Don't you be afraid that I'll save it and spare it and live idle on it. There won't be a penny of it left by Monday. I'll have to go to work same as if I'd never had it. It won't pauperize me, you bet. Just one good spree for myself and the missus, giving pleasure to ourselves and employment to others, and satisfaction to you to think it's not been throwed away. You couldn't spend it better.

HIGGINS (*taking out his pocket book and coming between* DOOLITTLE *and the piano*). This is irresistible. Let's give him ten. (*He offers two notes to the dustman.*)

DOOLITTLE. No, Governor. She wouldn't have the heart to spend ten; and perhaps I shouldn't neither. Ten pounds is a lot of money. It makes a man feel prudent like; and then goodbye to happiness. You give me what I ask you, Governor. Not a penny more, and not a penny less.

PICKERING. Why don't you marry that missus of yours? I rather draw the line at encouraging that sort of immorality.

DOOLITTLE. Tell her so, Governor: tell her so. I'm willing. It's me that suffers by it. I've no hold on her. I got to be agreeable to her. I got to give her presents. I got to buy her clothes something sinful. I'm a slave to that woman, Governor, just because I'm not her lawful husband. And she knows it too. Catch her marrying me! Take my advice, Governor: marry Eliza while she's young and don't know no better. If you don't you'll be sorry for it after. If you do, *she'll* be sorry for it after; but better her than you, because you're a man, and she's only a woman and don't know how to be happy anyhow.

HIGGINS. Pickering, if we listen to this man another minute, we shall have no convictions left. (*To* DOOLITTLE) Five pounds I think you said.

DOOLITTLE. Thank you kindly, Governor.

HIGGINS. You're sure you won't take ten?

DOOLITTLE. Not now. Another time, Governor.

HIGGINS (*handing him a five-pound note*). Here you are.

DOOLITTLE. Thank you, Governor. Good morning. (*He hurries to the door, anxious to get away with his booty. When he opens it he is confronted with a dainty and exquisitely clean young Japanese lady in a simple blue cotton kimono printed cunningly with small white jasmine blossoms.* MRS. PEARCE *is with her. He gets out of her way deferentially* [1] *and apologizes.*) Beg pardon, miss.

THE JAPANESE LADY. Garn! Don't you know your own daughter?

DOOLITTLE	*exclaiming*	Bly me! it's Eliza!
HIGGINS	*simul-*	What's that!
PICKERING	*taneously*	This!
		By Jove!

LIZA. Don't I look silly?

HIGGINS. Silly?

MRS. PEARCE (*at the door*). Now, Mr. Higgins, please don't say anything to make the girl conceited about herself.

HIGGINS (*conscientiously*). Oh! Quite right, Mrs. Pearce. (*To* ELIZA) Yes, damned silly.

MRS. PEARCE. Please, sir.

HIGGINS (*correcting himself*). I mean extremely silly.

LIZA. I should look all right with my hat on. (*She takes up her hat; puts it on; and walks across the room to the fireplace with a fashionable air.*)

HIGGINS. A new fashion, by George! And it ought to look horrible!

DOOLITTLE (*with fatherly pride*). Well, I never thought she'd clean up as good looking as that, Governor. She's a credit to me, ain't she?

LIZA. I tell you, it's easy to clean up here. Hot and cold water on tap, just as much as you like, there is. Woolly towels, there is; and a towel horse so hot, it burns your fingers. Soft brushes to scrub yourself, and a wooden bowl of soap smelling like primroses. Now I know why ladies is so clean. Washing's a treat for them. Wish they saw what it is for the like of me!

HIGGINS. I'm glad the bathroom met with your approval.

LIZA. It didn't. Not all of it, and I don't care who hears me say it. Mrs. Pearce knows.

HIGGINS. What was wrong, Mrs. Pearce?

MRS. PEARCE (*blandly*). Oh, nothing, sir. It doesn't matter.

LIZA. I had a good mind to break it. I didn't know which way to look. But I hung a towel over it, I did.

HIGGINS. Over what?

MRS. PEARCE. Over the looking glass, sir.

HIGGINS. Doolittle, you have brought your daughter up too strictly.

DOOLITTLE. Me! I never brought her up at all, except to give her a lick of a strap now and again. Don't put it on me, Governor. She ain't accustomed to it, you see. That's all. But she'll soon pick up your free-and-easy ways.

LIZA. I'm a good girl, I am; and I won't pick up no free-and-easy ways.

HIGGINS. Eliza, if you say again that you're a good girl, your father shall take you home.

LIZA. Not him. You don't know my father. All he come here for was to touch you for some money to get drunk on.

DOOLITTLE. Well, what else would I want money for? To put into the plate in church, I suppose. (*She puts out her tongue at him. He is so incensed by this that* PICKERING *presently finds it necessary to step between them.*) Don't you give me none of your lip; and don't let me hear you giving this gentleman any of it neither, or you'll hear from me about it. See?

HIGGINS. Have you any further advice to give her before you go, Doolittle? Your blessing, for instance.

DOOLITTLE. No, Governor. I ain't such a mug as to put up my children to all I know myself. Hard enough to hold them in without that. If you want Eliza's mind improved, Governor, you do it yourself with a strap. So long, gentlemen. (*He turns to go.*)

HIGGINS (*impressively*). Stop. You'll come regularly to see your daughter. It's your duty, you know. My brother is a clergyman, and he could help you in your talks with her.

---

[1] *deferentially* (dĕf'ẽr·ĕn'shăl·lĭ): respectfully.

DOOLITTLE (*evasively*). Certainly. I'll come, Governor. Not just this week, because I have a job at a distance. But later on you may depend on me. Afternoon, gentlemen. Afternoon, ma'am. (*He takes off his hat to* MRS. PEARCE, *who disdains the salutation and goes out. He winks at* HIGGINS, *thinking him probably a fellow-sufferer from* MRS. PEARCE'S *difficult disposition, and follows her.*)

LIZA. Don't you believe the old liar. He'd as soon you set a bulldog on him as a clergyman. You won't see him again in a hurry.

HIGGINS. I don't want to, Eliza. Do you?

LIZA. Not me. I don't want never to see him again, I don't. He's a disgrace to me, he is, collecting dust, instead of working at his trade.

PICKERING. What is his trade, Eliza?

LIZA. Taking money out of other people's pockets into his own. His proper trade's a navvy;[1] and he works at it sometimes too — for exercise — and earns good money at it. Ain't you going to call me Miss Doolittle any more?

PICKERING. I beg your pardon, Miss Doolittle. It was a slip of the tongue.

LIZA. Oh, I don't mind; only it sounded so genteel. I *should* just like to take a taxi to the corner of Tottenham Court Road and get out there and tell it to wait for me, just to put the girls in their place a bit. I wouldn't speak to them, you know.

PICKERING. Better wait 'til we get you something really fashionable.

HIGGINS. Besides, you shouldn't cut your old friends now that you have risen in the world. That's what we call snobbery.

LIZA. You don't call the like of them my friends now, I should hope. They've took it out of me often enough with their ridicule when they had the chance; and now I mean to get a bit of my own

---

[1] *navvy* (năv′ĭ): an unskilled or common laborer.

---

back. But if I'm to have fashionable clothes, I'll wait. I should like to have some. Mrs. Pearce says you're going to give me some to wear in bed at night different to what I wear in the daytime; but it do seem a waste of money when you could get something to show. Besides, I never could fancy changing into cold things on a winter night.

MRS. PEARCE (*coming back*). Now, Eliza. The new things have come for you to try on.

LIZA. Ah-ow-oo-ooh! (*She rushes out.*)

MRS. PEARCE (*following her*). Oh, don't rush about like that, girl. (*She shuts the door behind her.*)

HIGGINS. Pickering, we have taken on a stiff job.

PICKERING (*with conviction*). Higgins, we have.

UNDERSTANDING THE CHARACTERS

1. What reason does Eliza give for wanting lessons in speaking? How had she figured the amount she would pay for the instruction? Why does she want Higgins to know that she came in a taxi?

2. Why is Higgins willing to take her? What does Pickering promise to do? How does each man regard Eliza? Find passages that show the differences in their personalities.

3. How does Mrs. Pearce react to Eliza? On what points are Pickering and Mrs. Pearce in agreement? Does their point of view or Higgins' seem more natural to you? What does Higgins mean when he says, "Take care of the pence and the pounds will take care of themselves"?

4. Why does Alfred Doolittle come to see Higgins? How does he feel toward his daughter? What do you learn about Eliza from this visit? Is Doolittle a happy person? Why does he accept five pounds instead of the ten pounds that is offered?

5. Why is Eliza always saying, "I'm a good girl, I am"? Does she have any other virtue to which she can point at this time? Are there any indications that she may have potentialities for growth or change?

ACT III

It is MRS. HIGGINS' *at-home day. Nobody has yet arrived. Her drawing room, in a flat on Chelsea Embankment,[1] has three windows looking on the river; and the ceiling is not so lofty as it would be in an older house of the same pretension. The windows are open, giving access to a balcony with flowers in pots. If you stand with your face to the windows, you have the fireplace on your left and the door in the right-hand wall close to the corner nearest the windows.*

MRS. HIGGINS *was brought up on Morris and Burne Jones;[2] and her room, which is very unlike her son's room in Wimpole Street, is not crowded with furniture and little tables and knick-knacks. In the middle of the room there is a big ottoman; and this, with the carpet, the Morris wallpapers, and the Morris chintz window curtains and brocade covers of the ottoman and its cushions, supply all the ornament, and are much too handsome to be hidden by odds and ends of useless things. A few good oil paintings from the exhibitions in the Grosvenor Gallery thirty years ago (the Burne Jones, not the Whistler side of them) are on the walls. The only landscape is a Cecil Lawson on the scale of a Rubens. There is a portrait of* MRS. HIGGINS *as she was when she defied fashion in her youth in one of the beautiful Rossettian[3] costumes which, when caricatured by people who did not understand, led to the absurdities of popular estheticism in the eighteen-seventies.*

In the corner diagonally opposite the door MRS. HIGGINS, *now over sixty and long past taking the trouble to dress out of the fashion, sits writing at an elegantly simple writing table with a bell button within reach of her hand. There is a Chippendale[4] chair further back in the room between her and the window nearest her side. At the other side of the room, further forward, is an Elizabethan chair roughly carved in the taste of Inigo Jones.[5] On the same side a piano in a decorated case. The corner between the fireplace and the window is occupied by a divan cushioned in Morris chintz.*

It is between four and five in the afternoon.

The door is opened violently; and HIGGINS *enters with his hat on.*

MRS. HIGGINS (*dismayed*). Henry (*scolding him*)! What are you doing here today? It is my at-home day. You promised not to come. (*As he bends to kiss her, she takes his hat off, and presents it to him.*)

HIGGINS. Oh bother! (*He throws the hat down on the table.*)

MRS. HIGGINS. Go home at once.

HIGGINS (*kissing her*). I know, Mother. I came on purpose.

MRS. HIGGINS. But you mustn't. I'm serious, Henry. You offend all my friends. They stop coming whenever they meet you.

HIGGINS. Nonsense! I know I have no small talk, but people don't mind. (*He sits on the settee.*)

MRS. HIGGINS. Oh! don't they? Small talk indeed! What about your large talk? Really, dear, you mustn't stay.

HIGGINS. I must. I've a job for you. A phonetic job.

---

[1] *Chelsea* (chĕl'sĭ) *Embankment:* a metropolitan borough on the north bank of the Thames.

[2] *Morris and Burne Jones:* two members of a flourishing company that undertook church decoration, carving, stained glass, metalwork, paper-hangings, chintzes, and carpets. See page 459.

[3] *Rossettian:* in the simple, flowing style of dress found in Dante Gabriel Rossetti's paintings.

[4] *Chippendale:* a famous eighteenth-century cabinet maker.

[5] *Inigo Jones:* a seventeenth-century architect and designer.

MRS. HIGGINS. No use, dear. I'm sorry, but I can't get round your vowels; and though I like to get pretty postcards in your patent shorthand, I always have to read the copies in ordinary writing you so thoughtfully send me.

HIGGINS. Well, this isn't a phonetic job.

MRS. HIGGINS. You said it was.

HIGGINS. Not your part of it. I've picked up a girl.

MRS. HIGGINS. Does that mean that some girl has picked you up?

HIGGINS. Not at all. I don't mean a love affair.

MRS. HIGGINS. What a pity!

HIGGINS. Why?

MRS. HIGGINS. Well, you never fall in love with anyone under forty-five. When will you discover that there are some rather nice-looking young women about?

HIGGINS. Oh, I can't be bothered with young women. My idea of a lovable woman is something as like you as possible. I shall never get into the way of seriously liking young women. Some habits lie too deep to be changed. (*Rising abruptly and walking about, jingling his money and his keys in his trouser pockets*) Besides, they're all idiots.

MRS. HIGGINS. Do you know what you would do if you really loved me, Henry?

HIGGINS. Oh bother! What? Marry, I suppose?

MRS. HIGGINS. No. Stop fidgeting and take your hands out of your pockets. (*With a gesture of despair, he obeys and sits down again.*) That's a good boy. Now tell me about the girl.

HIGGINS. She's coming to see you.

MRS. HIGGINS. I don't remember asking her.

HIGGINS. You didn't. *I* asked her. If you'd known her you wouldn't have asked her.

MRS. HIGGINS. Indeed! Why?

HIGGINS. Well, it's like this. She's a common flower girl. I picked her off the curbstone.

MRS. HIGGINS. And invited her to my at-home!

HIGGINS (*rising and coming to her to coax her*). Oh, that'll be all right. I've taught her to speak properly, and she has strict orders as to her behavior. She's to keep to two subjects: the weather and everybody's health — Fine day and How do you do, you know — and not to let herself go on things in general. That will be safe.

MRS. HIGGINS. Safe! To talk about our health! About our insides! Perhaps about our outsides! How could you be so silly, Henry?

HIGGINS (*impatiently*). Well, she must talk about something. (*He controls himself and sits down again.*) Oh, she'll be all right: don't you fuss. Pickering is in it with me. I've a sort of bet on that I'll pass her off as a duchess in six months. I started on her some months ago; and she's getting on like a house on fire. I shall win my bet. She has a quick ear, and she's been easier to teach than my middle-class pupils because she's had to learn a complete new language. She talks English almost as you talk French.

MRS. HIGGINS. That's satisfactory, at all events.

HIGGINS. Well, it is and it isn't.

MRS. HIGGINS. What does that mean?

HIGGINS. You see, I've got her pronunciation all right; but you have to consider not only *how* a girl pronounces, but *what* she pronounces; and that's where —

[*They are interrupted by the* PARLOR MAID, *announcing guests.*]

THE PARLOR MAID. Mrs. and Miss Eynsford Hill. (*She withdraws.*)

HIGGINS. Oh Lord! (*He rises; snatches his hat from the table; and makes for the door; but before he reaches it his mother introduces him.*)

[MRS. *and* MISS EYNSFORD HILL *are the mother and daughter who sheltered from the rain in Covent Garden. The mother is well-bred, quiet, and has the habitual anxiety of straitened means. The daughter has acquired a gay air of being very much at home in society: the bravado of genteel poverty.*]

MRS. EYNSFORD HILL (*to* MRS. HIGGINS). How do you do? (*They shake hands.*)

MISS EYNSFORD HILL. How d'you do? (*She shakes.*)

MRS. HIGGINS (*introducing*). My son Henry.

MRS. EYNSFORD HILL. Your celebrated son! I have so longed to meet you, Professor Higgins.

HIGGINS (*glumly, making no movement in her direction*). Delighted. (*He backs against the piano and bows brusquely.*)

MISS EYNSFORD HILL (*going to him with confident familiarity*). How do you do?

HIGGINS (*staring at her*). I've seen you before somewhere. I haven't the ghost of a notion where; but I've heard your voice. (*Drearily*) It doesn't matter. You'd better sit down.

MRS. HIGGINS. I'm sorry to say that my celebrated son has no manners. You mustn't mind him.

MISS EYNSFORD HILL (*gaily*). I don't. (*She sits in the Elizabethan chair.*)

MRS. EYNSFORD HILL (*a little bewildered*). Not at all. (*She sits on the ottoman between her daughter and* MRS. HIGGINS, *who has turned her chair away from the writing table.*)

HIGGINS. Oh, have I been rude? I didn't mean to be.

[*He goes to the central window, through which, with his back to the company, he contemplates the river and the flowers in Battersea Park on the opposite bank as if they were a frozen desert.*]

[*The* PARLOR MAID *returns, ushering in* PICKERING.]

THE PARLOR MAID. Colonel Pickering. (*She withdraws.*)

PICKERING. How do you do, Mrs. Higgins?

MRS. HIGGINS. So glad you've come. Do you know Mrs. Eynsford Hill — Miss Eynsford Hill? (*Exchange of bows. The* COLONEL *brings the Chippendale chair a little forward between* MRS. HILL *and* MRS. HIGGINS, *and sits down.*)

PICKERING. Has Henry told you what we've come for?

HIGGINS (*over his shoulder*). We were interrupted, damn it!

MRS. HIGGINS. Oh Henry, Henry, really!

MRS. EYNSFORD HILL (*half rising*). Are we in the way?

MRS. HIGGINS (*rising and making her sit down again*). No, no. You couldn't have come more fortunately. We want you to meet a friend of ours.

HIGGINS (*turning hopefully*). Yes, by George! We want two or three people. You'll do as well as anybody else.

[*The* PARLOR MAID *returns, ushering* FREDDY.]

THE PARLOR MAID. Mr. Eynsford Hill.

HIGGINS (*almost audibly, past endurance*). God of Heaven! another of them.

FREDDY (*shaking hands with* MRS. HIGGINS). Ahdedo?

MRS. HIGGINS. Very good of you to come. (*Introducing*) Colonel Pickering.

FREDDY (*bowing*). Ahdedo?

MRS. HIGGINS. I don't think you know my son, Professor Higgins.

FREDDY (*going to* HIGGINS). Ahdedo?

HIGGINS (*looking at him much as if he were a pickpocket*). I'll take my oath I've met *you* before somewhere. Where was it?

FREDDY. I don't think so.

HIGGINS (*resignedly*). It doesn't matter, anyhow. Sit down.

[*He shakes* FREDDY'S *hand, and almost slings him on to the ottoman with his face to the windows; then comes round to the other side of it.*]

HIGGINS. Well, here we are, anyhow! (*He sits down on the ottoman next to* MRS. EYNSFORD HILL, *on her left.*) And now, what the devil are we going to talk about until Eliza comes?

MRS. HIGGINS. Henry! You are the life and soul of the Royal Society soirées; [1] but really you're rather trying on more commonplace occasions.

HIGGINS. Am I? Very sorry. (*Beaming suddenly*) I suppose I am, you know. (*Uproariously*) Ha, ha!

MISS EYNSFORD HILL (*who considers* HIGGINS *quite eligible matrimonially*). I sympathize. *I* haven't any small talk. If people would only be frank and say what they really think!

HIGGINS (*relapsing into gloom*). Lord forbid!

MRS. EYNSFORD HILL (*taking up her daughter's cue*). But why?

HIGGINS. What they think they ought to think is bad enough, Lord knows; but what they really think would break up the whole show. Do you suppose it would be really agreeable if I were to come out now with what *I* really think?

MISS EYNSFORD HILL (*gaily*). Is it so very cynical?

HIGGINS. Cynical! Who the dickens said it was cynical? I mean it wouldn't be decent.

MRS. EYNSFORD HILL (*seriously*). Oh! I'm sure you don't mean that Mr. Higgins.

HIGGINS. You see, we're all savages, more or less. We're supposed to be civilized and cultured — to know all about poetry and philosophy and art and science, and so on; but how many of us know even the meanings of these names? (*To* MISS HILL) What do *you* know of poetry? (*To* MRS. HILL) What do *you* know of science? (*Indicating* FREDDY) What does *he* know of art or science or anything else? What the devil do you imagine I know of philosophy?

MRS. HIGGINS (*warningly*). Or of manners, Henry?

THE PARLOR MAID (*opening the door*). Miss Doolittle. (*She withdraws.*)

HIGGINS (*rising hastily and running to* MRS. HIGGINS). Here she is, Mother. (*He

stands on tiptoe and makes signs over his mother's head to* ELIZA *to indicate to her which lady is her hostess.*)

[ELIZA, *who is exquisitely dressed, produces an impression of such remarkable distinction and beauty as she enters that they all rise, quite fluttered. Guided by* HIGGINS' *signals, she comes to* MRS. HIGGINS *with studied grace.*]

LIZA (*speaking with pedantic correctness of pronunciation and great beauty of tone*). How do you do, Mrs. Higgins? (*She gasps slightly in making sure of the H in* HIGGINS, *but is quite successful.*) Mr. Higgins told me I might come.

MRS. HIGGINS (*cordially*). Quite right. I'm very glad indeed to see you.

PICKERING. How do you do, Miss Doolittle?

LIZA (*shaking hands with him*). Colonel Pickering, is it not?

MRS. EYNSFORD HILL. I feel sure we have met before, Miss Doolittle. I remember your eyes.

LIZA. How do you do? (*She sits down on the ottoman gracefully in the place just left vacant by* HIGGINS.)

MRS. EYNSFORD HILL (*introducing*). My daughter Clara.

LIZA. How do you do?

CLARA (*impulsively*). How do you do? (*She sits down on the ottoman beside* ELIZA, *devouring her with her eyes.*)

FREDDY (*coming to their side of the ottoman*). I've certainly had the pleasure.

MRS. EYNSFORD HILL (*introducing*). My son Freddy.

LIZA. How do you do?

[FREDDY *bows and sits down in the Elizabethan chair, infatuated.*]

HIGGINS (*suddenly*). By George, yes! It all comes back to me! (*They stare at him.*) Covent Garden! (*Lamentably*) What a damned thing!

MRS. HIGGINS. Henry, please! (*He is about to sit on the edge of the table*) Don't sit on my writing table; you'll break it.

HIGGINS (*sulkily*). Sorry.

[*He goes to the divan, stumbling into the fender and over the fire irons on his way; extricating himself with muttered imprecations* [1]; *and finishing his disastrous journey by throwing himself so impatiently on the divan that he almost breaks it.* MRS. HIGGINS *looks at him, but controls herself and says nothing.*]

[*A long and painful pause ensues.*]

MRS. HIGGINS (*at last, conversationally*). Will it rain, do you think?

LIZA. The shallow depression in the west of these islands is likely to move slowly in an easterly direction. There are no indications of any great change in the barometrical situation.

FREDDY. Ha! ha! how awfully funny!

LIZA. What is wrong with that, young man? I bet I got it right.

FREDDY. Killing!

MRS. EYNSFORD HILL. I'm sure I hope it won't turn cold. There's so much influenza about. It runs right through our whole family regularly every spring.

LIZA (*darkly*). My aunt died of influenza, so they said.

MRS. EYNSFORD HILL (*clicks her tongue sympathetically*)!!!

LIZA (*in the same tragic tone*). But it's my belief they done the old woman in.

MRS. HIGGINS (*puzzled*). Done her in?

LIZA. Y-e-e-es, Lord love you! Why should *she* die of influenza? She come through diphtheria right enough the year before. I saw her with my own eyes. Fairly blue with it, she was. They all thought she was dead; but my father he kept ladling gin down her throat 'til she came to so sudden that she bit the bowl off the spoon.

MRS. EYNSFORD HILL (*startled*). Dear me!

LIZA (*piling up the indictment* [2]). What call would a woman with that strength in her have to die of influenza? What become of her new straw hat that should have come to me? Somebody pinched it; and what I say is, them as pinched it done her in.

MRS. EYNSFORD HILL. What does doing her in mean?

HIGGINS (*hastily*). Oh, that's the new small talk. To do a person in means to kill them.

MRS. EYNSFORD HILL (*to* ELIZA, *horrified*). You surely don't believe that your aunt was killed?

LIZA. Do I not! Them she lived with would have killed her for a hatpin, let alone a hat.

---

[1] *imprecations* (ĭm′prē·kā′shŭns): curses.

[2] *indictment* (ĭn·dīt′měnt): a statement charging someone with an offense.

MRS. EYNSFORD HILL. But it can't have been right for your father to pour spirits down her throat like that. It might have killed her.

LIZA. Not her. Gin was mother's milk to her. Besides, he'd poured so much down his own throat that he knew the good of it.

MRS. EYNSFORD HILL. Do you mean that he drank?

LIZA. Drank! My word! Something chronic.

MRS. EYNSFORD HILL. How dreadful for you!

LIZA. Not a bit. It never did him no harm what I could see. But then he did not keep it up regular. (*Cheerfully*) On the burst, as you might say, from time to time. And always more agreeable when he had a drop in. When he was out of work, my mother used to give him fourpence and tell him to go out and not come back until he'd drunk himself cheerful and loving-like. There's lots of women has to make their husbands drunk to make them fit to live with. (*Now quite at her ease*) You see, it's like this. If a man has a bit of a conscience, it always takes him when he's sober; and then it makes him low-spirited. A drop of booze just takes that off and makes him happy. (*To* FREDDY, *who is in convulsions of suppressed laughter*) Here! what are you sniggering at?

FREDDY. The new small talk. You do it so awfully well.

LIZA. If I was doing it proper, what was you laughing at? (*To* HIGGINS) Have I said anything I oughtn't?

MRS. HIGGINS (*interposing*). Not at all, Miss Doolittle.

LIZA. Well, that's a mercy, anyhow. (*Expansively*) What I always say is —

HIGGINS (*rising and looking at his watch*). Ahem!

LIZA (*looking round at him; taking the hint; and rising*). Well, I must go. (*They all rise.* FREDDY *goes to the door.*) So pleased to have met you. Good-by. (*She shakes hands with* MRS. HIGGINS.)

MRS. HIGGINS. Good-by.

LIZA. Good-by, Colonel Pickering.

PICKERING. Good-by, Miss Doolittle. (*They shake hands.*)

LIZA (*nodding to the others*). Good-by, all.

FREDDY (*opening the door for her*). Are you walking across the Park, Miss Doolittle? If so —

LIZA. Walk! Not bloody likely. (*Sensation.*) I am going in a taxi. (*She goes out.*)

[PICKERING *gasps and sits down.* FREDDY *goes out on the balcony to catch another glimpse of* ELIZA.]

MRS. EYNSFORD HILL (*suffering from shock*). Well, I really can't get used to the new ways.

CLARA (*throwing herself discontentedly into the Elizabethan chair*). Oh, it's all right, Mamma, quite right. People will think we never go anywhere or see anybody if you are so old-fashioned.

MRS. EYNSFORD HILL. I daresay I am very old-fashioned, but I do hope you won't begin using that expression, Clara. I have got accustomed to hear you talking about men as rotters, and calling everything filthy and beastly, though I do think it horrible and unladylike. But this last is really too much. Don't you think so, Colonel Pickering?

PICKERING. Don't ask me. I've been away in India for several years, and manners have changed so much that I sometimes don't know whether I'm at a respectable dinner table or in a ship's forecastle.

CLARA. It's all a matter of habit. There's no right or wrong in it. Nobody means anything by it. And it's so quaint, and gives such a smart emphasis to things that are not in themselves very witty. I find the new small talk delightful and quite innocent.

MRS. EYNSFORD HILL (*rising*). Well, after that, I think it's time for us to go.

[PICKERING *and* HIGGINS *rise.*]

CLARA (*rising*). Oh, yes! We have three at-homes to go to still. Good-by, Mrs. Higgins. Good-by, Colonel Pickering. Good-by, Professor Higgins.

HIGGINS (*coming grimly at her from the divan, and accompanying her to the door*). Good-by. Be sure you try that small talk at the three at-homes. Don't be nervous about it. Pitch it in strong.

CLARA (*all smiles*). I will. Good-by. Such nonsense, all this early Victorian prudery!

HIGGINS (*tempting her*). Such damned nonsense!

CLARA. Such bloody nonsense!

MRS. EYNSFORD HILL (*convulsively*). Clara!

CLARA. Ha! ha! (*She goes out radiant, conscious of being thoroughly up to date, and is heard descending the stairs in a stream of silvery laughter.*)

FREDDY (*to the heavens at large*). Well, I ask you — (*He gives it up, and comes to* MRS. HIGGINS.) Good-by.

MRS. HIGGINS (*shaking hands*). Good-by. Would you like to meet Miss Doolittle again?

FREDDY (*eagerly*). Yes, I should, most awfully.

MRS. HIGGINS. Well, you know my days.

FREDDY. Yes. Thanks awfully. Good-by. (*He goes out.*)

MRS. EYNSFORD HILL. Good-by, Mr. Higgins.

HIGGINS. Good-by. Good-by.

MRS. EYNSFORD HILL (*to* PICKERING). It's no use. I shall never be able to bring myself to use that word.

PICKERING. Don't. It's not compulsory, you know. You'll get on quite well without it.

MRS. EYNSFORD HILL. Only, Clara is so down on me if I am not positively reeking with the latest slang. Good-by.

PICKERING. Good-by. (*They shake hands.*)

MRS. EYNSFORD HILL (*to* MRS. HIGGINS). You mustn't mind Clara. (PICKERING, *catching from her lowered tone that this is not meant for him to hear, discreetly joins* HIGGINS *at the window.*) We're so poor! And she gets so few parties, poor child! She doesn't quite know. (MRS. HIGGINS, *seeing that her eyes are moist, takes her hand sympathetically and goes with her to the door.*) But the boy is nice. Don't you think so?

MRS. HIGGINS. Oh, quite nice. I shall always be delighted to see him.

MRS. EYNSFORD HILL. Thank you, dear. Good-by. (*She goes out.*)

HIGGINS (*eagerly*). Well? Is Eliza presentable? (*He swoops on his mother and drags her to the ottoman, where she sits down in Eliza's place with her son on her left.*)

[PICKERING *returns to his chair on her right.*]

MRS. HIGGINS. You silly boy, of course she's not presentable. She's a triumph of your art and of her dressmaker's; but if you suppose for a moment that she doesn't give herself away in every sentence she utters, you must be perfectly cracked about her.

PICKERING. But don't you think something might be done? I mean something to eliminate the sanguinary [1] element from her conversation.

MRS. HIGGINS. Not as long as she is in Henry's hands.

HIGGINS (*aggrieved*). Do you mean that *my* language is improper?

MRS. HIGGINS. No, dearest, it would be quite proper — say on a canal barge; but it would not be proper for her at a garden party.

HIGGINS (*deeply injured*). Well I must say —

PICKERING (*interrupting him*). Come, Higgins. You must learn to know yourself. I haven't heard such language as yours since we used to review the volunteers in Hyde Park twenty years ago.

HIGGINS (*sulkily*). Oh, well, if *you* say so, I suppose I don't always talk like a bishop.

[1] *sanguinary* (săng′gwĭ·nĕr′ĭ): bloody; a reference to Eliza's use of the slang term "bloody" in her conversation.

MRS. HIGGINS (*quieting Henry with a touch*). Colonel Pickering, will you tell me what is the exact state of things in Wimpole Street?

PICKERING (*cheerfully, as if this completely changed the subject*). Well, I have come to live there with Henry. We work together at my Indian Dialects, and we think it more convenient —

MRS. HIGGINS. Quite so. I know all about that: it's an excellent arrangement. But where does this girl live?

HIGGINS. With us, of course. Where *should* she live?

MRS. HIGGINS. But on what terms? Is she a servant? If not, what is she?

PICKERING (*slowly*). I think I know what you mean, Mrs. Higgins.

HIGGINS. Well, dash me if *I* do! I've had to work at the girl every day for months to get her to her present pitch. Besides, she's useful. She knows where my things are, and remembers my appointments and so forth.

MRS. HIGGINS. How does your housekeeper get on with her?

HIGGINS. Mrs. Pearce? Oh, she's jolly glad to get so much taken off her hands; for before Eliza came, *she* used to have to find things and remind me of my appointments. But she's got some silly bee in her bonnet about Eliza. She keeps saying "You don't think, sir," doesn't she, Pick?

PICKERING. Yes, that's the formula. "You don't think, sir." That's the end of every conversation about Eliza.

HIGGINS. As if I ever stop thinking about the girl and her confounded vowels and consonants. I'm worn out, thinking about her, and watching her lips and her teeth and her tongue, not to mention her soul, which is the quaintest of the lot.

MRS. HIGGINS. You certainly are a pretty pair of babies, playing with your live doll.

HIGGINS. Playing! The hardest job I ever tackled — Make no mistake about that, Mother. But you have no idea how frightfully interesting it is to take a human being and change her into a quite different human being by creating a new speech for her. It's filling up the deepest gulf that separates class from class and soul from soul.

PICKERING (*drawing his chair closer to* MRS. HIGGINS *and bending over to her eagerly*). Yes, it's enormously interesting. I assure you, Mrs. Higgins, we take Eliza very seriously. Every week — every day almost — there is some new change. (*Closer again*) We keep records of every stage — dozens of gramophone disks and photographs —

HIGGINS (*assailing her at the other ear*). Yes, by George! It's the most absorbing experiment I ever tackled. She regularly fills our lives up, doesn't she, Pick?

PICKERING. We're always talking Eliza.

HIGGINS. Teaching Eliza.

PICKERING. Dressing Eliza.

MRS. HIGGINS. What!

HIGGINS. Inventing new Elizas.

HIGGINS. *[speaking together]* You know, she has the most extraordinary quickness of ear:

PICKERING. *[speaking together]* I assure you, my dear Mrs. Higgins, that girl

HIGGINS. just like a parrot. I've tried her with every

PICKERING. is a genius. She can play the piano quite beautifully.

HIGGINS. possible sort of sound that a human being can make —

PICKERING. } HIGGINS. } PICKERING. } HIGGINS. } PICKERING. } HIGGINS. } PICKERING. } HIGGINS. } PICKERING.

We have taken her to classical concerts and to music halls; and it's all the same to her: she plays everything she hears right off when she comes home, whether it's Beethoven and Brahms or Lehar and Lionel Monckton; though six months ago, she'd never as much as touched a piano —

Continental dialects, African dialects, Hottentot clicks, things it took me years to get hold of; and she picks them up like a shot, right away, as if she had been at it all her life.

MRS. HIGGINS (*putting her fingers in her ears, as they are by this time shouting one another down with an intolerable noise*). Sh-sh-sh — sh! (*They stop.*)

PICKERING. I beg your pardon. (*He draws his chair back apologetically.*)

HIGGINS. Sorry. When Pickering starts shouting nobody can get a word in edgeways.

MRS. HIGGINS. Be quiet, Henry. Colonel Pickering, don't you realize that when Eliza walked into Wimpole Street, something walked in with her?

PICKERING. Her father did. But Henry soon got rid of him.

MRS. HIGGINS. It would have been more to the point if her mother had. But as her mother didn't something else did.

PICKERING. But what?

MRS. HIGGINS (*unconsciously dating herself by the word*). A problem.

PICKERING. Oh, I see. The problem of how to pass her off as a lady.

HIGGINS. I'll solve that problem. I've half solved it already.

MRS. HIGGINS. No, you two infinitely stupid male creatures! The problem of what is to be done with her afterwards.

HIGGINS. I don't see anything in that. She can go her own way, with all the advantages I have given her.

MRS. HIGGINS. The advantages of that poor woman who was here just now! The manners and habits that disqualify a fine lady from earning her own living without giving her a fine lady's income! Is that what you mean?

PICKERING (*indulgently, being rather bored*). Oh, that will be all right, Mrs. Higgins. (*He rises to go.*)

HIGGINS (*rising also*). We'll find her some light employment.

PICKERING. She's happy enough. Don't you worry about her. Good-by. (*He shakes hands as if he were consoling a frightened child, and makes for the door.*)

HIGGINS. Anyhow, there's no good bothering now. The thing's done. Good-by, Mother. (*He kisses her, and follows* PICKERING.)

PICKERING (*turning for a final consolation*). There are plenty of openings. We'll do what's right. Good-by.

HIGGINS (*to* PICKERING *as they go out together*). Let's take her to the Shakespeare exhibition at Earl's Court.

PICKERING. Yes, let's. Her remarks will be delicious.

HIGGINS. She'll mimic all the people for us when we get home.

PICKERING. Ripping. (*Both are heard laughing as they go downstairs.*)

MRS. HIGGINS (*rises with an impatient bounce, and returns to her work at the writing table. She sweeps a litter of disarranged papers out of her way; snatches a sheet of paper from her stationery case; and tries resolutely to write. At the third line she gives it up; flings down her pen; grips the table angrily and exclaims*). Oh, men! men!! men!!!

PROGRESS AND A PROBLEM

1. How much time has elapsed since the beginning of the experiment? Why does Higgins choose his mother's "at home" for Eliza's introduction to society? How would you describe the relationship between Higgins and his mother?

2. Point out the differences that you note between Mrs. Higgins and Mrs. Eynsford Hill. Describe the kind of life that Mrs. Eynsford Hill and her children live.

3. How much has Higgins accomplished in his education of Eliza? Compare Eliza now with the girl she was in Acts I and II. How is she received by Mrs. Higgins' guests? Do they recognize her? Does Eliza recognize them?

4. What is Mrs. Higgins' reaction to her son's experiment? How does she regard Eliza? In this act, do you detect a suggestion of a problem that may prove to be important later on? What is it?

ACT IV

The Wimpole Street laboratory. Midnight. Nobody in the room. The clock on the mantelpiece strikes twelve. The fire is not alight; it is a summer night.

Presently HIGGINS *and* PICKERING are heard on the stairs.

HIGGINS (*calling down to* PICKERING). I say, Pick. Lock up, will you? I shan't be going out again.

PICKERING. Right. Can Mrs. Pearce

go to bed? We don't want anything more, do we?

HIGGINS. Lord, no!

[ELIZA *opens the door and is seen on the lighted landing in opera cloak, brilliant evening dress, and diamonds, with fan, flowers, and all accessories. She comes to the hearth, and switches on the electric lights there. She is tired; her pallor contrasts strongly with her dark eyes and hair; and her expression is almost tragic. She takes off her cloak; puts her fan and flowers on the piano; and sits down on the bench, brooding and silent.* HIGGINS, *in evening dress, with overcoat and hat, comes in, carrying a smoking jacket which he has picked up downstairs. He takes off the hat and overcoat; throws them carelessly on the newspaper stand; disposes of his coat in the same way; puts on the smoking jacket; and throws himself wearily into the easy chair at the hearth.* PICKERING, *similarly attired, comes in. He also takes off his hat and overcoat, and is about to throw them on* HIGGINS' *when he hesitates.*]

PICKERING. I say, Mrs. Pearce will row if we leave these things lying about in the drawing room.

HIGGINS. Oh, chuck them over the bannisters into the hall. She'll find them there in the morning and put them away all right. She'll think we were drunk.

PICKERING. We are, slightly. Are there any letters?

HIGGINS. I didn't look. (PICKERING *takes the overcoats and hats and goes downstairs.* HIGGINS *begins half singing half yawning an air from* La Fanciulla del Golden West.[1] *Suddenly he stops and exclaims*) I wonder where the devil my slippers are!

[ELIZA *looks at him darkly; then rises suddenly and leaves the room.* HIGGINS *yawns again, and resumes his song.*

[PICKERING *returns, with the contents of the letter box in his hand.*]

PICKERING. Only circulars, and this coroneted billet-doux[2] for you. (*He throws the circulars into the fender, and posts himself on the hearthrug, with his back to the grate.*)

HIGGINS (*glancing at the billet-doux*). Moneylender. (*He throws the letter after the circulars.*)

[ELIZA *returns with a pair of large down-at-heel slippers. She places them on the carpet before* HIGGINS, *and sits as before without a word.*]

HIGGINS (*yawning again*). Oh Lord! What an evening! What a crew! What a silly tomfoolery! (*He raises his shoe to unlace it, and catches sight of the slippers. He stops unlacing and looks at them as if they had appeared there of their own accord.*) Oh! they're there, are they?

PICKERING (*stretching himself*). Well, I feel a bit tired. It's been a long day. The garden party, a dinner party, and the opera! Rather too much of a good thing. But you've won your bet, Higgins. Eliza did the trick, and something to spare, eh?

HIGGINS (*fervently*). Thank God it's over!

[ELIZA *flinches violently; but they take no notice of her; and she recovers herself and sits stonily as before.*]

PICKERING. Were you nervous at the garden party? *I* was. Eliza didn't seem a bit nervous.

HIGGINS. Oh, *she* wasn't nervous. I knew she'd be all right. No, it's the strain of putting the job through all these months that has told on me. It was interesting enough at first, while we were at the phonetics; but after that I got deadly sick of it. If I hadn't backed myself to do it I should have chucked the whole thing up two months ago. It was

---

[1] La Fanciulla del Golden West: *The Girl of the Golden West*, an opera by Puccini.

[2] *billet-doux* (bĭl'ả·doo'): a love letter.

a silly notion. The whole thing has been a bore.

PICKERING. Oh come! The garden party was frightfully exciting. My heart began beating like anything.

HIGGINS. Yes, for the first three minutes. But when I saw we were going to win hands down, I felt like a bear in a cage, hanging about doing nothing. The dinner was worse: sitting gorging there for over an hour, with nobody but a damned fool of a fashionable woman to talk to! I tell you, Pickering, never again for me. No more artificial duchesses. The whole thing has been simple purgatory.

PICKERING. You've never been broken in properly to the social routine. (*Strolling over to the piano*) I rather enjoy dipping into it occasionally myself. It makes me feel young again. Anyhow, it was a great success: an immense success. I was quite frightened once or twice because Eliza was doing it so well. You see, lots of the real people can't do it at all: they're such fools that they think style comes by nature to people in their position, and so they never learn. There's always something professional about doing a thing superlatively well.

HIGGINS. Yes, that's what drives me mad. The silly people don't know their own silly business. (*Rising*) However, it's over and done with; and now I can go to bed at last without dreading tomorrow.

[ELIZA'S *beauty becomes murderous.*]

PICKERING. I think I shall turn in too. Still, it's been a great occasion: a triumph for you. Good night. (*He goes.*)

HIGGINS (*following him*). Good night. (*Over his shoulder, at the door*) Put out the lights, Eliza; and tell Mrs. Pearce not to make coffee for me in the morning. I'll take tea. (*He goes out.*)

[ELIZA *tries to control herself and feel indifferent as she rises and walks across to the hearth to switch off the lights. By the time she gets there she* is on the point of screaming. She sits down in HIGGINS' *chair and holds on hard to the arms. Finally she gives way and flings herself furiously on the floor, raging.*]

HIGGINS (*in despairing wrath outside*). What the devil have I done with my slippers? (*He appears at the door.*)

LIZA (*snatching up the slippers, and hurling them at him one after the other with all her force*). There are your slippers. And there. Take your slippers, and may you never have a day's luck with them!

HIGGINS (*astounded*). What on earth — ! (*He comes to her.*) What's the matter? Get up. (*He pulls her up.*) Anything wrong?

LIZA (*breathless*). Nothing wrong — with *you.* I've won your bet for you, haven't I. That's enough for you. *I* don't matter, I suppose.

HIGGINS. *You* won my bet! You! Presumptuous insect! *I* won it. What did you throw those slippers at me for?

LIZA. Because I wanted to smash your face. I'd like to kill you, you selfish brute. Why didn't you leave me where you picked me out of — in the gutter? You thank God it's all over, and that now you can throw me back again there, do you? (*She crisps her fingers frantically.*)

HIGGINS (*looking at her in cool wonder*). The creature is nervous, after all.

LIZA (*gives a suffocated scream of fury, and instinctively darts her nails at his face*)!!

HIGGINS (*catching her wrists*). Ah! would you? Claws in, you cat. How dare you show your temper to me? Sit down and be quiet. (*He throws her roughly into the easy chair.*)

LIZA (*crushed by superior strength and weight*). What's to become of me? What's to become of me?

HIGGINS. How the devil do I know what's to become of you? What does it matter what becomes of you?

LIZA. You don't care. I know you don't

care. You wouldn't care if I was dead. I'm nothing to you — not so much as them slippers.

HIGGINS (*thundering*). *Those* slippers.

LIZA (*with bitter submission*). Those slippers. I didn't think it made any difference now.

[*A pause.* ELIZA *hopeless and crushed.* HIGGINS *a little uneasy.*]

HIGGINS (*in his loftiest manner*). Why have you begun going on like this? May I ask whether you complain of your treatment here?

LIZA. No.

HIGGINS. Has anybody behaved badly to you? Colonel Pickering? Mrs. Pearce? Any of the servants?

LIZA. No.

HIGGINS. I presume you don't pretend that *I* have treated you badly?

LIZA. No.

HIGGINS. I am glad to hear it. (*He moderates his tone*). Perhaps you're tired after the strain of the day. Will you have a glass of champagne? (*He moves toward the door.*)

LIZA. No. (*Recollecting her manners*). Thank you.

HIGGINS (*good-humored again*). This has been coming on you for some days. I suppose it was natural for you to be anxious about the garden party. But that's all over now. (*He pats her kindly on the shoulder. She writhes.*) There's nothing more to worry about.

LIZA. No. Nothing more for *you* to worry about. (*She suddenly rises and gets away from him by going to the piano bench, where she sits and hides her face.*) Oh God! I wish I was dead.

HIGGINS (*staring after her in sincere surprise*). Why? In heaven's name, why? (*Reasonably, going to her*) Listen to me, Eliza. All this irritation is purely subjective.

LIZA. I don't understand. I'm too ignorant.

HIGGINS. It's only imagination. Low spirits and nothing else. Nobody's hurting you. Nothing's wrong. You go to bed like a good girl and sleep it off. Have a little cry and say your prayers. That will make you comfortable.

LIZA. I heard your prayers. " Thank God it's all over! "

HIGGINS (*impatiently*). Well, *don't* you thank God it's all over? Now you are free and can do what you like.

LIZA (*pulling herself together in desperation*). What am I fit for? What have you left me fit for? Where am I to go? What am I to do? What's to become of me?

HIGGINS (*enlightened, but not at all impressed*). Oh *that's* what's worrying you, is it? (*He thrusts his hands into his pockets, and walks about in his usual manner, rattling the contents of his pockets, as if condescending to a trivial subject out of pure kindness.*) I shouldn't bother about it if I were you. I should imagine you won't have much difficulty in settling yourself somewhere or other, though I hadn't quite realized that you were going away. (*She looks quickly at him. He does not look at her, but examines the dessert stand on the piano and decides that he will eat an apple.*) You might marry, you know. (*He bites a large piece out of the apple and munches it noisily.*) You see, Eliza, all men are not confirmed old bachelors like me and the Colonel. Most men are the marrying sort (poor devils!); and you're not bad looking. It's quite a pleasure to look at you sometimes — not now, of course, because you're crying and looking as ugly as the very devil; but when you're all right and quite yourself, you're what I should call attractive. That is, to the people in the marrying line, you understand. You go to bed and have a good nice rest; and then get up and look at yourself in the glass; and you won't feel so cheap.

[ELIZA *again looks at him, speechless, and does not stir. The look is quite lost on him. He eats his apple with a dreamy expression of happiness, as it is quite a good one.*]

HIGGINS (*a genial afterthought occurring to him*). I daresay my mother could find some chap or other who would do very well.

LIZA. We were above that at the corner of Tottenham Court Road.

HIGGINS (*waking up*). What do you mean?

LIZA. I sold flowers. I didn't sell myself. Now you've made a lady of me I'm not fit to sell anything else. I wish you'd left me where you found me.

HIGGINS (*slinging the core of the apple decisively into the grate*). Tosh, Eliza. Don't you insult human relations by dragging all this cant about buying and selling into it. You needn't marry the fellow if you don't like him.

LIZA. What else am I to do?

HIGGINS. Oh, lots of things. What about your old idea of a florist's shop? Pickering could set you up in one. He's lots of money. (*Chuckling*) He'll have to pay for all those togs you have been wearing today; and that, with the hire of the jewelry, will make a big hole in two hundred pounds. Why, six months ago you would have thought it the millennium to have a flower shop of your own. Come! you'll be all right. I must clear off to bed. I'm devilish sleepy. By the way, I came down for something. I forget what it was.

LIZA. Your slippers.

HIGGINS. Oh, yes, of course. You shied them at me. (*He picks them up, and is going out when she rises and speaks to him.*)

LIZA. Before you go, sir —

HIGGINS (*dropping the slippers in his surprise at her calling him Sir*). Eh?

LIZA. Do my clothes belong to me or to Colonel Pickering?

HIGGINS (*coming back into the room as if her question were the very climax of unreason*). What the devil use would they be to Pickering?

LIZA. He might want them for the next girl you pick up to experiment on.

HIGGINS (*shocked and hurt*). Is *that* the way you feel toward us?

LIZA. I don't want to hear anything more about that. All I want to know is whether anything belongs to me. My own clothes were burnt.

HIGGINS. But what does it matter? Why need you start bothering about that in the middle of the night?

LIZA. I want to know what I may take away with me. I don't want to be accused of stealing.

HIGGINS (*now deeply wounded*). Stealing! You shouldn't have said that, Eliza. That shows a want of feeling.

LIZA. I'm sorry. I'm only a common ignorant girl; and in my station I have to be careful. There can't be any feelings between the like of you and the like of me. Please will you tell me what belongs to me and what doesn't?

HIGGINS (*very sulky*). You may take the whole damned houseful if you like. Except the jewels. They're hired. Will that satisfy you? (*He turns on his heel and is about to go in extreme dudgeon.[1]*)

LIZA (*drinking in his emotion like nectar, and nagging him to provoke a further supply*). Stop, please. (*She takes off her jewels.*) Will you take these to your room and keep them safe? I don't want to run the risk of their being missing.

HIGGINS (*furious*). Hand them over. (*She puts them into his hands.*) If these belonged to me instead of to the jeweler, I'd ram them down your ungrateful throat. (*He perfunctorily thrusts them into his pockets, unconsciously decorating himself with the protruding ends of the chains.*)

LIZA (*taking a ring off*). This ring isn't the jeweler's. It's the one you bought me in Brighton. I don't want it now. (HIGGINS *dashes the ring violently into the fireplace, and turns on her so threateningly that she crouches over the piano with her hands over her face, and exclaims*) Don't you hit me.

HIGGINS. Hit you! You infamous crea-

---

[1] *dudgeon* (dŭj'ŭn): angered feeling.

ture, how dare you accuse me of such a thing? It is you who have hit me. You have wounded me to the heart.

LIZA (*thrilling with hidden joy*). I'm glad. I've got a little of my own back, anyhow.

HIGGINS (*with dignity, in his finest professional style*). You have caused me to lose my temper — a thing that has hardly ever happened to me before. I prefer to say nothing more tonight. I am going to bed.

LIZA (*pertly*). You'd better leave a note for Mrs. Pearce about the coffee, for she won't be told by me.

HIGGINS (*formally*). Damn Mrs. Pearce; and damn the coffee; and damn you; and damn my own folly in having lavished hard-earned knowledge and the treasure of my regard and intimacy on a heartless guttersnipe. (*He goes out with impressive decorum, and spoils it by slamming the door savagely.*)

[ELIZA *smiles for the first time; expresses her feelings by a wild pantomime in which an imitation of* HIGGINS' *exit is confused with her own triumph; and finally goes down on her knees on the hearthrug to look for the ring.*]

A CRISIS

1. The experiment is finished and Higgins has won his bet. How does he react to his success? What do Higgins and Pickering have to say about the social routine? Do you think that Shaw means this as a criticism of society?

2. Eliza has been silent and brooding, but finally her " beauty becomes murderous." Why? How does Higgins first react to her outburst? What is really bothering her? When had this problem been suggested before? Is Higgins being honest in his response to Eliza? What effect does his response have on Eliza? Characterize Higgins in this scene.

3. At this point, what do you think Eliza's feelings for Higgins are? Can you justify what she says and does? Why is she smiling at the end of the scene?

ACT V

MRS. HIGGINS' *drawing room. She is at her writing table as before. The* PARLOR MAID *comes in.*

THE PARLOR MAID (*at the door*). Mr. Henry, ma'am, is downstairs with Colonel Pickering.

MRS. HIGGINS. Well, show them up.

THE PARLOR MAID. They're using the telephone, ma'am. Telephoning to the police, I think.

MRS. HIGGINS. What!

THE PARLOR MAID (*coming further in and lowering her voice*). Mr. Henry is in a state, ma'am. I thought I'd better tell you.

MRS. HIGGINS. If you had told me that Mr. Henry was not in a state it would have been more surprising. Tell them to come up when they've finished with the police. I suppose he's lost something.

THE PARLOR MAID. Yes, ma'am (*going*).

MRS. HIGGINS. Go upstairs and tell Miss Doolittle that Mr. Henry and the Colonel are here. Ask her not to come down till I send for her.

THE PARLOR MAID. Yes, ma'am.

[HIGGINS *bursts in. He is, as the* PARLOR MAID *has said, in a state.*]

HIGGINS. Look here, Mother! Here's a confounded thing!

MRS. HIGGINS. Yes, dear. Good morning. (*He checks his impatience and kisses her, while the* PARLOR MAID *goes out.*) What is it?

HIGGINS. Eliza's bolted.

MRS. HIGGINS (*calmly continuing her writing*). You must have frightened her.

HIGGINS. Frightened her! Nonsense! She was left last night, as usual, to turn out the lights and all that; and instead of going to bed, she changed her clothes and went right off. Her bed wasn't slept in. She came in a cab for her things before seven this morning, and that fool Mrs. Pearce let her have them without telling me a word about it. What am I to do?

MRS. HIGGINS. Do without, I'm afraid, Henry. The girl has a perfect right to leave if she chooses.

HIGGINS (*wandering distractedly across the room*). But I can't find anything. I don't know what appointments I've got. I'm — (PICKERING *comes in.* MRS. HIGGINS *puts down her pen and turns away from the writing table.*)

PICKERING (*shaking hands*). Good morning, Mrs. Higgins. Has Henry told you? (*He sits down on the ottoman.*)

HIGGINS. What does that fool of an inspector say? Have you offered a reward?

MRS. HIGGINS (*rising in indignant amazement*). You don't mean to say you have set the police after Eliza.

HIGGINS. Of course. What are the police for? What else could we do? (*He sits in the Elizabethan chair.*)

PICKERING. The inspector made a lot of difficulties. I really think he suspected us of some improper purpose.

MRS. HIGGINS. Well, of course he did. What right have you to go to the police and give the girl's name as if she were a thief, or a lost umbrella, or something? Really! (*She sits down again, deeply vexed.*)

HIGGINS. But we want to find her.

PICKERING. We can't let her go like this, you know, Mrs. Higgins. What were we to do?

MRS. HIGGINS. You have no more sense, either of you, than two children. Why —

[*The* PARLOR MAID *comes in and breaks off the conversation.*]

THE PARLOR MAID. Mr. Henry, a gentleman wants to see you very particular. He's been sent on from Wimpole Street.

HIGGINS. Oh, bother! I can't see anyone now. Who is it?

THE PARLOR MAID. A Mr. Doolittle, sir.

PICKERING. Doolittle! Do you mean the dustman?

THE PARLOR MAID. Dustman! Oh no, sir. A gentleman.

HIGGINS (*springing up excitedly*). By George, Pick, it's some relative of hers that she's gone to. Somebody we know nothing about. (*To the* PARLOR MAID) Send him up, quick.

THE PARLOR MAID. Yes, sir. (*She goes.*)

HIGGINS (*eagerly, going to his mother*). Genteel relatives! Now we shall hear something. (*He sits down in the Chippendale chair.*)

MRS. HIGGINS. Do you know any of her people?

PICKERING. Only her father. The fellow we told you about.

THE PARLOR MAID (*announcing*). Mr. Doolittle. (*She withdraws.*)

[DOOLITTLE *enters. He is brilliantly dressed in a new fashionable frock coat, with white waistcoat and gray trousers. A flower in his buttonhole, a dazzling silk hat, and patent leather shoes complete the effect. He is too concerned with the business he has come on to notice* MRS. HIGGINS. *He walks straight to* HIGGINS, *and accosts him with vehement [1] reproach.*]

DOOLITTLE (*indicating his own person*). See here! Do you see this? *You* done this.

HIGGINS. Done what, man?

DOOLITTLE. This, I tell you. Look at it. Look at this hat. Look at this coat.

PICKERING. Has Eliza been buying you clothes?

[1] *vehement* (vē′ĕ·mĕnt): furious.

DOOLITTLE. Eliza! Not she. Not half. Why would she buy me clothes?

MRS. HIGGINS. Good morning, Mr. Doolittle. Won't you sit down?

DOOLITTLE (*taken aback as he becomes conscious that he has forgotten his hostess*). Asking your pardon, ma'am. (*He approaches her and shakes her proffered hand.*) Thank you. (*He sits down on the ottoman, on* PICKERING'S *right.*) I am that full of what has happened to me that I can't think of anything else.

HIGGINS. What the dickens *has* happened to you?

DOOLITTLE. I shouldn't mind if it had only *happened* to me. Anything might happen to anybody and nobody to blame but Providence, as you might say. But this is something that you done to me. Yes, you, Henry Higgins.

HIGGINS. Have you found Eliza? That's the point.

DOOLITTLE. Have you lost her?

HIGGINS. Yes.

DOOLITTLE. You have all the luck, you have. I ain't found her; but she'll find me quick enough now after what you done to me.

MRS. HIGGINS. But what has my son done to you, Mr. Doolittle?

DOOLITTLE. Done to me! Ruined me. Destroyed my happiness. Tied me up and delivered me into the hands of middle class morality.

HIGGINS (*rising intolerantly and standing over* DOOLITTLE). You're raving. You're drunk. You're mad. I gave you five pounds. After that I had two conversations with you, at half a crown an hour. I've never seen you since.

DOOLITTLE. Oh! Drunk! am I? Mad! am I? Tell me this. Did you or did you not write a letter to an old blighter in America that was giving five millions to found Moral Reform Societies all over the world, and that wanted you to invent a universal language for him?

HIGGINS. What! Ezra D. Wannafeller! He's dead. (*He sits down again carelessly.*)

DOOLITTLE. Yes, he's dead; and I'm done for. Now did you or did you not write a letter to him to say that the most original moralist at present in England, to the best of your knowledge, was Alfred Doolittle, a common dustman.

HIGGINS. Oh, after your last visit I remember making some silly joke of the kind.

DOOLITTLE. Ah! you may well call it a silly joke. It put the lid on me right enough. Just give him the chance he wanted to show that Americans is not like us: that they recognize and respect merit in every class of life, however humble. Them words is in his blooming will, in which, Henry Higgins, thanks to your silly joking, he leaves me a share in his Pre-digested Cheese Trust worth three thousand a year on condition that I lecture for his Wannafeller Moral Reform World League as often as they ask me up to six times a year.

HIGGINS. The devil he does! Whew! (*Brightening suddenly*) What a lark!

PICKERING. A safe thing for you, Doolittle. They won't ask you twice.

DOOLITTLE. It ain't the lecturing I mind. I'll lecture them blue in the face, I will, and not turn a hair. It's making a gentleman of me that I object to. Who asked him to make a gentleman of me? I was happy. I was free. I touched pretty nigh everybody for money when I wanted it, same as I touched you, Henry Higgins. Now I am worrited; tied neck and heels; and everybody touches me for money. It's a fine thing for you, says my solicitor. Is it? says I. You mean it's a good thing for you, I says. When I was a poor man and had a solicitor once when they found a pram in the dust cart, he got me off, and got shut of me and got me shut of him as quick as he could. Same with the doctors: used to shove me out of the hospital before I could hardly stand on my legs, and nothing to pay. Now they finds out that I'm not a healthy man and can't live unless they looks after me twice a day. In the house I'm not let do a hand's turn for myself: somebody else must do it and touch me for it. A year ago I hadn't a relative in the world except two or three that wouldn't speak to me. Now I've fifty, and not a decent week's wages among the lot of them. I have to live for others and not for myself. That's middle class morality. *You* talk of losing Eliza. Don't you be anxious: I bet she's on my doorstep by this. She that could support herself easy by selling flowers if I wasn't respectable. And the next one to touch me will be you, Henry Higgins. I'll have to learn to speak middle class language from you, instead of speaking proper English. That's where you'll come in; and I daresay that's what you done it for.

MRS. HIGGINS. But, my dear Mr. Doolittle, you need not suffer all this if you are really in earnest. Nobody can force you to accept this bequest. You can repudiate it. Isn't that so, Colonel Pickering?

PICKERING. I believe so.

DOOLITTLE (*softening his manner in deference to her sex*). That's the tragedy of it, ma'am. It's easy to say chuck it; but I haven't the nerve. Which of us has? We're all intimidated. Intimidated, ma'am: that's what we are. What is there for me if I chuck it but the workhouse in my old age? I have to dye my hair already to keep my job as a dustman. If I was one of the deserving poor, and had put by a bit, I could chuck it; but then why should I, acause the deserving poor might as well be millionaires for all the happiness they ever has. They don't know what happiness is. But I, as one of the undeserving poor, have nothing between me and the pauper's uniform but this here blasted three thousand a year that shoves me into the middle class. (Excuse the expression, ma'am: you'd use it yourself if you had my provocation.) They've got you every way you turn: it's a choice between the Skilly of the workhouse and the Char Bydis [1] of the middle class; and I haven't the nerve for the workhouse. Intimidated! that's what I am. Broke. Bought up. Happier men than me will call for my dust, and touch me for their tip; and I'll look on helpless, and envy them. And that's what your son has brought me to. (*He is overcome by emotion.*)

MRS. HIGGINS. Well, I'm very glad you're not going to do anything foolish, Mr. Doolittle. For this solves the problem of Eliza's future. You can provide for her now.

DOOLITTLE (*with melancholy resignation*). Yes, ma'am: I'm expected to provide for everyone now, out of three thousand a year.

---

[1] *Skilly . . . Char Bydis:* Doolittle's distortion of Scylla (sĭl'ǎ) and Charybdis (kǎ·rĭb'dĭs), a dangerous rock and whirlpool on either side of a narrow strait between Sicily and Italy. The ancient Greeks personified them as two monsters, and they have come to symbolize two dangers between which it is almost impossible to steer a safe course.

HIGGINS (*jumping up*). Nonsense! He can't provide for her. He shan't provide for her. She doesn't belong to him. I paid him five pounds for her. Doolittle, either you're an honest man or a rogue.

DOOLITTLE (*tolerantly*). A little of both, Henry. Like the rest of us, a little of both.

HIGGINS. Well, you took that money for the girl; and you have no right to take her as well.

MRS. HIGGINS. Henry, don't be absurd. If you want to know where Eliza is, she is upstairs.

HIGGINS (*amazed*). Upstairs!!! Then I shall jolly soon fetch her downstairs. (*He makes resolutely for the door.*)

MRS. HIGGINS (*rising and following him*). Be quiet, Henry. Sit down.

HIGGINS. I —

MRS. HIGGINS. Sit down, dear; and listen to me.

HIGGINS. Oh very well, very well, very well. (*He throws himself ungraciously on the ottoman, with his face toward the windows.*) But I think you might have told us this half an hour ago.

MRS. HIGGINS. Eliza came to me this morning. She passed the night partly walking about in a rage, partly trying to throw herself into the river and being afraid to, and partly in the Carlton Hotel. She told me of the brutal way you two treated her.

HIGGINS (*bounding up again*). What!

PICKERING (*rising also*). My dear Mrs. Higgins, she's been telling you stories. We didn't treat her brutally. We hardly said a word to her; and we parted on particularly good terms. (*Turning on* HIGGINS) Higgins, did you bully her after I went to bed?

HIGGINS. Just the other way about. She threw my slippers in my face. She behaved in the most outrageous way. I never gave her the slightest provocation. The slippers came bang into my face the moment I entered the room — before I had uttered a word. And used perfectly awful language.

PICKERING (*astonished*). But why? What did we do to her?

MRS. HIGGINS. I think I know pretty well what you did. The girl is naturally rather affectionate, I think. Isn't she, Mr. Doolittle?

DOOLITTLE. Very tender-hearted, ma'am. Takes after me.

MRS. HIGGINS. Just so. She had become attached to you both. She worked very hard for you, Henry! I don't think you quite realize what anything in the nature of brain work means to a girl like that. Well, it seems that when the great day of trial came, and she did this wonderful thing for you without making a single mistake, you two sat there and never said a word to her, but talked together of how glad you were that it was all over and how you had been bored with the whole thing. And then you were surprised because she threw your slippers at you! *I* should have thrown the fire irons at you.

HIGGINS. We said nothing except that we were tired and wanted to go to bed. Did we, Pick?

PICKERING (*shrugging his shoulders*). That was all.

MRS. HIGGINS (*ironically*). Quite sure?

PICKERING. Absolutely. Really, that was all.

MRS. HIGGINS. You didn't thank her, or pet her, or admire her, or tell her how splendid she'd been?

HIGGINS (*impatiently*). But she knew all about that. We didn't make speeches to her, if that's what you mean.

PICKERING (*conscience-stricken*). Perhaps we were a little inconsiderate. Is she very angry?

MRS. HIGGINS (*returning to her place at the writing table*). Well, I'm afraid she won't go back to Wimpole Street, especially now that Mr. Doolittle is able to keep up the position you have thrust on her; but she says she is quite willing to meet you on friendly terms and to let bygones be bygones.

HIGGINS (*furious*). Is she, by George? Ho!

MRS. HIGGINS. If you promise to behave yourself, Henry, I'll ask her to come down. If not, go home; for you have taken up quite enough of my time.

HIGGINS. Oh, all right. Very well. Pick, you behave yourself. Let us put on our best Sunday manners for this creature that we picked out of the mud. (*He flings himself sulkily into the Elizabethan chair.*)

DOOLITTLE (*remonstrating*). Now, now, Henry Higgins! have some consideration for my feelings as a middle class man.

MRS. HIGGINS. Remember your promise, Henry. (*She presses the bell-button on the writing table.*) Mr. Doolittle, will you be so good as to step out on the balcony for a moment? I don't want Eliza to have the shock of your news until she has made it up with these two gentlemen. Would you mind?

DOOLITTLE. As you wish, lady. Anything to help Henry to keep her off my hands. (*He disappears through the window.*)

[*The* PARLOR MAID *answers the bell.* PICKERING *sits down in* DOOLITTLE'S *place.*]

MRS. HIGGINS. Ask Miss Doolittle to come down, please.

THE PARLOR MAID. Yes, ma'am. (*She goes out.*)

MRS. HIGGINS. Now, Henry, be good.

HIGGINS. I am behaving myself perfectly.

PICKERING. He is doing his best, Mrs. Higgins.

[*A pause.* HIGGINS *throws back his head; stretches out his legs; and begins to whistle.*]

MRS. HIGGINS. Henry, dearest, you don't look at all nice in that attitude.

HIGGINS (*pulling himself together*). I was not trying to look nice, Mother.

MRS. HIGGINS. It doesn't matter, dear.

I only wanted to make you speak.

HIGGINS. Why?

MRS. HIGGINS. Because you can't speak and whistle at the same time.

[HIGGINS *groans. Another very trying pause.*]

HIGGINS (*springing up, out of patience*). Where the devil is that girl? Are we to wait here all day?

[ELIZA *enters, sunny, self-possessed, and giving a staggeringly convincing exhibition of ease of manner. She carries a little workbasket, and is very much at home.* PICKERING *is too much taken aback to rise.*]

LIZA. How do you do, Professor Higgins? Are you quite well?

HIGGINS (*choking*). Am I — (*He can say no more*).

LIZA. But of course you are. You are never ill. So glad to see you again, Colonel Pickering. (*He rises hastily; and they shake hands.*) Quite chilly this morning, isn't it? (*She sits down on his left. He sits beside her.*)

HIGGINS. Don't you dare try this game on me. I taught it to you, and it doesn't take me in. Get up and come home, and don't be a fool.

[ELIZA *takes a piece of needlework from her basket, and begins to stitch at it, without taking the least notice of this outburst.*]

MRS. HIGGINS. Very nicely put, indeed, Henry. No woman could resist such an invitation.

HIGGINS. You let her alone, Mother. Let her speak for herself. You will jolly soon see whether she has an idea that I haven't put into her head or a word that I haven't put into her mouth. I tell you I have created this thing out of the squashed cabbage leaves of Covent Garden, and now she pretends to play the fine lady with me.

MRS. HIGGINS (*placidly*). Yes, dear; but you'll sit down, won't you?

[HIGGINS *sits down again, savagely.*]

LIZA (*to* PICKERING, *taking no apparent notice of* HIGGINS, *and working away deftly*). Will *you* drop me altogether now that the experiment is over, Colonel Pickering?

PICKERING. Oh, don't. You mustn't think of it as an experiment. It shocks me, somehow.

LIZA. Oh, I'm only a squashed cabbage leaf —

PICKERING (*impulsively*). No.

LIZA (*continuing quietly*). — but I owe so much to you that I should be very unhappy if you forgot me.

PICKERING. It's very kind of you to say so, Miss Doolittle.

LIZA. It's not because you paid for my dresses. I know you are generous to everybody with money. But it was from you that I learned really nice manners, and that is what makes one a lady, isn't it? You see it was so very difficult for me with the example of Professor Higgins always before me. I was brought up to be just like him, unable to control myself, and using bad language on the slightest provocation. And I should never have known that ladies and gentlemen didn't behave like that if you hadn't been there.

HIGGINS. Well!!

PICKERING. Oh, that's only his way, you know. He doesn't mean it.

LIZA. Oh, *I* didn't mean it either when I was a flower girl. It was only my way. But you see I did it, and that's what makes the difference after all.

PICKERING. No doubt. Still, he taught you to speak; and I couldn't have done that, you know.

LIZA (*trivially*). Of course. That is his profession.

HIGGINS. Damnation!

LIZA (*continuing*). It was just like learning to dance in the fashionable way. There was nothing more than that in it. But do you know what began my real education?

PICKERING. What?

LIZA (*stopping her work for a moment*). Your calling me Miss Doolittle that day when I first came to Wimpole Street. That was the beginning of self-respect for me. (*She resumes her stitching.*) And there were a hundred little things you never noticed, because they came naturally to you. Things about standing up and taking off your hat and opening doors —

PICKERING. Oh, that was nothing.

LIZA. Yes, things that showed you thought and felt about me as if I were something better than a scullery maid; though of course I know you would have been just the same to a scullery maid if she had been let into the drawing room. *You* never took off your boots in the dining room when I was there.

PICKERING. You mustn't mind that. Higgins takes off his boots all over the place.

LIZA. I know. I am not blaming him. It is his way, isn't it? But it made *such* a difference to me that you didn't do it. You see, really and truly, apart from the things anyone can pick up (the dressing and the proper way of speaking, and so on), the difference between a lady and a flower girl is not how she behaves, but how she's treated. I shall always be a flower girl to Professor Higgins, because he always treats me as a flower girl, and always will; but I know I can be a lady to you, because you always treat me as a lady, and always will.

MRS. HIGGINS. Please don't grind your teeth, Henry.

PICKERING. Well, this is really very nice of you, Miss Doolittle.

LIZA. I should like you to call me Eliza, now, if you would.

PICKERING. Thank you. Eliza, of course.

LIZA. And I should like Professor Higgins to call me Miss Doolittle.

HIGGINS. I'll see you damned first.

MRS. HIGGINS. Henry! Henry!

PICKERING (*laughing*). Why don't you slang back at him? Don't stand it. It would do him a lot of good.

LIZA. I can't. I could have done it once; but now I can't go back to it. Last night, when I was wandering about, a girl spoke to me; and I tried to get back into the old way with her, but it was no use. You told me, you know, that when a child is brought to a foreign country, it picks up the language in a few weeks and forgets its own. Well, I am a child in your country. I have forgotten my own language and can speak nothing but yours. That's the real break-off with the corner of Tottenham Court Road. Leaving Wimpole Street finishes it.

PICKERING (*much alarmed*). Oh! but you're coming back to Wimpole Street, aren't you? You'll forgive Higgins?

HIGGINS (*rising*). Forgive! Will she, by George! Let her go. Let her find out how she can get on without us. She will relapse into the gutter in three weeks without me at her elbow.

[DOOLITTLE *appears at the center window. With a look of dignified reproach at* HIGGINS, *he comes slowly and silently to his daughter, who, with her back to the window, is unconscious of his approach.*]

PICKERING. He's incorrigible, Eliza. You won't relapse, will you?

LIZA. No, not now. Never again. I have learnt my lesson. I don't believe I could utter one of the old sounds if I tried. (DOOLITTLE *touches her on her left shoulder. She drops her work, losing her self-possession utterly at the spectacle of her father's splendor*) A-a-a-a-a-ah-ow-ooh!

HIGGINS (*with a crow of triumph*). Aha! Just so. A-a-a-a-ahowooh! A-a-a-a-ahowooh! A-a-a-a-ahowooh! Victory! Victory! (*He throws himself on the divan, folding his arms, and spraddling arrogantly.*)

DOOLITTLE. Can you blame the girl? Don't look at me like that, Eliza. It ain't my fault. I've come into some money.

LIZA. You must have touched a millionaire this time, Dad.

DOOLITTLE. I have. But I'm dressed something special today. I'm going to St. George's, Hanover Square. Your stepmother is going to marry me.

LIZA (*angrily*). You're going to let yourself down to marry that low common woman!

PICKERING (*quietly*). He ought to, Eliza. (*To* DOOLITTLE) Why has she changed her mind?

DOOLITTLE (*sadly*). Intimidated, Governor. Intimidated. Middle class morality claims its victim. Won't you put on your hat, Liza, and come and see me turned off?

LIZA. If the Colonel says I must, I — I'll (*almost sobbing*) I'll demean [1] myself. And get insulted for my pains, like enough.

DOOLITTLE. Don't be afraid. She never comes to words with anyone now, poor woman! Respectability has broke all the spirit out of her.

PICKERING (*squeezing* ELIZA'S *elbow gently*). Be kind to them, Eliza. Make the best of it.

LIZA (*forcing a little smile for him through her vexation*). Oh well, just to show there's no ill feeling. I'll be back in a moment. (*She goes out.*)

DOOLITTLE (*sitting down beside* PICKERING). I feel uncommon nervous about the ceremony, Colonel. I wish you'd come and see me through it.

PICKERING. But you've been through it before, man. You were married to Eliza's mother.

DOOLITTLE. Who told you that, Colonel?

PICKERING. Well, nobody told me. But I concluded — naturally —

DOOLITTLE. No, that ain't the natural way, Colonel. It's only the middle class way. My way was always the undeserving way. But don't say nothing to Eliza. She don't know. I always had a delicacy about telling her.

PICKERING. Quite right. We'll leave it so, if you don't mind.

DOOLITTLE. And you'll come to the

[1] *demean* (dê·mēn′): lower, degrade.

church, Colonel, and put me through straight?

PICKERING. With pleasure. As far as a bachelor can.

MRS. HIGGINS. May I come, Mr. Doolittle? I should be very sorry to miss your wedding.

DOOLITTLE. I should indeed be honored by your condescension, ma'am; and my poor old woman would take it as a tremendous compliment. She's been very low, thinking of the happy days that are no more.

MRS. HIGGINS (rising). I'll order the carriage and get ready. (The men rise, except HIGGINS.) I shan't be more than fifteen minutes. (As she goes to the door ELIZA comes in, hatted and buttoning her gloves.) I'm going to the church to see your father married, Eliza. You had better come in the brougham [1] with me. Colonel Pickering can go on with the bridegroom.

[MRS. HIGGINS goes out. ELIZA comes to the middle of the room between the center window and the ottoman. PICKERING joins her.]

DOOLITTLE. Bridegroom! What a word! It makes a man realize his position, somehow. (He takes up his hat and goes toward the door.)

PICKERING. Before I go, Eliza, do forgive him and come back to us.

LIZA. I don't think Papa would allow me. Would you, Dad?

DOOLITTLE (sad but magnanimous). They played you off very cunning, Eliza, them two sportsmen. If it had been only one of them, you could have nailed him. But you see, there was two; and one of them chaperoned the other, as you might say. (To PICKERING) It was artful of you, Colonel; but I bear no malice. I should have done the same myself. I been the victim of one woman after another all my life; and I don't grudge you two getting the better of Eliza. I shan't interfere. It's time for us to go, Colonel.

_____
[1] brougham (broom): a light, closed carriage.

So long, Henry. See you in St. George's, Eliza. (He goes out.)

PICKERING (coaxing). Do stay with us, Eliza. (He follows DOOLITTLE.)

[ELIZA goes out on the balcony to avoid being alone with HIGGINS. He rises and joins her there. She immediately comes back into the room and makes for the door; but he goes along the balcony quickly and gets his back to the door before she reaches it.]

HIGGINS. Well, Eliza, you've had a bit of your own back, as you call it. Have you had enough? And are you going to be reasonable? Or do you want any more?

LIZA. You want me back only to pick up your slippers and put up with your tempers and fetch and carry for you.

HIGGINS. I haven't said I wanted you back at all.

LIZA. Oh, indeed. Then what are we talking about?

HIGGINS. About you, not about me. If you come back I shall treat you just as I have always treated you. I can't change my nature, and I don't intend to change my manners. My manners are exactly the same as Colonel Pickering's.

LIZA. That's not true. He treats a flower girl as if she was a duchess.

HIGGINS. And I treat a duchess as if she was a flower girl.

LIZA. I see. (She turns away composedly, and sits on the ottoman, facing the window.) The same to everybody.

HIGGINS. Just so.

LIZA. Like father.

HIGGINS (grinning, a little taken down). Without accepting the comparison at all points, Eliza, it's quite true that your father is not a snob, and that he will be quite at home in any station of life to which his eccentric destiny may call him. (Seriously) The great secret, Eliza, is not having bad manners or good manners or any other particular sort of manners, but having the same manner for all human souls. In short, behaving as if you were in Heaven, where there are no third class carriages, and one soul is as good as another.

LIZA. Amen. You are a born preacher.

HIGGINS (*irritated*). The question is not whether I treat you rudely, but whether you ever heard me treat anyone else better.

LIZA (*with sudden sincerity*). I don't care how you treat me. I don't mind your swearing at me. I don't mind a black eye: I've had one before this. But (*standing up and facing him*) I won't be passed over.

HIGGINS. Then get out of my way, for I won't stop for you. You talk about me as if I were a motor bus.

LIZA. So you are a motor bus. All bounce and go, and no consideration for anyone. But I can do without you; don't think I can't.

HIGGINS. I know you can. I told you you could.

LIZA (*wounded, getting away from him to the other side of the ottoman with her face to the hearth*). I know you did, you brute. You wanted to get rid of me.

HIGGINS. Liar.

LIZA. Thank you. (*She sits down with dignity.*)

HIGGINS. You never asked yourself, I suppose, whether *I* could do without *you*.

LIZA (*earnestly*). Don't you try to get round me. You'll *have* to do without me.

HIGGINS (*arrogant*). I can do without anybody. I have my own soul, my own spark of divine fire. But (*with sudden humility*) I shall miss you, Eliza. (*He sits down near her on the ottoman.*) I have learned something from your idiotic notions. I confess that humbly and gratefully. And I have grown accustomed to your voice and appearance. I like them, rather.

LIZA. Well, you have both of them on your gramophone and in your book of photographs. When you feel lonely without me, you can turn the machine on. It's got no feelings to hurt.

HIGGINS. I can't turn your soul on. Leave me those feelings, and you can take away the voice and the face. They are not you.

LIZA. Oh, you *are* a devil. You can twist the heart in a girl as easy as some could twist her arms to hurt her. Mrs. Pearce warned me. Time and again she has wanted to leave you, and you always got round her at the last minute. And you don't care a bit for her. And you don't care a bit for me.

HIGGINS. I care for life, for humanity; and you are a part of it that has come my way and been built into my house. What more can you or anyone ask?

LIZA. I won't care for anybody that doesn't care for me.

HIGGINS. Commercial principles, Eliza. Like (*reproducing her Covent Garden pronunciation with professional exactness*) s'yollin voylets [selling violets], isn't it?

LIZA. Don't sneer at me. It's mean to sneer at me.

HIGGINS. I have never sneered in my life. Sneering doesn't become either the human face or the human soul. I am expressing my righteous contempt for commercialism. I don't and won't trade in affection. You call me a brute because you couldn't buy a claim on me by fetching my slippers and finding my spectacles. You were a fool! I think a woman fetching a man's slippers is a disgusting sight. Did I ever fetch *your* slippers? I think a good deal more of you for throwing them in my face. No use slaving for me and then saying you want to be cared for. Who cares for a slave? If you come back, come back for the sake of good fellowship; for you'll get nothing else. You've had a thousand times as much out of me as I have out of you; and if you dare to set up your little dog's tricks of fetching and carrying slippers against my creation of a Duchess, Eliza, I'll slam the door in your silly face.

LIZA. What did you do it for if you didn't care for me?

HIGGINS (*heartily*). Why, because it was my job.

LIZA. You never thought of the trouble it would make for me.

HIGGINS. Would the world ever have been made if its maker had been afraid of making trouble? Making life means making trouble. There's only one way of escaping trouble, and that's killing things. Cowards, you notice, are always shrieking to have troublesome people killed.

LIZA. I'm no preacher; I don't notice things like that. I notice that you don't notice me.

HIGGINS (*jumping up and walking about intolerantly*). Eliza! You're an idiot. I waste the treasures of my Miltonic mind by spreading them before you. Once for all, understand that I go my way and do my work without caring twopence what happens to either of us. I am not intimidated, like your father and your stepmother. So you can come back or go to the devil — whichever you please.

LIZA. What am I to come back for?

HIGGINS (*bouncing up on his knees on the ottoman and leaning over it to her*). For the fun of it. That's why I took you on.

LIZA (*with averted face*). And you may throw me out tomorrow if I don't do everything you want me to?

HIGGINS. Yes, and you may walk out tomorrow if I don't do everything *you* want me to.

LIZA. And live with my stepmother?

HIGGINS. Yes, or sell flowers.

LIZA. Oh! if I only *could* go back to my flower basket! I should be independent of both you and father and all the world! Why did you take my independence from me? Why did I give it up? I'm a slave now, for all my fine clothes.

HIGGINS. Not a bit. I'll adopt you as my daughter and settle money on you if you like. Or would you rather marry Pickering?

LIZA (*looking fiercely round at him*). I wouldn't marry *you* if you asked me;

and you're nearer my age than what he is.

HIGGINS (*gently*). Than he is; not " than what he is."

LIZA (*losing her temper and rising*). I'll talk as I like. You're not my teacher now.

HIGGINS (*reflectively*). I don't suppose Pickering would, though. He's as confirmed an old bachelor as I am.

LIZA. That's not what I want, and don't you think it. I've always had chaps enough wanting me that way. Freddy Hill writes to me twice and three times a day, sheets and sheets.

HIGGINS (*disagreeably surprised*). Damn his impudence! (*He recoils and finds himself sitting on his heels.*)

LIZA. He has a right to if he likes, poor lad. And he does love me.

HIGGINS (*getting off the ottoman*). You have no right to encourage him.

LIZA. Every girl has a right to be loved.

HIGGINS. What! By fools like that?

LIZA. Freddy's not a fool. And if he's weak and poor and wants me, maybe he'd make me happier than my betters that bully me and don't want me.

HIGGINS. Can he *make* anything of you? That's the point.

LIZA. Perhaps I could make something of him. But I never thought of us making anything of one another; and you never think of anything else. I only want to be natural.

HIGGINS. In short, you want me to be as infatuated about you as Freddy? Is that it?

LIZA. No I don't. That's not the sort of feeling I want from you. And don't you be too sure of yourself or of me. I could have been a bad girl if I'd liked. I've seen more of some things than you, for all your learning. Girls like me can drag gentlemen down to make love to them easy enough. And they wish each other dead the next minute.

HIGGINS. Of course they do. Then what in thunder are we quarreling about?

LIZA (*much troubled*). I want a little kindness. I know I'm a common ignorant girl, and you a book-learned gentleman; but I'm not dirt under your feet. What I done (*correcting herself*) what I did was not for the dresses and the taxis. I did it because we were pleasant together and I come — came — to care for you; not to want you to make love to me, and not forgetting the difference between us, but more friendly like.

HIGGINS. Well, of course. That's just how I feel. And how Pickering feels. Eliza, you're a fool.

LIZA. That's not a proper answer to give me. (*She sinks on the chair at the writing table in tears.*)

HIGGINS. It's all you'll get until you stop being a common idiot. If you're going to be a lady, you'll have to give up feeling neglected if the men you know don't spend half their time sniveling over you and the other half giving you black eyes. If you can't stand the coldness of my sort of life, and the strain of it, go back to the gutter. Work till you are more a brute than a human being; and then cuddle and squabble and drink till you fall asleep. Oh, it's a fine life, the life of the gutter. It's real; it's warm; it's violent. You can feel it through the thickest skin; you can taste it and smell it without any training or any work. Not like Science and Literature and Classical Music and Philosophy and Art. You find me cold, unfeeling, selfish, don't you? Very well. Be off with you to the sort of people you like. Marry some sentimental hog or other with lots of money, and a thick pair of lips to kiss you with and a thick pair of boots to kick you with. If you can't appreciate what you've got, you'd better get what you can appreciate.

LIZA (*desperate*). Oh, you *are* a cruel tyrant. I can't talk to you. You turn everything against me; I'm always in the wrong. But you know very well all the time that you're nothing but a bully. You know I can't go back to the gutter, as you call it, and that I have no real friends in the world but you and the Colonel. You know well I couldn't bear to live with a low common man after you two; and it's wicked and cruel of you to insult me by pretending I could. You think I must go back to Wimpole Street because I have nowhere else to go but father's. But don't you be too sure that you have me under your feet to be trampled on and talked down. I'll marry Freddy, I will, as soon as he's able to support me.

HIGGINS (*sitting down beside her*). Rubbish! You shall marry an ambassador. You shall marry the Governor-General of India or the Lord-Lieutenant of Ireland, or somebody who wants a deputy-queen. I'm not going to have my masterpiece thrown away on Freddy.

LIZA. You think I like you to say that. But I haven't forgot what you said a minute ago, and I won't be coaxed round as if I was a baby or a puppy. If I can't have kindness, I'll have independence.

HIGGINS. Independence? That's middle class blasphemy. We are all dependent on one another, every soul of us on earth.

LIZA (*rising determinedly*). I'll let you see whether I'm dependent on you. If you can preach, I can teach. I'll go and be a teacher.

HIGGINS. What'll you teach, in heaven's name?

LIZA. What you taught me. I'll teach phonetics.

HIGGINS. Ha! ha! ha!

LIZA. I'll offer myself as an assistant to Professor Nepean.

HIGGINS (*rising in a fury*). What! That impostor! That humbug! That toadying ignoramus! Teach him *my* methods! *My* discoveries! You take one step in his direction and I'll wring your neck. (*He lays hands on her.*) Do you hear?

LIZA (*defiantly nonresistant*). Wring away. What do I care? I knew you'd strike me some day. (*He lets her go, stamping with rage at having forgotten himself, and recoils so hastily that he stumbles back into his seat on the ottoman.*) Aha! Now I know how to deal with you. What a fool I was not to think of it before! You can't take away the knowledge you gave me. You said I had a finer ear than you. And I can be civil and kind to people, which is more than you can. Aha! That's done you, Henry Higgins, it has. Now I don't care *that* (*snapping her fingers*) for your bullying and your big talk. I'll advertise it in the papers that your duchess is only a flower girl that you taught, and that she'll teach anybody to be a duchess just the same in six months for a thousand guineas. Oh, when I think of myself crawling under your feet and being trampled on and called names, when all the time I had only to lift up my finger to be as good as you, I could just kick myself.

HIGGINS (*wondering at her*). You impudent hussy, you! But it's better than sniveling; better than fetching slippers and finding spectacles, isn't it? (*Rising*) By George, Eliza, I said I'd make a woman of you; and I have. I like you like this.

LIZA. Yes, you turn round and make up to me now that I'm not afraid of you, and can do without you.

HIGGINS. Of course I do, you little fool. Five minutes ago you were like a millstone round my neck. Now you're a tower of strength, a consort battleship. You and I and Pickering will be three old bachelors together instead of only two men and a silly girl.

[MRS. HIGGINS *returns, dressed for the wedding.* ELIZA *instantly becomes cool and elegant.*]

MRS. HIGGINS. The carriage is waiting, Eliza. Are you ready?

LIZA. Quite. Is the Professor coming?

MRS. HIGGINS. Certainly not. He can't behave himself in church. He makes remarks out loud all the time on the clergyman's pronunciation.

LIZA. Then I shall not see you again, Professor. Good-by. (*She goes to the door.*)

MRS. HIGGINS (*coming to* HIGGINS). Good-by, dear.

HIGGINS. Good-by, Mother. (*He is about to kiss her, when he recollects something.*) Oh, by the way, Eliza, order a ham and a Stilton cheese, will you? And buy me a pair of reindeer gloves, number eights, and a tie to match that new suit of mine, at Eale & Binman's. You can choose the color. (*His cheerful, careless, vigorous voice shows that he is incorrigible.*)

LIZA (*disdainfully*). Buy them yourself. (*She sweeps out.*)

MRS. HIGGINS. I'm afraid you've spoiled that girl, Henry. But never mind, dear. I'll buy you the tie and gloves.

HIGGINS (*sunnily*). Oh, don't bother. She'll buy 'em all right enough. Good-by.

[*They kiss.* MRS. HIGGINS *runs out.* HIGGINS, *left alone, rattles his cash in his pocket; chuckles; and disports himself in a highly self-satisfied manner.*]

Feliks Topolski, whose line drawings appear throughout the play, was Shaw's favorite illustrator. His lively pen catches the humor and the shrewdness of Shavian characters and presents pictures that enlighten Shaw's witty style.

Of Polish ancestry, Topolski settled in England in 1935 and still lives there. He is primarily a painter, but he has also illustrated books and designed for the theater.

AN END AND A BEGINNING

1. Why do you think Eliza comes to Mrs. Higgins? What is Higgins' reaction to Eliza's disappearance?

2. Several months have passed since Alfred Doolittle followed his daughter to Henry Higgins' home. What has happened to him during this interval? How is Higgins responsible for what has happened? Through the character of Doolittle, what is Shaw saying about society?

3. How would you describe Eliza's meeting with Higgins and Pickering? Who is on the defensive? What are Eliza's feelings toward Pickering? Higgins? Her father? Find the best lines to illustrate Eliza's feelings. Compare Eliza now with the Eliza in each preceding act. Do you note any changes in Higgins in this final scene?

4. Higgins offers to adopt Eliza as his daughter and settle money on her; what other suggestions does he make? How does she react to each? What do you think Higgins' true feeling for Eliza is?

5. How is the situation at the end of the play the beginning of a new life for Eliza? Shaw ends the play without resolving the dilemma he has posed. What do you think will happen? If you are interested, read Shaw's prose sequel (in *Selected Plays of Bernard Shaw*, Dodd, Mead) in which he tells whom Eliza married, and why.

SHAW'S SATIRE

The humor of George Bernard Shaw always has a touch of satire — a sharp social lash that he flicks with superb skill. Satire, a device for exposing and discrediting vice or folly, was used by ancient Roman poets, and it has been developed into an effective and amusing literary art.

Satirists have moved from private animosity, or bitterness toward individuals, to elements in public life with which we all are concerned. All types of literature may be vehicles for satire. The spirit behind satirical writing, while it is always critical, ranges from lighthearted fun to angry denunciation.

1. *Pygmalion* is a satire on the false values of society. What classes is Shaw satirizing? What social standards does he criticize? According to Shaw, what is the most important thing each group or class does not have?

2. Make a list of the different aspects of society that Shaw satirizes in this play. How many of them do you think are justifiably ridiculed? In which instances do you disagree with Shaw's point of view?

3. Review the play, noticing what types of people are represented. For what purposes does Shaw use each of the following characters: Eliza, Higgins, Pickering, Mrs. Higgins, Mrs. Eynsford Hill, Clara, Freddy, Alfred Doolittle, Mrs. Pearce? To what extent are these characters individuals or representatives of types of people? What kind of people did Shaw admire? What kind did he dislike? Give definite evidence in support of your answers.

THE POWER OF WORDS

STAGE DIRECTIONS

Shaw is one playwright whose stage directions always are an integral part of the play. For the reader, his stage directions are an aid in visualizing the action of the characters, in understanding their attitudes, and in interpreting their personalities.

In Act II Higgins is described as acting and speaking *impetuously, peremptorily,* and *dogmatically*. In Act IV he thrusts his hands *perfunctorily* into his pockets and leaves the room with *impressive decorum*. In Act V Higgins is still, according to Shaw, an *arrogant, intolerant, incorrigible* person. What do these words mean? How do they clarify your impression of Higgins? Find words in the stage directions which help you visualize and understand other characters.

Riders to the Sea

JOHN MILLINGTON SYNGE 1871–1909

Off the bleak west coast of Ireland lie the little group of Aran Islands facing the unbroken sweep of the wind across the Atlantic Ocean. The tall cliffs of the islands, constantly beaten by heavy surf, have few safe harbors. Contact with the mainland is difficult, and the islanders lead a secluded and simple life, supporting themselves largely by mackerel fishing and the sale of seaweed containing iodine.

Probably the world at large would have known nothing about these islands had it not been for John Millington Synge (sĭng). He was a young Irishman, born near Dublin, whose ambition to write took him to the Continent to find inspiration in its literary atmosphere. In Paris he met William Butler Yeats, the great modern Irish poet, who gave him this advice: " Go to the Aran Islands. Live there as if you were one of the people themselves; express a life that has never found expression." Synge, following the suggestion, found not only the primitive life of fisherfolk but an Irish-English dialect of haunting poetic beauty.

With the materials he gathered in the Aran Islands and other parts of Ireland, Synge wrote a series of sketches and plays. Eventually they won for him a reputation as the most gifted among the many Irish playwrights contributing to the Abbey Theater in Dublin. The Abbey Players were one of the great moving forces in the " revival " of Irish culture at the turn of the century, when a new interest in old Celtic literature and language gave great impetus to the drive for Irish independence. These players still come to the United States at intervals; in the 1920's they largely inspired the " little theater " movement here.

Synge's untimely death at thirty-eight cut him off at the height of his career with only six plays to his credit. His most individual long play is the comedy, *The Playboy of the Western World*, full of quaint humor and rich imagery. Of his short plays, *Riders to the Sea* has won a secure place as a masterpiece. The poetry of its idiom (observe that it is in no sense the usual Irish brogue of the comic actor), the tragedy in the lives of its sea-bound natives, and the unforgettable character of old Maurya " keening " for her lost sons, combine in making it one of the greatest creations in Irish literature.

" Riders to the Sea" by John M. Synge. Reprinted by permission of John W. Luce and Company, and George Allen and Unwin Limited.

Characters

MAURYA, *an old woman*
BARTLEY, *her son*
CATHLEEN, *her daughter*
NORA, *a younger daughter*
Men and Women

SCENE. *An island off the coast of Ireland. Cottage kitchen, with nets, oilskins, spinning wheel, some new boards standing by the wall, etc. CATHLEEN, a girl of about twenty, finishes kneading cake, and puts it down in the pot oven by the fire; then wipes her hands, and begins to spin at the wheel. NORA, a young girl, puts her head in at the door.*

NORA (*in a low voice*). Where is she?
CATHLEEN. She's lying down, God help her, and maybe sleeping, if she's able.

[NORA *comes in softly, and takes a bundle from under her shawl.*]

CATHLEEN (*spinning the wheel rapidly*). What is it you have?
NORA. The young priest is after bringing them. It's a shirt and a plain stocking were got off a drowned man in Donegal.

[CATHLEEN *stops her wheel with a sudden movement, and leans out to listen.*]

NORA. We're to find out if it's Michael's they are; sometime herself will be down looking by the sea.
CATHLEEN. How would they be Michael's, Nora? How would he go the length of that way to the far north?
NORA. The young priest says he's known the like of it. "If it's Michael's they are," says he, "you can tell herself he's got a clean burial by the grace of God, and if they're not his, let no one say a word about them, for she'll be getting her death," says he, "with crying and lamenting."

[*The door which* NORA *half closed is blown open by a gust of wind.*]

CATHLEEN (*looking out anxiously*). Did you ask him would he stop Bartley going this day with the horses to the Galway fair?
NORA. "I won't stop him," says he, "but let you not be afraid. Herself does be saying prayers half through the night, and the Almighty God won't leave her destitute," says he, "with no son living."
CATHLEEN. Is the sea bad by the white rocks, Nora?
NORA. Middling bad, God help us. There's a great roaring in the west, and it's worse it'll be getting when the tide's turned to the wind.

[*She goes over to the table with the bundle.*]

Shall I open it now?
CATHLEEN. Maybe she'd wake up on us, and come in before we'd done. (*Coming to the table*) It's a long time we'll be, and the two of us crying.
NORA (*goes to the inner door and listens*). She's moving about on the bed. She'll be coming in a minute.
CATHLEEN. Give me the ladder, and I'll put them up in the turf loft,[1] the way she won't know of them at all, and maybe when the tide turns she'll be going down to see would he be floating from the east.

[*They put the ladder against the gable of the chimney;* CATHLEEN *goes up a few steps and hides the bundle in the turf loft.* MAURYA *comes from the inner room.*]

MAURYA (*looking up at* CATHLEEN *and speaking querulously*). Isn't it turf enough you have for this day and evening?
CATHLEEN. There's a cake baking at the fire for a short space (*throwing down the turf*) and Bartley will want it when the tide turns if he goes to Connemara.

[1] *turf loft:* loft or attic in which peat, or fuel, was stored.

[NORA *picks up the turf and puts it round the pot oven.*]

MAURYA (*sitting down on a stool at the fire*). He won't go this day with the wind rising from the south and west. He won't go this day, for the young priest will stop him surely.

NORA. He'll not stop him, Mother, and I heard Eamon Simon and Stephen Pheety and Colum Shawn saying he would go.

MAURYA. Where is he itself?

NORA. He went down to see would there be another boat sailing in the week, and I'm thinking it won't be long till he's here now, for the tide's turning at the green head, and the hooker's tacking from the east.

CATHLEEN. I hear someone passing the big stones.

NORA (*looking out*). He's coming now, and he in a hurry.

BARTLEY (*comes in and looks round the room; speaking sadly and quietly*). Where is the bit of new rope, Cathleen, was bought in Connemara?

CATHLEEN (*coming down*). Give it to him, Nora; it's on a nail by the white boards. I hung it up this morning, for the pig with the black feet was eating it.

NORA (*giving him a rope*). Is that it, Bartley?

MAURYA. You'd do right to leave that rope, Bartley, hanging by the boards. (BARTLEY *takes the rope.*) It will be wanting in this place, I'm telling you, if Michael is washed up tomorrow morning, or the next morning, or any morning in the week, for it's a deep grave we'll make him by the grace of God.

BARTLEY (*beginning to work with the rope*). I've no halter the way I can ride down on the mare, and I must go now quickly. This is the one boat going for two weeks or beyond it, and the fair will be a good fair for horses, I heard them saying below.

MAURYA. It's a hard thing they'll be saying below if the body is washed up and there's no man in it to make the coffin, and I after giving a big price for the finest white boards you'd find in Connemara.

[*She looks round at the boards.*]

BARTLEY. How would it be washed up, and we after looking each day for nine days, and a strong wind blowing a while back from the west and south?

MAURYA. If it wasn't found itself, that wind is raising the sea, and there was a star up against the moon, and it rising in the night. If it was a hundred horses, or a thousand horses you had itself, what is the price of a thousand horses against a son where there is one son only?

BARTLEY (*working at the halter, to* CATHLEEN). Let you go down each day, and see the sheep aren't jumping in on the rye, and if the jobber comes you can sell the pig with the black feet if there is a good price going.

MAURYA. How would the like of her get a good price for a pig?

BARTLEY (*to* CATHLEEN). If the west wind holds with the last bit of the moon let you and Nora get up weed enough for another cock for the kelp.[1] It's hard set we'll be from this day with no one in it but one man to work.

MAURYA. It's hard set we'll be surely the day you're drownd'd with the rest. What way will I live and the girls with me, and I an old woman looking for the grave?

[BARTLEY *lays down the halter, takes off his old coat, and puts on a newer one of the same flannel.*]

BARTLEY (*to* NORA). Is she coming to the pier?

NORA (*looking out*). She's passing the green head and letting fall her sails.

BARTLEY (*getting his purse and tobacco*). I'll have half an hour to go down, and you'll see me coming again in two days, or in three days, or maybe in four days if the wind is bad.

[1] *another . . . kelp:* another pile of seaweed. The sale of seaweed for chemical purposes was a source of income.

MAURYA (*turning round to the fire, and putting her shawl over her head*). Isn't it a hard and cruel man won't hear a word from an old woman, and she holding him from the sea?

CATHLEEN. It's the life of a young man to be going on the sea, and who would listen to an old woman with one thing and she saying it over?

BARTLEY (*taking the halter*). I must go now quickly. I'll ride down on the red mare, and the gray pony'll run behind me. The blessing of God on you.

[*He goes out.*]

MAURYA (*crying out as he is in the door*). He's gone now, God spare us, and we'll not see him again. He's gone now, and when the black night is falling I'll have no son left me in the world.

CATHLEEN. Why wouldn't you give him your blessing and he looking round in the door? Isn't it sorrow enough is on everyone in this house without your sending him out with an unlucky word behind him, and a hard word in his ear?

[MAURYA *takes up the tongs and begins raking the fire aimlessly without looking round.*]

NORA (*turning toward her*). You're taking away the turf from the cake.

CATHLEEN (*crying out*). The Son of God forgive us, Nora, we're after forgetting his bit of bread.

[*She comes over to the fire.*]

NORA. And it's destroyed he'll be going till dark night, and he after eating nothing since the sun went up.

CATHLEEN (*turning the cake out of the oven.*) It's destroyed he'll be, surely. There's no sense left on any person in a house where an old woman will be talking forever.

[MAURYA *sways herself on her stool.*]

CATHLEEN (*cutting off some of the bread and rolling it in a cloth, to* MAURYA). Let you go down now to the spring-well and give him this and he passing. You'll see him then and the dark word will be broken, and you can say, " God speed you," the way he'll be easy in his mind.

MAURYA (*taking the bread*). Will I be in it as soon as himself?

CATHLEEN. If you go now quickly.

MAURYA (*standing up unsteadily*). It's hard set I am to walk.

CATHLEEN (*looking at her anxiously*). Give her the stick, Nora, or maybe she'll slip on the big stones.

NORA. What stick?

CATHLEEN. The stick Michael brought from Connemara.

MAURYA (*taking a stick* NORA *gives her*). In the big world the old people do be leaving things after them for their sons and children, but in this place it is the young men do be leaving things behind for them that do be old.

[*She goes out slowly.* NORA *goes over to the ladder.*]

CATHLEEN. Wait, Nora, maybe she'd turn back quickly. She's that sorry, God help her, you wouldn't know the thing she'd do.

NORA. Is she gone round by the bush?

CATHLEEN (*looking out*). She's gone now. Throw it down quickly, for the Lord knows when she'll be out of it again.

NORA (*getting the bundle from the loft*). The young priest said he'd be passing tomorrow, and we might go down and speak to him below if it's Michael's they are surely.

CATHLEEN (*taking the bundle*). Did he say what way they were found?

NORA (*coming down*). " There were two men," says he, " and they rowing round with poteen [1] before the cocks crowed, and the oar of one of them caught the body, and they passing the black cliffs of the north."

CATHLEEN (*trying to open the bundle*). Give me a knife, Nora; the string's

---

[1] *poteen:* whisky manufactured illegally.

perished with the salt water, and there's a black knot on it you wouldn't loosen in a week.

NORA (*giving her a knife*). I've heard tell it was a long way to Donegal.

CATHLEEN (*cutting the string*). It is surely. There was a man in here a while ago — the man sold us that knife — and he said if you set off walking from the rocks beyond it, it would be seven days you'd be in Donegal.

NORA. And what time would a man take, and he floating?

[CATHLEEN *opens the bundle and takes out a bit of a stocking. They look at them eagerly.*]

CATHLEEN (*in a low voice*). The Lord spare us, Nora! isn't it a queer hard thing to say if it's his they are surely?

NORA. I'll get his shirt off the hook the way we can put the one flannel on the other. (*She looks through some clothes hanging in the corner.*) It's not with them, Cathleen, and where will it be?

CATHLEEN. I'm thinking Bartley put it on him in the morning, for his own shirt was heavy with the salt in it. (*Pointing to the corner*) There's a bit of a sleeve was of the same stuff. Give me that and it will do.

[NORA *brings it to her and they compare the flannel.*]

CATHLEEN. It's the same stuff, Nora; but if it is itself, aren't there great rolls of it in the shops of Galway, and isn't it many another man may have a shirt of it as well as Michael himself?

NORA (*who has taken up the stocking and counted the stitches, crying out*). It's Michael, Cathleen, it's Michael; God spare his soul, and what will herself say when she hears this story, and Bartley on the sea?

CATHLEEN (*taking the stocking*). It's a plain stocking.

NORA. It's the second one of the third pair I knitted, and I put up threescore stitches, and I dropped four of them.

CATHLEEN (*counts the stitches*). It's

that number is in it. (*Crying out*) Ah, Nora, isn't it a bitter thing to think of him floating that way to the far north, and no one to keen [1] him but the black hags that do be flying on the sea?

NORA (*swinging herself round, and throwing out her arms on the clothes*). And isn't it a pitiful thing when there is nothing left of a man who was a great rower and fisher, but a bit of an old shirt and a plain stocking?

CATHLEEN (*after an instant*). Tell me is herself coming, Nora? I hear a little sound on the path.

NORA (*looking out*). She is, Cathleen. She's coming up to the door.

CATHLEEN. Put these things away before she'll come in. Maybe it's easier she'll be after giving her blessing to Bartley, and we won't let on we've heard anything the time he's on the sea.

NORA (*helping* CATHLEEN *to close the bundle*). We'll put them here in the corner.

[*They put them into a hole in the chimney corner.* CATHLEEN *goes back to the spinning wheel.*]

NORA. Will she see it was crying I was?

CATHLEEN. Keep your back to the door the way the light'll not be on you.

[NORA *sits down at the chimney corner, with her back to the door.* MAURYA *comes in very slowly, without looking at the girls, and goes over to the stool at the other side of the fire. The cloth with the bread is still in her hand. The girls look at each other, and* NORA *points to the bundle of bread.*]

CATHLEEN (*after spinning for a moment*). You didn't give him his bit of bread?

[MAURYA *begins to keen softly, without turning round.*]

CATHLEEN. Did you see him riding down?

[MAURYA *goes on keening.*]

[1] *keen:* wail in mourning.

CATHLEEN (*a little impatiently*). God forgive you; isn't it a better thing to raise your voice and tell what you seen, than to be making lamentation for a thing that's done? Did you see Bartley, I'm saying to you.

MAURYA (*with a weak voice*). My heart's broken from this day.

CATHLEEN (*as before*). Did you see Bartley?

MAURYA. I seen the fearfulest thing.

CATHLEEN (*leaves her wheel and looks out*). God forgive you; he's riding the mare now over the green head, and the gray pony behind him.

MAURYA (*starts, so that her shawl falls back from her head and shows her white tossed hair; with a frightened voice*). The gray pony behind him.

CATHLEEN (*coming to the fire*). What is it ails you, at all?

MAURYA (*speaking very slowly*). I've seen the fearfulest thing any person has seen, since the day Bride Dara seen the dead man with the child in his arms.

CATHLEEN AND NORA. Uah.

[*They crouch down in front of the old woman at the fire.*]

NORA. Tell us what it is you seen.

MAURYA. I went down to the spring-well, and I stood there saying a prayer to myself. Then Bartley came along, and he riding on the red mare with the gray pony behind him. (*She puts up her hands, as if to hide something from her eyes.*) The Son of God spare us, Nora!

CATHLEEN. What is it you seen?

MAURYA. I seen Michael himself.

CATHLEEN (*speaking softly*). You did not, Mother; it wasn't Michael you seen, for his body is after being found in the far north, and he's got a clean burial by the grace of God.

MAURYA (*a little defiantly*). I'm after seeing him this day, and he riding and galloping. Bartley came first on the red mare; and I tried to say "God speed you," but something choked the words in my throat. He went by quickly; and,

"The blessing of God on you," says he, and I could say nothing. I looked up then, and I crying, at the gray pony, and there was Michael upon it — with fine clothes on him, and new shoes on his feet.

CATHLEEN (*begins to keen*). It's destroyed we are from this day. It's destroyed, surely.

NORA. Didn't the young priest say the Almighty God wouldn't leave her destitute with no son living?

MAURYA (*in a low voice, but clearly*). It's little the like of him knows of the sea. . . . Bartley will be lost now, and let you call in Eamon and make me a good coffin out of the white boards, for I won't live after them. I've had a husband, and a husband's father, and six sons in this house — six fine men, though it was a hard birth I had with every one of them and they coming to the world — and some of them were found and some of them were not found, but they're gone now, the lot of them. . . . There were Stephen, and Shawn, were lost in the great wind, and found after in the Bay of Gregory of the Golden Mouth, and carried up the two of them on the one plank, and in by that door.

[*She pauses for a moment, the girls start as if they heard something through the door that is half open behind them.*]

NORA (*in a whisper*). Did you hear that, Cathleen? Did you hear a noise in the northeast?

CATHLEEN (*in a whisper*). There's someone after crying out by the seashore.

MAURYA (*continues without hearing anything*). There was Sheamus and his father, and his own father again, were lost in a dark night, and not a stick or sign was seen of them when the sun went up. There was Patch after was drowned out of a currach [1] that turned over. I

---

[1] *currach* (kŭr'ăk): a small boat.

was sitting here with Bartley, and he a baby, lying on my two knees, and I seen two women, and three women, and four women coming in, and they crossing themselves, and not saying a word. I looked out then, and there were men coming after them, and they holding a thing in the half of a red sail, and water dripping out of it — it was a dry day, Nora — and leaving a track to the door.

[*She pauses again with her hand stretched out toward the door. It opens softly and old women begin to come in, crossing themselves on the threshold, and kneeling down in front of the stage with red petticoats over their heads.*]

MAURYA (*half in a dream, to* CATHLEEN). Is it Patch, or Michael, or what is it at all?

CATHLEEN. Michael is after being found in the far north, and when he is found there how could he be here in this place?

MAURYA. There does be a power of young men floating round in the sea, and what way would they know if it was Michael they had, or another man like him, for when a man is nine days in the sea, and the wind blowing, it's hard set his own mother would be to say what man was it.

CATHLEEN. It's Michael, God spare him, for they're after sending us a bit of his clothes from the far north.

[*She reaches out and hands* MAURYA *the clothes that belonged to* MICHAEL. MAURYA *stands up slowly, and takes them in her hands.* NORA *looks out.*]

NORA. They're carrying a thing among them and there's water dripping out of it and leaving a track by the big stones.

CATHLEEN (*in a whisper to the women who have come in*). Is it Bartley it is?

ONE OF THE WOMEN. It is surely, God rest his soul.

[*Two younger women come in and pull out the table. Then men carry in the* body of BARTLEY, *laid on a plank, with a bit of a sail over it, and lay it on the table.*]

CATHLEEN (*to the women, as they are doing so*). What way was he drowned?

ONE OF THE WOMEN. The gray pony knocked him into the sea, and he was washed out where there is a great surf on the white rocks.

[MAURYA *has gone over and knelt down at the head of the table. The women are keening softly and swaying themselves with a slow movement.* CATHLEEN *and* NORA *kneel at the other end of the table. The men kneel near the door.*]

MAURYA (*raising her head and speaking as if she did not see the people around her*). They're all gone now, and there isn't anything more the sea can do to me. . . . I'll have no call now to be up crying and praying when the wind breaks from the south, and you can hear the surf is in the east, and the surf is in the west, making a great stir with the two noises, and they hitting one on the other. I'll have no call now to be going down and getting holy water in the dark nights after Samhain,[1] and I won't care what way the sea is when the other women will be keening. (*To* NORA) Give me the holy water, Nora; there's a small cup still on the dresser.

[NORA *gives it to her.*]

MAURYA (*drops* MICHAEL'S *clothes across* BARTLEY'S *feet, and sprinkles the holy water over him*). It isn't that I haven't prayed for you, Bartley, to the Almighty God. It isn't that I haven't said prayers in the dark night till you wouldn't know what I'd be saying; but it's a great rest I'll have now, and it's time surely. It's a great rest I'll have now, and great sleeping in the long nights after Samhain, if it's only a bit of wet flour we do have to eat, and maybe a fish that would be stinking.

[1] *Samhain* (săm'hĭn): a Celtic feast.

[*She kneels down again, crossing herself, and saying prayers under her breath.*]

CATHLEEN (*to an old man*). Maybe yourself and Eamon would make a coffin when the sun rises. We have fine white boards herself bought, God help her, thinking Michael would be found, and I have a new cake you can eat while you'll be working.

THE OLD MAN (*looking at the boards*). Are there nails with them?

CATHLEEN. There are not, Colum; we didn't think of the nails.

ANOTHER MAN. It's a great wonder she wouldn't think of the nails, and all the coffins she's seen made already.

CATHLEEN. It's getting old she is, and broken.

[MAURYA *stands up again very slowly and spreads out the pieces of* MICHAEL'S *clothes beside the body, sprinkling them with the last of the holy water.*]

NORA (*in a whisper to* CATHLEEN). She's quiet now and easy; but the day Michael was drowned you could hear her crying out from this to the springwell. It's fonder she was of Michael, and would anyone have thought that?

CATHLEEN (*slowly and clearly*). An old woman will be soon tired with anything she will do, and isn't it nine days herself is after crying and keening, and making great sorrow in the house?

MAURYA (*puts the empty cup mouth downward on the table, and lays her hands together on* BARTLEY'S *feet*). They're all together this time, and the end is come. May the Almighty God have mercy on Bartley's soul, and on Michael's soul, and on the souls of Sheamus and Patch, and Stephen and Shawn (*bending her head*); and may He have mercy on my soul, Nora, and on the soul of everyone is left living in the world.

[*She pauses, and the keen rises a little more loudly from the women, then sinks away.*]

MAURYA (*continuing*). Michael has a clean burial in the far north, by the grace of the Almighty God. Bartley will have a fine coffin out of the white boards, and a deep grave surely. What more can we want than that? No man at all can be living forever, and we must be satisfied.

[*She kneels down again, and the curtain falls slowly.*]

AN IRISH TRAGEDY

1. As you read, did you imagine that you were seeing an actual performance of the play? How did you picture the cottage interior? In what ways do elements in the play itself — its date of writing (1904), its general tone, its geographic setting — influence your idea of how the play would look on a stage?

2. How do the opening speeches strike the note of tragedy immediately? At what point does the play reach its climax of emotion? Why does Maurya take the death of Bartley so quietly?

3. Point out how the dramatic devices of foreshadowing — hints of future events, suspense, uncertainty of outcome — are used in the play. What part does superstition play? What is the significance of the title?

4. Find examples of Irish local color. Study the idiom in which these islanders express themselves. What expressions are not found in standard English? What evidence is there that these people do farming on a small scale? that there is considerable poverty among them? that they have a strong neighborly feeling for one another?

REPORTING AND DRAMATIZATION

1. Read Eugene O'Neill's one-act tragedy *Ile* and compare it with this play as to the effect of the sea on a woman's life. Which is the more tragic? Which is the more appealing to you?

2. *Riders to the Sea* is an effective play for presentation if there are among you actors who can give an impressively serious performance, and who have mastered Irish ways of speaking. Try out members of the class with a few speeches.

The Old Lady Shows Her Medals

JAMES M. BARRIE

A one-act play
by a much-loved Scotsman
finds a new audience
through American television.

Photographs by George Joseph
from the CBS production of
The Old Lady Shows Her Medals.

JAMES M. BARRIE 1860–1937

No English writer has given more widespread delight to all ages and nations than the creator of *Peter Pan*, James M. Barrie. With Mary Martin as Peter Pan, this perennial favorite has been produced on Broadway and televised in color. While he excelled as a dramatist, Barrie is also known as a story writer and a novelist.

J. M. Barrie began life in a little Lowland village, called Kirriemuir on the map, but known as Thrums to Barrie fans. The amusing situations and racy speech of his old neighbors were recorded in *A Window in Thrums* when the author, far away from his village, was homesick. He left Scotland for England after receiving his master's degree from the University of Edinburgh when he was twenty-two. But fame shied away from him, and he said later that for three years he kept body and soul together with coffee and penny buns. Thrums won him rewards in the end, however. Many short stories and three novels based on village life brought him enthusiastic readers.

When his best-known novel, *The Little Minister*, was made into a successful play, Barrie turned his attention to the stage. With a fertile imagination, he was able to toss off play after play, once as many as three within a single year. His most popular comedies — *Quality Street, The Admirable Crichton,* and *What Every Woman Knows* — are frequently produced today in schools and colleges.

In 1913 Barrie was knighted by King George V for his marked contribution to British life and letters. His own college of Edinburgh presented him with a degree of Doctor of Letters in 1922, and made him Chancellor in 1930.

The following short play, set in London during the days of World War I, is typical of Barrie in many ways. It shows Scottish characters, in whose portrayal Barrie excelled. It blends humor and pathos, as do most of his plays. It contains the storylike and lengthy stage directions — in which playwright talks to reader — which are a trademark of Barrie plays. It shows his sympathetic portrayal of people in the humblest ranks of society, and illustrates the comment made about him that "his magic touch has ennobled and endeared the common things of life."

Characters

MRS. DOWEY
MRS. TWYMLEY
MRS. HAGGERTY
MRS. MICKLEHAM
THE REVEREND MR. WILLINGS
PRIVATE K. DOWEY

Three nice old ladies and a criminal, who is even nicer, are discussing the war over a cup of tea. The criminal, who is the hostess, calls it a dish of tea, which shows that she comes from Caledonia;[1] but that is not her crime.

They are all London charwomen,[2] but three of them, including the hostess, are what are called professionally " charwomen and" or simply " ands." An " and " is also a caretaker when required; her name is entered as such in ink in a registry book, financial transactions take place across a counter between her and the registrar, and altogether she is of a very different social status from one who, like MRS. HAGGERTY, *is a charwoman but nothing else.* MRS. HAGGERTY, *though present, is not at the party by invitation; having seen* MRS. DOWEY *buying the winkles,[3] she followed her downstairs — and so has shuffled into the play and sat down in it against our wish. We would remove her by force, or at least print her name in small letters, were it not that she takes offense very readily and says that nobody respects her. So, as you have slipped in, you can sit there,* MRS. HAGGERTY; *but keep quiet.*

There is nothing doing at present in the caretaking way for MRS. DOWEY, *our hostess; but this does not damp[4] her, caretaking being only to such as she an extra financially and a halo socially. If she had the honor of being served with an income-tax paper she would probably*

[1] *Caledonia* (kăl'ĕ·dōn′yȧ): Scotland.
[2] *charwomen:* cleaning women.
[3] *winkles:* small shellfish.
[4] *damp:* as used here, discourage.

"The Old Lady Shows Her Medals" by James Matthew Barrie, published by Charles Scribner's Sons. Reprinted by permission of the publishers.

fill in one of the nasty little compartments with the words " Trade — charring. Profession (if any) — caretaking." This home of hers (from which, to look after your house, she makes, occasionally, temporary departures in great style, escorting a barrow) is in one of those what-care-I streets that you discover only when you have lost your way; on discovering them your duty is to report them to the authorities, who immediately add them to the map of London. That is why we are now reporting Friday Street. We shall call it, in the rough sketch drawn for tomorrow's press, " Street in which the criminal resided "; and you will find MRS. DOWEY'S home therein marked with an X.

Her abode really consists of one room, but she maintains that there are two; so, rather than argue, let us say that there are two. The other one has no window, and she could not swish her old skirts in it without knocking something over; its grandest display is of tin pans and crockery on top of a dresser which has a lid to it; you have but to whip off the utensils and raise the lid, and, behold, a bath with hot and cold. MRS. DOWEY is very proud of this possession, and when she shows it off, as she does perhaps too frequently, she first signs to you with closed fist (funny old thing that she is) to approach softly.

She then tiptoes to the dresser and pops off the lid, as if to take the bath unawares. Then she sucks her lips, and is modest if you have the grace to do the exclamations.

In the real room is a bed, though that is putting the matter too briefly. The fair way to begin, if you love MRS. DOWEY, is to say to her that it is a pity she has no bed. If she is in her best form she will chuckle, and agree that the want of a bed tries her sore; she will keep you on the hooks, so to speak, as long as she can; and then, with that mouselike movement again, she will suddenly spring the bed on you. You thought it was a wardrobe, but she brings it down from the wall, and, lo, a bed. There is nothing else in her abode (which we now see to contain four rooms — kitchen, pantry, bedroom, and bathroom) that is absolutely a surprise; but it is full of " bits," every one of which has been paid ready money for and gloated over and tended until it has become part of its owner. Genuine Doweys, the dealers might call them, though there is probably nothing in the place except the bed that would fetch half a crown.

Her home is in the basement, so that the view is restricted to the lower half of persons passing overhead beyond the area stairs. Here at the window MRS.

DOWEY *sometimes sits of a summer eve-*
ning gazing, not sentimentally at a flow-
erpot which contains one poor bulb,
nor yearningly at some tiny speck of
sky, but with unholy relish at holes in
stockings, and the like, which are re-
vealed to her from her point of vantage.
You, gentle reader, may flaunt by, think-
ing that your finery awes the street; but
MRS. DOWEY *can tell (and does) that*
your soles are in need of neat repair.

Also, lower parts being as expressive
as the face to those whose view is thus
limited, she could swear to scores of the
passers-by in a court of law.

These four lively old codgers are hav-
ing a good time at the tea table, and wit
is flowing free. As you can see by their
everyday garments, and by their pails
and mops (which are having a little tea
party by themselves in the corner), it is
not a gathering by invitations stretching
away into yesterday. It is a purely in-
formal affair, so much more attractive
—don't you think? — than banquets
elaborately prearranged. You know how
they come about, especially in wartime.
Very likely MRS. DOWEY *met* MRS.
TWYMLEY *and* MRS. MICKLEHAM *quite*
casually in the street, and meant to do
no more than pass the time of day;
then, naturally enough, the word cam-

ouflage [1] *was mentioned and they got*
heated, but in the end MRS. TWYMLEY
apologized; then, in the odd way in
which one thing leads to another, the
winkleman appeared, and MRS. DOWEY
remembered that she had that pot of jam
and that MRS. MICKLEHAM *had stood*
treat last time; and soon they were all
three descending the area stairs, fol-
lowed cringingly by the HAGGERTY WOM-
AN.

They have been extremely merry, and
never were four hard-worked old ladies
who deserved it better. All a woman
can do in wartime they do daily and
cheerfully, just as their menfolk are do-
ing it at the Front; and now, with the
mops and pails laid aside, they sprawl
gracefully at ease. There is no intention
on their part to consider peace terms
until a decisive victory has been gained
in the field (Sarah Ann Dowey), until
the Kaiser is put to the rightabout (Em-
ma Mickleham) and singing very small
(Amelia Twymley).

At this tea party the lady who is to
play the part of MRS. DOWEY *is sure to*
want to suggest that our heroine has a

[1] *camouflage* (kăm′ oo·fläzh): in the old ladies'
time, a new and exciting word. It refers to various ways of disguising military equipment or
installations.

These four lively old codgers are having a good time at the tea table.

secret sorrow; namely, the crime. But you should see us knocking that idea out of her head! MRS. DOWEY *knows she is a criminal, but, unlike the actress, she does not know that she is about to be found out; and she is, to put it bluntly in her own Scotch way, the merriest of the whole clamjamfry. She presses more tea on her guests, but they wave her away from them in the pretty manner of ladies who know that they have already had more than enough.*

MRS. DOWEY. Just one more winkle, Mrs. Mickleham?

[Indeed there is only one more. But MRS. MICKLEHAM *indicates politely that if she took this one it would have to swim for it. The* HAGGERTY WOMAN *takes it long afterward when she thinks, erroneously, that no one is looking.* MRS. TWYMLEY *is sulking. Evidently someone has contradicted her. Probably the* HAGGERTY WOMAN.*]*

MRS. TWYMLEY. I say it is so.

THE HAGGERTY WOMAN. I say it may be so.

MRS. TWYMLEY. I suppose I ought to know: me that has a son a prisoner in Germany. *(She has so obviously scored that all good feeling seems to call upon her to end here. But she continues, rather shabbily.)* Being the only lady present that has that proud misfortune.

[The others are stung.]

MRS. DOWEY. My son is fighting in France.

MRS. MICKLEHAM. Mine is wounded in two places.

THE HAGGERTY WOMAN. Mine is at Salonaiky.[1]

[The absurd pronunciation of this uneducated person moves the others to mirth.]

MRS. DOWEY. You'll excuse us, Mrs. Haggerty, but the correct pronunciation is Salonikky.

THE HAGGERTY WOMAN *(to cover her confusion).* I don't think. *(She feels that even this does not prove her case.)* And I speak as one that has War Savings Certificates.

MRS. TWYMLEY. We all have them.

[The HAGGERTY WOMAN *whimpers, and the other guests regard her with unfeeling disdain.]*

MRS. DOWEY *(to restore cheerfulness).* Oh, it's a terrible war.

ALL *(brightening).* It is. You may say so.

MRS. DOWEY *(encouraged).* What I say is, the men is splendid; but I'm none so easy about the staff. That's your weak point, Mrs. Mickleham.

MRS. MICKLEHAM *(on the defense, but determined to reveal nothing that might be of use to the enemy).* You may take it from me, the staff's all right.

MRS. DOWEY. And very relieved I am to hear you say it.

[It is here that the HAGGERTY WOMAN *has the remaining winkle.]*

MRS. MICKLEHAM. You don't understand properly about trench warfare. If I had a map —

MRS. DOWEY *(wetting her finger to draw lines on the table).* That's the river Sommy.[2] Now, if we had barrages here —

MRS. TWYMLEY. Very soon you would be enfilded.[3] Where's your supports, my lady?

[MRS. DOWEY is damped.]

MRS. MICKLEHAM. What none of you grasps is that this is a artillery war —

[1] *Salonaiky:* her mispronunciation of Salonika (săl'ō·nē'kà), Greece, where a great naval battle took place in World War I.

[2] *Sommy:* her mispronunciation of the French river Somme (sôm), a scene of many conflicts in World War I.

[3] *enfilded:* her mispronunciation of enfiladed (ĕn'fĭ·lād'ĕd), a military term meaning "raked by gunfire."

THE HAGGERTY WOMAN (*strengthened by the winkle*). I say that the word is Salonaiky.

[*The others purse their lips.*]

MRS. TWYMLEY (*with terrible meaning*). We'll change the subject. Have you seen this week's *Fashion Chat*? (*She has evidently seen and devoured it herself, and even licked up the crumbs.*) The gabardine with accordion pleats has quite gone out.

MRS. DOWEY (*her old face sparkling*). My sakes! You tell me?

MRS. TWYMLEY (*with the touch of haughtiness that comes of great topics*). The plain smock has come in again, with silk lacing, giving that charming chic effect.

MRS. DOWEY. Oho!

MRS. MICKLEHAM. I must say I was always partial to the straight line (*thoughtfully regarding the want of line in* MRS. TWYMLEY'S *person*) though trying to them as is of too friendly a figure.

[*It is here that the* HAGGERTY WOMAN'S *fingers close unostentatiously upon a piece of sugar.*]

MRS. TWYMLEY (*sailing into the empyrean*[1]). Lady Dolly Kanister was seen conversing across the railings in a dainty *de jou.*[2]

MRS. DOWEY. Fine would I have liked to see her.

MRS. TWYMLEY. She is equally popular as maid, wife, and munition worker. Her two children is inset.[3] Lady Pops Babington was married in a tight tulle.

MRS. MICKLEHAM. What was her going-away dress?

MRS. TWYMLEY. A champagny cream

velvet with dreamy corsage. She's married to Colonel the Honorable Chingford — "Snubs," they called him at Eton.

THE HAGGERTY WOMAN (*having disposed of the sugar*). Very likely he'll be sent to Salonaiky.

MRS. MICKLEHAM. Wherever he is sent, she'll have the same tremors as the rest of us. She'll be as keen to get the letters wrote with pencils as you or me.

MRS. TWYMLEY. Them pencil letters!

MRS. DOWEY (*in her sweet Scotch voice, timidly, afraid she may be going too far*). And women in enemy lands gets those pencil letters and then stop getting them, the same as ourselves. Let's occasionally think of that.

[*She has gone too far. Chairs are pushed back.*]

THE HAGGERTY WOMAN. I ask you!

MRS. MICKLEHAM. That's hardly language, Mrs. Dowey.

MRS. DOWEY (*scared*). Kindly excuse. I swear to death I'm none of your pacifists.

MRS. MICKLEHAM. Freely granted.

MRS. TWYMLEY. I've heard of females that have no male relations, and so they have no man-party at the wars. I've heard of them, but I don't mix with them.

MRS. MICKLEHAM. What can the likes of us have to say to them? It's not their war.

MRS. DOWEY (*wistfully*). They are to be pitied.

MRS. MICKLEHAM. But the place for them, Mrs. Dowey, is within doors with the blinds down.

MRS. DOWEY (*hurriedly*). That's the place for them.

MRS. MICKLEHAM. I saw one of them today buying a flag. I thought it was very impudent of her.

MRS. DOWEY (*meekly*). So it was.

MRS. MICKLEHAM (*trying to look modest with indifferent success*). I had a letter from my son, Percy, yesterday.

---

[1] *empyrean* (ĕm'pĭ·rē'ăn): the highest part of heaven.

[2] *de jou* (dĕ zhōō): a dress "for play" (French).

[3] *inset:* Pictures of Lady Kanister's two children were apparently inserted into the larger picture of her.

MRS. TWYMLEY. Alfred sent me his photo.

THE HAGGERTY WOMAN. Letters from Salonaiky is less common.

[*Three bosoms heave, but not, alas,* MRS. DOWEY'S. *Nevertheless she doggedly knits her lips.*]

MRS. DOWEY (*the criminal*). Kenneth writes to me every week. (*There are exclamations. The dauntless old thing holds aloft a packet of letters.*) Look at this. All his.

[*The* HAGGERTY WOMAN *whimpers.*]

MRS. TWYMLEY. Alfred has little time for writing, being a bombardier.

MRS. DOWEY (*relentlessly*). Do your letters begin " Dear mother "?

" *Kenneth writes to me every week.*"

MRS. TWYMLEY. Generally.

MRS. MICKLEHAM. Invariable.

THE HAGGERTY WOMAN. Every time.

MRS. DOWEY (*delivering the knock-out blow*). Kenneth's begin " Dearest mother."

[*No one can think of the right reply.*]

MRS. TWYMLEY (*doing her best*). A short man, I should say, judging by yourself. (*She ought to have left it alone.*)

MRS. DOWEY. Six feet two — and a half.

[*The gloom deepens.*]

MRS. MICKLEHAM (*against her better judgment*). A kilty, did you tell me?

MRS. DOWEY. Most certainly. He's in the famous Black Watch.

THE HAGGERTY WOMAN (*producing her handkerchief*). The Surrey Rifles is the famousest.

MRS. MICKLEHAM. There you and the King disagrees, Mrs. Haggerty. His choice is the Buffs, same as my Percy's.

MRS. TWYMLEY (*magnanimously*). Give me the R.H.A.[1] and you can keep all the rest.

MRS. DOWEY. I'm sure I have nothing to say against the Surreys and the R.H.A. and Buffs; but they are just breeches regiments, I understand.

THE HAGGERTY WOMAN. We can't all be kilties.

MRS. DOWEY (*crushingly*). That's very true.

MRS. TWYMLEY (*it is foolish of her, but she can't help saying it*). Has your Kenneth great hairy legs?

MRS. DOWEY. Tremendous.

[*The wicked woman, but let us also say " Poor Sarah Ann Dowey." For, at this moment, enter Nemesis.[2] In other words, the less important part of a clergyman appears upon the stair.*]

MRS. MICKLEHAM. It's the reverent gent!

MRS. DOWEY (*little knowing what he is bringing her*). I see he has had his boots heeled.

[*It may be said of* MR. WILLINGS *that his happy smile always walks in front of him. This smile makes music of his life; it means that once again he has been chosen, in his opinion, as the central figure in romance. No one can well have led a more drab existence, but he will never know it; he will always think of himself, humbly though elatedly, as the chosen of the gods. Of*

[1] *Black Watch, Surrey Rifles, Buffs,* and *R.H.A.:* well-known British army regiments.

[2] *Nemesis* (něm′ě·sĭs): avenging fate (Greek mythology).

him must it have been originally written that adventures are for the adventurous. He meets them at every street corner. For instance, he assists an old lady off a bus and asks her if he can be of any further help. She tells him that she wants to know the way to Maddox the butcher's. Then comes the kind, triumphant smile; it always comes first, followed by its explanation, " I was there yesterday!" This is the merest sample of the adventures that keep MR. WILLINGS *up to the mark.*

[*Since the war broke out, his zest for life has become almost terrible. He can scarcely lift a newspaper and read of a hero without remembering that he knows someone of the same name. The Soldiers' Rest he is connected with was once a china emporium, and — mark my words — he had bought his tea service at it. Such is life when you are in the thick of it. Sometimes he feels that he is part of a gigantic spy drama. In the course of his extraordinary comings and goings he meets with Great Personages, of course, and is the confidential recipient of secret news. Before imparting the news he does not, as you might expect, first smile expansively; on the contrary, there comes over his face an awful solemnity, which, however, means the same thing. When divulging the names of the personages, he first looks around to make sure that no suspicious character is about, and then, lowering his voice, tells you, " I had that from Mr. Farthing himself — he is the secretary of the Bethnal Green Branch — H'sh . . ."*]

[*There is a commotion about finding a worthy chair for " the reverent," and there is also some furtive pulling down of sleeves; but he stands surveying the ladies through his triumphant smile. This amazing man knows that he is about to score again.*]

MR. WILLINGS (*waving aside the chairs*). I thank you. But not at all. Friends, I have news.

MRS. MICKLEHAM. News?

THE HAGGERTY WOMAN. From the Front?

MRS. TWYMLEY. My Alfred, sir?

[*They are all grown suddenly anxious — all except the hostess, who knows that there can never be any news from the Front for her.*]

MR. WILLINGS. I tell you at once that all is well. The news is for Mrs. Dowey.

" Now, now, ladies, good news doesn't kill."

MRS. DOWEY (*she stares*). News for me?

MR. WILLINGS. Your son, Mrs. Dowey — he has got five days' leave.

[*She shakes her head slightly, or perhaps it only trembles a little on its stem.*]

Now, now, good news doesn't kill.

MRS. TWYMLEY. We're glad, Mrs. Dowey.

MRS. DOWEY. You're sure?

MR. WILLINGS. Quite sure. He has arrived.

MRS. DOWEY. He is in London?

MR. WILLINGS. He is. I have spoken to him.

MRS. MICKLEHAM. You lucky woman.

[*They might see that she is not looking lucky, but experience has told them how differently these things take people.*]

MR. WILLINGS (*marveling more and more as he unfolds his tale*). Ladies, it is quite a romance. I was in the . . . (*He looks around cautiously, but he knows that they are all to be trusted.*) . . . in the Church Army quarters in Central Street, trying to get on the track of one or two of our missing men. Suddenly my eyes — I can't account for it — but suddenly my eyes alighted on a Highlander seated rather drearily on a bench, with his kit at his feet.

THE HAGGERTY WOMAN. A big man?

MR. WILLINGS. A great brawny fellow.

[*The* HAGGERTY WOMAN *groans.*]

" My friend," I said at once, " welcome back to Blighty." [1] I make a point of calling it Blighty. " I wonder," I said, " if there is anything I can do for you? " He shook his head. " What regiment? " I asked. (*Here* MR. WILLINGS *very properly lowers his voice to a whisper.*) " Black Watch, 5th Battalion," he said. " Name? " I asked. " Dowey," he said.

_____

[1] *Blighty* (blĭ′tĭ): British slang for home, much used by soldiers.

MRS. MICKLEHAM. I declare. I do declare.

MR. WILLINGS (*showing how the thing was done, with the help of a chair*). I put my hand on his shoulder as it might be thus. " Kenneth Dowey," I said, " I know your mother."

MRS. DOWEY (*wetting her lips*). What did he say to that?

MR. WILLINGS. He was incredulous. Indeed, he seemed to think I was balmy. But I offered to bring him straight to you. I told him how much you had talked to me about him.

MRS. DOWEY. Bring him here!

MRS. MICKLEHAM. I wonder he needed to be brought.

MR. WILLINGS. He had just arrived, and was bewildered by the great city. He listened to me in the taciturn Scotch way, and then he gave a curious laugh.

MRS. TWYMLEY. Laugh?

MR. WILLINGS (*whose wild life has brought him into contact with the strangest people*). The Scotch, Mrs. Twymley, express their emotions differently from us. With them tears signify a rollicking mood, while merriment denotes that they are plunged in gloom. When I had finished he said at once, " Let us go and see the old lady."

MRS. DOWEY (*backing, which is the first movement she has made since he began his tale*). Is he — coming?

MR. WILLINGS (*gloriously*). He has come. He is up there. I told him I thought I had better break the joyful news to you.

[*Three women rush to the window.* MRS. DOWEY *looks at her pantry door, but perhaps she remembers that it does not lock on the inside. She stands rigid, though her face has gone very gray.*]

MRS. DOWEY. Kindly get them to go away.

MR. WILLINGS. Ladies, I think this happy occasion scarcely requires you. (*He is not the man to ask of woman a* sacrifice that he is not prepared to make himself.) I also am going instantly.

[*They all survey* MRS. DOWEY, *and understand — or think they understand.*]

MRS. TWYMLEY (*pail and mop in hand*). I would thank none for their company if my Alfred was at the door.
MRS. MICKLEHAM (*similarly burdened*). The same from me. Shall I send him down, Mrs. Dowey?

[*The old lady does not hear her. She is listening, terrified, for a step on the stairs.*]

Look at the poor, joyous thing, sir. She has his letters in her hand.

[*The three women go.* MR. WILLINGS *puts a kind hand on* MRS. DOWEY'S *shoulder. He thinks he so thoroughly understands the situation.*]

MR. WILLINGS. A good son, Mrs. Dowey, to have written to you so often.

[*Our old criminal quakes, but she grips the letters more tightly.* PRIVATE DOWEY *descends.*]

Dowey, my friend, there she is, waiting for you, with your letters in her hand.
DOWEY (*grimly*). That's great.

[MR. WILLINGS *ascends the stair without one backward glance, like the good gentleman he is; and the* DOWEYS *are left together, with nearly the whole room between them. He is a great rough chunk of Scotland, howked out of her not so much neatly as liberally; and in his Black Watch uniform, all caked with mud, his kit and nearly all his worldly possessions on his back, he is an apparition scarcely less fearsome (but so much less ragged) than those ancestors of his who trotted with Prince Charlie [1] to Derby. He stands silent, scowling at the old lady, daring her to raise her*

[1] *Prince Charlie:* the Young Pretender to the British throne in the eighteenth century.

He is a great rough chunk of Scotland.

head; and she would like very much to do it, for she longs to have a first glimpse of her son. When he does speak, it is to jeer at her.]

DOWEY. Do you recognize your loving son, missis?

[" *Oh, the fine Scotch tang of him,*" *she thinks.*]

MRS. DOWEY (*trembling*). I'm pleased you wrote so often. ("*Oh, but he's raised,*" [2] *she thinks.*)

[*He strides toward her, and seizes the letters roughly.*]

DOWEY. Let's see them.

[2] *raised:* annoyed.

[There is a string round the package and he unties it, and examines the letters at his leisure with much curiosity. The envelopes are in order, all addressed in pencil to MRS. DOWEY, *with the proud words " Opened by Censor " on them. But the letter paper inside contains not a word of writing.]*

DOWEY. Nothing but blank paper! Is this your writing in pencil on the envelope? (*She nods, and he gives the matter further consideration.*) The covey [1] told me you were a charwoman. So I suppose you picked the envelopes out of wastepaper baskets, or such like, and then changed the addresses?

[She nods again; still she dare not look up, but she is admiring his legs. When, however, he would cast the letters into the fire, she flames up with sudden spirit. She clutches them.]

MRS. DOWEY. Don't burn them letters, mister.

DOWEY. They're not real letters.

MRS. DOWEY. They're all I have.

DOWEY (*returning to irony*). I thought you had a son?

MRS. DOWEY. I never had a man nor a son nor anything. I just call myself Missis to give me a standing.

DOWEY. Well, it's past my seeing through.

[He turns to look for some explanation from the walls. She gets a peep at him at last. Oh, what a grandly set-up man! Oh, the stride of him. Oh, the noble rage of him. Oh, Samson had been like this before that woman took him in hand.[2]]

DOWEY (*whirling round on her*). What made you do it?

MRS. DOWEY. It was everybody's war, mister, except mine. (*She beats her arms.*) I wanted it to be my war too.

DOWEY. You'll need to be plainer. And yet I'm d——d if I care to hear you, you lying old trickster.

[The words are merely what were to be expected, and so are endurable; but he has moved toward the door.]

MRS. DOWEY. You're not going already, mister?

DOWEY. Yes, I just came to give you an ugly piece of my mind.

MRS. DOWEY (*holding out her arms longingly*). You haven't gave it to me yet.

DOWEY. You have a cheek!

MRS. DOWEY (*giving further proof of it*). You wouldn't drink some tea?

DOWEY. Me! I tell you I came here for the one purpose of blazing away at you.

[It is such a roaring negative that it blows her into a chair. But she is up again in a moment, is this spirited old lady.]

MRS. DOWEY. You could drink the tea while you was blazing away. There's winkles.

DOWEY. Is there? (*He turns interestedly toward the table, but his proud Scots character checks him — which is just as well, for what she should have said was that there had been winkles.*) Not me. You're just a common rogue.

---

[1] *covey* (kŭv'ĭ): slang for *fellow.*

[2] *Samson . . . in hand:* In the Bible, Samson was betrayed to his enemies by Delilah, who sheared his hair — the source of his strength — while he slept.

(*He seats himself far from the table.*)
Now, then, out with it. Sit down! (*She
sits meekly; there is nothing she would
not do for him.*) As you char, I suppose
you are on your feet all day.

MRS. DOWEY. I'm more on my knees.

DOWEY. That's where you should be
to me.

MRS. DOWEY. Oh, mister, I'm willing.

DOWEY. Stop it. Go on, you accomplished liar.

MRS. DOWEY. It's true that my name is
Dowey.

DOWEY. It's enough to make me
change mine.

MRS. DOWEY. I've been charring and
charring and charring as far back as I
mind. I've been in London this twenty
years.

DOWEY. We'll skip your early days. I
have an appointment.

MRS. DOWEY. And then when I was
old the war broke out.

DOWEY. How could it affect you?

MRS. DOWEY. Oh, mister, that's the
thing. It didn't affect me. It affected
everybody but me. The neighbors
looked down on me. Even the posters,
on the walls, of the woman saying " Go,
my boy," leered at me. I sometimes
cried by myself in the dark. You won't
have a cup of tea?

DOWEY. No.

MRS. DOWEY. Suddenlike the idea
came to me to pretend I had a son.

DOWEY. You depraved old limmer! [1]
But what in the name of Old Nick made
you choose me out of the whole British
Army?

MRS. DOWEY (*giggling*). Maybe, mister, it was because I liked you best.

DOWEY. Now, now, woman.

MRS. DOWEY. I read one day in the
papers, " In which he was assisted by
Private K. Dowey, 5th Battalion, Black
Watch."

DOWEY (*flattered*). Did you, now!
Well, I expect that's the only time I was
ever in the papers.

MRS. DOWEY (*trying it on again*). I
didn't choose you for that alone. I read
a history of the Black Watch first, to
make sure it was the best regiment in
the world.

DOWEY. Anybody could have told you
that. (*He is moving about now in better
humor, and, meeting the loaf in his
stride, he cuts a slice from it. He is
hardly aware of this, but* MRS. DOWEY
knows.) I like the Scotch voice of you,
woman. It drumbles on like a hill burn. [2]

MRS. DOWEY. Prosen Water runs by
where I was born. Maybe it teached me
to speak, mister.

DOWEY. Canny, woman, canny.

MRS. DOWEY. I read about the Black
Watch's ghostly piper that plays proudly
when the men of the Black Watch do
well, and prouder when they fall.

DOWEY. There's some foolish story of
that kind. (*He has another careless slice
off the loaf.*) But you couldn't have been
living here at that time or they would
have guessed. I suppose you flitted? [3]

MRS. DOWEY. Yes, it cost me eleven
and sixpence.

DOWEY. How did you guess the *K* in
my name stood for Kenneth?

MRS. DOWEY. Does it?

DOWEY. Umpha.

MRS. DOWEY. An angel whispered it
to me in my sleep.

DOWEY. Well, that's the only angel in
the whole black business. (*He chuckles.*)
You little thought I would turn up!
(*Wheeling suddenly on her*) Or did
you?

MRS. DOWEY. I was beginning to
weary for a sight of you, Kenneth.

DOWEY. What word was that?

MRS. DOWEY. Mister.

[*He helps himself to butter, and she
holds out the jam pot to him; but he
haughtily rejects it. Do you think she
gives in now? Not a bit of it. He returns to sarcasm.*]

---

[1] *limmer:* Scotch for rascal.

[2] *burn:* Scotch for brook.
[3] *flitted:* moved.

DOWEY. I hope you're pleased with me now you see me.

MRS. DOWEY. I'm very pleased. Does your folk live in Scotland?

DOWEY. Glasgow.

MRS. DOWEY. Both living?

DOWEY. Ay.

MRS. DOWEY. Is your mother terrible proud of you?

DOWEY. Naturally.

MRS. DOWEY. You'll be going to them?

DOWEY. After I've had a skite [1] in London first.

MRS. DOWEY (*sniffing*). So she is in London!

DOWEY. Who?

MRS. DOWEY. Your young lady.

DOWEY. Are you jealyous?

MRS. DOWEY. Not me.

DOWEY. You needna be. She's a young thing.

MRS. DOWEY. You surprises me. A beauty, no doubt?

DOWEY. You may be sure. (*He tries the jam.*) She's a titled person. She is equally popular as maid, wife, and munition worker.

[MRS. DOWEY *remembers Lady Dolly Kanister, so familiar to readers of fashionable gossip, and a very leery expression indeed comes into her face.*]

MRS. DOWEY. Tell me more about her, man.

DOWEY. She has sent me a lot of things, especially cakes, and a worsted waistcoat, with a loving message on the enclosed card.

[*The old lady is now in a quiver of excitement. She loses control of her arms, which jump excitedly this way and that.*]

MRS. DOWEY. You'll try one of my cakes, mister?

DOWEY. Not me.

MRS. DOWEY. They're of my own making.

DOWEY. No, I thank you.

[*But with a funny little run she is in the pantry and back again. She pushes a cake before him, at sight of which he gapes.*]

MRS. DOWEY. What's the matter? Tell me, oh, tell me, mister!

DOWEY. That's exactly the kind of cake that her ladyship sends me.

[MRS. DOWEY *is now a very glorious old character indeed.*]

MRS. DOWEY. Is the waistcoat right, mister? I hope the Black Watch colors pleased you.

DOWEY. What-at! Was it you?

MRS. DOWEY. I daredna give my own name, you see, and I was always reading hers in the papers.

[*The badgered man looms over her, terrible for the last time.*]

DOWEY. Woman, is there no getting rid of you!

MRS. DOWEY. Are you angry?

[*He sits down with a groan.*]

DOWEY. Oh, hell! Give me some tea.

[*She rushes about preparing a meal for him, every bit of her wanting to cry out to every other bit, "Oh, glory,*

glory, glory!" For a moment she hovers behind his chair. "Kenneth!" she murmurs. "What?" he asks, no longer aware that she is taking a liberty. "Nothing," she says. "Just Kenneth," and is off gleefully for the tea caddy. But when his tea is poured out, and he has drunk a saucerful, the instinct of self-preservation returns to him between two bites.]

DOWEY. Don't you be thinking, missis, for one minute that you have got me.

MRS. DOWEY. No, no.

[On that understanding he unbends.]

DOWEY. I have a theater tonight, followed by a randy-dandy.[1]

MRS. DOWEY. Oho! Kenneth, this is a queer first meeting!

DOWEY. It is, woman — oh, it is — *(guardedly)* — and it's also a last meeting.

MRS. DOWEY. Yes, yes.

DOWEY. So here's to you — you old mop and pail. *Ave atque vale.*

MRS. DOWEY. What's that?

DOWEY. That means Hail and Farewell.

MRS. DOWEY. Are you a scholar?

DOWEY. Being Scotch, there's almost nothing I don't know.

MRS. DOWEY. What was you to trade?

DOWEY. Carter, glazier, orraman,[2] any rough jobs.

MRS. DOWEY. You're a proper man to look at.

DOWEY. I'm generally admired.

MRS. DOWEY. She's an enviable woman.

DOWEY. Who?

MRS. DOWEY. Your mother.

DOWEY. Eh? Oh, that was just protecting myself from you. I have neither father nor mother nor wife nor grandmama. *(Bitterly)* This party never even knew who his proud parents were.

MRS. DOWEY. Is that — *(gleaming)* — is that true?

DOWEY. It's gospel.

MRS. DOWEY. Heaven be praised!

DOWEY. Eh? None of that! I was a fool to tell you. But don't think you can take advantage of it. Pass the cake.

MRS. DOWEY. I daresay it's true we'll never meet again, Kenneth, but — but if we do, I wonder where it will be?

DOWEY. Not in this world.

MRS. DOWEY. There's no telling — *(leering ingratiatingly)* — it might be at Berlin.

DOWEY. Tod, if I ever get to Berlin, I believe I'll find you there waiting for me!

MRS. DOWEY. With a cup of tea for you in my hand.

DOWEY. Yes, and *(heartily)* very good tea too.

[He has partaken heavily; he is now in high good humor.]

MRS. DOWEY. Kenneth, we could come back by Paris!

DOWEY. All the ladies likes to go to Paris.

MRS. DOWEY. Oh, Kenneth, Kenneth, if just once before I die I could be fitted for a Paris gown with dreamy corsage!

DOWEY. You're all alike, old covey. We have a song about it. *(He sings)*:

Mrs. Gill is very ill,
    Nothing can improve her
But to see the Tuileries [3]
    And waddle through the Louvre.[4]

[No song ever had a greater success. MRS. DOWEY is doubled up with mirth. When she comes to — when they both come to, for they are a pair of them — she cries:]

MRS. DOWEY. You must learn me that *(and off she goes in song also)*:

---

[1] *randy-dandy:* a noisy frolic.
[2] *orraman:* one who does odd jobs.

[3] *Tuileries* (twē'lĕr·ĭz): famous royal palace in Paris.
[4] *Louvre* (loo'vr'): famous art gallery connected with the Tuileries.

Mrs. Dowey's very ill,
    Nothing can improve her.

DOWEY. Stop!

But dressed up in a Paris gown
    To waddle through the Louvre.

[*They fling back their heads. She points at him; he points at her.*]

MRS. DOWEY (*ecstatically*). Hairy legs!

[*A mad remark, which brings him to his senses; he remembers who and what she is.*]

DOWEY. Mind your manners! (*Rising*) Well, thank you for my tea. I must be stepping.

[*Poor* MRS. DOWEY, *he is putting on his kit.*]

" *Well, thank you for my tea.*"

MRS. DOWEY. Where are you living?
DOWEY. (*He sighs.*) That's the question. But there's a place called The Hut, where some of the 2nd Battalion are. They'll take me in. Beggars — (*bitterly*) — can't be choosers.
MRS. DOWEY. Beggars?
DOWEY. I've never been here before. If you knew (*a shadow comes over him*) what it is to be in such a place without a friend. I was crazy with glee, when I got my leave, at the thought of seeing London at last; but after wandering its streets for four hours, I would almost have been glad to be back in the trenches.

["*If you knew,*" *he has said, but indeed the old lady knows.*]

MRS. DOWEY. That's my quandorum too, Kenneth.

[*He nods sympathetically.*]

DOWEY. I'm sorry for you, you poor old body (*shouldering his kit*) but I see no way out for either of us.
MRS. DOWEY (*cooing*). Do you not?
DOWEY. Are you at it again!

[*She knows that it must be now or never. She has left her biggest guns for the end. In her excitement she is rising up and down on her toes.*]

MRS. DOWEY. Kenneth, I've heard that the thing a man on leave longs for more than anything else is a bed with sheets, and a bath.
DOWEY. You never heard anything truer.
MRS. DOWEY. Go into that pantry, Kenneth Dowey, and lift the dresser top, and tell me what you see.

[*He goes. There is an awful stillness. He returns, impressed.*]

DOWEY. It's a kind of a bath!
MRS. DOWEY. You could do yourself there pretty, half at a time.
DOWEY. Me?
MRS. DOWEY. There's a woman through the wall that would be very willing to give me a shakedown till your leave is up.
DOWEY. (*He snorts.*) Oh, is there!

[*She has not got him yet, but there is still one more gun.*]

MRS. DOWEY. Kenneth, look!

[*With these simple words she lets down the bed. She says no more; an effect like this would be spoiled by language. Fortunately he is not made of stone. He thrills.*]

" I'm just the commonest kind of old wifie myself."

DOWEY. Gosh! That's the dodge we need in the trenches.

MRS. DOWEY. That's your bed, Kenneth.

DOWEY. Mine? (*He grins at her.*) You queer old divert.[1] What can make you so keen to be burdened by a lump like me?

MRS. DOWEY. He! he! he! he!

DOWEY. I tell you, I'm the commonest kind of man.

MRS. DOWEY. I'm just the commonest kind of old wifie myself.

DOWEY. I've been a kick-about all my life, and I'm no great shakes at the war.

MRS. DOWEY. Yes, you are. How many Germans have you killed?

DOWEY. Just two for certain, and there was no glory in it. It was just because they wanted my shirt.

MRS. DOWEY. Your shirt?

DOWEY. Well, they said it was their shirt.

MRS. DOWEY. Have you took prisoners?

DOWEY. I once took half a dozen, but that was a poor affair too.

MRS. DOWEY. How could one man take half a dozen?

DOWEY. Just in the usual way. I surrounded them.

---

[1] *divert* (dĭ′vŭrt): slang for an odd or different person.

MRS. DOWEY. Kenneth, you're just my ideal.

DOWEY. You're easily pleased. (*He turns again to the bed.*) Let's see how the thing works. (*He kneads the mattress with his fist, and the result is so satisfactory that he puts down his kit.*) Old lady, if you really want me, I'll bide.

MRS. DOWEY. Oh! oh! oh! oh!

[*Her joy is so demonstrative that he has to drop a word of warning.*]

DOWEY. But, mind you, I don't accept you as a relation. For your personal glory you can go on pretending to the neighbors, but the best I can say for you is that you're on your probation. I'm a cautious character, and we must see how you'll turn out.

MRS. DOWEY. Yes, Kenneth.

DOWEY. And now, I think, for that bath. My theater begins at six-thirty. A cove I met on a bus is going with me.

MRS. DOWEY. (*She is a little alarmed.*) You're sure you'll come back?

DOWEY. Yes, yes. (*Handsomely*) I leave my kit in pledge.

MRS. DOWEY. You won't liquor up too freely, Kenneth?

DOWEY. You're the first (*chuckling*) to care whether I do or not. (*Nothing she has said has pleased the lonely man so much as this.*) I promise. Tod, I'm beginning to look forward to being wakened in the morning by hearing you cry, " Get up, you lazy swine." I've kind of envied men that had womenfolk with the right to say that.

[*He is passing to the bathroom when a diverting notion strikes him.*]

MRS. DOWEY. What is it, Kenneth?

DOWEY. The theater. It would be showier if I took a lady.

[MRS. DOWEY *feels a thumping at her breast.*]

MRS. DOWEY. Kenneth, tell me this instant what you mean. Don't keep me on the dumps.

[*He turns her around.*]

DOWEY. No, it couldn't be done.

MRS. DOWEY. Was it me you were thinking of?

DOWEY. Just for the moment (*regretfully*) but you have no style.

[*She catches hold of him by the sleeve.*]

MRS. DOWEY. Not in this, of course. But, oh, Kenneth, if you saw me in my merino! It's laced up the back in the very latest.

DOWEY. Hum (*doubtfully*) but let's see it.

[*It is produced from a drawer, to which the old lady runs with almost indecent haste. The connoisseur examines it critically.*]

DOWEY. Looks none so bad. Have you a bit of chiffon for the neck? It's not

bombs nor Kaisers nor Tipperary that men in the trenches think of; it's chiffon.

MRS. DOWEY. I swear I have, Kenneth. And I have a bangle,[1] and a muff, and gloves.

DOWEY. Ay, ay. (*He considers.*) Do you think you could give your face less of a homely look?

MRS. DOWEY. I'm sure I could.

DOWEY. Then you can have a try. But, mind you, I promise nothing. All will depend on the effect.

[*He goes into the pantry, and the old lady is left alone. Not alone, for she is ringed round by entrancing hopes and dreadful fears. They beam on her and jeer at her; they pull her this way and that. With difficulty she breaks through them and rushes to her pail, hot water, soap, and a looking glass.*]

[*Our last glimpse of her for this evening shows her staring — not discontentedly — at her soft old face, licking her palm, and pressing it to her hair. Her eyes are sparkling.*]

[*One evening a few days later* MRS. TWYMLEY *and* MRS. MICKLEHAM *are in* MRS. DOWEY'S *house, awaiting that lady's return from some fashionable dissipation. They have undoubtedly been discussing the war, for the first words we catch are:*]

MRS. MICKLEHAM. I tell you flat, Amelia, I bows no knee to junkerdom.[2]

MRS. TWYMLEY. Sitting here by the fire, you and me, as one to another, what do you think will happen after the war? Are we to go back to being as we were?

MRS. MICKLEHAM. Speaking for myself, Amelia, not me. The war has wakened me up to a understanding of my own importance that is really astonishing.

MRS. TWYMLEY. Same here. Instead

" *Have you a bit of chiffon for the neck?* "

---

[1] *bangle:* bracelet.

[2] *junkerdom:* the junkers, Prussian nobility; here means Germany's might.

of being the poor worms the like of you and me thought we was, we turns out to be visible departments of a great and haughty empire.

[*They are well under way, and with a little luck we might now hear their views on various passing problems of the day, such as the neglect of science in our public schools. But in comes the* HAGGERTY WOMAN, *and spoils everything. She is attired, like them, in her best; but the effect of her is that her clothes have gone out for a walk, leaving her at home.*]

MRS. MICKLEHAM (*with deep distaste*). Here's that submarine again.

[*The* HAGGERTY WOMAN *cringes to them, but gets no encouragement.*]

THE HAGGERTY WOMAN. It's a terrible war.
MRS. TWYMLEY. Is that so?
THE HAGGERTY WOMAN. I wonder what will happen when it ends?
MRS. MICKLEHAM. I have no idea.

[*The intruder produces her handkerchief, but does not use it. After all, she is in her best.*]

THE HAGGERTY WOMAN. Are they not back yet?

[*Perfect ladies must reply to a direct question.*]

MRS. MICKLEHAM. No. (*Icily*) We have been waiting this half-hour. They are at the theater again.
THE HAGGERTY WOMAN. You tell me! I just popped in with an insignificant present for him, as his leave is up.
MRS. TWYMLEY. The same errand brought us.
THE HAGGERTY WOMAN. My present is cigarettes.

[*They have no intention of telling her what their presents are, but the secret leaps from them.*]

MRS. MICKLEHAM. So is mine.

MRS. TWYMLEY. Mine too.

[*Triumph of the* HAGGERTY WOMAN. *But it is short-lived.*]

MRS. MICKLEHAM. Mine has gold tips.
MRS. TWYMLEY. So has mine.
THE HAGGERTY WOMAN (*need not say a word. You have only to look at her to know that her cigarettes are not gold-tipped. She tries to brazen it out, which is so often a mistake*). What care I? Mine is Exquisytos.

[*No wonder they titter.*]

MRS. MICKLEHAM. Excuse us, Mrs. Haggerty — if that's your name — but the word is Exquiseetos.
THE HAGGERTY WOMAN. Much obliged! (*Weeps.*)
MRS. MICKLEHAM. I think I heard a taxi.
MRS. TWYMLEY. It will be her third this week.

[*They peer through the blind. They are so excited that rank is forgotten.*]

THE HAGGERTY WOMAN. Much obliged! (*Weeps.*)
MRS. MICKLEHAM. A new astrakhan jacket he gave her, with Venus sleeves.
THE HAGGERTY WOMAN. Has she sold her gabardine coat?
MRS. MICKLEHAM. Not her! She has them both at the theater, warm night though it is. She's wearing the astrakhan — and carrying the gabardine, flung carelesslike over her arm.
THE HAGGERTY WOMAN. I saw her strutting about with him yesterday, looking as if she thought the two of them made a procession.
MRS. TWYMLEY. Hsh! (*Peeping*) Strike me dead — if she's not coming mincing down the stair, hooked on his arm!

[*Indeed it is thus that* MRS. DOWEY *enters. Perhaps she had seen shadows lurking on the blind, and at once hooked on to* KENNETH *to impress the visitors. She is quite capable of it.*

[*Now we see what Kenneth saw that afternoon five days ago when he emerged from the bathroom and found the old trembler awaiting his inspection. Here are the muff and the gloves and the chiffon, and such a kind old bonnet that it makes you laugh at once. I don't know how to describe it; but it is trimmed with a kiss, as bonnets should be when the wearer is old and frail. We must take the merino for granted until she steps out of the astrakhan. She is dressed up to the nines; there is no doubt about it. Yes, but is her face less homely? Above all, has she style? The answer is in a stout affirmative. Ask Kenneth. He knows. Many a time he has had to go behind a door to roar hilariously at the old lady. He has thought of her as a lark to tell his mates about by and by; but for some reason that he cannot fathom, he knows now that he will never do that.*]

MRS. DOWEY (*affecting surprise*). Kenneth, we have visitors!

DOWEY. Your servant, ladies.

[*He is no longer mud-caked and dour. A very smart figure is this Private Dowey; and he winks engagingly at the visitors, like one who knows that for jolly company you cannot easily beat charwomen. The pleasantries that he and they have exchanged this week! The sauce he has given them. The wit of MRS. MICKLEHAM'S retorts. The badinage of MRS. TWYMLEY. The neat giggles of the HAGGERTY WOMAN. There has been nothing like it since you took the countess in to dinner.*]

MRS. TWYMLEY. We should apologize. We're not meaning to stay.

MRS. DOWEY. You are very welcome. Just wait (*the ostentation of this!*) till I get out of my astrakhan — and my muff — and my gloves — and (*It is the bonnet's turn now*) my Excelsior.

[*At last we see her in the merino — a triumph.*]

MRS. MICKLEHAM. You've given her a glory time, Mr. Dowey.

DOWEY. It's her that has given it to me, missis.

MRS. DOWEY. Hey! hey! hey! hey! He just pampers me. (*Waggling her fists*) The Lord forgive us, but, this being the last night, we had a sit-down supper at a restaurant! (*Vehemently*) I swear by God that we had champagny wine. (*There is a dead stillness, and she knows very well what it means; she has even prepared for it.*) And to them as doubts my word — here's the cork. (*She places the cork, in its lovely gold drapery, upon the table.*)

MRS. MICKLEHAM. I'm sure!

MRS. TWYMLEY. I would thank you, Mrs. Dowey, not to say a word against my Alfred.

MRS. DOWEY. Me!

DOWEY. Come, come, ladies! (*In the masterful way that is so hard for women to resist*) If you say another word, I'll kiss the lot of you.

[*There is a moment of pleased confusion.*]

MRS. MICKLEHAM. Really, them sodgers!

THE HAGGERTY WOMAN. The kilties is the worst!

MRS. TWYMLEY (*heartily*). I'm sure we don't grudge you your treats, Mrs. Dowey; and sorry we are that this is the end.

DOWEY. Yes, it's the end. (*With a troubled look at his old lady*) I must be off in ten minutes.

[*The little soul is too gallant to break down in company. She hurries into the pantry and shuts the door.*]

MRS. MICKLEHAM. Poor thing! But we must run, for you'll be having some last words to say to her.

DOWEY. I kept her out long on purpose so as to have less time to say them in. (*He more than half wishes that he could make a bolt to a public house.*[1])

MRS. TWYMLEY. It's the best way. (*In the important affairs of life there is not much that anyone can teach a charwoman.*) Just a mere nothing — to wish you well, Mr. Dowey.

" *Just a mere nothing — to wish you well.*"

[*All three present him with the cigarettes.*]

MRS. MICKLEHAM. A scraping, as one might say.

THE HAGGERTY WOMAN (*enigmatically*). The heart is warm, though it may not be gold-tipped.

DOWEY. You bricks!

THE LADIES. Good luck, cocky.

DOWEY. The same to you. And if you see a sodger man up there in a kilt, he is one that is going back with me. Tell him not to come down, but — but to give me till the last minute, and then to whistle.

[*It is quite a grave man who is left alone, thinking what to do next. He tries a horse laugh, but that proves of no help. He says " Hell! " to himself, but it is equally ineffective. Then he opens the pantry door and calls.*]

DOWEY. Old lady.

[*She comes timidly to the door, her hand up as if to ward off a blow.*]

MRS. DOWEY. Is it time?

[*An encouraging voice answers her.*]

DOWEY. No, no, not yet. I've left word for Dixon to whistle when go I must.

MRS. DOWEY. All is ended.

DOWEY. Now, then, you promised to be gay. We were to help one another.

MRS. DOWEY. Yes, Kenneth.

DOWEY. It's bad for me, but it's worse for you.

MRS. DOWEY. The men have medals to win, you see.

DOWEY. The women have their medals, too. (*He knows she likes him to order her about, so he tries it again.*) Come here. No, I'll come to you. (*He stands gaping at her wonderingly. He has no power of words, nor does he quite know what he would like to say.*) God!

MRS. DOWEY. What is it, Kenneth?

DOWEY. You're a woman.

MRS. DOWEY. I had near forgot it.

[*He wishes he was at the station with Dixon. Dixon is sure to have a bottle in his pocket. They will be roaring a song presently. But in the meantime — there is that son business. Blethers,*[2] *the whole thing, of course — or mostly blethers. But it's the way to please her.*]

---

[1] *public house:* a tavern or bar.

[2] *Blethers:* nonsense.

DOWEY. Have you noticed you have never called me son?

MRS. DOWEY. Have I noticed it! I was feared, Kenneth. You said I was on probation.

DOWEY. And so you were. Well, the probation's ended. (*He laughs uncomfortably.*) The like of me! But if you want me you can have me.

MRS. DOWEY. Kenneth, will I do?

DOWEY (*artfully gay*). Woman, don't be so forward. Wait till I have proposed.

MRS. DOWEY. Propose for a mother?

DOWEY. What for no? (*In the grand style*) Mrs. Dowey, you queer carl,[1] you spunky tiddy, have I your permission to ask you the most important question a neglected orphan can ask of an old lady?

[*She bubbles with mirth. Who could help it, the man has such a way with him!*]

MRS. DOWEY. None of your sauce, Kenneth.

DOWEY. For a long time, Mrs. Dowey, you cannot have been unaware of my sonnish feelings for you.

MRS. DOWEY. Wait till I get my mop to you —

DOWEY. And if you're not willing to be my mother, I swear I'll never ask another. (*The old divert pulls him down to her and strokes his hair.*) Was I a well-behaved infant, Mother?

MRS. DOWEY. Not you, sonny — you were a rampaging rogue.

DOWEY. Was I slow in learning to walk?

MRS. DOWEY. The quickest in our street. He! he! he! (*She starts up.*) Was that the whistle?

DOWEY. No, no. See here. In taking me over you have, in a manner of speaking, joined the Black Watch.

MRS. DOWEY. I like to think that, Kenneth.

DOWEY. Then you must behave so

[1] *carl:* fellow or person.

that the ghost piper can be proud of you. 'Tion! (*She stands bravely at attention.*) That's the style. Now listen. I've sent in your name as being my nearest of kin, and your allowance will be coming to you weekly in the usual way.

MRS. DOWEY. Hey! hey! hey! Is it wicked, Kenneth?

DOWEY. I'll take the responsibility for it in both worlds. You see, I want you to be safeguarded in case anything hap —

MRS. DOWEY. Kenneth!

DOWEY. 'Tion! Have no fear. I'll come back, covered with mud and medals. Mind you have that cup of tea waiting for me.

[*He is listening for the whistle. He pulls her onto his knee.*]

MRS. DOWEY. Hey! hey! hey! hey!

DOWEY. What fun we'll have writing to one another! Real letters this time!

MRS. DOWEY. Yes.

DOWEY. It would be a good plan if you began the first letter as soon as I've gone.

MRS. DOWEY. I will.

DOWEY. I hope Lady Dolly will go on sending me cakes.

MRS. DOWEY. You may be sure.

[*He ties his scarf round her neck.*]

DOWEY. You must have been a bonny thing when you were young.

MRS. DOWEY. Away with you!

DOWEY. That scarf sets you fine.

MRS. DOWEY. Blue was always my color.

[*The whistle sounds.*]

DOWEY. Old lady, you are what Blighty means to me now.

[*She hides in the pantry again. She is out of sight of us, but she does something that makes* PRIVATE DOWEY *take off his bonnet. Then he shoulders his equipment and departs. That is he laughing coarsely with Dixon.*]

We have one last glimpse of the old lady — a month or two after Kenneth's death in action. It would be rosemary to us to see her in her black dress, of which she is very proud; but let us rather peep at her in the familiar garments that make a third to her mop and pail. It is early morning, and she is having a look at her medals before setting off on the daily round. They are in a drawer with the scarf covering them, and on the scarf a piece of lavender. First the black frock, which she carries in her arms like a baby. Then her War Savings Certificates, Kenneth's bonnet, a thin packet of real letters, and the famous champagne cork. She kisses the letters, but she does not blub over them. She strokes the dress, and waggles her head over the certificates and presses the bonnet to her cheeks, and rubs the tinsel of the cork carefully with her apron. She is a tremulous old 'un; yet she exults, for she owns all these things and also the penny flag on her breast. She puts them away in the drawer, the scarf over them, the lavender on the scarf. Her air of triumph well becomes her. She lifts the pail and the mop, and slouches off gamely to the day's toil.

. . . one last glimpse of the old lady . . .

INTERPRETER OF CHARACTER

1. How do Barrie's stage directions differ from the usual stage directions? How do they affect your interest in the play? How do they affect your understanding of the characters? How would they help actors? How might they hinder them?

2. Point out bits of humor in the opening conversation among the charwomen, especially their discussion of fashions. What apparently unimportant details of this discussion later prove to have bearing on the plot? Where do you first realize the nature of Mrs. Dowey's " crime "?

3. Show how each character in the play is made different in personality even though the part is very minor. What do you learn about British " class society " from this play?

4. Trace the steps in Kenneth's change of attitude. Is it made convincing? What are the most telling points in winning him over?

5. Study Mrs. Dowey's character carefully. What leads her to commit her " crime "? How would you characterize her feelings at the end of the play as she looks over her " medals "? In what way does she deserve them?

REPORTING AND DRAMATIZATION

1. Hold a panel or general discussion on this subject: the contrast between the mother-son relationship in *Riders to the Sea* and *The Old Lady Shows Her Medals*.

2. Act all or certain chosen parts of *The Old Lady Shows Her Medals*. Discuss how you would handle on the stage the short last scene for which there is no dialogue. How would you indicate the lapse of time? the fact that Kenneth has been killed? Would you try to supply any speech whatever for this scene? Why or why not?

READING LIST FOR MODERN DRAMA

Barrie, Sir James M., *Representative Plays*
    A good selection of Barrie's best.

Cerf, Bennett A. (editor), *Cavalcade*
    Good source for plays of sixteen famous British playwrights — especially Barrie, Maugham, Coward, Priestley, and Laurence Housman.

Coward, Noel, *Play Parade*

An omnibus of English social drama.

Eliot, T. S., *The Confidential Clerk*

A provocative play in blank verse about a financier whose aspirations are thwarted.

Fry, Christopher, *The Lady's Not for Burning*

A woman is accused of witchcraft in medieval England.

———, *The Dark Is Light Enough*

The value of human life and the error in using violence to redress wrong are the main themes of this three-act verse play.

Gallico, Paul, *The Snow Goose*

A strange World War II tale of a lonely man, his crippled benefactor, and the snow goose as a symbol of hope.

Galsworthy, John, *Plays*

Includes twenty-five successful plays of an outstanding playwright.

Gregory, Lady, *Seven Short Plays*

Outstanding choice of the Irish dramatist's short plays.

Kronenberger, Louis (editor), *Cavalcade of Comedy*

Among twenty-one brilliant time-tested comedies are those of Wilde, Shaw, Synge, Maugham, Kelly, O'Casey, and Coward.

Maugham, W. Somerset, *Quartet*

This book affords the experience of reading in a new form — a combination of four Maugham short stories with their accompanying screenplays by R. C. Sherriff.

Milne, A. A., *Four Plays*

Comedies of English social life.

O'Casey, Sean, *Selected Plays*

Among these eight plays which the author wants to survive him are *The Shadow of a Gunman, Juno and the Paycock,* and *The Plough and the Stars.*

———, *The Bishop's Bonfire*

Hilarious and tragic is the preparation for a worldly bishop's visit in this almost faultless play.

Rattigan, Terence, *The Winslow Boy*

A dramatic study of the effects of a long court trial on a middle-class family.

Shaw, George Bernard, *Nine Plays*

A representative list of Shaw's plays to enjoy, such as *The Devil's Disciple, Caesar and Cleopatra, Candida,* and *Saint Joan.*

Synge, John, *Playboy of the Western World*

An extravagant, boisterous play of Irish peasant life in which Christy finally confesses he is a fugitive, becomes a hero, and then has his game shattered.

Williams, Emlyn, *The Corn Is Green*

A play — made famous by Ethel Barrymore — about an understanding teacher among the miners of Wales.

GENERAL READING LIST FOR THE MODERN AGE

Campbell, Alexander, *The Heart of Africa*

The author, a Scot, has lived in Africa since 1937, and knows it thoroughly.

Colum, Padraic, *A Treasury of Irish Folklore*

Varied collection of stories, traditions, legends, humor, ballads, and songs of the Irish people.

Duff, Charles, *England and the English*

A little history, a little travel talk, and a little literature, with photographs.

Hunt, Sir John, *Conquest of Everest*

The Leader of the British group that climbed Mt. Everest in 1953 describes the exciting expedition.

Jeans, Sir James H., *Through Time and Space*

Clearly stated and easily understood descriptions of the physical universe make this a valuable book for young people.

Moorhead, Alan, *Rum Jungle*

An Australian journalist makes fascinating reading about this wild part of Australia, little known to most of us.

Morton, Henry C. V., *In Search of London*

Enjoy the familiar sights and the sensations experienced by this world traveler.

Thomas, Dylan, *Quite Early One Morning*

Twenty-five stories and a group of childhood reminiscences and descriptive essays.

Williams, R. E. (editor), *A Century of Punch Cartoons*

This collection from the pages of the famous humor magazine will show you what the English laugh at.

FOR LISTENING

A portion of *Pygmalion*, the first half of Act II, has been recorded and is available on *Many Voices 6B.*

GLOSSARY

Words that have been discussed in the Power of Words *sections throughout the text are included in this glossary. For definitions and other information about these words, refer to the pages indicated.*

A

abhorrèd (ăb·hôr'ĕd). *Poetic.* Hated; loathed.

abhorrent (ăb·hôr'ĕnt). Arousing strong dislike.

ablution (ăb·lū'shŭn). A washing or cleansing.

abysmal (à·bĭz'măl). Bottomless; profound.

acme (ăk'mē). *See page 582.*

adjuration (ăj'ŏō·rā'shŭn). *See page 506.*

admonition (ăd'mō·nĭsh'ŭn). Reproof; advice.

adroitly (à·droit'lĭ). Cleverly in use of hands or mental faculties.

aeon (ē'ŏn). An immeasurably long period of time.

affrayèd (à·frā'ĕd). *Archaic.* Frightened.

agility (à·jĭl'ĭ·tĭ). *See page 289.*

aliment (ăl'ĭ·mĕnt). Food.

allegory (ăl'ē·gō'rĭ). A story told by means of symbols, or abstract characters. *Adj.,* **allegorical** (ăl'ē·gŏr'ĭ·kăl).

alleviate (à·lē'vĭ·āt). Lighten or lessen trouble.

alliteration (à·lĭt'ĕr·ā'shŭn.) The use of a succession of words with the same initial letter.

allusions (à·lū'zhŭnz). Indirect references; hints.

ambrosian (ăm·brō'zhĭ·ăn). 1. Worthy of the gods. 2. Delighting the senses of taste or smell.

amenity (à·mĕn'ĭ·tĭ). Social courtesy.

amiability (ā'mĭ·à·bĭl'ĭ·tĭ). Good nature; friendliness.

amorous (ăm'ō·rŭs). Ardent in love.

amphibious (ăm·fĭb'ĭ·ŭs). Able to live or navigate both on land and in water.

amulet (ăm'ū·lĕt). A charm to ward off ill luck.

analytic (ăn'à·lĭt'ĭk), **analytical** (ăn'à·lĭt'ĭ·kăl). Able to separate a subject into its parts.

anesthetics (ăn'ĕs·thĕt'ĭks). Means of producing unconsciousness during an operation.

annihilation (à·nī'ĭ·lā'shŭn). Total destruction.

anticipatest (ăn·tĭs'ĭ·pāt'ĕst). *Poetic or archaic.* (You) prevent by prior action.

aperture (ăp'ĕr·tŭr). An opening; gap; hole.

apostate (à·pŏs'tāt). One who has forsaken a faith in which he once believed.

apostolical (ăp'ŏs·tŏl'ĭ·kăl). Pertaining to, or derived directly from, the apostles.

apothecaries (à·pŏth'ê·kĕr·ĭz). Those who prepare and sell drugs.

apparition (ăp'à·rĭsh'ŭn). A phantom or specter.

appellation (ăp'ĕ·lā'shŭn). A name or designation.

appraisal (à·prāz'ăl). An estimated value set on something. **appraising.** Determining the worth.

apprehensive (ăp'rē·hĕn'sĭv). 1. Quick to discern or grasp a matter. 2. Fearful.

apprising (à'prīz'ĭng). Informing.

apropos (ăp'rō·pō'). As suggested by; with respect to.

aqueduct (ăk'wē·dŭkt). A structure for conveying a large amount of flowing water.

archaic (är·kā'ĭk). Belonging to an earlier time; antiquated.

archangel (ärk'ān'jĕl). *See page 239.*

archenemy (ärch'ĕn'ê·mĭ). *See page 239.*

archives (är'kīvz). 1. Important records of a group. 2. A place for keeping such records.

argent (är'jĕnt). Silvery; shining.

argosy (är'gō·sĭ). A large ship or fleet.

aridity (à·rĭd'ĭ·tĭ). Dryness; lack of variety.

arras (ăr'ăs). Tapestry that is used as a wall covering.

articulating (är·tĭk'ū·lăt'ĭng). Speaking words distinctly.

artificer (är·tĭf'ĭ·sĕr). One who makes or devises. **The Great Artificer.** God the creator.

ascendancy (à·sĕn'dăn·sĭ). Domination; controlling power.

ascetic (à·sĕt'ĭk). Austere; pertaining to a life of self-denial.

asperity (ăs·pĕr'ĭ·tĭ). Harshness.

assignation (ăs'ĭg·nā'shŭn). An appointment for a meeting.

assizes (à·sīz'ĕz). County court.

assuage (à·swāj'). Soothe; lessen the sting.

astute (ăs·tūt'). Shrewd; discerning.

astrakhan (ăs'trà·kăn). 1. Long curled fur of young lambs. 2. A rough cloth imitating this fur.

atrocious (à·trō'shŭs). Savagely brutal.

atrophy (ăt'rō·fĭ). Become weak; seem to dry up and lose power.

audacity (ô·dăs'ĭ·tĭ). Boldness.

augurs (ô'gĕrz). Foretells.

avaricious (ăv'à·rĭsh'ŭs). Greedy for profits or gain.

avaunt (à·vônt'). *Archaic.* Begone.

averred (à·vûrd'). Declared positively.

avouches (à·vouch'ĕz). Asserts positively.

B

badinage (băd'ĭ·näzh'). Playful raillery or banter.

baggage (băg'ĭj). An artful, pert young woman.

baldric (bôl'drĭk). A belt worn over one shoulder to support a sword, horn, etc.

baleful (bāl'fŏŏl). Deadly in influence.

balustrade (băl'ŭs·trād'). A row of upright supports topped by a railing.

banality (bà·năl'ĭ·tĭ). An insipid, trite remark.

banns (bănz). Announcement in church of a couple's intention to marry.

banterers (băn'tĕr·ĕrz). Persons ridiculing each other good-naturedly.

āpe, chăotic, bâre, ăt, ăttend, ärt, flásk, átop; ēke, mẹrely, ĕlect, ĕcho, prudĕnt, doêr; ītem, ĭnn; rarĭty; ōde, ŏpaque, fôr, dŏt, lôft, cŏnfide; sōōn, tŏŏk; sour, toil; tūbe, ūnique, tûrn, sŭp, ŭntil.

baronetcy (băr'ŭn·ĕt·sĭ). The rank of baronet, between a knight and a baron, carrying the title Sir.

barrage (bá·räzh'). Heavy fire (often, of words).

beleaguered (bė·lē'gẽrd). Surrounded; besieged.

benignity (bė·nĭg'nĭ·tĭ). A kind, gentle disposition.

benison (bĕn'ĭ·z'n). Blessing.

betel (bē't'l). The nut of a climbing pepper vine, often chewed by natives of the Far East.

bibulous (bĭb'ū·lŭs). Addicted to drink.

bittern (bĭt'ẽrn). A variety of small heron notable for uttering booming sounds.

bizarre (bĭ·zär'). Odd; eccentric.

blanched (blȧncht). Whitened.

blatant (blā'tǎnt). Noisy; clamorous.

blazoned (blā'z'nd). Decorated with a coat of arms in bright colors.

bodements (bōd'mĕnts). Prophecies.

bombast (bŏm'băst). Inflated, pretentious language.

boon (bōōn). Archaic. A favor asked or granted.

bootless (bōōt'lĕs). Useless; profitless.

bourne (bōrn). Archaic. Boundary; limit.

boycott (boi'kŏt). A policy of withholding social or commercial intercourse to force a point.

bravado (brȧ·vä'dō). A pretense of bravery.

brinded (brĭn'dĕd). Archaic. Having dark streaks or spots on a light background.

buoyant (bōō'yǎnt). 1. Spritely. 2. Having the quality of a floating object.

burlesque (bûr'lĕsk'). An imitation which makes fun of some literary or dramatic work.

buttress (bŭt'rĕs). A projecting structure to support a wall.

C

cabined (kăb'ĭnd). Shut in; hampered.

cadence (kā'dĕns). Rhythmic measure.

cairns (kârnz). Mounds of stones used to mark a grave or significant location.

cajoled (kȧ·jōld'). Coaxed.

calumny (kăl'ŭm·nĭ). Slander.

cankering (kăng'kẽr·ĭng). Corroding; eating away.

capitulate (kȧ·pĭt'ū·lāt). Make terms of surrender.

caricature (kăr'ĭ·kȧ·tûr). See page 678.

carousing (kȧ·rouz'ĭng). Drinking in gay company.

cassock (kăs'ŭk). A long, close-fitting garment worn by the clergy.

cataclysm (kăt'ȧ·klĭz'm). A social or political upheaval.

catapult (kăt'ȧ·pŭlt). An ancient engine for hurling missiles against a wall.

catastrophe (kȧ·tăs'trō·fė). 1. A terrible disaster. 2. The conclusion of a dramatic tragedy.

catechising (kăt'ė·kīz·ĭng). Questioning fully, especially on religious doctrine.

caustic (kôs'tĭk). Sharp; satirical.

cavalcade (kăv'ǎl·kād'). A procession of persons on horseback.

celestial (sė·lĕs'chǎl). Heavenly; divine.

censer (sĕn'sẽr). A receptacle in which incense is burned.

certitude (sûr'tĭ·tūd). Sureness; certainty.

chasten (chās''n). Purify or refine.

chastise (chăs·tīz'). Punish.

chauntress (chôn'trĕs). Archaic. A singer.

checkmated (chĕk'māt'ĕd). 1. Defeated. 2. Blocked from making further progress, in the game of chess.

cherubim (chĕr'ū·bĭm). Pl. of cherub, the second rank of the angels of light.

circumscribed (sûr'kŭm·skrībd'). Limited.

circumspection (sûr'kŭm·spĕk'shŭn). Discreet conduct.

circumstantial (sûr'kŭm·stăn'shǎl). 1. Of, pertaining to, or derived from circumstances. 2. Secondary, incidental. 3. Full of details.

clarion (klăr'ĭ·ŭn). 1. A trumpet with clear shrill tones. 2. A call to action.

cloistered (klois'tẽrd). Secluded from the world.

cockney (kŏk'nĭ). 1. A person reared in the East End of London. 2. The dialect spoken by such a person.

codger (kŏj'ẽr) Colloquial. An odd or uncouth old person.

cohorts (kō'hôrts). 1. Troops of soldiers. 2. Colleagues or partners.

coign (koin). Corner.

colloquial (kǒ·lō'kwĭ·ǎl). Informal; conversational in style.

colloquies (kŏl'ō·kwĭz). Somewhat formal conversations.

comely (kŭm'lĭ) 1. Archaic. Decent. 2. Pleasing to the sight.

complacence (kǒm·plā'sĕns), complacency (kǒm·plā's'n·sĭ) 1. Self-satisfaction. 2. Good nature; affability.

compunction (kǒm·pŭngk'shŭn). Regret; a sense of guilt.

conciliate (kǒn·sĭl'ĭ·āt). To gain the good will of; make friendly. Adj., conciliatory (kǒn·sĭl'ĭ·ȧ·tō'rĭ). Tending to win favor.

concourse (kǒn'kōrs). 1. A gathering together of persons. 2. A main thoroughfare.

concurrence (kǒn·kûr'ĕns). Agreement.

condemnatory (kǒn·dĕm'nȧ·tō'rĭ). Disapproving.

conference (kǒn'fẽr·ĕns). See page 204.

conflagration (kǒn'flȧ·grā'shŭn). A raging fire.

confute (kǒn·fūt'). See page 204.

conjecture (kǒn·jĕk'tûr). Noun, supposition; theory. Verb, guess; suppose.

connoisseur (kǒn'ĭ·sûr'). One competent to pass critical judgment.

consummate (kǒn·sŭm'ĭt). Perfect; in the highest degree.

contentious (kǒn·tĕn'shŭs). Quarrelsome.

contradict (kǒn'trȧ·dikt'). See page 204.

cope (kōp). A long, capelike vestment.

copiously (kō'pĭ·ŭs·lĭ). Richly; fully.

coppice (kŏp'ĭs), or copse (kŏps). Thicket or grove of small trees.

cornice (kôr'nĭs). An ornamental molding around the wall of a room close to the ceiling.

covert (kŭv'ẽrt). A shelter; a protection.

coxcomb (kŏks'kōm). A conceited, silly man; a fop.

credulity (krė·dū'lĭ·tĭ). Readiness to believe without evidence. Adj., credulous (krĕd'ū·lŭs).

crone (krōn). A withered old woman.

cribbed (krĭbd). Confined to a small space.

---

bar; church; dog; ardŭous; fat; go; hear; jail; key; lame; meat; not; ring; pay; ran; see; shell; ten; there, thick; pastŭre; vast; wind; yes; zoo, zh = z in azure.

crossbow (krŏs'bō'). A medieval weapon for shooting arrows or stones from a bow.

crypt (krĭpt). An underground vault.

crystalline (krĭs'tăl·ĭn). Clear; transparent.

culinary (kū'lĭ·nĕr'ĭ). Pertaining to cooking.

culmination (kŭl·mĭ·nā'shŭn). Highest point; apex.

cumbrous (kŭm'brŭs). Heavy; burdensome.

cupola (kū'pō·là). A rounded roof.

cursory (kûr'sō·rĭ). Hurried; superficial.

cynic (sĭn'ĭk). One who disbelieves in the goodness or unselfishness of human motives. *Adv.*, **cynically** (sĭn'ĭ·kăl·ĭ).

D

dappled (dăp''ld). Spotted; flecked with clouds.

darkling (därk'lĭng). Being in the dark.

dauntless (dônt'lĕs). Bold; fearless.

dauphin (dô'fĭn). Formerly, title of the eldest son of the king of France.

debaucheries (dē·bôch'ẽr·ĭz). Drinking bouts; orgies.

debonair (dĕb'ō·nâr'). Courteous, graceful, and gay.

decussated (dē·kŭs'ăt·ĕd). Crossed in the form of an X.

deductive (dē·dŭk'tĭv). Pertaining to a method of reasoning from the general to the particular.

defamation (dĕf'à·mā'shŭn). Slander.

deferentially (dĕf'ẽr·ĕn'shăl·ĭ). Respectfully.

delectable (dē·lĕk'tà·b'l). Pleasing; delightful.

depreciated (dē·prē'shĭ·āt·ĕd). Belittled; undervalued.

deterrent (dē·tûr'ĕnt). That which prevents action because of fear.

dexterity (dĕks·tĕr'ĭ·tĭ). *See page* 288.

diametrically (dī'à·mĕt'rĭ·kăl·ĭ). As opposite as possible, like the two ends of a diameter.

dictum (dĭk'tŭm). An authoritative statement.

diffident (dĭf'ĭ·dĕnt). Shy; lacking confidence.

digression (dĭ·grĕsh'ŭn). A departure from the subject.

discrepancies (dĭs·krĕp'ăn·sĭz). Points of difference; inconsistencies.

discrimination (dĭs·krĭm'ĭ·nā'shŭn). 1. The ability to make careful selection. 2. Distinction in treatment, especially if unfair or injurious.

dislimned (dĭs·lĭmd'). *Poetic.* Became dim.

disreputabilities (dĭs·rĕp'ū·tà·bĭl'ĭ·tĭz). Low or dishonorable acts.

dissever (dĭ·sĕv'ẽr). Separate; cut off.

distempered (dĭs·tĕm'pẽrd). Afflicted with the plague.

documented (dŏk'ū·mĕnt'ĕd). Proved accurate by written or printed sources.

dogmatist (dŏg'mà·tĭst). One who states his beliefs positively, as if they were facts.

dolor (dō'lẽr). Pain; grief. *Adj.*, **dolorous** (dō'lẽr·ŭs). Mournful.

domicile (dŏm'ĭ·sĭl). Residence.

doughty (dou'tĭ). Strong; valiant.

dramatic monologue (mŏn'ō·lŏg). A poem in the first person revealing some dramatic moment in the speaker's life.

dynasty (dī'nàs·tĭ). A line of kings from the same family.

E

ecclesiastical (ĕ·klē'zĭ·ăs'tĭ·kăl). Pertaining to the church.

ecstasy (ĕk'stà·sĭ). Overwhelming joy or exultation. *Adj.*, **ecstatic** (ĕk·stăt'ĭk).

eerie (ē'rĭ). Weird; uncanny.

effeminacy (ĕ·fĕm'ĭ·nà·sĭ). Womanly gentleness and tenderness.

efficacy (ĕf'ĭ·kà·sĭ). Power to produce an effect. *Adj.*, **efficacious** (ĕf'ĭ·kā'shŭs).

effigies (ĕf'ĭ·jĭz). Pictured likenesses.

eglantine (ĕg'lăn·tīn). Honeysuckle.

elate (ē·lāt'). Exalted in spirit.

elegy (ĕl'ē·jĭ). A poem lamenting or honoring the dead.

elocutionary (ĕl'ō·kū'shŭn·ẽr'ĭ). Dramatic or orational in delivery.

emblazonings (ĕm·blā'z'n·ĭngz). Heraldic designs in bright colors.

embodiment (ĕm·bŏd'ĭ·mĕnt). A representation in bodily form of some abstract quality.

embowèd (ĕm·bō'ĕd). *Poetic.* Arched; vaulted.

emporium (ĕm·pō'rĭ·ŭm). Department store (British term).

encumber (ĕn·kŭm'bẽr). Impede; weigh down.

endu'th (ĕn·dūth'). *Poetic or archaic.* Endues; gives power to.

enigmatically (ē'nĭg·măt'ĭ·kăl·ĭ). In a puzzling manner.

entoiled (ĕn·toild'). Ensnared.

entrails (ĕn'trĕlz). Internal organs (often, of animals).

epic (ĕp'ĭk). A long narrative poem relating in dignified style the deeds of a national or mythical hero.

epitaph (ĕp'ĭ·tȧf). Inscription on a tomb.

epitomize (ē·pĭt'ō·mīz). Abridge; summarize.

equivocation (ē·kwĭv'ō·kā'shŭn). A double meaning used with intent to deceive; a lie. **equivocator** (ē·kwĭv'ō·kā'tẽr). One who deceives.

eremite (ĕr'ē·mīt). A hermit.

esplanade (ĕs'plà·nād'). An open space for promenading.

essences (ĕs'ĕn·sĕz). 1. Heavenly beings or substances. 2. Indescribable qualities.

estheticism (ĕs·thĕt'ĭ·sĭz'm). Devotion to principles of beauty and good taste.

ethereal (ē·thẽr'ē·ăl). Belonging to the misty, upper regions of space.

ethics (ĕth'ĭks). The science of moral duty and high character.

eucalyptus (ū·kà·lĭp'tŭs). A variety of myrtle tree yielding resinous gums.

evolution (ĕv'ō·lū'shŭn). The process of developing through a long series of slow changes.

execrable (ĕk'sē·krà·b'l). Very bad; detestable.

execrations (ĕk'sē·krā'shŭnz). Curses.

exemplary (ĕg·zĕm'plà·rĭ). Serving as a pattern worthy of imitation.

exhortations (ĕg'zôr·tā'shŭnz). Words of encouragement or inspiration.

exotic (ĕks·ŏt'ĭk). Foreign; belonging to another part of the world.

exponent (ĕks·pō'nĕnt). One who or that which exemplifies or represents.

āpe, chăotic, bâre, ăt, ȧttend, ärt, flásk, ȧtop; ēke, mẽrely, ĕlect, ĕcho, prudĕnt, doẽr; ītem, ĭnn, rarĭty; ōde, ȯpaque, fôr, dŏt, lôft, cŏnfide; sōon, tŏŏk; sour, toil; tūbe, ûnique, tûrn, sŭp, ŭntil.

F

façade (fȧ·säd′). The front of a building.
facetious (fȧ·sē′shŭs). *See page* 469.
facilitating (fȧ·sĭl′ĭ·tāt′ĭng). Making easier.
fakir (fȧ·kēr′). An Indian wonder-worker.
fallows (făl′ōz). Fields not sown with crops.
fealty (fē′ăl·tĭ). Fidelity, as to a feudal lord.
felicitous (fĕ·lĭs′ĭ·tŭs). Apt; happy; well expressed.
fell (fĕl). 1. Cruel. 2. A growth (of hair).
fenny (fĕn′ĭ). Living in a marsh.
fermenting (fĕr·mĕnt′ĭng). Secretly at work; seething.
ferret (fĕr′ĕt). An animal of the weasel family, kept for hunting rabbits and rats.
fillip (fĭl′ĭp). 1. A smart tap or blow. 2. Something serving to arouse and excite.
flagrant (flā′grănt). Conspicuously bad.
flambeau (flăm′bō). A flaming torch.
flamboyant (flăm·boi′ănt). Ornate; colorful.
flippant (flĭp′ănt). Pert; treating lightly that which should be respected.
foibles (foi′b'lz). Whims; peculiarities of disposition.
fops (fŏps). Silly, vain, overly fashionable men.
fossils (fŏs′ĭlz). Bones or impressions found in the soil of long-past ages.
frieze (frēz). 1. An ornamental band beneath the cornice of a building. 2. A coarse cloth.
fugitive (fū′jĭ·tĭv). Fleeting; likely to fade.
furtive (fûr′tĭv). Secret; stealthy. *Adv.*, **furtively.**
furze (fûrz). A spiny shrub of the bean family.

G

gambit (găm′bĭt). 1. A chess opening which sacrifices a piece to gain a later advantage. 2. An opening move.
garrulous (găr′ū·lŭs). Talkative.
gazetteer (găz′ĕ·tēr′). An officer appointed to write news.
genii (jē′nĭ·ī). Nature spirits having strong influence over other forms of nature. (*Pl. of* **genius**; *see footnote on page* 229.)
genuflect (jĕn′ū·flĕkt). Bend the knee, as in worship.
gibbet (jĭb′ĕt). Gallows from which criminals were hung in chains.
girded (gûrd′ĕd). 1. Clothed and belted. 2. Braced against difficulties.
gnomes (nōmz). A fabled race of dwarfs who lived under the earth.
gossamers (gŏs′ȧ·mērz). Cobwebs floating in air, used figuratively for delicate, imaginative productions of the mind. *Variant*, gossameres.
Gothic (gŏth′ĭk). 1. Pertaining to a style of architecture developed in the Middle Ages. 2. Pertaining to language forms used by Germanic groups.
gregarious (grĕ·gâr′ĭ·ŭs). *See page* 469.

grotesque (grō·tĕsk′). 1. Distorted for artistic effect. 2. Unnatural; abnormal.
guerdon (gûr′dŭn). Reward.
gullible (gŭl′ĭ·b'l). *Adj.*, easily duped or imposed upon. *Noun*, **gullibility** (gŭl′ĭ·bĭl′ĭ·tĭ).
gyrations (jī·rā′shŭnz). Whirling or rotating motions.

H

halberts (hăl′bērts). Pikes surmounted with battle-axes.
hallucination (hȧ·lū′sĭ·nā′shŭn). A belief that one sees an object not actually present.
hapless (hăp′lĕs). Unlucky.
haply (hăp′lĭ). By chance.
harangue (hȧ·răng′). *Noun*, a long speech, usually of a noisy, ranting nature. *Verb*, **harangue.**
harbinger (här′bĭn·jēr). Forerunner.
hautboys (hō′boiz). Old form of oboes (woodwind instruments).
heraldries (hĕr′ăld·rĭz). Signs and emblems used on coats of arms.
heretic (hĕr′ĕ·tĭk). One who rejects an established doctrine.
hermitage (hûr′mĭ·tĭj). A secluded retreat.
hierarchy (hī′ēr·är′kĭ). 1. A body of rulers of the church having different ranks. 2. A society based on ranks, one above the other.
hoardings (hōr′dĭngz). Billboards (British term).
hoary (hōr′ĭ). *See page* 279.
holocaust (hŏl′ō·kôst). Complete destruction by fire.
homage (hŏm′ĭj). Service to a superior in return for protection.
hoodwink (hōōd′wĭngk). Deceive.
horologist (hō·rŏl′ō·jĭst). A skilled clockmaker.
horoscope (hŏr′ō·skōp). Position of the stars by which one's future or character supposedly can be read.
Huguenot (hū′gĕ·nŏt). A French Protestant.
humanitarian (hū·măn′ĭ·târ′ĭ·ăn). *Adj.*, concerned with the welfare of mankind. *Noun*, one who is so concerned.
humors (hū′mērz). *Medieval and Elizabethan.* Whims; caprices; types of disposition.
hustings (hŭs′tĭngz). Platforms from which political campaign speeches are made.

I

iambic pentameter (ī·ăm′bĭk pĕn·tăm′ĕ·tēr). A line of poetry with five feet, each containing one unaccented syllable followed by one accented syllable.
idiosyncrasies (ĭd′ĭ·ō·sĭng′krȧ·sĭz). Peculiarities.
idyl or **idyll** (ī′dĭl). A simple description of rustic or pastoral life. *Adj.*, **idyllic** (ī·dĭl′ĭk).
ignominy (ĭg′nō·mĭn·ĭ). Disgrace. *Adj.*, **ignominious** (ĭg′nō·mĭn′ĭ·ŭs). Disgraceful.
illimitable (ĭl·lĭm′ĭt·ȧ·b'l). Incapable of being limited or measured.
illustrious (ĭ·lŭs′trĭ·ŭs). Noble; famous.
imminent (ĭm′ĭ·nĕnt). Threatening to occur immediately.

bar; church; dog; ardŭous; fat; go; hear; jail; key; lame; meat; not; ring; pay; ran; see; shell; ten; there, thick; pastūre; vast; wind; yes; zoo, zh = z in azure.

immobility (ĭm'mō·bĭl'ĭ·tĭ). Fixedness; lack of motion.

immunity (ĭ·mū'nĭ·tĭ). Freedom from any charge or punishment.

immured (ĭ·mūrd'). Protected by walls.

immutable (ĭ·mū'tá·b'l). Unchangeable.

impalpable (ĭm·păl'pá·b'l). Too delicate to be easily seen or felt.

impeccable (ĭm·pĕk'á·b'l). Without fault.

impecuniously (ĭm'pē·kū'nĭ·ŭs·lĭ). Habitually without money.

impediments (ĭm·pĕd'ĭ·mĕnts). Hindrances; obstacles.

imperceptible (ĭm'pēr·sĕp'tĭ·b'l). Not evident to the senses or mind; very slight.

imperturbability (ĭm'pēr·tûr·bá·bĭl'ĭ·tĭ). Serenity that cannot be disturbed.

impetus (ĭm'pē·tŭs). Driving force.

impious (ĭm'pĭ·ŭs). Lacking respect and piety.

implacable (ĭm·plā'ká·b'l). Not to be appeased or pacified.

importunate (ĭm·pôr'tṳ·nĭt). Urgent; insistent.

impotence (ĭm'pō·tĕns). Inability to bring about a result.

imprecations (ĭm'prē·kā'shŭnz). Curses.

impresario (ĭm'prä·sä'rĭ·ō). The manager or conductor of an opera or concert.

impunity (ĭm·pū'nĭ·tĭ). Freedom from punishment.

inaccessible (ĭn'ăk·sĕs'ĭ·b'l). Not to be reached.

inarticulate (ĭn'är·tĭk'ū·lát). Speechless; silent.

incalculable (ĭn·kăl'kū·lá·b'l). Impossible to judge or estimate.

incantation (ĭn'kăn·tā'shŭn). Magical words, chanted or recited.

incognito (ĭn·kŏg'nĭ·tō). With concealed identity.

incomparable (ĭn·kŏm'pá·rá·b'l). Without an equal; matchless.

incongruous (ĭn·kŏng'grōō·ŭs). Lacking in suitability or harmony.

incorrigible (ĭn·kŏr'ĭ·jĭ·b'l). Unruly; beyond correction or reform.

incredulous (ĭn·krĕd'ū·lŭs). Doubting; unbelieving. *Adv.,* **incredulously** (ĭn·krĕd'ū·lŭs·lĭ).

incriminating (ĭn·krĭm'ĭ·nāt'ĭng). Accusing; involving the writer in a fault or crime.

incumbent (ĭn·kŭm'bĕnt). *Adj.,* lying or reclining. *Noun,* one who holds an office.

indefatigable (ĭn'dē·făt'ĭ·gá·b'l). Tireless.

indict (ĭn·dīt'). Charge with an offense. *Noun,* **indictment** (ĭn·dīt'mĕnt). Accusation.

indomitable (ĭn·dŏm'ĭ·tá·b'l). Not to be subdued.

inductive (ĭn·dŭk'tĭv). Pertaining to a method of reasoning from the specific to the general, beginning from many different examples and arriving at a common rule.

indulgence (ĭn·dŭl'jĕns). A statement of forgiveness of sins before they were committed (Medieval Church).

indulgent (ĭn·dŭl'jĕnt). Lenient, as in allowing a child to follow his desires.

inexorable (ĭn·ĕk'sō·rá·b'l). Unyielding to entreaty. *Adv.,* **inexorably** (ĭn·ĕk'sō·rá·blĭ).

inexplicable (ĭn·ĕks'plĭ·ká·b'l). Puzzling; not capable of being explained. *Adv.,* **inexplicably** (ĭn·ĕks'plĭ·ká·blĭ).

inextinguishable (ĭn'ĕks·tĭng'gwĭsh·á·b'l). Not to be put out or overcome.

ingenuity (ĭn'jē·nū'ĭ·tĭ). *See page* 289.

ingenuous (ĭn·jĕn'ū·ŭs). *See page* 329.

ingle (ĭng'g'l). *Scot.* 1. Fire; blaze. 2. Fireplace.

inherent (ĭn·hĕr'ĕnt). Belonging to the nature or habit.

inimitable (ĭn·ĭm'ĭ·tá·b'l). Not capable of being imitated; matchless.

innumerable (ĭ·nū'mēr·á·b'l). Countless.

insinuate (ĭn·sĭn'ū·āt). Suggest artfully without a direct statement.

insupportable (ĭn'sŭ·pōr'tá·b'l). Not to be endured.

intangible (ĭn·tăn'jĭ·b'l). 1. Not capable of being touched. 2. Not clear to the mind.

interdict (ĭn'tēr·dĭkt). A ban of the Roman Catholic Church, refusing sacraments, etc., to a whole community or nation.

interstices (ĭn·tûr'stĭ·sĕz). Narrow spaces between things or parts.

intimidated (ĭn·tĭm'ĭ·dāt'ĕd). Made fearful.

intravenously (ĭn'trá·vē'nŭs·lĭ). Into a vein by injection.

introverted (ĭn'trō·vûrt'ĕd). Directed inward.

inured (ĭn·ūrd'). Accustomed to hard conditions.

invariably (ĭn·vâr'ĭ·á·blĭ). Always.

invective (ĭn·vĕk'tĭv). Violent accusation.

irony (ī'rō·nĭ). Ridicule or light sarcasm which implies the opposite of the literal sense of the words. *Adj.,* **ironical** (ī·rŏn'ĭ·kăl) or **ironic.**

irreconcilable (ĭr·rĕk'ŏn·sīl'á·b'l). Unwilling to change an opinion or to overlook an offense.

irrelevant (ĭr·rĕl'ē·vănt). Not appropriate to the subject.

irreparable (ĭ·rĕp'á·rá·b'l). Not to be repaired or remedied.

irreproachable (ĭr'rē·prōch'á·b'l). Above reproach; blameless.

irresistibly (ĭr'rē·zĭs'tĭ·blĭ). In a way that cannot be resisted or withstood.

irretrievably (ĭr'rē·trēv'á·blĭ). So that it cannot be recovered.

irrevocable (ĭ·rĕv'ō·ká·b'l). Incapable of being brought back or changed.

iteration (ĭt'ēr·ā'shŭn). Repetition.

itinerant (ī·tĭn'ēr·ănt). Traveling from place to place.

J

jargon (jär'gŏn). Lingo; the technical language or slang of a trade or profession.

jocund (jŏk'ŭnd). Cheerful; merry; lively.

joust (jŭst, joust, or jōost). *Verb,* fight on horseback in single combat. *Noun,* a tourney.

juniper (jōō'nĭ·pēr). An evergreen shrub whose berries have a pungent taste.

jurisprudence (jōōr'ĭs·prōō'dĕns). The science of law.

L

labyrinth (lăb'ĭ·rĭnth). A maze of intricate paths.

lagoon (lá·gōōn'). A shallow pool, usually communicating with the sea.

āpe, chȧotic, bâre, ăt, ȧttend, ärt, flȧsk, átop; ēke, mẽrely, ėlect, ĕcho, prudĕnt, doēr; ītem, ĭnn, rarĭty; ōde, ȯpaque, fôr, dŏt, lȯft, cŏnfide; sōon, tŏŏk; sour, toil; tūbe, ūnique, tûrn, sŭp, ŭntil.

languor (lăng'gẽr). Dullness; sluggishness.

lauch (läĸ). *Scot.* Laugh.

laudable (lôd'á·b'l). Praiseworthy.

levitation (lĕv'ĭ·tā'shŭn). The art of making heavy objects rise or float through the air without apparent means of support.

lexicographer (lĕk'sĭ·kŏg'rá·fẽr). A compiler of a dictionary.

liege (lēj). Overlord.

lighter (līt'ẽr). A large boat used to carry goods about a harbor.

lineament (lĭn'é·á·mĕnt). The outline of the face or contour of the body.

linnet (lĭn'ĕt). A small finch of the Old World.

lintel (lĭn't'l). A horizontal span over a door.

literati (lĭt'é·rā'tī). Men of letters.

litigation (lĭt'ĭ·gā'shŭn). A law suit.

lorries (lŏr'ĭz). Large, low trucks.

livid (lĭv'ĭd). Ashen; the color of bruised flesh.

lucent (lū'sĕnt). Radiant; brilliant.

lucid (lū'sĭd). Clear; easily understood.

luminous (lū'mĭ·nŭs). 1. Shining; giving off light. 2. Enlightened; intelligent.

lustrous (lŭs'trŭs). Shining with reflected light because of a polished surface.

lute (lūt). A stringed instrument with a pear-shaped body.

M

madrigals (măd'rĭ·gálz). Love songs.

magisterially (măj'ĭs·tẽr'ĭ·ál·ĭ). With the manner of a magistrate, an important public official.

malevolence (má·lĕv'ô·lĕns). Ill will.

malignity (má·lĭg'nĭ·tĭ). Bad influence; evil.

manifesto (măn'ĭ·fĕs'tō). A public declaration of the intentions of a government.

manna (măn'á). Divinely supplied food.

mantling (măn'tlĭng). Becoming covered with a top surface. The word may be used for foam on ale, scum on a pool, a blush on the cheek, etc.

marionettes (măr'ĭ·ô·nĕts'). 1. Puppets usually operated by strings from above. 2. Persons completely under the control of another person.

marquetry (mär'kĕ·trĭ). Inlaid wood.

masque or **mask** (másk). A form of drama emphasizing music, poetry, dancing, and costuming.

mattocks (măt'ŭks). Implements for digging.

meandering (mē·ăn'dẽr·ĭng). Winding; turning.

mendacity (mĕn·dăs'ĭ·tĭ). A lie; quality of telling lies.

mercenary (mûr'sē·nẽr'ĭ). *Adj.*, acting merely for money. *Noun*, a soldier who sells his services to an army not of his own country.

metaphor (mĕt'á·fẽr). A figurative comparison of unlike things. *Adv.*, **metaphorically** (mĕt'á·fŏr'ĭ·kál·ĭ). Figuratively speaking.

metaphysical (mĕt'á·fĭz'ĭ·kál). Pertaining to abstract philosophy; apart from material objects.

mettle (mĕt''l). Temperament involving vigorous spirit, fortitude, and courage.

mezzotint (mĕz'ô·tĭnt). An engraving on copper or steel.

miasma (mī·ăz'má). Unhealthy night mists from swamps.

mien (mēn). Air; demeanor; bearing.

millennium (mĭ·lĕn'ĭ·ŭm). Period of greatest happiness and prosperity (derived from Bible prophecy of a thousand years during which Christ will reign on earth).

minions (mĭn'yŭnz). Favorites.

mobile (mō'bĭl). Easily moved; expressive.

molestation (mō'lĕs·tā'shŭn). Annoyance; interference.

moly (mō'lĭ). A wondrous herb of secret power, mentioned by ancient writers.

momentous (mô·mĕn'tŭs). Of great importance or significance. *Noun*, **momentousness**.

monetarily (mŏn'é·tẽr'ĭ·lĭ). In terms of money.

monitors (mŏn'ĭ·tẽrz). Those who give advice and warning.

monologue (mŏn'ô·lŏg). A long speech by one person. (*See also* **dramatic monologue**.)

monumental (mŏn'ù·mĕn'tál). 1. Serving as a monument. 2. Massive and lasting.

mortified (môr'tĭ·fīd). 1. Deadened, poisoned, as flesh after a wound. 2. Embarrassed.

motley (mŏt'lĭ). 1. Costume of varied colors worn by a jester. 2. Variegated by many differing elements, as a throng.

mountebank (moun'tē·băngk). 1. One who sells quack medicines. 2. Any boastful and unscrupulous pretender.

multifoliate (mŭl'tĭ·fō'lĭ·át). Having many leaves.

multiplex (mŭl'tĭ·plĕks). Manifold; having many.

mummers (mŭm'ẽrz). Merrymakers at Christmas time; actors.

munificence (mù·nĭf'ĭ·sĕns). Generosity.

N

naïveté (nä·ēv·tā'). Artless, unaffected simplicity.

nether (nĕth'ẽr). Lower.

newt (nūt). A small, lizardlike creature.

niggard (nĭg'ẽrd). A stingy person.

nocturnal (nŏk·tûr'nál). Nightly.

noisome (noi'sŭm). Disgusting; offensive to the senses.

nomadic (nō·măd'ĭk). Roving; wandering.

nostalgic (nŏs·tăl'jĭk). Homesick.

novice (nŏv'ĭs). 1. One who has just entered a religious order. 2. A beginner in any field.

nymph (nĭmf). *See page 115.*

O

obdurate (ŏb'dù·rát; *poetic*, ŏb·dū'rát). Hard-hearted; unyielding.

oblivious (ŏb·lĭv'ĭ·ŭs). Completely unaware of surroundings.

obsequious (ŏb·sē'kwĭ·ŭs). Fawning; currying favors.

obsolete (ŏb'sô·lēt). Not in present use.

octoroon (ŏk'tô·rōōn'). Child of a quadroon and a white person, having one-eighth Negro blood.

offal (ŏf'ál). Refuse; rubbish.

officious (ô·fĭsh'ŭs). Meddlesome.

ogling (ō'glĭng). Casting flirtatious glances.

ominous (ŏm'ĭ·nŭs). Foreshadowing evil.

Omnipotent (ŏm·nĭp'ô·tĕnt). *See page 239.*

omniscient (ŏm·nĭsh'ĕnt). *See page 239.*

---

bar; church; dog; ardǔous; fat; go; hear; jail; key; lame; meat; not; ring; pay; ran; see; shell; ten; there, thick; pastǔre; vast; wind; yes; zoo, zh = z in azure.

opiate (ō'pĭ·āt). *Noun,* a drug producing sleep. *Adj.,* sleep-inducing.

opulence (ŏp'ū·lĕns). Wealth.

oracles (ŏr'à·k'lz). Mediums by which the future is revealed.

orangery (ôr'ĕnj·rĭ). A greenhouse for raising oranges.

oratorio (ŏr'à·tō'rĭ·ō). A dramatic text, usually on a Biblical theme, set to music with instrumental accompaniment.

oratory (ŏr'à·tō'rĭ). A place for prayer.

orb (ôrb). 1. A sphere surmounted by a cross, held by a monarch as a symbol of power. 2. *Adj.,* **orbèd** (ôrb'ĕd). *Poetic.* Shaped like a sphere.

ostentation (ŏs'tĕn·tā'shŭn). Proud show.

overcredulous (ō'vĕr·krĕd'ū·lŭs). Ready to believe anything without sufficient evidence.

P

pagan (pā'găn). *Noun,* a heathen; especially one who believed in the ancient Greek and Roman gods. *Adj.,* pertaining to such a person or his beliefs.

palatable (păl'ĭt·à·b'l). Pleasing to the taste.

palisade (păl'ĭ·sād'). A fence of stakes for protection.

palpitated (păl'pĭ·tāt'ĕd). Fluttered; quivered.

paradox (păr'à·dŏks). An assertion apparently absurd or self-contradictory, but really true.

paragon (păr'à·gŏn). A model; a type of perfection.

parody (păr'ō·dĭ). An imitation of the style and language of an author with comic effect. *Verb,* **parodied** (păr'ō·dĭd). Mimicked the style in ridicule.

paroxysm (păr'ŏk·sĭz'm). A sharp attack (of pain).

parricide (păr'ĭ·sīd). Murder of a parent.

pastoral (păs'tō·răl). Pertaining to rural life or the life of shepherds.

patriarchal (pā'trĭ·är'kăl). Like an ancient father or head of a tribe.

pavilion (pà·vĭl'yŭn). A tentlike top; a canopy.

pawn (pôn). The chessman of lowest rank.

pedantic (pē·dăn'tĭk). Overly precise.

pendent (pĕn'dĕnt). Hanging.

pentameter (pĕn·tăm'ê·tēr). A line of poetry containing five feet or accents.

penury (pĕn'ū·rĭ). Extreme poverty.

perennial (pēr·ĕn'ĭ·ăl). 1. *Noun,* a plant that comes up each year. 2. *Adj.,* appearing afresh from time to time.

perfunctorily (pēr·fŭngk'tō·rĭ·lĭ). In a routine manner without interest or zeal.

periwig (pĕr'ĭ·wĭg). An elaborate powdered wig worn in the eighteenth century.

periwinkle (pĕr'ĭ·wĭng'k'l). A trailing evergreen with blue and white flowers.

permeated (pûr'mê·āt'ĕd). Spread throughout.

pernicious (pēr·nĭsh'ŭs). Injurious; deadly.

pertinaciously (pûr'tĭ·nā'shŭs·lĭ). Stubbornly; steadfastly.

perturbation (pûr'tēr·bā'shŭn). State of being distressed or agitated.

pestilent (pĕs'tĭ·lĕnt). Troublesome; endangering peace and morals.

phantasies (făn'tà·sĭz). Dreams; imaginings. *Adj.,* **phantasmal** (făn·tăz'măl). Unreal, like a dream.

philosophical (fĭl'ō·sŏf'ĭ·kăl). Being like a philosopher — wise, temperate, calm.

philosophy (fĭ·lŏs'ō·fĭ). Literally, the love of wisdom. A body of principles underlying the study of any subject.

phonetician (fō'nê·tĭsh'ăn). One versed in the science of speech sounds.

phonetics (fō·nĕt'ĭks). The science of speech sounds as elements of language. *Adj.,* **phonetic.**

phosphorus (fŏs'fō·rŭs). A substance that shines in the dark.

physic (fĭz'ĭk). Word formerly used for any medicine.

piquancies (pē'kăn·sĭz). Delightful, stimulating qualities.

plebeian (plê·bē'yăn). *Noun,* the lowest class in ancient Roman society; hence, a person of low class. *Adj.,* inferior; common.

poignant (poin'yànt). Piercing the emotions; touching.

polysyllabic (pŏl'ĭ·sĭ·lăb'ĭk). Having more than three syllables.

pomegranate (pŏm'grăn'ĭt). A tropical thick-skinned reddish berry about the size of an orange; also the tree. Both are very decorative.

ponderous (pŏn'dēr·ŭs). Weighty.

popish (pōp'ĭsh). Of the Roman Catholic Church (an uncomplimentary usage).

postern (pōs'tērn). *Rare.* A back door or gate.

posthumous (pŏs'tû·mŭs). Published after the author's death. *Adv.,* **posthumously.**

potation (pō·tā'shŭn). The act of drinking.

potent (pō'tĕnt). *See page 239.*

potentates (pō'tĕn·tāts). Monarchs or other persons wielding great power over others.

potential (pō·tĕn'shăl). Possible.

precedence (prê·sēd'ĕns). The order observed by persons of different rank on ceremonial occasions.

precedent (prĕs'ê·dĕnt). An act which authorizes future acts of a similar nature.

precocious (prê·kō'shŭs). Exceptionally early in mental development. *Noun,* **precocity** (prê-kŏs'ĭ·tĭ).

predestined (prê·dĕs'tĭnd). Destined or determined beforehand.

preferment (prê·fûr'mĕnt). Advancement.

prelates (prĕl'ĭts). Dignitaries of the church.

preponderance (prê·pŏn'dēr·ăns). Superiority of influence, power, force, or weight.

presumptuous (prê·zŭmp'tû·ŭs). Overbold; taking undue liberty.

prithee (prĭth'ē). *Archaic.* I pray thee.

probity (prō'bĭ·tĭ). Virtue; uprightness.

prodigies (prŏd'ĭ·jĭz). 1. Extraordinary persons. 2. Remarkable acts.

prodigious (prō·dĭj'ŭs). Extraordinary in bulk, quality, or degree.

prolific (prō·lĭf'ĭk). Producing abundant results.

propitiated (prō·pĭsh'ĭ·āt'ĕd). Appeased or rendered favorable.

prostrate (prŏs'trāt). Thrown down with face on the ground.

āpe, chảotic, bâre, ăt, ẩttend, ärt, flảsk, ảtop; ēke, mẹrely, êlect, ĕcho, prudĕnt, doẽr; ītem, ĭnn, rarĭty; ōde, ŏpaque, fôr, dŏt, lŏft, cŏnfide; sōon, tŏŏk; sour, toil; tūbe, ūnique, tûrn, sŭp, ŭntil.

provocation (prŏv'ŏ·kā'shŭn). Cause of irritation or anger.

provocative (prŏ·vŏk'a·tĭv). Stimulating; arousing thought or argument.

proximity (prŏks·ĭm'ĭ·tĭ). Nearness.

pseudonym (sū'dŏ·nĭm). Name assumed by an author; pen name.

psychiatry (sī·kī'a·trĭ). The medical specialty dealing with mental disorders.

psychology (sī·kŏl'ŏ·jĭ). The science which treats of the mind and human behavior in any of its aspects. *Adj.*, psychological (sī'kō·lŏj'ĭ·kăl).

pugnacious (pŭg·nā'shŭs). *See page* 469.

pulverize (pŭl'vẽr·īz). Grind to powder.

pungent (pŭn'jĕnt). Sharply pricking; piercing.

Q

quadrant (kwŏd'rănt). Nautical instrument for measuring the height of the sun.

quatrain (kwŏt'rān). A stanza of four lines.

quittance (kwĭt'ăns). Discharge.

R

ravined (răv'ĭnd). Seized by violence.

recalcitrant (rē·kăl'sĭ·trănt). Rebellious.

recantation (rē'kăn·tā'shŭn). Public withdrawal of a previous opinion.

redundant (rē·dŭn'dănt). Unnecessary; superfluous.

refectory (rē·fĕk'tŏ·rĭ). *Adj.*, pertaining to a dining hall in a monastery.

reft (rĕft). *Archaic.* Robbed.

refulgent (rē·fŭl'jĕnt). Brilliant; splendid.

regicide (rĕj'ĭ·sīd). The killing of a king.

regime (rå·zhēm'). Governmental system.

regression (rē·grĕsh'ŭn). Setback; a return to former undesirable conditions.

reiterated (rē·ĭt'ẽr·āt'ĕd). Repeated many times.

relevant (rĕl'ē·vănt). Applying to the case in hand; having bearing on.

reminiscent (rĕm'ĭ·nĭs'ĕnt). Reminding one of something previously known.

Renaissance (rĕn'ē·zäns'). Revival of interest in ancient classics during the fourteenth to sixteenth centuries.

replicas (rĕp'lĭ·kaz). Reproductions; close copies.

reprobate (rĕp'rŏ·bāt). Scoundrel.

reprobation (rĕp'rŏ·bā'shŭn). 1. Severe disapproval; censure. 2. Rejection by God's decree.

reticulated (rē·tĭk'ū·lāt'ĕd). Having crossed fibers, as in a network.

ribaldries (rĭb'ăld·rĭz). Coarse jests.

roisterers (rois'tẽr·ẽrz). Noisy, destructive merrymakers.

Romanesque (rō'măn·ĕsk'). A form of architecture between the Roman and the Gothic, characterized by the rounded arch.

roseate (rō'zē·ăt). Rose-colored; hence, happy, pleasant.

rotunda (rō·tŭn'da). 1. A round building, usually with a dome. 2. A large round room inside such a building.

ruminating (rōō'mĭ·nāt'ĭng). Musing; pondering

runagate (rŭn'a·gāt). Deserter; vagabond.

russet (rŭs'ĕt). A group of browns varying from reddish to red-yellow.

S

sacrilegious (săk'rĭ·lē'jŭs). Sinning against something sacred.

saffron (săf'rŭn). A deep orange color.

salvers (săl'vẽrz). Trays.

satiate (sā'shĭ·āt). Fully satisfied. *Noun*, satiety (sa·tī'ĕ·tĭ). State of being overfed.

satire (săt'īr). Ridicule of human follies and vices. *Adj.*, satiric (sa·tĭr'ĭk) or satirical. *Verb*, satirize (săt'ĭ·rīz).

scission (sĭzh'ŭn). Division; split.

scrupulous (skrōō'pū·lŭs). Careful; exact.

scurrilous (skŭr'ĭ·lŭs). Coarsely abusive. *Noun*, scurrility (skŭ·rĭl'ĭ·tĭ).

scutcheon (skŭch'ŭn). A field on which a coat of arms is emblazoned. A shielded scutcheon is shaped like a shield.

sear (sēr). Dry; withered.

sedan (sē·dăn'). A portable chair borne on poles by two men.

senility (sē·nĭl'ĭ·tĭ). Infirmity of old age.

sensual (sĕn'shōō·ăl). Pertaining to the physical sense, as of hearing.

sensuous (sĕn'shōō·ŭs). Appealing pleasurably to the senses.

sequestered (sē·kwĕs'tẽrd). Retired; secluded.

seraph (sĕr'ăf). An angel of the highest rank.

shoaling (shōl'ĭng). Gradually becoming shallow.

shoughs (shŏks). *Archaic.* Shaggy dogs.

shrieve (shrēv). *Archaic.* Hear confession and give absolution.

simile (sĭm'ĭ·lē). A figure of speech by which two unlike things are shown to have some point of similarity, usually expressed by *like* or *as.*

solicitations (sŏ·lĭs'ĭ·tā'shŭnz). Appeals; entreaties.

solicitude (sŏ·lĭs'ĭ·tūd). Attentive care.

solitudinous (sŏl'ĭ·tū'dĭ·nŭs). Lonely.

somnolence (sŏm'nō·lĕns). Drowsiness.

sonorousness (sŏ·nō'rŭs·nĕs). Quality of loud, full sound.

sophistical (sŏ·fĭs'tĭ·kăl). Apparently true, but really false. *Noun*, sophistry (sŏf'ĭs·trĭ). Subtly deceptive reasoning.

sordid (sôr'dĭd). Base; despicable.

spasmodically (spăz·mŏd'ĭ·kăl·ĭ). With sudden spurts of energy or violence.

specious (spē'shŭs). Apparently true and just, but in reality false.

spontaneity (spŏn'ta·nē'ĭ·tĭ). Natural energy without force or restraint. *Adj.*, spontaneous (spŏn·tā'nē·ŭs).

static (stăt'ĭk). Motionless; not progressing.

staunchless (stônch'lĕs). Not to be stopped.

stimuli (stĭm'ū·lī). Things that stir into activity; incentives.

strategist (străt'ē·jĭst). One well versed in the science and art of military command.

suavity (swăv'ĭ·tĭ). Poise and polished manners.

---

bar; church; dog; ardǔous; fat; go; hear; jail; key; lame; meat; not; ring; pay; ran; see; shell; ten; there, thick; pastŭre; vast; wind; yes; zoo, zh = z in azure.

subaltern (sŭ·bôl'tẽrn). An officer below the rank of captain.
sublimated (sŭb'lĭ·māt'ĕd). Refined; elevated.
subordination (sŭ·bôr'dĭ·nā'shŭn). Obedience to authority of higher rank.
subtile (sŭb'tĭl). Penetrating; wily.
subtle (sŭt''l). Marked by insight, perception, and fine shades of thought.
succor (sŭk'ẽr). Aid; assistance.
suffice (sŭ·fīs'). Satisfy; be enough.
sumptuous (sŭmp'tṳ·ŭs). Luxurious; splendid.
surcease (sûr·sēs'). End.
surfeited (sûr'fĭt·ĕd). Fed or given too much.
surmise (sûr·mīz'). A guess; a supposition.
surplice (sûr'plĭs). An outer garment of white linen worn over a cassock by a clergyman.
susceptible (sŭ·sĕp'tĭ·b'l). Easily influenced.
swain (swān). See page 115.
swound (swound) or swowne (swoun). Archaic variations of swoon, a fainting spell.
sylphs (sĭlfs). Imaginary beings inhabiting the air.
sylvan (sĭl'văn). Pertaining to life in the woods or forest.
symbol (sĭm'bŭl). A visible object used as a sign of an abstract idea. Adj., symbolic (sĭm·bŏl'ĭk).
symmetry (sĭm'ĕ·trĭ). Equal balance between two sides of an object.
symposium (sĭm·pō'zĭ·ŭm). A conference at which a particular subject is discussed and opinions are gathered.
synonym (sĭn'ô·nĭm). A word having nearly the same meaning as another word. Adj., synonymous (sĭ·nŏn'ĭ·mŭs).

T

taciturn (tăs'ĭ·tûrn). Silent.
tawdry (tô'drĭ). Showy; without good taste.
temporal (tĕm'pô·răl). Civil or political as distinguished from spiritual.
tenets (tĕn'ĕts). Doctrines; beliefs.
tenterhooks (tĕn'tẽr·hŏoks'). Used with on, in suspense, under strain.
terminology (tûr'mĭ·nŏl'ô·jĭ). The technical or special terms in any field of study.
terrestrial (tĕ·rĕs'trĭ·ăl). Of the world; of the earth.
thralls (thrôlz). Archaic. Slaves; bondmen.
throstle (thrŏs''l). Scot. A thrush.
tillage (tĭl'ĭj). The operation of tilling land.
tinct (tĭngkt). Delicately colored. Noun, tincture (tĭngk'tṳr). A substance that gives delicate color.
tippet (tĭp'ĕt). A scarf or scarflike garment of fur, cloth, etc.
titillating (tĭt'ĭ·lāt'ĭng). Tickling.
tortuous (tôr'tṳ·ŭs). Winding.
transcendent (trăn·sĕn'dĕnt). Beyond experience.
transitory (trăn'sĭ·tō'rĭ). Fleeting.
transmutation (trăns'mṳ·tā'shŭn). Change.
travesty (trăv'ĕs·tĭ). Burlesque; mockery.
treatise (trē'tĭs). A systematic exposition of facts and principles involved in any subject.
trenchèd (trĕn'chĕd). Poetic or archaic. Cut deep like a trench.

trilogy (trĭl'ô·jĭ). A group of three literary compositions having some similarity, though each is a separate and complete unit.
troubadour (trōo'bà·dŏor). 1. A French poet-singer of the eleventh to thirteenth centuries. 2. A singer of love lyrics.
truckling (trŭk'lĭng). Currying favor.
tumid (tū'mĭd). Swollen.
tumultuous (tṳ·mŭl'tṳ·ŭs). Agitated; stormy.
turbid (tûr'bĭd). Clouded; muddled.
turbulent (tûr'bṳ·lĕnt). Restless; violent.

U

ultimatum (ŭl'tĭ·mā'tŭm). The final terms offered by either party in a dispute; a determined stand.
uncompromisingly (ŭn·kŏm'prô·mīz'ĭng·lĭ). Firmly; in an unyielding manner.
uncouth (ŭn·kōoth'). 1. Unfamiliar; strange. 2. Boorish; not versed in the manners of society.
undivulged (ŭn'dĭ·vŭljd'). Not revealed; secret.
unimpeachable (ŭn'ĭm·pēch'à·b'l). Blameless; unquestionable.
unintelligible (ŭn'ĭn·tĕl'ĭ·jĭ·b'l). Not to be understood.
unlineal (ŭn·lĭn'ê·ăl). Not of the same family or line of descent.
unostentatiously (ŭn'ŏs·tĕn·tā'shŭs·lĭ). Without show; quietly.
unperturbed (ŭn'pẽr·tûrbd'). Undisturbed; unworried.
unpremeditated (ŭn'prĕ·mĕd'ĭ·tāt'ĕd). Spontaneous; not planned beforehand.
unsavory (ŭn·sā'vẽr·ĭ). 1. Unpleasant to smell or taste. 2. Having a bad reputation.
urbane (ûr·bān'). Polite; at ease in society.

V

vantage (vàn'tĭj). A position of superiority or advantage.
vaporous (vā'pẽr·ŭs). Full of vapor or fog.
vassal (văs'ăl). 1. In the feudal system, one who gives his allegiance to an overlord in return for protection. 2. A lover devoted to his lady-love.
vaunteth (vônt'ĕth). Poetic or archaic. Speaks boastfully. Adj., vaunting. Boasting.
vehement (vē'ĕ·mĕnt). Furious.
venerable (vĕn'ẽr·à·b'l). Commanding respect, usually because of age or dignified position. Noun, veneration (vĕn'ẽr·ā'shŭn). Respect.
verdurous (vûr'dṳr·ŭs). Covered with green vegetation.
vermeil (vûr'mĭl). Poetic form of vermilion (vẽr·mĭl'yŭn). Bright red.
vernacular (vẽr·năk'ū·lẽr). Native or commonly spoken language.
vernal (vûr'năl). Belonging to spring.
versatility (vûr'sà·tĭl'ĭ·tĭ). Ability along many lines of effort. Adj., versatile (vûr'sà·tĭl).
vestige (vĕs'tĭj). A trace.
vexation (vĕks·ā'shŭn). Annoyance; irritation.
vilifying (vĭl'ĭ·fī'ĭng). Slandering.
villein (vĭl'ĭn). A free peasant of medieval days.

āpe, chāotic, bâre, ăt, ăttend, ärt, flàsk, átop; ēke, mẽrely, ĕlect, ĕcho, prudĕnt, doẽr; ītem, ĭnn, rarĭty; ōde, ôpaque, fôr, dŏt, lôft, cônfide; sōon, tŏŏk; sour, toil; tūbe, ûnique, tûrn, sŭp, ŭntil.

vintage (vĭn′tĭj). A season's produce of wine.
virago (vĭ·rā′gō). A quarrelsome woman.
vivacity (vī·văs′ĭ·tĭ). Liveliness; sprightliness.
vociferation (vō·sĭf′ĕr·ā′shŭn). Loud speaking.
voluble (vŏl′ū·b'l). Speaking fluently.
voluptuous (vō·lŭp′tū·ŭs). Delightful to the senses. *Noun*, voluptuousness (vō·lŭp′tū·ŭs·nĕs). Desire for sensual pleasure.
vouchsafed (vouch·sāft′). Granted; bestowed.

W

waived (wāvd). Set aside; gave up a claim to.
wanton (wŏn′tŭn). *Adj.*, gay; lighthearted. *Verb*, play; fly freely.
wassail (wŏs′'l). 1. A spiced wine or ale of ancient times. 2. A feast at which healths were drunk.
ween (wēn). *Archaic.* Suppose; imagine.

weltering (wĕl′tĕr·ĭng). Wallowing; soaking in a liquid.
wench (wĕnch). A girl.
whetstone (hwĕt′stōn′). A stone for sharpening edged tools.
wimple (wĭm′p'l). A folded cloth worn over the head and neck by women in the Middle Ages.
wist (wĭst). *Archaic. See page 393.*
wizened (wĭz′'nd). Withered; shriveled.
wonted (wŭnt′ĕd). Accustomed.
woof (wo͞of). The cross thread in a woven fabric.
woofèd (wo͞of′ĕd). *Poetic.* Woven.
wot (wŏt). *Archaic.* Know.

Y

yeoman (yō′măn). A freeholder, a common man of the most respectable class.

---

bar; church; dog; ardŭous; fat; go; hear; jail; key; lame; meat; not; ring; pay; ran; see; shell; ten; there, thick; pastūre; vast; wind; yes; zoo, zh = z in azure.

British Money

Throughout this book you will come across references to British money. This section will help you to understand the British money system and to have some way of comparing British and American money.

Although there have been many units of exchange through the years, the beginnings of the modern British system go back to A.D. 775 when Offa, king of Mercia, issued silver pennies. It took 240 of these pennies to weigh a pound. Shortly after the Norman Conquest of 1066 something very close to the modern system was already established, though Latin names were used: the pound was called the *libra* (from which the symbol £ comes); this was worth 20 shillings (called *solidi*, symbol s.); and the shilling was worth 12 pence (called *denarii*, symbol d.). These symbols are used in two ways in writing out sums of money. Five pounds, six shillings, and sixpence, for example,

may be written £5.6s.6d. or £5/6/6.

Through the nineteenth century until 1914 the pound was worth about $4.86. Its value fluctuated through the changing conditions of the next decades. In 1939 its value was fixed at $4.03, and in 1949 the pound was devalued to its present $2.80. The table below gives approximate values of British money in 1912, when *Pygmalion* was written, and today.

You will come across other names for units of money: a *sovereign* is a gold coin worth a pound; a *guinea*, for which there is no coin now, is worth 21 shillings; a *florin* is a coin worth 2 shillings. Two small denominations, now seldom used, are the *halfpenny* (called hā′ penny) and the *farthing*, worth a quarter of a penny. The *groat*, now obsolete, was worth fourpence.

Some slang terms for money are: *quid* —pound; *tanner* — sixpence; *bob* — shilling; *copper* — penny.

1912		*Today*
$4.86	*1 pound (20 shillings)*	*$2.80*
.60	*half a crown (2½ shillings)*	*.35*
.24	*shilling (12 pence)*	*.14*
.12	*sixpence*	*.07*
.02	*1 penny*	*.01*

INDEX

A Becket, Thomas, 52, 68, 69
"Acme" (Galsworthy), 577
Addison, Joseph, 264, 267, 684; life, 293–94; selections, 295–303
"Afterward" (Hardy), 538
Albert, Prince, 452, 454, 456
"Alexander's Feast, or the Power of Music" (Dryden), 252
Alfred, King, 34, 36, 50, 52
"All Yankees Are Liars" (Knight), 593
American Revolution, 268, 269, 349
"Amoretti" (Spenser), 111–12
Anglo-Saxon Chronicle, 34
Anglo-Saxon Period, 28–49; introduction, 28–36; time chart, 33; map, 35; reading list, 47; The Growth of the English Language, 48–49; selections, 36–47
Anglo-Saxons, 28, 30–33, 34, 50–51
Anne, Queen, 264
"Apostrophe to the Ocean" (Byron), 412
Arnold, Matthew, 350, 458, 459; life, 507; selection, 507–08
Arthur, King, 30, 54, 58
Attlee, Clement, 555
Auden, W. H., 556, 620, 621; life, 653; selections, 654–56
Augustan Age, 262
Augustine, 33
Austen, Jane, 344, 345, 346, 347, 371

Bacon, Francis, 104, 109, 213, 684; life, 202–03; selection, 203–04
"Ballad of East and West, The" (Kipling), 547
Ballads, Early English and Scottish, 59–65
"Banks o' Doon, The" (Burns), 333
"Bannockburn" (Burns), 334
"Barrel Organ, The" (Noyes), 639
Barrie, James M., 346, 556, 713; life, 780; selection, 778–800
"Battle of Blenheim, The" (Southey), 446
Battle of Hastings, 50
Beardsley, Aubrey, 459
Bede, Venerable, 34
Bennett, Arnold, 346, 347
Beowulf, 31, 34, 342; selections from, 39–47
Bible, 58; see also *King James Bible*
Bill of Rights, 212

"Birthday, A" (C. Rossetti), 510
Blake, William, 269; life, 329–30; selections, 330–31
"Blow, Blow, Thou Winter Wind" from *As You Like It* (Shakespeare), 123
"Bonny Barbara Allan," 62
"Boot and Saddle" (Browning), 492
Boswell, James, 262, 268, 665; life, 306; selections, 308–15
Bowen, Elizabeth, 347
"Break, Break, Break" (Tennyson), 484
"Bright Star! Would I Were Steadfast As Thou Art" (Keats), 429
Brontë, Charlotte, 344, 345, 346, 347
Brontë, Emily, 344, 345, 346, 347
Brooke, Rupert, life, 644; selections, 644–46
Browning, Elizabeth Barrett, 452; life, 489; selections, 490-91
Browning, Robert, 452, 458, 459, 712; life, 489; selections, 491–99
"Bugle Song, The" (Tennyson), 478
Bunyan, John, 214; life, 239–40; selection, 241–45
Burke, Edmund, 268, 352
Burns, Robert, 269, 350, 351, 371; life, 331–32; selections, 332–41
"But the Greatest of These Is Charity" (I Corinthians 13), 206
Butler, Samuel, 216
Byron, Lord (George Gordon), 351, 352; life, 403–04; selections, 404–14

Caedmon, 34
Caesar, Julius, 29
Callaghan, Morley, 347
Calvin, John, 102
Canterbury, 34, 52
Canterbury Tales, The (Chaucer), 52; selections from, 69–93
Carlyle, Thomas, 452, 458, 684; life, 460–61; selection, 461–64
Carroll, Lewis, 460; life, 511; selection, 512–13
Cary, Joyce, 347
Cavalier poets, 214, 217
Cavaliers, 211
Caxton, William, 94, 109
Celts, 28, 51

Charles I, 211, 212
Charles II, 104, 212, 214
Chaucer, Geoffrey, 52, 58; life, 68; selections, 69–93
Chesterton, G. K., life, 631; selections, 632–35
Chivalry, 53–54
Churchill, Sir Winston, 31, 555; life, 701–02; selections, 702–09
Classicism, 348
"Clod and the Pebble, The" (Blake), 331
"Cloud, The" (Shelley), 416
Coleridge, Samuel Taylor, 348, 350, 351, 352, 371, 459; life, 372; selections, 373–92
Collins, Wilkie, 344
"Composed upon Westminster Bridge" (Wordsworth), 361
Congreve, William, 216
Conrad, Joseph, 346, 347, 556, 559; life, 566; selection, 566–76
"Consecration, A" (Masefield), 636
"Constant Lover, The" (Suckling), 219
"Cooking Picnics" from *Delight* (Priestley), 685
"Coquette's Heart, The" from *The Spectator* (Addison), 300
"Cotter's Saturday Night, The" (Burns), excerpts, 337–41
"Counsel to Girls" (Herrick), 218
Coward, Noel, 714
Cromwell, Oliver, 211, 212, 458
"Crossing the Bar" (Tennyson), 487
Crusades, 53

Dahl, Roald, 560; life, 604; selection, 604–11
Danes, 30, 34, 50, 51
"Darkling Thrush, The" (Hardy), 539
Darwin, Charles, 458
"Death Be Not Proud" (Donne), 221
"Death of Gandhi, The" (Sahgal), 678
"Definitions from Johnson's *Dictionary*," 307
Defoe, Daniel, 264, 269, 343, 347; life, 289; selection, 289–92
De la Mare, Walter, 620; life, 627; selections, 627–29
Delight (Priestley), selections from, 685–88
Deserted Village, The (Goldsmith), selection from, 316–23

Picture Acknowledgments

pp. 28–29: British Information Service; pp. 50–51: Pierpont Morgan Library; pp. 56, 128: Drawings by C. Walter Hodges from The Globe Restored, courtesy of Ernest Benn, Ltd.; pp. 100–01: Metropolitan Museum of Art; p. 118: Ginn and Company; p. 126: From Hellas, courtesy of J. J. Augustin; pp. 293, 372, 403, 427: National Portrait Gallery, London; p. 361: N. R. Farbman, courtesy of LIFE magazine © 1950 Time, Inc.; pp. 552–53: British Information Service; pp. 648, 653, 656: Photos by Rollie McKenna.